Contemporary Authors®

NEW REVISION SERIES

ISSN 0275-7176

Contemporary Authors®

A Bio-Bibliographical Guide to
Current Writers in Fiction, General Nonfiction,
Poetry, Journalism, Drama, Motion Pictures,
Television, and Other Fields

NEW REVISION SERIES
volume 83

Detroit
San Francisco
London
Boston
Woodbridge, CT

Staff

Scot Peacock, *Senior Editor and Project Manager*

Simone Sobel, *Assistant Project Editor*

Amy Francis, John Jorgenson, *Senior Content Editor*s

Katy Balcer, Regie A. Carlton, Elizabeth A. Cranston, Dwayne D. Hayes, *Content Editors*

Anja Barnard, Thomas Wiloch, *Associate Content Editors*

Kristen A. Dorsch, *Assistant Content Editor*

Susan M. Trosky, *Managing Editor*

Victoria B. Cariappa, *Research Manager*

Andrew Guy Malonis, Barbara McNeil, Gary J. Oudersluys. Maureen Richards, *Research Specialists*

Wendy K. Festerling, Tamara C. Nott, Tracie A. Richardson, Corrine A. Stocker, Cheryl L. Warnock, *Research Associates*

Phyllis J. Blackman, Tim Lehnerer, Patricia L. Love, *Research Assistants*

Library of Congress Catalog Card Number 62-52046
ISBN 0-7876-3093-4
ISSN 0275-7176
Printed in the United States of America

10 9 8 7 6 5 4 3 2 1

Contents

Preface vii

CA Numbering System and
Volume Update Chart xi

Authors and Media People
Featured in This Volume xiii

Author Listings 1

Indexing note: All *Contemporary Authors* entries are indexed in the *Contemporary Authors* cumulative index, which is published separately and distributed twice a year.

As always, the most recent *Contemporary Authors* cumulative index continues to be the user's guide to the location of an individual author's listing.

Preface

Contemporary Authors (*CA*) provides information on approximately 100,000 writers in a wide range of media, including:

- Current writers of fiction, nonfiction, poetry, and drama whose works have been issued by commercial publishers, risk publishers, or university presses (authors whose books have been published only by known vanity or author-subsidized firms are ordinarily not included)

- Prominent print and broadcast journalists, editors, photojournalists, syndicated cartoonists, graphic novelists, screenwriters, television scriptwriters, and other media people

- Authors who write in languages other than English, provided their works have been published in the United States or translated into English

- Literary greats of the early twentieth century whose works are popular in todays high school and college curriculums and continue to elicit critical attention

A *CA* listing entails no charge or obligation. Authors are included on the basis of the above criteria and their interest to *CA* users. Sources of potential listees include trade periodicals, publishers' catalogs, librarians, and other users.

How to Get the Most out of *CA*: Use the Index

The key to locating an author's most recent entry is the *CA* cumulative index, which is published separately and distributed twice a year. It provides access to *all* entries in *CA* and *Contemporary Authors New Revision Series* (*CANR*). Always consult the latest index to find an authors most recent entry.

For the convenience of users, the *CA* cumulative index also includes references to all entries in these Gale literary series: *Authors and Artists for Young Adults, Authors in the News, Bestsellers, Black Literature Criticism, Black Writers, Children's Literature Review, Concise Dictionary of American Literary Biography, Concise Dictionary of British Literary Biography, Contemporary Authors Autobiography Series, Contemporary Authors Bibliographical Series, Contemporary Literary Criticism, Dictionary of Literary Biography, Dictionary of Literary Biography Documentary Series, Dictionary of Literary Biography Yearbook, DISCovering Authors, DISCovering Authors: British, DISCovering Authors: Canadian, DISCovering Authors: Modules* (including modules for Dramatists, Most-Studied Authors, Multicultural Authors, Novelists, Poets, and Popular/Genre Authors), *Drama Criticism, Hispanic Literature Criticism, Hispanic Writers, Junior DISCovering Authors, Major Authors and Illustrators for Children and Young Adults, Major 20th-Century Writers, Native North American Literature, Poetry Criticism, Short Story Criticism, Something about the Author, Something about the Author Autobiography Series, Twentieth-Century Literary Criticism, World Literature Criticism,* and *Yesterday's Authors of Books for Children.*

A Sample Index Entry:

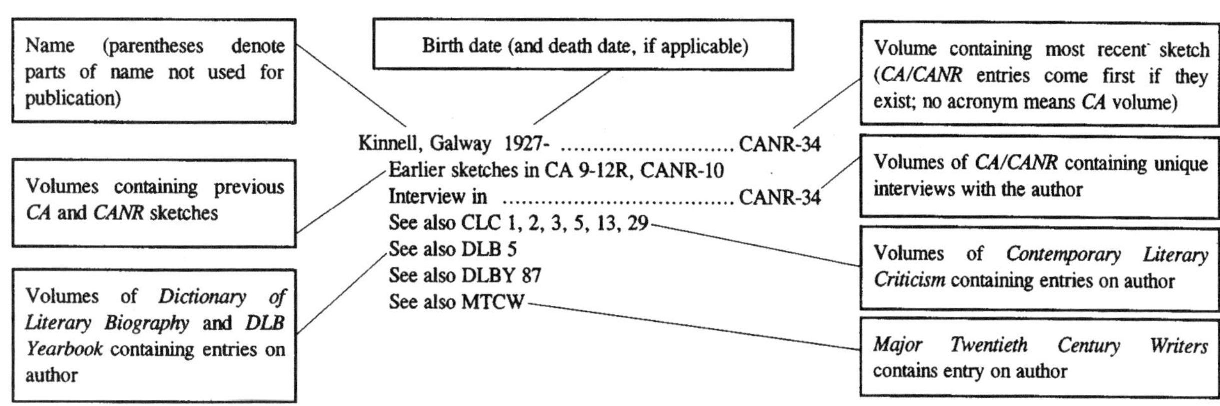

How Are Entries Compiled?

The editors make every effort to secure new information directly from the authors; listees' responses to our questionnaires and query letters provide most of the information featured in *CA.* For deceased writers, or those who fail to reply to requests for data, we consult other reliable biographical sources, such as those indexed in Gale's *Biography and Genealogy Master Index,* and bibliographical sources, including *National Union Catalog, LC MARC,* and *British National Bibliography.* Further details come from published interviews, feature stories, and book reviews, as well as information supplied by the authors' publishers and agents.

An asterisk (*) at the end of a sketch indicates that the listing has been compiled from secondary sources believed to be reliable but has not been personally verified for this edition by the author sketched.

What Kinds of Information Does An Entry Provide?

Sketches in *CA* contain the following biographical and bibliographical information:

- **Entry heading:** the most complete form of author's name, plus any pseudonyms or name variations used for writing

- **Personal information:** author's date and place of birth, family data, ethnicity, educational background, political and religious affiliations, and hobbies and leisure interests

- **Addresses:** author's home, office, or agent's addresses, plus e-mail and fax numbers, as available

- **Career summary:** name of employer, position, and dates held for each career post; resume of other vocational achievements; military service

- **Membership information:** professional, civic, and other association memberships and any official posts held

- **Awards and honors:** military and civic citations, major prizes and nominations, fellowships, grants, and honorary degrees

- **Writings:** a comprehensive, chronological list of titles, publishers, dates of original publication and revised editions, and production information for plays, television scripts, and screenplays

- **Adaptations:** a list of films, plays, and other media which have been adapted from the author's work

- **Work in progress:** current or planned projects, with dates of completion and/or publication, and expected publisher, when known

- **Sidelights:** a biographical portrait of the author's development; information about the critical reception of the author's works; revealing comments, often by the author, on personal interests, aspirations, motivations, and thoughts on writing

- **Interview:** a one-on-one discussion with authors conducted especially for *CA*, offering insight into authors' thoughts about their craft

- **Autobiographical Essay:** an original essay written by noted authors for *CA*, a forum in which writers may present themselves, on their own terms, to their audience

- **Photographs:** portraits and personal photographs of notable authors

- **Biographical and critical sources:** a list of books and periodicals in which additional information on an author's life and/or writings appears

Obituary Notices in *CA* provide date and place of birth as well as death information about authors whose full-length sketches appeared in the series before their deaths. The entries also summarize the authors' careers and writings and list other sources of biographical and detah information.

Related Titles in the *CA* Series

Contemporary Authors Autobiography Series complements *CA* original and revised volumes with specially commissioned autobiographical essays by important current authors, illustrated with personal photographs they provide. Common topics include their motivations for writing, the people and experiences that shaped their careers, the rewards they derive from their work, and their impressions of the current literary scene.

Contemporary Authors Bibliographical Series surveys writings by and about important American authors since World War II. Each volume concentrates on a specific genre and features approximately ten writers; entries list works written by and about the author and contain a bibliographical essay discussing the merits and deficiencies of major critical and scholarly studies in detail.

Available in Electronic Formats

CD-ROM. Full-text bio-bibliographic entries from the entire *CA* series, covering approximately 100,000 writers, are available on CD-ROM through lease and purchase plans. The disc combines entries from the *CA, CANR,* and *Contemporary Authors Permanent Series* (*CAP*) print series to provide the most recent author listing. The *CA CD-ROM* is searchable by name, title, subject/genre, nationality/ethnicity, personal data, and as well as by using Boolean logic. The disc is updated every six months. For more information, call 1-248-699-4253.

Contemporary Authors is also available on CD-ROM from SilverPlatter Information, Inc.

Online. The *Contemporary Authors* database is made available online to libraries and their patrons through online public access catalog (OPAC) vendors. Currently, *CA* is offered through Ameritech Library Services' Vista Online (formerly Dynix).

GaleNet. *CA* is available on a subscription basis through GaleNet, an online information resource that features an easy-to-use end-user interface, the powerful search capabilities of the BRS/Search retrieval software, and ease of access through the World-Wide Web. For more information, call 1-248-699-4253.

Magnetic Tape. *CA* is available for licensing on magnetic tape in a fielded format. The database is available for internal data processing and nonpublishing purposes only. For more information, call 1-248-699-4253.

Suggestions Are Welcome

The editors welcome comments and suggestions from users on any aspect of the *CA* series. If readers would like to recommend authors for inclusion in future volumes of the series, they are cordially invited to write the Editors at *Contemporary Authors*, Gale Group, 27500 Drake Rd., Farmington Hills, MI 48331-3535; or call at 1-248-699-4253; or fax at 1-248-699-8054.

CA Numbering System and Volume Update Chart

Occasionally questions arise about the *CA* numbering system and which volumes, if any, can be discarded. Despite numbers like "29-32R," "97-100" and "178," the entire *CA* print series consists of only 189 physical volumes with the publication of *CA* Volume 179. The following charts note changes in the numbering system and cover design, and indicate which volumes are essential for the most complete, up-to-date coverage.

CA First Revision

- 1-4R through 41-44R (11 books)
  Cover: Brown with black and gold trim.
  There will be no further First Revision volumes because revised entries are now being handled exclusively through the more efficient *New Revision Series* mentioned below.

CA Original Volumes

- 45-48 through 97-100 (14 books)
  Cover: Brown with black and gold trim.
- 101 through 179 (79 books)
  Cover: Blue and black with orange bands.
  The same as previous *CA* original volumes but with a new, simplified numbering system and new cover design.

CA Permanent Series

- *CAP*-1 and *CAP*-2 (2 books)
  Cover: Brown with red and gold trim.
  There will be no further Permanent Series volumes because revised entries are now being handled exclusively through the more efficient *New Revision Series* mentioned below.

CA New Revision Series

- CANR-1 through CANR-83 (83 books)
  Cover: Blue and black with green bands.
  Includes only sketches requiring significant changes; **sketches are taken from any previously published *CA, CAP,* or *CANR* volume.**

If You Have:	You May Discard:
CA First Revision Volumes 1-4R through 41-44R and *CA Permanent Series* Volumes 1 and 2.	*CA* Original Volumes 1, 2 ,3, 4 Volumes 5-6 through 41-44
CA Original Volumes 45-48 through 97-100 and 101 through 179	**NONE:** These volumes will not be superseded by corresponding revised volumes. Individual entries from these and all other volumes appearing in the left column of this chart may be revised and included in the various volumes of the *New Revision Series.*
CA New Revision Series Volumes *CANR*-1 through *CANR*-83	**NONE:** The *New Revision Series* does not replace any single volume of *CA*. Instead, volumes of *CANR* include entries from many previous *CA* series volumes. All *New Revision Series* volumes must be retained for full coverage.

A Sampling of Authors and Media People Featured in This Volume

Stephen E. Ambrose
Ambrose is the author of several books that explore historical figures, battles, and foreign policy. He won a National Book Award from the Freedom Foundation for *Eisenhower: Soldier, General of the Army, President-Elect, 1890-1952.* Ambrose, whose works also include *Nixon: The Education of a Politician, 1913-1962* and *The Victors: Eisenhower and His Boys—The Men of World War II,* saw his book *Undaunted Courage: Meriwether Lewis, Thomas Jefferson, and the Opening of the American West* become a best-seller. He served as an historical consultant on the 1998 film *Saving Private Ryan.*

Tom Brokaw
Brokaw, a broadcast journalist who has been the anchor of *NBC Nightly News* since 1982, is the author of 1998's *The Greatest Generation*, a work that gives tribute to those Americans who saw the United States through the Great Depression and World War II and who helped lead the nation towards postwar prosperity. The book, which also examines some of the injustices of the time and what was done to fight them, features numerous interviews with both obscure and famous individuals, including an interview with former President George Bush.

Lanny J. Davis
Davis, an attorney who was special counsel to President Bill Clinton from 1996-98, is the author of *Truth to Tell: Tell It Early, Tell It All, Tell It Yourself: Notes from My White House Education*, a book that reveals Davis' efforts to deal with the media as improper campaign financing allegations fell upon the Clinton administration. Among his other works are *The Emerging Democratic Majority* and the coauthored *Negotiating Computer Contracts.*

Radclyffe Hall
Hall, an award-winning English writer, was the author of several poetry collections and novels, such as the 1928 novel for which she is best known, *The Well of Loneliness,* a formerly controversial work that was one among the first of the modern literary works to feature a same-sex relationship between women. Hall's other works include *Twixt Earth and Stars: Poems, Poems of the Past and Present,* and the novel *Adam's Breed,* for which she earned a 1927 Femina-Vie Heureuse Prize.

Yusef Komunyakaa
Komunyakaa, an educator and an award-winning poet, penned the collection *Neon Vernacular: New and Selected Poems,* which earned him in 1994 both a Pulitzer Prize for poetry and a Kingsley Tufts Poetry Award from Claremont Graduate School. *Neon Vernacular*, like his other works of poetry, utilizes various images—some of which reflect aspects of his own life—that include images of the southern United States and its culture, of blues and jazz music, of blacks living in a white world, and of war in Southeast Asia.

Bobbie Ann Mason
A writer of novels and short stories that feature her native Kentucky and the conflicts experienced by its people between such opposites as traditionalism and modernity, Mason has seen her 1985 novel *In Country*, which depicts a teenage girl haunted by the effects of the Vietnam War on her family's life years after the war has ended, adapted to film. The writer, among whose other works are *Shiloh and Other Stories* and *Feather Crowns,* both of which are award winners, is also the author of 1999's *Clear Springs: A Memoir.*

Thomas Mofolo
Regarded as the first major author of modern African literature, Mofolo wrote, along with two other novels in his lifetime, the 1925 novel *Chaka,* which is among the most significant African works of the twentieth century and a book that is often praised as ranking among the great works of world literature. *Chaka,* which combines African verse and mythology, Christian philosophy, and Western literature, portrays the Zulu leader Chaka in what could be deemed a story of good versus evil.

Alexei Maximovich Peshkov
Peshkov, a former Russian novelist, dramatist, short story writer, essayist, autobiographer, diarist, poet, and journalist, was known to many as Maxim Gorky. Seen as one of the first advocates of socialist realism in literature, he portrayed the Russian working class sympathetically. Among the works of this author are the short story collection *Creatures that Once Were Men,* the novel *Mat',* the play *Na dne,* and the autobiography *Detstvo.*

A

**** Indicates that a listing has been compiled from secondary sources believed to be reliable, but has not been personally verified for this edition by the author sketched.***

ABBOT, Rick
See SHARKEY, John Michael

* * *

ADAMS, Barbara
See GARDNER, Virginia (Marberry)

* * *

ADAMS, Harold 1923-

PERSONAL: Born February 20, 1923, in Clark, SD; son of Lafayette Elihu (in sales) and Wilda (a homemaker; maiden name, Dickey) Adams; married Betty Skogsberg, September 10, 1949 (divorced April 17, 1965); children: Wendy. *Education:* University of Minnesota, B.A., 1950. *Avocational interests:* "My avocational interests include travel to England, Europe, Mexico, Puerto Rico, Colombia, and the Virgin Islands. I'm a compulsive letter writer, journal keeper, and a very amateur photographer."

ADDRESSES: Home—2916 Greenwood Rd., Minnetonka, MN 55343. *Agent*—Ivy Fischer Stone, Fifi Oscard Associates, Inc., 19 West 44th St., New York, NY 10036.

CAREER: The Sloan Company, St. Paul, MN, warehouse manager, 1953-57; Better Business Bureau of Minneapolis, Minneapolis, MN, assistant manager, 1957-65; Charities Review Council of Minnesota, Minneapolis, MN, executive director, 1965-88; writer, 1988—. *Military service:* U.S. Army, 1943-45; became staff sergeant.

MEMBER: National Book Critics Circle, American Crime Writer's League, Author's Guild, Minneapolis United Way Associates (secretary/treasurer, 1974-88).

AWARDS, HONORS: Private Eye Writers of America Shamus award, 1992; Minnesota Book Award, 1993.

WRITINGS:

"CARL WILCOX" SERIES

Murder, Ace Books (New York City), 1981.
Paint the Town Red, Ace Books, 1982.
The Missing Moon, Ace Books, 1983.
The Naked Liar, Mysterious Press (New York City), 1985.
The Fourth Widow, Mysterious Press, 1986.
The Barbed Wire Noose, Mysterious Press, 1987.
The Man Who Met the Train, Mysterious Press, 1988.
The Man Who Missed the Party, Mysterious Press, 1989.
The Man Who Was Taller than God, Walker (New York City), 1992.
A Perfectly Proper Murder, Walker, 1993.
A Way with Widows, Walker, 1994
The Ditched Blonde, Walker, 1995.
Hatchet Job, Walker, 1996.
The Ice Pick Artist, Walker, 1997.
No Badge, No Gun, Walker, 1998.

Contributor of short stories to *The Mysterious West,* edited by Tony Hillerman, HarperCollins, 1994, and *Murder for Father,* edited by Martin H. Greenberg, 1994.

OTHER

When Rich Men Die, Doubleday, 1987.

SIDELIGHTS: Harold Adams is known for his stylistically sharp dialogue, complex characterizations, wry humor, and evocation of the Dakotas and small-town life in the Depression era. All but one of his mystery novels star Carl Wilcox, an ex-convict who first turns to crime-solving only because he is afraid that murders committed in his town will be pinned on him. Reviewers have compared the series admiringly to the work of such masters of crime fiction as James M. Cain and Jim Thompson. Many critics have expressed delight over the Wilcox series. "Adams is as natural a writer as Wilcox is a detective," states Susan L. Clark in *Armchair Detective,* "both play fair with clues, both have authentic voices and understandings of the complexities of place and time, and both clearly like doing things right."

Wilcox comes from Corden, South Dakota, a town of approximately 1,300 people, and a number of the crimes he solves takes place there. Corden has a "superb, claustrophobic, small-town atmosphere," according to a critic for *Booklist,* and Wilcox is its black sheep, a womanizer and a drifter among hard-working, upstanding farmers. At the same time, observes William Malloy in *Twentieth-Century Crime and Mystery Writers,* Wilcox has "the personal moral code endemic to [mystery writer Raymond] Chandler's ilk—which drives him to seek justice for the oppressed and powerless, and allows the reader to side with him over his calvinistic fellow Cordenites." Wilcox makes his living as a sign painter, but in times of crisis he also pitches in as the town's lone detective and hotelier. Though crimes seem to come Wilcox's way—Chicago mobsters hide stolen loot in Corden, a ten-year high school reunion brings about foul play—his ability to get at the truth is not haphazard. Wilcox conducts himself like Philip Marlowe—even speaking in "snappy *film noir* dialogue," notes a reviewer for *Booklist*—and has "no pretensions about his skills as a Sherlock Holmes or Dupin," Adams explains in *Twentieth-Century Crime and Mystery Writers.* Adams says further of Wilcox, "He solves crimes by talking with people involved and depending on his instincts about suspects and their motivations."

Part of the success of the Wilcox series is the in-depth and colorful characterization Adams brings both to his detective and the many victims and suspects. Clark contends that Adams's work "gives a richer picture of human emotions and choices than do most contemporary mysteries." Wilcox himself is certainly a standout, "just enough of a cross between tender and tough to be believable," says a *Publishers Weekly* critic in a review of *The Ditched Blonde.* When he has to, Wilcox gets himself out of deadly situations with such original weapons as a ladder, a toilet tank cover, and a dead cornstalk. The books also abound with people like Arthur Foote, "an old smelly dog that was yours and you felt sorry for him but kind of wished he'd die so you'd be [rid] of him," or the widow of a con man who, according to a critic for *Library Journal,* is "hard as nails and fun to read about." Malloy writes that Adams "turns even characters who appear briefly into three-dimensional beings."

In the Carl Wilcox series, Adams also delivers a compelling, Depression-era atmosphere. Many critics have remarked upon the complementary relationship between Wilcox's narration, his characters' dialogue, and the bleak Dakota background. "The characters in Adams's long-running series wear the ways and views of their era with a natural, convincing grace," states a *Publishers Weekly* contributor in a piece on *The Ice Pick Artist.* The same publication's review of *The Ditched Blonde* notes that Wilcox's "deliberately barren prose manages to echo the times and the terrain with remarkable effect." Malloy praises "Adams's laconic prose style" as "perfectly suited to his prosaic Dakota landscape." Another *Publishers Weekly* critique, of *No Badge, No Gun,* calls Adams's writing "spare as a Dakota sky" and adds that it "contains more complexity and substance than most mystery writers achieve with the normal genre arsenal of noir atmospherics and anxiety-ridden psychologizing."

Some of Wilcox's realism may also come from the fact that he has a real-life archetype, Adams's own ne'er-do-well uncle. For whatever reason, Adams's books have, as Clark writes, an "almost uncanny sense of time and place." Comments Malloy, "The Adams novels may also be read with a healthy nostalgic appreciation. Adams spent his boyhood in this milieu, and the books brilliantly delineate a time before the small western and Midwestern farming communities withered away, bled by declining populations and failing businesses along Main Street. If the mysteries in the Carl Wilcox novels were not as fine as they are, Adams would still be remembered for what he remembers."

Adams told *CA:* "I became a disciplined writer when I realized in middle age that nothing else I could do gave me true satisfaction. I became a published writer out of sheer persistence and application. The key for me was getting up so early no one else would bother me until I'd put in my hour or more every day. My advice to would-be writers is, don't ever say you'll write when you have the time. If you really want to write, you make the time. When asked how I sold my first book, I replied, 'it was easy; I just wrote the book and took ten years selling it. And between times wrote more books.' Three of my first books sold were rejected at least a dozen times each before acceptance of *Murder.* I believe there are an unconscionable number of capable writers in the mystery field and it makes the competition murder. I don't resent that, however, because I enjoy reading them."

BIOGRAPHICAL/CRITICAL SOURCES:

BOOKS

Twentieth-Century Crime and Mystery Writers, 3rd edition, St. James Press (Chicago), 1991.

PERIODICALS

Armchair Detective, winter, 1988; winter, 1990; winter, 1995.
Booklist, June 1, 1985; June 15, 1986; April 15, 1987; June 1, 1987; August, 1994, p. 2025; September 1, 1995, p. 44; November 15, 1996, p. 573.
Kirkus Reviews, August 1, 1995.
Library Journal, June 1, 1985, p. 147; May 1, 1987, p. 86; September 1, 1994, p. 219; August, 1995, p. 124.
Minneapolis Star and Tribune, January 26, 1988.
Minneapolis-St. Paul Magazine, September, 1987.
New York Times Book Review, December 13, 1998, p. 28.
Publishers Weekly, August 24, 1992, p. 66; July 5, 1993, p. 65; July 18, 1994, p. 238; July 24, 1995, p. 49; October 14, 1996, p. 67; September 8, 1997, p. 61; September 7, 1998, p. 88.
Vinyl Arts, September, 1987.*

* * *

A GENTLEWOMAN
See MOORE, Doris Langley

* * *

AMBROSE, Stephen E(dward) 1936-

PERSONAL: Born January 10, 1936, in Decatur, IL; son of Stephen Hedges (a family physician) and Rosepha (Trippe) Ambrose; married Judith Dorlester, 1957 (deceased, 1966); married Moira Buckley, 1967; children: Stephanie (Tubbs), Barry Halleck, Andrew, Grace, Hugh. *Ethnicity:* "English." *Education:* University of Wisconsin, B.S., 1957, Ph.D., 1963; Louisiana State University, M.A. *Politics:* Republican. *Religion:* Protestant. *Avocational interests:* Canoes, woodworking, mountain hiking.

ADDRESSES: Home and Office—606 Hauser, Helena, MT 59601.

CAREER: Louisiana State University in New Orleans (now University of New Orleans), assistant professor, 1960-64, professor, 1971-89, Alumni Distinguished Professor of History, 1982-95, Boyd Professor of History, 1989-95, professor emeritus, 1995—; founder of the Eisenhower Center, 1983, director, 1983-95, director emeritus, 1995—; Johns Hopkins University, Baltimore, MD, associate professor, 1964-69; U.S. Naval War College, Newport, RI, Ernest J. King Professor of Maritime History, 1969-1970; Kansas State University, Manhattan, Dwight D. Eisenhower Professor of War and Peace, 1970-71. Visiting assistant professor, Louisiana State University, Baton Rouge, 1963-64; Mary Ball Washington Professor, University College, Dublin, Ireland, 1981-82; visiting professor, University of California, Berkeley, 1986; Howard Johnson Visiting Professor of Military History, Army War College, 1989; senior fellow, Rutgers Center for Historic Analysis, 1993. Founder and president, National D-Day Museum, New Orleans. *Military service:* Reserve Officer Training Corps.

MEMBER: American Committee on World War II (member, board of directors), American Historical Association, American Military Institute (member, board of directors; member, board of trustees, 1971-74), Conference on History of Second World War (member of American Committee), SANE (member, board of directors), Society for American Historians of Foreign Relations, Southern Historical Association, Lewis and Clark Heritage Trail Foundation (member, board of directors), Big Blue Athletic Association, Chi Psi.

AWARDS, HONORS: Eisenhower: Soldier, General of the Army, President-elect, 1890-1952, won the Freedom Foundation's National Book Award.

WRITINGS:

Halleck: Lincoln's Chief of Staff, Louisiana State University Press (Baton Rouge), 1962.
Upton and the Army, Louisiana State University Press, 1964.

Duty, Honor, and Country: A History of West Point, Johns Hopkins Press (Baltimore, MD), 1966.

Eisenhower and Berlin, 1945: The Decision to Halt at the Elbe, Norton (New York City), 1967.

The Supreme Commander: The War Years of General Dwight D. Eisenhower, Doubleday (New York City), 1970.

Rise to Globalism: American Foreign Policy since 1938, Penguin (New York City), 1971, eighth edition (with Douglas G. Brinkley), 1997.

General Ike: Abeline to Berlin (juvenile), Harper (New York City), 1973.

Crazy Horse and Custer: The Parallel Lives of Two American Warriors, illustrations by Kenneth Francis Dewey, Doubleday, 1975.

(With Richard H. Immerman) *Ike's Spies: Eisenhower and the Espionage Establishment,* Doubleday, 1981.

(With Immerman) *Milton S. Eisenhower: Educational Statesman,* Johns Hopkins University Press, 1983.

Eisenhower: Soldier, General of the Army, President-elect, 1890-1952 (Book of the Month Club choice; also see below), Simon & Schuster (New York City), 1983.

Eisenhower: The President (also see below), Simon & Schuster, 1984.

Pegasus Bridge: 6 June, 1944, Allen & Unwin (London, England), 1984, Simon & Schuster, 1985.

Nixon: The Education of a Politician, 1913-1962, Simon & Schuster, 1987.

Nixon: The Triumph of a Politician, 1962-1972 (Book of the Month Club alternate), Simon & Schuster, 1989.

Eisenhower: Soldier and President (condensed version of *Eisenhower: Soldier and President,* Simon & Schuster, 1990.

Nixon: The Ruin and Recovery of a Politician, 1973-1990, Simon & Schuster, 1991.

Band of Brothers: E Company, 506th Regiment, 101st Airborne, from Normandy to Hitler's Eagle's Nest, Simon & Schuster, 1992.

D-Day, June 6, 1944: The Climactic Battle of World War II, Simon & Schuster, 1994.

Undaunted Courage: Meriwether Lewis, Thomas Jefferson, and the Opening of the American West, Simon & Schuster, 1996.

Americans at War (essays), University Press of Mississippi (Jackson), 1997.

Citizen Soldiers: The U.S. Army from the Normandy Beaches to the Bulge to the Surrender of Germany, Simon & Schuster, 1997.

The Victors: Eisenhower and His Boys—The Men of World War II, Simon & Schuster, 1998.

Lewis & Clark: Voyage of Discovery, photographs by Sam Abell, National Geographic Society (Washington, DC), 1998.

Comrades, Brothers, Fathers, Heroes, Brothers, Sons, Pals, illustrated by Jon Friedman, Simon & Schuster, 1999.

EDITOR

A Wisconsin Boy in Dixie, University of Wisconsin Press (Madison), 1961.

Institutions in Modern America: Innovation in Structure and Process, Johns Hopkins Press, 1967.

(Assistant editor) Alfred Chandler, editor, *The Papers of Dwight David Eisenhower: The War Years,* five volumes, Johns Hopkins Press, 1970.

(With James A. Barber Jr.) *The Military and American Society,* Free Press (New York City), 1972.

Dwight D. Eisenhower, *The Wisdom of Dwight D. Eisenhower: Quotations from Ike's Speeches and Writings, 1939-1969,* Eisenhower Center, 1990.

(With Gunter Bischof) *Eisenhower and the German POWs: Facts against Falsehood,* Louisiana State University Press, 1992.

C. L. Sulzberger, *American Heritage New History of World War II: Revised and Updated,* Viking (New York City), 1997.

(With Douglas G. Brinkley) *Witness to America: An Illustrated Documentary History of the United States from the Revolution to Today,* HarperCollins (New York City), 1999.

OTHER

Also author of a television documentary, *Eisenhower: Supreme Commander,* British Broadcasting Corporation, 1973. Author of biweekly column, *Baltimore Evening Sun,* 1968—. Author of introduction for Ronald Lewin, *Hitler's Mistakes,* Morrow, 1987, and *Handbook on German Military Forces,* Louisiana State University Press, 1990. Contributor to *The Harry S Truman Encyclopedia,* edited by Richard S. Kirkendall, G. K. Hall (Boston), 1989, and *What If? The World's Foremost Military Historians Imagine What Might Have Been: Essays,* edited by Robert Cowley, Putnam (New York City), 1999. Authenticator, *New Standard Encyclopedia,* 1994. Contributor of reviews and articles to numerous journals and newspapers, including *American Heritage, American History Illustrated, American Historical Review, Foreign Affairs, Harvard Magazine, Historic New Orleans Collection Quarterly, Journal of Contemporary History, Times Literary Supplement, New York Times Book Review, Prologue: Quarterly of the National Archives, Quarterly Journal of Military*

History, and *U.S. News and World Report.* Contributing editor of *Quarterly Journal of Military History.* Member of board of editors of *Military Affairs.* Interviewee on television documentary *Lewis & Clark: The Journey of the Corps of Discovery,* produced by Ken Burns and Dayton Duncan, 1997. Historical consultant on feature film *Saving Private Ryan,* directed by Steven Spielberg, 1998.

Ambrose's *Duty, Honor, and Country: A History of West Point* has been translated into Spanish; *Eisenhower: The President, Eisenhower: Soldier, General of the Army, President-elect, 1890-1952,* and *Pegasus Bridge: 6 June, 1944,* have been translated into French; *Crazy Horse and Custer: The Parallel Lives of Two American Warriors* has been translated into German and Italian; *The Supreme Commander: The War Years of General Dwight D. Eisenhower* has been translated into Norwegian, Spanish and Romanian; *Eisenhower: Soldier and President* has been translated into French, German and Russian; and *Rise to Globalism: American Foreign Policy since 1938,* has been translated into Arabic, Norwegian, Romanian, Spanish, and Turkish. An abridged edition of *Ike's Spies: Eisenhower and the Espionage Establishment* was translated into French and published under the title *"Les Services Secrets d'Eisenhower."* DreamWorks TV is developing a miniseries based on *Citizen Soldiers: The U.S. Army from the Normandy Beaches to the Bulge to the Surrender of Germany.*

SIDELIGHTS: Historian and biographer Stephen E. Ambrose has written about generals, presidents, explorers, major military battles, and foreign policy in his twenty-plus books, always demonstrating an uncommon ability to bring history and historical actors to vivid life. Ambrose had already had a productive and distinguished career when events of the late 1990s brought him increased fame: *Undaunted Courage: Meriwether Lewis, Thomas Jefferson, and the Opening of the American West* became a best-seller, and Ambrose served as an historical consultant on Steven Spielberg's 1998 film *Saving Private Ryan,* which contributed to a surge of interest in his books on World War II. Ambrose, who retired in 1995 as a University of New Orleans professor, is also well known for his multi-volume biographies of Presidents Dwight D. Eisenhower and Richard M. Nixon. Ambrose labored for nearly twenty years on the Eisenhower volumes and ten years on the Nixon volumes, both times with results that critics praised for meticulous research and balance.

Ambrose grew up in Whitewater, Wisconsin. A high-school football captain and prom king, he went to the University of Wisconsin in Madison, where he decided to major in history. After receiving his B.A. in 1957, Ambrose moved on to the master's program at Louisiana State University, returning to the University of Wisconsin to receive his Ph.D. in history in 1963. During graduate school, Ambrose published a biography of General Henry Halleck, who had served as chief of staff to President Abraham Lincoln. A few years later, when Ambrose was working as an assistant professor at Louisiana State University, he received a phone call from an admirer of the book. The caller was former President Dwight D. Eisenhower.

"I was flabbergasted," Ambrose told *New York Times Book Review* contributor Herbert Mitgang. President Eisenhower told Ambrose that he liked the author's book, had thought about writing a work on Halleck himself, and wondered if the historian would come to his Gettysburg, Pennsylvania, home to talk; he also asked Ambrose if he would be interested in working on the Eisenhower papers. Ambrose recalled: "I told him, Born January 18, 1935, in New York, NY, 'General, I'd prefer to write your biography.' He replied, 'I'd like to have you any way I can.' " So began Ambrose's long association with the life and reputation of President Eisenhower, an association that allowed him to produce a multi-volume set of edited papers, a biography of Milton Eisenhower (the president's brother), two books on Eisenhower's military career (*Eisenhower and Berlin, 1945: The Decision to Halt at the Elbe* and *The Supreme Commander: Eisenhower*), an analysis of Eisenhower's relationship with the espionage community, and the two-volume biography.

In the introduction to *Eisenhower: Soldier, General of the Army, President-elect, 1890-1952,* Ambrose describes Eisenhower as "decisive, well disciplined, courageous, dedicated . . . intensely curious about people and places, often refreshingly naive, fun-loving—in short a wonderful man to know or be around." Despite his clear liking for the former president, most reviewers found that Ambrose developed an even-handed portrait of the man who is widely perceived to have been, in the words of *Time* reviewer Donald Morrison, both a "canny leader who brilliantly outmaneuvered subordinates and statesman," and a "mediocre President . . . slow of wit and out of touch with the currents of upheaval swirling beneath the calm surface of the 1950s." In reconciling these two views, Ambrose "has provided the most complete and objective work yet on the general who became President," wrote Drew Middleton in the *New York Times Book Review. New Yorker* contributor Naomi Bliven said that the biography "offers the beguiling mixture of nostalgia and illumination we find in old newsreels, along with an abundance of themes for reflection."

Reviewers praised Ambrose's reassessment of a president who had been reviled as a bumbling, inefficient leader, a President who, in the words of Chicago's *Tribune Books* reviewer Richard Rhodes, "golfed too much, knew little and did nothing." Ambrose acknowledges such public perception, wrote Henry Brandon in the *Washington Post Book World,* but his biography portrays Eisenhower as "a man in charge if not always in control, a born leader and a deft pilot who knows how to weather storms." In volume two, *Eisenhower: The President,* Ambrose highlights the fact that "Ike," as he was affectionately known, kept his country out of war for eight turbulent years, stood up to a burgeoning military-industrial complex, and managed to maintain domestic economic prosperity.

Though most reviewers praised Ambrose for his equanimity, some thought that he failed to advance a compelling interpretation of the voluminous data he compiled. *Los Angeles Times Book Review* contributor Kenneth Reich complained that the book was too restrained. "It seems sad," he wrote, "when someone has obviously put in so much effort yet fails to go beyond even-handedness. . . . [This] biography of Eisenhower emerges as a dull parade of data." Ivan R. Dee, writing in the Chicago's *Tribune Books,* said that the problem was that "a reader can arrive at opposite judgments about Eisenhower's performance based upon the evidence Ambrose presents," pointing to Eisenhower's handling of civil rights, the U-2 spying incident, and Middle Eastern politics as examples of failed leadership which Ambrose does not acknowledge.

After nearly twenty years of writing about one of the most loved American presidents, Ambrose turned his attention to a man he said had once been "the most hated and feared man in America," President Richard M. Nixon. A number of writers had penned psychological portraits of Nixon that attempted to account for his seeming cruelty, his terrific drive to succeed, and his failure to admit fault for the Watergate controversy and his subsequent resignation in the face of impeachment proceedings. But by 1987, no one had written a carefully researched scholarly biography on the most controversial president of the twentieth century. With *Nixon: The Education of a Politician, 1913-1962,* the first of three volumes, Ambrose wrote that kind of biography. *Washington Post Book World* reviewer Richard Harwood echoed the praise of many critics in noting Ambrose's ability to "examine with a surgeon's neutrality all the cliches and stereotypical assumptions about the character of this strange and fascinating man." Political analyst Sidney Blumenthal wrote in the *New Republic* that "Ambrose has written the standard, a middle point of reference, around which all Nixonia may be organized."

In three volumes, Ambrose follows Nixon from his humble beginnings in Yorba Linda, California, to his academic success at Duke University, to his bitter 1950 Senate campaign, to his troubled tenure as Eisenhower's vice president, and finally to his rise to and fall from the presidency of the United States. Along the way, Ambrose debunks many of the myths about Nixon, picturing Nixon's childhood as happy, not sad, showing that Nixon's opponents initiated the mud-slinging for which he became known, and demonstrating that the political dirty work Nixon performed while vice president to Eisenhower was done at the president's insistence. The final volume, *Nixon: Ruin and Recovery,* follows the resuscitation of the former president's reputation throughout the 1980s. *Spectator* reviewer Anthony Howard wrote that Ambrose "has crowned the edifice of his impressive trilogy with an admirably fair-minded last volume covering easily the most controversial aspect of what was already a singularly resilient political career." Throughout the three volumes, Ambrose does not excuse Nixon for the excesses that characterized his political career nor does he attempt to provide a explanation of what motivated Nixon to behave as he did; instead, he shows what happened and lets the reader decide.

Ambrose's reluctance to offer insights into Nixon's motivations frustrated some reviewers. *New York Times* reviewer Christopher Lehmann-Haupt complained that "there is something passive about the way Mr. Ambrose tells Mr. Nixon's story. He seems always confined by context, praising his subject for this, condemning him for that. He lacks the lift of a driving thesis." Ronald Steel, writing in the *New York Times Book Review,* echoed this appraisal, suggesting that Ambrose "is better at providing information than at delving into the dark recesses of character." And Gary Wills, whose own *Nixon Agonistes* attempted to probe the dark recesses of Nixon's character, thought that Ambrose's concern for the facts made him overlook an essential undercurrent in Nixon's life.

Edward Z. Friedenberg saw Ambrose's hesitancy to pass judgment on Nixon in a slightly different light. Writing in the Toronto *Globe and Mail,* he claimed that "Ambrose seems largely content to explain the hostility Nixon aroused in terms of his personality," but contended that "Nixon's enemies hated not merely the man but his (and his country's) policies." Thus Ambrose's equanimity led him to excuse the most sinister elements of Nixon's presidency: his policy toward Vietnam, and his willingness to do whatever it took to win. R. W. Apple Jr. wrote in the *New York Times Book Review,* however, that "it is Mr. Ambrose's achievement to immerse himself in Mr. Nixon's life and keep his cool. . . . The result is a portrait that is all its subject is not: evenhanded and thoroughly reliable." Ambrose himself told *New York Times Book Review* contributor Alex Ward, "I make no claim to finding the key to the man—he's so complicated that it would take Shakespeare to do him justice."

Ambrose turned to less controversial material with his 1992 *Band of Brothers,* a history of the military exploits of Company E, 506th Parachute Infantry Regiment, 101st Airborne Division during their numerous engagements in World War II. Ambrose based his book on the stories he collected from the surviving members of the company as part of his work for the Eisenhower Center at the University of New Orleans. The soldiers told Ambrose of their predawn drop behind enemy lines on D-Day and of their eventual capture of German leader Adolf Hitler's beloved retreat, "Eagle Nest." The result, wrote *New York Times Book Review* contributor and combat veteran Harry G. Summers Jr., is "a harrowing story," that captures "the true essence of a combat rifle company." *Times Literary Supplement* reviewer M. R. D. Foot asserted that the book "is full of insights into the nature of comradeship, as well as brutally frank description: noise, stench, discomfort, hunger and fear are all there, tied together in a masterly narrative flow."

Ambrose continued with World War II subject matter in *D-Day, June 6, 1944: The Climactic Battle of World War II.* Ambrose drew on soldiers' oral histories on file at the Eisenhower Center and accounts from other eyewitnesses to tell the story of the landing of Allied troops to face the German army along the coast of France's Normandy region. He deals with the strategies and personalities of the commanders, Eisenhower and German Field Marshal Erwin Rommel, but the stories of ordinary soldiers form the heart of the book. "The descriptions of individual ordeals on the bloody beach of Omaha make this book outstanding," enthused Raleigh Trevelyan in the *New York Times Book Review.* Trevelyan noted that Ambrose cited Cornelius Ryan's 1959 work, *The Longest Day,* as an inspiration for his book. "Like that account, *D-Day, June 6, 1944,* is mostly about people, but goes even further in evoking the horror, the endurance, the daring and, indeed, the human failings at Omaha Beach and other places among the Calvados coastline," Trevelyan observed. *New Leader* contributor William L. O'Neill found it "unlikely" that any other historian "will produce a book like *D-Day, June 6, 1944,* with its wealth of detail, absorbing vignettes, and rich anecdotal material." Ambrose, he added, "brings to his new work the narrative drive, thorough research and muscular prose he is justly famous for." In the *National Forum,* Leah Rawls Atkins pronounced the book "the definitive account of America's landing on the French coast," adding "*D-Day* is not a quick read, but it is a satisfying one. The bloody tales of carnage are thankfully relieved by Ambrose's selection of humorous anecdotes and perceptive quotations that linger in the reader's mind."

Undaunted Courage brought Ambrose additional accolades. Ambrose had been long fascinated by Meriwether Lewis and William Clark's exploratory journey to from St. Louis to the Pacific Ocean. He had read the pair's journals in 1975, and since then he had visited numerous sites along Lewis and Clark's trail. He had wanted to write about the expedition for years and decided to do so after becoming convinced there was sufficient fresh material available to warrant a new biography of Lewis (he found out another well-regarded historian was planning a book on Clark). *Undaunted Courage,* therefore, is a comprehensive study of Lewis as well as his 1804-1806 trek with Clark and their party to the Pacific and back through an expanse of land the United States had just acquired from France in the Louisiana Purchase. President Thomas Jefferson hoped the land would contain an all-water route to the Pacific; Lewis and Clark found that no such route existed, but they did bring back a plethora of information about the new territory. The expedition turned out to be the pinnacle of Lewis's life; he subsequently was a failure as governor of the Louisiana territory, and he suffered from alcohol abuse and depression. He killed himself at age 35 in 1809. (Ambrose finds no evidence that Lewis's death was not a suicide but, as some have suggested, a murder.)

"A remarkably balanced historian, Ambrose is neither a revisionist nor an apologist," remarked Malcolm Jones Jr. in his *Newsweek* review of *Undaunted Courage.* For instance, Jones noted, Ambrose shows that Lewis was not always honest with the Indians the party encountered but still maintained a degree of respect for them. "Here and elsewhere, Ambrose weighs shortcomings against positive attributes and ultimately presents us with a convincing hero," the critic averred. In the *New York Times Book Review,* Alvin M. Josephy Jr. reported that Lewis emerges "as an outstanding explorer and hero, fair, energetic, beloved by his men and greatly self-disciplined, but also occasionally impetuous and arrogant, and possessed of a flaring temper that could get him into trouble." *Yale Review* contributor Howard Lamar likewise praised Ambrose's portrait of Lewis: "Ambrose with good reason not only rescues Meriwether Lewis from two centuries of obscurity but presents him as a fascinating, complex, strong, contradictory individual. What Ambrose has done is to make Lewis a real person, a hero who was at once a frontiersman and near poet." What's more, Lamar related, Ambrose "portrays Thomas Jefferson as a more shrewd, highly political, and tough figure than we usually encounter in American texts. For Ambrose, Jefferson was a practical political standing midway between the opposite categories of dreamer and schemer." In *Wild West,* Dale Walker lauded Ambrose's analysis of Lewis's relationship with Jefferson, his mentor; this "has never been explored so deeply," Walker asserted. Walker also complimented Ambrose's "meticulous reconstruction" of Lewis and Clark's journey, saying, "all the joys and miseries of that greatest exploration in our history come to life in the author's measured prose." Lamar summed up the book by declaring that the well-known story of the expedition "is so well told by Ambrose that it seems a fresh, new saga. *Undaunted Courage* may well remain the most effectively narrated American adventure story to appear in this decade."

Ambrose's association with Lewis and Clark continued as he contributed text to a photography book covering the pair's route and appeared in Ken Burns's documentary film about the expedition. He also returned, though, to the subject of World War II, with *Citizen Soldiers: The U.S. Army from the Normandy Beaches to the Bulge to the Surrender of Germany* and *The Victors: Eisenhower and His Boys—The Men of World War II. Citizen Soldiers* chronicles the final eleven months of the war in Europe through interviews with the men who served on the front lines—and who had often been neglected by historians who focused on their leaders. "Almost no one except the surviving participants has any comprehension of the vicious, unrelenting, blood-stained conflict that continued through every day and every night of the 11 months from D-Day to the German surrender on V-E Day," observed Charles W. Bailery in a *Washington Monthly* review of the book. "*Citizen Soldiers* fills that gap. In the process, Ambrose has produced not only an authoritative history but a powerful and painful anti-war testament as well." Carlo D'Este, writing in the *New York Times Book Review,* thought that "in Ambrose's capable hands, the bloody and dramatic battles fought in northwest Europe in 1944-45 come alive as never before." Among other things, D'Este noted, Ambrose details how not only bullets and grenades but also frostbite and disease were dangerous enemies of ordinary soldiers, and he decries the military's racial segregation and—in some aspects—its inefficiency. Added Malcolm Jones Jr. in *Newsweek:* "Without ever questioning the necessity of fighting, Ambrose provides one of the best looks yet at the dark side of the 'good' war." D'Este concluded, " 'Citizen Soldiers' is an unforgettable testament to the World War II generation."

In *The Victors,* Ambrose draws on his previous World War II books to produce a portrait of the U.S. Army from Eisenhower's appointment to lead the forces in Europe through the end of the war. Because of this, "Ambrose fans will have a distinct sense of deja vu," remarked Nathaniel Tripp in the *New York Times Book Review.* "Still, there is a lot to be said for having it all under one cover, for combining Ambrose's compelling portrait of Eisenhower's leadership with the vivid experiences of the infantrymen, and following the campaign from conception to conclusion." This has a downside as well, Tripp contended, as "in the compression of thousands of pages from his earlier books into just under 400 here, many illuminating and insightful details have been lost and jingoism comes to the fore." *National Review* contributor Josiah Bunting III, however, felt that Ambrose had done exactly what he set out to do: to demonstrate "that the essential goodness of a moral, democratic society makes of its citizens military defenders who will triumph over enemies whose soldiers are the product of totalitarian, racist, and authoritarian regimes. Ambrose accomplishes this with great power."

BIOGRAPHICAL/CRITICAL SOURCES:

PERIODICALS

Chicago Tribune, March 24, 1985.
Commonweal, April 24, 1998, p. 13.
Fortune, August 8, 1994, p. 108.
Globe and Mail (Toronto), March 16, 1985; July 25, 1987; November 4, 1989.
London Review of Books, July 4, 1985, pp. 5-6.
Los Angeles Times, February 13, 1981.
Los Angeles Times Book Review, November 4, 1984; June 21, 1987, p. 12; October 15, 1989; November 24, 1991, pp. 4, 11.
Maclean's, June 6, 1994, p. 56.
Nation, February 28, 1972.
National Forum, fall, 1994, p. 45.
National Review, December 21, 1998, p. 60.
New Leader, March 5, 1990, pp. 16-17; June 6, 1994, p. 12.
New Orleans Magazine, December, 1998, p. 56.

New Republic, July 6, 1987, pp. 30-34.
Newsweek, April 27, 1987; February 19, 1996, p. 70; August 26, 1996, p. 46; November 17, 1997, p. 89.
New Yorker, July 1, 1985, pp. 95-97.
New York Review of Books, May 6, 1971.
New York Times, April 23, 1987; November 9, 1989.
New York Times Book Review, October 4, 1970, p. 5; September 19, 1983; December 9, 1984, pp. 1, 46-47; April 28, 1985; April 26, 1987; November 12, 1989, pp. 1, 65-66; November 24, 1991, pp. 3, 25; September 6, 1992, p. 11; May 29, 1994, p. 1; March 10, 1996, p. 9; December 21, 1997, p. 10; November 22, 1998, p. 14.
People Weekly, July 1, 1996, p. 101; November 3, 1997, p. 17; January 19, 1998, p. 34.
Publishers Weekly, January 22, 1996, p. 50.
Spectator, July 4, 1987, pp. 32-33; February 1, 1992, p. 32.
Time, October 3, 1983, pp. 79-80; May 4, 1987, p. 101; November 6, 1989, pp. 100-102; November 24, 1997, p. 108.
Times Literary Supplement, June 1, 1967, p. 486; November 5, 1971, p. 1398; February 8, 1985, p. 135; December 25, 1987, p. 1424; August 21, 1992, p. 20.
Tribune Books (Chicago), October 16, 1983; October 7, 1984, pp. 1, 24; April 12, 1987, p. 3; July 19, 1992, p. 6.
Washington Monthly, December, 1997, p. 49.
Washington Post Book World, September 11, 1983, pp. 1, 4; September 30, 1984; May 3, 1987; November 12, 1989, pp. 1, 13; November 10, 1991, p. 5.
Wild West, December, 1966, p. 74.
Yale Review, October, 1997, p. 146.*

* * *

ATKINS, Jack
See HARRIS, Mark

B

BARON, J. W.
See KRAUZER, Steven M(ark)

* * *

BENJAMIN, David
See SLAVITT, David R(ytman)

* * *

BEVIS, James
See CUMBERLAND, Marten

* * *

BLAKE, Sally
See SAUNDERS, Jean

* * *

BONNER, Terry Nelson
See KRAUZER, Steven M(ark)

* * *

BROCKWAY, (Archibald) Fenner 1888-1988

PERSONAL: Born November 1, 1888, in Calcutta, India; died April 28 (one source says April 29), 1988, in Hertfordshire, England; son of William George (a missionary) and Frances Elizabeth (Abbey) Brockway; married Lilla Harvey-Smith, 1914; married second wife, Edith Violet King, January, 1946; children: (first marriage) Audrey (Mrs. James Wood), Joan (Mrs. Sam Pover), Olive; (second marriage) Christopher. *Education:* Attended School for the Sons of Missionaries (now Eltham College). *Politics:* Socialist. *Religion:* Universalist.

CAREER: Writer or editor in Manchester and London, England, on staffs of *Examiner, Christian Commonwealth, Labour Leader,* 1907-17; Labour member of Parliament for East Leyton, 1929-31, for Eton and Slough, 1950-88. Independent Labour Party, organizing secretary, 1922, general secretary, 1928, 1933-39, chairman, 1931-33, political secretary, 1939-46, resigned, 1946, and returned to Labour Party. Sentenced to three terms in prison under Military Service Act, 1916-17. Joint secretary, British Committee of Indian National Congress, 1919; chairman, No More War Movement and War Resister's International, 1923-28; executive member, Labour and Socialist International, 1926-31; chairman, British Center for Colonial Freedom, 1942-47; member, International Committee of Socialist Movement for United Europe, 1947-52; first chairman, Congress of Peoples against Imperialism, 1948-88; chairman, Movement for Colonial Freedom, 1954-88; chairman, British Asian and Overseas Socialist Fellowship, 1959-88; vice chairman, Campaign for Nuclear Disarmament, 1964-88; executive member, Anti-Apartheid Movement, 1964-88; chairman, British Council for Peace in Vietnam, 1965.

AWARDS, HONORS: Order of Republic of Tunisia; honorary chief, Kikuyu Tribe, Kenya.

WRITINGS:

Labour and Liberalism, National Labour Press, 1913.

The Devil's Business (one-act comedy), National Labour Press, 1915, new edition, Independent Labour Party Publication Department, 1926.

Is Britain Blameless?, with a letter by G. Bernard Shaw, National Labour Press, 1915.

Socialism for Pacifists, National Labour Press, 1917.

The Recruit (one-act play), National Labour Press, 1919.

Non-Cooperation in Other Lands, Tagore & Co., 1921.

(With Stephen Hobhouse) *English Prisons Today: Being the Report of the Prison System Enquiry Committee,* Macmillan, 1922.

A Week in India—and Three Months in an Indian Hospital, New Leader, 1928.

A New Way with Crime, Williams & Norgate, 1928.

The Indian Crisis, Gollancz, 1930.

Hungry England, Gollancz, 1932.

(With Harry Pollitt) *Which Way for Workers?,* Communist Party of Great Britain, 1932.

The Bloody Traffic, Gollancz, 1933.

Will Roosevelt Succeed?: A Study of Fascist Tendencies in America, G. Routledge & Sons, 1934.

Purple Plague: A Tale of Love and Revolution (novel), Low, 1935.

Workers' Front, Secker & Warburg, 1938.

Pacifism and the Left Wing, Pacifist Publicity Unit, 1938.

Inside the Left: Thirty Years of Platform, Press, Prison and Parliament, Allen & Unwin, 1942, post-war edition, 1947.

(With Frederic Mullally) *Death Pays a Dividend,* Gollancz, 1944.

German Diary, Gollancz, 1946.

Socialism over Sixty Years: The Life of Jowett of Bradford, 1864-1944, Allen & Unwin, 1946.

Bermondsey Story: The Life of Alfred Salter, Allen & Unwin, 1949.

Why Mau Mau?, Movement for Colonial Freedom, 1953.

African Journeys (autobiographical), Gollancz, 1955.

1960: Africa's Year of Destiny—A Political Guide to a Continent in Crisis, Movement for Colonial Freedom, 1960.

Red Liner: A Novel in TV Form, Lawrence & Wishart, 1962.

Outside the Right (autobiography), with a lost play by G. Bernard Shaw, Allen & Unwin, 1963.

African Socialism, Dufour, 1963.

(With H. Fennell) *Immigration: What Is the Answer?,* Routledge & Kegan Paul, 1965.

(With Wendy Campbell-Purdie) *Woman against the Desert,* Gollancz, 1967.

This Shrinking Explosive World: A Study of Race Relations, Epworth, 1967.

(Contributor) *The International Trade in Armaments Prior to World War II* (includes *The Bloody Traffic*), introduction by Richard Dean Burns, Garland (New York City), 1972.

The Colonial Revolution, Hart-Davis, MacGibbon (London), 1973.

Towards Tomorrow: The Autobiography of Fenner Brockway, Hart-Davis, MacGibbon, 1977.

Britain's First Socialists: The Levellers, Agitators, and Diggers of the English Revolution, Quartet Books (London), 1980.

98 Not Out, Quartet Books, 1986.

PAMPHLETS

India and Its Government, Labour Publishing Co., 1921.

How to End War: The I.L.P. View on Imperialism and Internationalism, Independent Labour Party, 1925.

Make the Workers Free!: The Industrial Policy of the I.L.P., International Labour Party Publication Department, 1925.

Socialism—with Speed!: An Outline of the I.L.P. "Socialism in Our Time" Proposals, International Labour Party Publication Department, 1928.

(With E.R.A. Seligman and Scott Nearing) *Resolved: That Capitalism Offers More to the Workers of the World than Socialism or Communism,* Rand Book Store, 1930.

The I.L.P. and the Crisis, International Labour Party Publication Department, 1931.

A Socialist Plan for Unemployment, International Labour Party Publication Department, 1931.

Hands off the Railmen's Wages!, International Labour Party Publication Department, 1931.

The Coming Revolution, Independent Labour Party, 1932.

Socialism at the Cross-Roads: Why the I.L.P. Left the Labour Party, Independent Labour Party, 1932.

(With others) *Socialism Can Defeat Nazism,* Independent Labour Party, 1940.

The Way Out, Independent Labour Party, 1942.

The C.O. and the Community, Fellowship of Conscientious Objectors, 1943.

Empire in Crisis: A Survey of Conditions in the British Colonies Today, Peace News, 1953.

(With Richard Acland) *Waging Peace,* Peace News, 1954.

British Protectorates—Key to South African Freedom, Union of Democratic Control, 1957.

Author of weekly article on colonial affairs published in ten countries. Editor, *India,* 1919, *New Leader,* 1926-29, 1931-46.

SIDELIGHTS: A politician, activist, and author, Fenner Brockway fought all his life for the causes of socialism, peace, Indian and African independence, and nuclear disarmament. First elected to the British Parliament's House of Commons in 1929 as a member of the Labour party, Brockway was active in establishing links with Socialist groups in other countries. He also helped found the Campaign for Nuclear Disarmament, taking part in many protest marches. Though he advocated the abolition of the House of Lords because it represented to him a last bastion of special privilege, Brockway was created a life peer by Queen Elizabeth II in 1964, and thus gained a seat in the House of Lords. He wrote novels and plays as well as political works, including *Labour and Liberalism, English Prisons Today: Being the Report of the Prison System Enquiry Committee, Purple Plague: A Tale of Love and Revolution, Pacifism and the Left Wing,* an autobiography titled *Towards Tomorrow,* and *98 Not Out.*

BIOGRAPHICAL/CRITICAL SOURCES:

BOOKS

Brockway, Fenner, *Towards Tomorrow: The Autobiography of Fenner Brockway,* Hart-Davis, 1977.
Brockway, Fenner, *98 Not Out,* Quartet Books, 1986.
Macnair, John, *Beloved Rebel,* Allen & Unwin, 1955.

OBITUARIES:

BOOKS

The Writers Directory: 1988-1990, St. James Press, 1988.

PERIODICALS

Globe and Mail (Toronto), April 30, 1988.
Los Angeles Times, April 30, 1988.
New York Times, May 1, 1988.
Times (London), April 30, 1988.
Washington Post, April 30, 1988.*

BROKAW, Thomas John 1940-
(Tom Brokaw)

PERSONAL: Known professionally as Tom Brokaw; born February 6, 1940, in Webster, SD; son of Anthony Orville (a construction worker) and Eugenia (a clerk; maiden name, Conley) Brokaw; married Meredith Lynn Auld (a proprietor and developer of toy store chain), August 17, 1962; children: Jenifer Jean, Andrea Brooks, Sarah Auld. *Education:* University of South Dakota, B.A., 1962. *Avocational interests:* Jogging, backpacking, mountain climbing, skiing, tennis, jazz.

ADDRESSES: *Home*—New York, NY. *Office*—National Broadcasting Co., 30 Rockefeller Plaza, New York, NY 10022.

CAREER: KTIV, Sioux City, Iowa, newscaster, weatherman, and staff announcer, 1960-62; KMTV, Omaha, NE, morning news editor, 1962-65; WSB-TV, Atlanta, GA, news editor and anchor, 1965-66; KNBC-TV, Los Angeles, CA, reporter and anchor, 1966-73, National Broadcasting Co. (NBC-TV), White House correspondent and anchor of Saturday evening news, 1973-76, co-host of *Today* show, 1976-81, co-anchor, then sole anchor, of *NBC Nightly News,* 1982—. Lecturer in television news at Yale University, New Haven, CT, 1978-79. Member of board of trustees of Norton Simon Museum of Art, Pasadena, CA.

MEMBER: American Federation of Television and Radio Artists (director, 1968-72), Reporters Committee for Freedom of the Press (member of board of advisers), Sierra Club, Sigma Delta Chi.

AWARDS, HONORS: Golden Mike Award from Radio and Television News Association of Southern California; L.H.D. and alumni achievement award, both from University of South Dakota; honorary doctoral degrees from Syracuse University and Washington University, St. Louis.

WRITINGS:

UNDER NAME TOM BROKAW

The Greatest Generation Random House (New York City), 1998.

Contributor of articles to newspapers and magazines, including *New York Times, New York Daily News, Los Angeles Times, Diversions, Backpacker,* and *Family Weekly.* Author of introductions to various volumes, including *NBC News/Rand McNally World Atlas and Almanac.*

SIDELIGHTS: In 1984, Tom Brokaw, anchor of the *NBC Nightly News,* visited France's Normandy region to prepare a documentary on the fortieth anniversary of the D-Day landings of Allied troops there. That trip and a return visit in 1994, for the fiftieth anniversary of D-Day, inspired Brokaw's first book, *The Greatest Generation,* in which he pays tribute to the Americans who saw their country through the Great Depression and World War II, and laid the groundwork for the nation's postwar prosperity. This generation, he writes in the book, is "the greatest generation any society has ever produced."

When *The Greatest Generation* was published in 1998, Brokaw had already had a long and successful career in broadcast journalism. In July, 1981, Brokaw, then forty-one, signed a contract with the National Broadcasting Co. (NBC) that promised to make him the youngest person ever to anchor a nightly network news program. For Brokaw, then host of NBC's *Today* show, the decision marked the end of a dramatic and highly publicized courtship in which each of the three major television networks attempted to convince him to sign on as anchor of their respective evening news programs. "At one point I would have bet the family farm he would go to CBS, then I was sure it was ABC," commented Jane Pauley, Brokaw's *Today* show co-host, when negotiations were finally complete. "Last week it seemed clear he wasn't packing his bags, but this week he was so mysterious and dark I thought ABC had offered him the crown, robe and scepter," she told *People.* "In a way it was the most emotional thing I have done since I decided to get married," Brokaw informed *Time* after renewing his contract with NBC.

Plans for the revamped *NBC Nightly News* stipulated that Brokaw would report the news from New York City, while Roger Mudd, whose former title was "chief Washington correspondent," would remain in Washington, D.C., and be billed as Brokaw's co-anchor. John Chancellor, former sole anchor of the news program, would do occasional commentaries and special projects. Brokaw and Mudd, who assumed their new duties in April of 1982, were hailed by some as the Huntley-Brinkley of the 1980s, causing John J. O'Connor of the *New York Times* to observe: "Clearly, Mr. Brokaw and Mr. Mudd are accomplished television journalists. Will they become the Huntley and Brinkley of the 1980's? They would be better off concentrating on becoming the Mudd and Brokaw of this decade." Within a year, NBC executives decided the two-anchor arrangement was not working, and they removed Mudd as co-anchor in 1983. Brokaw, since then sole anchor, has scored coups including an exclusive interview with Soviet leader Mikhail Gorbachev in 1987, and has reported such major stories as the fall of the Berlin Wall in 1989 and the bombing at the Olympic games in Atlanta in 1996. He has also endured ratings fluctuations, occasional criticism of his style, and a threatened libel suit by a man who was too quickly named as a suspect in the Atlanta bombing (and who eventually was cleared), but he has emerged with a great deal of popularity and respect. In 1999 *People Weekly* described him as "one of the most trusted faces in TV journalism" and "the unflappable anchorman" who "has spent the last 16 years taking the nation coolly through controversy, triumph and tragedy."

Brokaw's unfaltering ascent in broadcast journalism began in 1960, when he was hired by KTIV, a Sioux City, Iowa, television station. Two years later (after receiving a degree in political science from the University of South Dakota) Brokaw began working for KMTV in Omaha, Nebraska. In 1965 he moved to Atlanta, Georgia, where he served for a year as news editor and anchorman for WSB-TV. Brokaw was in Atlanta during a time when, as writer Lyn Tornabene put it, "the South was a civil-rights war zone covered by only a few network correspondents. Events were exploding faster than the Eastern press could get to them, and NBC needed help from its local affiliates. Where the battle was thickest, they got Brokaw." "It was so dangerous, a lot of people [reporters] kept coming back," Brokaw recalled. "Our man said, 'Get me the hell out, they're shooting people. I don't want any part of it.' I said, 'Well, I'll go.' I went down and worked around-the-clock with a single cameraman," he told *Rolling Stone.* That national exposure served Brokaw well—it brought him to the attention of network officials—and by 1966 he was in Los Angeles working as an anchorman for KNBC-TV.

In Los Angeles, he found himself again in the center of historic events. There were racial riots in Watts, student protests at the University of California, Berkeley, a growing antiwar movement, and, in 1968, the assassination of Robert Kennedy. Brokaw "reported incessantly," noted Thompson, "even though his anchor responsibilities did not demand it." During that time, Brokaw reflected, "I lived in the vortex. . . . California was an important story. I was the first television reporter I know of who went to Haight-Ashbury. I stumbled on it in my coat and tie, my trench coat, and I was about the same age as many of the kids who were there. I couldn't believe it. I did a number of stories and felt I was caught between two tides. I was *fascinated* by the Haight. There was a kind of daring about these kids that I didn't have in my soul. . . . I was so ambitious and so intent, I couldn't quite identify with the freedom of their behavior and their absolute lack of discipline about where they wanted to go within the establishment. I was trying to fight my way up through it, and they were oblivious to it."

In 1972, while covering the national political conventions, Brokaw met John Chancellor, who reportedly told him that it was time for him to "grow up and leave that cushy job in California." A few months later, Brokaw accepted NBC's offer to serve as their White House correspondent. "Once again, his timing was perfect," marveled Thompson. "It was the summer of Watergate, and the Nixon White House was the world's biggest story." Brokaw encountered some resistence from the established White House press corps, who viewed "this kid from L.A." with skepticism; but he soon managed to impress them. Eventually, reported Tony Schwartz in the *New York Times,* Brokaw was "widely credited with finally making NBC competitive with CBS News and Dan Rather on the Watergate story."

In 1974 NBC offered Brokaw a job as co-host of their *Today* show. Brokaw declined the offer, partially because he didn't want to do commercials, but also because he didn't want to leave Washington in the middle of Watergate. Two years later, when NBC extended the invitation again (this time without the stipulation that Brokaw do commercials) Brokaw accepted. However, the adjustment from Washington correspondent to *Today* show co-host was not an easy one for him to make. "I came right off the White House beat covering the resignation of the president of the United States, going with Gerald Ford to Vladivostok and China, and the next thing I knew I was talking to Dr. Art Ulene about fingernails," he explained to Thompson. "I was a dreadful *Today* correspondent for a time."

Brokaw joined *Today* at a time when the show's long-held ratings lead was being seriously challenged by *Good Morning America,* ABC's early-morning counterpart. Over the course of Brokaw's tenure with *Today,* NBC made a number of changes in the program's cast and format in attempts to boost ratings. While the competition between the two programs remained fierce, television critics continued to pronounce *Today* the superior program, citing, for instance, Brokaw's authoritative delivery of news and his journalistic expertise. He "exudes equal probity and stalwartness whether he's telling us about the Iran-Iraq war or the problems of battered husbands," asserted Francine du Plessix Gray in a *Vogue* article about the early-morning programs and their various hosts. Observers have also commented on Brokaw's seemingly unending supply of energy. One example of this was chronicled by Thompson, who wrote: "On the day [Anwar] Sadat was shot, Brokaw did his usual two hours of *Today,* had approximately an hour off-camera, then did six hours of commentary with John Chancellor before flying directly to Cairo. There, he labored as NBC's chief correspondent for five days prior to Sadat's funeral, which he covered. On Sunday he flew back to New York, and on Monday morning he was back on *Today.*"

In 1981, a few months before Brokaw's *Today* show contract was due to expire, speculation on what he would do next began to rage. "I think he could do anything," ABC news division president Roone Arledge was quoted as saying in the *New York Times.* "He's proved that he's a good anchor on 'Today,' he did a fine job on Election night, and he's an excellent reporter." Discussing the pros and cons of anchoring an evening news program, Brokaw told the *New York Times:* "It's certainly the most visible job, perhaps the most glamorous in the public mind, and in most instances the most financially rewarding. But it's not necessarily the most professionally fulfilling. You're often tied to a studio as an anchor, and you can't get your hands on that much material, which is what I really like to do." However, he continued, "It's a position that brings with it power and influence, and that can prove to be pretty tempting."

Brokaw finally put an end to speculation by announcing his decision to remain with NBC, and in April, 1982, made his debut, with Mudd, as co-anchor of the *NBC Nightly News.* In addition to his on-the-air duties, Brokaw spends a substantial portion of each day tracking down news stories, "using every connection and wile to nail them down." He also helps decide which stories will be aired on any given night, and, according to Thompson, "Brokaw throws considerable weight in the making of that decision." Indeed, these off-camera aspects of his new position seemed to dispel many of Brokaw's initial reservations about the job. Perhaps for this reason critics like Tony Schwartz of the *New York Times* felt that "for Mr. Brokaw, who has thrived since his childhood in South Dakota on 'Showing people how the world works,' the anchor job—with its attendant power, prestige and visibility—represents the ideal forum."

The Greatest Generation gave him a different type of forum. Brokaw interviewed nearly fifty people, both famous and obscure, about their experiences in the war and their contributions to the postwar United States. His famous interviewees include former President George Bush, columnist Art Buchwald, ex-U.S. Senator Bob Dole, and former *Washington Post* editor Ben Bradlee. His lesser-known subjects include Gertrude "Trudy" Elion, who was able to get work in a science laboratory only after male scientists had gone to war and went on to develop anti-cancer drugs and win a Nobel Prize in Medicine. "The stories are the book," observed David Brudnoy in the *National Review*. "The book is about more than the combat abroad; it's about the home front, too, about those, like Tom Brokaw's own father, who did duty stateside, men and women whose mundane tasks facilitated the war effort."

Brokaw deals with not only what was admirable about this generation but also some of the injustices of the time, such as the treatment of blacks, Latinos, and Japanese-Americans. When discussing these problems, though, Brokaw emphasizes what members of the World War II generation did to fight bigotry—not how some of their number practiced it. This tendency to accentuate the positive brought some negative comments from reviewers. "Why give credit for civil rights legislation and Medicare to an entire cohort, rather than to the liberals who backed these reforms—particularly when the reforms were opposed by conservative veterans of World War II?" asked Michael Lind in the *New York Times Book Review*. Lind also complained that Brokaw embraces "the myth that World War II was uncontroversial," when in fact many Americans, at least before the Japanese attack on Pearl Harbor, opposed U.S. entry into the conflict. An *Economist* critic derided the book's "flat style, sugared with small-town sentimentality" and its lack of attention to what the United States's allies did to help win the war. But the critic added, "For all that, the quiet courage and plain decency of many of the people Mr. Brokaw describes make up for these limitations."

Other reviewers, too, found the book's flaws balanced by its virtues. According to Brudnoy, even with "a certain amount of revisionist pontificating" and "a tendency now and then to moralize Brokaw nonetheless succeeds in demonstrating (if not totally proving) his point about the generation's superb qualities." And Lind remarked, "Brokaw succeeds in his goal of memorializing the experiences of representative Americans in the deadliest war in history. In 'The Greatest Generation,' he has compiled a moving scrapbook as a tribute to the members of the World War II generation to whom we Americans and the world owe so much."

BIOGRAPHICAL/CRITICAL SOURCES:

PERIODICALS

Christian Science Monitor, September 3, 1976; April 2, 1982.
Cosmopolitan, August, 1982.
Economist, April 10, 1999, p. 5.
National Review, February 8, 1999, p. 53.
New Republic, April 23, 1984, p. 20.
Newsweek, September 1, 1980; March 9, 1981; April 12, 1982.
New York Times, September 10, 1980; January 25, 1981; May 23, 1981; July 14, 1981; December 19, 1981; January 22, 1982; April 7, 1982.
New York Times Book Review, December 27, 1998.
People Weekly, July 13, 1981; August 5, 1983, p. 58; April 28, 1986, p. 95; February 1, 1988, p. 62; January 18, 1999.
Rolling Stone, May 13, 1982.
Time, December 1, 1980; July 13, 1981; September 28, 1981; August 8, 1983, p. 56; December 14, 1987, p. 68; February 17, 1997, p. 76.
Vogue, December, 1980.*

* * *

BROKAW, Tom
See BROKAW, Thomas John

* * *

BRYANT, Margaret M. 1900-1993

PERSONAL: Born December 3, 1900, in Trenton, SC; died June 14, 1993, in Clemson, SC; daughter of John Lee and Harriet (Yonce) Bryant. *Education:* Winthrop College, A.B., 1921; Columbia University, A.M., 1925, Ph.D., 1931; summer student at University of Virginia, 1922, University of Michigan, 1939, University of Wisconsin, 1943, 1944, and Indiana University, 1946. *Politics:* Democrat. *Avocational interests:* Theatre, travel.

CAREER: Held teaching and administrative positions at various elementary and secondary schools in South Carolina, Kansas, West Virginia, and New York, 1921-25; Chowan College, Murfreesboro, NC, head of English department, 1925-26; Hunter College (now Hunter College of the City University of New York), New York City, member of faculty, 1926-33; City University of New York, Brooklyn College, Brooklyn, NY, 1930-71, began as instructor, became professor of English, acting chairman of department, 1940-41, chairman, 1941-44, Graduate School and University Center, New York City, 1938-71, began as assistant professor, became professor. Visiting professor, University of Vermont, summer, 1947, University of Arkansas, summer, 1948, New School for Social Research, fall, 1948, University of Utah, summer, 1949, University of Colorado, summer, 1950, University of Uppsala, Handelshoegskola, and University of Stockholm, 1950-51, Columbia University, 1952-53, 1955-56, and Rutgers University, summer, 1962; distinguished professor, Winthrop College, summer, 1973. Member, English Graduate Union (Columbia University). Trustee, Virginia Gildersleeve International Fund for University Women.

MEMBER: International Linguistic Association (vice president, 1969-72; president, 1972-73; member of executive council, 1973-76; member of advisory council, 1976-93), International Federation of University Women, International Folk Music Council, International Society for General Semantics, International Association of University Professors of English, Modern Humanities Research Association (member of American committee, 1960-65), Philological Society of England, National Folk Festival Association, American Society of Geolinguistics (member of executive council, 1975-93; president, 1979-80), Linguistic Society of America, National Council of Teachers of English (member of board of directors, 1946-60; chairman of current English usage committee, 1947-60; member of executive committee, 1948-50; chairman of college section, 1948-50), American Association of University Professors, College English Association, English Institute, American Association of University Women (New York City branch; vice president, 1951-55; president, 1955-59; member of board of directors, 1960-93), Modern Language Association of America, American Dialect Society (chairman of committee on proverbial sayings, 1944-93; member of executive council, 1952-54), American Folklore Society (member of council, 1946-60), American Name Society (vice president, 1955-57; president, 1958-59, 1974-75; first vice president, 1973-74), College Council of English of the Central Atlantic States (president, 1942-44; member of executive committee, 1944-46), New York Folklore Society (vice president, 1949-52), New York Council of Teachers of English (vice president, 1943-44; president, 1944-45; member of executive committee, 1946-53), New York College English Association (member of executive committee, 1952-56), Medieval Club of New York (president, 1973-75), Phi Beta Kappan Graduates in New York (vice president, 1971-74; president, 1974-76), Phi Kappa Phi.

AWARDS, HONORS: American Council of Learned Societies grant, 1939; gold medal from Columbia University, 1941, for distinguished service in alumni association of graduate schools; Society of General Semantics scholarship, 1945; honorary fellow, American-Scandinavian Foundation, 1950-51; Mary Mildred Sullivan Award from Winthrop College, 1956; American Association of University Women, Founder's Day citation, 1962, Eightieth Anniversary citation, 1966, Woman of Achievement award (from New York City branch), 1969; D.Litt., Cedar Crest College, 1966; L.H.D., Winthrop College, 1968; D.H., Francis Marion College, 1979; D.Litt., Northern Michigan University, 1979.

WRITINGS:

English in the Law Courts, Columbia University Press, 1930, 2nd edition, Ungar, 1962.

(With J. R. Aiken) *Psychology of English,* Columbia University Press, 1940, 2nd edition, Ungar, 1962.

(Compiler with R. H. Barker and C. T. Ernst) *Prose Pieces,* Crofts, 1941.

A Functional English Grammar, Heath, 1945, 2nd edition, 1959.

Proverbs and How to Collect Them, American Dialect Society, 1945.

Modern English and Its Heritage, Macmillan, 1948, 2nd edition, 1962.

(With M. L. Howe, P. R. Jenkins, and Helen Munn) *English at Work,* Scribner, 1953.

(Editor) *Current American Usage,* Funk, 1962.

(Author of introduction) Richard H. Thornton, *An American Glossary,* three volumes, 2nd edition, Ungar, 1962.

(Contributor) Gary Tate, editor, *Reflections on High School English,* University of Tulsa, 1966.

Modern English Syntax, Seibido (Tokyo), 1976.

(Contributor) E. P. Sewell and B. M. Rogers, editors, *Confronting Crisis,* UTA Press, 1979.

(With K. Sonoda) *The Development of General and English Linguistics Studies in Japan,* New York University, 1981.

A Story of Achievement, edited by Katsuaki Horiuchi and Koji Sonada, Kenkyusha (Tokyo), 1990.

Also author of *A Dictionary of American Proverbs.* Contributor to *Encyclopedia Americana* and *Encyclopedia International.* Contributor of more than one hundred articles and reviews to scholarly journals, including *American Speech, College English, New York Folk-*

lore Quarterly, American Poet, Names, Teachers College Journal, Quarterly Journal of Speech, and *Study of Current English.* Member of advisory board, *American Speech,* 1943-44, 1960-61, 1977-79, *College English,* 1947-50, and *Standard College Dictionary* and *World Book Encyclopedia Dictionary,* 1963; member of general advisory committee, Thorndike-Barnhart dictionaries, 1950-93; member of editorial board, *Names* (journal of American Name Society), 1952-55, 1959-65; member of editorial advisory board, Funk and Wagnalls dictionaries, 1956-63.

SIDELIGHTS: Margaret M. Bryant, who taught English at several institutions throughout the 1920s, spent the majority of her career at Brooklyn College (now Brooklyn College of the City University of New York), where she started as an instructor in 1930. The linguist, educator, and author eventually rose to the positions of professor and head of the English department. Her numerous publications include *English in the Law Courts, A Functional English Grammar, Modern English and Its Heritage, The Development of General and English Linguistics Studies in Japan,* which she co-authored, and *A Dictionary of American Proverbs.* Bryant was editor of books such as *Current American Usage* and was also a member of the editorial advisory boards of the *World Book Encyclopedia* and Thorndike-Barnhart and Funk & Wagnalls dictionaries. Throughout her academic career she held leadership positions in various professional societies.

BIOGRAPHICAL/CRITICAL SOURCES:

BOOKS

Bryant, Margaret M., *A Story of Achievement,* edited by Katsuaki Horiuchi and Koji Sonada, Kenkyusha, 1990.

OBITUARIES:

PERIODICALS

New York Times, June 18, 1993, section D, p. 16.*

C

CANDY, Edward
See NEVILLE, B(arbara) Alison (Boodson)

* * *

CARLISE, Carris
See PEMBERTON, Margaret

* * *

CHESTOR, Rui
See COURTIER, S(idney) H(obson)

* * *

CHLAMYDA, Jehudil
See PESHKOV, Alexei Maximovich

* * *

CHRISTIAN, Frederick H.
See NOLAN, Frederick William

* * *

CLARESON, Thomas D(ean) 1926-1993

PERSONAL: Born August 26, 1926, in Austin, MN; died July 6, 1993, in Wooster, OH; son of Thomas Albert and Ruth (Dalager) Clareson; married Alice Super, December 23, 1954; children: Thomas Frederic Reade. *Education:* University of Minnesota, B.A., 1946; Indiana University, M.A., 1949; University of Pennsylvania, Ph.D., 1956. *Religion:* Presbyterian. *Avocational interests:* Travel, basketball, photography, cinema, and the magazines and films of the 1930s and 1940s.

CAREER: Fiction House, Inc., New York, NY, staff writer, 1946; New Mexico College of Agriculture and Mechanic Arts (now New Mexico State University), Las Cruces, instructor in English, 1949-50; H. L. Yoh Co., Philadelphia, PA, technical writer and editor, intermittently, 1950-54; University of Maryland Overseas Program, Northeast Air Command, instructor in English and speech, 1953; Norwich University, Northfield, VT, instructor in English, 1954-55; College of Wooster, Wooster, OH, 1955-93, began as instructor, professor of English, 1967-93, chairperson of department, 1984-86. Chairman of first Modern Language Association of America Conference on Science Fiction, 1958, and of various other annual conferences, 1964-84.

MEMBER: American Studies Association, Modern Language Association of America (member of executive committee of section of popular culture, 1976-80; member of delegate assembly, 1982-84), Science Fiction Research Association (first president, 1970-76), Science Fiction Writers of America, Popular Culture Association, College English Association (member of executive committee, 1969-71; vice president, 1974-75; president of Ohio chapter, 1975-76).

AWARDS, HONORS: Danforth Foundation grants, summers, 1959 and 1961; American Philosophical Society grants, 1960, 1964, and 1966-67; National Endowment for the Humanities grant, 1976; Pilgrim Award, Science Fiction Research Association, 1977; Martha Kinney Cooper Ohioana Library Association Citation, 1985, for "his study of science fiction literature, editorship of *Extrapolation: A Journal of Science Fiction and Fantasy,* and his publications."

WRITINGS:

(Editor) *Science and Society: Midcentury Readings,* Harper, 1961.
(Editor with Warren D. Anderson) *Victorian Essays,* Kent State University Press, 1967.
Science Fiction: The Other Side of Realism, Bowling Green University, 1971.
Science Fiction Criticism: An Annotated Checklist, Kent State University Press, 1972.
(Editor) *A Spectrum of Worlds,* Doubleday, 1972.
(General editor) "Science Fiction Periodicals" series (microfilm), Greenwood Press, 1975, second series published as "Science Fiction Periodicals: 1926-1978," 1978.
(Editor) *Voices for the Future: Essays on Major Science Fiction Writers,* Bowling Green University, Volume 1, 1976, Volume 2, 1979, Volume 3 (with Thomas L. Wymer), 1984.
(Editor) *Many Futures, Many Worlds: Theme and Form in Science Fiction,* Kent State University Press, 1977.
Robert Silverberg: A Primary and Secondary Bibliography, G. K. Hall, 1983.
Robert Silverberg, Starmont House, 1983.
Science Fiction in America, 1870s-1930s: An Annotated Bibliography of Primary Sources, Greenwood Press, 1984.
Some Kind of Paradise: The Emergence of American Science Fiction, Greenwood Press, 1985.
(General editor) "Early Science Fiction Novels" series (microfiche), Greenwood Press, 1985.
Frederik Pohl, Starmont House, 1987.
Understanding Contemporary American Science Fiction: The Formative Periodical (1926-1970), South Carolina University Press, 1990.
(Author of introduction) James Gunn, *The Listeners,* Easton Press, 1991.

Contributor of chapters to numerous books, including *Anatomy of Wonder: Science Fiction,* edited by Neil Barron, Bowker, 1976, 3rd edition, 1987; *Teaching Science Fiction: Education for Tomorrow,* edited by Jack Williamson, Owlswick Press, 1980; *Science Fiction, Fantasy, and Weird Fiction Magazines,* edited by Marshall B. Tymn and Mike Ashley, Greenwood Press, 1986; and *Science Fiction Roots and Branches: Contemporary Critical Approaches,* edited by Rhys Garnett and E. J. Ellis, Macmillan, 1990. Also contributor to *Academic American Encyclopedia,* Grolier, 1985. Editor, *Extrapolation: A Journal of Science Fiction and Fantasy,* 1959-90; member of editorial board, *Victorian Poetry,* 1967-84, and *Journal of Popular Culture,* 1971-93.

SIDELIGHTS: Also an editor and author, Thomas D. Clareson taught English at the College of Wooster for thirty-eight years before retiring in 1993. His main area of research was science fiction, which he believed had a legacy reaching back into American literature for hundreds of years. The author and editor of numerous books on science fiction, Clareson attempted to establish the genre as a literary form equal in importance to the realistic novel. Clareson's 1984 publication, *Science Fiction in America, 1870s-1930s: An Annotated Bibliography of Primary Sources,* was described by Marvine Howe in the *New York Times* as "a standard reference in the field." He also wrote *Science Fiction: The Other Side of Realism* and *Some Kind of Paradise: The Emergence of American Science Fiction,* and edited a number of books including the three-volume work *Voices for the Future: Essays on Major Science Fiction Writers.* In 1959 Clareson founded the scholarly science fiction journal *Extrapolation,* which he edited for more than thirty years, and during the 1970s he served as the first president of the Science Fiction Research Association.

Clareson told *CA:* "A main part of my efforts as a writer and editor has been to show that science fiction belongs to a literary tradition going back to the seventeenth and eighteenth centuries, and that it deserves wider academic attention than it has received in the past. The basic problem results from the general neglect of popular fiction, perhaps especially in the first half of the twentieth century. Too often, literary critics have seemed to divorce the reading audience from the general, continuing body of fiction by creating and imposing an artificial canon of acceptable writers. Melville was ignored by contemporary critics, while for a time Faulkner's novels were allowed to go out of print. More recently, it has been Hemingway's turn to be pushed aside by many critics.

"Not only do critical opinions change," Clareson adds, "but sometimes it seems as though critics are afraid of living writers. Past neglect of popular fiction, as well as the magazines and publishing houses which issued much of it, has caused the loss of data invaluable to the literary and social historian.

"The myths which shape the public imagination derive from popular fiction, whether from the printed page, or cinema and TV. As a form of literary expression, science fiction opens up thematically some of the most important problems we face as a society or as individuals, and it affords the writer an escape from the too-often confining (and time-worn) patterns of literary realism. We have been storytellers throughout history, and I believe that science fiction tells us more about the potentials and limitations of being human than does any other contemporary literary form."

OBITUARIES:

PERIODICALS

New York Times, July 9, 1993, p. D18.*

* * *

CLEVE, John
See HALDEMAN, Jack C(arroll) II

* * *

CONKLE, E(llsworth) P(routy) 1899-1994

PERSONAL: Born July 10, 1899, in Peru, NE; died from a lung infection, February 18, 1994, in Austin, TX; son of Elza Green and Mary Estella (Prouty) Conkle; married Virginia Carroll McNeal; children: Ellsworth Prouty Conkle II, Alice Elena Conkle Cogdell. *Education:* University of Nebraska, A.B., 1921, A.M., 1923, additional study, 1931-32; Yale University, graduate study, 1926-28; University of Iowa, Ph.D., 1936.

CAREER: High school principal in Comstock, NE, 1921-22; University of North Dakota, Grand Forks, instructor in English, 1923-26; University of Delaware, Newark, assistant professor of English, 1928-30; University of Iowa, Iowa City, assistant professor of speech, 1936-39; University of Texas, Austin, associate professor, 1939-45, professor of drama, 1945-73, professor emeritus, 1973. Guest professor of playwriting, University of Alberta, beginning 1945.

MEMBER: Sigma Tau Delta, Purple Mask (University of Iowa).

AWARDS, HONORS: Guggenheim fellowship, 1930; Rockefeller fellowships, 1935-36 and 1945; University of Texas graduate school research grant, 1966; D.Litt. from University of Nebraska, 1970.

WRITINGS:

PLAYS; ALL PUBLISHED BY SAMUEL FRENCH, EXCEPT AS NOTED

Crick Bottom Plays: Five Mid-Western Sketches (includes one-act plays: *Minnie Field,* produced in New Haven, CT, at Yale University, 1928; *Things Is That-a-Way,* produced at Yale University, 1930; *Sparkin; Warter-Wucks;* and *Lection*), 1928.

The Owl and the Two Young People: A One-Act Play for Two Boys, 1934.

Loolie and Other Short Plays (includes one-act plays: *P'taters in the Spring,* produced in Iowa City, IA, at University of Iowa, 1933; *Little Granny Graver,* produced at University of Iowa, 1936; *Loolie; The Owl and the Young Men; Lace;* and *Madge*), 1935.

The Juber-Bird: A Small Play for Small Boys, 1936.

In the Shadow of a Rock: A Drama in Three Acts (produced at University of Iowa, 1933), 1937.

Two Hundred Were Chosen: A Play in Three Acts (produced in New York at 48th Street Theatre, 1937), 1937.

Prologue to Glory: A Play in Eight Scenes Based on the New Salem Years of Abraham Lincoln (produced at Maxine Elliott Theatre, 1938), 1938.

We'd Be Happy Otherwise (one-act), Dramatists Play Service, 1939.

Five Plays (includes *Paul and the Blue Ox,* produced at University of Iowa, 1939; *Johnny Appleseed,* produced in Austin, TX, at University of Texas, 1940; *Bill and the Widow Maker,* produced at University of Texas, 1942; *The Delectable Judge,* produced in Washington at Arena Theatre, 1951; and *Forty-Nine Dogs in the Meathouse*), 1947.

A China-handled Knife: A One-Act Play about Abe Lincoln, 1949.

Son-of-a-Biscuit Eater: Comedy in One Act, 1958.

Granny's Little Cheery Room: A Comedy in One Act, 1960.

Kitten in the Elm Tree: A Comedy in One Act, 1962.

Lots of Old People Are Really Good for Something: A Comedy in One Act, 1964.

The Jewel in Papa's Crown: A Play in One Act, I. E. Clark (Schlenburg, TX), 1990.

UNPUBLISHED PLAYS

"Oxygenerator," produced at Pasadena Playhouse, 1931.

"The Mayor of Sherm Center," produced at University of Iowa, 1932.

"The Lovings," produced at University of Iowa, 1933.

"The 'Nitiated," produced at University of Iowa, 1933.

"Gold Is Where You Don't Find It," produced at University of Texas, 1939.
"What D'You Call It?," produced at Provincetown Playhouse, 1940.
"They Die for Peace," produced at University of Texas for Office of Civilian Defense, 1943.
"Afternoon Storm," produced at Maxine Elliott Theatre, 1948.
"Don't Lose Your Head," produced in London at Saville Theatre, 1950.
"No More Wars but the Moon," produced at University of Texas, 1956.
"No Time for Heaven," produced at University of Texas, 1961.
"Quest for an Answer," produced at University of Texas, 1963.
"Way down in the Paw-Paw Patch," produced in Arlington, NJ, by Producing Actors' Co., 1963.

OTHER

(Contributor) John Gassner, editor, *Twenty-five Best Plays of the Modern American Theatre: Early Series,* Crown, 1949.
(Contributor) Margaret Mayorga, editor, *Best Short Plays of 1958-1959,* Beacon Press, 1959.
(Contributor) Irwin J. Zachar, editor, *Plays as Experience: One-Act Plays for the Secondary School,* Odyssey, 1962.

Author of radio drama series *Honest Abe,* fifty two episodes, Columbia Broadcasting System (CBS), 1942. Co-author, with Ray Middleton, of television drama *Day's End,* National Broadcasting Co. (NBC-TV), 1952. Also author of play, *Fraeulein Klauber,* privately printed, and of other unpublished plays, *Th' Young Feller from Omaha, Chief Sittum Bull, Chickadee, If You Can't Eat Fish without Tenderloin, Papa Never Done Nothing . . . Much, Incident at Eureka Bumps, Muletail Prime, The Least One, Arbie, the Bug Boy, Poor Old Bongo, A Bauble for the Baby, The Reticent One, Heaven Is Such a Long Time to Wait, Lavender Gloves,* and *Day's End.* Contributor of articles, essays, and short stories to periodicals, including *English Journal, Players Magazine,* and *Theatre Arts.*

ADAPTATIONS: Conkle's play, *Prologue to Glory,* was adapted for television.

SIDELIGHTS: E. P. Conkle was a prolific dramatist whose works were published and produced extensively in the 1930s and 1940s. Also an educator, Conkle began his career as a high school principal in 1921, switching to work as a teacher of English at the University of North Dakota and later at the University of Delaware. He taught speech at the University of Iowa for three years before embarking upon thirty-four years in the department of theater and dance at the University of Texas in Austin. A successful dramatist, he had several plays produced on Broadway, including *Prologue to Glory: A Play in Eight Scenes Based on the New Salem Years of Abraham Lincoln* in 1938. Before his retirement in 1973, Conkle wrote dozens of plays, such as *A China-Handled Knife, Son-of-a-Biscuit Eater,* and *Kitten in the Elm Tree.* He also wrote radio and television dramas.

OBITUARIES:

PERIODICALS

New York Times, February 23, 1994, p. A16.*

* * *

COPLAND, Aaron 1900-1990

PERSONAL: Born November 14, 1900, in Brooklyn, NY; died of respiratory failure, December 2, 1990, in North Tarrytown, NY; son of Harris Morris and Sarah (Mittenthal) Copland. *Education:* Studied piano under Leopold Wolfson, Victor Wittgenstein, Clarence Adler, and (briefly) Ricardo Vines; studied composition with Rubin Goldmark, 1917-21, with Nadia Boulanger at Fontainbleau School of Music, 1921, and in Paris, 1921-24.

CAREER: Composer of music for orchestra, ballet, stage, films, chamber music, and voice, 1920-90; pianist. Lecturer on contemporary music at New School for Social Research, 1927-37; teacher of composition, and Charles Eliot Norton Professor of Poetry at Harvard University, 1951-52; chairman of faculty and head of composition, Berkshire Music Center; public lecturer throughout the United States. Organizer with Roger Sessions, of Copland-Sessions Concerts, 1928-31; founder of American Festival of Contemporary Music at Yaddo, 1932. Piano soloist with New York Philharmonic, Boston Symphony, and Los Angeles Philharmonic; conductor of own works with other orchestras in United States, Europe, Mexico, and South America; pianist and conductor on government-sponsored tours of Latin American countries, 1941, 1947. Vice president, Koussevitsky Music Foundation; president of Edward MacDowell Association; director of Walter W. Naumburg Music Foundation, American Music Center.

MEMBER: National Institute of Arts and Letters, American Academy of Arts and Letters, American Society of Composers, Authors and Publishers, League of Composers (director), International Society for Contemporary Music (director); Royal Academy of Music, Royal Society of Arts (both London), Accademia Nazionale di Santa Cecilia (Rome).

AWARDS, HONORS: Guggenheim Foundation, first composer to receive fellowship, 1925, renewed, 1926; RCA Victor Co., $5,000 award for *Dance Symphony,* 1930; Pulitzer Prize in music and New York Music Critics Circle Award for *Appalachian Spring,* 1945; New York Music Critics Circle Award for *Third Symphony,* 1946; Oscar, Academy of Motion Picture Arts and Sciences, for musical score for *The Heiress,* 1950; American Academy of Arts and Letters Gold Medal for Music, 1956; Edward MacDowell Medal, 1961; Presidential Medal of Freedom, 1964; Kennedy Center Award, 1979, for lifetime contributions to culture and the performing arts. Honorary degrees included Mus. D., Princeton University, 1956, Oberlin College, 1958, Illinois, Wesleyan University, 1958, Temple University, 1959, University of Hartford, 1959; H.H.D., Brandeis University, 1957, Harvard University, 1961, Syracuse University of Rhode Island, 1964.

WRITINGS:

What to Listen for in Music, McGraw, 1939, revised edition, 1957.
Our New Music, McGraw, 1941, revised edition, Norton, 1968.
Music and Imagination, Harvard University Press, 1952.
Copland on Music, Doubleday, 1960.
(With Vivian Perlis) *Copland: 1900 through 1942,* St. Martin's (New York City), 1987.
(With Perlis) *Copland: Since 1943,* St. Martin's, 1989.

MUSIC; ALL PUBLISHED BY BOOSEY AND HAWKS

Cortege Macabre, 1923.
Symphony for Organ and Orchestra, 1924.
Music for the Theatre, 1925.
Dance Symphony, 1925.
Piano Concerto, 1926.
First Symphony, 1928.
Symphonic Ode, 1929.
Short Symphony, 1933.
Statements, 1934.
El Salon Mexico, 1936.
Music for Radio, 1937.
Outdoor Overture, 1938.
Billy the Kid (ballet), 1938.
Our Town (film), 1940.
John Henry, 1940.
Quiet City (play), 1940.
Music for the Movies (film scores), 1942.
Lincoln Portrait, 1942.
Rodeo (ballet), 1942.
Danzon Cubano, 1942.
Fanfare for the Common Man, 1942.
Appalachian Spring (ballet), 1944.
Third Symphony, 1946.
The Red Pony (film), 1948.
Preamble for a Solemn Occasion, 1949.
The Tender Land (opera), 1954.
Inscape, 1968.
Canticle of Freedom, 1968.
Prelude, from First Symphony, 1968.
Ceremonial Fanfare: For Brass Ensemble, 1974.
Three Latin-American Sketches, 1975.
Threnodies: I and II, for Flute/Alto Flute and String Trio, 1977.
Midsummer Nocturne: Piano Solo, 1978.
Duo: For Violin and Piano, 1979.
Pastorale, High Voice and Piano, 1979.
Quatre Motets pour un Choeur Mixte . . . Capelle, 1979.
Three Moods: For Piano Solo, 1981.
Piano Album, edited by Leo Smit, 1981.

Published works also include music for string orchestra, chamber music, band music, choral music, various instrumental and vocal compositions, mainly published by Boosey and Hawkes.

SIDELIGHTS: Deemed one of the most influential composers of the twentieth century, Aaron Copland was also a conductor, lecturer, and author. Copland helped popularize classical music in the United States with his pieces for orchestra, ballet, stage, films, and voice. Copland's music possessed a distinctly American accent as a result of his combinations of unique sounds and influences, including cowboy tunes, folk songs, and hymns. With works such as *Billy the Kid, Rodeo, El Salon Mexico, Lincoln Portrait,* and *Fanfare for the Common Man,* Copland won popular appeal and received critical acclaim. His honors included a Pulitzer Prize in 1944 for his ballet score of *Appalachian Spring,* an Academy Award in 1950 for the musical score of the film *The Heiress,* the Presidential Medal of Freedom in 1964, and a Kennedy Center Award in 1979 for his lifetime contributions to culture and the performing arts. Throughout his career, Copland also organized concerts for emerging artists, promoted new music, and served as a mentor for many composers at the onset of their careers. Although he virtually stopped composing after 1970, Copland continued to conduct, lecture, and write books; his titles include *What to Listen for in Music, Our New Music, Music and Imagination,* and *Copland on Music.* He also collaborated with Vivian Perlis on two volumes of his autobiography, *Copland: 1900 through 1942,* and *Copland: Since 1943.*

BIOGRAPHICAL/CRITICAL SOURCES:

BOOKS

Berger, Arthur, *Aaron Copland,* Oxford University Press, 1953.
Copland, Aaron, and Vivian Perlis, *Copland: 1900 through 1942,* St. Martin's, 1987.
Copland and Perlis, *Copland: Since 1943,* St. Martin's, 1989.
Smith, Julia, *Aaron Copland: His Work and Contribution to American Music,* Dutton, 1955.
Vasiliu, Mircea, *Aaron Copland, His Life,* Holt, Rinehart & Winston (New York City), 1969.

OBITUARIES:

BOOKS

Celebrity Register, 5th edition, Gale, 1990.

PERIODICALS

New York Times, December 3, 1990.
Times (London), December 4, 1990.*

* * *

COULSON, Juanita (Ruth) 1933-
(John Jay Wells, a pseudonym)

PERSONAL: Surname is pronounced "*Col*-son"; born February 12, 1933, in Anderson, IN; daughter of Grant Elmer (a tool and die maker) and Ruth Margaret (Oemler) Wellons; married Robert Stratton Coulson (a writer), August 21, 1954; children: one boy, Bruce Edward. *Education:* Ball State University, B.S., 1954, M.A., 1961. *Politics:* Independent. *Religion:* Unitarian Universalist.

CAREER: Writer. Art editor and publisher of *Yandro* (science fiction magazine), 1953—. Elementary school teacher, 1954-55; collator, Heckman's Bookbindery, North Manchester, IN, 1955-57; publisher, *SFWA Forum,* two years; freelance writer, 1963—.

MEMBER: Science Fiction Writers of America.

AWARDS, HONORS: Joint nominee with husband, Robert S. Coulson, for Hugo Award, World Science Fiction Convention, 1960-64, 1966-67, for best amateur science fiction magazine, *Yandro,* and joint winner with R. S. Coulson, Hugo Award, 1965, for *Yandro;* Ralph Holland Memorial Award, Fan Art Show, twentieth World Science Fiction Convention, 1962; co-Fan Guest of Honor, with R. S. Coulson, thirtieth World Science Fiction Convention, 1972.

WRITINGS:

SCIENCE FICTION

Crisis on Cheiron, Ace Books (New York City), 1967.
The Singing Stones, Ace Books, 1968.
The Secret of Seven Oaks, Berkley Publishing (New York City), 1972.
Door into Terror, Berkley Publishing, 1972.
Stone of Blood, Ballantine (New York City), 1975.
Unto the Last Generation, Laser Books (New York City), 1975.
Space Trap, Laser Books, 1976.
Fear Stalks the Bayou, Ballantine, 1976.
Dark Priestess, Ballantine, 1977.
The Web of Wizardry, Del Rey Books (New York City), 1978.
Fire of the Andes, Ballantine, 1979.
The Death God's Citadel, Del Rey Books, 1980.
Star Sister, Del Rey Books, 1990.

"CHILDREN OF THE STARS" SERIES; PUBLISHED BY DEL REY BOOKS

Tomorrow's Heritage, 1981.
Outward Bound, 1982.
Legacy of Earth, 1989.
The Past of Forever, 1989.

OTHER

Also author of *Intersection Point,* 1976. Contributor to books, including *The Comic-Book Book,* edited by Richard A. Lupoff and Don Thompson, Arlington House (New York City), 1973; *Star Trek: The New Voyages,* edited by Sandra Marshak and Myrna Culbreath, Bantam (New York City), 1976; and *Goldmann Fantasy Foliant III,* edited by Peter Wilfert, Wilhelm Goldmann Verlag, 1985. Contributor to anthologies, including *Tales of Witch World IV,* edited by Andre Norton, and *Women at War,* Tor, 1996. Also contributor to periodicals, sometimes under pseudonym John Jay Wells, including *Fantasy and Science Fiction.* Art editor and publisher of Science Fiction Writers of America's *Forum* magazine, 1971-72.

Many of Coulson's books have been translated into German.

SIDELIGHTS: "I have been writing fiction since before I could write," Juanita Coulson told *Twentieth-Century Science-Fiction Writers.* Coulson explained that her mother encouraged the young storyteller by transcribing her tales for her. By the time Coulson was eight, she was using her own typewriter. Despite her early start, Coulson did not seek publication until she was in her thirties, when she wrote the story "Another Rib" in collaboration with science-fiction author Marion Zimmer Bradley. Since then she has written more than a dozen novels of various genres, including women's literature, historic romance, fantasy, and science fiction.

Coulson and her husband Robert also edit their own publication, *Yandro,* which is referred to by science-fiction enthusiasts as a "fanzine"—an amateur science-fiction magazine published by those interested in the genre—and is one of the longest-running large fanzines in the world.

Coulson explained to *CA,* "In recent years, our amateur magazine *Yandro* has virtually ceased publication, due to increasing pressure of freelance writing. Originally, *Yandro* served as our forum, and that of our fellow science-fiction and fantasy enthusiasts. Now we have acquired broader outlets—not to say considerably more profitable ones. My husband's interest in reviewing has been transferred to several professional periodicals, and I have been able to concentrate my creative focus on the writing of novels."

Coulson's first two novels, *Crisis on Cheiron* and *The Singing Stones,* deal with alien planets struggling under economic or political exploitation. "In both novels," wrote R. E. Briney in *Twentieth-Century Science-Fiction Writers,* "the alien environment is well thought out and convincingly portrayed." Briney added that the "scientific underpinnings" reflect Marion Zimmer Bradley's influence on Coulson's work.

Coulson said, "Prior to the eighties, my work lay in the fields of women's genre, action/adventure-oriented Science Fiction and fantasy. When I was commissioned to write the *Children of the Stars* series for Del Rey Books, I was forced into a very different mode. [This series follows several generations of the Saunder family, focusing especially on three siblings who take differing stands on Earth's extraterrestrial expansion.] Following the dictum of 'stick to what you know—or can extrapolate from what you know,' I had never attempted even the fringes of so-called 'hard science' fiction. My degrees are in the 'soft sciences,' not astrophysics and computer technology, etc. However, I was able to pick the brains of a number of highly trained friends employed in those fields. The results apparently are satisfactory; numerous readers, also qualified in high-tech industries, have complimented me not only on the characters and stories I have created but on the technological 'scenery' in the backgrounds of those books. It has certainly been the most challenging task of my writing career—to date. Now I would like to make the swing back to the quite different genre of fantasy adventure."

Two of Coulson's fantasy-adventure short stories, "Wizard of Death" and "The Dragon of Tor-Nali," and two novels, *The Web of Wizardry* and *The Death God's Citadel,* all share the same fantasy-world setting. Briney describes this setting as one "in which sorcery and the presence of supernatural beings are facts of everyday existence. The backgrounds (geographical, cultural, and linguistic) are worked out in detail." Speaking of her two specialties, Coulson said, "Style and background requirements vary enormously in the science-fiction and fantasy specialties, but the basics of solid characterizations and a narrative the reader can become involved in are constants. In that regard, I've found that storytelling in novel form really is the same; and I hope it continues to be indefinitely, for *my* enjoyment as well as the reader's."

BIOGRAPHICAL/CRITICAL SOURCES:

BOOKS

Watson, Noelle, and Paul E. Schellinger, editors, *Twentieth-Century Science-Fiction Writers,* third edition, St. James Press (Chicago), 1991.

PERIODICALS

Locus, May, 1989, p. 46; November, 1989, p. 54; April, 1990, pp. 25, 35.
Science Fiction Chronicle, April, 1990, p. 34.
Science Fiction Review, November, 1981.*

COULSON, Robert 1924-

PERSONAL: Born July 24, 1924, in New Rochelle, NY; son of Robert Earl (a lawyer) and Abby (Stewart) Coulson; married Cynthia Cunningham, October 15, 1960; children: Cotton Richard, Dierdre, Crocker, Robert Cromwell, Christopher. *Education:* Yale University, B.A., 1949; Harvard University, LL.B., 1953.

ADDRESSES: Home—9 Reginald St., Riverside, CT. *Office*—American Arbitration Association, 140 West 51st St., New York, NY 10020.

CAREER: Admitted to the State Bars of New York and Massachusetts, 1954; Whitman, Ransom, & Coulson (law firm), New York City, associate, 1955-61; Littlefield, Miller, & Cleaves (law firm), New York City, partner, 1961-63; American Arbitration Association, New York City, executive vice president, 1963-71, president, 1991-94 (retired in 1994). Youth Consultation Service of New York, president, 1970; Federation of Protestant Welfare Agencies, president, 1982-84, chairman, 1985-87, member of board of directors. Member of boards of directors of International Council for Commercial Arbitration and Fund for Modern Courts. New York State Division of Youth, consultant, 1961-63.

MEMBER: American Bar Association, American Society of Association Executives (chief association executive), New York City Bar Association (secretary, 1960-62), New York Society of Association Executives, New York Yacht Club, Riverside Yacht Club (CT).

AWARDS, HONORS: D.Sc., Bryant University, 1985; D.LL., Hofstra University, 1987.

WRITINGS:

(Editor) *Racing at Sea,* Van Nostrand, 1959.
How to Stay out of Court, Crown, 1969.
Labor Arbitration: What You Need to Know, American Arbitration Association, 1973, 4th revised edition, 1988.
Business Arbitration: What You Need to Know, American Arbitration Association, 1980, 3rd revised edition, 1986.
The Termination Handbook: A Book for Those on Both Sides of the "Firing Line," Free Press, 1981.
Fighting Fair: Family Mediation Will Work for You, Collier Macmillan, 1983.
Professional Mediation of Civil Disputes, American Arbitration Association, 1984.
Arbitration in the Schools, American Arbitration Association, 1986.
Alcohol, Drugs, and Arbitration, American Arbitration Association, 1987.
Empowered at Forty: How to Negotiate the Best Terms and Time of Your Retirement, Harper Business, 1990.
Police under Pressure: Resolving Disputes, Greenwood Press (Westport, CT),1993.
Family Mediation: Managing Conflict, Resolving Disputes, Jossey-Bass Publishers (San Francisco), 1996.

Also author of *Business Mediation,* 1987, and *ADR in America,*1994.

Contributor to professional journals.

BIOGRAPHICAL/CRITICAL SOURCES:

PERIODICALS

Library Journal, May 15, 1988, p. 76.
National Association of Secondary School Principals Bulletin, December,1986, p. 123.
Social Science Quarterly, June, 1985, p. 470.
Social Work, July, 1985, p. 379.
Wall Street Journal, February 3, 1992, p. A10.*

* * *

COURTIER, S(idney) H(obson) 1904-1974 (Rui Chestor)

PERSONAL: Born January 28, 1904, in Kangaroo Flat, Victoria, Australia; died 1974; son of Sidney Ernest and Maud McKenzie (Hobson) Courtier; married Audrey Jennie George, December 28, 1932; children: Colin, Brian, Lynne (Mrs. Graham Main). *Education:* University of Melbourne, Certificate in Education (first honors). *Politics:* Liberal ("in Australian politics, Conservative"). *Religion:* Methodist.

CAREER: Teacher in primary schools of Victoria, Australia, then principal for twelve years of Melbourne schools that were used for teacher training; retired in 1969. Lecturer on literary subjects at teacher colleges; judge in short story competitions. *Military service:* Australian Imperial Forces, 1942-44.

MEMBER: International PEN (president of Melbourne branch, 1954-57, 1958-61), British Crime Writers' Association, Masons.

WRITINGS:

NOVELS; ALL PUBLISHED BY HAMMOND, HAMMOND, EXCEPT AS INDICATED

The Glass Spear, A. A. Wyn, 1950.
Gold for My Fair Lady, A. A. Wyn, 1951.
One Cried Murder, Rinehart, 1954.
(With R. G. Campbell) *The Mudflat Million,* Angus & Robertson, 1955.
Come Back to Murder, 1957.
Now Seek My Bones, 1957.
A Shroud for Unlac, 1958.
Death in Dream Time, 1959.
Gently Dust the Corpse, 1960.
Let the Man Die, 1961.
Swing High Sweet Murder, 1962.
Who Dies for Me?, 1962.
A Corpse Won't Sing, 1964.
Mimic a Murderer, 1964.
The Ringnecker, 1965.
A Corpse at Least, 1966.
See Who's Dying, 1967.
Murder's Burning, Random House, 1967.
No Obelisk for Emily, Jenkins, 1970.
Ligny's Lake, Simon & Schuster, 1971.
Some Village Borgia, R. Hale, 1971.
Dead If I Remember, R. Hale, 1972.
Into the Silence, R. Hale, 1973.
Listen to the Mocking Bird, R. Hale, 1974.
A Window in Chungking, R. Hale, 1975.
The Smiling Trip, R. Hale, 1976.

Also author of short stories "Run for Your Life" and "Island of No Escape," which appear in anthologies. Contributor of about two hundred short stories to magazines in Australia, United States, Great Britain, and other European countries; some of the short stories were published under the pseudonym Rui Chestor.

SIDELIGHTS: The cultural richness and unique environment of S. H. Courtier's native Australia provided the background and setting for much of his work. Courtier wrote only mystery novels, with two exceptions: a comedy, *The Mudflat Million,* written with Ronald G. Campbell, and *Gold for My Fair Lady,* an historical novel about gold mining set in Courtier's home town of Kangaroo Flat.

Abandoned tunnels—a feature of the gold-digging town in which Courtier grew up—figure prominently in *Come Back to Murder* and *Murder's Burning.* The dangerous wilds of Queensland's McGorrie's Island integrate well into the plot of *Now Seek My Bones. Death in Dream Time* is heavily influenced by Australian aboriginal myths and is generally considered one of Courtier's best works. Many of Courtier's books have been issued in German translation by Wilhelm Goldmann Verlag.

BIOGRAPHICAL/CRITICAL SOURCES:

BOOKS

Henderson, Lesley, editor, *Twentieth-Century Crime and Mystery Writers,* third edition, St. James Press (Chicago), 1991.

PERIODICALS

Armchair Detective, spring, 1986, p. 189.
Australian Book Review, September, 1993, p. 55.
Books and Bookmen, July, 1965, p.32; August, 1970, p. 28.
Library Journal, July, 1968, p. 530; September 15, 1968, p. 3335, July,1971, p. 2351.
New York Times Book Review, July 28, 1968, p. 18; December 1, 1968, p.46; October 17, 1971, p. 30.
Publishers Weekly, April 29, 1968, p. 77; April 19, 1971, p. 46.
Times Literary Supplement, September 14, 1967, p. 824.*

* * *

COUTO, Nancy Vieira 1942-

PERSONAL: Legal name, Nancy Lee Couto; born June 11, 1942, in New York, NY; daughter of Edward (in bread sales) and Angelina (Vieira) Couto; married Joseph A. Martin (a teacher), August 13, 1988. *Education:* Bridgewater State College, B.S., 1964; Cornell University, M.F.A., 1980. *Politics:* Democrat.

ADDRESSES: *Home*—508 Turner Place, Ithaca, NY 14850.

CAREER: Elementary schoolteacher in Dartmouth, MA, 1964-65; National Academy of Sciences, Washington, DC, staff assistant, 1967-68; General- American Life Insurance Co., San Francisco, CA, claims representative, 1968-72; Sperry-Univac, San Francisco, secretary, 1972-73; WTEV-6, New Bedford, MA, executive secretary, 1975-78; Cornell University, Ithaca, NY, lecturer in English, 1980-82; Cornell University Press, Ithaca, secondary rights assistant, 1981-82, subsidiary rights manager, 1982—; poet. Gives readings of her works.

MEMBER: Poets and Writers, Associated Writing Programs.

AWARDS, HONORS: Academy of American Poets Prize, 1980; KAC Second Poetry Award, *Kansas Quarterly,* 1982-83; fellow, Creative Artists Public Service, 1982-83, and National Endowment for the Arts, 1987; Agnes Lynch Starrett Prize, University of Pittsburgh Press, 1989.

WRITINGS:

The Face in the Water, University of Pittsburgh Press, 1990.

Work represented in anthologies, including *New Voices,* Academy of American Poets, 1984. Contributor of poems to journals, including *Poetry Northwest, Prairie Schooner, Hudson Review, American Poetry Review, Chiaroscuro,* and *Milkweed Chronicle.*

SIDELIGHTS: Nancy Vieira Couto told *CA:* "I wrote my first poem at the age of five to celebrate the birth of my baby brother."

BIOGRAPHICAL/CRITICAL SOURCES:

PERIODICALS

Booklist, November 15, 1990, p. 596.
Publishers Weekly, November 2, 1990, p. 69.
University Press Book News, June, 1991, p. 38.*

* * *

COWAN, Peter (Walkinshaw) 1914-

PERSONAL: Born November 4, 1914, in Perth, Western Australia, Australia; son of Norman Walkinshaw and Marie (Johnson) Cowan; married Edith Howard, June 18, 1941; children: Julian Walkinshaw. *Education:* University of Western Australia, Nedlands, B.A. (English), 1941, Diploma in Education, 1946. *Avocational interests:* Nature and wildlife conservation, particularly in Australia.

ADDRESSES: Home—149 Alfred Rd., Mount Claremont, Western Australia, Australia. *Office*—English Department, University of Western Australia, Nedlands, Western Australia, Australia.

CAREER: Clerk, farm laborer, and casual worker in Australia, 1930-39, and teacher, 1941-42; University of Western Australia, Nedlands, part-time teacher, 1946-50; Scotch College, Swanbourne, Western Australia, senior English master, 1950-62; University of Western Australia, senior tutor in English, 1964-79. *Military service:* Royal Australian Air Force, 1943-45.

AWARDS, HONORS: Commonwealth literary fellowship, 1963, to write *Seed;* Australian Council for the Arts fellowship, 1975 and 1980; honorary research fellow, University of Western Australia Department of English, 1979, 1982; Order of Australia, A.M., 1987; Patrick White Award, 1992; honorary D.Phil., Edith Cowan University (Perth), 1995.

WRITINGS:

SHORT STORIES

Drift, Reed & Harris, 1944.
The Unploughed Land, Angus & Robertson, 1958.
The Empty Street, Angus & Robertson, 1965.
The Tins and Other Stories, University of Queensland Press, 1973.
(With others) *New Country,* edited by Bruce Bennett, Fremantle Arts Centre Press, 1976.
Mobiles, Fremantle Arts Centre Press, 1979.
A Window in Mrs. X's Place, Penguin, 1986.
Voices, Fremantle Arts Centre Press, 1988.

NOVELS

Summer, Angus & Robertson, 1964.
Seed, Angus & Robertson, 1966.
The Color of the Sky, Fremantle Arts Centre Press, 1986.
The Hills of Apollo Bay, Fremantle Arts Centre Press, 1989.
The Tenants, Fremantle Arts Centre Press, 1994.

EDITOR

Short Story Landscape: The Modern Short Story (anthology), Longman, Green, 1964.
(With Bruce Bennett) *Spectrum One: Narrative Short Stories,* Longman, 1970.
(With Bennett) *Spectrum Two: Modern Short Stories,* Longman, 1970.
Today: Short Stories of Our Time, Longman, 1971.

A Faithful Picture: The Letters of Eliza and Thomas Brown at York in the Swan River Colony, 1841-1852, Fremantle Arts Centre Press, 1977.
A Unique Position: A Biography of Edith Dircksey Cowan 1861-1932, University of Western Australia Press (Nedlands), 1978.
A Colonial Experience: Swan River 1839-88 from the Diary and Reports of Walkinshaw Cowan, privately printed, 1979.
(With Bennett and Hay) *Spectrum Three: Experimental Short Stories* (anthology), Longman Cheshire, 1979.
(With Bennett and Hay) *Perspectives One* (short stories), Longman Cheshire, 1985.
Impressions: West Coast Fiction 1829-1988, Freemantle Arts Center Press, 1989.

OTHER

Maitland Brown: A View of Nineteenth-Century Western Australia (biography), Fremantle Arts Centre Press, 1988.
Editor; with Bruce Bennett, John Hay, and Susan Ashford)*Western Australian Writing: A Bibliography,* 1990.
(Contributor) *This Is Australia,* Hamlyn, 1975.
(Contributor) *The Literature of Western Australia,* edited by Bennett, University of Western Australia Press, 1979.

SIDELIGHTS: "My writings may have been concerned as much with place as with people," said Peter Cowan. The place is Australia, and Cowan believes his frequent theme of isolation is "enforced by the Australian landscape." He added, "I am deeply involved in everything to do with the physical Australia."

Cowan began his career writing short stories, preferring the genre for its technical demands, which, he feels, "are high, and seldom met." In addition, short stories, in his opinion, better capture "something of the fragmentary nature of today's living." He has, however, expanded his writing to include novels.

Critics found Cowan's first two attempts, *Summer* and *Seed,* less than successful. John Barnes, writing for *Contemporary Novelists,* noted that Cowan "is not skilled at creating personalities or at suggesting the social facts of life," skills which, as Barnes pointed out, are precisely what is needed in Cowan's type of "rather old-fashioned, realistic novel." Of Cowan's third book, however, Barnes wrote: "*The Color of the Sky* has the formal integrity and the imaginative vigour which the previous novels lacked."

The narrator in *The Color of the Sky* is, in Barnes words, "a familiar enough Cowan creation—a man on his own, trying to make sense of his experience." In Cowan's stories, the reader encounters people alone, especially middle-aged men, who are disillusioned with their marriages, their families, and their commonplace lives. Some turn to murder; others seek fulfillment in sexual love. But in the end, Barnes concludes, Cowan's "human beings are no more than transitory figures in an enduring and inhospitable landscape."

BIOGRAPHICAL/CRITICAL SOURCES:

BOOKS

Barnes, John, *An Australian Selection,* Angus & Robertson, 1974.
Bennett, Bruce, editor, *The Literature of Western Australia,* University of Western Australia Press, 1979.
Bennett, Bruce, and Susan Miller, editors, *Peter Cowan: New Critical Essays,* University of Western Australia Press, 1992.
Contemporary Novelists, sixth edition, St. James Press (Detroit),1996.
Cowan, Peter, *A Window in Mrs. X's Place,* introduction by Bruce Bennett, Penguin, 1986.
Hewett, Dorothy, editor, *Sandgropers,* University of Western Australia Press, 1973.
Jones, Evan, editor, *Commonwealth Literary Fund Lectures,* Australian National University Press, 1961.
Reference Guide to Short Fiction, St. James Press (Detroit),1994.

PERIODICALS

Australian Book Review, February, 1994, p. 12.
Meanjin Quarterly, no. 2, 1960; no. 2, 1966.
Times Literary Supplement, June 19, 1987.
Westerly, no. 3, 1973.*

* * *

CREW, Gary 1947-

PERSONAL: Born September 23, 1947, in Brisbane, Queensland, Australia; son of Eric (a steam engine driver) and Phyllis (a milliner; maiden name, Winch) Crew; married Christine Joy Willis (a teacher), April 4, 1970; children: Rachel, Sarah, Joel. *Education:* Attended Queensland Institute of Technology; University of Queensland, diploma of civil engineering drafting, 1970, B.A., 1979, M.A, 1984.

ADDRESSES: Home—Green Mansions, 66 Picnic St., Enoggera, Queensland 4051, Australia. *Agent*—c/o Reed Australia, P.O. Box 460, Port Melbourne, Victoria 3027, Australia.

CAREER: McDonald, Wapner & Priddle, Brisbane, Queensland, Australia, senior draftsman and drafting consultant, 1962-72; Everton Park State High School, Brisbane, English teacher, 1974-78; Mitchelton State High School, Brisbane, English teacher, 1978-81; Aspley High School, Brisbane, subject master in English, 1982; Albany Creek High School, Brisbane, subject master in English and head of English department, 1983-88; Queensland University of Technology, Brisbane, creative writing lecturer, 1989—.

MEMBER: Australian Society of Authors.

AWARDS, HONORS: Book of the Year Award, Children's Book Council of Australia, and Alan Marshall Prize for Children's Literature, both 1991, both for *Strange Objects; Lucy's Bay* was shortlisted for the Children's Book Council of Australia's picture book of the year, 1993.

WRITINGS:

NOVELS

The Inner Circle, Heinemann Octopus, 1985.
The House of Tomorrow, Heinemann Octopus, 1988.
Strange Objects, Heinemann Octopus, 1990, Simon & Schuster (New York City), 1993.
No Such Country, Heinemann Octopus, 1991, Simon & Schuster, 1994.
Among Others, Heinemann Octopus, 1993.
Inventing Anthony West, University of Queensland Press (St. Lucia, Queensland),1994.

CHILDREN'S STORY BOOKS

Tracks, illustrated by Gregory Rogers, Lothian, 1992.
Lucy's Bay, illustrated by Rogers, Jam Roll Press, 1992.
The Figures of Julian Ashcroft, illustrated by Hans DeHaas, Jam Roll Press, 1993.
First Light, illustrated by Peter Gouldthorpe, Lothian, 1993.
The Watertower, Ekare and Crocodile Books, 1994.
Angel's Gate, Simon & Schuster, 1995.
Bright Star, illustrated by Anne Spudvilas, Kane/Miller Book Publishers (Brooklyn, NY), 1997.

Also author of *Caleb, Dark House,* and *Gulliver in the South Seas,* illustrated by John Burge. Contributor of short stories to anthologies, including *Hair Raising,* edited by Penny Matthews, Omnibus, 1992, and *The Blue Dress,* edited by Libby Hathorn, Heinemann, 1992. Contributor to books, including *At Least They're Reading! Proceedings of the First National Conference of the Children's Book Council of Australia,* Thorpe, 1992, and *The Second Authors and Illustrators Scrapbook,* Omnibus Books, 1992. Contributor to periodicals, including *Australian Author, Magpies,* and *Reading Time.*Heinemann Octopus, series editor, 1990—.Heinemann Octopus, series editor, 1990—.

ADAPTATIONS: The story "Sleeping over at Lola's" was adapted as a radio play by the Australian Broadcasting Commission; a film adaptation of *Strange Objects* was scheduled for production by Zoic Films of Australia.

SIDELIGHTS: The novels of Australian writer Gary Crew have received critical acclaim for achieving two qualities that are difficult to combine: they have been declared intricate and enriching examples of literary writing, and they are also accessible to young readers. "His novels epitomize young adult literature in Australia to date," wrote Maurice Saxby in *The Proof of the Pudding.* "They successfully combine popular appeal with intellectual, emotional, psychological and spiritual substance." Crew's books often explore the history of Australia, but he finds that it is his own personal history that often drives his fiction. "Perhaps more than other mortals, it is the writer of children's fiction who suffers most from the desire to return to the past," he wrote in an essay in *Magpies.* "I know I cannot entirely abandon my own past. Once I would have longed to; I would have given anything to at least redress, at best forget, the forces that shaped me—but, as I grow older, and more confident in my art, I am not so certain. . . . A writer who cannot remember must produce lean fare. And surely, a children's writer who cannot remember is no writer at all."

Crew's past begins in Brisbane, Australia, where he was born in 1947. In his *Magpies* essay, Crew recalled that he "spent most of my childhood with the local kids racing around the neighbourhood," but there was also a sadder aspect to the author's early years. Crew began to suffer from poor health as a youngster, describing himself in a speech published in *Australian Author* as "a sickly, puny child." As a result, his rambunctious adventures soon gave way to calmer pursuits. "My mother says that I was a very quiet child, and my earliest memories suggest that she is right," Crew once commented. "I was always happiest by myself, reading, drawing, or making models. I never did like crowds or noise."

Crew's illness also forced him to spend a lot of time in hospitals or confined to the house, but this experience later benefited his writing in at least two ways. It first allowed him much time to read. In *Magpies,* Crew recalled that he and his sister read "anything," and this interest in books continued into adulthood, providing him with a solid literary background.

A second benefit of Crew's illness was that it brought him in closer contact with an influential setting that would later be featured in one of his books. "A significant period of my childhood had been spent at my great-grandmother's house in Ipswich, to the west of Brisbane," Crew related in *Australian Author.* "My great-grandmother was bedridden in this house; my widowed grandmother cared for her. Because I was always sick, there seemed to be some logic in packing me off to join them." Recalling the location in *The Second Authors and Illustrators Scrapbook,* Crew wrote that "this house was wonderful, with verandas all around, and a great big mango tree growing right up against it. We could climb over the rail and drop onto the branches of the mango. This house gave me the main idea for my second novel, *The House of Tomorrow.*" In that novel Crew writes of a teenage boy, Danny, who has difficulty coping with the increased pressures in his life. Searching for a means to order and understand the world around him, Danny finds solace in the house that is modeled on the home in Ipswich. As the author explained it in *Australian Author,* "In *The House of Tomorrow* my great-grandmother's house re-established a sense of place and belonging in a young boy's life."

Crew's stays in Ipswich had other benefits, as well. "My first public attempts at writing were letters sent from my great-grandmother's house to my parents," he wrote in *The Second Authors and Illustrators Scrapbook,* and writing and drawing later became important elements in his life. "Until I went to high school, I never seemed to be especially good at anything," Crew once remarked, "but at fifteen years old, I realized that I could write and draw—but that was about all I could do well!"

Despite his desire to continue his studies, Crew's drawing abilities and his family's economic status soon led him in another direction. "My parents had very little money," he commented, "so I left school at sixteen to become a cadet draftsman, working for a firm of engineers. I hated this, and at twenty-one I returned to college to matriculate by studying at night; then I went to university. All this time I was earning a living as a draftsman, but had decided to be a teacher of English because I loved books so much." Crew soon proved his abilities as a student, and he valued the opportunity to continue his delayed education. "I don't think anyone was ever more comfortable at uni[versity] than I was," he told *Scan* interviewer Niki Kallenberger, "—it was most wonderful! I would have done all the assignments on the sheets! It was a feeling of being totally at home and I was a changed person."

It was not until after he became a high school English teacher that Crew began writing fiction, and then only at the urging of his wife. "Christine cut out a piece from the paper advertising a short story contest which I entered virtually as a joke," he told Kallenberger. The story placed in the contest and later won a best short story of the year contest. Crew then turned to novels for young adults and drew inspiration from the students in his English classes. "I guess my first novels came out of my experience as a high school teacher," he once remarked. "I saw so many teenagers who were confused and unhappy—about themselves and the world around them." His first book, *The Inner Circle,* turned on the relationship between a black teenager, Joe, and a white one, Tony, who form a bond despite their racial differences. Saxby, analyzing the novel in *The Proof of the Pudding,* found that *The Inner Circle* is "above all, a well-told story incorporating many of the concerns of today's teenagers. The theme of personal and racial reintegration and harmony is inherent in the plot and reinforced through symbolism." The book has enjoyed great popularity in Australia, and English and Canadian editions have also been published. Crew has been pleased by its success but believes there are several flaws in the novel. "I'm not a fool in regard to approaching the book critically myself and I know the book's got phenomenal weaknesses," he told Kallenberger. "But I also see it as being a remarkable publishing oddity because it's so accessible to kids and its use in the classroom continues to astound me."

Crew's enjoyment of academic study—and research in particular—has influenced his fiction writing process. He is not an author who sits at a desk and waits for inspiration to visit him; instead, Crew actively seeks out information about a subject and collects the materials in a journal. As he told Kallenberger, a typical journal contains "clippings, drawings, scrappy notes I write to myself. I just keep it all in a carton and throw in anything, even books, that's broadly relevant. . . . It all goes in there and if it's a rainy day I'll look at it." Crew has also conducted computer searches to gain information on subjects, and he often employs his artistic skills in preparation for writing a book. "I think that drawing people and places before I write about them prevents me from having writer's block, and allows me to write smoothly without interruptions," he related in *The Second Authors and Illustrators Scrapbook.* "These jottings are quick and rough but they mean a great deal to me when I come to write the episode they represent; they serve as mental reminders."

Crew's explorations of Australian history began with his third novel, *Strange Objects.* The novel's hero, Stephen Messenger, is a sixteen-year-old boy who discovers a leather-bound journal and other mysterious objects in a cave. The relics are believed to have belonged to two survivors from the *Batavia,* a ship that wrecked off the coast of Australia in 1629. These relics provide Messenger with a direct link to his country's earliest European inhabitants, and they provide Crew with a means of addressing the relationship between the Europeans and the aboriginal peoples who were the original inhabitants of the Australian continent. As is the case in several of Crew's books, *Strange Objects* forces the reader to consider some unpleasant aspects of the European conquest of the island and is often critical of the colonists who settled in Australia. Commenting on *Strange Objects* in *Reading Time,* Crew wrote that the book is "intended to challenge the reader to examine what has happened in our past, to re-assess what forces shaped this nation—and the effect the white invasion has had on the original inhabitants of this country."

Crew finds that, like many other things, his interest in the past stems from his childhood. When he received the Book of the Year Award from the Children's Book Council of Australia for *Strange Objects,* Crew explained the influence of his early years. "The origins of *Strange Objects* are founded deep in my memory," he stated in his acceptance speech, later published in *Reading Time.* "During the never ending sunshine of my childhood in the 50's, my parents would regularly take me and my sister Annita to the Queensland Museum. . . . Here we were able to stare goggle-eyed and open-mouthed at mummies stolen-away from the Torres Strait Islands, bamboo headhunters' knives complete with notches from every head taken and other so-called 'cannibal' artifacts. . . . When I had been made wiser by my studies, I began to understand the colonist's fear of the Indigene [or aborigines] as The Other, and to appreciate fully the fantastical and ever-changing phenomenon we call 'history.' "

Crew has further explored the legacy of Australia's past in his novel *No Such Country,* which takes place in the fictional setting of New Canaan and concerns the fate of the White Father, a priest who enjoys great power in the village. Joan Zahnleiter, writing about the book in *Magpies,* noted that "the Father uses his knowledge of a particularly evil event in the past of New Canaan to blackmail superstitious fisherfolk into accepting him as the Messiah who controls their lives with his great book." Zahnleiter also found that "the book has deeply religious concepts embedded in it so that a working knowledge of the Bible enriches the reading of it. However it is a story which works well for the reader without that knowledge."

In addition to his novels, Crew has published story books for young children such as *Tracks* and *Lucy's Bay,* both including illustrations by Gregory Rogers. In *Tracks,* a young boy ventures into the strange, night-time world of the jungle, making many unusual and beautiful discoveries. *Lucy's Bay* concerns a boy, Sam, whose sister drowns while he is taking care of her. Several years later, Sam returns to the scene of the tragedy in an attempt to come to terms with his feelings. A *Reading Time* review found *Lucy's Bay* to be "a beautiful piece of descriptive writing which places in perspective Sam's grief for his sister against the ceaseless rhythm of nature."

The Watertower and *Caleb,* which Crew wrote incollaboration with illustrator Steven Woolman, also are aimed at a young audience. In *The Watertower,* two boys from Australia's outback keep cool by swimming in an abandoned watertower. But there is something sinister about the watertower and its effect on folks, it even transforms one character's appearance. *Caleb* is the story of an odd, quiet child prodigy who is obsessed with insects. In a review of *Caleb* in *Magpies,* Michael Gregg observed that in both *The Watertower* and *Caleb* the authors "[seek] to redefine our notion of the picture book." For example, *The Watertower*'s twisting plot is mirrored in the layout of the book's text. The story opens with the words printed sideways on the page so that the book must be read on its side. And as *The Watertower* progresses and its plot unwinds, the text shifts so that the book must be completed upside down.

Looking ahead to future projects, Crew believes that his personal experiences will continue to play a large role in his books. "As a writer, I am not done with looking inward," he explained in *Australian Author.* "There is much for me still to find in my house of fiction; in those fantastical inner rooms of childhood from which, I imagine, some choose never to emerge." And in each book he writes, Crew has definite aims regarding his young audience. "My main objective in writing is to open the minds of my readers," he has remarked, "to say 'the world can be a wonderful place—its possibilities are open to you and your imagination.' "

BIOGRAPHICAL/CRITICAL SOURCES:

BOOKS

At Least They're Reading! Proceedings of the First National Conference of the Children's Book Council of Australia, Thorpe, 1992.
Authors & Artists for Young Adults, Volume 17, Gale (Detroit), 1995.
Children's Literature Review, Volume 52, Gale, 1997.
Saxby, Maurice, *The Proof of the Pudding,* Ashton, 1993.
The Second Authors and Illustrators Scrapbook, Omnibus Books, 1992.

PERIODICALS

Australian Author, autumn, 1992, pp. 24-27.
Booklist, June 1, 1993, p. 1812; May 1, 1994, p. 1594.
Horn Book Magazine, March-April, 1996, p. 205.
Magpies, May, 1991, p. 22; July, 1991, p. 37; September, 1991, pp. 17-19; March, 1992, p. 34; July, 1992, pp. 5-8; March, 1996, p. 12.
Papers: Explorations in Children's Literature, August, 1990, pp. 51-58; April, 1992, pp. 18-26.
Publishers Weekly, May 31, 1993, p. 55; May 30, 1994, p. 57; August 7, 1995, p. 461.
Reading Time, vol. 35, no. 3, 1991, pp. 11-12; Vol. 35, no. 4, 1991, pp. 4-5; Vol. 37, no. 2, 1992, p. 20.
Scan, November, 1990, pp. 9-11.
School Librarian, May, 1995, p. 63; November, 1996, p. 150.*

* * *

CREWS, Donald 1938-

PERSONAL: Born August 30, 1938 in Newark, NJ; son of Asa (a railroad trackman) and Marshanna (a dressmaker; maiden name, White); married Ann Jonas (an author, artist, and designer), January 28, 1964; children: Nina Melissa, Amy Marshanna. *Education:* Cooper Union for the Advancement of Science and Art, graduated 1959.

ADDRESSES: Home—New York, NY.

CAREER: Freelance artist, photographer, and designer.

AWARDS, HONORS: One of Fifty Books of the Year, American Institute of Graphic Arts, 1968, for *We Read: A to Z;* chosen by Children's Book Council for Children's Book Showcase, 1974, for *Eclipse: Darkness in Daytime;* Notable Book citation, American Library Association (ALA), 1978, and Caldecott Honor Book, 1979, both for *Freight Train;* American Institute of Graphic Arts Book Show selection, 1979, for *Rain;* Notable Book citation, ALA, 1980, and Caldecott Honor Book, 1981, both for *Truck;* one of the ten best illustrated books, *New York Times,* 1986, for *Flying.*

WRITINGS:

FOR CHILDREN; AND ILLUSTRATOR

We Read: A to Z, Harper, 1967.
Ten Black Dots, Scribner, 1968.
Freight Train, Greenwillow, 1978.
Truck, Greenwillow, 1980.
Light, Greenwillow, 1981.
Harbor, Greenwillow, 1982.
Carousel, Greenwillow, 1982.
Parade, Greenwillow, 1983.
School Bus, Greenwillow, 1984.
Bicycle Race, Greenwilow, 1985.
Flying, Greenwillow, 1986.
Bigmama's, Greenwillow, 1991.
Shortcut, Greenwillow, 1992.
Sail Away, Greenwillow, 1995.
Night at the Fair, Greenwillow, 1997.
Cloudy Day/Sunny Day, Harcourt, 1999.

ILLUSTRATOR

Harry Milgrom, *ABC Science Experiments,* Crowell-Collier Press, 1970.
J. Richard Dennis, *Fractions Are Parts of Things,* Crowell, 1971.
Milgrom, *ABC of Ecology,* Macmillan, 1972.
Franklyn M. Branley, *Eclipse: Darkness in Daytime,* Crowell, 1973.
Robert Kalan, *Rain,* Greenwillow, 1978.
Kalan, *Blue Sea,* Greenwillow, 1979.
Dorothy de Wit, editor, *The Talking Stone: An Anthology of Native American Tales and Legends,* Greenwillow, 1979.
Paul Giganti Jr., *How Many Snails?: A Counting Book,* Greenwillow, 1988.
Paul Giganti Jr., *Each Orange Had Eight Slices: A Counting Book,* Greenwillow,1992.
Patricia Lillie, *When This Box Is Full,* Greenwillow, 1993.
George Shannon, *Tomorrow's Alphabet,* Greenwillow, 1995.
Miriam Schlein, *More Than One,* Greenwillow, 1996.

SIDELIGHTS: Donald Crews, award winning author-illustrator of children's books, grew up in New Jersey, one of four children. Crews was surrounded by artistic influences throughout his early life. As a young boy he drew inspiration from his mother, a skilled craftswoman who often involved him and his siblings in artistic projects. Crews commented, "I've drawn and sketched as long as I can remember." Summers at his grandparents' farm in Florida provided added inspiration. Steam trains passed near the farm and Crews' fascination with them is evident in some of his books. The creative atmosphere at home and the memories of his annual trips to the farm played a prominent part in Crews' development as an artist.

Crews' college studies in art design earned him a position on the magazine staff of *Dance* as assistant art director and later a job at New York City's Will Burton Studios. Drafted into the Army in the early sixties, Crews developed his first book, *We Read: A to Z,* while stationed in Germany. Crews explained that it was not intended for publication, but as a "pacer" or "freshener" for art directors looking at his portfolio. It wasn't until several years after his tour of duty, when the book was published in 1967, that he won high praise for its innovative teaching approach through a strong graphic medium. He continued working as a freelance artist and illustrator until he won a Caldecott Honor Book award in 1979 for his picture book *Freight Train.* Having achieved national recognition, Crews focused his talent on being a picture book artist and numerous awards followed.

Kay E. Vandergrift, in her critique of *Freight Train* for *Twentieth-Century Children's Writers,* wrote, "*Freight Train* roars through the pages moving right through the book into children's memories." *Truck,* Crews' second Honor Caldecott Book, was likewise praised by *New York Times Book Review* critic Harold C. K. Rice. Rice wrote that the images in the book "are all brilliantly conveyed in simple, almost two-dimensional shapes that have the impact and celebratory joy of 1940's travel posters seen by a post-pop artist."

Although most of Crews' books employ similar illustration techniques, each story explores one specific subject. Crews said, "I attempt to isolate an area of interest and to involve my readers in my excitement about that area." Vandergrift concluded, "Bold illustrations with simple texts, an ability to see things from a child's perspective, and the development of the sensitive cyc of the reader are characteristic of Donald Crews' work."

BIOGRAPHICAL/CRITICAL SOURCES:

BOOKS

Children's Literature Review, edited by Gerard J. Senick, Gale, Volume 7, 1984.
Something about the Author, edited by Diane Telgen, Gale, Volume 76, 1994.
Twentieth-Century Children's Writers, 4th edition, edited by Laura Standley Berger, St. James Press, 1995.

PERIODICALS

Booklist, March 1, 1996, p. 1179.
Horn Book Guide, spring, 1997, p. 11.
Horn Book Magazine, September/October, 1995, p. 587.
Library Journal, April, 1996, p. 118.
Publishers Weekly, April 1, 1996, p. 76; October 7, 1996, p. 75.*

* * *

CREWS, Judson (Campbell) 1917-
(Cerise Farallon)

PERSONAL: Born June 30, 1917, in Waco, TX; son of Noah George (a nurseryman) and Tommie (Farmer) Crews; married Mildred Tolbert (a photographer and writer), October 19, 1947 (divorced January, 1980); children: Anna Bush, Carole Judith. *Education:* Baylor University, A.B., 1941, M.A. (with honors), 1944, study in fine arts, 1946-47; University of Texas at El Paso, graduate study, 1967. *Politics:* None. *Religion:* None.

ADDRESSES: Home—2323 Kathryn Southeast, #531, Albuquerque, NM 87106-3456.

CAREER: Landscape architect in Waco, TX, 1936-39; publisher of Motive Press, Waco, TX, and Este Es Press, Taos, NM, 1946-66; El Paso Country Child Welfare Unit, caseworker, 1966-67; Taos *Star, El Crepusculo,* and Taos News Publishing Co., printer, 1948-66; Wharton Junior College, Wharton, TX, instructor in sociology and psychology, 1967-70; Community Mental Health Service, Gallup, NM, psychological counselor and community services coordinator, 1970-71; University of New Mexico Branch College, Gallup, lecturer in sociology, 1971-72; State School for Girls, Chillicothe, MO, director of intensive care unit,

1973; University of Zambia, Lusaka, lecturer in social development studies, 1974-78. *Military service:* U.S. Army Medical Corps, 1942-44.

MEMBER: Yale Library Associates, Rio Grande Writers Association.

WRITINGS:

POETRY

Psalms for a Late Season, Iconograph Press, 1942.
No Is the Night, privately printed, 1949.
A Poet's Breath, privately printed, 1950.
Come Curse the Moon, privately printed, 1952.
The Anatomy of Proserpine, privately printed, 1955.
The Wrath Wrenched Splendor of Love, privately printed, 1956.
The Heart in Naked Hunger, Motive Book Shop, 1958.
To Wed beneath the Sun, privately printed, 1958.
The Ogres Who Were His Henchmen, Hearse Press, 1958.
Inwade to Briney Garth, Este Es Press (Taos, N.M.), 1960.
(Contributor) Fred Baver, compiler, *River,* River Spring, 1960.
The Feel of the Sun and Air upon Her Body, Hearse Press, 1960.
A Unicorn When Needs Be, Este Es Press, 1963.
Hermes Past the Hour, Este Es Press, 1963.
(Contributor) Louis Untermeyer, editor, *An Uninhibited Treasury of Erotic Poetry,* Dial, 1963.
Selected Poems, Renegade Press, 1964.
You, Mark Antony, Navigator upon the Nile, privately printed, 1964.
Angels Fall, They Are Towers, Este Es Press, 1965.
(With Wendell B. Anderson; under real name and under pseudonym Cerise Farallon) *Three on a Match,* privately printed, 1966.
The Stones of Konarak, American Poets Press, 1966.
(Contributor) A. W. Stevens, editor, *Poems Southwest,* Prescott College Press, 1968.
(Contributor) Robert L. Williams, compiler, *Mehy in His Carriage,* Summit Press, 1968.
(Contributor) Lawrence Ferlinghetti, editor, *City Lights Anthology,* City Lights, 1974.
(Contributor) Paul Foreman and Joanie Whitebird, editors, *Travois: An Anthology of Texas Poetry,* Thorp Springs Press, 1976.
Nations to Nations, Cherry Valley, 1976.
Nolo Contendere, edited by Joanie Whitebird, preface by Robert Creeley, Wings Press, 1978.
Modern Onions and Sociology, St. Valentine's Press, 1978.
Roma a Fat At, Instantaneous Centipede Publications, 1979.
Gluons, Q, Namaste Press, 1979.
The Noose, a Retrospective: Four Decades, edited by Larry Goodell and John Brandi, Duende Press, 1980.
If I, Wormwood Review Press (Stockton, CA), 1981.
The Clock of Moss, edited by Carol Berge and Dale Boyer, Ahsahta, 1983.
Against All Wounds, Trout Creek Press (Parkdale, OR), 1987.
Henry Miller and My Big Sur Days, Yergin Press, 1992.

Also author of *A Sheaf of Christmas Verse,* published by Three Hands (Washington, DC).

OTHER

The Southern Temper, Motive Book Shop, 1946.
(With Wendell B. Anderson and wife Mildred Crews) *Patocinio Barela: Taos Wood Carver,* privately printed, 1955, revised edition, Taos Recordings and Publications, 1962.

Contributor to approximately 350 periodicals, including *Beloit Poetry Journal, Poetry Now, Wormwood Review, Puerto del Sol,* and *Southwestern American Literature.*

WORK IN PROGRESS: Three new collections of poetry.

SIDELIGHTS: Judson Crews once told *CA* that during "an earlier phase [of my career], I was involved in editing and publishing several avant-garde magazines of the thirties, forties, and fifties. They ranged from *Vers Libre,* which lasted over two years, to *Taos,* a deluxe magazine of the arts which was a one-shot deal. In addition to the two above, *Motive, The Flying Fish, Suck-Egg Mule, The Deer and Dachshund, Poetry Taos,* and *The Naked Ear* were my sole responsibility. I was more than slightly involved with *Crescendo,* edited by Scott Greer, and *Gale,* edited by Jay Waite."

Crews later wrote *CA:* "I studied English and classical versification for two years, but in my own practice I have never regretted that I have chosen contemporary models for closest study. Any perceptive reviewer of my books will readily note two or three obvious influences on my work (William Carlos Williams, Wallace Stevens), but often enough two or three which simply do not apply (Sylvia Plath, Charles Olson); all seem to have missed the deep and lasting influence, quite early, of some of Delmore Schwartz's earliest and best work, or for that matter, James Agee.

"I disavow all formalist aspects of 'the [surrealistic] movement'—yet it is clear that the essential effect of my best and most characteristic work achieves an interface with the borderline of exceptional feelings and experiencings that may be most usefully thought of as the surreal.

"Thematically, my subjects extend to the entire range of human verities. But the one ever-recurring motif is the erotic, often explicit, in 'the naming of parts.' This work does not fit so very easily in the 'poetry of love' genre with much of the work of e. e. cummings or Robert Graves, or for that matter Kenneth Rexroth and Kenneth Patchen.

"The over-riding project of most of my sixties has been a personal memoir begun in Africa in 1976. I worked regularly through most of the small hours of the morning on this project for seven years. I gave up the writing of poetry during this period. I worked exclusively from memory completing some 9,500 pages of narrative, bringing the story up to my mid-thirties.

"However, as I continued writing about the 1950s, I began to feel a greater and greater need for literal accuracy concerning my impressions of peoples and events in such a recent time. Earlier, I had been willing to rely on 'symbolic' accuracy, feeling-tones—the way it was to me. This change of approach was not total—I had no wish and no intention to 'research' my own life. But I did require access to my archives for the late fifties and early sixties housed in the Harry Ransom Humanities Research Center at the University of Texas. Here I ran into an impregnable wall in the form of several Catch 22s—conditions which I could not meet without grant money, a research assistant, and secretarial help. I have been stalled by a bureaucracy.

"I returned to the writing of poetry in 1982, and in the first three months produced a hundred poems from which Carol Berge culled *The Clock of Moss* collection."

Extensive archives of Crew's materials, including manuscripts and letters, are at University of Texas, Austin, University of California, Los Angeles, Yale University, University of Zambia, and University of New Mexico.

BIOGRAPHICAL/CRITICAL SOURCES:

BOOKS

Anderson, Wendell B., *The Heart's Precision: Judson Crews and His Poetry,* edited by Jefferson P. Selth, Dumont Press (Carson, CA), 1994.

Contemporary Poets, 6th edition, St. James Press (Detroit), 1996.

PERIODICALS

A.B. Bookman's Weekly, December 20, 1965, p. 2389.

Library Journal, December 15, 1983, p. 2299.

Poetry, June, 1966, p. 191; September, 1966, p. 408; June, 1967, p. 186.

Poetry Now, Volume VI, number 6, 1982.

Western American Literature, fall, 1984, p. 240.*

* * *

CROMIE, Robert (Allen) 1909-

PERSONAL: Born February 28, 1909, in Detroit, MI; son of Robert and Annie Gertrude (Crosby) Cromie; married Alice Louise Hamilton, May 22, 1937; children: Michael, Richard, Barbara, James. *Education:* Oberlin College, A.B., 1930. *Avocational interests:* Photographic memorabilia, golf.

ADDRESSES: Home—23849 West Erhart Rd., Grayslake, IL 60030.

CAREER: Pontiac Daily Press, Pontiac, MI, reporter, 1935; *Pontiac News,* Pontiac, reporter, 1936-37; *Chicago Tribune,* Chicago, IL, reporter, 1937-42, war correspondent, 1942-46, news reporter, 1946-48, sportswriter, 1948-60, book editor, 1960-69, daily columnist, 1969-74. Host of *Book Beat,* WTTW-TV, Chicago, 1963-79, of *The Cromie Circle,* WGN-TV, Chicago, 1969-82, and of *About Books and Writers,* National Public Radio, 1982—.

MEMBER: Authors Guild, Authors League of America, American Federation of Television and Radio Artists, Society of Midland Authors, Chicago Arts Club, Chicago Press Club.

AWARDS, HONORS: Emmy Award, National Academy of Television Arts and Sciences (Chicago branch), 1966; Irita Van Doren Award, American Booksellers Association, 1968; Peabody Award for *Book Beat* television program, 1969.

WRITINGS:

The Great Chicago Fire, McGraw, 1959, illustrated edition, Rutledge Hill Press, 1994.
(Reviser) Mark Harris, *New Angles on Putting and Chip Shots,* Reilly & Lee, 1960.
(With Joseph Pinkston) *Dillinger: A Short and Violent Life,* McGraw, 1962.
(Editor) *Par for the Course: A Golfer's Anthology,* Macmillan, 1964.
Golf for Boys and Girls, Follett, 1965.
(Editor) *Where Steel Winds Blow: Poets on War,* McKay, 1968.
(With Archie Lieberman) *Chicago in Color,* Hastings House, 1969.
(With Herman Kogan) *The Great Fire: Chicago, 1871,* Putnam, 1971.
(With Lieberman) *Chicago,* Rand McNally, 1980.
A Short History of Chicago, Lexikos, 1984.
Chicago: A Celebration, photographs by Archie Lieberman, Rand McNally (Chicago), 1990.
(Editor) *Illinois Trivia,* Rutledge Hill Press (Nashville, TN),1992.

Also author, with Art Haug, of *Chicago,* Ziff-Davis. Contributor of articles to golf magazines; contributor to popular periodicals; contributor of light verse to *Saturday Evening Post.*

SIDELIGHTS: A *Variety* writer notes that the Chicago public television station that produces the *Book Beat* series had some difficulty selling the NET network on the show because of the large number of book review-interview shows already on the air in many cities. However, "NET became interested in the Cromie show when authors began reporting and complaining that Cromie was the only one of the interviewers who had obviously read all of the book under discussion. . . . More than just a literary man, Cromie brings a widely-diversified journalistic background to his interviews that allows him to put the book and author in a wider perspective."

Cleveland Amory in *TV Guide* writes that "the average author is a difficult interview subject. All too often he exhibits that one unpardonable combination—nervousness and ego together. A man becomes an author, Somerset Maugham once said, because he is the kind of man who thinks of what he should have said on the way home from the party. We have often thought of that line as we watched some interview program and saw some author mumbling along. During one program, however, we never think of it. It is Robert Cromie's *Book Beat,* telecast out of Chicago on some 150 educational stations. Mr. Cromie is strictly upbeat—a cheerful, gentle man. A refugee from the sports desk, he is, compared to the average literary critic, no intellectual giant. Compared to the average TV host, however, he is a think tank."

BIOGRAPHICAL/CRITICAL SOURCES:

PERIODICALS

A.B. Bookman's Weekly, March 6, 1972, p. 860; August 8, 1994, p. 466.
Booklist, March 1, 1969, p. 727; January 1, 1981, p. 612; January1, 1985, p. 614.
Library Journal, October 15, 1965, p. 4636; January 1, 1969, p. 87; Febrauary 15, 1969, p. 893; May 15, 1969, p. 2074; March 1, 1985, p. 88.
Publishers Weekly, November 4, 1968, p. 44.
Tribune Books (Chicago), October 25, 1992, p. 8.
TV Guide, February 15, 1969.
Variety, October 14, 1970.*

* * *

CROMPTON, Richmal
See LAMBURN, Richmal Crompton

* * *

CULLETON, Beatrice 1949-

PERSONAL: Born August 27, 1949, in St. Boniface, Manitoba, Canada; daughter of Louis and Mary Clara (Pelletier) Mosionier; married William F. Culleton (a truck driver), divorced; married George Moehring; children: William J., Deborah E. *Education:* Attended George Brown College, 1970, and Banff School of Fine Arts, 1983.

ADDRESSES: *Home*—79 Cameron St., Winnipeg, Manitoba, Canada R2L 1W2. *Office*—Pemmican Publications, Inc., 411504 Main St., Winnipeg, Manitoba, Canada R3B 1B8.

CAREER: Wahn, Mayer & Smith (law firm), Toronto, Ontario, accounting clerk, 1970-72; Joseph J. Marek (law firm), Winnipeg, Manitoba, bookkeeper, 1973-77; homemaker, 1977-83; Pemmican Publications, Inc., Winnipeg, manager and publisher, 1983—; Native

Earth Performing Arts (Toronto), playwright-in-residence.

MEMBER: Manitoba Writers Guild, Association of Manitoba Book Publishers (past president), Ma Mawi Wi Chi Itata Centre, Inc., Coalition on Native Child Welfare.

WRITINGS:

In Search of April Raintree (novel), Pemmican Publications, 1983, revised school edition published as *April Raintree,* 1984.

Spirit of the White Bison (juvenile), Pemmican Publications, 1985.

Also author of the play *Night of the Trickster* and the film-script *Walker.*

SIDELIGHTS: Beatrice Culleton told *CA:* "I am Metis (part Indian, part white). Due to my parents' alcoholism, I grew up in non-native foster homes, as did my two sisters and my older brother. Before I began writing, I lived happily enough in white society, and I had nothing to do with native people or native issues. My brother once told me that my sisters and I were like apples, red on the outside, white on the inside. I was so naive about native issues that I used to think that assimilation was the solution to native problems! When I was fourteen one of my sisters committed suicide and in October of 1980 my oldest sister committed suicide. That's when I decided to write a book; there had been two suicides in my family, the rest of my family members were alcoholics, and we had to be raised in foster homes. I wanted to know why: Was it because we were natives?

"*In Search of April Raintree* is the story of two Metis sisters, Cheryl and April Raintree. They grow up in foster homes, but because April can pass for white and Cheryl cannot and does not desire to do so, they grow apart. In their adult years April distances herself from Cheryl and her Metis heritage. Cheryl tries to convince April to accept who they are, but it is only after Cheryl's suicide that April fully accepts being a native person."

Agnes Grant, writing in *Canadian Literature,* succinctly stated Culleton's reason for writing *In Search of April Raintree:* catharsis. The story's prose is simple and reflects, in Grant's words, "the barren formative years" of Culleton's own upbringing. In her critique for *Native Literature in Canada: From the Oral Tradition to the Present,* Penny Petrone wrote, "While *April Raintree* is depressing, it is elevated from melodramatic cliche by its daring honesty and its energy." Grant concluded, "If this book is judged by whether it works to good effect, communicates, moves us, or makes us see, then it must stand as one of the most scathing indictments of Canadian society that has ever been written."

Culleton said, "After *In Search of April Raintree* was published, I began to be drawn into the native community and issues, particularly the child welfare issues. I learned then that assimilation had been the cause of native problems. By being honest about my feelings in my writing, I had told the stories of many native people, and non-native people could also relate to the stories.

"I know I will never win awards for my literary abilities, or lack of them, and if I did, it would be due to an editor. However, my novel has been used for different courses at universities and colleges, and high school teachers began using it as well. Because of a rape scene and some of the language, the Native Education Branch of Manitoba Education asked if I would revise the book for high school use. Some people feel I should not have bent to the pressure of censorship, but I felt the book was important enough to make it available to high schools. There are not enough materials like this available to readers in the seventh-to-tenth-grade levels.

"Because I had grown up under the threat of nuclear annihilation, I had always been concerned about this issue, though I had never been an activist. *Spirit of the White Bison* came about after I watched the animated *Watership Down,* which was about rabbits. I figured we ought to have a native animation and decided to write a story about a bison. The book is about the near-destruction of the bison: why it occurred and how the advancement of weapons made it possible to happen so quickly. My beliefs in different social and political issues are based more on instinct than on actual knowledge. If I write about an issue, I try to bring forth common sense, and I hope that readers will at least stop to think about what I've written. *Spirit of the White Bison* was my small contribution to the peace movement.

"The most important thing that writing has done for me is to force me to learn, but I never write to teach people. My aim is to provide a good, entertaining story."

BIOGRAPHICAL/CRITICAL SOURCES:

BOOKS

Native North American Literature, Gale (Detroit, MI), 1994.

PERIODICALS

Books in Canada, February, 1984, p. 30.
Canadian Author and Bookman, fall, 1985.
Canadian Literature, spring, 1990, pp. 124, 168.
Emergency Librarian, November, 1985, p. 45; March/April, 1986.
Maclean's, April 21, 1986.
Quill and Quire, November, 1983, p. 20.*

* * *

CULLINAN, Patrick 1932-

PERSONAL: Born May 21, 1932, in Pretoria, South Africa. *Education:* Magdalen College, Oxford, B.A., M.A. (Italian and Russian), 1953.

ADDRESSES: *Office*—Silver Spring, Hout Bay Road, Constantia 7800, South Africa.

CAREER: Freelance writer, 1963—. Farmer and saw miller, eastern Transvaal, 1953-79; Co-founder of Bateleur Press; *The Bloody Horse,* editor, 1980-81; University of the Western Cape, lecturer in English, 1982-92.

AWARDS, HONORS: Olive Schreiner award, 1980; Pringle prize, 1983, 1984, 1990; Sanlam Literary award, 1989.

WRITINGS:

POETRY

The Horizon Forty Miles Away, Polygraph (Johannesburg, South Africa), 1973.
The White Hall in the Orchard and Other Poems, David Philip (Cape Town, South Africa), 1984.
Selected Poems 1961-1991, Artists' Press (Johannesburg), 1992.
Selected Poems, 1961-1994, Snailpress (Plumstead, South Africa), 1994.

OTHER

Robert Jacob Gordon 1743-1795: The Man and His Travels at the Cape (biography), Winchester-Struik (Cape Town), 1992.

Also author of poetry *Today Is Not Different,* 1978.

SIDELIGHTS: Patrick Cullinan's early life afforded him the somewhat unusual combination of an excellent British education in European cultures and literature and a South African national identity. Cullinan was born in South Africa, into a colonial family dynasty established by his grandfather, Sir Thomas Cullinan. Although Cullinan's father had little appreciation for his son's poetic tendencies, he sent the boy to England to be educated first at Charterhouse and then at Oxford. Upon returning to his homeland at the age of twenty-one, Cullinan acknowledged, "I have an enormous amount of Europe in my make-up." Nonetheless, he confirmed, "I [am] an African and always [will] be."

Cullinan's study of Italian, French, and Russian literature provides a broad base for his writings. Roy Macnab, writing in *Contemporary Poets,* noted that Cullinan's work "reveals a sophistication and modernism which gives it a dimension far beyond the local." While Cullinan's poems express his interest in South Africa's history, especially his interest in some of its early European explorers, he is primarily a metaphysical poet, asking questions of a philosophical nature. Cullinan also explores, in Macnab's words, "the nature of poetry, how and why it is written." These concerns set Cullinan's poetry apart from the writings of his South African contemporaries, which are often politically oriented.

BIOGRAPHICAL/CRITICAL SOURCES:

BOOKS

Contemporary Poets, sixth edition, St. James Press (Detroit, MI), 1996.

PERIODICALS

Times Literary Supplement, May 10, 1985, p. 527; June 4, 1993, p.14.*

* * *

CUMBERLAND, Marten 1892-1972 (R. Laugier, Kevin O'Hara; James Bevis, a joint pseudonym)

PERSONAL: Born July 23, 1892, in London, England; son of Alfred (a member of the London Stock Exchange) and Ada Frances (Fletcher) Cumberland; married Kathleen Walsh, November 28, 1928. *Education:* Attended Cranleigh School, Surrey, England.

CAREER: Ran away from home and stock exchange job at eighteen; trained as wireless operator and went to sea on an Argentine ship in 1913; after service in British Merchant Navy, 1914-18, his short stories brought offer of assistant editorship of *New Illustrated* (weekly paper), London, England; when paper failed, joined staff of *Harmsworth Encyclopaedia,* London, 1919-20, resigning to become one of first advertising consultants, 1920-22; assistant fiction editor of Sir Edward Hulton Press (later Allied Newspapers), London, 1922-24; freelance writer in England, Paris, France, and Dublin, Ireland, 1924-72.

WRITINGS:

(With Raymond Harrison) *The New Economics,* Cecil Palmer, 1922, 2nd edition, Stanley Nott, 1936.
(With B. V. Shann) *Behind the Scenes* (novel), Cecil Palmer, 1923, 2nd edition, published under joint pseudonym James Bevis, 1933.
(With Shann) *Loaded Dice,* Methuen, 1926, 2nd edition, published under joint pseudonym James Bevis, 1933.
(With Michael Joseph) *How to Write Serial Fiction,* Henry Holt, 1928, published as Part 4 of omnibus volume *The Complete Writing for Profit,* Hutchinson, 1930.
(With Granville Hill) *Spoils and Stratagems* (one-act play), G. Hill, 1931.
The Sin of David (novel), Selwyn & Blount, 1932.
(With Shann) *Murder at Midnight,* Mellifont, 1935.
Birds of Prey, Gramol, 1937.
Climbing (three-act comedy; produced in London, 1937, then United States), W. H. Baker, 1937.
The Testing of Tony, Macdonald, 1943.

MYSTERY NOVELS

The Perilous Way, Jarrolds, 1926.
The Dark House, Gramol, 1935.
The Devil's Snare, Gramol, 1935.
The Imposter, Gramol, 1935.
Shadowed, Mellifont, 1936.
Someone Must Die, Hurst & Blackett, 1940.
Questionable Shape, Hurst & Blackett, 1941.
Quislings over Paris, Hurst & Blackett, 1942.
The Knife Will Fall, Hurst & Blackett, 1943, Doubleday, Doran, 1944.
Everything He Touched, Macdonald, 1945.
Not Expected to Live (originally known as "*The Lorrain-Prad Affair*"), Hurst & Blackett, 1945.
Steps in the Dark, Doubleday, Doran, 1945.
A Dilemma for Dax, Doubleday, 1946, published as *Hearsed in Death,* Hurst & Blackett, 1947.
A Lovely Corpse, Hurst & Blackett, 1946.
Darkness as a Bride, Hurst & Blackett, 1947.
Hate Will Find a Way, Doubleday, 1947, published as *And Worms Have Eaten Them,* Hurst & Blackett, 1948.
And Then Came Fear, Doubleday, 1948.
The Crime School, Eldon, 1949.
The Man Who Covered Mirrors, Doubleday, 1949.
Policeman's Nightmare, Doubleday, 1949.
The House in the Forest, Doubleday, 1950, published as *Confetti Can Be Red,* Hurst and Blackett, 1951.
On the Danger List, Hurst & Blackett, 1950.
Fade out the Stars, Doubleday, 1952.
Grave Consequences, Doubleday, 1952, published as *Booked for Death,* Hurst & Blackett, 1952.
One Foot in the Grave, Hurst & Blackett, 1952.
Etched in Violence, Hurst & Blackett, 1953, McGraw, 1955.
Nobody Is Safe, Doubleday, 1953, published as *Which of Us Is Safe?,* Hurst & Blackett, 1953.
The Frightened Brides, Hurst & Blackett, 1954.
Unto Death Utterly, Hurst & Blackett, 1954, McGraw, 1955.
The Change Is Murder, Hurst & Blackett, 1955.
Lying at Death's Door, Hurst & Blackett, 1956.
Far Better Dead!, Hutchinson, 1957.
Hate for Sale, British Book Centre, 1957.
Out of This World, Hutchinson, 1958.
Murmurs in the Rue Morgue, London House & Maxwell, 1959.
Remains to Be Seen, Hutchinson, 1960.
There Must Be Victims, Hutchinson, 1961.
Attention! Saturnin Dax!, Hutchinson, 1962.
Postscript to a Death, Hutchinson, 1963.
Hate Finds a Way, Hutchinson, 1964.
The Dice Were Loaded, Hutchinson, 1965.
No Sentiment in Murder, Hutchinson, 1966.

MYSTERY NOVELS UNDER PSEUDONYM KEVIN O'HARA

The Customer's Always Wrong, Hurst & Blackett, 1951.
Exit and Curtain, Hurst & Blackett, 1952.
Sing, Clubman, Sing!, Hurst & Blackett, 1952.
Always Tell the Sleuth, Hurst & Blackett, 1953.
It Leaves Them Cold, Hurst & Blackett, 1954.
Keep Your Fingers Crossed, Hurst & Blackett, 1955.
The Pace That Kills, Hurst & Blackett, 1955.
Danger: Women at Work, John Long, 1958.
Women Like to Know, Jarrolds, 1958.
And Here Is the Noose, John Long, 1959.
Well, I'll Be Hanged!, John Long, 1960.
Taking Life Easy, John Long, 1961.
If Anything Should Happen, John Long, 1962.
Don't Tell the Police, John Long, 1963.
Don't Neglect the Body, John Long, 1964.

It's Your Funeral, John Long, 1966.

OTHER PLAYS PRODUCED

Inside the Room, London, 1934.
(Adaptor from the French) Louis Verneuil, *No Ordinary Lady,* London, 1936.
Men and Wife, London, 1937.
Believe It or Not, London, 1938.
(With Claude Houghton) *Baxter's Second Wife,* London, 1949.

Also author of ballet, *The Golden Bell of Ko,* with music by Aloys Fleischmann, produced at Cork Opera House. Stories included in Edward O'Brien's *Best Short Stories of the Year* series, Dodd, 1927-32, and in *Best Detective Stories of the Year,* Faber, 1933.

Contributor of verse, short stories, and essays to *New Age* (and later to *New English Weekly*), some under pseudonym R. Laugier, 1920-39; humorous essays to *Daily Herald* (London), 1921; short stories and *A Paris Letter,* to *Daily Dispatch* (Manchester), 1930-31; stories and essays to *Ideas,* and stories to *Truth,* both for a twenty-year period; serials to King Features Syndicate, *Montreal Standard,* and *Toronto Star;* reviews, stories, and articles to *Dublin Magazine* for ten years.

Also contributor at various times to most London newspapers, and to *Men Only, Argosy, Adelphi, Everybody's Weekly, Theatrical World, Strand, Mystery Stories Magazine* (United States), *Lilliput, Irish Digest, Time and Tide, Crimnology, Kilkenny,* and other magazines; short stories and plays to Radio Eireann.

ADAPTATIONS: Inside the Room was sold to Ambassador Films in England and was adapted for television production in America.

SIDELIGHTS: Despite the considerable international success of his detective novels, Marten Cumberland considered himself essentially a man of the theatre. He first became aware of this leaning in 1932 and set about writing ten hours a day until two years later when the London production of "Inside the Room" established his reputation as a playwright. He wrote plays until his death, but believed that the interruption of the war took the edges off his full potential as a playwright.

"A dramatist was knocked out by War II," he said, "and started writing this stuff." The "stuff" Cumberland was referring to were his thirty-some-odd detective novels featuring French Commissaire Saturnin Dax and his thriller series about the half-Argentinian, half-Irish, London-based private eye, Chico Brett. In *Twentieth-Century Crime and Mystery Writers,* Mary Ann Grochowski called the Dax mysteries well-written "intellectual puzzlers," noting they are generally intricate in plot, though slow in action. Cumberland took an entirely different approach in the Brett series. Grochowski described these stories as apparently simple cases in which Brett "inevitably finds himself embroiled in a tangled web of passionate crime."

Cumberland's thrillers have appeared in thirty countries in fifteen languages. More than a million and a half of the Dax stories have been sold in Germany alone in the past decade and as many of the Brett books in less time. Eleven of the Dax stories have borne the Doubleday Crime Club imprint.

BIOGRAPHICAL/CRITICAL SOURCES:

BOOKS

Twentieth-Century Crime and Mystery Writers, second edition, St. Martin's Press (New York City), 1985.*

* * *

CUMMING, Primrose Amy 1915-

PERSONAL: Born April 7, 1915, in Isle of Thanet, England; daughter of Arthur Somerville and Emily Christin (Heath) Cumming. *Education:* Educated privately. *Politics:* Liberal. *Religion:* "Christian in the broadest sense." *Avocational interests:* Countryside, horses (riding, breeding, and schooling), gardening, flower arranging, music, handiwork.

ADDRESSES: Home—Wynberg, Sandhurst, Hawkhurst, Kent, England.

CAREER: Writer. *Military service:* Auxiliary Territorial Service, 1940-45.

WRITINGS:

JUVENILES

Doney, Country Life, 1934.
Spider Dog, Country Life, 1936.
Silver Snaffles, Blackie & Son, 1937.
The Silver Eagle Riding School, A. & C. Black, 1938.
Rachel of Romney, Country Life, 1939.
The Wednesday Pony, Blackie & Son, 1939.

Ben: The Story of a Cart-Horse, Dent, 1939.
Silver Eagle Carries On, A. & C. Black, 1940.
The Chestnut Filly, Blackie & Son, 1940.
Owls Castle Farm, A. & C. Black, 1942.
The Great Horses, Dent, 1946.
Trouble at Trimbles, Country Life, 1949.
Four Rode Home, Dent, 1951.
Rivals to Silver Eagle, A. & C. Black, 1954.
No Place for Ponies, Dent, 1954, published as *The Mystery Pony,* Criterion, 1957.
The Deep Sea Horse, Dent, 1956.
The Flying Horseman, Dent, 1959.
The Mystery Trek, Dent, 1964.
Foal of the Fjords, Dent, 1966.
Penny and Pegasus, Dent, 1969.

Regular contributor of scripts to pictorial magazines and annuals.

SIDELIGHTS: Born in 1915, and growing up in a rural farming community in England without electricity, running water, or a telephone in her home, Primrose Amy Cumming filled her days with reading and exploring the countryside. She was inspired by the everyday dramas of country life and by special events, such as annual fairs, traveling circuses, and bands of gypsies who sometimes camped nearby. Cumming began recording her thoughts on paper at an early age and was published while still a teenager.

Cumming's first book, *Doney,* was inspired by a pony owned by one of her friends. Other "pony books" followed, and she purchased a pony of her own from the proceeds of her first book. Cumming became one of the original practitioners of this popular genre that Marcus Crouch, writing for *Twentieth-Century Children's Writers,* referred to as "books about pony-worship and pony-mad children."

For over thirty years Cumming wrote of the exploits of children and ponies. However, as Crouch pointed out, "Cumming was always aware of the dangers of becoming identified with a limited byway of literature." Thus she has made more than one conscious departure from her established niche. Cumming said, "I have widened my field to include ballet dancers, gymnasts and young explorers, even car, engine and elephant characters, a cornet-player and a bagpiper." Yet, she acknowledged, horses still "manage to push their noses into my books even when I have meant to concentrate on humans." In *Ben: The Story of a Cart-Horse,* Cumming collaborated with photographer Harold Burdekin to document the life of a working farm horse. *The Great Horses* is a fictional representation of three historic periods which show the descent of the draft horse from the warhorses brought to England by the conquering Normans.

Cumming told *CA:* "I write for children to try to interest them in the country things that enthralled me as a child—and still do. After over forty years it is very rewarding to find one's books are being passed down the generations as family heirlooms." Four of Cumming's books have been translated into Swedish.

BIOGRAPHICAL/CRITICAL SOURCES:

BOOKS

Something about the Author, Volume 24, Gale (Detroit, MI), 1981.
Twentieth-Century Children's Writers, fourth edition, St. James Press (Detroit, MI), 1995.

PERIODICALS

Books and Bookmen, August, 1969, p. 46; January, 1970, p. 40.
Times Literary Supplement, May 19, 1966, p. 437.*

* * *

CUMMINGS, Jack
See CUMMINGS, John W(illiam), Jr.

* * *

CUMMINGS, John W(illiam), Jr. 1940-
(Jack Cummings)

PERSONAL: Born March 30, 1940, in Fort Lauderdale, FL; son of John William (a realtor) and Jeanne (a realtor; maiden name, Jones) Cummings; married Gloria Lopez (a travel agent), October 31, 1963; children: Robert, Anne Marie. *Education:* University of Florida, A.A., 1959; attended Wofford College, 1960; Drake College, B.S./B.A., 1962; graduate studies at University of Liege and University of Madrid. *Religion:* Methodist.

ADDRESSES: Home—3111 Northeast 22nd St., Fort Lauderdale, FL 33305.

CAREER: Realtor, 1964—. President of Investment Division of Fort Lauderdale Board of Realtors, 1966,

1972; member of board of directors of Fort Lauderdale Symphony Orchestra, 1974; director of Fort Lauderdale Junior Achievement, 1976. *Military service:* U.S. Air Force, 1961.

MEMBER: National Association of Realtors, National Association of Real Estate Editors, Fort Lauderdale Toastmasters Club (president, 1973).

WRITINGS:

The Ultimate Game (novel), Major Books, 1976.

UNDER NAME JACK CUMMINGS

The Venture (novel), Charter House Publishers, 1978.
Complete Guide to Real Estate Financing, Prentice-Hall, 1978, revised edition, 1979.
Lauderdale Run (novel), Manor Books, 1979.
Complete Handbook of How to "Farm" Real Estate Listings and Sales, Prentice-Hall, 1979.
Successful Real Estate Investing for the Single Person, Playboy Press, 1980.
Cashless Investing in Real Estate, Playboy Press, 1982, revised edition published as *$1,000 Down Can Make You Rich,* Prentice-Hall, 1985.
Creative Investing in Real Estate, H. Pierce & Co., 1982.
Real Estate Financing Manual, Prentice-Hall, 1986.
The Guide to Real Estate Exchanging, Wiley, 1991.
The Business Travel Survival Guide, Wiley, 1991.
The Thirty-Six Hour Real Estate Investing Course, McGraw, 1992.
The Real Estate Investor's Answer Book, McGraw, 1994.

OTHER

Also author of *This Condo'll Kill Ya,* a two-act play, and *Cocaine Alley,* a screenplay.

SIDELIGHTS: In *Successful Real Estate Investing for the Single Person,* Jack Cummings advises unmarried persons of all ages and circumstances on the many advantages of real estate ownership. He recommends particularly the tax advantage and inflation protection offered single people by such investment. Convinced that neither lack of money nor lack of spouse ought to prevent home ownership, Cummings offers a wide range of investment opportunities for unmarried people, including condominiums, houses, apartment complexes, vacant land, and commercial and recreational property. Alan Wolfe, member of *Nation*'s editorial board, describes *Successful Real Estate Investing for the Single Person* as "a guidebook to the illicit, a set of rules about how to procreate and multiply in a world of ever-changing real estate transactions," and, in his examination of five other real estate investment titles which appeared in the expanding economy of the early 1980s, judged Cummings's book "the most interesting of the lot."

In *Cashless Investing in Real Estate,* Cummings presents forty techniques which allow a buyer to purchase property without using any of his own money. Cummings explains the advantages and pitfalls of each method he suggests and illustrates them with case histories.

Cummings once told *CA:* "My motivation has been to express things as I feel them and to allow my mind to be visible on paper in as structured and clear a form as possible. My past has allowed me to travel extensively and to have had many varied experiences on which to draw as a temper and backdrop for my work. I believe that no matter the kind of writing, it must be entertaining.

"I speak Spanish, understand French, and am conversant in English, although I was once nearly deterred from being a writer by a mindless university professor who said that since I couldn't spell worth a 'dam,' I should consider a non-writing profession. Editors have since told me that a writer's gift isn't the properly spelled word but the picture the words placed on paper depict."

Cummings adds that he lectures frequently throughout the world and spends eight to ten weeks each year on board cruise lines as a speaker on numerous topics. He told *CA* that on one cruise he "provided several lectures that combined the history of wine development with wine tastings of Spanish wine and brandy."

BIOGRAPHICAL/CRITICAL SOURCES:

PERIODICALS

Booklist, August, 1991, p. 2094.
Library Journal, August, 1991, p. 130.
Nation, May 16, 1981.*

* * *

CUMMINGS, Ray(mond King) 1887-1957

PERSONAL: Born August 30, 1887, in New York, NY; died of a stroke, January 23, 1957, in Mount Vernon,

NY; married Janet Matheson (divorced); married Gabrielle Wilson; children: (first marriage) Harry Matheson; (second marriage) Elizabeth Starr Hill. *Education:* Attended Princeton University.

CAREER: Writer, 1919-57. Early occupations included gold prospecting, working on oil fields and orange plantations; worked as an editor for Thomas Alva Edison, 1914-19.

WRITINGS:

SCIENCE FICTION NOVELS

The Girl in the Golden Atom, Methuen, 1922, Harper, 1923.
The Man Who Mastered Time, McClurg, 1929.
The Sea Girl, McClurg, 1930.
Tarrano the Conqueror, McClurg, 1930.
Brigands of the Moon, McClurg, 1931.
Into the Fourth Dimension, Swan, 1943.
The Shadow Girl, Swan, 1946, Ace, 1962.
The Princess of the Atom, Avon, 1950.
The Man on the Meteor, Swan, 1952.
Beyond the Vanishing Point, Ace, 1958.
Wandl, the Invader, Ace, 1961.
Beyond the Stars, Ace, 1963.
A Brand New World, Ace, 1964.
The Exile of Time, Avalon, 1964.
Explorers into Infinity, Avalon, 1965.
Tama of the Light Country, Ace, 1965.
Tama, Princess of Mercury, Ace, 1966.
The Insect Invasion, Avalon, 1967.

Contributor of over seven hundred and fifty short stories under various pseudonyms to numerous periodicals.

SIDELIGHTS: Ray Cummings was a popular author of science fiction, detective and horror stories whose work is little known today except among collectors of pulp magazines. His first and most successful novel, *The Girl in the Golden Atom,* is about a man who discovers a drug which allows him to change size and have incredible adventures on a world that exists on an atom of gold. A number of Cummings' novels after the publication of *The Girl in the Golden Atom,* such as *Explorers into Infinity, The Princess of the Atom,* and *Beyond the Vanishing Point,* were based on this concept of a size-altering drug. The best Cummings novels, noted Erich S. Rupprecht in the *Dictionary of Literary Biography,* are his earlier works, which are "often clear, spare, and straightforward." After publishing numerous books based on variations of his first idea, the author's writing became repetitious, careless, and cliched, according to Rupprecht. But although the critic points out that "it would be easy to sneer at Cumming's work today," he also recognizes that "had it not been for pioneers like Cummings writing in the early decades of the century and helping to popularize this new genre, it is doubtful whether science fiction would have achieved the success it now enjoys."

BIOGRAPHICAL/CRITICAL SOURCES:

BOOKS

Dictionary of Literary Biography, Volume 8: *Twentieth-Century American Science Fiction Writers,* Gale (Detroit, MI), 1981.

(Sketch reviewed by daughter, Elizabeth Starr Hill)

* * *

CURTIS, Tony 1946-

PERSONAL: Born December 26, 1946, in Carmarthen, Wales; son of Leslie Thomas (a mechanic) and Doris Elizabeth (Williams) Curtis; married Margaret Blundell (a teacher), March 30, 1971; children: Gareth, Bronwen. *Education:* University College of Swansea, University of Wales, B.A. (with honors), 1969; Goddard College, M.F.A., 1980.

ADDRESSES: Home—Pentwyn, 55 Colcot Rd., Barry CF6 8BQ, Wales.

CAREER: Grammar school, Wilmslow, England, assistant teacher, 1969-71; grammar school, Maltby, England, second in charge of English, 1971-74; Polytechnic of Wales, Pontypridd, senior lecturer in English, 1974—. Founder of Edge Press, 1977. Chairman of the Welsh Academy, 1984—; director of Cardiff Literature Festival, 1986.

MEMBER: Yr Academi Gymreig (executive member, 1977-82).

AWARDS, HONORS: Eric Gregory Award, Society of Authors, 1972, for poetry; Young Poet's Prize, Welsh Arts Council, 1974; poetry prize, Stroud Festival, 1980, for "Jack Watts," and 1981, for "Affairs"; winner of 1984 national poetry competition.

WRITINGS:

POETRY

Walk Down a Welsh Wind, Phoenix Pamphlet Poets Press, 1972.
Album, Christopher Davies, 1974.
(With Duncan Bush and Nigel Jenkins) *Three Young Anglo-Welsh Poets,* Welsh Arts Council, 1974.
(Editor) *Pembrokeshire Poems,* Pembrokeshire Handbooks, 1975.
Carnival, Alun, 1978.
Preparations, Gomer Press, 1980.
(Editor) *The Art of Seamus Heaney,* Poetry Wales Press, 1982, second revised edition, Dufour, 1985.
Letting Go, Poetry Wales Press, 1983.
Selected Poems, 1970-85, Poetry Wales Press, 1986.
Poems Selected and New, Story Line Press, 1986.
(Editor) *The Poetry of Snowdonia,* Seren Books (Chester Springs, PA), 1989.
Taken for Pearls: New Poems, Seren, 1993.
War Voices, Seren, 1995.

OTHER

Islands (one-act play), first broadcast by British Broadcasting Corp. (BBC-Radio Wales), March 26, 1975.
Out of the Dark Woods (stories), Edge Press, 1977.
Dannie Abse (monograph), University of Wales Press, 1985.
(Editor with Cliff James) *Writing in Wales: A Resource Pack,* Welsh Academy, 1985.
(Editor) *Wales: The Imagined Nation* (essays in cultural and national identity), Poetry Wales Press, 1986.
(Editor with Sian James) *Love from Wales: An Anthology,* Seren, 1991.
(Editor) *How Poets Work,* Seren, 1996.

Editor of *Madog Arts,* 1977-81.

WORK IN PROGRESS: Throwing the Punch, a book of selected stories; *How to Study a Contemporary Poem,* for Macmillan.

SIDELIGHTS: Tony Curtis told *CA:* "I believe that one can be taught to write. We in the United Kingdom have lagged behind the United States in this respect. However, one has to keep returning to one's own feelings and needs, and weighing one's work against those criteria despite critical or commercial pressures. A really serious writer ought to be able to go into areas of experience without restraint and to explore his or her reaction to those experiences in the most suitable medium."

BIOGRAPHICAL/CRITICAL SOURCES:

PERIODICALS

Times Literary Supplement, March 6, 1981; March 2, 1984; June 13, 1986.*

* * *

CUSHING, Peter (Wilton) 1913-1994

PERSONAL: Born May 26, 1913, in Kenley, Surrey, England; died of cancer, August 11, 1994, in Canterbury, England; son of George Edward (a quantity surveyor) and Nellie Maria (a homemaker; maiden name, King) Cushing; married Violet Helen Beck, April 10, 1943 (died January 14, 1971). *Education:* Attended Guildhall School of Music and Drama. *Religion:* Church of England. *Avocational interests:* Nature study, social history, and watercolor painting.

CAREER: Surveyor's assistant with Coulsdon and Purley Urban District Council, England, c. 1934; professional actor, 1935-94. Appeared in nearly one hundred films, including *Vigil in the Night,* 1939; *A Chump at Oxford,* 1941; *Hamlet,* Universal, 1948; *Moulin Rouge,* 1951; *Black Knight,* 1954; *The End of the Affair,* Columbia, 1955; *Alexander the Great,* United Artists, 1956; *Magic Fire,* Republic, 1956; *Time without Pity,* 1956; *Abominable Snowman,* Twentieth Century-Fox, 1957; *The Curse of Frankenstein,* 1957; *The Revenge of Frankenstein,* Columbia, 1958; *The Horror of Dracula,* Universal International, 1958; *John Paul Jones,* Warner Bros., 1959; *The Hound of the Baskervilles,* United Artists, 1959; *The Mummy,* 1959; *The Brides of Dracula,* Universal, 1960; *The Sword of Sherwood Forest,* Columbia, 1961; *The Naked Edge,* United Artists, 1961; *Cash on Demand,* Columbia, 1962; *Night Creatures,* Universal, 1962; *The Man Who Finally Died,* 1962; *Fury at Smuggler's Bay,* Embassy, 1963; *The Evil of Frankenstein,* Universal, 1964; *The Gorgon,* Columbia, 1965; *Dr. Terror's House of Horrors,* Paramount, 1965; *She,* Metro-Goldwyn-Mayer, 1965; *The Skull,* Paramount, 1965; *Dr. Who and the Daleks,* Continental, 1966; *Daleks—Invasion Earth 2150 A.D.,* 1966; *Frankenstein Created Woman,* Twentieth Century-Fox, 1967; *Island of Terror,* Universal, 1967; *Some May Live,* 1967; *The Night of the Big Heat,* 1967; *The Torture Garden,* Columbia, 1968; *Corruption,* Columbia, 1968.

Frankenstein Must Be Destroyed, Warner Bros., 1970; *Scream and Scream Again,* American International Pictures, 1970; *The House That Dripped Blood,* Cinerama, 1971; *The Vampire Lovers,* 1971; *Dracula A.D. 1972,* Warner Bros., 1972; *Fear in the Night,* Hammer Films, 1972; *Asylum,* Cinerama, 1972; *The Creeping Flesh,* Columbia, 1972; *I, Monster,* 1972; *Nothing but the Night,* 1972; *Panico en el Transiberiano,* 1972; *Tales from the Crypt,* 1972; *Horror Express,* Scotia International, 1973; *Dynasty of Fear,* Hammer Films, 1973; *And Now the Screaming Starts,* 1973; *The Satanic Rites of Dracula,* 1973; *From beyond the Grave,* 1973; *Frankenstein and the Monster from Hell,* Paramount, 1974; *Count Dracula and His Vampire Bride,* 1974; *La Grande Trouille,* 1974; *The Beast Must Die,* Cinerama, 1975; *The Legend of the Werewolf,* Tyburn Films, 1975; *Dracula and the Seven Golden Vampires,* 1975; *Almost Human,* 1975; *At the Earth's Core,* American International, 1976; *Call Him Mr. Shatter,* 1976; *Trial by Combat,* 1976; *Star Wars,* Twentieth Century-Fox, 1977; *Shock Waves,* 1977; *Die Standarte,* 1977; *The Uncanny,* Astral Films, 1978; *Arabian Adventure,* Associated Film Distributors, 1979; *The Ghoul,* Tyburn Films, 1981; *Monster Island,* 1981; *Sword of the Valiant,* Cannon Films, 1983; *The House of the Long Shadows,* 1983; *Top Secret!,* Paramount, 1984; *Bloodsuckers,* VCL Communications, 1985; *Biggles,* Yellowbill Productions, 1985; *Cone of Silence,* 1985; *Battleflag; Hitler's Son; Touch of the Sun; Black Jack; Violent Playground; Suspect; The Flesh and the Friends; The Devil's Agent; The Hell-Fire Club; The Frighten Bed Island; Death's Head Moth; Doctors Wear Scarlet; The Bride of Fengriffen; The Revenge of Dr. Death; Tender Dracula; The Devil's People;* and *Death Corps.*

Performed in television roles, including Professor Copeland in *Helen Keller: The Miracle Continues,* 1984, and Sherlock Holmes in *The Masks of Death,* 1984.

MEMBER: Royal Society for the Protection of Birds, National Trust.

AWARDS, HONORS: National Television Award for outstanding actor of the year from *Daily Mail,* 1954; Best Performance Award from Guild of Television Producers and Directors, 1955, for his role in *1984;* Television Top Ten Award for best actor from *News Chronicle,* 1956; Licorne d'or Award of France, 1973, for his role in *Tales from the Crypt;* named to the order of the British Empire, 1989.

WRITINGS:

Peter Cushing: An Autobiography, Weidenfeld & Nicolson, 1986.

Past Forgetting: Memoirs of the Hammer Years, Weidenfeld & Nicolson, 1988.

SIDELIGHTS: Actor and author Peter Cushing was best known for his roles in a series of horror films produced by Great Britain's prolific Hammer studio, including *The Curse of Frankenstein, The Horror of Dracula, The Evil of Frankenstein, Dr. Terror's House of Horrors,* and *Tales from the Crypt.* After studying at the Guildhall School of Music and Drama, Cushing made his stage debut in 1935 and later joined Sir Laurence Olivier's Old Vic repertory company. In 1948 he played the role of Osric in Olivier's acclaimed film version of *Hamlet* and subsequently appeared in a number of other films and on television before beginning his affiliation with Hammer in 1957. Thereafter Cushing became—with Christopher Lee and Vincent Price—one of Hammer's central players, creating convincingly sinister characters and earning praise for his polished acting style. Cushing won several awards for acting, and was named to the order of the British Empire in 1989. Cushing also wrote two books about his life, *Peter Cushing: An Autobiography* and *Past Forgetting: A Memoir of the Hammer Years.*

BIOGRAPHICAL/CRITICAL SOURCES:

BOOKS

Del Vecchio, Deborah, and Tom Johnson, *Peter Cushing: The Gentle Man of Horror and His 91,* McFarland & Co. (Jefferson, NC), 1992.

Miller, Mark A., *Christopher Lee and Peter Cushing and Horror Cinema: A Filmography of Their 22 Collaborations,* McFarland, 1995.

OBITUARIES:

PERIODICALS

Chicago Tribune, August 12, 1994, sec. 3, p. 12.

Los Angeles Times, August 12, 1994, p. A26.

New York Times, August 12, 1994, p. A21.

Times (London), August 12, 1994, p. 17.

Washington Post, August 12, 1994, p. B6.*

D

D'AGUIAR, Fred 1960-

PERSONAL: Born February 2, 1960, in London, England. *Education:* University of Kent at Canterbury, B.A. (with honors), 1985.

ADDRESSES: *Home*—England and the United States. *Agent*—Curtis Brown Ltd., 10 Astor Place, New York, NY 10003.

CAREER: Cambridge University, Cambridge, England, visiting fellow, 1989-90; Amherst College, Amherst, MA, visiting writer, 1992-94; Bates College, Lewiston, ME, assistant professor of English, 1994-95; University of Miami, Coral Gables, FL, professor of English, 1995—. Trained and worked as a psychiatric nurse.

AWARDS, HONORS: Minority Rights Group award, 1983; University of Kent T. S. Eliot prize, 1984; G.L.C. literature award, 1985; Guyana Prize for Poetry from the Guyanese government, 1989, for *Mama Dot* and *Airy Hall;* David Higham First Novel Award from the Book Trust (London, England), 1995, for *The Longest Memory;* Whitbread Award from the Booksellers Association of Great Britain and Ireland, 1995, for *The Longest Memory.*

WRITINGS:

Mama Dot (poems), Chatto & Windus (London), 1985.
Airy Hall (poems), Chatto & Windus, 1989.
Sweet Thames (teleplay), BBC 2, 1992.
1492 (radio), BBC Radio 3, 1992.
British Subjects (poems), Bloodaxe (Newcastle upon Tyne), 1993.
Rain (teleplay), BBC 2, 1994.
The Longest Memory (novel), Pantheon (New York), 1995.
A Jamaican Airman Foresees His Death (play), Methuen (London), 1995.
Dear Future (novel), Pantheon (New York), 1996.

Also editor, with others, of *The New British Poetry,* Paladin Grafton (London), 1988; fiction, nonfiction, and poetry have appeared in numerous periodicals and anthologies.

SIDELIGHTS: Fred D'Aguiar told *CA:* "I was born in London, grew up in Guyana, and then returned to England for my teen and adult years. My poetry and prose deal with these two landscapes. Add to that a U.S. experience and a black perspective. For me, imaginative writing is about historical recovery and finding forms to shape memory. Discovery is a part of the equation, too. The oxygen for all this is love and loss."

When he was not quite two years old, D'Aguiar's parents sent him from London to Guyana, to be reared by his grandmother, Mama Dot, and a multi-cultural extended family that lived in a big house called Airy Hall forty miles outside the capital of Georgetown. D'Aguiar's first book, a poetry collection titled *Mama Dot,* is a series of occasional poems based on the composite character of his two grandmothers (the second lived in Georgetown). The image of woman as mother or grandmother is central in the poems and is developed in the multi-shaped metaphor of Mama Dot. The first part of the book comprises fourteen Mama Dot poems with titles such as "Oracle Mama Dot," "Mama Dot's Treatise," and "Carnival Mama Dot." The poet fuses the mythic and the quotidian qualities of the grandmother figure, and through her he connects to an African past—a connection that has been compelling and central in the work of many Caribbean writers of African ancestry, including Derek Wolcott. God-like,

Mama Dot's words and gestures create, punish, and heal. Simultaneously she is a no-nonsense, practical Caribbean woman. The second section, "Roots Broadcasts," contains eleven poems less tightly tied by theme and metaphor than those in the first section. Although they deal to some extent with experiences of metropolitan alienation, they never really depart from Guyana as the beginning and end of D'Aguiar's consciousness. The third section of the book, one long poem called "Guyana Days," completes the cycle with the poet's adult return to the country of his youth and confirms a central theme, that only by a return to childhood can the child in man mature.

D'Aguiar's first novel, *The Longest Memory,* tells the story of a young slave who tries to escape from a Virginia plantation but whose own father betrays him. Many critics noted D'Aguiar's ability to create a powerful emotional impact with relatively few words and a restrained style. *New York Times* contributor Michael Ross credited the author's "impressive economy of style." A *Kirkus Reviews* writer called *The Longest Memory* "a small book with the emotional impact of a wide-screen blockbuster." *Booklist* s Brad Hooper ranked the book with Toni Morrison's *Beloved,* then added that "no fiction collection can do without it."

Dear Future, D'Aguiar's second novel, also revolves around a tragic incident involving two male family members. This time, the hero, Red Head, is hit on the head with an axe at the age of nine. The unwitting perpetrator is his uncle. This second novel was less enthusiastically received than the first. Christopher Atamian, in the *New York Times,* wrote that D'Aguiar "never lets us penetrate deeply enough into his characters' motivations and desires." Brad Hooper, again writing for *Booklist,* called *Dear Future* "less cohesive and compelling" than its predecessor.

BIOGRAPHICAL/CRITICAL SOURCES:

BOOKS

Contemporary Poets, 6th edition, St. James Press, 1996.

Dictionary of Literary Biography, Volume 157: *Twentieth-Century Caribbean and Black African Writers,* 3rd Series, Gale, 1996.

PERIODICALS

Booklist, December 15, 1994, pp. 735, 743; August 19, 1996, p.1880.

Kirkus Reviews, November 1, 1994, p. 1428; August 1, 1996, p.1071.

Los Angeles Times Book Review, March 5, 1995, p. 6; February 4, 1996, p. 11.

Nation, January 13, 1997, p. 32.

New York Times Book Review, May 7, 1995, p. 26; March 24, 1996, p. 28; November 10, 1996, p. 56.*

* * *

DALY, Maureen 1921-
(Maureen Daly McGivern)

PERSONAL: Born March 15, 1921, in Castlecaufield, County Tyrone, Ulster, Ireland; naturalized U.S. citizen; daughter of Joseph Desmond (a salesman) and Margaret (Mellon-Kelly) Daly; married William P. McGivern (a writer), December 28, 1946 (died, November, 1983); children: Megan (deceased), Patrick. *Education:* Rosary College, B.A., 1942. *Politics:* Democrat.

ADDRESSES: Home—73-305 Ironwood St., Palm Desert, CA 92260. *Agent*—Eleanor Wood, Blassingame, McCauley, and Wood, 432 Park Ave. S., Suite 1205, New York, NY 10016.

CAREER: Writer, 1938—. *Chicago Tribune,* Chicago, IL, reporter and columnist, 1941-44; Chicago City News Bureau, Chicago, reporter, 1941-43; *Ladies' Home Journal,* Philadelphia, PA, associate editor, 1944-49; *Saturday Evening Post,* Philadelphia, PA, consultant to editors, 1960-69; *Desert Sun,* Palm Desert, CA, reporter and columnist, 1987—. Screenwriter for Twentieth Century-Fox. Lecturer on foreign lands and emerging nations.

MEMBER: PEN, Mystery Writers of America, Writers Guild of America (West).

AWARDS, HONORS: Scholastic magazine's short story contest, third prize, 1936, for "Fifteen," first prize, 1937, for "Sixteen"; O. Henry Memorial Award, 1938, for short story "Sixteen"; Dodd, Mead Intercollegiate Literary Fellowship Novel Award, 1942, and Lewis Carroll Shelf Award, 1969, both for *Seventeenth Summer;* Freedoms Foundation Award, 1952, for "humanity in reporting"; Gimbel Fashion Award, 1962, for contribution to U.S. fashion industry through *Saturday Evening Post* articles; *Redbook*'s ten great books for teens, 1987, for *Acts of Love.*

WRITINGS:

YOUNG ADULT FICTION

Seventeenth Summer, Dodd, 1942, illustrated edition, 1948.
Sixteen and Other Stories, illustrated by Kendall Rossi, Dodd, 1961.
Acts of Love, Scholastic, 1986.
First a Dream, Scholastic, 1990.

YOUNG ADULT NONFICTION

Smarter and Smoother: A Handbook on How to Be That Way, illustrated by Marguerite Bryan, Dodd, 1944.
What's Your P.Q. (Personality Quotient)?, illustrated by Ellie Simmons, Dodd, 1952, revised edition, 1966.
Twelve around the World, illustrated by Frank Kramer, Dodd, 1957.
Spanish Roundabout (travel), Dodd, 1960.
Moroccan Roundabout (travel), Dodd, 1961.

ADULT NONFICTION

The Perfect Hostess: Complete Etiquette and Entertainment for the Home, Dodd, 1950.
(Under name Maureen Daly McGivern; with husband, William P. McGivern) *Mention My Name in Mombasa: The Unscheduled Adventures of an American Family Abroad,* illustrated by Kramer, Dodd, 1958.
(With W. P. McGivern) *A Matter of Honor,* Arbor House, 1984.

JUVENILE

Patrick Visits the Farm (fiction), illustrated by Simmons, Dodd, 1959.
Patrick Takes a Trip (fiction), illustrated by Simmons, Dodd, 1960.
Patrick Visits the Library (fiction), illustrated by Paul Lantz, Dodd, 1961.
Patrick Visits the Zoo (fiction), illustrated by Sam Savitt, Dodd, 1963.
The Ginger Horse (fiction), illustrated by Wesley Dennis, Dodd, 1964.
Spain: Wonderland of Contrasts (nonfiction), Dodd, 1965.
The Small War of Sergeant Donkey (fiction), illustrated by Dennis, Dodd, 1966.
Rosie, the Dancing Elephant (fiction), illustrated by Lorence Bjorklund, Dodd, 1967.

EDITOR

My Favorite Stories (young adult), Dodd, 1948.
Profile of Youth (adult), Lippincott, 1951.
My Favorite Mystery Stories (young adult), Dodd, 1966.
(And author of introduction) *My Favorite Suspense Stories* (young adult), Dodd, 1968.

Also author of "High School Career Series," Curtis Publishing Co., 1942-49. Writer with husband of scripts for television series, including *Kojak,* and of screenplay, *Brannigan.* Work represented in several textbooks and anthologies. Contributor of over two hundred articles to numerous periodicals, including *Vogue, Mademoiselle, Cosmopolitan, Woman's Day, Scholastic, Woman's Home Companion,* and *Redbook.* Daly's papers are housed in a permanent collection at the University of Oregon Library.

WORK IN PROGRESS: Indian Summer, a story of a young Hollywood stunt woman and a young man just off the Morongo Reservation outside Palm Springs; *Hollywood People,* an adult novel about contemporary Hollywood based on Daly's experience working there.

ADAPTATIONS: The film rights to *Seventeenth Summer* were purchased by Warner Bros. in 1949; *The Ginger Horse* was filmed by Walt Disney Studios; Daly's short story, "You Can't Kiss Caroline," has also been dramatized.

SIDELIGHTS: Maureen Daly is an accomplished and prolific writer who throughout her career has successfully bridged genres and print mediums making her name recognizable by young and old. In addition to numerous works for young adults, including her bestselling novel, *Seventeenth Summer,* Daly has also written three books of nonfiction for adults and several tales for young children. She has also reported for and penned columns for the *Chicago Tribune* and *Desert Sun,* authored screenplays for films and television, and contributed over two hundred articles to periodicals.

Daly began her writing career at an early age. She was fifteen when a story she entered in *Scholastic* magazine's short story contest won third prize. The next year, her English teacher submitted another work written by Daly to the contest. This time, Daly's "Sixteen," a tale about a boy and a girl who meet at a skating rink, was awarded first prize. Since *Scholastic* first printed Daly's story in 1938, "Sixteen" has been included in over three hundred anthologies and published in twelve different languages. The story is also in Daly's collection *Sixteen and Other Stories.* "Even now, when I get checks from the reprint of' Sixteen,' it's like seeing an old friend from 1938," Daly commented to an interviewer for *Publishers Weekly.*

The following year, when she was seventeen years old, Daly started working on a story about a small town boy and girl who fall in love. Finally finishing the novel during her senior year at college, Daly sent the manuscript of *Seventeenth Summer* to a publisher who immediately accepted it for publication. The book quickly became a bestseller, making Daly a successful author at the age of twenty-one. *Seventeenth Summer* has remained in print for nearly half a century, selling more than a million copies worldwide. Though originally released as a adult title, *Seventeenth Summer* is now credited as one of the first novels to begin defining the genre of young adult literature.

Reviewers praise *Seventeenth Summer* for its sensitive portrayal of the many and varied emotions and facets involved in young, first love. Set in a rural Wisconsin town, *Seventeenth Summer* follows the sweet and innocent romance of two teenagers as they experience all the joys and tribulations that are so commonly felt by most adolescents when they discover love for the first time. "*Seventeenth Summer,* perhaps captures better than any other novel the spirit of adolescence," states Dwight L. Burton in *English Journal.* Burton goes on to note: "More than just a love story of two adolescents, *Seventeenth Summer,* with its introspection and fine mastery of the scene, portrays the adolescent validly in several of his important relationships—with his family, with his age mates, and, very important, with himself. In each of these three aspects, Miss Daly is discerning."

In her review of *Seventeenth Summer,* Edith H. Walton writes in the *New York Times Book Review:* "Lyrically young and breathless, *Seventeenth Summer* deals with one of the oldest themes in the world, the theme of first love, and deals with it in a fashion which is so unhackneyed and so fresh that one forgets how often the same story has been told before. . . . Completely up to date in its idiom and its atmosphere, vividly authentic in a warm and homely way, it seems to me to be as unpretentiously good a first novel as any one could ask. . . . Simply, eloquently, Maureen Daly tells one how youth in love really feels—how it felt yesterday and how it feels today."

"My first and most widely published novel, *Seventeenth Summer,* was written in a spurt of creativity and emotion because I was so wildly and vividly happy about love and life at a particular time in my existence," Daly explains to *CA.* "I knew that euphoria and hope could not last (and it didn't) and I wanted to get all that fleeting excitement down on paper before it passed, or I forgot the true feelings. Lucky I did. I have never felt so hopeful since. It was not until the reviews came out (and the royalties came in) that I realized I had recorded universal emotions and joys—and people would want to read about them year after year."

Although *Seventeenth Summer* caused quite a stir in the publishing field, Daly decided to complete her university studies and resolved to pursue a career in journalism. While still a college senior, Daly accepted a job as a reporter covering the police beat for the *Chicago Tribune.* Working as a reporter challenged Daly's writing skills. As she reveals in *Publishers Weekly:*"I had to work really hard to keep all the details straight, when I called from the scene of news stories. I was so afraid they would fire a question at me and I wouldn't have the answer. Often I'd be standing in phone booths with sweat pouring down my back."

In addition to reporting on crime for the *Chicago Tribune,* Daly also reviewed books and wrote an advice column for the paper's Sunday magazine. Aimed at teenagers, Daly's column, "On the Solid Side," was so popular the paper soon ran the column three times a week. Later, "On the Solid Side" was syndicated to more than a dozen newspapers. A collection of these articles was published as *Smarter and Smoother* in 1944. By the following year, the book had gone into it ninth printing. A critic for *Virginia Kirkus* suggests that "parents should be thankful to Maureen Daly for she gives all the advice and counsel that teenagers think is sermonizing from parents, but that they'll lap up in this form."

Since her first job as a reporter in Chicago, Daly has worked for several respected publications, such as the *Ladies' Home Journal* and the *Saturday Evening Post,* earning awards and a reputation as a talented and thoroughly professional journalist. In addition to her work as a reporter, columnist, and associate editor, Daly has also written hundreds of articles on a wide variety of topics. Many of these articles explored one of her favorite subjects—travel and foreign lands.

Daly's interest in travel accelerated in 1949, when she left her job as associate editor for *Ladies' Home Journal,* moved to Europe, and began work as a freelance writer. Accompanied by her husband, William McGivern, and their two-year-old daughter, Megan, Daly spent time in Paris, Rome, Dublin, London, and Spain. She reported on the important issues of the day and interviewed many famous people, including Eleanor Roosevelt and Harry Truman. Her son, Patrick, was born during Daly's early years in Europe. The family returned to the United States to live when Daly's children were teenagers.

Daly's years traveling and living in Europe were the inspiration for her several books on travel, including her own family's personal experiences in *Mention My Name in Mombasa: The Unscheduled Adventures of an American Family Abroad.* Written with her husband, Daly introduces her readers to many of the quaint places and captivating people her family encountered during their travels. A writer for *Virginia Kirkus* called *Mention My Name in Mombasa* "charming." The critic went on to comment: "Writing with intelligence, sympathy and humor, interested in people rather than scenery, the authors tell of fishermen and babysitters, flowers and artists, bulls and bullfighting, friendly servants, food good and bad, palaces and hotels. Lengthy but never dull, neither a guidebook nor a study of social conditions, the book should appeal to all kinds of travelers, those who go to far places and those who dream of them, and to students of social life outside the United States."

While *Mention My Name in Mombasa* is considered adult nonfiction, Daly has also shared many of her travel experiences with young readers in *Spain: Wonderland of Contrasts* and with young adults in *Twelve around the World, Spanish Roundabout,* and *Moroccan Roundabout.* In the *New York Times Book Review,* Lavinia R. Davis states that *Spanish Roundabout* "is not a guide book in the usual sense. It is, rather, a cohesive series of profiles and sketches of Spain drawn from affection, experience and compassion. . . . [The] emphasis is on people in contemporary Spain. Family life, bull-fighting, religious observances, cooking and teenage mores are described so skillfully and with such a complete lack of condescension that the reader cannot help sharing the author's enthusiasm and eager curiosity."

In 1986, Daly returned to the genre of literature that made her a bestselling author with *Acts of Love.* Another young adult novel, *First a Dream,* followed in 1990. As in her first novel for young adults, *Seventeenth Summer,* Daly once again provides her readers with a sweet love story that involves many of the experiences and emotions young people realize on their road to maturity. Both these books tell of the wonders and magic that are known only once in a lifetime—when love is discovered for the first time. Describing Daly as "the spiritual grandmother of the young adult novel," Richard Peck notes in the *Los Angeles Times* that "well before the term 'YA' [Young Adult] was coined [Daly] wrote the perennial best-seller, *Seventeenth Summer.* With *Acts of Love* she returns after 44 years to the sort of love story she pioneered when she was herself a YA."

In correspondence with *CA,* Daly shared her thoughts on writing: "I write more than one kind of book. In travel books I try to put down what I see, feel and learn as vividly and memorably as the experiences that have occurred to me. In fiction I am an entertainer but sometimes a sad one. The stories, the fictionalized versions of real life, are often melancholy but sometimes there is a joy, and a relief, in just sharing a human adventure.

"Writing is my kind of freedom, the chance to look outward as well as inward. It is an excellent excuse for curiosity, for traveling, studying, and just staring at other people and other scenes. I am constantly plagued by 'need to know,' not just to stockpile lists of facts and statistics but to have some understanding of what it is like to be someone else, or live somewhere else. So I travel to 'see' and write to 'think' and find out about myself and other people I meet—or invent."

BIOGRAPHICAL/CRITICAL SOURCES:

BOOKS

Contemporary Literary Criticism, Volume 17, Gale, 1981.

Something about the Author Autobiograpy Series, Volume 1, Gale, 1986.

PERIODICALS

Chicago Tribune, September 1, 1986.

English Journal, September, 1951.

Los Angeles Times, October 11, 1986.

New York Times Book Review, May 3, 1942; July 12, 1942; July 24, 1960.

Publishers Weekly, June 27, 1986.

Virginia Kirkus, March 1, 1944; July 15, 1958.*

* * *

DANIEL, Glyn (Edmund) 1914-1986 (Dilwyn Rees)

PERSONAL: Born April 23, 1914, in Lampeter Velfrey, Pembrokeshire, England; died December 13,

1986; son of John (a schoolmaster) and Mary Jane (Edmunds) Daniel; married Ruth Langhorne, 1946. *Education:* Attended University College, University of Wales, 1931-32; St. John's College, Cambridge, B.A. (with first class honors), 1935; Cambridge University, M.A., 1938, PhD., 1939. *Avocational interests:* Travel, walking, swimming, food, wine, writing detective novels.

CAREER: Archaeologist, educator, broadcaster, author, and editor; Cambridge University, Cambridge, England, fellow of St. John's College, 1938-45, faculty assistant lecturer, 1945-48, university lecturer in archaeology, 1948-74, Disney Professor of Archaeology, 1974-81, professor emeritus, 1981-86. St. John's College, steward, 1946-55. University of Edinburgh, Munro Lecturer, 1954; British Academy, Rhys Lecturer, 1954; University of Edinburgh, O'Donnell Lecturer, 1956; University of Birmingham, Josiah Mason Lecturer, 1956; University College, Cardiff, Gregynog Lecturer, 1968; University College of North Wales, Ballard-Matthews Lecturer, 1968; University of Aarhus, visiting professor, 1968; University of Hull, Ferrens Professor, 1969; Harvard University, George Grant MacCurdy Lecturer, 1971. Anglia Television Ltd. and Antiquity Publications Ltd., director; Cambridge Arts Theatre, director and trustee. *Military service:* Royal Air Force, intelligence officer, 1940-45; became wing commander.

MEMBER: Society of Antiquaries (fellow), Instituto Italiano di Preistoria e Protostoria (honorary member), British Academy (fellow), German Archaeological Institute (corresponding fellow), Jutland Archaeological Society (corresponding member), South Eastern Union of Scientific Societies (president, 1955), Bristol and Gloucestershire Archaeological Society (president, 1962-63), United Oxford and Cambridge University Club.

AWARDS, HONORS: Knight (first class) of the Dannebrog, 1961; Litt.D., Cambridge University, 1962.

WRITINGS:

The Three Ages: An Essay on Archaeological Method, Cambridge University Press, 1943.

(Under pseudonym Dilwyn Rees) *The Cambridge Murders* (novel), Gollancz, 1945.

A Hundred Years of Archaeology, Duckworth, 1950, revised edition published as *A Hundred and Fifty Years of Archaeology,* 1975.

The Prehistoric Chamber Tombs of England and Wales, Cambridge University Press, 1950.

(With Stuart Piggott) *A Picture Book of Ancient British Art,* Cambridge University Press, 1951.

(Under pseudonym Dilwyn Rees) *Welcome Death* (novel), Gollancz, 1954, Dodd, 1955, reprinted, Hamilton, 1972.

Who Are the Welsh?, British Academy, 1954.

Lascaux and Carnac, Lutterworth, 1955, revised and enlarged edition published as *The Hungry Archaeologist in France: A Travelling Guide to Caves, Graves, and Good Living in the Dordogne and Brittany,* Faber, 1963.

(With others) *Myth or Legend?* (broadcasts), Macmillan, 1955, Capricorn Books, 1968.

(With Thomas George Eyre Powell) *Barclodiad y Gawres: The Excavation of a Megalithic Chamber Tomb in Anglesey, 1952-53,* Liverpool University Press, 1956.

The Megalith Builders of Western Europe, Hutchinson, 1958, Praeger, 1959.

(Editor of translation) Raymond Block, *Die Etrusker,* M. DuMont Schauberg, 1960.

The Prehistoric Chamber Tombs of France: A Geographical, Morphological, and Chronological Survey, Thames & Hudson, 1960.

The Idea of Prehistory, C. A. Watts, 1962, World Publishing, 1963.

The Pen of My Aunt, Merry Boys (Cambridge), 1962.

(With Sean P. O'Riordain) *New Grange and the Bend of the Boyne,* Praeger, 1964.

(Editor with Idris Llewelyn Foster) *Prehistoric and Early Wales,* Routledge & Kegan Paul, 1965.

Oxford Chicken Pie, Merry Boys, 1966.

Man Discovers His Past, Duckworth, 1966, Crowell, 1968.

The Origins and Growth of Archaeology, Penguin, 1967, Crowell, 1968.

(With J. D. Evans) *The Western Mediterranean,* Cambridge University Press, 1967.

The First Civilizations: The Archaeology of Their Origins, Crowell, 1968.

Archaeology and the History of Art, University of Hull Press, 1970.

Megaliths in History, Thames & Hudson, 1972.

(Editor with R. F. Paget) *Central Italy: An Archaeological Guide,* Noyes Data, 1973.

(Editor) Margaret Guido, *Southern Italy: An Archaeological Guide,* Noyes Data, 1973.

La France de la prehistoire, Tallandier, 1973.

(With Piggott and Charles McBurney) *France before the Romans,* Thames & Hudson, 1974.

Cambridge and the Back-Looking Curiosity: An Inaugural Lecture, Cambridge University Press, 1976.

(Editor) *The Illustrated Encyclopedia of Archaeology,* Macmillan, 1978.

(Editor) *Towards a History of Archaeology,* Thames & Hudson, 1981.

A Short History of Archaeology, Thames & Hudson, 1981.

Some Small Harvest (autobiography), Thames & Hudson, 1986.

(With Paul Bahn) *Ancient Places: The Prehistoric and Celtic Sites of Britain,* photographs by Anthony Gascoigne, Constable (London), 1987.

Writing for Antiquity: An Anthology of Editorials from Antiquity, introduced by Philip Howard, Thames and Hudson (New York City), 1992.

Also the general editor of "Ancient Peoples and Places" series, Thames & Hudson, beginning 1958. Contributor to *Nation, Natural History,* and archaeological journals. Editor, *Antiquity,* beginning 1958.

SIDELIGHTS: Glyn Daniel was an internationally known archaeologist who devoted his energies to popularizing the field, as well as to conducting disciplined research in it, his specialty being the study of megalithic chamber tombs. Daniel was particularly admired for his role, along with Mortimer Wheeler, in establishing the British Broadcasting Corporation's television program *Animal, Vegetable, Mineral?.* In a London *Times* review of Daniel's autobiography, *Some Small Harvest,* Peter Ackroyd explains: "Relentlessly middlebrow it may have been, but *Animal, Vegetable, Mineral?* was nevertheless responsible for a whole generation of young children who wanted to be nothing other than archaeologists." Daniel further popularized the field through his numerous books, lectures, and radio and television broadcasts.

In the more scholarly sense, Daniel taught archaeology at Cambridge University; he joined the faculty of St. John's College, Cambridge, in 1938, acted as Disney Professor of Archaeology there from 1974 to 1981, and later became professor emeritus. Colin Renfrew elaborates in his *Times* obituary for Daniel that the archaeologist "was an innovator in at least two ways. He was the first systematic historian of archaeology, at any rate in the English language. His pioneering *The Three Ages* laid the foundation for the first coherent account of the history of the subject, *A Hundred Years of Archaeology* [later revised as *A Hundred and Fifty Years of Archaeology*]. . . . This body of work gave several generations of students and scholars their first appreciation that archaeology and prehistory are about ideas, not simply about things, and that ideas are produced by people who are themselves the products of their time." Apart from archaeology, Daniel penned two detective novels, *The Cambridge Murders* and *Welcome Death,* under the pseudonym Dilwyn Rees.

BIOGRAPHICAL/CRITICAL SOURCES:

BOOKS

Cunliffe, Barry, John D. Evans, and Colin Renfrew, editors, *Antiquity and Man: Essays in Honor of Glyn Daniel,* Thames & Hudson, 1981.

Daniel, Glyn, *Some Small Harvest* (autobiography), Thames & Hudson, 1986.

PERIODICALS

Booklist, September 15, 1979.

Natural History, November, 1968.

Spectator, June 9, 1950.

Times (London), September 25, 1986.

Times Literary Supplement, June 9, 1950; May 2, 1968; April 9, 1982; November 21, 1986.

OBITUARIES:

BOOKS

Evans, John D., Barry Cunliffe, and Colin Renfrew, editors, *Antiquity and Man: Essays in Honour of Glyn Daniel,* Thames & Hudson, 1981.

The Oxford Companion to Literature of Wales, Oxford University Press, 1986.

PERIODICALS

Times (London), December 15, 1986; December 20, 1986.*

* * *

DARNTON, John (Townsend) 1941-

PERSONAL: Born November 20, 1941, in New York, NY; son of Byron (a newsman) and Eleanor (an editor; maiden name, Choate) Darnton; married Nina Lieberman, August 21, 1966; children: Kyra, Liza, James. *Education:* Attended University of Paris IV (Sorbonne) and Alliance Francaise, Paris, 1960-61; University of Wisconsin, B.A., 1966. *Politics:* Democrat.

ADDRESSES: *Office*—New York Times, Foreign Desk, 229 West 43rd St., New York, NY 10036.

CAREER: *New York Times,* New York City, copy boy, news clerk, and news assistant, 1966-68, city reporter,

1968-69, CT correspondent, 1969-70, chief suburban correspondent, 1970-71, night rewriter, 1971-72, reporter for New York City fiscal crisis, 1972-75, correspondent in Lagos, Nigeria, 1976-77, and Nairobi, Kenya, 1977-79, bureau chief in Warsaw, Poland, 1979-82, and Madrid, Spain, 1982-84, deputy foreign editor, 1984-86, metropolitan editor, 1987-91, news editor, 1991-93, London bureau chief, 1993—. Correspondent and narrator for film, *Spain: Ten Years After.* Member of board of directors, New York State Associated Press.

MEMBER: Century Association, French American Institute.

AWARDS, HONORS: George Polk Award, Long Island University, 1979 and 1982, for foreign reporting; Pulitzer Prize in international reporting, Columbia University Graduate School of Journalism, 1982, for dispatches from Poland.

WRITINGS:

Neanderthal (novel), Random House (New York City), 1996.

Also author of *The Fat Lady Sings,* a film script about the Polish underground, and the introduction to *A Day in the Life of Spain.* Contributor to the *Readers Digest* and other periodicals. Also contributor to *Assignment America: A Collection of Outstanding Writing From the New York Times* and *About Men: Reflections on the Male Experience.*

SIDELIGHTS: Pulitzer Prize winning journalist John Darnton also won the George Polk award in 1978 for his reports from Africa. In an article titled "Nigeria's Dissident Superstar," Darnton covers the politically controversial career of Fela Anikulapo-Kuti, whose songs are highly critical of the Nigerian government. The article proved to be so embarrassing to the government that Darnton was expelled from the country. In 1982, Darnton also received the George Polk award for his coverage of the political unrest in Poland. As the Warsaw bureau chief for the *New York Times,* he chronicled the rise of the industrial trade union Solidarity, and the wave of optimism which eventually swept away the Polish communist government. In a 1980 *New York Times* article, titled "Sixty Days That Shook Poland," Darnton discusses the struggle between Solidarity and the Polish government, detailing the workers' strike, which was lead by Lech Walesa to protest the rise in meat prices. Other articles followed, such as "Polish Awakening," which describes the intellectual, cultural, and spiritual renaissance that was the legacy of Solidarity's activities, and the less optimistic "Poland: Still Defiant," which examines the communist government's attempts to suppress the trade union movement by declaring martial law in December, 1981.

The award-winning journalist began writing novels, with the publication *Neanderthal* in 1996. The plot involves the discovery of two currently existing tribes of Neanderthals, and the scientists who study them, and work to keep them free from the intrusions of twentieth-century civilization. Edwin B. Burgess, in *Library Journal,* claims that Darnton's first novel "is very Indiana Jonesish," while Ian Tattersal in a *Time* magazine review comparing Darnton's *Neanderthal* to William Morrow's *Almost Adam,* suggests that both books are "pure fantasy constructs" and that "neither [author] even attempts to exploit the promising device of confronting human with almost human to explore the essence of our uniqueness as a species." Nevertheless, Tattersall admits that *Neanderthal* "might make an adequate companion on a plane ride."

BIOGRAPHICAL/CRITICAL SOURCES:

PERIODICALS

Detroit News, April 13, 1982.
Library Journal, May 15, 1996, p. 83.
New York Times, July 24, 1977; April 13, 1982; May 13, 1996, p. B2.
New York Times Book Review, April 14, 1996, p. 8.
Time, May 27, 1996, p. 79.*

* * *

DAVIS, Harold Eugene 1902-1988

PERSONAL: Born 1902, in Girard, OH; died of cancer (one source says pneumonia), September 13, 1988, in Chevy Chase, MD; son of Henry E. and Catherine (Zeller) Davis; married Audrey Hennen, 1929; children: Barbara Lee Davis Owen. *Education:* Western Reserve University (now Case Western Reserve University), student, 1923-24, Ph.D., 1933; Hiram College, B.A., 1924; University of Chicago, M.A., 1927. *Religion:* Disciples of Christ. *Avocational interests:* Music (violin), poetry, and woodworking.

CAREER: Hiram College, Hiram, OH, professor, 1927-47, dean, 1944-47; Office of Inter-American Affairs, Washington, DC, director, division of education and teacher aids, 1943-45; U.S. Army University, Biarritz, France, instructor in Latin American history, 1945-46; American University, Washington, DC, professor of Latin American history and government, 1947-63, dean, College of Arts and Sciences, 1953-58, University Professor, 1963-73, University Professor emeritus, 1973. Fulbright lecturer in American history, University of Chile, 1959; visiting professor at India School of International Studies, 1965-66, and at University of West Virginia, Oberlin College, Western Reserve University (now Case Western Reserve University), and Johns Hopkins University. Lectured on Latin American subjects at various universities and organizations, including Inter-American Defense College, United States Foreign Service Institute, Washington International Center, National University of Mexico. Member of Governor's Commission on the History of Ohio. Representative of Hiram College in Cooperative Study in General Education, 1938-40. Consultant to colleges.

MEMBER: American Historical Association, Inter-American Council, American Political Science Association, American Society of International Law, Institute on History of Law (Buenos Aires; corresponding member), American Peace Society (director), Inter-American Indianist Institute, Societe des Americanistes, Ohio Academy of History (president, 1937), Garfield Society, Cosmos Club (Washington).

AWARDS, HONORS: Washington Evening Star grant for research in Latin American social thought, 1958; faculty author award, American University, 1950; distinguished service award from Inter-American Council, 1978, and Ohio Academy of History, 1978; certificate for distinguished service from Office of Inter-American Affairs; Order of Colon, Dominican Republic.

WRITINGS:

Garfield of Hiram, Historical Society (Hiram, OH), 1931.

Makers of Democracy in Latin America, H. W. Wilson, 1945, reprinted, Cooper Square, 1968.

(Contributor) *Twentieth-Century Political Thought,* Philosophical Publishing, 1946.

(Contributor) *Origins and Consequences of World War II,* Dryden, 1948.

A History of America: Civilization in the Western Hemisphere, American University Press, 1948.

Latin American Leaders, H. W. Wilson, 1949, reprinted, Cooper Square, 1968.

Social Science Trends in Latin America, American University Press, 1950.

The Americas in History, Ronald, 1953.

(Contributor) *Contemporary Social Science,* Volume I, Stackpole, 1953.

(Contributor) *The Caribbean: Contemporary Trends,* University of Florida Press, 1953.

(Contributor) *The Development of Historiography,* Stackpole, 1954.

(With others) *Government and Politics in Latin America,* Ronald, 1958.

Material and Spiritual Factors in American History, American University Language Center, 1958.

Latin American Social Thought, University Press of Washington, 1961, 2nd edition, 1967.

(With Harold A. Durfee) *The Teaching of Philosophy in Universities of the United States,* Pan American Union, 1965.

(Editor) Samuel Guy Inman, *Inter-American Conferences, 1826-1954,* University Press of Washington, 1965.

History of Latin America, Ronald, 1968.

Hinsdale of Hiram: The Life of Burke Aaron Hinsdale, Pioneer Educator, University Press of Washington, 1971.

Latin American Thought: A Historical Introduction, Louisiana State University Press, 1972.

Revolutionaries, Traditionalists, and Dictators in Latin America, Cooper Square, 1973.

(With others) *Latin American Foreign Policies: An Analysis,* Johns Hopkins University Press, 1975.

(With others) *Latin American Diplomatic History: An Introduction,* Louisiana State University Press, 1977.

History and Power: The Social Relevance of History, University Press of America, 1983.

Contributor to *Encyclopedia Americana, Encyclopaedia Britannica, Collier's Encyclopedia, World Book Encyclopedia, and Dictionary of American History.* Also author of notes for a dictionary of Ohio Indian place names, 1979. Contributor of over one hundred articles to journals including *Inter-American Law Review, Latin American Research Review, Americas, Journal of Inter-American Studies, World Affairs,* and *Hispanic American Historical Review.* Editorial consultant to *Jefferson Encyclopedia.* Member of board of editors, *World Affairs.*

SIDELIGHTS: Harold Eugene Davis was a member of the American University faculty from 1947 until his retirement as professor emeritus in 1973. He served the university in a variety of posts, including professor in the schools of international studies and government and public administration, dean of the College of Arts and Sciences, and director of the university's language center. Prior to joining the American University staff, Davis taught at Hiram College, where he also served as chairman of the division of social studies and dean of administration. Davis was a devoted educator; he told *CA:* "All of my professional life and all of my writing, in one way or another, have been devoted to enriching my teaching. . . . I am pleased to have a considerable number of . . . students who have followed in my footsteps. . . . My epitaph, which I have written out and circulated to a few friends, with a collection of my poems, is: 'He lived to teach, and hoped to leave behind the loving flame of knowledge in some mind.'" Among Davis's many publications are *The Americas in History; Latin American Social Thought; Revolutionaries, Traditionalists, and Dictators in Latin America;* and more than one hundred articles contributed to reference books and professional journals.

OBITUARIES:

BOOKS

The Writers Directory: 1988-1990, St. James Press, 1988.

PERIODICALS

New York Times, September 18, 1988.
Washington Post, September 17, 1988.*

* * *

DAVIS, Lanny J(esse) 1945-

PERSONAL: Born December 12, 1945, in Jersey City, NJ; son of Mortimer (a dentist) and Frances (Goldberg) Davis; married Elaine Joyce Charney, December 18, 1966; children: Marlo, Seth. *Education:* Yale University, B.A., 1967, LL.B., 1970.

ADDRESSES: Home—11812 Selfridge Rd., Silver Spring, MD 20906. *Office*—2550 M St., N.W., Washington, DC 20037. *Agent*—Timothy Seldes, Russell & Volkening, 551 Fifth Ave., New York, NY 10017.

CAREER: Admitted to the Bar of the state of Connecticut, 1970, and the District of Columbia, 1972; member of staff of Senator Abraham Ribicoff, 1968, and of Senator Edmund Muskie, Washington, DC, 1970-72; Yale Law School, assistant instructor in legal research, 1971-72; Patton, Boggs & Blow, Washington, DC, attorney, 1975—. Democratic candidate for U.S. House of Representatives from Eighth District of Maryland, 1974, 1976. Washington Suburban Transit Commission, chairman, 1981-82, vice chairman, 1983; Montgomery County Commission on Reorganization of County Governments, chairman, 1987. Special counsel to President Bill Clinton, 1996-98.

MEMBER: American Bar Association (member of computer law, science, and technology sector committee, 1980—, and chairman of subcommittee on computer contracts, 1981—); District of Columbia Bar Association (chairman of computer law division, 1985-86; vice chairman, 1987); Connecticut Bar Association; Federal Bar Association.

WRITINGS:

The Emerging Democratic Majority, Stein & Day (New York City), 1974.
(With others) *A User's Guide to Computer Contracting: Forms, Techniques, and Strategies,* Prentice-Hall (Englewood Cliffs, NJ), 1984.
(With Charles B. Ortner) *Negotiating Computer Contracts,* Law and Business (New York City), 1984.
(With Don A. Allen) *Allen & Davis on Computer Contracting: A User's Guide With Forms and Strategies,* Prentice-Hall, 1992.
Truth to Tell: Tell It Early, Tell It All, Tell It Yourself: Notes from My White House Education, Free Press (New York City), 1999.

Contributor to *Washington Post* and *Washington Monthly.* Contributing editor of *Democratic Review.*

SIDELIGHTS: In his fourteen months as special counsel to President Bill Clinton, Lanny J. Davis was assigned to deal with the media as allegations of improper campaign financing came to light. He details his efforts to manage the press's handling of these reports—to put the administration's desired "spin" on the stories—in *Truth to Tell: Tell It Early, Tell It All, Tell It Yourself: Notes from My White House Education.*

For all the negative connotations of the term "spin control," Davis maintains that this process, when handled correctly, does not involve deceit. A good spin doctor, he says, seeks to "minimize the damage" by placing negative news in its proper context and by pointing out to the press any positive aspects of the situation. "Bad spinning," he contends, tries to evade media inquiries and cover up less-than-flattering facts, and it "is not only dishonest, it is ineffective." He notes that he and press secretary Mike McCurry released documents on campaign finance to the media at the same time they released them to Congressional investigators, on the theory that it was "better that we put the story out ourselves, with plenty of opportunity to answer questions and to characterize the documents favorably, or at least accurately." They also leaked certain facts to reporters whom they felt would write balanced, context-filled, comprehensive articles—what Davis terms "predicate" stories—that would influence how the rest of the media handled the news.

John W. Dean, who had served as counsel to President Richard Nixon, praised Davis's book in the *New York Times Book Review.* "Can a former White House aide write an informative book about the scandal control operations without betraying the President and First Lady?" Dean asked. "If you're Lanny J. Davis, special counsel to President Clinton from December 1996 through January 1998, yes. His autobiographical examination of what worked and what didn't is exposition, not expose." *Truth to Tell,* Dean continued, "is a book for people curious about the machinery of the Presidency, the ways of politics and what takes place behind the headlines."

In a piece for the *National Review,* Dick Morris, who was an adviser to Clinton for many years, found *Truth to Tell* "a relatively truthful, insightful, and complete account of how the administration fought to keep the facts about its various scandals from the public." However, he asserted that in television appearances, Davis "offers the same cover-ups he rightly deplores in print. It's as if, having written his memoir, Davis has not read it." Because of this, Morris characterized Davis as "two Lannys—Book Lanny and TV Lanny." Morris added, "Actually, Davis isn't entirely forthcoming even in *Truth to Tell.* He writes almost entirely in the passive voice"—a device that, according to Morris, allows him to state that decisions were made but not who made them. "So we are left with the big question, What role did Bill Clinton play in his administration's many cover-ups? We don't know, precisely. Does either Lanny?"

BIOGRAPHICAL/CRITICAL SOURCES:

PERIODICALS

Insight on the News, August 11, 1997.
National Review, July 12, 1999, p. 54.
New York Times Book Review, May 23, 1999, p. 18.
Publishers Weekly, April 26, 1999, p. 61.
Washington Monthly, May, 1999, p. 38.*

DAWE, (Donald) Bruce 1930-

PERSONAL: Born February 15, 1930, in Geelong, Australia; son of Alfred (a laborer) and Mary Ann (Hamilton) Dawe; married Gloria Desley, January 1, 1964; children: Brian, Jamie, Katrina, Melissa. *Education:* University of Queensland, B.A., 1969, M.A., 1975, Ph.D., 1980; University of New England, Litt.B., 1973. *Religion:* Roman Catholic.

ADDRESSES: Home—30 Cumming St., Toowoomba, Queensland, Australia 4350.

CAREER: Worked as a laborer, postman, and gardener. Institute College of Advanced Education, Toowoomba, Australia, lecturer in literature, 1971-78, senior lecturer and teaching fellow, 1979-89, associate professor, 1990-93. *Military service:* Royal Australian Air Force, 1959-68; became sergeant.

AWARDS, HONORS: Myer Award for poetry, 1966, for *A Need of Similar Name,* and 1969, for *An Eye for a Tooth;* Ampol Arts Award for Creative Literature, 1967; Dame Mary Gilmore Medal, 1971, for *Condolences of the Season;* Grace Leven Poetry Prize, 1978, and Braille Book of the Year award, 1979, both for *Sometimes Gladness: Collected Poems, 1954-1978;* Patrick White Literary Award for contributions to Australian poetry, 1980; Christopher Bremmer Award, 1984; Order of Australia, 1992; honorary D. Litt., University of Southern Queensland, 1995.

WRITINGS:

No Fixed Address, Cheshire (Melbourne, Australia), 1962.
A Need of Similar Name, Cheshire, 1965.
An Eye for a Tooth, Cheshire, 1968.
Beyond the Subdivision, Cheshire, 1969.
Heat-Wave, Sweeny Reed (Melbourne), 1970.
Condolences of the Season, Cheshire, 1971.
Bruce Dawe Reads from His Own Work, University of Queensland Press (St. Lucia, Australia), 1971.
(Editor) *Dimensions,* McGraw (New York City), 1974.
Just a Dugong at Twilight, Cheshire, 1975.
Sometimes Gladness: Collected Poems, 1954-1978, Longman Cheshire, 1979, 4th edition published as *Sometimes Gladness: Collected Poems, 1954-1993,* 1993.
Five Modern Comic Writers, Darling Downs Institute of Advanced Studies(Toowoomba, Australia), 1981.
Over Here, Harv! and Other Stories, Penguin (Melbourne and Harmondsworth, Australia), 1983.
Selected Poems, Longman (London), 1984.

Towards Sunrise: Poems, 1979-1986, Longman Cheshire, 1986.

(Editor) *Speaking in Parables: A Reader,* Longman Cheshire, 1987.

Bruce Dawe: Essays and Opinions, edited by Ken Goodman, Longman Cheshire, 1990.

This Side of Silence: Poems 1987-1990, Longman Cheshire, 1990.

Mortal Instruments: Poems 1990-1995, Longman, 1995.

SIDELIGHTS: "Bruce Dawe was certainly the most central and pivotal poet in Australia during the decade of the 1960s," writes Thomas W. Shapcott in *Contemporary Poets.* The poems in Dawe's first collection, *No Fixed Address,* celebrate the lives of suburban Australians and echo the rhythms of their speech. Subsequent collections address more diverse subject matter, including political and social issues, especially abortion. But, Shapcott says, "The best poems . .. still capture the laconic sage of the backyard larrikin turned Head of the Family, with an occasional day off." Shapcott recommends *Sometimes Gladness: Collected Poems 1954-1978* as "perhaps the most successful book of verse by a contemporary Australian poet."

Clive James, writing in the *Times Literary Supplement,* asserts that Dawe's poetry "sounds easy . . . but it represents a feat of strength." James praises Dawe's ability to show his country's relationship to, and assimilation of, American culture. "Dawe was the first Australian poet to take measure of the junk media and find poetry in their pathos," James continues. "He wrote better about the Vietnam War than any other poet, including American poets; and he could do so because he wrote better about television."

Dawe told *CA:* "One of the reasons why the use of various verse forms may help me to capture something of the evanescence of the contemporary Australian idiom is that the use of various traditional rhyme-forms and some metrical regularity together with elements of the contemporary scene and idiom provide a 'mix' of past and present in an acceptable form overall.

"I never *consciously* chose the dramatic monologue form—it just occurred as a form frequently enough to confirm its possibilities. I am sure this is the general way things happen—forms choose us.

"Regional poetry is not (as in the United States) a very obvious and characteristic kind of poetry here, Australian society being culturally and linguistically far more homogeneous than American—urban and rural are the significant 'regions' rather than the Southwest, West, Midwest, East, etc. This is one of our greatest losses, I feel, artistically."

BIOGRAPHICAL/CRITICAL SOURCES:

BOOKS

Contemporary Poets, 6th edition, St. James Press, 1996.

Kuch, Peter, *Bruce Dawe,* Oxford University Press (New York City), 1995.

PERIODICALS

Australian Book Review, February, 1991, p. 35.

Times Literary Supplement, November 27-December 3, 1987.*

* * *

DAWIDOWICZ, Lucy S(childkret) 1915-1990

PERSONAL: Born June 16, 1915, in New York, NY; died of cancer, December 5 (one source says December 6), 1990, in New York, NY; daughter of Max and Dora (Ofnaem) Schildkret; married Szymon M. Dawidowicz, January 3, 1948. *Education:* Hunter College (now Hunter College of the City University of New York), B.A., 1936; Columbia University, M.A., 1961.

CAREER: Institute for Jewish Research, New York City, assistant to research director, 1940-46; American Jewish Joint Distribution Committee, Germany, educational officer for displaced persons' camps, 1946-47; American Jewish Committee, New York City, research analyst, 1950-68, director of research, 1968-69; Yeshiva University, New York City, associate professor, 1969-74, professor of history, 1974-78, Paul and Leah Lewis Chair in Holocaust Studies, 1970-75, Eli and Diana Zborowski Chair in Interdisciplinary Holocaust Studies, 1976-90. Visiting professor, Stanford University, 1981, and State University of New York at Albany, 1982.

MEMBER: American Historical Association, American Jewish Historical Society, Conference of Jewish Social Studies, Association for Jewish Studies.

AWARDS, HONORS: Yivo Institute for Jewish Research fellow, 1938-39; National Foundation for Jewish Culture award, 1965; Memorial Foundation for Jewish

Culture awards, 1968, 1973, 1974; Atran Foundation award, 1971; John Slawson Fund for Research Teaching and Education award, 1972; Gustave Wurzweiler Foundation award, 1974; Guggenheim Foundation fellowship, 1976; Anisfield-Wolf prize, 1976, for *The War Against the Jews, 1933-1945;* L.H.D., Kenyon College and Hebrew Union College, both 1978, Monmouth College, 1982, Yeshiva University and Spertus College, both 1983.

WRITINGS:

(With Leon J. Goldstein) *Politics in a Pluralist Democracy,* American Jewish Committee, 1963.

(Editor with Joshua A. Fishman and others) *For Max Weinreich on His Seventieth Birthday: Studies in Jewish Languages, Literature and Society,* Mouton, 1964.

(Editor and author of historical introduction) *The Golden Tradition: Jewish Life and Thought in Eastern Europe,* Holt, 1967.

The War against the Jews, 1933-1945, Holt, 1975.

A Holocaust Reader, Behrman, 1976.

The Jewish Presence: Essays on Identity and History, Holt, 1977.

The Holocaust and the Historians, Harvard University Press, 1981.

On Equal Terms: Jews in America 1881-1981, Holt, 1982.

From That Place and Time: A Memoir, 1938-1947, Norton, 1989.

What Is the Use of Jewish History?: Essays, Schocken Books (New York City), 1992.

Contributor to periodicals, including *Commentary, New York Times Book Review,* and *Times Literary Supplement.*

SIDELIGHTS: Lucy S. Dawidowicz was one of America's leading Holocaust historians, an educator and writer whose books are notable for their sharp criticism of U.S. and European foreign policy, particularly as it related to the treatment of the Jews during World War II. Dawidowicz argued in her scholarly works that the annihilation of Jews was as important to German dictator Adolf Hitler as his goal of conquering Europe during World War II, and bitterly disputed other historians' claims that Jews had failed to mount an active resistance to Nazi atrocities due to passivity and cowardice.

Dawidowicz was a witness to anti-Semitism while she lived in Poland in the late 1930s, and wrote of the subject in her book *From That Place and Time: A Memoir, 1938-47.* She returned to Europe after World War II to help Jewish survivors re-establish schools and libraries, also recovering collections of books stolen by the Nazis. Dawidowicz was a professor of history at Yeshiva University, where she held the Eli and Diana Zborowski Chair in Interdisciplinary Holocaust Studies beginning in 1976.

One of Dawidowicz's best-known books is *The War against the Jews, 1933-1945,* described by Irving Howe in the *New York Times Book Review* as "a major work of synthesis, providing for the first time a full account of the holocaust not merely as it completed the Nazi vision but as it affected the Jews of eastern Europe." As Howe further points out: "It is a work committed to the sovereignty of fact, free of metaphysical decoration; and emerging out of an awareness that no theory about the holocaust can be as important as a sustained confrontation with the holocaust itself. Austere and disciplined, this book comes to seem an exemplar of that Jewish belief—or human delusion—that somehow there may still be a moral use in telling what it meant to live and die in the 20th century."

The main thesis of *The War against the Jews,* Dawidowicz once indicated in a letter to *CA,* "is that Hitler's ideological goals—the annihilation of the Jews and German racial purity—determined his political and military goals, that is, the drive towards war and for world domination, a thesis not shared by those who view Hitler as a conventional, if despotic leader." In addition, "the author is also concerned with the nature of Jewish experience as well as the successful Nazi experiment in mass murder," stated *New Republic* critic Marie Syrkin. "Consequently this history, without special pleading, by its very content, offers answers to such nagging questions as: why did the Jews not resist? What was the role of the Jewish councils? . . . Particularly useful is [Dawidowicz's] analysis of the inner structure of the [eastern-European Jewish] ghettoes and the various organized attempts at self-help and education to prevent the lapse into chaos, which was part of the Nazi program for Jewish debasement—the prelude to extermination."

The author took a critical look at some of her peers in *The Holocaust and the Historians,* an examination of what the author felt was the neglect of serious Holocaust studies since the war. *New York Times* reviewer John Leonard considered the book "tendentious." "Anyone who looks at American textbooks will agree at least partly with [the author]," noted Leonard. "The Holocaust gets short shrift in our schools, although not in our literature, theater, movies and television. But . . . not all historians can be enlisted as partisans or accessories of national policy; think of France and Russia; consult the Western Marxists. It simply isn't true that the immediate postwar years in the Soviet Union 'were the most cruel period in Russian history'; think of the 1930s."

New York Times Book Review critic Telford Taylor also cited inaccuracies in *The Holocaust and the Historians,* but judged that, "for the most part, [the book] embodies high standards of scholarship. The analysis is shrewd and generally fair, and the comparisons often brilliantly perceptive. The work as a whole is a valuable contribution to the literature of the Second World War and the Holocaust." Martin Gilbert wrote in *Commentary* that this "short but closely argued book performs a major service." *The Holocaust and the Historians* is "a thought-provoking analysis and meaningful work," a *West Coast Review of Books* critic concluded.

BIOGRAPHICAL/CRITICAL SOURCES:

BOOKS

Dawidowicz, Lucy S., *The Holocaust and the Historians,* Harvard University Press, 1981.

Dawidowicz, *From That Place and Time: A Memoir, 1938-1947,* Norton, 1989.

PERIODICALS

Commentary, December, 1981; January, 1983.

Journal of Modern History, June, 1983.

New Republic, May 17, 1975.

New York Times, March 4, 1967; June 12, 1975; July 25, 1977; September 3, 1981.

New York Times Book Review, April 20, 1975; July 24, 1977; January 24, 1982.

Washington Post Book World, July 10, 1977.

West Coast Review of Books, December, 1981.

OBITUARIES:

BOOKS

Who's Who in America, 46th edition, Marquis, 1990.

PERIODICALS

Chicago Tribune, December 8, 1990.

Los Angeles Times, December 7, 1990.

New York Times, December 6, 1990.

Time, December 17, 1990.

Washington Post, December 7, 1990.*

DAWLISH, Peter
See KERR, James Lennox

*   *   *

DEE, Johnny
See KRAUZER, Steven M(ark)

*   *   *

DERFLER, (Arnold) Leslie 1933-

PERSONAL: Born January 11, 1933, in New York, NY; son of David (a salesman) and Ruth (Zarelnik) Derfler; married Gunilla Akesson, June 24, 1962; children: Ingrid, Linnea, Astrid, Elin. *Education:* City College (now City College of the City University of New York), B.A., 1954; University of Chicago, graduate study, 1956; Columbia University, M.A., 1957, Ph.D., 1962.

ADDRESSES: Office—Department of History, Florida Atlantic University, Boca Raton, FL 33432.

CAREER: City College of the City University of New York, New York, NY, lecturer, 1960-62; Carnegie-Mellon University, Pittsburgh, PA, 1962-68, began as assistant professor, became associate professor; University of Massachusetts—Amherst, associate professor, 1968-69; Florida Atlantic University, Boca Raton, professor of history, 1969—, chairman of department, 1978—. *Military service:* U.S. Army, 1954-56.

MEMBER: American Historical Association, Societe d'Histoire Moderne, Society for French Historical Studies.

AWARDS, HONORS: Carnegie Falk grant-in-aid; Fulbright travel grant; American Council of Learned Societies grant; American Philosophical Society grant; Koren Prize of the Society for French Historical Studies, 1964; National Endowment for the Humanities fellowship, 1971-72.

WRITINGS:

The Dreyfus Affair: Tragedy of Errors, Heath (Boston), 1963.

The Third French Republic: 1870-1940, Van Nostrand (New York City), 1966.

Socialism Since Marx: A Century of the European Left, St. Martin's (New York City), 1973.

(Editor) *Alexandre Millerand: The Socialist Years,* Mouton (The Hague, Nethlerands), 1977.

President and Parliament: A Short History of the French Presidency, University Presses of Florida (Boca Raton), 1983.

(Editor) *An Age of Conflict: Readings in Twentieth-Century European History,* Harcourt (San Diego), 1990.

Paul Lafargue and the Founding of French Marxism, 1842-1882, Harvard University Press (Cambridge, MA), 1991.

Paul Lafargue and the Flowering of French Socialism, 1882-1911, Harvard University Press, 1998.

Contributor to journals, including *International Review of Social History, Revue d'Histoire Moderne,* and *Historical Abstracts.*

SIDELIGHTS: Leslie Derfler has written extensively on French history and socialism, including two volumes on the life of Paul Lafargue, Karl Marx's disciple and son-in-law, who helped introduce Marxism to France. The books cover, respectively, the first forty and last thirty years of Lafargue's life: *Paul Lafargue and the Founding of French Marxism, 1842-1882,* and *Paul Lafargue and the Flowering of French Socialism, 1882-1911.* In a review of the latter, *London Review of Books* contributor Susan Watkins pronounces it "diligently researched in four languages although occasionally faltering in the narration." Lafargue was born in 1842 in Cuba, the son of part-African owners of a coffee plantation. After Spain, Cuba's colonial master, put down an uprising on the island in 1851, the Lafargue family moved to Bordeaux, France. Rebelling against middle-class conservatism, Paul Lafargue embraced leftist politics as a medical student in Paris in the 1860s. At a student conference in Belgium he gave a speech endorsing "war on God," leading to his expulsion from his university. He resumed his studies in London, where he met Marx. He quickly became enthralled by Marx's socialist philosophy and by Laura, the most attractive of the three Marx daughters; Marx, for his part, looked on Lafargue as a son.

Lafargue became active in Marx's International Working Men's Association and wrote extensively on Marxism. He and Laura moved to France after their marriage, and he took part in the effort to set up a revolutionary government, the Paris Commune, in 1871. The Commune was short lived, but its veterans set up a new leftist party a decade later. Lafargue continued writing and speaking out on Marxism as a remedy for the troubles of the working people. In the 1890s he fell somewhat out of favor, as younger activists called for an evolving version of Marxist philosophy, not the stagnant one they saw touted by Lafargue. Nevertheless, Lafargue remained part of the circle of prominent socialists, entertaining many of them at a country home near Paris that he purchased in 1895 with money left him by Marx's colleague Friedrich Engels. He committed suicide in 1911, leaving a note in which he stated his wish to avoid the infirmities of old age. Laura joined him in taking a lethal dose of poison. Watkins notes that "Lafargue's suicide shocked the Left and dimmed his reputation in the decades after his death," but adds that his influence has made itself felt in French socialist and progressive movements throughout the twentieth century.

BIOGRAPHICAL/CRITICAL SOURCES:

PERIODICALS

American Historical Review, February, 1985; June, 1992.

London Review of Books, May 13, 1999, pp. 19-21.*

* * *

DONINGTON, Robert 1907-1990

PERSONAL: Born May 4, 1907, in Leeds, England; son of George Caulton (a teacher) and Ellen (Lowry) Donington; died 1990; married Gloria Rose (a musicologist; died, 1975); children: Jenny, Laura, Charles, Janie. *Education:* Queen's College, Oxford, B.A., 1930, B.Litt., 1946; studied music privately under Arnold Dolmetsch, H. K. Andrews, R. O. Morris, and Egon Wellesz. *Avocational interests:* Collecting antique clocks, country walks.

CAREER: Played at Haslemere Festivals and was secretary of the Dolmetsch Foundation in the early 1930's; as Leverhulme research fellow, scored and catalogued seventeenth-century English music for viols, 1934-36; member of English Consort of Viols, 1935-39, and London Consort, 1950-60; member of teaching staff of Trinity College of Music, London, England, 1948-60, and Attingham Summer School of Music, 1950-60; founder and director of Donington Consort, 1956-61; University of Pittsburgh, Pittsburgh, PA, visiting Andrew Mellon Professor of Music, 1961-62; did research, writing, and broadcasting in London, 1962-64; University of Iowa, Iowa City, visiting professor, 1964-66, professor of music, 1966-73. Visiting professor, Yale University, 1970-71; summer faculty member of visiting professor of music at Stanford University, 1961, 1964, University of Washington, Seattle, 1962, University of Southern California, 1964, Rutgers University, 1968; visiting professor at City University of New York, autumn, 1969, and State University of New York at Buffalo, 1972-74. In addition his own concerts, performed at Elizabethan Festival in Berlin, 1948, Festival of Britain, 1951, Purcell-Handel celebrations in England, 1959, and Carmel Bach Festival, Carmel, CA, 1961, 1971; director of recordings of Purcell in Paris and British Council recordings in London; has played in films and on numerous British Broadcasting Corp. and other broadcasts and television shows.

MEMBER: American Musicological Society (member of council, 1967-69, 1970-72), Royal Musical Association, International Musicological Society, Galpin Society (founder-member), Viola da Gamba Society, Stradivarius Association (member of honorary committee), International Bach Society (honorary member), Royal Academy of Music (honorary member), Royal Academy of Music (honorary member), Analytical Psychology Club (vice-chairman, 1960-61).

AWARDS, HONORS: Leverhulme research fellowship, 1935-36; Grand Prix du Disque, 1948; Grand Prix de l'Academie Charles Cros, 1949; Fellowes Memorial Fund grant, 1958; Composition Prize of Viola da Gamba Society, 1961; guest fellow, Jonathan Edwards College, Yale University, 1970-71; Commander of the Order of the British Empire, 1979.

WRITINGS:

The Work and Ideas of Arnold Dolmetsch (booklet), Dolmetsch Foundation, 1932.

(With Edgar Hunt) *A Practical Method for the Recorder,* two volumes, Oxford University Press, 1935.

(With Barbara Donington) *The Citizen Faces War,* Gollancz, 1936.

The Instruments of Music, Methuen, 1949, 4th revised edition, 1970.

The Connoisseur Period Guides, Connoisseur, Book I: *Music and Musical Instruments in the Tudor Period, 1500-1603,* 1956, Book II: *Music and Musical Instruments in the Stuart Period, 1603-1714,* 1957, Book III: *Music and Musical Instruments in the Regency Period, 1810-1830,* 1958, Book IV: *Music and Musical Instruments in the Early Victorian Period, 1830-1860,* 1958.

Music for Fun (quiz book), Hutchinson, 1960.

Tempo and Rhythm in Bach's Organ Music, Hinrichsen Edition, 1960.

(With Margaret Donington) *Scales, Arpeggios and Exercises for the Recorder,* Oxford University Press, 1961.

Wagner's "Ring" and Its Symbols: The Music and the Myth, St. Martin's, 1963, 3rd edition, 1975.

The Interpretation of Early Music, St. Martin's 1963, 3rd edition, 1974.

(Author of foreword) Francesco Geminiani, *A Treatise of Good Taste in the Art of Musick,* DaCapo Press, 1969.

A Performer's Guide to Baroque Music, Faber, 1973, Scribner, 1974.

String-Playing in Baroque Music, Scribner, 1977.

The Opera, Harcourt, 1978.

The Rise of the Opera, Scribner, 1981.

Music and its Instruments, Methuen (New York City), 1982.

Baroque Music: Style and Performance: A Handbook, Norton, 1982.

Opera and its Symbols: The Unity of Words, Music, and Staging, Yale University Press, 1990.

CONTRIBUTOR

Unofficial British Peace Aims (booklet), National Peace Council, 1942.

Imogen Holst, editor, *Henry Purcell, 1659-1695,* Oxford University Press, 1959.

Ian Kemp, editor, *Michael Tippett: A Symposium on His Sixtieth Birthday,* Faber, 1965.

Denis Arnold and Nigel Fortune, editors, *The Monteverdi Companion,* Faber, 1968.

H. C. Robbins Landon and Roger E. Chapman, editors, *Studies in Eighteenth-Century Music: A Tribute to Karl Geiringer on His Seventieth Birthday,* Oxford University Press, 1970.

MUSICAL COMPOSITIONS

(Editor) *English Fantasies for Viols,* Schott, 1949.

(Editor with Walter Emery) Henry Purcell, *Two Trio Sonatas,* Novello, 1959.

Suite No. I for Three or More Violins, Elkin, 1960.

Suite No. II for Three or More Violins, Elkin, 1964.

Contributor of about sixty articles to *Grove's Dictionary of Music and Musicians,* 5th edition, Macmillan, 1954, and to *Encyclopedia Britannica, Pitman's Popular Encyclopaedia, Collier's Encyclopedia, Book of Knowledge, Larousse Dictionnaire de Musique, Die Musik in Geschichte und Gegenwart, Enciclopedia della Musica,* and *Encyclopedia of Music and Musicians.* Contributor of articles and reviews to *Listener, New Statesman, Times Literary Supplement,* and music journals. Editor, *Cherwell,* 1927-29, and *Consort,* 1934-38.

SIDELIGHTS: A musician, educator, and author, Robert Donington wrote several influential books in his field over the course of a career that spanned fifty years. *Wagner's "Ring" and Its Symbols: The Music and the Myth* examined the operas of German composer Richard Wagner in terms of Jungian psychology and became the basis of several new performances of Wagner's opera cycle; *The Interpretation of Early Music,* considered a seminal work, helped revive interest in Elizabethan music. Among his other writings are *The Instruments of Music, String-Playing in Baroque Music, The Opera,* and *The Rise of Opera.* Donington played viol in a number of ensembles and led his own consort from 1956 to 1961. He taught at institutions such as Trinity College of Music, the University of Pittsburgh, and University of Iowa. Donington was interested in analytical psychology, "especially as a tool for studying works of art," and in neoplatonic symbolism, "especially for my studies of early opera." In 1979, Donington was named a Commander of the Order of the British Empire.

OBITUARIES:

BOOKS

Baker's Biographical Dictionary of Musicians, 7th edition, Schirmer, 1984.

PERIODICALS

Times (London), January 26, 1990.*

* * *

DOUGLAS, Ellen
See HAXTON, Josephine Ayres

E

EISENSTEIN, Phyllis 1946-

PERSONAL: Born February 26, 1946, in Chicago, IL; daughter of Irving (a grocer) and Sylvia (Davidson) Kleinstein; married Alex Eisenstein (an artist and writer), September 8, 1966. *Education:* Attended University of Chicago, 1963-66; University of Illinois at Chicago Circle, B.A., 1981. *Avocational interests:* Anthropology, archaeology, mythology, astronomy, old movies.

ADDRESSES: Home—Chicago, IL.

CAREER: Writer. Grocery stock clerk and butcher, 1963-65; Columbia College of Chicago, Chicago, IL, teacher of fiction writing, 1977-80, 1989-91.

MEMBER: Science Fiction Writers of America (Nebula trustee,1976-81), Authors Guild.

AWARDS, HONORS: Balrog award, 1978.

WRITINGS:

SCIENCE FICTION NOVELS

Born to Exile, Arkham, 1978.
Shadow of Earth, Dell, 1979.
In the Hands of Glory, Pocket Books, 1981.
In the Red Lord's Reach, Signet, 1989.

FANTASY NOVELS

Sorcerer's Son, del Rey, 1979.
The Crystal Palace, Signet, 1988.

OTHER

(Compiler and editor, with Alexander Eisenstein) *Stars My Destination: Alfred Bester,* Vintage Books (New York City), 1996.

Contributor to anthologies such as *Best from Fantasy and Science Fiction,* Twentieth Series, Doubleday, 1973; *Best Science Fiction of the Year,* Dutton, 1976; *Year's Best Fantasy,* DAW Books, 1978; and *Best Science Fiction of the Year,* Dutton, 1979. Also contributor to *New Dimensions, Shadows,* and *Whispers,* and to science fiction magazines, including *Analog, Galaxy, Magazine of Fantasy and Science Fiction, Asimov's Science Fiction Magazine, Cavalier,* and *Twilight Zone.*

SIDELIGHTS: Phyllis Eisenstein told *St. James Guide to Fantasy Writers:* "I never intended to be a fantasy writer. Rather, my goal, from the age of eight, was to be a science-fiction writer, thereby writing in the genre I loved best. But I always enjoyed fantasy. Some of my earliest reading was of the Andrew Lang color-coded fairy-tale books, which led me on to Grimm, Perrault, and others. And by the time I was ten or eleven, I had read most of Edgar Allen Poe's fiction, which made for an interesting balance. I was reading the science-fiction magazines and the Groff Conklin anthologies by then, and it was becoming clear to me that science fiction and fantasy were a continuum—a spectrum, with sf at the violet end, fantasy at the red end, and a whole array of hard-to-categorize stories in the middle.

"When the old *Twilight Zone* TV show came on the air, I saw that it spanned that spectrum, and it confirmed my feeling that there were no hard and fast barriers, that I could write in any color of the spectrum and still be in the same universe. One result of that feeling is that some of my stories are those hard-to-categorize creatures, those in-betweeners that might be science fiction or might be fantasy. But some are solidly in the fantasy end of the spectrum. With all that material from the Western European folkloric tradition absorbed in my formative reading years, it was almost inevitable that some fantasy ideas would leap out of my imagination and demand to be put down on paper. Important human questions were explored in that folkloric tradition—including questions of morality, identity, loyalty, compulsion—and they remain worth exploring, whether in a traditional, a modern, or a futuristic context.

"My own work in the fantasy arena tends to focus on the problems of individuals rather than on world-spanning events. I am interested in the outsider, the alienated, the reluctant sorcerer, the seeker for a lost heritage—people searching for their places in the scheme of things, and for whatever happiness they can snatch from an indifferent universe. My stories also frequently concern the lust for power, and the sense of responsibility that must contend with it, the perils of obsessive hatred, and the emptiness of revenge. At least, these things can be found in my work. All of these aspects of the human condition speak to me much more strongly than any supposed struggle between abstract Good and Evil, so I leave that larger canvas' to others."

Eisenstein's first novel, *Born to Exile,* introduces Alaric, the main character of that book and of *In the Red Lord's Reach.* Alaric was discovered alone on a hillside when he was a baby (albeit with a severed hand grasping his ankle), and was soon found to have magical powers. He is fifteen when *Born to Exile* begins, and the book tells of his quest to unearth his past—an antidote, he hopes, to the loneliness he feels in the superstitious society in which he lives.

In *St. James Guide to Fantasy Writers,* Mike Ashley wrote that the best of Eisenstein's novels combine "convincing characterization with well developed story lines steeped solidly in myth and magic, resulting in a body of work that is rare but impressive." Ashley singled out *Sorcerer's Son* for praise. *Sorcerer's Son* introduces another sequence of fantasy books, this one featuring Cray Omeru. Cray's mother is a sorceress; his father, he believes, is a wandering knight named Gildrum. Like Alaric, Cray's quest is to find and know his father.

BIOGRAPHICAL/CRITICAL SOURCES:

BOOKS

St. James Guide to Fantasy Writers, St. James Press, 1996.

PERIODICALS

Magazine of Fantasy and Science Fiction, October, 1991, p. 71.
Publishers Weekly, October 14, 1988, p. 68; June 2, 1989, p. 79.
Science Fiction Chronicle, December, 1988, p. 45.*

* * *

EKLUND, Gordon (Stewart) 1945-

PERSONAL: Born July 24, 1945, in Seattle, WA; son of Alfred James (a dental technician) and DeLois (Stewart) Eklund; married Dianna Jean Mylarski, March 12, 1969 (separated); children: two sons. *Education:* Attended Contra Costa College, San Pablo, CA, 1973-75.

ADDRESSES: *Home*—6305 East D. St., Tacoma, WA 98403. *Agent*—Kirby McCauley, 220 East 26th St., New York, NY 10010.

CAREER: Worked at numerous odd jobs in the San Francisco area, 1967-71; writer, principally of science fiction, 1968—. *Military service:* U.S. Air Force; became sergeant.

MEMBER: Science Fiction Writers of America, Lilapa.

AWARDS, HONORS: Nebula Award nomination, Science Fiction Writers of America, 1971, for first published short story, "Dear Aunt Annie"; Nebula Award for best science fiction novelette, 1975, for *If the Stars Are Gods.*

WRITINGS:

The Eclipse of Dawn, Ace Books, 1971.
A Trace of Dreams, Ace Books, 1972.
Beyond the Resurrection, Doubleday, 1973.
(Contributor) Robert Silverberg, editor, *Chains of the Sea: Three Original Novellas of Science Fiction,* T. Nelson, 1973.
(Contributor) Terry Carr, editor, *Universe 3,* Random House, 1973.

(Contributor) Lester Del Ray, editor, *Best Science Fiction Stories of the Year,* Ace Books, 1973.
All Times Possible, DAW Books, 1974.
(With Poul Anderson) *The Inheritors of Earth,* Chilton, 1974.
(Contributor) Donald A. Wollheim, editor, *The 1974 Annual World's Best Science Fiction,* DAW Books, 1974.
Serving in Time, Laser Books, 1975.
Falling Toward Forever, Laser Books, 1975.
The Grayspace Beast, Doubleday, 1976.
(Contributor with Gregory Benford) Carr, editor, *Universe 6,* Popular Library, 1976.
Dance of the Apocalypse, Laser Books, 1976.
(With Benford) *If the Stars Are Gods,* Putnam, 1977.
(Contributor) Carr, editor, *Universe 8,* Popular Library, 1978.
The Starless World, Bantam, 1978.
Devil World, Bantam, 1979.
(With Benford) *Find the Changeling,* Dell, 1980.
The Garden of Winter, Berkley Publishing, 1980.
Lord Tedric: Space Pirates #2, Ace Books, 1980.
(With Smith) *Lord Tedric III: Black Knight of the Iron Sphere,* Ace Books, 1981.
A Thunder on Neptune, W. Morrow (New York City),1989.

Contributor to science fiction magazines, including *Galaxy, Fantasy and Science Fiction, Analog Science Fiction/Science Fact, Amazing Stories,* and *Fantastic.*

SIDELIGHTS: The Science Fiction Writers of America nominated Gordon Eklund for the Nebula award in 1971 on the strength of his first published story. In "Dear Aunt Annie," which appeared in a 1970 issue of *Fantastic* magazine, a robot columnist advises unlucky lovers of the future. American life in the future was the most frequent subject of Eklund's work of the seventies, notes *Dictionary of Literary Biography Yearbook* contributor Mark Lidman. The 1971 novel *The Eclipse of Dawn* portrays presidential election politics in a 1988 nuclear-war-damaged America; *All Times Possible* follows leftist revolutionary hero Tommy Bloom as he creates a New America in an alternate time-line that runs parallel to that of actual history, which remains unchanged; and *Beyond the Resurrection,*"set in a future complete with automated cars and mindless professional soldiers, . . . looks at the frightening aspects of genetic engineering and the moral issues involved, [having at] the center of attention an outsider alienated from the mainstream of humanity," Lidman reports.

These books brought their author more acclaim than later books, says the essayist, who identifies the zenith of Eklund's literary popularity as the novelette *If the Stars Are Gods.* Co-authored with astrophysicist Gregory Benford, the Nebula Prize winner compares the glory-seeking aspirations behind human space travel to those of wisdom-seeking aliens who hope to find guidance from a benevolent Sun. By the end of the story, hero Bradley Reynolds, who is an ambassador of sorts to the aliens, identifies with the alien view. Together they meet disappointment when it is learned, after "communing" with the Sun, that its core is cold, and its benevolence not equal to their hopes.

Two later projects—two Star Trek adventures *(The Starless World* and *Devil World)* "seem to be commercial rather than artistic efforts," writes Lidman, who concludes by saying, "it is hoped that Eklund can recover the enthusiasm and involvement with his work that made him one of science fiction's most promising figures in the 1970s."

Shortly after the Star Trek books, Eklund launched his Lord Tedric series with *Lord Tedric* and *Space Pirates.* The books were conceived and written with E. E. Smith, and in them the battle between good and evil is fought on a grand scale. Like Superman, Lord Tedric was born in some other world that he has forgotten and has superhuman powers on Earth. Tedric's understanding of his gifts and his destiny comes gradually, however. According to *Twentieth-Century Science-Fiction Writers* contributor Peter Lynch, Tedricis not meant to be as realistic a character as Bradley Reynolds in *If the Stars Are Gods.*

"Eklund has a rare ability to project alternative outcomes for the United States, the world, and the cosmos," writes Lynch. "He ranges from sarcastic pessimism in *The Eclipse of Dawn* to . . . total cosmic liberation (communication with the stars) in *If the Stars Are Gods.*"

BIOGRAPHICAL/CRITICAL SOURCES:

BOOKS

Carr, Terry, editor, *Universe 6,* Popular Library, 1976.
Dictionary of Literary Biography Yearbook: 1983, Gale, 1984.
Twentieth-Century Science-Fiction Writers, 3rd edition, St. James Press, 1991.

PERIODICALS

Analog Science Fiction/Science Fact, June, 1976.
Library Journal, May 15, 1973; October 1, 1974; September 15,1976.

Magazine of Fantasy and Science Fiction, June, 1972, August, 1973, October, 1975.
New York Times Book Review, March 27, 1977; February 11, 1990.
Publishers Weekly, December 4, 1972, April 8, 1974, September 23, 1974, June 28, 1976; October 20, 1989.
Times Literary Supplement, June 16, 1978.*

* * *

ELGIN, (Patricia Anne) Suzette Haden 1936-

PERSONAL: Born November 18, 1936, in Louisiana, MO; daughter of Gaylord Lloyd (a lawyer) and Hazel (a teacher; maiden name, Lewis) Wilkins; married Peter Haden, 1955 (deceased); married George Elgin (a sales manager), 1964; children: (first marriage) Michael, Rebecca, Patricia; (second marriage) Benjamin. *Education:* Attended University of Chicago, 1954-56; Chico State College (now California State University, Chico), B.A., 1967; University of California, San Diego, M.A., 1970, Ph.D., 1973. *Avocational interests:* Theology ("particularly seen as a discipline . . . religious language, for example"), guitar, singing.

ADDRESSES: Home—P.O. Box 1137, Huntsville, AR 72740. *Agent*—James Byron, P.O. Box 2389, Hollywood, CA 90028.

CAREER: Writer. ETV (channel 9), Redding, CA, performer on folk music show and folk guitar instruction show, 1966-68; Chico Conservatory of Music, Chico, CA, instructor, 1967-68; adult education teacher of French, 1968-69; teacher of guitar and music theory, 1969-70; University of California at San Diego, La Jolla, teacher of basic linguistics for Apache field methods, summer, 1971; San Diego State University, San Diego, CA, associate professor of linguistics, 1972-80, associate professor emeritus, 1980—; Ozark Center for Language Studies, Huntsville, AR, founder and director, and publisher of newsletter, *The Lonesome Node,* 1980—.Worked as translator and interpreter for American Bar Association Committee on World Peace through Law. Has worked as a consultant.

MEMBER: Science Fiction Writers of America, Science Fiction Poetry Association, Association of Women in Psychology, National Council of Teachers of English, Loving Kindness (president).

AWARDS, HONORS: Academy of American Poets Award, University of Chicago, 1955; Eugene Saxon Memorial Trust fellowship in poetry from *Harper's,* 1958.

WRITINGS:

PUBLISHED BY PRENTICE-HALL, EXCEPT AS INDICATED

(Contributor) John Kimball, editor, *Syntax and Semantics,* two volumes, Academic Press, 1972.
(With John T. Grinder) *Guide to Transformational Grammar: History, Theory, Practice,* Holt Rinehart, 1973.
What Is Linguistics?, 1973, 2nd edition, 1979, workbook published as *Beginning Linguistics Workbook,* 1974.
Pouring Down Words (English textbook), 1975.
A Primer of Transformational Grammar for Rank Beginners, National Conference of Teachers of English, 1975.
The Gentle Art of Verbal Self-Defense, 1980.
More on the Gentle Art of Verbal Self-Defense, Prentice Hall (Englewood Cliffs, NJ), 1983.
A First Grammar and Dictionary of Latin, SF3, 1984.
The Last Word on the Gentle Art of Verbal Self-Defense, Prentice Hall Press (New York City), 1987.
Success With the Gentle Art of Verbal Self-Defense, Prentice Hall, Business and Professional Division (Englewood Cliffs, NJ), 1989.
Staying Well with the Gentle Art of Verbal Self-Defense, Prentice Hall, 1990.
(With Rebecca Haden) *A Celebration of Ozark English: A Collection of Articles from the "Lonesome Node"—1980 to 1990,* OCLS Press (Huntsville, AR), 1991.
Genderspeak: Men, Women, and the Gentle Art of Verbal Self-Defense, J. Wiley (New York City), 1993.
The Gentle Art of Written Self-Defense Letter Book: Letters in Response to Triple-F Situations, Prentice Hall,1993.
BusinessSpeak: Using the Gentle Art of Verbal Persuasion to Get What You Want at Work, McGraw-Hill (New York City),1995.
You Can't Say That to Me!: Stopping the Pain of Verbal Abuse: An 8-Step Program, Wiley, 1995.
The Gentle Art of Communicating with Kids, Wiley, 1996.
How to Disagree without Being Disagreeable: Getting Your Point Across with the Gentle Art of Verbal Self-Defense, J. Wiley, 1997.
Try to Feel It My Way: New Help for Touch Dominant People and Those Who Care About Them, Wiley, 1997.

How to Turn the Other Cheek and Still Survive in Today's World, T. Nelson (Nashville, TN), 1997.

SCIENCE FICTION NOVELS

The Communipaths (also see below), Ace Books, 1970.
Furthest (also see below), Ace Books, 1971.
At the Seventh Level (also see below), Daw Books,1972.
Star-Anchored, Star-Angered, Doubleday, 1979.
Communipath Worlds (collection including *The Communipaths, Furthest,* and *At the Seventh Level*), Pocket Books, 1981.
The Ozark Trilogy (includes *Twelve Fair Kingdoms, The Grand Jubilee,* and *And Then There'll Be Fireworks;* Science Fiction Book Club alternate selection), Doubleday, 1981.
Native Tongue, DAW, 1984; Women's Press (London), 1985.
Yonder Comes the Other End of Time, DAW, 1986.
Native Tongue II: The Judas Rose, DAW, 1987; as *The Judas Rose,* Women's Press, 1988.

Contributor of articles and reviews to linguistics journals and to *Mother Earth News.*

SIDELIGHTS: Suzette Haden Elgin is a linguist whose science-fiction novels deal with, in her words to *Twentieth-Century Science-Fiction Writers,* "problems of communication as they are now and as they are likely to develop in the future. "Communication is explored in all its forms, from telepathy (nearly as common as eyesight among Elgin's characters) to poetry (battles are waged over bad verse). The novels divide into three series: the Communipath books, the Ozark trilogy, and the series that begins with *Native Tongue* and its sequel.

The Communipath novels take place in the distant future and range over various planets inhabited by humanoids. The series' pivotal character is Agent Coyote Jones who has both outstanding strengths (projective telepathy is a specialty) and weaknesses (he is "mind-deaf," a handicap that is rare in his time). In *Star-Anchored, Star-Angered,* Jones is assigned to investigate a female messiah named Drussa Silver and her followers. In *Furthest,* a character who has been groomed for a life as a "psychic concubine" rebels against her role.

Bernadette Bosky wrote in *Twentieth-Century Science-Fiction Writers,* "Much of the charm of the Ozark trilogy comes from the familiar strangeness, and strange familiarity, of alien equivalents of the modern-American Ozark culture Elgin knows well, including mules, 'actually telepathic, but generally uncommunicative aliens who fly by magic'; and the Grannies, 'a powerful social class, able to perform household magic and known for their folksy and fiery form of speech.' " In Bosky's estimation, Elgin's plotting skills show improvement in the Ozark trilogy, marked by complex, tightly written stories in which everything that happens turns out to be significant. "The narrative voice gets more sure and the characters get both more human and more powerful," Bosky added.

In the series that begins with *Native Tongue,* Elgin's future counterparts, interspecies linguists, are both powerful and hated. Vitally important at a time of interplanetary commerce, the linguists have become an inbred priestly class, marrying within clans and training their children as translators during their early years, when language acquisition is relatively easy. Another interesting aspect of the time is that the idea of women's rights is nothing but a vague legend; men have complete authority over women.

Bosky summed up by calling Elgin a significant author, one whose books "present the reader with an enticing blend of readability and challenging (often provoking) insights concerning serious issues."

Elgin writes: "A great deal of my time, and much of my writing, is devoted to an attempt to destroy the Romantic Love Ethic of our culture, which I see as the major barrier to male/female communication, the major obstacle to women's liberation, and a blasted nuisance generally." Her linguistic specialty is Amerindian languages, especially Navajo, Kumeyaay (a California Indian language), and Hopi.

BIOGRAPHICAL/CRITICAL SOURCES:

BOOKS

Twentieth-Century Science-Fiction Writers, 3rd edition, St. James Press, 1991.

PERIODICALS

Analog, January 5, 1981, p. 163; February 1, 1982, p. 142; June, 1994, p. 161.
Locus, December, 1993, p. 25; March, 1994, p. 54.
Publishers Weekly, April 23, 1979, p. 79; April 17, 1981, p. 51; June22, 1984, p. 84; December 12, 1994, p. 59; December 4, 1995, p. 61.
Voice Literary Supplement, October, 1984, p. 18.*

ELLERBECK, Rosemary (Anna L'Estrange, Nicola Thorne, Katherine Yorke)

PERSONAL: Born in Cape Town, South Africa. *Education:* London School of Economics, B.S.

ADDRESSES: Home—96 Townshend Court, Mackennal St., London NW86LD, England.

CAREER: Editor, until 1976; writer, 1976—.

WRITINGS:

NOVELS

Inclination to Murder, Hodder & Stoughton, 1965, reprinted, 1985.
Hammersleigh, McKay, 1976.
Rose, Rose, Where Are You?, Coward, 1978.

NOVELS; UNDER PSEUDONYM ANNA L'ESTRANGE

Return to Wuthering Heights (historical novel), Pinnacle Books, 1977.

NOVELS; UNDER PSEUDONYM NICOLA THORNE

The Girls, Random House, 1967.
Bridie Climbing, Ace Books, 1974.
In Love, Quartet, 1974.
A Woman Like Us, St. Martin's, 1979.
The Perfect Wife and Mother, St. Martin's, 1981.
Sisters and Lovers (historical novel), Doubleday, 1982, published in England as *The Daughters of the House,* May-flower Books, 1982.
Cashmere (historical novel), Doubleday, 1982, published in England as *Where the Rivers Meet,* Granada, 1982.
Affairs of Love (historical novel), Doubleday, 1983.
The Enchantress Saga (based on *The Enchantress, Lady of the Lakes,* and *Falcon Gold;* also see below), Grafton Books, 1985.
Never Such Innocence, Grafton Books, 1985.
Yesterday's Promises, Grafton Books, 1986.
Bright Morning, Grafton Books, 1986.
A Place in the Sun, Grafton Books, 1987.
Champagne, Bantam Press (New York City), 1989.
Bird of Passage, Curley Pub (South Yarmouth, MA), 1991.
Champagne Gold, HarperCollins (London and New York City), 1992.
The Rector's Daughter, Heinemann (London), 1992.
Worlds Apart, G.K. Hall (Thorndike, ME), 1997.
Repossession, Thorndike Press (Thorndike, ME), 1997.
Rules of Engagement, Thorndike Press (Thorndike, ME), 1997.
The Good Samaritan, Thorndike Press (Thorndike, ME), 1999.

NOVELS; UNDER PSEUDONYM KATHERINE YORKE

The Enchantress, Pocket Books, 1979.
Falcon Gold, Futura, 1980; Pinnacle, 1981.
Lady of the Lakes, Futura, 1982.
A Woman's Place, Macdonald, 1983.
The Pair Bond, Macdonald, 1984.
Swift Flows the River, Macdonald, 1988.
The People of This Parish, Heinemann, 1991.
A Wind in Summer, Heinemann, 1991.

Also author of *Pride of Place,* 1988; *Silk: A Novel,* 1993; *Profit and Loss,* 1994; and *Trophy Wife,* 1995.

SIDELIGHTS: Rosemary Ellerbeck wrote *CA:* "My first novel was published in 1965. It was a thriller and apart from two 'gothics' was never followed by another, though I am listed in *Romance and Gothic Writers.* I do enjoy an element of mystery and suspense in most things I write, I must say—the idea that things are never as they seem.

"For a short time I abandoned novel writing and went into business as a small-time publisher. This was largely a fiasco because of insufficient backing. I discovered I was a better novelist than a businesswoman, though I did have some very good ideas, also a great sympathy for and interest in writers which made them want to keep in touch with me long after the business folded. I began to write full time in 1976. At first I did editorial jobs to eke out a living. Happily in the eighties I have started to be very successful. My first real success was *Where the Rivers Meet,* which was published in the United States as *Cashmere.* That was on the bestseller list in Great Britain for quite a long time.

"In 1983 I started on an epic work which I completed in the summer of 1986. It didn't start off as an epic, just as a novel; but at the end, it was four volumes long and the time span was from 1898 to 1967. I could have gone on and on, but I was becoming obsessed by the main family, the Askhams, who dominate the series of novels that I call the 'Askham Chronicles: 1898-1967' [which includes *Never Such Innocence, Yesterday's Promises, Bright Morning,* and *A Place in the Sun*]. Luckily, I just happened to be free, and wondering what to do next, when my agent was approached by the Booker conglomerate. They wanted to link a book with a television series that was then being hatched on the other side of the Channel simply called 'Champagne.' I had been suggested to them as the best person to do it, which was very flattering—also very fortunate for me as I am both a Francophile and I love champagne! That's what I'm working on now. As for the future, I hope that after the publication of over twenty novels, I can have a little time in the sun myself—maybe from the results of 'Champagne'! Who knows?"

An earlier Ellerbeck novel of interest is *Hammersleigh,* one of several of the author's novels that mix history and the supernatural. It tells a tale of forbidden love between a monk, Abbot Roderick, and Agatha, Prioress of Hammersleigh. Roderick goes abroad to ask permission to marry Agatha, who dies mysteriously. Then the story leaps forward five hundred years, and the tragic couple begins to haunt Karen Blackwood, a widow, and Hugh Fullerton, the master of Hammersleigh Hall.

Repossession, published in 1997, also has an air of the supernatural. Englishwoman Helen Tempest has moved from the suburbs to a remote country house because of her husband's new job. She isn't happy about the move, and the house only makes things worse. There are "bad vibrations" about. Perhaps it's just because the house was repossessed and the previous owners forced out. Or perhaps it's something more spine-chilling, having to do with the body buried under the house. *Booklist* reviewer Ilene Cooper praised *Repossession,* calling it "a well-paced psychological thriller" populated by well-drawn characters.

Ellerbeck also has written a sequel to Emily Bronte's *Wuthering Heights,* titled *Return to Wuthering Heights.* The sequel's structure is similar to that of the original, and Ellerbeck made a studied effort to recreate Bronte's style. Beginning where the original story ends, with the marriage of Hareton Earnshaw and Cathy (Catherine Earnshaw's daughter), the sequel finds Cathy falling in love with Captain Jack Ibbotson, the tenant at Wuthering Heights. Cathy then discovers that Jack is Heathcliff 's illegimate son. She dies giving birth to Antony, her son by Jack, and the child is brought up by Hareton. Years later, Jack marries Margaret, the daughter Cathy bore to Hareton. Jack constantly compares Margaret to her mother, however, and mistreats her. It is Antony and his wife, Jessica, who end up at Wuthering Heights. P. Campbell wrote in *Twentieth-Century Romance and Historical Writers,*" *Return to Wuthering Heights* is an extremely well written book, if a little confusing. For those readers unfamiliar with the original Bronte work, the relationships will probably be extremely confusing." Acknowledging that it would be a difficult challenge to write a novel that measures up to the original work, Campbell nevertheless called the sequel "an extremely credible work."

BIOGRAPHICAL/CRITICAL SOURCES:

BOOKS

Twentieth-Century Romance and Historical Writers, 3rd edition, St. James Press, 1994.

PERIODICALS

Booklist, January 1, 1997.
Times Literary Supplement, January 2, 1981.
Washington Post Book World, December 5, 1982.*

* * *

ELLIN, E(lizabeth) M(uriel) 1905-

PERSONAL: Born March 22, 1905, in Waiuku, New Zealand; daughter of Ernest Morely (a farmer) and Edith (Sorby) Ellin. *Education:* Educated in Auckland, New Zealand.

ADDRESSES: Home—42 Beach Rd., Castor Bay, Auckland 9, New Zealand.

CAREER: "Jack of all trades . . . here, there and anywhere."

WRITINGS:

The Children of Clearwater Bay (juvenile; illustrated by Garth Tapper), Macmillan, 1969.
The Greenstone Axe (juvenile; illustrated by Elizabeth Sutherland), Stockton House, 1975.

SIDELIGHTS: E. M. Ellin grew up on a farm in northern New Zealand, which provides the setting for both her books. Both are stories of children growing up in times past and facing dangerous situations. Well-researched historical details, authentic characters, and simple prose make her books highly readable.

In *The Children of Clearwater Bay* the six Cameron children, ages two to fourteen, must summon resourcefulness, courage, and endurance in the face of disaster. "[I]n common with their counterparts in *The Greenstone Axe,"* wrote Dorothy Butler in *Twentieth-Century Children's Writers,* "they demonstrate a proper balance of anxiety evoked by consciousness of their own immaturity, and determination to do the best in the circumstances." Praising Ellin's "capacity for bringing characters alive and bestowing credibility on the action," Butler concluded that, in both Ellin's books, "The result is entertainment of a high order."

BIOGRAPHICAL/CRITICAL SOURCES:

BOOKS

Twentieth-Century Children's Writers, 4th edition, St. James Press, 1995.

PERIODICALS

Times Literary Supplement, October 16, 1969.*

* * *

ENRIGHT, D(ennis) J(oseph) 1920-

PERSONAL: Born March 11, 1920, in Leamington, Warwickshire, England; son of George (a postman) and Grace (Cleaver) Enright; married Madeleine Harders, November 3, 1949; children: Dominique. *Education:* Downing College, Cambridge, B.A. (with honors), 1944, M.A., 1946; University of Alexandria, D. Litt., 1949.

ADDRESSES: Home—35A Viewfield Rd., London SW18 5JD, England. *Agent*—Watson, Little Ltd., Suite 8, 26 Charing Cross Road, London WC2H ODG, England.

CAREER: Poet, novelist, essayist, and editor. University of Alexandria, Alexandria, Egypt, assistant lecturer in English, 1947-50; University of Birmingham, Birmingham, England, extramural lecturer, 1950-53; Koonan University, Kobe, Japan, visiting professor, 1953-56; Free University of Berlin, Berlin, Germany, visiting professor, 1956-57; Chulalongkorn University, Bangkok, Thailand, British Council Professor, 1957-59; University of Singapore, Singapore, professor of English, 1960-70; *Encounter* (magazine), London, England, co-editor, 1970-72; Chatto & Windus Ltd. (publishers), London, director, 1974-82. Honorary professor of English, Warwick University, 1975-80.

MEMBER: Royal Society of Literature (fellow).

AWARDS, HONORS: Cholmondeley Award for Poetry, British Society of Authors, 1974; Queen's Gold Medal for Poetry, 1981; D.Lett., University of Warwick, 1982; D.Univ., University of Surrey, 1985; Order of the British Empire, 1991.

WRITINGS:

POETRY

Season Ticket, Editions du Scarabee (Alexandria), 1948.
The Laughing Hyena and Other Poems, Routledge & Kegan Paul, 1953.
Bread Rather than Blossoms, Secker & Warburg, 1956.
The Year of the Monkey, Koonan University, 1956.
Some Men Are Brothers, Chatto & Windus (London), 1960.
Addictions, Chatto & Windus, 1962.
The Old Adam, Chatto & Windus, 1965.
Unlawful Assembly, Wesleyan University Press, 1968.
Selected Poems, Chatto & Windus, 1969.
The Typewriter Revolution and Other Poems, Library Press, 1971.
In the Basilica of the Annunciation, Poem-of-the-Month Club, 1971.
Daughters of Earth, Chatto & Windus, 1972.
Foreign Devils, Covent Garden Press, 1972.
The Terrible Shears: Scenes from a Twenties Childhood, Chatto & Windus, 1973, Wesleyan University Press, 1974.
Rhyme Times Rhyme (juvenile), Chatto & Windus,1974.
Sad Ires, Chatto & Windus, 1975.
(Contributor) *Penguin Modern Poets 26: Dannie Abse, D. J. Enright, Michael Longley,* Penguin, 1975.
Paradise Illustrated, Chatto & Windus, 1978.
A Faust Book, Oxford University Press, 1979.
Collected Poems, Oxford University Press, 1981, revised and enlarged edition published as *Collected Poems, 1987,* 1987.
Instant Chronicles: A Life, Oxford University Press, 1985.
Selected Poems, 1990, Oxford University Press, 1990.
Under the Circumstances: Poems and Proses, Oxford University Press, 1991.
Old Men and Comets, Oxford University Press, 1993.

NOVELS

Academic Year, Secker & Warburg, 1955, Oxford University Press, 1985.
Heaven Knows Where, Secker & Warburg, 1957.
Insufficient Poppy, Chatto & Windus, 1960.
Figures of Speech, Heinemann, 1965.
The Joke Shop (juvenile), McKay, 1976.
Wild Ghost Chase (juvenile), Chatto & Windus, 1978.

Beyond Land's End (juvenile), Chatto & Windus, 1979.

The Way of the Cat, HarperCollins, 1992.

ESSAYS

Literature for Men's Sake, Kenkyusha Ltd. (Tokyo), 1955.

The Apothecary's Shop: Essays on Literature, Secker & Warburg, 1957, Dufour, 1959.

Conspirators and Poets, Dufour, 1966.

Man Is an Onion: Reviews and Essays, Chatto & Windus, 1972, Library Press, 1973.

A Mania for Sentences, Chatto & Windus, 1983, David Godine, 1985.

The Alluring Problem: An Essay on Irony, Oxford University Press, 1986.

Fields of Vision: Essays on Literature, Language, and Television, Oxford University Press, 1988.

EDITOR

(And author of introduction) *Poetry of the 1950s: An Anthology of New English Verse,* Kenkyusha Ltd. (Tokyo), 1955.

(With Takamichi Nimomiya) *The Poetry of Living Japan,* Grove, 1957.

(With Ernest de Chickera) *English Critical Texts: Sixteenth-Century to Twentieth-Century,* Oxford University Press, 1962.

(And author of introduction) John Milton, *A Choice of Milton's Verse,* Faber, 1975.

(And author of introduction) Samuel Johnson, *The History of Rasselas, Prince of Abyssinia,* Penguin, 1976.

(And author of introduction) *The Oxford Book of Contemporary Verse, 1945-80,* Oxford University Press, 1980.

(And author of introduction) *The Oxford Book of Death,* Oxford University Press, 1983.

(And author of introduction), *Fair of Speech: The Uses of Euphemism,* Oxford University Press, 1985.

(And author of introduction) *The Faber Book of Fevers and Frets,* Faber, 1989, published as *Ill at Ease,*1990.

(With David Rawlinson) *The Oxford Book of Friendship,* Oxford University Press, 1991.

Marcel Proust, *The Captive* [and] *The Fugitive*, revised edition, Modern Library, 1993.

Proust, *Time Regained,* Modern Library, 1993.

(And author of introduction) *The Oxford Book of the Supernatural,* Oxford University Press, 1994.

OTHER

A Commentary on Goethe's "Faust", New Directions Press, 1949.

The World of Dew: Aspects of Living Japan, Secker & Warburg, 1955, Dufour, 1959.

Robert Graves and the Decline of Modernism (text of lecture), Craftsman Press (Singapore), 1960.

Memoirs of a Mendicant Professor (autobiography), Chatto & Windus, 1969.

Shakespeare and the Students, Chatto & Windus, 1970.

(Translator, with Madeleine Enright) *Nature Alive,* by Colette Portal, Chatto and Windus, 1980.

(Translator and reviser, with Madeleine Enright) *In Search of Lost Time,* by Marcel Proust, Chatto and Windus, and Random House (New York), 1992.

Interplay: A Kind of Commonplace Book, Oxford University Press (New York City), 1995.

Telling Tales, Oxford University Press, 1997.

Contributor to *Encounter, Scrutiny, Listener, New York Review of Books, Observer, London Review of Books,* and *Times Literary Supplement.*

SIDELIGHTS: D. J. Enright is known for his quiet, almost casual poetry. "Enright's form," M. L. Rosenthal observes in *The New Poets: American and British Poetry since World War II,* "is usually very flat and conversational, approaching in a way the 'minimal' style of Robert Creeley, and though actually the poetry is intellectually oriented the statement is kept as simple as possible." Speaking of the collection *The Terrible Shears: Scenes from a Twenties Childhood,* Dan Jacobson notes in the *New Statesman* that "many of the poems have the appearance of being as casual as they can be without lapsing into prose; they are given to unrhymed, conjunctional line-endings, broken rhythms, and a deliberate avoidance of sonority. Yet one does not feel for a moment that they have been easy to write. Candour is never easily come by."David Bromwich writes in the *Nation* that "the plainness of forms leads into a peculiarly stringent mode of vision, so that the most important notes are those struck most quietly."

A large number of Enright's poems are about the Far East, where he taught for a number of years, and often contain social commentary. "Many of [Enright's] Eastern poems," Douglas Dunn explains in the *New Statesman,* "conjure situations of the underdog beset by politicians." Enright's numerous poems about Japan, Philip Gardner remarks in *Contemporary Literature,* are not "testimonials to the Japan of the tourist brochures, the Japan of cherry blossom, Mount Fuji, Kyoto temple, Noh, Tea Ceremony, Flower Arrangement, and Zen.

All these aspects appear, but as a background." Gardner emphasizes Enright's "concern for individuals rather than governments" and his depictions of "a Japan of overpopulation, poverty, landslides, suicides, [and] streetwalkers."

The collection *The Terrible Shears* concerns Enright's childhood in England. "Enright shows us vividly," a reviewer for the *Times Literary Supplement* states, "what it was like to grow up in a particular town in circumstances of poverty and an atmosphere of disease and death." Jacobson writes, "In the face of the large facts of death and poverty, the poems in this collection have the courage to speak repeatedly of the enduring littleness of a child's bewilderment and shame. Hence it is a measure of their painful exactness and truth that they should often be extremely funny. . . . But the funnier they are, the more poignant they are, too." A later collection, *Instant Chronicles: A Life,* deals largely with Enright's years as a self-described "mendicant professor" in Asia and elsewhere. Reviewing the book in the *New York Times Book Review,* John W. Aldridge writes, "At his best—as he clearly is here—Mr. Enright displays a remarkable gift for detecting the diabolical edge to the ordinary. . . . He is interested not in grandiose generalizations about the human condition, not in mankind but in men and women, not in grief but in griefs, particularly the suffering of those incurably exploited by an untouchable authority, human beings sentenced for life to the jails of the uncivilized."

Reviewing Enright's *Collected Poems, 1987* for the *New York Times,* John Gross observes that "critics have sometimes described Mr. Enright's poetry, rather sniffily, as lightverse. Certainly he isn't a heavy poet; but he is a more seriouspoet than many of his more portentous colleagues, and the best way to approach him is to set distinctions between 'heavy' and 'light' to one side. If you do, you will find that his work yields innumerable pleasures and satisfactions."Enright's *Selected Poems, 1990* and Jacqueline Simms' *Life by Other Means: Essays on D. J. Enright* were published simultaneously to honor his seventieth birthday. In *Life by Other Means,* Simms collected numerous compositions written on Enright and his work. Many of the essayists in *Life by Other Means* remark repeatedly on the poet's use of irony and, in Douglas Dunn's words, his "grimly waggish" wit. In his essay, John Bayley praises Enright's fusion of "the literary and the domestically ordinary." In his review of both *Selected Poems* and *Life by Other Means,* Michael Walters writes in the *Times Literary Supplement* that he agrees with the view of essayist P. N. Furbank that Enright's "attitude toward writing and himself as a writer is both earnest and throwaway." Walters observes that Enright, at seventy, was still in his prime.

Throughout his career, Enright has supplemented verse with prose. All four of his novels are about British academics in foreign lands. According to Blake Morrison in the *Times Literary Supplement,* Enright's first novel, *Academic Year,* was greeted as "an Alexandrian *Lucky Jim*" by a *Daily Telegraph* reviewer when it first appeared in 1955. On its reissue a generation later as part of Oxford University Press's "Twentieth Century Classics" series, Morrison stated that *Academic Year*"is a novel which gives pleasure not at the level of its plot (whichis less a sequence of events than a series of setpieces taking us through the academic year), but the wry, ironic, authorial voice rumbling below."

Enright's nonfiction has brought him recognition as a witty critic of literature and television. *A Mania for Sentences* brings together many of his essays on literature. Reacting to Enright the essayist in the *New York Times Book Review,* Aldridge notes: "As a critic he is widely and deeply read and extremely eclectic in his tastes. . . . He represents, in short . . . the old-style practical critic and man of letters who knows and loves books and who can write about them with style, vigor and precision." "All in all," Aldridge summarizes, "D. J. Enright is a welcome reminder that poetry and criticism find their vitality not in theories but in the experiences of personal life and history." In the *Washington Post Book World,* Bob Halliday writes that Enright's *A Mania for Sentences* "straddles the divide between criticism and entertainment, and readers who follow his leads will discover the special virtues of books which may have been out of range for a more seriously didactic sensibility."

Enright has enlarged his public following by serving as editor for widely-read anthologies, including *The Oxford Book of Friendship* and *The Oxford Book of Death,* two compilations of quotations. Anthony Burgess, in the *Times Literary Supplement,* calls *The Oxford Book of Death* "mostly very heartening and sometimes even hilarious" in spite of its grim subject matter, and "one of the liveliest publications of the half-year." Anatole Broyard, in the *New York Times,* says, "[Enright's] editorial comments are among the best things in *The Oxford Book of Death,*" which includes quotations from Ludwig Wittgenstein, Sigmund Freud, Samuel Johnson, Virginia Woolf, and William James. Going from death to mere illness, Enright has edited *The Faber Book of Fevers and Frets,* which Roy Porter in the *Times Literary Supplement* terms "something altogether more ambitious than a rehash of drolleries about doctors: a superb book of embodiment, a documentation of our painful experience of the flesh—solid, sullied, sordid, absurd." Porter concludes that "reading, no less than writing, possesses a healing power."

Interplay: A Kind of Commonplace Book, published in 1995, is Enright's contribution to a genre in which Thomas Jefferson, W. H. Auden, E. M. Forster and many others have dabbled. A commonplace book is a collection of short texts that offer lasting insights; in most cases some are by the author and the rest are drawn from a variety of other writers. The texts may all address a single subject (Jefferson's deal with government), or a wide spectrum of topics, as in Enright's book. *New York Times Book Review* critic William H. Pritchard wrote, "It is testimony to Mr. Enright's brilliance as a resourceful entertainer that his book mainly incites toward quotation, toward reading passages aloud to another person or rereading to oneself by way of catching the trouvailles missed first time through. He's always surprising in that he inevitably manages to top the quite good piece of observation he's just finished making."

BIOGRAPHICAL/CRITICAL SOURCES:

BOOKS

Contemporary Literary Criticism, Gale, Volume 4, 1975, Volume 8, 1978, Volume 31, 1985.
Contemporary Poets, 6th edition, St. James Press, 1996.
Dictionary of Literary Biography, Volume 27: *Poets of Great Britain and Ireland, 1945-1960* Gale, 1984.
Enright, D. J., *Memoirs of a Mendicant Professor,* Chatto & Windus, 1969.
O'Connor, William Van, *The New University Wits and the End of Modernism,* Southern Illinois University Press, 1963.
Rosenthal, M. L., *The New Poets: American and British Poetry since World War II,* Oxford University Press, 1967.
Simms, Jacqueline, editor, *Life by Other Means: Essays on D. J. Enright,* Oxford University Press, 1990.
Something about the Author, Volume 25, Gale, 1981.
Walsh, William, *D. J. Enright: Poet of Humanism,* Cambridge University Press, 1974.

PERIODICALS

Books and Bookmen, November, 1973; October, 1978.
Commonweal, December 1, 1967.
Contemporary Literature, winter, 1965, pp. 100-111; autumn, 1976.
Economist, January 18, 1969; October 22, 1994, p. 106.
Globe & Mail (Toronto), August 29, 1987; May 19, 1990; May 11, 1991, p. 7.
Hudson Review, summer, 1969.
Listener, September 5, 1968; August 20, 1970; November 20, 1975.
Los Angeles Times Book Review, October 2, 1983, p. 2.
Nation, December 6, 1971, p. 599.
New Lugano Review, Volume 3, numbers 1-2, 1977.
New Republic, October 13, 1973.
New Statesman, June 18, 1965; September 28, 1973, p. 432; June 28, 1974, p. 927; May 19, 1978.
Newsweek, August 1, 1983, p. 69.
New York Review of Books, March 31, 1966.
New York Times, June 30, 1983; December 1, 1987, p. 25.
New York Times Book Review, February 13, 1972; April 6, 1975; June 19, 1983, p. 3; November 3, 1985, p. 28; February 11, 1996, p. 33.
Observer, November 20, 1966; December 18, 1994, p. 20; January 8, 1995, p. 14.
Poetry, April, 1973; February, 1976.
Punch, April 7, 1965.
Saturday Review, March 15, 1969.
Spectator, August 25, 1973; October 7, 1995, p. 44.
Times (London), February 27, 1964; June 2, 1983; August 18, 1983; August 17, 1985; October 9, 1986; February 5, 1990.
Times Educational Supplement, June 16, 1978.
Times Literary Supplement, March 18, 1965; July 29, 1965; June 9, 1972; June 8, 1973, p. 646; December 10, 1976; September 26, 1980, p. 1059; May 6, 1983, p. 499; September 9, 1983, p. 951; April 12, 1985, p. 399; June 7, 1985, p. 649; November 29, 1985, p. 1371; October 17, 1986, p. 1151; October 9, 1987, p. 1121; December 23, 1988, p. 1413; December 8, 1989, p. 1367; March 9, 1990, p. 248; May 3, 1991, p. 5; August 16, 1991, p. 24; July 22, 1994, p. 24; November 4, 1994, p. 8; January 26, 1996, p. 25.
Washington Post Book World, September 23, 1973; July 10, 1983, p. 6; June 23, 1985, p. 3; January 26, 1986.*

* * *

ENRIGHT, Elizabeth 1909-1968

PERSONAL: Born September 17, 1909, in Oak Park, IL; died June 8, 1968; daughter of Walter J. (a political cartoonist) and Maginel (a magazine illustrator; maiden name, Wright) Enright; married Robert Marty Gillham (an advertising man and television executive), April 24, 1930; children: Nicholas Wright, Robert II, Oliver. *Education:* Studied at Edgewood School, Greenwich, CT, at Art Students League of New York, 1927-28, in Paris, 1928, and at Parsons School of Design.

CAREER: Began as magazine illustrator but started writing the stories to accompany her drawings and eventually stopped illustrating; author of books for children and of short stories for adults, appearing in *New Yorker* and other national magazines and published as collections. Lecturer in creative writing at Barnard College, 1960-62, and at writing seminars at Indiana University, University of Connecticut, and University of Utah.

MEMBER: Authors League of America, Pen and Brush Club.

AWARDS, HONORS: John Newbery Medal of American Library Association, 1939, for *Thimble Summer; New York Herald Tribune* Children's Spring Book Festival Award, 1957, for *Gone-Away Lake;* named by American Library Association as U.S. nominee for International Hans Christian Andersen Award, 1963, for outstanding literary quality of complete works; *Tatsinda* was an Honor Book in *New York Herald Tribune* Children's Spring Book Festival, 1963; LL.D., Nasson College, 1966.

WRITINGS:

JUVENILE FICTION; ALL SELF-ILLUSTRATED FROM 1935 TO 1951

Kintu: A Congo Adventure, Farrar, 1935.
Thimble Summer, Farrar, 1938.
The Sea Is All Around, Farrar, 1940.
The Saturdays, Farrar, 1941, Puffin Books (New York), 1997.
The Four-Story Mistake, Farrar, 1942, Puffin Books,1997.
Then There Were Five, Farrar, 1944, Puffin Books,1997.
The Melendy Family, three volumes in one (containing *The Saturdays, The Four-Story Mistake,* and *Then There Were Five*), Rinehart, 1947.
A Christmas Tree for Lydia, Rinehart, 1951.
Spiderweb for Two: A Melendy Maze, Rinehart, 1951,Puffin Books, 1997.
Gone-Away Lake, Harcourt, 1957, illustrated by Beth and Joe Krush, Harcourt Brace Jovanovich (San Diego, CA), 1987.
Return to Gone-Away, Harcourt, 1961, illustrated by Beth and Joe Krush, Harcourt Brace Jovanovich, 1987.
Tatsinda (fairy tale), Harcourt, 1963, illustrated by Katie Thamer, Harcourt Brace Jovanovich, 1987.
Zeee (fairy tale), Harcourt, 1965, illustrated by Susan Gaber, Harcourt Brace Jovanovich, 1993.

ADULT STORY COLLECTIONS

Borrowed Summer and Other Stories, Rinehart, 1946 (published in England as *The Maple Tree and Other Stories,* Heinemann, 1947).
The Moment Before the Rain, Harcourt, 1955.
The Riddle of the Fly and Other Stories, Harcourt, 1959.
Doublefields: Memories and Stories (autobiographical sketches, short stories, and one novella), Harcourt, 1966.

ILLUSTRATOR

Marian King, *Kees,* Harper, 1930.
Nellie M. Rowe, *The Crystal Locket.*
Albert Whitman, circa 1931.
Marian King, *Kees and Kleintje,* Albert Whitman, 1934.

Many of Enright's short stories were first published in *New Yorker,* but others appeared in *Ladies' Home Journal, Cosmopolitan, Mademoiselle, Redbook, Yale Review, Harper's McCall's,* and *Saturday Evening Post.* Her stories were included in *Prize Stories: The O. Henry Awards,* 1946, 1949, 1951, 1955, 1958, and 1960, and *Best American Short Stories,* 1950, 1952, and 1954. Contributor of reviews of children's books to *New York Times.*

SIDELIGHTS: Elizabeth Enright, an only child, was born in Illinois but grew up in New York City, Wisconsin (where her uncle, Frank Lloyd Wright, had a farm), and Nantucket. The stories in her books often borrow people, places, and happenings from her own childhood and from her son's early years.

Kintu: A Congo Adventure began as a series of drawings at a time when Enright was an illustrator. She had the idea to write a story around the pictures, and came up with a narrative about an African boy, the son of a chief, who goes into the jungle to conquer his fear of it. The fact that the writing turned out to be more exciting than the drawing determined the course her career was to take.

It was in her second book, the Newbery medal winner *Thimble Summer,* that Enright began to use more familiar subject matter. The book tells of a young girl's happy summer on a Midwestern farm. In fact, Enright wrote the story while visiting Wright's Wisconsin farm during a summer of drought. In the book, summer begins with oppressive heat, and nine-year-old Garnet Linden's father fears for his crops. Garnet finds a silver thimble in the swimming hole, and coincidentally the rains come, saving the crops. The rest of the novel describes a series of minor adventures—barn building, hitchhiking, and pig raising—made fully credible for the reader by the depiction of Garnet's hopes and fears and by Enright's descriptions of the rich country landscape. The vividness of Enright's descriptions won much praise. In *Thimble Summer* and the books to follow, Enright demonstrated her ability to capture not only a child's sense of the epiphanies afforded by nature but also her alertness to the sounds and smells of familiar objects—screen doors banging, brown soap reeking. A *New York Times Book Review* critic wrote: "There is the flavor of real life in this story, expressed with charm and humor."

The Sea Is All Around is similar in style and scope to *Thimble Summer,* focusing on the experiences of a single heroine. This time, though, the setting is Pokenick Island, modeled on Nantucket, and the time is winter. Young Mab Kendall is visiting her childless Aunt Belinda and fears a long, lonely winter. Mab eventually discovers the Crocker children, and together they hatch the schemes and secrets that keep children and readers alike occupied.

In the four books about the Melendy family—*The Saturdays, The Four-Story Mistake, Then There Were Five,* and *Spiderweb for Two*— Enright deals with a group of fully developed characters. The Melendys capture the world of the 1940s, when holidays were major family events. Charisse Gendron wrote in *Dictionary of Literary Biography* that "Enright's deft characterizations of young boys, her ear for juvenile repartee, and her sense of the drama of children's play assume new proportions, with the result that these and the Gone-away books offer more to adolescent readers than does *Thimble Summer.* In *The Saturdays* ten-year-old Randy (short for Miranda), twelve-year-old Rush, their older sister Mona, and their younger brother Oliver pool their allowances so that each Saturday during the winter one of them can afford to do something special in New York City. The book follows their escapades, some of which are more successful than others. Destinations range from a beauty parlor to the opera.

The Gone-away Lake books of the late 1950s introduce two new families, the Blakes and the Jarmans. They are more modern and more typical than the Melendys. In *Gone-Away Lake* ten-year-old Portia Blake and her younger brother Foster spend the summer in the country with their Aunt and Uncle Jarman and their cousin Julian. While exploring a swamp that was once a resort area, Portia and Julian discover a cluster of decayed Victorian summer cottages where Minnehaha Cheever and Pindar Payton, elderly recluses, maintain their turn-of-the-century way of life. The children and the old people become fast friends, and the former fix up one of the old cottages for a clubhouse.

Enright's last two children's books are less realistic and more like fairy tales. *Tatsinda* is about a blonde, brown-eyed girl in a land of white-haired, blue-eyed people. She must overcome prejudice to win the heart of a prince. *Zeee* is a tiny, misanthropic fairy whose houses are continually destroyed by careless human beings but whose spirit is soothed when a little girl befriends her.

"The world of Enright's children's books is basically a secure one," wrote Gendron, "in which risks and sorrows are short-term rather than everlasting. . . . Enright's most original contribution to children's literature remains her humorous and lyrical description of characters."

BIOGRAPHICAL/CRITICAL SOURCES:

BOOKS

Children's Literature Review, Volume 4, Gale, 1982.
Dictionary of Literary Biography, Volume 22: *American Writers for Children, 1900-1960,* Gale, 1983.
Haviland, Virginia, *Children and Literature: Views and Reviews,* Scott, Foresman, 1973.
Twentieth-Century Children's Writers, 4th edition, St. James Press, 1995.

PERIODICALS

Library Journal, June 15, 1965, p. 2883; September 15, 1966, p. 4134.
New York Times Book Review, August 21, 1938, p. 10; June 13, 1965, p. 24; June 5, 1966, p. 43; November 20, 1966, p. 62.
School Library Journal, July, 1991, p. 56.*

ENSLEY, Evangeline 1907-
(Evangeline Walton)

PERSONAL: Born November 24, 1907, in Indianapolis, IN; daughter of Marion Edmund and Wilna Eunice (Coyner) Ensley. *Education:* Studied under private tutors. *Avocational interests:* Dancing (ballroom and ballet), opera, travel, history, mythology.

ADDRESSES: *Home*—2130 East Water St., Tucson, AZ 85719.

CAREER: Writer.

MEMBER: National Association of American Pen Women, Society of Friends, Opera Guild of Southern Arizona.

WRITINGS:

UNDER PSEUDONYM EVANGELINE WALTON

The Virgin and the Swine: The Fourth Branch of the Mabinogi (fantasy novel based on Welsh myth), Willett, Clark, 1936, published as *The Island of the Mighty,* Ballantine, 1970.

Witch House, Arkham, 1945, Collier Books (New York City), 1991.

The Cross and the Sword (historical novel), Bouregy & Curl, 1956 (published in England as *Son of Darkness,* Hutchinson, 1957).

The Children of Llyr (fantasy novel based on the Second Branch of the *Mabinogion*), introduction by Lin Carter, Ballantine, 1971.

The Song of Rhiannon: The Third Branch of the Mabinogion (fantasy novel based on Welsh myth), introduction by Carter, Ballantine, 1972.

The Prince of Annwn: The First Branch of the Mabinogion (fantasy novel based on Welsh myth), Ballantine, 1974.

"*Above Ker-Is*" (short story), published in *The Fantastic Imagination II: An Anthology of High Fantasy,* edited by Robert H. Boyer and Kenneth J. Zahorski, Avon, 1978.

The Sword Is Forged (first novel in trilogy based on Theseus myth), Timescape, 1984.

"The Mistress of Kaer-Mor" (short story), published in *The Phoenix Tree: An Anthology of Myth Fantasy,* edited by Boyer and Zahorski, Avon, 1980. Work represented in other anthologies, including *Elsewhere.* Author of stories, including "At the End of the Corridor" and "The Chinese Woman," several essays, and unpublished works, including a verse-drama, "Swan-Wife," a novel, *Prince of the Air,* and a children's book, *The Forest That Would Not Be Cut Down.*

SIDELIGHTS: A storyteller since childhood, Evangeline Ensley drew upon a lifelong interest in mythology for her highly praised adaptations of ancient Celtic tales. Her best-known works, published under the pseudonym Evangeline Walton, are based on the medieval Welsh myths collectively called the *Mabinogion* (or *Mabinogi,* a term that scholars believe means "a tale of a hero's youth"). Of the twelve tales that comprise the *Mabinogion,* Walton adapted the first four—known as the Four Branches—for her novels *Prince of Annwn, The Children of Llyr, The Song of Rhiannon,* and *The Virgin and the Swine.* According to a *Fantasy Review* critic, Walton's tetralogy established the author as "one of fantasy's major writers—and brought her special esteem for her ability to humanize historical and mythological subjects with eloquence, humor, and compassion."

Though Walton's *Mabinogion* novels are separate tales focusing on the adventures of several characters, together they relate the history of the Welsh hero Pryderi. In *Prince of Annwn,* Pwyll, the central character, makes a bargain with the Prince of Annwn (Death) and must go to the land of the dead to fight a dangerous otherworld lord. Later he courts and wins the beautiful Rhiannon of the Birds, who becomes his queen and subsequently bears Pryderi. *The Children of Llyr* focuses on Pwyll's friend Manawyddan, who, along with his brother King Bran and two other male siblings, attempts to rescue his sister from her cruel husband, an Irish monarch. Awar ensues, and of the five siblings only Manawyddan survives. In *The Song of Rhiannon* Walton reveals that Manawyddan is Pryderi's true father—to provide an heir for his impotent friend Pwyll, Manawyddan had assumed Pwyll's shape and impregnated Rhiannon. *The Virgin and the Swine* concludes the tetralogy with the deeds of Gwydion, a canny, ambitious magician who ultimately kills Prince Pryderi.

A unifying feature of the tetralogy, judged C. W. Sullivan III in *Fantasy Review,* is that Walton "sees . . . traces of a matrilineal and matriarchal system in the Four Branches, and she develops these traces into a major aspect of her four novels. "For instance, Sullivan pointed out, in *The Children of Llyr* Walton "includes a strong storyline involving patrilineal succession in a previously matrilineal system." Gwydion, for example, inherits a kingdom because he is the son of a king's sister. Gwydion's sister's children would in turn be his heirs, but Gwydion wants a son—and wants his son to succeed him—so he sleeps with his sister; the child can thus inherit under either system.

The matrilineal/patrilineal theme becomes "part of a larger conflict," Sullivan asserted, "between the Old Tribes and the New Tribes." In Sullivan's opinion Walton suggests that Pwyll's people, "with their belief in fatherhood,. . . and patrilineal succession—are the New Tribes, the people whose ideas are the New Ways." Gwydion's people, in contrast, "are developed in Walton's novels as matriarchal and matrilineal, without knowledge of fatherhood." Sullivan conceded that because Gwydion defeats Pwyll's son in *The Virgin and the Swine* it might seem that the Old Tribes defeat the New, but "Gwydion's actions imply that he has adopted the belief in fatherhood and patrilineal succession." The New Tribes "may go home in military defeat," Sullivan allowed, "but they have changed the people of the Old Tribes forever."

Sullivan summed up Walton's *Mabinogion* work with praise: "She has, in effect, taken ancient materials and breathed new life into them by casting them in a form appropriate to the twentieth century." Sullivan also approved the author's many additions to the text, noting, "The material she adds has the same rough, dramatic quality as the original so that there is no change in tone. Moreover, the material she adds is consistent with what we know of the Celtic peoples—what they believed as well as how they lived—so that her additions ring 'true' on the deeper levels found in all traditional materials, especially myths." *Fantasy Review* editor Bob Collins compared Walton's books favorably to those of J.R.R. Tolkien, judging that "her work is just as original, just as fresh and potent, and far, far better written." And in his book *Imaginary Worlds,* fantasy author-editor-historian Lin Carter observed, "In Miss Walton's hands the crude, loosely-spun narrative achieves heroic stature as it attains beautifully controlled form"; he declared Walton "one of the three or four finest artists working in fantasy today."

Walton came to earn praise such as Carter's after many years, reading widely and writing a few little-known books. Studying under a tutor in her childhood because she suffered recurring pneumonia, Walton "learned more about literature and history than most of [her] former classmates" learned in school, she surmised in a *Fantasy Review* interview. She also read extensively from several libraries, and in the mid-1930's she began to write, using the pseudonym Evangeline Walton. In *Fantasy Review* she recalled adopting the name of her Walton ancestors, who had Native American blood, because "I considered them the most picturesque branch of my ancestry—at least the only one that had any recent connection with pagan idol worshippers." Walton's first book, *The Virgin and the Swine,* was published in 1936, but it received little attention and remained largely unknown until a fan presented it to Carter for inclusion in a Ballantine adult fantasy book series in 1970. The novel's success, under the new title *The Island of the Mighty,* led to the first publication of the other *Mabinogion* books.

Among the books Walton discovered in her library excursions were those of the Celtic Twilight writers. The term "Celtic Twilight," originally the title of a story collection by William Butler Yeats, has come to represent the preservation of poetic, mystical vision in the Scottish, Welsh, and especially Irish peoples in the late nineteenth and early twentieth centuries. During this period, known as the Irish Renaissance, Irish writers seized on ancient Celtic legends to help develop a national literary consciousness. The revived legends became the root of most of Walton's writings.

Walton drew on Greek myth, however, for her 1984 fantasy, *The Sword Is Forged,* the first volume in a proposed trilogy about the Greek hero Theseus. In the *Washington Post Book World* Somtow Sucharitkul described the work as "a historical novel which seriously attempts to reconstruct a viable Bronze Age from archaeological, anthropological, and mythological sources." The book explores the love-hate relationship between Theseus and the Amazon queen Antiope and, according to Sucharitkul, "the relationship becomes a symbol for the clash between the dying matriarchal society and the newly ascendant sky-father-figure cult . . . never so tellingly personalized as in this novel." Judging the Amazons "superbly imagined," Sucharitkul also commended Walton's "gritty realism" and "vivid characterization" and concluded that the book is "an important work . . . the first fresh treatment of this much-treated subject in some time."

INTERVIEW:

CA interviewed Evangeline Walton by telephone on September 9, 1985, at her home in Tucson, Arizona.

CA: You began composing stories when you were five or six. What prompted that serious storytelling urge at such a young age?

WALTON: I think it was just a desire to use my imagination. One feels one's powers coming sometimes, I suppose, and doesn't know what they're for. I was always a child who wanted to have people read aloud to me, and I evidently became seized with a desire to make my own stories.

CA: Being educated by tutors rather than having conventional schooling seems to have worked very much in your favor.

WALTON: Well, I didn't have friends to grow up with, of course, but I wouldn't have had in any case, since I had to be out of school so much every winter on account of the pneumonia I had back East. It was really my great-aunt who acted as my tutor. She had been a schoolteacher.

CA: And you were allowed to read pretty much what you liked?

WALTON: Yes, outside of the essential school subjects.

CA: Did you know fairly early that mythology would provide the inspiration for your best-known books?

WALTON: I didn't realize that before my late teens, anyway, and I'm not sure I actually realized it *then,* but that was when I fell in love with the Celtic Twilight.

CA: Is that when you read The Mabinogion?

WALTON: Yes. I read everything Irish I could get hold of, but I didn't dare write about those things with A. E., [William Butler] Yeats, and James Stephens already doing it, and I thought at the time that *The Mabinogion* was virgin territory. I didn't know anything about Kenneth Morris.

CA: Did you know at once that you wanted to write about those characters, or was there a lot more reading and study before that happened?

WALTON: Actually, the books began in the first place with my visualizing the scene where Gwydion finds his son in eagle form and sings him down out of the tree. It was thinking what James Stephens could do with a scene like that that made me decide to try it myself, and then everything followed.

CA: How fortunate you were to find such an inspiration.

WALTON: Yes. Stephens was both poet and novelist. He wrote just two novels on mythological subjects, *Deirdre* and *In the Land of Youth.* He had meant to turn the whole Ulster Cycle epic into a set of novels, but he didn't live to do that. But those two books he did get written on mythology were practically the bible of my teens and twenties.

CA: There seems to be some disagreement about the meaning of the word Mabinogion. *What's your feeling about its derivation?*

WALTON: Mab—later *map*—is a Welsh word for son, akin, I suppose, to the Gaelic *mac.* The Welsh themselves call the four tales the Four Branches of the *Mabinogi,* but *Mabinogion,* though less correct, is easier to say. I must admit I don't really know the Welsh language; I wish I did.

CA: Did you learn any other languages for your work on your books?

WALTON: No, I didn't. I often wished I did know them. When I studied the witchcraft subjects, for instance, so many of the older documents were in Latin. I had had high-school Latin, but it was all so respectable; I didn't know the words used in witchcraft.

CA: Your books attracted little popular notice until The Virgin and the Swine, *originally published in 1936, was republished as* The Island of the Mighty *in 1970. What led to its rediscovery and republication*?

WALTON: Paul Spencer, who was at that time running a magazine on [novelist] James Branch Cabell, read the book and enjoyed it. James Branch Cabell himself, apparently, didn't like it; at the time it first came out, my publisher sent him a copy, but we never heard anything. But Paul Spencer was very fond of it and loaned it to Lin Carter [a fantasy author, editor, and historian] to read, and then Lin Carter brought it to Ballantine. At the time, they thought I was dead. That seems to be a recurring delusion. A few years ago I went to a convention at which I was told I was dead. Anyway, Ballantine started to publish the book and then found out to their surprise that I had renewed the copyright and therefore must be alive. So then we made a deal. They thought it was very nice of me not to sue, and I felt it was very nice of them to be publishing the book.

CA: Were the following three books of the series pretty much already written at the time The Island of the Mighty *was published by Ballantine*?

WALTON: I had the manuscripts. You see, I wrote this thing backwards. In the beginning, I didn't intend to do anything but what is now *The Island of the Mighty,* but then it seemed that it would be nice to follow that up. For some reason, the First Branch, my *Prince of*

Annwn, 1974, is the one with which I always had the most trouble. It sounds easiest, because it's the only one that conforms to the boy-meets-girl formula, yet in some ways it was hardest to handle. But Ballantine, having published three, felt that they should have the fourth, so I finally gave it to them, and they liked it.

CA: Was it difficult to achieve the voice and style you used in those books?

WALTON: I shudder now when I remember that I once thought of using *thee* and *thou* instead of *you.* One has to work at anything. I was at a convention in Phoenix last week where [fantasy author] Nancy Springer was guest of honor, and we were talking. She said it seemed to be so impossible for people to believe that authors work, and that's true. Outsiders never seem to believe that our work is just the same as putting in a day on any other job.

CA: In the foreword to The Island of the Mighty *you thanked Professor Robinson of Harvard for a special translation of some difficult source material. Where do most of the difficulties lie in dealing with the early sources and languages?*

WALTON: I only had Lady Charlotte Guest's translation to work from; that was my main trouble. I have been told since that there was an Everyman's translation that would have been accurate, but I didn't know it at the time. Of course Lady Charlotte wrote in Victorian days. She really knew what she was about, but she couldn't afford to say it; she had to whirl over all the sexy parts during the transformation of Gwydion and his brother in punishment for the rape of Goewyn. In her version, you can't tell what happened. I made a good guess, but I had to get confirmation from Professor Robinson before I dared go ahead with it.

CA: We don't think today about a time when people didn't realize men had a part in making babies. That was one of the interesting aspects of your stories: this idea was gaining some credence among the younger people, but the elders were scornful of it.

WALTON: People have to find out everything. I had never heard of it until I read Sir John Rhys's books. I got it from his *Celtic Folklore, Welsh and Manx,* which was reprinted a few years ago. That was my main source of material. At the time, there weren't many books on Welsh folklore available in English.

CA: Reading your Mabinogion *books, one has the feeling that the characters are as much real as mythical. Is this an impression that comes from the earlier sources, or another dimension that you've given them in the retelling?*

WALTON: It's simplest to say that I considered *The Mabinogion* a skeleton, and I worked to put flesh and blood on it. I didn't have my own copies of Lady Guest's books—those I used belonged to the Indianapolis Public Library—so I typed out a twenty-six-page copy of her translation of the Fourth Branch to work from. Those 26 pages made my 312-page book. You can see how much I added.

CA: In the April, 1985, English Journal, *[critic] John Herman says you suggest in your books that "in our ability to use the creative power of our imagination we have fallen from a higher estate and are now unable to see the magic that surrounds us." Did you come to believe in the kind of magic that some of your characters practice?*

WALTON: I wouldn't expect to transform anybody into something else, but I think that the Welsh name for magicians—men of illusion and fantasy—itself shows that a good deal of illusion was involved in such magic. In my books, I treat everything as a question of development. The world passes through certain stages and then goes on to others.

CA: Do you find in studying the early source material that fact and myth are sometimes intertwined?

WALTON: It seems to me they are tremendously, but there are so many different theories as to which is myth and which is fact that everybody has to reach his or her own conclusions. Nothing can be proved, I fear.

CA: That must make for some problems.

WALTON: It makes for problems, but when your own imagination selects the explanation that fits in and the creative part really begins, then it's soaring joy for a little while.

CA: The Sword Is Forged, *published in 1983, is the first of your Theseus books, which I understand were delayed in publication because Mary Renault's books on the same material happened to be published just when yours were about to be. How much rewriting was necessitated by the publication of her books?*

WALTON: I have never read hers, I have no doubt they're great, but I take care never to read anything anybody else does on a subject I'm handling.

CA: Have you acquired quite a library of your own in the process of researching your subjects?

WALTON: Yes. The books threaten to make me move out of the house. I have great masses of them. Of course the ones I rely on most for my work, the research books, are usually hard to get hold of, and I have to go to the library. I use the university library most of the time here in Tucson.

CA: You've been in Tucson for forty years now. Is it a good place for writing?

WALTON: I think a good place for writing has to be made by one's own mood, though certainly Arizona has helped me a great deal. During my last year in Indiana, I wasn't able to breathe from my nose between November and April because of allergies. Though the word didn't mean very much to me then, I became fully acquainted with it after moving down here.

CA: How do you feel about being considered primarily a fantasy writer?

WALTON: So long as my characters can have flesh and blood, I really prefer the freedom of fantasy. Of course I added a few fantasy touches to *The Sword Is Forged* which I wouldn't have used if people hadn't expected them of me.

CA: Do you get a lot of fan mail?

WALTON: Not a lot; I never did. I get letters every so often, and of course one gets them from all ages and types, and all are very welcome.

CA: Do you find that you have a larger following among college-age people?

WALTON: It seems to me that young people take to my books more than the middle-aged. Of course it's always unwise to generalize, but it has surprised me, since my books have a rather feminist tone, that it's more often young men who write me about them than young women. I didn't suppose that young women of this generation were shy, but I was talking with a young woman at one of the conventions, and she said, "Well, I won't bother you any longer." I certainly didn't intend to give her any impression that she was bothering me, so shyness may have been the explanation. It is a quality I share, though.

CA: Your Quaker belief seems to have had a great effect on your approach to history and to your work.

WALTON: Yes, that's true. I'm not an orthodox anything now, but I notice that the Quaker humanitarianism sticks even when people have ceased to hold orthodox beliefs.

CA: Are there periods in modern history that are particularly interesting to you?

WALTON: I will read a good historical novel of any period, and I like a good mystery to lose myself with.

CA: Are the other Theseus novels coming out very soon?

WALTON: I hope they will. I had to have major surgery twice in 1983, and I've been greatly slowed by that. I'm just getting back into real working order.

CA: A few of your short stories have been published in anthologies. Are there plans for the publication of other short writings?

WALTON: I fear not. All my short stories were written by the time I was twenty-one. Three have come out now in anthologies, and two others have been lost. There was a contest at one time, and I was just getting over the flu and sent off my only copies without Xeroxing them. I found out later that the editor herself had the flu too, and the deadline was extended, so the hurry was unnecessary. Two of those stories got lost somehow; there was a shake-up when the publisher changed hands.

CA: Do you have specific writing plans beyond the Theseus books?

WALTON: There are two other books I would like to go over. I had a Gothic novel ready just when the Gothic craze expired, and I'd like to get that out someday. And then there's a children's story I once wrote for a young cousin, *The Forest That Would Not Be Cut Down.* That's the only title that expresses it, and yet it's too long to be used, I'm afraid. This forest has a magical ability to protect itself which, unfortunately, real forests lack.

CA: Is there any advice you'd offer aspiring writers?

WALTON: Find out all you can about your subject, and then work. And I mean work!

BIOGRAPHICAL/CRITICAL SOURCES:

BOOKS

Carter, Lin, *Imaginary Worlds,* Ballantine, 1973.

St. James Guide to Fantasy Writers, St. James Press, 1996.

PERIODICALS

English Journal, October, 1977; April, 1985.
Fantasy Review, March, 1985.
Locus, June, 1991.
Saturday Review, November 4, 1972.
School Library Journal, June, 1994.
Science Fiction Review, August, 1983.
Washington Post Book World, July 31, 1983.*

* * *

ENSLIN, Theodore (Vernon) 1925-

PERSONAL: Born March 25, 1925, in Chester, PA; son of Morton Scott (a professor) and Ruth May (a teacher; maiden name, Tuttle) Enslin; married Mildred Marie Stout, August 1, 1945 (divorced June 6, 1961); married Alison Jane Jose, September 14, 1969; children: (first marriage) Deirdre, Jonathan Morton; (second marriage) Jacob Hezekiah. *Education:* Private study of musical composition with Nadia Boulanger and Francis Judd Cooke.

ADDRESSES: *Home*—R.F.D. Box 289, Kansas Rd., Milbridge, ME 04658.

CAREER: Full-time writer.

MEMBER: American Foundation for Homeopathy.

AWARDS, HONORS: Niemann Award, 1955, for weekly newspaper column, "Six Miles Square," in *Cape Codder;* Hart Crane Award, 1969, for *To Come, to Have Become;* National Endowment for the Arts fellowship, 1976-77.

WRITINGS:

POETRY

The Work Proposed, Origin Press, 1958.
New Sharon's Prospect (also see below), Origin Press, 1962.
The Place Where I Am Standing, Elizabeth Press, 1964.
This Do [and] *The Talents,* El Corno Emplumado (Mexico), 1966.
New Sharon's Prospect [and] *Journals,* Coyote's Journal, 1966.
To Come, to Have Become, Elizabeth Press, 1966.
The Dependencies, Caterpillar, 1966.
Characters in Certain Places, Wine Press, 1967.
The Diabelli Variations, and Other Poems, Matter Books, 1968.
2/30-6/31: Poems, 1967, Vermont Stoveside Press, 1968.
Agreement and Back: Sequences, Elizabeth Press, 1969.
Forms, Elizabeth Press, Part 1: *The First Dimensions,* 1970, Part 2: *The Tessaract,* 1971, Part 3: *The Experiences,* 1972, Part 4: *The Fusion,* 1972, Part 5: *Coda,* 1973.
The Poems, Elizabeth Press, 1970.
Views 1-7, Maya, 1970.
The Country of Our Consciousness: Selected Poems, Sand Dollar, 1971.
Etudes, Elizabeth Press, 1972.
With Light Reflected: Poems, 1970-1972, Sumac Press, 1973.
Views, Elizabeth Press, 1973.
In the Keeper's House, Salt-Works, 1973.
The Swamp Fox, Salt-Works, 1973.
Fever Poems, Blackberry Press, 1974.
The Last Days of October, Salt-Works, 1974.
The Mornings, Shaman Drum Press, 1974.
Sitio, Granite Publications, 1974.
The Median Flow: Poems, 1943-1973, Black Sparrow Press, 1975.
Synthesis 1-24, North Atlantic Books, 1975.
Laendler, Elizabeth Press, 1975.
Some Pastorals: A New Year's Cycle for Jake, Salt-Works 1975.
Carmina, Salt-Works, 1976.
Papers, Elizabeth Press, 1976.
Ascensions, Black Sparrow Press, 1977.
Circles, Great Raven Press, 1977.
Concentrations, Salt-Works, 1977.
The Further Regions, Pentagram, 1977.
Tailings, Pentagram, 1978.
Ranger, North Atlantic Books, Volume 1, 1978, 2nd revised edition, 1980, Volume 2, 1980.
May Fault, Great Raven, 1979.
Opus 31 #3, Pentagram, 1979.
A Root in March, University of Maine Press, 1979.
16 Blossoms in February, Blackberry Press, 1979.
Ranger, Ranger 2, 2 volumes, North Atlantic, 1979-1980.
The Flare of Beginning Is in November, Jordan Davies, 1980.
Star Anise, Pentagram, 1980.
The Fifth Direction, Pentagram, 1980.
Two Geese, Pentagram, 1980.
Axes 52, Ziesing Bros., 1981.
In Duo Concertante, Pentagram, 1981.

Markings, Membrane Press, 1981.
Opus O, Membrane Press, 1981.
(With others) *Knee Deep in the Atlantic,* Pentagram, 1981.
Processionals, Salt-Works, 1981.
September's Bonfire, Potes and Poets Press, 1981.
(Translator from the Greek) Pindar and Calimachus, *Fragments/Epigrammata,* Salt-Works, 1982.
(Editor) *F.P.,* Ziesing Bros., 1982.
A Man in Stir, Pentagram, 1983.
To Come Home (To), Great Raven, 1983.
Meditations, Potes and Poets Press, 1983.
Passacaglia, Beehive Press, 1983.
Grey Days, Last Straw Press, 1984.
Songs w/out Notes, Salt-Works, 1984.
(With Keith Wilson) *Meeting at Jal,* Southwestern American Literature Association, 1985.
For Mr. Walters, Master Mechanic, Shirt Pocket Press, 1985.
I Am You Are, Green River, 1985.
Music for Several Occasions, Membrane Press, 1985.
The Path Between, Blackberry, 1986.
The Waking of the Eye, Stingy Artist/Last Straw Press, 1986.
Case Book, Potes and Poets Press, 1988.
From Near the Great Pine, Spoon River, 1989.
Love and Science, Light and Dust, 1990.
Gamma UT, Tel-Let, 1992.
A Sonare, Longhouse, 1994.

PROSE

Mahler, Black Sparrow Press, 1975.
The July Book, Sand Dollar Press, 1976.
Two Plus Twelve (short stories), Salt-Works, 1979.

OTHER

Author of play, *Barometric Pressure 29.83 and Steady,* first produced in New York at Hardware Poets Theatre, October, 1965. Editor of *The Selected Poems of Howard McCord 1961-1971,* Crossing Press, 1975. Author of weekly newspaper column, "Six Miles Square," in *Cape Codder,* 1949-56. Contributor of poems to periodicals.

SIDELIGHTS: Seamus Cooney, writing in *Contemporary Poets,* noted similarities between Theodore Enslin's poetry and that of both Cid Corman and Robert Frost. Cooney noted that Enslin's work was first published in *Origin,* a magazine that Corman edited, and that Corman also published Enslin's first book. "Both write spare, quiet, post-Williams poems grounded in a shared respect for the otherness and autonomy of natural things and a distrust of the romantic ego," Cooney observed. But, he added, Enslin's poems require careful reading and special attention to lineation and sound in order to mine their full meaning.

Readers are given an insider's view of Enslin's writing method in *New Sharon's Prospect,* where they will find, alongside the poems, the prose notes that Enslin condensed to create them.

Forms is a five-volume, open-structure poem that was written over a period of sixteen years. While Cooney found it, on first reading, to be less rewarding than Enslin's short poems, he also noted that Enslin's best work suggests that the long work deserves further reading.

As for the similarities to Frost, Cooney wrote: "Enslin's work is filled with the people, places, and things of rural New England, where he lives. If at times it reminds you of a Frost landscape, it is free of Frost's often intrusive personality."

Enslin once told *CA:* "It is always very tempting to say more than one should concerning those things that are dearest and closest. I will try to avoid that, and simply hope that the record is in the work itself. In the past few years I have found myself drawn more and more to the musical possibilities of the poem, and I mean this in quite literal terms. For me, poetry and music are one art. The greatest compliment that anyone could pay me: 'He was a composer who happened to use words.' "

BIOGRAPHICAL/CRITICAL SOURCES:

BOOKS

Contemporary Authors Autobiography Series, Volume 3, Gale, 1986.
Contemporary Poets, 6th edition, St. James Press, 1996.

PERIODICALS

American Book Review, January, 1986, p. 22.
Small Press, October, 1988, p. 77.*

* * *

EPHRON, Nora 1941-

PERSONAL: Born May 19, 1941, in New York, NY; daughter of Henry (a writer) and Phoebe (a writer;

maiden name, Wolkind) Ephron; married Dan Greenburg (a writer), April 9, 1967 (divorced); married Carl Bernstein (a journalist), April 14, 1976 (divorced); married Nicholas Pileggi (a writer), 1987; children: (second marriage) Jacob, Max. *Education:* Wellesley College, B.A., 1962.

ADDRESSES: Agent—Lynn Nesbit, International Creative Management, 40 West 57th St., New York, NY 10019.

CAREER: Author and screenwriter. *New York Post,* New York City, reporter, 1963-68; freelance journalist, 1968-72; *Esquire* magazine, New York City, columnist and contributing editor, 1972-73; *New York* magazine, New York City, contributing editor,1973-74; *Esquire,* senior editor and columnist, 1974-76.

AWARDS, HONORS: Penney-Missouri award from University of Missouri Journalism School and J. C. Penney & Co., 1973; D.H.L. from Briarcliff College, 1974; with Alice Arlen, nomination for best original screenplay, American Academy of Motion Picture Arts and Sciences, 1984, for *Silkwood;* nomination for best original screenplay, American Academy of Motion Picture Arts and Sciences, 1989, for *When Harry Met Sally . . .*

WRITINGS:

Wallflower at the Orgy (collection of articles), Viking, 1970.

Crazy Salad: Some Things about Women (collection of articles), Knopf, 1975.

Perfect Gentleman (television movie), CBS-TV, 1978.

Scribble, Scribble: Notes on the Media (collection of columns), Knopf, 1979.

Heartburn (novel; also see below), Knopf, 1983.

(With Alice Arlen) *Silkwood* (screenplay), Twentieth Century-Fox, 1983.

Heartburn (screenplay; adapted from her novel), Paramount Pictures, 1986.

When Harry Met Sally . . . (screenplay), Castle Rock Entertainment, 1989.

(With Arlen) *Cookie* (screenplay), Warner Brothers, 1989.

My Blue Heaven (screenplay), Warner Brothers, 1990.

Nora Ephron Collected, Avon Books, 1991.

(With sister, Delia Ephron; also director) *This Is My Life* (screenplay; based on the novel by Meg Wolitzer), Twentieth Century-Fox, 1992.

(With David S. Ward and Jeff Arch; also director) *Sleepless in Seattle,* Tri-Star Pictures, 1993.

Also co-author of the following screenplays: *Modern Bride* and *Maggie,* both with Arlen; *Mixed Nuts,* with Delia Ephron, produced in 1994; *Michael,* with Delia Ephron, Pete Dexter, and Jim Quinlan, produced in 1996. Director of the film *You've Got Mail,* produced in 1998. Contributor of short stories, essays, and reviews to numerous magazines.

SIDELIGHTS: Nora Ephron is no stranger to public scrutiny. In the early 1960s, her parents, writers Henry and Phoebe Ephron, based their successful play, *Take Her, She's Mine,* on their eldest daughter's letters home from Wellesley College. Later, Nora Ephron gained a reputation as an acerbic, often autobiographical reporter and columnist, regularly writing for such publications as *New York* magazine and *Esquire.* Finally, Ephron chronicled her much-publicized breakup with second husband Carl Bernstein in her novel *Heartburn,* which she later adapted for the screen.

Heartburn tells the story of Rachel Samstat, a well-known cookbook author, who discovers while she is seven months pregnant with their second child that her political columnist husband is having an affair with an elegant socialite. The plot, which mirrors the circumstances of Ephron's own divorce, has been criticized for its obviously autobiographical origins. "How could [Ephron] publish a *roman* so shamelessly *a clef,* exposing the warts, peccadilloes and worse of family, ex-husbands and friends?" wrote Art Seidenbaum of the *Los Angeles Times Book Review.* "How awfully lucky for those who treat them badly . . . that when journalists get mad they reach for a typewriter instead of a gun," observed Grace Glueck in the *New York Times Book Review.*

Ephron defended her right to use material from her own life as inspiration for a novel. "I've always written about my life," Ephron explained to Stephanie Mansfield in a *Washington Post* interview coinciding with the release of *Heartburn.* "That's how I grew up. 'Take notes. Everything is copy.' All that stuff my mother said to us. I think it would have been impossible for me to go through the end of my marriage and not written about it, because although it was the most awful thing I've ever been through . . . it was by *far* the most interesting."

Other critics found the novel and its screenplay adaptation witty and realistic. Calling the film "*seriously* funny," *Washington Post* writer Paul Attanasio finds it profoundly intimate, as well. "You feel as if you were there, and it happened to you, and its heroism, the heroism of everyday life, is yours," Attanasio writes. "Long after the chatter has abated,"observes *Time* magazine's Stefan Kanfer, "*Heartburn* will be providing insights and laughter. . . . [As] Nora Ephron is about to learn, leaving well is the best revenge."

Ephron's next screenplay, *Silkwood,* tells the story of activist Karen Silkwood, a worker in a plutonium fuel rod plant who uncovers evidence of slipshod manufacturing procedures but dies shortly thereafter in a car accident that many speculated was more than accidental. Based on a true story, the film won a nomination for best original screenplay from the American Academy of Motion Picture Arts and Sciences. Although he found the mix of fact and fiction problematic, *New York Times* critic Vincent Canby also remarked that "perhaps for the first time in a popular movie has America's petrochemical-nuclear landscape been dramatized, and with such anger and compassion." Other critics found the film's interpretation of the circumstances surrounding Silkwood's death disturbing. "The film cannot supply the truth because no one really knows the truth," states Sheila Benson in the *Los Angeles Times.*

Ephron's 1989 comedy *When Harry Met Sally. . .* was a success with critics and fans alike. Following the twelve-year friendship and eventual courtship of a modern New York couple, the film blends witty one-liners with startlingly accurate observations about the dating scene. Calling the screenplay a "genial update" of the 1940s "screwball comedies" popularized by actors Spencer Tracy and Katharine Hepburn, *Washington Post* writer Rita Kempley notes that the caustic *Heartburn* must have assuaged Ephron's anger and left her "free to be funny again." The screenplay, Kempley writes, "seems sweet and savage both, remarkably frank about the selfish and often mean-spirited attitudes—particularly men's—that otherwise responsible single people take on in their encounters." The film's dialogue, notes *Los Angeles Times* critic Sheila Benson, consists of "splendid, risible exchanges that fly by with the speed and delicacy of a great badminton game."

Ephron made her directorial debut in 1992 with *This Is My Life,* a comedy which she wrote with her sister, Delia. *New York Times* reviewer Janet Maslin found the screenplay witty, full of "small, wry touches," and a "distinctive comic style." Ephron's directing, she added, produced a single vision of New York Life that "even at its most generous and funny manages to retain a penetrating clarity." Ephron attributes the film's accurate portrayal of family relationships, particularly sisters' bonds, to her collaboration with her own sister. "It's really about sisters," says Ephron in the *New York Times.* "It was also material I knew should be emotional and gentle, and because of that [Delia] was the person to write it with."

Ephron, who's seen nine of the scripts she's written (or co-written) produced, acknowledges the collaborative nature of script-writing in general. "When a movie comedy works, it starts with a script, then you get a director who adds, and an actor who adds, and it gets funnier and funnier," she told Allessandra Stanley of the *New York Times.* In an interview with John Blades of the *Chicago Tribune,* Ephron added, "The truth is that all the input in the world doesn't mean that much on movies because the director makes most of the creative decisions and if you expect it to be your movie you're in for a real shock. But if you get really lucky with the director, it's your movie, too."

BIOGRAPHICAL/CRITICAL SOURCES:

BOOKS

Authors in the News, Volume 2, Gale, 1976.
Contemporary Literary Criticism, Gale Volume 17, 1981, Volume 31, 1985.
Current Biography Yearbook 1990, H. W. Wilson, 1990, p.216.
Ephron, Nora, *Scribble, Scribble,* Knopf, 1979.
Ephron, *Heartburn,* Knopf, 1983.
Newsmakers, 1992 Cumulation, Gale, 1992.

PERIODICALS

Chicago Tribune, November 4, 1979; December 14, 1983; July 25, 1986; July 12, 1989; February 13, 1990; August 20, 1990.
Commonweal, June 18, 1976.
Critic, August 15, 1978.
Detroit Free Press, July 22, 1986; July 30, 1986.
Entertainment Weekly, June 23, 1995, p. 68; January 10, 1997, p. 41; June 13, 1997, 71.
Globe and Mail (Toronto), May 26, 1984; July 15, 1989.
Houston Post, November 4, 1975.
Los Angeles Times, December 14, 1983; July 25, 1986; July 14, 1989; July 27, 1989; August 23, 1989; August 20, 1990.
Los Angeles Times Book Review, April 17, 1983; March 10, 1991, p. 10; August 18, 1996, p. 15.
Ms., November, 1975.
New Republic, May 23, 1983; March 30, 1992, p. 26; March 3, 1997, p. 30.
Newsweek, April 24, 1978; April 11, 1983; July 28,1986, p. 70.
New York, March 14, 1983; May 9, 1983.

New York Times, December 14, 1983; July 25, 1986; July 9, 1989; July 12, 1989; August 23, 1989; September 17, 1989; February 18, 1990; August 18, 1990; January 24, 1991; February 16, 1992, p. 22; February 21, 1992, p. C8.
New York Times Book Review, June 27, 1975; July 13, 1975; April 16, 1978; April 24, 1983.
People, January 14, 1980.
Time, May 29, 1978; April 11, 1983; August 4, 1986, p.71.
Times (London), September 15, 1983.
Times Literary Supplement, September 16, 1983, p. 1001.
Tribune Books Chicago, April 17, 1983.
Washington Post, March 30, 1983; April 25, 1983; December 14, 1983; July 25, 1986; July 12, 1989; August 24, 1989; August 25, 1989; August 18, 1990.*

* * *

ETS, Marie Hall 1893-1984

PERSONAL: Born December 16, 1893, in North Greenfield, WI; daughter of Walter Augustus (doctor turned minister) and Mathilde (Carhart) Hall; married Milton Rodig, November 30, 1917 (died in World War I, January, 1918); married Harold Norris Ets (a physician), June 6, 1930 (died June, 1943). *Education:* Attended Lawrence College, 1911-12, New York School of Applied and Fine Art, 1912-13, and Chicago School of Civics and Philanthropy (now School of Social Service Administration, University of Chicago); University of Chicago, Ph.B., 1924, also graduate study; Art Institute of Chicago, study with Frederick V. Poole; Columbia University, graduate study. *Politics:* Liberal.

CAREER: D. N. & E. Waters & Co., San Francisco, CA, artist, 1917-18; U.S. Navy Department, Waukegan, IL, member of staff of Law Enforcement Division for girls, 1918-19; United Charities, Chicago, IL, student caseworker, 1919; Chicago Commons Social Settlement House, Chicago, volunteer resident, 1919-29; author-illustrator, primarily of children's books, 1935-84. Organizer of child health clinic, American Red Cross foreign service, Pilsen, Czechoslovakia, 1921-22; investigator for U.S. Coal Commission in West Virginia and Illinois, 1923. Had one-man show of original drawings, Columbia Teachers College, 1963; work has also been exhibited in group shows and is represented in several permanent collections.

MEMBER: Authors League, Authors Guild.

AWARDS, HONORS: New York Herald Tribune Children's Book Festival Awards, 1947, for *Oley the Sea Monster,* and 1963, for *Gilberto and the Wind;* Hans Christian Andersen Award, 1956, for *Play with Me;* Caldecott Medal, 1960, for *Nine Days to Christmas;* Kerlan Award, University of Minnesota, 1975.

WRITINGS:

JUVENILE, EXCEPT AS INDICATED; ALL PUBLISHED BY VIKING, EXCEPT AS INDICATED

Mister Penny, 1935.
The Story of a Baby, 1939.
In the Forest, 1944, published as *In the Forest: Story and Pictures,* Puffin Books (New York City), 1978.
(With Ellen Tarry) *My Dog Rinty,* 1946.
Oley the Sea Monster, 1947.
Little Old Automobile, 1948.
Mr. T. W. Anthony Woo, 1951.
Beasts and Nonsense, 1952.
Another Day, 1953.
Play with Me, 1955.
Mister Penny's Race Horse, 1956.
Cow's Party, 1958.
(With Aurora Labastida) *Nine Days to Christmas,* 1959.
Mister Penny's Circus, 1961.
Gilberto and the Wind, 1963.
Automobiles for Mice, 1964.
Just Me, 1965, with illustrations by the author, Puffin Books, 1978.
Bad, Good Boy, Crowell, 1967.
Talking without Words: I Can, Can You?, 1968.
Rosa: The Life of an Italian Immigrant (adult biography), University of Minnesota Press, 1970.
Elephant in a Well, illustrated by the author, 1972.
Jay Bird, illustrated by the author, 1974.

Manuscript collected at University of Minnesota, Minneapolis.

SIDELIGHTS: As a child, Marie Hall Ets moved around a lot with her rather large family; she was the fourth of six children, three boys and three girls. Her talent as an artist was evident as early as the first grade, when she began studying art with a group of adults. Still, she was very much a normal child. As she once explained, "The happiest memories of my childhood are of summers in the north woods of Wisconsin. I loved to run off by myself into the woods and watch for the deer with their fawns, and for porcupines, badgers, turtles, frogs and huge pine snakes and sometimes a bear or a copperhead or a skunk." These very memories inspired a number of her books.

In 1939, Ets published an educational book without precedent. *The Story of a Baby* tells of pre- and post-natal infant development. Ets wrote the book and sketched the drawings herself after research into medical resources and personal interviews. Ruth Irvine, in *Elementary English,* described it as a book parents and children could enjoy together, as it satisfies a child's curiosity in language the child understands." Ets considered this book her most significant addition to the canon of children's literature.

As a result of her career as a social worker, Ets personally answered the need for good books about minority children. *My Dog Rinty* takes place in Harlem and is about an African-American boy and his mischievous dog. Although it is a playful story with a happy ending, Irvine found that it was weighed down by a social message about slums, which she felt was out of place in a children's book. Another book about minorities (in this case, Mexicans living in the United States) is *Nine Days to Christmas,* for which Ets won the Caldecott Medal.

According to *Twentieth-Century Children's Writers* contributor James E. Higgins, Ets used silly names, slapstick comedy, and mischievous characters to engage her readers so that she could teach them lessons about life. Her stories often show love and patience for all creatures.

Although few of Ets' titles are still in print, Karen Nelson Hoyle in *Dictionary of Literary Biography* explained that in their day, they were "heralded as much-needed additions to children's literature." At the time, more than half of Ets' books were translated into several foreign languages; others were included in teaching kits or served as the basis for filmstrips, recordings, and cassette tapes.

May Massee, Ets' editor at Viking, in an article for *Horn Book Magazine,* explained her success by saying, "Marie Hall Ets is a brave and delightful woman with a wonderful sense of humor and play, great talent as an artist and writer, and just plain genius, the greatest and most demanding gift of all."

BIOGRAPHICAL/CRITICAL SOURCES:

BOOKS

Children's Literature Review, Volume 33, Gale, 1994..
Dictionary of Literary Biography, Volume 22: *American Writers for Children, 1900-1960,* Gale, 1983.
Twentieth-Century Children's Writers, 4th edition, St. James Press, 1995.

PERIODICALS

Christian Science Monitor, May 23, 1960.
Elementary English, May 10, 1958, pp. 259-65.
Horn Book Magazine, August, 1960, pp. 278-82.
Nation, December 15, 1969, p. 672.
New York Times Book Review, November 5, 1967, p. 63; November 3, 1968, p. 69.
Sunday Post-Crescent (Appleton, WI), January 8, 1967.
Times Literary Supplement, November 24, 1966, p. 1083.*

* * *

EURICH, Alvin C(hristian) 1902-1987

PERSONAL: Surname is pronounced Ur-ik; born June 14, 1902, in Bay City, MI; died May 27, 1987, in New York, NY; son of Christian Henry (a shoe merchant) and Hulda (Steinke) Eurich; married second wife, Nell P. Hutchinson (an educator), March 15, 1953; children: Juliet Ann, Donald Alan. *Education:* North Central College, Naperville, IL, B.A., 1924; University of Maine, M.A., 1926; University of Minnesota, Ph.D., 1929. *Religion:* Protestant.

CAREER: University of Minnesota, Minneapolis, 1929-37, began as assistant professor, professor of educational psychology, 1936-37, assistant to the president, 1935-36, assistant dean of College of Education, 1936-37; Northwestern University, Evanston, IL, professor of education, 1937-38; Stanford University, Stanford, CA, professor of education, 1938-44 (on leave, 1942-44), academic vice president, 1944-45, vice president, 1945-48, acting president, 1948; State University of New York, Albany, first president 1949-51; Ford Foundation, New York, NY, vice president of Fund for the Advancement of Education, 1951-64, director, 1952-87, executive director of Education Division, 1958-64; Academy for Educational Development, New York, NY, president, 1963-87. President of Aspen Institute of Humanistic Studies, 1963-67. Visiting fellow, Clare College, University of Cambridge, 1967; visiting professor at various universities. U.S. government posts included director of Consumer Division, Office of Price Administration, 1942; member of President Truman's Commission on Higher Education, Personnel Policy Committee of the Hoover

Commission, President Kennedy's Task Force on Education, National Committee on Libraries, and Committee on International Exchange of Persons. Chairman of U.S. delegation to UNESCO (General Conference, Paris, 1968, and of U.S. National Commission for UNESCO; chairman of advisory committee, Haile Selaissee University (Ethiopia); planning adviser to University of Patras (Greece); educational adviser to Libya; Consultant to Office of the Surgeon General, National Aeronautics and Space Administration, Agency for International Development, and Peace Corps. Vice-chairman of board of Educational Facilities Laboratories. Trustee of Lovelace Foundation for Medical Education and Penn Mutual Life Insurance Co. *Military service:* U.S. Naval Reserve, director of Standard and Curriculum Division, Bureau of Naval Personnel, 1942-44; became commander.

MEMBER: American Association for the Advancement of Science (fellow; member of council, 1941-45), American Psychological Association (fellow), American Educational Research Association (vice president, 1944; president, 1945), Sigma Xi, Phi Delta Kappa, Cosmos Club (Washington, DC), Century Association and University Club (both New York), Bohemian Club (San Francisco), Cactus Club (Denver), Athenaeum (London).

AWARDS, HONORS: Distinguished Achievement Award, University of Minnesota, 1951; New York Academy of Public Education Annual Award, 1963. Honorary degrees from Hamline University, 1944, North Central College, 1949, Alfred University, 1949, Clarke University, 1950, Miami University 1951, New School for Social Research, 1952, University of Florida, 1953, Yeshiva University, 1954, University of Redlands, 1960, Akron University, 1960, University of Maine, 1965, Albion College, 1965, University of Miami (FL), 1968, Fairfield University, 1971.

WRITINGS:

The Reading Abilities of College Students: An Experimental Study, University of Minnesota Press, 1931.
(Editor) *The Changing Educational World,* University of Minnesota Press, 1931.
(With Howard A. Carroll) *Educational Psychology,* Heath, 1935.
(With James E. Wert) *Applications for Federal Aid at Minnesota Colleges,* University of Minnesota, 1937.
(With Eric C. Wilson) *In 1936* (news summary of the year), Holt, 1937.
(With Wilson) *In 1937,* Holt, 1938.
(With C. Robert Pace) *Follow-up Study of Minnesota Graduates from 1928-1936,* Commission of Educational Research, University of Minnesota, 1938.
(Editor) *General Education in the American College,* University of Chicago Press, 1939.
(With J. Paul Leonard) *An Evaluation of Modern Education,* Appleton, 1942.
Looking Ahead to Better Education in Missouri: A Report on Organization, Structure, and Financing of Schools and Junior Colleges (field study), Academy for Educational Development (New York), 1966.
(Editor) *Campus 1980: The Shape of the Future in American Higher Education,* Delacorte, 1968.
(With Lucien B. Kinney and Sidney G. Tickton) *The Expansion of Graduate and Professional Education during the Period 1966 to 1980: A Summary of Findings and Conclusions,* Academy for Educational Development, 1969.
Reforming American Education: The Innovative Approach to Improving Our Schools and Colleges, Harper, 1969.
(Editor) *High School 1980: The Shape of the Future in American Secondary Education,* Pitman, 1970.
(Editor) *Major Transitions in the Human Life Cycle,* Lexington Books (Lexington, MA), 1981.

Also author, with Melvin E. Haggerty, of *Minnesota Reading Examination for College Students,* University of Minnesota Press.

CONTRIBUTOR

Studies in College Examinations, University of Minnesota Press, 1934.
The General College Curriculum as Revealed by Examinations, University of Minnesota Press, 1937.
Federal Aid to College Students, University of Minnesota Press, 1937.
Guidance in Education Institutions, Public School Publishing, 1938.
General Education in the American College, Public School Publishing, 1939.
Social Education, Macmillan, 1939.
The Improvement of College Instruction, University of Chicago Press, 1940.
Encyclopedia of Educational Research, Macmillan, 1941.

Editor of Farrar and Rinehart "Series in Education." Originator and compiler with Wilson of tri-annual "Current Affairs Test" for *Time,* 1935-55, and "Contemporary Affairs Test" for American Council on Education. Contributor of more than three hundred articles to *Atlantic Monthly, Saturday Review, Nation, Vital Speeches,* and other periodicals.

SIDELIGHTS: An educator and author, Alvin C. Eurich held a number of professorial and administrative posts at several universities, among them the University of Minnesota, Northwestern University, Stanford University, and the State University of New York. He was an executive of several private organizations, including the Ford Foundation, the Academy for Educational Development, which he also founded, and the Aspen Institute for Humanistic Studies. In addition, Eurich served in a number of U.S. government posts for several different administrations beginning in 1942. His writings include *The Reading Abilities of College Students: An Experimental Study, Reforming American Education: The Innovative Approach to Improving Our Schools and Colleges,* and psychological and achievement tests, among them *Time* magazine's "Current Affairs Test." Two of the titles Eurich co-authored are *Educational Psychology* and *An Evaluation of Modern Education.* Books he edited include *The Changing Educational World, General Education in the American College,* and *Campus 1980: The Shape of the Future in American Higher Education.* Eurich also contributed articles to psychological and educational books and journals and to general periodicals, including *Atlantic Monthly, Saturday Review, Nation,* and *Vital Speeches.* Additionally, he was education editor of a New York publishing company during the early 1940s. In 1951 the University of Minnesota awarded him its Distinguished Achievement Award. Eurich received numerous additional awards and more than thirteen honorary degrees.

OBITUARIES:

PERIODICALS

Current Biography, August, 1987.*

* * *

EVANS, Lee
See FORREST, Richard (Stockton)

F

FANTINI, Mario D. 1927-1989

PERSONAL: Born c.1927 in Philadelphia, PA; died of cancer, October 6, 1989, in Woodland Hills, CA. *Education:* Temple University, B.S., 1957, M.A., 1958; Harvard University, C.A.G.S., 1960, Ed.D., 1961.

CAREER: Worked as an elementary school teacher, and high school teacher, of mentally retarded and emotionally disturbed children; Syracuse University, Syracuse, NY, senior research associate, and director of urban teacher preparation program, school social work program, and scholastic rehabilitation program for emotionally disturbed children, 1962-64; Ford Foundation, New York, NY, program officer, beginning 1965; State University of New York at New Paltz, project director of grant to establish regional cooperation, beginning 1972, faculty exchange scholar, beginning 1974; professor and dean of education at University of Massachusetts, Amherst, 1976-87. Adjunct professor at Antioch College, Open University, Walden University, and Inter-American University of Puerto Rico; lecturer at Harvard University and Yale University; member of advisory board at University San Francisco and Kent State University. Member of National Advisory Council of Supplementary Centers and Services, 1968; adjunct member of National Commission on Resources for Youth. Demonstration teacher in public schools in Philadelphia, PA; staff director of special projects for Syracuse public schools. Testified before Kerner Commission on Civil Disorders; guest on television and radio programs; consultant to Institute for the Advancement of Urban Education and National committee for Citizens in Education.

MEMBER: American Association of School Administrators, Association for Supervision and Curriculum Development, Phi Delta Kappa.

WRITINGS:

(With Gerald Weinstein) *Toward a Contact Curriculum,* Anti-Defamation League, B'nai B'rith, 1967.

Taking Advantage of the Disadvantaged (monograph), Ford Foundation, 1967.

Alternatives for Urban School Reform (monograph), Ford Foundation, 1968.

(With Weinstein) *The Disadvantaged: Challenge to Education,* Harper, 1968.

(With Weinstein) *Making Urban Schools Work,* Holt, 1968.

(With Milton A. Young) *Designing Education for Tomorrow's Cities,* Holt, 1968.

(With Marilyn Gittell and Richard Magat) *Community Control and the Urban School,* Praeger, 1970.

(With Weinstein) *Toward Humanistic Education: A Curriculum of Affect,* Praeger, 1970.

(With Gittell) *Decentralization: Achieving Reform,* Praeger, 1973.

Public Schools of Choice: A Plan for the Reform of American Education, Simon & Schuster, 1974.

What's Best for the Children?: Resolving the Power Struggle between Parents and Teachers, Doubleday, 1974.

Alternative Education: A Source Book for Parents, Teachers, Students, and Administrators, Doubleday, 1976.

(Editor with Rene Cardenas) *Parenting in a Multicultural Society,* Longman (New York City), 1980.

(Editor with Robert L. Sinclair) *Education in School and Nonschool Settings,* National Society for the Study of Education (Chicago, IL), 1985.

Regaining Excellence in Education, Merrill (Columbus, OH), 1986.

CONTRIBUTOR

Arthur B. Shostak, editor, *Sociology in Action,* Dorsey, 1960.

Lester and Olui Crow, editors, *Mental Hygiene for Teachers,* Macmillan, 1963.

Readings in the Methods of Education, Odyssey, 1964.

A. Harry Passow, editor, *Teaching and Learning in Depressed Areas,* Teachers College Press, 1966.

(Author of foreword) Marilyn Gittell, *Participants and Participation,* Praeger, 1967.

Alvin Taffler, editor, *The Schoolhouse in the City,* Praeger, 1968.

Edmund C. Short, editor, *Contemporary Thought on Public School Curriculum Leadership,* W.C. Brown, 1968.

(Author of foreword) Naomi Levine, *The School Crisis,* Popular Library, 1969.

Troy V. McKelvey and Austin D. Swanson, editors, *Urban School Administration,* Sage Publications, 1969.

Gittell and Alan G. Hevesi, editors, *The Politics of Urban Education,* Praeger, 1969.

Ronald and Beatrice Gross, editors, *Radical School Reform,* Simon & Schuster, 1969.

Schools for the Seventies, Center for the Study of Instruction, National Education Association, 1970.

(Author of foreword) Francesco Cordasco, Maurie Hillson, and Henry A. Bullock, editors, *The School in the Social Order: A Sociological Introduction to Educational Understanding,* International Textbook Co., 1970.

Richard L. Hart and J. Galen Saylor, editors, *Student Unrest: Threat or Promise?,* Association for Supervision and Curriculum Development, 1970.

Arthur W. Foshay, editor, *The Professional as an Educator,* Teachers College Press, 1970.

J. A. Lauwerys and D. G. Scanlon, editors, *The World Yearbook of Education,* 1970.

Education in Cities, Harcourt, 1970.

Louis J. Rubin, editor, *Improving In-Service Education,* Allyn & Bacon, 1971.

Richard B. Heidenreich, editor, *Urban Education,* College Readings, Inc., 1971.

Roy P. Fairfield, editor, *Humanistic Frontiers in American Education,* Prentice-Hall, 1971.

(Author of preface) Dennis L. Roberts II, editor, *Planning Urban Education,* Educational Technology Publications, 1972.

(Author of foreword) James Haskins, *Black Manifesto for Education,* Morrow, 1973.

John M. Raynor, compiler, *Cities, Communities, and the Young,* Routledge & Kegan Paul, 1973.

Francis A. J. Ianni, editor, *Conflict and Change in Education,* Scott, Foresman, 1974.

Harvey F. Clarizio, editor, *Contemporary Issues in Educational Psychology,* Allyn & Bacon, 2nd edition (Fantini was not included in 1st edition), 1974.

William Cave and Mark Chesler, editors, *Sociology of Education,* Macmillan, 1974.

John Johansen and other editors, *American Education,* W.C. Brown, 2nd edition (Fantini was not included in 1st edition), 1975.

Also co-editor of *Alternative Education: Resources for Improving Education.* Also contributor to *The Formative Process: Early Childhood Education, Challenge and Choice in American Education, Children of the Cities, The Social Cultural Foundations of Education,* and *Development in Adolescence, and Contemporary Adolescence: Readings.* Contributor: C. Glenn Hass, editor, *Readings in Curriculum,* Allyn & Bacon, 3rd edition (Fantini was not included in earlier editions); Malcolm Provus, editor, *Trainers of Teacher Trainers,* University Press of Virginia; and Ianni, editor, *Education and Social Problems,* Scott Foresman.

Contributor to *World Book Encyclopedia,* and of articles and reviews to newspapers, education journals, and popular magazines, including *Saturday Review.* Member of editorial board of *Principal.*

SIDELIGHTS: A proponent of educational reform, Mario D. Fantini was instrumental in decentralizing the public school systems in New York City, Los Angeles, and Washington, D.C., beginning in the 1960s. Formerly a public school teacher and educator of mentally and emotionally impaired children, he was named program officer of the Ford Foundation's Fund for the Advancement of Education in 1965. Fantini later served as dean of the education faculty at the State University of New York at New Paltz and, from 1976 to 1987, as professor and dean of education at the University of Massachusetts at Amherst. The educator, administrator, and editor contributed numerous writings in the field of education, including *The Disadvantaged: Challenge to Education,* with Gerald Weinstein; *Decentralization: Achieving Reform,* with Marilyn Gittell; *Public Schools of Choice: A Plan for the Reform of American Education; Alternative Education: A Source Book for Parents, Teachers, Students, and Administrators;* and *Regaining Excellence in Education.* In addition, Fantini co-edited *Alternative Education: Resources for Improving Education.*

OBITUARIES:

PERIODICALS

Los Angeles Times, October 11, 1989.
New York Times, October 12, 1989.*

* * *

FARALLON, Cerise
See CREWS, Judson (Campbell)

* * *

FATCHEN, Max 1920-

PERSONAL: Born August 3, 1920, in Adelaide, South Australia, Australia; son of Cecil William (a farmer) and Isabel (Ridgway) Fatchen; married Jean Wohlers (a teacher), May 15, 1942; children: Winsome Genevieve, Michael John, Timothy James. *Education:* Attended high school in South Australia. *Religion:* Methodist. *Avocational interests:* Fishing, travel.

ADDRESSES: *Home*—15 Jane Street, Smithfield, South Australia 5114, Australia. *Agent*—John Johnson Ltd., 45-47 Clerkenwell Green, London EC1R0HT, England.

CAREER: *Adelaide News* and *Sunday Mail,* Adelaide, South Australia, journalist and special writer, 1946-55; *Advertiser,* Adelaide, journalist, 1955- 84, literary editor, 1971-81, special writer, 1981-84. *Military service:* Royal Australian Air Force, 1940-45.

MEMBER: Order of Australia.

AWARDS, HONORS: Book of the Year Younger Honor, Children's Book Council of Australia, 1988, for *A Paddock of Poems;* Advance Australia Award for literature, South Australia section, 1991; Walkley Award nomination, 1995; commendation, Children's Book Council of Australia, for *The River Kings;* Runner-up, Book of the Year Award, Children's Book Council of Australia, for *The Spirit Wind.*

WRITINGS:

JUVENILE FICTION

The River Kings, illustrated by Clyde Pearson, Hicks Smith (Sydney, Australia), 1966, St. Martin's (New York City), 1968.
Conquest of the River, illustrated by Pearson, Methuen (London), 1970.
The Spirit Wind, illustrated by Trevor Stubley, Methuen, 1973.
Chase through the Night, illustrated by Graham Humphreys, Methuen, 1977.
The Time Wave, illustrated by Edward Mortelmans, Methuen, 1978.
Closer to the Stars, Methuen, 1981.
Had Yer Jabs?, Methuen, 1987.
Pass Me a Poem, Omnibus (New York), 1989.

POETRY

Songs for My Dog and Other People, illustrated by Michael Atchison, Kestrel, 1980.
Wry Rhymes for Troublesome Times, illustrated by Atchison, Kestrel, 1983.
A Paddock of Poems, illustrated by Kerry Argent, Puffin (New York City), 1987.
A Pocketful of Rhymes, illustrated by Argent, Omnibus, 1989.
A Country Christmas, illustrated by Timothy Ide, Omnibus, 1990.
The Country Mail Is Coming: Poems from Down Under, illustrated by Catherine O'Neill, Joy Street Books, 1990.
(With Colin Thiele) *Tea for Three,* illustrated byCraig Smith, Moondrake, 1994.
Peculiar Rhymes and Lunatic Lines, illustrated by Lesley Bisseker, Orchard Books (New York City), 1995.

Contributor of light verse to the *Denver Post.*

VERSE; ILLUSTRATED BY IRIS MILLINGTON

Drivers and Trains, Longman (London), 1963.
Keepers and Lighthouses, Longman, 1963.
The Plumber, Longman, 1963.
The Electrician, Longman, 1963.
The Transport Driver, Longman, 1965.
The Carpenter, Longman, 1965.

ADULT COLLECTIONS

Peculia Australia: Verses, privately printed, 1965.
Just Fancy, Mr. Fatchen! A Collection of Verse, Prose and Fate's Cruel Blows, Rigby (Adelaide), 1967.
Forever Fatchen, Advertiser (Adelaide), 1983.
Mostly Max, illustrated by Michael Atchison, Wakefield Press, 1995.

ADAPTATIONS: *Chase through the Night* was adapted as a television series by Independent Productions,

1983; *The River Kings* was adapted as a television miniseries by Prospect Productions and broadcast by Australian Broadcasting Corporation, 1991.

SIDELIGHTS: As a native Australian and journalist, Max Fatchen has traveled and lived throughout Australia. In his fiction and poetry for children, Fatchen shares his experiences and celebrates the Australian people and landscape. His adventure novels for teens, including *The River Kings* and *Chase through the Night,* and his poetry collections for younger readers, such as *Songs for My Dog and Other People* and *The Country Mail Is Coming: Poems from Down Under,* provide readers with an understanding of the land and language of Australia and the lives of young people there while addressing universal concerns and themes as well.

Fatchen wants his readers, he once explained, "to be standing beside me or running beside me, breathless with interest as we clamber up some old riverbank or hang onto a rail in the wild sea. A book is a voyage and I don't just want my readers to be passengers anxious to get off because they feel seasick with all the words, but eager members of the crew shouting, 'land ho' when we sight the islands of imagination. . . . Stories must be honest, and honest stories are not always happy, but they can be moving, vivid, arresting, so that you never want to put them down. . . . That's what I want my stories to be."

During his years as a journalist for Australian newspapers, Fatchen discovered remote parts of his native land that fascinated him with their beauty. He recalled how he flew with "surveyors among the islands of the Gulf of Carpenteria" and "with helicopter pilots across swamps where the geese rose in living carpets or past muddy estuaries, where the seagoing crocodiles, drawn up like small canoes, lifted their heads as we came down low to buzz them as we passed.

"When I traveled along the Australian river, the Murray, with old riverboat men, again the feeling of the landscape, the movement of the river, the birds that congregated in small families on the long sandspit, and the river towns tucked around the bends all found their way into my books. When I was at sea with the trawler men, getting more stories for my paper, I watched the conflict between men and the sea, enjoyed the yarns in the fo'castle, wedged myself in the corner of the wheelhouse as the great grey-bearded waves went roaring past in the Australian bight."

Fatchen's adventure novels for teens draw upon his intimate knowledge of Australian history and geography. In several books, he wrote of the maritime life in old Australia. Set in nineteenth-century Australia, *The River Kings* concerns thirteen-year-old Shawn, who runs away from home to find work on the boats that trade goods up and down the Murray River. According to *Library Journal* contributor Joseph L. Buelna, Fatchen combined humor and "suspense" in an "entertaining mixture." *The River Kings* was adapted for Australian television in 1991. Shawn's further adventures on the Murray River are chronicled in *Conquest of the River,* which a *Times Literary Supplement* critic describes as a "tough racy book."

The Spirit Wind is, according to *Twentieth-Century Children's Writers* contributor Barbara Ker Wilson, "a much deeper and more ambitious work" than Fatchen's first two novels. "[T]he strain of poetry and mysticism emerges strongly, linked to Aboriginal lore through the character of Nunganee, an outcast from his tribe because he once 'sang' a man's death." The book's main character is fifteen-year-old Jarl Hansen, a deckhand on a squarerigger sailing from Norway to Australia. Jarl jumps ship in South Australia to escape Mate, the ship's sadistic captain. His fate ends up entangled with that of Nunganee, Mate, and the ship when the mysterious Spirit Wind blows of up a fierce night-time storm.

Encounters with kidnappers figure into the stories of two of Fatchen's more popular titles. In *The Time Wave,* Josef, the son of a millionaire, takes a vacation on a Pacific island that is periodically flooded by a gigantic wave. After he and his new friend Gina are kidnapped, the children attempt to escape their captors while the threat of the destructive wave looms over the island. *The Time Wave* contains some suspenseful moments. As the *Junior Bookshelf* critic noted, the scene in which a professional killer chases the children is "nerve-shattering" and "really quite something." *Chase through the Night* also involves a kidnapping. This time, Petra and her mother become the hostages of the thieves they have recognized. When they are taken to the small town where Petra's friend Ray lives, Ray tricks the thieves and foils their plans. Although *Times Literary Supplement* contributor David Bartlett complained about the story's "stereotyped characters," Margery Fisher, writing in *Growing Point,* admired the author's skillful use of setting and the "unity of atmosphere and plot."

Aside from his adventure fiction for children, Fatchen also writes poetry for a young audience. In the collection *Wry Rhymes for Troublesome Times,* for example, nonsense poems voice complaints about parents, aunts, and authority figures and describe the poet's pet peeves.

Other poems toy with traditional nursery rhymes. According to *School Librarian* reviewer Colin Mills, Fatchen is "at his best with word play and mild satire" in this work. Similarly, *Songs for My Dog and Other People,* as *School Librarian* critic Marcus Crouch asserted, maintains the perspective of an Australian child but is "quite complex" technically, and Fatchen "handles rhymes and rhythms with professional ease."

The forty-one poems in *The Country Mail Is Coming* explore life in rural Australia as well as new babies, dinosaurs, haunted shipwrecks, and the letters in the mailman's bag. Although, as Ellen Fader related in *Horn Book,* the poems include Australian words like "takeaway," "heeler," and "bathers" that non-Australians might not understand, the meanings of the poems "are never obscured." Kathleen Whalin concluded in *School Library Journal* that *The Country Mail Is Coming* is "energetic" and "illuminating."

While Fatchen's books allow Australian children to take pride in their country's natural beauty and diverse cultures, they also inform other children about Australia. Fatchen told *CA:* "I am particularly interested in writing for children, and my children's verse is read throughout the English speaking world. I like children for their frankness and enthusiasm when they enjoy my work. I enjoy their criticisms too. They are very wise people." Fatchen once invited his readers to join him for adventure: "Come aboard my book. We're sailing in five minutes!"

BIOGRAPHICAL/CRITICAL SOURCES:

BOOKS

Something about the Author Autobiography Series, Volume 20, Gale, 1995.

Twentieth-Century Children's Writers, 4th edition, St. James Press, 1995.

PERIODICALS

Booklist, April 1, 1990, p. 1548.

Emergency Librarian, March, 1995, p. 20.

Growing Point, October, 1977, pp. 3185-86.

Horn Book, May/June, 1990, pp. 342-43.

Junior Bookshelf, February, 1979, p. 50.

Kirkus Reviews, September 1, 1968, p. 978.

Library Journal, November 15, 1968, pp. 4412-13.

School Librarian, March, 1979, p. 54; June, 1981, p. 143; March, 1984, p. 61; August, 1995, p. 115.

School Library Journal, August, 1990, p. 153.

Times Literary Supplement, December 11, 1970, p. 1457; December 2, 1977, p. 1412.*

FATIO, Louise 1904-

PERSONAL: Born August 18, 1904, in Lausanne, Switzerland; daughter of Alfred and Elisa (Chenevard) Fatio; married Roger Antoine Duvoisin (a writer and illustrator of children's books), July 25, 1925 (died 1980); children: Roger, Jacques. *Education:* Attended boarding school in Basel and College des Jeunes Filles in Geneva. *Avocational interests:* Growing flowers, the animals on their land, music, reading.

ADDRESSES: Home—P.O. Box 116, Gladstone, NJ 07934.

CAREER: Began to gather ideas for her own books while helping her husband with his writing for children.

MEMBER: Authors Guild.

AWARDS, HONORS: The Happy Lion received first prize for a juvenile book from the West German Government, 1956 (it was published in German, 1955).

WRITINGS:

ALL ILLUSTRATED BY HUSBAND, ROGER DUVOISIN

The Christmas Forest, Aladdin Books, 1950.

Anna, the Horse, Aladdin Books, 1951.

The Happy Lion, Whittlesey House, 1954.

The Happy Lion in Africa, Whittlesey House, 1955.

A Doll for Maria, Whittlesey House, 1957.

The Happy Lion Roars, Whittlesey House, 1957.

The Three Happy Lions, Whittlesey House, 1959.

The Happy Lion's Quest, Whittlesey House, 1961.

Red Bantam, Whittlesey House, 1963.

The Happy Lion and the Bear, Whittlesey House, 1964.

The Happy Lion's Vacation, McGraw, 1967.

The Happy Lion's Treasure, McGraw, 1971.

The Happy Lion's Rabbits, McGraw, 1973.

Hector Penguin, McGraw, 1974.

Marc and Pixie and the Walls in Mrs. Jones's Garden, McGraw, 1975.

Hector and Christina, McGraw, 1977.

The Happy Lioness, McGraw-Hill, 1980.

SIDELIGHTS: Louise Fatio's best-known works are the Happy Lion books illustrated by her husband, Roger Duvoisin. The Happy Lion is a gentle, compassionate creature who lives in a zoo but gets to come and go as he pleases, courtesy of the zookeeper's son, Francois. In addition to being friendly and helpful, the Happy Lion, in the first book, is also lonely. In the second book, *The Happy Lion Roars,* this problem is solved when he meets his mate. In *The Happy Lion in Africa* he learns that home is where we live, not where we came from.

Fatio told *CA:* "*The Happy Lion* was inspired by a true story I read in a French newspaper during one of our trips to France. A friendly, well-fed lion had escaped from a circus which had set up its tent in a small French town. People screamed and ran off in all directions when they saw the good lion stroll through their streets. The lion was saved when the circus owner brought him back to the circus. I loved that newspaper article."

Twentieth-Century Children's Writers contributor Rebecca J. Lukens wrote of Fatio's work, "These direct, straightforward stories with little imagery or stylistic complexity . . . have warmth and acceptance in their tone: they are important as comfortable affirmations of love and loyalty."

BIOGRAPHICAL/CRITICAL SOURCES:

BOOKS

Lee Bennet Hopkins, *Books Are by People,* Citation, 1969.
Twentieth-Century Children's Writers, 4th edition, St. James Press, 1995.

PERIODICALS

Book World, October 1, 1967.
Learning, April, 1985.
New York Times Book Review, January 21, 1968; November 8, 1970.
School Library Journal, December, 1975; April, 1978.
Times Literary Supplement, June 17, 1965; July 2, 1971; March 29, 1974.
Young Reader's Review, November, 1967.*

* * *

FAULKNOR, Cliff(ord Vernon) 1913-
(Pete Williams)

PERSONAL: Born March 3, 1913, in Vancouver, British Columbia, Canada; son of George Henry and Rhoda Anne Faulknor; married Elizabeth Harriette Sloan, August 21, 1943; children: Stephen Edward Vernon, Noreen Elizabeth. *Education:* University of British Columbia, B.S.A. (with honors), 1949. *Politics:* "A little right of centre." *Religion:* Protestant.

ADDRESSES: Home—403-80 Point McKay Cr. NW, Calgary, Alberta T3B 4W4, Canada.

CAREER: Affiliated with Royal Bank of Canada, beginning 1929; also worked with lumber companies, and as an assistant ranger for British Columbia Forest Service; British Columbia Department of Lands and Forests, Land Utilization Research and Survey Division, Victoria, British Columbia, Canada, land inspector, 1949-54; *Country Guide* (national farm monthly), Calgary, Alberta, Canada, associate editor, 1954-75; McKinnon, Allen & Associates, Calgary, accredited appraiser, 1976—; member of Alberta Land Compensation Board, 1978—. *Military service:* Royal Canadian Artillery, Victoria, gunner, 1937-39; Canadian Army, Water Transport, 1939-45; became sergeant.

MEMBER: Agricultural Institute of Canada, Appraisal Institute of Canada, Writers' Union of Canada, Canadian Farm Writers' Federation, Alberta Farm Writers' Association (past president).

AWARDS, HONORS: Awards from Canadian Farm Writers Federation, 1961, 1962, 1968, 1969, 1973, 1974, and 1975; Pacific Northwest Writers Conference award, 1963, for short story; Canadian Children's Book Award, Little, Brown, 1964, for *The White Calf; Pen and Plow* was named best nonfiction book by an Alberta writer, 1976; Vicky Metcalf Award, 1979, for contributions to Canadian literature.

WRITINGS:

YOUNG ADULT FICTION

The White Calf, illustrated by Gerald Tailfeathers, Little, Brown (Boston, MA), 1965.
The White Peril, Little, Brown, 1966.
The In-Betweener, Little, Brown, 1967.
The Smoke Horse, McClelland & Stewart (Toronto), 1968.
West to Cattle Country, McClelland & Stewart, 1975.
Johnny Eagleclaw, cover and design and illustrations by Richard A. Conroy, John LeBel Enterprises, 1982.

OTHER

The Romance of Beef, Public Press, 1967.
Pen and Plow, Public Press, 1976.
Turn Him Loose!, Western Producer Prairie Books, 1977.
Alberta Hereford Heritage, Advisor Graphics, 1981.

Contributor to anthologies, including *Chinook Arch,* Co-op Press, 1967; *Western Profiles,* Alberta Education, 1979; *Transitions,* Alberta Education, 1979; and *The Alberta Diamond Jubilee Anthology,* Hurtig, 1979. Former columnist, under pseudonym Pete Williams, for *Country Guide;* former freelance columnist for *Victoria Times.* Contributor of articles and short stories to numerous magazines and newspapers, including *Toronto Star Weekly, Liberty, Canadian Geographic Journal,* and *Cattlemen.*

SIDELIGHTS: Cliff Faulknor's adventure stories for young adults are noted for their action-based plots and accurate historical details. The author's best known work, the trilogy beginning with *The White Calf,* portrays the coming of age of a young Blackfoot Indian brave during the middle of the nineteenth century, just as the encroachment of whites into Indian territory begins to pose a threat to their way of life.

As *The White Calf* opens, Eagle Child, age twelve, finds an orphaned albino buffalo calf, a creature so rare that tribal legend holds it as a symbol of good luck. While Eagle Child spends the summer of his twelfth year learning the skills necessary to become a brave, heal so raises the calf until the time when it can be set free to roam with the herd. Critics note that the calf symbolizes Eagle Child's journey to manhood. Janice R. Scott writes in a *Library Journal* review that the details of Blackfoot ways, including hunting buffalo and performing rituals, would likely "appeal to adventure-minded boys." A reviewer in *Times Literary Supplement* highlights the realistic portrayal of Faulknor's Indian characters. "In a simple prose with no false note," according to the critic, Faulknor presents characters who are "alive and real," offering "exciting" descriptions of hunting, inter-tribal warfare, and performances of tribal rituals.

"The events are exciting, and the details of Blackfoot life are authentic, but [*The White Calf*] suffers a little from the presence of two heroes"—Eagle Child and his brother War Bonnet—according to John Robert Sorfleet in *Twentieth-Century Children's Writers.* Its sequel, *The White Peril,* however, offers the advantages of the earlier book, including excitement and realistic detail, claims Sorfleet, without introducing the possible problem of reader-identification presented by dual heroes. In *The White Peril,* which takes place five years after the earlier book, Eagle Child's buffalo has become a rogue killer that must be destroyed, and the increasing presence of white settlers threatens the survival of the tribe. While a critic in *Kirkus Reviews* feels that "the theme of the disintegration of the tribe is stronger than the story can support," and complains of the lack of a sympathetic central character, Sorfleet comments: "The book contains a realistic admixture of sadness and joys, with the coming of the whites viewed from an Indian perspective."

In what Sorfleet calls "a fitting conclusion to the trilogy,"*The Smoke Horse* brings Eagle Child to full manhood when he learns the quality of mercy. Faulknor relies again on the action of hunting and fighting scenes to fill out a story that Sorfleet dubs "well-crafted and gripping, with many flashes of Faulknor's subtle humour and adept dialogue." Of the highly praised historical background of his adventures, Faulknor told *Twentieth-Century Children's Writers:* "As for the story setting and background information, I research this very carefully. And if I am dealing with the past, my story must be true to the history of that period, and the setting must be as it was during that period."

A 1982 title for young adults, *Johnny Eagleclaw,* is set in western Canada during the early part of the twentieth century. *Johnny Eagleclaw* presents the story of a young Indian's struggle to succeed on the rodeo circuit despite discrimination and the dangers of the work. Critics highlighted the interest of the details about life on the rodeo circuit, and in a review in *Books in Canada* Mary Ainslie Smith praised Faulknor's "sensitive portrayal" of his protagonist's attempts to overcome prejudice.

Faulknor once commented: "When I was a youth, I could idle away a whole summer's day on some beach without a twinge of conscience, just listening to the music of the waves or watching galleon-like cumulus clouds moving across the sky. Later, I was somehow inveigled into taking what is often referred to as higher 'education' and soon fell prey to the work ethic demon. In that grinding process and the various careers which followed, the boy on the beach was lost. But I found him again, or at least apart of him, when I began to write adventure stories for juveniles. I did not plan any of these stories. My daily journalistic chores gave me about all the planning I could stomach. With my juveniles, I just sat down at my typewriter and put my characters into motion. If any new ones appeared I tossed them into the pot and stirred. The characters themselves did the rest. As they went about their lives they took me with them. I recommend this as a cure to those who feel that they are growing old in heart."

BIOGRAPHICAL/CRITICAL SOURCES:

BOOKS

Twentieth-Century Children's Writers, St. James Press, 3rd edition, 1989, 4th edition, 1995.

PERIODICALS

Books in Canada, December, 1982, p. 11.
Journal of Reading, December, 1982, p. 221.
Kirkus Reviews, May 15, 1965, p. 499; October 1, 1966, p. 1054.
Library Journal, October 15, 1965, p. 4615; June 15, 1967, p. 2449.
Times Literary Supplement, November 24, 1966, p. 1069; March 14, 1968, p. 263.*

* * *

FAUSET, Jessie Redmon 1884- 1961

PERSONAL: Born April 27, 1884 (some sources say 1882 or 1886), in Snow Hill, NJ; died of heart disease, April 30, 1961, in Philadelphia, PA; daughter of Redmon (a minister) and Annie (Seamon) Fauset; married Herbert Harris, 1929. *Education:* Cornell University, B.A., 1905; University of Pennsylvania, M.A.; attended Sorbonne, University of Paris.

CAREER: Teacher of French at high schools in Washington, DC, and New York City; literary editor of *The Crisis,* New York City, 1919-26, and *Brownie's Book,* 1920-21; novelist, critic, and poet.

MEMBER: Phi Beta Kappa.

WRITINGS:

There Is Confusion (novel), Boni & Liveright, 1924, with a new foreword by Thadious M. Davis, Northeastern University Press (Boston), 1989.
Plum Bun (novel), Mathews & Marrot (London), 1928, published as *Plum Bun: A Novel without a Moral,* introduction by Deborah E. McDowell, Pandora Press (Boston), 1985.
The Chinaberry Tree (novel), Frederick A. Stokes, 1931, published as *The Chinaberry Tree: A Novel of American Life and Selected Writings,* with a new foreword by Marcy Jane Knopf, Northeastern University Press, 1995.
Comedy, American Style (novel), Frederick A. Stokes, 1933, introduction by Thadious M. Davis, G.K. Hall (New York City), 1994.

Contributor of poems, short stories, and essays to periodicals, including *The Crisis* and *Brownie's Book.*

SIDELIGHTS: The first black female to be graduated from Cornell University, Fauset taught French at an all-black high school in Washington, D.C., until 1919 when sociologist W.E.B. DuBois asked her to move to New York City to work for *The Crisis* magazine, of which he was editor. As literary editor, Fauset published the works of many Harlem Renaissance writers, such as Countee Cullen, Langston Hughes, George Schuyler, Claude McKay, and Jean Toomer, as well as her own writings. Fauset also edited and was the primary writer for another of W. E. B. DuBois' projects, *Brownie's Book,* a magazine for black children.

Fauset wrote poetry, essays, short stories, and novels, most of which portrayed black life in a prejudice-wrought world. Her last novel, *Comedy, American Style,* is considered her most direct statement about the various effects of racial discrimination. The main character, Olivia Cary, is a woman who, because of the prejudice she encounters, hates being black and vainly desires to be white. Her passionate and futile desires threaten to destroy her, while at the same time her husband and son are proud of their heritage and exemplify the richness of black culture.

Fauset's novels received largely mixed reviews, some critics feeling the author unrealistically characterized her subjects. In *Black Writers of the Thirties,* for example, James O. Young commented: "The black middle class was not an invalid subject for fiction, but Miss Fauset's idealized treatment of it had little redeeming value. . . . [Instead] of presenting a serious, realistic interpretation of middle-class black life, as she professed to do, Miss Fauset concocted a highly idealized romance. Her characters are not real human beings, they are idealizations of what the Negro middle class conceived itself to be." And Gerald Sykes, reviewing *The Chinaberry Tree,* wrote in *Nation:* "[It] attempts to idealize [the] polite colored world in terms of the white standards that it has adopted. . . . When she parades the possessions of her upper classes and when she puts her lovers through their Fauntleroy courtesies, she is not only stressing the white standards that they have adopted; she is definitely minimizing the colored blood in them. This is a decided weakness, for it steals truth and life from the book. Is not the most precious part of a Negro work of art that which is specifically Negroid, which none but a Negro could contribute?" Despite her "artistic errors," however, Sykes found "Fauset has a rare understanding of people and their motives. . . . Inspired by the religious motive which so many Negro writers seem to feel, she has simply been trying to justify her world to the world at large. Her mistake has consisted in trying to do this in terms of the white standard."

On the other hand, in a review of Fauset's *Comedy, American Style,* Hugh M. Gloster hailed Fauset's "description of the lives and difficulties of Philadelphia's colored elite" as "one of the major achievements of American Negro fiction." And Joseph J. Feeney defended Fauset's portrayal of blacks, claiming in his *CLA Journal* article that critics "who speak of her middle-class respectability and her 'genteel lace-curtain romances' miss the dark world of prejudice, sadness, and frustration just below the surface of her novels. There are two worlds in Jessie Fauset: the first is sunlit, a place of pride, talent, family love, and contentment; the other world is shadowed by prejudice, lost opportunities, a forced choice between color and country." Feeney continued: "Miss Fauset, through structure and content has offered a far more complex and harrowing portrait of American black life than the critics have recognized. She is far more than a conventional writer of middle-class romances, and her reputation must be revised accordingly. . . .She was not a major writer. But she cannot be dismissed as 'vapidly genteel' or 'sophomoric.' In the construction of her novels and in her vision of the Negro world, she displayed a sensibility which comprehended tragedy, sardonic comedy, disillusioned hopes, slavery, prejudice, confusion, and bitterness against America."

BIOGRAPHICAL/CRITICAL SOURCES:

BOOKS

Robert Bone, *The Negro Novel in America,* Yale University Press, 1965.

Contemporary Literary Criticism, Volume 19, 1981; Volume 54, 1989; Gale.

Dictionary of Literary Biography, Volume 51: *Afro-American Writers from the Harlem Renaissance to 1940,* Gale, 1987.

Hugh M. Gloster, *Negro Voices in American Fiction,* University of North Carolina Press, 1948.

McLendon, Jacuelyn Y., *The Politics of Color in the Fiction of Jessie Fauset and Nella Larsen,* University Press of Virginia (Charlottesville, VA), 1995.

Schomburg Center Guide to Black Literature, Gale, 1996.

Sylvander, Carolyn Wedin, *Jessie Redmon Fauset, Black American Writer,* Whitston Pub. Co. (Troy, NY), 1981.

Wall, Cheryl A., *Women of the Harlem Renaissance,* Indiana University Press (Bloomington, IN), 1995.

James O. Young, *Black Writers of the Thirties,* Louisiana State University Press, 1973.

PERIODICALS

African American Review, summer, 1996, p. 205.

Booklist, February 15, 1996, p. 982.

CLA Journal, December, 1974; June, 1979.

Ebony, February, 1949, August, 1966.

New Republic, July 9, 1924; April 10, 1929.

Nation, July 27, 1932.

New Statesman, August 9, 1985, p. 27.

New York Times Book Review, November 19, 1933.

Saturday Review of Literature, April 6, 1929.

Voice Literary Supplement, March, 1987, p. 14.*

* * *

FEDERMAN, Raymond 1928-

PERSONAL: Born May 15, 1928, in Paris, France; immigrated to United States, 1948, naturalized citizen, 1953; son of Simon (a painter) and Marguerite (Epstein) Federman; married Erica Hubscher, September 14, 1960; children: Simone Juliette. *Education:* Columbia University, B.A. (cum laude), 1957; University of California, Los Angeles, M.A., 1959, Ph.D. in French, 1963. *Avocational interests:* Cinema, theater, jazz.

ADDRESSES: Home—46 Four Seasons W., Eggertsville, NY 14226. *Office*—State University of New York at Buffalo, Buffalo, NY 14260.

CAREER: University of California, Santa Barbara, assistant professor, 1962-64; State University of New York at Buffalo, associate professor of French, 1964-68, professor of French and comparative literature, 1968-73, professor of English and comparative literature, 1973-1990, distinguished professor of English and comparative literature, 1990—, Melodia E. Jones Chair of Literature, 1994—. Visiting professor, University of Montreal, 1970, and Hebrew University, Jerusalem, 1982-83. Jazz saxophonist, 1947-50. Co-editor of *MICA* (literary magazine), 1960-63; contributing editor of *American Book Review;* member of editorial board of *Jewish Publication Society* and *Buff.* Member of board of directors, Coordinating Council of Literary Magazines, 1976-79, and of Hallwalls, 1980—. Co-director, Fiction Collective, 1977-80. Fiction judge for CAPS, 1980. *Military service:* U.S. Army, 82nd Airborne Division, 1951-54; served in Korea and Japan; became sergeant.

MEMBER: Modern Language Association of America, American Association for the Studies of Dada and Surrealism, PEN American Center, Samuel Beckett Society (honorary trustee), Phi Beta Kappa.

AWARDS, HONORS: Grants from State University of New York, New York State Research Foundation, and the Asia Foundation; Guggenheim fellowship, 1966-67; Frances Steloff prize, 1971, and *Panache* Experimental Fiction Prize, 1972, both for *Double or Nothing;* Pushcart anthology prize, 1977; Camargo Foundation fellowship, 1977; Fulbright fellowship to Israel, 1982-83; National Endowment for the Arts fellowship, 1985; New York State Foundation for the Arts fellowship, 1986; American Book Award, 1986, for *Smiles on Washington Square;* DAAD fellowship (Berlin Artist Program), 1989-90, in residence in Berlin Germany.

WRITINGS:

POETRY

(Translator) F. J. Temples, *Postal Cards,* Noel Young, 1964.
Among the Beasts/Parmi les Monstres (bilingual), Editions Millas-Martin (Paris), 1967.
Me Too, West Coast Poetry Review, 1975.
Duel, Stopover Press, 1991.
Now Then, Editions Isele, 1992.

NOVELS

Double or Nothing, Swallow Press, 1971.
Amer Eldorado, Editions Stock (Paris), 1974.
Take It or Leave It, Fiction Collective, 1976.
The Voice in the Closet/La Voix dans le cabinet de Debarras (bilingual), Coda, 1979.
The Twofold Vibration, Indiana University Press, 1982.
Smiles on Washington Square, Thunder's Mouth, 1985.
To Whom It May Concern, Fiction Collective, 1990.
A Version of My Life, Maro Verlag, 1993.

OTHER

Journey to Chaos: Samuel Beckett's Early Fiction, University of California Press, 1965.
(Editor and translator) Yvonne Caroutch, *Paysages provisoires/Temporary Landscapes* (bilingual), Stamperia di Venizia, 1965.
(With John Fletcher) *Samuel Beckett: His Work and His Critics,* University of California Press, 1970.
(Editor) *Cinq Nouvelles* (collected fiction), Appleton-Century-Crofts, 1970.
(Editor) *Surfiction: Fiction Now and Tomorrow* (essays), Swallow Press, 1975, revised edition, 1981.
(Editor with Tom Bishop) *Samuel Beckett: Cahier de L'Herne,* Editions de L'Herne, 1976.
(Editor with Lawrence Graver) *Samuel Beckett: The Critical Heritage,* Routledge & Kegan Paul, 1979.
(Translator with Genevieve James) Michel Serres, *Detachment,* Ohio University Press, 1989.
Playtexts/Spieltexts, LCB-DAAD (Berlin), 1990.
Critifiction: The Way of Literature (essays), State University of New York Press, 1993.

Contributor to numerous books and anthologies, including *On Contemporary Literature, Samuel Beckett Now, Essaying Essays, Pushcart Prize Anthology II, The Wake of the Wake, Bright Moments,* and *Imaged Words and Worded Images.* Also contributor of fiction and poetry to numerous periodicals, including *Partisan Review, Chicago Review, Tri-Quarterly, Paris Review,* and *North American Review.* Contributor of articles and essays to *French Review, Modern Drama, Film Quarterly, Comparative Literature,* and many other periodicals.

ADAPTATIONS: The Voice in the Closet was adapted into a full-length modern ballet under the title *Project X.* All of Federman's novels have been adapted into radio plays and broadcast in German by the Bayerischer Rundfunk (Bavarian Radio) in Munich.

SIDELIGHTS: A bilingual novelist, poet, critic, and translator, Raymond Federman attempts in his novels to redefine fiction, calling the developing form "surfiction." "Building on the work of Joyce, Celine, Beckett, and other twentieth-century masters, his fictions are fascinating constructs that combine a brilliant style, unorthodox typography, and a masterful new approach to the development of characters and literary structure," declares Welch D. Everman in the *Dictionary of Literary Biography Yearbook: 1980.* "Unlike the traditional novel, these works are not intended to be representations of events; they are events in their own right, language events that reflect on their own mode of becoming and that, in effect, critique themselves. . . . Federman questions the very nature of fiction, the fiction writer, and the reality that the writer's language is supposed to represent."

The reality that affected Federman's life most strongly was the Nazi Holocaust. In the summer of 1942, the Gestapo entered his family's apartment, taking his parents and his two sisters to the death camps; Raymond, whom his parents hid in a closet, escaped. Although Federman's fiction is experimental in form, its contents grapple with the experience of death and survival that marked the author while he was young. Questioning the validity of autobiography and fiction alike, Federman creates autobiographical fictions, and does so in a language, English, that he learned as an adult. Federman's first book of poems, *Among the Beasts/Parmi les Monstres,* is a crucial text in his canon, the earliest literary version of his Holocaust experience. His subsequent fictions, according to Everman, rewrite this "original text."

Federman's first novel, *Double or Nothing,* is a multilayered, bleakly comic work whose plot focuses on a young French immigrant who lost his family in the concentration camps. The immigrant's story is told by a would-be author who narrates his own life as well as that of the young immigrant. Comments on the writing process are intertwined with the narrative. At least two additional voices are added to the layering, producing a potentially infinite regression of narrators. Typography is of central importance to the novel, for each page is a complete visual unit. "Humor is one of Federman's key tools," Everman points out. "The style is frantic and purposely paradoxical, and often the reader laughs not so much at the antics of the characters as at his own confusion in the face of this convoluted text."

Take It or Leave It, Federman's second novel in English, is an extended reworking of his French novel *Amer Eldorado.* A note on the title page calls it an "exaggerated second-hand tale." The plot concerns a young French immigrant in the American Army, Frenchy, who has thirty days to travel from Fort Bragg, North Carolina, to a ship that will take him to Korea, but who must first travel north to upstate New York to retrieve some crucial papers. The digressive story is told by a nameless narrator who is interrupted by faceless audience members and literary critics. "*Take It or Leave It* is a text which constitutes, contradicts, and erases itself, as it constitutes, contradicts, and erases the voices which it produces and by which it is produced," Everman says.

The Voice in the Closet/La Voix dans le cabinet Debarras, Federman's bilingual novel of 1979, marks a shift in the author's work while preserving his preoccupation with form. Federman sets himself a strict form, consisting of twenty pages with eighteen lines per page and sixty-eight characters per line. From this constricted form—which parallels the physical constriction of a closet—emerges the voice of a boy hiding in a closet while the Nazis take away his family. The voice speaks to a writer named federman (with a lowercase "f "), who has repeatedly tried and failed to tell the boy's story. Critic Peter Quartermain, writing in the *Chicago Review,* calls *The Voice in the Closet* "a compelling book indeed. . . . [It] astonishes partly because nothing in Federman's previous work . . . prepares us for the obsessive immediacy of this. This book may be a one-shot, perhaps, but in it Federman has come to do what over a generation ago D. H. Lawrence enjoined readers as well as writers to do: trust the tale."

The English version of *The Voice in the Closet* is part of Federman's 1982 novel, *The Twofold Vibration.* Here, typography and style are more traditional than in most of Federman's earlier work. The novel's setting is New Year's Eve, 1999. In a persistently self-reflexive style, the narrator, an old man whose history contains many parallels with Federman's, tells the story of his life. Meanwhile, two characters named Namredef and Moinous, who serve as doubles for the narrator, argue about the way the story ought to be told. Reviewing the book for the *Times Literary Supplement,* Brian Morton comments: "For the first time with any success, Federman . . . combines a sense of time and consequence with the spatial concerns of radical postmodernist fiction. . . . If this is not what John Gardner called 'metafiction for the millions,' it is at least an entertaining and salutary journey through the darker and more troubled outlands of contemporary history and fiction."

Smiles on Washington Square was published in 1985, and once again features a character named Moinous who bears resemblances to Federman. Moinous, a French-born naturalized American who has served in Korea, is out of work in New York City. At a political rally, he meets—or perhaps does not meet—Sucette, the leftist daughter of a wealthy New England family. Sucette, who is studying creative writing at Columbia University, begins to write stories about a man named Moinous. Two weeks later, they may or may not meet again; indeed, the whole love story may belong to Sucette's creative writing efforts. Reviewing the book for the *Los Angeles Times Book Review,* Allen Boyer terms it "more of a teasing exercise than a novel—long on intellect, but short on flesh and bone. . . . The book could be called subdued or spare, but precious would be a better term. Instead of sensation, passion, or plot, it offers a suggestion that life and art are necessarily related, competitive and tentative—and this idea is hardly new." Alan Cheuse, in the *New York Times Book Review,* was more appreciative, saying, "In this new work of fiction [Federman] appears intent on compressing and compacting his story. . . . The result is much more charming and readable than anything else of his in English. . . . Basically, the novel succeeds because of its appealing voice, something resembling Moinous's 'English with a French Accent.' "

Federman once told *CA:* "I write to gain my freedom and hopefully to liberate my readers from all conventions. Anything goes because meaning does not precede language, language produces meaning. There is as much value in making nonsense as there is in making sense; it's simply a question of direction." Of his work, Federman once commented, "My entire writing career has been a Journey to Chaos."

Several of Federman's books have been translated into Polish, German, French, Portuguese, Italian, Spanish, Japanese, Chinese, Hungarian, Romanian, Hebrew, and Dutch.

BIOGRAPHICAL/CRITICAL SOURCES:

BOOKS

Contemporary Authors Autobiography Series, Volume 8, Gale, 1989.
Contemporary Literary Criticism, Gale, Volume 6, 1976, Volume 47, 1988.
Contemporary Novelists, 6th edition, St. James Press, 1996.
Dictionary of Literary Biography Yearbook: 1980, Gale, 1981.
Federman, Raymond, *Take It or Leave It,* Fiction Collective, 1976.
Hartl, Thomas, *Raymond Federman's Real Fictitious Discourses: Formulating Yet Another Paradox,* Edward Mellen Press (Lewiston, NY), 1995.
Pearce, Richard, *The Novel in Motion: An Approach to Modern Fiction,* Ohio State University Press, 1983.

PERIODICALS

American Book Review, March-April, 1981, pp. 10-12; January-February, 1982, pp. 2-3; November-December, 1983, p. 7; September-October, 1986, pp. 22-23; August, 1996, p. 5.
Boundary 2, fall, 1976, pp. 153-165.
Chicago Review, summer, 1977, pp. 145-149; autumn, 1980, pp. 65-74.
Chicago Tribune Book World, September 2, 1982.
Fiction International, numbers 2-3, 1974, pp. 147-150.
Los Angeles Times Book Review, February 9, 1986, p. 4.
Michigan Quarterly Review, winter, 1974.
Modern Fiction Studies, winter, 1994, p. 857.
New Republic, July 11, 1970, p. 23.
New York Times Book Review, January 23, 1966, p. 4; October 1, 1972, pp. 40-41; September 15, 1974, p. 47; November 7, 1982, pp. 12, 26; November 24, 1985, p. 24.
North American Review, March, 1986, pp. 67-69.
Saturday Review, January 22, 1972, p. 67.
Times Literary Supplement, May 5, 1966, p. 388; October 12, 1973, p. 1217; December 3, 1982, p. 1344.
Yale Review, spring, 1983, pp. 12-13.*

* * *

FIDLER, Kathleen (Annie) 1899-1980

PERSONAL: Born August 10, 1899, in Coalville, Leicestershire, England; died in August, 1980; daughter of Francis and Sarah H. B. (Ellison) Fidler; married James Hutchison Goldie (a banker), 1930 (deceased); children: Agnes M. (Mrs. Michael H. McTaggart), Francis James. *Education:* St. Mary's College, Bangor, North Wales, 1918-20, Board of Education Teacher's Certificate, 1920. *Politics:* Conservative. *Religion:* Presbyterian. *Avocational interests:* Gardening and the theatre.

CAREER: Writer for children. St. Paul's Girls' School, Wigan, Lancashire, England, headmistress, 1924-30; Scot Lane Evening Institute, Wigan, headmistress, 1925-30; Authors' Panel for Schools Broadcasting in Scotland, scriptwriter, 1938-62. Speaker on writing at libraries and schools.

MEMBER: Society of Authors, PEN (Scottish branch), Soroptimist Club.

AWARDS, HONORS: Moscow Film Festival award, 1967, for *Flash the Sheep Dog,* on which a motion picture was based; *Haki the Shetland Pony* was listed as one of Child Study Association's children's books of the year, 1970.

WRITINGS:

JUVENILES

The Borrowed Garden, Lutterworth, 1944.
St. Jonathan's in the Country, Lutterworth, 1945, revised edition, 1952.
Fingal's Ghost (based on radio play), John Crowther, 1945.
The Kathleen Fidler Omnibus, Collins, 1946.
White Cockade Passes, Lutterworth, 1947.
Mysterious Mr. Simister, Lutterworth, 1947.

Mr. Simister Appears Again, Lutterworth, 1948.
Mr. Simister Is Unlucky, Lutterworth, 1949.
Guest Castle, Lutterworth, 1949.
I Rode with the Covenanters, Lutterworth, 1950.
(With Lennox Milne) *Stories from Scottish Heritage,* three volumes, Chambers, 1951.
The White-Starred Hare and Other Stories, Lutterworth, 1951.
To the White North: The Story of Sir John Franklin, Lutterworth, 1952.
Fedora the Donkey, Lutterworth, 1952.
Stallion from the Sea, Lutterworth, 1953.
Pete, Pam and Jim, the Investigators, Lutterworth, 1954.
The Bank House Twins, Lutterworth, 1955.
The Droving Lad, Lutterworth, 1955.
The Man Who Gave Away Millions: The Story of Andrew Carnegie, Lutterworth, 1955, Roy, 1956.
Mr. Punch's Cap, Lutterworth, 1956.
Lanterns over the Lune, Lutterworth, 1958.
(With Jack Gillespie) *The McGills at Mystery Farm,* Lutterworth, 1958.
(With Gillespie) *More Adventures of the McGills,* Lutterworth, 1959.
Escape in Darkness, Lutterworth, 1961.
The Little Ship Dog, Lutterworth, 1963.
The Desperate Journey, Lutterworth, 1964.
New Lamps for Old (reader), Oliver & Boyd, 1965.
Flash the Sheep Dog (also see below), Lutterworth, 1965.
Police Dog, Lutterworth, 1966.
Adventure Underground (reader), Oliver & Boyd, 1966.
Forest Fire (reader), Oliver & Boyd, 1966.
Flash the Sheep Dog (screenplay; based on book of same title), British Broadcasting Corp., 1967.
The Boy with the Bronze Axe, Chatto, Boyd & Oliver, 1968, illustrated by Edward Mortelmans, Penguin (Baltimore), 1975.
Haki the Shetland Pony (also see below), illustrated by Victor G. Ambrus, 1968, Rand McNally, 1970.
Treasure of Ebba, Lutterworth, 1968.
Mountain Rescue Dog, Lutterworth, 1969.
School at Sea, Epworth, 1970.
The Gold of Fast Castle, Lutterworth, 1970.
Flodden Field, September 9, 1513, Lutterworth, 1970.
Haki the Shetland Pony (teleplay; based on book of same title), BBC-TV, 1971.
The Thames in Story, Epworth, 1971.
Diggers of Lost Treasure, Epworth, 1972.
The Forty-five and Culloden, July 1745 to April 1746, Lutterworth, 1973.
Stories of Old Inns, Epworth, 1973.
Pirate and Admiral: The Story of John Paul Jones, Lutterworth, 1974.
Turk, the Border Collie, Lutterworth, 1975.
(With Dr. Ian Morrison) *Wrecks, Wreckers and Rescuers,* illustrated by Ian Morrison, Lutterworth, 1976.
The Railway Runaways, Blackie & Son, 1977.
The Lost Cave, Blackie & Son, 1978.
Seal Story, Lutterworth, 1979.
Pablos and the Bull, Blackie & Son, 1979.
The Ghosts of Sandeel Bay, Blackie & Son, 1981.

"BRYDON FAMILY" SERIES

The Brydons at Smuggler's Creek, Lutterworth, 1946, edition with new illustrations, 1952.
More Adventures of the Brydons, Lutterworth, 1947, edition with new illustrations, 1952, revised edition, Knight Books, 1971.
The Brydons Go Camping, Lutterworth, 1948.
The Brydons Do Battle, Lutterworth, 1949.
The Brydons in Summer, Lutterworth, 1949, revised edition, Knight Books, 1971.
The Brydons Look for Trouble, Lutterworth, 1950.
The Brydons in a Pickle, Lutterworth, 1950.
Surprises for the Brydons, Lutterworth, 1950.
The Brydons Get Things Going, Lutterworth, 1951, revised edition, Knight Books, 1971.
The Brydons Hunt for Treasure, Lutterworth, 1951.
The Brydons Catch Queer Fish, Lutterworth, 1952.
The Brydons Stick at Nothing, Lutterworth, 1952.
The Brydons Abroad, Lutterworth, 1953.
The Brydons on the Broads, Lutterworth, 1955, revised edition, Knight Books, 1971.
Challenge to the Brydons, Lutterworth, 1956.
The Brydons at Blackpool, Lutterworth, 1960.
The Brydons Go Canoeing, Lutterworth, 1963.

"HERITAGE OF BRITAIN" SERIES

Tales of the North Country, Lutterworth, 1952.
Tales of London, Lutterworth, 1953.
Tales of the Midlands, Lutterworth, 1954.
Tales of Scotland, Lutterworth, 1956.
Look to the West: Tales of Liverpool, Lutterworth, 1957.
Tales of the Islands, Lutterworth, 1959.
Tales of Pirates and Castaways, Lutterworth, 1960.
Tales of the West Country, Lutterworth, 1961.
True Tales of Treasure, Lutterworth, 1962.
Tales of the South Country, Lutterworth, 1962.
True Tales of Escapes, Lutterworth, 1965.
True Tales of Mystery, Lutterworth, 1967.
True Tales of Castles, Lutterworth, 1969.

"DEAN FAMILY" SERIES

The Deans Move In, Lutterworth, 1953.
The Deans Solve a Mystery, Lutterworth, 1954.
The Deans Follow a Clue, Lutterworth, 1954.
The Deans Defy Danger, Lutterworth, 1955.
The Deans Dive for Treasure, Lutterworth, 1956.
The Deans to the Rescue, Lutterworth, 1957.
The Deans' Lighthouse Adventure, Lutterworth, 1959.
The Deans and Mr. Popple, Lutterworth, 1960.
The Deans' Dutch Adventure, Lutterworth, 1962.

OTHER

Also author of numerous radio plays for the BBC-Radio program *Children's Hour* and for BBC-Radio schools' programs.

SIDELIGHTS: Kathleen Fidler began writing for the entertainment of her own children. In fact, she once told *Twentieth-Century Children's Writers* that the "Brydon Family" series "reflected my own happy and simple family life." As her children grew up, her writing reflected the expansion of their interests, along with her own. For example, many of her trips abroad (including an archaeological dig) and several of her books, such as *The Boy with the Bronze Axe* and *Treasure of Ebba,* were inspired by her interest in history and archaeology. Topics for Fidler's children's books include everything from family adventures to historical fiction to animal stories.

In fact, Fidler's animal stories are among her most popular. Many of them, such as *Police Dog, Mountain Rescue Dog, Turk, the Border Collie,* and *Flash the Sheep Dog,* feature canine heroes. In these books, the main characters are hard-working dogs who possess very human qualities. However, *Haki the Shetland Pony* is more about a relationship between an animal and its owner. In this story a fifteen-year-old boy named Adam and his pony, Haki, win an award for performing tricks at the fair. A circus owner on tour through Scotland offers to buy the pony, and hires Adam in the process. Adam and Haki get to see the world together, as they travel with the circus. Fidler's books are described as full of enthusiasm for the people and places of her native England. An example of this is her "Heritage of Britain" series, for which she collected stories, folklore, and anecdotes about historic England. *The Desperate Journey* tells the story of a Scottish family dealing with the challenges of poverty. At the beginning of Britain's industrial era, they sail to Canada in search of a better life. Enthusiastic stories of historic battles are told in *Flodden Field, September 9, 1513* and *The Forty-five and Culloden, July 1745 to April 1746.*

Fidler remains known for her portrayals of ordinary characters (people or animals) in somewhat extraordinary situations. She kept her stories realistic, but exciting. Later in life she wrote stories with her grandchildren in mind, and enjoyed staying in touch with children by speaking at schools and libraries.

BIOGRAPHICAL/CRITICAL SOURCES:

BOOKS

Twentieth-Century Children's Writers, 4th edition, St. James Press, 1995.

PERIODICALS

Booklist, April 1, 1971, p. 663.
New Statesman, November 12, 1971, p. 667.
Observer, December 7, 1975, p. 32.
Publishers Weekly, September 28, 1970, p. 80.
Times Literary Supplement, December 9, 1965, p. 1134; June 6, 1968, p. 581; October 22, 1971, p. 1344; December 8, 1972, p. 1500.

OBITUARIES:

BOOKS

Something about the Author, Volume 45, Gale, 1986.*

* * *

FIGES, Eva 1932-

PERSONAL: Surname is pronounced Fie-jess; born April 15, 1932, in Berlin, Germany; daughter of Emil Eduard (a businessman) and Irma (an artist; maiden name, Cohen) Unger; married John George Figes, July 10, 1954 (divorced, 1963); children: Catherine Jane, Orlando Guy. *Education:* Queen Mary College, University of London, B.A. (with honors), 1953. *Politics:* "Left wing (undogmatic)." *Religion:* None.

ADDRESSES: *Home*—24 Fitzjohns Ave., London NW3 5NB, England. *Agent*—Rogers, Coleridge & White, Ltd, 20 Powis Mews, London W11 1JN, England; Elaine Markson, 64 Greenwich Avenue, New York, NY 10011.

CAREER: Longmans, Green & Co., Ltd., London, England, editor, 1955-57; Weidenfeld & Nicolson, Ltd.,

London, editor, 1962-63; Blackie & Son, Ltd., London, editor, 1964-67; writer, 1967—; Macmillan Women Writers series, co-editor, 1987—.

MEMBER: Writers' Guild.

AWARDS, HONORS: Guardian fiction prize, 1967, for *Winter Journey;* C. Day Lewis fellowship, 1973; Arts Council fellowship, 1977-79; Society of Authors traveling scholarship, 1988; fellow, Queen Mary and Westfield College, 1990.

WRITINGS:

NOVELS

Equinox, Secker & Warburg, 1966.
Winter Journey, Faber, 1967.
Konek Landing, Faber, 1969.
B, Faber, 1972.
Days, Faber, 1974.
Nelly's Version, Secker & Warburg, 1977.
Waking, Pantheon, 1982
Light, Pantheon, 1983.
The Seven Ages, Hamish Hamilton, 1987.
Ghosts, Hamish Hamilton, 1988.
The Tree of Knowledge, Sinclair-Stevenson, 1990.
The Tenancy, Sinclair-Stevenson, 1993.
The Knot, Sinclair-Stevenson (London), 1996.

NONFICTION

Patriarchal Attitudes, Stein & Day, 1970, published as *Patriarchal Attitudes: Women in Society,* Faber, 1970, new edition, MacMillan, 1986.
Tragedy and Social Evolution, John Calder, 1976.
Little Eden: A Child at War (autobiography), Faber, 1978.
Sex and Subterfuge: Women Novelists to 1850, Macmillan, 1982.

CHILDREN'S STORIES

(Translator) *The Musicians of Bremen: Retold,* Blackie & Son, 1967.
The Banger, Lion Press, 1968.
Scribble Sam: A Story, McKay, 1971.

OTHER

(Translator) *The Gadarene Club,* by Martin Walser, Longmans, Green, 1960.
(Translator) *The Old Car,* by Elisabeth Borchers, Blackie (London), 1967.
(Translator) *He and I and the Elephants,* by Bernhard Grzimek, Deutsch-Thames and Hudson (London) and Hill and Wang (New York), 1967.
(Translator) *Little Fadettes,* by George Sand, Blackie, 1967.
(Translator) *A Family Failure,* by Renate Rasp, Calder & Boyars, 1970.
(Translator) *The Deathbringer,* by Manfred von Conta, Calder and Boyars (London), 1971.

Contributor to the *London Observer, Publishers Weekly,* and the *New Review;* contributor to anthologies, including *Woman on Woman,* 1970, *Beyond the Words: Eleven Writers in Search of a New Fiction,* 1975, and *Women's Letters in Wartime, 1450-1945,* Harper Collins, 1993.

SIDELIGHTS: Critics have found novelist Eva Figes's focus on the inner lives of her characters, as well as her rendering of time in fiction, to recall the work of novelist Virginia Woolf. Peter Conradi, in the *Dictionary of Literary Biography,* wrote: "Figes seems sometimes to be painfully relearning lessons which are implicit in the brilliant innovations of Virginia Woolf more than fifty years earlier. Figes shares a commonly held view . . . that the novel must . . . primarily explore the neglected world of the self."

Figes was born to Jewish parents in Berlin, Germany, in 1932 and fled with her family to London when Adolf Hitler rose to power late in the 1930s. In an interview with Michele Field in *Publishers Weekly,* she commented that "it gave me my first moral problem, being told by my parents that the Germans had to be wiped out as a nation because they were so wicked. I kept saying, 'But we're Germans,' and was told, 'No, we're not Germans, we're Jewish.' " Figes chronicled her childhood experiences in her 1978 autobiography *Little Eden: A Child at War.*

Figes first received critical notice with her 1967 novel *Winter Journey,* a depiction of twenty-four hours in the solitary life of an elderly man. Monica Foot of *Books and Bookmen* considered the work "finely and powerfully written" and felt it "is not easy to read or assimilate. But it sticks in the memory like a burr." Although believing some of the novel's allusion "too literary," a *Times Literary Supplement* reviewer called the book a "tight, biting little commentary" and concluded that *Winter Journey* "captures with great sensitivity the lonely indignities of old age." Stephen Wall of the *Observer Review* agreed that several allusions appeared "unnecessarily literary" but approved of Figes's treatment of the stream-of-consciousness technique. Wall commented that *Winter Journey* "is a short book, but its slenderness is nevertheless the product of an authentic talent."

Patriarchal Attitudes, Figes' historical analysis of male dominance and the subjugation of women in marriage—as well as in other social, political, and intellectual contexts—has come to be regarded as a classic of feminist literature. The study is "full of very interesting observations," according to Kathy Mulherin of *Commonweal.* And although Mulherin objected that "the end does not live up to the rest . . . the last chapter is muddled and empty," she nevertheless regarded *Patriarchal Attitudes* as "a good book." Writer Gore Vidal observed in *New York Review of Books* that *Patriarchal Attitudes* "can be set beside John Stuart Mill's celebrated review of the subject [*The Subjection of Women,* 1869] and not seem shoddy or self-serving."

Carol Rumens described the structure of Figes's seventh novel, *Waking,* in the *Times Literary Supplement:* "Echoing perhaps the Shakespearean 'seven stages' [espoused by Jacques in *As You Like It*], there are seven chapters, each dedicated to a different stage of a woman's life—from idyllic early childhood to final illness. Each 'age' begins with the experience of waking from a night's sleep, a useful fictional device which allows the central character to be unusually receptive to exploration of an inner world." A London *Times* critic called the novel "brilliant," adding: "The insights are poignant and funny. The revelations are tender and cruel. The observations are incisive and profound. . . . There is only one line of dialogue in the whole of the book, yet by some miracle the voices of the characters are distinctive and clear." But Rumens perceived several weaknesses in *Waking,* one of which was that "it never quite solves the dilemma of whether the unnamed figure is to represent suffering Everywoman or to emerge as truly individualized." Another was that, because many of the images used in the novel are archetypal, they seemed somewhat predictable. Lastly, Rumens claimed that the book (which is eighty-eight pages in length) seemed "too short, too small to fulfill its potential. It looks almost as if the narrative has been ruthlessly cut, perhaps through a wish to conform to the seven ages prototype." Nevertheless, Rumens considered *Waking* a "sorrowful and often beautifully written work that raises painful questions about women's place in the family and society."

Calling Figes's next novel, *Light,* "a stronger, more vivid and far more interesting" work than *Waking,* Joyce Carol Oates wrote in the *New York Times Book Review:* "Eva Figes's luminous prose poem of a novel . . . is clearly descended from [Virginia] Woolf 's great experimental novels. Technique is all or nearly all in this fastidiously wrought narrative of a day in the life of Claude Monet in the summer of 1900." Michael Kernan, a contributor to the *Washington Post Book World,* called *Light* "beautifully crafted," commenting that even the reader who is unfamiliar with Monet and his works will find it "enough to see into the mind of an artist . . . surrounded . . . by the riotous flowers, by the loves and griefs and flitting concerns of the people about him, by the evanescent light that bathes them."

Similarly, *The Tree of Knowledge* provides a fictionalized account of an historical character. The marriages and children of poet John Milton are featured in what *New York Times Book Review* contributor Linda Simon referred to as "a feminist reading of both Milton and his times." Simon noted that Figes creates "a world in which women's aspirations had no means of fulfillment, a world peopled by powerless, voiceless women and powerful, articulate—but blind—men."

BIOGRAPHICAL/CRITICAL SOURCES:

BOOKS

Contemporary Literary Criticism, Volume 31, Gale, 1985.
Contemporary Novelists, 6th edition, St. James Press, 1996.
Dictionary of Literary Biography, Volume 14: *British Novelists since 1960,* Gale, 1983.

PERIODICALS

Books and Bookmen, June, 1967.
Choice, May, 1987; October, 1991.
Commonweal, April 2, 1971.
Los Angeles Times, September 23, 1983; February 13, 1987; January 22, 1989. *Los Angeles Times Book Review,* September 25, 1988; March 31, 1991.
Ms., March, 1987.
New Statesman, May 23, 1986; September 25, 1987; May 13, 1988.
New York Review of Books, July 22, 1971; May 14, 1982.
New York Times, February 23, 1982.
New York Times Book Review, April 28, 1968; February 28, 1982; October 16, 1983; February 22, 1987; August 16, 1987; September 25, 1988; January 8, 1989; June 16, 1991.
Observer, May 4, 1986; May 15, 1988; September 23, 1990; March 21, 1993; November 27, 1994; March 17, 1996.

Observer Review, April 9, 1967.
Publishers Weekly, January 16, 1987; July 22, 1988.
Times (London), January 22, 1981.
Times Literary Supplement, April 27, 1967; July 31, 1970; January 23, 1981; August 26, 1983; May 16, 1986; June 3-9, 1988; October 19, 1990; March 26, 1993; March 15, 1996.
Village Voice, January 24, 1989.
Washington Post, October 2, 1988.
Washington Post Book World, March 13, 1982; October 23, 1983; February 21, 1987; October 2, 1988; April 7, 1991.*

* * *

FIGUEROA, John
FIGUEROA, John J(oseph Maria)

* * *

FIGUEROA, John J(oseph Maria) 1920-

PERSONAL: Born August 4, 1920, in Kingston, Jamaica; immigrated to England, 1979, dual British and Jamaican citizenship; son of Rupert Aston (in insurance sales) and Isclena (a teacher; maiden name, Palomino) Figueroa; married Dorothy Grace Murray Alexander (a teacher and author), August 3, 1944; children: Dorothy Anna Jarvis, Catherine, J. Peter, Robert P. D., Mark F. E., Esther M., Thomas Theodore (deceased). *Education:* George's College (Kingston, Jamaica), 1931-37; College of the Holy Cross, A.B. (cum laude), 1942; London University, teacher's diploma, 1947, M.A., 1950; graduate study at University of Indiana—Bloomington, 1964. *Religion:* Catholic. *Avocational interests:* Travel, Creole linguistics, cricket, Caribbean studies, music, painting, lay theology and liturgy.

ADDRESSES: Home—77 Station Rd., Woburn Sands, Buckinghamshire MK17 8SH, England.

CAREER: Water Commission, Kingston, Jamaica, clerk, 1937-38; teacher at secondary schools in Jamaica, 1942-46, and London, England, 1946-48; University of London, Institute of Education, London, lecturer in English and philosophy, 1948-53; University College of the West Indies, Kingston, senior lecturer, 1953-57, professor of education, 1957-73, dean of faculty of education, 1966-69; University of Puerto Rico, Rio Piedras and Cayey, professor of English and consultant to the president, 1971-73; El Centro Caribeno de Estudios Postgraduados, Carolina, Puerto Rico, professor of humanities and consultant in community education, 1973-76; University of Jos, Jos, Nigeria, professor of education and acting dean, 1976-80; Bradford College, Yorkshire, England, visiting professor of humanities and consultant in multicultural education, 1980; Open University, Milton Keynes, England, member of Third World studies course team, 1980-83; Manchester Education Authority, Manchester, England, adviser on multicultural studies, West Indian language and literature, and Caribbean heritage students, 1983-85; fellow at Warwick University's Center of Caribbean studies, 1988. British Broadcasting Corporation, London, sports reporter and general broadcaster for programs including *Reflections*" and poetry readings, 1946-60. Consultant to Ford and Carnegie foundations; consultant to Organization of American States and to West Indian governments. External examiner, Africa and West Indies. Has lectured and read his poetry in Africa, Canada, Europe, South America, the United Kingdom, and the United States.

MEMBER: Linguistic Society of America, Caribbean Studies Association, Society for the Study of Caribbean Affairs, Athenaeum Club.

AWARDS, HONORS: British Council fellowship, 1946-47; Carnegie fellowship, 1960; L.H.D. from College of the Holy Cross, 1960; Guggenheim fellowship, 1964; Lilly Foundation grant, 1973; Institute of Jamaica Medal, 1980; Gold medal Bourg-en-Bresse for poetry about L'Eglise du Brou, 1990; Musgrave Silver medal for contribution to literature, 1993; Rockefeller fellowship to Villa Serbelloni, Como, Italy, 1993.

WRITINGS:

POETRY

Blue Mountain Peak (poetry and prose), Gleaner, 1944.
Love Leaps Here, [privately printed], 1962.
Ignoring Hurts: Poems (includes "Cosmopolitan Pig" and "The Grave Digger"), introduction by Frank Getlein, Three Continents Press, 1976.
The Chase 1941-1989, Peepal Tree Press (Leeds), 1991.
The Project, art by Kirk Albert, lettering by Bob Lappan, Paradox Press (New York City), 1996.

EDITOR

Caribbean Voices: An Anthology of West Indian Poetry, Evans, Volume 1: *Dreams and Visions,* 1966, second edition, 1982, Volume 2: *The Blue Horizons,* 1970, published in one volume, Evans, 1971, Luce, 1973.

Society, Schools, and Progress in the West Indies, Franklin Book Co., 1971.

(And author of introduction) Sonny Oti, *Dreams and Realities: Six One-Act Comedies,* J. West, 1978.

(With Donald E. Herdeck and others) *Caribbean Writers: A Bio- Bibliographical Critical Encyclopedia,* Three Continents, 1979.

An Anthology of African and Caribbean Writing in English, Heinemann, 1982.

Third World Studies: Caribbean Sampler, Open University Press, 1983.

OTHER

Staffing and Examinations in British Caribbean Secondary Schools: A Report of the Conference of the Caribbean Heads, Evans, c. 1964.

(Author of introduction) Edgar Mittelhoelzer, *A Morning at the Office,* Heinemann, 1974.

(With David Sutcliffe) *System in Black Language,* Taylor & Francis, 1992.

Author with Ed Milner of television plays, "St. Lucia: Peoples and Celebrations" series, British Broadcasting Corporation, 1983—. Translator of works by Horace. Contributor to *Poems from the West Indies,* edited by Jose A. Jarvis, Kraus Reprint, 1954; *Whose Language?,* 1985, and *The Caribbean in Europe,* Cass, 1986; contributor to periodicals, including *Commonweal, Dorenkamp, London Magazine, Universities Quarterly, Caribbean Studies, Cross Currents, Caribbean Quarterly,* and *Commonwealth Essays and Studies.* General editor of "Caribbean Writers" series for Heinemann. Editor of recording, *Poets of the West Indies Reading Their Own Works,* Caedmon, 1972.

SIDELIGHTS: West Indian poet and scholar John J. Figueroa is known for his original verse, the anthologies he has edited, and his critical and academic writings. He draws on classical literature, such as the poetry of Virgil, Sappho, and Horace (whom he has translated), as well as on the rhythms of Jamaican speech and calypso music for his poems, which at their best are regarded as sensual, spiritual, and unusually well crafted.

In *Contemporary Poets,* Howard Sergeant described Figueroa as a poet who "is acutely aware of the physical world and responds to contrasts in color and even to contrasts in modes of living. He constantly seems to be relating one thing to another, the known to the unfamiliar, darkness to light, and rough to smooth." Sergeant divides Figueroa's work into the following five broad categories: reflective poems, poems with a religious theme, insight poems arising out of experience in other countries, personal and anecdotal poems, and translations. Sergeant concludes his observations by noting that such poems as "On Hearing Dvorak's New World Symphony," "Other Spheres," "Green Is the Color of Hope," "The Three Epiphanies," and "From the Caribbean with Love" demonstrate that Figueroa's best work is in reflective and philosophical poetry.

Figueroa commented: "It has been good to have grown up with and to have been part of the development and flowering of Caribbean literature, painting, and music. But it is a pity that there is so little appreciation of the *variety* as well as the achievement in these fields. People are much too quick to look for something they call identity, and to disown anyone who does not abjectly follow the tribe on the grounds that right or wrong doesn't matter—all that matters is whether it's 'one of us' who is involved.

"I have also been very lucky to have traveled and lived among various peoples in Africa, Europe, and the Americas, and to have seen the kinds of space explorations which have not, alas, made it clearer to dwellers on the Earth that caring for one's neighbor is not 'other worldly' but an imperative for life, and for living more abundantly."

BIOGRAPHICAL/CRITICAL SOURCES:

BOOKS

Contemporary Poets, 6th edition, St. James Press, 1996.

PERIODICALS

Times Literary Supplement, January 28, 1972.

World Literature Today, spring, 1977; spring, 1993, p. 429.*

* * *

FINCH, Robert (Charles) 1943-

PERSONAL: Born June 16, 1943, in North Arlington, NJ; son of Charles Wesley (a chemical supervisor) and Fritzi (a university bookstore manager; maiden name, Wasserburger) Finch; married Elizabeth Ann Wolford (a trust officer), September 19, 1964; children: Christopher, Katherine. *Education:* Harvard College, A.B. (cum laude), 1967; Indiana University, M.A., 1969. *Politics:* Independent. *Avocational interests:* Choral singing, chamber music, clamming, walking, sailing, bicycling, cross-country skiing, cooking, family.

ADDRESSES: Home and Office—R.R. 1 Red Top Rd., Brewster, MA 02631.

CAREER: Oregon State University, Corvallis, instructor in English, 1969-71; carpenter in Brewster, MA, 1971-75; freelance writer, 1975—; Cape Cod Museum of Natural History, Cape Cod, MA, director of publications, 1982-86. *Orion Nature Quarterly,* advisory board member; Brewster Conservation Commission, co-chair, 1980-87; Brewster Land Acquisition Commission, co- chair, 1984-87; Cape Cod Community College, West Barnstable, MA, part-time instructor, 1972-74.

MEMBER: Chatham Chorale (board member, 1988—).

AWARDS, HONORS: Conservationist of the Year, Brewster Conservation Trust, 1986 and 1987; commendation, Association for the Preservation of Cape Cod and United States Environmental Protection Agency, 1987; Environmental Service Award, Massachusetts Association of Conservation Commissions, 1989.

WRITINGS:

Common Ground: A Naturalist's Cape Cod (essays), illustrations by Amanda Cannell, David Godine, 1981.

The Primal Place, Norton, 1983.

Outlands: Journeys to the Outer Edges of Cape Cod (essays), David Godine, 1986.

(Editor with John Elder) *The Norton Book of Nature Writing,* Norton, 1990.

The Cape Itself, photographs by Ralph S. MacKenzie, Norton, 1991.

Cape Cod National Seashore Handbook, National Park Service, 1992.

(Editor) *A Place Apart: A Cape Cod Reader,* Norton (New York City), 1993.

Cape Cod: Its Natural and Cultural History: A Guide to Cape Cod National Seashore, Massachusetts, National Park Service, U.S. Department of the Interior (Washington, DC), 1993.

The Smithsonian Guides to Natural America: Southern New England—Massachusetts, Connecticut, and Rhode Island, photography by Jonathan Wallen, preface by Thomas E. Lovejoy, Smithsonian Books (Washington, DC), 1996.

Editor of an anthology of Cape Cod literature, Norton, in press. Advisory editor and contributor to *On Nature: Essays on Nature, Landscape, and Natural History,* edited by Daniel Halpern, North Point, 1987. Contributor to anthologies, including *Penguin Book of Contemporary American Essays,* 1989; *Words from the Land,* 1988; *Bread Loaf Anthology of Contemporary American Essays,* 1989; and *The Norton Reader,* 1992. Author of introductions to books, including Henry David Thoreau's *Cape Cod,* Parnassus Imprints, 1984, Aldo Leopold's *Sand County Almanac,* Oxford, 1987, and Henry Williamson's *Tarka the Otter,* Beacon Press, 1990. Author of weekly columns for several Cape Cod Newspapers, 1975-82; editor of *The Cape Naturalist,* 1973-82. Contributor to periodicals, including *New England Monthly, New York Times, New Age Journal, Washington Post, Boston Globe, Family Circle, Georgia Review, Antaeus,* and *Orion Nature Quarterly.*

ADAPTATIONS: Soundings: A Cape Cod Notebook, a recording of the author reading selections from his work, was released on audiocassette by Audio Press, 1989.

SIDELIGHTS: Robert Finch is a New England-area writer, specializing in nature and conservation topics. His columns for newspapers in the Cape Cod, Massachusetts area were the basis of his first book, *Common Ground: A Naturalist's Cape Cod.* The work, a collection of essays, is structured around the author's observations of the natural landscape and wildlife in his community. *New York Times* critic Christopher Lehmann-Haupt praised Finch's writing as "first-rate," remarking that the volume "avoid[s] the pitfalls of preciousness and inertness that so often cripple nature writing." The critic added that "*Common Ground* is an unusual specimen of the endangered species of attractive, well-made books."

In his second work, *The Primal Place,* Finch again takes a close look at the natural and human history of his immediate neighborhood on Cape Cod, examining how the two are intertwined. The reader accompanies him as his feet and thoughts wander, ruminating on the cyclical nature of wildlife and seasons, clamming on the shore, or passing several hours in a rowboat on a pond. In the *New York Times Book Review,* Alec Wilkinson commented that "[Finch's] temperament is introspective, his prose fleshy, sometimes poetic, sometimes sentimental and occasionally rhapsodic." Finch's third book, *Outlands: Journeys to the Outer Edges of Cape Cod,* follows the author even further on his exploratory outings. He relates incidents—nearly being swept away by the tide during a storm or facing a panicked herd of seals. Many of these essays center around humanity's specific relation to the environment, and the idea that people are also at the mercy of its capriciousness. *New York Times* critic Lehmann-Haupt noted that Finch's writing "gives us readers a tactile sense of the land that mere esthetic appreciation usually fails to do."

Finch told *CA:* "Most of my published writing has been rooted in the Cape Cod landscape; however, the issues raised by our relationship to nature here seem universal ones. It has been helpful to me to work in an area with a rich literary tradition; in particular, the books of John Hay (my neighbor) helped show me the possibilities of the genre. In recent years I have become increasingly interested in the assumptions and unspoken questions underlying most nature writing, e.g., what constitutes our deepest attraction to nature and what is the relationship of human values, language, and concepts to natural experience. I have also become increasingly interested in Newfoundland and its people and am eager to explore some of these questions in a very different landscape."

BIOGRAPHICAL/CRITICAL SOURCES:

PERIODICALS

Los Angeles Times Book Review, July 3, 1994, p. 9.
New York Times, July 17, 1981; June 27, 1986.
New York Times Book Review, August 2, 1981, p. 13; July 31, 1983, p. 8.
Publishers Weekly, May 30, 1986, p. 52; February 23, 1990, p. 212; April 26, 1993, p. 67.
Washington Post Book World, May 13, 1990, p. 13; May 31, 1992, p. 8.*

* * *

FINE, Anne 1947-

PERSONAL: Born December 7, 1947, in Leicester, England; daughter of Brian (a chief scientific experimental officer) and Mary Laker; married Kit Fine (a university professor), 1968; children: two daughters. *Education:* University of Warwick, B.A. (with honors), 1968.

ADDRESSES: *Home*—County Durham, England. *Agent*—Murray Pollinger, 222 Old Brompton Rd., London SW5 0BZ, England.

CAREER: English teacher at Cardinal Wiseman Girls' Secondary School, 1968-70; Oxford Committee for Famine Relief, Oxford, England, assistant information officer, 1970-71; Saughton Jail, Edinburgh, Scotland, teacher, 1971-72; freelance writer, 1973—. Volunteer for Amnesty International.

AWARDS, HONORS: *Guardian/Kestrel* Award nominations, 1978, for *The Summer-House Loon,* 1983, for *The Granny Project,* and 1987, for *Madame Doubtfire;* Scottish Arts Council Book Award, 1986, for *The Killjoy; Observer* Prize for Teenage Fiction nomination, 1987, for *Madame Doubtfire;* Smarties (6-8) Award, 1989, for *Bill's New Frock; Guardian* Award for Children's Fiction, 1989, and Carnegie Medal, 1990, both for *Goggle Eyes;* Children's Author of the Year, British Book Awards, 1990; School Library Journal Best Book of the year and International Reading Association Young Adult Choice citations, 1991, for *My War with Goggle-Eyes;* Carnegie Medal, 1992, and Whitbread Children's Novel award, 1993, both for *Flour Babies;* Whitbread Children's Book of the year, 1996, for *The Tulip Touch.*

WRITINGS:

FICTION FOR CHILDREN

The Summer-House Loon, Methuen, 1978, Crowell, 1979.
The Other, Darker Ned, Methuen, 1979.
The Stone Menagerie, Methuen, 1980.
Round behind the Ice-House, Methuen, 1981.
The Granny Project, Farrar, Straus, 1983.
Scaredy-Cat, illustrated by Vanessa Julian-Ottie, Heinemann, 1985.
Anneli the Art Hater, Methuen, 1986.
Madame Doubtfire, Hamish Hamilton, 1987, published as *Alias Madame Doubtfire,* Little, Brown, 1988.
Crummy Mummy and Me, illustrated by David Higham, Deutsch, 1988.
A Pack of Liars, Hamish Hamilton, 1988.
My War with Goggle Eyes, Little, Brown, 1989 (published in England as *Goggle Eyes,* Hamish Hamilton, 1989).
Stranger Danger?, illustrated by Jean Baylis, Hamish Hamilton, 1989.
Bill's New Frock, illustrated by Philippe Dupasquier, Methuen, 1989.
A Sudden Puff of Glittering Smoke, illustrated by Adriano Gon, Picadilly Press, 1989.
Only a Show, illustrated by Valerie Littlewood, Hamish Hamilton, 1990.
A Sudden Swirl of Icy Wind, illustrated by Higham, Picadilly Press, 1990.

The Country Pancake, illustrated by Dupasquier, Methuen, 1990.
Poor Monty, illustrated by Clara Vulliamy, Clarion Books, 1991.
A Sudden Glow of Gold, Picadilly Press, 1991.
The Book of the Banshee, Hamish Hamilton, 1991, Little, Brown, 1992.
The Worst Child I Ever Had, illustrated by Vulliamy, Hamish Hamilton, 1991. *Design-A-Pram,* Heinemann, 1991.
The Angel of Nitshill Road, Methuen, 1992.
The Same Old Story Every Year, Hamish Hamilton, 1992.
The Haunting of Pip Parker, Walker, 1992.
The Chicken Gave It to Me, illustrated by Cynthia Fisher, Joy Street (Boston), 1993.
Flour Babies, Little, Brown (Boston), 1994.
The Diary of a Killer Cat, illustrated by Steve Cox, Puffin, 1996.
Countdown, illustrated by Higham, Heinemann, 1996.
How to Write Really Badly, illustrated by Dupasquier, Methuen, 1996.
Care for Henry, illustrated by Paul Howard, Walker, 1997.

OTHER

The Granny Project (play; based on her story), Collins, 1986.
The Killjoy (adult novel), Bantam (London), 1986, Mysterious Press, 1987.
Taking the Devil's Advice (adult novel), Viking, 1990.
In Cold Domain, Viking, 1994.
Step by Wicked Step: A Novel, Little, Brown, 1996.
The Tulip Touch: A Novel, Little, Brown, 1997.

Also author of radio play *The Captain's Court Case,* 1987. Contributor of short stories to periodicals.

SIDELIGHTS: In such children's books as *The Summer-House Loon, Alias Madame Doubtfire,* and *My War with Goggle-Eyes,* novelist Anne Fine brings a keen comic insight to bear on family problems. "I was brought up in the country, in a family of five girls, including one set of triplets," Fine once related. "My husband was brought up in a family of six boys, including twins. Family relationships have always interested me and it is with the close members of their families that the characters in my books are either getting, or not getting, along."

Fine's first book, *The Summer-House Loon,* presents teenager Ione Muffet, the daughter of a blind college professor who is sometimes oblivious to her. The novel portrays a single, farcical day in Ione's life as she attempts to match her father's secretary with an intelligent yet fumbling graduate student. Calling the novel "original and engaging . . . , mischievous, inventive and very funny," *Times Literary Supplement* writer Peter Hollindale praises Fine for "a fine emotional delicacy which sensitively captures, among all the comic upheaval, the passionate solitude of adolescence." *The Summer-House Loon* is "not just a funny book, although it is certainly that," Marcus Crouch of *Junior Bookshelf* likewise comments. "Here is a book with deep understanding, wisdom and compassion. It tosses the reader between laughter and tears with expert dexterity."

A sequel, *The Other, Darker Ned,* finds Ione organizing a charity benefit for famine victims. "Through [Ione's] observations of other people" in both these works, Margery Fisher comments in *Growing Point,* "we have that delighted sense of recognition which comes in reading novels whose characters burst noisily and eccentrically out of the pages." While these books "are not for everyone, requiring a certain amount of sophistication," Anthea Bell remarks in *Twentieth-Century Children's Writers,* for readers "in command of that sophistication they are stylishly lighthearted entertainment."

Some of Fine's next novels directly examine such social issues as homelessness and care of the elderly. *The Stone Menagerie,* in which a boy discovers that a couple is living on the grounds of a mental hospital, is "devised with a strict economy of words, an acute sense of personality and a shrewd, ironic humour that once more shows Anne Fine to be one of the sharpest and humorous observers of the human condition writing today for the young," Fisher writes in *Growing Point.* And in using humor while "tackling the aged and infirm," Fine's *The Granny Project* "against all the odds contrives to be both audacious and heart- warming," Charles Fox remarks in *New Statesman.* The story of how four siblings conspire to keep their grandmother out of a nursing home by making her care a school assignment, *The Granny Project* is "mordantly funny, ruthlessly honest, yet compassionate in its concern," Nancy C. Hammond notes in *Horn Book.*

Alias Madame Doubtfire brings a more farcical approach to a serious theme, this time the breaking up of a family. "Novels about divorce for children are rarely funny," Roger Sutton observes in the *Bulletin of the Center for Children's Books,* but Fine's work "will have readers laughing from the first page." To gain more time with his children, out-of-work actor Daniel poses as Madame Doubtfire, a supremely capable housekeeper, and gets a job in his ex-wife Miranda's household. Miranda remains blind to her housekeeper's identity while the children quickly catch on, leading to several amusing incidents. But "beneath the farce, the story deals with a serious subject," Mark Geller states in *New York Times Book Review:* "the pain children experience when their parents divorce and then keep on battling." "The comedy of disguise allows the author to skate over the sexual hates and impulses inherent in the situation without lessening the candour of her insights into the irreconcilable feelings of both adults and children," Fisher concludes. "Readers of the teenage novel, weary of perfunctory blue-prints of reality, should be thankful to Anne Fine for giving them such nourishing food for thought within an entertaining piece of fiction."

Crummy Mummy and Me and *A Pack of Liars* "are two more books whose prime intent is to make young people laugh," Chris Powling of the *Times Educational Supplement* observes. "Both exploit the standard comic techniques of taking a familiar situation, turning it on its head, and shaking it vigorously to see what giggles and insights fall into the reader's lap." *A Pack of Liars* recounts how a school assignment to write to a pen pal turns into a mystery of sorts, while *Crummy Mummy and Me* presents a role-reversal in the relationship between an irresponsible mother and her capable daughter. "Details of the plots, though neatly worked out, may sometimes seem a little farfetched in the abstract," Bell notes; "in practice, however, the sheer comic verve of the writing carries them off." Powling agrees, commenting that "once again the narrative shamelessly favours ingenuity over plausibility on the pretty safe assumption that a reader can't complain effectively while grinning broadly." Both books, the critic concludes, "offer welcome confirmation that humour is closer to humanity than apostles of high seriousness care to admit."

In *My War with Goggle-Eyes,* Fine offers yet another "comic yet perceptive look at life after marriage," Ilene Cooper states in *Booklist.* From the opening, in which young Kitty relates to a schoolmate how her mother's boyfriend "Goggle-Eyes" came into her life, "to the happy-ever-after-maybe ending, Fine conveys a story about relationships filled with humor that does not ridicule and sensitivity that is not cloying," Susan Schuller comments in *School Library Journal.* In showing how Kitty gradually learns to accept her mother's new relationship, "Anne Fine writes some of the funniest—and truest—family fight scenes to be found," Sutton observes in *Bulletin of the Center for Children's Books.* The result is "a book that is thoroughly delightful to read," Schuller concludes.

Fine has also written fiction for adults, including the award-winning novel *The Killjoy.* Unlike the sharply witty portraits of family life of her children's books, *The Killjoy* "is an unsettling tale of suspense and a horrific psychological study of a suffering, deformed man," as Elena Brunet describes it in the *Los Angeles Times Book Review.* In detailing the twisted, increasingly debasing relationship between a physically scarred professor and a student, Fine "never falters," *New York Times* critic John Gross comments. "You feel that every aspect of the drama has been thought through and fully imagined, that every detail belongs in its place." "Fine happily eschews generalisations in favour of a zest for understanding human particulars," Valentine Cunningham comments in the *Observer.* "It promises great fictional things to come."

BIOGRAPHICAL/CRITICAL SOURCES:

BOOKS

Authors & Artists for Young Adults, Volume 20, Gale, 1997.

Children's Literature Review, Volume 25, Gale, 1991, pp. 27-36.

Something about the Author Autobiography Series, Volume 15, Gale, 1993.

Twentieth-Century Children's Writers, 3rd edition, 1989; 4th edition, 1995; St. James Press.

PERIODICALS

Booklist, April 15, 1989, p. 1465.

Bulletin of the Center for Children's Books, April, 1988, p. 155; May, 1989, p. 222.

Growing Point, September, 1980, p. 3756; September, 1987, p. 4858; September, 1988, p. 5037; May, 1990, pp. 5343-44.

Horn Book, October, 1983, p. 573.

Junior Bookshelf, August, 1978, pp. 202-203.

Los Angeles Times Book Review, March 13, 1988, p. 14.

New Statesman, December 2, 1983, p. 26; May 2, 1986, p. 27; June 5, 1987, p. 35.

New York Times, March 27, 1987, p. 21.

New York Times Book Review, May 1, 1988, p. 34; May 22, 1994, p. 23; June 5, 1994, p. 27; December 4, 1994, p. 69.

New Yorker, May 18, 1987, p. 119.

Observer, May 4, 1986, p. 23; December 20, 1987, p. 20; April 3, 1988, p. 43; April 2, 1989, p. 44; May

13, 1990, p. 58; November 24, 1991, p. 8; July 10, 1994, p. 18; July 17, 1994, p. 15; November 20, 1994, p. 11; April 13, 1997, p. 18.
School Library Journal, June, 1988, p. 104; May, 1989, p. 104.
Spectator, July 4, 1987, pp. 34-36.
Times Educational Supplement, June 3, 1988, p. 49.
Times Literary Supplement, July 7, 1978, p. 767; November 20, 1981, p. 1355; March 29, 1985, p. 354; June 22, 1990, p. 674; November 4, 1994, p. 24.
Wilson Library Bulletin, February, 1990, pp. 84-85.*

* * *

FLYNN, Robert (Lopez) 1932-

PERSONAL: Born April 12, 1932, in Chillicothe, TX; son of James Emmitt (a farmer and stockperson) and Gladys (Wilkinson) Flynn; married Jean Sorrels (a librarian and biographer), June 1, 1953; children: Deirdre Siobhan Flynn Bass, Brigid Erin (deceased). *Education:* Baylor University, B.A., 1954, M.A., 1956. *Politics:* "Independent (but Democrat since Nixon)." *Religion:* Baptist.

ADDRESSES: Agent—Agnes Birnbaum, Blecker Associates, 532 LaGuardia, No. 617, New York, NY 10012.

CAREER: Gardener-Webb College, Boiling Springs, NC, instructor, 1957-59; Baylor University, Waco, TX, assistant professor, 1959-63; Trinity University, San Antonio, TX, assistant professor of drama, became professor and novelist-in-residence, 1963—. *Military service:* U.S. Marine Corps, 1950-52; became corporal.

MEMBER: Writers Guild of America, PEN, Texas Institute of Letters (president, 1992-94).

AWARDS, HONORS: Special Jury Award, Theatre of Nations, 1964, for *Journey to Jefferson;* Jesse Jones Award, Texas Institute of Letters, and Western Heritage Award, Cowboy Hall of Fame, both 1968, for *North to Yesterday;* Spur Award, Western Writers of America, for *Wanderer Springs.*

WRITINGS:

North to Yesterday, Knopf (New York City), 1963.
In the House of the Lord, Knopf, 1968.
The Sounds of Rescue, The Signs of Hope, Knopf, 1970.
And Holy Is His Name, Dimension (Denville, NJ), 1983.
Seasonal Rain and Other Stories, Corona (San Antonio, TX), 1984.
Wanderer Springs: A Novel, Texas Christian University Press (Fort Worth), 1987.
A Personal War in Vietnam, Texas A & M University Press (College Station), 1989.
When I Was Just Your Age, University of North Texas Press, 1990.
The Last Klick: A Novel, Baskerville (Dallas), 1994.
Living with the Hyenas: Short Stories, Texas Christian University Press, 1995.

Also author of *The Stars in Their Courses* and *The Devils Tiger,* both 1996. Author of play, *Journey to Jefferson,* produced by Dallas Theater Center, 1964, and of television script, "Cowboy Legacy," for American Broadcasting Company (ABC-TV). Author of short storiespublished in *Saturday Evening Post* and other periodicals.

SIDELIGHTS: Twentieth-Century Western Writers contributor Mark Busby called Robert Flynn's *North to Yesterday* a masterpiece, citing several reasons for the accolade: "Firstly, it is beautifully written, full of excellent description and incisive characterization. Secondly, it demonstrates a comic genius not oftenfound previously in literature about the West. Thirdly, its ambivalence toward the passing of the older western values connects it with some of the best post-World War II works about the West, books William Bloodworth calls "Literary" or "Off-Trail Westerns," such as Larry McMurtry's *Horseman, Pass By* and Edward Abbey's *The Brave Cowboy,* as well as the "New Westerns" of the 1960s like Thomas Berger's *Little Big Man* and E. L. Doctorow's *Welcome to Hard Times.* Finally its combined use of a journey, a regional setting, individual characters' obsessions, and a comic treatment of human folly becoming heroic suggests its imaginative connection with William Faulkner's *As I Lay Dying.* Flynn, in fact, won a Special Jury award, Theater of Nations, for his 1964 adaptation of Faulkner's *As I Lay Dying* called *Journey to Jefferson.*

Brian Garfield called *North to Yesterday* "a powerful first novel . . . a thoughtful, tragicomic parable of all America . . . and ungentle satire on the foolishness of those who live in the past, as well as the blindness of those who turn their backs on it."

A *Best Sellers* critic gave similarly high praise to *The Sounds of Rescue, The Signs of Hope:* "Despite the fact that my natural reading interest would strongly deter me from reading this or any other 'war' novel I was hooked on the first paragraph of this book and read it through in an almost uninterrupted single sitting. I read totally immersed, with pity, horror, pain, compassion, disbelief, . . . wishing I had never started, unable to stop. This is a moving and, I suspect, unforgettable story of a man revealed to his very marrow, to the deepest center of his *self,* an average young man, no hero, no superman."

A *Publishers Weekly* review of *Living with the Hyenas* called Flynn's prose "bare and simple . . . a joy to read," but criticized the stories for stereotypical characters and endings in which the author is "pushing for meaning, rather than allowing it to emerge organically."

BIOGRAPHICAL/CRITICAL SOURCES:

BOOKS

Twentieth-Century Western Writers, 2nd edition, St. James Press, 1991.

PERIODICALS

Best Sellers, June 15, October 1, 1970.
Library Journal, March 15, 1994.
New York Times Book Review, June 25, 1967; March 30, 1969; October 11, 1987; October 29, 1995.
Publishers Weekly, September 12, 1986; August 7, 1987; September 1, 1989; September 4, 1995.
Saturday Review, July 22, 1967.
Time, October 5, 1970.*

* * *

FORD, R(obert) A(rthur) D(ouglass) 1915-
(Robert A. D. Ford)

PERSONAL: Born January 8, 1915, in Ottawa, Ontario, Canada; son of Arthur Rutherford (a journalist) and May Lavinia (Scott) Ford; married Maria Thereza Gomes, June 27, 1946 (deceased). *Education:* University of Western Ontario, B.A., 1938; Cornell University, M.A., 1939.

ADDRESSES: *Home*—La Poivriere, Randan 63310, France.

CAREER: *Gazette,* Montreal, Quebec, reporter, 1938; Cornell University, Ithaca, NY, instructor in history, 1938-40; Canadian Department of External Affairs, Ottawa, Ontario, third secretary, 1940-41; Canadian Embassy, Rio de Janeiro, Brazil, third secretary, 1941-45; Canada House, London, England, second secretary, 1945-46, first secretary, 1947-49; Canadian Embassy, Moscow, Soviet Union, second secretary, 1946-47; Canadian Department of External Affairs, Ottawa, first secretary for United Nations Affairs, 1949-51; Canadian Embassy, Moscow, charge d'affaires, 1951-54; Canadian Department of External Affairs, Ottawa, head of European division, 1954-57; ambassador to Columbia, 1957-58, ambassador to Yugoslavia, 1959-61, ambassador to United Arab Republic (now Arab Republic of Egypt) and the Sudan, 1961-63, ambassador to the Soviet Union in Moscow, 1964-80, dean of diplomatic corps in Moscow, 1971-80, and ambassador to Mongolia, 1974-80. Special advisor to the Canadian Government on East-West relations, 1980-84; member of the Independent Commission on Disarmament and Security Issues (Palme Commission), 1980; board member, International Institute of Geopolitics; advisor, Canadian Institute for Global Security.

MEMBER: League of Canadian Poets, France-Canada Association, Cercle des Ecrivains Bourbonnais.

AWARDS, HONORS: Governor General's Award, 1957, for *A Window on the North;* D.Litt. from University of Western Ontario, 1965; Companion of Order of Canada, 1971; gold medal from Professional Institute of Public Service of Canada, 1971; LL.D. from University of Toronto, 1987.

WRITINGS:

POETRY

A Window on the North, Ryerson, 1956.
The Solitary City: Poems and Translations, McClelland & Stewart, 1969.
Holes in Space, Hounslow Press, 1979.
Needle in the Eye: Poems New and Selected, Mosaic, 1983.
Doors, Words and Silence, Mosaic, 1985.
Dostoyevsky and Other Poems, Mosaic, 1989.
Coming from Afar: Selected Poems, McClelland & Stewart, 1990.

CONTRIBUTOR TO ANTHOLOGIES

Canadian Poetry in English, Ryerson, 1954.
Penguin Book of Canadian Verse, Penguin (London), 1958.

Also contributor to *The Oxford Book of Canadian Verse in English and French, Twentieth-Century Canadian Poetry,* and *Modern Canadian Verse.*

UNDER NAME ROBERT A. D. FORD

Our Man in Moscow: A Diplomat's Reflections on the Soviet Union, University of Toronto Press, 1989.
Diplomate et Poete a Moscow, Editions Collignon, 1990.
A Moscow Literary Memoir, University of Toronto, 1995.

Contributor to *Encounter, Malahat Review, Maryland Quarterly, Canadian Forum, Montreal Gazette, Financial Post,* and *Foreign Affairs.* Works have been translated into Russian, French, Spanish, and Portuguese.

OTHER

(Translator) *Russian Poetry: A Personal Anthology,* Mosaic, 1986.

SIDELIGHTS: R. A. D. Ford considers himself a diplomat first and a poet second. Having spent much of his life outside the borders of his Canadian homeland, he is not easily grouped with other contemporary Canadian poets. He told *CA:* "A very active diplomatic career limited the amount of time I had for poetry, but it also extended my horizons, exposing me to the misery of the world—Colombia, Yugoslavia, Egypt, Sudan, what was then the USSR. This had the effect of creating a pessimistic view of the world and mankind, and is reflected in my verse." Also reflected in his poetry is Ford's lifelong battle with "a form of muscular atrophy which has helped to shape a rather somber view of the world," according to Ford. This sadness permeates Ford's poems, which are often set in the arctic wastes of Canada and Russia. Although Ford is not a prolific writer, his poetry is distinct. Stanley W. Lindberg wrote in *Contemporary Poets,* "These are quiet, serious poems, lyric rather than dramatic, but always restrained. They explore the edges of emotion, seldom taking risks. They offer little irony, less of the comic, and very few surprises, yet they are consistently competent, sincere, and quietly rewarding."

In addition to his original verse, Ford has also published a number of translated poems, many of which are included in his volume *Russian Poetry: A Personal Anthology.* "I was completely bilingual in French and had learned Latin, German, and Russian at school," he told *CA.* "I subsequently added Serbo-Croation, Portuguese, Spanish, and Italian." In the author's note included in his book *A Window on the North,* he explains that his goal in translating poetry is "to make of each adaptation as fine or even finer a poem in his (the translator's) own language," a goal which often requires the taking of "considerable liberties with the verse form and rhyme in order to transmit the spirit of the original." Lindberg found the translations to be true to the original spirit of the works, and to demonstrate poetic abilities not always apparent in Ford's own restrained verse.

Russian verse, in particular, has often been the subject of Ford's interpretation. He once told *CA:* "The richness of Russian literature, and above all Russian poetry . . . is so little appreciated because of the difficulty of the language." He later told *CA:* "The 20th century poets who have most influenced me are Eliot, Auden, William Carlos Williams, Garcia Lorca, Rilke, Eluard, and the great Russians—Pasternak, Akhmatova, Tsvetaeva, and Esenin."

BIOGRAPHICAL/CRITICAL SOURCES:

BOOKS

Dictionary of Literary Biography, Gale, Volume 88: *Canadian Writers, 1920-1959, Second Series,* 1989.
Ford, R. A. D., *A Window on the North,* Ryerson, 1956.
Ford, *Needle in the Eye,* Mosaic, 1983.

PERIODICALS

Choice, September, 1989, p. 204.
Globe and Mail (Toronto), October 13, 1984.
World Literature Today, spring, 1996, p. 428.*

* * *

FORD, Robert A. D.
See FORD, R(obert) A(rthur) D(ouglass)

* * *

FOREST, Antonia

PERSONAL: Born in London, England.

ADDRESSES: *Office*—c/o Faber & Faber Ltd., Three Queen Sq., London WC1N 3AU, England.

CAREER: Author of books for young people.

AWARDS, HONORS: Commendation from British Library Association, 1961, for *Peter's Room;* 1963, for *Thursday Kidnapping.*

WRITINGS:

JUVENILE; PUBLISHED BY FABER, EXCEPT AS NOTED:

Autumn Term, illustrated by Marjorie Owens, 1948.
The Marlows and the Traitor, illustrated by Doritie Kettlewell, 1953.
Falconer's Lure: The Story of a Summer Holiday, illustrated by Tasha Kallin, 1957.
End of Term, 1959, Puffin, 1978.
Peter's Room, 1961.
The Thursday Kidnapping, 1963, Coward, 1965.
The Thuggery Affair, 1965.
The Ready-made Family, 1967.
The Player's Boy, 1970.
The Players and the Rebels, 1971.
The Cricket Term, 1974.
The Attic Term, 1976.
Run Away Home, 1982.

SIDELIGHTS: Antonia Forest was born in London, England. As an only child, she was brought up with a next-door family of seven who became her best friends, although she later admitted that "this gave me a certain skepticism about the real-life joys of being one of a large family." As a child she studied ballet and won poetry society medals for verse-speaking. She also acted in school and university plays, "being better if allowed to be either comic or sinister."

There was never a time when Forest did not intend to be a professional writer, and the first book in her Marlow series was published in 1948. The books focus on the lives of the Marlow children and most of the stories take place during the holidays, when they are not in school. The family is upper middle-class, and the stories make reference to servants, parties, and private chapels. Anne W. Ellis of *Twentieth-Century Children's Writers* declared *Peter's Room* to be the "most original and outstanding plot in the series." In the story, one of the sisters is assigned an essay on the Brontes' life or work. All of the children consequently become interested in the Bronte kingdoms of Gondol and Angria to the extent that they create their own kingdom of Angora, which occupies them for the entire Christmas break. This story won Forest a commendation from the British Library Association in 1961.

A lifelong interest in ships and the sea is reflected in many of Forest's books. One such book is *Run Away Home,* a Marlow book with a running-away theme in which a sailing accident heightens the suspense. While writing *Run Away Home* Forest took "a crash course in dinghy sailing in the interests of verisimilitude." She found it "exhausting, but wildly enjoyable."

Four of the Marlow stories take place while school is in session, and these, according to Ellis, are the ones for which Forest will be remembered. This is because there are inventive variations that set these stories apart from other authors' books about school-aged children. In these stories, the Marlow twins seem doomed never to achieve their academic aspirations. In one episode, one of the girls, Nick, tries to run away, only to be sent immediately back to school by her older brother without ever being missed in class. Ellis concluded, "Dramatics perhaps occupy an undue proportion of certain plots, but this is acceptable to the wariest reader because of Forest's enthusiastic details."

Only one of Forest's books is not about the Marlow family—*The Thursday Kidnapping,* which was commended by the Library Association.

BIOGRAPHICAL/CRITICAL SOURCES:

BOOKS

Twentieth-Century Children's Writers, 4th edition, St. James Press, 1995.

PERIODICALS

Observer, December 3, 1967, p. 26; November 28, 1976, p. 31.
Times Literary Supplement, December 9, 1965, p. 1143; November 30, 1967, p. 1150; December 11, 1970, p. 1457; October 1, 1976, p. 1243.*

* * *

FORESTER, C(ecil) S(cott) 1899- 1966

PERSONAL: Born August 27, 1899, in Cairo, Egypt; died April 2, 1966; son of George (a government official) and Sarah (Troughton) Forester; married Katherine Belcher, 1926 (divorced, 1944); married Dorothy Foster, 1947; children: (first marriage) John, George. *Education:* Studied medicine at Guy's Hospital.

CAREER: Novelist. Wrote film scripts in Hollywood for part of each year, 1932-39; worked as a correspondent in Spain, 1936-37, and covered the Nazi occupation of Czechoslovakia in Prague; was a member of the British Information Service, 1939-40.

MEMBER: Athenaeum Club, Savage Club (London), Century Club (New York).

AWARDS, HONORS: James Tait Black Memorial Prize, 1939, for *A Ship of the Line.*

WRITINGS:

"HORATIO HORNBLOWER" SERIES

Beat to Quarters, Little, Brown, 1937, published in England as *The Happy Return,* M. Joseph, 1937.
A Ship of the Line, Little, Brown, 1938.
Flying Colours, Little, Brown, 1939.
Captain Horatio Hornblower (contains three novels, *Beat to Quarters, Ship of the Line,* and *Flying Colours;* illustrated by N. C. Wyeth), Little, Brown, 1939.
Commodore Hornblower, Little, Brown, 1945.
Lord Hornblower, Little, Brown, 1946.
Mr. Midshipman Hornblower, Little, Brown, 1950.
Lieutenant Hornblower, Little, Brown, 1952.
Hornblower and the Atropos, Little, Brown, 1953.
Hornblower Takes Command (selections from *Beat to Quarters* and *Hornblower and the Atropos;* edited by G. P. Griggs; illustrated by Geoffrey Whittam), Little, Brown, 1953.
Admiral Hornblower in the West Indies, Little, Brown, 1958.
Young Hornblower, Three Complete Novels: Mr. Midshipman Hornblower, Lieutenant Hornblower, Hornblower and the Atropos, Little, Brown, 1960.
Hornblower and the Hotspur, Little, Brown, 1962.
The Indomitable Hornblower: Commodore Hornblower, Lord Hornblower, [and] Admiral Hornblower in the West Indies, Little, Brown, 1963.
The Hornblower Companion (illustrated by Samuel H. Bryant), Little, Brown, 1964.
Hornblower's Triumph (selections from *Commodore Hornblower* and *Lord Hornblower;* edited by G. P. Griggs; illustrated by G. Whittam), Little, Brown, 1965.
Hornblower in Captivity (selections from *A Ship of the Line* and *Flying Colours;* edited by Griggs; illustrated by Whittam), Little, Brown, 1965.
Hornblower during the Crisis, and Two Stories: Hornblower's Temptation and The Last Encounter (unfinished novel), Little, Brown, 1967.

PLAYS

U 97, Lane (London), 1931.
Nurse Cavell, Lane, 1951.

OTHER

"The Paid Piper" (short story), Methuen, 1924.
A Pawn among Kings, Methuen, 1924.
Napoleon and His Court (biography), Methuen, 1924.
Josephine, Napoleon's Empress (biography), Dodd, 1925.
Payment Deferred, J. Lane, 1926.
Victor Emmanuel II and the Union of Italy, Dodd, 1927.
One Wonderful Week, Bobbs-Merrill, 1927, published in England as *The Wonderful Week,* J. Lane, 1927.
Love Lies Dreaming, Bobbs-Merrill, 1927.
The Daughter of the Hawk, Bobbs-Merrill, 1928, published in England as *The Shadow of the Hawk,* J. Lane, 1928.
Louis XIV, King of France and Navarre (biography), Methuen, 1928.
Single-Handed, Putnam, 1929, published in England as *Brown on Resolution,* J. Lane, 1929.
Lord Nelson (biography), Bobbs-Merrill, 1929.
The Voyage of the Annie Marble, J. Lane, 1929.
Plain Murder, J. Lane, 1930.
The Annie Marble in Germany, J. Lane, 1930.
Two-and-Twenty, D. Appleton, 1931.
Death to the French, J. Lane, 1932.
The Gun (novel), Little, Brown, 1933.
The Peacemaker, Little, Brown, 1934, M. Joseph (London), 1974.
The African Queen, Little, Brown, 1935.
Marionettes at Home, M. Joseph, 1936.
The General, Little, Brown, 1936, Nautical and Aviation Pub. Co. (Annapolis, MD), 1982.
The Earthly Paradise, M. Joseph, 1940.
To the Indies, Little, Brown, 1940.
The Captain from Connecticut, Little, Brown, 1941.
Poo-Poo and the Dragons (children's story; illustrated by Robert Lawson), Little, Brown, 1942.
Rifleman Dodd [and] The Gun: Two Novels of the Peninsular Wars, Readers Club, 1942.
The Ship, Little, Brown, 1943.
The Sky and the Forest, Little, Brown, 1948.
Randall and the River of Time, Little, Brown, 1950.
(Editor) John Porrit Wetherell, *The Adventures of John Wetherell,* Doubleday, 1953, with an introduction by Forester, M. Joseph (London), 1994.
The Barbary Pirates (children's story; illustrated by Charles J. Mazoujian), Random House, 1953.
The Nightmare, Little, Brown, 1954.
The Good Shepherd (Book-of-the-Month Club selection), Little, Brown, 1955.
The Age of Fighting Sail: The Story of the Naval War of 1812, (history), Doubleday, 1956, published in England as *The Naval War of 1812,* M. Joseph, 1957.

The Last Nine Days of the Bismarck, Little, Brown, 1959, also published as *Sink the Bismarck!,* Bantam Books, 1959, published in England as *Hunting the Bismarck,* M. Joseph, 1959.
Long before Forty (autobiography), Little, Brown, 1967.
The Man in the Yellow Raft (short stories), Little, Brown, 1969.
Gold from Crete (short stories), Little, Brown, 1970.
The Hostage (selections from *The Nightmare*), New English Library, 1970.

ADAPTATIONS: All of the following were adapted as motion pictures: *Payment Deferred* by Metro-Goldwyn-Mayer, 1932; *Eagle Squadron,* 1942; *The Commandos* as *The Commandos Strike at Dawn* by Columbia Pictures, 1943; *The African Queen* by United Artists, 1951, and Horizon Pictures, 1981; *Captain Horatio Hornblower* by Warner Brothers, 1951; *Brown on Resolution* as *Sailor of the King* by Twentieth-Century Fox, 1953; *The Gun* as *The Pride and the Passion* by United Artists, 1957; and *Sink the Bismarck!* by Twentieth-Century Fox, 1960. *The African Queen* was adapted as a television special for CBS, aired March 18, 1977.

SIDELIGHTS: Cecil Scott Forester was born in Cairo, Egypt, but spent most of his childhood in England. Forester and his brothers attended a public school, since his father could ill afford to privately educate five children, and were motivated to earn scholarships for their further education. The school Forester attended was academically strong, so although it was unusual for even a single scholarship to be won by a student in a school, Forester and a dozen or so others from his school managed to earn them. This was a particular accomplishment for Forester, who was a few years younger than his classmates. The result was a thorough and accelerated academic education.

Around 1926, Forester traveled along the rivers of England, France, and Germany in a dinghy with his first wife, Katherine Belcher. The author kept a log of his journey, which was later published as *The Voyage of the Annie Marble.*

Although Forester never won a major literary award, his obituary was featured on the front page of the *New York Times.* Perhaps this was because his books sold eight million copies during his career, and his hero of historical fiction, Captain Horatio Hornblower, became a household name. Much of Hornblower's appeal came from the realism in which he was portrayed. In a review of *Beat to Quarters,* Alexander Laing of *New York Herald Tribune Books* commented, "I know of no other book in which the behavior and character of a typical, competent naval officer of the period are so tellingly presented." Fletcher Pratt of *Saturday Review of Literature* likened Forester's Hornblower series to the work of Rudyard Kipling. Not until Ian Fleming's James Bond captured the attention of the American public was Hornblower's status as the hero of escapist fiction challenged. Sanford Sternlicht of *Twentieth-Century Romance and Historical Writers* observed, "Hornblower was a hero of and for the World War II generation, and Bond was the darling of the Cold War generation."

One of Forester's best-known works is *The African Queen,* the adaptation of which is now considered a classic of American cinema. When it was published in 1935, it was well received among critics. Amy Loveman of *Saturday Review of Literature* wrote that Forester "has sufficient skill in characterization, sufficient psychological subtlety, to lift his story above the general run of adventure yarns, and enlist interest in his hero and heroine as personalities and not mere lay figures on which to hang excitement." While critics agreed that certain aspects of the story are a bit implausible, they agreed Forester makes it worth the reader's while to set that aside. In *New York Times Book Review,* Percy Hutchison concluded, "The credulity of the reader may be stretched here and there, but, having given himself to the tale, as one must always give one's self up wholeheartedly to romance or eschew it altogether, he will go on. Suspended again and again in midair, he will find pleasure in the suspense, a device of which Mr. Forester again and again proves himself a master."

Although an attack of arteriosclerosis left him a semi-invalid later in life, Forester continued to write historical novels.

BIOGRAPHICAL/CRITICAL SOURCES:

BOOKS

Contemporary Literary Criticism, Volume 35, Gale, 1985.
Forester, C. S., *Long before Forty,* Little, Brown, 1967.
Sternlicht, Sanford, *C.S. Forester,* Twayne Publishers (Boston), 1981.
Twentieth-Century Romance and Historical Writers, 3rd edition, St. James Press, 1994.

PERIODICALS

Christian Science Monitor, August 2, 1962.
Los Angeles Times Book Review, April 22, 1990; July 28, 1991; August 23, 1992.

Newsweek, July 9, 1956; September 1, 1958.
New Yorker, September 28, 1968; June 26, 1997.
New York Herald Tribune Books, April 11, 1937.
New York Times, March 6, 1968.
New York Times Book Review, February 10, 1935; April 6, 1952; April 3, 1955; November 12, 1967; November 3, 1968; June 22, 1969; November 15, 1970.
Observer, August 7, 1966; December 3, 1967.
Saturday Evening Post, July 6, 1946; March 6, 1948.
Saturday Review of Literature, February 9, 1935; September 28, 1946.
Times Literary Supplement, September 16, 1965; September 14, 1967.
Washington Post Book World, March 9, 1980; August 26, 1984; September 22, 1985.

OBITUARIES:

PERIODICALS

New York Times, April 3, 1966; *Time,* April 8, 1966; *Illustrated London News,* April 9, 1966; *Newsweek,* April 11, 1966; *Britannica Book of the Year,* 1967.*

* * *

FORREST, Katherine V(irginia) 1939-

PERSONAL: Born April 20, 1939, in Windsor, Ontario, Canada; adopted daughter of Leland Wilson McKinlay and Mary Elizabeth Gilhuly. *Education:* Attended Wayne State University, Detroit, and University of California, Los Angeles.

ADDRESSES: Home—P.O. Box 25115, Los Angeles, CA 90025.

CAREER: Writer. Senior fiction editor for Naiad Press.

MEMBER: International PEN.

AWARDS, HONORS: Lambda Literary Award for *The Beverly Malibu* and *Murder by Tradition.*

WRITINGS:

Curious Wine, Naiad Press (Tallahassee, FL), 1983.
Daughters of a Coral Dawn, Naiad Press, 1984.
Amateur City, Naiad Press, 1984.
An Emergence of Green, Naiad Press, 1986.
Murder at the Nightwood Bar, Naiad Press, 1987.
Dreams and Swords, Naiad Press, 1988.
The Beverly Malibu, Naiad Press, 1990.
Murder by Tradition, Naiad Press, 1991.
(Editor, with Barbara Grier) *The Erotic Naiad: Love Stories by Naiad Press Authors,* Naiad, 1992.
(Editor, with Barbara Grier) *The Romantic Naiad: Love Stories by Naiad Press Authors,* Naiad, 1993.
Flashpoint, Naiad, 1994.
(Editor, with Barbara Grier) *The Mysterious Naiad: Love Stories by Naiad Press Authors,* Naiad, 1994.
Liberty Square, Berkley Prime Crime (New York City), 1996.
Apparition Alley: A Kate Delafield Mystery, Berkley Prime Crime, 1997.

SIDELIGHTS: Katherine V. Forrest is best known for her police series featuring lesbian detective Kate Delafield. Forrest told *CA:* "All my work is directed primarily to a lesbian audience. . . . My objective in this series is to present entertaining fiction and also a lesbian life in process—a woman in a high-visibility job who must deal with her sexual identity in a totally homophobic atmosphere."

In *Amateur City,* the first novel in the series, Forrest introduces her character as an independent, self-confident woman who does not shy away from the opportunity for a romantic interlude while working on a case. However, because she is not openly homosexual, she has to be careful about keeping her professional life as separate from her personal life as possible. At work, she is diligent and patient, with an eye for detail and sympathy for victims and their families.

Another book in the series is *The Beverly Malibu.* Delafield and her partner Ed Taylor are working on a gruesome murder case in which the victim is a Hollywood director. Forrest brings in an eccentric array of characters and sub-plots, including Delafield's emotional and sexual involvement with two of the suspects. To the end, the reader is kept guessing at the outcome of this intriguing story.

In *Murder by Tradition,* Delafield is given the case of the murder of a young homosexual man. She finds herself so embroiled in the case that her career and personal life are threatened as she is, for the first time, facing the possibility of exposure.

A more recent addition to the series is *Liberty Square,* where Delafield attends a reunion with her U. S. Marines buddies, with whom she served in Vietnam. While catching up with them, she realizes that they have now experienced the same outcast status she understands so well. Delafield is a dynamic character who grows and changes as the series progresses. Patricia Holt of the *San Francisco Chronicle* wrote that "half the fun of reading the Delafield mysteries lies in watching Kate change: as she deals with such issues as child abuse, breast cancer, homophobia, LAPD infighting and racism."

Besides her Delafield series, Forrest has published other thematically complex novels. *Curious Wine* is a romantic fantasy about two women in love, and Forrest brings in themes of exploration, love, discovery, and passion. Holt called *Curious Wine* "a kind of classic in contemporary lesbian literature for its open and unapologetic depiction of sexuality and intimacy among women." A science-fiction novel, *Daughters of a Coral Dawn,* tells the story of the women of Cybele who have left Earth in search of a world without men. *An Emergence of Green* considers the many themes of lesbian identity, including jealousy, indecision, doubt, and loyalty.

BIOGRAPHICAL/CRITICAL SOURCES:

BOOKS

Gay and Lesbian Literature, St. James Press, 1994.

PERIODICALS

Armchair Detective, fall, 1991, p. 478.

Booklist, April 1, 1987, p. 1179; November 1, 1989, p. 527; September 1, 1991, p. 32.

New York Times Book Review, December 10, 1989, p. 41; September 15, 1991, p. 25.

Publishers Weekly, February 27, 1987, p. 159; June 14, 1991, p. 47; August 12, 1996, p. 68.*

* * *

FORREST, Richard (Stockton) 1932-
(Lee Evans, Rebecca Morgan, Stockton Woods)

PERSONAL: Born May 8, 1932, in Orange, NJ; son of Williams Kraemer and Georgia (Muller) Forrest; married Frances Anne Reese, December 20, 1952 (divorced May, 1955); married Mary Bolan Brumby (a nurse), May 11, 1955 (separated, 1995); children: (first marriage) Richard; (second marriage) Christopher, Remley, Katherine, Mongin, Bellamy. *Education:* Attended New York Dramatic Workshop, 1950, and University of South Carolina, 1953-55. *Politics:* Democrat. *Religion:* Unitarian Universalist.

ADDRESSES: Home—8912 Ewing Dr., Bethesda, MD 20817. *Agent*—Phyllis Westburg, Harold Ober Associates, Inc., 40 East 49th St., New York, NY 10017.

CAREER: Playwright, 1955-58; Lawyers Title Insurance Corp., Richmond, VA, state manager, 1958-68; Chicago Title Insurance Co., Chicago, IL, vice-president, 1969-72; freelance writer, 1972—. Vice-president of Connecticut Board of Title Underwriters. *Military service:* U.S. Army, Rangers, 1951-53; served in Korea; became staff sergeant.

MEMBER: Mystery Writers of America, Authors Guild, Authors League of America.

AWARDS, HONORS: Edgar Allan Poe Award, Mystery Writers of America, 1975, for *Who Killed Mr. Garland's Mistress?;* Porgie Award for best original paperback, *West Coast Review of Books,* for *The Laughing Man.*

WRITINGS:

MYSTERY NOVELS

Who Killed Mr. Garland's Mistress?, Pinnacle Books (New York City), 1974.

The Killing Edge, Tower Publications (New York City), 1980.

Lark, New American Library (New York City), 1986.

"LYON AND BEA WENTWORTH" MYSTERY SERIES

A Child's Garden of Death, Bobbs-Merrill (New York City), 1975.

The Wizard of Death, Bobbs-Merrill, 1977.

Death through the Looking Glass, Bobbs-Merrill, 1978.

The Death in the Willows, Holt (New York City), 1979.

Death at Yew Corner, Holt, 1981.

Death under the Lilacs, St. Martin's (New York City), 1985.

Death on the Mississippi, St. Martin's, 1989.

The Pied Piper of Death, St. Martin's, 1997.

UNDER PSEUDONYM STOCKTON WOODS

The Laughing Man, Fawcett (New York City), 1980.

Game Bet, Fawcett, 1981.

The Man Who Heard Too Much, Fawcett, 1983.

(With wife, Mary Forrest) *The Complete Nursing Home Guide,* Facts on File (New York City), 1990.

(With M. Forrest) *Retirement Living,* Facts on File, 1991.

OTHER

Also author of the plays *Cry for the Spring, The Meek Cry Loud,* and *The Sandhouse.* Author of the "Lexi Lane Nautical Mystery" series under the pseudonym Rebecca Morgan and the "Randy Holden Aeronautical Adventure" series under the pseudonym Lee Evans. Contributor of short stories to periodicals, including *Northeast Magazine, Ellery Queen Mystery Magazine,* and *Mystery Monthly.*

Several editions of Forrest's work have been published in Finnish, French, German, Italian, and Swedish. His manuscript collection is part of the Twentieth-Century Archives at Mungar Memorial Library, Boston University, Boston.

SIDELIGHTS: Richard Forrest's crime novels combine the classic puzzle plotting of traditional mysteries with the element of corruption common in detective novels. His portrayal of human pain on an individual and personal level further distinguishes his work from that of previous authors. Susan Baker of *Twentieth-Century Crime and Mystery Writers* noted that "Forrest presents this mixture [of mystery novels, detective novels, and individual human pain] in consistently graceful prose and adds reasonably restrained moments of sex and violence." Most of Forrest's novels are about Lyon Wentworth, a children's author and former English professor. He is also a keen amateur mystery-solver who works with the chief of the Murphysville police, Rocco Herbert, whom he met in the military while serving in Korea. Wentworth's wife, Bea, is a successful, independent politician and feminist. Her access to inside information frequently comes in handy during her husband's investigations. Bea's aide is Kimberly Ward, who led welfare mothers in a protest, met Mrs. Wentworth, and stayed to work for her. Forrest's characters intentionally do not fit into neat stereotypes. He prefers to call the reader's attention to the assumptions of stereotypes rather than perpetuate them. Wentworth's relationship with Herbert, for instance, is not characterized by the macho exchanges one might expect based on their history together; both Wentworth and Herbert display brains and brawn. Forrest's mobsters are not stereotypical pinstriped goons, either. One of them reads Proust and another has created a home in the style and spirit of a Japanese haven. Forrest creates such characters not to lecture his readers, but to make subtle social comments.

In the character of Wentworth, Forrest frequently reveals something about himself. In describing Wentworth's children's books, Forrest tells about his own reasons for writing and the appeal of the murder mystery genre. Wentworth's doctoral dissertation was written on the subject of violence in Victorian children's literature. Baker observed, "Not surprisingly, then, he is conscious of the power of literature to exorcize fears, to render private terrors manageable." Wentworth's books, like Forrest's novels, tell stories of victory over monsters. Forrest, however, came to writing along a different path than Wentworth, who studied and then taught literature before dedicating himself to a writing career. Forrest told *CA* that he "spent early years as a playwright until [a] growing family made business a necessity. Resigned [my] position as vice-president of major insurance company on [my] fortieth birthday to write full time—why not?"

Baker summed up Forrest's work as "well-written, with thoroughly realized backgrounds and persuasively likeable characters. Occasionally in the earliest books, the machinery of planning creaks a bit too obviously, but the care and craft with which Forrest approaches his writing have led to increasing subtlety. There is nothing slapdash here; above all, Richard Forrest writes *thoughtful* mysteries, socially conscious and emotionally satisfying."

BIOGRAPHICAL/CRITICAL SOURCES:

BOOKS

Twentieth-Century Crime and Mystery Writers, 3rd edition, St. James Press, 1991.

PERIODICALS

Chicago Tribune Book World, April 19, 1981.
New York Times Book Review, March 8, 1981.
Publishers Weekly, December 12, 1980.
Washington Post Book World, January 18, 1981.*

* * *

FRANKLYN, Ross
See HARDY, Francis Joseph

FRASER, Ronald (Angus) 1930-

PERSONAL: Born December 9, 1930, in Hamburg, Germany; British citizen; son of Alexander and Janey Fraser; married; children: one son and one daughter.

ADDRESSES: *Home*—16 Evangelist Rd., London NW5 1UB, England. *Office*—*New Left Review,* 7 Carlisle St., London W1V 6NL, England. *Agent*—Tessa Sayle, 11 Jubilee Pl., London SW3, England.

CAREER: Foreign correspondent for Reuters News Agency, 1952-57; editor of *New Left Review;* writer.

WRITINGS:

(Editor) *Work: Twenty Personal Accounts,* Penguin, Volume 1, 1968, Volume 2, 1969.

In Hiding: The Life of Manuel Cortes, Pantheon, 1972.

Tajos: The Story of a Village on the Costa del Sol, Pantheon, 1973, published in England as *The Pueblo: A Mountain Village on the Costa del Sol,* Allen Lane, 1973.

Blood of Spain: An Oral History of the Spanish Civil War, Pantheon, 1979, published in England as *Blood of Spain: The Experience of Civil War, 1936-1939,* Allen Lane, 1979.

(With Pierre Broue and Pierre Vilar) *Metodologia historica de la guerra y revolucion espanolas,* Fontamara (Barcelona), 1980.

In Search of a Past: The Rearing of an English Gentleman, 1933- 1945, Atheneum, 1984, published in England as *In Search of a Past: The Manor House, Amnersfield, 1933-1945,* Verso, 1984.

(With others) *Nineteen Sixty-eight: A Student Generation in Revolt,* Pantheon, 1988.

SIDELIGHTS: Journalist and historian Ronald Fraser is well known for his books of oral history, particularly those about Spain. In his 1972 book, *In Hiding: The Life of Manuel Cortes,* Fraser tells of a Spanish man who had been a supporter of the Republican government before it was defeated by Francisco Franco's rebel army during the civil war of 1936 to 1939. Faced with execution for his political beliefs, Cortes hid in his own home for thirty years, aided by his wife and daughter. After Franco declared a general amnesty in 1969, Cortes was finally able to leave his house. Based on Fraser's interviews with the Cortes family, the book reveals the repression and lack of forgiveness that characterized Franco's regime. Critics praised the author's narrative style, noting the tension and drama that Fraser is able to create. Arthur Miller, writing in the *New York Times Book Review,* commented that "in the mountain of books about [the Spanish Civil War] there cannot be another so brief and yet so complete, so unguarded and yet so subtle, so movingly human as this." For *Tajos: The Story of a Village on the Costa del Sol,* Fraser interviewed the inhabitants of Tajos, a rural village in Southern Spain. Conducted during the 1960s, the interviews reveal a community that was poor and struggling to understand the wave of modernization that had overcome Spain at the time. Critics responded favorably to the book and to the author's simple, straightforward presentation of his material.

Fraser continued his study of the Spanish Civil War in *Blood of Spain: An Oral History of the Spanish Civil War.* By presenting accounts of people of varying social, economic, and political backgrounds, Fraser offers what critics called an unsurpassed range of Spanish expression about the war. The Republican side, which consisted of the parties of the Left and included the left-leaning government, was hindered in its war effort by conflict within its ranks over the issue of a social revolution. The smaller leftist parties such as the Trotskyist and Anarchist parties were determined that a social revolution, complete with nationalization of industries and land, should take place in those areas controlled by the Republican side. The Communist party, though, was convinced that the Republicans should first defeat Franco's rebels and regain control over the entire country before carrying out a revolution. The accounts from Republican supporters reveal the extent to which this infighting weakened the Republic's chances of subduing the rebels. Within the rebel side, by contrast, Franco was able to silence all who disagreed with him—especially other army officers—and thereby present a unified front against the Republic. The accounts from Franco's side reveal how his supporters were convinced that the military rebellion was needed to protect private property, end leftist attacks on the Catholic church—long a dominant landholder in a country where few owned land—and restore order to Spain.

Reviewers praised the book as a long-awaited answer to how Spaniards view their civil war, since the majority of first-hand accounts of the war have been written by foreigners—the most well known of whom are British writer George Orwell, American writer Ernest Hemingway, and French writer Andre Malraux. After Franco died in 1975, many Spaniards began to openly discuss the war. Writing in the *Washington Post Book World,* Bernard M. W. Knox noted that "for nearly forty years no Spanish voice was raised to talk about the war except the strident official voice of the regime. In this book the silence is broken; people who held their tongues in fear for decades here pour out their memories, their sorrows and fears, their judgments . . . on what went wrong." Other reviewers commended Fraser for exploring a wide spectrum of issues important in the war—the desire of some for radical social change, the power and importance of the Catholic church, and the brutal retributions committed by both sides—and for offering a broad range of viewpoints about those issues. *Saturday Review* contributor James Sloan Allen commented that the differing accounts allow the author to present "the bewildering variety of forces and alliances" that existed without simplifying the conflict. Paul Preston of the *New York Times Book Review* summed up critical reaction to *Blood of Spain* by calling the book "a moving and original work that will immediately take its place among the dozen or so truly important books about the Spanish conflict."

In his 1984 book, *In Search of a Past: The Rearing of an English Gentleman, 1933-1945,* Fraser turned his attention from Spain to his own life. In an attempt to better understand his childhood, he interviewed servants, cooks, and gardeners who worked at the country estate where he was raised. Fraser combines these interviews with his own observations about his past, many of which the author formulated after going through psychoanalysis. The accounts reveal an unhappy household in which Fraser's parents, ill-suited for one another, engaged in affairs and eventually divorced. The period during World War II—in which his father fought—was a turning point for Fraser's family, for when his father returned from the war his mother took the children and moved out of the house. The book is more than a personal memoir, though, since Fraser uses the interviews to examine the nature of the class system that existed in England at that time. The servants relate how Fraser's parents, especially his father, treated them with disdain and a lack of respect; the servants therefore did their jobs and kept to themselves without expecting any gratitude for their work. Critics praised Fraser for combining the interviews with his own recollections. Writing in the *Observer,* Paul Bailey noted that the book "is wholly engrossing—social history viewed from the angle of deep personal anguish." Other reviewers commended the honest and forthright way in which Fraser delves into his past. *New York Times Book Review* contributor Edward Mendelson called *In Search of a Past* a "calm, subtle, often beautiful book, one that makes peace with old catastrophes."

BIOGRAPHICAL/CRITICAL SOURCES:

BOOKS

Fraser, Ronald, *In Search of a Past: The Rearing of an English Gentleman, 1933-1945,* Atheneum, 1984.

PERIODICALS

Choice, March, 1986.
New Republic, March 8, 1980.
New Statesman, December 21, 1984.
New York Review of Books, August 10, 1972.
New York Times, July 1, 1972; December 11, 1973.
New York Times Book Review, July 9, 1972; June 17, 1979; February 17, 1985.
Observer (London), January 27, 1985; May 8, 1994.
Saturday Review, September 2, 1972; January 12, 1974; July 21, 1979.
Spectator, November 17, 1984.
Time, July 2, 1979.
Times Literary Supplement, January 25, 1974; December 14, 1979; April 15, 1988.
Washington Post Book World, June 10, 1979.*

* * *

FRIEDBERG, Gertrude (Tonkonogy) 1908-1989

PERSONAL: Born March 17, 1908, in New York, NY; died of cancer, September 17, 1989; daughter of George and Sylvia Tonkonogy; married Charles K. Friedberg (a cardiologist); children: Richard, Barbara. *Education:* Wellesley College; Barnard College, B.A.

CAREER: Substitute teacher of mathematics in New York City public schools, 1964-1989. Free-lance writer.

WRITINGS:

Three Cornered Moon (play), Samuel French, 1933.
Town House (play), adaptation of stories by John Cheever, produced in New York, 1948.
(Contributor of five stories) *Short Story Two,* Scribner, 1959.
The Revolving Boy (science fiction novel), Doubleday, 1966.

Contributor of short stories to *Atlantic, Harper's, Esquire, Magazine of Fantasy and Science Fiction,* and other magazines. Work represented in anthology *The*

Woman Who Lost Her Names, edited by Julia Wolf Mazow, Harper, 1980.

SIDELIGHTS: In Gertrude Friedberg's *The Revolving Boy,* the main character, Derv, is a superhuman boy who was born to astronauts in a weightless atmosphere far from the earth and has abilities to be his own radiometer and compass. Due to the unusual circumstances of his birth, he was able to align himself with a signal from a distant solar system; this alignment keeps him oriented, so he is always winding himself around to maintain the direction. For example, when he is in bed, he does somersaults to offset the earth's rotation. After Derv's birth, his parents fake a fatal boating accident in order to establish a new life where they can escape the publicity of Derv's birth. As Derv grows up, the parents experience both fear and amazement at the development of their son's ability. As an adult, Derv loses his signal, and he and his wife must determine if it has been terminated. A major theme of this novel is the discovery of and communication with another civilization. While interesting in its premise and plot development, Judith Snyder of *Twentieth-Century Science-Fiction Writers* found the scientific elements lacking. She wrote: "Freidberg's scientific projections are mostly erroneous. . . . She overestimated the speed of change to electronic devices in the homes of the 1970s. Her scientific research can also be faulted, since she has failed to take into account some of the properties of radio signals. . . ."

"The Short and Happy Life of George Frumkin," published in 1963, is a satirical short story about the use of artificial organs. George is ninety-seven years old and suffers not only from a small problem with his artificial heart, but also from boredom and lack of motivation to finish rewriting the second act of his play. In the story, most doctors are also electricians, so Dr. Stebbins is called in to evaluate George's problem. The doctor switches George to house current while he prepares the new battery, and George is full of creative and sexual energy. However, when Dr. Stebbins puts him on battery power again, George is back to his old mindset. Snyder called this story an "entertaining spoof" and a "gem, undoubtedly Freidberg's best science fiction effort."

More of a science fantasy, "For Whom the Girl Waits," published in 1972, is a story of double identities. It takes place in a high school where Louis Demperi is a substitute teacher who always assumes the identity of the teacher he is temporarily replacing. He runs into trouble, however, when he substitutes for Koppinger, and finds that every afternoon after school, a beautiful girl waits for him. He becomes disoriented about whom he is supposed to be and then realizes that someone else has assumed his identity. He carries on as Koppinger, but when the girl rejects him, he dies in an auto accident. Because someone else has taken on his identity, he remains, in a sense, still living.

As a general overview of Friedberg's work, Snyder concluded that she "wrote in a simple, unpretentious style and in general organized her material chronologically. She excelled in the handling of women's characters, which suggests that her work might have been more successful if the central characters had been women instead of men."

BIOGRAPHICAL/CRITICAL SOURCES:

PERIODICALS

Kirkus Reviews, July 15, 1966, p. 717.
Library Journal, October 15, 1966, p. 5262.
Magazine of Fantasy & Science Fiction, January, 1967, p. 67.
Publishers Weekly, March 18, 1968, p. 56.
School Library Journal, September, 1988, p. 121.
Times Literary Supplement, March 2, 1967, p. 172.

OBITUARIES:

BOOKS

Contemporary Science Fiction Authors II, Gale, 1979.

PERIODICALS

New York Times, September 20, 1989.*
—Sketch by Jennifer Bussey

* * *

FRIESNER, Esther M. 1951-

PERSONAL: Born July 16, 1951, in New York, NY; daughter of David R. (a teacher) and Beatrice (a teacher; maiden name, Richter) Friesner; married Walter Stutzman (a software engineer), December 22, 1974; children: Michael Jacob, Anne Elizabeth. *Education:* Vassar College, B.A. (cum laude), 1972; Yale University, M.A., 1975, Ph.D., 1977.

ADDRESSES: Home—53 Mendingwall Circle, Madison, CT 06443. *Agent*—Richard Curtis Literary Agency, 171 East 74th Street, New York, NY 10021.

CAREER: Writer. Yale University, New Haven, CT, instructor in Spanish, 1977-79, and 1983.

MEMBER: Science Fiction Writers of America.

AWARDS, HONORS: Named Outstanding New Fantasy Writer by *Romantic Times,* 1986; Best Science Fiction/Fantasy Titles citation, *Voice of Youth Advocates,* 1988, for *New York by Knight.*

WRITINGS:

FANTASY NOVELS

Harlot's Ruse, Popular Library, 1986.
New York by Knight, New American Library, 1986.
The Silver Mountain, Popular Library, 1986.
Elf Defense, New American Library, 1988.
Druid's Blood, New American Library, 1988.
Sphynxes Wild, New American Library, 1989.
Gnome Man's Land (first volume in trilogy), Ace, 1991.
Harpy High (second volume in trilogy), Ace, 1991.
Unicorn U (third volume in trilogy), Ace, 1992.
Yesterday We Saw Mermaids, Tor Books, 1992.
Wishing Season (young adult), Atheneum, 1993.
Majik by Accident, Ace, 1993.
(With Laurence Watt-Evans) *Split Heirs,* Tor Books, 1993.
Majyk by Hook or Crook, Ace, 1994.
Majyk by Design, Ace, 1994.
Blood Muse: Timeless Tales of Vampires in the Arts, Donald I. Fine, 1995.
The Psalms of Herod, White Wolf, 1995.
The Sherwood Game, Pocket Books, 1995.
Child of the Eagle: A Myth of Rome, Baen Books, 1996.
The Sword of Mary, White Wolf, 1996.

SCIENCE FICTION

Warchild (Star Trek Deep Space Nine, No. 7), Pocket Books, 1994.
To Storm Heaven (Star Trek the Next Generation, No. 46) Pocket Books, 1997.

"CHRONICLES OF THE TWELVE KINGDOMS" SERIES; FANTASY NOVELS

Mustapha and His Wise Dog, Avon, 1985.
Spells of Mortal Weaving, Avon, 1986.
The Witchwood Cradle, Avon, 1987.
The Water King's Laughter, Avon, 1989.

"DEMONS" SERIES; FANTASY NOVELS

Here Be Demons, Ace, 1988.
Demon Blues, Ace, 1989.
Hooray for Hellywood, Ace, 1990.

OTHER

Also author of *Alien Pregnant by Elvis,* 1994.

SIDELIGHTS: "Esther M. Friesner," writes Fred Lerner in *Voice of Youth Advocates,* "has established herself as one of the most prolific writers of fantasy fiction, and one of the funniest." She overturns many of the conventions of modern and traditional fantasy in books ranging from *New York by Knight,* in which a dragon and his armored pursuer bring their ages-old battle to the streets of modern-day New York, and *Elf Defense,* in which a mortal woman seeks to escape her marriage to the king of Elfhame by hiring a divorce lawyer, to the "Gnome Man's Land" trilogy—where Tim Desmond, a high-school student from a single- parent home, must cope not only with adolescence but with successive invasions of "little people" from folklore, as well as exotic monsters and gods. Friesner's works, Lerner continues, "open new territory. She has made a specialty of ferreting out obscure creatures from the mythologies and demonologies of the world and turning them loose on unsuspecting places like Brooklyn, New Haven, and Hollywood."

Friesner herself was born and raised in Brooklyn, where she attended high school. She later went on to Vassar College, studying Spanish and drama, and Yale University, where she earned her Masters and doctoral degrees in classical Spanish literature, specializing in the works of playwright Lope de Vega. "I always knew that I wanted to write," Friesner told an interviewer. "I was trying to get published while I was in college, but it wasn't until I was in grad school that I got very serious about it. . . . The first time I got an encouraging rejection slip (saying 'We are not buying this, but this is why') was from George Scithers of *Isaac Asimov's Science Fiction Magazine.* I continued to send to him and he continued to send me back rejection slips, but always telling me what was wrong. Finally I made my first sale to *IASFM* as a result of his encouragement. That was a short story, but I got into writing full-length fantasy thanks to a group at Yale." In the Yale grad school, Friesner related, was a published science fiction author—Shariann Lewitt— who was working on a fantasy novel. "We saw her building a whole world," Friesner explained, "working out all the details on a big legal pad she had. This was quite different from writing a short story. I thought, 'Oh, building a world. I get to be God! How nice. I'm going to try that.' And that was how I got started on fantasy novels.

"The novel I wrote from my first world-building was actually the second book I sold," Friesner relates. "It was *Spells of Mortal Weaving,* in the 'Chronicles of the Twelve Kingdoms' series." Friesner's first published book was *Mustapha and His Wise Dog,* an Arabian Nights-style adventure "enlivened by an exotic and evocative fantasy setting, and a pair of captivating characters," declares Don D'Ammassa in *Twentieth-Century Science-Fiction Writers.* The series, continued in *The Witchwood Cradle* and *The Water King's Laughter,* follows the struggles of various mortals through several generations to overthrow Morgeld, an evil demigod. "Although Friesner followed traditional forms for the most part in this series," D'Ammassa concludes, "her wry humor and gift for characterization marked her early as someone to watch."

Friesner originally conceived the "Chronicles of the Twelve Kingdoms" as a twelve-volume high fantasy series. But, she explained, she also wanted to try some ideas about characterization that were not traditional in the high fantasy genre. "I wanted to have characters that were not just good and evil," she told an interviewer. "There are several villains in the series, but the main one is the demigod-type known as Morgeld. Morgeld was half-god but he was also half of another kind of creature, a night spirit. I tried to explain why he was so horrible, to give a reason for him being so villainish and, in fact, give him a chance to redeem himself from his evil. Most people, unless they are really unbalanced mentally, do not do evil things without a reason. Their reasons seems perfectly good and perfectly justified to them, and they go ahead and do atrocious things in the belief that they are doing the right thing. In *The Witchwood Cradle,* the villain shows up as something other than villainish, while you actually get to see a hero that is not always perfectly sterling silver pure. There can be a lot of mercilessness behind being a hero, and by the end of that book I had pretty well established the point that *you can't just accept this guy is the good guy in the white hat.* I think that comes out of the real world too. A lot of people want to believe that so-and-so is our flawless leader, and if our flawless leader all of a sudden decides to do something that isn't right, they will follow it anyway: *our leader is good, therefore everything our leader does must be good, and we must do it; we must not question.*"

"I don't think that I have a particular cause in writing fantasy," Friesner stated. "I just try to make it interesting and also to say a few things that I feel need to be said. For instance, in *Gnome Man's Land* . . . I was speaking about the suppression of people's ethnic heritage. In fact, I pointed out how this could get a little dangerous, because every culture has its own domestic spirits. Now, America is a melting pot of ethnicity, so while you can have an American who is predominantly Irish, you often have people who really aren't predominantly anything, and then all the little spirits from their different ethnic backgrounds will fight over them. In America the only little domestic spirits kids ever learn about are in the story 'The Shoemaker and the Elves,' which draws on a British tradition. The kids don't realize that there are the *hinzelmaenner,* little people myths from Germany, and they don't know about the *duende* in the Hispanic culture. The little people of Hawaii are quite active even today—it's still an active belief."

In addition to the warring ethnic spirits, the protagonist, Tim Desmond, has to deal with his own personal problems: getting through high school, living in a single-parent family—his father disappeared one evening on his way to buy a paper—and stabilizing a relationship with his girlfriend. Tim also has to fend off the lusty attentions of his own personal spirit, the Desmond family banshee. "A lot of the modern American perception of the elfin community in general is very sanitized—you know, Santa's little helpers happily making toys and shoes and whatever—but traditionally most otherworldly sprites were incredibly sexy creatures," Friesner explained. "They did not invite the ladies to come and join them just to have a cup of tea. In addition, there's a whole history of changelings and elfin babies with mortal mothers, and on the other side, the women of Elfhame stealing men. I think the Irish hero Oisin was taken away to the Land of Youth by a woman, a female elf. The ballad of Tam Lyn tells of a mortal man who has been stolen away by the Queen of Elves. He takes a mortal lover who winds up pregnant by him and she saves him from becoming Elfland's tithe to hell, from being sacrificed by the elves to hell. These are not nice elves, so having an amorous banshee is pretty much in keeping with the spirit of the otherworldly creatures."

Friesner views humor as an important ingredient in her works, but not necessarily the defining one. "Humor can make you think, and therefore can be very, very dangerous," she warned. "There is a long tradition of humorists being regarded as very dangerous people. I think that a country that can stand humorists has got an open mind and is willing to take chances, because humor can be devastating—it can make you stop and question things that you accepted before. But if the humor doesn't arise naturally out of the plot, the story's going to resemble one of the really bad sitcoms. Good humor, and good writing in general, should seem to be pretty natural. There is a lot of humor that does arise out of day to day situations; in fact, humor shows up in places that you wouldn't believe, in some of the most ghastly situations. In times like those laughter could be the saving of us."

Several of Friesner's works also use historical figures and settings. "I have always loved history," she once told an interviewer. "History is full of incredible trashy gossip that has been legitimized, because it is history: great stories, the things that people did and how they got around to doing them, how they justified them, and some of the things that they actually said. I have learned from some of this. . . . In *Sphynxes Wild* I used the Roman Emperors from my old reading of Suetonius. With *Druid's Blood* . . . I had a perfectly justified way of getting some of my favorite characters from English history together. I finally got to use Spanish history for my first hardback, called *Yesterday We Saw Mermaids.* The title is a direct quote from the diary of the first voyage of Christopher Columbus. He wrote, 'Yesterday we saw mermaids. They are not as beautiful as we have been led to believe.' And you know what he saw—manatees (adorable animals but they have got a face that would make a train take a dirt road). I thought 'Well, what would happen if indeed they saw mermaids but it's not Christopher Columbus who sees it, it's the ship that got there ahead of him.' Now in history when Columbus got to the New World and discovered the native Americans, a whole chunk of years passed during which the Europeans were debating whether the natives were human or not. 'Do they have souls or not? Because if we decide they are not human and do not have souls, then we can do whatever we want to them without any fear.' Well, finally the Europeans published the *Dialogue of the Dignity of Man,* in which they decided 'Oh, well, I guess they do have souls.' They kept on being pretty awful to the natives anyway, in spite of the excellent work of a number of churchmen who kept saying, 'What are you doing? These are human beings, they have souls and we must save their souls.' (If they didn't have their souls saved, they were still semi-fair game.) So that was my little ax to grind with Columbus and the *are they human* people."

"When I write," Friesner explained, "I try to make the story so interesting that I wouldn't mind rereading it myself. This is actually a very good thing. It's important to interest your readers because if you don't you won't have readers anymore. But if you don't interest yourself in what you're writing. . . . Well, the process of going from the first draft to the published book takes an awfully long time. You will have to look at that story and those characters a lot— you'll have to do another draft, perhaps even a third, then the editor will go over it, then the copy editor. Every time you're going to be reading the same words. If they aren't good words, you're going to get the feeling of being trapped at a party with people you don't like.

"Now my husband Walter is a published writer too. He is the person who pushed me to go from the typewriter to the computer for writing. Now whenever I have a problem with the computer I don't reach for the manual; I just say, 'Oh *hon*ey!' And a few years back, while we were sitting around just joking about these ads on TV—the ones for Ronco or Ginsu blades that will cut through anything, or for Elvis Presley's Greatest Hits—we started to write a fantasy parody titled 'But Wait, There's More,' which was later published. He contributed as much as I did. Again, recently I was asked to participate in an anthology called *Whatdunnit: Science Fiction Mysteries.* The editor gave me my choice of scenarios but I said, 'Could I please have Walter help me on this, because he's a mystery fan?' (I'm the one who looks at the last page to find out who done it and then decides if I'm going to read the book or not.) I did the actual writing but Walter was the plotter. Now I'm trying to drag him into writing a full length science mystery with me. I'm also going to try and drag our poor innocent thirteen-year-old son in. He's becoming a young computer expert and he likes to do computer gaming and I'd like to make the project a family thing. I may drag my daughter in at some point, too. The cat is still safe."

BIOGRAPHICAL/CRITICAL SOURCES:

BOOKS

Authors & Artists for Young Adults, Volume 10, Gale, 1993.

Twentieth-Century Science-Fiction Writers, 3rd edition, St. James, 1991.

PERIODICALS

Analog, December, 1989, pp. 184-185; September, 1991, pp. 166-167; March, 1993, p. 162; April, 1994, p. 169; October, 1994, p. 161; December, 1994, p. 161; February, 1997, p. 145.

Locus, April, 1989, pp. 25-27; January, 1990, p. 25; September, 1992, p. 33; September, 1993, p. 31.

Magazine of Fantasy & Science Fiction, July, 1995, p. 32.

Science Fiction Chronicles, June, 1990, p. 37; October, 1991, p. 41.
Voice of Youth Advocates, April, 1991, p. 42; December, 1991, p. 294.
Washington Post Book World, November 29, 1992, p. 11.*

* * *

FRY, Rosalie Kingsmill 1911-

PERSONAL: Born April 22, 1911, on Vancouver Island, British Columbia, Canada; daughter of Lindsay Bowring (an engineer) and Edith Alice (Finch) Fry. *Education:* Attended school in Swansea, Wales, and then Central School of Arts and Crafts, London, England, 1929-34. *Politics:* Conservative (Tory). *Religion:* Anglican.

ADDRESSES: Home—1 Mountain Cottage, Llandybie, Ammanford, Wales.

CAREER: Writer and illustrator. Designer of Christmas cards. *Military service:* Women's Royal Naval Service, 1939-45.

MEMBER: Society of Authors.

WRITINGS:

SELF-ILLUSTRATED, EXCEPT AS INDICATED

Bumblebuzz, Dutton, 1938.
Ladybug Ladybug!, Dutton, 1940.
Bandy Boy's Treasure Island, Dutton, 1941.
Baby's Progress Book, W. H. Smith, 1944.
Lost in the Dew, W. H. Smith, 1944.
Many Happy Returns (birthday book), W. H. Smith, 1944.
Adventure Downstream, Hutchinson, 1946.
In a Rock Pool, Hutchinson, 1947.
Cherrywinkle, Hutchinson, 1951.
The Little Gipsy, Hutchinson, 1951.
Pipkin Sees the World, Dutton, 1951, published in England as *Pipkin the Woodmouse,* Dent, 1953.
Two Little Pigs (readers), three books, Hutchinson, 1953.
Cinderella's Mouse and Other Fairy Tales, Dutton, 1953.
Deep in the Forest, Hutchinson, 1955, Dodd, 1956.
The Wind Call, Dutton, 1955.
Lucinda and the Painted Bell, Dent, 1956, published as *A Bell for Ringleblume,* Dutton, 1957.
Child of the Western Isles, Dent, 1957, published as *Secret of the Ron Mor Skerry* (Junior Literary Guild selection), Dutton, 1959.
Secret of the Forest, Hutchinson, 1958.
Matelot, Little Sailor of Britanny, Dutton, 1958, published in England as *Lucinda and the Sailor Kitten,* Dent, 1959.
Fly Home, Colombina, Dutton, 1960.
The Mountain Door, Dent, 1960, Dutton, 1961.
Princess in the Forest, Hutchinson, 1961.
The Echo Song (Junior Literary Guild selection), Dutton, 1962.
The Riddle of the Figurehead, Dutton, 1963.
September Island, illustrated by Margery Gill, Dutton, 1965.
The Castle Family, illustrated by Margery Gill, Dent, 1965, Dutton, 1966.
Promise of the Rainbow, illustrated by Robin Jacques, Farrar, Straus, 1965.
Whistler in the Mist, illustrated by Robin Jacques, Farrar, Straus, 1968.
Gypsy Princess, illustrated by Philip Gough, Dutton, 1969.
Snowed Up, illustrated by Robin Jacques, Farrar, Straus, 1970.
Mungo, Farrar, Straus, 1971, illustrated by Velma Ilsley, Farrar, Straus, 1972.
Secrets, Dent, 1973.
The Secret of Roan Inish, Hyperion Paperbacks for Children (New York City), 1995.

Illustrator of *The Water Babies* in Dutton's "Children's Illustrated Classics," and of other books published by Dent, Dutton, and Hutchinson. Stories included in several anthologies. Contributor of articles and illustrations to *Lady, Parents', Collins' Children Annual, Countryman,* and *Country Life,* of stories to British Broadcasting Corp. and Radio Eireann programs.

Manuscript collection at University of Southern Mississippi in Hattiesburg, in the de Grummond Collection.

ADAPTATIONS: The Secret of Ron Mor Skerry was adapted as a film titled *The Secret of Roan Inish,* directed by John Sayles and released in 1994.

SIDELIGHTS: In *Something about the Author Autobiography Series,* Rosalie Kingsmill Fry described the creative impulse that compels her to write: "Suddenly, out of nowhere, an idea takes shape in my mind. I see it clearly like a tiny, vivid picture and I know at once that a story is there, waiting to be developed. It is always an exciting moment. You cannot *make* an idea, it simply comes, and then you have to work on it. I always see the settings of my stories very clearly and wonder if this is because I have lived most of my life in beautiful places."

Although trained as an artist, Fry wrote her own children's books as a forum for her illustrations. As she explained, "A childhood love of drawing grew into a decision to illustrate children's books. But when I had completed a course at a London art school I was faced with the fact that I didn't know a single author who might write a book for me to illustrate! So there was nothing for it but to write my own." Her stories often feature unlikely characters, such as hawk moths (*Cherrywinkle*), crabs (*In a Rock Pool*), and a fairy child (*The Wind Call*).

Fry's earliest work was aimed at a very young audience, but with *Pipkin Sees the World,* she branched out to eight- and nine-year-old audiences. The story and the accompanying illustrations reflect the author's love of nature and its creatures, and portray Pipkin (a live toy) in a sentimental, and sometimes humorous, light.

In *Deep in the Forest,* the main characters are Katinka, a spirited child, and a snuggly bear cub named Jokle. Katinka is a typical little girl, playing house, loving her pet, and exploring her surroundings. She is also responsive to the beauty of the countryside.

The children who star in her books gradually get older as Fry becomes more experienced as a writer. She wrote three books about Lucinda, who is eight years old, and whose travels with her artist parents expose her to the art and lore of Brittany and Italy. Then, starting with *The Echo Song,* her characters are all ten years old or older. Gwen Marsh wrote in *Twentieth-Century Children's Writers,* "In these later works, which no longer draw upon fantasy, her style is still a model of clarity: thoughtful and telling details make the plots absorbing and convincing, and the characters and settings have a charm that appeals strongly to children, especially girls entering their teens."

Secrets are often used as technique not only to delight children's natural curiosity and love of suspense, but, as Marsh observed, to "provide a significant aid in a child's progress towards a strong self-image." In *Gypsy Princess,* a secret eventually tells Zilda, the heroine, who she is. When she discovers a secret passage leading to an old gypsy wagon, Zilda finds her name carved underneath the wagon with the words "My princess." As it turns out, the gypsy who once lived in the wagon vowed to return some day to give it to the rightful owner, a princess. Zilda learns the story of her dead parents, and learns that to her father, she was a princess.

Fry draws from her own surroundings for her books, so it is no coincidence that Fry owns a gypsy wagon like the one described in *Gypsy Princess.* When she is writing about a particular place, especially abroad, she usually spends several weeks in the area, sometimes doing the first draft on the spot. She expanded on her use of familiar settings: "I live and work in a small cottage in the lovely Welsh countryside and many of my books are set in or around this area. . . . I also have an isolated wooden hut in the hills, which is a wonderful place in which to work during the summer months. It is the setting for *Whistler in the Mist,* much of which was written up there on the verandah. This little hut provides endless material for articles as well as stories."

BIOGRAPHICAL/CRITICAL SOURCES:

BOOKS

Something about the Author Autobiography Series, Volume 11, Gale, 1991.

Twentieth-Century Children's Writers, 4th edition, St. James Press, 1995.

PERIODICALS

Booklist, July 15, 1966, p. 1086.

Christian Science Monitor, November 4, 1965, p. 86; November 7, 1968, p. 1047; January 2, 1971, p. 19; January 30, 1978, p. 15.

New York Times Book Review, August 15, 1965, p. 28.

Times Literary Supplement, December 9, 1965, p. 1131; June 26, 1969, p. 699; July 2, 1971, p. 775.*

* * *

FULLER, Roy (Broadbent) 1912- 1991

PERSONAL: Born February 11, 1912, in Failsworth, Lancashire, England; died September 27, 1991, in London, England; son of Leopold Charles (a factory manager) and Nellie (Broadbent) Fuller; married Kathleen Smith, 1936; children: John (a writer). *Education:* Attended Blackpool High School, Lancashire.

CAREER: Poet, novelist, and critic. Qualified as solicitor, 1934; staff member of various legal firms, 1934-38; Woolwich Equitable Building Society, London, assistant solicitor, 1938-58, solicitor, 1958-69, director,

1969-88; Oxford University, professor of poetry, 1968-73. Building Societies Association, London, chair of Legal Advisory Panel, 1958-69, vice president, 1969-91. Member of board of Governors, British Broadcasting Corp. (BBC), 1972-79. Member, Poetry Book Society, London, chairman, 1960-68; Arts Council of Great Britain, and chairman of Literature Panel, 1976-77; member, Library Advisory Council, 1977-79. *Military service:* Royal Navy, 1941-46; Royal Naval Volunteer Reserve, lieutenant.

AWARDS, HONORS: Royal Society of Literature fellow, 1958; Arts Council Poetry Award, 1959; Duff Cooper Memorial Prize for Poetry, 1968; Queen's Gold Medal for Poetry, 1970; Commander, Order of the British Empire, 1970; Cholmondeley Award for poetry, 1980; honorary M.A., Oxford University; honorary D.Litt., University of Kent, Canterbury, 1986.

WRITINGS:

FOR CHILDREN

Savage Gold: A Story of Adventure, illustrated by Robert Medley, Lehmann (London), 1946, new edition illustrated by Douglas Hall, Hutchinson Educational, 1960.

With My Little Eye, illustrated by Alan Lindsay, Lehmann, 1948, Macmillan (New York City), 1957.

Catspaw, illustrated by David Gollins, Alan Ross (London), 1966.

Seen Grandpa Lately? (verse), illustrated by Joan Hickson, Deutsch (London), 1972.

Poor Roy (verse), illustrated by Nicolas Bentley, Deutsch, 1977.

The Other Planet and Three Other Fables, illustrated by Paul Peter Piech, Keepsake Press (Surrey), 1979.

More about Tompkins and Other Light Verse, Tragara Press (Edinburgh), 1981.

(With Barbara Giles and Adrian Rumble) *Upright, Downfall* (verse), Oxford University Press (Oxford), 1983.

The World through the Window: Collected Poems for Children, illustrated by Nick Duffy, Blackie (Glasgow), 1989.

POETRY FOR ADULTS

Poems, Fortune (London), 1940.

The Middle of a War, Hogarth Press (London), 1942.

A Lost Season, Hogarth Press, 1944.

Epitaphs and Occasions, Lehmann, 1949.

Counterparts, Verschoyle (London), 1954.

Brutus's Orchard, Deutsch, 1957, Macmillan, 1958.

Collected Poems 1936-1961, Dufour (Philadelphia), 1962.

Buff, Dufour, 1965.

New Poems, Dufour, 1968.

Off Course, Turret (London), 1969.

To an Unknown Reader, Poem-of-the-Month Club (London), 1970.

Song Cycle from a Record Sleeve, Sycamore Press (Oxford), 1972.

Tiny Tears, Deutsch, 1973.

An Old War, Tragara Press, 1974.

Waiting for the Barbarians: A Poem, Keepsake Press, 1974.

From the Joke Shop, Deutsch, 1975.

The Joke Shop Annexe, Tragara Press, 1975.

An Ill-governed Coast, Ceolfrith Press (Sunderland), 1976.

Re-treads, Tragara Press, 1979.

The Reign of Sparrows, London Magazine Editions (London), 1980.

The Individual and His Times: A Selection of the Poetry of Roy Fuller, edited by V. J. Lee, Athlone Press (London), 1982.

House and Shop, Tragara Press, 1982.

As from the Thirties, Tragara Press, 1983.

Mianserin Sonnets, Tragara Press, 1984.

New and Collected Poems 1934-1984, Secker and Warburg (London), 1985.

Subsequent to Summer, Salamander Press (London), 1985.

Outside the Canon, Tragara Press, 1986.

Consolations, Secker and Warburg, 1987.

Available for Dreams, Collins, 1989.

Contributor to books, including *Pergamon Poets 1,* edited by Evan Owen, Pergamon Press, 1968; and *Penguin Modern Poets 18,* Penguin, 1970.

FICTION FOR ADULTS

The Second Curtain, Verschoyle, 1953, Macmillan, 1956.

Fantasy and Fugue, Verschoyle, 1954, Macmillan, 1956, published as *Murder in Mind,* Academy (Chicago), 1986.

Image of a Society, Deutsch, 1956, Macmillan, 1957.

The Ruined Boys, Deutsch, 1959, published as *That Distant Afternoon,* Macmillan, 1957.

The Father's Comedy, Deutsch, 1961.

The Perfect Fool, Deutsch, 1963.

My Child, My Sister, Deutsch, 1965.

The Carnal Island, Deutsch, 1970.

Omnibus (contains *With My Little Eye, The Second Curtain,* and *Fantasy and Fugue*), Carcanet (Manchester), 1988.
Stares, Sinclair-Stevenson, 1990.

NONFICTION FOR ADULTS

Owls and Artificers: Oxford Lectures on Poetry, Deutsch, 1971, Library Press (LaSalle, IL), 1971.
Professors and Gods: Last Oxford Lectures on Poetry, Deutsch, 1973, St. Martin's Press (New York City), 1974.
Souvenirs (memoirs), London Magazine Editions, 1980.
Vamp till Ready: Further Memoirs, London Magazine Editions, 1982.
Home and Dry: Memoirs 3, London Magazine Editions, 1984.
Twelfth Night: A Personal View, Tragara Press, 1985.
The Strange and the Good: Collected Memoirs, Collins Harvill (London), 1989.
Spanner and Pen: Post-War Memoirs, Sinclair- Stevenson, 1991.

EDITOR

Byron for Today, Porcupine Press (Philadelphia), 1948.
(With Clifford Dyment and Montagu Slater) *New Poems 1952,* Joseph, 1952.
The Building Societies Acts 1874-1960: Great Britain and Northern Ireland, Franey, 1957, 6th edition, 1962.
Supplement of New Poetry, Poetry Book Society, 1964.
Fellow Mortals: An Anthology of Animal Verse, illustrated by David Koster, Macdonald & Evans, 1981.
(With John Lehmann) *The Penguin New Writing 1940-1950: An Anthology,* Penguin, 1985.

Legal correspondent for *Building Societies' Gazette.* Contributor to periodicals, including *Listener, New Statesman,* and *Times Literary Supplement.*

Fuller's papers are housed in manuscript collections at the Brotherton Collection, Leeds University, the State University of New York, Buffalo, and the British Library, London.

SIDELIGHTS: According to Stephen Spender in *Dictionary of Literary Biography,* Roy Fuller is the norm against which "other poets of the past thirty years may be judged." Clear, lucid verses were Fuller's trademark, something that became unfashionable in the later twentieth century. Fuller was also a well-respected novelist, turning his hand to stories about sensitive individuals fighting against the forces of an uncaring society or corporation. Less well known are Fuller's works for young readers. In the four fiction books and the five collections of poetry he wrote for a juvenile audience, Fuller explored many of the same themes and with much the same linguistic sophistication as his adult works. "There is no talking-down to a youthful audience here," Peter Reading commented in the *Times Literary Supplement* in a review of Fuller's collected poems for children, *The World through the Window.*

Fuller was a family man involved in corporate life, serving for thirty years as a solicitor for a British savings and loan association. He once described his life as "part managerial, part poetic," and he balanced both aspects well enough to leave behind, at his death in 1991, a body of work including thirty-one volumes of poetry, nine novels, eleven nonfiction works, and a score of edited works and reviews.

Born into a lower-middle-class home in Failsworth, Lancashire, in 1912, Fuller was one of two children, and his father worked as manager of a rubber-proofing mill. With the death of his father when he was only eight, Fuller and his family moved to Blackpool. At sixteen Fuller was articled, or apprenticed, to a solicitor from whom he learned the law, and by age twenty-one he passed his qualifying law exams. As quoted in *Dictionary of Literary Biography,* Fuller described his background as "provincial . . . [and] unliterary" and his schooling as "uninspired . . . [and] truncated." He worked for various law firms, married in 1936, and by the time of the outbreak of World War II had moved his family to the outskirts of London where he took a post with the Woolwich Equitable Building Society. Except for serving in the Royal Navy during the war, Fuller remained with this firm until his retirement in 1968 and stayed in Blackheath, a London suburb, until his death.

During the war, Fuller worked in the newly emerging field of radar and spent several years in Kenya as a radar technician. He had already begun to write poetry before the war and published his first volume in 1939. But it was during the war years that he gained some renown with *The Middle of a War* and *A Lost Season.* Influenced by W. H. Auden and Stephen Spender, these early poems are characterized by a liberal political slant—Fuller considered himself a Marxist at the time—and a concern for the individual in modern technological society. Some critics have mentioned these two volumes as among the best war poetry of the time.

With the end of the war and his return to England, Fuller wrote his first fiction. His son, John, later a poet in his own right, stimulated Fuller to write books for younger readers. The first of these, *Savage Gold: A Story of Adventure,* revolves around two young boys who become involved in a rivalry between two mining companies. Alan Edwin Day, writing in *Twentieth-Century Children's Writers,* characterized *Savage Gold* as "well told" and with "a fast and exciting pace." In 1948, Fuller wrote his first mystery novel, *With My Little Eye.* Its youthful protagonist, Frederick French, the only son of a county judge, plays detective with a courtroom murder trial. Both literate and sophisticated, the book is "in its small way a perfect example of a modern crime story," according to Julian Symons, writing in *Mortal Consequences: A History—From the Detective Story to the Crime Novel.* But it is this very sophistication that bothered Day. For Day, this sophistication and plot complexity were too much for young readers: "We can only conclude that Fuller sadly misdirected his inventiveness," Day noted. In the same article, Fuller himself commented that "though writing for children has always given me a certain sense of freedom, I have never thought of my children's books as 'written down' to an audience. Indeed, I have erred the other way."

As his son grew up, Fuller's inspirations changed, and he returned to adult fiction and poetry for almost twenty years. During this time he secured his reputation with such poetry collections as *Epitaphs and Occasions, Counterparts,* and *Brutus's Orchard.* Of *Epitaphs and Occasions,* a reviewer for *Times Literary Supplement* wrote, "He has ruthlessly simplified his verse-forms to enable his writing, without change of tone, to move easily through very different kinds of theme, while the meaning remains transparent. Mr. Fuller's latest manner is perhaps over-reminiscent in style of early Auden, possibly also of the colloquial Byron." Years later, another reviewer for *Times Literary Supplement* would review *Brutus' Orchard,* concluding, "The major achievement of this volume are the nineteen mythological sonnets that close it. Here the sustaining passions of men, as gods—love, hate, lust, ambition, art, jealousy—are scrutinized and compared in a series of finely wrought images." By the 1960s Fuller was considered one of the foremost British poets of his time. He also continued his experiments in the mystery fiction genre in the 1950s with *The Second Curtain* and *Fantasy and Fugue.* James Sandoe compared these books for *New York Herald Tribune of Books,* observing, "[*Fantasy and Fugue*] is at least as exciting and as disturbing as [Roy Fuller's first crime novel] *The Second Curtain* and by that token one of the more considerable mysteries in this or any other season. Like its predecessor it has the haunting quality of those entertainments with which Graham Greene expressed his alertness to the Thirties."

By the late 1960s both Fuller's poetry and prose had reached a new and more personal level, exploring themes of death, loss, aging, and the role of the artist. Much of the poetry is infused with a quiet and suburban enjoyment of nature, as well, influenced by back-garden musings at his home in Blackheath. *Collected Poems* and *The Individual and His Times* are considered by some critics to be touchstones of this middle to late period of Fuller's poetic development. His novels also took on more private, personal themes, as in *My Child, My Sister,* which Fuller considered his best structured poetry.

With retirement from Woolwich Equitable in 1968, Fuller's public life did not diminish. He had just published *New Poems,* a collection which a *Times Literary Supplement* reviewer claimed would "force one into asking severely moral questions, of art and of oneself. That they do so in such a disquieting way is, quite apart from their great skill, a sign of their importance." Fuller became a professor of poetry at Oxford University and served as governor on the board of the British Broadcasting Corporation (BBC). It was during this part of his career that Fuller returned to children's books. "The separation in time between the two groups of children's books," Fuller explained in *Twentieth-Century Children's Writers,* "is to be accounted for by the fact that I was stimulated to write them first by my son's childhood, then my grandchildren's." Fuller's first return to juvenile fiction was *Catspaw,* in which his character Victoria wanders into a land populated only by dogs who are continually worried about the machinations of the country called Pussia, populated only by cats—an allegory of the Cold War, then at its height.

With the publication of *Seen Grandpa Lately?,* Fuller made his first verse contribution to children's literature. Judith Nichols, writing in *Books for Your Children,* commented on the "gentle pleasures" of this volume. In part comic and nonsensical, the volume also contains serious poems exploring many of Fuller's adult themes such as death and loss. Throughout the 1970s, Fuller made further periodic sallies into juvenile fiction and verse. A second volume of children's verse, *Poor Roy,* appeared in 1977, followed by a book of stories, *The Other Planet and Three Other Fables,* in 1979. Fuller's output for young readers in the 1980s was confined to verse: *More about Tompkins and Other Light Verse* in 1981 and *Upright, Downfall* in 1983. The latter was written with two other poets, which, according to a reviewer for *Book Report,* provides "a broad range of experience, discovery and delight."

New and Collected Poems 1934-1984 successfully reintroduced the poet to a new generation of adult readers. Other volumes of poetry followed, *Consolations* and *Available for Dreams* among them. He also wrote several volumes of memoirs as well as making a return to fiction with the 1990 *Stares,* which Lachlan Mackinnon, writing in the *Times Literary Supplement,* called a "frightening and memorable novel." Fuller's verse for children was gathered together in *The World through the Window: Collected Poems for Children* in 1989. Peter Reading, in his *Times Literary Supplement* review of the collection, noted that it "is at once enjoyable and informative" but also that because of its "wit, imagery, sophistication" it would probably not find the wide readership that other simpler texts do. An *Observer Review* writer commented on Fuller's "light and genial touch" evident in his collected poems, while Nichols, in *Books for Your Children,* concluded that *The World through the Window* would be "an ideal opportunity to catch up" on Fuller's work.

BIOGRAPHICAL/CRITICAL SOURCES:

BOOKS

Contemporary Authors Autobiography Series, Volume 10, Gale, 1991.
Contemporary Literary Criticism, Gale, Volume 28, 1974, Volume 4, 1975.
Dictionary of Literary Biography, Gale, Volume 15: *British Novelists, 1930-1959,* 1983, Volume 20: *British Poets, 1914-1945,* Gale, 1983.
Powell, Neil, *Roy Fuller: Writer and Society,* Carcanet (Manchester, England), 1995.
Smith, Steven E., *Roy Fuller: A Bibliography,* Ashgate Pub. Co. (Brookfield, VT), 1996.
Twentieth-Century Children's Writers, 4th edition, St. James Press, 1995.

PERIODICALS

Book Report, May-June, 1986, p. 36.
Books for Your Children, spring, 1990, p. 19.
New York Herald Tribune Book Review, August 19, 1956, p. 9.
New York Times Book Review, April 13, 1986, p. 38.
Observer (London), September 5, 1965, p. 26; June 23, 1985, p. 23; February 8, 1987, p. 28; March 22, 1987, p. 27; April 23, 1989, p. 44; November 11, 1990, p. 67; March 10, 1991, p. 61; October 24, 1993, p. 23.
Observer Review, August 6, 1989, p. 40.
Times Literary Supplement, December 30, 1949, p. 858; January 3, 1958, p. 9; October 3, 1968, p. 1134; November 1, 1985, p. 1223; April 25, 1986, p. 450; March 6, 1987, p. 244; June 23, 1989, p. 694; December 1, 1989, p. 1344; January 11, 1991, p. 17; February 1, 1991, p. 21; June 4, 1993, p. 26.

OBITUARIES:

PERIODICALS

Los Angeles Times, September 30, 1991, p. A20.
Times (London), September 28, 1991, p. 14.
Washington Post, September 29, 1991, p. B7.*

G

GALLAGHER, Patricia

PERSONAL: Born in Lockhart, TX; daughter of Frank (in construction), and Martha (Rhody) Bienek; married James D. Gallagher (a television engineer; died, 1966); children: James C. *Education:* Attended Trinity University, San Antonio, TX, 1951. *Avocational interests:* Traveling, reading, and gardening.

ADDRESSES: Home—3111 Clearfield Dr., San Antonio, TX78230. *Agent*—Scott Meredith Literary Agency, Inc., 845 Third Ave., New York, NY 10022.

CAREER: Writer, 1949—. Limited operator for KTSA-Radio, 1950-51; has appeared on television and radio programs in Texas, Charleston, SC, and other cities. Member of advisory council for *San Antonio* magazine.

MEMBER: Authors Guild, Authors League of America, Romance Writers of America, Golden Triangle Writers Guild.

WRITINGS:

NOVELS

The Sons and the Daughters, Messner, 1961.
Answer to Heaven, Avon,1964.
The Fires of Brimstone, Avon, 1966.
Shannon, Avon, 1967.
Shadows of Passion, Avon, 1971.
Summer of Sighs, Avon, 1971.
The Thicket, Avon,1974.
Castles in the Air, Avon, 1976.
Mystic Rose, Avon, 1977.
No Greater Love, Avon, 1979.
All for Love, Avon, 1981.
Echoes and Embers, Avon,1983.
Love Springs Eternal, Berkley Publishing (New York), 1985.
On Wings of Dreams, Berkley Publishing, 1985.
A Perfect Love, Berkley Publishing, 1987.

SIDELIGHTS: Patricia Gallagher wrote *CA:* "I've been interested in writing since childhood, wrote short stories in high school, and walked three miles each way to the Public Library. 'Making it' was a long hard struggle, writing on a small portable on my kitchen table between the chores of housewife and mother, and often late at night when my family was asleep, and the kitchen was the quietest place in the house."

Castles in the Air is Gallagher's best-known work. It is the story of Devon, a post-Civil War woman trying to make her way north so she can pursue a career as a journalist. On her way, she encounters Keith, a wealthy man who takes advantage of her; yet they fall madly in love. Although he is married, their relationship lasts five years before she decides to accept a marriage of convenience to another man. Although she sets out to prove that women have an array of choices beyond getting married and having children, ultimately, she fails. George Walsh, in *Twentieth-Century Romance and Historical Writers,* wrote of Gallagher, "She presents situation, leaves moral reflection to her readers. And this interest in something beyond a conventional romantic plot, this use of romantic devices to convey her own themes, is common to many of her novels." Despite his criticisms of her inconsistent skill with language and dialogue, Walsh concluded that Gallagher has the potential to "set a standard against which other romance novelists will be measured." In fact, *Castles in the Air* has been used as a text at Penn State University and was rated by students as second only to *Gone with the Wind.*

Gallagher's works have been published in French, German, Spanish, Portuguese, Italian, Dutch, Danish, Swedish, and Norwegian.

BIOGRAPHICAL/CRITICAL SOURCES:

BOOKS

Twentieth-Century Romance and Historical Writers, 3rd edition, St. James Press, 1994.

PERIODICALS

Affaire de Coeur, September, 1987.
Bride's Magazine, February-March, 1983.
Dallas News, April 16, 1961; May 27, 1976.
Houston Post, April 1, 1962; June 1,1976.
Publishers Weekly, November 30, 1984.
Romantic Times, September, 1987.
San Antonio Light, May 23,1976.
San Antonio Magazine, October, 1976.*

* * *

GALVIN, Brendan 1938-

PERSONAL: Born October 20, 1938, in Everett, MA; son of James Russell (a letter carrier) and Rose (McLaughlin) Galvin; married Ellen Baer, August 1, 1968; children: Kim, Peter, Anne Maura. *Education:* Boston College, B.S., 1961; Northeastern University, M.A.,1964; University of Massachusetts at Amherst, M.F.A., 1967, Ph.D., 1970.

ADDRESSES: Home—P.O. Box 54, Durham, CT 06422; P.O. Box 383, Truro, MA 02666. *Office*—Department of English, Central Connecticut State University, Stanley St., New Britain, CT 06050.

CAREER: Northeastern University, Boston, MA, instructor in English,1963- 65; Slippery Rock State College, Slippery Rock, PA, assistant professor of English, 1968-69; Central Connecticut State University, New Britain, assistant professor, 1969-74, associate professor, 1974-80, professor of English, 1980—. Founder and director of Connecticut Writers Conference; visiting writer, Connecticut College, 1975-76; affiliated with Wesleyan- Suffield Writer-Reader Conference, 1977-78, Martha's Vineyard Poetry Seminar, 1986; Coal Royalty Visiting Chair in creative writing, University of Alabama, Tuscaloosa, spring, 1993.

AWARDS, HONORS: Fine Arts Work Center fellowship, 1971; National Endowment for the Arts creative writing fellowship, 1974, 1988; Artist Foundation fellowship, 1978; New England Film Festival, first prize, 1978, for *Massachusetts Story;* Connecticut Commission on the Arts fellowship, 1981, 1984; Guggenheim fellow, 1988; Sotheby Prize, Arvon Foundation, 1988; Levinson Prize, *Poetry* magazine, 1989; O. B. Hardison Jr. Poetry Prize, Folger Shakespeare Library, 1991; Outstanding Academic Book, American Library Association, 1993, for *Saints in Their Ox-Hide Boat;* Chavity Randall Citation, International Poetry Forum, 1994.

WRITINGS:

POETRY

The Narrow Land, Northeastern University Press (Boston), 1971.
The Salt Farm, Fiddlehead, 1972.
No Time for Good Reasons, University of Pittsburgh Press (Pittsburgh, PA), 1974.
The Minutes No One Owns, University of Pittsburgh Press, 1977.
Atlantic Flyway, University of Georgia Press (Athens, GA), 1980.
Winter Oysters, University of Georgia Press, 1983.
A Birder's Dozen, Ampersand Press (Princeton, NJ), 1984.
Seals in the Inner Harbor, Carnegie-Mellon University Press (Pittsburgh, PA), 1985.
Raising Irish Walls (chapbook) Ampersand Press, 1989.
Wampanoag Traveler: Being, in Letters, the Life and Times of Loranzo Newcomb, American and Natural Historian, Louisiana State University Press (Baton Rouge, LA), 1989.
Great Blue: New and Selected Poems, University of Illinois Press (Champaign, IL), 1990.
OuterLife: The Poetry of Brendan Galvin, edited by Martha Christina, Ampersand Press, 1991.
Early Returns, Carnegie-Mellon University Press,1992.
Saints in Their Ox-Hide Boat, Louisiana State University Press, 1992.
Islands (chapbook) Druid City Press (Tuscaloosa, AL), 1993.
Sky and Island Light, Louisiana State University Press, 1995.
Hotel Malabar, University of Iowa Press (Iowa City, IA), 1998.

OTHER

Massachusetts Story (documentary film script), produced by Gordon Massingham, 1978.

Today You Will Meet the Love of Your Life (poetry video), Connecticut Public TV, 1987-88.

Also author of short stories, reviews, and books on poetic theory. Contributor to numerous periodicals, including *American Review, Atlantic, Connecticut English Journal, Georgia Review, Harper's, Hudson Review, Massachusetts Studies in English, Nation, New Republic, New Yorker, Paris Review, Ploughshares, Poetry, Sewanee Review,* and *Shenandoah.* Editor with George Garrett of *Poultry: A Magazine of Voice,* 1981—.

SIDELIGHTS: Brendan Galvin told *CA:* "I began writing little stories on the kitchen floor when I was maybe nine or ten, using Disney characters in badly plotted one-pagers, and in high school received my first rejection when the faculty advisor to the student newspaper didn't believe I'd written the poems I submitted. I was a tackle on the football team, and I think he thought I took them from someone on the bus to school.

"Later, as a biology major at Boston College, I sometimes wrote at the back of a laboratory while my peers cut into a turtle's plastron to get at its terrified heart. Biology gave me a vocabulary I use in my poems without self-consciousness, so it's not unusual for me to use a word like 'meniscus.'

"I was accepted at two dental schools, but decided on a master's degree in English, instead. At Northeastern University I took a poetry-writing course with Wallace Stevens scholar Samuel French Morse, who encouraged me to try for publication, and in the following year the *Atlantic* accepted two poems. I continued to write and publish at the University of Massachusetts, where I earned an M.F.A. in Creative Writing and a Ph.D., with a dissertation on Theodore Roethke.

"Robert Frost, Theodore Roethke, Robert Lowell, James Dickey, Elizabeth Bishop, James Wright, Richard Wilbur, Galway Kinnel, and D. H. Lawrence are just a few of the poets I admire deeply and keep returning to in my reading. In addition I read a lot of fiction and history, natural history, and folklore.

"I continue to write about the natural world I live in at my home in the woods above a Cape Cod salt marsh. I accept the fact that my poems are 'under peopled,' but am not perplexed by it. In many respects I'm a private person to whom the politics of literary reputation seem both a waste of time and an appalling example of our present-day lack of shame.

"Around the time I turned fifty, I walked into my study one afternoon and the autumn sun was falling through the skylight onto my open notebook. A pen was lying beside the notebook. Sounds like a scene from a bad movie, I know, but my first thought was, 'That's the most beautiful sight in the world!' I wonder how many people my age feel that way about the tools of their trade. That moment convinced me I'd chosen the right life, and I'm still deeply pleasured by feeling the poem grow under my fingertips. I believe the world exists so that writers can write about it."

Galvin's poetry is characterized by a sense of geographic place and personal heritage, and a keen interest in the landscapes, the fauna and flora, of the world about him. Some of his specific themes have included the country versus the city, the exploitation of workers, and the victimization of children. More generally, Galvin can be seen as a poet who celebrates the beauty of the natural world, making use of images from that world to explore human relationships: familial, interpersonal, social, and historical.

Writing in a precise yet lyrical free verse, influenced by his early work in metric forms, Galvin's voice interweaves the literary with the conversational, often borrowing from the local speech patterns of his native Cape Cod. He also makes use of scientific terminology, reflecting his lifelong interest in the natural sciences. His imagery tends to be realistic, firmly rooted in the direct experience of the senses, particularly the visual. Additional elements that make Galvin's poetry distinctive are its use of serio-comic effects and traditional narrative techniques.

Galvin's first book, *The Narrow Land,* deals with seasons along the Atlantic Coast. His second, *The Salt Farm,* broadens his range of topics, including poems about animals, the loss of loved ones, and the burning of an abandoned factory. In both books, Galvin's preference for the rural over the urban, the beauties of nature over the "the paranoia of supermarkets," is clearly expressed.

By the mid-seventies, Galvin had established his poetic reputation with publication in such major venues as *Harper's, Atlantic Monthly,* and *New Yorker.* His third book, and first major collection, *No Time for Good Reasons,* brought together forty-six poems, the best of ten years' work.

It received critical praise for its inventiveness, its organic use of language, and its sense of humor. In his next collection, *The Minutes No One Owns,* Galvin further developed his vision and deepened the texture of his language. Both of these books, as their titles indicate, are concerned with the passage of time, another of Galvin's recurrent themes.

Galvin's fifth collection, *Atlantic Flyway,* presents an example of why he has described his own work as "under peopled." Birds play a significant role in poems throughout this book, and human characters are often described in avian terms. Galvin also begins to explore his own heritage in *Atlantic Flyway,* including poems about a journey in search of his ancestral home, about his grandfather, and about the Irish potato famine.

Wampanoag Traveler: Being, in Letters, the Life and Times of Loranzo Newcomb, American and Natural Historian further demonstrates Galvin's interest in history and natural history, and as the author has stated, involved research in both fields. It also extends his narrative approach to poetry by creating an entire book-length story set in the eighteenth century. *Wampanoag Traveler* relates the tale of Loranzo Newcomb, who gathers seeds and other specimens in the New World for shipment to the Royal Society in England. It is told in fourteen sections, each an imaginary letter written by Newcomb, thirteen to the Society and a final letter addressed directly to the reader. Snake bites, hummingbirds, a trained alligator, and fiddler crabs are among the subjects covered, every one serving as a starting point for Newcomb's ponderings on a variety of themes, from unrequited love to the destruction of the environment. In the final letter, a discussion of apples, Galvin examines the question of history itself. Writing in *Poetry,* Ben Howard criticizes the book for it's lack of thematic unity, and states: "Galvin's project is ambitious, but the power of the book lies less in its grand design than in its compelling local effects." Glyn Maxwell, in the *Times Literary Supplement,* attributes the success of the poem to "Newcomb's voice, the intelligence and humanity that Galvin breathes into this lonesome scientist."

Composed of sixty poems from eight previous collections, along with twenty new poems, *Great Blue: New and Selected Poems* provides a representative selection of Galvin's work. In the title poem of the book, a near-mystical parallel is drawn between the great blue heron and Galvin's mother, both of whom are seen as guardian spirits. Here one can also find poems about animals, folklore, nature, art, history, holiday rituals, Galvin's Irish ancestry, and other subjects. In *Shenandoah,* X. J. Kennedy praises the selection as "tightly-winnowed" and goes on to say that he is grateful for many of the poems "forthrightness, intensity and originality." Writing in *Prairie Schooner,* Philip Paradis describes *Great Blue* as "an outstanding collection by a major contemporary poet," and states that "Galvin's style with its lyricism, earthiness, penchant for irony, and realistic clear-sightedness suggests he is certainly acquainted with the wellsprings of Irish poetry."

In *Saints in Their Ox-Hide Boat,* Galvin returns to the book-length story format of *Wampanoag Traveler.* This tale centers on an actual historical character, his own namesake, the sixth-century Irish monk, Brendan the Navigator. Background for the poem relies heavily on the medieval *Voyage of St. Brendan,* which tells of a small fishing boat, manned by Brendan and other monks, that may well have sailed all the way to the New World. Galvin's version, however, is primarily a fictitious account, in which he creates personalities for Brendan and the other monks and adds adventures of his own. The premise of the book is that Brendan, as an old man, is dictating an account of his voyage to a young scribe in order to correct misconceptions about it. Phoebe-Lou Adams, in *Atlantic Monthly,* states: "Mr. Galvin's highly distinctive style blends legend, folktale, psychological reconstruction, and gritty commonplace into its own poetic coherence." Fred Chappel, in the *Georgia Review,* says: "This work is a true narrative poem even by my persnickety standards, and a fascinating story it is."

Galvin once wrote: "I grew up on Cape Cod and in a suburb of Boston, and these two poles have affected my work strongly, in that my poems are full of imagery from the sea, the land, austere and muted, of the outer Cape, and the urban blight that infects humans who come in contact with it, especially through their work, most of which is unfulfilling and worthless." Elsewhere, he has written "the true risk [in writing poetry] is presenting felt expressions of the way things are, statements that move the inner life of the hearer because they offer him a truth deeper than one he previously knew."

George Garrett notes in the *Dictionary of Literary Biography* that "whether he is being serious or funny, or, as is usual, a combination of both, it appears that Galvin is facing up to the desperate elements in nature as well as in social and private situations; he is working out crucial events with strokes both bold and delicate."

BIOGRAPHICAL/CRITICAL SOURCES:

BOOKS

Christina, Martha, editor, *OuterLife: The Poetry of Brendan Galvin,* Ampersand Press, 1991.

Contemporary Authors Autobiography Series, Volume 8, Gale, 1991.
Contemporary Poets, 6th edition, St. James Press, 1996.
Critical Survey of Poetry, Salem Press (Englewood Cliffs, NJ), 1982.
Dictionary of Literary Biography, Volume 5: *American Poets since Word War II,* Gale, 1980.

PERIODICALS

American Book Review, January-February, 1982.
American Poetry Review, January-February, 1979.
Atlantic Monthly, June, 1992, p. 128.
Cimarron Review, April, 1993.
Georgia Review, fall, 1990; summer, 1992, pp. 376-79.
Hudson Review, spring, 1981.
New Review, May-June, 1992.
Parnassus, Volume 17, number 2, 1993; Volume 18, number 1, 1993.
Pembroke Magazine, spring, 1988.
Pittsburgh Quarterly, winter, 1994.
Ploughshares, Volume IV, 1978.
Poetry, June, 1977; September, 1990, pp. 353-54; January, 1993, pp. 229-30.
Prairie Schooner, spring, 1993, pp. 168-73.
Publishers Weekly, April 28, 1989, p. 72; December 30, 1996, p. 61.
Shenandoah, winter, 1991, pp. 115-20.
Southern Humanities Review, winter, 1994, pp. 91-93.
Stand, spring, 1992, p. 30.
Tar River Poetry, fall, 1987; fall, 1992.
Texas Review, spring, 1988.
Three Rivers Poetry Journal, Volumes 19-20, 1982.
Times Literary Supplement (London), May 31, 1991, p. 11.
Washington Times, April 26, 1992.*

* * *

GANDER, Forrest 1956-

PERSONAL: Born January 21, 1956, in Barstow, CA; son of James Forrest Cockerille Jr.(a bar owner) and Ruth Clare Caulsen (a teacher); married C. D. Wright (a poet), 1983; children: Brecht Wright. *Education:* Received B.S. and B.A. from College of William and Mary; received M.A. from San Francisco State University; attended Brown University.

ADDRESSES: Home—351 Nayatt Road, Barrington, RI 02806-4336.

CAREER: Providence College, Providence, RI, associate professor, 1985—. Also serves as editor for Lost Road Publishers, Barrington, RI.

AWARDS, HONORS: National Endowment for the Arts fellowship in poetry, 1989.

WRITINGS:

Rush to the Lake, Alice James Books, 1988.
Eggplants and Lotus Root, Burning Deck, 1991.
(With Carmen Boullosa) *Poetry and Translation,* Wayland Collegium Brown University, 1992.
Lynchburg, University of Pittsburgh Press, 1993.
(Editor) *Mouth to Mouth: Poems by 12 Contemporary Mexican Women,* Milkweed Editions, 1993.
Deeds of Utmost Kindness, Wesleyan/University Press of New England, 1994.
Science and Steepleflower, New Directions (New York City), 1998.

SIDELIGHTS: Forrest Gander told *CA:* "Along with my two young sisters, I was brought up in Virginia by my mother, an ebullient, dedicated school teacher. She delighted in reading to me Edgar Allan Poe and Carl Sandburg, and she translated her love of the natural world into a remarkable tolerance (considering that all four of us lived in a two-bedroom apartment) for my childhood menageries of leeches, snakes, salamanders, turtles, and rodents. My father, James Forrest Cockerille Jr., owned a bar called the Mod Scene in Greenwich Village, and my sisters and I sometimes spent summers with him. Then, in 1972, when I was a high school sophomore, a handsome, morally exemplary banker, Walter J. Gander, asked for my mother's hand and we were all adopted into his family of two boys.

"I had been overly praised for my poetry from an early age, and it wasn't until I was in college that someone (Professor Donald Jenkins) kindly told me that my poems were not good. Though I was majoring in geology, I took courses enough to double major in English. Among them, workshops with Peter Klappert exposed me to an ardent poet who in turn introduced me to contemporary and modernist poets I had been reading only haphazardly.

"In 1979, by chance, my mother found a spot on my right scapula that turned out to be a third-stage melanoma. I had already lost my spleen, appendix, tonsils, and adenoids, and had been operated on for a hernia. I would later lose lymph nodes around my groin. During this last major surgery in the hospital, a deep seriousness visited upon me, and I determined that I would throw myself into poetry, and that my love for geology would be corollary to that overriding devotion.

"To get as far away from those regional influences with which I was already familiar, and because I could afford graduate school in the state of my birth, I went to San Francisco where the Language Poets were holding forth at 80 Langton Street and where there were poetry readings and arguments in cafes around the city every night.

"It was a fabulously exciting time. While I worked in a methadone clinic, I lived in a breathtaking apartment on Potrero Hill overlooking the Mission, and I spent as many hours as I could exploring the Marin headlands. I met C. D. Wright in The Poetry Center at San Francisco State University, where I was systematically reading through the library, and eventually I apprenticed myself to Lost Road Publishers, the book press she edited. With money we both saved, we decided somewhat capriciously to move to Mexico and to publish a series of books from there.

"In Mexico I began to write my first good poems. I also began a correspondence with writers there that formed the foundation for my anthology *Mouth to Mouth: Poems by 12 Contemporary Mexican Women.*

"My own first book, *Rush to the Lake,* was published by Alice James Books in 1988.The central long poem of that collection, 'Sumo,' developed from notes and photographs I had taken on a trip to Japan during the sumo training season. This poem became the first in a series of long poems that I began to write. Looking at a single subject for an extended time, I found the long poem prodded me to develop radical formal strategies. To keep the poem from repeating itself, I had to approach the material from various angles in different, but generative forms.

"In 1991, my sui generis long poem, *Eggplants and Lotus Root,* was published by Burning Deck. In this book, beautifully designed by Rosmarie Waldrop and Pam Rehm, I intended to acknowledge three primary spheres of influence on our species: sex, aesthetics, and violence. And I wanted to exercise distinctive forms of consciousness, separating out the emotive, the descriptive, and the meditative, and weaving these three strands horizontally across the poem to suggest a three-dimensional space for desire and loss. *Eggplants and Lotus Root* was, in part, a response to my physiological father's recent death.

"As C. D. Wright and I spent more and more time in Arkansas, her home state, renting a cabin in Hog Jaw near Lead Hill, I became more obsessed with landscape as an event. I wrote a long poetic libretto to Robert Johnson, making pilgrimages to Robinsonville and Three Forks, Mississippi, and to the music room at the Library of Congress where I listened to out takes of Johnson's recordings which were commercially unavailable at that time. This poem, 'Life of Johnson upside Your Head,' became the foundation of *Lynchburg,* a book of poems focused on the landscape of the rural South.

"On the heels of *Lynchburg, Deeds of Utmost Kindness* was published in 1994. It, too, is concerned with landscape, but divers ones. Consisting of a prelude and six long poems, *Deeds of Utmost Kindness* exposes varied rhythms of thought and illustrates how different logics work in the metaphoric structures of changing places. Formally innovative, the poems might be read as a curious travelogue in which the traveller's own foreignness, the 'I' not the 'you,' is most deeply mysterious. In one of the sequences, *The Blue Rock Collection,* poetic structures are based on the characteristics of the mineral, crystal, or rock of the title. Quartz crystals, for instance, are translucent and hexagonal, and the poem titled 'Yellow Quartz' is composed of six lines and makes reference to the passage of light through windows.

"Since 1982, the year we went to Mexico, I have continued with C. D. Wright to co-edit Lost Roads Publishers, a literary book press. This year we are bringing out our fortieth title, Kamau Brathwaite's incendiary *Trench Town Rock.* Publishing has been a spiritually rewarding, if time-consuming activity by which we have been able to promote the work of such admirable writers as Arthur Sze, Phillip Foss, Myra Sklarew, Keith Waldrop, John Taggart, Sharon Doubiago, Frank Stanford, Fanny Howe, and Donald Berger, among others."

BIOGRAPHICAL/CRITICAL SOURCES:

PERIODICALS

Bloomsbury Review, March, 1994, p. 3.
Publishers Weekly, January 10, 1994, p. 58.
Virginia Quarterly Review, summer, 1994, p. 101.
World Literature Today, spring, 1994, p. 348.*

* * *

GANN, Ernest Kellogg 1910- 1991

PERSONAL: Born October 13, 1910, in Lincoln, NE; died December 21, 1991, of kidney failure; son of

George Kellogg and Caroline (Kupper) Gann; married Eleanor Michaud, 1933 (divorced); married Dodie Post, 1966; children: (first marriage) George, Steven, Polly. *Education:* Culver Military Academy; Attended Yale University, 1930-32. *Politics:* Republican. *Religion:* Protestant.

CAREER: Author and screen writer. *Military service:* U.S. Army Air Forces, Air Transport Command, 1942-46; became captain; received Distinguished Flying award.

MEMBER: Press Club (San Francisco), Quiet Birdmen.

AWARDS, HONORS: National Association of Independent Schools Award for *The High and the Mighty,* 1954; award, Pacific Northwest Booksellers, 1973; Aviation Journalist of the Year, Ziff-Davis Publishing, 1975; Inspirational Award, Western Aerospace Association, 1977.

WRITINGS:

Sky Roads, Crowell (New York), 1940.
All American Aircraft, Crowell, 1941.
Getting Them into the Blue, Crowell, 1942.
Island in the Sky, Viking, 1944.
Blaze at Noon, Holt, 1946.
Benjamin Lawless, Sloane, 1948.
Fiddler's Green, Sloane, 1950.
The High and the Mighty, Sloane, 1952.
Soldier of Fortune, Sloane, 1954.
Trouble with Lazy Ethel, Sloane, 1957.
Twilight for the Gods, Sloane, 1958.
Fate Is the Hunter, Simon & Schuster, 1961.
Of Good and Evil, Simon & Schuster, 1963.
In the Company of Eagles, Simon & Schuster, 1966.
The Song of the Sirens, Simon & Schuster, 1968.
The Antagonists, Simon & Schuster, 1971.
Band of Brothers, Simon & Schuster, 1973.
Ernest K. Gann's Flying Circus, Macmillan, 1974.
A Hostage to Fortune (autobiography), Knopf, 1978.
Brain 2000, Doubleday, 1980.
The Aviator, G.K. Hall (Boston), 1981.
The Magistrate: A Novel, Arbor House (New York City), 1982.
Gentlemen of Adventure, Arbor House, 1983.
The Triumph: A Novel, Simon & Schuster (New York City), 1986.
The Bad Angel, Arbor House, 1987.
The Black Watch: The Men Who Fly America's Secret Spy Planes, Random House (New York City), 1989.

SCREENPLAYS; ALL BASED ON HIS NOVELS

The Raging Tide (based on *Fiddler's Green*), Universal, 1951.
Island in the Sky, Warner Brothers, 1953.
The High and the Mighty, Warner Brothers, 1954.
Soldier of Fortune, Twentieth Century-Fox, 1955.
Twilight for the Gods, J. Arthur Rank, 1957.

SIDELIGHTS: Ernest Kellogg Gann's books about pilots and flying are highly popular with pilots around the world. His painstaking attention to aeronautical accuracy has been noted as one reason for this popularity. In his research for *Band of Brothers,* for instance, Gann interviewed pilots, airline officials, and traffic controllers in both Europe and Asia. "A lot of pilots read my stuff," he told the *Seattle Post-Intelligencer,* "and I knew it had to be absolutely as accurate as I could make it."

One of Gann's early novels, *The High and Mighty* is about a passenger plane on its way to San Francisco when it encounters serious problems. The story is not only about the technical aspects of the flight, but about the passengers and crew aboard, who are dealing with the tough questions that facing death can bring. Coleman Rosenberger, in *New York Herald Tribune,* praised Gann's ability to give the reader an early sense of something ominous. Rosenberger observed, "Mr. Gann's examination of character under stress, coupled with the superbly sustained suspense of the plane's fight for survival, makes a dramatic novel which is likely to catch and hold the attention of almost any reader."

In 1961 Gann published an autobiographical work called *Fate Is the Hunter.* Critics expressed enthusiasm in their reviews. Martin Caidin wrote in *New York Times Book Review,* "It is a tribute to Mr. Gann that in his review of his own stirring years in the skies, the reader is often quick to forget that this is not fiction. Mr. Gann's subtle technique of drawing the reader into his scenes establishes a rapport between pilots and nonfliers that is rare, indeed." Caidin identified Gann's candor as one of the many strengths of the book. The reader finds that Gann is "sharing the secrets as well as the great beauties of flight." V. S. Pritchett, in a review for *New Statesman,* described the men in Gann's book as "quiet, unoppressive heroes." Further, Pritchett commended Gann's choice of content as suspenseful, interesting, and mysterious. Pritchett concluded, "Mr. Gann is a writer saturated in his subject; he has the skill to make every instant sharp and important and we catch the fever to know that documentary writing does not often invite."

Critics were less impressed with the 1966 novel *In the Company of Eagles.* A reviewer for *The New Yorker* described it as "extremely disappointing," noting that although the main characters are brave and appealing, Gann's attention to demonstrating their technical skill and competence is lacking. Brian Garfield, in *Saturday Review,* described the main characters as "curiously distant" and "little more than mouthpieces for the weary statement that war is hell." Garfield, however, remained optimistic: "We are not, this time, in the cockpit with Ernest Gann. The vitality is no longer there; the best one can do is wait, and hope, for Gann's next novel."

Gann went on to successfully publish a dozen more novels, many with screenplays. One of his novels, *The Aviator,* was described by David Salisbury of *Christian Science Monitor* as "reminiscent of Antoine St. Exupery's 'Night Flight.' " Salisbury wrote that the plot was very suspenseful and the characters were so interesting that he wished they were more developed. Michael Malone of *New York Times Book Review* enjoyed the nostalgic feel of the novel, likening it to the feel of *Saturday Evening Post.*

BIOGRAPHICAL/CRITICAL SOURCES:

BOOKS

Contemporary Literary Criticism, Volume 23, Gale, 1983.

Twentieth-Century Romance and Historical Writers, 3rd edition, St. James Press, 1994.

PERIODICALS

Best Sellers, January 1, 1974.

Chicago Tribune, December 22, 1991.

Christian Science Monitor, January 30, 1975; March 18, 1981.

Flying, April, 1974.

Los Angeles Times Book Review, October 10, 1982; January 22, 1984.

New Statesman, May 16, 1969.

New Yorker, October 29, 1966.

New York Times, October 17, 1966; December 21, 1991, p. 26.

New York Times Book Review, November 27, 1966; October 27, 1968; February 14, 1971; April 5, 1981; January 22, 1984; March 25, 1984.

Saturday Review, December 24, 1966; April 29, 1972.

Seattle Post-Intelligencer, December 23, 1974.

Spectator, June 5, 1976.

Time, September 25, 1978.

Times (London), December 30, 1991, p. 14.

Washington Post, December 21, 1991, p. B6.

World Journal Tribune, October 10, 1966.*

* * *

GANNETT, Ruth Stiles 1923-

PERSONAL: Born August 12, 1923, in New York, NY; daughter of Lewis Stiles (a book reviewer) and Mary (Ross) Gannett; married H. Peter Kahn (a professor and artist), March 21, 1947; children: Charlotte, Margaret, Sarah, Hannah, Louise, Catherine, Elizabeth. *Education:* Vassar College, B.A., 1944.

ADDRESSES: *Home*—309 Mitchell St., Ithaca, NY 14850.

CAREER: Medical technician, Boston City Hospital; radar research technician, MIT, Cambridge; Children's Book Council, New York, staff member. Author of children's books.

AWARDS, HONORS: First prize in medium-age children's category, *New York Herald Tribune* Children's Spring Book Festival, 1948, for *My Father's Dragon.*

WRITINGS:

ALL PUBLISHED BY RANDOM HOUSE

My Father's Dragon (Junior Literary Guild selection), 1948, illustrations by Ruth Chrisman Gannett, Knopf, (New York City), 1987.

The Wonderful House-Boat Train, 1949.

Elmer and the Dragon (Junior Literary Guild Selection), 1950, illustrations by Ruth Chrisman Gannett, Knopf, 1987.

The Dragons of Blueland (Junior Literary Guild selection), 1951, illustrations by Ruth Chrisman Gannett, Knopf, 1987.

Katie and the Sad Noise, 1961.

Three Tales of My Father's Dragon, illustrated by Ruth Chrisman Gannett, Random House (New York City), 1998.

Manuscript collections at Emporia State University in Kansas (May Massee Collection) and University of Minnesota in Minneapolis (Kerlan Collection).

SIDELIGHTS: Ruth Stiles Gannett told *CA:* "I do not write for children so much as for my own pleasure. Of course, I am happy if children like the stories. When I was little I went to a school where we all (teachers and children) assumed that writing was fun, and I still do think so. My books have come out that happy childhood."

The Wonderful House-Boat Train is a story about a retired railroad engineer, Pops Pops, and his four grandchildren, who are all looking for a home. *Twentieth-Century Children's Writers* contributor Mae Durham Roger was disappointed because the story "is more deliberate and lacks the quality that is associated with a natural, creative flow." *Katie and the Sad Noise,* a beginner's book, is about a little girl who hears peculiar noises. When she tells her parents, they become so worried that they talk to Katie's teachers. Suspense builds, and ends with a Christmas surprise.

Gannett's trilogy, *My Father's Dragon, Elmer and the Dragon,* and *The Dragons of Blueland,* is a blend of childlike straightforwardness and a sense of the fantastic. In *My Father's Dragon,* Gannett demonstrates her understanding of little boys through the character of Elmer, who decides to go to Wild Island to free the baby dragon. *Elmer and the Dragon* continues his adventure with humor and nonsense as elements of a child's world. Gannett's attention to detail is indicative of her understanding of a child's curiosity. She describes food, history, and the contents of a treasure chest in a lively style. In the final installment of the trilogy, *The Dragons of Blueland,* Elmer and the baby dragon, Boris, set off on their final adventure to rescue Boris's family from a cave. The conclusion is appropriate for a saga meant to reflect the world and imagination of a child. Gannett's mother did the illustrations for the trilogy, Roger wrote that "they complement the text so that there is not only reading but visual pleasure."

BIOGRAPHICAL/CRITICAL SOURCES:

BOOKS

Twentieth-Century Children's Writers, 4th edition, St. James Press, 1995.

PERIODICALS

Booklist, January 1, 1987, p. 708.
Horn Book Magazine, January, 1995, p. 90.
Reading Teacher, October, 1987, p. 43.
School Library Journal, November, 1997, p. 69.
Washington Post Book World, January 11, 1987, p. 13; May 8, 1988, p. 16.*

GARD, Robert Edward 1910-1992

PERSONAL: Born July 3, 1910, in Iola, KS; died December 7, 1992, in Madison, WI; son of Samuel Arnold and Louisa Maria (Ireland) Gard; married Maryo Kimball, June 7, 1939; children: Maryo Gwendolyn, Eleanor Copeland. *Education:* University of Kansas, B.A., 1934; Cornell University, M.A., 1938.

CAREER: Writer. University of Kansas, Lawrence, instructor, 1934-37; Cornell University, Ithaca, NY, instructor, 1940-43; University of Wisconsin, Madison, assistant professor, 1945-48, associate professor, 1948-55, professor, 1955-92; Duell, Sloan, & Pearce, New York City, field director, 1958-60. Director of the New York State Playwriting Project, 1938-43, and of the Alberta, Canada, Folklore and Local History Project, 1943-45; participant in the Survey of Cultural Arts, Great Britain, 1953; trustee of the National Theatre Conference, 1958-62, and of the Foundation of Integrated Education, 1961-92; Fulbright professor, University of Helsinki, 1959-60, visiting professor, 1963; U.S. delegate to the World Theatre Congress, Vienna, Austria, 1961; president, Wisconsin House Publications, Madison, 1969; co-founder, Dale Wasserman Professional Playwright Development Laboratory, Rhinelander, WI, 1976.

MEMBER: National Theatre Conference, American Educational Theatre Association, American National Theatre and Academy, Wisconsin Academy of Sciences, Arts, and Letters (president, 1976-77), Wisconsin Arts Foundation and Council (president, 1957-59), Wisconsin Regional Writers Association (president, 1961-64), Pi Kappa Alpha.

AWARDS, HONORS: Service award from Department of Speech, University of Kansas, 1958; Gold Medal of Honor from the Finnish Theatre, 1961; distinguished service award from the International Institute of Milwaukee, 1964; Governor's award for creativity, 1967; Wisconsin local history award; citation from the Wisconsin Academy of Sciences, Arts, and Letters.

WRITINGS:

Raisin' th' Devil: A Comedy of Schoharie Country, American Agriculturist, 1940.
(Editor with Alexander M. Drummond) *The Lake Guns of Seneca and Cayuga, and Eight Other Plays of Upstate New York,* Cornell University Press, 1942.
Johnny Chinook: Tall Tales and True From the Canadian West (legends), Longmans, Green, 1945, new edition, Tuttle, 1967.

Wisconsin Is My Doorstep: A Dramatist's Yarn Book of Wisconsin Lore (legends), Longmans, Green, 1948.

(With Drummond) *The Cardiff Giant,* Cornell University Press, 1949.

Midnight: Rodeo Champion (juvenile), illustrated by C. W. Anderson, Duell, Sloan, 1951.

Grassroots Theater: A Search for Regional Arts in America, University of Wisconsin Press, 1955.

A Horse Named Joe (juvenile), illustrated by C. W. Anderson, Duell, Sloan, 1956.

Scotty's Mare (juvenile), illustrated by Aaron Bohrod, Duell, Sloan, 1957.

(Contributor) David H. Stevens, editor, *Ten Talents in the American Theatre,* University of Oklahoma Press, 1957.

The Big One, Duell, Sloan, 1958.

Run to Kansas (juvenile), illustrated by Alan Moyler, Duell, Sloan, 1958.

(With Gertrude S. Burley) *Community Theatre: Idea and Achievement,* Duell, Sloan, 1959.

(With Leland G. Sorden) *Wisconsin Lore, Antics, and Anecdotes of Wisconsin People and Places,* Duell, Sloan, 1962.

Devil Red (juvenile), illustrated by Richard W. Lewis, Duell, Sloan, 1963.

The Error of Sexton Jones, Duell, Sloan, 1964.

(With Spencer A. Gard) *The Early Background of the Gard Family in America,* [Iola, KS], 1965.

(With Marston Balch and Pauline B. Temkin) *Theater in America: Appraisal and Challenge for the National Theatre Conference,* Dembar Educational Research Services, 1968.

(With David Semmes) *America's Players,* Seabury, 1967.

(With Sorden) *The Romance of Wisconsin Place Names,* October House, 1968.

This Is Wisconsin, Wisconsin House, 1969.

(With others) *The Arts in the Small Community: A National Plan,* [Madison, WI], 1969.

(With Helen O'Brien) *Act Nine: Plays for Youth,* Wisconsin House, 1970.

University Madison, U.S.A., Wisconsin House, 1970.

Down in the Valleys: Wisconsin Back Country Lore and Humor, Wisconsin House, 1971.

Wild Goose Marsh: Horicon Stopover, Wisconsin House, 1972.

(Editor with Elaine Reetz) *The Trail of the Serpent: The Fox River Valley* (legends), Madison House, 1973.

Wisconsin Sketches, edited by Mark E. Lefebvre, Wisconsin House, 1973.

(With Allen Crafton) *A Woman of No Importance* (novel), Wisconsin House, 1974.

Wild Goose Country: Horicon Marsh to Horseshoe Island, Wisconsin House, 1975.

(Editor with others) *We Were Children Then: Ninety Wisconsin Writers Age Sixty to Ninety-Six,* Wisconsin House, 1976.

(With August Derleth and Jesse Stuart) *The Only Place We Live,* edited by Mark E. Lefebvre, wood engravings by Frank Utpatel, Wisconsin House, 1976.

(With David Harrison Stevens) *A Time of Humanities: An Oral History,* edited by Robert Yahnke, Wisconsin Academy of Sciences, Arts and Letters (Madison, WI), 1976.

(Editor with Joan Sullivan) *Frost Blossoms: Yarns and Impressions of Stoughton and Regional Life and Adventures,* assistance by Rita and Irving Quale, decoration by Rita Quale, University of Wisconsin Extension (Madison, WI), 1978.

Coming Home to Wisconsin, Stanton & Lee (Madison, WI), 1982.

Beyond the Thin Line, Prairie Oak Press (Madison, WI), 1992.

Also author of *Innocence of Prairie,* 1978, and *My Land, My Home, My Wisconsin,* with Maryo Gard, 1978.

SIDELIGHTS: An educator and author, Robert Edward Gard was particularly interested in folklore and drama. Gard began his career as an instructor at several institutions, including Cornell University in Ithaca, New York, before becoming a professor at the University of Wisconsin at Madison, where he taught until his retirement. Active in the community, Gard was a member of several organizations including the Wisconsin Arts Foundation and Council and the Wisconsin Regional Writers Association. Gard was the author of more than forty books, including *The Lake Guns of Seneca and Cayuga, and Eight Other Plays, Wisconsin Is My Doorstep: A Dramatists Yarn Book of Wisconsin Lore, The Big One, The Error of Sexton Jones, Innocence of Prairie,* and with Allen Crafton, *A Woman of No Importance.* Gard also wrote for children, including *A Horse Named Joe* and *Scotty's Mare.*

In reviewing Gard's *Wisconsin Is My Doorstep,* a *San Francisco Chronicle* critic observed: "*Wisconsin Is My Doorstep* is a collection of Wisconsin Folk Tales old and new. They are cast in a remarkably readable dramatic form that is closer to radio script than any other recognizable type of composition. In them, the author . . . retained the spirit and aim of folklore, which is to divert and often to amuse the audience. . . ."

Gard's contributions to children's literature include *Midnight: Rodeo Champion,* which was reviewed by a *New York Herald Tribune Book Review* critic: "The style is crisp and authentic, the rodeo lore fascinating, the characterization excellent, and the illustrations by an expert [C. W. Anderson]."

BIOGRAPHICAL/CRITICAL SOURCES:

BOOKS

Gard, Robert E., *Coming Home to Wisconsin,* Stanton & Lee, 1982.

PERIODICALS

New York Herald Tribune Book Review, May 13, 1951.
San Francisco Chronicle, May 30, 1948.

OBITUARIES:

PERIODICALS

Chicago Tribune, December 8, 1992, sec. 1, p. 10.*

* * *

GARDNER, Virginia (Marberry) 1904-1992 (Barbara Adams, Jane Logan)

PERSONAL: Born June 27, 1904, in Sallisaw, Indian Territory (now Oklahoma); died January 5, 1992, in San Diego, CA; daughter of John Carnall (a banker) and Gertrude (Boltwood) Gardner; married Jerome Butler, December 17, 1927 (divorced, 1934; deceased); married M. Marion Marberry (a writer), July 9, 1937 (divorced, 1945; died, 1968); children: John Marberry. *Education:* University of Missouri, B.J., 1924.

CAREER: Affiliated with *Pawhuska Daily Journal, Ponca City News,* and *Fort Smith Times-Record,* all 1924-25; *Kansas City Post,* Kansas City, MO, reporter, 1926; *St. Louis Times,* St. Louis, MO, reporter, 1927-28; *Chicago Tribune,* Chicago, IL, general assignment reporter, 1929-40; Federated Press, Washington, DC, bureau manager and author of "Washington Scene" column, 1942-43; *New Masses,* Washington, DC, head of bureau, 1943-47; *Daily People's World,* San Francisco, CA, reporter and political columnist with Los Angeles bureau, 1947-51; writer, 1951-92. Executive secretary of Citizens Committee for Harry Bridges, 1941-42.

WRITINGS:

Washington War Wreckers, Federated Press, 1942.
The Rosenberg Story, Masses & Mainstream, 1954.
"Friend and Lover": The Life of Louise Bryant, Horizon Press, 1982.

Contributor of articles to magazines, including *Jubilee, Catholic Digest, Masses and Mainstream,* and *Science and Society.* Contributor to newspapers under the pseudonyms Barbara Adams and Jane Logan.

SIDELIGHTS: A journalist and author, Virginia Gardner was known for her investigative articles for the *Chicago Tribune* during the 1930s, including an expose of health risks to workers at a radium watch dial plant. She was also a reporter for the *Daily Worker* and *New Masses,* and contributed to several other newspapers under the pseudonyms Barbara Adams and Jane Logan. Her collected articles on the trial and execution of suspected Soviet spies Julius and Ethel Rosenberg were published as the book *The Rosenberg Story.*

Gardner once told *CA:* "I consider myself an Okie-Arkie, a term once used derisively in California. I was born in the Indian Territory, and when I was two years old my father was transferred back to Fort Smith, Arkansas, where I was brought up.

"At seventy-nine I have lived longer than anyone in my family. My mother died at age forty, when I was five; my father at fifty-hour. Had my mother lived she would have finished a history of the Cherokee nation. Her diaries were filled with sketches of Indians. My mother and grandmother were feminists, inspired by certain speakers at the Chautauqua, a regular summer feature in Ottawa, Kansas, where they lived. I too am a feminist.

"When I started out on newspapers most city editors seemed to be enraged at the very idea of journalism schools, and I learned to conceal the fact that I was a product of one. In fact, I felt it safer never to mention that I had gone to college. So when I was asked by Bob Lee of the *Chicago Tribune* to tell him about my education, I said, 'I went to the public schools of Fort Smith, Arkansas.' How far did I get? Had I finished high school? Yes. Had I ever been to college? I admitted that I had. Where? The University of Missouri. He brightened: 'Ever have any journalism courses there?' I blurted out: 'Yes, but I wasn't any good at them.' He persisted until he unearthed the fact that I was a bachelor of journalism. Then he told me that only the previous week Colonel R. R. McCormick had put through the rule that only graduates of journalism schools could be considered for jobs in the editorial department."

Gardner's biography of Louise Bryant, *"Friend and Lover,"* establishes its subject as a person in her own right. Critics noted that Gardner showed Bryant's stamina as an activist and the tragedy of her last years in this well-documented book, thus freeing her from the shadow of her famous husband, John Reed, without impinging on his reputation. As Alden Whitman explained in a *Philadelphia Inquirer* review, "Gardner's account of Bryant's life is careful and thoughtful. In establishing Bryant as a woman in her own right, the book in no way diminishes the importance of John Reed, nor does it overpraise its subject. . . . [Gardner made] us realize that there was more to Bryant than a beautiful face and a bewitching smile."

Reviewers praised Gardner for capturing Bryant as a feminist who actively pursued equality and liberty. Michael Edmonds, for one, claimed in the *Milwaukee Journal* that *"Friend and Lover* is an engrossing book that reveals the courage, power and intelligence of a woman determined to fight for justice and equality in her personal and public lives." For instance, three years before meeting Reed, Bryant campaigned for women's suffrage in Oregon. She became a daring foreign correspondent for the Hearst International News Service and the King Features Syndicate, for she thwarted danger—including counter-revolutionary uprisings—to cover events during the Russian Revolution. Bryant also interviewed world figures such as Mussolini and Lenin. In fact her *Mirrors of Moscow* is a collection of sympathetic portraits of Soviet leaders.

Bryant's other writings evidence her concern for the quality of human life. *Six Red Months in Russia,* for example, illustrates the effect of the October Revolution on ordinary people. Now critics consider this work a necessary companion to Reed's famous *Ten Days That Shook the World.*

Bryant's commitment to personal freedom extended into her marriage with Reed. Each led independent careers, and both engaged in extramartial affairs. For her part, Bryant maintained long-term relationships with playwright Eugene O'Neill and painter Andrew Dasburg; Reed, however, carried on more casual affairs.

After Reed's death, Bryant married William Christian Bullitt. She also contracted an incurable disease, adiposis dolorosa. Gardner contended that the combination of this last unhappy marriage and the painful illness drove Bryant to alcoholism, which led to her decay. Thus, *Chicago* writer Herman Kogan noted that "Gardner not only amply fill[ed] out the portrait of this mercurial woman but also challenge[d] calumnies that have appeared about her in earlier works about Reed and his times." Kogan considered this the biography's strength.

Other reviewers applauded Gardner's impressive twelve years of research, her documentation, and her affection for her subject. As Kimbark MacColl explained in *Northwest Magazine,* "Louise Bryant obviously was a hero to the author, but such a bias does not diminish either the quality or the legitimacy of her work. The book is well-documented with an extensive bibliography."

BIOGRAPHICAL/CRITICAL SOURCES:

BOOKS

Casey, Robert J., *Such Interesting People,* Bobbs-Merrill, 1943.

MacDougall, Curtis D., *A College Course in Reporting for Beginners,* Macmillan, 1932.

Murray, George, *The Madhouse on Madison Street,* Follett, 1965.

Ross, Ishbel, *Ladies of the Press: The Story of Women in Journalism by an Insider,* Harper, 1936.

PERIODICALS

Chicago, March, 1983.

Milwaukee Journal, December 19, 1982.

Northwest Magazine, February 6, 1983.

Philadelphia Inquirer, January 9, 1983.

Washington Post Book World, February 13, 1983.

OBITUARIES:

PERIODICALS

Chicago Tribune, February 5, 1992, section 3, p. 12.*

* * *

GASKIN, Catherine 1929-

PERSONAL: Born April 2, 1929, in Dundalk, Ireland; daughter of James (an engineer) and Mary (Harrington) Gaskin; married Sol Cornberg, 1955. *Education:* Educated at Holy Cross College, Sydney, Australia. *Avocational interests:* Music.

ADDRESSES: Home—Ballyma cahara, Wicklow, County Wicklow, Ireland; and White Rigg, East Ballaterson, Maughold, Isle of Man.

CAREER: Novelist.

WRITINGS:

This Other Eden, Collins, 1947.
With Every Year, Collins, 1949.
Dust in the Sunlight, Collins, 1950.
All Else Is Folly, Harper, 1951.
Daughter of the House, Harper, 1952.
Sara Dane, Lippincott, 1955.
Blake's Reach, Lippincott, 1958.
Corporation Wife, Doubleday, 1960.
I Know My Love, Doubleday, 1962.
The Tilsit Inheritance, Doubleday, 1963.
The File on Devlin, Doubleday, 1965.
Edge of Glass, Doubleday, 1967.
Fiona, Doubleday, 1970.
A Falcon for a Queen, Doubleday, 1972.
The Property of a Gentleman, Doubleday, 1974.
The Lynmara Legacy, Doubleday, 1976.
The Summer of the Spanish Woman, Doubleday, 1977.
Family Affairs, Doubleday, 1980.
Promises, Doubleday, 1982.
The Ambassador's Women, Scribner (New York City), 1986.
The Charmed Circle, Scribner, 1989.

ADAPTATIONS: The File on Devlin was adapted for dramatic presentation on *Hall of Fame,* National Broadcasting Company, Inc., November 21, 1969.

SIDELIGHTS: Catherine Gaskin told *CA:* "I still work with the idea to entertain and think that an honourable enough motive. The work gets harder as I get older, but it must not appear to the reader to be hard. I make great efforts to appear effortless. A hermit-like existence here on the Isle of Man and in Ireland suits my working routine, which is haphazard, but necessarily solitary. Socializing seems to be done in London and New York."

Gaskin has occupied a unique niche in the genre of romance fiction. While her stories take on gothic elements such as a disputed inheritance, forbidden love, strangers, ancestral homes, and family secrets, they are set in modern times. An example is *Corporation Wife,* a novel about four women in a small town that is overtaken by an industrial company. Two of the women are newly arrived wives of executives, and the other two are natives. Gaskin explores the ways each of them adapts to the pressures brought on by the presence of the corporation. In *Twentieth-Century Romance and Historical Writers,* Geoffrey Sadler observed, "Her [Gaskin's] touch is sure, romance and tragedy made part of a convincing social scene, the characters perfectly and subtly realized."

The gothic emphasis on family and ancestral homes is evident in *The Property of a Gentleman* and *The Lynmara Legacy.* The former is set in the world of art auctioneering, and the heroine falls in love with the heir to a mansion. The discovery of a skeleton and art treasures brings about action which leads to the book's violent denouement. The heroine of *The Lynmara Legacy* is typical in that she is independent and determined. Sadler found Gaskin's later sagas diminished by the intrusive use of gothic elements in comparison to these earlier works in which they are so balanced and neatly integrated.

Gaskin has also published historical romance titles, but critics are less satisfied with them than with her modern gothics. *Sara Dane* is a story about a servant girl who attains wealth and power in colonial Australia. The movement of the novel is from one crisis to the next, with prospective lovers coming and going. Sadler wrote, "Though immensely popular, *Sara Dane* lacks the sense of solid reality that marks even the earliest of Gaskin's contemporary novels." Comparing Sara to Susan Taite, the sophisticated fashion editor in *All Else Is Folly,* Sadler described Sara as a character in a novel, whereas Susan seems like a living person. He went on to generalize that "Although they are exciting period tales, they do not possess the depth of penetration found in other works."

Read by audiences around the world, Gaskin's novels have been published in eleven languages, including Hebrew, Turkish, and Japanese.

BIOGRAPHICAL/CRITICAL SOURCES:

BOOKS

Twentieth-Century Romance and Historical Writers, 3rd edition, St. James Press, 1994.

PERIODICALS

Los Angeles Times Book Review, March 19, 1989.
New York Times Book Review, September 12, 1965.
Observer, October 24, 1965; December 17, 1972; October 30, 1977.
Times Literary Supplement, January 17, 1975; February 10, 1978.
Washington Post Book World, August 3, 1980.*

GLATZER, Nahum Norbert 1903-1990

PERSONAL: Born March 25, 1903, in Lemberg, Austria; immigrated to United States, 1938, naturalized citizen, 1944; died after several days in a coma, February 27, 1990, in Tucson, AZ; son of Daniel (a businessman) and Rose (Gottlieb) Glatzer; married Anne Stiebel (a teacher); children: Daniel Franz, Judith Eve Wechsler. *Education:* University of Frankfurt, Ph.D., 1931. *Religion:* Jewish.

CAREER: University of Frankfurt, Frankfurt am Main, Germany, lecturer in Jewish philosophy, 1932-33; Bet Sefer Reali, Haifa, Palestine (now Israel), instructor in Bible, 1933-37; The College of Jewish Studies (now Spertus College of Judaica), Chicago, IL, instructor in Bible, 1938-43; Hebrew Teachers College (now Hebrew Collge), Boston, MA, professor of Talmud, 1943-47; Yeshiva University, New York, NY, professor of history, 1948-50; Brandeis University, Waltham, MA, professor of Jewish history, 1950-73, chairman of department of Near Eastern and Judaic Studies, 1957-69; Boston University, Boston, professor of religion, 1973-90. Editor, Schocken Books, Inc., 1945-90. Seminar associate, Columbia University, 1960-63; visiting professor, University of California, Los Angeles, 1967, 1974.

MEMBER: American Academy for Jewish Research (fellow), Leo Baeck Institute (fellow; member of board of directors), Jewish Publication Society (member of editorial board), American Society for the Study of Religion, American Academy of Arts and Sciences (fellow).

AWARDS, HONORS: Guggenheim fellow, 1959-60; Dr. honoris causa, Brandeis University, 1973; B'nai B'rith Prize for Literary Excellence, 1973; Doctor of Laws, University of Southern California, 1981.

WRITINGS:

Untersuchungen zur Geschichtslehre der Tannaiten, Schocken Verlag (Berlin), 1933.

Geschichte der talmudischen Zeit, Schocken Verlag, 1937.

Kizur toldoth Yisrael, Beth Sefer Reali Press (Haifa), 1947.

Hillel the Elder: The Emergence of Classical Judaism, B'nai B'rith Hillel Foundations, 1956, revised edition, Schocken, 1966.

Anfaetige des Judentums: Eine Einfuehrung, G. Mohn (Guetersloh), 1966.

Essays in Jewish Thought, University of Alabama Press, 1978.

The Loves of Franz Kafka, Schocken Books, 1986.

The Memoirs of Nahum N. Glatzer, edited and presented by Michael Fishbane and Judith Glatzer Wechsler, Hebrew Union College Press (Cincinnati, OH), 1997.

EDITOR, EXCEPT AS INDICATED

(Compiler with Ludwig Strauss) *Sendung und Schicksal: Aus dem Schrifttum des nachbiblischen Judentums,* Schocken Verlag, 1931, published as *Sendung und Schicksal des Judetitums,* Hegner, 1969.

(Compiler) *Gespraeche der Weisen: Aus taltnudisch-midraschischen Texten,* Schocken Verlag, 1935.

(Compiler) Mosche ben Maimon, *Moses Maimonides: Ein systematischer Querschnitt durch sein Werk,* Schocken Verlag, 1935.

Flavius Josephus, *Jerusalem and Rome: The Writings of Josephus,* Meridian Books, 1940.

(And translator) Moses ben Maimon, *Maimonides Said: An Anthology,* Jewish Book Club (New York), 1941.

In Time and Eternity: A Jewish Reader, Schocken, 1946, 2nd revised edition, 1961.

The Language of Faith: A Selection from the Most Expressive Jewish Prayers, Schocken, 1967.

Samuel J. Agnon, *Days of Awe,* Schocken, 1948.

Hammer on the Rock: A Short Midrash Reader, Schocken, 1948.

S. D. Goldschmidt, *Passover Haggadah: Introduction and Commentary,* Schocken, 1953, revised edition, 1969.

Franz Rosenzweig: His Life and Thought, Farrar, Straus, 1953, revised edition, Schocken, 1961.

Franz Rosenzweig, *Understanding the Sick and the Healthy,* Noonday, 1954.

Rosenzweig, *On Jewish Learning,* Schocken, 1955, revised edition, 1965.

Leopold and Adelheid Zunz: An Account in Letters, 1815-1885, East & West Library, 1958.

Franz Rosenzweig, [Tel-Aviv], 1959.

The Rest Is Commentary: A Source Book of Judaic Antiquity (also see below), Beacon Press, 1961.

Franz Kafka, *Parables and Paradoxes,* Schocken, 1961.

(And abridger) Emil Schuerer, *A History of the Jewish People in the Time of Jesus,* Schocken, 1961, revised edition, 1963.

(And author of introduction) *Faith and Knowledge: The Jew in the Medieval World* (also see below), Beacon Press, 1963.

Leopold Zunz: Jude-Deutscher-Europaeer, J.C.B. Mohr, (Tuebingen), 1964.

(And author of introduction) *The Dynamics of Emancipation: The Jew in the Modern Age* (also see below), Beacon Press, 1965.

Martin Buber, *The Way of Response,* Schocken, 1966.

Martin Buber, *On Judaism,* Schocken, 1967.

Martin Buber, *On the Bible,* Schocken, 1969.

(Compiler) *The Dimensions of Job: A Study and Selected Readings,* Schocken, 1969.

(Compiler and author of introduction) *The Judaic Tradition* (includes revisions of *The Rest Is Commentary, Faith and Knowledge,* and *The Dynamics of Emancipation*), Beacon Press, 1969.

Agnon, *Twenty-one Stories,* Schocken, 1970.

Flavius Josephus, *The Second Jewish Commonwealth,* Schocken, 1970.

Kafka, *The Complete Stories,* Schocken, 1971.

Philo Judaeus, *The Essential Philo,* Schocken, 1971.

I Am a Memory Come Alive (documentary biography of Kafka), Schocken, 1974.

Kafka, *Letters to Ottla and the Family,* translated by Richard and Clara Winston, Schocken Books, 1982.

(With Paul Mendes-Flohr) *The Letters of Martin Buber: A Life of Dialogue,* translated by Richard and Clara Winston and Harry Zohn, Schocken, 1991.

CONTRIBUTOR

Aus unbekannten Schriften, Lambert Schneider (Heidelberg), 1928.

Paul Lazarus Gedenkbuch, [Jerusalem], 1951.

Der Friede: Idee und Venvirklichung (Leschnitzer Festschrift), [Heidelberg], 1951.

Ale Ayyin (Schocken Festschrift), [Jerusalem], 1952.

The Scrolls and the New Testament, Harper, 1957.

Between East and West, [London], 1958.

Yuval Shay (Agnon Jubilee Volume), Ramat Gan, 1958.

Hokmat Yisrael be-Maarav Europa, Ogen, 1958.

Zion in Jewish Literature, Herzl, 1961.

Politische Ordnung und menschlichte Existenz (Voegelin Festschrift), [Munich], 1962.

P. A. Schilpp and M. Friedman, editors, *Martin Buber,* [Germany], 1963, translation published as *The Philosophy of Martin Buber,* Open Court, 1965.

Great Jewish Thinkers of the Twentieth Century, B'nai B'rith, 1963.

Hugo Hahn Jubilee Volume, Habonim, 1963.

Brandeis Judaica Texts and Studies, Volumes II-III, Harvard University Press, 1964.

Arthur A. Cohen, editor, *Arguments and Doctrines: A Reader of Jewish Thinking in the Aftermath of the Holocaust,* Harper, 1970.

OTHER

(Author of foreword) *Flavius Josephus, The Great Roman-Jewish War,* Harper, 1960.

(Author of introduction to 2nd edition of German translation) Robert T. Hertord, *The Pharisees,* Macmillan, 1924, published as *Die Pharisaeer,* 2nd edition, [Cologne], 1961.

(Author of foreword) J. M. Guyau, *The Non-Religion of the Future,* 2nd edition, Schocken, 1962.

Also contributor to *Encyclopaedia Britannica, Jewish Book Annual, Grolier Encyclopedia,* and *Encyclopaedia Judaica.* Contributor to journals in Germany, United States, and Israel. Contributing editor, *Judaism.*

SIDELIGHTS: An educator, publisher, translator, editor, and author, Nahum Norbert Glatzer was a noted scholar of Jewish religious history. During his career, he taught at institutions in Europe and the United States, including University of Frankfurt, Bet Sefer Reali in Israel, and Yeshiva, Brandeis, and Boston universities. A founder of Schocken books, Glatzer wrote *Hillel the Elder: The Emergence of Classical Judaism* and *Essays in Jewish Thought,* and among works he edited for Schocken are *In Time and Eternity: A Jewish Reader, Faith and Knowledge: The Jew in the Medieval World,* and Franz Kafka's *Letters to Ottla and the Family.* Glatzer edited and translated writings by Moses ben Maimon in *Maimonides Said: An Anthology.*

BIOGRAPHICAL/CRITICAL SOURCES:

BOOKS

Glatzer, Nahum N., *The Memoirs of Nahum N. Glatzer,* edited and presented by Michael Fishbane and Judith Glatzer Wechsler, Hebrew Union College Press, 1997.

Introductions to Texts and Responses: Essays Presented to N. N. Glatzer, E. J. Brill, 1975.

PERIODICALS

Commonweal, September 5, 1969; March 12, 1971.

Judaism, Volume 12, number 2, 1963.

New York Times Book Review, March 15, 1970; January 17, 1982.

Village Voice Literary Supplement, March, 1982.

OBITUARIES:

PERIODICALS

Chicago Tribune, March 4, 1990.

New York Times, March 1, 1990.*

* * *

GLUBB, John Bagot 1897-1986
(Glubb Pasha)

PERSONAL: Born April 16, 1897, in Preston, England; died March 17, 1986, in Mayfield, Sussex, England; son of Frederick Manley (a general in the British Army) and Frances Letitia (Bagot) Glubb; married Muriel Rosemary Forbes, August 20, 1938; children: Godfrey, Naomi, Mary, John. *Education:* Attended Royal Military Academy at Woolwich, 1914-15. *Religion:* Church of England.

CAREER: British Army, Royal Engineers, regular officer, served on western front in France and Belgium, 1915-18, in Iraq, 1920-26, resigned as captain; administrative inspector, Iraq Government, 1926-30; Transjordan (now Jordan) Army, officer in command of desert area, 1930-38, chief of staff of Arab Legion, 1938-56, retired as lieutenant general; free-lance writer and lecturer.

AWARDS, HONORS: Military Cross, World War I; Knight Commander of the Bath; Commander of the Order of St. Michael and St. George; Distinguished Service Order; Order of the British Empire, Rafidain (Iraq); Knight of the Order of St. John of Jerusalem; Order of Istiqlal, first class, and Order of Nahdha, first class (both Jordan); Lawrence Memorial Medal; Livingston Memorial Medal, Royal Asiatic Society; Burton Memorial Medal, Royal Scottish Geographical Society.

WRITINGS:

(With Henry Field) *The Yezidis, Sulubba, and Other Tribes of Iraq and Adjacent Regions,* G. Banta, 1943.

The Story of the Arab Legion, Hodder & Stoughton, 1948, Da Capo Press, 1976.

(Author of foreword) Godfrey Lias, *Glubb's Legion,* Evans Brothers, 1956.

A Soldier with the Arabs, Harper, 1957.

Britain and the Arabs: A Study of Fifty Years, 1908 to 1958, Hodder & Stoughton, 1959.

War in the Desert: An R.A.F. Frontier Campaign, Hodder & Stoughton, 1960, Norton, 1961.

The Great Arab Conquests, Hodder & Stoughton, 1963, Prentice-Hall, 1964.

The Empire of the Arabs, Hodder & Stoughton, 1963, Prentice-Hall, 1964.

The Course of Empire: The Arabs and Their Successors, Hodder & Stoughton, 1965, Prentice-Hall, 1966.

The Lost Centuries: From the Muslim Empires to the Renaissance of Europe, 1145-1453, Hodder & Stoughton, 1966, Prentice-Hall, 1967.

Syria, Lebanon and Jordan, Walker & Co., 1967.

The Mixture of Races in the Eastern Arab Countries (lecture), Blackwell Bookshop, 1967.

The Middle East Crisis: A Personal Interpretation, Hodder & Stoughton, 1967.

A Short History of the Arab Peoples, Stein & Day, 1969.

The Life and Times of Muhammad, Stein & Day, 1970.

Peace in the Holy Land: An Historical Analysis of the Palestine Problem, Hodder & Stoughton, 1971.

Soldiers of Fortune: The Story of the Mamlukes, Stein & Day, 1973.

The Way of Love, Troy University Press, 1974.

Haroon Al Rasheed and the Great Abbasids, Hodder & Stoughton, 1976.

Into Battle: A Soldier's Diary of the Great War, Cassell, 1977.

(Author of foreword) *A Moorish Calendar: From the Book of Agriculture of Ibn al-Awam,* translated by Philip Lord, edited and illustrated by Peter Lord, Black Swan Press (Wantage, UK), 1978.

The Fate of Empires and Search for Survival, Blackwood (Edinburgh), 1978.

Arabian Adventures: Ten Years of Joyful Service, Cassell (London), 1978.

A Purpose for Living, S.P.C.K. (London), 1980.

The Changing Scenes of Life: An Autobiography, Quartet Books (London), 1983.

SIDELIGHTS: A military officer, educator, and author, John Bagot Glubb is best remembered as commander of the Arab Legion and a rival in reputation to Lawrence of Arabia. Glubb began his military career as a member of the British Army, serving in France and Belgium from 1915 to 1918 and then in Iraq from 1920 to 1926. He then resigned his position as captain to become an administrative inspector for the Iraqi Government. By that time fluent in Arabic and an expert on Arab history and culture, Glubb developed tactics to help the Bedouin tribes combat terrorism; his exploits were renowned and he became known to the Bedouins as *Abu Hunaik*—Father of the Little Jaw—an allusion to a war wound he received. Glubb eventually became one of the most powerful men in the Middle East, earning the appellation pasha, a title of high respect, and transforming the Arab Legion (a desert army of Bedouins that later became the Jordanian Army) into one of the best armies of the Arab countries. With their long skirts and hair the desert fighters were dubbed "Glubb's girls" by the British, and under his leadership the Bedouin troops scored the only major victory over Israel in the Palestine war of 1948. Glubb was a legend by the time he left the Middle East in 1956 and subsequently turned to lecturing and writing. He was the author of numerous books, including *The Story of the Arab Legion; Britain and the Arabs: A Study of Fifty Years, 1908 to 1958; The Great Arab Conquests; The Course of Empire: The Arabs and Their Successors; Peace in the Holy Land: An Historical Analysis of the Palestine Problem;* and *Into Battle: A Soldier's Diary of the Great War.*

Glubb's thirteenth book on the military and political history of the Islamic empires, *The Life and Times of Muhammad,* "reveals the simple and open reflections of the soldier-author," James M. Murphy wrote in a review for *Best Sellers.* "This is not the work of a professional historian. Had it been so it would have been a worthless book. By Glubb's own confession, it is a popular work." C. M. Woodhouse called the book "more than a mere biography" and explained: "Fourteen years ago Sir John Glubb was dismissed from his post as Commander of the Arab Legion with peremptory and brutal discourtesy. . . . Such treatment as Glubb Pasha received in the country of his adoption would have led to a blood-feud lasting many generations if he had been himself a Jordanian. This is just one symptom of the gulf which separates even so sympathetic an observer as Sir John from the people he [knew] so well. He [wrote] from the point of view of an outsider who [could] profoundly understand and brilliantly interpret their philosophy of life, but [did] not share it."

BIOGRAPHICAL/CRITICAL SOURCES:

BOOKS

Glubb, John Bagot, *Arabian Adventures: Ten Years of Joyful Service,* Cassell, 1978.

Glubb, *Into Battle: A Soldier's Diary of the Great War,* Cassell, 1978.

Glubb, *The Changing Scenes of Life: An Autobiography,* Quartet Books, 1983.

Lias, Godfrey, *Glubb's Legion,* foreword by Glubb, Evans Brothers, 1956.

Lunt, James D., *Glubb Pasha, a Biography: Lieutenant-General Sir John Bagot Glubb, Commander of the Arab Legion, 1939-1956,* Harvill Press (London), 1984.

Royle, Trevor, *Glubb Pasha,* Abacus (London), 1993.

PERIODICALS

Best Sellers, June 1, 1970.
Library Journal, June 1, 1969; March 15, 1970.
New Yorker, March 30, 1968.
Spectator, March 28, 1970.

OBITUARIES:

PERIODICALS

Chicago Tribune, March 19, 1986.
Newsweek, March 31, 1986.
New York Times, March 18, 1986.
Times (London), March 18, 1986.*

* * *

GLUBB PASHA
See GLUBB, John Bagot

* * *

GOITEIN, S(helomo) D(ov) 1900-1985
(Solomon Dob Fritz Goitein)

PERSONAL: Born April 3, 1900, in Burgkunstadt, Germany; died of a heart attack, February 6, 1985, in Princeton, NJ; came to United States in 1957; son of Eduard E. (a rabbi) and Frida (Braunschweiger) Goitein; married Theresa Gottlieb (a teacher of eurhythmics), July 16, 1929; children: Ayala (Mrs. Amirav Gordon), Ofra (Mrs. Baruch Rosner), Elon. *Education:* University of Frankfurt on the Main, Ph.D., 1923. *Religion:* Jewish. *Avocational interests:* Calisthenics, hiking.

CAREER: School teacher in Haifa, Israel, 1923-27; Hebrew University, Jerusalem, Israel, instructor, 1928-32, assistant professor, 1933-46, associate professor, 1947-48, professor of Islamic history, 1949-57, director of School of Oriental Studies, 1949-56; University of Pennsylvania, Philadelphia, professor of Arabic, 1957-71; Institute for Advanced Study, School of History, Princeton, NJ, visitor, 1971-85. Senior education officer of Mandatory Government of Palestine, 1938-48.

MEMBER: American Philosophical Society, Mediaeval Academy of America (fellow), American Academy for Jewish Research (fellow), American Oriental Society (president, 1969-70), Conference on Jewish Social Studies, Middle Eastern Studies Association, Israel Oriental Society (president, 1949-57).

AWARDS, HONORS: Recipient of grants from American Philosophical Society, 1958, 1961, Ulmann Foundations, 1959, Social Science Research Council, 1962, 1968-69, and Guggenheim Memorial Foundation, 1965-66, 1971-73; L.H.D., University of Chicago, 1971, University of Pennsylvania, 1982, and Gratz College; D.H.L., Jewish Theological Seminary of America, 1973; Haskins Medal, Mediaeval Academy of America, 1973; Ben-Zvi Institute Prize, 1973; Levi Della Vida Medal, University of California, 1975; Harvey Prize, Technion, Haifa, 1980; lifetime annual stipend, John D. and Catherine T. MacArthur Foundation, 1983.

WRITINGS:

From the Land of Sheba: Tales of the Jews of Yemen, translation by Christopher Fremantle, Schocken, 1947, revised edition, 1973.
Jews and Arabs: Their Contacts through the Ages, Schocken, 1955, revised edition, 1974.
Studies in Islamic History and Institutions, E. J. Brill, 1966.
A Mediterranean Society: The Jewish Communities of the Arab World as Portrayed in the Documents of the Cairo Geniza, University of California Press, Volume I: *Economic Foundations,* 1968, Volume II: *The Community,* 1971, Volume III: *The Family,* 1978, Volume IV: *Daily Life,* Volume V: *The Individual,* Volume VI (with Paula Sanders): *Cumulative Indices. Letters of Medieval Jewish Traders,* Princeton University Press, 1974.
Palestinian Jewry in Early Islamic and Crusader Times, Ben Zvi Institute (Jerusalem), 1980.
The Yemenites: History, Communal Organization, Spiritual Life, Ben Zvi Institute, 1982.

AS SOLOMON DOB FRITZ GOITEIN

Jemenica: Sprichwoerter und Redensarten aus Zentral-Jemen, Kommissionsverlag von O. Harrassowitz, 1934.
Baladhuri: Arab Historian, Hebrew University Press, 1936.
Travels in Yemen, Hebrew University Press, 1941.
Hora-at ha-ivrit be-Erets Yisrael, Yavneh Publishing, 1945.
Ha-Islam shel Muhammad, Hebrew University, 1956.
(Author of introduction) Carl Rathjens, *Jewish Domestic Architecture in San'a, Yemen,* Luzac & Co., 1957.
The Mentality of the Middle Class in Mediaeval Islam, Centre pour l'Etude des Problems du Monde Musulman Contemporain (Brussels, Belgium), 1961.

Also author of *Hora-at ha-TaNakh be-vet ha-sefer,* 1942, *Shete masot al sefer Yirmiyah,* 1952, Umanut ha-sipur ba-Mikra, 1955, *Iyunim be-Mikra,* 1957, *Ha-Mishpat ha-muslimi bi-Medinat Yisrael,* 1957, *Hora-at ha-TaNakh,* 1957, *The Geniza Collection at the University Museum of the University of Pennsylvania,* 1958, *Sidre hinnukh,* 1962, *Hora-at ha-Ivrit,* 1967 and *Iyunim ba-Mikra,* 1967. Also editor and translator of *Masa'ot Habshush,* by Hayyim Habshush, 1939.

SIDELIGHTS: S. D. Goitein, a Hebraic and Arabic scholar and a leading authority on Islamic culture, immigrated to Palestine (now Israel) in 1923 to become head of the Department of Education of the Palestine Mandate. In 1949 he accepted the post of director of the School of Oriental Studies at the Hebrew University in Jerusalem. Goitein came to the United States in 1957 and was professor of Arabic at the University of Pennsylvania until 1971, when he became associated with the Institute for Advanced Study in Princeton, New Jersey. In 1983 the educator and author received a lifetime annual stipend from the John D. and Catherine T. MacArthur Foundation. Goitein, who sometimes published under the name Solomon Dob Fritz Goitein, wrote numerous books on the Middle East, including *From the Land of Sheba: Tales of the Jews of Yemen; Jews and Arabs: Their Contacts Through the Ages; Letters of Medieval Jewish Traders; Palestinian Jewry in Early Islamic and Crusader Times; The Yemenites: History, Communal Organization, Spiritual Life;* and *The Geniza Collection at the University Museum of the University of Pennsylvania.*

According to Charles Issawi in *Commentary,* Volume I of Goitein's series *A Mediterranean Society* is a "particularly valuable" study. "It is based on one of the richest archieval sources available on medieval Islam, the Geniza documents. . . . The existence of the Geniza has been known since 1864, and its contents have been scattered over four continents, but it remained for Professor Goitein to realize its potential value for economic history. . . . Ten years of intensive work in libraries ranging from Leningrad and Jerusalem to Cambridge and New York, and a lifetime devoted to Semitic studies and research on Oriental Jewish communities, have enabled Goitein to make one of the most important contributions to medieval Islamic and Jewish history." Goitein's series, Issawi continued, is "an incomparable mine of information and a rich storehouse of historical interpretation." In a review of Volume II of the series for *Commentary,* Erich Isaac wrote that Goitein's "monumental researches" resulted in a "fascinating recounting" of Mediterranean society. And a *Commonweal* reviewer believed Goitein's *Jews and Arabs* "is the kind of book one should have read years ago. . . . There are many historical indications in these pages as to why Jews and Arabs are so similar in some areas, so dissimilar in others."

"My lifework has had one main purpose," Goitein told *CA,* "[namely,] to help Jews and Arabs to understand their own civilizations, as well as the relations between the two, more completely. My occupation with the gigantic work of the Muslim historian al-Baladhuri provided me with an excellent opportunity to penetrate into the life of a most genuine Arab society. My study of the Jews of Yemen, those most Jewish and most Arab of all Jews, revealed important aspects of Judaec-Arabic symbiosis. Research in the Cairo Geniza (letters and documents from the tenth through the thirteenth centuries written mostly in Judaec-Arabic) has resulted thus far in seven [books], portraying a Mediterranean, mostly middle class, world of almost modern mobility and lively contacts between the various religious and racial groups. However, the increasingly oppressive discrimination of non-Muslims and all that went with it led to the eclipse of that society by the end of the thirteenth century." In all these studies, Goitein concluded, "My lifelong preoccupation with biblical literature, society, and thought provided a firm foundation."

BIOGRAPHICAL/CRITICAL SOURCES:

BOOKS

Attal, Robert, *A Bibliography of the Writings of Professor S. D. Goitein,* Institute of Asian and African Studies, Hebrew University, 1975.

Morag, Shelomo, Issachar Ben-Ami, and Norman A. Stillman, editors, *Studies in Judaism and Islam: Presented to Shelomo Dov Goitein on the Occasion of His Eightieth Birthday by His Students, Colleagues, and Friends,* Magnes Press, Hebrew University (Jerusalem), 1981.

PERIODICALS

American Historical Review, April, 1974; June, 1975; October, 1979.
Archaeology, January, 1979.
Commentary, May, 1968; September, 1973.
Commonweal, December 6, 1974.
Economist, March 9, 1974.
Journal of Economic History, June, 1969.
Speculum, July, 1973; July, 1976.

OBITUARIES:

PERIODICALS

Chicago Tribune, February 12, 1985.
New York Times, February 10, 1985.
Times (London), February 15, 1985.*

* * *

GOITEIN, Solomon Dob Fritz
See GOITEIN, S(helomo) D(ov)

* * *

GOLDSTEIN, Israel 1896-1986

PERSONAL: Born June 18, 1896, in Philadelphia, PA; died April 11, 1986, in Tel Aviv, Israel; son of David (a sexton) and Fanny (Silver) Goldstein; married Bertha Markowitz, July 21, 1918; children: Avram, Vivian (Mrs. Paul Olum). *Education:* University of Pennsylvania, B.A., 1914; Columbia University, M.A., 1917; Jewish Theological Seminary of America, rabbi, 1918. *Politics:* Liberal Party of New York.

CAREER: Ordained rabbi, 1918; Congregation B'nai Jeshurun, New York, NY, rabbi, 1918-61, rabbi emeritus, 1961-86. President, Jewish Conciliation Board of America, 1930-68, honorary president, 1969-86; delegate to World Zionist Congress, 1935-61; member, National Labor Relations Board, 1935; president, Albert Einstein Foundation of Higher Learning, Inc., 1946; founder, Brandeis University, 1946; president, World Confederation of General Zionists, 1947-56, co-chairman, 1956-72, honorary president, 1972-86; United Jewish Appeal, national co-chairman, 1947-48, member of national cabinet and co-chairman of New York Campaign, 1951-86; president, Jewish Restitution Successor Organization, 1950-86; chairman of Western Hemisphere Executives, United Jewish Congress, 1950-59; first chairman, Amidar Israel National Housing Co., 1950; member of board of governors, Hebrew University of Jerusalem, 1950-86, and Haifa University, 1970-86; member of executive committee, Weizmann Institute of Science, Rehovot, Israel, 1950-86; Israel Bond Drive, member of board of governors, 1951-86, chairman of New York executive committee, 1951-61; council member, National Bank of Israel, 1953-86; vice president, Conference of Jewish Organizations on Material Claims against Germany and Austria, 1953-61; chairman, Israel's Tenth Anniversary Celebration in the United States, 1958; world chairman, Keren Hayesed United Israel Appeal, 1961-71; president, World Association of Hebrew Union, 1963-73; chairman, Jerusalem Artists House, 1965-70; chairman of Jerusalem Council, Israel-American Friendship League, 1969-74; chairman, World Bible Center, Jerusalem, 1973-86; member of board of directors, Israel Philharmonic Orchestra, 1965-71; president, New York Board of Jewish Ministers, 1926-28; member of commission on immigration and naturalization, Department of Labor, 1921; member, Citizens Committee on Unemployment Relief, 1930-33; public representative, U.S. Department of Labor, 1935-40. Lecturer at Jewish Theological Seminary of America, 1928; professor, University of Judaism, 1954.

MEMBER: World Jewish Congress (honorary vice president, 1959-86), World Zionist Organization (treasurer), American Jewish Congress (president, 1951-58; honorary president, 1958-86), American Jewish Historical Society, Jewish Academy of Arts and Sciences, Zionist Organization of America (president, 1943-45), Synagogue Council of America (president), Young Judea (president), Jewish Agency of Executives (treasurer, 1949-50), Americans and Canadians in Israel (honorary president, 1961-86), Israel Interfaith Commission (honorary president, 1970-86), American Liberal Party (honorary vice-chairman, 1950-60), Phi Beta Kappa.

AWARDS, HONORS: D.H.L., 1927, and D.D., 1945, Jewish Theological Seminary of America; L.H.D., Brandeis University, 1958; LL.D., New York University, 1961; D.H.L. from Chicago College of Jewish Studies, 1961, Dropsie University, 1971, and Gratz College, 1973; Ph.D., Hebrew University of Jerusalem, 1971. The following have been named in honor of Goldstein: Children's Nursing Home, by British War Relief Society, England; Children's Home, Lyon, France; Immigrant's Hostel, Tel Aviv, Israel; Youth Village, Jerusalem, 1950; tract of land in Israel, by Jewish National Fund of America; Hebrew University of Jerusalem Synagogue, 1956; chair in practical theology, Jewish Theological Seminary of America, 1958; chair in history of Zionism and modern Israel, Hebrew University of Jerusalem, 1967.

WRITINGS:

A Century of Judaism in New York, 1825-1925, Congregation B'nai Jeshurun, 1930.
Toward a Solution, Putnam, 1940.
Mourners Devotions, Bloch, 1946.
Brandeis University: Chapter of Its Founding, Bloch, 1951.
American Jewry Comes of Age, Bloch, 1956.
Transition Years, Rubin Mass (Jerusalem), 1963.
Israel at Home and Abroad, Rubin Mass, 1972.
Jewish Justice and Conciliation: History of the Jewish Conciliation Board of America, 1930-1968, and a Review of Jewish Juridical Autonomy, preface by Simon Agranat, Ktav Pub. House (New York City), 1981.
My World as a Jew: The Memoirs of Israel Goldstein, Herzl Press (New York City), 1984.
Jewish Perspectives: Selected Addresses, Sermons, Broadcasts, and Articles, 1915-1984, edited and annotated by Gabriel A. Sivan, Keter Pub. House (Jerusalem), 1985.

Also author of *Shana b'Yisrael* (title means "A Year in Israel"), 1949. Contributor to *Encyclopaedia Britannica Yearbook, Universal Jewish Encyclopedia,* and *Encyclopedia Hebraica.*

SIDELIGHTS: A Much-honored leader of the Zionist movement in the United States, Israel Goldstein helped found Brandeis University, in Waltham, Massachusetts, in 1946, and was among the founders of what is now the National Conference of Christians and Jews. Goldstein was rabbi at Congregation B'nai Jeshurun in Manhattan, the oldest synagogue of the conservative branch of American Judaism, from 1918 to 1960, when he retired and moved to Israel. He also served as a top executive of many Zionist organizations, including the Jewish National Fund, the Zionist Organization of America, the American Jewish Congress, the World Zionist Organization, and the Jewish Agency. Other posts held by Goldstein included national co-chairman of the United Palestine Appeal and of the United Jewish Appeal, both fund-raising agencies to buy land in Palestine for Jewish agricultural settlement, and vice president of the Conference of Jewish Organizations on Material Claims against Germany after World War II. Goldstein also wrote many books about American Jewry and Jewish ethics, including *American Jewry Comes of Age, Israel at Home and Abroad,* and *Jewish Justice and Conciliation,* and contributed articles to several encyclopedias. His memoirs, two volumes titled *My World as a Jew,* were published in 1984.

BIOGRAPHICAL/CRITICAL SOURCES:

BOOKS

Goldstein, Israel, *My World as a Jew: The Memoirs of Israel Goldstein,* Herzl Press, 1984.

Schneiderman, H., editor, *Two Generations in Perspective,* Monde Publications, 1957.

OBITUARIES:

BOOKS

The Writers Directory: 1984-1986, St. James Press, 1983.

PERIODICALS

Chicago Tribune, April 13, 1986.
Los Angeles Times, April 13, 1986.
Newsweek, April 21, 1986.
New York Times, April 13, 1986.
Times (London), May 1, 1986.
Washington Post, April 13, 1986.*

* * *

GORDON, Vivian V(erdell) 1934-1995 (Satiafa)

PERSONAL: Born April 15, 1934, in Washington, DC; died of amyotrophic lateral sclerosis ("Lou Gehrig's Disease"), March, 1995, in Albany, NY; daughter of Thomas and Susie Verdell; married Ronald Clayton Gordon (divorced); children: Ronald Clayton Jr., Susan Gordon Akkad. *Education:* Virginia State University, B.S., 1955; University of Pennsylvania, M.A., 1957; University of Virginia, Ph.D., 1974.

CAREER: Women's Christian Alliance Child Welfare Agency, Philadelphia, PA, social worker, 1956-57; Library of Congress Legislative Reference Service, Washington, DC, research assistant, 1957, education and social analyst, 1957-63; U.S. House of Representatives Committee on Education and Labor, Washington, DC, coordinator of research, 1963; Upward Bound Project, University of California, Los Angeles, assistant director, 1966-67; California State College (now California State University, Los Angeles), director of Education Participation in Community Program, 1967-69; University of Virginia, Charlottesburg, teaching assistant, 1971-73, assistant professor and department chairperson, 1973-79, associate professor of sociology, 1979-84; State University of New York at Albany, associate professor of African and Afro-American Studies, 1987-95. Black scholar-in-residence, Gettysburg College, 1978; visiting Black scholar, Ball State University, 1981; visiting professor, Wellesley College, 1987. Coordinator of the National Council for Black Studies Student Contest, 1984-89; and consultant to Albany Annual Critical Black Issues Conference.

MEMBER: National Council for Black Studies, Association of Black Sociologists, Association of Black Women Historians.

AWARDS, HONORS: Outstanding Service Award, Parents Association of Jordan High School, 1968; Bethune-Roosevelt Award, Society of Artemas of the University of Virginia, 1974, for outstanding contributions to race relations at the university; Martin Luther King Award, Alpha Phi Alpha, 1982, for service to students; Award for Distinguished Service to Students and Community, National Association for the Advancement of Colored People (NAACP) branch of the University of Virginia, 1983; Distinguished Service to Students Award, Council of Black Students Organizations at the University of Virginia, 1984; Outstanding Service to African Students, State University of New York African Students Association, 1985; Albany Black Arts and Culture Award, 1985; Outstanding Black Woman, State University of New York, 1989; Outstanding Service to Black Students, State University of New York, 1989; Martin Luther King Service Award, 1990.

WRITINGS:

The Self-Concept of Black Americans, University Press of America, 1977.
Lectures: Black Scholars on Black Issues, University Press of America, 1979.
Black Women, Feminism and Black Liberation: Which Way?, Third World Press, 1984.
Kemet and Other Ancient African Civilizations, Third World Press, 1991.
(With Lois Smith Owens) *Think about Prisons and the Criminal Justice System* (part of the "Think" series), Walker, 1992.

Also author of *Dark Women and Others,* under the pseudonym Satiafa. Author of educational publications for the Legislative Reference Service, Council of State Governments, and United States Government Printing Office, 1958-62. Member of the editorial board, *Negro Education Review,* 1985-86.

SIDELIGHTS: A social worker, educator, and author, Vivian V. Gordon was known for her studies and writings of black families and feminism. She began her career as a social worker in 1956, before working at the Library of Congress as a research assistant and analyst. Gordon's early career in Washington, D.C., also included stints with the U.S. House of Representatives Committee on Education and Labor and as a writer with the U.S. Government Printing Office. Gordon later spent time as an educator, teaching at the University of Virginia, Charlottesburg, from 1971 through 1984, and at the State University of New York at Albany, serving as associate professor of African and Afro-American Studies and chairperson of the Africana Studies department. Gordon was the coordinator of the National Council for Black Studies Student Contest from 1984 to 1989. She was also a member of the editorial board of *The Negro Education Review* between 1985 and 1986.

Several honors were bestowed on Gordon, such as the Award for Distinguished Service to Students and Community from the NAACP branch of the University of Virginia; Outstanding Service to African Students, 1985, and Outstanding Black Woman, 1989, both from the State University of New York; and the Martin Luther King Service Award in 1990.

Gordon produced many studies, centering on subjects from driver's education to prisons. In *Black Women, Feminism and Black Liberation: Which Way?,* she had the opportunity to unite many of her areas of knowledge, methodologies, and concerns. "The author," wrote Beverly H. Robinson in *The Black Scholar,* "conduct[ed] a systematic analysis of those issues with which Black women and Black men have grappled since the emergence of the so-called women's liberation movement." Those issues include coalition politics and how they bear upon any alliance of black and white women within the movement, the strong identification between white women and white men, and the cause and effect relationship between the Civil Rights movement and the emergence of Women's Studies.

Ironically, that latter connection resulted in the attempted erasure, in academia, of any difference between black women's and white women's problems. Gordon's historical review reveals this to be a damaging mistake. Her contemporary research with a sample of black women, moreover, showed them connecting their own liberation with the liberation of the entire African American community—male and female, upper and lower class. Unification of that community, through education and bridge-building, is and should be the black woman's priority, she concluded.

In noting that Gordon's conclusions agreed with many other black feminist writings, Robinson commented that the book is still a valuable addition to those previous views. Gordon's long career allowed her to experience social problems which affect black Americans from a wide range of perspectives—that of a social worker, researcher and analyst, and educator. "Vivian Gordon," concluded Robinson, "analyzed all of the possible issues that must be considered for the development of a theoretical perspective on political alternatives for Black women."

BIOGRAPHICAL/CRITICAL SOURCES:

PERIODICALS

Black Scholar, March, 1985.*

OBITUARIES:

PERIODICALS

New York Times, March, 1995.*

* * *

GORKY, Maxim
See PESHKOV, Alexei Maximovich

* * *

GOULD, Jean R(osalind) 1919-1993

PERSONAL: Born May 25, 1919, in Greenville, OH; died of cancer of the jaw, February 8, 1993, in Perrysburg, OH; daughter of Aaron J. and Elsie (Elgutter) Gould; divorced. *Education:* Attended University of Michigan for two years; University of Toledo, A.B., 1937. *Politics:* Reform Democrat. *Avocational interests:* Politics, gardening, watercolor painting, and cooking.

CAREER: Freelance writer, 1941-93. Amalgamated Clothing Workers Union, National Education Office, New York, NY, editorial and rewrite work, part-time, 1952-62; National Opinion Research Center, Princeton, NJ, research and public opinion work. Guest lecturer, Elgin Community College, Elgin, IL; lecturer, International Writers Conference, Hofstra University, Hemstead, NY, 1984. County committeewoman, Democratic Party, 1961-62. Member of advisory board, Virginia Center for the Creative Arts, 1978-93.

MEMBER: Authors Guild, Authors League of America, International PEN, Phi Kappa Phi.

AWARDS, HONORS: Thomas A. Edison Award and prize for special excellence in contributing to character development of children, 1959, for *That Dunbar Boy;* Huntington Hartford Foundation, fellowship, 1962, for work on Robert Frost book; fellowship at Yaddo, 1964, and Huntington Hartford Foundation, 1965, both for biographical studies of American playwrights; Ossabaw Island Foundation fellowships, 1968 and 1976; Radio Network Book Reviews "Oppie" Award for best biography of the year, 1969, Ohioana Library Association award, 1969, and American Association of University Women special award, 1970, all for *The Poet and Her Book: A Biography of Edna St. Vincent Millay;* National Book Award nomination, 1975, for *Amy: The World of Amy Lowell and the Imagist Movement;* Virginia Center for the Creative Arts fellowships, 1978, 1979, 1983, 1984, and 1985, for studies of American women poets; MacDowell Colony fellowship, 1982; *Modern American Women Poets* was the English Speaking Union's Books-Across-the-Sea selection for 1985.

WRITINGS:

FOR YOUTH

Fairy Tales, Whitman, 1944.
Miss Emily (biography of Emily Dickinson), Houghton, 1946.
Jane (biography of Jane Austen), Houghton, 1947.
Young Thack (biography of William Makepeace Thackeray), Houghton, 1949.
Sidney Hillman, Houghton, 1952.
Fisherman's Luck, Macmillan, 1954.
That Dunbar Boy (biography of Paul Laurence Dunbar), illustrated by Charles Walker, Dodd, 1958.

FOR ADULTS

(Editor and contributor) *Homegrown Liberal,* Dodd, 1954.
Young Mariner Melville (Literary Guild selection), Dodd, 1956.
A Good Fight: F.D.R.'s Conquest of Polio, Dodd, 1960.
Winslow Homer: A Portrait, Dodd, 1962.
Robert Frost: The Aim Was Song, Dodd, 1964.
Modern American Playwrights, Dodd, 1966.
The Poet and Her Book: A Biography of Edna St. Vincent Millay, Dodd, 1969.
Walter Reuther: Labor's Rugged Individualist, Dodd, 1972.
Amy: The World of Amy Lowell and the Imagist Movement, Dodd, 1975.
American Women Poets: Pioneers of Modern Poetry, Dodd, 1980.
Modern American Women Poets, Dodd, 1985.

Member of editorial board, *National Forum,* 1978.

SIDELIGHTS: Jean R. Gould received her undergraduate degree from the University of Toledo and went on to write literary biographies for young readers on such notables as novelist Herman Melville and black poet Paul Lawrence Dunbar. After traveling to New York City in the early 1950s, she worked as an editor and writer at the Amalgamated Clothing Workers Union. In the 1960s she began a string of biographies for adults, including *The Story of F. D. R.'s Conquest of Polio,* which concerns President Franklin Delano Roosevelt, *Winslow Homer: A Portrait, Robert Frost: The Aim Was Song,* and *The Poet and Her Book: A Biography of Edna St. Vincent Millay.* She was nominated for a National Book Award in 1975 for *Amy: The World of Amy Lowell and the Imagist Movement.*

Gould told *CA:* "To use an old phrase, which will surely date me, I was injected, if not born, with 'printer's ink in my veins.' My family was in the minor publishing business from the time I was six years old. They printed [or] published theater programs for years, plus an entertainment guide and a weekly paper. My mother wrote poetry and editorials; my aunt was a newspaperwoman for fifty years. So quite naturally, I began writing when I was about ten years old. My first effort was a play which I not only wrote, but directed and played the lead. My first writing 'job' was as assistant editor to my mother. A creative urge resulted in short stories, fairy tales, and plays for children. Several of the last were included in *Best Plays for Young Readers* in various years of the fifties. I always thought I would write novels and plays, but became known as a biographer instead. [This was] quite by accident.

"Because I wrote poetry, I loved reading it, and through a rare, truly literary professor [of] both seventeenth-century and contemporary poetry, I came under the spell of Emily Dickinson. A good many books had already been written about the New England mystic-poet, but none for young readers. So I wrote *Miss Emily,* which, after some hesitation, Houghton accepted and published. It was unexpectedly successful and stayed in print a long time. Since publishers, like movie producers, always want more of a successful [genre], I became a biographer. As might be expected, I have written more biographies of poets than of other figures of note; but my collective work *Modern American Playwrights* proved very successful and led to [my] . . . project on modern American poets, which at first was to have dealt with both sexes. However, since 'women's lib' and the E.R.A. have become so prominent, it was suggested by my publishers that I confine my subjects to women responsible for the evolution of modern poetry. Then I discovered the vast number of women writing poetry today and being recognized for their work on the same level as men. So two books became necessary instead of a single volume.

"Having written and published eighteen books, with few exceptions biographies or biographical studies, I decided it was time to write my own story, and have begun to write an autobiography. It will deal in part with a childhood concerned in surmounting my handicap (paralysis at or near birth), my 'salad days' as a writer, and some of the most striking adventures in dealing with the well-known figures who were my subjects."

BIOGRAPHICAL/CRITICAL SOURCES:

PERIODICALS

Best Sellers, July 1, 1972; January, 1976.
Book World, May 18, 1969.
Los Angeles Times, February 14, 1986.
Los Angeles Times Book Review, August 3, 1980.
New Republic, December 6, 1975.
New York Herald Tribune Book Review, May 11, 1952.
New York Herald Tribune Weekly Book Review, May 11, 1947.
New York Times, April 28, 1946.
New York Times Book Review, September 20, 1964.
Saturday Review, June 7, 1969.
Saturday Review of Literature, September 28, 1946.
Villager, April 20, 1961.

OBITUARIES:

BOOKS

The Writers Directory: 1990-1992, St. James Press, 1990.

PERIODICALS

New York Times, February 12, 1993, p. B7.
School Library Journal, April, 1993, p. 24.*

* * *

GRAHAM, Sheilah 1904-1988

PERSONAL: Birth-given name, Lily Shiel; born c. 1904 in London, England; immigrated to United States, 1933, naturalized citizen, August, 1947; died of congestive heart failure, November 17 (one source says November 18), 1988, in West Palm Beach, FL; married John Graham Gilliam (a military officer and agent for an iron and steel manufacturer), c. 1926 (divorced June, 1937); married Trevor C. L. Westbrook (an aircraft manufacturer), 1941 (divorced, 1946); married third husband, February, 1953 (divorced c. 1955); children: (second marriage) Wendy (Mrs. Donald Fairey), Robert. *Education:* Attended Royal Academy of Dramatic Art.

CAREER: Performer in musical comedies on the London stage, beginning with *One Damn Thing After Another,* 1927; began contributing articles about the stage to London periodicals, including *Daily Mail;* freelance writer in New York City for *Mirror* and *Evening Journal,* 1933-34; North American Newspaper Alliance (NANA), New York City, author of syndicated Hollywood column "Hollywood Today," 1935-40, war correspondent in England, 1940-45, author of syndicated Hollywood columns "Hollywood Today," "Hollywood Everywhere," and "Speaking for Myself," 1945-70; author of syndicated column "Speaking Frankly" for Bell-McClure Syndicate, 1970-88; *Hollywood Citizen-News,* Los Angeles, CA, author of movie column, 1970-88. Conducted television interviews with stars, 1951-55, and own radio show; wrote daily gossip column for *Daily Variety,* 1952-53, and monthly piece for *Photoplay;* appeared in film *College Confidential,* 1960.

WRITINGS:

Gentleman—Crook, Rich & Cowan, 1933.
(With Gerold Frank) *Beloved Infidel: The Education of a Woman,* Holt, 1958.
The Rest of the Story, Coward, 1964.
College of One, Viking, 1967.
Confessions of A Hollywood Columnist, Morrow, 1969, published in England as *Scratch an Actor: Confessions of a Hollywood Columnist,* W. H. Allen, 1970.
The Garden of Allah, Crown, 1970.
A State of Heat, Grosset, 1972.
How to Marry Super Rich; or, Love, Money, and the Morning After, Grosset, 1974, published in England as *For Richer, for Poorer: The Truth Behind Some of the World's Most Fabulous Marriages,* W.H. Allen, 1975.
The Real F. Scott Fitzgerald Thirty-five Years Later, Grosset, 1976.
The Late Lily Shiel, Grosset, 1978.

My Hollywood: A Celebration and a Lament, M. Joseph (London), 1984.

Hollywood Revisited: A Fiftieth Anniversary Celebration, St. Martin's Press (New York City), 1985.

ADAPTATIONS: A film version of *Beloved Infidel,* screenplay by Sy Bartlett and starring Gregory Peck and Deborah Kerr, was released by Twentieth Century-Fox in 1959.

SIDELIGHTS: In its heyday, Sheilah Graham's syndicated Hollywood column was carried by more than 180 newspapers in the United States and abroad. *Time* magazine noted that by 1964 Graham had "deposed Hopper and Parsons as doyenne of the Hollywood columnists" in an era when a gossip reporter's opinion could make or break a movie or a star. Even when the interest in Hollywood began to wane in subsequent decades with the decline of the studio/star system, Graham's columns remained popular as her pursuit of the "beautiful people" became more global. The columnist also wrote a number of best-selling books about her life, career, and romances, particularly her four-year affair with novelist F. Scott Fitzgerald.

Graham's journalistic influence belied her humble beginnings: she was born Lily Shiel in a London slum around 1908 and entered a London orphanage by the age of six. At seventeen Graham was working as a toothbrush demonstrator at a Holborn department store, where she captured the attention of Major John Graham Gilliam, a man twenty-five years her senior and of superior social standing. The two married, and Gilliam encouraged Lily to pursue a career as a musical-comedy performer on the London stage, where she had a measure of success. It was at this time that she adopted the name Sheilah Graham. It was also at this time that she began her journalism career, contributing articles about the stage to various London periodicals.

In 1933 Graham moved to New York City in hopes of expanding her writing opportunities. She free-lanced for a while, and in 1935 was offered the position of syndicated Hollywood columnist for the North American Newspaper Alliance (NANA). She remained in that post for the next thirty-five years, with a five-year hiatus as a war correspondent in England during World War II. In 1970 Graham moved her affiliation to Bell-McClure, continuing her observations on Hollywood, show business, the international social scene, and women's concerns. The columnist also appeared frequently on television and radio programs and wrote articles for a number of popular periodicals.

Graham's job in the film capital allowed her to mingle with the "watched" and the "talked-about" and ultimately to become one of them; her affair with F. Scott Fitzgerald was another factor that helped precipitate this rise to celebrity. Graham met the novelist at a Hollywood party in 1937. The two fell immediately in love, and she remained with Fitzgerald until late 1940 when he died in her arms. During Fitzgerald's last years, a period of emotional traumas and financial setbacks, Graham encouraged the author to continue writing for the movies and begin his book about Hollywood, *The Last Tycoon.* The heroine of the novel, Kathleen, was modeled after Graham. Fitzgerald's attentions, at the same time, developed in the young columnist a sense of sophistication and assurance and an intimacy with reading and the liberal arts. "I was never a mistress," Graham wrote in one autobiography, *The Rest of the Story.* "I was a woman who loved Scott Fitzgerald for better or worse until he died."

Graham's books are largely autobiographical, exploring her career as a Hollywood columnist, her observations on the "beautiful people," and her relationship with Fitzgerald. In her first best-seller, *Beloved Infidel,* Graham described her rise from London orphan to Hollywood journalist. Yet the bulk of the book recounts her meeting with Fitzgerald and their ensuing four-year romance.

Edmund Wilson wrote in the *New Yorker* that *Beloved Infidel* is "the very best portrait of Fitzgerald that has yet been put into print," revealing incidents never before related. Other critics agreed, noting that while the first part of the book read like a confession magazine, those parts dealing with Fitzgerald were frank and warm. A review in the *Times Literary Supplement* reflected the book's general critical reception: "Miss Graham's description of their turbulent but deeply touching love affair could have foundered on many shoals, both hidden and obvious. Miraculously she avoid[ed] them, and in her story of their time together she manage[d] to tell almost all there can be to know without once offending against taste, loyalty or good manners. . . . She [wrote] of him with a haunting tenderness that is never cloying. . . . [Fitzgerald] grows to life in her hands in a way that even his excellent biographer never achieved, and a many-sided portrait—of the lover, the writer, the teacher, the drinker—emerges."

An autobiographical sequel, *The Rest of the Story,* followed *Beloved Infidel.* In it Graham told of her life post-Fitzgerald: about her marriages, children, and journalism career. The sequel was not as successful as its predecessor, and in 1967 Graham returned to the subject of her life with Fitzgerald in another publication, *A College of One*. This time her recollections emphasized the Pygmalion-Galatea aspect of their relationship, with the book presenting the entire curriculum that Fitzgerald had prepared for Graham's liberal arts education and describing his method of teaching. Warren Coffey explained in *Commonweal:* "[Graham's] education had ended when she left the orphanage as a girl, and she lived in constant dread of making the slip that would betray her ignorance and her slum origins. . . . She couldn't tell anybody about the agonies this caused her for fear of being taunted. But she did tell Fitzgerald, and when he realized how vulnerable she was in the matter, he undertook to educate her." And Graham herself recalled a premonition upon meeting Fitzgerald that said, "Here is the person for whom you have been searching so desperately, who will give you comfort and love and anguish, and the education for which you have longed."

Some critics wondered whether the subject matter of *A College of One* was too scholarly to appeal to the general reader and speculated that perhaps its curiosity value had been overestimated. One *Times Literary Supplement* reviewer pointed out that the papers that largely comprised the book had been available in the Princeton University library for several years already, and Roderick Nordell of the *Christian Science Monitor* remarked that this book of "scholar's morsels" was presenting material already integrated into literary history. Yet both reviewers, along with others, conceded that much could be gleaned about Fitzgerald from the lists, lectures, and notes presented within Graham's context. "[*A College of One*] has a bitty quality which turns out to be its chief fascination," wrote A.S. Byatt in *New Statesman*. "There is more of Fitzgerald the man and the artist to be got from Miss Graham's gobbets and lists and chatter and her honorably recorded response to her teacher."

In addition, the *Times Literary Supplement* reviewer was moved by Graham's compelling reasons for writing *A College of One*. "Miss Graham took her education as seriously as Fitzgerald planned it," he interpreted, "and it is her earnest attempt to fulfill his wishes, together with her honest regard for what he taught her, that gives this book its touching quality." And Nordell reiterated that sentiment: "Certainly the College of One was a magnificent thing for one human being to do for another. . . . [The reader] can hardly fail to be touched by a star pupil's determination to keep from oblivion some last artifacts of her beloved, tortured Mr. Chips."

Feeling that she had essentially exhausted the subject of Fitzgerald, Graham next wrote *Confessions of a Hollywood Gossip Columnist,* a collection of profiles of Hollywood giants, past and present. "Miss Graham lets go with personal opinion on individual and collective film types, both Hollywood and international," Robert B. Frederick synopsized in *Variety*. "It's gossip of the first order and even those individuals whom she personally likes and admires get the rug pulled from under them when the occasion demands."

Other critics acknowledged that *Confessions* did hold a prurient fascination and that it would have great appeal for the gossip-column crowd. "[This] look at Hollywood in its Gotterdammerung twilight is crammed with goodies—" Liz Smith of *Book World* quipped, "33 years of impressions, twice-told and new tales, mountainous items made from the molehills of gossip-mongering, rough and realistic anecdotes, and the columnist's own conclusions." "The conclusions," she added, "are mostly first-rate; Miss Graham comes up with telling analyses of her subjects." Yet Judith Crist wondered in the *New York Times Book Review* whether a regular follower of Hollywood could find anything new or truly revealing in Graham's opinion-based book; and both reviewers took issue with the author's prose style, which Smith concluded "is mawkish, pretentious, selfconscious, cryptic, and sometimes simply incredibly weird."

Graham followed *Confessions* with *The Garden of Allah,* an examination of the Hollywood bungalow hotel by that name which was the habitation of the film capital's writers and actors for thirty-two years. Among its visitors were such notables as Ernest Hemingway, Robert Benchley, Dorothy Parker, and Fitzgerald, as well as Graham herself. The *Atlantic* labeled Graham's approach to her subject as "solemnly indiscriminate enthusiasm proper to a gossip columnist," and Robert Berkvist noted in the *New York Times Book Review* that "Miss Graham catalogues the guest list in chapter-loads of the most unrelated snippets since the night the Yellow Pages hit the fan."

Still Berkvist admitted that when Graham related her own personal recollections, her book became an oddly moving and fitting tribute to a place and an era that was unmatched anywhere. And Carroll Carroll insisted in *Variety* that "you don't care very much if the connective fiber of her yarn about the fascinating old caravansary is as flimsy as a spider's weaving. [Graham made] it hold from page to page with a sizing of classic anecdotes about the early denizens of Tinseltown-on-the-Freeway."

In Graham's next autobiographical installment, *A State of Heat,* the author exposed how she used sex "to get all I wanted out of life." She related intimate details of her numerous love affairs and conjectured how other female celebrities used their feminine charms to snare wealthy husbands. Nora Ephron condemned Graham's sex memoir/manual in the *New York Times Book Review:* "I would like to attribute its candor to Miss Graham's long career as a gossip columnist but I'm afraid it all has more to do with bad taste. . . . [Her] writing is as astonishing as the indiscriminate details she subjects us to. . . . Miss Graham [suffered] from a lack of. . . a Selectivity Index."

The Real Scott Fitzgerald appeared in 1976, several years after Graham had written *Beloved Infidel* and *College of One.* Yet the author felt the need to address the many 'misconceptions and errors" about the novelist that had arisen since her earlier books; she also felt that *Beloved Infidel* had been too romanticized, and that she was "obliged to tell the accurate story" of their lives together. Critics found little new or laudable in this third Fitzgerald volume.

Graham presented *The Late Lily Shiel* two years later. In that autobiographical work she recalled the earliest segments of her life, relating in detail her Cinderella rise from London slumdweller to successful musical-comedy star and budding journalist. The author related her story in novelistic style—in the third person and the past tense. "She [had] the meticulousness of a too-thorough diarist," Janet Maslin commented in the *New York Times,* "and little knack for emphasizing what's special about her story."

Yet Maslin also admitted that, intrinsically, Graham's social success chronicle is an arresting one and that "her story remains lively, even when it's turgidly told." A *New Yorker* critic concurred: "Miss Graham peppers her clunky prose with misplaced punctuation; nevertheless, this is an interesting, and not always flattering, self-portrait of an ambitious young woman with an instinct for social survival."

BIOGRAPHICAL/CRITICAL SOURCES:

BOOKS

Fairey, Wendy W., *One of the Family,* Norton (New York City), 1992.

Graham, Sheilah, *Hollywood Revisited: A Fiftieth Anniversary Celebration,* St. Martin's Press, 1985.

Graham, S., *My Hollywood: A Celebration and a Lament,* M. Joseph, 1984.

Westbrook, Robert, *Intimate Lies: F. Scott Fitzgerald and Sheilah Graham: Her Son's Story,* HarperCollins (New York City), 1995.

PERIODICALS

Atlantic Monthly, December, 1970.

Best Sellers, June 4, 1964; April 1, 1969; September, 1976.

Book Week, March 5, 1967.

Book World, April 6, 1969.

Christian Science Monitor, March 23, 1967.

Commonweal, April 14, 1967.

Listener, June 1, 1967; November 25, 1976.

Manchester Guardian, July 31, 1959.

Miami Herald, October 29, 1974.

New Statesman, August 1, 1959; July 14, 1967.

New York Times Book Review, March 30, 1969; January 3, 1971; April 23, 1972.

New York Times, December 1, 1978.

New Yorker, January 24, 1959; January 1, 1979.

Spectator, July 24, 1959.

Time, May 29, 1964.

Times Literary Supplement, July 31, 1959; June 29, 1967.

Variety, March 26, 1969; April 16, 1969; March 25, 1970; July 8, 1970; August 12, 1970; October 28, 1970; October 6, 1971.*

OBITUARIES:

BOOKS

The Writers Directory: 1988-1990, St. James Press, 1988.

PERIODICALS

Chicago Tribune, November 19, 1988.

Los Angeles Times, November 19, 1988.

New York Times, November 19, 1988.

Washington Post, November 19, 1988.*

* * *

GREENE, Felix 1909-1985

PERSONAL: Born May 21, 1909, in Berkhamsted, England; died of cancer, June 15, 1985, in Mexico; son of Edward and Eva (Stutzer) Greene; married Elena Lindeman; children: Anne. *Education:* Attended Cambridge University, two years. *Avocational interests:* Reading, walking.

CAREER: Office of the Prime Minister, London, England, political worker, 1931-33; senior official for British Broadcasting Corp. (BBC) in London and the United States, 1932-40, head of offices in New York, NY, five years; freelance radio and television commentator, filmmaker, and lecturer on international affairs, 1940-85.

MEMBER: Royal Institute of International Affairs, Society for Anglo-Chinese Understanding (vice president), PEN.

AWARDS, HONORS: First prize, Melbourne International Film Festival, for *China!*; British Film Academy nomination for best feature-length documentary, 1968, for "Inside North Vietnam"; received honorary doctorate for his work towards creating understanding between the people of America and the Far East.

WRITINGS:

What's Really Happening in China?, City Lights, 1960.
Awakened China: The Country Americans Don't Know, Doubleday, 1961, published as *China: The Country Americans Are Not Allowed to Know,* Ballantine, 1962, published in England as *The Wall Has Two Sides: A Portrait of China Today,* J. Cape, 1962.
Let There Be a World, Fulton, 1963.
A Curtain of Ignorance: How the American Public Has Been Misinformed about China, Doubleday, 1964.
Viet Nam! Viet Nam!, Fulton, 1966.
The Enemy: Notes on Imperialism and Revolution, J. Cape, 1970, published as *The Enemy: What Every American Should Know about Imperialism and Revolution,* Random House, 1971.
Peking, Mayflower Books, 1978.

Films include interviews with Chou En-lai, 1960, 1963, and 1972, Ho Chi Minh, 1965, Chairman Hua Guofeng, 1979, and Vice-Chairman Deng Xiaoping, 1979, as well as the documentaries *China!,* 1963, *Peking Symphony Orchestra,* 1963, *Inside North Vietnam,* 1967, and *One Man's China* (series of eight films on different aspects of modern China), broadcast by the BBC and distributed in the United States by Time-Life Films, 1972.

SIDELIGHTS: Felix Greene's work, first as a correspondent for the British Broadcasting Corporation (BBC) and later as a freelance writer and filmmaker, took him to virtually every country in the world. One of the journalist's favorite destinations was China; he visited there some sixteen times, occasionally for periods as long as six months. Accompanied by a film crew consisting only of his wife (the sound recorder) and his daughter (the production assistant), Greene (the cameraman) began each new China film project with one major goal in mind: to provide the West with what he believed was a more realistic and positive view of modern-day China than was portrayed in the past.

In 1960, for example, Greene obtained a filmed interview with Premier Chou En-lai, the first such interview ever granted by a Chinese leader. A subsequent project, the 1963 film *China!,* was the first full-length documentary on that country made by a Westerner since the Communist revolution; another extended visit in 1972 furnished Greene with enough material for eight more films, each on a different aspect of contemporary life in China.

Despite these and many other films to his credit, Greene told *CA* that he considered himself "more of an author than a filmmaker." In many cases, though, reviewers (especially American reviewers) criticized his written work for what they considered to be a one-sided approach to the subject matter. Greene attributed their negative reaction to the overall political climate of the 1960s and early 1970s. He explained: "When my books *Awakened China* and *A Curtain of Ignorance* were written, the prevailing attitude towards China was one of extreme hostility—at least in the United States. Almost nothing even remotely positive about China could be written without being challenged as subversive. A Gallup poll of that period indicated that the public considered China as a far more dangerous enemy than even the Soviet Union. It is a strange fact that virtually nothing that these books contained would today be challenged either in fact or in spirit. . . . [As for *Viet Nam! Viet Nam!,*] this again was published before the full enormity of that war had become apparent to world opinion. . . . Nothing written in that book would today be questioned."

In discussions on *Awakened China* dating back to 1961, for example, many reviewers praised Greene's attempt to report on such a long-neglected topic, but they also criticized him for glossing over or entirely omitting facts unfavorable to his thesis. As Tillman Durdin of the *New York Times Book Review* wrote: "[Greene] produced a book that consistently errs, by commission and omission, in favor of the Communist regime but which, on the other hand, effectively portrays successful, dynamic aspects of the New China that Americans should acknowledge and know better. . . . *Awakened China,* though well-written and bright with perceptive passages, is simply not a balanced and objective work."

Takashi Oka of the *Christian Science Monitor* believed that "many . . . conversations, notably about restrictions on criticism in a Communist society, show that Mr. Greene was by no means one-sidedly impressed by all he saw. Nevertheless the total impact of the book is disturbing, for one feels that beside the many things which Mr. Greene did see and record there were others which he passed by. And there is misinformation as well."

The *Guardian*'s Frank Edmead remarked: "Travellers to China, particularly if they know anything of the anarchy and wickedness of Kuomintang rule, must find infuriating the more lurid stories printed in Western newspapers. But often their burning desire to counteract these stories betrays them into partisanship equally unacceptable in the opposite way, and their purpose is defeated. So it is with [*Awakened China*]."

Though the *Saturday Review*'s Gerald Clark admitted to a few reservations about Greene's personal convictions, he decided that the author's main purpose in writing *Awakened China* was "to get the 'feel' of the land in the big sense, its feverish sense of strength and possibility, the dedication of the young people, the patriotic pride and hopes for the future. And this he [did] admirably well." *New York Herald Tribune Books* critic J. Tuzo Wilson felt that regardless of any bias present in *Awakened China,* "those who most hate communism and who most fear China should logically be those to study this and other first hand accounts most carefully." And the *Spectator*'s Nicholas Wollaston simply stated: "The facts of China's prodigious advance cannot be drummed too often into the ears of a complacent West, and Mr. Greene [had] several notable qualifications which make [*Awakened China*] the most valuable account since Edgar Snow exploded his *Red Star over China* twenty-five years ago."

Greene's subsequent works encountered objections quite similar to those raised in connection with *Awakened China.* Commenting on *A Curtain of Ignorance,* an examination of media coverage of China, a critic in *Book Week* wrote: "It is not possible, without matching his research, to refute Greene as he picks and chooses his way through mountains of old newspapers and magazines, but one wonders how representative his selection of quotations is. The press is not fettered or monolithic. It has its wild men, and the author quotes some of them at length. . . . [But] despite its lopsidedness, there is truth in the small hard core of Greene's argument. The press has never reported China well. Greene could have demonstrated this convincingly with a less biased and partisan approach."

H. L. Boorman of the *New York Times Book Review* felt that "many of the points made by Mr. Greene are both valid and worthy of emphasis. Yet the net effect of this book is as misleading as the type of writing on China that its author condemn[ed]. . . . Unfortunately, Mr. Greene . . . laced his negative case on China reporting with more impatience than perspective. Had he taken the time to produce a shorter and less polemical book, the purposes which stimulated his writing might have been better served."

But *Best Sellers* critic W. M. Moses noted: "[Greene pointed] out that our news media have apparently relied to a great extent on the reports of refugees who probably have an axe to grind, on press releases and reports emanating from Chiang Kai-shek's headquarters on Formosa and on information furnished by the 'China Lobby' which has had almost unlimited funds with which to attempt to mold American public opinion. . . . [*A Curtain of Ignorance*] presents a severe indictment of our Federal administration. . . . [It also] presents an even more severe indictment of all of our news media. . . . It is a thought provoking book in which the author's conclusions are well documented."

The *New Republic*'s James Gilbert described *The Enemy,* Greene's study of revolution and the link between capitalism and imperialism (written from a Marxist-Leninist point of view), as "a statement of faith and the documentation of what must have been the reason for the author's decision to join the revolutionary struggle." But, said Gilbert, the book ultimately fails "because the author, as he [admitted, saw] no need to present the good as well as the bad aspects of capitalism. In one stroke he thus [tossed] out the complexities and convert[ed] his indictment to rhetoric." Another critic wrote in *New Statesman:* "This book is a piece of wartime propaganda, and hence it can perhaps be forgiven for containing a fair proportion of rhetorical exaggeration. . . . What is lacking in Greene's whole analysis of imperialism is any sense of the complexities of this subject. . . . [He chose] a subject of first importance; but he [wrote] a second-rate book."

A *Times Literary Supplement* reviewer agreed that the author's "moral indictment is not in the least assisted by the simplistic Marxism with which Mr. Greene [felt] obliged to back it. For what he [got] from Marx [was] not science but demonology." Nevertheless, the reviewer concluded, "Mr. Greene [was] a reporter of immense reputation, and the reputation is wholly justified; here [in *The Enemy*] he [built] up a crescendo of invective on the basis of official statistics and some terrifying, self-destructive quotations. . . . Almost everything Mr. Greene [had] to say is true and important."

BIOGRAPHICAL/CRITICAL SOURCES:

PERIODICALS

Best Sellers, September 15, 1964.
Book Week, September 6, 1964.
Chicago Sunday Tribune, September 24, 1961.
Christian Science Monitor, September 20, 1961.
Guardian, February 2, 1962.
New Republic, May 29, 1971.
New Statesman, February 2, 1962; December 11, 1970.
New York Herald Tribune Books, October 1, 1961.
New York Times Book Review, September 10, 1961; August 23, 1964.
New York Times, May 26, 1965.
Saturday Review, September 9, 1961.
Spectator, January 12, 1962.
Times Literary Supplement, May 25, 1967; March 19, 1971.

OBITUARIES:

PERIODICALS

Chicago Tribune, June 28, 1985.
New York Times, June 27, 1985.
Washington Post, June 30, 1985.*

* * *

GUY, Rosa (Cuthbert) 1928-

PERSONAL: Born September 1, 1928, in Trinidad; came to United States in 1932; daughter of Henry and Audrey (Gonzales) Cuthbert; married Warner Guy (deceased); children: Warner. *Education:* Attended New York University; studied with the American Negro Theater.

CAREER: Writer, 1950—. Lecturer.

MEMBER: Harlem Writer's Guild (founder and former president).

AWARDS, HONORS: American Library Association's Best Book for Young Adults citation, 1973, for *The Friends,* 1976, for *Ruby,* 1978, for *Edith Jackson,* 1979, for *The Disappearance,* and 1981, for *Mirror of Her Own;* Child Study Association of America's Children's Book of the Year, 1973, for *The Friends* and 1986, for *Paris, Pee Wee and Big Dog; New York Times* Outstanding Book of the Year, 1973, for *The Friends* and 1979, for *The Disappearance; School Library Journal*'s Best of the Best Books, 1979, for *The Friends;* New York Public Library's Books for the Teen Age citation, 1980, for *The Disappearance,* and 1980, 1981, and 1982, for *Edith Jackson;* Coretta Scott King Award, 1982, for *Mother Crocodile;* Parents' Choice Award for Literature from the Parents' Choice Foundation, 1983, for *New Guys around the Block;* Other Award (England), 1987, for *My Love, My Love; or, The Peasant Girl;* first prize at Cabourg, France, festival, 1988, for *My Love, My Love; or, The Peasant Girl.*

WRITINGS:

Bird at My Window (novel), Lippincott, 1966.
(Editor) *Children of Longing* (anthology), Holt, 1971.
The Friends (first book in trilogy for young adults), Holt, 1973.
Ruby (second book in trilogy for young adults), Viking, 1976.
Edith Jackson (third book in trilogy for young adults), Viking, 1978.
The Disappearance (novel), Delacorte, 1979.
Mirror of Her Own (novel), Delacorte, 1981.
(Translator and adapter) Birago Diop, *Mother Crocodile: An Uncle Amadou Tale from Senegal* (story), illustrated by John Steptoe, Delacorte, 1981.
A Measure of Time (novel), Holt, 1983.
New Guys around the Block (novel), Delacorte, 1983.
Paris, Pee Wee and Big Dog (novel), Gollancz, 1984, Delacorte, 1985.
My Love, My Love; or, The Peasant Girl (novel; also see below), Holt, 1985.
Bird at My Window, Schocken, 1987.
And I Heard a Bird Sing (novel), Delacorte, 1987.
The Ups and Downs of Carl Davis III (novel), Delacorte, 1989.
Billy the Great (novel), illustrated by Caroline Binch, Delacorte, 1992.
The Music of Summer (novel), Delacorte, 1992.
(Afterword) Iriving Burgie, compiler, *Caribbean Carnival: Songs of the West Indies,* illustrated by Frane Lessac, Tambourine Books (New York City), 1992.
The Sun, the Sea, a Touch of the Wind, Dutton (New York City), 1995.

Also author of one-act play, *Venetian Blinds,* 1954; author of *Time Out in Haiti* and *Summer of 1985.* Author of documentary film about her novel *The Friends for Thames Television. Contributor to periodicals, including Cosmopolitan* and *Freedomways.*

ADAPTATIONS: Thames Television produced *Documentary of "The Friends"* in 1984. The 1990 Broadway musical *Once on This Island* was based on Guy's novel *My Love, My Love; or, The Peasant Girl.*

SIDELIGHTS: Rosa Guy often writes about black teenagers, but her topics hold universal appeal. One of Guy's publishers indicated that her "literary themes stem from the fact that she is a black and a woman." About the success of her work, Katherine Paterson observes in the *Washington Post Book World* that "a great strength of Guy's work is her ability to peel back society's labels and reveal beneath them highly individual men and women."

Critics often comment on the intensity of her characters. In the *Times Literary Supplement* Brian Baumfield describes Guy's novel *Edith Jackson* as "a vigorous, uncompromising" book, with characters who "live and breathe and are totally credible. The West Indian speech may prove difficult for some, but it is a raw novel of urgency and power, which readers of sixteen and older will find a moving experience." *New York Times Book Review* critic Selma G. Lanes comments that in *New Guys around the Block,* "the reader cannot resist rooting for" the book's protagonist "with his intelligence and growing self-awareness, as he negotiates the booby traps of a difficult life." Alice Walker writes in the *New York Times Book Review* that central to Guy's novel *The Friends* is "the fight to gain perception of one's own real character; the grim struggle for self-knowledge and the almost killing internal upheaval that brings the necessary growth of compassion and humility *and courage,* so that friendship (of any kind, but especially between those of notable economic and social differences) can exist."

A Measure of Time is a departure from Guy's youth fiction. Stuart Schoffman of the *Los Angeles Times* states that it "is a black *Bildungsroman* in the tradition of Claude McKay, Ralph Ellison and James Baldwin, a sharp and well-written meld of storytelling and sociology. Which is to say it is hardly an Alger tale, or if anything a bitter parody." Susan Isaacs, in the *New York Times Book Review,* characterizes the heroine, Dorine, as "a brash and intelligent guide; her observations about people and places are funny, pointed and often moving." Isaacs further notes "the other characters in this novel do not come to life. . . . Only Dorine stands on her own—she and the Harlem setting are vividly described, filled with life and a pleasure to read about."

Guy returned to her stories about the young in *The Ups and Downs of Carl Davis III.* The story is a "witty, sometimes bitter romp with a very spirited boy" sent from his home in New York City to live with his grandmother in Spoonsboro, South Carolina, according to a *Washington Post Book World* reviewer. With *My Love, My Love: Or, The Peasant Girl* Guy retells the Hans Christian Andersen story of *The Little Mermaid* in a Caribbean setting. The inspiration for the Broadway musical *Once on This Island, My Love, My Love,* like all of Guy's prose, "derives much of its undeniable appeal" from the author's "ability to capture the rhythm and color of Caribbean speech," a *Los Angeles Times Book Review* critic remarked.

BIOGRAPHICAL/CRITICAL SOURCES:

BOOKS

Children's Literature Review, Volume 13, Gale, 1987.

Contemporary Literary Criticism, Volume 26, Gale, 1983.

Dictionary of Literary Biography, Volume 33: *Afro-American Fiction Writers after 1955,* Gale, 1984.

Twentieth-Century Young Adult Writers, 1st edition, St. James Press, 1994.

PERIODICALS

Los Angeles Times, August 24, 1983.

New York Times Book Review, November 4, 1973; July 2, 1978; December 2, 1979; October 4, 1981; August 28, 1983; October 9, 1983, November 2, 1986; February 17, 1991; April 21, 1991; June 7, 1992; November 8, 1992.

Times Educational Supplement, June 6, 1980.

Times Literary Supplement, September 20, 1974; December 14, 1979; July 18, 1980; August 3, 1984.

Variety, October 22, 1990.

Washington Post, January 9, 1966.

Washington Post Book World, November 11, 1979; May 14, 1989.*

H-I

HADLEY, Lee 1934-1995
(Hadley Irwin, a joint pseudonym)

PERSONAL: Born October 10, 1934, in Earlham, IA; died of cancer, August 22, 1995 in Madrid, IA; daughter of Oren B. (a farmer) and Pearle Hadley. *Education:* Drake University, B.A., 1956; University of Wisconsin-Madison, M.A., 1961.

ADDRESSES: *Home*—R.R. 1, Madrid, IA 50156.

CAREER: Writer. Younkers of Des Moines (department store), Des Moines, IA, copywriter, 1955-58; high school English teacher in De Soto, IA, 1959-60, and Monmouth, NJ, 1962-65; Ocean County Community College, Toms River, NJ, instructor in English, 1965-68; Iowa State University, Ames, began as assistant professor, 1969, associate professor of English, 1980-92, professor of English, 1992-95. Author of children's books, beginning collaboration with Ann Irwin in 1979.

AWARDS, HONORS: Honor Book Award, Jane Addams Peace Association, 1981, for *We Are Mesquakie, We Are One;* Society of Midland Authors Award, 1982, for *Moon and Me;* Notable Children's Trade Book in the Field of Social Studies Award from joint committee of the National Council on Social Studies and Children's Book Council, and Best Young Adult Book Award from American Library Association, both 1982, for *What about Grandma?,* and both 1985, for *Abby, My Love;* Children's Choice Book Award, joint committee of Children's Book Council and International Reading Association, 1986, for *Abby, My Love;* Library of Congress Children's Book of the Year list, 1987, for *Kim/Kimi.*

WRITINGS:

JUVENILE; WITH ANN IRWIN, UNDER JOINT PSEUDONYM HADLEY IRWIN

The Lilith Summer, Feminist Press, 1979.
We Are Mesquakie, We Are One, Feminist Press, 1980.
Bring to a Boil and Separate, Atheneum, 1980.
Moon and Me, Macmillan, 1981.
What about Grandma?, Atheneum, 1982.
I Be Somebody, Macmillan, 1984.
Abby, My Love, Macmillan, 1985.
Kim/Kimi, Macmillan, 1987.
So Long at the Fair, Macmillan, 1988.
Can't Hear You Listening, Macmillan, 1990.
The Original Freddie Ackerman, M. K. McElderry Books (New York City), 1992.
Jim Dandy, M. K. McElderry Books, 1994.
Sarah with an H, M. K. McElderry Books, 1996.

OTHER; WITH ANN IRWIN, UNDER JOINT PSEUDONYM HADLEY IRWIN

Writing Young Adult Novels, Writer's Digest Books, 1988.

Many of the Hadley Irwin books have been published in other countries, including Holland, Germany, and France.

ADAPTATIONS: *The Lilith Summer* was released with a teaching guide by Aims, 1984; *Abby, My Love* was adapted as a "CBS Schoolbreak Special" in 1988.

SIDELIGHTS: Lee Hadley and Ann Irwin wrote under the joint pseudonym Hadley Irwin. Hadley and Irwin met in 1973 when both were employed as English professors at Iowa State University. Their first collaborations consisted of professional writings for the university; since they worked so well together, they eventually decided to try and write a novel together. Over the years, Hadley Irwin became a personality in her own right, complete with a personal history (in fact, when Hadley and Irwin gave lectures, an empty chair for Hadley Irwin was placed in front of the audience). Many of Hadley and Irwin's books deal with difficult themes, such as incest, divorce, and prejudice. Because they respected their young audience, the two authors tried to deal with these issues as honestly as possible. In an interview with *Something about the Author Autobiography Series* (*SAAS*), Hadley and Irwin wrote: "Hadley Irwin believes that, like life, no matter how coincidental events may seem, stories are a matter of cause and effect. Her books do not always end happily ever after because the 'ever after' is impossible to see; it is always ahead in the unknown future. She is more interested in life in the present tense—its ups and downs, hills and valleys that, over time, seem to even out."

Both Lee Hadley and Ann Irwin grew up in Iowa. Hadley came from a family of four children. She spent most of her early career as a high school teacher. After finishing her M.A. degree, Hadley began teaching college courses. Eventually, she became a professor of English at Iowa State University. Irwin also came from a family of four children. Like Hadley, Irwin taught high school for a number of years. In 1970, she became an associate professor of English at Iowa State, where she remained until her retirement.

The idea for their first novel, *The Lilith Summer,* came after the two writers noticed an article in a local newspaper about an elderly woman who was going to be allowed to remain in her own home, even though the county had condemned it. The woman was pictured hugging a young woman, her social worker. Hadley and Irwin were struck by the mixture of pride and pain that showed in the lines on the older woman's face, and decided to capture her character in a story. Able to meet only on weekends, they tried working on separate parts of the story independently and then getting together weekly to review their efforts. However, this method seemed too slow, and the spark that they had felt in other projects didn't seem to be there. It was then that they discovered "Hadley Irwin." They started working on every page together, and found the process to be more satisfying than working separately. Irwin once told *CA,* "The result is that a given line or paragraph does not belong to either Lee or Ann, but to someone who is a better writer than either of us. There is another advantage—no ego involvement in chopping out the bad lines that inevitably appear."

In *The Lilith Summer,* the twelve-year-old narrator tells the story of a seventy-seven-year-old woman with whom she spends the summer as a companion. Praised by reviewers for their sensitive plot and for the high quality of their writing, Irwin and Hadley were encouraged to pursue their course; Hadley Irwin was on her way to becoming a well-known author of novels for young adults.

We Are Mesquakie, We Are One was published a year later, in 1980. Distinguished with the Jane Addams Peace Association Honor Book designation, Hadley Irwin's second novel takes place in 1837, when the Mesquakie Indians of Tama, Ohio, were forced from their lands by the U.S. government. Hidden Doe, a young Mesquakie girl, is taught the many traditions of her people; when she is forced to move to Kansas with her tribe, Hidden Doe helps to preserve her cultural heritage. Along with other Mesquakie, she saves the relocation money given to her by the government and eventually buys back a portion of the land her tribe was forced to abandon. Reviews were mixed, but Gale Eaton of *School Library Journal* concluded, "The prose is patterned and a bit remote, but the historical predicament of the people, portrayed with more sorrow than bitterness, gives the book impact." Hadley Irwin also focused on a historical subject in *Jim Dandy,* in which motherless Caleb runs away from home after his distraught father sells a young horse the boy has raised. The buyers are U.S. Army officers led by General Custer. And in another historical novel, *I Be Somebody,* Anson, a ten-year-old descendant of freed slaves, finds his people still attempting to flee from prejudice. The novel takes place in a close-knit African American community in turn-of-the-century Oklahoma.

Several of Hadley Irwin's novels explore social issues that affect modern teens. In *Bring to a Boil and Separate,* thirteen-year-old Katie attempts to deal with the emotional fallout of her parents' divorce while struggling with her own inner confusion as a budding adolescent. A growing friendship with Marti helps Katie separate herself from her parents' emotional situation and focus on her own needs. Denise M. Wilms of *Booklist* wrote that Katie's "true-sounding dialogue and internal monologue brightly display her contemporary character—one energetic enough to sweep readers right along the story's erratic path." In 1982's *What about Grandma?* sixteen-year-old Rhys's hopes of a fun summer vacation are shattered. Helping her mom take care of her independent but fragile Grandmother Wyn is stressful, due in part to her mother's wish that Wyn be placed in a nursing home. When her mother begins to interfere with a developing romance between Rhys and an older man named Lew, the mood at home becomes even more strained. Sari Feldman reviewed the book for *Voice of Youth Advocates,* writing, "This novel is wonderful. The three generations of women are distinct and their relationships well developed." In *So Long at the Fair,* teen suicide is the focus as Joel tries to come to terms with the death of a young classmate. Cathryn M. Mercier praised the novel in a *Five Owls* review as "a poignant story of an aching adolescent challenged to muster the inner strength necessary to cope with the unfair complexities of living and caring."

Inspired by a letter from a reader, *Abby, My Love* tackles the volatile issue of sexual abuse within a family and intervention by an outsider. In *Kim/Kimi,* a young Asian-American woman faces her confusion about her identity in a small town where no one else looks like her family. Discovering the truth about the father she never knew gives her a sense of pride. Here Hadley Irwin addresses issues of racism, including the imprisonment of Japanese-American citizens during World War II. Racism is also at the core of *Sarah with an H,* Hadley Irwin's last novel. In this case, however, racism takes the form of anti-Semitism as Marti sees a new classmate harassed because she is Jewish.

Hadley and Irwin enjoyed being collaborators, largely because the arrangement allowed them to share ideas. They tried to write eight pages every day. Hadley and Irwin described their writing persona for *SAAS* by noting that "most of Hadley Irwin's life revolves around writing, probably because she has always been in love with words. . . . [She] loves books. . . . She respects librarians because they do so much to encourage kids to read. . . . We remember that one of her characteristics which we like best is her sense of humor, probably because it matches ours."

For Hadley and Irwin, writing was more than merely putting words on paper; it was also a learning process. "The value of writing, whether for adults or children, lies in trying to create beauty through printed words. The best one can hope for is an approximation of those abstractions, but the attempt is worth the risk. Even in failure there is much to be learned. Writing means putting words on paper in the most careful way one can and hoping that the reader will receive them with the same awareness."

BIOGRAPHICAL/CRITICAL SOURCES:

BOOKS

Children's Literature Review, Volume 40, Gale, 1996.
Holtz, Sally Holmes, editor, *Sixth Book of Junior Authors,* H. W. Wilson, 1989.
Something about the Author Autobiography Series, Volume 13, Gale, 1992.
Twentieth-Century Young Adult Writers, 1st edition, St. James Press, 1994.

PERIODICALS

Booklist, April 1, 1980, p. 1128; September 1, 1996, p. 119.
Children's Literature Association Quarterly, fall, 1992, p. 5.
Publishers Weekly, October 7, 1996, p. 77.
School Library Journal, January, 1981, p. 62; February, 1997, p. 103.
Voice of Youth Advocates, August, 1982, p. 32; May, 1994, p. 116.

PERIODICALS

New York Times, August 26, 1995, p. 9.
Washington Post, August 25, 1995, p. C6.*

* * *

HAIG-BROWN, Roderick (Langmere) 1908-1976

PERSONAL: Born February 21, 1908, in Lancing, Sussex, England; died October 9, 1976, in Campbell River, British Columbia, Canada; son of Alan Roderick (an Army officer) and Violet M. (Pope) Haig-Brown; married Anne Elmore (a high school librarian), January 20, 1934; children: Valerie Joan, Mary Charlotte, Alan Roderick, Evelyn Celia. *Education:* Attended Charterhouse School, Godalming, England.

CAREER: Naturalist and author. Logger, guide, fisherman, and trapper in Washington State and British Columbia, 1926-30, and 1931-34; Family and Children's Court, Campbell River, judge, 1941-75. University of Victoria (British Columbia), chancellor, 1971-73. Federal Electoral Boundary Commission, commissioner, 1965-66, member, 1972-73, and 1975; International Salmon Commission, member, 1970-76. Member, Federal Saltwater Sports Advisory Committee. Consultant, National Film Board, Canadian Broadcasting Company, and Vancouver Public Aquarium. *Military service:* Canadian Army, 1939-45; served overseas; became major; assigned to Royal Canadian Mounted Police, 1944.

MEMBER: Authors Guild, Canadian Writers Association, Society of Authors.

AWARDS, HONORS: Canadian Library Association medals, 1947, for *Starbuck Valley Winter,* and 1963, for *The Whale People;* Governor General's Award, 1948, for *Saltwater Summer;* LL.D., University of British Columbia, 1952; Crandall Conservation Trophy, 1955; National Award in Letters, University of Alberta, 1956; Barien Library Award, 1964, for *Fisherman's Fall;* Vicky Metcalf Award (juvenile writing), 1965; Conservation Award, Trout Unlimited, 1965; J. B. Harkin Award, 1977.

WRITINGS:

Silver: The Life Story of an Atlantic Salmon, A. & C. Black, 1931, illustrated by Gordon Allen, Lyons and Burford (New York City), 1989.

Pool and Rapid, J. Cape, 1932.

Ki-Yu: A Story of Panthers, Houghton, 1934, revised edition published as *Panther: The Story of a North American Mountain Lion,* Collins, 1967.

The Western Angler: An Account of Pacific Salmon and Western Trout in British Columbia, Derrydale, 1939.

Return to the River: The Story of the Chinook Run, Morrow, 1941, published as *Return to the River: The Classic Story of the Chinook Run and of the Men Who Fish It,* with a new introduction by Steve Raymond, Lyons and Burford, 1997.

Timber: A Novel of Pacific Coast Loggers, Morrow, 1942, published as *Timber,* introduction by Glen A. Love, Oregon State University Press, (Corvallis, OR), 1993.

Starbuck Valley Winter, Morrow, 1943.

A River Never Sleeps (autobiography), Morrow, 1946, illustrated by Louis Darling, introduction by Steve Raymond, Lyons and Burford, 1991.

Saltwater Summer, Morrow, 1948.

On the Highest Hill, Morrow, 1949, introduction by Laurence Ricou, Oregon State University Press, 1994.

Measure of the Year, Morrow, 1950, introduction by George Woodcock, Lyons and Burford, 1990.

Fisherman's Spring, Morrow, 1951, illustrated by Louis Darling, N. Lyons Books, 1988.

Mounted Police Patrol, Morrow, 1954.

Fisherman's Winter, Morrow, 1954, illustrated by Louis Darling, Nick Lyons Books, 1989.

Captain of the Discovery: The Story of Captain George Vancouver, Macmillan, 1956.

Fabulous Fishing in Latin America: Your Guide to the 60 Best Fishing Areas in Mexico, the Caribbean, Central and South America, Pan American World Airways, 1956.

Fisherman's Summer, Morrow, 1959, illustrated by Louis Darling, Nick Lyons Books, 1989.

(Contributor) *The Face of Canada,* Clarke, Irwin, 1959.

The Farthest Shores, Longmans, Green, 1960.

The Living Land: An Account of the Natural Resources of British Columbia, Macmillan, 1961.

Fur and Gold, Longmans, Green, 1962.

The Whale People, Collins, 1962.

(Contributor) Anthony Netboy, editor, *The Pacific Northwest,* Doubleday, 1963.

A Primer of Fly-Fishing, Morrow, 1964.

Fisherman's Fall, Morrow, 1964, Nick Lyons Books (New York City), 1987.

(Contributor) J. M. S. Careless and R. Craig Brown, editors, *The Canadians,* Macmillan, 1967.

(With Ralph Wahl) *Come Wade the River,* Superior Publishing, 1971.

The Salmon, Fisheries Marine Service, 1974.

The Master and His Fish: From the World of Roderick Haig-Brown, University of Washington Press, 1981.

Writings and Reflections: From the World of Roderick Haig-Brown, University of Washington Press, 1982.

To Know a River: A Haig-Brown Reader, edited by Valerie Haig-Brown, introduction by Thomas McGuane, Lyons and Burford, 1996.

Also contributor to numerous periodicals, including *Atlantic Monthly, Sports Illustrated,* and *Life.*

Manuscript collection at University of British Columbia Library in Vancouver.

SIDELIGHTS: Roderick Haig-Brown was well known for his numerous writings about the Canadian wilderness. In books such as *Fisherman's Spring* and *The Living Land,* he mixed scientific facts with almost poetic descriptions of his adopted country; in novels such as *Saltwater Summer* and *On the Highest Hill,* Haig-Brown explored the complex, and sometimes unhealthy, relationship between man and nature. All of Haig-Brown's work stressed the need for conservation of natural resources, whether these resources be wildlife or the land itself. In an article for *Canadian Children's Literature,* Heather Kirk noted that the author "challenged children to think hard about life and to feel profoundly by presenting them with a complete view of the world to which they could relate which was exciting yet sobering."

Haig-Brown's extensive knowledge of fish and their habits informs *Return to the River: The Story of the Chinook Run* (1941). Concerned with the life cycle of the Columbia River salmon, the book is strongly didactic. It urges the necessity of preserving the rivers on which the salmon runs depend and reveals the impact on the salmon of the newly completed Bonneville dam.

Logging and trapping provide the backgrounds for the novels *Timber* (1942), which deals with the working conditions and the mentality of loggers; and for *Starbuck Valley Winter* (1943), an appealing boy's story about how young Don Morgan achieves maturity during a winter spent running his own wilderness trap line. Anne T. Eaton reviewed *Starbuck Valley Winter* for *New York Times Book Review,* where she wrote, "The book is full of the feeling of out-of-doors; the scent of pine and fir; the motion of swift, dark rivers breaking into 'white water'; the life of wild animals that are fierce and cunning and brave and also beautiful. Quietly and without effort the author brings his characters to life."

During the 1950s Haig-Brown began to study and write about the history of his adopted homeland, first in *Captain of the Discovery: The Story of Captain George Vancouver* (1956), an account of the British explorer for young readers. His research also led to other projects, including *The Land Is Bright,* a series of CBC-Radio broadcasts on West Coast history, parts of which were subsequently published as *The Farthest Shores* (1960) and *Fur and Gold* (1962). Haig-Brown's interests in conservation and in Western history converge in *The Living Land: An Account of the Natural Resources of British Columbia* (1961). His admiration for the region's natives prompted *The Whale People* (1962), a sympathetic fictional portrayal of a boy's development to manhood in a coastal fishing and whaling tribe. *Canadian Children's Literature* reviewer Carole Gerson commented, "The characters speak simply, without the symbols or metaphors that well-meaning white writers often put into Indian mouths. . . ." She went on to observe, "Haig-Brown may be guilty of idealizing the spiritual side of Hotsath life, but his romantic tendencies are somewhat balanced by his descriptions of physical and psychological distress." Even more impressed with the main character, Atlin, was Heather Kirk, another reviewer for *Canadian Children's Literature,* who praised Haig-Brown's "remarkable, even poetic vision of perfect integration between self, nature, and society."

BIOGRAPHICAL/CRITICAL SOURCES:

BOOKS

Contemporary Literary Criticism, Volume 21, Gale, 1982.

Dictionary of Literary Biography, Volume 88: *Canadian Writers, 1920-1959, Second Series,* Gale, 1989.

Lingren, Arthur James, *Fly Patterns of Roderick Haig-Brown,* F. Amato (Portland, OR), 1993.

Robertson, Anthony, *Above Tide: Reflections on Roderick Haig-Brown,* Harbour (Madeira Park, BC, Canada), 1984.

Twentieth-Century Children's Writers, 4th edition, St. James Press, 1995.

Twentieth-Century Western Writers, 2nd edition, St. James Press, 1991.

PERIODICALS

British Columbia Library Quarterly, July, 1958.

Canadian Children's Literature, numbers 31-32, 1983, pp. 113-15; number 51, 1988, pp. 25-42.

Choice, May, 1982, p. 1284.

Globe and Mail (Toronto), June 22, 1991.

New York Times Book Review, November 14, 1943, p. 6; June 29, 1975, p. 20.

Times Literary Supplement, November 30, 1967, p. 1157.

Washington Post Book World, September 5, 1982, p. 12.*

* * *

HAILEY, Oliver 1932-1993

PERSONAL: Born July 7, 1932, in Pampa, TX; died of liver cancer, January 23, 1993, in Studio City, CA; son of Oliver D. (a butcher) and Hallie May (Thomas) Hailey; married Elizabeth Ann Forsythe (a writer), June 25, 1960; children: Elizabeth Kendall, Melinda Brooke. *Education:* University of Texas, Main University (now University of Texas at Austin), B.F.A., 1954; Yale University, M.F.A., 1962. *Politics:* Democrat. *Religion:* Protestant. *Avocational interests:* Travel.

CAREER: Playwright. *Dallas Morning News,* Dallas, TX, feature writer, 1957-59; Theater-by-the-Sea, Matunuck, RI, playwright-in-residence, 1962; Play-Pix Productions, New York City, consultant, 1963-65; head writer for television series *Love of Life,* Columbia Broadcasting System (CBS), 1970; story editor for television series *McMillan and Wife,* National Broadcasting Corp. (NBC), 1972-74; creative consultant for syndicated television series *Mary Hartman, Mary Hartman,* Tandem Productions, 1976; co-producer of television series *Another Day,* CBS, 1977; developer of television series *Love, Sidney* (based on his teleplay *Sidney Shorr*), NBC, 1982. Instructor at University of California, Los Angeles, 1974, and California State Polytechnic Institute, 1979. *Military service:* U.S. Air Force, Strategic Air Command, 1954-57; became first lieutenant; captain in the Reserve.

MEMBER: Writers Guild of America, West, Dramatists Guild.

AWARDS, HONORS: Phyllis S. Anderson fellowship in playwriting, 1961-62; Drama Desk-Vernon Rice Award, 1963, for *Hey You, Light Man!;* Certificate of Merit, Los Angeles Drama Critics Circle, 1973, for *Father's Day;* Emmy nomination for outstanding writing in a limited series or special from American Academy of Television Arts and Sciences and Writers Guild of America Award for outstanding comedy written for television, both 1982, both for *Sidney Shorr;* National Commission on Working Women award, 1982.

WRITINGS:

PLAYS

Child's Play: A Comedy for Orphans, produced in New Haven, CT, at Yale University, 1962.

Home by Hollywood, produced in New London, CT, at Mitchell College, 1964.

First One Asleep, Whistle (produced on Broadway at Belasco Theatre, 1966), S. Fischer Verlag, 1967.

Who's Happy Now? (three-act; first produced in Los Angeles, CA, at Mark Taper Forum, 1967; produced Off-Broadway at Village South Theatre, November 17, 1969; produced on *Theatre in America* series, PBS-TV, 1975), Random House, 1969.

Hey You, Light Man! (two-act; first produced in Lawrence, KS, at University of Kansas, 1961; produced Off-Broadway at Mayfair Theatre, 1963), Dramatists Play Service, 1970.

Picture, Animal, Crisscross: Three Short Plays (*Picture* and *Animal* produced together Off-Off-Broadway at Caffe Cino, 1965; *Crisscross* produced in Los Angeles, CA, at Evergreen Theatre, 1970), Dramatists Play Service, 1970.

Orphan, produced in Los Angeles at Evergreen Stage, 1970.

Father's Day (two-act; first produced in Los Angeles, CA, 1970; produced on Broadway at Golden Theatre, 1971), Dramatists Play Service, 1971.

Continental Divide (three-act; produced in Washington, DC, at Washington Theatre Club, 1970), Dramatists Play Service, 1973.

For the Use of the Hall (two-act; first produced in Providence, RI, at Trinity Square Theatre, 1974; produced Off-Off-Broadway at Playwrights Horizon, 1977; produced on *Hollywood Television Theatre* series, PBS-TV, 1975), Dramatists Play Service, 1976.

And Where She Stops Nobody Knows, produced in Los Angeles at Mark Taper Forum, 1976.

And Furthermore, produced in Pittsburgh, 1977.

Triptych, produced in Los Angeles at Mark Taper Forum Lab, 1978.

I Can't Find It Anywhere, produced in Louisville, KY, at Actors Theatre, 1979.

Red Rover, Red Rover (two-act; produced in Minneapolis, MN, at Cricket Theatre, 1977; produced Off-Off-Broadway at Park Royal Theatre, 1983), Dramatists Play Service, 1979.

I Won't Dance (two-act; first produced in Buffalo, NY, at Studio Arena Theatre, 1980; produced on Broadway at the Helen Hayes Theatre, 1981), Samuel French, 1982.

And Baby Makes Two, produced in Los Angeles, 1981.

About Time (short play; produced in Los Angeles at Back Alley Theatre, 1982), Dramatists Play Service, 1983.

The Father (adapted from the play by August Strindberg; produced in Philadelphia, PA, at the Philadelphia Drama Guild, 1984), Dramatists Play Service, 1984.

Round Trip, produced in Kalamazoo, MI, at Kalamazoo College, 1984.

Kith and Kin (two-act), Dramatists Play Service, 1988.

The World and His Wife, produced in Los Angeles at the Tamarind Theater, 1993.

Also author of plays *Twenty-four Hours: AM and PM,* 1983, and *The Bar off Melrose,* 1988, and of television scripts, including three episodes of *Bracken's World,* NBC, nine episodes of *McMillan and Wife,* NBC, 1972-74, and scripts for *Family* and *The Cosby Show.* Also author of two television movies, *Sidney Shorr,* NBC, 1981, and *Isabel's Choice,* CBS, 1981. Also co-author of feature film *Just You and Me, Kid,* 1979.

Contributor to anthologies, including *Three Plays from the Yale School of Drama,* edited by John Gassner, Dutton, 1964, *Collision Course,* edited by Edward Parone, Random House, 1968, *Showcase One: Plays from the Eugene O'Neill Foundation,* edited by John Lahr, Grove, 1969, and *New Theatre for Now,* edited by Parone, Delta, 1971.

SIDELIGHTS: Oliver Hailey's plays enjoyed nationwide success in university and regional playhouses, but did not catch the eyes of critics that might have given him more commercial exposure during his lifetime. Hailey approached writing as a means of interpreting the world. He told *Contemporary Dramatists,* "My plays are primarily the attempt to take a serious theme and deal with it comedically. Though the idea for a particular play often begins as something quite serious, I try not to start writing until I have found a comic point of view for the material . . . because, finally, my plays are an attempt to entertain—and when they cease to entertain—no matter how important' what I am trying to say—they fail as plays."

Written and first produced at Yale, *Hey You, Light Man!* juxtaposes the commonplace setting of the domestic world with the role-playing of the stage. Ashley Knight is an actor who runs away from his family and takes up residence on a stage set. He encounters a young widow who has been inadvertently locked in the theater after falling asleep during the previous performance. Her husband had been a stagehand who was killed by falling equipment, and she lost all three of her children at a national park where one fell into a waterfall, one fell off a mountain, and the third was taken away by a bear. Because her experience has been with the illusions of the stage, she has hope for the future. Leonard Fleischer of *Contemporary Dramatists* wrote that Hailey's overuse of the themes of illusion and reality weakens the play, and the introduction of intentionally odd characters seems strained. Still, he concluded, "His dialogue achieves the intended poetic effect, and his tender concern for his odd couple results in some touching moments." *First One Asleep, Whistle* is similar to *Hey You, Light Man!* in its portrayal of the differences between stage life and real life. The central figure is a television commercial actress whose daughter is by a man other than her husband and who has an affair during the course of the play with an immature actor who is separated from his wife. At the end, the lovers part (as they do in *Hey You, Light Man!*) but the actress gains a sense of independence in the realization that she can get along without a man. Fleischer wrote, "While Hailey avoids a sentimental happy' ending, his characters are never very interesting and the play remains at the level of a semi-sophisticated soap opera."

Who's Happy Now? is set in Texas in the years spanning 1941 to 1955. The play depicts a young man's confusion at his parents' strange relationship, and his desire to be a songwriter despite his father's ridicule. The father, a butcher, is a crude and stubborn man who has kept his wife and mistress happy even though his son has tried to meddle. The mistress is a widowed waitress whose husband died in a freak accident, and whose respect for her lover never falters. As in previous works, Hailey utilizes the device of contrasting the stage with the lives of the characters. The hero of *Who's Happy Now?* tries to express to his mother, through drama, how he feels about his parents. The parallels to Hailey's own life are not coincidental. Hailey called *Who's Happy Now?* his "most autobiographical" play, and explained to *Contemporary Dramatists,* "There had been nothing particularly funny about my childhood—and yet I felt that to tell the story without a comic perspective was to put upon the stage a story too similar to many that had been seen before. With the comic perspective came the opportunity for a much fresher approach to the material—and also, strangely, it allowed me to deal with the subject on a much more serious level than I would have risked otherwise."

Fleischer deemed *Father's Day* Hailey's best play, although it only ran for one performance on Broadway. The play is about three divorced couples coming together for brief Father's Day visits. The story reveals something about the conflicting desires of the women, who simultaneously want independence and security. Fleischer observed, "The comic tone on the surface barely conceals the pathos of their situation, and the play has a toughminded quality normally absent in a conventional sex comedy." Hailey is sympathetic toward his characters and refrains from passing judgment. At the end of the play, Hailey makes reference to Chekhov's *The Three Sisters,* implying a parallel. "While *Father's Day* lacks the depth and resonance of Chekhov's work," wrote Fleischer, "its tenderness and its willingness to understand the bitterness and frustration of unfulfilled lives make the parallel not altogether inapt."

BIOGRAPHICAL/CRITICAL SOURCES:

BOOKS

Contemporay American Dramatists, St. James Press, 1994.

Contemporary Dramatists, 5th edition, St. James Press, 1993.

PERIODICALS

Los Angeles Times, May 7, 1983.
New York Times, June 22, 1979; May 11, 1981.

OBITUARIES:

PERIODICALS

Los Angeles Times, January 25, 1993, p. A20.
New York Times, January 24, 1993, p. 34; January 25, 1993, p. B7.
Washington Post, January 26, 1993, p. D8.*

* * *

HAINES, Pamela Mary 1929-

PERSONAL: Born November 4, 1929, in Harrogate, England; daughter of Harry Beeley (a lawyer) and Muriel (Armstrong) Burrows; married Anthony Haines (a physician), June 24, 1955; children: Charlotte Haines Brignall, Lucy, Nicholas, Hal, Emily. Deceased. *Education:* Newnham College, Cambridge, M.A., 1952.

CAREER: Writer, 1971-87.

MEMBER: International PEN, Society of Authors.

AWARDS, HONORS: New writing prize from *Spectator,* 1971, for story, "Foxy's Not at Home"; young writers award from Yorkshire Arts Society, 1975, for *Tea at Gunter's.*

WRITINGS:

NOVELS

Tea at Gunter's, Heinemann, 1974.
A Kind of War, Heinemann, 1976.
Men on White Horses, Collins, 1978.
The Kissing Gate (Book-of-the-Month Club alternate selection), Doubleday, 1981.
The Diamond Waterfall, Doubleday, 1984.
The Golden Lion, Scribners, 1986.
Daughter of the Northern Fields, Collins, 1987.

SIDELIGHTS: Pamela Mary Haines' novels are characterized by recurring themes, including the advent of womanhood in a young girl's life, the struggle for independence from the past, and the idealization of a flawed object of love. In *Tea at Gunter's,* the heroine, Lucy, strives toward self-realization while her mother continues to live in a false world characterized by idealized memories of Lucy's stepbrother. Lucy falls in love only to find that freedom from her mother comes at a high price. Geoffrey Sadler of *Twentieth-Century Romance and Historical Writers* wrote that *Tea at Gunter's* is a "poised, subtle work" and "the most perfect of Haines' creations, the author displaying a mastery of tone and considerable psychological penetration." Edwina matures into womanhood in Edwardian Yorkshire in *Men on White Horses.* As in *Tea at Gunter's,* the heroine's selfhood is threatened by her mother. As Edwina gets older, however, the threat comes from a schoolmate instead. Traumatized by the tragic death of her secret love, Edwina turns to music and the sea, which Haines uses to symbolize music.

In *A Kind of War,* Haines plumbs the psyches of three women of different generations who have one thing in common—their lives are devoid of satisfying relationships. The novel tells each of the women's stories, from past to present, showing what they have in common as well as their fundamental differences.

The Kissing Gate adds elements of a gothic romance to the psychological nuances of Haines' previous novels as it follows three generations of the Rawson family. The kissing gate serves as a symbol of love and death and marks the starting point of the relationships between the Rawsons and the aristocratic Inghams. While Sadler declared *The Kissing Gate* Haines' most impressive novel, he conceded, "There are flaws in the fabric—too many unhappy marriages, unfortunate accidents, fortuitous deaths—but interest is sustained to such an extent that they are scarcely noticed." Novels following *The Kissing Gate* resemble it in that they span multiple generations. *The Diamond Waterfall* follows three women from the Edwardian era to 1945. *The Golden Lion* is a pre-war story of a Sicilian girl raised by a family in Yorkshire, and her subsequent relationship with her own adopted daughter. These novels also address the repression of violence and sexuality in proper societies. Haines tells the story of Christabel, Branwell Bronte's daughter, in *Daughter of the Northern Fields.* The destructive nature of illicit love is the theme, and Haines utilizes a narrative form that recalls the Bronte novels.

Haines has been praised for her ability to effectively capture the feel of the periods in which her stories are set. Sadler commented on her body of work: "Her grasp of character is sure, her dialogue superb. Her books present the essence of life, its tragedy leavened by sharp flashes of humour. With a clear but sympathetic eye she depicts the transient joys, the harrowing griefs, the slow poignant awakening of love."

BIOGRAPHICAL/CRITICAL SOURCES:

BOOKS

Twentieth-Century Romance and Historical Writers, 3rd edition, St. James Press, 1994.

PERIODICALS

Washington Post, May 16, 1981.*

* * *

HALDEMAN, Jack C(arroll) II 1941-
(John Cleve, a joint pseudonym)

PERSONAL: Born December 18, 1941, in Hopkinsville, NY; son of Jack C. Haldeman; married Alice, 1965 (marriage ended); married 1975; wife's name, Vol; children: two daughters. *Education:* Attended University of Oklahoma at Norman, 1960-63; Johns Hopkins University, B.S. (life science), 1973.

ADDRESSES: Home—P.O. Box 969, Port Richey, FL 33568. *Agent*—Eleanor Wood, Blassingame, McCauley, and Wood, 111 8th Ave., Suite 1501, New York, NY 10001.

CAREER: Johns Hopkins University School of Hygiene and Public Health, Baltimore, MD, research assistant, 1963-68; University of Maryland Hospital, MD, medical technician, 1968-73; freelance sports and science fiction writer. Has also worked variously as a statistician, photographer, and printer's devil. Served as chair of Discon II.

MEMBER: Washington Science Fiction Association (president).

WRITINGS:

NOVELS

Vector Analysis, Berkley (New York), 1978.
Perry's Planet, Bantam (New York), 1980.
(With Joe Haldeman) *There Is No Darkness,* Ace (New York), 1983.
(With wife, Vol Haldeman and Andrew J. Offutt, under joint pseudonym John Cleve) *The Fall of Winter,* Baen (New York), 1985.
(With Harry Harrison) *Bill, the Galactic Hero, on the Planet of Zombie Vampires,* Avon (New York), 1991.
(With Jack Dann) *Echoes of Thunder* (published with *Run for the Stars* by Harlan Ellison), Tor (New York), 1991.
(With Dann) *High Steel,* Tor, 1993.
(Author of introduction) Reed Manning, *Earthly Pleasures: The Erotic Science Fiction,* Circlet Press (Boston, MA), 1996.

Also author of *Spaceways #11: The Iceworld Connection,* 1983. Contributor of short stories to numerous anthologies, including *The Far Side of Time,* edited by Roger Elwood, Dodd (New York), 1974; *Alternities,* edited by David Gerrold and Stephen Goldin, Dell (New York), 1974; *Stellar 2,* edited by Judy-Lynn del Rey, Ballantine (New York), 1976; *Astronauts and Androids,* edited by Isaac Asimov, Dale (New York), 1977; *Black Holes and Bug Eyed Monsters,* edited by Asimov, Dale, 1977; *Comets and Computers,* edited by Asimov, Dale, 1978; *Nightmares,* edited by Charles L. Grant, Doubleday (New York), 1978; *TV: 2000,* edited by Asimov, Martin H. Greenberg, and Charles G. Waugh, Fawcett (New York), 1982; and *Shadows 7,* edited by Grant, Doubleday (New York), 1984. Contributor of short stories to periodicals, including *Amazing, Analog, Fantastic, Isaac Asimov's Science Fiction Magazine,* and *Omni.*

SIDELIGHTS: Although Jack C. Haldeman describes himself as a "traditional" science fiction writer, his work in the genre is unique in that he is one of few authors who combine science fiction and sports themes. Included among his many futuristic, sometimes humorous, sports stories are "Louisville Slugger," which pits humans against Arcturians in a baseball game to decide the future of mankind; "The Agony of Defeat" and "Thrill of Victory," both of which feature a robotic football team; and "Thirty Love," about a tennis player's advantageous ability to foresee where his opponent's next shot will land. The prolific storywriter has also demonstrated his talents in numerous stories outside the arena of sports, receiving critical praise for tales such as "Songs of Dying Swans," about the demise of a genetically-altered people, and "What Weighs 8000 Pounds and Wears Red Sneakers," a comical story about a family who finds their front yard to be an elephant graveyard. Haldeman established himself as a novelist in 1978 with the publication of *Vector Analysis,* which is set on a space research ship. As the ship's crew begin collecting various alien creatures, they are attacked by a mind-altering illness. Protagonist Rob MacGregor, a biologist who has studied vectors (pathogen-transmitting organisms), rallies to discover a remedy to save his researchers, the woman he loves, and himself. A *Publishers Weekly* reviewer judged Haldeman's first novel "fast-moving" and stated that Haldeman "succeeds in creating tension and suspense." *Analog* contributor Spider Robinson similarly deemed *Vector Analysis* "a satisfying, balanced novel."

Haldeman also earned high marks with his novel *The Fall of Winter,* set on the planet Frost, an ice world. While one group of space pioneers seeks to inhabit the planet, it becomes apparent that another group is working to counter their efforts by altering the atmospheric conditions. As the battle for control of Frost continues, protagonist Roger Trent fights both the opposing scientists and some bizarre and devastating physical changes he is experiencing in his own body. This suspense story, according to a *Science Fiction Chronicle* reviewer, has "a more complex plot" and "better characterization" than Haldeman's previous efforts.

Haldeman has written several novels with collaborators, including *There Is No Darkness,* which he produced with his brother, noted science fiction author Joe Haldeman, and *Echoes of Thunder* and *High Steel,* written with Jack Dann. The latter story, set in the twenty-second century, concerns the exploitation of a Native American nation by huge corporations that manufacture space weapons. When they discover the Native Americans have an inherent ability to design and construct their weapons at high altitudes, the corporations begin drafting them, achieving for themselves a cache of low-paid, but extremely intelligent and talented laborers, while at the same time depleting the reservations of their men. One Native American, a medicine man named John Stranger, is particularly valuable to the corporations, but eventually becomes a savior, of sorts, to his people. A critic in *Kirkus Reviews* noted that *High Steel* contains "many impressive and tantalizing parts."

BIOGRAPHICAL/CRITICAL SOURCES:

BOOKS

Twentieth-Century Science-Fiction Writers, St. Martin's, 1981.

Twentieth-Century Science-Fiction Writers, 3rd edition, St. James Press, 1991.

PERIODICALS

Analog, November, 1979, p. 177; November, 1985, p. 179; February, 1994, pp. 159-162.

Kirkus Reviews, October 15, 1978, p. 1154; May 15, 1993, p. 629.

Library Journal, December 1, 1978, p. 2447.

Locus, May, 1991, p. 45; July, 1991, p. 19; August, 1993, pp. 29, 50.

Publishers Weekly, October 23, 1978, p. 92; June 21, 1993, p. 90.

Science Fiction Chronicle, July, 1985, p. 45.

Voice of Youth Advocates, February, 1986, p. 393.*

* * *

HALE, Kathleen 1898-

PERSONAL: Born May 24, 1898, in Scotland; daughter of Charles Edward and Ethel Alice Aylmer (Hughes) Hale; married Douglas McClean (a doctor), 1926 (died, 1967); children: two sons. *Education:* Attended Manchester School of Art, Reading University College of Art, Central School of Arts and Crafts, London, and East Anglican School of Painting and Drawing. *Avocational interests:* Painting.

ADDRESSES: Home—Tod House, Forest Hill, Oxford, England.

CAREER: Author and illustrator. Worked for the Ministry of Foods, England, 1917; after the war, held various jobs such as caring for children, mending, and collecting bad debts for a window cleaner; later began designing book jackets and posters; wrote and illustrated stories for *Child Education.* Her works have been exhibited at numerous galleries, including Grosvenor Galleries, Vermont Gallery, and Leicester Galleries; designed mural for Festival of Britain schools section, 1951.

MEMBER: Society of Industrial Arts (fellow), Society of Authors, Chelsea Arts Club.

WRITINGS:

ALL SELF-ILLUSTRATED

Henrietta: The Faithful Hen, Transatlantic, 1943.

Manda, J. Murray, 1952, Coward, 1953.

Henrietta's Magic Egg, Allen & Unwin, 1973.

"ORLANDO" SERIES; SELF-ILLUSTRATED

Orlando the Marmalade Cat: A Camping Holiday, Scribner, 1938.

Orlando's Evening Out, Penguin, 1941.

Orlando's Home Life, Penguin, 1942.
Orlando the Marmalade Cat Buys a Farm, Transatlantic, 1942.
Orlando the Marmalade Cat Becomes a Doctor, Transatlantic, 1944.
Orlando the Marmalade Cat: His Silver Wedding, Transatlantic, 1944.
Orlando's Invisible Pyjamas, Transatlantic, 1947, new edition, J. Murray, 1964.
Orlando the Marmalade Cat Keeps a Dog, Transatlantic, 1949.
Orlando the Marmalade Cat: A Trip Abroad, Country Life, 1949.
Orlando the Judge, J. Murray, 1950.
Orlando the Marmalade Cat: A Seaside Holiday, Country Life, 1952.
Orlando's Zoo, J. Murray, 1954.
Orlando the Marmalade Cat: The Frisky Housewife, Country Life, 1956.
Orlando's Magic Carpet, J. Murray, 1958.
Orlando the Marmalade Cat Buys a Cottage, Country Life, 1963.
Orlando and the Three Graces, J. Murray, 1965.
Orlando the Marmalade Cat Goes to the Moon, J. Murray, 1968.
Orlando the Marmalade Cat and the Water Cats, J. Cape, 1972.

ILLUSTRATOR

Mary Rachel Harrower, *I Don't Mix Much with Fairies,* Eyre & Spottiswode, 1928.
M. R. Harrower, *Plain Jane,* Coward, 1929.
Puss in Boots, Houghton, 1951.

SIDELIGHTS: Much of Kathleen Hale's early life was in distinct contrast to the books for which she is known. Her father, Charles Edward Hale, died when she was five. When her mother, Ethel Alice Aylmer Hale, was unable to care for her three children, they were separated. Hale went to live with her grandparents and an insensitive aunt, by whom she felt terribly neglected, especially emotionally. After her mother was able to bring the children together again in Manchester in 1907, Hale never found the loving family for which she yearned and that she wrote about in the Orlando books. Her outlet was art, a talent inspired at an early age by the works of Edmund Dulac and Arthur Rackham, though her drawings did not resemble theirs. After World War I her artwork was exhibited in a series of shows and reproduced in art journals. In 1926 she married Douglas McClean, a bacteriologist, and soon after began designing book jackets and illustrating children's books. Hale then turned to writing her own children's books, creating an imaginative vision of what she thought a family should be.

Today Hale is known principally for the Orlando the Marmalade Cat series. Perhaps what is most extraordinary about this series is its longevity. It began in 1938 with *Orlando the Marmalade Cat: A Camping Holiday* and concluded in 1972 with *Orlando the Marmalade Cat and the Water Cats.* The texts for the nineteen books of the series grew longer and longer, at first to match the aging of Hale's two children, for whom the first books were written. In addition, the stories grew more and more fantastic, adding magic carpets and even—during 1968—a trip to the moon. But neither Orlando nor his wife, Grace, nor the three kittens, Tinkle, Pansy, and Blanche, ever change; their ages seem to be eternally fixed.

Like so many children's books, Hale's books began as stories for the author's children. After Hale's second son, Nicholas, was born in 1933, she grew tired of the children's literature that she found available. She found inspiration in the family cat. In fact, much of the Orlando series is based on Hale's family life. The early books were based upon trips that she and her husband had taken—camping in the country and a trip to the coast of France. *Orlando the Marmalade Cat Buys a Farm* (1942) is based on a farm located near Hale's home, and the story benefits from her farm experience during World War I. *Orlando the Marmalade Cat Buys a Cottage* (1963) deals with Hale's own house. Orlando himself is modeled upon Hale's husband.

The books were influenced by Jean de Brunhoff's Babar books and, in fact, have much the same format. But while the Babar books are still enjoying a lively existence, the Orlando series has faded from popularity. The usual forces for this kind of decline are not evident here: the books are not especially tied to a particular time. Perhaps the books have faded because of a want of invention; there is no sense that each book represents some new idea on the part of the author, some new way of handling material that is potentially delightful. In fact, the Orlando books become progressively less interesting as the fantasy is stretched further and the interplay between the human and feline worlds is pushed further from the center.

Yet these books did survive for almost a generation. Perhaps their two strongest elements are their vision of the life of the family and their insistence upon normality in a world filled with the unexpected. No matter what the situation, Orlando and his family end up together and at some sort of peace. At the end of *Orlando the Marmalade Cat Becomes a Doctor* (1944) Orlando and Grace purchase and run a hospital. The narrator observes, "However busy Grace might be, she never allowed a day to pass without spending an hour with her kittens. She called them to her and they gathered round beneath the magnolia blossom in the Maternity ward to hear the wonderful stories she was waiting to tell them. Sometimes they romped with the insects, or they discussed the day's events, and they always ended by falling asleep and dreaming of each other." No matter how hectic the books might be—and they are remarkably hectic—they end on a peaceful note.

In the Orlando series readers find a satisfying union of the human and feline worlds, unity of place that provides a credible and attractive context for the adventure, a sense of restraint in holding back a too elaborate fantasy. The cats' adventures and chores are intimately tied to the life of the farm, and the humor and delight of the book lie in how cats perform human chores. The full illustrations mirror the changing of the seasons and reflect the complexity of farm life, while at the same time exploiting the potential humor in personifying animals. Orlando's family works successfully and playfully together, so that every item in the book hangs together.

BIOGRAPHICAL/CRITICAL SOURCES:

BOOKS

Dictionary of Literary Biography, Volume 160: *British Children's Writers, 1914-1960,* Gale, 1996.
Twentieth-Century Children's Writers, 4th edition, St. James Press, 1996.

PERIODICALS

Christian Science Monitor, December 12, 1947.
New Statesman, June 2, 1972; November 9, 1973.
New York Herald Tribune, July 15, 1951.
New York Times, November 30, 1947.
Observer, December 10, 1978; May 22, 1994.
Times Literary Supplement, July 2, 1971; April 28, 1972; November 23, 1973.
Washington Post Book World, February 10, 1991.*

* * *

HALL, Aylmer
See HALL, Norah E. L.

HALL, Norah E. L. 1914-
(Aylmer Hall)

PERSONAL: Born April 24, 1914, in Surrey, England; daughter of S. Lyle and E. F. (Hall) Cummins; married Robert Aylmer Hall (a company director), October, 1938; children: John James, Julia K. A. *Education:* St. Hugh's College, Oxford, B.A. (with honors), 1935.

ADDRESSES: *Home*—28 Burghley Rd., London SW 19, England. *Agent*—Winant, Towers Ltd., 14 Clifford's Inn, London EC4A 1DA, England.

CAREER: New Commonwealth Institute, London, England, personal assistant to the secretary, 1936; Royal Institute of International Affairs, London, assistant press librarian, 1937-39; Ministry of Information, Research Division, London, chief press librarian, 1939-40; writer, 1947—.

WRITINGS:

(Editor) *The Chronology of the Second World War,* Royal Institute of International Affairs, 1947.

CHILDREN'S BOOKS; ALL UNDER PSEUDONYM AYLMER HALL

The Mystery of Torland Manor, Harrap, 1952.
The Admiral's Secret, Harrap, 1953.
The K. F. Conspiracy, Harrap, 1955.
The Sword of Glendower, Methuen, 1960, published as *The Search for Lancelot's Sword,* Criterion, 1962.
The Devilish Plot, Hart-Davis, 1965.
The Tyrant King: A London Adventure, London Transport Board, 1967.
The Marked Man, Hart-Davis, 1967.
Colonel Bull's Inheritance, Macmillan (London), 1968, Meredith Corp., 1969.
Beware of Moonlight, Macmillan (London), 1969, Thomas Nelson, 1970.
The Minstrel Boy, Macmillan (London), 1970.

SIDELIGHTS: Norah E. L. Hall began writing with her husband using the pseudonym of Aylmer Hall. Norah Hall explained in *Twentieth-Century Children's Writers,* "The first five books by Aylmer Hall were written at the instigation of, and in collaboration with, my husband, as serial stories for our small son at his preparatory school. Later, when my husband's job became too demanding, I was a solo performer with a very good and helpful trainer. The last books, all set in Ireland, from which my family comes, were inspired by our acquiring a country refuge in West Cork, but their historical setting has been very carefully prepared."

While the early Hall books are considered too dated for modern audiences, the heroes of the stories are noteworthy. They reflect many of the stereotypical qualities of the upper-middle-class public-school characters of the post-war era, but they have an added dimension of self-doubt and fear. When they succeed, it is not before they nearly fail, which sets these characters apart from most other schoolboy protagonists of the time, who were brash and fearless. Hall's heroes ultimately succeed as a result of their adherence to a code of conduct, which becomes more personally significant to them as a result of the conflicts in the story. Michael Mannering confronts ex-Nazi opportunists in *The Admiral's Secret,* but does so with uneasiness and anxiety. Michael is older and more confident in *The K. F. Conspiracy,* in which a border war inspires mixed feelings of elation and insecurity.

Hall's later works, set in Ireland, exhibit a more natural flow of action and dialogue. Where her earlier works show the value of codes of conduct, her later works portray such codes as rather shallow. Instead, value is placed on mutual love and respect. Sean Daly in *Minstrel Boy* finds that the creeds of all those around him are ultimately weak and useless, whereas his own humbler creed enables him to endure betrayal, torture, and hunger. His beliefs are different because they are rooted in his deepening love for a woman. The young Irish hero of *Colonel Bull's Inheritance* finds himself in the midst of four rival factions in the eighteenth century. Myles McDowell commented on *Colonel Bull's Inheritance* in *Twentieth-Century Children's Writers:* "This is indeed a very workmanlike novel, for the complicated elements of plot are cleverly mixed and balanced in a story that never for a moment loses its line and clarity."

BIOGRAPHICAL/CRITICAL SOURCES:

BOOKS

Twentieth-Century Children's Writers, 4th edition, St. James Press, 1995.

PERIODICALS

Booklist, February 15, 1971, p. 493.
Kirkus Reviews, September 15, 1970, p. 1048.
New Statesman, May 24, 1968, p. 694; October 31, 1969, p. 624.
Times Literary Supplement, June 17, 1965, p. 514; May 25, 1967, p. 446; March 14, 1968, p. 254; June 6, 1968, p. 580; December 4, 1969, p. 1385.*

* * *

**HALL, Oakley (Maxwell) 1920-
(O. M. Hall, Jason Manor)**

PERSONAL: Born July 1, 1920, in San Diego, CA; son of Oakley M. and Jessie (Sands) Hall; married Barbara Edinger, June 28, 1945; children: Oakley III, Mary, Tracy, Sara. *Education:* University of California, Berkeley, B.A., 1943; University of Iowa, M.F.A., 1950. *Politics:* Democrat.

ADDRESSES: Home—P.O. Box 2101, Olympic Valley, CA 95730. *Agent*—Don Congdon Associates, 177 East 70th St., New York, NY 10021.

CAREER: University of Iowa Writer's Workshop, staff member, 1950-52; Squaw Valley Community of Writers, founding director, 1969, executive director, 1986—; University of California, Irvine, writer-in-residence, 1967-69, professor of English, 1968-90, director of programs in writing, 1968-89, professor emeritus, 1990—. *Military service:* U.S. Marine Corps, 1939-45.

MEMBER: San Francisco Writers Round Table, Squaw Valley Community of Writers (Olympic Valley, CA), member of board of directors.

AWARDS, HONORS: Pulitzer Prize nomination, 1958, for *Warlock;* Silver Medal, Commonwealth of San Francisco, 1958; National Endowment for the Arts grant, 1975, 1979; Golden Spur, Western Writers of America, 1982; Wrangler Award for magazine piece "How the River Roars"; National Cowboy Hall of Fame, 1989; San Diego Historical Society's Author Award, 1997; PEN Center USA West Award of Honor, 1998.

WRITINGS:

UNDER NAME O. M. HALL

Murder City, Farrar, Straus, 1949.
So Many Doors, Random House, 1950.
The Corpus of Joe Bailey, Viking, 1953.
Maridios Beach, Viking, 1955.
Warlock, Viking, 1958.
The Downhill Racers, Viking, 1963, Scribner, 1988.

The Pleasure Garden, Viking, 1966.
A Game for Eagles, Morrow, 1970.
Report from Beau Harbor, Morrow, 1971.
The Adelita, Doubleday, 1975.
The Bad Lands, Atheneum, 1978.
Lullaby, Atheneum, 1981.
The Children of the Sun, Atheneum, 1983.
The Coming of the Kid, Harper, 1985.
Apaches, Simon & Schuster, 1986.
The Art and Craft of Novel Writing, Writer's Digest Books, 1989.
Separations, University of Nevada Press, 1997.
Ambrose Bierce and the Queen of Spades, University of California Press, 1998.

Also author of libretto for *Angle of Repose,* an opera based on the book by Wallace Stegner, 1976.

UNDER PSEUDONYM JASON MANOR

Too Dead to Run, Viking, 1953.
The Red Jaguar, Viking, 1954.
The Pawns of Fear, Viking, 1955.
The Tramplers, Viking, 1956.

Contributor of short stories to *Playboy* and to *TriQuarterly, Antioch Review,* and other literary magazines.

ADAPTATIONS: Warlock was filmed by Twentieth Century-Fox in 1959; *The Downhill Racers* was filmed by Paramount in 1969 as *Downhill Racer* with Robert Redford.

SIDELIGHTS: Oakley Hall writes historical and contemporary novels, generally with Western settings, about people who face ordinary and extraordinary challenges. Wirt Williams comments that Hall "has always had an X-ray penetration of social orders, big and little, and the keenest sensitivity to their nuances and subtleties. And he has always had a skill with plot that was absolutely dangerous."

Report from Beau Harbor, Bernard Weinstein notes in *Best Sellers,* "never sacrifices the humanity of its characters to shallow opportunism," and "perceives this country in depth as well as in breadth . . . [cutting] deeply into the marrow of upper-middle-class America with the scalpel of skepticism." Martin Levin of the *New York Times Book Review* contends that "[Hall] establishes a painfully recognizable social climate . . . bound together with a storyteller's sense and an adhesive of bitter humor," while *Book World*'s Sara Blackburn observes that "Hall . . . has a rare gift for depicting those moments during which people grow and change."

The Bad Lands, set in Dakota Territory during the 1880s, deals with range wars and the influx of the small farmers and ranchers into the territory. Ross Thomas of the *Washington Post* notes that "although he tries very hard indeed, Hall does not quite capture either the essence or the flavor of the time and place about which he writes." *Newsweek*'s Peter S. Prescott took a more positive position, commenting, "The great pleasure . . . of any mythic fiction is that we already know the story before we have begun it: We read for confirmation."

In his depiction of a troubled couple reunited in *Lullaby* just before their son falls from a bridge and faces possible permanent brain damage, Hall ventured into a world of black magic and ancient curses. This horror story, says Rick DeMarinis in the *Chicago Tribune Book World,* is "an impressive novel by a master of the form. It is a tale rich with believable characters involved in an occult detective story that keeps the reader on edge. . . . Oakley Hall . . . has given us a strong moral allegory for our times." However, Richard Rhodes, writing for the *New York Times Book Review,* finds the novel "too earnest to be taken simply as entertainment and a little too mechanical to be taken completely seriously. . . . Like its title, Oakley Hall's book swings somewhere between a bedtime story and a serious attempt to pierce the human and cultural darkness." In the *Los Angeles Times,* Roger Dionne comments, "Mostly the novel is about guilt and the confrontation of past sins. . . . However, the themes don't mesh; they remain out of focus; and held together with such tenuous mythological threads, they carry little conviction." The *Washington Post Book World*'s Christopher Schemering pronounces it "all very dark, psychological, insular . . . and without a cathartic conclusion, finally tedious."

In *The Children of the Sun,* Hall creates a fictionalized epic of the sixteenth-century Spanish explorer Cabeza de Vaca and three of his men, survivors of the expedition of Panfilo de Narvaez, a rival of Cortes, in the American Southwest and Mexico. These men have become healers and defenders of the Indians that the Conquistadores had brutalized, but they are unable to work any lasting good for them in the face of Spanish greed for gold. David M. Walsten states in the *Chicago Tribune Book World,* "Oakley Hall is a facile storyteller, but there is precious little here to relieve his accounts of slaughter, brutality, torture, venereal agonies, and disfigurement or death by smallpox, historic or otherwise." *Washington Post* writer Robert W. Smith gives Hall good grades for accuracy of detail and notes that "his prose moves, though he has a tendency to overwrite and lacks the restraint that lies just this side of art. . . . But on its own terms as a sprawling saga with little sag, this is an enjoyable reading adventure for a long summer afternoon." Diane Cole, writing for the *New York Times Book Review,* declares, "Doomed quests are the stuff that heroic tales are made of, and in *The Children of the Sun* Oakley Hall has transformed the feats of real-life adventurers into an adventurous and impressive fiction." Grover Sales of the *Los Angeles Times* calls attention to Hall's "exhaustive knowledge of Mexican history and folklore, a superb literary style and a burning passion for his subjects that sears on every page."

Hall's more recent novels focus on the time period of Billy the Kid. In *The Coming of the Kid,* Hall satirizes the legendary Billy the Kid, naming his villain Big Mac, which *Detroit News* reviewer Robert Mayer finds distracting and irritating. Further, Mayer says, "Trying at once to be a tall tale, an adventure, a comic novel and an allegory, *The Coming of the Kid* succeeds at none of these. The characters never come to life; the concept has been done better."

Apaches, which also involves a Billy the Kid-like character, is filled with Indians and cowboys, cavalry and Mexicans, strong-willed women and a hero who searches for a better life in the old west. As Matt Schudel observes in the *Washington Post Book World:* "Hall does not really rise beyond the genre of the western novel, and *Apaches* is at least 100 pages too long, but he writes with clarity and a clipped eloquence. . . . Writing like that knocks the boots off Louis L'Amour and Zane Grey, and by creating solid characters in a gritty, believable world, Oakley Hall gives formula fiction a good name." As Sales comments: "Hall is among our most absorbing, as well as our most underrated, novelists."

BIOGRAPHICAL/CRITICAL SOURCES:

BOOKS

Twentieth-Century Western Writers, 2nd edition, St. James Press, 1991.

PERIODICALS

Best Sellers, December 1, 1970; November 1, 1971.
Book World, January 2, 1972.
Chicago Tribune Book World, May 16, 1982; June 26, 1983.
Detroit News, February 16, 1986.
Hudson Review, spring, 1967.
Kenyon Review, Volume 30, number 1, 1968.
Los Angeles Times, March 31, 1982; July 7, 1983.
Los Angeles Time Book Review, January 26, 1986; August 10, 1986.
New York Times Book Review, October 17, 1971; May 14, 1978; March 28, 1982; October 23, 1983; December 23, 1984; July 20, 1997.
Newsweek, June 5, 1978.
Variety, December 24, 1969.
Washington Post, May 20, 1978; August 9, 1983.
Washington Post Book World, March 7, 1982; August 8, 1986.*

* * *

HALL, (Marguerite) Radclyffe 1886- 1943

PERSONAL: Born in 1886, in Bournemouth, Hampshire, England; died of cancer, October 7, 1943, in London, England; companion of Ladye Mabel Batten, 1908-1916; companion of Una Troubridge, 1916-43. *Education:* Attended King's College, London; educated in Germany. *Religion:* Catholic.

CAREER: Writer. Society for Psychical Research, Council member, 1916-24.

AWARDS, HONORS: James Tait Black Memorial Prize, 1927; Femina-Vie Heureuse Prize, 1927, for *Adam's Breed;* Eichelbergher Humane Award Gold Medal, c. 1926.

WRITINGS:

POETRY

'Twixt Earth and Stars: Poems, John and Edward Bumpus (London), 1906.
A Sheaf of Verses: Poems, John and Edward Bumpus, 1908.
Poems of the Past and Present, Chapman and Hall (London), 1910.
Songs of Three Counties, and Other Poems, Chapman and Hall, 1913.
The Forgotten Island, Chapman and Hall, 1915.

NOVELS

The Forge, Arrowsmith (London), 1924.
The Unlit Lamp, Cassell (London), 1924, reprinted with a new introduction by Zoe Fairbairns, Virago (London), 1981.

A Saturday Life, Arrowsmith, 1925, reprinted with a new introduction by Alison Hennegan, Penguin (New York), 1989.

Adam's Breed, Cassell, 1926, reprinted with a new introduction by Hennegan, Penguin, 1986.

The Well of Loneliness, J. Cape (London), 1928, reprinted with a new introduction by Hennegan, Penguin, 1982, with a commentary by Havelock Ellis, Anchor Books (New York City), 1990.

The Master of the House, J. Cape, 1932.

The Sixth Beatitude, Heinemann (London), 1936.

OTHER

Policeman of the Land: A Political Satire, Sophistocles Press, 1928.

Miss Ogilvy Finds Herself (short stories), Heinemann, 1934.

Your John: The Love Letters of Radclyffe Hall, edited and with an introduction by Joanne Glasgow, New York University Press (New York City), 1997.

SIDELIGHTS: Radclyffe Hall is perhaps best known for her 1928 novel, *The Well of Loneliness,* one of the first modern literary works whose plot concerned a same-sex relationship between women. Despite its laudatory critical reception, Hall's book was the subject of a ban under Britain's Obscene Libel Act, but scholars today consider it one of the premiere fictional portrayals of contemporary gay and lesbian life, a sensitive work that helped open doors of cultural acceptance for later writers.

Hall was born into a wealthy family in Hampshire, England, in 1886. Raised as a boy by her emotionally unstable parents, she was known as "John" to her friends and found security and support in her maternal grandmother, who encouraged the young girl's creative gifts. After receiving a large inheritance at the age of seventeen, Hall attended King's College in London and spent a year abroad in Germany. An accomplished amateur musician, she often wrote lyrics to accompany her compositions, and at the urging of her grandmother published some of this writing as a volume of verse entitled *'Twixt Earth and Stars* in 1906.

Around this time Hall became acquainted with Ladye Mabel Batten, a literary figure who became her companion and mentor for several years to follow. In these early years preceding World War I, Hall produced several other volumes of poetry, including *A Sheaf of Verses* and *Songs of Three Counties, and Other Poems,* works noteworthy for their frank expressions of passion between women. In *Radclyffe Hall at the Well of Loneliness: A Sapphic Chronicle,* scholar Lovat Dickson wrote of the good influence Batten was on the shy Hall, encouraging her writing and remaining a steady companion. The critic noticed the improvement from Hall's debut to the publication of *A Sheaf of Verses,* remarking that "for the first time, with increasing confidence and power, the passion of those first years of their association is struck for all to hear." During this period Hall had become a Catholic, like Batten, and her new faith was to become an integral element in her later works of fiction. Batten encouraged Hall to branch out into fiction, and the writer's first foray into this genre came with the 1924 publication of *The Forge.* However, Batten had passed away in 1916, and the grieving Hall felt in part responsible, since the writer had developed a romantic interest in Batten's niece, Una Troubridge.

The Unlit Lamp, Hall's second novel, was also published in 1924 and is seen by scholars as a thematic precursor to *The Well of Loneliness.* Much more subtle in its addressing of same-sex romance, the work's possibly scandalous subject matter was so restrained that little was mentioned of it in reviews. The novel is the tale of a young Julia Ogden and her affection toward her tutor, Elizabeth Rodney. Ogden's increasing devotion to Rodney incenses her mother, and the conflict this presents in the Ogden family is the basis for the novel. The two younger women dream of leaving their small coastal town for London in order to pursue a university education, but the plans are continually waylaid due to financial considerations or the interference of the manipulative, emotionally needy Mrs. Ogden. Yet "the mother is no ogre," observed Stephen Brook in an essay on Hall for *The Spectator,* "which is why the portrait is so brilliant." Brook termed the novel "a powerful and detailed portrayal not just of Lesbian love, but of how the emotional needs of three flawed women are finally irreconcilable." It had taken Hall two years to write *The Unlit Lamp,* and another two years to find a publisher for it. "It is by the standards of the time a good first novel," wrote Dickson in *Radclyffe Hall at the Well of Loneliness,* "conveying with noticeable skill for a beginner subtleties in human relationships that could only have been observed by someone of acute sympathies."

Hall's 1926 novel, *Adam's Breed,* is the story of a young man besieged by a collective guilt about the excess consumption of modern society, and is a reflection of her compassion for the plight of animals. By this time Hall and Troubridge, the wife of a naval officer, had become involved in a long-term relationship. Troubridge, who later penned the biography *The Life of Radclyffe Hall,* wrote of her lover's compassion for animals and Hall's difficulty in accepting their often cruel treatment at the hands of humans, recalling that the writer "taught me to appreciate the rights of animals and conferred on me the painful privilege of the 'seeing eye,' until in the end I also could not fail to remark on the underfed or overloaded horse or ass, the chained and neglected dog, the untamed bird in the dirty, cruelly tiny cage." The protagonist of *Adam's Breed* is a young headwaiter of Italian descent, Gian-Luca, who is sickened by the gorging he witnesses nightly by wealthy patrons of the restaurant; he is also acutely aware of the plight of animals he sees mistreated in everyday life. The pressure builds until Gian-Luca flees the city to live simply in the woods, but again becomes despondent when the pony he has befriended is captured for manual labor.

Hall had originally wished to title *Adam's Breed* "Food," but her publisher feared that it would be mistaken for a cookbook. Before its publication, informed Dickson in *Radclyffe Hall at the Well of Loneliness,* she told friends that after watching a waiter in a restaurant struggle to keep his tables appeased that she "would like to write a novel about the life of a waiter who becomes so sick of food that he allows himself nearly to die of starvation." When *Adam's Breed* appeared in print, a *New York Times Book Review* contributor found both praiseworthy elements as well as some flaws, noting "the first part of the book moves along with a great deal of interest," but the critic went on to remark that "the last part of the book degenerates into high-falutin' sentimentalism. . . . It seems predetermined and does not ring true."

Hall's landmark novel, *The Well of Loneliness,* appeared in print in 1928. The proclivities of its protagonist are explicit, and the passions depicted toward other female characters in the novel are also frank. Some details are autobiographical: the heroine's parents wished for a boy while the mother was expecting, and thus named the baby girl Stephen. Hall herself was raised as a boy and went by the nickname John for much of her life. As a young girl, Stephen develops a crush on one of the maids of the household, an incident which the scholar Dickson noted had also taken place in Hall's own youth. As a young girl, Stephen feels that she is not like other young girls, and finds herself more drawn to masculine pursuits; like Hall, the protagonist is an accomplished equestrienne. As she enters young adulthood, she sees the folly of pursuing heterosexual relations, especially after a swain—with whom she feels only a brotherlike affinity—proclaims his love for her and she feels obligated to send Martin away. Stephen later becomes enmeshed in a quasi-relationship with a married woman in the small town in which they live; when Stephen's mother learns of the affair, she condemns her daughter harshly.

As *The Well of Loneliness* continues, Stephen enlists in a service corps for women when World War I breaks out and meets Mary, who is young, somewhat naive, and soon completely devoted to Stephen. The two return to Stephen's family estate, and their passion is not consummated quickly, "even though [Mary] makes no secret of her desire for it," wrote Dickson in *Radclyffe Hall at the Well of Loneliness.* "The strain on both of them is intense. Although the language in which this protracted restraint is presented is novelettish, the sense of strain is vividly conveyed, and the reader sees some of the handicaps of perversion," Dickson noted.

When Martin returns and falls in love with Mary, Stephen relinquishes her paramour unto him at the conclusion of *The Well of Loneliness,* knowing that Mary "cannot stand the social isolation of her life with Stephen, would have grown bitter at the judgments Stephen has the strength to rise above, for she has no work of her own as Stephen does," as Jane Rule pointed out in *Lesbian Images,* "no identity of her own." It is this self-sacrifice that may have been what Hall wished to convey, that sexual "inverts," while not concerned with reproducing themselves for posterity, may indeed be of a higher spiritual and moral nature than non-inverts. Secondarily, Hall may have also chosen to portray those whom nature had made inverts as objects of compassion, because societal mores might never allow them to lead happy, fulfilling—and prejudice-free—lives. In the end, Stephen beseeches God to "Give us also the right to our existence."

After its publication in 1928, *The Well of Loneliness* was publicly condemned by a writer for the *Sunday Express* and a trial soon followed. Hall lost the case and the novel was banned in England; in a later case in a New York court the obscenity charges were dropped. Critical reaction to the novel was mixed, and was often tied in with a defense of it due to the controversy. Leonard Woolf, part of the influential British literary circle known as the Bloomsbury Group and husband to novelist Virginia, commented in *The Nation and The Athenaeum* that Hall's novel "is written with understanding and frankness, with sympathy and feeling," but charged that as a work of literary merit, it fell short. Woolf termed *The Well of Loneliness* "formless and therefore chaotic. . . . It is emotionally that the book loses way, and a sign of this is Miss Hall's use of language. At the beginning the language is alive; the style is not brilliant or beautiful, but it is quick and vivid. . . . But as the book goes on, life and emotion die out of the language, and Miss Hall drops into journalese or the tell-tale novelist's cliches when she wants to heighten the emotion."

Novelist and literary critic Rebecca West, one of Hall's contemporaries, also found fault artistically with the author's use of language, remarking in the *Bookman* that the novelist seemed to be inciting a feeling of sentimentalism in the reader. Such pandering to popular taste, West claimed, made it hard to defend *The Well of Loneliness* on purely artistic merit in the courts. Conversely, in her book *The School of Femininity: A Book for and about Women as They Are Interpreted through Feminine Writers of Yesterday and Today,* Margaret Lawrence praised the author's "mystical sensitivity to tone. Her phrasing shows it. Her words are put down in relation to their sounds set against other sounds. She produces by this means a disturbing emotional effect." In the *International Journal of Sexology,* Clifford Allen also lauded *The Well of Loneliness,* granting that while its author "may have had faults in style . . . on no occasion did she indulge in dishonesty, never did she describe things falsely or cast a gloss over what was real. She never pretended that homosexuality led to other than unhappiness. It was her very honesty which led to her book's being banned."

Hall penned two other novels before ill health curtailed her writing in the years before her death. In 1932, she published *The Master of the House,* the story of a man whose life paralleled that of Jesus Christ. The critic Lawrence, writing in *The School of Femininity,* deemed it an appropriate companion to *The Well of Loneliness.* "While the heroine in the one book lives the life of a man within the body of a woman, the man in the other book lives the life of a Christ within the body of a mortal," Lawrence wrote. "Neither of them has any concern with normal experience. They should be kept together and read together. They are part of the same mysterious saga." Many elements of *The Master of the House* correspond to the life of Christ as presented in the Bible: Christophe is the son of a carpenter and his wife, Jouse and Marie; his cousin Jan, like John the Baptist, will remain a close confidant through adulthood. Hall set her updated version of the Biblical tale shortly before the outbreak of World War I, and the two men are sent to Palestine to defend it against the Turkish army. There Christophe is ambushed and his journey to death closely follows Christ's procession to the cross.

Dickson, writing in *Radclyffe Hall at the Well of Loneliness,* observed that Hall's attempt to retell the story of Christ in a modern atmosphere "diminishes the glory and the brightness that myth has attached to it. . . . One sees, looking at it from this distance, that the book in fact fails through over-earnestness, a mood antipathic to the time in the early thirties when it was published." L. A. G. Strong, critiquing *The Master of the House* for the *Spectator* at the time of its publication, declared that if divorced from the Biblical comparison the novel would hold up on its own, but that "by adding this weight of symbolism to it, [Hall] makes it totter dangerously."

Hall's seventh and final novel, *The Sixth Beatitude,* appeared in 1936. It is the story of a poor woman, Hannah Bullen, whose somewhat unconventional life (she is unmarried, but mother to two) in a small English seaside town is marked by poverty and strife within her immediate family. The title of the work refers to the Roman Catholic notion of purity of mind and chastity of heart, and Hall attempts to portray the goodness of her protagonist despite the squalor of her surroundings. A 1936 review of the novel in the *Times Literary Supplement* noted that "Hall certainly conveys, without any special pleading or attitudinizing, the native richness of speech and character that can exist in a row of old hovels in an old town, the warmth that somehow makes the dirt, cold and bickering bearable." Gwen Leys, critiquing *The Sixth Beatitude* for *New York Herald Tribune Books,* noted that the author's characterizations of the peripheral figures of Bullen's life "give this story its bite, its fight and its character," yet concluded that "Hall is relentlessly determined to be grim."

Hall died of cancer in 1943. Although *The Well of Loneliness* is often cited as seminal to modern gay and lesbian fiction, the rest of her novels and poetry have often been overshadowed by the scandal that is associated with her best-known title—yet they also evince many of the same themes and convictions important to her. "The work of Radclyffe Hall . . . is serious, profound and beautiful work, in no way doctrinaire, yet thoroughly indoctrinated," wrote Lawrence in an essay titled "Priestesses" in *The School of Femininity.* "Her emotion is still yet deep. She is like a quiet pool of great depth. She is ageless. . . . She is preoccupied with the mysteries, as the priestesses were, and she pities the human race as it passes them by for things that can be added up and multiplied and subtracted and divided."

BIOGRAPHICAL/CRITICAL SOURCES:

BOOKS

Baker, Michael, *Our Three Selves: A Life of Radclyffe Hall,* Hamish Hamilton (London), 1985.

Castle, Terry, *Noel Coward and Radclyffe Hall: Kindred Spirits,* Columbia University Press (New York City), 1996.

Cline, Sally, *Radclyffe Hall: A Woman Called John,* Overlook Press (New York City), 1998.
Dickson, Lovat, *Radclyffe Hall at the Well of Loneliness: A Sapphic Chronicle,* Scribner (New York), 1975.
Gay and Lesbian Literature, St. James Press, 1994.
Glasgow, Joanne, editor and author of introduction, *Your John: The Love Letters of Radclyffe Hall,* New York University Press (New York City), 1997.
Lawrence, Margaret, *The School of Femininity: A Book for and about Women as They Are Interpreted through Feminine Writers of Yesterday and Today,* Frederick A. Stokes, 1936.
O'Rourke, Rebecca, *Reflecting on The Well of Loneliness,* Routledge (New York City), 1989.
Rule, Jane, *Lesbian Images,* Doubleday (New York), 1975.
Troubridge, Una, *The Life of Radclyffe Hall,* Citadel (New York), 1973.
Twentieth-Century Literary Criticism, Volume 12, Gale, 1984.
Twentieth-Century Romance and Historical Writers, 3rd edition, St. James Press, 1994.

PERIODICALS

Bookman, January, 1929.
International Journal of Sexology, Volume 4, 1950.
Life and Letters, October, 1928, pp. 329-341.
The Nation and The Athenaeum, August 4, 1928, p. 593.
New Republic, September 18, 1929, pp. 132-133.
New Statesman, September 13, 1968, pp. 321-322.
New York Herald Tribune Books, April 26, 1936, p. 10.
New York Times Book Review, May 23, 1926, pp. 9, 17.
Publishers Weekly, December 30, 1996, p. 47.
Spectator, February 7, 1981, pp. 21-23.
Times Literary Supplement, April 18, 1936, p. 333.*

* * *

HALL, Roger (Leighton) 1939-

PERSONAL: Born January 17, 1939, in Woodford Wells, Essex, England; immigrated to New Zealand, 1958, naturalized citizen, 1981; son of Sidney L. (an insurance official) and Agnes Hilda (a teacher; maiden name, Feurstahler) Hall; married Mavis Dianne Sturm (an airline hostess), January 20, 1968; children: Philippa Anne, Simon Leighton. *Education:* Wellington Teachers College, teaching diploma, 1963; Victoria University of Wellington, M.A. (honors), 1967.

ADDRESSES: Home—298 York Place, Dunedin, New Zealand. *Office*—English Department, University of Otago, P.O. Box 56, Dunedin, New Zealand. *Agent*—Casarotto Company Ltd., National House, 60-66 Wardour St., London W1V 3HP, England.

CAREER: Writer. Berhampore School, Wellington, New Zealand, teacher, 1966 and 1968-69; University of Otago, Dunedin, New Zealand, teaching fellow, 1979-91. *On Camera* (television program), New Zealand Broadcasting Company, interviewer, 1970-71; New Mexico State University, guest artist, 1983; lecturer. New Zealand State Literary Fund Advisory Committee, member, 1980-82; Fortune Theatre Board, chairman, 1983-85; founder of Monitor. Worked variously in insurance, in factories, as a wine waiter, and as a public servant.

MEMBER: PEN, New Zealand Scriptwriters Guild.

AWARDS, HONORS: Feltex nomination, TV Writer of the Year, New Zealand, 1974 and 1975; Queen Elizabeth II Arts Council travel grant, 1975; Robert Burns fellow, University of Otago, 1977 and 1978; Comedy of the Year, Society of West End Theatre Awards, 1979, for *Middle-Age Spread;* Fulbright fellow, 1982; New Year's Honours, Queen's Service Order for community services, 1987.

WRITINGS:

PLAYS

Glide Time (two-act; produced in Wellington, New Zealand, 1976), Victoria University Press, 1977.
Middle-Age Spread (two-act; produced in Wellington, 1977, produced in the West End, 1979, produced in Washington, DC, 1983), Victoria University Press, 1978, Samuel French, 1980.
State of the Play (two-act; produced in Wellington, 1978), Victoria University Press, 1979.
Cinderella (pantomime), produced in Dunedin, New Zealand, 1978.
Prisoners of Mother England (two-act; produced in Wellington, 1979), Playmarket, 1980.
Robinhood (pantomime), produced in Auckland, New Zealand, 1980.
Fifty-Fifty (two-act; produced in Auckland, 1981), Victoria University Press, 1982.
The Rose (one-act), produced in Auckland, 1981.
Hot Water (two-act; produced in Auckland, 1982), Victoria University Press, 1983.

Footrot Flats (two-act musical; adapted from Murray Ball's cartoon strip of the same title), music by Philip Norman, lyrics by A. K. Grant, produced in Christchurch, New Zealand, 1983.

Multiple Choice (two-act), produced in Las Cruces, NM, 1983.

Dream of Sussex Downs (two-act; adapted from Anton Chekhov's play *The Three Sisters*) produced in Auckland, 1986.

Love off the Shelf (two-act musical), music by Norman, lyrics by Grant, produced in Dunedin, 1986, produced in Southampton, England, 1987.

The Hansard Show (two-act show), music and lyrics by John Drummond and Nigel Eastgate, produced in Wellington, 1986.

The Share Club (two-act), produced in Dunedin, 1987.

After the Crash (two-act), produced in Dunedin, 1988.

Mr. Punch (one-act), produced in Dunedin, 1989.

You Must Be Crazy, produced in Wellington, 1989.

Conjugal Rites (two-act), produced in Palmerston North, 1990.

Making It Big, music by Norman, produced in Dunedin, 1991.

Also author of stage revues, including *Gone to Lunch, Knickers,* and *The Last Half-Crown;* and of children's plays.

CHILDREN'S FICTION

Captain Scrimshaw in Space, Rigby (Adelaide), 1979.

How the Crab Got a Hard Back, Rigby, 1979.

Sam, Max, and Harold Meet Dracula, Nelson Price (Wellington), 1990.

Penguin Trouble, Nelson Price, 1991.

My Aunt Mary Went Shopping, Ashton Scholastic (Auckland), 1991.

OTHER

By Degrees (play), 1993.

Mum's Photo (children's book), 1993.

Author of television screenplays, including *Clean-Up, The Bach,* and *Some People Get All the Luck;* and of radio plays, including *The Quiz, Hark Hark the Harp,* and *Last Summer;* writer for numerous television series, including *Gliding On,* based on his play *Glide Time, Neighborhood Watch,* and *Conjugal Rites.* Contributor to periodicals, including *New Zealand Listener* and *New Zealand Book World.*

ADAPTATIONS: Middle-Age Spread was adapted as a full-length feature film of the same title, directed by John Reid.

SIDELIGHTS: Described as the most successful playwright in New Zealand, Roger Hall is given credit for boosting the popularity of theatre among the country's citizens. Although he writes plays in a variety of categories, his comedies and musicals have won him the most attention and have been internationally produced. When Bill Lennox wrote in the *New Zealand Listener* that "Hall seems to entertain first and stimulate second," he capsulized the reason for reviewers' mixed reception of the playwright. Hall's light-hearted spoofs on human behavior are sometimes faulted for their strictly popular appeal and lack of commentary on sociopolitical matters. Hall responded to such criticism in Leonard Radic's Melbourne *Age* article, stating that "it's a curious thing to have written a play that people flock to, and because they do, it's a mark against it." Giving reason for the writer's popularity among audiences, Lennox noted Hall's exceptional ability to portray the ordeals of ordinary people and added that he allows his audience the opportunity for "looking and laughing at themselves but not feeling threatened as a result."

Two of Hall's most performed plays, *Glide Time* and *Middle-Age Spread,* focus on the everyday lives of middle-class people. *Glide Time* satirizes the work practices of employees in a public service office and, due to its favorable reputation in the theatre, was adapted as a long-running New Zealand television series, *Gliding On.* Rosemary Beresford in the *New Zealand Listener* commented that "*Glide Time*'s mixture of comedy and pathos, its simple language and its recognisable characters drew people into the theatres in a way that few other New Zealand plays had done." Hall's popularity was heightened with the release of his next play, *Middle-Age Spread,* a comedy depicting the anxieties of three couples who, in the midst of mid-life crises, discuss their troubles at a dinner party. The play's success in New Zealand spurred an award-winning West End production, which was described by Harold Hobson in *Drama* as "delightful entertainment." A subsequent American premiere of *Middle-Age Spread* received mixed reviews from two *Washington Post* critics; although David Richards called the production "awfully flat," reviewer Lloyd Grove was prompted to declare that Hall, who deftly portrays mid-life malaise, "may be New Zealand's John Updike."

In *Glide Time,* Hall touched upon the theme of seeking refuge from an increasingly bleak domestic life that is the result of cultural displacement. Hall expanded this idea in *Prisoners of Mother England.* The main characters are eight migrants headed for New Zealand, where they dream of walking the Milford Track, fishing, and living inexpensively in a land of opportunity and people who are very much like them. The assimilation process, however, shatters their delusions. Howard McNaughton wrote in *Contemporary Dramatists,* "This play, broadly autobiographical, frankly acknowledged the migrant perspective that informs much of Hall's best satire." Anther play dealing with the migration theme is *Dream of Sussex Downs,* an adaptation of Chekhov's *The Three Sisters. Hall told CA:* "I like writing most forms of drama for stage and television. Comedy is my favorite because you can say everything.

"I write because I really enjoy it; when it's going well, really going well, there's nothing like it. From the outside people walk past me and see me at the word processor and it must look pretty dull, but inside I'm having a tremendous time. Days when I don't write, I'm fairly grumpy about it. I have to do a bit each day; even if I'm not physically writing, in my head I am."

BIOGRAPHICAL/CRITICAL SOURCES:

BOOKS

Contemporary Dramatists, 5th edition, St. James Press, 1993.

PERIODICALS

Age (Melbourne), September 15, 1986.
Drama, January, 1980, pp. 34-35 and 47-48.
New Statesman, January 15, 1988, p. 29.
New Zealand Listener, August 23, 1980, pp. 14-15; August 9, 1986, p. 39.
Washington Post, May 17, 1983; May 20, 1983.*

* * *

HARDY, Francis Joseph 1917-
(Ross Franklyn, Frank J. Hardy)

PERSONAL: Born March 21, 1917, in Southern Cross, Victoria, Australia; married Rosslyn Couper, 1939; children: one son, two daughters. *Education:* Attended state schools.

ADDRESSES: Office—c/o State Mutual, 521 5th Ave., 17th Fl., New York, NY 10175.

CAREER: Has worked variously as a cartoonist, seaman, journalist, trade union organizer, and farm laborer. Freelance writer, lecturer, songwriter, and television personality. Co-founder, Australian Society of Authors, 1968-74. *Military service:* Australian Army, 1941-46.

MEMBER: Australian Society of Authors, Realist Writers Group, Carringbush Writers (president, 1980-83), Realist Writers Group (president, 1945-74).

AWARDS, HONORS: Logic award, 1972, for a television script; Television Society award, 1973; three Literature Board grants; A.N.A. Literature award (with others), 1980, for *Who Shot George Kirkland?*

WRITINGS:

NOVELS

(As Ross Franklyn) *Power without Glory,* Realist (Melbourne), 1950.
The Four-Legged Lottery, Laurie (London), 1958.
The Outcasts of Foolgarah, Allara (Melbourne), 1971.
But the Dead Are Many: A Novel in Fugue Form, Bodley Head (London), 1975.
Who Shot George Kirkland? A Novel about the Nature of Truth, Arnold (Melbourne), 1981.
The Obsession of Oscar Oswald [with] *"Warrant of Distress" by Oscar Oswald,* Pascoe (Carleton, Victoria), 1983.

Novels also published under the name variation Frank J. Hardy.

SHORT STORIES

The Man from Clinkapella and Other Prize-winning Stories, Realist, 1951.
Legends from Benson's Valley, Laurie, 1963, with "The Eviction of Erine Lyle" published as *It's Moments Like These,* Gold Star (Melbourne), 1972.
The Yarns of Billy Borker, Reed (Sydney), 1965.
Billy Borker Yarns Again, Nelson (Melbourne), 1967.
The Great Australian Lover and Other Stories, Nelson, 1972.
(With Athol George Mulley) *The Needy and the Greedy: Humorous Stories of the Racetrack,* Libra (Canberra), 1975.
(With Fred Trueman) *You Nearly Had Him That Time and Other Cricket Stories,* S. Paul (London), 1978.
A Frank Hardy Swag, edited by Clement Semmler, Harper (Sydney), 1982.
The Loser Now Will Be Later to Win, Pascoe, 1985.
Hardy's People: Stories of Truthful Jones, Pascoe, 1986.
Journey into the Future (travel), Australasian Book Society (Melbourne), 1952.

The Hard Way: The Story behind "Power without Glory" (nonfiction), Laurie, 1961.
The Unlucky Australians (nonfiction), Nelson, 1968, revised edition, Gold Star, 1972.
Great Australian Legends, Hutchinson (Surry Hills, New South Wales), 1985.
Retreat Australian Fair, and Other Great Australian Legends, Hutchinson, 1990.
Faces in the Street: An Epic Drama (play), Stained Wattle Press (Westgate, New South Wales), 1990.
Mary Lives! (play), Currency Press, 1992.

Author's work has been translated into several languages. Also author of plays *Black Diamonds,* 1956; *The Ringbolter,* 1964; and *Who Was Harry Larsen?,* 1985. Author of numerous television scripts. Author's works are collected in the Australian National Library, Canberra.

ADAPTATIONS: Power without Glory was adapted as an Australian television series, 1976.

SIDELIGHTS: Author Francis Joseph Hardy first made a name for himself in his native Australia with the novel, *Power without Glory,* which Hardy initially published and distributed himself in 1950, after publishing houses shied from the book due to its controversial nature. Indeed, only months after reviews of *Power without Glory* reached the Australian papers, Hardy found himself involved in a libel suit. Citing the novel as a thinly disguised attack on millionaire John Wren, Wren's wife sued Hardy over his fictionalization of her as the adulterous character Nellie West. Finally acquitted after the nine-month-long trial, Hardy was transformed into an international celebrity; *Power without Glory* has since been reprinted several times, was translated into several languages, and has been adapted into a television series in the mid-1970s.

Born in 1917 and raised in the Victoria community of Bacchus Marsh, which he would later fictionalize as "Benson's Valley" in several short story collections, Hardy left school as soon as he reached adolescence and was employed variously as a farm worker, a road construction crew worker, and as a seaman. The sufferings of Australia's working class during the Depression era prompted the idealistic young Hardy to join the Communist Party in 1939; he would repeatedly reflect upon the inequities of society in his short fiction, as well as in novels such as 1975's *But the Dead Are Many: A Novel in Fugue Form,* which while taken to task by Peter Ackroyd in the *Spectator*—"Here is a creature which had long been thought extinct, but which has now been discovered in Australia: the solemn novel of the brow-beating species"—was hailed by Van Ikin in *Contemporary Novelists* as "one of the major works of Australian literature in the 1970s."

While Hardy's novels most often treat serious topics—*The Four-Legged Lottery* focuses on the corruption in the horse racing industry, *But the Dead Are Many* confronts the suicide of a left-wing intellectual, and *Who Shot George Kirkland?* traces the path of a journalist investigating the veracity of his sources after breaking a damning story—he is also known for his short fiction. "The Load of Wood," included in 1982's *A Frank Hardy Swag,* is considered among the classic Australian short stories, and the poignant depictions of rural life during the Depression collected in *Legends from Benson's Valley* reflect his ear for speech and respect for character. Reflecting a more humorous side, Hardy's creation of the character Billy Borker, an imaginative, good-timing Aussie with a knack for storytelling, breathed life into a traditional rural stereotype and the short stories in *The Yarns of Billy Borker* and *Billy Borker Yarns Again* have gained a large following.

In *The Hard Way,* published in 1981, Hardy reflects upon his early fame as the author of *Power without Glory,* describes gathering information for his novel while working in Melbourne during the late 1940s, and depicts the turmoil of his months in court over the novel. In later years, Hardy again showed the strong social conscience reflected in his earlier works. The 1983 novel *The Obsession of Oscar Oswald* is a condemnation of the machinations of twentieth-century financiers, lawyers, and collection companies through casting a fresh perspective on the predictions of dystopian novelist George Orwell. Accompanying the novel is the booklet *Warrant of Distress,* a tract purported by Hardy to be written by the novel's protagonist. Well known as a lecturer, journalist, playwright, and television celebrity, Hardy has continued to entertain Australians with his far-reaching interests and to illuminate for readers what he perceives as the economic fallout that results from living in a capitalist society.

BIOGRAPHICAL/CRITICAL SOURCES:

BOOKS

Contemporary Novelists, 6th edition, St. James Press, 1996.

PERIODICALS

Spectator, August 9, 1975, p. 149.
Times Educational Supplement, June 14, 1985, p. 28.

Times Literary Supplement, August 1, 1975, p. 865.*

* * *

HARDY, Frank J.
See HARDY, Francis Joseph

* * *

HARDY, Lyndon (Maurice) 1941-

PERSONAL: Born April 16, 1941, in Los Angeles, CA; married Joan Taresh, 1966; children: two. *Education:* California Institute of Technology, B.S. (in physics), 1962; University of California, Ph.D. (in high-energy physics), 1966.

CAREER: Engineer, TRW Systems, Redondo Beach, CA, beginning 1966; writer.

WRITINGS:

FANTASY NOVELS

Master of the Five Magics, Del Rey (New York), 1980.
Secret of the Sixth Magic, Del Rey, 1984.
Riddle of the Seven Realms, Del Rey, 1988.

SIDELIGHTS: The increased popularity of fantasy fiction over the last few decades has created a hungry market. As a result, many novels seem to utilize the same themes and devices repeatedly. Lyndon Hardy, on the other hand, avoids the overly convenient use of limitless magic in his books, opting instead for magic that must conform to a code of rules. Hardy commented to *St. James Guide to Fantasy Writers,* "My magical universe is one in which the laws of magic are rigorously defined, rather than omnipotent powers that have no bounds." His approach to magic is evident in *Master of the Five Magics,* the beginning of his Arcadia series. The five magics are thaumaturgy (a type of magic in which two substances are eternally joined), alchemy, magic, sorcery, and wizardry, and each has its own unique qualities. In the novel, Alodar is an apprentice thaumaturge whose explorations of the various schools of magic introduce the reader to their distinctions. When Alodar decides against thaumaturgy as a career, he begins a personal journey in which he seeks masters of other types of magic, learning all he can from each of them. Eventually, he chooses to pursue wizardry and the art of controlling demons. From here, the story follows Alodar as he matures and grows in power as a wizard. In the end, Alodar reaches an amazing conclusion: his quest is actually to find in himself an Archimage, a master of all five magics.

The next book in the series is *Secret of the Sixth Magic,* where readers meet Melizar, a being whose presence seems to cancel out magical effects, and Jemidon, an adult man who wants to learn sorcery, despite his being too old to apprentice. It is Jemidon who connects the appearance of Melizar with the weakening of all types of magic. With the fate of the world in his hands, Jemidon travels to Melizar's land, where a different magic, metamagic, governs. This knowledge alone is sufficient for Jemidon's mission, and he returns to his own world to restore order. Like Alodar, Jemidon finds himself a stronger and wiser person by the end of the story.

The final installment in the series is *Riddle of the Seven Realms.* The hero is a scoundrel, Kestrel, whose actions lead him into adventure that affects not only his life, but the future of the world. While trying to defraud a witch, Kestrel inadvertently opens a passage between worlds, letting in a djinn whom Kestrel then uses to trick several wizards. They in turn chase Kestrel into the domain where Alodar is an Archimage. Alodar sends Kestrel and the djinn on a journey through several universes. Don D'Ammassa wrote in *St. James Guide to Fantasy Writers,* "Once again, Hardy's ability to superimpose a system of logic on patterns of magic is the high point of the book, which is diversely inventive and filled with remarkable ideas and exotic settings."

BIOGRAPHICAL/CRITICAL SOURCES:

BOOKS

St. James Guide to Fantasy Writers, St. James Press, 1996.

PERIODICALS

School Library Journal, January, 1985, p. 92.
Science Fiction Chronicle, January, 1985, p. 35.*

* * *

HARDY, W(illiam) G(eorge) 1895-1979

PERSONAL: Born February 3, 1895, in Oakwood, Ontario, Canada; died in 1979; son of George William (a farmer) and Anne (White) Hardy; married Llewella May Sonley, September 9, 1919 (deceased); children: Helen Elizabeth Dickinson, George Evan, Margaret Ann Simpson. *Education:* University of Toronto, B.A., 1917, M.A., 1920; University of Chicago, Ph.D., 1922. *Avocational interests:* Sports.

CAREER: University of Toronto, Toronto, Ontario, lecturer in classics, 1918-20; University of Alberta, Edmonton, Alberta, lecturer, 1920-22, assistant professor, 1922-28, associate professor, 1928-33, professor of classics, 1933-64, professor emeritus, 1964-79, head of department, 1938-64. President of Alberta Amateur Hockey Association, 1932-33, Canadian Amateur Hockey Association, 1938-40, and Ligue Internationale de Hockey sur Glace, 1948-51. Edmonton Little Theatre, president, 1930, and producer of its plays for four years. Speaker or guest on about one thousand radio and television programs in Canada.

MEMBER: Canadian Authors' Association (president, 1950-52; council member), Classical Association of Canada (council member).

AWARDS, HONORS: National Award in Letters, University of Alberta, 1962; L.L.D. from University of Alberta, 1964; Order of Canada, 1973.

WRITINGS:

Abraham: Prince of Ur, Dodd, 1935.
Turn Back the River, Dodd, 1938.
All the Trumpets Sounded, Coward, 1942.
Education in Alberta, Calgary Herald, 1946.
The Unfulfilled, Appleton, 1952.
The City of Libertines, Popular Library, 1957.
(Editor-in-chief) *The Alberta Golden Jubilee Anthology,* McClelland & Stewart, 1959.
From Sea unto Sea: Canada 1850-1920 (history), Doubleday, 1960.
The Greek and Roman World, Schenkman, 1962, revised edition, 1970.
Our Heritage from the Past, McClelland & Stewart, 1964.
Journey into the Past, McClelland & Stewart, 1965.
Origins and Ordeals of Western Civilization, Schenkman, 1966.
(Editor) *Alberta: A Natural History,* M. G. Hurtig, 1967.
The Scarlet Mantle: A Novel of Julius Caesar, Macmillan, 1978.
The Bloodied Toga: A Novel of Julius Caesar, Macmillan, 1979.

Author of radio plays. Contributor of more than two hundred short stories and articles to *Canadian Home Journal, Star Weekly, Maclean's, Collier's, Saturday Evening Post, Tomorrow, Strand,* and other periodicals.

SIDELIGHTS: W. G. Hardy's early works focus on Canadian social commentary. *The Unfulfilled,* for instance, considers relations between Canada and the United States. Though they deal with controversial issues such as sexuality, these books did not create any waves. Instead, it was Hardy's historical literature that captured the attention of readers.

Hardy is best known for his "Roman Trilogy," which consists of *The City of Libertines, The Scarlet Mantle: A Novel of Julius Caesar,* and *The Bloodied Toga: A Novel of Julius Caesar. The City of Libertines* centers on the decadence of Roman life in the final years of the Republic. Especially significant to the plot is the poet Catallus' worship of "Lesbia" (actually Clodia Pulcher), who is unfaithful to him. Clodia's brother was at the center of a scandal involving a religious rite forbidden to men. Hardy compares him and the other manipulative libertines to modern political figures and events. Julius Caesar's middle life is the subject of *The Scarlet Mantle.* Caesar is shown in his military roles as warrior and renegade. For contrast, Hardy created the character of Fadius, a lowly soldier. Through his eyes, Caesar's effects on Rome and its people are witnessed. Finally, in *The Bloodied Toga,* the last years of Caesar's life are examined, including his relationship with Cleopatra. Hardy's extensive background in the classics enabled him to comfortably recount historical events and discuss famous historical figures.

BIOGRAPHICAL/CRITICAL SOURCES:

BOOKS

Twentieth-Century Romance and Historical Writers, 3rd edition, St. James Press, 1994.*

* * *

HARRINGTON, John W(ilbur) 1918- 1986

PERSONAL: Born March 28, 1918, in Berwyn, IL; died April 16, 1986; son of John L. and Florence Fonda Harrington; married Ethel O'Brien, June, 1941 (deceased); married Emma Dodge, 1978; children: (first marriage) Tor (deceased), Tara Lau. *Education:* Virginia Polytechnic Institute and State University, B.S., 1940; University of North Carolina at Chapel Hill, M.S., 1946, Ph.D., 1948.

CAREER: Amerada Petroleum Corp., OK, geologist, 1948; Lone Star Gas Co., TX, geologist, 1948-49; Southern Methodist University, Dallas, TX, associate professor of geology, 1949-56; worked as a consulting geologist, 1956-63; Wofford College, Spartanburg, SC, professor of geology, 1963-81, professor emeritus, 1981-86. Consulting geologist; writer.

MEMBER: Geological Society of America (fellow), American Association of Petroleum Geologists, American Geophysical Union, History of Science Society.

WRITINGS:

To See a World, Mosby, 1973.
Discovering Science, Houghton, 1981.
Dance of the Continents: Adventures with Rocks and Time, J. P. Tarcher, 1983.

BIOGRAPHICAL/CRITICAL SOURCES:

PERIODICALS

Booklist, March 1, 1983, p. 849.
Kirkus Reviews, January 1, 1983, p. 45; February 1, 1983, p. 128.
Library Journal, March 1, 1983, p. 506; March 1, 1984, p. 431.
School Library Journal, August, 1983, p. 84.
Science Books & Films, November, 1983, p. 77.*

Date of death provided by wife, Emma Dodge Harrington.

* * *

HARRINGTON, Joseph Daniel 1923-

PERSONAL: Born September 29, 1923, in Boston, MA; son of James Patrick (a carpenter) and Anastatia (Lee) Harrington; married Bette Lou Allan, December 29, 1945 (divorced); married Virginia Clark, January 15, 1953 (divorced); married Carol Elizabeth Webster (a dining room manager), April 29, 1978; children: (second marriage) Sheila Frances, Polly Patricia, Matthew Joseph. *Education:* Attended high school in Boston, MA *Politics:* "Anarchist."

ADDRESSES: Home and Office—P.O. Box 1322, Hallandale, FL 33009.

CAREER: U.S. Navy, career enlisted man, 1942-63, retiring as chief petty officer; writer and editor for U.S. Government, 1963-64; Harrington Associates (national employment agency for military men entering private industry), Washington, DC, president, 1964-71; carpenter, 1971-77; writer, 1977—.

MEMBER: Fleet Reserve Association.

AWARDS, HONORS: Essay prizes from U.S. Naval Institute, 1952, for "Wanted—5000 Middlemen," 1953, for "Evaluating Enlisted Men's Performance," and 1955, for "Every Weapon to the Fray."

WRITINGS:

Kaiten: The Story of Japan's Human Torpedos, Ballantine, 1962, reprinted as *Suicide Submarine,* 1979.
Rendezvous at Midway: The Story of the "U.S.S. Yorktown" and the Japanese Carrier Fleet, John Day, 1968.
I-Boat Captain: The Story of Japan's Submarines at War (Literary Guild's Military Book Club selection), Major Books, 1976.
Yankee Samurai: The Secret Role of Nisei in America's Pacific Victory (Literary Guild's Military Book Club selection; first volume in trilogy), Pettigrew Enterprises, 1979.
The Bad, Bad Banzai Boys: The Story of the 442nd Regimental Combat Team (second volume in trilogy), Pettigrew Enterprises, 1980.

SIDELIGHTS: Joseph Daniel Harrington's interest in naval history began when he was working on a historical project for the Navy's public information department. *Yankee Samurai* involved interviews with some fifteen hundred Japanese-American veterans of World War II, fifteen thousand miles of travel, and extensive research in archives. It covers events and attitudes long kept secret by government officials and agencies: the prison camps and occupation, the discrimination and prejudice focused on these American citizens, and what they did in the post-War years.

Harrington comments: "The aim of my trilogy (and my life) is to demonstrate that hate, vindictiveness, prejudice, and discrimination are a WASTE, and that the civilized human being trying to lead a decent life just has no place for them in it. I have consistently (and successfully) challenged 'official' versions, and kind of wish that my fellow citizens would develop a general healthy skepticism."

BIOGRAPHICAL/CRITICAL SOURCES:

PERIODICALS

Japan Times, November 19, 1978.
Miami Herald, April 5, 1979.*

* * *

HARRIS, Aurand 1915-1996

PERSONAL: Born July 4, 1915, in Jamesport, MO; died of cancer on May 6, 1996, in Manhattan, NY; son of George Dowe (a physician) and Myrtle (a drama teacher; maiden name, Sebastian) Harris. *Education:* University of Kansas City (now University of Missouri-Kansas City), A.B., 1936; Northwestern University, M.A., 1939; graduate study at Columbia University, 1945-47.

CAREER: Children's playwright. Teacher of drama at public schools in Gary, IN, 1939-41; William Woods College, Fulton, MO, head of drama department, 1942-45; Grace Church School, New York City, instructor in drama, 1946-77; University of Texas at Austin, lecturer in drama, beginning 1978. Lecturer at Columbia University Teachers College, summers, 1958-63, Western Connecticut State College, summer, 1976, University of Kansas, fall, 1980, California State University, Northridge, spring, 1982, Indiana University-Purdue University at Indianapolis, 1985, New York University, 1990-92. Playwright-in-residence at University of Florida, 1972, University of Kansas, Lawrence, 1979, University of Texas, Austin, 1976-84, Young Audiences, Cleveland, fall, 1981-84, New Orleans Public Schools, winter, 1984, Birmingham, AL, Public Schools, 1984, Columbus Public Schools, Columbus, OH, 1984, Children's Educational Theatre, Salem, OR, 1984, and American School of Madrid, Spain, 1986. Director at Cleveland Play House, fall, 1982-84, Nebraska Theatre Caravan, fall, 1982, Youtheatre, Ft. Wayne, IN, fall, 1983, and Shanghai Childrens Art Theatre, Republic of China, 1987; director and designer at summer theatres in Cape May, NJ, 1946, Bennington, VT, 1947, Peaks Island, ME, 1948, and Harwich, MA, 1963-82.

MEMBER: American Alliance of Theatre and Education, Institute for Advanced Studies in Theatre Arts (advisory board), Children's Theater Association of America.

AWARDS, HONORS: Seattle Junior Programs Playwrighting award, 1945, 1946, 1950, 1952, 1956, 1958, 1960; John Golden Award from Columbia University, 1945, for *Circus Day;* Midwestern Writers Conference, 1947; Anderson Award from Stanford University, 1948, for *Missouri Mural;* Marburg Prize from Johns Hopkins University, 1956; Birmingham Junior Programs award, 1958, 1960, 1962; Junior League of New Jersey award, 1960; NorthShore Music Theatre award, 1966; Noratio Alger Newsboy Award, 1967, for *Rags to Riches;* Chorpenning Cup from American Theatre Association, 1967 and 1985, for "continued contributions to the field of children's drama in the writing of superior plays for young audiences"; creative writing fellowship from National Endowment for the Arts, 1976; Ohio Theatre Alliance Award, 1984, for "outstanding achievement in the theatre"; American Theatre Association fellow, 1985; Alumni Achievement Award, University of Missouri, 1987; Sara Spencer Award, 1988, for outstanding contribution to children's theatre; Distinguished Service Award from Southwest Theatre Association, 1988; American Alliance of Theatre and Education award, 1990, for best children's play; Alumni Merit Ward from Northwestern University, 1991; D.H.L. from University of Indiana, 1991.

WRITINGS:

PLAYS

Ladies of the Mop (one-act), Baker, 1945.
The Doughnut Hole (three-act), Samuel French, 1947.
The Moon Makes Three (three-act), Samuel French, 1947.
Madam Ada (three-act), Samuel French, 1948.
And Never Been Kissed (three-act; adapted from the novel by Sylvia Dee), Samuel French, 1950.
We Were Young That Year (three-act), Samuel French, 1954.
Young Black Beauty: A Dramatization of the Novel "Black Beauty" by Anna Sewell, Anchorage Press (New Orleans, LA), 1996.

CHILDREN'S PLAYS

Once upon a Clothesline (four-act; produced in Fulton, MO, 1944), Baker, 1945.
Seven League Boots (three-act; produced in Cleveland, OH, 1947), Baker, 1948.
Circus Day (three-act; produced in Seattle, WA, 1948), Samuel French, 1949, revised edition published as *Circus in the Wind,* 1960.
Pinocchio and the Indians (three-act; produced in Seattle, 1949), Samuel French, 1949.
Simple Simon; or, Simon Big-Ears (three-act; produced in Washington, DC, 1952), Anchorage Press, 1953.

Buffalo Bill (three-act; produced in Seattle, 1953), Anchorage Press, 1954.

The Plain Princess (three-act; adapted from the book by Phyllis McGinley; produced in Kalamazoo, MI, 1954), Anchorage Press, 1955.

The Flying Prince (two-act; first produced in Washington, DC, 1965; revised and produced in Ft. Wayne, IN, 1983), Samuel French, 1958, revised edition, Anchorage Press, 1985.

Junket: No Dogs Allowed (three-act; adapted from the story by Anne H. White; produced in Louisville, KY, 1959), Anchorage Press, 1959.

The Brave Little Taylor (three-act; produced in Charleston, WV, 1960), Anchorage Press, 1961.

Pocahontas (two-act; produced in Birmingham, AL, 1961), Anchorage Press, 1961.

Androcles and the Lion (also see below; two-act; produced in New York City, 1964), Anchorage Press, 1964.

Rags to Riches (also see below; two-act; adapted from stories by Horatio Alger; produced in Harwich, MA, 1965), Anchorage Press, 1966.

Pinocchio and the Fire-Eater (one-act; produced in Gary, IN, 1940), McGraw, 1967.

A Doctor in Spite of Himself (two-act; adapted from a play by Moliere; produced in New York City, 1966) Anchorage Press, 1968.

The Comical Tragedy or Tragical Comedy of Punch and Judy (also see below; two-act; produced in Atlanta, GA, 1969), Anchorage Press, 1970.

Just So Stories (three-act; adapted from stories by Rudyard Kipling; produced in Tallahassee, FL, 1971), Anchorage Press, 1971.

Ming Lee and the Magic Tree (one-act), Samuel French, 1971.

Steal Away Home (also see below; two-act; adapted from the story by Jane Kristof; produced in Louisville, 1972), Anchorage Press, 1972.

Peck's Bad Boy (also see below; three-act; adapted from the novel by George Wilbur Peck; produced in Harwich, 1973), Anchorage Press, 1974.

Yankee Doodle (also see below; two-act; produced in Austin, TX, 1975), Anchorage Press, 1975.

Star-Spangled Salute (two-act; produced in Harwich, 1975), Anchorage Press, 1975.

Six Plays for Children, edited by Coleman A. Jennings (contains *Androcles and the Lion, Rags to Riches, Punch and Judy, Steal Away Home, Peck's Bad Boy,* and *Yankee Doodle*), University of Texas Press, 1977.

Robin Goodfellow (two-act; produced in Harwich, 1974), Anchorage Press, 1977.

A Toby Show (three-act; produced in Austin, 1978), Anchorage Press, 1978.

Ralph Roister Doister (one-act; adapted from a play by Nicholas Udel), Baker, 1978.

Cyrano de Bergerac (one-act; adapted from the play by Edmund Rostand), Baker, 1979.

The Romancers (one-act; adapted from the play by E. Rostand), Baker, 1979.

Candida (one-act; adapted from the play by George Bernard Shaw), Baker, 1979.

The Arkansaw Bear (three-act; produced in Austin, 1977), Anchorage Press, 1980.

Fashion (one-act; adapted from the play by Anne Cara Mowatt), Baker, 1981.

Treasure Island (three-act; adapted from the novel by Robert Lewis Stevenson; produced in Northridge, CA, 1983), Anchorage Press, 1983.

The Magician's Nephew (three-act; adapted from the novel by C. S. Lewis; produced in Austin, 1984), Dramatic Publishing Company, 1984.

Ride a Blue Horse (three-act; produced in Indianapolis, IN, 1985), Anchorage Press, 1986.

Huck Finn's Story (three-act; adapted from the novel *Huckleberry Finn* by Mark Twain; produced in Akron, OH, 1987) Anchorage Press, 1988.

Monkey Magic (three-act; produced in Honolulu, HI, 1989), Anchorage Press, 1990.

OTHER

(Co-editor and contributor) *Plays Children Love* (anthology), Doubleday, 1981, Volume 2, St. Martin's Press, 1988.

(Co-editor and contributor) *Short Plays of Theatre Classics* (anthology), Anchorage Press, 1991

Contributor to *Give Them Roots and Wings,* American Theatre Association, 1972, and *Children and Drama,* Logman, 1977, revised edition, 1981. Also contributor of plays to numerous anthologies, including *Twenty Plays for Young People, Contemporary Children's Theatre, Dramatic Literature for Children, and Theatre for Youth.* Contributor to *Childrens Literature Quarterly, Youth Theatre Journal,* and *Asian Theatre Journal.*

Manuscript collection at Arizona State University in Tempe.

SIDELIGHTS: Aurand Harris is remembered as a prolific children's playwright and the author of a version of the classic *Androcles and the Lion,* which has been performed over nine thousand times. In fact, most of Harris's children's plays are based on fairy tales and legends. Harris began his forty-year career as an author in 1945, while teaching drama at William Woods College in Fulton, Missouri, where his first children's work, *Once Upon a Clothesline,* a four-act play, was produced. Between 1946 and 1977, Harris served as a drama instructor at Grace Church School in New York City. Harris's plays have been translated into twenty languages, and he has received many honors, including a creative writing fellowship from the National Endowment for the Arts.

Harris told *CA:* "I write plays for youth theatre because I like theatre, I like children, and I like what children like in the theatre—a good story, interesting characters, visual excitement and beauty, suspense, music, and comedy. In youth theatre there is the freedom to write in any style or use any appropriate dramatic form. There is the challenge of breaking new ground. And there is the reward of the spontaneous applause of a young, critical, and appreciative audience. There is also the practical side. Children's theatre is one area in American drama that is growing both in quality and quantity, which means a present and increasing market for good scripts.

"With the exception of a few professional companies, I think the best children's drama is produced in regional theatres across the nation. There is no 'Little Broadway' for a children's playwright, which is healthy. Instead of being bound by the provincial tastes of a New York Broadway, childrens' theatre is a part of the varied tastes, demands, and mores of the entire country.

"I am proud to be part of a growing movement in American drama and have no regrets about giving up a promising career of writing for adults. I once suggested to the late Pulitzer Prize-winning playwright William Inge that he write a play for youth theatre. Inge replied, 'I have nothing to say to children.' In the same manner, perhaps I have nothing to say to adults. But happily I do have many stories to 'show and tell' to children."

Reba and Bonnie Churchill of the *Los Angeles Times* noted Harris's habit of traveling throughout the country to work with classroom teachers to instruct grade school children on the art of playwriting. Although Harris also taught playwriting to college students, he told the Churchills that "his great love is teaching youngsters, 'to keep in touch with the children I write for. Their imagination, freedom, enthusiasm continually amazes and delights me.' " As Harris told the reporters, playwriting is "a motivational tool to teach children to read and write. When a youngster writes a play, it puts him in charge of something he has created. It also trains him to think logically, to use his imagination and to read, write and speak, in what some teachers call basic oral and written English."

Coleman A. Jennings commented on the playwright's career in *Twentieth-Century Children's Writers,* describing Harris as "America's most-produced children's theatre playwright. His plays, constantly produced since the late 1940s, have enormously enriched the literature of American children's theatre."

BIOGRAPHICAL/CRITICAL SOURCES:

BOOKS

Swortzell, Lowell, *The Theatre of Aurand Harris: America's Most Produced Playwright for Young Audiences, His Career, His Theories, His Plays: Including Fifteen Complete Plays by Aurand Harris,* Anchorage Press, 1996.

Twentieth-Century Children's Writers, 4th edition, St. James Press, 1995.

PERIODICALS

Los Angeles Times, December 26, 1984.

OBITUARIES:

PERIODICALS

Chicago Tribune, May 10, 1996, section 3, p. 9.
Los Angeles Times, May 9, 1996, p. A31.
New York Times, May 8, 1996, p. D21.
Washington Post, May 13, 1996, p. D6.*

* * *

HARRIS, Christie (Lucy) Irwin 1907-

PERSONAL: Born November 21, 1907, in Newark, NJ; immigrated to Canada in 1908; daughter of Edward (a farmer) and Matilda (Christie) Irwin; married Thomas Arthur Harris (a Canadian immigration officer), February 13, 1932; children: Michael, Moira (Mrs. Donald Johnston), Sheilagh (Mrs. Jack Simpson), Brian, Gerald. *Education:* Attended University of British Columbia, 1925. *Religion:* Church of England.

ADDRESSES: Home—302-975 Chilco St., Vancouver, British Columbia, Canada V6G 2R5.

CAREER: Novelist, author of historical fiction, short stories, and plays especially for young people. Teacher in British Columbia, 1926-32; freelance writer for Canadian Broadcasting Corp. Radio, 1936-63; *British Columbia News Weekly,* women's editor, 1951-57.

MEMBER: Writers' Union of Canada.

AWARDS, HONORS: First award in educational radio and television competitions in Columbus, OH, for school radio series, *Laws for Liberty*; Book of the Year for Children medal from Canadian Association of Children's Librarians, 1967, for *Raven's Cry;* Vicki Metcalf Award, 1973, 1982; Canadian Association of Children's Librarians, 1977, International Board on Books for Young People (IBBY) honor list citation, both for *Mouse Woman and the Vanished Princess;* Children's Literature Prize from Canada Council, 1980, Canadian Library Association Book of the Year runner-up citation, 1981, and Amelia Frances Howard-Gibbon Award, 1981, all for *The Trouble with Princesses;* member of the Order of Canada, 1981.

WRITINGS:

PUBLISHED BY ATHENEUM, EXCEPT AS INDICATED

Cariboo Trail, Longmans, Green, 1957.
Once upon a Totem, 1963.
You Have to Draw the Line Somewhere, illustrations by daughter, Moira Johnston, 1964.
West with the White Chiefs, 1965.
Raven's Cry, illustrations by Bill Reid, foreword by Robert Davidson and Margaret B. Blackman, 1966.
Confessions of a Toe Hanger, 1967.
Forbidden Frontier, 1968.
Let X Be Excitement, 1969.
(With Johnston) *Figleafing through History: The Dynamics of Dress,* 1971.
Secret in the Stlalakum Wild, 1972.
(With husband, Thomas Arthur Harris) *Mule Lib,* McClelland & Stewart, 1972.
Once More upon a Totem, 1973.
Sky Man on the Totem Pole?, 1975.
Mystery at the Edge of Two Worlds, 1979.
The Trouble with Princesses, 1980.
The Trouble with Adventures, illustrations by Douglas Tait, 1982.
Something Weird Is Going On, Orca, 1994.

"MOUSE WOMAN" SERIES; PUBLISHED BY ATHENEUM

Mouse Woman and the Vanished Princesses, 1976.
Mouse Woman and the Mischief-Makers, 1977.
Mouse Woman and the Muddleheads, 1979.

OTHER

Also author of twelve adult plays, juvenile stories, and radio scripts, including several hundred school programs. Women's editor, *A S & M News.*

SIDELIGHTS: A diversified writer with many books to her credit, Christie Irwin Harris is noted and respected most for her works depicting Indian legends and the Canadian West. As a child, Harris grew up in a log cabin in British Columbia, and this region of western Canada is the chief source of Harris's material.

Kenneth Radu explains in *Canadian Children's Literature: A Journal of Criticism and Review:* "Indian folklore and mythology have quite clearly made their imprint upon Mrs. Harris's imagination. Her finest work is directly concerned with the Indian life and legends of the Northwest. *Raven's Cry* . . . remains a singularly moving paean to the now extinct Haida civilization of the Queen Charlotte Islands. Fully and accurately researched, *Raven's Cry* portrays the complexities and uniqueness of the Haida culture with insight, wonder, and compassion. Mrs. Harris's view is neither sentimental, romantic, nor patronizing. She reports Haida life as it was lived on the islands with the clear eye and honesty of the sympathetic chronicler."

The Republic of Childhood: A Critical Guide to Canadian Children's Literature in English author Sheila Egoff also recognizes Harris's talent for interpreting Indian legends. "The potential for children's literature inherent in the Indian legends is most fully realized by Christie Harris in *Once upon a Totem,*" Egoff writes. "Other collections may have more charm, or a more fluid style, but the legends chosen by Harris and her interpretation of them are outstanding in that they seek quietly to illuminate universal values. The stories are very much a part of early Indian life and very much a part of today."

Priscilla L. Moulton notes in *Horn Book Magazine* that Harris has "rediscovered and reproduced a dignified and inspiring picture of [Haida] culture in a work of epic proportions [*Raven's Cry*]. Painstaking research and intense absorption in anthropological details have enabled the author to write with rare commitment and involvement from the Haida point of view. . . . Dealing as it does in a highly artistic and complicated manner with the whole range of human emotion and character, it makes demands of the reader but rewards him with new understanding of the forces that shape civilizations. . . . This distinguished work, probably classified as fiction, will occupy a respected position in historical, anthropological, and story collections."

Critics often cite Harris's sensitivity in portraying Indian tales as one reason for her large and loyal readership. It has been said that she makes the myths or legends come alive, and many of the young readers, in turn, better understand the ways of their Indian brothers. For example, S. Yvonne MacDonald of *In Review* believes that *Raven's Cry* and *Forbidden Frontier* "combine the author's knowledge of Indian folklore and custom with historical fact to describe the collision between European white man's civilization and Indian culture. Harris writes with sympathy for the Indians, apparently determined to tell their side of the story. . . . This knowledge of legend and folklore seems to me to be the author's main strength, whether in her collections of myths or in her novels."

While it has been written that Harris writes all her books with sensitivity, realism, and a strong respect for history, it also has been suggested that it is her sense of humor that makes her books an enjoyable learning experience for her readers. Kenneth Radu contends that "the hallmark of [Harris's] style is good-humored briskness which carries the story along in an uncomplicated, well-placed narrative." Critic Priscilla L. Moulton writes in another review published in *Horn Book Magazine* that she feels that Harris usually writes with "an abundance of humor—a rare quality in exploration accounts." And in her *Washington Post* review of *You Have to Draw the Line Somewhere,* Margaret Sherwood Libby notes that "Harris has achieved a minor miracle, a romance-career story that is sparkling and well written, filled with humor that springs naturally from character and situation."

Readers and critics alike have also delighted in Harris's books for the sometimes unusual, often comical, and almost always life-like characters she creates. A perfect example of her use of a strong, dominant character to carry her message is offered by S. Yvonne MacDonald. She writes that *Mouse Woman and the Vanished Princesses,* a "collection of legends from the mythology of the Northwest Coast Indians of Canada, is uniquely linked through the character of Mouse Woman, a Narnauk or Supernatural Being. . . . The stories are clearly and lyrically told, with perhaps the most distinctive quality being the characterizations of the Narnauks. Harris manages to evoke the magical and essentially alien World of the Supernaturals and also its familiarity to the Indians, for these spirits were a daily part of their lives."

New York Times Book Review critic Benjamin Capps explains in a review of *West with the White Chiefs* that "the journal of two Englishmen . . . who crossed western Canada in 1863 is the basis for this fictionalized account of a perilous trip through little-known, difficult land. . . . Comic relief is supplied by a roguish Irishman, a ridiculous, helpless freeloader who intrudes into the party and makes the journey with the explorers. He quotes Latin aphorisms, is generally unavailable for any work, always makes outrageous demands on the others. He is a wonderful creation, a delightful contrast to the hard-working, serious Indians and Englishmen." And Sriani Fernando of *In Review* writes in an article about *The Trouble with Princesses* that "within each story, the characters are distinctive and adequately developed. The difference in impetus—depending on whether the protagonists resort to wit, cunning or magic to achieve their ends—lends variety to the stories."

Besides tales of Indian lore and adventures in western Canada, Harris is also the author of other books for young people. Several of her books are based on the experiences of her own family. For example, *Let X Be Excitement* is based on the life of her oldest son, Michael (Ralph to Harris's readers). Julie Losinski writes that in *Let X Be Excitement* "for Ralph, discovering his life's occupation meant finding a job that offered intellectual challenge and satisfied his love of excitement and the outdoors. . . . Ralph's satisfaction in doing what comes naturally, combined with a sense of humor, results in a appealing zest for living. Readers (boys particularly) facing career decisions will empathize with Ralph, and enjoy, even though they may not be able to equal, his adventures." In *Confessions of a Tow Hanger,* comments Shirley Ellison of *Profile,* "Mrs. Harris ventured once more into family collaboration to tell the story of her younger daughter, Sheilagh. . . . The humorous but poignant account of the 'ordinary' middle child in a talented family is now the favourite reading of Sheilagh's own daughters." Ellison continues to explain that Harris's *You Have to Draw the Line Somewhere* "recreates the story of her older daughter, Moira, a fashion artist. It was undertaken at Moira's suggestion." Helen M. Kovar of *School Library Journal* notes that *You Have to Draw the Line Somewhere* "is the story of a young Canadian girl who aspires to become a *Vogue* fashion artist. The British Columbia setting is refreshing and the style is humorous. . . . It is a frank picture of the non-glamorous side of fashion art and modeling and the amount of work necessary to become first-rate in either profession. With a light touch the story offers depth and mature values. . . . This has much more to offer than most girls' fiction."

BIOGRAPHICAL/CRITICAL SOURCES:

BOOKS

Contemporary Literary Criticism, Volume 12, Gale, 1980.

Dictionary of Literary Biography, Volume 88: *Canadian Writers, 1920-1959,* Gale, 1989.

Egoff, Sheila, *The Republic of Childhood: A Critical Guide to Canadian Children's Literature in English,* 2nd edition, Oxford University Press, 1975.

Something about the Author Autobiography Series, Volume 10, Gale, 1990.

Twentieth-Century Children's Writers, 4th edition, St. James Press, 1995.

PERIODICALS

American Museum of Natural History, November, 1967.

Canadian Children's Literature, number 2, 1975; number 5, 1976; number 6, 1976; number 51, 1988, pp. 6-24; summer, 1994, pp. 5-15.

Horn Book Magazine, April, 1963; June, 1964; June, 1965; October, 1966; April, 1968; April, 1975.

In Review, autumn, 1975; autumn, 1976; August, 1980.

Kirkus Review, March 1, 1973; March 15, 1975; April 15, 1976.

New York Times Book Review, May 12, 1963; April 4, 1965.

Profile, 1971.

Quill & Quire, December, 1994, p. 33.

School Library Journal, April, 1964; September, 1969.

Scientific American, December, 1966.

Voice of Youth Advocates, August, 1993, p. 152.

Washington Post, May 17, 1964.*

* * *

HARRIS, Hyde
See HARRIS, Timothy Hyde

* * *

HARRIS, Mark 1922-
(Jack Atkins, Willis J. Ingram, Henry Martha, Alex Washington, Jack R. Wright)

PERSONAL: Born Mark Harris Finkelstein, November 19, 1922, in Mount Vernon, NY; son of Carlyle and Ruth (Klausner) Finkelstein; name legally changed; married Josephine Horen, March 17, 1946; children: Hester Jill, Anthony Wynn, Henry Adam. *Education:* University of Denver, B.A., 1950, M.A., 1951; University of Minnesota, Ph.D., 1956.

ADDRESSES: Office—Department of English, Arizona State University, Tempe, AZ 85287.

CAREER: Newsman for *Daily Item,* Port Chester, NY, 1944, *PM,* New York City, 1945, and International News Service, St. Louis, MO, 1945-46; writer for *Negro Digest* and *Ebony* in Chicago, IL, 1946-51; member of English department faculty, University of Minnesota, Minneapolis, 1951-54, San Francisco State College (now University), San Francisco, CA, 1954-68, Purdue University, West Lafayette, IN, 1967-70, California Institute of the Arts, Valencia, 1970-73, Immaculate Heart College, Los Angeles, CA, 1973-74, and University of Southern California, Los Angeles, 1974-75; University of Pittsburgh, Pittsburgh, PA, professor of English, 1975-80; Arizona State University, Tempe, AZ, professor of English, 1980-94. Fulbright professor, University of Hiroshima, 1957-58; visiting professor, Brandeis University, 1963. Made survey of teaching of English in Sierra Leone, for Peace Corps, 1965, and survey of educational television for Carnegie Corp., 1966. U.S. delegate, Dartmouth Conference, Kurashiki, Japan, 1974.

MEMBER: San Francisco Art Commission, 1961-64. *Military service:* U.S. Army, 1943-44.

AWARDS, HONORS: Ford Foundation grant for residence with Actor's Workshop, 1960; National Institute of Arts and Letters award for published work showing creative achievement, 1961; Guggenheim Foundation grants, 1965-66, for autobiography, *Twenty-one Twice,* and 1974; National Endowment for the Arts grant, 1966; D.H.L., Illinois Wesleyan University, 1974.

WRITINGS:

NOVELS, EXCEPT AS INDICATED

Trumpet to the World, Reynal & Hitchcock, 1946.

City of Discontent: An Interpretive Biography of Vachel Lindsay, Being Also the Story of Springfield, Illinois, U.S.A., and of the Love of the Poet for That City, That State, and That Nation, Bobbs-Merrill (New York City), 1952, published as *City of Discontent,* with a foreword by Laurence Goldstein, University of Illinois Press (Urbana), 1992.

Something about a Soldier, Macmillan (New York City), 1957.

Wake Up, Stupid, Knopf (New York City), 1959.

Friedman & Son (play; first produced in San Francisco by Actors Workshop, 1962), published with autobiographical preface, Macmillan, 1963.

(Editor and author of preface) *Selected Poems of Vachel Lindsay,* Macmillan, 1963.

(Author of preface) Henry B. Fuller, *With the Procession,* University of Chicago Press (Chicago), 1965.

(Editor and contributor) *Public Television: A Program for Action,* Harper (New York City), 1967.

The Goy, Dial (New York City), 1970.

Killing Everybody, Dial, 1973.

(Editor with wife, Josephine Harris, and daughter, Hester Harris) *The Design of Fiction* (story collection), Crowell (New York City), 1976.

Short Work of It: Selected Writings by Mark Harris (collection), University of Pittsburgh Press (Pittsburgh), 1980.

(Editor) *The Heart of Boswell: Six Journals in One Volume* (reader), McGraw (New York City), 1980.

Saul Bellow: Drumlin Woodchuck (nonfiction) University of Georgia Press (Athens), 1980.

Lying in Bed, McGraw, 1984.

Speed, D. I. Fine (New York City), 1990.

The Tale Maker, D. I. Fine, 1994.

Diamond: Baseball Writings of Mark Harris, D. I. Fine, 1994.

"HENRY WIGGEN" SERIES

The Southpaw, by Henry W. Wiggen: Punctuation Freely Inserted and Spelling Greatly Improved by Mark Harris, Bobbs-Merrill, 1953, published with autobiographical preface, Charter Books, 1963.

Bang the Drum Slowly, by Henry W. Wiggen: Certain of His Enthusiasms Restrained by Mark Harris, Knopf, 1956, published as *Bang the Drum Slowly,* Dell, 1974.

A Ticket for a Seamstich, by Henry W. Wiggen: But Polished for the Printer by Mark Harris, Knopf, 1957.

Henry Wiggen's Books, Volume 1, Avon (New York City), 1977.

It Looked Like for Ever, McGraw, 1979.

AUTOBIOGRAPHY

Mark the Glove Boy; or, the Last Days of Richard Nixon, Macmillan, 1964, published with a new afterword by the author, Curtis Books, 1972.

Twenty-one Twice: A Journal, Little, Brown, 1966.

Best Father Ever Invented: The Autobiography of Mark Harris, Dial, 1976.

The Man That Corrupted Hadleyburg (television play; adaptation of the story by Mark Twain), broadcast in 1980, published in *The American Short Story 2,* edited by Calvin Skaggs, Dell (New York City), 1980.

Also author of screenplay, *Bang the Drum Slowly* (adaptation of his novel), 1973, and of television plays *Boswell for the Defence,* 1983, and *Boswell's London Journal,* 1984. Contributor to books, including *The Living Novel,* edited by Granville Hicks, Macmillan, 1957; *The Potential of Woman,* edited by Farber and Wilson, McGraw, 1963; and *How We Live,* edited by Rust Hills, Macmillan, 1968. Contributor of articles, fiction, and reviews to numerous periodicals, including *Life, Esquire, Harper's Bazaar, Sports Illustrated, Virginia Quarterly Review, New Republic, Nation,* and *New York Times Book Review.*

Manuscript collection in University of Delaware Library in Newark.

ADAPTATIONS: Excerpts from *Best Father Ever Invented, Bang the Drum Slowly, It Looked Like for Ever, Something about a Soldier,* and *Lying in Bed* have been recorded by Harris for American Audio Prose Library (Columbia, MO), 1987; *Bang the Drum Slowly* was produced as a film, adapted for television by Arnold Schulman and produced on *U.S. Steel Hour,* December 26, 1956, and adapted as a play, produced at the Next Theatre in Evanston, IL, 1992; *Something about a Soldier* was adapted for the stage by Ernest Kinoy and produced by the Theater Guild in 1962.

SIDELIGHTS: Mark Harris's best-known works are those in the series of novels centering around pitcher Henry Wiggen of the fictional New York Mammoths baseball team. These books, as reviewers are quick to point out, are not simple sports stories, although they certainly do contain plenty of baseball action. In this series Harris, according to Donald Hall of the *New York Times Book Review,* "uses material that we normally associate with the sports pages and by skill and compassion enlarges what he touches until he reveals us to ourselves—our ordinary, universal lives."

The first book in the "Henry Wiggen" series, *The Southpaw,* introduces the main character and moves him from his home-town ball team into the big leagues. With the help of Wiggen's superb pitching skill, the Mammoths win the World Series, and the young left-hander is named Most Valuable Player. Along the way, Harris portrays a highly complex character whose insight and sensitivity set him apart from the typical hero of many sports novels. In a *Saturday Review* article, E. J. Fitzgerald writes: "Mr. Harris's novelistic achievement is a considerable one. He has taken a long, serious, and penetrating look at American mores and morals. And he has done this while telling a highly dramatic, colorful, and absorbingly exciting action story." Harry Sylvester of the *New York Times* says that "even those whose knowledge of baseball is elemental will find the book worth reading. For let there be no doubt about it, this is a distinguished and unusual book." When *The Southpaw* first appeared in 1953, a *San Francisco Chronicle* reviewer proclaimed it "the best 'serious' baseball novel ever published."

Harris's next baseball book, *Bang the Drum Slowly,* has proven to be his most popular work, especially since its 1973 production as a motion picture starring Robert De Niro and Michael Moriarty. Although Harris is somewhat perturbed at being known primarily as "the author of *Bang the Drum Slowly,*" many critics insist that it is his best novel. The book picks up Henry Wiggen three years after his first pennant-winning season in the big leagues; he has had a few mediocre years since then and has made the transition from hot young "phenom" to seasoned veteran. The Mammoths are once again racing for the pennant, and it is on this struggle that most of the baseball action is concentrated. But at the same time we find that Wiggen's catcher, Bruce Pearson, is dying from Hodgkin's disease, and the underlying theme of the book deals with the reactions of the various team members as one by one they become aware of this fact. Like *The Southpaw,* this book succeeds on two levels. As Robin Gottlieb notes in the *New York Herald Tribune Book Review,* "Henry's dead-pan vernacular account of life in the dugout is refreshing, lively, and often uproariously funny"; and at the same time, "his reactions to his doomed friend are poignant and profoundly touching." In a 1956 *San Francisco Chronicle* review, William German wrote: "People who go around asking each other who are the important new American writers could do worse than answer with the name of Mark Harris. He's pretty new, and he's very important."

After two Henry Wiggen novels that dealt with serious issues, Harris attempted a lighter tone in *A Ticket for a Seamstich.* Although Wiggen is still the narrator, or chronicler, in this book he is no longer the main character; the action centers mainly on Bruce Pearson's replacement, Piney Woods, and on the seamstich, a young woman who works her way across the country in order to see the Mammoths—and particularly her hero, Woods—play baseball. *A Ticket for a Seamstich* has been praised for its humor and, like all of the baseball novels, for its realistic use of language, but it has been heavily criticized for its failure to measure up to its predecessors. Robert Cromie of the *Chicago Sunday Tribune* writes: "This latest report on the strange doings of the Mammoths baseball team is not—in our view—in the same league with the earlier ones. . . . The writing is there, the amusing phrases are there, but the rest is sawdust and fails to convince." William German says that "on the whole it looks to us in the stands as if Henry Wiggen is beginning to tire in the late innings. Take care, Mark Harris. Go have a conference on the mound. If need be, derrick him." And William Hogan of the *San Francisco Chronicle* feels that "Harris-Wiggen had a bad day, even a bad season, on this one. The story about a seamstress from out West who catches up with her idols, The Mammoths, might have been written as a television script."

After leaving Henry Wiggen for more than twenty years, Harris revives the character in *It Looked Like for Ever.* Wiggen is now thirty-nine years old and has lost his fastball, he won only three games last year, and in the first chapter of the book he is passed over for a manager's job and is released as a player. This novel, as Donald Hall points out, "is not so much about baseball as about aging, just as *Bang the Drum Slowly* was not so much about baseball as it was about dying." A *Publishers Weekly* reviewer, however, finds that the book fails to achieve the depth of the earlier Wiggen books, writing that "beyond the humor and baseball satire, there is little else, and readers who were moved by the tragedy of *Bang the Drum Slowly* may well be disappointed by this effort." But Hall feels that in this book Harris "remains entertaining, using the pop character of Henry Wiggen to make intelligent moral generalities. . . . Writing like Harris's helps us to understand, even to withstand disaster—Vietnam, the meaningless death of the young, an enlarged prostate gland and, in an earlier work of art, the failure of Mudville's Casey."

Harris has also won the respect of reviewers for his work outside of the Henry Wiggen series. *Speed* is lauded as "an accomplished coming-of-age novel" by a *Publishers Weekly* reviewer. It tells the story of the narrator and his youth in Mount Vernon, New York—Harris's own hometown. The narrator's brother, nicknamed Speed, is more intelligent, better looking, and morally superior to him, yet he is socially handicapped by a severe stutter. This speech impediment causes most of the world to regard Speed as slow-witted, but the narrator is one of the few that recognizes his brother's many gifts. This situation is typical of the irony that permeates the book. According to Jeff Silverman in *Los Angeles Times Book Review,* "Through the sheer strength and beauty of Harris' writing, most of the irony works."

A fine writing style gives "the feel of a classic" to Harris's 1994 novel, *The Tale Maker,* according to a *Kirkus Reviews* contributor. The plot of this book concerns the intertwined fates of Rimrose, a talented but financially unsuccessful writer, and his college classmate Kakapick, an amoral character who becomes a literary critic and scholar. Jealous of Rimrose's real talent, Kakapick sets out to sabotage the other man's life. According to the *Kirkus Reviews* writer, it is "a wry, self-referential story" that "abounds in satirical insights into the natures of the creative mind, writing, editing, publishing, and criticism." Michael E. Ross comments in the *New York Times Book Review* that *The Tale Maker* offers "sly and whimsical comments on everything from revisionist education to the nature of literature."

In an essay published in *Contemporary Authors Autobiography Series,* Harris comments: "I . . . grow wild with rage at the way the world is run. I care for nothing more than staying home and writing out my proposals for a new heaven and a new earth. My writing began in anger and continues to be sustained by anger. . . . I cannot imagine my not being a writer, and I am almost unable to imagine my not working for a university and living in its environment. My particular burrow is the Department of English. In my novel *Wake Up, Stupid,* my hero Lee Youngdahl wrestled with the question whether the university was the right place for a writer to live. For me, at least, no other place would have been possible. I have taken advantage of the university system of tenure to write freely and to speak freely. In anybody's ordinary everyday business or corporation I'd have been fired in an hour, as my Chair at Arizona State University tried to fire me."

BIOGRAPHICAL/CRITICAL SOURCES:

BOOKS

Contemporary Authors Autobiography Series, Volume 3, Gale, 1986.
Contemporary Literary Criticism, Volume 19, Gale, 1981.
Contemporary Novelists, 6th edition, St. James Press, 1996.
Dictionary of Literary Biography, Volume 2: *American Novelists since World War II,* Gale, 1978.
Dictionary of Literary Biography Yearbook: 1980, Gale, 1981.

PERIODICALS

Armchair Detective, spring, 1986, p. 176.
Kirkus Reviews, April 1, 1994, p. 421.
Los Angeles Times Book Review, December 9, 1990, p. 9; June 26, 1994, p. 6.
New York Times Book Review, August 25, 1985, p. 28; September 23, 1990, p. 25; July 24, 1994, p. 18.
Publishers Weekly, June 29, 1990, p. 86; July 25, 1991, p. 49.
Tribune Books (Chicago), September 30, 1990, p. 6; June 19, 1994, p. 1.

OTHER

Mark Harris Interview with Kay Bonetti (sound recording), American Audio Prose Library, 1987.*

* * *

HARRIS, Timothy Hyde 1946-
(Hyde Harris)

PERSONAL: Born July 21, 1946, in Los Angeles, CA; son of Donald and Mary Helen (an artist; maiden name, McDermott) Harris; married Mary Bess Walker (a film director), March 21, 1980. *Education:* Peterhouse College, Cambridge, B.A. (with honors), 1969, M.A., 1974. *Politics:* Independent. *Religion:* "Pagan." *Avocational interests:* Travel (Europe and Africa), competitive saber fencing, spearfishing, skin diving, tennis (junior champion of Portugal, 1963).

ADDRESSES: Home—1053 1/2 South Genesee Ave., Los Angeles, CA 90019. *Agent*—Stuart Miller, Stuart Miller Agency, 4444 Riverside Dr., Burbank, CA 91505.

CAREER: Sailor, carpenter, and house painter, 1964—.

MEMBER: Writers Guild of America (West).

WRITINGS:

NOVELS

Kronski/McSmash, M. Joseph, 1969, Doubleday, 1970.
Steelyard Blues, Bantam, 1972.
Kyd for Hire, Dell, 1978, published in England under name Hyde Harris, Gollancz, 1978.
American Gigolo, Delacorte, 1979.
Goodnight and Goodbye, Delacorte, 1979.
Heat Wave, Dell, 1979.

SCREENPLAYS

Cheaper to Keep Her, Regal Productions, 1980.

French Kiss, Universal, 1980.

SIDELIGHTS: Timothy Harris has enjoyed success writing screenplays as well as novels. His two Thomas Kyd books (*Kyd for Hire* and *Good Night and Good-Bye*) are crime novels that have been aligned with the tradition of Dashiell Hammett, Raymond Chandler, and Ross MacDonald. According to Walter Albert of *Twentieth-Century Crime and Mystery Writers,* Harris has distanced himself from trite "hard-boiled" detective stories, instead voicing his admiration for Chandler's "deadpan poetics" and Patricia Highsmith's "insight and misanthropy." In *Kyd for Hire,* the title character does not think much of his life but sees his first case through simply because of his disdain for the criminal he is tracking. As in the works of Chandler and MacDonald, Harris builds a story from a family's dubious past. Harris utilizes a classic crime story device by ending the novel with a wrap-up speech delivered to a room full of suspects. Harris does, however, leave his unique mark on his novel, which he ends with a twist.

In *Good Night and Good-Bye,* the plot is more elaborate. Kyd becomes overly taken with Laura Cassiday, who is caught up in the game playing of the movie industry. Albert commented on the thematic complexity of the story: "*Good Night and Good-Bye,* as well as being an unusually powerful Hollywood private-eye novel, also draws on unresolved tensions of the Vietnam conflict in ways that were not to be examined in the crime novel for several years."

BIOGRAPHICAL/CRITICAL SOURCES:

BOOKS

Twentieth-Century Crime and Mystery Writers, 3rd edition, St. James Press, 1991.

PERIODICALS

Los Angeles Times, February 27, 1980.
New Republic, March 4, 1978, p. 40.
New York Times Book Review, October 7, 1979, p. 35.
Observer, November 6, 1977, p. 29.*

* * *

HASZARD, Patricia Moyes 1923-

PERSONAL: Born January 19, 1923, in Bray, Ireland; daughter of Ernst (a judge in the Indian Civil Service) and Marion (Boyd) Pakenham-Walsh; married John Moyes (a photographer), 1951 (divorced, 1959); married John S. Haszard (an official of the International Monetary Fund), October 13, 1962 (died 1994). *Politics:* Liberal (non-party). *Religion:* Church of England. *Avocational interests:* Skiing, sailing, good food and wine, travel.

ADDRESSES: Home—P.O Box 1, Virgin Gorda, British Virgin Islands, West Indies. *Agent*—Curtis Brown, Ltd., Haymarket House, 28/29 Haymarket, London, SW1Y 4SP England.

CAREER: Writer. Peter Ustinov Productions, Ltd., London, England, secretary, 1947-53; *Vogue,* London, assistant editor, 1954-58. *Military service:* British Women's Auxiliary Air Force, Radar Section, 1940-45; became flight officer.

AWARDS, HONORS: Edgar Allan Poe Award from Mystery Writers of America, 1970, for *Many Deadly Returns.*

WRITINGS:

UNDER NAME PATRICIA MOYES

Time Remembered (play; first produced in London, 1954; produced in New York, 1957), Methuen, 1955.
Dead Men Don't Ski, Collins (London), 1959, Rinehart (New York City), 1960.
(With Peter Ustinov and Hal E. Chester) *School for Scoundrels* (screenplay), Continental Pictures, 1960.
Down among the Dead Men, Holt (New York City), 1961, published in England as *The Sunken Sailor,* Collins, 1961.
Death on the Agenda, Holt, 1962.
Murder a la Mode, Holt, 1963.
Falling Star, Holt, 1964.
Johnny under Ground, Collins, 1965, Holt, 1966.
Murder by 3's (omnibus volume of mystery novels), Holt, 1965.
Murder Fantastical, Holt, 1967.
Death and the Dutch Uncle, Holt, 1968.
Helter-Skelter (juvenile), Holt, 1968.
Many Deadly Returns, Holt, 1970, published in England as *Who Saw Her Die?,* Collins, 1970.
Seasons of Snows and Sins, Holt, 1971.
The Curious Affair of the Third Dog, Holt, 1973.
After All, They're Only Cats, Curtis Books, 1973.
Black Widower, Holt, 1975.
The Coconut Killings, Holt, 1977, published in England as *To Kill a Coconut,* Collins, 1977.

How to Talk to Your Cat, Holt, 1978.
Who Is Simon Warwick?, Collins, 1978, Holt, 1979.
Angel Death, Holt, 1980.
A Six-Letter Word for Death, Holt, 1983.
Night Ferry to Death, Holt, 1985.
Black Girl, White Girl, Holt, 1989.
Twice in a Blue Moon, Holt, 1993.
Who Killed Father Christmas and Other Seasonable Demises, Crippen & Landrew, 1996.

Contributor of short stories and articles to *Women's Mirror, Evening News* (London), *Writer, Ellery Queen's Mystery Magazine,* and other publications.

Moyes's books have been translated into fifteen languages.

ADAPTATIONS: The short stories "A Sad Loss" and "Hit and Run" were made into episodes of the British television program *Tales of the Unexpected. Black Girl, White Girl* was adapted to audio, 1993.

SIDELIGHTS: Many historians argue that World War II saw the end of the Golden Age of the detective novel. For evidence, they point out that many of the well-known authors of the genre died around this time, others turned to different genres, and still others declined in skill. Yet, there are some contemporary authors who have upheld the tradition of the detective novel, and Patricia Moyes is one. A *New York Times Book Review* critic described her as "one of the brightest contemporary practitioners of the puzzle-and-plot whodunit." Her background in writing for movies and the stage has given her the ability to create believable dialogue with a natural flow. To engage her reader, she provides clues and false leads throughout her books, and sometimes concludes with a plot twist. Moyes told *Twentieth-Century Crime and Mystery Writers,* "Really, all I can say about my work is that I try to write the sort of books that I enjoy reading—that is, I write for my own pleasure and never try to appeal to a particular market. My preference is for mystery stories that are well-plotted (and never cheat the reader), that are ingenious, and amusing rather than vicious, and that are placed in a setting which the author clearly knows well, and peopled with characters who are more than dummies to be pushed around by the exigencies of the plot. I know that this sets a high standard, and I can't honestly pretend that I always achieve it—but I do try. . . . Frankly, I would sooner divert people than put their souls through an emotional meat-grinder, and I have long ago stopped apologizing for not being a serious' writer."

Moyes' series character is Henry Tibbett, who works in Scotland Yard. He began as Chief Inspector and has become Detective Chief Superintendent. Although criminals underestimate him, he is skillful at detecting hidden crimes and solving them with his trademark rational approach. Tibbett's wife, Emmy, is also involved in many of the mysteries, although she relies more on her intuition than logic. Together they solve crimes of Scotland Yard as well as mysteries they encounter in their own lives, such as while they are on vacation. Jean M. White of the *Washington Post Book World* called the Tibbetts a "thoroughly engaging couple" and praised Moyes's "talent for overlaying mystery with witty, sophisticated social comment." Writing in the *New York Times Book Review,* Newgate Callendar saw Moyes as "carrying on the traditions of the classical British mystery." Similarly, Anthony Boucher, writing for the same publication, stated that "Moyes is so good with people and professions and milieus that her books . . . keep reminding one more and more of the best work of [Ngaio] Marsh and [Margery] Allingham and other exemplary products of the Golden Thirties."

BIOGRAPHICAL/CRITICAL SOURCES:

BOOKS

Twentieth-Century Crime and Mystery Writers, 3rd edition, St. James Press, 1991.
Twentieth-Century Young Adult Writers, 1st edition, St. James Press, 1994.

PERIODICALS

Armchair Detective, winter, 1997.
Listener, April 7, 1977; January 11, 1979.
Los Angeles Times Book Review, October 6, 1985.
New York Times Book Review, July 26, 1964; May 31, 1970; February 22, 1981; May 16, 1982; October 15, 1989.
Observer (London), July 5, 1970; February 6, 1977.
Saturday Review, December 25, 1971.
Spectator, August 18, 1973.
Times Literary Supplement, August 13, 1964; July 16, 1970; November 12 1971; October 3, 1980; June 20, 1986; June 1, 1990.
Washington Post Book World, November 18, 1973; July 20, 1975; January 21, 1979.*

* * *

HAVIS, Allan 1951-

PERSONAL: Born September 26, 1951, in New York, NY; son of Meyer (in business) and Estelle (Heitner)

Havis; married Cheryl Riggins in 1982. *Education:* City College of the City University of New York, B.A., 1973; Hunter College of the City University of New York, M.A., 1976; Yale University, M.F.A., 1980. *Avocational interests:* Foreign travel, horseback and motorcycle riding.

ADDRESSES: Agent—William Craver, Writers & Artists, 19 West 44th St., Ste. 1000, New York, NY 10036.

CAREER: Guggenheim Museum, New York City, film instructor, 1974-76; Case Western Reserve University, writer-in-residence, 1976; *Our Town,* New York, theater critic, 1977; Foundation of the Dramatist Guild, New York City, playwriting instructor, 1985-87; Ulster County Community College, Stone Ridge, NY, playwriting instructor, 1985-87; Stone Ridge, New York, playwriting instructor, 1986-88; Old Dominion University, Norfolk, VA, playwriting instructor, 1987; Sullivan County Community College, Loch Sheldrake, NY, playwriting instructor, 1987; University of California, San Diego, professor of theatre, 1988—.

MEMBER: Circle Rep Writers Lab, Literary Managers and Dramaturgs of America (LMDA).

AWARDS, HONORS: John Golden Award for playwriting from Hunter College, 1974 and 1975; Marc A. Klein Award, Case Western Reserve University, 1976, for *Oedipus Again;* Foundation of the Dramatist Guild/CBS Award, 1985; Playwrights USA Award (HBO grant), 1986, for *Morocco;* National Endowment for the Arts fellowship, 1986; Rockefeller fellowship, 1987; Guggenheim fellowship, 1987; New York State Foundation for the Arts fellowship, 1987; Edward Albee Foundation for the Arts fellowship, 1987; Kennedy Center/American Express Production grant, 1987; MacDowell residency fellowship, 1988; McKnight fellowship, 1989; Hawthornden fellowship, 1989; University of California faculty summer fellowship, 1989; California Arts Council playwriting fellowship, 1991; Bellagio Center/Rockefeller fellowship, 1991; Camargo fellowship (France), 1993.

WRITINGS:

PLAYS, EXCEPT AS NOTED

The Boarder and Mrs. Rifkin (two-act), first produced in New York City at Hunter Playwrights, December, 1974.

Oedipus Again (two-act), first produced in Cleveland, OH, at Case Western Reserve University, February, 1976.

Watchmaker, produced in New York, 1977.

Heinz, produced in New Haven, CT, 1978.

Interludes (one-act), first produced in New Haven, CT, at Yale Center Cabaret, December, 1978.

Family Rites (one-act), first produced in New Haven, CT, at Yale Drama School, December, 1979.

Albert the Astronomer (juvenile novel), Harper (New York City), 1979.

Holy Wars, produced in Cambridge, MA, 1984.

The Road from Jerusalem, first produced in Cambridge, MA, at American Repertory Theatre, 1984.

Morocco (first produced in Cambridge, MA, at American Repertory Theatre, 1984), published in *Plays in Process,* Volume 6, number 5, Theatre Communications Group (New York City), 1985.

Einstein for Breakfast, produced in New York, 1986.

Haut Gout (first produced in Norfolk, VA, at Virginia State Company, 1987), published in *Plays in Process,* Volume 8, number 5, Theatre Communications Group, 1987.

Mink Sonata (two-act), first produced at BACA Downtown, New York City, 1986.

Duet for Three, first produced at West Bank Cafe, New York City, 1986.

Mother's Aria, first produced at West Bank Cafe, New York City, 1986.

Hospitality, first produced in Philadelphia, PA, at Philadelphia Theatre Company, 1988.

A Daring Bride, first produced in New Haven, CT, at Long Wharf Theatre, 1990.

Lilith (first produced in New York City, at Home for Contemporary Arts, 1990), Broadway Play Publishing (New York City), 1991.

Heaven & Earth (radio play), first produced by LA Theatre Works, 1991.

Ladies of Fisher Cove, first produced in New York City, at Ohio Theatre, 1993.

Adoring the Madonna, first produced in New York City, at Circle Rep Lab, 1994.

A Vow of Silence, Penguin (New York City), 1996.

SIDELIGHTS: Allan Havis' plays are dark, bizarre, and often disturbing. In *Contemporary Dramatists,* M. Elizabeth Osborn regarded him as a "cryptic storyteller" whose work is Kafkaesque. The main character is typically a well-to-do white Jewish man who finds himself simultaneously repulsed and lured by the Other, often a woman or a dark man. In the end, the white man never wins. Havis draws on the familiar tensions of sex and race to demonstrate the plight of the white American male whose dominance is weakening. Osborn observed, "Whether or not a formal investigation is taking place, dialogue is filled with the threat of attack, the tension of defense."

The scope of Havis' plays is as unexpected as his strange style. *Morocco* is a cat-and-mouse story in which Kempler, a Jewish architect, must arrange for his wife's release from a Moroccan jail after she has been charged with prostitution. In the first act, Havis heightens tension by making the jailer appear completely evil, while making Kempler and his wife appear faultless and victimized. In the second act, however, the audience begins to suspect that perhaps their first impressions were not at all accurate. In the final act, Kempler returns to the jailer, confessing to the murder of his wife, who later arrives to pick up her husband. A final exchange between the wife and the jailer reveals that they have been working together all along. In *Haut Gout,* a wealthy Jewish doctor travels to Haiti to do research and meets the fictional ruler of the island, Le Croix. Havis endows Le Croix with traits subject to prejudice; he is a communist, a heroin addict, and a homosexual with AIDS. The doctor becomes entangled in a net woven of Le Croix's unwelcome sexual advances and pressure from Latch, a State Department official, to kill Le Croix. After administering a lethal injection to the ruler, the doctor returns home with an empty spirit. In the final scene, Le Croix shows up with his attendant, a woman purported to be able to raise the dead, and they poison the doctor.

Mink Sonata is one of Havis' most absurd plays, and it begins with a lighter tone than most of his work. The story is about a wealthy father and his strained relationship with his daughter. She has an alter ego who is confident and attractive, and whose presence allows otherwise-taboo sexual fantasies to surface. *Lilith* provides a modern-day setting for a version of the Adam, pre-Eve Lilith, and Eve story. As in *Mink Sonata,* Havis introduces comedic elements rarely found in his plays.

Havis told *CA:* "In several of my plays I have attempted to build a drama without the mechanics of predictable plotting. I wanted to deal with little scenes, as if I were working in a film editing room, organizing old anticlimatic dialogues, putting them together in stories that begin harmlessly and end wickedly. These plays were meant to stir and shock the casual audience. These plays were also an experiment in economy. I wanted to take out as much verbiage as possible, leaving only essential dialogue that comes from looking inside people's minds and hearts."

BIOGRAPHICAL/CRITICAL SOURCES:

BOOKS

Contemporary American Dramatists, St. James Press, 1994.

Contemporary Dramatists, 5th edition, St. James Press, 1993.*

* * *

HAXTON, Josephine Ayres 1921-
(Ellen Douglas)

PERSONAL: Born July 12, 1921, in Natchez, MS; daughter of Richardson (an engineer) and Laura (a homemaker; maiden name, Davis) Ayres; married Kenneth Haxton, January 12, 1945 (divorced); children: Richard, Ayres, Brooks. *Education:* Attended Randolph Macon Women's College, 1938-39; University of Mississippi, B.A., 1942.

ADDRESSES: Home and office—1600 Pine St., Jackson, MS 39202. *Agent*—Robert L. Rosen Associates, 7 West 51st St., New York, NY 10019.

CAREER: Writer. Northeast Louisiana University, Monroe, writer-in- residence, 1976-79; University of Mississippi, Oxford, writer-in-residence, 1982—; University of Virginia, Charlottesville, writer-in-residence, spring, 1984. Faculty member of Faulkner Symposium, University of Mississippi, 1980. Welty Professor, Millsaps College, Jackson, spring, 1988. Guest reader and lecturer at University of Michigan, Louisiana State University, and other colleges and universities.

AWARDS, HONORS: Short story "On the Lake" included in O. Henry collection, 1961; Houghton Mifflin fellowship, 1961, and best novel of the year citation, *New York Times,* both for *A Family's Affairs;* five best works of fiction citation, *New York Times,* 1963, for *Black Cloud, White Cloud;* National Book Award finalist, National Book Committee, 1973, for *Apostles of Light;* National Endowment for the Humanities fellowship, 1976; Mississippi Institute of Arts and Letters Award (literature), 1979, for *The Rock Cried Out,* and 1983, for *A Lifetime Burning;* grants from National Educational Association for *The Rock Cried Out* and *Can't Quit You, Baby;* fiction award, Fellowship of Southern Writers, 1989, for body of work.

WRITINGS:

COLLECTIONS; UNDER PSEUDONYM ELLEN DOUGLAS

Black Cloud, White Cloud: Two Novellas and Two Stories (fairy tales), Houghton, 1963, illustrated by

Elizabeth Wolfe, University Press of Mississippi (Jackson), 1989.

The Magic Carpet, University Press of Mississippi, 1987.

NOVELS; UNDER PSEUDONYM ELLEN DOUGLAS

A Family's Affairs, Houghton, 1962.

Where the Dreams Cross, Houghton, 1968.

Apostles of Light, Houghton, 1973, with an introduction by Elizabeth Spencer, Banner Books (Jackson, MS), 1994.

The Rock Cried Out, Harcourt, 1979.

A Lifetime Burning, Random House, 1982.

Can't Quit You, Baby, Atheneum, 1988.

Also contributor to periodicals, including *Harper's, New York Times Book Review, Esquire, New Yorker,* and *New Republic.*

SIDELIGHTS: Writing as Ellen Douglas, Josephine Ayres Haxton has created a fictional Mississippi county in which many of her novels and stories take place. Called Homochito County, it is the setting for Douglas's fourth novel, *The Rock Cried Out*—a tale that explores the Southern staples of "secret love, unrevealed parentage, miscegenation, hatred, revenge and murder," reported Doris Grumbach in the *Washington Post Book World.* "Some of the elements are gothic," she continued, "but in Ellen Douglas's talented hands the story unfolds slowly, believably, without the piled-up, exclamatory haste of the gothic novel."

The narrator of *The Rock Cried Out* is an ex-hippie who returns to his native Chickasaw Ridge to reconnect with the land and his past. His serenity is shattered, however, when another native son returns and stirs up buried information about a gory car accident that took place several years ago, at the height of the town's civil rights and Ku Klux Klan activities. Jonathan Yardley wrote in the *New York Times Book Review* that it is Douglas's "admirably sensitive treatment" of "the corrosive effect upon whites and their families of massive, violent reaction to the civil-rights movement . . . that gives *The Rock Cried Out* its true distinction." Yardley further explained that "the author does not present this as an apology; it's an attempt, to me a persuasive one, at explanation."

A *New Yorker* critic noted that in *The Rock Cried Out* "Miss Douglas achieves . . . an illuminating portrait of an exceptionally troubled region and era." Grumbach concurred, calling the book "a valuable and impressive fictional portrait. Here we are brought to know, poignantly, a time, a young man's loss of innocence, a civilization's endurance despite the menace of outside forces and, most of all, a place," she added. And Yardley concluded: "Miss Douglas knows her fellow Mississippians well, and her exploration of their hearts and lives is at once passionate and clinical. She will have nothing of evasions and deceptions; she forces all of her characters to confront the legacy of their past head-on. She writes very well and thinks very clearly. *The Rock Cried Out* is powerful and disturbing. It should secure Ellen Douglas's place in the literature of the South."

In *A Lifetime Burning* Douglas takes a departure from her Southern narratives, presenting her fifth novel in the form of a diary of a sixty-two-year-old Southern woman—a literature professor named Corinne—who bitterly tries to make sense of her life. Corinne's discovery of her husband's love affair has forced a lifetime of past hurts and confusions to resurface; she professes to write the diary for the illumination of her grown children, but her real need is to piece together an existence that holds meaning for her. Susan Isaacs, writing in the *New York Times Book Review,* observed that "Corinne is engaging and credibly drawn. Because she is so intelligent and literate, Corinne can express her hurt eloquently. . . . It is fascinating to watch Corinne expose herself as she peels off layers of lies and facile explanation."

Because the diary shifts back and forth between dream and reality, invention and confession, the reader can never be sure of the "truth" of Corinne's revelations. "Lies, distortions, deceptions, evasions—these are essential to the maintenance of the delicate fabric of which family and society are made," explained Yardley in a second *Washington Post Book World* review. He continued: "This, as I interpret it, is the central theme of *A Lifetime Burning:* we are separate beings and cannot be otherwise, we are mysteries to each other and will always be. In order to keep the structure of our lives intact, it is necessary to withhold the full truth: we invent ourselves for others—and, perhaps, for ourselves." The critic deemed the book "a splendid piece of writing . . . [Douglas's] finest novel." Expressing similar praise, Isaacs stated that, while the book has "too many literary" moments when "technique overpower[s] characterization," it "is for the most part a beautifully constructed work of fiction." She added that "Ellen Douglas has all the qualities a reader could ask of a novelist: depth, emotional range, wit, sensitivity and the gift of language. *A Lifetime Burning* is a fine showcase for her talents."

As daunting as it was to follow such critically-acclaimed novels as *The Rock Cried Out* and *A Lifetime Burning,* Douglas managed to win over the critics again with *Can't Quit You, Baby.* It is the story of two middle-aged women: Cornelia, a deaf, privileged white woman, and Julia, her black servant of fifteen years. Cornelia learns about Julia's horrific past, which brings up her own memories of crisis. When tragedy affects both women, their roles change and their relationship deepens. Sharon Sloan Fiffer commented in *Chicago Tribune:* "Douglas has used a distinctive style in this book, injecting the narrator's character into the text and asking questions of the reader—questions that serve the Brechtian purpose of jolting the reader out of his or her private world. . . . It is a risky technique, but one that Ellen Douglas handles with great skill. *Can't Quit You, Baby,* her sixth novel, is a wonder." In his review for *New York Times Book Review,* Alfred Uhry connected this novel with the tradition of Southern literature. He wrote, "Faulkner, O'Connor, McCullers, Welty and almost all the writers of the region have dealt with white versus black. . . . One of the more interesting and subtle war zones is the middle-class white kitchen. Here the hostilities are often camouflaged by shared household chores and idle gossip. . . . Such a dance is at the heart of the author's sad and deeply felt new novel, *Can't Quit You, Baby,* her first in six years." Uhry concluded that the novel is "a haunting examination of the lives of two memorable women." It is not, however, a book intended for a strictly female audience, as Carolyn See of *Los Angeles Times Book Review* noted: "Cornelia's downfall is a direct result of her self-imposed self-deception. For Julia it is more of the same, a senseless disaster that finally forces her family to call upon their white folks. The hatred that blazes out from this transaction is brilliantly conceived, but so is the love, and makes this far more than just a women's novel."

BIOGRAPHICAL/CRITICAL SOURCES:

BOOKS

Contemporary Novelists, 6th edition, St. James Press, 1996.

PERIODICALS

Esquire, May, 1973.
Los Angeles Times Book Review, July 11, 1988.
New York Times Book Review, February 18, 1973; September 23, 1979; November 25, 1979; October 31, 1982; July 10, 1988.
New Yorker, March 3, 1973; October 8, 1979.
Newsweek, March 5, 1973.
Observer (London), June 13, 1983.
Time, April 15, 1974.
Times Literary Supplement, July 20, 1990.
Tribune Books (Chicago), November 6, 1988.
Washington Post Book World, September 9, 1979; December 9, 1979; October 31, 1982; September 9, 1990.*

* * *

HAYAKAWA, S(amuel) I(chiye) 1906-1992

PERSONAL: Born July 18, 1906, in Vancouver, British Columbia, Canada; died of a stroke, February 27, 1992, in Greenbrae, CA; naturalized U.S. citizen; son of Ichiro (an import-export merchant) and Tora (Isono) Hayakawa; married Margedant Peters, May 29, 1937; children: Alan, Mark, Wynne. *Education:* University of Manitoba, B.A., 1927; McGill University, M.A., 1928; University of Wisconsin, Ph.D., 1935. *Politics:* Republican. *Avocational interests:* Fishing, scuba diving, fencing, tap dancing, Japanese cooking, collecting jazz records, African sculpture, and Chinese ceramics.

CAREER: University of Wisconsin, Madison, assistant instructor in English, 1930-36, instructor in English in English Extension Division, 1936-39; Armour Institute (now Illinois Institute of Technology), Chicago, IL, instructor, 1939-40, assistant professor, 1940-42, associate professor of English, 1942-47; University of Chicago, Chicago, IL, lecturer in University College, 1950-55; San Francisco State College (now San Francisco State University), San Francisco, CA, professor of English, 1955-68, acting president, 1968-69, president, 1969-73, president emeritus, 1973-92; U.S. Senate, Washington, DC, senator from California, 1977-83, served on Senate Committee on Agriculture, Nutrition, and Forestry, Senate Budget and Human Resources Committee, Senate Foreign Relations Committee, and Senate Small Business Committee. Served on U.S. Senate Republican Policy Committee and National Republican Senatorial Committee. Certified psychologist in California, 1959. Claude Bernard Lecturer at Institute of Experimental Medicine and Surgery, University of Montreal, 1959; Alfred P. Sloan Visiting Professor, Menninger School of Psychiatry, 1961. Columnist, Register & Tribune syndicate, 1970-76; former supervisor of editorial board, Funk & Wagnalls Standard Dictionaries.

MEMBER: International Society for General Semantics (president, 1949-50), American Association for the Advancement of Science (fellow), American Psychological Association (fellow), American Sociological Association, American Anthropological Association, Modern Language Association of America, American Dialect Society, National Council of Teachers of English, U.S. English, Consumers Union of the United States (director, 1953-55), Royal Society of Arts, Society for the Psychological Study of Social Issues, Institute of Jazz Studies (director), Press and Union League (San Francisco), Pannonia Athletic Club, Bohemian Club.

AWARDS, HONORS: D.F.A., California College of Arts and Crafts, 1956; Claude Bernard Medal for Experimental Medicine and Surgery, University of Montreal, 1959; Litt.D., Grinnell College, 1967; L.H.D., Pepperdine University, 1972; LL.D., The Citadel, 1972.

WRITINGS:

(Editor with Howard Mumford Jones) *Oliver Wendell Holmes: Representative Selections,* American Book Co., 1939.

Language in Action: A Guide to Accurate Thinking (Book-of-the-Month Club selection), Harcourt, 1941, completely revised edition published as *Language in Thought and Action* (with Basil H. Pillard), Harcourt, 1949, 4th edition (with Arthur Asa Berger and Arthur Chandler), 1978, with Alan R. Hayakawa, with an introduction by Robert MacNeil, Harcourt, 1990.

(Contributor) *Middle English Dictionary,* University of Michigan Press, 1952.

(Editor) *Language, Meaning, and Maturity: Selections from "ETC: A Review of General Semantics," 1943-53* (also see below), Harper, 1954.

(Editor) *Our Language and Our World: Selections from "ETC: A Review of General Semantics," 1953-58* (also see below), Harper, 1959.

Symbol, Status, and Personality, Harcourt, 1963.

(Editor and author of foreword) *The Use and Misuse of Language: Selections from "ETC: A Review of General Semantics"* (contains *Language, Meaning, and Maturity* and *Our Language and Our World*), Fawcett, 1964.

(Editor) *Funk & Wagnalls Modern Guide to Synonyms and Related Words,* Funk, 1968, published as *Reader's Digest Use the Right Word: A Modern Guide to Synonyms and Related Words,* Reader's Digest Association, 1968, new edition published in England as *Cassell's Modern Guide to Synonyms and Related Words,* Cassells, 1971.

Modern Guide to Synonyms and Related Words, Verlag Darmstaedter Blatter Schwartz, 1969.

Quotations from Chairman S. I. Hayakawa, [San Francisco], 1969.

(Editor with William Dresser) *Dimensions of Meaning,* Bobbs-Merrill, 1970.

Through the Communication Barrier: On Speaking, Listening, and Understanding, edited by Arthur Chandler, Harper, 1979.

Indonesia, Thailand, the Philippines, and Taiwan: A Report to the Committee on Foreign Relations, United States Senate, U.S. Government Printing Office (Washington, DC), 1980.

United States Relations with ASEAN (Thailand, Indonesia, Malaysia, Singapore, and the Philippines), Hong Kong, and Laos: A Report to the Committee on Foreign Relations, United States Senate, U.S. Government Printing Office, 1982.

Africa Revisited: A Report to the Committee on Foreign Relations, United States Senate, U.S. Government Printing Office, 1982.

Choose the Right Word: A Modern Guide to Synonyms, Perennial Library, 1987.

SOUND RECORDINGS

On Defining the Self, Big Sur Recordings, 1963.

The Conditions of Creativity, Big Sur Recordings, 1963.

The Fully Functioning Personality, Big Sur Recordings, 1964.

Language: Key to Human Understanding, Jeffrey Norton, 1974.

OTHER

Contributor to *New Republic, Harper's, Poetry, Sewanee Review,* and other periodicals. Columnist for *Defender* (Chicago), 1942-47; founder and editor, *ETC: A Review of General Semantics,* 1943-70.

SIDELIGHTS: As a scholar, university administrator, senator, and proponent of the English language, S. I. Hayakawa demonstrated an ability to deal with problems directly and decisively, but more significantly, as former U.S. President Ronald Reagan suggested in *Esquire,* he revealed his "unique ability to communicate." Hayakawa first caught public attention in 1941 with the publication of his best seller, *Language in Action: A Guide to Accurate Thinking,* a study of semantics, or meaning in language. "In his . . . book," related Fred C. Kelly in the *Saturday Review of Literature,* "Hayakawa gives many examples of the human tendency to confuse mere words with objects." For instance, Kelly added: "When we tackle social problems, we're likely to follow signal words or labels and disregard modifying circumstances. We act as if any word or combination of words that sounds true *must* be true." The result, Hayakawa points out in his book, is that "undue regard for words makes us tend to permit words to act as barriers between us and reality instead of as guides to reality."

In offering his views on language in action, wrote Otis Ferguson in the *New Republic,* Hayakawa "speaks with patience and a ready intelligence of the function of language, its use and misuse, the laws of double-intention and result by which it may and should be analyzed." "The book is not devoted to explaining words with more words," observed Kelly, "but to showing how human beings react, sometimes sanely, sometimes unsanely, both to the words they hear and to the words they use themselves." In his review, written just before the United States entry into World War II, Kelly commented that "Hayakawa makes it clear that ability to recognize truth—or to recognize a lie—when one hears it or sees it, is of vital importance in this day of propaganda and censorship."

Hayakawa made extensive revisions to *Language in Action* and the new edition was published in 1949 as *Language in Thought and Action.* As Stuart Chase explains in the *Nation,* semanticists hypothesize "that many of the difficulties in which *homo sapiens* finds himself today are not due to human cussedness but to failure clearly to see his world. The language he uses creates entities out there which are not there, and vice versa." In presenting this study to the general reader, "Hayakawa examines each of these difficulties with wit and profundity, bringing to bear the latest findings of semantics, and of the sciences upon which it relies. He has produced perhaps the best book yet on the whole subject, and one of the most readable," concluded Chase.

Hayakawa's concern with the capacity of language to obscure reality is expressed in another book, *Through the Communication Barrier: On Speaking, Listening, and Understanding.* "The central thrust of these essays is the explanation of the way we use and respond to language and how what we use shapes our lives and our beliefs," observed Thomas A. Wassmer in *Best Sellers.* And, added the reviewer: "Each one of these essays is short and packed with insights." *Library Journal* contributor Alice Davison found them "engaging and unpretentious . . . expressing very broad, commonsense views about human interaction." In its entirety, the book "provides a strong testament to Hayakawa's philosophy that a better understanding of our reactions to language would lead to many fewer misunderstandings in the world," noted Reagan in his *Esquire* review. "This is an excellent book," maintained Wassmer, "provocative and stimulating in small doses or large."

Aside from his scholarly and popular writings, Hayakawa made his name known in the world of politics and policy making. He entered the public arena during the turbulent fall of 1968 when he was named president of San Francisco State College. Student demands had forced the resignations of his two predecessors and rioting had forced the school's closing. Hayakawa stood firm in the face of militant threats. By meeting reasonable student demands while retaining administrative authority, he succeeded in reopening the college. "He was enshrined forever as a man who dared stand up to the anarchy that seemed to be engulfing the nation," wrote Leroy Aarons in *People.*

Hayakawa resigned from San Francisco State College in 1973 to run for the United States Senate, but a California election regulation postponed his bid until the 1976 election. He earned the Republican nomination over two opponents, then defeated incumbent John V. Tunney in a close race. As a senator, Hayakawa quickly drew attention, both for his unorthodox style and for his stance on certain issues. He told *People*'s reporter: "I always seem to have some little area, whether it is wearing a tam-o'shanter, riding a motorcycle or carrying a walking stick, that says to myself and others, 'I am an individual.' " As a legislator, wrote Aarons, he saw "himself as a moral philosopher on questions of government and social structure."

He was critical of welfare, unionism, and affirmative action. He explained to Aarons: "If you're ignorant and lazy and can't do arithmetic and then sit around and complain that there are no opportunities, you're not seeing the world as it really is." His interests were education, youth labor, and Africa. "Sensing a vacuum in knowledge about Africa in the Senate," noted Aarons, "Hayakawa wangled a 12-day excursion to Rhodesia, South Africa, Botswana and Kenya. . . . [He] interviewed government and rebel leaders and returned full of information and prescriptions for policy changes."

Upon his retirement from the Senate in 1982, Hayakawa campaigned to make English the official language of the United States. As William F. Buckley Jr. noted in the *National Review,* the constitutional amendment the former senator has proposed reads: "1) The English language shall be the official language of the United States. 2) Neither the United States nor any State shall make or enforce any law which requires the use of any language other than English. . . ." His political action group, U.S. English, actively pursued the repeal of a portion of the Votings Rights Act that calls for non-English ballots in some areas. "We can speak any language we want at the dinner table," Hayakawa was quoted in a *Newsweek* report, "but English is the language of public discourses, of the marketplace and of the voting booth." In an interview in *Macleans,* he pointed to the legal precedents: "Do not forget that the naturalization laws of the United States require that you learn to read, write and speak English in ordinary usage. That requirement is right there in the law." And, added Hayakawa, rather than excluding other cultures, having English as the common language of all Americans has in the past enriched culture. He said in the interview, "Because we have this line of communication with our [English] language, we absorb what every other culture brings to our civilization."

BIOGRAPHICAL/CRITICAL SOURCES:

PERIODICALS

Best Sellers, August, 1979.
Esquire, April 24, 1979.
Library Journal, April 1, 1979.
Macleans, October 8, 1984.
Nation, January 3, 1942; November 12, 1949.
National Review, June 26, 1981.
New Republic, December 1, 1941.
Newsweek, January 20, 1975; June 7, 1976; November 15, 1976; January 9, 1984.
People, October 2, 1978.
Saturday Review of Literature, November 22, 1941.
Time, June 21, 1976.

OBITUARIES:

BOOKS

Who's Who in America, 46th edition, Marquis, 1990.

PERIODICALS

Chicago Tribune, February 28, 1992, section 1, p. 11; March 1, 1992, section 2, p. 6.
Detroit Free Press, February 28, 1992, p. B4.
Los Angeles Times, February 28, 1992, p. A1.
New York Times, February 28, 1992, p. B6.
Times (London), February 29, 1992, p. 15.
Washington Post, February 28, 1992, p. D4.*

HAYWOOD, Carolyn 1898- 1990

PERSONAL: Born January 3, 1898, in Philadelphia, PA; died of a stroke, January 11, 1990, in Philadelphia, PA; daughter of Charles and Mary Emma (Cook) Haywood. *Education:* Attended Pennsylvania Academy of the Fine Arts.

CAREER: Writer, illustrator, and portrait and mural painter. Teacher at Friends Central School, Philadelphia, PA; assistant in studio of Violet Oakley.

MEMBER: Pennsylvania Academy of the Fine Arts (fellow), Philadelphia Water Color Club.

AWARDS, HONORS: Boys' Clubs of America Junior Book Award, 1956, for *Eddie and His Big Deals;* named Distinguished Daughter of Pennsylvania, by governor, 1967; Utah children's Book Award, 1981.

WRITINGS:

SELF-ILLUSTRATED JUVENILES

"B" Is for Betsy, Harcourt, 1939
Two and Two Are Four, Harcourt, 1940.
Betsy and Billy, Harcourt,.
Primrose Day, Harcourt, 1942.
Back to School with Betsy, Harcourt, 1943.
Here's a Penny, Harcourt,.
Betsy and the Boys, Harcourt, 1945.
Penny and Peter, Harcourt.
Little Eddie, Morrow.
Penny Goes to Camp, Morrow, 1948
Eddie and the Fire Engine, Morrow, 1949, illustrated by Betsy Lewin, Beech Tree Books, 1992.
Betsy's Little Star, Morrow, 1950.
Eddie and Gardenia, Morrow, 1951
The Mixed-Up Twins, Morrow, 1952.
Eddie's Pay Dirt, Morrow, 1953.
Betsy and the Circus, Morrow, 1954.
Eddie and His Big Deals, Morrow, 1955.
Betsy's Busy Summer, Morrow, 1956.
Eddie Makes Music, Morrow, 1957.
Betsy's Winterhouse, Morrow, 1958.
Eddie and Louella, Morrow, 1959.
Annie Pat and Eddie, Morrow, 1960.
Snowbound with Betsy, Morrow, 1962.
Here Comes the Bus, Morrow, 1963.
Eddie's Green Thumb, Morrow, 1964.
Robert Rows the River, Morrow, 1965.
Eddie, the Dog Holder, Morrow, 1966.
Betsy and Mr. Kilpatrick, Morrow, 1967.
Ever-Ready Eddie, Morrow, 1968.
Taffy and Melissa Molasses, Morrow, 1969.

Merry Christmas from Betsy, Morrow, 1970.
Eddie's Happenings, Morrow, 1971.
Away Went the Balloons, Morrow, 1973.
"C" Is for Cupcake, Morrow, 1974.
Eddie's Valuable Property, Morrow, 1975.

JUVENILES

A Christmas Fantasy, illustrations by Glenys and Victor Ambrus, Morrow, 1972.
A Valentine Fantasy, illustrations by G. and V. Ambrus, Morrow, 1976.
Betsy's Play School, illustrations by James Griffin, Morrow, 1977.
Eddie's Menagerie, illustrations by Ingrid Fetz, Morrow, 1978.
The King's Monster, illustrations by V. Ambrus, Morrow, 1980.
Halloween Treats, illustrations by Victoria de Larrea, Morrow, 1981.
Santa Claus Forever, illustrations by V. Ambrus, Morrow, 1982.
Make a Joyful Noise: Bible Verses for Children, illustrations by Lane Yerkes, Westminster, 1983.
Happy Birthday from Carolyn Haywood, illustrations by Wendy Watson, Morrow, 1984.
Summer Fun, illustrations by Julie Durrell, Morrow, 1986.
How the Reindeer Saved Santa, illustrated by Victor Ambrus, Morrow (New York City), 1986.
Hello, Star, illustrated by Julie Durrell, Morrow, 1987.
Eddie's Friend Boodles, illustrations by Catherine Stock, Morrow, 1991.

OTHER

Also illustrator and calligrapher of *Book of Honor,* a collection of the biographies of Pennsylvania women. Contributor to *Jack and Jill.*

ADAPTATIONS: The audio cassette version of *Santa Claus Forever* was produced by Random House in 1985.

SIDELIGHTS: An educator, artist, illustrator, and writer, Carolyn Haywood was best known for her series of children's books about the characters Betsy and Eddie, most of which she illustrated herself. Betsy and Eddie are average children who are dealing with problems that readers themselves might have, though the problems are complex enough to give the stories a great deal of interesting action. The first book of the series, *"B" Is for Betsy,* about the little girl's first year of school, was published in 1939. The lengthy series covers many entertaining aspects of a little girl's childhood, while the "Eddie" series describes the adventures of a growing boy. In *Eddie's Menagerie,* ten-year-old Eddie Wilson lands a job as a volunteer store detective at a pet shop. A *Booklist* reviewer wrote that "Haywood's warm, humorous style hits the mark, once again, as an enjoyable story children can relate to."

Merry Christmas from Betsy combines two new Christmas episodes with eight other Christmas chapters from earlier Betsy books by Haywood. A *Center for Children's Books Bulletin* reviewer noted that "as always, the simplicity and realism of Miss Haywood's writing are appealing." Although not part of the series, another Christmas book, *Santa Claus Forever,* met with critical acclaim. In this seasonal tale, Santa Claus becomes disenchanted with his job after a series of freak accidents such as a chimney brick falling and hitting him, and his suit getting singed in someone's fireplace. But when he sees the man who proposes to replace him and hears his dubious plans for improvements, Santa changes his mind about retiring. As a reviewer for *Bulletin of the Center for Children's Books* put it, "The humor and sentiment of pictures and story, and the happy solution to a problem should make this Christmas tale a great favorite with the read-aloud audience."

Critics cite Haywood's talent for capturing the everyday events of childhood as the reason for her enduring popularity. In particular, Anne Pellowski of *Horn Book* praised the author's "uncanny ability in observing children and somehow in getting their speech, their actions, and their interactions expressed in a simple, natural style." Haywood's books have been translated into Norwegian, French, German, and Japanese, and her works are represented in the Pennsylvania Academy of Fine Arts' permanent collection.

BIOGRAPHICAL/CRITICAL SOURCES:

BOOKS

Children's Literature Review, Volume 22, Gale, 1991.
Hopkins, Lee Bennett, *More Books by More People,* Citation, 1974.
Twentieth-Century Children's Writers, 4th edition, St. James Press, 1995.

PERIODICALS

Booklist, September 15, 1978.
Bulletin of the Center for Children's Books, October, 1983.
Center for Children's Books Bulletin, November, 1970.
Christian Science Monitor, May 2, 1973.

Horn Book, January-December, 1947; January-December, 1948; December, 1962; December, 1963; February, 1965; April, 1973.

OBITUARIES:

PERIODICALS

New York Times, January 12, 1990.
Washington Post, January 15, 1990.*

* * *

HIBBERD, Jack 1940-

PERSONAL: Born April 12, 1940, in Warracknabeal, Australia; son of James George (a plumber) and Moira (a singer; maiden name, Richardson) Hibberd; married first wife, Jocelyn, February 8, 1969 (divorced, 1976); married Evelyn Krape (an actress and singer), January 3, 1978; children: (first marriage) Lillian Margaret, James Benjamin; (second marriage) Samuel Spike Mendel. *Education:* University of Melbourne, M.B.B.S., 1964.

ADDRESSES: Home—87 Turner St., Abbotsford, Victoria 3067, Australia. *Agent*—Almost Managing, P.O. Box 34, Carlton, Victoria 3053, Australia.

CAREER: Writer. Physician in general practice in Australia, 1965-66, 1970- 73, 1986—; registrar, St. Vincent's Hospital, Department of Social Medicine, Melbourne, Australia, 1967. Member of Australian Performing Group; Australia Council, member of Theatre Board, 1977-79; Melbourne Writers' Theatre, president, 1984-86.

AWARDS, HONORS: Australia Council fellowships, 1973, 1977, 1981.

WRITINGS:

Brain Rot (also see below), first produced in Carlton, Australia, 1967.
White with Wire Wheels, first produced in Melbourne, Australia, 1970.
(Co-author) *Marvelous Melbourne,* first produced in Melbourne, 1970.
Klag, first produced in Melbourne, 1970.
Customs and Excise, first produced in Carlton, 1970, produced as *Proud Flesh,* 1972.
Aorta, first produced in Melbourne, 1971.
Flesh, first produced in Carlton, 1972.
Women! (adaptation of a play by Aristophanes), first produced in Carlton, 1972.
A Stretch of the Imagination (first produced in Carlton, 1972), Currency Press, 1973.
Captain Midnight VC (first produced in Carlton, 1973); music by Lorraine Milne, foreword by Humphrey McQueen, Yackandandah, 1984.
The Les Darcy Show (first produced in Adelaide, Australia, 1973; also see below), Scribe, 1979.
The Architect and the Emperor of Assyria (adaptation of a play by Fernando Arrabel), first produced in Carlton, 1974.
Dimboola: A Wedding Reception Play (also see below; first produced in Carlton; bound with *The Last of the Knucklemen*), Penguin, 1974.
Peggy Sue (first produced in Carlton, 1974; revised version produced in Melbourne, 1983), Yackandandah, 1982.
A Toast to Melba (also see below), first produced in Adelaide, Australia, 1976.
Three Popular Plays (contains *One of Nature's Gentlemen, A Toast to Melba,* and *The Les Darcy Show*), Outback Press, 1976.
The Overcoat (adaptation of a story by Nikolai Gogol), first produced in Carlton, 1976.
(Translator) Charles Baudelaire, *Le Vin des amants: Poems from Baudelaire,* Gryphon Books, 1977.
Mothballs, first produced in Melbourne, 1981.
(With Garrie Hutchinson) *The Barracker's Bible,* illustrated by Noel Counihan and Barry Dickens, McPhee Gribble (Melbourne), 1983.
(With John Timlin) *Goodbye Ted,* Yackandandah, 1983.
Liquid Amber (also see below), first produced in Melbourne, 1984.
A Country Quinella with Damboola (includes *Liquid Amber*) Penguin, 1984.
Squibs (a collection of microplays from *Brain Rot* and short plays; includes *Asian Oranges, A League of Nations, The Three Sisters* [a parody of Anton Chekhov's story of the same title], and *Death of a Traveller* [a parody of Arthur Miller's play *Death of a Salesman*]), Phoenix (Brisbane, Australia), 1984.
(Adapter) Guy de Maupassant, *Odyssey of a Prostitute* (first produced in Melbourne, Australia, 1984), published in *Outrider,* Volume 2, number 1, 1985.
Memoirs of an Old Bastard: Being a Portrait of a City, an Epicurean Chronicle, Fantasia and Search, McPhee Gribble, 1989.
Duets (plays; contains *The Old School Tie* and *Glycerine Tears* [also see below]), Yackandandah, 1989.
The Life of Riley, Heinemann (Australia), 1990.
Perdita, McPhee Gribble, 1992.

Dimboola [and] *Liquid Amber* (revised versions), Penguin (Australia), 1994.

Also author of unpublished and unproduced plays, including *The Last Days of Epic J. Remorse,* 1969; *A Man of Many Parts,* 1980; *Smash Hit!,* 1980, *Medical Follies,* 1993, *Trios,* 1993, and *Hotel Paradiso, 1956,* 1994. Work represented in anthologies, including *Buzo, Hibberd, Romeril: Four Australian Plays* (includes *White with Wire Wheels* and *Who*), Penguin, 1970. Works published in periodicals include: *Memoirs of a Carlton Bohemian,* published in *Meanjin 3,* 1977; *Sin,* 1978, and *Glycerine Tears* and *Malarky Barks,* 1982, all published in *Meanjin 4; Lavender Bags,* published in *Aspect,* number 25, 1982; and *Death Warmed Up,* published in *Scripsi,* Volume 2, number 4, 1984. Editor of special performing arts edition of *Meanjin 4,* 1984. Author of wine column for *Age,* 1986—.

Hibberd's manuscripts are housed in the Australian Collection, Australian National Library, Canberra, Australian Capital Territory; Melbourne University Archives; La Trobe Library, Melbourne; and Eunice Hanger Collection, Fryer Library, University of Queensland.

SIDELIGHTS: As a playwright, Jack Hibberd's philosophy is that the stage provides a distinct experience of communal celebration, and is also a metaphor for life itself. He once told *CA:* "My plays are non-autobiographical and generally anti-naturalistic. My ambition is to write bizarre comedies that depict the sad, mad paradoxes of contemporary existence within and without Australia. Major influences on my work are vaudeville and popular demotic comedy, the theatre of the absurd, Bertolt Brecht, German expressionism, Baudelaire, and the French symbolists." Because of his refusal to write plays since 1984 (in protest of the envy and discrimination that he feels are dominating theater), his popularity in Australia remains strong.

Hibberd's early works were explorations for the playwright to find his own voice and style. In *Who?,* Hibberd applied the influences of Pinter and Beckett to a tribal Australian setting. The theme is violence as it is directed at someone who leaves the tribe, at women, and at attempted refinements of the crude tribal lifestyle. The same themes are present in his first full-length play, *White with Wire Wheels.* According to Paul McGillick of *Contemporary Dramatists, A Stretch of the Imagination* is Hibberd's most important early work. It is a monodrama, a play performed by one person in which the character reenacts his or her life story for his or her own edification, not the audience's. In *A Stretch of the Imagination,* this character is Monk O'Neill, a reclusive man living in Australia's outback. O'Neill considers the nature of existential alienation and how it results in the worst of humanity, ranging from soccer hooligans to Hitler. Because of the universality of this play, it has been performed worldwide, despite the difficulties of translating the Australian cultural references and dialect. Also enjoyed by international audiences is *Dimboola,* the result of Hibberd's desire to create a form that involves audience participation. Such a form manifests his belief in theater as a social celebration. The play is a wedding reception, and is even performed in a reception hall instead of a theater. The audience comprises the guests, sitting at tables, actually being served food and drink. The play considers the rituals of weddings, comparing Catholic and Presbyterian traditions.

As an established playwright, Hibberd has adapted the work of other writers he admires. He refers to his adaptation of Nikolai Gogol's *The Overcoat* as "a theatrical somersault and half-pike from the springboard of Gogol's insane prose." *Odyssey of a Prostitute* is one of Hibberd's seven monodramas, and according to McGillick, his best play after *A Stretch of the Imagination.* It is an adaptation of a Maupassant story about a country girl forced to turn to prostitution, described by McGillick as "essentially a farce with a dark underbelly, celebrating the theatre as entertainment but seeing it also as a metaphor for a menacingly unpredictable universe." As a mature writer, Hibberd has moved toward themes that are less Australian in tone and style. He applies more universal settings and uses the Australian vernacular not as his characters' means of communication, but as a way of differentiating a character. Hibberd remarked to *CA* in 1988: "Over the last ten years I have been less concerned to write specifically of Australian experience but more sweepingly of human conduct in a context of comico-tragic formal experiment, especially in my monodramas and other theatrical sorties into the actor-audience farce."

BIOGRAPHICAL/CRITICAL SOURCES:

BOOKS

Contemporary Australian Drama, Currency Press, 1981.

Contemporary Dramatists, 5th edition, St. James press, 1993.

Fitzpatrick, Peter, *After the Doll,* Edward Arnold (London), 1979.

McGillick, Paul, *Jack Hibberd,* Rodopi, 1988.

PERIODICALS

Quadrant, March, 1979.*

* * *

HILD, Jack
See PRESTON, John

* * *

HILL, Douglas (Arthur) 1935-
(Martin Hillman)

PERSONAL: Born April 6, 1935, in Brandon, Manitoba, Canada; son of William (a locomotive engineer) and Cora (a nurse; maiden name, Smith) Hill; married Gail Robinson (a poet and author), April 8, 1958 (divorced, 1978); children: Michael Julian. *Education:* University of Saskatchewan, B.A. (with honors), 1957; University of Toronto, graduate study, 1957-59.

ADDRESSES: Home—Flat 2, 16 Haslemere Rd., London N8 9QX, England. *Agent*—Bolt & Watson, 8-12 Old Queen Street, Storey's Gate, London SW1H 9HP, England.

CAREER: Freelance writer, 1959—; Aldus Books Ltd., London, England, editor, 1962-64. Science fiction adviser to Rupert Hart-Davis, 1966-68, Mayflower Books, 1969-71, J. M. Dent & Sons, 1972-74, and to Pan Books, 1974-80.

MEMBER: Writers Guild of Great Britain, British Science Fiction Association.

AWARDS, HONORS: Received grants from the Canada Council of Arts, 1966, 1968, 1969, and 1970; Parents' Choice Award, 1987, for *Blade of the Poisoner.*

WRITINGS:

(With Pat Williams) *The Supernatural,* Hawthorn, 1965.
The Peasants' Revolt, Jackdaw, 1966.
(Editor) *The Way of the Werewolf,* Panther, 1966.
(Editor, and contributor under pseudonym Martin Hillman) *Window on the Future* (anthology), Hart-Davis, 1966.
The Opening of the Canadian West, John Day, 1967.
(Editor) *The Devil His Due* (anthology), Hart-Davis, 1967.
John Keats, Morgan-Grampion, 1968.
Magic and Superstition, Hamlyn, 1968.
Regency London, Macdonald, 1969.
Georgian London, Macdonald, 1970.
Return from the Dead, Macdonald, 1970.
(Under pseudonym Martin Hillman) *Bridging a Continent,* Aldus, 1971.
(Editor, and contributor under pseudonym Martin Hillman) *Warlocks and Warriors* (anthology), Mayflower, 1971.
Fortune Telling, Hamlyn, 1972.
The Scots to Canada, Gentry, 1972.
The Comet, Wildwood House, 1973.
Northern Ireland, Cambridge University Press, 1974.
(With others) *Witchcraft, Magic, and the Supernatural,* Octopus, 1974.
(With wife, Gail Robinson Hill) *Coyote the Trickster,* Chatto & Windus, 1975.
The English to New England, Gentry, 1975.
(Editor) *The Shape of Sex to Come* (anthology), Pan Books, 1975.
The Exploits of Hercules, Piccolo, 1977.
(Editor) *"Tribune" 40* (anthology), Quartet, 1977.
Fortune Telling, Hamlyn, 1978.
Galactic Warlord, Atheneum (New York City, 1980.
The Illustrated Faerie Queen (prose abridgement), Newsweek Books, 1980.
Alien Worlds (anthology), Heinemann, 1981.
Deathwing over Veynaa, Atheneum, 1981.
Day of the Starwind, Atheneum, 1981.
Young Legionary: The Earlier Adventures of Keill Randor, V. Gollancz (London), 1982.
Planet of the Warlord, Atheneum, 1982.
The Huntsman, Atheneum, 1982.
Have Your Own Extraterrestrial Adventure, Sparrow, 1983.
Warriors of the Wasteland, Atheneum, 1983.
Alien Citadel, Atheneum, 1984.
Exiles of ColSec, Atheneum, 1984.
ColSec Rebellion, Atheneum, 1985.
The Caves of Klydor, Atheneum, 1985.
How Jennifer (and Speckle) Saved the Earth, illustrated by Andre Amstutz, Heinemann, 1986.
(Editor) *Planetfall,* Oxford University Press, 1986.
Blade of the Poisoner, M.K. McElderry Books (New York City), 1987.
Goblin Party, illustrated by Paul Demayer, Gollancz, 1988.
Master of Fiends, M.K. McElderry Books, 1988.
The Fraxilly Fracas, Gollancz, 1989.
The Moon Monsters, illustrated by Jeremy Ford, Barron's (New York City), 1989.
The Colloghi Conspiracy, Gollancz, 1990.

Penelope's Pendant, illustrated by Annabel Spenceley, Pan-Macmillan, 1990; illustrated by Steve Johnson, Doubleday, 1990.
Unicorn Dream, Heinemann, 1992.
The Lightless Dome, Pan, 1993.
The Voyage of Mudjack, Methuen, 1993.
The Leafless Forest, Pan, 1994.
The World of the Stiks, Transworld, 1994.
Penelope's Protest, Pan, 1994.
(Editor) *The Baked Apple?: Metropolitan New York in the Greenhouse,* New York Academy of Sciences (New York City), 1996.
Witches and Magic-Makers, photographs by Alex Wilson, Knopf (New York City), 1997.

Also author of *Penelope's Peril,* 1995, and *Galaxy's Edge,* 1996. Poems represented in anthologies, including *Poetmeat Anthology of British Poetry,* edited by Dave Cunliffe, Screeches Publications, 1965; *Young British Poets,* edited by Jeremy Robson, Poesie Vivante (Geneva), 1967; and *Poems from Poetry and Jazz in Concert,* edited by Robson, Souvenir Press, 1969. Contributor of poems, book reviews, and articles to periodicals, including *Ambit, Akros, Adam International Review, Canadian Forum, Encounter, Poetry Review, New Statesman, New Worlds, Guardian, Books and Bookmen, Mayfair, Times Literary Supplement,* and *Toronto Star.* Regular columnist and literary editor of *Tribune* (London), 1971—.

SIDELIGHTS: Douglas Hill's range of writing includes folklore, occultism, science, science fiction for adults and young people, and work as both an editor and publisher's consultant. Discussing the pressures of his work, Hill told *CA:* "Diversity seems the keynote—and now extending it into different sorts of children's fiction, science fiction, and so on, while maintaining a considerable output of literary journalism, nonfiction articles, and occasional nonfiction books. [It] often seems [I work] an eight-day week and a twenty-five-hour day, but it's still the best way to live and to earn a living that I know."

Hill's first book, *The Supernatural* (1965), initiated a long line of nonfiction books on history, the supernatural, popular folklore, literary biography, and other topics. During the 1970s, Hill spent more time writing science fiction. Like many science-fiction writers, Hill's fascination with the genre began in childhood when he was a self-proclaimed addict of Buck Rogers, Flash Gordon, and other science-fiction heroes of the time. "When I began writing SF for young readers—after some ten years and nearly twenty books of adult nonfiction—I felt it had to be a simple enough process," Hill noted in *The Writer.* "I could clearly remember what I liked reading when I was twelve or thirteen, so I set out to write along those lines." He began writing space adventures because "as a kid I had liked reading about adventures on other worlds; I'd had an idea for an interplanetary hero with a particular problem and purpose; and I was encouraged by the fact that television and films were creating a huge audience for space adventure, even in 1977 B.S.W. (Before Star Wars)."

The battle of good versus evil, as well as fast action and strong central characters, are trademarks of Hill's science fiction, which includes two trilogies. Hill's "Huntsman" trilogy comprises *The Huntsman, Warriors of the Wasteland,* and *Alien Citadel.* In this trilogy, Hill's hero, Finn, leads the fight against an alien dictatorship, the Slavers, who rule the world after a holocaust and are determined to destroy the remains of humanity left on Earth. The "ColSec" trilogy (*Exiles of ColSec, The Caves of Klydor,* and *ColSec Rebellion*) tells the story of a group of five young people from a chaotic, oppressed future Earth who try to establish a colony on the planet of Klydor. In the conclusion of the trilogy, the governors of Earth who sent the young people to Klydor (in hopes they would not survive) arrive for an inspection and find, to their disbelief, the group very much alive. Allied with Lathan, an explorer supposedly lost in space, the young people strand the governors on the planet and return to Earth to rally a force of rebels and evacuate them to Klydor, a base from which to fight the tyrannous ColSec organization.

Hill has also published poetry. In fact, his first professional sale as a writer was a poem. His verse has been included in several poetry anthologies as well as numerous periodicals. In *Contemporary Poets,* Hill described his dominant themes as "loneliness, fear, the minor and less minor horrors of 20th-century human relationships—with a scattering of love poems, comic poems and exercises in various degrees of human rhetoric."

BIOGRAPHICAL/CRITICAL SOURCES:

BOOKS

Contemporary Poets, St. James Press, 1973.
Twentieth-Century Young Adult Writers, 1st edition, St. James Press, 1994.

PERIODICALS

Magazine of Fantasy and Science Fiction, June, 1967, p. 37.

New Statesman, December 24, 1965, p. 1005; July 15, 1966, p. 101; October 7, 1977, p. 480.

New York Times Book Review, May 22, 1966, p. 6.

Observer, November 21, 1965, p. 26; November 30, 1980, p. 36; November 29, 1981, p. 27; November 28, 1982, p. 31.

Times Literary Supplement, December 30, 1965, p. 1219; December 7, 1967, p. 1177; February 27, 1969, p. 218; May 15, 1969, p. 541; November 20, 1981, p. 1361; April 13, 1984, p. 414.

Writer, January, 1984, p. 15.*

* * *

HILLMAN, Martin
See HILL, Douglas (Arthur)

HUDSON, Michael
See KUBE-MCDOWELL, Michael P(aul)

* * *

INGRAM, Willis J.
See HARRIS, Mark

* * *

INNES, Jean
See SAUNDERS, Jean

* * *

IRWIN, Hadley
See HADLEY, Lee

J

JOHNSON, Mike
See SHARKEY, John Michael

* * *

JOKEMEISTERS
See KRAUZER, Steven M(ark)

* * *

JONES, Madison (Percy, Jr.) 1925-

PERSONAL: Born March 21, 1925, in Nashville, TN; son of Madison Percy and Mary Temple (Webber) Jones; married Shailah McEvilley, February 5, 1951; children: Carroll (Mrs. John S. Lofty), Madison III, Ellen, Michael, Andrew. *Education:* Vanderbilt University, A.B., 1949; University of Florida, A.M., 1951, graduate study, 1951-53. *Avocational interests:* Hunting, fishing, sailing, sculpturing.

ADDRESSES: Agent—Harold Matson Company, Inc., 276 Fifth Avenue, New York, NY 10001.

CAREER: Farmer and horse trainer in Cheatham County, TN, during the 1940s; instructor in English at Miami University, Oxford, OH, 1953-54, and at University of Tennessee, Knoxville, 1955-56; Auburn University, Auburn, AL, assistant professor, 1956-68, professor of English, 1968-87, alumni writer-in-residence, 1966-87, distinguished faculty lecturer, 1980, currently professor emeritus. *Military service:* U.S. Army, Corps of Military Police, 1944-45; served in Korea.

MEMBER: Fellowship of Southern Writers, Alabama Academy of Distinguished Authors.

AWARDS, HONORS: Sewanee Review fellow, 1954; Alabama Library Association Book Award, 1967; Rockefeller fellow, 1968; Guggenheim fellow, 1973-74; Lytle Prize, 1992, for short fiction.

WRITINGS:

NOVELS

The Innocent, Harcourt (New York City), 1957.
Forest of the Night, Harcourt, 1960.
A Buried Land, Viking (New York City), 1963.
An Exile, Viking, 1967, published as *I Walk the Line,* Popular Library (New York City), 1970.
A Cry of Absence, Crown (New York City), 1971.
Passage through Gehenna, Louisiana State University Press (Baton Rouge), 1978.
Season of the Strangler, Doubleday (New York City), 1982.
Last Things, Louisiana State University Press, 1989.
An Exile, illustrated by Dean Bornstein, Frederic C. Beil (Savannah), 1990.
To the Winds: A Novel, Longstreet Press (Atlanta), 1996.
Nashville 1864: The Dying of the Light: A Novel, J. S. Sanders (Nashville),1997.
(With Thomas Davidson Dow) *History of the Tennessee State Dental Association,* Tennessee State Dental Association, 1958.

Author's work is represented in the anthologies *Best American Short Stories, 1953,* edited by Martha Foley, and *Stories of the Modern South,* edited by Benjamin Forkner and Patrick Samway. Contributor of short stories to *Perspective, Sewanee Review, Arlington Quarterly,* and *Delta Review.* Jones's manuscripts are collected at Emory University and Auburn University.

ADAPTATIONS: An Exile was filmed in 1970 as *I Walk the Line.*

SIDELIGHTS: Although Madison Jones has a devoted and enthusiastic following in certain (mostly Southern) circles, widespread critical and popular acclaim have proved elusive through much of his career. In the eyes of his admirers, however, he has been favorably compared to the classic Greek tragedians as well as to more "modern" writers. Ovid Pierce notes in the *New York Times Book Review* that "outside of Faulkner, few writers have been able to command such a range of country with so much atmospheric detail . . . nor have they been able to capture so well the air of defeat over forgotten little towns." As a stylist, praise has also come Jones's way. Called "clean, spare, and subtle" by David Payne in *Washington Post Book World,* Jones "offers us those little epiphanies of altered perspective that constitute fresh seeing." For the most part, Jones has made use of traditional themes, what Jonathan Yardley calls in *Partisan Review* "good, solid, 'Southern' material": small towns, fundamentalism, moonshine, racial tension, and loyalty to the Confederacy. Guilt—or hubris—and retribution are common preoccupations, as is the conflict between past and present and the destruction that can result when people refuse to accept what cannot be changed. The typically Southern concerns of place, community, and history also figure prominently in Jones's fictional world.

The Innocent, published in 1957, introduces themes of innocence corrupted by experience and the insinuation of past evils upon the present, as well as a symbolic and allegorical quality that would also mark Jones's later work. The protagonist of Jones's first novel, Duncan Welsh, seeks to break with his past transgressions committed during a seven-year residency in the North and start a new life after he inherits farmland near his boyhood home in rural Tennessee. An allegory of the Agrarian movement of the first half of the twentieth century in which a Southern economy based on farming rather than industry was championed, *The Innocent* portrays the battle of idealism over reality. Welsh, an agrarian, tries to create an idealized pastoral community, but ultimately his hubris causes his downfall. Symbolism abounds: Welsh's growing obsession is reflected by his Godlike but futile attempts to stop the extinction of a breed of horse; meanwhile he must confront the more sinister side of his own nature in the person of a local moonshiner who ultimately involves him in murder.

Jones's second novel, *Forest of the Night,* is set in the American frontier during the early part of the nineteenth century. Jonathan Cannon, an innocent, albeit enlightened, product of the philosophy of Rousseau, Paine, and Jefferson, follows the Natchez Trail from Nashville to Natchez, Mississippi, in hopes of discovering men living untouched by civilization in a Rousseauian "state of nature." What he discovers instead are the outlaw Harpe brothers—brutal, psychotic killers whom Jonathan eventually comes to resemble in his effort to survive. Jones's protagonist "becomes the very thing he abhorred in theory," notes Sandy Cohen in the *Dictionary of Literary Biography.* "Eventually, Cannon, like John Locke and Edmund Burke, comes to the conclusion that society is a civilizing force."

"The story is largely imagined," Jones explains to *CA,* describing the historic backdrop of *Forest of the Night.* "There is a little about the Harpe brothers on record, but very little. We know what kind of men they were and a few things they did, but we don't even know with certainty what their end was. But I hope this much is clear: the virgin forest has become a forest of the night for the enlightened hero and the confrontation issues in the near extinction of his real humanity. It's the fatality of badly misreading the nature of things."

A Buried Land, considered one of Jones's best novels, echoes the themes of *Forest of the Night,* but in a more modern setting. Taking place in the Tennessee River Valley as the historic Tennessee Valley Authority dam projects were reshaping the Southern landscape, the novel follows a young attorney as he returns to the land of his youth, intent upon changing those around him to accommodate his more sophisticated attitudes. "He attempts," notes M. E. Bradford in *Contemporary Novelists,* "to bury the old world (represented by a girl who dies aborting his child) under the waters of the TVA; but its truths (and their symbol) rise to haunt him back into abandoned modes of thought and feeling."

Jones's fifth novel, 1971's *A Cry of Absence,* tells the story of Hester Glenn, a well-to-do, middle-aged woman whose obsession with decorum and "tradition" cause her to reject the changes taking place in the South during the post- World War II years. After learning that her youngest son was instrumental in stoning a young black civil-rights activist to death, Hester at first denies his involvement, then suppresses the evidence. Eventually, however, as her old-fashioned attitudes become less and less acceptable to her peers, Hester is forced to reassess both her own and her son's behavior. Joseph Catinella of *Saturday Review* attributes the success of *A Cry of Absence* to Jones's mastery of the tragic style. In short, he writes, reading *A Cry of Absence* is particularly affecting "not only because racial conflicts still exist but because Mr. Jones dramatically places our national turmoil in a poignant framework. Seldom have I found a novel this formal in structure, one so perfectly plotted and harmoniously designed, such a moving experience." The result, declares Catinella, is "a novel that in many respects is an astonishing technical performance by an impressive artist, a writer whose Southern themes transcend their region and embody universal truths."

Jones's next novel, *Passage through Gehenna,* tells the story of the fall of Jud Rivers, a young man who decided early in life to renounce sin and live as an ascetic. He is lured away, however, by three hedonistic sinners, and then saved when a young woman, Hannah, literally dies for his sins, and frees him from his new-found evil ways. Highly allegorical and symbolic, this novel is "less successful than its predecessors," according to Cohen. She compares the novel to Faulkner's *A Fable* because the characters represent ideas rather than people, and thus are not sharply drawn or developed.

Last Things, published in 1989, takes the modern South as its setting. While living conditions may have improved with time, the ills of modern society—adultery, drug trafficking, murder, cynicism, and an increasing sense of alienation, to name a few—have more than cancelled out such improvements. Through the moral breakdown of a poor white Southerner named Wendell Corbin, Jones illustrates contemporary society's efforts to discard the moral precepts that once cemented the country's social fabric. As with his other works, *Last Things* mirrors Jones's view that, as Cohen explains, "not only will innocence always be corrupted by experience but . . . the innocent deserve some blame for their ignorance of the reality of evil."

In *Contemporary Novelists,* Jones discussed the themes at work in his fiction: "Generally, on a more obvious level, my fiction is concerned with the drama of collisions between past and present, with emphasis upon the destructive elements involved. More deeply, it deals with the failure, or refusal, of individuals to recognize and submit themselves to inevitable limits of the human condition."

Jones consistently sets his fiction in a Southern locale; as he once told *CA:* "I feel a strong attachment for the country of my childhood. Most people do in the South, probably more than people from other parts of the nation. Our sense of history has a lot to do with that, and for me as a writer this attachment to place has been indispensable. The familiar place offers inspiration and images to embody my ideas. Some images I remember from my childhood, and they retain a certain mystery for me.

"I could, of course, have seen fields of briars and buckbushes stretching to the horizon in other places. But I saw them in Tennessee, and for me they will always be associated with the country of my childhood. I hope that the mystery I feel in connection with the remembered images has been retained in my fiction."

BIOGRAPHICAL/CRITICAL SOURCES:

BOOKS

Contemporary Authors Autobiography Series, Volume 11, Gale, 1990.
Contemporary Literary Criticism, Volume 4, Gale, 1975.
Contemporary Novelists, 6th edition, St. James Press, 1996.
Dictionary of Literary Biography, Volume 152: *American Novelists since World War II,* Gale, 1995.

PERIODICALS

American Book Review, October, 1979.
Chicago Sunday Tribune, February 24, 1957.
Commonweal, March 22, 1957; August 9, 1963.
Harper's, October, 1967.
New Republic, June 26, 1971.
New York Herald Tribune Book Review, March 13, 1960.
New York Herald Tribune Books, May 19, 1963.
New York Times, March 10, 1957; June 24, 1971.
New York Times Book Review, September 3, 1967; July 4, 1971; September 24, 1989, p. 48.
Partisan Review, spring, 1973, p. 291.
Saturday Review, February 23, 1957; July 10, 1971.
Southern Humanities Review, spring, 1991, pp. 194-96.
Time, February 25, 1957; June 21, 1971.
Times Literary Supplement, October 4, 1957.
Washington Post, January 27, 1982.
Washington Post Book World, July 18, 1971; October 15, 1989, pp. 4, 11.*

* * *

JUSSAWALLA, Adil (Jehangir) 1940-

PERSONAL: Born April 8, 1940, in Bombay, India; married Veronik Jussawalla, 1971; children: one stepdaughter. *Education:* Attended Cathedral School,

1947-56; attended Architectural Association School of Architecture, London, 1957-58; attended Felsham House, 1958-60; University College, Oxford University, M.A., 1964.

ADDRESSES: Home—Palm Springs, Flat R2, Cuffe Parade, Bombay 400 005, India.

CAREER: Greater London Council, supply teacher, 1965; International Language Centre, London, language teacher, 1965-69; language teacher at various colleges in Bombay, 1970-72; St. Xavier's College, Bombay, lecturer in English language and literature, 1972-75; International Writing Program, University of Iowa, Iowa City, member, 1976; *Indian Express,* Bombay, book reviews editor, 1980-81; *Express Magazine,* Bombay, literary editor, 1980-82; *Science Age,* Bombay, literary editor, 1983-87; *Debonair,* Bombay, literary editor, 1987-89, editor, 1989—.

WRITINGS:

POETRY

Land's End, Writers Workshop (Calcutta), 1962.
Missing Person, Clearing House (Bombay), 1976.

OTHER

(Editor) *New Writing in India,* Penguin (London), 1974.
(Editor with Eunice de Souza) *Statements: An Anthology of Indian Prose in English,* Orient Longman (Bombay), 1976.

Also author of television scripts, including *Train to Calcutta,* 1970, and *War,* 1989.

SIDELIGHTS: Adil Jussawalla's poetry centers on themes of alienation and the unreality of city life, as well as dilemmas of identity and experience. Devindra Kohli of *Contemporary Poets* noted that although Jussawalla is not a prolific poet, "his is a significant voice that has assimilated the influence of Ezra Pound and T.S. Eliot." His poetry is harsh at times, describing the alienation of an Indian middle-class intellectual in a foreign land, as he does in *Land's End.* The same persona appears in the setting of post-independence India in *Missing Person.*

Land's End contains poems written abroad and describes the misery of exile. The first poem is "Seventeen" and was written when Jussawalla was that age. The poem describes replacing sensual vitality with "a cold assumption of arrogance." The reason for this is never made clear, however, in either *Land's End* or *Missing Person.* "November Day" criticizes nineteenth-century English romanticism, including an allusion to Shelley's "Ode to the West Wind" which is ironic, intended to emphasize the futility of human endeavor. The title poem of *Missing Person* is written in an impersonal style and explores the effects of colonialism. The poem also addresses the marginalization of India's middle-class intellectuals, a group of people who remain passive in the face of decadence and, according to the poet, need to strive toward self-assertiveness and renewal.

BIOGRAPHICAL/CRITICAL SOURCES:

BOOKS

Contemporary Poets, 6th edition, St. James Press, 1996.*

* * *

JUSTER, Norton 1929-

PERSONAL: Born June 2, 1929, in Brooklyn, NY; son of Samuel H. (an architect) and Minnie (Silberman) Juster; married Jeanne Ray (a graphic designer), August 15, 1964; children: Emily. *Education:* University of Pennsylvania, B. of Arch., 1952; University of Liverpool, graduate study, 1952-53. *Avocational interests:* Cooking, gardening, bicycling, reading.

ADDRESSES: Home—259 Lincoln Ave., Amherst, MA 01002. *Office*—Juster/Pope/Frazier Associates, 9 Ashfield Rd., Shelburne Falls, MA 01370. *Agent*—Sterling Lord Literistic, 1 Madison Ave., New York, NY 10010.

CAREER: Juster & Gugliotta, New York City, architect, 1960-68; Pratt Institute, Brooklyn, NY, professor of environmental design, 1960-70; Juster/Pope/Frazier Associates, Shelburne Falls, MA, architect, 1969—; Hampshire College, Amherst, MA, professor, 1970-92, emeritus professor of design, 1992—. *Military service:* U.S. Naval Reserve, Civil Engineer Corps, active duty, 1954-57.

AWARDS, HONORS: Fulbright fellowship, 1952-53; Ford Foundation grant, 1960-61; National Academy of Arts and Sciences award for outstanding achievement, 1968-69; Guggenheim fellowship, 1970-71; George G. Stone Center for Children's Books Seventh Recognition of Merit, 1971.

WRITINGS:

FOR CHILDREN

The Phantom Tollbooth, illustrated by Jules Feiffer, Random House, 1961.

The Dot and the Line: A Romance in Lower Mathematics, Random House, 1963.

Alberic the Wise and Other Journeys, illustrated by Domenico Gnoli, Pantheon, 1965, illustrated by Leonard Baskin, Picture Book Studios, 1992.

Otter Nonsense, Philomel, 1982.

As: A Surfeit of Similes, illustrated by David Small, Morrow, 1989.

FOR ADULTS

Stark Naked: A Paranomastic Odyssey, Random House, 1970.

So Sweet to Labor: Rural Women in America, 1865-1895, Viking, 1979.

(Editor) *A Woman's Place: Yesterday's Rural Women in America,* Fulcrum Publishing, 1996.

ADAPTATIONS: The Dot and the Line was produced as an animated short film by Metro-Goldwyn-Mayer (MGM) in 1965; *The Phantom Tollbooth* was produced as an animated full-length feature film by MGM in 1970.

SIDELIGHTS: Norton Juster, an architect and professor of design, is best known to children and adults alike as the author of *The Phantom Tollbooth,* a work which the *New York Times Book Review*'s Diane Manuel recalls "turned children's librarians on their ears" when it was published in 1961. Today, *The Phantom Tollbooth* is considered a modern classic of children's literature.

"As *Pilgrim's Progress* is concerned with the awakening of the sluggardly spirit," writes Emily Maxwell in the *New Yorker,* "*The Phantom Tollbooth* is concerned with the awakening of the lazy mind." Milo is the owner of just such a mind; he is bored by just about everything—his toys, his house, and especially his schoolwork. After class one day, Milo finds a large package waiting for him; it is labeled "One Genuine Turnpike Tollbooth," for use by "Those Who Have Never Traveled in Lands Beyond." Intrigued, he sets up the tollbooth and, driving his small electric car, passes through. In an instant, Milo is transported to an unfamiliar road in the Kingdom of Wisdom.

The kingdom, he discovers, is made up of Dictionopolis, the land of words, and Digitopolis, the land of numbers. These lands are ruled by feuding brothers—King Azaz the Unabridged and the Mathemagician—who constantly argue over which are better, words or numbers. Peace in the Kingdom of Wisdom has been maintained by the kings' adopted sisters, Rhyme and Reason; however, the sisters have recently been exiled from the kingdom and are being held captive in the Mountains of Ignorance. Milo is persuaded by the only slightly malevolent witch Faintly Macabre to bring Rhyme and Reason back to the kingdom.

The creatures and colleagues Milo encounters in the Kingdom of Wisdom humorously demonstrate the many quirks of the English language: there are his traveling companions, the giant, insectile Humbug, and the watchdog Tock (whose body is a large alarm clock); there are the noisy Dischord and Dynne, and the insidious Terrible Trivium; as well as the Gross Exaggeration, the Threadbare Excuse, and the blowhard Overbearing Know-It-All. The travelers dine on "ragamuffins" and "rigamarolls" in Dictionopolis, while in Digitopolis they nibble on plus signs to fill up and minus signs to become hungry again. *Atlantic Monthly*'s Charlotte Jackson notes that *The Phantom Tollbooth,* "besides being very amusing, has a quality that will quicken young minds and encourage readers to pursue pleasures that do not depend on artificial stimulation." With its wordplay and fantastic characters, Juster's book has often been compared to another classic, Lewis Carroll's *Alice in Wonderland.* But, Maxwell stresses, *The Phantom Tollbooth*" remains triumphantly itself, lucid, humorous, full of warmth and real invention." Maxwell describes her initial reading of *The Phantom Tollbooth* as "my first experience of opening a book with no special anticipation and gradually becoming aware that I am holding in my hands a newborn classic, still sticky from its crysalis."

Because it is a modern morality play in the vein of the "Everyman" dramas, many critics have argued that *The Phantom Tollbooth* is too sophisticated for young readers. "The ironies, the subtle play on words will be completely lost on all but the most precocious children," comments Miriam Mathes in the *Library Journal,* while a critic for the *Saturday Review* opines: "I'm inclined to think it is largely an adult book [for it] goes above the head of its intended audience—the 'lazy' mind." The *New York Times Book Review*'s Ann McGovern, however, believes wholeheartedly in the universal appeal of *The Phantom Tollbooth:* "To those who might wonder whether children will grasp Mr. Juster's subtleties, I can only quote one well-read eleven-year-old who reported it 'the cleverest book I've ever read.' Youngsters who drive through the tollbooth with Milo will probably, in the midst of their laughter, digest some important truth of life."

Juster has delivered over the years several more allegorical children's tales, including *The Dot and the Line* and *Alberic the Wise.* His most recent book for children, 1989's *As: A Surfeit of Similes,* is probably closest to *The Phantom Tollbooth* in style. In this book, two gentlemen travel the world by any means available in order to collect similes; some (like "slow as ketchup" and "hot as a griddle") are relatively mundane, while others ("clever as paint," "tight as a suture," and "reassuring as a dentist's smile") are refreshingly original. Though she describes its premise as "slim as an isthmus," Manuel lauds Juster's latest tale: "At a time when knock-knock and elephant jokes are sinking to new lows in elementary-school circles . . . [*As*] is the kind of book that could help to sell youngsters on the devilish delights of well-turned phrases."

Before moving to Amherst, Massachusetts, in 1980, Juster and his family lived on a rural farm. While working to restore and run their property, Juster was taken aback by the amount of sheer labor involved in maintaining a farm. He became curious as to how early American farmers—and, in particular, farm women—managed the burdens of farm work. His research into the subject yielded 1979's *So Sweet to Labor: Rural Women in America, 1865-1895,* a collection of essays, letters, and poetry written by, to, and about farm women. This collection "evokes the concrete struggles, deeply held cultural values and the blind spots of nineteenth-century rural women," praises Milton Cantor in *Nation.* Juster's documents "tell us something about the fragility and chanciness of life in rural America and about the part played by those whom history has swept into the darkened corners of our national past." Though Sharon Congdon of the *Washington Post Book World* points out that *So Sweet to Labor* "is plagued with problems," such as poor editing and a too-heavy reliance upon the late-1800s periodical *The Household* as a source, she asserts that Juster's "message is sound." Cantor concludes: "Juster's collection is a realistic and balanced sampling, and enlarges our understanding of the still mostly uncharted history of farm women."

BIOGRAPHICAL/CRITICAL SOURCES:

BOOKS

Fourth Book of Junior Authors and Illustrators, H. W. Wilson, 1978.

St. James Guide to Fantasy Writers, St. James Press, 1996.

Twentieth-Century Children's Writers, 3rd edition, St. James Press, 1989.

Twentieth-Century Young Adult Writers, 1st edition, St. James Press, 1994.

PERIODICALS

Atlantic Monthly, December, 1961, p. 120.

Chicago Tribune, December 17, 1961, p. 7.

Commonweal, November 10, 1961, p. 186.

Library Journal, January 15, 1962, p. 332.

Los Angeles Times Book Review, March 26, 1989, p. 8.

Nation, September 8, 1979, pp. 187-188.

New Statesman, December 21, 1962, p. 907.

New Yorker, November 18, 1961, pp. 222-224; December 4, 1965, p. 236; September 24, 1979, pp. 162-163.

New York Herald Tribune, November 12, 1961, p. 14.

New York Review of Books, December 9, 1965, p. 38.

New York Times Book Review, November 12, 1961, p. 35; November 14, 1982, p. 43; October 22, 1989, p. 35.

Saturday Review, January 20, 1962, p. 27; January 22, 1966, p. 45.

School Library Journal, April, 1989.

Spectator, November 9, 1962, p. 732.

Time, December 15, 1961, p. 89; March 22, 1971.

Times Literary Supplement, November 23, 1962, p. 892; November 24, 1966, p. 1089.

Washington Post Book World, February 3, 1980, p. 10; May 14, 1989, p. 15; January 10, 1993, p. 11.*

K

KAHL, Virginia 1919-

PERSONAL: Born February 18, 1919, in Milwaukee, WI; daughter of Arthur H. and Frieda (Krause) Kahl. *Education:* Milwaukee-Downer College, B.A., 1940; University of Wisconsin, M.S.L.S., 1957.

ADDRESSES: Office—Alexandria Public Library, Alexandria, VA.

CAREER: Milwaukee Public Library, Milwaukee, WI, library assistant, 1942-48; U.S. Army, Special Services Section, librarian in Berlin, Germany, 1948-49, and Salzburg, Austria, 1949-55; Madison Public Schools, Madison, WI, school librarian, 1958-61; Menomonee Falls Public Library, Menomonee Falls, WI, library director, 1961-68; Alexandria Public Library, Alexandria, VA, branch librarian, 1971—, coordinator of public services, 1977—. Teaches writing and illustrating of children's books at George Washington University.

MEMBER: National League of American Pen Women, Children's Book Guild (Washington, DC).

AWARDS, HONORS: New York Herald Tribune Spring Book Festival Award Honor Book, 1954, for *Away Went Wolfgang; New York Herald Tribune* Spring Book Festival Award Honor Book, 1955, and Lewis Carroll Shelf Award, 1972, both for *The Duchess Bakes a Cake.*

WRITINGS:

ALL SELF-ILLUSTRATED CHILDREN'S BOOKS; ALL PUBLISHED BY SCRIBNER

Away Went Wolfgang, 1954.
The Duchess Bakes a Cake, 1955.
Maxie, 1956.
Plum Pudding for Christmas, 1956.
Habits of Rabbits, 1957.
Droopsi, 1958.
(With Edith Vacheron) *Voici Henri,* 1959.
The Perfect Pancake, 1960.
(With Vacheron) *Encore Henri,* 1961.
The Baron's Booty, 1963.
How Do You Hide a Monster?, 1971.
Gunhilde's Christmas Booke, 1972.
Giants, Indeed!, 1974.
Gunhilde and the Halloween Spell, 1975.
How Many Dragons Are Behind the Door?, 1977.
Whose Cat Is That?, 1979.

ADAPTATIONS: The Duchess Bakes a Cake was adapted to filmstrip with record or cassette by Miller-Brody.

SIDELIGHTS: Virginia Kahl's children's books possess a simple humor, easily understood by very young readers. Kahl uses slapstick and humor derived from exaggeration and chaos. One of her best-known books is *The Duchess Bakes a Cake.* The Duchess is a humorous character whose efforts at the simplest tasks result in ridiculous ordeals. When she bakes a cake, she puts in so much yeast that she is trapped on top of the cake as it rises toward the sky. With thirteen children in the family, however, her rescue is simply a matter of everyone eating the cake down. Donnarae MacCann of *Twentieth-Century Children's Writers* attributed the success of this story to "the clarity with which silliness and logic have been joined," the Duchess' scatter-brained personality, the easy rhyme, and words that are new to small children (such as "pummel," "catapult," and "minstrel").

The Duchess appears again in *The Baron's Booty* and *The Habits of Rabbits.* In the first, kidnappers find themselves unprepared for the behavior of the children they have taken, and in the second, rabbits reproduce at an alarming rate. MacCann noted that "these are ideal vehicles for the Duchess character and for employing a popular motif of folktales—the central role of the youngest family member."

A dog is the title character in *Away Went Wolfgang.* The story is about an overzealous milk-cart dog who spills the milk in his enthusiasm to deliver it. The solution produces a different saleable product: butter. In Wolfgang, Kahl creates a figure of devotion, energy, and youth. According to MacCann, some of Kahl's books do not live up to the creativity and charm of so many of her stories. The title character of *Maxie,* another dog, is an explicit moralizer rather than a lively and endearing character like Wolfgang. *Gunhilde's Christmas Booke* provides an explanation of Christmas customs to non-Christian characters. Despite the lighthearted nature of the text, MacCann found this book predictable and uninspired.

Kahl told *CA:* "I believe that everyone who writes for children finds his own level. For me, it is the picture book age group; and I've never been tempted to write for an older child. So, happily for me, the problems that have surfaced in the past couple of decades are of no concern. I plumb no murky depths, leave no story with [the] ending unresolved. Mine are simple books for simple folk, and I love to do them.

"Little children should enjoy their books. As long as possible, let them live in a world where characters are basically good, incidents are funny or exciting, and the story ultimately satisfying. I hope that the children who read my books have put them down with sighs of contentment, knowing that their expectations of cheerful uncomplicated tales with happy endings have been vindicated."

Kahl notes that she has always been a compulsive reader, especially of art history, cookbooks, mysteries, travel, and biography. Her second great interest is animals—she owns seven cats and would have other creatures, if possible. She "emphatically hates anyone who shoots, traps, poisons, hurts, or destroys wolves or eagles or prairie dogs or whales or seals, who lets oil spill onto beaches to destroy wildfowl, puts industrial wastes into streams and lakes, destroys forests, defaces mountains, or bulldozes his way across the landscape in the name of profit or progress."

BIOGRAPHICAL/CRITICAL SOURCES:

BOOKS

Something about the Author, Volume 48, Gale, 1987.

Twentieth-Century Children's Writers, 4th edition, St. James Press, 1995.

PERIODICALS

Horn Book, August, 1971, p. 375; October, 1975, p. 453.

New York Times Book Review, May 1, 1977, p. 28.

School Library Journal, October, 1975, p. 91; September, 1977, p. 110; October, 1979, p. 141.

Washington Post Book World, April 8, 1979, p. L2; July 8, 1979, p. E5.*

* * *

KAHN, Herman 1922-1983

PERSONAL: Born February 15, 1922, in Bayonne, NJ; died of a heart attack, July 7, 1983, in Chappaqua, NY; son of Abraham and Yetta (Koslowsky) Kahn; married R. Jane Heilner (a mathematician), March 21, 1953; children: Deborah Yetta Cunningham, David Joshua. *Education:* University of California, Los Angeles, B.A., 1945; California Institute of Technology, M.A., 1948. *Politics:* Member of Democratic Party; conservative.

CAREER: Rand Corp., Santa Monica, CA, mathematician, 1948-60; Hudson Institute, Croton-on-Hudson, NY, director, beginning 1961. Research associate, Princeton University's Center of International Studies, 1958. Member of the board of Hudson Institute, Hudson Research Services, Advanced Computer Techniques, and Hudson of Canada. *Military service:* U.S. Army, 1943-45.

MEMBER: Council on Foreign Relations, Center for Inter-American Relations, American Political Science Association, Phi Beta Kappa, Phi Mu Epsilon.

AWARDS, HONORS: Ph.D., University of Puget Sound and Worchester Polytechnic Institute, both 1976.

WRITINGS:

Application of Monte Carlo, Rand Corporation, 1954.

On Thermonuclear War, Princeton University Press, 1962, Greenwood, 1978.

Thinking about the Unthinkable, Horizon Press, 1962.

(Editor with Anthony Wiener) *Crises and Arms Control,* Hudson Institute, 1962.

On Escalation, Praeger, 1965.

The Alternative World Futures Approach, Hudson Institute, 1966.

(With Carl Dibble) *Notes on the Choice of a Basic National Security Policy,* Hudson Institute, 1967.

(With Wiener) *The Year 2,000: A Framework for Speculation on the Next 33 Years,* Macmillan, 1967.

Can We Win in Vietnam?, Praeger, 1968.

On Thermonuclear War: Three Lectures and Some Suggestions, Free Press, 1969.

The Emerging Japanese Superstate: Challenge and Response, Prentice-Hall, 1970.

Why ABM?, Prentice-Hall, 1970.

(With Garrett Scalera) *Basic Issues and Potential Lessons of Vietnam,* Hudson Institute, 1970.

(With B. Bruce-Briggs) *Things to Come: Thinking about the '70s and '80s,* Macmillan, 1972.

(With Chris Morgan) *Some World Economic and Population Scenarios for the 21st Century,* Hudson Institute, 1972.

(Editor) *The Future of the Corporation,* Mason & Lipscombe, 1974.

(With William M. Brown) *A World Turning Point, and a Better Prospect for the Future,* Hudson Institute, 1975.

(With Lewis A. Dunn) *Trends in Nuclear Proliferation: 1975-1995,* Hudson Institute, 1976.

(With Leon Martel and Brown) *The Next 200 Years: A Scenario for America and the World,* Morrow, 1976.

(With Brown) *Long-term Prospects for Developments in Space,* Hudson Institute, 1977.

(With Jane Newitt) *The Schools' Community Roles in the Next Ten Years: An Outsider Perspective,* U. S. Department of Health, Education and Welfare, 1977.

World Economic Development: 1979 and Beyond, Westview Press, 1979.

(With Thomas Pepper) *The Japanese Challenge: The Success and Failure of Economic Success,* Crowell, 1979.

(With Pepper) *Will She Be Right?: The Future of Australia,* University of Queensland Press, 1980.

The Coming Boom: Economic, Political, and Social, Simon & Schuster, 1982.

(Editor with Julian L. Simon) *The Resourceful Earth: A Response to Global 2000,* Blackwell, 1984.

Thinking about the Unthinkable in the 1980s, Simon & Schuster, 1984.

SIDELIGHTS: Herman Kahn, the late futurist, author, mathematician, physicist, political scientist, and director of the conservative Hudson Institute "think tank," was "a pioneer in the art of using mathematical and scientific tools to predict the future," according to Walter Isaacson in *Time.* "But above all," Isaacson noted, "he was a provocateur in the sedate world of ideas, a futurist who attempted, in his own words, 'to cope with history before it happens.' "

Kahn, a self-described "free-thinking intellectual," rose to national prominence in the early 1960s with publication of his controversial books *On Thermonuclear War* and *Thinking about the Unthinkable.* In these works he argued in a matter-of-fact way that nuclear war was possible—even probable—and so the United States should make plans to fight and win such a conflict. While this view understandably caused an uproar, and reportedly led film director Stanley Kubrick to pattern the title character of his classic 1964 anti-war film *Dr. Strangelove* after Kahn, the resulting celebrity gave him an opportunity to expound on a wide range of other important issues. "One of Kahn's major intellectual contributions to . . . strategic thought [was] the writing of 'scenarios,' a technique for stretching the imagination to contemplate extensions of current tendencies and potentialities perhaps for gauging in advance otherwise unexpected possibilities," Richard Kostelanetz observed in *Master Minds: Portraits of Contemporary American Artists and Intellectuals.*

Kahn began his career in the late 1940s with the Rand Corporation, which was engaged at the time in secret work for the U.S. Air Force. Initially apprehensive about working for Rand, Kahn soon discovered that he enjoyed it. "They were doing what I always wanted—making integrated studies of important questions and pontificating on a range of issues," he told Kostelanetz. Nonetheless, Kahn remained uncertain about the direction of his career. While at Rand, he obtained a real estate broker's license, lectured, and wrote an intended Ph.D. dissertation on the Monte Carlo Theory of mathematical probability. Kahn's quest for a doctorate was thwarted, however, because the California Institute of Technology had a policy against accepting commercially-sponsored studies for graduate degree standing. As a result, Kahn abandoned academia and had the work published by Rand as his first book, *Applications of Monte Carlo.*

In the early 1950s Kahn turned his attention to economic and political matters. His changing intellectual interests were mirrored in a shift in his duties at Rand, where he moved from his office in the physics division to working as a roving consultant for a number of in-house projects. This being the height of the Cold War between the United States and the former USSR, one of these projects was a study of America's civil defense system. The result, Rand Report R-322-RC, titled *A Study of Non-Military Defense,* was released in 1958. Years later, Kahn told Kostelanetz that it was this Rand project, as well as his co-directorship of the strategic Air Force Project, that inspired him to write *On Thermonuclear War.* That book, written in 1959, grew out of a series of lectures Kahn gave during a year he spent as a Research Associate at Princeton University's Center of International Studies.

On Thermonuclear War was the first book to discuss openly the likely effects of nuclear war under various circumstances. Conventional wisdom held that any type of nuclear war would annihilate both superpowers; Kahn pointed out that there were many scenarios in which one or both combatants would survive. He argued that these scenarios needed to be studied, because the Soviet Union might decide to go to war if convinced that their survival potential was high. Further, he argued, if "we have a posture which might result in 40 million dead in a general war, and as a result of poor planning, apathy, or other causes, our posture deteriorates and a war occurs with 80 million dead, we have suffered an additional disaster, an *unnecessary* additional disaster that is almost as bad as the original disaster." .

Before *On Thermonuclear War* was published, public discussion of nuclear war was timid. Because of its willingness to discuss an uncomfortable subject, Kahn's book provoked an intense reaction. While no one debated the book's importance, critics and commentators either praised Kahn for his dispassionate logic or condemned him for minimizing the dangers of nuclear war, and thus making it more likely to happen. Jerome Spingarn of the *New York Times Book Review,* for example, termed *On Thermonuclear War*"a landmark in the literature of military strategy and power-oriented diplomacy"; while Fred Greene of the *New Republic* chided Kahn for basing his theories on what Greene believed were outdated estimates contained in a 1958 Rand civil defense study. James R. Newman, an editor of *Scientific American* magazine, was even more adamant, denouncing *On Thermonuclear War* as "a moral tract on mass murder: how to plan it, how to commit it, how to get away with it, how to justify it . . . permeated with a bloodthirsty irrationality." When Kahn attempted to reply to these charges, the magazine declined to publish his letter.

The controversy surrounding *On Thermonuclear War* spurred public interest in the book. Initial hardcover sales were in excess of 40,000 copies, an exceptional sale for an academic study intended for a narrow audience of military and civilians interested in strategic issues. Buoyed by this success and disillusioned with his work at Rand, Kahn resigned in the summer of 1961. He joined a group of colleagues in establishing the Hudson Institute, a conservatively-oriented, non-profit "think tank" at Croton-on-Hudson, New York. Kahn became the first director of the Institute, which was set up to do inter-disciplinary freelance research into what he termed "important issues, not just urgent ones."

Some of these important issues had been raised in *On Thermonuclear War,* and his next two books dealt with many of the same themes. *Thinking about the Unthinkable* was a collection of essays which represented Kahn's effort to clarify his ideas about nuclear war and to correct the mistaken impression that in his cool, logical methodology he was somehow advocating the use of nuclear weapons. "To act intelligently we must learn as much as we can about the risks. We may thereby be able better to avoid nuclear war," he wrote in the book. "Even if [the probability of war] were as low as one in fifty a year, the annual risk would be too high—an even chance that there would be a war before the year 2000."

In *On Escalation* Kahn proposed a sophisticated signaling system by which the nuclear superpowers could convey their political and military intentions without disastrous misunderstanding. At the core of Kahn's thinking was what Kostelanetz described as "a metaphoric escalation-ladder of forty-four rungs." Michael Howard, writing in the *Bulletin of Atomic Scientists,* noted that "it must constantly be remembered in reading his study . . . exactly how specialized it is, and how large is the area both of strategy and of politics to which [these] concepts are very largely irrelevant." Stefan Possony, writing in the *National Review,* had a different perspective. "Kahn is provocative, informative, and witty," Possony stated. "He is a good phrase-maker. He is also absolutely honest and, for the most part, constructive. And he excels at his real job, which is to build abstract models for the benefit of the strategists."

After three books about thermonuclear war, Kahn began to turn his attentions to other concerns. He had always been fascinated by economics and politics, and while he maintained his interest in strategic military issues (and published several more books and studies on aspects of the subject) he began devoting more and more of his time to topics related to economic development and the impact of technology. These studies resulted in Kahn co-authoring or editing numerous reports and studies for Hudson Institute clients and writing commercial books which stirred public debate.

In 1967, for example, he and Hudson Institute colleague Anthony Wiener co-authored *The Year 2000: A Framework for Speculation on the Next 33 Years,* an attempt to predict in a general way the state of the planet at the millennium. In 1970, Kahn wrote *The Emerging Japanese Superstate: Challenge and Response,* which foresaw a coming boom in the Japanese economy long before most other Western observers had even considered the prospect of such a development. Then, in 1979, at a time when it had become fashionable to look to Japan as the model for economic and corporate development, Kahn confounded most observers—and the Japanese themselves—with *The Japanese Challenge,* a book arguing that the Japanese economy needed serious readjustment to maintain its momentum.

Kahn expressed a more characteristic optimism in *World Economic Development: 1979 and Beyond* and *The Coming Boom: Economic, Political and Social.* In these books he postulated that unless bad luck or bad management prevented it, technology would allow the world to overcome many of the problems it faced. Particularly in *The Coming Boom,* Kahn argued that the economic trends were such that worldwide prosperity was inevitable. "One of the reasons we expect relatively high and sustained growth rates through the 1980's and 1990's," Kahn wrote in the book, "is that a whole host of new technologies and technological improvements are now ripe for large-scale exploitation." His predictions of low inflation, higher productivity and an easing of energy shortages—as well as the phenomenal 400 percent rise of the stock market during the 1980s—came to pass within a few short years of the book's publication. *The Coming Boom* was, in the words of *Time* reviewer R. Z. Sheppard, "a call to optimism."

"I'm against ignorance," Kahn once told a *New York Times* interviewer. "I'm against sloppy, emotional thinking. I'm against fashionable thinking." This approach to his work led Kahn into areas of research consistently ahead of his time, allowing him to map new terrains of thought. Kostelanetz saw Kahn's writings "as a succession of attempts to create concepts and coin words and phrases—indeed, an entire critical language—appropriate to historically unprecedented situations." Thomas Bell, president of the Hudson Institute at the time of Kahn's death in 1983, told the *New York Times* about his friend and associate. "For a man who many people said had one of the world's great intellects, an incredibly high I.Q., he was a very gregarious person, the kind of guy you liked to talk to, to have over for dinner," Bell remembered. "He was funny. He had a sense of humor, and he didn't take himself so seriously that you couldn't deal with him. He got a huge enjoyment out of what he was doing."

BIOGRAPHICAL/CRITICAL SOURCES:

BOOKS

Contemporary Issues Criticism, Gale, Volume 1, 1982.

Herzog, Arthur, *The War-Peace Establishment,* Harper, 1965.

Kahn, Herman, *On Thermonuclear War,* Princeton University Press, 1962.

Kahn, Herman, *Thinking about the Unthinkable,* Horizon Press, 1962.

Kahn, Herman, *The Coming Boom: Economic, Political, and Social,* Simon & Schuster, 1982.

Kostelanetz, Richard, *Master Minds: Portraits of Contemporary American Artists and Intellectuals,* Macmillan, 1969.

PERIODICALS

Bulletin of the Atomic Scientists, October, 1965, pp. 25-26.

Critic, fall, 1976, pp. 73-75.

Dun's Review, December, 1976.

Economist, April 16, 1977, p. 123; September 8, 1979, pp. 120-121.

Esquire, September, 1962.

Journal of Conflict Resolution, March, 1971, pp. 55-70.

Life, December 5, 1968.

Los Angeles Times Book Review, July 15, 1979, p. 1; December 2, 1984, p. 17.

Nation, January 14, 1961, pp. 34-35.

National Review, July 13, 1965, pp. 601-603; January 30, 1968, pp. 90-92; November 17, 1970, pp. 1216-1218.

Nation's Business, July, 1973.

New Republic, February 27, 1961, pp. 16-17; August 18, 1979, pp. 35-36.

New Statesman, May 12, 1961, p. 754; September 10, 1965, pp. 364-365; April 26, 1968, pp. 552-553.

Newsweek, July 4, 1976.

New York, August 9, 1976.

New York Herald Tribune Magazine, July 4, 1965.

New York Review of Books, July 15, 1965, pp. 8-10.

New York Times, August 13, 1982; September 19, 1982.

New York Times Book Review, January 1, 1961, p. 3; May 8, 1979, p. 9; June 10, 1979, p. 12; August 5, 1979, p. 9.

New York Times Magazine, December 1, 1968.

Reader's Digest, April, 1973.
Saturday Review, February 4, 1961, pp. 17-19; February 10, 1968, pp. 36-37.
Science, February 5, 1971, pp. 467-468.
Scientific American, March, 1961.
Sociology: Review of New Books, November-December, 1979, pp. 20-21.
Der Spiegel, April 3, 1967.
Time, August 16, 1982, p. 66.
Times (London), February 17, 1983.
Tribune Books (Chicago), October 6, 1984, p. 37.
U.S. News & World Report, December 21, 1959, p. 54; February 8, 1971; March 12, 1973.
Washington Post, September 20, 1982, p. C2.
Washington Post Book World, May 20, 1979, p. 5; September 9, 1984, p. 4; September 22, 1985, p. 13.

OBITUARIES:

BOOKS

The Writer's Directory: 1982-1984, Gale, 1981.

PERIODICALS

Chicago Tribune, July 9, 1983.
London Times, July 9, 1983.
Los Angeles Times, July 8, 1983.
New York Times, July 8, 1983.
Time, July 18, 1983.
Washington Post Book World, July 8, 1983.*

* * *

KAHN, James 1947-

PERSONAL: Born December 30, 1947, in Chicago, IL; son of Alfred J. (a physician) and Judith (an artist; maiden name, Pesmen) Kahn; married Jill Alden Littlewood (an illustrator), August 30, 1975; children: one daughter. *Education:* University of Chicago, B.A., 1970, M.D., 1974.

ADDRESSES: Agent—Jane Jordan Browne, Multimedia Product Development, Inc., 410 South Michigan Ave., Suite 724, Chicago, IL 60605.

CAREER: University of Wisconsin—Madison, intern, 1974-75; Los Angeles County Hospital, Los Angeles, CA, emergency medicine resident, 1976-77; University of California, Los Angeles, emergency medicine resident, 1978-79; Rancho Encino Hospital, Los Angeles, emergency room physician, 1978—; writer. Worked as consultant to Steven Spielberg for film *E.T.*

MEMBER: American College of Emergency Physicians.

WRITINGS:

(With Jerome McGann) *Nerves in Patterns* (poems), X Press, 1978.
Diagnosis: Murder (mystery), Carlyle, 1978.
World Enough and Time (first novel in "New World" science-fiction trilogy), Ballantine, 1980.
Time's Dark Laughter (second novel in "New World" trilogy), Ballantine, 1982.
A Pig Too Far (teleplay for "St. Elsewhere" series), National Broadcasting Co., 1983.
Timefall (third novel in "New World" trilogy), St. Martin's, 1987.
The Echo Vector (suspense novel), St. Martin's, 1988.

SCREENPLAY NOVELIZATIONS

Poltergeist, Warner Books, 1982.
Return of the Jedi, Ballantine, 1983.
Indiana Jones and the Temple of Doom, Ballantine, 1984.
The Goonies, Warner Books, 1985.
Poltergeist II, Warner Books, 1986.
Star Wars: Return of the Jedi, Ballantine, 1995.

OTHER

Also author of teleplays for *E/R* series, CBS-TV, 1984-85. Contributor of stories to magazines, including *Playboy.*

SIDELIGHTS: Dr. James Kahn is a trauma specialist and author of science fiction and film novelizations. He began his writing career with the "New World" trilogy, which consists of *World Enough and Time, Time's Dark Laughter,* and *Timefall.* In the first novel, Kahn's writing style is marked by his love of words and inclusion of poetic quotations. The novel is about Rose and Dicey, who are kidnapped from their husbands, the centaur Beauty and the human Scribe Josh. Beauty and Josh set out together to find their wives. Their companions are the cat/human Isis, the Flutterby (a giant butterfly) Humbelly, the Neuroman Jasmine, and the scholarly Vampire Lon. Their quest is not completely successful—Dicey dies after being lured by a vampire—but Rose is rescued from a Neuroman intelligence experiment.

Kahn develops minor themes of history and legend in *World Enough and Time.* Jasmine lectures on the past and helps the centaur understand that, like other talking animals, his species is a recent genetic creation by humans. Kahn uses his medical training in discussing the vampires and the Neuroman quest for long life by a process that destroys all body tissue, leaving nerve cells which are placed in an artificial body.

The second book in the trilogy, *Time's Dark Laughter,* is about a cyclic universe that ends and begins again whenever human genetic manipulation yields semi-divine beings. Because these beings possess knowledge of the universe but lack understanding of morality and power, they must be destroyed. Josh and Rose from the previous novel appear as the central figures. The final installment, *Timefall,* introduces the premise that the first two books were based on a seventy-million-year-old diary owned by a mental patient, Joshua Green. The diaries belong to him because in a past incarnation he left them for his future self to find millions of years later.

Kahn spent six days on the set of the film *E.T.: The Extra-Terrestrial* helping director Steven Spielberg with the scenes in which E.T. is dying and then is resuscitated. While on the set, Kahn noticed that the famed director had a copy of his first novel, *World Enough and Time;* after introducing himself as its author, Kahn was offered a chance to work on the novelization of another film, *Poltergeist.* Since then Kahn has added the book versions of many other Spielberg projects to his credits, as well as two other fiction titles. Marilyn K. Nellis of *Twentieth-Century Science-Fiction Writers* commented that, of the novelizations, *Poltergeist* is the most interesting. Kahn used his knowledge of ESP research from medical school along with his background in myth to describe astral planes and their inhabitants, most notably the figures of the shadow, the tree, and the flame. Nellis wrote that Kahn's handling of these elements is congruent with accounts of occult experience and well above the level of the rest of the film material.

Kahn's novelization of *The Return of the Jedi* is more focused on landscape descriptions than characterization, whereas *Indiana Jones* draws more heavily on characterization techniques.

About his writing, Kahn once told *CA:* "I'm basically a storyteller. I stretch for metaphors at times, but only if they make good stories themselves. The way the story is told is the art, the craft, the game of it—what makes the writing (and reading) fun." He added that he "would like to be a man of letters, involved in all literary forms—the novel, short story, essay, screenplay, and poetry." Kahn has achieved almost all of these, for he has written several scripts for the television medical shows *St. Elsewhere* and *E/R.* As he commented to Marian Smith Holmes in a *People* interview, "I'm following in the tradition of doctor writers. I see myself as a cross between Chekhov, Conan Doyle, and Michael Crichton." Despite his success, Kahn remains dedicated to medicine: "It's very exciting," he said of his specialty, trauma medicine, to the *Chicago Tribune*'s Arthur Shay. "Saving someone from certain death or preserving an arm or leg someone else might have amputated, saving a child or just alleviating pain—all these are why I trained as a doctor."

BIOGRAPHICAL/CRITICAL SOURCES:

BOOKS

Twentieth-Century Science-Fiction Writers, 3rd edition, St. James Press, 1991.

PERIODICALS

Chicago Tribune, August 22, 1983.
Los Angeles Times Book Review, December 6, 1987.
New York Times Book Review, April 26, 1987.
People, October 4, 1982.*

* * *

KAMM, Josephine (Hart) 1905-1989

PERSONAL: Born December 30, 1905, in London, England; died August 31, 1989; daughter of Percy M.C. (a lawyer) and Hilda (Marx) Hart; married George Emile Kamm (deceased), April 4, 1929; children: Antony. *Education:* Triangle Secretarial College, London, 1923.

CAREER: British Commonwealth Union, London, shorthand typist, 1924-26; Empire Industries Association, assistant secretary, 1926-29; British Ministry of Information, London, literary and administrative posts, 1939-45; Central Office of Information, London, senior information officer, 1946. Fawcett Library, London, member of Committee of Management, 1967-75. Writer.

MEMBER: National Book League (former member of council), International PEN (executive member, London Center), Society of Authors.

AWARDS, HONORS: Isaac Siegel Juvenile Award of Jewish Book Council of America, 1962, for *Return to Freedom.*

WRITINGS:

All Quiet at Home (novel), Longmans, Green, 1936.
Disorderly Caravan (novel), Harrap, 1938.
Nettles to My Head (novel), Duckworth, 1939.
Progress towards Self-Government in the British Colonies, Fosh & Cross, 1945.
Peace, Perfect Peace (novel), Duckworth, 1947.
Come, Draw This Curtain (novel), Duckworth, 1948.
Abraham: A Biography, Union of Liberal & Progressive Synagogues, 1948.
Gertrude Bell: Daughter of the Desert, Vanguard, 1956, published as *Daughter of the Desert: The Story of Gertrude Bell,* Bodley Head, 1956.
How Different from Us: A Biography of Miss Buss and Miss Beale, Bodley Head, 1958.
Hope Deferred: Girls' Education in English History, Methuen, 1965.
Rapiers and Battleaxes: The Women's Movement and its Aftermath, Humanities, 1966.
Indicative Past: A Hundred Years of the Girls' Public Day School, Allen & Unwin, 1971.
(Editor) Charles Dickens, *A Tale of Two Cities,* Collins (London), 1973.
John Stuart Mill in Love, Gordon-Cremonesi, 1977.

JUVENILES

African Challenge: The Story of the British in Tropical Africa, Thomas Nelson, 1946.
He Went with Captain Cook, Harrap, 1952.
Janet Carr: Journalist, Bodley Head, 1953.
They Served the People, Bodley Head, 1954.
Student Almoner, Bodley Head, 1955.
Men Who Served Africa, Harrap, 1957.
Leaders of the People, Abelard, 1959.
The Story of Sir Moses Montefiore, Vallentine, Mitchell, 1960.
The Story of Mrs. Pankhurst, Methuen, 1961, published as *The Story of Emmeline Pankhurst,* Meredith Corp., 1968.
Return to Freedom, Abelard, 1962.
Out of Step, Brockhampton Press, 1962.
Malaya and Singapore, Longmans, Green, 1963.
Malaria Ross, Methuen, 1963, Criterion, 1964.
A New Look at the Old Testament, Gollancz, 1965, published as *Kings, Prophets and History: A New Look at the Old Testament,* McGraw, 1966.
Young Mother, Duell, Sloan & Pearce, 1965.
The Story of Fanny Burney, Methuen, 1966, Meredith Corp., 1967.
The Hebrew People: A History of the Jews from Biblical Times to the Present Day, Gollancz, 1967, published as *The Hebrew People: A History of the Jews,* McGraw, 1968.
Joseph Paxton and the Crystal Palace: A Story Biography, Methuen, 1967.
No Strangers Here, Constable, 1968.
First Job, Brockhampton Press, 1969, 2nd edition, 1971.
Explorers into Africa, Crowell, 1970.
Where Do We Go from Here?, Brockhampton Press, 1972.
The Starting Point, Brockhampton Press, 1972.
Runaways, Hodder & Stoughton, 1978.
The Slave Trade, Evans Brothers, 1980.

SIDELIGHTS: Josephine Kamm established a career as an author of young adult fiction while the genre was still in its infancy. Eileen Dunlop of *Twentieth-Century Young Adult Writers* commented that although Kamm's novels are outdated for contemporary audiences, her work was "a response to the challenge of writing for young adults" when there was little if any precedent in America or Britain. In addition to pioneering the young adult genre itself, Kamm was also a forerunner in the themes and situations she depicted. Her books address single parenthood, interracial relationships, adoption, and marrying young. Her best known book, *Young Mother,* tells the story of a pregnant schoolgirl. Although Kamm was in her fifties when she published it, her portrayal of the girl's experiences has been praised for its bravery and honesty. Kamm also wrote two "career novels" intended to give teenage girls ideas about professional possibilities. While these two books, *Janet Carr: Journalist* and *Student Almoner,* were more focused on conveying career information than character development, they were important in Kamm's progress as a young adult writer.

In the 1950s Kamm wrote several biographies for young audiences, including *They Served the People, Men Who Served Africa, Leaders of the People,* and *The Story of Sir Moses Montefiore.* Dunlop noted that in *Daughter of the Desert,* a biography of British scholar Gertrude Bell, Kamm shows the insight and scholarship that mark her biographies for adults. She put her research skills to use in creating her one historical novel, *Return to Freedom,* an award-winning book about Oliver Cromwell's attempts to prohibit Jewish settlers in England. Commenting on this book, Dunlop wrote, "Although the narrative is initially slowed down by more historical detail than present-day teenagers find palatable, the story is unusual and told with both skill and sympathy. The character of Cromwell, not superficially attractive, is particularly well-drawn."

BIOGRAPHICAL/CRITICAL SOURCES:

BOOKS

Something about the Author, Volume 24, Gale, 1981.
Twentieth-Century Young Adult Writers, 1st edition, St. James Press, 1994.

PERIODICALS

Best Sellers, December 1, 1968.
Book World, March 17, 1968.
Books and Bookmen, July, 1968; June, 1970; July, 1975; April, 1978.
New Statesman, April 30, 1965; September 16, 1966; May 26, 1967.
New York Times Book Review, November 7, 1965; May 1, 1966; October 16, 1977.
Observer, March 21, 1965; June 26, 1966; January 1, 1978; December 3, 1978.
Times Literary Supplement, May 6, 1965; December 9, 1965; May 19, 1966; July 14, 1966; May 25, 1967; January 25, 1968; June 6, 1968; June 26, 1969; August 14, 1970; March 10, 1972; April 4, 1975; January 13, 1978; September 29, 1978.*

* * *

KANE, Henry Bugbee 1902-1971

PERSONAL: Born January 8, 1902, in Cambridge, MA; died, 1971; children: one son, one daughter. *Education:* Attended Massachusetts Institute of Technology.

CAREER: Worked in a variety of fields, including lighting engineering, kitchen design, advertising, and public relations; Massachusetts Institute of Technology, Cambridge, director of alumni fund, 1940-66; author, photographer, and illustrator for adult and juvenile magazines and books. *Military service:* Served in the U.S. Navy as a flier.

AWARDS, HONORS: The Tale of a Wood was chosen by the *New York Times* as one of the best illustrated children's book of the year, 1962.

WRITINGS:

The Alphabet of Birds, Bugs, and Beasts (self-illustrated), Houghton, 1938.
Wings, Legs, or Fins (self-illustrated), Knopf, 1965.
Four Seasons in the Woods (self-illustrated), Knopf, 1968.
A Care for Nature, Norton, 1971.

"WILD WORLD TALES" SERIES; ALL SELF-ILLUSTRATED; ALL PUBLISHED BY KNOPF

The Tale of the Whitefoot Mouse, 1940.
The Tale of the Bullfrog, 1941.
The Tale of the Promethea Moth, 1942.
The Tale of the Crow, 1943.
The Tale of the White-Faced Hornet, 1943.
The Tale of the Wild Goose, 1946.
Wild World Tales: The Tale of the Mouse, the Moth, and the Crow, 1949.
The Tale of a Meadow, 1959.
The Tale of a Pond, 1960.
The Tale of a Wood, 1962.

ILLUSTRATOR

Sally Carrighar, *One Day on Beetle Rock,* Knopf, 1944.
Henry David Thoreau, *Thoreau's Walden: A Photographic Register,* Knopf, 1946.
John James Rowlands, *Cache Lake Country,* Norton, 1947.
Thoreau, *Maine Woods,* Norton, 1950.
Thoreau, *Cape Cod,* Norton, 1951.
Thoreau, *Walden,* Norton, 1951.
David Thompson Watson McCord, *Far and Few,* Little, Brown, 1952.
Carrighar, *Icebound Summer,* Knopf, 1953.
Edwin Way Teale, *wilderness World of John Muir,* Houghton, 1954.
Thoreau, *Concord and the Merrimac,* Little, Brown, 1954.
Bud Helmericks, *Arctic Hunter,* Little, Brown, 1955.
McCord, *Take Sky,* Little, Brown, 1962.
Dudley Cammett Lunt, *The Woods and the Sea: Wilderness and Seacoast Adventures in the State of Maine,* Knopf, 1965.
McCord, *All Day Long: Fifty Rhymes of the Never Was and Always Is,* Little, Brown, 1966.
Louise and Norman Dyer Harris, *Flash: The Life Story of a Firefly,* Little, Brown, 1966.
McCord, *For Me to Say: Rhymes of the Never Was and Always Is,* Little, Brown, 1970.
McCord, *One at a Time: Poems,* Little, Brown, 1977.

SIDELIGHTS: Henry Bugbee Kane became interested in drawing and photography as a child. He pursued his interest in the arts as an avocation until his retirement in 1966. The author's early books in the "Wild World Tales" series examine the life-cycles of various insects, birds, and animals. The later books in the series look at plant and animal life from a small boy's viewpoint.

BIOGRAPHICAL/CRITICAL SOURCES:

PERIODICALS

Booklist, May 15, 1969; February 1, 1972.
Books, April 20, 1941.
Christian Science Monitor, November 3, 1960.
Kirkus Reviews, August 15, 1971.
Library Journal, October 1, 1971.
New York Times, May 11, 1941.
New York Times Book Review, February 6, 1966.
Saturday Review, February 22, 1969.

OBITUARIES:

PERIODICALS

New York Times, February 16, 1971.*

* * *

KAPLAN, Johanna 1942-

PERSONAL: Born December 29, 1942, in New York, NY; daughter of Max (a teacher) and Ruth (a social worker; maiden name Duker) Kaplan. *Education:* University of Wisconsin, Madison; New York University, B.A., 1964; Columbia University, M.A., 1966. *Politics:* Democrat. *Religion:* Jewish.

ADDRESSES: *Home*—411 West End Ave., New York, NY 10024. *Office*—P.S. 106, 1450 Madison Ave., New York, NY 10029. *Agent*—Russell & Volkening, 551 Fifth Ave., New York, NY 10017.

CAREER: Teacher of emotionally disturbed children in New York City Public Schools and at Mount Sinai Hospital, New York, NY, 1966—.

MEMBER: Authors Guild, PEN.

AWARDS, HONORS: New York State Council on the Arts grant, 1973; National Endowment for the Arts grant, 1973; National Book Award nomination and Jewish Book Award from Jewish Book Council, both 1976, for *Other People's Lives;* Wallant award and Jewish Book Award, both 1981; Smilen-*Present Tense* award, 1981.

WRITINGS:

Other People's Lives, Knopf, 1975.
O My America!: A Novel, Harper and Row (New York City), 1980.

Contributor of short stories and reviews to *Commentary* and to *Harper's.*

SIDELIGHTS: Johanna Kaplan's fiction explores Jewish life in New York City. She is especially interested in the fully Americanized generation that grew up in the 1940s and 1950s, and her characters tend to be a blend of tradition and individuality. Kaplan's writing career began in the early 1970s when fiction about American-Jewish life was so abundant that even critics were tiring of the subject matter. Still, Kaplan's stories captured the attention of the literary world. "It doesn't seem possible that any literary vitality can still be squeezed out of Jewish life in the Bronx," said Pearl K. Bell for *New Leader.* Yet Bell conceded that Johanna Kaplan's stories in *Other People's Lives* "abundantly prove that the chicken soup has not yet turned into water."

In *Dictionary of Literary Biography,* Peter Shaw wrote: "Kaplan's stories, published between 1969 and 1973 and collected in her first book, *Other People's Lives* (1975), deal with secular, middle-class family life in New York City. In them Kaplan is often concerned with the relationship between the generations and with differing attitudes toward the Jewish experience. The members of Kaplan's fictional older generation include both foreigners and native-born Americans, both Jews and non-Jews. All of the characters were alive during World War II and have been touched by it to one degree or another. The children come to terms with this past in their own sometimes comic, sometimes melancholy ways." Bell commented on the characters in *Other People's Lives:* "[Kaplan] has a sharp but affectionate eye for ultra-liberal hypocrites and upwardly mobile families that finally make it from Intervale Avenue to Mount Vernon, so their snotty children can brag: 'I don't live in the disgusting Bronx any more.' " A reviewer for *Book List* described the book as "sardonically fitful perceptions in brief and at length of alien cultures."

Discussing the stories in *Other People's Lives,* Shaw wrote: "In 'Sickness,' a child's experience of the Jewish past is restricted to the romanticized versions that she finds in her history books on the one hand, and on the other to her mother's recollections of a Polish childhood. While home from school for a few weeks on account of illness, Miriam observes the life of her Bronx apartment house. Images of the heroic Jewish past from her books interweave with the concerns of the partly immigrant population of the building. Kaplan's comic talent, which flowers in her novel, *O My America!,* is evident in the speech and behavior of the heroine's mother, her schoolmates, and their parents. By the end of the story, though, the naively presented past of the young girl's books has played through her sensibility in such a way as to lend a historical and even tragic significance to the mundane, daily existence of the apartment house.

"The collection's title novella, 'Other People's Lives,' employs the oddly revealing point of view of an unwanted, maladjusted young girl who has been sent to live with an eccentric bohemian family on New York's Upper West Side. The household consists of a middle-aged German immigrant wife, Maria, her American ballet-dancer husband who is in the hospital dying, her seven-year-old son, and the neighbors in their apartment house who constantly wander in and out of the family's life. The young boarder tends to view these 'other people's lives' in the light of her lonely need, yet her conception of them proves to be a profound one.

"Although the milieu of 'Other People's Lives' is Jewish, Maria is not. Yet her neighbors' jokes about her German past, which must be steeped in Anti-Semitism, have the surprising effect of casting her experience in the context of twentieth-century displacement and exile. As a result this non-Jewish character becomes the vehicle for giving significance to the Jewish experience.

"The stories collected in *Other People's Lives* originally appeared in *Commentary* and *Harper's* magazines. The volume was nominated for a National Book Award and for the Ernest Hemingway Foundation Award and won the Jewish Book Award for fiction in 1976.

"In some ways Kaplan's novel, *O My America!* (1980), represents a departure from her previous fiction. Its central character, New York Jewish intellectual Ezra Slavin, is at once more intellectual and more flamboyant than her earlier characters. Also, the historical sweep of his life story is broader and the political and intellectual issues that he raises are more explicit than any she dealt with before. Born in 1910, Slavin was a young radical in the 1930s, a skeptic with regard to World War II, and a critic of conformity in the 1950s. Then, as a result of his championing of youth and opposition to the Vietnam War, he is taken as a media hero in the 1960s. His story amounts to the biography of a representative of his generation. Reviewers noted the resemblance between Slavin's career and that of the social critic Paul Goodman, among others."

Shaw concluded: "Johanna Kaplan's work bears comparison with that of her contemporaries Jerome Charyn, Robert Kotlowitz, Jay Neugeboren, Hugh Nissenson, and Cynthia Ozick. It is her distinction both to have rendered closely the speech and thought patterns of characters drawn from contemporary life and at the same time to have consistently viewed their lives in the context of Jewish tradition. Kaplan's relationship to that tradition is suggested by her remark in acceptance of the Jewish Book Award in 1976 that she could never forget the obligation impressed on her in youth 'to benefit and answer to the common good.' Her fiction holds to this imperative even when most critical of the Jewish tradition from which it derives."

Since 1968 Johanna Kaplan has been employed as a teacher of mentally disturbed children in the psychiatry department of Mount Sinai Hospital in New York.

BIOGRAPHICAL/CRITICAL SOURCES:

BOOKS

Contemporary Novelists, 6th edition, St. James Press,1996.

Dictionary of Literary Biography, Volume 28: *Twentieth-Century American-Jewish Fiction Writers,* Gale, 1984.

PERIODICALS

Booklist, March 1, 1975.

Kirkus Reviews, February 1, 1975.

Nation, April 12, 1980.

New Leader, June 9, 1975.

New Yorker, February 18, 1980.

New York Times Book Review, January 13, 1980; October 18, 1981.*

KASPER, Walter 1933-

PERSONAL: Born March 5, 1933, in Heidenheim, Germany; son of Josef and Theresia (Bacher) Kasper. *Religion:* Roman Catholic.

ADDRESSES: Home—Schwabstrasse 65, D-7400 Tuebingen 1, Germany. *Office*—University of Tuebingen, Liebermeisterstrasse 12, D-7400 Tuebingen 1, Germany.

CAREER: University of Muenster, Muenster, Germany, professor, 1964-70; University of Tuebingen, Tuebingen, Germany, professor, 1970—. Consultor, German Bishops Conference; Bishop of Rottenburg-Stuttgart, Germany.

WRITINGS:

Einfuehrung in den Glauben, Matthias-Gruenewald-Verlag, 1972, translation by David Smith published as *Introduction to Christian Faith,* Paulist Press, 1981.

Jesus der Christus, Matthias-Gruenewald-Verlag, 1974, translation published as *Jesus the Christ,* Paulist Press, 1977.

Zur Theologie der christlichen Ehe, Matthias-Gruenewald-Verlag, 1977, translation published as *The Theology of Christian Marriage,* Crossroad Publishing, 1980.

Der Gott Jesu Christi, Matthias-Gruenewald-Verlag, 1982, translation published as *The God of Jesus Christ,* Crossroad, 1984.

Faith and the Future, Crossroad Publishing, 1982.

God's Time for Mankind, Franciscan Herald, 1983.

The Church's Confession of Faith: A Catholic Catechism for Adults, Ignatius Press, 1987.

The Christian Understanding of Freedom and the History of Freedom in the Modern Era, Marquette University Press (Milwaukee, WI),1988.

Transcending All Understanding: The Meaning of Christian Faith Today, Ignatius Press (San Francisco, CA), 1989.

Theology and Church, Crossroad, 1989.

(With Raymond E. Brown and Gerald O'Collins) *Faith and the Future: Studies in Christian Eschatology,* Paulist Press, 1994.

SIDELIGHTS: In addition to authoring books on Catholic theology and modern life, Bishop Walter Kasper has also taught theology at the university level. He is the bishop of Rottenburg-Stuttgart, Germany, and is an active and vocal member of the German Catholic community. In 1993, Kasper and two other German bishops released a controversial letter on the issue of remarried parishioners. It addressed the theological and practical complications of administering the Sacrament to those who were divorced and remarried. In an interview with James S. Torrens for *America,* Kasper commented on his book *Jesus the Christ:* "I have sought to take the concrete, human Jesus, the so-called historical Jesus, seriously, and to show how from this concrete Jesus the theological statement derives that he is the Christ, the Messiah or, later, the Son of God. My whole Christology is thus constructed on a correspondence between the earthly Jesus and the confessional statement of the church about this earthly Jesus. . . . I wanted simply to show that the results of historical-critical research, which at that time was hotly discussed, could build a bridge to the high-christological statements of the early church, not only to ground them but also to help us understand them, to fill them with life and thereby to bring them closer to people of today."

Kasper believes that the notion of self-liberation has characterized contemporary European life. He commented on this in his interview with Torrens, stating, "If you take emancipation in a radical sense, it is certainly not compatible with the basic Christian understanding, because man as a creature cannot emancipate himself from God. Further, as Christians we cannot emancipate ourselves from salvation history and from our tradition of faith. . . . My aim in thc book [*Jesus the Christ*] was to understand redemption as a setting-free. . . . I believe that thereby, on the one hand, we can grasp the justifiable desire for modern, contemporary emancipation; but at the same time we can, and even must, criticize and surpass it. In other words we cannot purely and simply be totally emancipated people in today's modern or post-modern sense, and at the same time Christians."

BIOGRAPHICAL/CRITICAL SOURCES:

PERIODICALS

America, January 22, 1983, p. 57; October 8, 1994, p. 20; February 10, 1996, p. 9.

Choice, July, 1977, p. 699.

Library Journal, June 15, 1980, p. 1397.

Times Literary Supplement, April 8, 1977, p. 434.*

* * *

KAY, Jackie

See KAY, Jacqueline Margaret

KAY, Jacqueline Margaret 1961-
(Jackie Kay)

PERSONAL: Born November 9, 1961, in Edinburgh, Scotland; children: one son. *Education:* University of Stirling, B.A. (honors in English), 1983.

ADDRESSES: Home—20 Townsend Road, London N15 4NT, England. *Agent*—Pat Kavanagh, Peters Fraser & Dunlop, 503/4 The Chambers, Chelsea Harbour, London SW10 0XF, England.

CAREER: Writer. Writer-in-residence, Hammersmith, London, 1989-91.

AWARDS, HONORS: Eric Gregory Award, 1991; Scottish Arts Council Book Award, 1991, for *The Adoption Papers;* Saltire First Book of the Year Award, 1991, for *The Adoption Papers;* Forward Prize, 1992, for *The Adoption Papers;* Signal Poetry Award, 1993, for *Two's Company;* Somerset Maugham Award for *Other Lovers.*

WRITINGS:

UNDER NAME JACKIE KAY

The Adoption Papers (poetry), Bloodaxe (Newcastle upon Tyne, England), 1991.
That Distance Apart (chapbook), Turret (London), 1991.
Two's Company (poetry for children), Puffin (London), 1992.
Other Lovers (poetry), Bloodaxe, 1993.
Three Has Gone (poetry for children), Blackie Children's (London), 1994.
Bessie Smith, Absolute (New York City), 1997.
Trumpet (novel), Pantheon (New York City), 1999.

SIDELIGHTS: Jackie Kay is a "vigorously individual" writer, in the words of *Contemporary Women Poets* contributor Philip Hobsbaum. Her body of work encompasses poetry that deals with subjects such as love and childhood difficulties in simple, straightforward language, in addition to a study of blues singer Bessie Smith and a well-received first novel, *Trumpet,* about a female jazz musician who passes for male.

In her first poetry collection, *The Adoption Papers,* Kay, an adoptee, writes from the points of view of a birth mother, an adoptive mother, and a daughter. "We hear the voices quite distinctively," observes Hobsbaum, adding that "the plainness of diction . . . gives a sense of authenticity." Kay displays a "child's-eye view" in her poetry, he notes. In "My Grandmother's Houses," a poem in *The Adoption Papers,* Kay describes a house in which "rooms lead off like an optopus's arms" from a seemingly enormous hallway; in "The Year of the Letter," from *Other Lovers,* she conveys the joy a book-loving child finds in the library. "Kay is able to get across what happens to a child with considerable atmosphere," Hobsbaum declares, but he feels Kay is not equally successful in portraying adult emotions and experiences. When she writes about a mother, he contends, it "is a child's idea of a mother"; additionally, her discussion of the life of her African ancestors under slavery looks at this topic as a child might. *New Statesman and Society* critic Peter Forbes, however, offers no such reservations, and he lauds Kay's handling of the adult topic of romantic love in *Other Lovers.* Kay, he says, has "bravado . . . but also the kind of fierce tenderness you need to animate the timeless love lyric."

In the opinion of some critics, Kay's experience as a poet informs her first novel, *Trumpet,* which a *Publishers Weekly* reviewer calls an "intense and poetic narrative" about a musician named Joss Moody, who lived as man, married a woman and adopted a son with her, and was revealed to be a woman only after her death. The novel was inspired by the true story of Billy Tipton, born Dorothy, a journeyman jazz player who passed as a man for more than 50 years, married five times, and adopted several children. In 1989, paramedics trying to save a dying Tipton discovered the musician was a woman. Moody differs from Tipton in numerous ways; in addition to having had one wife instead of five, Moody is black and Scottish while Tipton was white and American. Also, Moody's wife knows her husband's true gender; Tipton's wives claimed to have been fooled.

Kay tells Moody's story from various viewpoints, including Moody's wife, mother, and grown son; an unsympathetic prospective biographer; and a fellow musician. This approach, according to *Advocate* reviewer Carol Anshaw, "serve[s] the story well, for what is a show without its audience, a disguise without those fooled by it?" While noting that "some voices ring truer than others and wear better," Anshaw adds that "these opposing points of view set up the truly intriguing (and somewhat underexplored in this novel) question about a life played out in drag. Is this really a disguise after all? Is gender limited to physicality, or can it be superseded by desire and reinvention?" An *Economist* contributor notes that *Trumpet*'s divergent characters are motivated in differing ways by love and remarks that "Ms. Kay takes her readers through the various voices of love—rough and lyrical, simple and sophisticated—with perfect assurance." The *Publishers Weekly* critic concludes, "In the end, the mysteries of Joss's life remain ambiguous, but his courage . . . and his legacy of love, provide the haunting motif of this richly evocative narrative."

BIOGRAPHICAL/CRITICAL SOURCES:

BOOKS

Contemporary Women Poets, St. James Press (Detroit), 1998.

PERIODICALS

Advocate, March 16, 1999, p. 63.
Economist, March 6, 1999, p. 80.
Entertainment Weekly, May 21, 1999, p. 70.
New Statesman and Society, November 26, 1993, p. 43.
Publishers Weekly, December 21, 1998, p. 50.*

* * *

KEFALA, Antigone 1935-

PERSONAL: Born May 28, 1935, in Braila, Romania; married Robert Kerr, 1959 (divorced 1963); married Usher Weinrauch, 1964 (divorced 1976). *Education:* Victoria University, B.A., 1958, M.A., 1960.

ADDRESSES: Home—12 Rose St., Annandale, New South Wales 2038, Australia.

CAREER: Writer. New South Wales Department of Education, Sydney, teacher of English, 1961-68; University of New South Wales, administrative assistant, 1968-69; Australia Council for the Arts, Sydney, arts administrator, 1971-87.

WRITINGS:

POETRY

The Alien, Makar Press (Brisbane), 1973.
Thirsty Weather, Outback Press (Melbourne), 1978.
European Notebook, Hale and Iremonger (Sydney), 1988.
Absence: New and Selected Poems, Hale and Iremonger, 1992.

NOVELS

The First Journey, Wild and Woolley (Sydney), 1975.
The Island, Hale and Iremonger, 1984.
Alexia: A Tale of Two Cultures (for children), illustrated by Warwick Hatton, John Ferguson (Sydney), 1984.

SIDELIGHTS: Antigone Kefala's development as a writer has been deeply influenced by her exposure to various languages. As a child she lived in Romania, she learned to speak Greek in Greece, and she began writing in English while attending an Australian university. Although she once understood poetry in a musical sense, she now understands it more as an architectural form that allows truth to be perceived. In poetry and prose, Kefala writes sparingly and intensely. She endeavors to strike the perfect balance between language and meaning.

The Alien and *Thirsty Weather* were groundbreaking books in terms of publications by writers for whom English is a second language. When they were published in the 1970s, there were very few serious books by such authors despite the number of people living in Australia whose backgrounds were in other languages. Readers find a unique voice in Kefala, who is bitter but not hostile in her sharp observations. Judith Rodriguez of *Contemporary Poets* observed, "Taking in images as light as skeletal leaves and yet invested with symbolic weight, readers in fact learn a new language for themselves and their places. . . ."

BIOGRAPHICAL/CRITICAL SOURCES:

BOOKS

Contemporary Poets, 6th edition, St. James Press, 1996.

PERIODICALS

Australian Book Review, June,1996, p. 67.
World Literature Today, winter, 1994, p. 210; autumn, 1996, p. 1037.*

* * *

KEITH, Harold (Verne) 1903-1998

PERSONAL: Born April 8, 1903, in Lambert, Oklahoma Territory (now Oklahoma); died February 23, 1998; son of Malcolm Arrowwood (a grain buyer) and Arlyn (Kee) Keith; married Virginia Livingston, August 20, 1931; children: John Livingston, Kathleen

Ann. *Education:* Attended Northwestern State Teachers College (now Northwestern State College); University of Oklahoma, B.A., 1929, M.A., 1938, special courses in professional writing, 1953-56. *Politics:* Independent. *Religion:* Episcopalian. *Avocational interests:* Long-distance running, quail hunting, trout fishing, singing in a barbershop quartet.

CAREER: Amorita Consolidated School System, Amorita, OK, seventh-grade teacher, 1922-23; *Daily Oklahoman, Oklahoma City, Tulsa World, Kansas City Star,* and *Oklahoma World-Herald,* sports correspondent, 1922-29; Red Star Milling Co., Hutchinson, KS, assistant to grain buyer, 1929-30; University of Oklahoma, Norman, sports publicity director, 1930-69.

MEMBER: College Sports Information Directors of America (president, 1964-65), National Collegiate Athletic Association (member of public relations committee, 1960-69), Norman Kiwanis Club (member of board of directors for eleven years).

AWARDS, HONORS: Helms Foundation Sports Publicist of Year, 1950; John Newbery Medal for the most distinguished contribution to literature for American children, 1958, and Lewis Carroll Shelf Award, 1964, both for *Rifles for Watie;* Arch Ward Memorial Trophy for outstanding achievement in sports publicity, 1961; *New York Times* Best Book citation, 1965, for *Komantcia;* Charlie May Simon Award, 1973, for *The Runt of Rogers School;* Western Heritage Award, 1975, and Spur Award, both for *Susy's Scoundrel;* Western Heritage Award for *The Obstinate Land.* Oklahoma Lifetime Achievement Book Award; member of Oklahoma Writer's Hall of Fame.

WRITINGS:

JUVENILE; ALL PUBLISHED BY CROWELL (NEW YORK CITY), EXCEPT AS INDICATED

Boys' Life of Will Rogers, illustrated by Karl S. Woerner, 1936, revised edition published as *Will Rogers, A Boy's Life: An Indian Territory Childhood,* Levite of Apache Publishing (Norman, OK), 1991.
Sports and Games (Junior Literary Guild selection), 1940.
Shotgun Shaw: A Baseball Story, illustrated by Mabel Jones Woodbury, 1949.
A Pair of Captains, illustrated by Woodbury, 1951.
Rifles for Watie, 1957.
Komantcia (novel about Comanche Indians), Levite of Apache Publishing, 1965, 2nd edition, 1991.
Brief Garland, 1971.
The Runt of Rogers School, Lippincott (Philadelphia, PA), 1971.
The Bluejay Boarders, illustrated by Harold Berson, 1972.
Go Red, Go!, illustrated by Ned Glattauer, Nelson (Nashville, TN), 1972.
Susy's Scoundrel, illustrated by John Schoenherr, 1974.
The Obstinate Land, 1977.
The Sound of Strings: Sequel to Komantcia, Levite of Apache Publishing, 1992.

OTHER

Sports and Games, Crowell, 1941, revised edition, 1960.
Oklahoma Kickoff: An Informal History of the First Twenty-five Years at the University of Oklahoma, & of the Amusing Hardships that Attended Its Pioneering (on football), privately printed, 1948, University of Oklahoma Press, 1978.
(With Wilkinson's players of the University of Oklahoma football team) *Forty-seven Straight: The Bud Wilkinson Era at Oklahoma,* University of Oklahoma Press, 1984.
The Obstinate Land (novel), Levite of Apache (Norman, OK), 1993.

Contributor of sports fiction to *American Boy* and *Bluebook,* sports articles to *Esquire* and *Saturday Evening Post.*

Keith's manuscript collections are housed at Northwestern State College Library, Alva, OK, and University of Oklahoma Library, Norman, OK.

SIDELIGHTS: As the child of a grain buyer, Harold Verne Keith moved enough times to attend nine different schools. This appears to have either satisfied any wanderlust he may have had or developed a deep love of Oklahoma, because he lived there for more than sixty years. As a writer, Keith followed the rule of writing about the familiar; he enjoyed a successful career built on books for boys about sports, history, and America's heartland. His books are noted for their accuracy and attention to detail. A thorough researcher, Keith once commented that he drew material for *The Runt of Rogers School* partly from talks with "five runtish Oklahomans who won their spurs as athletes . . . and several elementary school football coaches." For *Rifles for Watie,* his Newbery-winning book about the Civil War set in Oklahoma, he interviewed twenty-two veterans of that conflict, each nearly one hundred years old. His material came primarily from his involvement in sports, both personally and professionally, and from his fascination with local history.

Keith's first book, *Boys' Life of Will Rogers,* grew out of his master's thesis on Rogers' father, Clem Rogers, and his influence on Oklahoma history. The inspiration for *Komantcia,* based on the true story of a young Spaniard's captivity by the Comanches in 1865, came from Keith's extensive reading about "these fascinating people," as he once called them, "as well as [from] personally visiting several Comanches still living in Oklahoma, one of them, Topay, seventh and last living wife of War Chief Quanah Parker." *Oklahoma Kickoff* is a history of another kind: an account of the first twenty-five years of University of Oklahoma football. The later book *Forty-Seven Straight* is a biography of Oklahoma football coach Bud Wilkinson as told by his players and by Keith.

In the years before his retirement, Keith wrote at night and on weekends. *Rifles for Watie* was a five-year labor that led him to compare writing to long-distance running: "You had to learn to punish yourself and keep going even after you grew dead tired. But each night I sat down to write, I felt enthusiasm about this story. I never grew tired of it nor doubted for a moment that it would be accepted," he explained in an interview in the *Wilson Library Bulletin.* The novel's plot involves a young Union soldier, Jefferson Davis Bussey, who spies behind Confederate lines to find a Cherokee, Stand Watie, who is intercepting rifles intended for the Union Army. Jeff is captured by the Confederates and successfully pretends to be one of them for a time, thus learning, as Zena Sutherland notes in *Twentieth-Century Children's Writers,* that "his enemies . . . are young men much like himself." In this "substantial historical fiction," as Sutherland and May Hill Arbuthnot call it in *Children and Books,* Keith presents "unforgettable characters . . . and all the hunger, dirt and weariness of war to balance the heroism." In his Newbery Medal acceptance speech for *Rifles for Watie,* Keith credited his professional writing experience at the University of Oklahoma for teaching him the skills that critics found so evident in the book.

When he retired from the University of Oklahoma, Keith no longer had to fit his writing into the hours he was away from work. At that time he explained his new writing schedule: "I like to start writing early in the morning and work steadily for four hours, then join my friends for a long-distance run, then drive home for a short nap, then return to my library sanctum to work two additional hours in the afternoon. . . . I compose by hand-writing and triple space on the typewriter, and my first drafts are as rough as you'll find anywhere."

Among his own favorite authors Keith named Charles Dickens, O. Henry, and Mark Twain.

BIOGRAPHICAL/CRITICAL SOURCES:

BOOKS

Arbuthnot, May Hill, and Zena Sutherland, *Children and Books,* 8th edition, Harper Collins, 1991, p. 436.
Carlson, G. Robert, *Books and the Teen-Age Reader,* Harper, 1967.
Hack, Charlotte S., editor, *Newbery and Caldecott Medal Books: 1956-1965,* Horn Book, 1965.
Something about the Author, Volume 74, Gale, 1993.
Twentieth-Century Children's Writers, 3rd edition, St. Martin's, 1989.
Twentieth-Century Young Adult Writers, 1st edition, St. James Press, 1994.

PERIODICALS

Booklist, December 15, 1990.
Horn Book, August, 1958.
Roundup Quarterly, spring, 1992; fall, 1992.
Small Press Book Review, November, 1991.
Social Studies, November, 1991.
Wilson Library Bulletin, June, 1958.

OBITUARIES:

PERIODICALS

Atlanta Journal and Constitution, February 26, 1998.*

* * *

KELLEY, Leo P(atrick) 1928-

PERSONAL: Born September 10, 1928, in Wilkes-Barre, PA; son of Leo A. and Regina (Caffrey) Kelley. *Education:* New School for Social Research, B.A., 1957.

ADDRESSES: *Home*—702 Lincoln Blvd., Long Beach, NY 11561.

CAREER: McGraw-Hill Book Co., New York, NY, 1959-69, began as copywriter, became advertising and promotion manager; free-lance writer, 1969—.

MEMBER: Western Writers of America, Science Fiction Writers of America, Mystery Writers of America, Mensa.

AWARDS, HONORS: Short story "The Traveling Man" was nominated for a Nebula Award.

WRITINGS:

SCIENCE FICTION

The Counterfeits, Belmont Books, 1967.
Odyssey to Earthdeath, Belmont Books, 1968.
The Accidental Earth, Belmont Books, 1970.
Time Rogue, Lancer, 1970.
Brother John (based on a screenplay by Ernest Kinoy), Avon, 1971.
The Coins of Murph, Berkley Publishing, 1971.
(Contributor) Robert Hoskins, editor, *Infinity 3,* Lancer, 1972.
Mindmix, Fawcett, 1972.
Time: 110100, Walker & Co., 1972 (published in England as *The Man from Maybe,* Coronet, 1974).
Deadlocked, Fawcett, 1973.
The Earth Tripper, Fawcett, 1973.
Mythmaster, Dell, 1973.

JUVENILE SCIENCE FICTION

(Editor) *Themes in Science Fiction: A Journey into Wonder,* McGraw-Hill, 1972.
(Editor) *Fantasy: The Literature of the Marvelous,* McGraw-Hill, 1973.
(Editor) *The Supernatural in Fiction,* McGraw-Hill, 1973.
The Time Trap: Pacesetters, Children's Press, 1978.
Night of Fire and Blood, illustrated by Ed Diffenderfer, Fearon-Pitman, 1979.
Star Gold, Children's Press, 1979.

"GALAXY 5" SERIES

Dead Moon (also see below), Fearon-Pitman, 1979.
Goodbye to Earth (also see below), Fearon-Pitman, 1979.
King of the Stars (also see below), Fearon-Pitman, 1979.
On the Red World (also see below), Fearon-Pitman, 1979.
Vacation in Space (also see below), Fearon-Pitman, 1979.
Where No Sun Shines (also see below), Fearon-Pitman, 1979.
Galaxy 5 Science Fiction Series (contains *Dead Moon, Goodbye to Earth, King of the Stars, On the Red World, Vacation in Space,* and *Where No Sun Shines*), with teacher's guide, Fearon-Pitman, 1979.

"SPACE POLICE" SERIES

Backward in Time (also see below), Fearon-Pitman, 1979.
Death Sentence (also see below), Fearon-Pitman, 1979.
Earth Two (also see below), Fearon-Pitman, 1979.
Prison Satellite (also see below), Fearon-Pitman, 1979.
Sunworld (also see below), Fearon-Pitman, 1979.
Worlds Apart (also see below), Fearon-Pitman, 1979.
Space Police (contains *Backward in Time, Death Sentence, Earth Two, Prison Satellite, Sunworld,* and *Worlds Apart*), with teacher's guide, Fearon-Pitman, 1979.

WESTERN NOVELS

Luke Sutton: Outlaw, Doubleday (New York City), 1981.
Johnny Tall Dog, Pitman Learning, 1981.
Luke Sutton: Gunfighter, Doubleday, 1982.
Luke Sutton: Indian Fighter, Doubleday, 1982.
Luke Sutton: Avenger, Doubleday, 1983.
Luke Sutton: Outrider, Doubleday, 1984.
Luke Sutton: Bounty Hunter, Doubleday, 1985.
Morgan, Doubleday, 1986.
Luke Sutton: Hired Gun, Doubleday, 1987.
The Last Cowboy, David S. Lake Publishers, 1988.
Thunder Gods' Gold, M. Evans (New York City), 1988.
Luke Sutton, Lawman, Doubleday, 1989.
Luke Sutton, Mustanger, Doubleday, 1990.
Bannock's Brand, Doubleday, 1991.

"CIMARRON" SERIES; PUBLISHED BY NEW AMERICAN LIBRARY

Cimarron in the Cherokee Strip, 1983.
Cimarron and the Border Bandits, 1983.
Cimarron and the Bounty Hunters, 1983.
Cimarron and the Elk Soldiers, 1983.
Cimarron and the Hanging Judge, 1983.
Cimarron Rides the Outlaw Trail, 1983.
Cimarron in the No Man's Land, 1984.
Cimarron on Hell's Highway, 1984.
Cimarron and the High Rider, 1984.
Cimarron and the Medicine Wolves, 1984.
Cimarron and the Vigilantes, 1984.
Cimarron and the War Women, 1984.
Cimarron and the Bootleggers, 1984.
Cimarron and the Gun Hawks' Gold, 1985.
Cimarron and the Prophet's People, 1985.

Cimarron and the Scalp Hunters, 1985.
Cimarron and the Hired Guns, 1986.
Cimarron and the Red Earth People, 1986.

OTHER

A Man Named Dundee, Doubleday, 1988.

Contributor of stories and poetry to numerous periodicals, including *Alfred Hitchcock's Mystery Magazine, Gallery, Magazine of Fantasy and Science Fiction, Saint Mystery Magazine, Swank,* and *Worlds of If.*

SIDELIGHTS: Leo P. Kelley is an accomplished writer in the two genres of Western fiction and science fiction. He first established his reputation with numerous science-fiction titles, but today he is best known for his Luke Sutton and Cimarron Western series. David Whitehead of *Twentieth-Century Western Writers* attributed the success of Kelley's frontier stories to "their fast pace and wealth of wilderness lore."

Kelley introduced himself to readers of Westerns with *Luke Sutton: Outlaw,* which blends traditional Western elements and modern ones. The character of Sutton is heroic—he is quick with a gun and his fists, attractive to women, able to withstand pain, and capable of living in the wild. His quest is to find the four men who killed his brother. In each of the Sutton novels, Kelley explores a different aspect of the Old West; Whitehead noted that this gives the stories "a rather episodic feel . . . as if we are really only witnessing a series of interesting but often pointless incidents in Sutton's life." In *Luke Sutton: Indian Fighter,* Sutton has already slain two of his brother's killers (one in the first book, and another in *Luke Sutton: Gunfighter*), and his quest leads him to the Black Hills. He loses everything he owns in a buffalo stampede, then makes a raft to take him into the hills, where he meets an old muleskinner whom he offers to help. When the man is badly injured, he signs his livestock over to Sutton. In a nearby mining town, Sutton discovers the whereabouts of Johnny Loud Thunder, one of the men he is seeking; but when he sets out to find him he is captured and forced to work with slaves in a mine. He manages to escape and track down and eventually kill Loud Thunder, fighting in the Battle of Little Big Horn along the way.

In Kelley's second Western series, he adds sex to the mix of historical detail, Western lore, and adventure. Whitehead observed that the Cimarron series lacks much of the credibility of the Sutton series, largely due to the fantasy-based nature of these Westerns in which imaginative bedroom scenes interrupt whatever else is happening in the story. The main character, Cimarron, wears a scar on his face from when his father punished him by burning him with a branding iron. He leaves home at a young age and becomes an outlaw. He changes, however, when he robs a small town and shoots the marshal, who turns out to be his father. Vowing to turn his life around, he goes to work for Judge Isaac C. Parker (in *Cimarron and the Hanging Judge*), and makes a life of tracking down outlaws and bringing them to justice. His adventures bring him in contact with all sorts of people, including Belle Starr (in *Cimarron Rides the Outlaw Trail*) and a religious cult leader (in *Cimarron and the Prophet's People*).

Before he achieved his stature as a Western writer, Kelley was a science-fiction writer. His first novel, *Counterfeits,* is a story about Earth's invasion by aliens whose planet has been destroyed. Because they are able to take on any shape, their resolve to destroy human civilization is especially threatening. George Kelley of *Twentieth-Century Science-Fiction Writers* found that this book distinguishes itself from the alien invasion formula by concluding with an attempt at a plausible reconciliation. In *The Accidental Earth,* Earth is separated from an alternate Earth by a time wall. When an accident brings the two Earths into contact, a secret weapon (Photon Spray) severs the link, safely separating the two Earths. George Kelley noted: "Although the conclusion is hackneyed space opera, the beginning and middle sections of the novel feature some of Kelley's best writing." *The Coins of Murph* is set in a post-holocaust society that worships Joseph Murphy, a chief programmer of the past. On surviving tapes, Murphy blames the holocaust on bad decisions, which leads the society to the conclusion that decisions should be based on chance. Subsequently, issues are decided by tossing coins.

Kelley commented to *Something about the Author,* "Science-fiction authors have always been very much concerned with tomorrow. But, as authors, their concern encompasses an additional dimension not always shared by everyone, at least not to the same degree. They are deeply concerned with the events that may result from actions taken by men today. Such authors observe the behavior of men in the world today and they speculate on how that behavior may determine the nature and character of the not too distant future. . . . Science-fiction stories are not necessarily written to predict the future although many such stories have predicted it with surprising accuracy. Instead, the science-fiction story attempts to portray the writer's vision of such subjects as interstellar travel or war in the future. *Vision* is the key word here. . . . No story succeeds that does not affect its readers. To be affected by a story means simply that the reader's thoughts and emotions must be stirred. It is this stirring of thoughts and emotions that encourages readers to turn to literature for a sharpened insight into life."

BIOGRAPHICAL/CRITICAL SOURCES:

BOOKS

Something about the Author, Volume 32, Gale, 1983.

Twentieth-Century Science-Fiction Writers, 3rd edition, St. James Press, 1991.

Twentieth-Century Western Writers, 2nd edition, St. James Press, 1991.

PERIODICALS

Booklist, September 15, 1985, p. 108; January 1, 1989, p. 752; March 1, 1989, p. 1092.

Library Journal, July, 1986, p. 109; December, 1988, p. 133; January, 1991, p. 152.

Publishers Weekly, November 11, 1988, p.42.

Roundup Review, spring, 1991, p. 49.*

* * *

KELLEY, William Melvin 1937-

PERSONAL: Born November 1, 1937, in New York, NY; son of William (an editor) and Narcissa Agatha (Garcia) Kelley; married Karen Isabelle Gibson (a designer), December, 1962; children: Jessica, Ciratikaiji. *Education:* Attended Harvard University, 1957-61.

ADDRESSES: *Office*—P.O. Box 2658, New York, NY 10027.

CAREER: Free-lance writer and photographer. Writer in residence, State University of New York at Geneseo, spring, 1965; instructor, New School for Social Research, 1965-67; guest lecturer in American literature, University of Paris, Nanterre, 1968; guest instructor, University of West Indies, Mona, 1969-70.

AWARDS, HONORS: Dana Reed Prize from Harvard University, 1960; Bread Loaf Scholar, 1962; John Hay Whitney Foundation Award and Rosenthal Foundation Award, 1963, both for *A Different Drummer; Transatlantic Review* Award, 1964, for *Dancers on the Shore;* fiction award from Black Academy of Arts and Letters, 1970, for *Dunfords Travels Everywheres.*

WRITINGS:

FICTION

A Different Drummer (novel), Doubleday, 1962, with a foreword by David Bradley, Anchor Books, 1989.

Dancers on the Shore (short stories), Doubleday, 1964, reprinted (introduction by Mel Watkins), Howard University Press, 1984.

A Drop of Patience (novel), Doubleday, 1965.

dem (novel), Doubleday, 1967, reprinted with an introduction by Willie E. Abraham, Collier Books, 1969.

Dunfords Travels Everywheres (novel), Doubleday, 1970.

CONTRIBUTOR TO ANTHOLOGIES

Langston Hughes, editor, *The Best Short Stories by Negro Writers: An Anthology from 1899 to the Present,* Little, Brown, 1967.

Richard Kostelanetz, editor, *The Young American Writers,* Funk, 1967.

James A. Emanuel and Theodore Gross, editors, *Dark Symphony: Negro Literature in America,* Free Press, 1968.

Edward Margolies, editor, *Native Sons: A Critical Study of Twentieth- Century Negro American Authors,* Lippincott, 1968.

Arnold Adoff, editor, *Brothers and Sisters: Modern Stories by Black Americans,* Macmillan, 1970.

Lettie J. Austin, Lewis W. Fenderson, and Sophia P. Nelson, editors, *The Black Man and the Promise of America,* Scott, Foresman, 1970.

Bradford Chambers and Rebecca Moon, editors, *Right On!: Anthology of Black Literature,* New American Library, 1970.

John Henrik Clarke, editor, *Harlem: Voices from the Soul of Black America,* New American Library, 1970.

Charles L. James, editor, *From the Roots: Short Stories by Black Americans,* Dodd, 1970.

Francis E. Kearns, editor, *Black Experience: An Anthology of American Literature for the 1970's,* Viking, 1970.

Darwin T. Turner, editor, *Black American Literature: Essays, Poetry, Fiction, Drama,* Merrill, 1970.

Houston A. Baker, Jr., editor, *Black Literature in America,* McGraw-Hill, 1971.

Arthur P. Davis and J. Saunders Reddings, editors, *Cavalcade: Negro American Writing from 1760 to the Present,* Houghton, 1971.

Nick Aaron Ford, editor, *Black Insights: Significant Literature by Black Americans, 1760 to the Present,* Ginn, 1971.

Richard K. Barksdale and Kenneth Kinnamon, editors, *Black Writers of America: A Comprehensive Anthology,* Macmillan, 1972.

Abraham Chapman, editor, *New Black Voices,* New American Library, 1972.

Richard A. Long and Eugenia W. Collier, editors, *Afro-American Writing: An Anthology of Prose and Poetry,* New York University Press, 1972.

William Smart, editor, *Women and Men, Men and Women,* St. Martin's, 1975.

OTHER

"Excavating Harlem" (video), produced by Manhattan Cable/Channel D, 1988.

Contributor to periodicals, including *Accent, Canto, Jazz and Pop, Mademoiselle, Negro Digest, New York Times Magazine, Partisan Review, Playboy, Quilt, River Styx, Urbanite,* and *Works in Progress.*

SIDELIGHTS: The fiction of William Melvin Kelley published between 1962 and 1970—spanning the most tumultuous years of the civil rights movement— displays the author's evolving perceptions of black and white in American society. Kelley's fiction undergoes noticeable transformations from his first novel, *A Different Drummer,* supportive of nonviolence as a means to effect social change, to his later works, which become increasingly experimental in structure and more vehemently critical of social injustice. Kelley begins with "a vision of racial coexistence," explains Valerie M. Babb in the *Dictionary of Literary Biography,* yet as he "became more aware of the systematic degradation of blacks throughout American history, the themes and concerns of his writing took on a more radical stance. He shifted from characters making quiet protests to regain their lost dignity to characters angrily avenging past wrongs." This progression in Kelley's fiction offers a paradigm to changes within the 1960s civil rights movement itself. "In his personal development, we can see a chapter of our nation's history," contends Babb, "and in his literary development, we can note some of the clearest articulations of American culture at the time."

Kelley's four novels, along with his short story collection *Dancers on the Shore,* are often collectively examined as a saga of contemporary Afro-American experience. Robert Bone notes in *New York Times Book Review* that Kelley's "books are unified in over-all design," comparing the effect to a "reverse" variation on William Faulkner's Yoknapatawpha County legend: "an epic treatment of American history from a Negro point of view." Jill Weyant similarly comments in *CLA Journal:* "The purpose of writing a serious saga . . . is to depict impressionistically a large, crowded portrait, each individual novel presenting enlarged details of the whole, each complete in itself, yet evoking a more universal picture than is possible in a single volume." Weyant elaborates that the "Kelley saga is an attempt to redefine the Complete Man and to overturn inaccurate racial stereotypes that, in Kelley's opinion, have too long held sway." Kelley himself has commented on a goal of interrelatedness in his fiction, telling Roy Newquist in *Conversations:* "Perhaps I'm trying to follow the Faulknerian pattern although I guess it's really Balzacian when you connect everything. I'd like to be eighty years old and look up at the shelf and see that all of my books are really one big book."

Throughout his fiction, Kelley emphasizes the worth and intrinsic rights of humans as individuals. Babb comments on the early stages of Kelley's outlook: "In the beginning stages of his writing career, Kelley saw that to be black in America was an amalgam of many experiences, yet many white and even black leaders sought to view black consciousness as a single entity. The individual has an obligation, Kelley believed, to focus more on 'what we really are: human beings, not simply members of a race.' " This belief exists behind the title of Kelley's first novel, *A Different Drummer,* recalling the famous lines of Henry David Thoreau: "If a man does not keep pace with his companions, perhaps it is because he hears a different drummer. Let him step to the music which he hears, however measured or far away." Hugh J. Ingrasci comments on the resilience of Kelley's concept of individuality: "The world Kelley portrays . . . projects a life of possibilities, one wherein the struggle to eliminate racial inequities is viable, but only for the individual who hammers away at exploitation with one irresistible conviction: that each human person has too great a value to allow others to regard him as a mere social commodity." It matters little, Ingrasci continues, if one "wins his battle with the society he finds. . . . It is his belief that he is humanly equal to anyone else that has set him free, and not the prospect of attaining social justice."

In the preface to his short story collection *Dancers on the Shore,* Kelley likewise emphasizes an approach to writing that focuses on the individual. He criticizes those who would lump all black authors into a single category, the "Negro literary ghetto," as he describes it. "An American writer who happens to have brown skin faces this unique problem," Kelley explains: "Solutions and answers to the Negro Problem are very often read into his work. At the instant they open his book, the readers begin to search fervently, and often with honest concern, for some key or answer to what is happening today between black and white people in America." Kelley likewise applies an emphasis on individuality to his own characters: "At this time, let me say for the record that I am not a sociologist or a politician or a spokesman. Such people try to give answers. A writer, I think, should ask questions. He should depict people, not symbols or ideas disguised as people."

Critical response to Kelley's individual books has been divided. He is often cited for maintaining a controlled and calculated distance from his subject matter, yet at times is criticized for writing too facilely, or—in seeming contradiction to his stated intentions—from too ideological a perspective. Regarding *Dancers on the Shore,* Louis Rubin, Jr., comments in *New York Herald Tribune Book Week* that Kelley's stories "bear all the earmarks of having been written while the author was still searching for his true subject" and that they suffer in two main areas: "Either they are underdeveloped, with the author having worked only at the surface of his material, or else (and sometimes at the same time) they are content with presenting aspects of what Mr. Kelley said he wasn't going to try to solve, The Negro Problem." Michele Murray in *Commonweal,* on the other hand, praises Kelley's perspective in *Dancers on the Shore,* writing that the stories benefit from "a fineness that comes from the *tone* of the telling—very spare, very quiet, very honest." Kelley's third book, *A Drop of Patience,* similarly received mixed comments. The story of a black jazz musician who is blind, *A Drop of Patience* "is a moving, painful and stinging experience," writes David Boroff in *New York Times Book Review:* "Kelley's prose is tight and spare, the novel's anger and bitterness straining against the stripped-down language." He concludes, however, that Kelley's main character is "in the end . . . too simple a figure, a slice of folklore rather than a convincing human being." Likewise, Whitney Balliett in *New Yorker,* although in praise of Kelley's going "about his work calmly" while working with subject matter that can "turn well-meaning novelists into polemicists," comments on over-ideologized characters: "Kelley's characters . . . tend to spring from his ideas, rather than the other way around. If he were to press deeper into the ordinary hearts he writes of, instead of forcing them to grow on intellectual trellises, he would help us to know our own hearts."

Kelley's fourth book, the novel *dem,* takes a distinctly radical approach in communicating the destructive influences of racism in America. An "overt satire of the ways of white people," according to Bone, Kelley's novel is the story of a white couple who, through a rare fertilization process, become the parents of twin boys, one white and one black. Calling the book "a jarring surprise," Henry S. Resnik in *Saturday Review* describes *dem*'s major characters: "The protagonist, Mitchell Pierce, is upper-middle-class white, an advertising copy-writer, emotionally and sexually impotent, a travesty of a man. His wife, Tam, is a domineering bitch whose principal characteristics are her penchant for ridicule and her preoccupation with her hairdo." Resnick adds: "The book is an angry, if not always original, portrait of American society. . . . Kelley is not only angry at savagery, racism, emasculation, and matriarchy; he takes a good hard crack at our slim hold on reality."

As with Kelley's previous fiction, some reviewers objected to a level of superficiality in the novel. Dan Jaffe remarks in *Prairie Schooner:* "The texture of the language, the settings, and the dialogue, give the reader a sense of life, of the alienation of a confused white man who suspects he is on the periphery of a life-rhythm more natural and substantial than his own. Unfortunately, the rest of the novel is slick and stagey by comparison." Frank C. Shapiro comments in *Book World* that the main character of *dem* is not quite believable: "There are good scenes in this unsatisfying book, and good writing, too, but on the whole, reading *dem* is like watching a basketball player, in perfect form, fake out a guard, arch for a pivot shot, and miss." Bone, however, praises Kelley's use of satire to effectively communicate his message: "[Kelley's] present mood is bitter, disillusioned, alienated to the point of secession from American society. The expatriate impulse, however, has found in satire a controlling form. Kelley's images are able to encompass his negative emotions. The result is a sharp increase in perception for the victims of his satire." Babb commends Kelley's innovative approach in that it "represents a reordering of the social history of America. Rather than having blacks as the victims, in [*dem*] it is the whites who suffer as Kelley parodies their traditions and their values. . . . Kelley suggests that white America is sterile in the values it pursues and is consciously, deliberately cruel."

Kelley's next novel, *Dunfords Travels Everywheres,* is his most experimental. "Inspired by *Finnegans Wake* and the problem [James] Joyce faced as an Irish writer within a larger English context," notes Babb, "*Dunfords Travels Everywheres* is constructed from a language derived from Bantu, Pidgin English, and Harlem argot, among other forms of black speech." In the novel, Kelley combines this experimental, collective language ("Langleash") with that of standard English prose to relate the internal exploration of Chig Dunford, a contemporary Harvard-educated black. In his self-exploration, Dunford comes upon an aspect of himself embodied in a character named Carlyle Bedlow, a Harlem-raised black; these twin aspects of the same person converge along common bonds that are understood through their secret language. Michael Wood explains in *New York Review of Books:* "In the half-gibberish of their dreams, represented in the novel by Joycean metalanguage,. . . they know the truth which escapes them in waking life—shown here by Kelley in more conventional prose, as a place of assassinations and deceit, where slaves are suddenly encountered on a lower deck of a modern liner, where vast competing conspiracies, secret societies of whites against blacks and vice versa, are glimpsed beneath the surfaces of an innocent-looking world." Dunford emerges as a far-reaching representative of the Afro-American, according to David Galloway in *The Black American Short Story in the Twentieth Century: A Collection of Critical Essays:* "Just as Joyce's hero, H. C. E., metamorphoses into 'Here comes Everybody,' so Dunford is a kind of 'everybody' traveling everywhere—Harlem spade, Ivy League Negro, crook and cowboy and lover and artist and pilgrim."

Regarding *Dunfords Travels Everywheres* critical opinion was again divided on Kelley. Wood comments that like Joyce, Kelley "as a black American and a writer, is caught in the language and culture of an enemy country, and his use of *Finnegans Wake* reflects a legitimate distress: it is a mockery both of 'good English' and of black manglings of it." Wood concludes, however, that "the effort looks in the wrong direction. The experimental idiom is ingenious, but it is, also, thin and obscure." On the other hand, Christopher Lehmann-Haupt notes in *New York Times* that the "black form of the dream language of James Joyce's *Finnegans Wake* . . . has released in Kelley a creative exuberance that was being choked with bitterness in his last book." Although Lehmann-Haupt agrees that some aspects of the novel "seem curiously cryptic and incomplete," he commends Kelley for "the way the 'real' surface is undermined, so that finally it threatens to splinter into hallucination at every moment. Chief among the myriad themes . . . is that the way to the black man's roots is not over Harlem and out, but back to the streets of the ghetto and in through its language."

Regarding possible political statements in his fiction, Kelley remarked in his 1967 *Conversations* interview: "I simply want to try to write good books. It isn't that I'm naive, that I'm trying to divorce myself from the racial struggle, but I don't think it should enter into my art in such a way that my writing becomes propagandistic. If my novels are so strongly tied to the times the book would have no reason to live once the present struggles are over—if indeed, they ever will be over. I want my books to have reason to exist." Galloway comments that, as enduring literature, Kelley's novels and short stories "manage to carve a reasonably secure niche for themselves within the American system; the trials to which they are submitted have as much to do with being human as they do, specifically, with being black." Galloway notes a particular relevance of Kelley's fiction: "The dilemma he frequently underscores is that the black's destiny is in many ways indistinguishable from the destiny of the entire post-modern American society, but that participation in such a destiny must not be allowed to submerge entirely the ethnic, cultural, and personal identity of the black."

BIOGRAPHICAL/CRITICAL SOURCES:

BOOKS

Bruck, Peter, editor, *The Black American Short Story in the Twentieth Century: A Collection of Critical Essays,* Gruener, 1977.

Contemporary Literary Criticism, Volume 22, Gale, 1982.

Contemporary Novelists, 6th edition, St. James Press, 1996.

Dictionary of Literary Biography, Volume 33: *Afro-American Fiction Writers after 1955,* Gale, 1984.

Kelley, William Melvin, *Dancers on the Shore,* Doubleday, 1964.

Kelley, *dem,* Doubleday, 1967.

Kelley, *Dunfords Travels Everywheres,* Doubleday, 1970.

Littlejohn, David, *Black on White,* Grossman, 1966.

Newquist, Roy, editor, *Conversations,* Rand McNally, 1967.

Whitlow, Roger, *Black American Literature: A Critical History,* Nelson Hall, 1973.

Williams, Sherley Anne, *Give Birth to Brightness,* Dial, 1972.

PERIODICALS

America, April 17, 1965.

American Literature, January, 1973.

Best Sellers, April 15, 1964; April 15, 1965; October 1, 1970.

Booklist, July 1, 1962.
Book World, October 22, 1967.
CLA Journal, December, 1975.
Commonweal, July 3, 1964.
Critique: Studies in Modern Fiction, fall, 1984.
Esquire, August, 1963.
Harper's, December, 1969.
Negro Digest, October, 1962; January, 1967; March, 1967; May, 1968; November, 1969.
Newsweek, April 12, 1965.
New Yorker, May 22, 1965.
New York Herald Tribune Books, June 17, 1962.
New York Herald Tribune Book Week, March 22, 1964.
New York Review of Books, March 11, 1971.
New York Times, April 9, 1965, September 7, 1970.
New York Times Book Review, June 17, 1962; May 2, 1965; September 24, 1967; November 8, 1970.
Partisan Review, spring, 1968.
Prairie Schooner, spring, 1968.
Reporter, May 21, 1964.
Saturday Review, April 17, 1965; October 28, 1967.
Studies in Black Literature, summer, 1971; fall, 1972; winter, 1974; fall, 1975.
Times Literary Supplement, March 17, 1966.*

* * *

KELLY, James Plunkett 1920-
(James Plunkett)

PERSONAL: Born May 21, 1920, in Dublin, Ireland; son of Patrick and Cecilia (Cannon) Kelly; married Valerie Koblitz, September, 1945, children: Valerie Cecilia (Mrs. Michael Murdoch), Ross, James, Vadim. *Education:* Attended Dublin College of Music and Municipal College of Music. *Religion:* Roman Catholic. *Avocational interests:* Listening to and performing on the violin and viola, walking in the country, learning about Ireland, especially its writers, literature, and legends.

ADDRESSES: Home—County Wicklow, Ireland. *Office*—Radio Telefis Eireann, Donnybrook, Dublin 4, Ireland. *Agent*—A. D. Peters, 10 Buckingham St., London WC2 N6BU, England.

CAREER: Worked as clerk and as trade union secretary; assistant head of drama for Radio Eireann, 1955-60; program head (features) for Telefis Eireann, 1960-71; with Radio-Telefis Eireann, 1971—. Governor of Royal Irish Academy of Music, 1950-55.

MEMBER: Irish Academy of Letters, Music Association of Ireland.

AWARDS, HONORS: Jacobs television award, 1964, 1966; *Yorkshire Post* award for literature, 1970.

WRITINGS:

UNDER PSEUDONYM JAMES PLUNKETT

The Trusting and the Maimed and Other Irish Stories, Hutchinson, 1959, revised edition, 1969.
Strumpet City, Delacorte, 1969.
The Gems She Wore, Hutchinson, 1972, Holt, 1973.
Farewell Companions, Hutchinson, 1977.
Collected Short Stories, Poolbeg Press (Dublin), 1977.
The Boy on the Back Wall and Other Essays, Poolbeg Press, 1987.
The Circus Animals, Hutchinson, 1990.

Author of *The Risen People,* a three-act play, first performed in Abbey Theatre, Dublin, Ireland, 1958, published by the Irish Writers' Co-operative in 1978.

SIDELIGHTS: James Plunkett Kelly, who writes as James Plunkett, has great affection for Dublin, where he has lived his entire life. *Strumpet City* takes place in Dublin during the tense years before World War I and describes the plight of the working class, especially in relation to trade unions. The central figure, Barney Mulhall, is based on the real-life trade union leader Barney Conway, who was the right-hand man of political activist Jim Larkin. Plunkett once served as a trade union official, and his characters are drawn from those experiences. In addition to the working class, Plunkett depicts other segments of society, including the middle-class lives of the Bradshaws and the priestly lives of Fathers Giffley and O'Connor. As the book closes, Plunkett demonstrates his belief in the basic decency of human beings.

Farewell Companions is set in the inter-war years, and regards the generation that finds itself in a country that has broken free from its British shackles. The story focuses on Tom McDonagh and his hope for an independent Ireland rather than the Ireland of his parents' generation. Plunkett incorporates political considerations into the narrative; there is an ongoing debate between sentimental nationalism and international socialism. Trevor Royle of *Contemporary Novelists* wrote, "Once again, the description of Dublin and the delineation of Irish working-class life is faultless, equaled only by Plunkett's uncanny ability to create a gallery of vivid characters, each with a story to tell." The conclusion proves unsatisfying for many readers, as Tom turns away from worldly issues and instead takes holy orders.

Dublin's post-war years are the subject of *The Circus Animals.* The book describes bleak years of economic and political upheaval. The central characters are Frank and Margaret McDonagh, a young married couple trying to adapt to married life in a changing, restrictive Ireland where Catholicism is becoming out of place. Frank is a political cartoonist and struggles to maintain his identity as he is drawn into conflict with the more conservative segments of Irish politics. Royle noted, "Plunkett is particularly good at revealing his characters' feelings and at presenting them in a plausible way. Even his priests and nuns possess a rounded humanity despite the fact that they are portrayed as basically unsympathetic characters."

BIOGRAPHICAL/CRITICAL SOURCES:

BOOKS

Contemporary Novelists, 6th edition, St. James Press, 1996.

PERIODICALS

New Statesman, May 2, 1969, p. 630; September 16, 1977, p. 375.
New Yorker, October 25, 1969, p. 190.
New York Times Book Review, November 9, 1969, p. 69.
Observer, April 27, 1969, p. 30; September 11, 1977, p. 25; September 9, 1990, p. 55.
Times Literary Supplement, May 22, 1969, p. 549; August 4, 1972, p. 926; December 9, 1977, p. 1456; December 21, 1990, p. 1382.
Washington Post Book World, September 14, 1969, p. 12.*

* * *

KERR, James Lennox 1899-1963 (Peter Dawlish, Lennox Kerr)

PERSONAL: Born July 1, 1899, in Paisley, Renfrewshire, Scotland; died March 11, 1963; son of John and Sarah (Mathers) Kerr; married Elizabeth Lamorna Birch, 1932; children: one son. *Education:* Educated in Paisley, Renfrewshire, Scotland.

CAREER: Writer. Worked as gold prospector; member of British Mercantile Marine, 1919-29 and 1939-42. *Military service:* Royal Naval Volunteer Reserve, 1915-19 and 1942-46.

WRITINGS:

Back Door Guest, Bobbs-Merrill, 1930, reprinted, Arno, 1974.
Old Ship (novel), Constable, 1930, Macmillan, 1931.
Glenshiels (novel), John Lane, 1932.
(Editor) *On, and Under, the Ocean Wave* (juvenile), Thomas Nelson, 1933.
Ice, a Tale of Effort (novel), John Lane, 1933.
The Young Steamship Officer, Thomas Nelson, 1933.
The Blackspit Smugglers (novel), Thomas Nelson, 1935.
Woman of Glenshiels (novel), Collins, 1935.
The Fool and the Tractor (novel), Collins, 1936.
The Eye of the Earth (juvenile), Thomas Nelson, 1936.
Cruising in Scotland: The Log of the Migrant, Collins, 1938.
The Eager Years: An Autobiography, Collins, 1940.
(Editor) Aylward Edward Dingle, *A Modern Sinbad,* Harrap, 1948.
(Editor with David James) *Wavy Navy by Some Who Served* (nonfiction), Harrap, 1950.
(Editor) *Touching the Adventures of Merchantmen in the Second World War* (nonfiction), 1953.
The Great Storm, Being the Authentic Story of the Loss at Sea of the Princess Victoria and Other Vessels Early in 1958, Harrap, 1954.
(With Wilfred Granville) *The R.N.V.R.: A Record of Achievement,* Harrap, 1957.
Wilfred Grenfell: His Life and Work, Dodd, 1959.
The Unfortunate Ship: The Story of H. M. Troopship Birkenhead, Harrap, 1960.
Harbour Spotter, Newman Neame, 1962.
The Yachtsman's Log and Astronomical Position Line Formula, privately printed, 1963.

FOR CHILDREN, ALL AS PETER DAWLISH; ALL PUBLISHED BY OXFORD UNIVERSITY PRESS, EXCEPT AS INDICATED

The First Tripper, 1947.
North Sea Adventure, 1949.
Aztec Gold, 1951.
MacClellan's Lake, 1951.
The Bagodia Episode, 1953.
Young Drake of Devon, 1954.
He Went With Drake, Harrap, 1955.
Way for a Sailor, 1955.
Martin Frobisher, 1956.
The Sea Story Omnibus, Collins, 1956.
Sailors All, Basil Blackwell, 1957.
The Race for Gowrie Bay, 1959.

Johnno, the Deep-Sea Diver: The Life Story of Diver John Johnstone, Watts, 1960.
The Boy Jacko, 1962.
The Royal Navy, 1963.
The Seas of Britain, Benn, 1963.
The Merchant Navy, 1966.

"PEG-LEG" SERIES

Captain Peg-Leg's War, 1939.
Captain Peg-Leg and the Fur Pirates, 1939.
Captain Peg-Leg and the Invaders, 1940.
Captain Peg-Leg Swaps the Sea, 1940.

"DAUNTLESS" SERIES

Dauntless Finds Her Crew, 1947.
Dauntless Sails Again, 1948.
Dauntless and the Mary Baines, 1949.
Dauntless Takes Recruits, 1950.
Dauntless Sails In, 1952.
Dauntless in Danger, 1954.
Dauntless Goes Home, 1960.

SIDELIGHTS: James Kerr drew from his experiences as a professional sailor to create many of his books for adults and children. His tales of the sea and ships are filled with adventure and humor and provide much practical information on boating.

The author's popularity was established with the publication of his "Dauntless" series of children's books. These stories relate the various adventures encountered by schoolboys who recondition a fishing boat. Alan Edwin Day of *Twentieth-Century Children's Writers* commented, "Dawlish's own extensive marine experience and know-how were evident on every page, and no boy with salt in his veins could resist the authentic tang of the sea." Another series of sea stories featured the burly skipper Captain Peg-Leg. Kerr also became one of the first authors to market a career book for young people with the publication of *The First Tripper.*

For adults, Kerr wrote biographies in addition to his usual nautical fare. His biographies include a detailed account of the life of Wilfred Grenfell, a medical missionary who served in Labrador and Newfoundland, and the story of Johnno, a deep-sea diver from Liverpool who finds adventure on the seas near Australia and the East Indies.

BIOGRAPHICAL/CRITICAL SOURCES:

BOOKS

Twentieth-Century Children's Writers, 4th edition, St. James Press, 1995.

PERIODICALS

Bookman, March, 1931.
New York Evening Post, March 22, 1930.
New York Herald Tribune Books, August 3, 1930.
New York Herald Tribune Book Review, December 27, 1959.
New York Times Book Review, March 30, 1930; March 1, 1931.*

* * *

KERR, (Anne-) Judith 1923-

PERSONAL: Born June 14, 1923, in Berlin, Germany; naturalized British citizen, 1947; daughter of Alfred Kerr (a well-known German writer and drama critic); married Nigel Kneale (a writer), 1954; children: one son, one daughter. *Education:* Attended Central School of Arts and Crafts, 1945.

ADDRESSES: Office—c/o William Collins Sons & Co. Ltd., 14 St. James Place, London SW1A 195, England.

CAREER: Writer and illustrator. Worked as textile designer and teacher, 1946-53; reader, scriptwriter, and editor for BBC-TV, 1953-58. *Wartime service:* Worked as secretary for Red Cross in London, England, 1941-45.

WRITINGS:

JUVENILE; ALL SELF-ILLUSTRATED

The Tiger Who Came to Tea, Coward, 1968.
Mog, the Forgetful Cat, Collins, 1970, Parents' Magazine Press, 1972.
When Hitler Stole Pink Rabbit, Collins, 1971, Coward, 1972.
When Willy Went to the Wedding, Collins, 1972, Parents' Magazine Press, 1973.
The Other Way Round, Coward, 1975.
Mog's Christmas, Collins, 1976, Collins, 1977.
A Small Person Far Away, Collins, 1978.
Mog and the Baby, Collins, 1980.
Mog in the Dark, Collins, 1983; Larousse (New York), 1984.

Mog and Me, Collins, 1984.
Mog's Family of Cats, Collins, 1985.
Mog's Amazing Birthday Caper, Collins, 1986.
Mog and Bunny, Collins, 1988; Knopf (New York City), 1988.
Mog and Barnaby, Collins, 1991, published as *Look Out, Mog!,* Random House, 1991.
How Mrs. Monkey Missed the Ark, Collins, 1992.
The Adventures of Mog, Collins, 1993.
Mog on Fox Night, HarperCollins, 1993.

OTHER

Also author of *Baby Animals, Favorite Things,* and *My Home,* all 1985 and *Mog in the Garden,* 1994.

ADAPTATIONS: Mog, the Forgetful Cat was adapted to audio in 1992.

SIDELIGHTS: Judith Kerr's books arise out of the fabric of her life. The picture books were originally created for her children, and many of the ideas came from them and from her husband. Her juvenile books deal with World War II and her own childhood as a refugee from Nazi Germany. She relates the changes and disasters of this period in an easily understood style. Her childhood in Switzerland, France, and England was so different from the way her children grew up that she wanted to give them a glimpse of her experiences. Kerr commented on *When Hitler Stole Pink Rabbit* to *Something about the Author:* "I wrote the book for my children, who have often asked what it was like to lose one's home, one's country, and even one's language. I wanted to explain that it was not nearly as bad as it sounded—that given good parents and a bit of luck one can cope with such difficulties and even enjoy the process. But perhaps even more than this, I wanted to write something about my parents. They were the very opposite of the parents in pioneer stories, for instance the admirable Laura Ingalls Wilder books. Unlike Laura Ingalls' splendidly practical parents, my mother could neither cook nor sew, my father had absolutely no understanding of money. He was a writer and she a musician and no two people could have been less fitted for the very practical everyday difficulties which we encountered. And yet, because they were marvelous people, we managed. In spite of all the trouble and tragedies around us, my brother and I probably had a happier and more satisfying childhood than most."

When Hitler Stole Pink Rabbit features nine-year-old Anna and her family who have left Hitler's Germany for Switzerland, France, and finally England where they settle permanently. Although unable to fully grasp the political events responsible for her family's flight from Germany, Anna bravely accepts the drastic changes in her life. The only time she is traumatized is when she is briefly separated from her parents. As Kerr did, Anna enjoys an unsettled but ultimately happy childhood as a result of the strength and love of the family. Critic Lore Segal of *Washington Post Book World* claimed that Kerr "is good at showing how in a child's world—and an adult's too—the little businesses of life overshadow the monstrous ones: The Reichstag burns, but will Anna's friend Elsbeth buy a wooden Yo-Yo which works best or the tin one which is a lovely color?" An *Economist* critic further observed that "Hitler is still a fact of life that most parents find they have to explain to their young. Anti-Semitism is another. This excellent . . . novel . . . will go a long way to help the questioning child understand some of what happened during those years."

The Other Way Around continues the story begun in *When Hitler Stole Pink Rabbit.* In the book, Anna is eighteen and fully assimilated into English society. She deals with emerging issues of independence as she fills the roles of daytime secretary and nighttime art student. Experiences of love, success, failure, work, and creativity contribute to her maturity. At the same time, she is very concerned about her parents in their reduced existence. Christopher Wordsworth asserted that "the triumph of the novel is its avoidance of sententiousness. . . . Almost alarmingly evocative, tinged with quiet wisdom, it touches tellingly on the pecking order of the refugee community and the sadness when one generation adapts and another is left marooned."

The extensive Mog series is inspired by the Kerrs's family cat. This series is aimed at a much younger audience than the autobiographical World War II books about Anna. Consequently, they are much lighter and have simple plots for beginning readers. The title character was first introduced in *Mog, the Forgetful Cat,* a story describing Mog's need for affection. When Mog saves the day, the family realizes how special Mog is to them. In *Mog and Bunny* the family is ready to get rid of Mog's favorite toy bunny until they see how much Mog loves it. A dog named Barnaby disrupts Mog's day in *Look Out, Mog!*

BIOGRAPHICAL/CRITICAL SOURCES:

BOOKS

Something about the Author, Volume 24, Gale, 1981.
Twentieth-Century Children's Writers, 4th edition, St. James Press, 1995.

PERIODICALS

Economist, December 18, 1971.

London Times Literary Supplement, April 4, 1975.

New Statesman, March 5, 1971; May 23, 1975.

New Yorker, December 2, 1972.

New York Times Book Review, December 28, 1975; December 11, 1977.

Observer, November 29, 1970; December 8, 1974; March 30, 1975; September 28, 1980.

Times Literary Supplement, October 3, 1968; December 11, 1970; October 22, 1971; April 4, 1975; December 10, 1976.

Washington Post Book World, May 7, 1972; April 8, 1979; November 5, 1989.*

* * *

KERR, Lennox
See KERR, James Lennox

* * *

KIRST, Hans Hellmut 1914-1989

PERSONAL: Born December 5, 1914, in Osterode, East Prussia (now Poland); died of heart failure, February 23, 1989, in Bremen, Germany; son of Johannes (a policeman) and Gertrud (Golldack) Kirst; married Ruth Mueller, December 14, 1962; children: one daughter. *Education:* Educated in Osterode, East Prussia. *Politics:* Social-Liberal. *Religion:* Roman Catholic.

CAREER: Writer, 1947-89. Worked as gardener, bricklayer, and road builder; writer for *Muendnner Meikuer. Military service:* German Army, 1933-45; served in Poland, France, and Russia; became first lieutenant.

MEMBER: PEN, Authors Guild, Mark Twain Society (honorary member).

AWARDS, HONORS: Edgar Allan Poe Award, 1965, for *The Night of the Generals.*

WRITINGS:

NOVELS; ALL GERMAN EDITIONS PUBLISHED BY K. DESCH, EXCEPT AS NOTED

Wir nannten ihn Galgenstrick, 1950, translation by Richard Winston and Clara Winston published as *The Lieutenant Must Be Mad,* Harcourt, 1951.

Sagten Sie Gerechtigkeit, Captain?, 1952, revised edition published as *Letzte Station Camp 7,* 1966, translation by J. Maxwell Brownjohn published as *Last Stop Camp Seven,* Coward, 1969.

Aufruhr in einer kleinen Stadt, 1953.

Die letzte karte spielt der Tod, 1955, translation by Brownjohn published as *The Last Card,* Pyramid Publications, 1967 (published in England as *Death Plays the Last Card,* Fontana, 1968).

Null-acht fuenfzehn, three volumes, 1954-55, translation by Robert Kee published as *Zero Eight Fifteen,* Weidenfeld & Nicolson, 1955-57, Volume I: *Null-act fuenfzehn in der Kaserne,* 1954, translation published as *The Strange Mutiny of Gunner Asch,* 1955, published as *The Revolt of Gunner Asch,* Little, Brown, 1956, Volume II: *Null-acht fuenfzehn im Krieg,* 1954, translation published as *Forward, Gunner Asch!,* Little, Brown, 1956 (published in England as *Gunner Asch Goes to War,* 1956), Volume III: *Null-acht fuenfzehn bis zum Ende,* 1955, translation published as *The Return of Gunner Asch,* Little, Brown, 1957.

Gott schlaeft in Masuren, 1956.

Keiner kommt davon, 1957, translation by Richard Graves published as *The Seventh Day,* Doubleday, 1959 (published in England as *No One Will Escape,* Weidenfeld & Nicolson, 1959).

Mit diesen meinen Haenden, 1957.

Kultura 5 und der Rote Morgen, 1958.

Glueck laesst sich nicht kaufen, 1959.

Fabrik der Offiziere, 1960 (also see below), translation by Kee published as *The Officer Factory,* Collins, 1962, Doubleday, 1963.

Kameraden, 1961, translation by Brownjohn published as *Brothers in Arms,* Collins, 1965, Harper, 1967.

Die Nacht der Generale, 1962 (also see below), translation by Brownjohn published as *The Night of the Generals,* Harper, 1963.

Null-acht fuenfzehn heute, 1963, translation by Brownjohn published as *What Became of Gunner Asch,* Harper, 1964.

Aufstand der Soldaten: Roman des 20 Juli 1944, 1965 (also see below), translation by Brownjohn published as *Soldiers' Revolt,* Harper, 1966 (published in England as *The Twentieth of July,* Collins, 1966).

Die Woelfe, 1967, translation by Brownjohn published as *The Wolves,* Coward, 1968 (published in England as *The Fox of Maulen,* Collins, 1968).

Kein Vaterland, 1968, translation by Brownjohn published as *No Fatherland,* Coward, 1970 (published in England as *Undercover Man,* Collins, 1970).

Faustrecht, 1969, translation by Brownjohn published as *The Adventures of Private Faust,* Coward, 1971 (published in England as *Who's in Charge Here?,* Collins, 1971).

Soldaten, Offiziere, Generale (contains *Aufstand der Soldaten, Fabrik der Offiziere,* and *Die Nacht der Generale*), 1969.

Held im Turm, 1970, translation by Brownjohn published as *Hero in the Tower,* Coward, 1972.

Verdammt zum Erfolg, 1971, translation by Brownjohn published as *Damned to Success,* Coward, 1973 (published in England as *A Time for Scandal,* Collins, 1973).

Verurteilt zur Wahrheit, 1972, translation by Brownjohn published as *A Time for Truth,* Coward, 1974.

Verfolgt vom Schicksal, 1973.

Alles hat seinen Preis, Hoffmann & Campe, 1974, translation by Brownjohn published as *Everything Has Its Price,* Coward, 1976 (published in England as *A Time for Payment,* Collins, 1976).

Die Naechte der langen Messer, Hoffmann & Campe, 1975, translation by Brownjohn published as *The Nights of the Long Knives,* Coward, 1976.

Generals-Affaeren, Bertelsmann, 1977, translation by Brownjohn published as *The Affairs of the Generals,* Coward, 1979.

Null-acht fuenfzehn in der Partei, Bertelsmann, 1978, translation by Brownjohn published as *Party Games,* Simon & Schuster, 1980.

Der Nachkriegssieger, Bertelsmann, 1979.

Der unheimliche Freund, Heyne, 1979.

Hund mit Mann: Bericht ueber einen Freund, Bertelsmann, 1979.

Ausverkauf der Helden, Bertelsmann, 1980; translation by Brownjohn published as *Heroes for Sale,* Collins, 1982.

Eine Falle aus Papier, Heyne, 1981.

Bedenkliche Begegnung, Heyne, 1982.

Geld, Geld, Geld, Heyne, 1982.

Die gefaehrliche Wahrheit, Heyne, 1984.

Die seltsamen Menschen von Maulen: Heitere Geschichten aus Ostpreussen, Blanvalet 1984.

Blitzmaedel, Blanvalet, 1984.

Das Schaf in Wolfspelz, Busse Seewald, 1985.

Der unheimliche Mann Gottes: Eine heitere Erzaehlung aus Ostpreussen, Blanvalet, 1987.

OTHER

Bilanz der Traumfabrik, Bruckmann, 1963.

Deutschland, deine Ostpreussen: Ein Buch voller Vorurteile, Hoffmann & Campe, 1968.

Heinz Ruehmann: Ein biographischer Report, Kindler, 1969.

(With David Hamilton and Heinz Edelmann) *Das Udo-Juergens-Songbuch,* Juncker, 1970.

Gespraeche mit meimen Hund Anton, K. Desch, 1972.

Die Katzen von Caslano, Hoffmann & Campe, 1977.

Ende '45, Bertelsmann, 1982.

Also author of *Twilight of the Generals.*

ADAPTATIONS: The Night of the Generals was adapted to film and released by Columbia Pictures in 1967.

SIDELIGHTS: Hans Hellmut Kirst is considered by some to have been an analyst of the burden of Nazism on postwar Germany, delving into and retelling the stories of the not-too-distant past. He wrote from a position of knowledge in this respect, having served for many years in the German Army both before and during World War II. As one who reminded his countrymen of things they would just as soon forget, Kirst has been described as a conscience for his people. Other critics, however, view him more as a skillful storyteller, adept at writing tightly constructed, suspenseful, adventure-filled novels.

Much of Kirst's fiction is based on fact. Born in the village of Osterode in East Prussia (now part of Poland), he felt early the impact of war. His father was a prisoner of war in Russia during World War I, and Kirst was five when he saw him for the first time. Kirst grew up in a highly nationalistic part of Germany where young men were encouraged to enter military service. At age eighteen he enlisted in the German Army and eventually became a first lieutenant. The author once remarked: "During all those years people acted like idiots. One had to do one's duty as 'a good German.' One did not really know one was in a club of murderers. You have to pay for being involved with criminals." While training officer candidates during World War II, Kirst was captured by American troops and imprisoned for eight months. Following his release, he began writing books and movie reviews, becoming a full-time writer in 1947.

Kirst originally gained international prominence for his trilogy *Zero Eight Fifteen.* The title refers to the serial number of a German machine gun, and the story follows the life of Gunner Asch, a low-ranking soldier, in his resistance to the military machine. This is a basic motif that recurs in many of his novels: the lowly soldier, the common man, in conflict with the generals, the representatives of the establishment. In the first volume of the trilogy, which is generally considered to be the best, Kirst presents a picture of barrack and army life before the onset of World War II. In the second and third volumes the scenes shift variously from the Russian front to a German base during the war and then recount the military occupation of Germany.

Reviewers have praised Kirst most highly for his craftsmanship and his skills as a storyteller and satirist. Other critics, however, have described his books as escape literature and charged him with over-simplifying the events surrounding the Third Reich. A reviewer for *New Statesman and Nation,* for instance, called *Revolt of Gunner Asch* a "sparkling little satire. It is a closed story, carefully written and shaped round a few characters. . . . It is all very lively and spry, done with a nice, light, dry touch." But in his review for the *New York Times,* Frederic Morton stated his reservations about the book: The character Asch "jousts entertainingly with the absurdities of the Nazi military code but somehow fails to really grapple with its malevolence. His warfare against 08-15 toilet-kit inspections is shrewd and funny, but for all his unusual discernment, he remains unaware of the concentration camps and the storm troopers' nightsticks among which he must have grown up. Hidden away among the comic riches of this novel are things that call for more bite and less jest, that are fit for brooding, not for laughter."

Similar comments were made about another novel, *The Wolves.* The story presents the rivalry between German nationalists and an independent man of high principles, Materna. He joins the Nazis, seeming to conform, but as William Hill observed in *Best Sellers,* "Every concession he makes to the regime somehow turns into a joke against it. . . . There is about the story an aura of unreality because it does not seem to take into account the thoroughness and brutality of the Nazi regime and does not recognize the totality of the second world war." Gertrud Bauer Pickar, in her remarks for *Books Abroad,* praised Kirst for his quick-moving adventure story, but contended that "there is a singular lack of concern with the broader implications. The superficial treatment of the political aspects arises in part from the emphasis on the regional elements, which localize both the roots and impact of the political activity and preclude universal treatment." Kirst disagreed with this critique. He commented in a *Publishers Weekly* interview, "If you look at a drop of water under the microscope you see the structure of the universe, and if you look at what the local Nazis were saying and doing in Osterode, you can see what was going to happen later."

Whether or not the critics approved of his books, the general public has been accepting. Kirst's books have been translated into twenty-eight languages, and *The Night of the Generals* was made into a movie in 1967. A Columbia Pictures release, it starred Peter O'Toole, Omar Sharif, Christopher Plummer, and Joanna Pettet. The *New York Times* remarked that it was "efficiently constructed and played," but that it was also melodramatic and not very "sophisticated and articulate about the crime of war."

Kirst once reflected on the reception of his novels in Germany: "Here the right thinks my view of the Third Reich is erroneous; the left thinks I don't feel enough guilt. In fact, 98 percent of the Germans stood behind the Nazis, and the young read me to find out why their parents did it. . . . I wanted to show the human tragedy, to show what history can do to men."

BIOGRAPHICAL/CRITICAL SOURCES:

BOOKS

Dictionary of Literary Biography, Volume 69: *Contemporary German Fiction Writers, First Series,* Gale, 1988.

Twentieth-Century Crime and Mystery Writers, 3rd edition, St. James Press, 1991.

PERIODICALS

Best Sellers, July 15, 1968.

Books Abroad, spring, 1968.

New Statesman, August 2, 1968; July 10, 1970; April 9, 1971; March 23, 1979.

New Statesman and Nation, July 9, 1955.

New Yorker, July 23, 1966; July 1, 1967; December 20, 1976.

New York Times, March 4, 1956; February 22, 1965; February 3, 1967.

New York Times Book Review, July 17, 1966; June 25, 1967; August 4, 1968; August 3, 1969; October 1, 1972; June 3, 1973; November 17, 1974; May 2, 1976.

Observer, September 5, 1965; July 28, 1968; June 18, 1972; February 10, 1980.

Publishers Weekly, June 10, 1968; September 2, 1977.

Saturday Review, August 2, 1969.

Time, April 28, 1967.

Times Literary Supplement, August 8, 1968; April 10, 1969; January 3, 1975.

Washington Post Book World, June 21, 1970; June 10, 1973.

OBITUARIES:

PERIODICALS

Chicago Tribune, February 24, 1989.

Los Angeles Times, February 24, 1989.

New York Times, February 24, 1989.
Times (London), February 25, 1989.
Washington Post, February 25, 1989.*

* * *

KLAUSE, Annette Curtis 1953-

PERSONAL: Born June 20, 1953, in Bristol, England; came to the United States, June, 1968; daughter of Graham Trevor (a radiologist) and Mary Frances (maiden name, Kempe) Curtis; married Mark Jeffrey Klause (a library assistant), August 11, 1979. *Education:* University of Maryland, B.A., 1976, M.L.S., 1978. *Politics:* "Sometimes." *Religion:* "Never." *Avocational interests:* Reading science fiction, fantasy, and horror; collecting first editions, limited editions, and chapbooks of science fiction, fantasy, and horror; attending science fiction conventions.

ADDRESSES: *Home*—Hyattsville, MD. *Office*—c/o Bantam Doubleday Dell, 1540 Broadway, New York, NY 10036.

CAREER: Various positions for library contracting companies, Montgomery County, MD, Department of Public Libraries, 1981—; Silver Spring Community Libraries, Department of Public Libraries, Silver Spring, MD, children's librarian I, 1981; Montgomery County Department of Public Libraries, substitute librarian, 1981-82; Kensington Park Community Library, Kensington Park, MD, part-time children's librarian I, 1982-84; Bethesda Regional Library, Bethesda, MD, full-time children's librarian I, 1984-89; Olney Community Library, Olney, MD, head of children's services, 1989-91; Kensington Park Community Library, head of children's services, 1991-92; Aspen Hill Community Library, Rockville, Maryland, head of children's services, 1992—. Writer.

MEMBER: American Library Association (ALA), Association of Library Services to Children, Young Adult Library Services Association.

AWARDS, HONORS: American Library Association (ALA) Best Book for Young Adults and Best Book for Reluctant Readers, 1990, *School Library Journal* Best Book, 1990, Booklist Best Book and Editor's Choice, 1990, Best Book of the Year Honor Book, Michigan Library Association Young Adult Division, 1990, Maryland Library Association Black-eyed Susan award for grades six through nine, 1992-93, California Young Reader Medal, young adult category, 1993, Sequoyah Young Adult Book Award, Oklahoma Library Association, 1993, and South Carolina Library Association Young Adult Award, all for *The Silver Kiss; Alien Secrets* was named an ALA Notable Book for Children, a *Booklist* Editor's Choice, one of the *School Library Journal Best Books,* and one of New York Public Library's 100 Best Children's Books, all 1993.

WRITINGS:

The Silver Kiss, Delacorte Press, 1990.
Alien Secrets, Delacorte Press, 1993.
Blood and Chocolate, Delacorte Press, 1997.

Also author of short stories, including "Librarians from Space," published in *The U*n*a*b*a*s*h*e*d Librarian,* number 51, 1984; and "The Hoppins," published in *Short Circuits,* edited by Donald Gallo, Delacorte, 1992. Author of poetry published in *Takoma Park Writers 1981,* Downcounty Press, 1981; *Cat's Magazine; Aurora; Visions;* and others. Contributor of articles to professional journals; contributor of book reviews to *School Library Journal,* 1982-94.

SIDELIGHTS: Annette Curtis Klause broke new ground in young adult literature with *The Silver Kiss,* a book that is at once "sexy, scaring, and moving," according to Roger Sutton writing in the *Bulletin of the Center for Children's Books.* A vampire love story, Klause's first novel is a darkly seductive thriller with heart and message.

Born in Bristol, England, in 1953, Klause became fascinated with grisly things at an early age. "My mother read and sang to me," Klause explained. "But my daddy used to sit me on his lap and tell me the plots to gangster and monster movies. I knew all about Boris Karloff, Bela Lugosi, Jimmy Cagney, and Edward G. Robinson before I ever saw any of their movies." Her father also let her speak to Willoughby, an imaginary little boy who lived down his throat.

When she was seven, Klause and her family moved north to Newcastle-upon-Tyne. She recalls that her first experience with creative writing occurred when she was incapacitated with a twisted ankle at age eight or nine. Klause wrote a poem about her mother ironing and decided from then on to save all her poems in a notebook. Soon she was writing and illustrating her own books, mostly about a cat and the kittens she has. At age ten she and a neighborhood friend began making up plays and performing them on a tape recorder. "The plays usually involved some kind of humorous mistake," Klause recalled, "like a woman calling up a plant nursery instead of a nursery school for her child."

It was also about this time when Klause wrote her first (unpublished) bit of horror, *The Blood Ridden Pool of Solen Goom.* Each of the chapters ended with ". . . and more blood flowed into the blood ridden pool of Solen Goom." Increasingly she read fantasy and science-fiction books, in addition to Mark Twain and, as she got older, the beatnik books of Jack Kerouac. "I wanted desperately to be a beatnik," she remembered. She also read her first vampire book at age fourteen: Jane Gaskell's *The Shiny Narrow Grin,* which was Klause's initial inspiration for her first novel many years later. "I was smitten by the pale young man who appeared in a few suspenseful scenes," Klause related, "and became mesmerized with the whole concept of vampires." Initially, Klause responded to this fascination by writing poetry, which she described as "a pretentious, overwritten, dreadful sequence of poems interspersed with prose called *The Saga of the Vampire*[also unpublished]." These early writings would later become invaluable for Klause when she set out on the journey of her first novel.

Klause's life was distinctly changed when she was fifteen and her father moved the family to Washington, DC, for career reasons. In high school Klause continued writing poetry. After finishing college in 1976, Klause went on to graduate school in library science. She took poetry workshops in college, but poetry was soon replaced by short stories once she graduated and started working in libraries. Klause began sending her work out to magazines, collecting numerous rejection letters. Several of her poems and a short story were published in anthologies and small magazine reviews, but it took several years of concerted effort to find her voice and her audience.

"I finally took a writing workshop with Larry Callen, a well-known children's writer," Klause noted. "I knew I wanted to write for young people. I'm still working through my own adolescence, so it seemed appropriate. I continued with further ones. I still go to the writing group Larry Callen introduced me to, and often chuckle about how an idea or action will affect the people in my group even as I am writing." Klause soon graduated from short stories, and with the help and encouragement of Callen, set to work on a novel. "I wanted to write for teenagers, so I thought back to what I liked to read at that age. In a way, I stole from myself with *The Silver Kiss,* because I looked at my old writing notebooks and found the vampire poem I had written as a teenager, and I realized I had some good ideas in that poem. So I just borrowed them."

Although the main characters were lifted from Klause's own adolescent poems, the plot was contemporary and, according to some critics, daring for a young adult title. The story of a seventeen-year-old girl whose world is in turmoil, *The Silver Kiss* blends horror, suspense, and romantic longing. Zoe's mother is dying of cancer, her father is too upset to provide consolation to his daughter, and her best friend is moving away. A series of murders have rocked Zoe's town: women found with their throats slashed and drained of blood.

However, the teen still ventures to her favorite park at night to think and dream. There she first catches a glimpse of an eerily handsome, silver-haired boy who changes her life. Simon, as Zoe comes to learn, is a vampire, alive for centuries, and on the trail of his own brother—the one who has been responsible for the recent murders and also the one who killed Simon's mother three centuries ago. Simon has tracked this brother through the ages, seeking vengeance. Drawn to Zoe, he feels a glimmer of life because of this attraction and helps her understand her own feelings about her mother's imminent death. In the process she learns to understand her own loneliness and fears. In return she helps him find his brother, and ultimately to end his own tormented existence. The pull between Zoe and Simon is strongly sensual, full of the dark passions of the vampire legend.

"The book was a couple of years in the writing," Klause acknowledged. "Then another two for rewriting and marketing. A couple of editors liked it early on, but told me that the vampire was much more convincing than Zoe. Which is understandable: I sympathize more with the Simon character, the outsider." Finally, a former editor of *School Library Journal* for whom Klause had written reviews and who had since moved into publishing at Delacorte saw the manuscript and wanted to publish it. "He called me at work," Klause recalled, "and I figured here was another rejection. When he said Delacorte wanted to publish it, I thought I would float away."

Even in galleys at the 1990 American Library Association conference, the book was causing a stir. Writing in the *Wilson Library Bulletin,* Cathi MacRae found that *The Silver Kiss*"marries every surefire ingredient of [young-adult] appeal with literary vision and graceful style . . . Klause's fluid writing style casts its own spells. Zoe's 'quiet poetry suffused with twilight and questions' is Klause's own, and the passionate intensity of her writing will draw YA readers as surely as Simon drew Zoe." In addition, Molly Kinney, writing in *School Library Journal,* called the work "a well-drawn, powerful, and seductive novel," and added, "The climax is a roller-coaster ride in reality, the macabre, death, and love."

Klause moved on to a blending of science fiction and mystery genres for her second book. "I think there may be something of the masochist in me," Klause joked. "With *The Silver Kiss* I needed to do some preliminary research into vampire lore, but I had read so much of it already that I was fairly well steeped in it. With *Alien Secrets* it was completely different. I had to create an entire new world. I had to extrapolate what life would be like when the story takes place—what events had occurred on Earth and how people would think and act in my new world. I had to do astronomical research to find out how people would travel through space, in what sequence and through which galaxies. And I had to track down a likely star that might have habitable planets around it." But the book itself does not contain a lot of complex, scientific jargon or data. At heart, it is a mystery and another outsider story. "That is the trick," Klause explained. "To do all this research so that I am completely immersed in my make-believe world to the point where the reader believes in it as well. You don't use all the research. It's like an iceberg. It's the stuff below the surface that makes the setting real."

Alien Secrets tells the story of Puck, a thirteen-year-old earthling on her way to visit her parents on the planet Shoon. Expelled from her private school in England, Puck is carrying plenty of emotional luggage with her. Aboard the space ship she meets Hush, a native of Shoon. Hush has problems, as well, for someone has pilfered a precious statue that Hush was returning to his planet. Together the two search the spaceship to find the statue, are caught up in all sorts of intrigues involving murder and smuggling, and finally are able to work through their problems, helping each other reach greater self-understanding in the process. "It's *Murder on the Orient Express,* space style," deemed Roger Sutton, writing in *Bulletin of the Center for Children's Books.* "*Alien Secrets* demonstrates Klause's versatility and affirms her talent," Donna L. Scanlon wrote in *Voice of Youth Advocates,* adding, "Klause assembles a sympathetic and well rounded cast of characters." Susan L. Rogers in *School Library Journal* mentioned that Puck's "experiences with alien friends and enemies provide lessons applicable to the changing relationships between races and ethnic groups here on Earth as well." In addition, Maeve Visser Kroth told *Horn Book* readers that Klause "uses her setting to explore themes of imperialism and oppression of native peoples," and called *Alien Secrets* "a rich, exciting story."

"I always felt like an outsider growing up," Klause said. "I was the one with red hair, the one always staring out the window. I am interested in outsiders and what we can all learn from them. In my vampire book, Simon is definitely the outsider, but Zoe learns from him. It's the same with Puck and Hush. The alien helps Puck to come to terms with herself. I call it my outsider-as-catalyst theory." Klause does not start out with theme or message, though; it grows naturally out of the story. "You can't force the theme," Klause said. "It has to come naturally. Because of my background as the odd kid out in England and a foreigner in the United States, I find I often deal with the positive aspects of difference. Different is good. People contribute to life and society in different ways, but everybody has something to contribute."

Blood and Chocolate takes werewolves as its subject, and the outsider theme is central once again. The main character, Vivian Gandillon, is a teenager in a family of werewolves. Unimpressed by the other teenage werewolves in her pack, she falls for a boy at her school named Aiden. As Vivian wrestles with the decision of whether or not to tell Aiden what she is, a murder threatens her pack. Caught between two worlds, Vivian is forced to deal with her divided sense of loyalty. A reviewer for *Booklist* wrote that *Blood and Chocolate* "can be read as feminist fiction, as smoldering romance, as a rites of passage novel, or as a piercing reflection on human nature."

As with all her books, Klause's work on *Blood and Chocolate* began with research into the subject as a sort of psychic preparation. "I like to howl for a few minutes before starting to write it," she commented while working on the novel, "just to get in the mood. I am asked to speak at schools quite frequently, to talk about my books and writing. At one assembly, I had the entire student body start to howl with me. It was very therapeutic. With *The Silver Kiss* some editors said I was pushing the envelope, whatever that means. But with my werewolf book, I just might break it." Klaus added: "What I really want to do with my books is change the way readers look at themselves and the world around them. To confirm the right to be different."

BIOGRAPHICAL/CRITICAL SOURCES:

BOOKS

Klause, Annette Curtis, interview with J. Sydney Jones for *Something about the Author,* Volume 79, Gale, 1995.

Twentieth-Century Young Adult Writers, 1st edition, St. James Press, 1994.

PERIODICALS

Booklist, June 1, 1997, p. 1694.

Bulletin of the Center for Children's Books, September, 1990, p. 10; September, 1993, p. 15.

Horn Book, September-October, 1993, pp. 599-600.

New York Times Book Review, April 21, 1991, p. 33.

Publishers Weekly, July 27, 1990, p. 236; July 5, 1993, p. 74.

School Library Journal, September, 1988, pp. 120-123; September, 1990, p. 255; September, 1993, p. 233.

Voice of Youth Advocates, April, 1993, p. 20; August, 1993, pp. 165-166.

Wilson Library Bulletin, December, 1990, pp. 124-125; March, 1991, p. 4.*

* * *

KOMUNYAKAA, Yusef 1947-

PERSONAL: Surname is pronounced "koh-mun-yah-kuh"; born April 29, 1947, in Bogalusa, LA; son of a carpenter; married Mandy Sayer (a novelist and short story writer), 1985. *Education:* University of Colorado, B.A., 1975; Colorado State University, M.A., 1979; University of California, Irvine, M.F.A., 1980.

ADDRESSES: Office—English Dept., 442 Ballantine Hall, Indiana University, Bloomington, IN 47405.

CAREER: New Orleans Public Schools, elementary teacher; University of New Orleans—Lakefront, instructor in English and poetry; Colorado State University, associate instructor of English composition, 1976-78; University of California, Irvine, teaching assistant in poetry, writing instructor for remedial English composition, 1980; University of New Orleans, instructor in English composition and American literature, 1982-84; poet-in-the-schools, New Orleans, 1984-85; Indiana University at Bloomington, visiting assistant professor of English, 1985-86, associate professor of English and African-American Studies, 1986-93, professor of English and African-American Studies, 1993—; University of California, Berkeley, visiting professor of English, fall, 1991, Holloway lecturer, spring, 1992. *UCCA* and *Riverrun,* University of Colorado, editor, 1973-75; *Gumbo: A Magazine for the Arts,* co-editor and publisher, 1976-79; *Indiana Review,* administrative consultant; *Callaloo,* Johns Hopkins University, advisor. *Military service:* U.S. Army, 1965-67, served in Vietnam as an information specialist and as editor of the *Southern Cross,* a military newspaper; received the Bronze Star.

AWARDS, HONORS: Rocky Mountain Writers Forum, First Place Poetry award, 1974, 1977; Fine Arts Work Center Writing fellowship, Provincetown, 1980-81; National Endowment for the Arts Creative Writing fellowship, 1981-82, 1987-88; Louisiana Arts fellowship, 1985; San Francisco Poetry award, 1986, for *I Apologize for the Eyes in My Head;* American Library Association Best Books for Young Adults selection, 1988, and The Dark Room Poetry prize, 1989, both for *Dien Cai Dau;* University of Massachusetts, Boston, Thomas Forcade award, 1990; *Kenyon Review* award for literary excellence, 1991; *Village Voice* Twenty-Five Best Books selection, 1992, for *Magic City;* Pulitzer Prize for poetry, and Kingsley Tufts Poetry Award, Claremont Graduate School, both 1994, both for *Neon Vernacular: New and Selected Poems.*

WRITINGS:

POETRY

Dedications and Other Darkhorses, RMCAJ, 1977.

Lost in the Bonewheel Factory, Lynx House Press (Amherst, MA), 1979.

Copacetic, Wesleyan University Press (Middletown, CT), 1984.

I Apologize for the Eyes in My Head, Wesleyan University Press, 1986.

Toys in a Field, Black River Press, 1986.

Dien Cai Dau, Wesleyan University Press, 1988.

February in Sydney (chapbook), Matchbooks, 1989.

Magic City, Wesleyan University Press/University Press of New England, 1992.

Neon Vernacular: New and Selected Poems, Wesleyan University Press/University Press of New England, 1993.

OTHER

(Editor with Sascha Feinstein) *The Jazz Poetry Anthology,* Indiana University Press (Bloomington), 1991.

(Translator, with Martha Collins) *The Insomnia of Fire* by Nguyen Quang Thieu, University of Massachusetts Press, 1995.

(Editor with Feinstein) *The Second Set: The Jazz Poetry Anthology, Volume 2,* Indiana University Press, 1996.

Contributor to anthologies, including *The Morrow Anthology of Younger American Poets,* and *Carrying the Darkness,* edited by W. D. Ehrhart. Contributor of poetry and reviews to periodicals, including *Black American Literature Forum, Beloit Poetry Journal, Chameleon, Colorado Quarterly, Free Lance, Poetry Now,* and *African American Review.* Former editor of *Gumbo.*

SIDELIGHTS: In his poetry, Yusef Komunyakaa weaves together the elements of his own life in short lines of vernacular to create complex images of life in his native Louisiana and the jungles of Vietnam. From his humble beginnings as the son of a carpenter, Komunyakaa has traveled far to become a scholar, professor, and prize-winning poet. In 1994, he claimed the Pulitzer Prize and the $50,000 Kingsley Tufts Poetry Award for his *Neon Vernacular: New and Selected Poems.* "In the pantheon of poet stereotypes—the vitriolic, passionate drunkard is one; the wry, acerbic loner another—Mr. Komunyakaa . . . is more the dreamy intellectual," Bruce Weber notes in the *New York Times,* "a Wordsworthian type whose worldly, philosophic mind might be stirred by something as homely and personal as a walk in a field of daffodils." Weber continues, "His poems, many of which are built on fiercely autobiographical details—about his stint in Vietnam, about his childhood—deal with the stains that experience leaves on a life, and they are often achingly suggestive without resolution."

In *Neon Vernacular: New and Selected Poems,* Komunyakaa pulls together all of the most powerful strands of his poetic vision. The images are those of the South and its culture, of blacks living in a white world, of war in Southeast Asia, of cities pulsing to the blues and jazz. The language is simple, laid out in short lines. Diann Blakely Shoaf observed in the *Bloomsbury Review,* "The short-lined poem, a staple of the Deep Image movement, has seemed stale and tiresome in recent years, as too often it has been shaped by poets who equate the line with a unit of syntax." Yet, the reviewer continues, "Komunyakaa mostly avoids this pitfall, in part because of his sensitive and well-tuned ear, in part because he knows that a short line as well as a long one should possess both content and integrity." Combining his deeply personal images and his seemingly effortless presentation, Komunyakaa crafts a "neon vernacular." As Robyn Selman puts it in a *Voice Literary Supplement* review, "Most of Yusef Komunyakaa's poems rise toa crescendo, like that moment in songs one or two beats before the bridge, when everything is hooked-up, full-blown."

In *Copacetic,* Komunyakaa returns "to his boyhood and early manhood," observes Kirkland C. Jones in a *Dictionary of Literary Biography* profile. "These poems examine folk ideas, beliefs, sayings, and songs, and the terminology of blues and jazz." *I Apologize for the Eyes in My Head* takes the poet and his reader "from lost love in the city to loved ones and friends lost to the evils of slavery and Jim Crowism in the Deep South," adds Jones. In these poems, "Komunyakaa continues his fascination with ghosts reflected in life's looking glasses, with images of skeletons, and with other symbols of mortality and life's fragility.""Komunyakaa shows us racism revealing itself in the most ordinary ways," *Booklist* reviewer Pat Monaghan writes of *Magic City,* "the connections between people and their land, sex finding beautiful expression in hard times."

In the late 1960s, Komunyakaa served as a correspondent for Army publications in Vietnam. Although he uses images from this experience in many of his works, the poet deals directly with the war in his collection *Dien Cai Dau.* The title means "crazy" in Vietnamese and was used by locals to refer to American soldiers fighting in their country. In the opinion of Kirkland C. Jones, "Komunyakaa's Vietnam poems rank with the best on that subject. He focuses on the mental horrors of war—the anguish shared by the soldiers, those left at home to keep watch, and other observers, participants, objectors, who are all part of the 'psychological terrain.' " The poems in this volume also explore issues of race and sex: "Komunyakaa writes sensitively about the difficulties of being a black American soldier fighting alongside white men," observes Wayne Koestenbaum in the *New York Times Book Review,* "and of American servicemen's sexual relations with Vietnamese women."

In these poems of Vietnam, Komunyakaa uses his characteristic style to tangle together the natural and the man-made, the Southeast Asian landscape and the war. In the words of *Bloomsbury Review* contributor Samuel Maio, "Komunyakaa, through his simple and vernacular diction, his evocative images and chronicled experiences, successfully provides us with glimpses into the mind of a *dien cai dau,* often quite aptly named, the insanity of Vietnam measuring against (and similarly affecting) its principles, as these terrifying poems—

drawn by the precise hand of an unerring craftsman—make so strikingly clear." Koestenbaum remarks that the poet's casual juxtaposition of nature and war belie the artistry at work. "Though his tersely-phrased chronicles, like documentary photographs, give us the illusion that we are facing unmediated reality, they rely on a predictable though powerful set of literary conventions." He adds, "The book works through accretion, not argument; the poems are all in the present tense, which furthers the illusion that we are receiving tokens of a reality untroubled by language."

BIOGRAPHICAL/CRITICAL SOURCES:

BOOKS

Contemporary Literary Criticism, Volume 94, Gale, 1997.
Contemporary Literary Criticism Yearbook 1994, Volume 86, Gale, 1995.
Contemporary Poets, 6th edition, St. James Press, 1996.
Dictionary of Literary Biography, Volume 120: *American Poets since World War II, Third Series,* Gale, 1992, pp. 176-179.

PERIODICALS

Bloomsbury Review, May/June, 1990, p. 27; November, 1993, p. 11.
Booklist, October 1, 1992, p. 231.
New York Times, April 16, 1994, p. A21; May 2, 1994, p. C11.
New York Times Book Review, October 4, 1987, p. 24; September 24, 1989, p. 50.
Poetry, June, 1993, pp. 167-70.
Village Voice, January 12, 1993, p. 80.
Voice Literary Supplement, December, 1992, p. 14; June, 1993, p. 6.*

* * *

KOUTOUKAS, H. M. 1947-

PERSONAL: Born June 4, 1947, in Endicott, NY; son of Harilabie and Agnes (Dailey-Ogden) Koutoukas; married Theodora Sangree (a countess), June 1, 1964; married H. K. Klein (a critic), June 11, 1968; children: Antigone, Medea, Linn, Christopher-Swan. *Education:* Attended Harper College, Binghamton, NY; attended New School for Social Research, 1962-65, and Middleton College, 1964-65; Universalist Life Church, Modesto, CA, Ph.D. *Religion:* Greek Orthodox.

ADDRESSES: *Office*—c/o Judson Church, Washington Square, New York, NY 10012. *Agent*—Nino Karlweis, 250 East 65th St., New York, NY 10021.

CAREER: Dramatist and director. Pioneer in Off-Off Broadway movement; chairperson of drive to build Caffe Cino, New York City; founder of Chamber Theatre Group, New York City, and Supper Theatre concepts. Associated with Electric Circus and other theatre groups in New York City.

MEMBER: New York Playwrights Strategy.

AWARDS, HONORS: National Arts Club Award, 1962; Obie Award, *Village Voice,* 1965; Professional Theatre Wing Award.

WRITINGS:

The Compleat Anthology of Lesbian Humour, Beau Rivage (New York City), 1983.

PLAYS

The Last Triangle, produced in New York City, 1965.
Tidy Passions; or, Kill, Kaleidoscope, Kill, produced in New York City, 1965.
All Day for a Dollar; or, Crumpled Christmas, produced Off-Off Broadway at Caffe Cino, 1966.
Medea, produced in New York City, 1966.
Only a Countess May Dance When She's Crazy (also see below), produced in New York City, 1966.
Pomegranada, produced in New York City, 1966.
With Creatures Make My Way, produced in New York City, 1967.
(And director) *When Clowns Play Hamlet,* produced in New York City, 1967.
View from Sorrento, produced in New York City, 1967.
Howard Kline Trilogy, produced in New York City, 1968.
A Letter from Colette, produced Off-Off Broadway at Judson Poets' Theatre, 1969.
Christopher at Sheridan Squared, produced Off-Off Broadway at Performance Garage, 1971.
Grandmother Is in the Strawberry Patch, produced Off-Off Broadway at La Mama Experimental Theatre, 1974.
(With others) *French Dressing* (revue), produced in New York City, 1974.
One Man's Religion, produced Off-Off Broadway at La Mama Experimental Theatre, 1975.

The Pinotti Papers, produced Off-Off Broadway at La Mama Experimental Theatre, 1975.
(And director) *Star Followers in an Ancient Land,* produced Off-Off Broadway at La Mama Experimental Theatre, December, 1975.
The Legend of Sheridan Square, produced in New York City, 1976.
(And director) *Turtles Don't Dream,* produced in New York City, 1977.
(And director) *Too Late for Yogurt,* produced in New York City, 1978.
The Butterfly Encounter, produced in New York City, 1978.
A Hand Job for Apollo, produced in New York City, 1988.
When Lightning Strikes Twice (two-play performance containing *Awful People Are Coming Over So We Must Be Pretending to Be Hard at Work and Hope They Will Go Away* and *Only a Countess May Dance When She's Crazy*), produced in New York City at Charles Ludlam Theater, January, 1991.

OTHER

Work is represented in anthologies, including *The Off-off Broadway Playbook,* Bobbs-Merrill (Indianapolis, IN), 1972; and *More Plays from Off-off Broadway,* edited by Michael T. Smith, Bobbs-Merrill, 1972. Also the author of *Pope Jean.*

SIDELIGHTS: H. M. Koutoukas once told *CA:* "I have learned from strangers and wish to wander and report on the darker side of life's areas."

Michael T. Smith of *Contemporary Dramatists* noted that Koutoukas' plays "have a special tone and flavor that are all his own and immediately recognizable." The playwright tends to use verse in his plays, and the characters and situations are generally elaborate and imaginative. Smith noted, "Most of his plays are designated 'camps' rather than drama or comedies, and the style is flamboyantly romantic, idiosyncratic, sometimes self-satirizing, full of private references and inside jokes, precious, boldly aphoristic, and disdainful of restrictions of sense, taste, or fashion. Koutoukas is perhaps the last of the aesthetes." His plays concern characters who are deformed, perverse, or rejected and have become too bizarre to carry on ordinary lives. At the same time, they express feelings of human tenderness and vulnerability. One example is the title character of *Medea,* who was played by a man in Koutoukas' production of the play. Set in a Laundromat, this version of the classic Greek play depicts a woman from an expressive and primitive culture who is caught in the civilized society of the Greeks. Koutoukas has also written about witches in *Tidy Passions; or, Kill, Kaleidoscope, Kill,* a sexually neutral person who consummates an undying love for a lobster in *With Creatures Make My Way,* the love between an aging woman and a young man in *A Letter from Colette,* and Greenwich Village in *Christopher at Sheridan Squared.*

Koutoukas is known for bringing drama to settings other than theaters, including art galleries, concert halls, churches, coffee houses, and even living rooms of wealthy patrons in need of entertainment for guests. Writing in *Vogue,* John Gruen explained that "Koutoukas is deeply involved in assaulting the theatrical traditions and conventions of Off-Off-Broadway. He had invented Chamber Theater—theater that takes place in people's living rooms. Koutoukas wishes to return to the eighteenth century when theatricals in great private halls were taken for granted. He goes to extreme lengths to assure a proper milieu for his productions, usually a large living room. His patrons, or hosts, give him complete freedom, carte blanche in the way he stages his plays. Koutoukas also exercises complete control over his audiences. The *Howard Kline Trilogy* was staged in a private room that allowed only twelve persons in the audience . . . by choice. Koutoukas sends out a questionnaire to all persons wishing to see his plays. Potential guests must answer 60 per cent of these questions on theater lore correctly in order to gain admittance. Only a small percentage gets to see a Koutoukas play."

Koutoukas' production slowed down considerably after the 1970s, and he now focuses on acting. As a member of the Ridiculous Theatrical Company, he has traveled to New York and London, earning acclaim for his performances in the plays of Charles Ludlam.

BIOGRAPHICAL/CRITICAL SOURCES:

BOOKS

Contemporary American Dramatists, St. James Press, 1994.
Contemporary Dramatists, 5th edition, St. James Press, 1993.

PERIODICALS

New York Times, January 14, 1991.
Show Business, August 30, 1969.
Vogue, March 1, 1969, pp. 114, 116.*

KRAUSS, Ruth (Ida) 1911-1993

PERSONAL: Born July 25, 1911, in Baltimore, MD; died July 10, 1993, in Westport, CT; daughter of Julius and Blanche (Rosenfeld) Krauss; married David Johnson Leisk (a writer and illustrator under pseudonym Crockett Johnson), c. 1940 (died July 11, 1975). *Education:* Attended Peabody Institute of Music, New School for Social Research, Maryland Institute of Art, and Columbia University; Parsons School of Fine and Applied Art, bachelor's degree.

CAREER: Writer; also conducted poetry workshops.

MEMBER: Authors League of America, PEN.

AWARDS, HONORS: Caldecott Medal honor book citations for *The Happy Day,* 1950, and *A Very Special House,* 1954.

WRITINGS:

FOR CHILDREN

A Good Man and His Good Wife, illustrated by Ad Reinhardt, Harper (New York City), 1944, revised edition, illustrated by Marc Simont, 1962.

The Carrot Seed, illustrated by Crockett Johnson, Harper, 1945.

The Great Duffy, illustrated by Richter, Harper, 1946.

The Growing Story, illustrated by Phyllis Rowand, Harper, 1947.

Bears, illustrated by Rowand, Harper, 1948.

The Big World and the Little House, illustrated by Simont, H. Schuman (New York City), 1949.

The Happy Day, illustrated by Simont, Harper, 1949.

The Backward Day, illustrated by Simont, Harper, 1950.

I Can Fly (verse), illustrated by Mary Blair, Simon & Schuster (New York City), 1950.

The Bundle Book, illustrated by Helen Stone, Harper, 1951.

A Hole Is to Dig: A First Book of First Definitions, illustrated by Maurice Sendak, Harper, 1952.

A Very Special House, illustrated by Sendak, Harper, 1953.

How to Make an Earthquake, illustrated by Johnson, Harper, 1954.

I'll Be You and You Be Me, illustrated by Sendak, Harper, 1954.

Charlotte and the White Horse, illustrated by Sendak, Harper, 1955.

(With Johnson) *Is This You?,* illustrated by Johnson, W. R. Scott (New York City), 1955.

I Want to Paint My Bathroom Blue, illustrated by Sendak, Harper, 1956.

The Birthday Party, illustrated by Sendak, Harper, 1957.

Monkey Day, illustrated by Rowand, Harper, 1957.

Somebody Else's Nut Tree, and Other Tales from Children, illustrated by Sendak, Harper, 1958.

A Moon or a Button: A Collection of First Picture Ideas, illustrated by Remy Charlip, Harper, 1959.

Open House for Butterflies, illustrated by Sendak, Harper, 1960.

Mama, I Wish I Was Snow; Child, You'd Be Very Cold, illustrated by Ellen Raskin, Atheneum (New York City), 1962.

A Bouquet of Littles (verse), illustrated by Jane Flora, Harper, 1963.

Eyes, Nose, Fingers, Toes, illustrated by Elizabeth Schneider, Harper, 1964.

The Little King, The Little Queen, The Little Monster; And Other Stories You Can Make up Yourself, self-illustrated, Albert Whitman (Chicago), 1966.

The Happy Egg, illustrated by Johnson, Scholastic (New York City), 1967.

This Thumbprint: Words and Thumbprints, self-illustrated, Harper, 1967.

What a Fine Day For . . . (verse), music by Al Carmines, illustrated by Charlip, Parents Magazine Press (New York City), 1967.

I Write It (verse), illustrated by Mary Chalmers, Harper, 1970.

Everything under a Mushroom (verse), illustrated by Margot Tomes, Four Winds Press (New York City), 1973.

Little Boat Lighter Than a Cork, illustrated by Esther Gilman, Magic Circle Press (Connecticut), 1976.

Somebody Spilled the Sky (verse), illustrated by Eleanor Hazard, Greenwillow (New York City), 1979.

Poems for People, Morrow, 1979.

Minestrone: A Ruth Krauss Selection (verse), self-illustrated, Greenwillow, 1981.

Big and Little, illustrated by Mary Szilagyi, Scholastic, 1987.

Also author of *Love Poems for Children,* 1986. Contributor to textbooks and anthologies.

POEM-PLAYS FOR ADULTS

The Cantilever Rainbow, illustrated with woodcuts by Antonio Frasconi, Pantheon (New York City), 1965.

There's a Little Ambiguity Over There among the Bluebells, and Other Theatre Poems, illustrated by

Marilyn Harris, Something Else Press (New York City), 1968.

If Only (produced Off-Off Broadway at Judson Poets' Theatre), Toad Press (Eugene, OR), 1969.

Under Twenty, Toad Press, 1970.

Love and the Invention of Punctuation, Bookstore Press (Lenox, MA), 1973.

This Breast Gothic, Bookstore Press, 1973.

Under Thirteen, Bookstore Press, 1976.

If I Were Freedom, produced in Annandale-on-Hudson, NY, at Bard College, 1976-77.

Re-examination of Freedom (produced in Boston at Boston University, 1976-77), Toothpaste Press (West Branch, IA), 1981.

When I Walk I Change the Earth, Burning Deck (Providence, RI), 1978.

Small Black Lambs Wandering in the Red Poppies, produced in New York City, 1982.

Ambiguity 2nd, produced in Boston, 1985.

Also author of *A Beautiful Day,* produced Off-Off Broadway at Judson Poets' Theatre, *Newsletter, In a Bull's Eye, Pineapple Play, Quartet, A Show, a Play—It's a Girl!, Onward, Duet; or, Yellow Umbrella,* and *Drunk Boat.*

OTHER

Contributor of poetry to periodicals, including *Harper's, New World Writing, Plumed Horn, Kulchur, Locus Solus,* and *Chelsea Review.*

A collection of Krauss's manuscripts is at Dupont School, Wilmington, DE.

ADAPTATIONS: The Carrot Seed and *A Hole Is to Dig: A First Book of First Definitions* were both adapted to books with audio.

SIDELIGHTS: A well-respected and prolific writer of children's stories, Ruth Krauss is renowned for works that display humor, cleverness, and an awareness of the thoughts, desires, and language of young children. Her most popular creations are picture books with brief texts that present a simple, undeniable truth as seen from a child's perspective. She was one of the earliest authors to observe and record the language of young people, using their words and ideas to create such ground-breaking books as *A Hole Is to Dig: A First Book of First Definitions,* her first collaborative effort with illustrator Maurice Sendak. Krauss disappointed some critics, however, who observed that her unique and clever manner might be unappreciated by small children, while others felt that her texts are more buoyed by the talent of her illustrators than by her own efforts. Still, Krauss's influence on children's literature is extensive, and her humorous, whimsical, and creative portrayal of a child's world earned her a lasting reputation. Prabha Gupta Sharma of *Dictionary of Literary Biography* observed, "A measure of the appeal of her books lies in the fact that they are in great demand from children's collections in libraries."

Commenting on some of Krauss's best-known books for children, Sharma wrote, "Ruth Krauss's first work, *A Good Man and His Good Wife* (1944), illustrated by Ad Reinhardt, is a folktale about a married couple and their domestic life. The story of a child's confidence in the planting and growing of a carrot, her second book, *The Carrot Seed,* has a brief text, though each sentence or line carries an image, perfect for picture books. *The Growing Story* (1947) follows a child's observations of his own growth and his comparison of it to the growth of plants and animals. At first disappointed that he is not growing, he tries on his winter clothes from the year before and realizes that they no longer fit.

"From this initial stage of writing mainly for entertainment, Krauss progressed to more inward-looking books in the 1950s. In 1952 she published *A Hole Is to Dig: A First Book of First Definitions,* based on the humorous, unexpected definitions children often give things and actions they do not understand. With illustrations by Maurice Sendak this was a landmark book. The observations that 'a face is so you can make faces,' 'a dream is to look at the night and see things,' 'dogs are to kiss people,' or 'mud is to jump in and slide and yell doodlee doodlee doo' make reading the book a funny and touching experience." Critics responded eagerly to this book, which a reviewer for *Bulletin of the Children's Book Center* called "an unusual and exciting book with all the elements of a true classic." Ellen Lewis Buell of *New York Times Book Review* concluded that it is "a revelation to grown-ups as to children's impressions." She even suggested that the book might serve as a starting point for a game of questions "which would set children to thinking."

Sharma continued: "Whereas her earlier books had been well received by readers and critics, the late 1950s was a transition period for Krauss, and her works received mixed reviews. . . . After this period Ruth Krauss's work began to reflect more of her poetic talent. *Open House for Butterflies* (1960), written in childlike, descriptive sentences and illustrated by Sendak, was praised more for its amusing miniature line drawings than for its text. *Mama, I Wish I Was Snow; Child You'd Be Very Cold* (1962) is a translation of a Spanish poem in which a mother and child converse, the child wishing impossible things and the mother providing sensible reasons why such desires might not be as pleasant as anticipated. The woodcut illustrations by Ellen Raskin complement the text, though some critics thought the book was not relevant for most American children. In *Everything under a Mushroom* (1967), a big beige mushroom stands at the center of each two-page spread, and above it runs a line of rhyming words, such as 'little one little two little cow little moo,' while below it a group of children are drawn acting out and commenting on the illustrations above. A world of whimsy is created, but according to [Karla Kuskin of] *New York Times Book Review,* 'the pages were laid out confusingly and there was no path for the eye to follow with ease.' "

In addition to her work as a children's book author, Krauss was also an illustrator and an author of poem-plays for the theater. She commented in *Something about the Author,* "The work in the poetry and the theater are fusing into one with the books for young people. Things that were considered far-out, like my 'news items,' are accepted by children now. They are attuned to it. Still there are some things that children don't have the background for understanding the allusions and references contained. A lot of my poems have been produced on stage as part of musicales, such as at the Judson Poets' Theatre. Some of the poems that were considered so advanced have been included in the Ginn & Co. textbooks and anthologies collected by David Kerdian. . . . *The Cantilever Rainbow* was considered too sophisticated for kids. My work has a lot of humor in it, I hope, whereas most modern poets are so serious."

BIOGRAPHICAL/CRITICAL SOURCES:

BOOKS

Barbara Bader, *American Picturebooks from "Noah's Ark" to "The Beast Within,"* Macmillan, 1976.
Children's Literature Review, Volume 42, Gale, 1997.
Dictionary of Literary Biography, Volume 52: *American Writers for Children since 1960: Fiction,* Gale, 1986, pp. 228-32.
Something about the Author, Volume 30, Gale, 1983.
Twentieth-Century Children's Writers, 3rd edition, 1989; 4th edition, 1995, St. James Press.

PERIODICALS

Bulletin of the Children's Book Center, September, 1952.
Christian Science Monitor, May 13, 1954.
Los Angeles Times Book Review, February 25, 1990.
Nation, August 25, 1969.
New York Herald-Tribune Book Review, May 30, 1954; November 14, 1954.
New York Times Book Review, September 7, 1952; May 5, 1974; April 29, 1979.
Saturday Review, July 16, 1960.

OBITUARIES:

PERIODICALS

New York Times, July 15, 1993, p. D22.*

* * *

KRAUZER, Steven M(ark) 1948-
(J. W. Baron, Adam Lassiter, Don Pendleton; joint pseudonyms Johnny Dee, JokeMeisters, Owen Rountree; Terry Nelsen Bonner, a house pseudonym)

PERSONAL: Born June 9, 1948, in Jersey City, NJ; son of Earl (in business) and Bernice Krauzer. *Education:* Yale University, B.A., 1970; University of New Hampshire, M.A., 1974.

ADDRESSES: Home—13 September Dr., Missoula, MT 59802. *Agent*—Ginger Barber, Virginia Barber Literary Agency, Inc., 353 West 21st St., New York, NY 10011.

CAREER: Writer.

MEMBER: Authors Guild, Mystery Writers of America, Writers Guild of America (West).

WRITINGS:

Cocaine Wars (screenplay), New Horizon Picture Corp., 1985.
(With others) *Sweet Revenge* (screenplay), Concorde Pictures, 1987.
Frame Work (novel), Bantam (New York City), 1989.
Brainstorm (novel), Bantam, 1991.
Rojak's Rule (novel), Pocket Books (New York City), 1992.
Kayaking: Waterwater and Touring Basics (nonfiction; a Trailside Series Guide), introduction by John Viehman, W. W. Norton (New York City), 1995.
(With Peter Stark) *Winter Adventure: A Complete Guide to Winter Sports* (nonfiction), W. W. Norton, 1995.

"HOLT" WESTERN SERIES

God's Country, Fawcett (New York City), 1993.
Winter of the Wolf, Fawcett, 1994.

UNDER PSEUDONYM J. W. BARON

Blaze (western novel), Pinnacle (New York City), 1983.

UNDER HOUSE PSEUDONYM TERRY NELSEN BONNER

The Diggers, Dell/Emerald (New York City), 1983.

UNDER JOINT PSEUDONYM JOHNNY DEE

(With Cheryl Krauzer and Michael J. Sherwood), *You Gotta Be Kidding* (jokebook), St. Martin's (New York City), 1991.

UNDER JOINT PSEUDONYM "THE JOKEMEISTERS"

(With C. Krauzer and Sherwood), *The Jokemeisters* (jokebook), St. Martin's, 1990.

"DENNISON'S WAR" SERIES; ACTION-ADVENTURE NOVELS UNDER PSEUDONYM ADAM LASSITER

Dennison's War, Bantam, 1984.
Conte's Run, Bantam, 1985.
Hell on Wheels, Bantam, 1985.
King of the Mountain, Bantam, 1985.
Triangle, Bantam, 1985.
Snowball in Hell, Bantam, 1986.

UNDER PESUDONYM DON PENDLETON

Double Crossfire, Gold Eagle (New York), 1982.
Terrorist Summit, Gold Eagle, 1982.
Renegade Agent, Gold Eagle, 1982.
Brothers in Blood, Gold Eagle, 1983.

"CORD" SERIES OF WESTERN NOVELS; WITH WILLIAM KITTREDGE UNDER JOINT PSEUDONYM OWEN ROUNTREE

Cord, Ballantine (New York City), 1982.
Cord: The Nevada War, Ballantine, 1982.
Cord: The Black Hills Duel, Ballantine, 1983.
Cord: Gunman Winter, Ballantine, 1983.
Cord: Hunt the Man Down, Ballantine, 1984.
Cord: King of Colorado, Ballantine, 1984.
Cord: Gunsmoke River, Ballantine, 1985.
Cord: Paradise Valley, Ballantine, 1986.
Cord: Brimstone Basin, Ballantine, 1986.

EDITOR WITH KITTREDGE

Great Action Stories, New American Library (New York City), 1977.
The Great American Detective, New American Library, 1978.
Stories into Film, Harper (New York City), 1978.

OTHER

Contributor to books, including *That Awesome Space,* edited by E. Richard Hart, Westwater (Boulder City, NV), 1982. Contributor of articles, stories, and reviews to magazines, including *Armchair Detective, Cavalier, Far West, Rocky Mountain,* and *Triquarterly.* Author of monthly column, "Almanac," *Outside* magazine, 1992-94. Guest editor with Kittredge of *Triquarterly,* number 48, 1980.

SIDELIGHTS: In the nine-book Cord series of adventure novels, written with William Kittredge under the joint pseudonym Owen Rountree, Steven M. Krauzer explores the Western milieu. The series protagonist, Cord, is an outlaw whose partner is, surprisingly, a Mexican woman named Chi. The sexual tension between the two is an ongoing issue, but they have the foresight to resist each other.

Cord: The Nevada War is set during a range war in which Cord and Chi become involved in an effort to overthrow a powerful land baron. Their life of crime often strains the relationship between Cord and Chi, and in this novel Chi almost turns her back on Cord until his brother intervenes. In *Los Angeles Times Book Review,* Kristiana Gregory observed that another book in the series, *Cord: King of Colorado,* displays "much color" and includes "interesting facts on miners, millionaires and other frontier fortunes."

John L. Wolfe of *Twentieth-Century Western Writers* commented that one of Krauzer's particular strengths is his characterization of men, whether they are ruthless villains or simple bartenders. Cord is a complicated and paradoxical character; he is a corrupt outlaw, yet he devotes much time to helping those in need. Wolfe suggested that the appeal of the series may be not only the action, but also the depth of the characters, whose personal flaws are not concealed. Wolfe observed, "Krauzer's view of the Western frontier is that of a timeless plateau, where arguments are settled with guns, knives, and fists. . . . Krauzer is at his best when describing scenes of emotional conflict, when his writing pulls what is fundamentally a formulaic series out of its rut, and his abilities in this area are probably underrated."

BIOGRAPHICAL/CRITICAL SOURCES:

BOOKS

Twentieth-Century Western Writers, 2nd edition, St. James Press, 1991.

PERIODICALS

Locus, October, 1991.
Los Angeles Times, February 10, 1986.
Los Angeles Times Book Review, November 11, 1984, p. 12.
Magazine of Fantasy and Science Fiction, October, 1991.
Publishers Weekly, November 9, 1984; March 7, 1987.
Voice of Youth Advocates, June, 1992.*

* * *

**KUBE-MCDOWELL, Michael P(aul) 1954-
(Michael Hudson)**

PERSONAL: Surname is pronounced "Cue-bee"; born August 29, 1954, in Philadelphia, PA; son of John F. (a sales engineer) and L. Patricia (an office administrator; maiden name, Deich) McDowell; married Karla Jane Kube (a systems analyst and computer programmer), December 12, 1975 (divorced, 1987); children: Matthew T. *Education:* Michigan State University, B.A. (with high honors), 1976; Indiana University-Bloomington, M.S., 1981. *Politics:* Independent.

ADDRESSES: Home—409 Sunset Blvd., Goshen, IN 46526. *Office*—P.O. Box 1141, Goshen, IN, 46526. *Agent*—Russell Galen, Scott Meredith Literary Agency, 845 Third Ave., New York, NY 10022.

CAREER: Science and mathematics teacher at public schools in Middlebury, IN, 1976-83; Miles Laboratories, Elkhart, IN, instructor, 1978-80; *South Bend Tribune,* South Bend, IN, book reviewer, 1981—; *Truth,* Elkhart, IN, correspondent, 1982-84; Goshen College, instructor, 1984-85; Laurel T.V., Inc., New York, screenwriter, 1985-86; Clarion SF Workshop, East Landing, MI, instructor, 1990.

MEMBER: Writers Guild East, Science Fiction Writers of America, L-5 Society, Planetary Society, Nature Conservancy.

AWARDS, HONORS: Presidential distinguished teacher, 1985; guest of honor at Inconjunction V, 1985; guest of honor at Phoenixcon of Atlanta, 1987; nomination for Philip K. Dick Memorial Award, 1986, for novel *Emprise.*

WRITINGS:

(With Robert Silverberg and Norman Spinrad) *After the Flames* (novella), Baen Books, 1985.
Isaac Asimov's Robot City: Odyssey, Publishing, 1986.
(Under pseudonym Michael Hudson) *Thieves of Light,* Berkley Publishing, 1987.
Alternities, Ace Books (New York City), 1988.
The Quiet Pools, Ace Books, 1990.
Exile, Ace Books, 1992.
Before the Storm (Star Wars, Book One of the Black Fleet Crisis), Demco Media, 1996.
Shield of Lies (Star Wars, Book Two of the Black Fleet Crisis), Demco Media, 1996.
Tyrant's Test (Star Wars, Book Three of the Black Fleet Crisis), Bantam, 1997.
(With Arthur C. Clarke) *The Trigger,* Bantam, 1999.

"THE TRIGON DISUNITY" SERIES:

Emprise, Berkley Publishing, 1985.
Enigma, Berkley Publishing, 1986.
Empery, Berkley Publishing, 1987.

Work represented in anthologies, including *Perpetual Light,* edited by Alan Ryan, Warner, 1982; *Aliens and Outworlders,* edited by Shawna McCarthy, Dial, 1983; *The Year's Best Horror Stories: XI,* edited by Karl Edward Wagner, DAW Books, 1983. Writer for television series *Tales from the Darkside,* 1984-86. Contributor of stories to magazines, including *Analog, Amazing Stories, Magazine of Fantasy and Science Fiction, If, Rod Serling's Twilight Zone,* and *Isaac Asimov's Science Fiction.*

ADAPTATIONS: Isaac Asimov's Robot City: Odyssey was adapted to audio in 1990. *Before the Storm* and *Shield of Lies* were adapted to audio in 1996 by Bantam Doubleday Dell, and *Tyrant's Test* was adapted in 1996 by Bantam Books Audio.

SIDELIGHTS: Michael P. Kube-McDowell is a writer whose work is best categorized as cosmic science fiction, a subgenre exemplified by the work of Arthur C. Clark. A sense of wonder about the universe permeates cosmic science fiction stories, which generally span great distances of space and time. Kube-McDowell's career as an author began with the publication of short stories, many of which are included in science-fiction anthologies. Prior to the release of his first novel, he also wrote and adapted screenplays for television.

Kube-McDowell's first novel, *Emprise,* introduces the Trigon Disunity series, which is set in the future and spans one thousand years. In *Emprise,* humans send a spaceship to greet alien visitors only to discover that the aliens are actually human. In the next book in the series, *Enigma,* a human is taken by energy-beings and learns that thousands of years ago an Earth race colonized other worlds until it was destroyed by a more powerful alien race which is preparing to return. *Empery* continues the story as the humans attempt a preemptive strike in an effort to save humankind. D. Douglas Fratz of *Twentieth-Century Science-Fiction Writers* commented, "These novels, like most of Kube-McDowell's science fiction, are often primarily involved in political struggles between various factions of characters."

The Quiet Pools is Kube-McDowell's best-known novel to date. Set on a future Earth, the story describes dire conditions as a result of overpopulation. Controversy surrounds a project to build a spaceship large enough to safely carry ten thousand men and women to a place beyond the solar system. While many regard the project as the last hope for humankind, a covert group violently opposes the plan. Kube-McDowell suggests that there is a genetic tendency toward exploration of new frontiers. Consequently, those who possess the trait will travel through space while those without it stay on Earth despite the fact that resources are depleted. Fratz observed, "It is a powerful and moving hypothesis, aimed at the very heart and soul of the doctrine of science fiction."

"I consider myself a child of the sixties," Kube-McDowell informed *CA,* "a person whose adult outlook was shaped by the powerful currents of political activism and technological optimism then coursing through society. When I examine my present-day interests and attitudes, I find echoes of the dawn of the space age, of the peace movement, of the struggle to liberate blacks and women from social bondage. For some reason, the period encompassing the Chicago Seven, Woodstock, Kent State, Watergate, and the assassinations of the two Kennedys and Martin Luther King is more vivid to me than more recent history.

"That part of my world view not traceable to the influences listed above comes in large part from science. Though I am not a scientist, I attempt to employ a ratiocinative and synthetic approach to problem-solving. I endeavor to temper my expectations of humanity with the realities which limit what we can do and be. Astronomy has given me a picture of our unprivileged place in the universe; biology, an understanding of the struggle between the rigid determinism of the genes and the flexible programming of the brain.

"Out of this mixture, I have evolved a viewpoint which might be called skeptical meliorism. Recent cynicism to the country, I believe that the human prospect is still very bright and the future still very much in our control. As H. G. Wells wrote at the turn of the century, 'All this world is heavy with the promise of greater things.' However, there is nothing certain about progress, no matter how generously defined. Because we have the capacity to choose, we also have the opportunity to choose badly. There are no grounds on which to expect the naked ape suddenly to shed all its well-known flaws and foibles.

"Even so, I believe that the human species has a long and interesting future lying ahead of it—a future in which we will both achieve great deeds and commit terrible misdeeds in the course of learning more about ourselves and the universe we inhabit. The balance between the positive and the negative is being shaped by the decisions we make today and by our perceptions of what is possible. In my writing, I attempt to deal in human terms with this mixture of caution and hope, with the striving of the individual for fulfillment in the face of challenges posed by a growing, evolving culture."

BIOGRAPHICAL/CRITICAL SOURCES:

BOOKS

Twentieth-Century Science-Fiction Writers, 3rd edition, St. James Press, 1991.

PERIODICALS

Analog, February, 1984; March, 1988; July, 1989.
Los Angeles Times Book Review, July 29, 1990.
Magazine of Fantasy and Science Fiction, May, 1987; August, 1987; December, 1987.
New York Times Book Review, July 8, 1990.
Publishers Weekly, April 11, 1986; September 2, 1988; April 20, 1990.
Tribune Books (Chicago), July 15, 1990.*

KUHN, Thomas S(amuel) 1922-1996

PERSONAL: Born July 18, 1922, in Cincinnati, OH; died of cancer, June 17, 1996 in Cambridge, MA; son of Samuel L. (an industrial engineer) and Minette (Stroock) Kuhn; married Kathryn Louise Muhs, November 27, 1948 (divorced September, 1978); children: Sarah, Elizabeth, Nathaniel Stroock. *Education:* Harvard University, S.B. (summa cum laude in physics), 1943, A.M., 1946, Ph.D., 1949.

CAREER: U.S. Office of Scientific Research and Development, civilian employee at Harvard University, Cambridge, MA, 1943-44, and in Europe, 1944-45; Harvard University, junior fellow, 1948-51, instructor, 1951-52, assistant professor of general education and history of science, 1952-56; University of California, Berkeley, assistant professor of history and philosophy, 1956-58, associate professor, 1958-61, professor of history of science, 1961-64; Princeton University, Princeton, NJ, professor of history of science, 1964-68, M. Taylor Pyne Professor of the History of Science, 1968-79; Massachusetts Institute of Technology, Cambridge, professor of philosophy and history of science, 1979-83, professor emeritus, 1984-96. Director of project, Sources of History for Quantum Physics, sponsored by the American Physical Society and American Philosophical Society, 1961-64; member of Institute for Advanced Study, 1972-79.

MEMBER: American Academy of Arts and Sciences, History of Science Society (president), American Philosophical Society, American Historical Association, Social Science Research Council (member of board of directors, 1964-66), National Academy of Sciences, American Association for the Advancement of Science, Academie Internationale d'Histoire des Sciences (membre effectif), Phi Beta Kappa, Sigma Xi.

AWARDS, HONORS: Guggenheim fellow, 1954-55; Center for Advanced Study in the Behavioral Sciences fellow, 1958-59; LL.D., University of Notre Dame, 1973; Howard T. Behrman Award, Princeton University, 1977; American Book Award nomination, 1980, for *The Essential Tension: Selected Studies in Scientific Tradition and Change;* History of Science Society Sarton Medal, 1982; Society for Social Studies of Science Bernal Award, 1983.

WRITINGS:

The Copernican Revolution: Planetary Astronomy in the Development of Western Thought, Harvard University Press, 1957, 2nd edition, 1959.

The Structure of Scientific Revolutions, University of Chicago Press, 1962, 2nd edition, 1964.

(With J. L. Heilbron, P. L. Forman, and Lini Allen) *Sources for History of Quantum Physics,* American Philosophical Society, 1967.

The Essential Tension: Selected Studies in Scientific Tradition and Change, University of Chicago Press, 1977.

Black-Body Theory and the Quantum Discontinuity, 1894-1912, Oxford University Press, 1978.

CONTRIBUTOR

I. B. Cohen, editor, *Isaac Newton's Papers and Letters on Natural Philosophy,* Harvard University Press, 1958.

Marshall Clagett, editor, *Critical Problems in the History of Science,* University of Wisconsin Press, 1959.

Harry Woolf, editor, *Quantification: A History of Measurement in the Natural and Social Sciences,* Bobbs-Merrill, 1961.

B. Barber and W. Hirsch, editors, *The Sociology of Science,* Free Press of Glencoe, 1961.

C. W. Taylor and F. Barron, editors, *Scientific Creativity: Its Recognition and Development,* Wiley, 1963.

A. C. Crombie, editor, *Scientific Change,* Basic Books, 1963.

Cohen and R. Taton, editors, *Melanges Alexandre Koyre,* Volume II: *L'Aventure de l'esprit,* Hermann, 1964.

The Trouble with the Historical Philosophy of Science, Harvard University, 1992.

OTHER

Member of board of editors, *Dictionary of Scientific Biography,* 1964-96. Contributor to *Encyclopedia of the Social Sciences,* 1968; also contributor to *Isis, Science,* and to symposium volumes.

SIDELIGHTS: Thomas S. Kuhn was a respected historian and philosopher of science who is best remembered for his insights into scientific revolutions. Kuhn's work emphasizes both the history of scientific inquiry and the role of science in society. His first exposure to the history of science came as an assistant to James B. Conant in a course designed to present science to nonscientists. He stated that he was attracted to this field "by the great difference between the image of science provided by historical study, on the one hand, and by scientific training or philosophy of science, on the other."

While a graduate student at Harvard University, Kuhn devised the theory that revolutionary changes in scientific thought occur based on society's view at a given time in history. His best-known book, *The Structure of Scientific Revolutions,* fully develops this idea. In it, Kuhn argues that the conventional view of progress in science bears almost no relation to how science actually progresses. According to the conventional view, scientists construct theories from firm, neutral facts, test their theories against new data, and gradually—over years and centuries—accommodate new evidence. Kuhn maintains that what really happens is that some prevailing view of nature undergoes a radical "paradigm shift," a revolution in thought comparable to one in politics. Such a change alters the kinds of experiments scientists perform, the instruments they use, the form of questions they ask, even the types of problems considered important. Isaac Newton and Albert Einstein are only two of the scientists cited by Kuhn as having ushered in major paradigm shifts.

The reception of *The Structure of Scientific Revolutions* was mixed. Philosophically, the model was criticized for describing scientific revolution as the outcome of psychological and social causes rather than pragmatic ones. On the other hand, many academics praise the book for its far-reaching ideas. Gary Gutting of *Thinkers of the Twentieth Century* noted that "Kuhn's major work, *The Structure of Scientific Revolutions,* has been the most widely influential academic book of the last twenty years." Robert Kanigel of *Los Angeles Times Book Review* agreed, explaining that it "almost overnight changed how many scientists imagined science worked. . . . Each year, hundreds of scholarly treatises cite it. . . . And while, narrowly speaking, the book deals only with the physical sciences, its ideas are, as one critic has put it, 'so seductive' that scholars in economics, political science and sociology have applied them to their own fields."

BIOGRAPHICAL/CRITICAL SOURCES:

BOOKS

Andersson, Gunnar, *Criticism and the History of Science: Kuhn's, Lakatos's, and Feyrabend's Criticisms of Critical Rationalism,* E.J. Brill (New York City), 1994.

Barnes, Barry, *T.S. Kuhn and Social Science,* Columbia University Press, 1982.

Horwich, Paul, *World Changes: Thomas Kuhn and the Nature of Science,* MIT Press, 1993.

Hoyningen-Huene, Paul, *Reconstructing Scientific Revolutions: Thomas S. Kuhn's Philosophy of Science,* University of Chicago Press, 1993.

Schultz, William R., *Genetic Codes of Culture?: The Deconstruction of Tradition by Kuhn, Bloom, and Derrida,* Garland (New York City), 1994.

Stove, D.C., *Popper and After: Four Modern Irrationalists,* Pergamon Press (Oxford, NY), 1982.

Thinkers of the Twentieth Century, 2nd edition, St. James Press, 1987.

PERIODICALS

American Spectator, December, 1991.
Callaloo, winter, 1987.
Choice, April, 1987.
Isis, March, 1994.
Los Angeles Times Book Review, December 19, 1982.
SciTech Book News, June, 1987.

OBITUARIES:

PERIODICALS

Los Angeles Times, June 21, 1996, p. A22.
New York Times, June 19, 1996, p. B7.
Physics Today, December, 1996, p. 74.
Washington Post, June 20, 1996, p. C5.*

* * *

KUPPNER, Frank 1951-

PERSONAL: Born in 1951, in Glasgow, Scotland . *Education:* Attended University of Glasgow, became qualified electronics engineer.

ADDRESSES: *Agent*—c/o Polygon, 22 George Sq., Edinburgh EH8 9LF, Scotland.

CAREER: Engineer and writer.

WRITINGS:

POETRY

A Bad Day for the Sung Dynasty, Carcanet (Manchester), 1984.

The Intelligent Observation of Naked Women, Carcanet, 1987.

Everything Is Strange, Carcanet, 1994.

Second Best Moments of Chinese History, Carcanet, 1997.

NOVELS

Ridiculous! Absurd! Disgusting!, Carcanet, 1989.
A Very Quiet Street, Polygon (Edinburgh), 1989.
A Concussed History of Scotland, Polygon, 1990.
Something Very Like Murder, Polygon, 1994.
Life on a Dead Planet, Polygon, 1997.

SIDELIGHTS: Frank Kuppner's career began during the resurgence of Scottish poetry in the 1980s. This rise was part of a reaction against the Scottish Renaissance of the 1920s through the 1970s. Kuppner's first collection, *A Bad Day for the Sung Dynasty,* consists of five hundred unrhymed quatrain stanzas described by Maurice Lindsay of *Contemporary Poets* as "a succession of Chinese-like cameos."

Kuppner's next collection, *The Intelligent Observation of Naked Women,* is similar to *A Bad Day for the Sung Dynasty* in style, containing a short introductory poem and four lengthy poems, all in unrhymed quatrains. Lindsay commented on one of the poems, "An Old Guide Book to Prague," noting that it "achieves its remarkable effect partly by the many detailed images accurately observed with almost photographic detachment and partly by the fact that so many of his lines mark off their own word-picture."

In the novel *Life on a Dead Planet,* the narrator walks through a city in the evening, letting his imagination range freely. He looks into windows and imagines what happens inside, and he creates life stories for the women he meets. While telling this story, Kuppner makes observations of human behavior as he depicts a single life amidst a busy world.

BIOGRAPHICAL/CRITICAL SOURCES:

BOOKS

Contemporary Poets, 6th edition, St. James Press, 1996.

PERIODICALS

London Review of Books, February 23, 1995, p. 26.
Observer, June 25, 1989, p. 45.
Times Literary Supplement, November 30, 1984, p. 1393; July 24, 1987, p. 805; October 20, 1989, p. 1164; November 16, 1990, p. 1232.
Village Voice Literary Supplement, November, 1987, p. 18.*

KURLAND, Michael (Joseph) 1938- (Jennifer Plum)

PERSONAL: Born March 1, 1938, in New York, NY; son of Jack (a manufacturer) and Stephanie (a dress designer; maiden name, Yacht) Kurland; married Rebecca Jacobson, 1976. *Education:* Attended Hiram College, 1955-56, University of Maryland, 1959-60, foreign study in Germany, 1960-61, and Columbia University, 1963-64. *Politics:* Whig. *Religion:* Secular Humanist. *Avocational interests:* Politics, bear baiting, barn storming, lighter-than-air craft, carnivals, vaudeville, science fiction incunabula.

ADDRESSES: Home—New York, NY. *Agent*—Richard Curtis Associates, 340 East 66th St., New York, NY 10021.

CAREER: Full-time writer, 1963—. News editor, KPFK-Radio, Los Angeles, CA, 1966; High school English teacher in Ojai, CA, 1968; managing editor, *Crawdaddy Magazine,* 1969; editor, Pennyfarthing Press, San Francisco and Berkley, CA, 1976—. Occasional director of plays for Squirrel Hill Theatre, 1972—. *Military service:* U.S. Army, Intelligence, 1958-62.

MEMBER: Authors Guild, Authors League of America, Mystery Writers of America, Science Fiction Writers of America, Institute for Twenty-First-Century Studies, Baker Street Irregulars, Computer Press Association.

AWARDS, HONORS: Edgar scroll from Mystery Writers of America, 1971, for *A Plague of Spies,* and 1979, for *The Infernal Device;* American Book Award nomination, 1979, for *The Infernal Device.*

WRITINGS:

FICTION

(Under pseudonym Jennifer Plum) *The Secret of Benjamin Square,* Lancer Books, 1972.
The Whenabouts of Burr, DAW Books, 1975.
Pluribus, Doubleday, 1975.
Tomorrow Knight, DAW Books, 1976.
The Princes of Earth, Thomas Nelson, 1978.
The Infernal Device, New American Library, 1978.
The Last President, William Morrow, 1980.
Psi Hunt, Berkley (New York), 1980.
(With H. Beam Piper) *Death by Gaslight,* New American Library, 1982.
Gashopper, Doubleday, 1987.
Ten Little Wizards (for young adults), Berkley, 1987.

Perchance, New American Library, 1988.
A Study in Sorcery, Ace, 1989.
Button Bright, Berkley, 1990.
Too Soon Dead, St. Martin's Press, 1997.
The Girls in the High-Heeled Shoes, St. Martin's Press, 1998.

PUBLISHED BY PYRAMID PUBLICATIONS, EXCEPT AS NOTED

(With Chester Anderson) *Ten Years to Doomsday,* 1964.
Mission: Third Force, 1967.
Mission: Tank War, 1968.
Mission: Police Action, 1969.
A Plague of Spies, 1969.
The Unicorn Girl, 1969.
Transmission Error, 1971.
Star Griffin, Doubleday (Garden City, NY), 1987.

NONFICTION

The Spymaster's Handbook, Facts on File (New York City), 1988.
World Espionage: A Historical Encyclopedia, Facts on File, 1993.
A Gallery of Rogues: Portraits in True Crime, Prentice-Hall General Reference (New York City), 1994.
How to Solve a Murder: The Forensic Handbook, Macmillan (New York City), 1995.
How to Try a Murder: The Armchair Lawyer's Handbook, Macmillan, 1997.

EDITOR

Avram Davidson, *The Redward Edward Papers,* Doubleday, 1978.
The Best of Avram Davidson, Doubleday, 1979.
(From H Beam Piper's unfinished manuscript) *First Cycle,* Ace Books, 1982.

OTHER

Author of editorials for *National Examiner,* 1966, and of "Impropa-Ganda" column in *Berkeley Barb,* 1967. Contributor to *Worlds of Tomorrow.*

SIDELIGHTS: Michael Kurland is an author of science-fiction novels and short stories whose steady production has resulted in more than thirty books. Richard A. Lupoff of *Twentieth-Century Science-Fiction Writers* observed, "Kurland is highly adept at creating societies which are compellingly believable and populating them with vivid and sympathetic characters. His style is lively, warm, and highly informal. His stories are told with rapidity of pace and great variety of setting and incident." Kurland's first novel was a collaborative effort with Chester Anderson. *Ten Years to Doomsday* concerns a planet with only a decade to prepare for a planned invasion. In order to defend themselves from the attack, the people determine that they must change their feudal state to an industrial and technological one. Kurland says that this novel is intended as a parody of the works of Poul Anderson. Lupoff commented, "Either as a parody or in its own right, the book is fairly successful."

Kurland told *CA* that "*The Unicorn Girl* is part of a unique trilogy, the middle work of a linked three-book opus with three different authors. The first [is] *The Butterfly Kid* by Chester Anderson, and the third [is] *The Probability Pad* by T. A. Waters." *The Butterfly Kid* includes the three authors as characters in a comical plot involving an alien invasion of a bohemian community in the 1960s. *The Unicorn Girl* continues with the same themes and characters, although it was less successful than the first part of the trilogy.

The protagonist of *Transmission Error* is likable, resourceful, and witty but constantly finds himself in difficult situations. For example, he is inadvertently taken to an alien planet where he faces a potential life of slavery. Although he escapes this threat, he soon finds himself faced by others. Lupoff pointed to *Transmission Error* as an illustration of the weakness of many of Kurland's novels. He explained, "Their major flaw is a failure—whether by the author or his protagonist—to grapple with and satisfactorily resolve problems. The 'solutions' offered are almost invariably flight rather than confrontation."

Pluribus is regarded as Kurland's most successful science-fiction novel. Set in a future barbaric United States, the novel is replete with vivid imagery such as the horse-drawn Highway Patrol cruiser that carries the protagonist away after his arrest. *The Princes of Earth,* which Lupoff deemed "favorably comparable to standard [Robert] Heinlein juveniles," contains typical Kurland elements—future societies, characters, and movement from problem to problem. The author also utilizes satire, as in his parody of the Church of Scientology.

BIOGRAPHICAL/CRITICAL SOURCES:

BOOKS

Something about the Author, Volume 48, Gale, 1987.
Twentieth-Century Science-Fiction Writers, 3rd edition, St. James Press, 1991.

PERIODICALS

Analog, August, 1989, p. 175.
Armchair Detective, spring, 1989, p. 201.
New York Times Book Review, August 31, 1980, p. 17.
Publishers Weekly, June 2, 1975, p. 56; November 13, 1978, p. 61; March 21, 1980, p. 54; February 6, 1987, p. 88; November 11, 1988, p. 50.
Washington Post Book World, June 1, 1980, p. 10.*

L

La FLESCHE, Francis 1857(?)-1932

PERSONAL: Born December 25, 1857 (some sources say 1860), in Omaha, NE; native name Zhogaxe (Woodworker); died September 5, 1932, near Macy, NE; son of Joseph (an Omaha chief also known as Estamaza, or Iron Eye) and Elizabeth Esau (Tainne) La Flesche; married Alice Mitchell, June, 1877 (died, 1878); married Alice Cline, August, 1879 (divorced, 1884); married Rosa Bourassa, 1906 (divorced, 1908). *Education:* Received degree from National University Law School, 1892.

CAREER: Served as an interpreter for Chief Standing Bear, Thomas Henry Tibbles, and Susette La Flesche (Francis's half-sister) on a speaking tour of cities in the eastern United States, 1879-80; Bureau of Indian Affairs, Washington, DC, interpreter and advisor, 1881-c. 1910; affiliated with the Bureau of American Ethnology of the Smithsonian Institution, 1910-30; writer.

AWARDS, HONORS: Fellow, American Association for the Advancement of Science; honorary Doctor of Laws, University of Nebraska, 1926.

WRITINGS:

The Middle Five: Indian Boys at School (autobiography), Small, Maynard (Boston), 1900, reprinted with a foreword by David A. Baerreis, University of Wisconsin Press (Madison), 1963.

Who Was the Medicine Man? Address by Francis La Flesche (of the Omaha Tribe) (speech), Hampton Institute Press, 1905.

"Right and Left in Osage Ceremonies" (essay), in *Holmes Anniversary Volume,* J.W. Bryan, 1916.

The Osage Tribe: The Rite of Vigil, Thirty-Ninth Annual Reports of the Bureau of American Ethnology, 1917-18.

The Osage Tribe: Two Versions of the Child Naming Rite, Forty-Third Annual Report of the Bureau of American Ethnology, 1925-26.

The Osage Tribe: Rite of Waxobe and Shrine Degree, Forty-Fifth Annual Report of the Bureau of American Ethnology, 1927-28.

(With Alice C. Fletcher) *The Omaha Tribe,* University of Nebraska Press (Lincoln), 1972 (originally published in the 27th Annual Report of the Bureau of American Ethnology, 1911).

The Osage Tribe: Rite of the Chiefs; Sayings of the Ancient Men, Johnson Reprint Corp. (New York), 1970 (originally published in the 36th Annual Report of the Bureau of American Ethnology, c. 1921).

Omaha Bow and Arrow-Makers, Imprensa Nacional (Rio de Janeiro, Brazil), 1924.

A Dictionary of the Osage Language, United States Government Printing Office (Washington), 1932, revised edition edited and introduced by W. David Baird, Indian Tribal Series (Phoenix), 1975.

War Ceremony and Peace Ceremony of the Osage Indians, United States Government Printing Office (Washington), 1939.

(Edited by James W. Parins and Daniel F. Littlefield, Jr.) *Ke-Ma-Ha: The Omaha Stories of Francis La Flesche,* University of Nebraska Press, 1995.

(Edited by Garrick A. Bailey) *The Osage and the Invisible World: From the Works of Francis La Flesche,* University of Oklahoma Press, 1995.

Collaborative role in Alice C. Fletcher's *A Study of Omaha Indian Music,* Peabody Museum of American Archaeology and Ethnology (Cambridge), 1893. Creator of the opera *Da-o-ma,* 1912; the essay "Death and Funeral Customs" was published in the *Journal of American Folklore.* Published essays in journals such as *Indian Leaders, Southern Workman,* and *American Anthropologist.*

SIDELIGHTS: Francis La Flesche was one of the first Native Americans to establish a noteworthy career as a researcher and writer of scholarly books. This achievement was all the more remarkable in view of the fact that he had only a few years of primary and secondary education at an Indian mission school, followed many years later by academic training in law while working as a clerk for the federal government in Washington, DC. With the aid of his extraordinary family and his devoted friend Alice Fletcher, he became a widely respected ethnologist.

La Flesche was born on the Omaha Reservation, near the present city of Omaha, Nebraska, the son of Joseph La Flesche and Elizabeth Esau. In his childhood and adolescence, he shared in many of the traditional tribal activities and rituals, including several of the last great buffalo hunts. His father, of half-Omaha and half-French ethnicity, was the last principal chief of the Omaha tribe. Still, he was determined that all of his children should learn to live in the white man's world. Francis' mother, a full-blooded Omaha, was the second of at least three wives of Joseph. Francis was the half-brother of the first Native American physician, Susan La Flesche Picotte, and of Indian rights activist Susette La Flesche. He traveled with Susette on speaking engagements, where she (and probably he) met Henry Wadsworth Longfellow, who, according to Jarold Ramsey of *Dictionary of Literary Biography,* "effused that Susette *was* Minnehaha—thus helping to launch her own remarkable career as a writer, speaker, and champion of Indian rights."

The closest personal, as well as professional, relationship of La Flesche's life was with Alice Fletcher, a woman twenty years his senior with whom he developed a kinship. She became crippled with rheumatism in the early 1880s and La Flesche became her close associate and interpreter. He provided not only physical help in her frequent travels to Indian reservations but also assistance in her studies of the life of the Plains Indians and her efforts to improve the condition of Native Americans in general. He did much of the research over a period of twenty years that ultimately resulted in the monumental study *The Omaha Tribe,* published in 1911 with Fletcher as co-author. He was particularly skilled at persuading elderly tribal leaders of the Omaha to reveal the words and ceremonies of the ancient tribal rituals, which were rapidly dying out. Following the publication of *The Omaha Tribe,* he turned his scholarly research to the Osage tribe, a group closely related to the Omahas.

In 1900 La Flesche published *The Middle Five,* an autobiographical sketch of his school days at the Omaha Indian mission school. Ramsey commented, "This delightful book—which has never been out of print since its first appearance—quickly became a classic of Native American childhood biography, alongside Charles Eastman's contemporaneous *Indian Boyhood* (1902). . . . Although La Flesche's account of his school days is unsentimental, it is also richly evocative of cherished memories of escapades and schoolboy pranks and intense friendships—the narrative ends with the tragic illness and death of his best friend, 'Brush,' an orphan for whom the school was home. Of special importance for La Flesche's scholarly and literary career are episodes of forbidden after-hours traditional storytelling and singing of Anglo hymns and Omaha songs."

In 1910 La Flesche transferred from the Office of Indian Affairs to the Bureau of American Ethnology in the Smithsonian Institution. There he could devote his full time to exhaustive research on the Osage tribe, the first results of which appeared in 1921 in *The Osage Tribe: Rite of the Chiefs; Sayings of the Ancient Men.* Hartley Alexander of *American Anthropologist* described the Osage volumes as "the most complete single record of the ceremonies of any native American Indian people." Later products of his studies included a monumental *A Dictionary of the Osage Language,* published in 1932, and *War Ceremony and Peace Ceremony of the Osage Indians,* published posthumously in 1939.

BIOGRAPHICAL/CRITICAL SOURCES:

BOOKS

Dictionary of Literary Biography, Volume 175: *Native American Writers of the United States,* Gale, 1997.
Native North American Literature, Gale, 1994.
Notable Native Americans, Gale, 1995.

PERIODICALS

American Anthropologist, new series 35, 1933, p. 328.
Choice, June, 1996, p. 1689.
Library Journal, March 1, 1995, p. 105.
Reference and Research Book News, May, 1996, p. 10.
Western Historical Quarterly, autumn, 1996, p. 408.*

LAKE, David J(ohn) 1929-

PERSONAL: Born March 26, 1929, in Bangalore, India; naturalized Australian citizen; son of William George (a merchant) and Norah (Babington) Lake; married Marguerite Ferris, December 30, 1964; children: Sarah; stepchildren: Margarita, Anne, David. *Education:* Trinity College, Cambridge, B.A., 1952, M.A., 1956; University College of North Wales, diploma in linguistics, 1965; University of Queensland, Ph.D., 1974. *Politics:* "Liberal/environmentalist." *Religion:* "Taoist/agnostic."

ADDRESSES: Home—7 Eighth Ave., St. Lucia, Brisbane, Queensland 4067, Australia. *Office*—Department of English, University of Queensland, St. Lucia, Brisbane, Queensland 4067, Australia. *Agent*—Valerie Smith, 538 East Harford St., Milford, PA 18337.

CAREER: Assistant master, Sherrardswood School, Welwyn Garden City, Hertfordshire, England, 1953-58, and St. Albans Boys Grammar School, Hertfordshire, 1958-59; teacher of English, Saigon University, Vietnam, 1959-61, for Thai Government, Bangkok, Thailand, 1961-63, and Chiswick Polytechnic, London, England, 1963-64; Jadavpore University, Calcutta, India, reader in English and teacher, 1965-67; University of Queensland, Brisbane, Australia, lecturer, 1967-72, senior lecturer, 1973-76, reader in English, 1977—. *Military service:* British Army, gunner in Royal Artillery, 1948-49.

MEMBER: Anti-Slavery and Aboriginals Protection Society of London (life member).

AWARDS, HONORS: Ditmar Award for best Australian science fiction, 1977, for *Walkers on the Sky,* and 1982, for *The Man Who Loved Morlocks: A Sequel to the Time Machine as Narrated by the Time Traveller.*

WRITINGS:

John Milton: Paradise Lost, Mukhopadhyay, 1967.
Greek Tragedy, Excelsus Academy, 1969.
Hornpipes and Funerals (poems), University of Queensland Press, 1973.
The Canon of Thomas Middleton's Plays: Internal Evidence for the Major Problems of Authorship, Cambridge University Press, 1975.

SCIENCE FICTION NOVELS

Walkers on the Sky, DAW, 1976, revised edition, John M. Fontana, 1978.
The Right Hand of Dextra, DAW, 1977.
The Wildings of Westron, DAW, 1977.
The Gods of Xuma; or, Barsoom Revisited, DAW, 1978.
The Fourth Hemisphere, Void, 1980.
The Man Who Loved Morlocks: A Sequel to the Time Machine as Narrated by the Time Traveller, illustrated by Steph Campbell, Hyland House, 1981.
The Ring of Truth, Cory & Collins, 1982.
Warlords of Xuma, DAW, 1983.

FANTASY NOVELS

The Changelings of Chaan, Hyland House, 1985.
West of the Moon, Hyland House, 1988.

OTHER

Editor of two new critical editions of H.G. Wells' novels: *The First Men in the Moon,* 1995, and *The Invisible Man,,* 1996, both published by Oxford University Press.

Contributor to books, including *Rooms of Paradise,* edited by Lee Harding, Quartet Books, 1978; *Envisaged Worlds,* edited by Paul Collins, Void, 1978; *Alien Worlds,* edited by Collins, Void, 1979; *Transmutations,* edited by Rob Gerrand, Outback Press, 1979; and *Distant Worlds,* edited by Collins, Cory & Collins, 1981. Also contributor to *Notes and Queries, Extrapolation, Science Fiction Studies,* and *Wellsian.*

SIDELIGHTS: David Lake is a novelist who utilizes science fiction as a means of escape as he seeks spiritual answers to his own pessimism. Michael J. Tolley of *Twentieth-Century Science-Fiction Writers* observed, "If Earth is the City of Destruction in a godless universe, where may hope be found? In his novels Lake catapults small colonies of survivors to distant, wondrous planets, and new Jerusalem is actually built foursquare on Dextra." The two Dextra novels, *The Right Hand of Dextra* and *The Wildings of Westron,* demonstrate a complementary duality reminiscent of William Blake's *Songs of Innocence* and *Songs of Experience. The Right Hand of Dextra* depicts a state of innocence in which New Earthmen find their Puritan ways somewhat altered by the naivet of other species. *The Wildings of Westron,* however, depicts a feudal world characterized by anguish and hopelessness. Set thousands of years after *The Right Hand of Dextra,* the story tells of the necessity for all humankind to perish to make a New Earth on Dextra possible. While many humans agree to be transformed from human to Dextran, those who do not must be slain. The reason for the mass destruction is the inferiority of humans, as Tolley explained: "There is no hope in human flesh because it is closed; Dextran flesh, however, is open, unsecret, allowing telepathic understanding of one another." A similar belief is presented in *The Gods of Xuma,* in which humans are deemed unfit for space travel, but only the truly evil are killed.

The Changelings of Chaan and *West of the Moon* are fantasies for a young-adult audience. Tolley noted that adolescent readers who enjoy the works of C.S. Lewis "should find them [Lake's fantasies] at least as charming and thoughtful as the best of the Narnia books. Both use the pleasant conceit of advancing their young heroes to a higher world. . . ." In *The Changelings of Chaan,* the protagonist must embark on a journey to the Silver World (where the gods live) before he can return to Chaan. The novel demonstrates Lake's knowledge of Indian society and religious legends. In *West of the Moon,* orphans Megan and Mark are lured to Middleworld by an evil king and his magician.

Lake told *Twentieth-Century Science-Fiction Writers,* "The main influences on my writing are probably H.G. Wells and C.S. Lewis, and the clash between these two authors' values. I follow Wells and Lewis in writing SF that deliberately borders on fantasy. Elves may appear wearing spacesuits. The same themes also appear in my poems, some of which are in fact close to being SF. I am also strongly influenced by my early background as a child in India under the old British Raj. I know how it feels to be an invader in a vast, different culture." In addition to Wells and Lewis, Lake cites William Blake as an influence, along with his interest in astronomy, biology, and other sciences. He commented to *CA* that in his novels, the "main preoccupations are beauty, sex, and religion, and in general the predicament of being a rational animal."

BIOGRAPHICAL/CRITICAL SOURCES:

BOOKS

Twentieth-Century Science-Fiction Writers, 3rd edition, St. James Press, 1991.

PERIODICALS

Fantasy Review, February, 1986, p. 23.*

LAMBURN, Richmal Crompton 1890-1969 (Richmal Crompton)

PERSONAL: Born November 15, 1890, in Bury, Lancashire, England; died January 11, 1969; daughter of Edward John Sewell (a clerk in Holy Orders) and Clara (Crompton) Lamburn. *Education:* Royal Holloway College, London, B.A. (honors), 1914 (Driver scholar, 1914). *Politics:* Conservative. *Religion:* Church of England.

CAREER: St. Elphin's School, Darley Dale, Derbyshire, England, classical mistress, 1914-17; Bromley High School, Bromley, Kent, England, classical mistress, 1917-24; writer, 1922-69. *Military service:* Volunteer in Auxiliary Fire Service, Bromley, during World War II.

MEMBER: Authors' Society, National Book League.

WRITINGS:

ALL AS RICHMAL CROMPTON; "JUST WILLIAM" SERIES FOR CHILDREN; ALL PUBLISHED BY GEORGE NEWNES, EXCEPT AS INDICATED

Just William, 1922.
More William, 1923.
William Again, 1923.
William—the Fourth, 1924.
Still—William, 1925.
William—The Conqueror, 1926.
William—in Trouble, 1927.
William—the Outlaw, 1927.
William—the Good, 1928.
William, 1929.
William—the Bad, 1930.
William's Happy Days, 1930.
William's Crowded Hours, 1931.
William—the Pirate, 1933.
William—the Rebel, 1933.
William—the Gangster, 1934.
William—the Detective, 1935.
Sweet William, 1936.
William—the Showman, 1937.
William—the Dictator, 1938.
William and the A.R.P., 1939, reissued as *William's Bad Resolution,* 1956.
Just William: The Story of the Film, 1939.
William and the Evacuees, 1940, reissued as *William the Film Star,* 1956.
William Does His Bit, 1941.
William Carries on, 1942.
William and the Brains Trust, 1945.
Just William's Luck, 1948.

William—the Bold, 1950.
William and the Tramp, 1952.
William and the Moon Rocket, 1954.
William and the Artist's Model (play), J. Garnet Miller, 1956.
William and the Space Animal, 1956.
William's Television Show, 1958, abridged edition, 1965.
William—the Explorer, 1960.
William's Treasure Trove, 1962.
William and the Witch, 1964.
William and the Monster, illustrated by Peter Archer and Thomas Henry, Armada, 1965.
William—the Ancient Briton, illustrated by Archer and Henry, Armada, 1965.
William—the Cannibal, illustrated by Archer and Henry, Armada, 1965.
William—the Globetrotter, illustrated by Archer and Henry, Armada, 1965.
William and the Pop Singers, 1965.
William and the Masked Ranger, 1966.
William the Superman, 1968.
William the Lawless, 1970.

OTHER CHILDREN'S BOOKS AS RICHMAL CROMPTON

Jimmy, George Newnes, 1949.
Jimmy Again, George Newnes, 1951.
Jimmy the Third, illustrated by Lunt Roberts, Armada, 1965.

NOVELS; ALL AS RICHMAL CROMPTON

The Innermost Room, Andrew Melrose, 1923.
The Hidden Light, Hodder & Stoughton, 1924.
Anne Morrison, Jarrolds, 1925.
The Wildings, Hodder & Stoughton, 1925.
David Wilding, Hodder & Stoughton, 1926.
Dread Dwelling, Boni & Liveright, 1926 (published in England as *The House,* Hodder & Stoughton, 1926).
Enter—Patricia, George Newnes, 1927.
Millicent Dorrington, Hodder & Stoughton, 1927.
Leadon Hill, Hodder & Stoughton, 1928.
The Thorn Bush, Hodder & Stoughton, 1928.
Roofs Off!, Hodder & Stoughton, 1928.
The Four Graces, Hodder & Stoughton, 1929.
Abbot's End, Hodder & Stoughton, 1929.
Blue Flames, Hodder & Stoughton, 1930.
Naomi Godstone, Hodder & Stoughton, 1930.
Portrait of a Family, Macmillan, 1931.
The Odyssey of Euphemia Tracy, Macmillan, 1932.
Marriage of Hermione, Macmillan, 1932.
The Holiday, Macmillan, 1933.
Chedsy Place, Macmillan, 1934.
The Old Man's Birthday, Macmillan, 1934, Little, Brown, 1935.
Quartet, Macmillan, 1935.
Caroline, Macmillan, 1936.
There Are Four Seasons, Macmillan, 1937.
Journeying Wave, Macmillan, 1938.
Merlin Bay, Macmillan, 1939.
Steffan Green, Macmillan, 1940.
Narcissa, Macmillan, 1941.
Mrs. Frensham Describes a Circle, Macmillan, 1942.
Weatherley Parade, Macmillan, 1944.
Westover, Hutchinson, 1946.
The Ridleys, Hutchinson, 1947.
Family Roundabout, Hutchinson, 1948.
Frost at Morning, Hutchinson, 1950.
Linden Rise, Hutchinson, 1952.
The Gypsy's Baby, Hutchinson, 1954.
Four in Exile, Hutchinson, 1955.
Matty and the Dearingroydes, Hutchinson, 1956.
Blind Man's Buff, Hutchinson, 1957.
Wiseman's Folly, Hutchinson, 1959.
The Inheritor, Hutchinson, 1960.

SHORT STORY COLLECTIONS UNDER PSEUDONYM RICHMAL CROMPTON:

Kathleen and I, and Of Course, Veronica, Hodder & Stoughton, 1926.
A Monstrous Regiment, Hutchinson, 1927.
Mist, and Other Stories, Hutchinson, 1928.
The Middle Things, Hutchinson, 1928.
Felicity—Stands By, George Newnes, 1928.
Sugar and Spice, Ward, Lock, 1929.
Ladies First, Hutchinson, 1929.
The Silver Birch, and Other Stories, Hutchinson, 1931.
First Morning, Hutchinson, 1936.

ADAPTATIONS: *Just William* was adapted to film in 1939 by Associated British. *Jimmy* has been adapted to audio.

SIDELIGHTS: Richmal Crompton Lamburn's "Just William" books about an eleven-year-old boy were originally written for adults but were enjoyed by children so much that they came to be classified as children's fiction. The title character of William Brown was first introduced to readers in short stories in *Home* and *Happy* magazines. Many of these short pieces were recreated as books, and as a result the series is episodic, with almost every book able to stand alone. Lamburn drew many of her ideas from her childhood memories of her brother and from her later memories of her nephew. Mary Cadogan of *Twentieth-Century Chil-*

dren's Writers commented that the William books appeal to readers of varying ages and tastes because the stories work on different levels. Even young readers who do not appreciate the irony and subtlety of the early books are able to enjoy the ridiculous situations in which William finds himself. When Lamburn began to tailor the books to children instead of adults, she dispensed with much of the satire but did so without sacrificing the stories' characteristic inventiveness.

In the 1920s William emerged as a new type of protagonist. Whereas most children in books of that era are honorable and well-behaved, William is lazy, untidy, often defiant, and not always truthful. Yet Lamburn depicts him as likeable and appealing rather than loathsome. Cadogan noted, "William's boisterous proclivities seem natural and require no justification (though he is always complaining that grown-ups misunderstand his good intentions). He is the ultimate unbookish, adventurous, outdoor child." William's family is well-to-do and genteel, making his non-conformity even more pronounced.

The fact that Lamburn was a supporter of women's suffrage makes her characterization of female characters somewhat surprising. Cadogan observed that Lamburn's women and girls are often stereotypes, such as William's mother, who darns socks and passively agrees with her husband's statements. The character of William's sister Ethel is developed as little more than a flirtatious young girl. On the other hand, six-year-old Violet Elizabeth Bott is a precocious child in whom William often meets his match.

Lamburn's efforts to create other young characters were less successful than the William books. The character of Jimmy is younger than William, and his series lasted only three books. *Kathleen and I, and, of Course, Veronica* features Veronica whose antics were described by Cadogan as "merely cute," and *Enter—Patricia* and *Felicity Stands By* are young adult heroines rather than juveniles.

BIOGRAPHICAL/CRITICAL SOURCES:

BOOKS

Scutte, David, *William-The Immortal: An Illustrated Bibliography,* D. Schutte (Midhurst), 1993.

Something about the Author, Volume 5, Gale, 1973.

Twentieth-Century Children's Writers, 4th edition, St. James Press, 1995.

Williams, Kay, *Just Richmal: The Life and Work of Richmal Crompton Lamburn,* Genesis Publications Ltd. (Guildford), 1986.

PERIODICALS

London Review of Books, December 1, 1983, p. 27.

New Statesman, May 16, 1969, p. 702; December 16, 1983, p. 40.

Observer, February 13, 1977, p. 35.

Variety, January 29, 1969.*

* * *

LAMPITT, Dinah 1937-

PERSONAL: Born March 6, 1937, in Essex, England; daughter of Edgar Robert and Ena (Hardy) Daniels; married L. F. Lampitt (a journalist and writer), November 28, 1959 (died, 1981); children: Amanda Valentine, Brett Robert. *Education:* Attended Polytechnic of Central London. *Politics:* Socialist. *Religion:* "Still considering."

ADDRESSES: *Home*—Fairlight Cottage, Rushers Cross, Mayfield, Sussex TN20 6PU, England. *Agent*—Shirley Russell, Rupert Crew Ltd., Kings Mews, London WC1N 2JA, England.

CAREER: Worked as junior writer for *Woman* magazine, 1954-55; assistant to the news editor of London *Times,* 1956-57; assistant to the fiction editor of London *Evening News,* 1957-59; free-lance writer, 1960s-1980s; writer. Director of plays and musicals, including *Lock Up Your Daughter, Oliver!, Pickwick, Cabaret, Half a Sixpence,* and *The Crucible,* for southern England theater groups.

MEMBER: Society of Authors.

WRITINGS:

NOVELS

Sutton Place, Muller, 1983.

The Silver Swan, Muller, 1984.

Fortune's Soldier, Muller, 1985.

To Sleep No More, M. Joseph, 1987; St. Martin's Press (New York), 1988.

Pour the Dark Wine, M. Joseph, 1989.

The King's Women, New English Library (London), 1991; New American Library (New York), 1993.

As Shadows Haunting, New English Library, 1993; New American Library, 1994.

Novellas serialized in *Woman's Realm* include *The Moonlit Door, The Gemini Syndrome, The Staircase,* and *The Anklets.* Contributor of articles to *She* and *Woman's World,* short stories to *Prima,* and serials to *Woman's Own.*

SIDELIGHTS: Dinah Lampitt told *CA:* "I started to write when I was five but burned all my early work, including six novels, because it was all awful. My husband's forced retirement owing to ill health brought about the need to earn hard cash. My first novel, the first I submitted, was thus finished and published. The best motivation for any career is the need to eat!"

In her novels Lampitt combines her interests in history and the supernatural. As she explained to *Twentieth-Century Romance and Historical Writers,* "My historical novels are not all they would appear to be, for an element of the supernatural, a dalliance with the paranormal, haunts the pages of each and every one. Painstakingly researched, vividly bringing to life the people and events of the past, they all have a gothic quality that has earned me an ever-increasing readership. Recently reviewed as 'the best writer' of my kind, my fascination with the world unseen continues unabated."

The Sutton Place Trilogy focuses on a house and estate cursed by Queen Edith, the neglected wife of Edward the Confessor. In the first installment, *Sutton Place,* the eldest Weston son, Francis, comes under the effects of the curse as he is accused of adultery with Anne Boleyn and executed. The people living in Sutton Place witness the appearances of ghosts of people doomed by the curse as well as visions of future inhabitants of the estate. *The Silver Swan* concerns Sutton Place in the eighteenth century. The title refers to Melior Mary, the beautiful Weston heiress. In childhood her hair turns white from frequent malevolent visitations by ghosts. As an adult, she discovers a secret that enables her to retain her unsurpassed youthful beauty. In the end, however, the curse overcomes her and she dies alone as the house falls to ruin. *Fortune's Soldier* tells how the Westons lose their fortune as a result of the rundown estate. Consequently, the heir, John Joseph, becomes an Austrian soldier. He and a close friend are in love with the same woman, making this the most melodramatic book in the trilogy. Pamela Cleaver of *Twentieth-Century Romance and Historical Writers* wrote that in all three of the books "a gripping story is told, and the doom-laden atmosphere is deliciously spine-chilling."

To Sleep No More is set in a fourteenth-century Sussex village. The three main characters are the brother of the Archbishop of Canterbury, his young wife, and the Gascon squire who loves her. These characters all meet untimely deaths after which their spirits are restless. In the seventeenth century, they are reincarnated only to die again as a result of their implication in a witch trial. A century later, they are reincarnated again, this time as outlaws involved in smuggling.

The Tudors are the focus of *Pour the Dark Wine,* a novel in which Lampitt suggests two intriguing theories. The first is that Edward VI was born to Jane Seymour by a caesarian section that cost the young woman her life. The second theory is that Queen Elizabeth I remained the "Virgin Queen" due to a physical malformation.

Commenting on Lampitt's fiction in general, Cleaver wrote that she "is at home in all periods she writes about, having a sure hand with the details of the social life of the past. Although her writing is occasionally a little too lush and fulsome, her stories are always absorbing, and well worth reading."

BIOGRAPHICAL/CRITICAL SOURCES:

BOOKS

Twentieth-Century Romance and Historical Writers, 3rd edition, St. James Press, 1994.

PERIODICALS

Books, July, 1987, p. 28.
Kirkus Reviews, March 15, 1988, p. 392.
Kliatt Young Adult Paperback Book Guide, May, 1995, p. 16.*

* * *

LAMPLUGH, Lois 1921-

PERSONAL: Surname is pronounced "Lamploo"; born June 9, 1921, in Barnstaple, Devonshire, England; daughter of Aubrey Penfound and Ruth (Lister) Lamplugh; married Lawrence Carlile Davis (a sales representative), September 24, 1955; children: Susan Ruth, Hugh Lawrence. *Education:* B.A. (with honors), Open University, 1978. *Avocational interests:* Listening to music (especially Italian opera), gardening, walking.

ADDRESSES: *Home*—Springside, Bydown, Swimbridge, Devonshire EX32 0QB, England. *Agent*—A. P. Watt Ltd., 26/28 Bedford Row, London WC1R 4HL, England.

CAREER: Writer. Jonathan Cape Ltd., London, England, member of editorial staff, 1946-57; former part-time teacher at school for maladjusted boys. *Military service:* Served in Auxiliary Territorial Service, World War II.

MEMBER: P.E.N., Society of Authors, West Country Writers Association.

WRITINGS:

The Stream Way, Golden Galley Press, 1948.
The Quarry Hare (poetry), privately printed, 1976.
Barnstaple: Town on the Taw, Phillimore, 1983.
A History of Ilfracombe, Phillimore, 1984.
Minehead and Dunster, Phillimore, 1987.
Take Off from Chivenor, Badger Books, 1990.
The Shadowed Man: Henry Williamson 1895-1977, Exmoor Press (Dulverton), 1991.
A Look at the Past of Swimbridge, privately printed, 1993.
Lundy: Island without Equal, Mark Young (Swimbridge, Devon), 1993.
Parson Jack Russell of Swimbridge, privately printed, 1994.

JUVENILES

Nine Bright Shiners, J. Cape, 1955.
The Pigeongram Puzzle, J. Cape, 1955, Verry, 1960.
Vagabonds' Castle, J. Cape, 1957, Verry, 1965.
Rockets in the Dunes, J. Cape, 1958.
The Sixpenny Runner, J. Cape, 1960.
Midsummer Mountains, J. Cape, 1961.
The Rifle House Friends, Deutsch, 1965.
The Linhay on Hunter's Hill, Deutsch, 1966.
The Fur Princess and Fir Prince, Dent, 1969.
(With Peter Dickinson) *Mandog,* BBC Publications, 1972.
Sean's Leap, Deutsch, 1979.
The Winter Donkey, Deutsch, 1980.
Falcon's Tor, Deutsch, 1984.
Sandrabbit, Wellspring, 1991.

OTHER

Also author of television documentary *The Old Navigator,* 1967; half-hour documentary *Coleridge,* Harlech Television, 1966; and more than 300 five-minute stories for television, including "Honeyhill" series, Harlech Television, 1967-70.

SIDELIGHTS: Lois Lamplugh writes books for older children about children their age. Her earliest books feature adventurous plots, while the appeal of her later stories lies in careful attention to the detail of everyday life. The themes of her books often relate to issues of personal growth, change, and decision making. *The Winter Donkey,* for example, is about a boy named Matthew who lives in a small community and ponders the outside world with curiosity and uncertainty. He feels torn between the comfortable family life of his childhood and the possibilities of new people and places. Alison Sage of *Twentieth-Century Children's Writers* commented, "Lamplugh concentrates on the interior life of her characters, and their complex and fragile emotions are extremely compelling. . . . Probably best enjoyed by a contemplative child or even adult, her books yield more on a second or even third reading."

A country child, Lamplugh still prefers country living, noting "for all that, I wrote my first children's books when I was living and working in London—perhaps a form of escape, since they were set in North Devon." She wrote a great deal of unpublished work, mainly novels and verse, in her teens and had a book accepted for publication by Faber in 1942. It was an account of her experiences in the Auxiliary Territorial Service, and the War Office withheld approval of publication on the grounds that it would discourage recruiting. The manuscript remains unpublished.

Sean's Leap arose from Lamplugh's experience of teaching at a school for maladjusted boys and was written "at intervals between courses [she was taking at the Open University] on 'Renaissance and Reformation,' 'The Nineteenth Century Novel,' and 'Twentieth Century Poetry.'" The story is about a boy named Sean who runs away from the Island of Brytherne. Sage deemed the book the "best of Lamplugh's work."

Lamplugh believes "the outlook for children's books in England is poor at present, with the cuts in spending affecting the buying of books for schools and children's libraries, and this is why I've been at work on books on the history of places in southwest England in recent years," in addition to a "first attempt" at biography with a book on the life of children's author Henry Williamson. "Williamson," Lamplugh related, is "an obvious choice of subject, as he was a friend of my parents from 1923, and I possess a collection of letters from him written to them and, later, to myself."

Lamplugh told *CA:* "It is possible that I became a writer simply because I happened to spend the first eighteen years of my life in or near the village of Georgeham [where] in the 1920s Henry Williamson was living—for part of the time in a cottage he rented from my grandmother. (He wrote most, if not all, of *Tarka the Otter* in that cottage.)"

BIOGRAPHICAL/CRITICAL SOURCES:

BOOKS

Something about the Author, Volume 17, Gale, 1979.
Twentieth-Century Children's Writers, 4th edition, St. James Press, 1995.

PERIODICALS

School Library Journal, December, 1984.
Times Literary Supplement, March 30, 1984.*

* * *

LANGLEY, Noel 1911-1980

PERSONAL: Born December 25, 1911, in Durban, South Africa; became U.S. citizen, 1961; died November 4, 1980, in Desert Hot Springs, CA; son of Aubrey and Dora Langley; married Naomi Mary Legate, 1937 (divorced, 1954); married Pamela Deeming, 1959; children: (first marriage) three sons, two daughters. *Education:* University of Natal, B.A.

CAREER: Author, playwright, and writer-director of films produced in Britain and United States. *Military service:* Canadian Navy, 1943-45; became lieutenant.

MEMBER: Writers Guild of America West.

AWARDS, HONORS: Donaldson Award (shared with Robert Morley), 1948, for *Edward, My Son.*

WRITINGS:

Cage Me a Peacock (also see below), Barker, 1935, Morrow, 1937, reprinted, Penguin Books/Methuen, 1960.
There's a Porpoise Close behind Us, Barker, 1936, reprinted, Penguin, 1961, published as *So Unlike the English,* Morrow, 1937.
The Tale of the Land of Green Ginger, Morrow, 1937, revised edition published as *The Land of Green Ginger,* illustrated by Edward Ardizzone, Penguin Books, 1966, reprinted, 1982.
Hocus Pocus, Methuen, 1941.
The Music of the Heart, Barker, 1946, reprinted, Mayflower, 1969.
The Cabbage Patch, Barker, 1947.
Nymph in Clover, Barker, 1948.
The True and Pathetic Story of Desbarollda the Waltzing Mouse, Drummond, 1948.
The Inconstant Moon, Barker, 1949.
(With Hazel Pynegar) *Somebody's Rocking My Dreamboat,* Barker, 1949.
Tales of Mystery and Revenge, Barker, 1950, reprinted, Mayflower, 1969.
(With Pynegar) *Cuckoo in the Dell,* Barker, 1951.
The Rift in the Lute, Barker, 1952.
Where Did Everybody Go?, Barker, 1960.
The Loner, Triton, 1967.
Edgar Cayce on Reincarnation, edited by Hugh Lynn Cayce, Hawthorn, 1968.
A Dream of Dragonflies, Macmillan, 1970.
(Editor) Jasper Swain, *On the Death of My Son,* Turnstone Books, 1974.

PLAYS

Farm of Three Echoes (first produced in London, 1935; produced in New York at Cort Theatre, November, 1939), French, 1940.
Three Plays: Farm of Three Echoes, For Ever, Friendly Relations (also see below), Miles, 1936.
Little Lambs Eat Ivy: A Light Comedy in Three Acts, (first produced, 1947; also produced as *The Walrus and the Carpenter*), Samuel French, 1950, reprinted, Mayflower, 1969.
(With Robert Morley) *Edward, My Son* (first produced in New York at Martin Beck Theatre, September, 1948; also see below), French, 1948.
The Burning Bush (adaptation), first produced in New York at Erwin Piscator Dramatic Workshop, December, 1949.
An Elegance of Rebels: A Play in Three Acts, Barker, 1960.

Also author of plays *Queer Cargo,* 1934, *For Ever,* 1934, *Friendly Relations, No Regrets,* 1937, *Cage Me a Peacock* (musical adaptation of his own book), 1948, *The Gentle Rain,* and *Married Alive,* 1952.

SCREENPLAYS

Maytime, Metro-Goldwyn-Mayer (MGM), 1936.
The Wizard of Oz, MGM, 1939.
Florian, MGM, 1940.
Unexpected Uncle, RKO, 1941.
I Became a Criminal, Warner Brothers, 1947, originally entitled *They Made Me a Fugitive,* also entitled *They Made Me a Criminal.*
Adam and Evalyn, Universal, 1949, originally entitled *Adam and Evelyne.*
Edward, My Son, MGM, 1948.

(With W. Somerset Maugham and R. C. Sherriff) *Trio,* Paramount, 1950.
Tom Brown's Schooldays, United Artists, 1951.
A Christmas Carol, United Artists, 1951, originally entitled *Scrooge.*
Ivanhoe, MGM, 1952.
Pickwick Papers, Mayer-Kingsley, 1952.
Knights of the Round Table, MGM, 1953.
The Prisoner of Zenda, MGM, 1953.
The Adventures of Sadie, 20th Century-Fox, 1954, originally entitled *Our Girl Friday.*
Svengali, MGM, 1954.
The Vagabond King, Paramount, 1956.
The Search for Bridey Murphy, Paramount, 1956.
The Circle, Kassler Films, 1957, originally entitled *The Vicious Circle.*

Also author of screenplays *Queer Cargo, Shadows of Fire, Father Knows Best,* and *Snow White and the Three Stooges,* for 20th Century-Fox, the last released in Britain as *Snow White and the Three Clowns.*

SIDELIGHTS: Noel Langley was a successful writer of satirical fiction and screenplays, including adaptations of classics. His original works include *Cage Me a Peacock,* a satirical book in which Langley offers a new version of the Rape of Lucretia. The central character is a peasant girl who makes the best of two worlds by living a bigamous life as she moves up the ranks of the Roman Army. The entertainment industry provides the context for Langley's wit in *There's a Porpoise Close behind Us,* which is set amid London theater life, and *Hocus Pocus,* which takes aim at the Hollywood film industry. Langley's familiarity with Hollywood came from his years of work as a screenwriter. He wrote the screenplays for *The Wizard of Oz,* for Alistair Sims's *Scrooge* (based on Charles Dickens' *A Christmas Carol*), and for *The Search for Bridey Murphy,* which he also directed.

Langley was only twenty-six years old when producer Mervyn LeRoy asked him to write the film script for the MGM movie *The Wizard of Oz.* Langley had already established himself as one of Hollywood's fastest scriptwriters—he produced a shooting script for the Nelson Eddy-Jeanette MacDonald hit picture *Maytime* in less than four days—and he produced a forty-three page adaptation of the novel by L. Frank Baum in only eleven days. Many of Langley's changes remain in the final version of the film; he introduced the Kansas farmhands who later appear in Oz as the Scarecrow and Tin Woodman, and Miss Gulch, the alter ego of the Wicked Witch of the West.

Fantasy readers remember Langley for the children's novel *The Tale of the Land of Green Ginger.* The book is a sequel to the traditional story of Aladdin and opens with the birth of his son, Abu Ali. Amazingly, the day-old infant describes his grandmother as a button-nosed tortoise, and Aladdin summons the genie for advice. The genie tells him that the child has been chosen to rescue a magician who created the floating Land of Green Ginger for himself. The magician has inadvertently turned himself into a button-nosed tortoise, however, and must wait to be rescued. As an adult, Abu Ali embarks on a journey to find a wife and rescue the magician. After much adventure, he wins the hand of Silver Bud and liberates the magician. Maureen Speller of *St. James Guide to Fantasy Writers* noted, "Langley's theatrical interests show up particularly strongly in this novel, which is constructed much along the lines of a traditional pantomime, including traditional pantomime villains and rescue from a nasty fate in the nick of time, not to mention a love of increasingly preposterous names."

BIOGRAPHICAL/CRITICAL SOURCES:

BOOKS

Harmetz, Aljean, *The Making of "The Wizard of Oz,"* new edition, Delta, 1989.
St. James Guide to Fantasy Writers, St. James Press, 1996.

PERIODICALS

Booklist, June 15, 1989.
Kirkus Reviews, February 1, 1971.
Library Journal, March 1, 1968; July, 1971.
New York Times, May 10, 1936; March 28, 1937; March 8, 1953.
Publishers Weekly, February 15, 1971.
Times Literary Supplement, December 14, 1935; December 18, 1937.
Washington Post Book World, August 13, 1989.

OBITUARIES:

BOOKS

Something about the Author, Volume 25, Gale, 1981.*

LANGTON, Jane (Gillson) 1922-

PERSONAL: Born December 30, 1922, in Boston, MA; daughter of Joseph Lincoln (a geologist) and Grace (Brown) Gillson; married William Langton (a physicist), 1943; children: Christopher, David, Andrew. *Education:* Attended Wellesley College, 1940-42; University of Michigan, B.S., 1944, M.A., 1945; Radcliffe College, M.A., 1948; Boston Museum School of Art, graduate study, 1958-59. *Politics:* Democrat.

ADDRESSES: *Home*—9 Baker Farm Rd., Lincoln, MA 01773.

CAREER: Writer. Teacher of writing for children at Graduate Center for the Study of Children's Literature, Simmons College, 1979-80, and at Eastern Writers' Conference, Salem State College. Teacher of suspense novel writing at Radcliffe Seminars, 1981. Prepared artwork and visual material for *Discovery,* an educational program in the natural sciences, WGBH-Channel 2, Boston, 1955-56. Volunteer worker for school and church.

MEMBER: Phi Beta Kappa.

AWARDS, HONORS: Edgar Award nomination, Mystery Writers of America, 1962, for *The Diamond in the Window;* Newbery Honor Book Award, Children's Services Division of American Library Association, 1980, and American Book Award nomination, 1982, both for *The Fledgling;* Nero Wolfe Award, 1984, and Edgar Award nomination, Mystery Writers of America, 1985, both for *Emily Dickinson Is Dead.*

WRITINGS:

JUVENILES

The Majesty of Grace, Harper, 1961, published as *Her Majesty, Grace Jones,* 1972.
The Diamond in the Window, Harper, 1962.
The Swing in the Summerhouse, Harper, 1967.
The Astonishing Stereoscope, Harper, 1971.
The Boyhood of Grace Jones, Harper, 1972.
Paper Chains, Harper, 1977.
The Fledgling, Harper, 1980.
The Fragile Flag, Harper, 1984.
The Hedgehog Boy (picture book), illustrated by Ilse Plume, Harper, 1985.
Salt: From a Russian Folktale (picture book), illustrated by Plume, Hyperion Press, 1992.
The Queen's Necklace: A Swedish Folktale, illustrated by Plume, Hyperion Press, 1994.

ADULT SUSPENSE NOVELS

The Transcendental Murder, Harper, 1964, published as *The Minuteman Murder,* Dell, 1976.
Dark Nantucket Noon, Harper, 1975.
The Memorial Hall Murder, Harper, 1978.
Natural Enemy, Ticknor & Fields, 1982.
Emily Dickinson Is Dead, St. Martin's, 1984.
Good and Dead, St. Martin's, 1986.
Murder at the Gardner, St. Martin's, 1988.
The Dante Game, Viking, 1991.
God in Concord, Viking, 1992.
Divine Inspiration: A Homer Kelly Mystery, Viking, 1993.
The Shortest Day: Murder at the Revels, Viking, 1995.
Dead as a Dodo: A Homer Kelly Mystery, Viking, 1996.
The Face on the Wall: A Homer Kelly Mystery, Viking, 1998.

OTHER

Contributor to *Acts of Light,* New York Graphic Society, 1980. Former children's book reviewer for *New York Times Book Review.*

Manuscripts in the Kerlan Collection at University of Minnesota in Minneapolis and at Boston University.

ADAPTATIONS: The following titles were adapted to audio: *Good and Dead,* 1993; *Divine Inspiration: A Homer Kelly Mystery,* 1995; and *The Shortest Day: Murder at the Revels,* 1996.

SIDELIGHTS: Jane Langton once told *CA:* "My books start with an interest in a place. This has been most often Concord, Massachusetts, with its several layers of history, both from revolutionary times and from nineteenth-century transcendental times. But it is the present time, littered about with the past, that I seem to want to write about. Putting real children (as real as I can make them) into a real setting (as real as I can copy it) and then pulling some sort of fantasy out of that litter of the past that lies around them—this is what particularly interests me.

"I am lucky [to be] living in the town next to Concord. We go there very often for shopping, and [while] walking or driving one is wading through air which to me seems thick with meaning. The thing I am most afraid of is making a muddle of too many things which are not pulled together into a single unit. But the thing I like best is taking a great many things and managing them all somehow in one fist like a complicated sort of cat's cradle."

Langton is known for her mysteries as well as her novels for young adults. The appeal of her stories to younger audiences lies in their three-dimensional characters involved in intriguing adventures that lead to personal growth. Pat Pflieger of *Twentieth-Century Young Adult Writers* noted, "Whether chronicling Grace Jones's bumpy journey into adolescence or the mystical adventures of the Hall family, Langton's works glow with a sense of history, place, and the value placed on the individual spirit." The ongoing saga of the Hall family is told in five books that also relate transcendentalist history: *The Diamond in the Window, The Astonishing Stereoscope, The Swing in the Summerhouse, The Fledgling,* and *The Fragile Flag.* The main characters of the Hall family are Eddy, Eleanor, their uncle Freddy, and their cousin Georgie. Pflieger praised Langton for creating such believable and unique adolescent characters. In the first book Eddie and Eleanor have magical dreams in which they are the toys of Louisa May Alcott and her sisters, and mice in Henry David Thoreau's cabin on Walden Pond.

Langton often depicts the free-thinking Hall family in contrast to other members of the community who are complacent and conformist. Pflieger commented, "The works are, in effect, transcendentalist novels. The Hall family, unique and somewhat shabby, eschews monetary treasures for the greater riches of warm hearts and wide-ranging minds. The words of Thoreau and of Ralph Waldo Emerson echo through the novels in the conversations of Freddy, a great—if unhinged—transcendentalist scholar." In *The Fragile Flag,* Georgie is inspired to act on her concern for the world and lead a children's crusade to persuade the President of the United States to cancel his new "Peace Missile." *New York Times* reviewer Nicholas Lemann described the book as "completely charming" and added, "the portrayals of the children themselves are so effortless and true that it seems momentarily impossible that other writers could find it difficult to endow characters that young with distinctive personalities."

The theme of individualism is particularly prominent in the books featuring Grace Jones. In *The Boyhood of Grace Jones,* for example, she rejects playing with dolls and giggling at boys in favor of wearing the top of her father's World War I naval uniform and imagining herself having adventures on the high seas.

BIOGRAPHICAL/CRITICAL SOURCES:

BOOKS

Carr, John C., *The Craft of Crime,* Houghton, 1983.
Something about the Author, Volume 68, Gale, 1992.
Something about the Author Autobiography Series, Volume 5, Gale, 1988.
Twentieth-Century Young Adult Writers, 1st edition, St. James Press, 1994.

PERIODICALS

Armchair Detective, winter, 1997.
Los Angeles Times Book Review, April 21, 1991.
New Yorker, August 13, 1984.
New York Times, May 21, 1978.
New York Times Book Review, August 20, 1967; September 28, 1980; May 16, 1982; November 11, 1984; March 24, 1991; June 21, 1992; December 10, 1995.
Newsweek, December 3, 1984.
Times Literary Supplement, December 4, 1969; April 16, 1970.
Tribune (Chicago), March 3, 1991.
Washington Post Book World, May 11, 1980; December 21, 1980; June 17, 1984; January 13, 1985.*

* * *

LANSDALE, Joe R(ichard) 1951-
(Ray Slater)

PERSONAL: Born October 28, 1951, in Gladewater, TX; son of Alcee Bee (a mechanic) and Reta (in sales; maiden name, Wood) Lansdale; married Cassie Ellis, June 25, 1970 (divorced, 1972); married Karen Ann Morton, August 25, 1973; children: (second marriage) Keith Jordan, Kasey JoAnn. *Education:* Attended Tyler Junior College, 1970-71, University of Texas at Austin, 1971-72, and Stephen F. Austin State University, 1973, 1975, 1976.

ADDRESSES: *Home and Office*—113 Timber Ridge, Nacogdoches, TX 75961. *Agent*—Barbara Puechner, 3121 Portage Rd., Bethlehem, PA 18017.

CAREER: Transportation manager, Goodwill Industries, 1973-75; custodian, Stephen F. Austin State University, Nacogdoches, TX, 1976-80; foreman, LaBorde Custodial Services, Nacogdoches, 1980-81; writer, 1981—. Also worked variously as a bouncer, bodyguard, factory worker, carpenter, ditch digger, plumber's helper, and karate instructor.

MEMBER: Horror Writers of America (vice president, 1987-88), Western Writers of America (treasurer, 1987).

AWARDS, HONORS: Bram Stoker Award, Horror Writers of America, 1988, 1989; American Horror award, 1989; British Fantasy Award, 1989, for novella.

WRITINGS:

MYSTERY/SUSPENSE NOVELS

Act of Love, Zebra (New York City), 1981, CD Publications (Edgewood, MD), 1993.
The Nightrunners, Dark Harvest (Arlington Heights, IL), 1987.
Cold in July (also see below), Bantam (New York City), 1989.
Savage Season (also see below), Bantam, 1990.
Lansdale's Limited Edition: Cold in July & Savage Season, (as boxed set), Ziesing (Shingletown, CA), 1990.
Mucho Mojo, Mysterious Press (New York City), 1994.
The Two-Bear Mambo, Mysterious Press, 1995.

SCIENCE-FICTION/FANTASY/HORROR NOVELS

The Drive In: A B-Movie with Blood and Popcorn, Made in Texas, Bantam, 1988.
The Drive In 2: Not Just One of Them Sequels, Bantam, 1989.
Batman: Captured by the Engines, Warner (New York City), 1991.
On the Far Side of the Cadillac Desert with Dead Folks (chapbook), Roadkill Press (Denver, CO), 1991.
Terror on the High Skies (juvenile), Little, Brown (Boston), 1992.

WESTERN NOVELS

(Under pseudonym Ray Slater) *Texas Night Riders,* Leisure Press (Champaign, IL), 1983.
Dead in the West, Space & Time Books (New York City), 1986.
The Magic Wagon, Doubleday (New York City), 1986.
Jonah Hex: Two-Gun Mojo, DC Comics (New York City), 1994.
The Two-Bear Mambo, Mysterious Press (New York City), 1995.
Bad Chili, Mysterious Press, 1997.

SHORT STORIES

By Bizarre Hands, Ziesing, 1989.
Stories by Mama Lansdale's Youngest Boy, Pulphouse (Eugene, OR), 1991.
Best Sellers Guaranteed, Ace (New York City), 1993.
A Fist Full of Stories (and Articles), Cemetery Dance Publications, 1996.
Atomic Chili: The Illustrated Joe R. Lansdale, Mojo Press, 1997.
Writer of the Purple Rage, Carrol & Graf, 1997.

Also author of *The Steel Valentine,* 1991; *Tight Little Stitches in a Dead Man's Back,* 1992; *The Lone Ranger and Tonto,* 1996; and *The Good, the Bad, and the Indifferent: Early Stories and Commentary,* 1997.

EDITOR

Best of the West, Doubleday, 1986.
The New Frontier: Best of the West 2, Doubleday, 1989.
(With Pat Lo Brutto) *Razored Saddles,* Dark Harvest, 1989.
(With wife, Karen Lansdale) *Dark at Heart,* Dark Harvest, 1992.

OTHER

(Contributor) *Tarzan: The Lost Adventure,* Del Rey, 1997.

Also contributor to several anthologies, including *Fears,* 1984, and *Book of the Dead,* Bantam, 1989. Contributor of articles, stories, and reviews to magazines including *Horror Show, Modern Stories, Espionage,* and *Mike Shayne.*

SIDELIGHTS: Joe R. Lansdale once told *CA:* "The Martian series by Edgar Rice Burroughs got me started, and I've been writing my own stories ever since. My work ranges from popular to literary. I believe the purpose of fiction is to entertain. Enlightening the reader is nice, but secondary. If you don't have a good tale to tell, no one is listening anyway.

"My preferred genre is the fantastic, but suspense runs a close second, followed by mystery, westerns, and the mainstream. Actually, much of my work and intended work is a combination of these things. I am also interested in screenplays, and hope to work in that medium on occasion.

"I like all kinds of horror and fantasy writing, especially the contemporary horror tale. I am not too fond, though, of the vague ending that seems so popular in many publications today. Much of what I write, although it is called horror, is really just oddball or weird fantasy, perhaps never becoming scary, but certainly striking a note of the unusual."

Horror, fantasy, science fiction, mystery, suspense, Western: Lansdale's fiction encompasses all of the above, frequently combining several genres in the same story or novel while at the same time defining a distinctive voice of its own. Writing in *New York Times Book Review,* Daniel Woodrell characterized Lansdale's work as "country noir," likening him to such authors as James M. Cain and Erskine Caldwell. (Lansdale, himself, has listed Cain as a major influence.) The "country" in this case is East Texas, where Lansdale was born, raised, and continues to reside. The "noir" refers to the dark vision of human nature and contemporary life that pervades nearly all of his work. Other writers that Lansdale mentions as influential include Ray Bradbury, Robert Bloch, Flannery O'Connor, Dashiell Hammett, Raymond Chandler, and Richard Matheson. Lansdale departs from these literary icons, however, on at least two counts, each of which reflects one of his stated non-literary influences: B-movies and comic books. No matter the genre in which he is writing, graphic horror and violence are usually present. No matter how dark the vision he is rendering, satirical and humorous elements often abound.

Author of well over one hundred stories, Lansdale first made his mark in short fiction. "I prefer the short-story medium," he told Stanley Wiater in *Dark Dreamers: Conversations with the Masters of Horror.* "I think if I could make a living as a short-story writer, I would do that primarily." Lansdale's stories began appearing widely in both commercial and alternative publications by the late 1970s. Some of this work is collected in *By Bizarre Hands* and *Stories by Mama Lansdale's Youngest Boy. Best Sellers Guaranteed* combines the stories from the second collection with "The Events Concerning a Nude Fold-Out Found in a Harlequin Romance," a previously anthologized novella. Writing in *Locus,* Ed Bryant described *Best Sellers Guaranteed* as "a first-rate retrospective, particularly of Lansdale's earlier career." He went on to characterize "Lansdale's strong suit" as "whacked-out humorous melodrama with a distinctive voice (East Texas) and a keen sense of place (ditto)." Writing in *Bloomsbury Review,* Bryant also credited Lansdale with having "a universal grasp of humankind's terrors."

Lansdale's novels began appearing in the early 1980s. Although marketed within particular genres, they transcend traditional genre definitions. Typical of a Lansdale Western is *Dead in the West.* Set in pioneer days in Mud Water, Texas (a fictionalized version of Lansdale's own Gladewater), it relates a series of events involving animated corpses that would seem more at home in a contemporary horror tale than in a Western. The more recent *Magic Wagon,* set in East Texas in 1909, tells of a traveling medicine show that includes a wrestling chimpanzee and the corpse of Wild Bill Hickok. Writing on *The Magic Wagon* for *New York Times Book Review,* Anne Roston offered another example of how Lansdale's work defies simple categorization: "Behind this entertaining and seemingly innocent Western . . . lies a subtle discussion of racism and the myths people create for themselves."

Prime examples of Lansdale's science fiction and fantasy/horror fiction can be found in *The Drive In: A B-Movie with Blood and Popcorn, Made in Texas,* and *The Drive In 2: Not Just One of Them Sequels.* In the first novel, the patrons of a Texas drive-in movie are whisked into another universe where the horror films they have been watching and the drive-in itself become the sum of their reality. Scenes of rape, cannibalism, and necrophilia are portrayed. In the sequel, the patrons leave the drive-in to enter the strange world surrounding it, where they encounter both dinosaurs and vampires. Richard Gehr in *Village Voice* saw these two books as "semiparodistic novels" that "turn the horror spectacle upon itself."

Lansdale's mystery and suspense novels tend to adhere more closely to genre conventions. *Savage Season,* set in the nineties, relates the story of Hap Collins, a sixties draft-dodger who is lured by his ex-wife Trudy into a scheme to locate stolen money at the bottom of the Sabine River in East Texas. Accompanied by his friend Leonard, a gay Vietnam veteran, Hap must eventually confront the nefarious gang with whom Trudy has become involved. Liz Currie in *Armchair Detective* wrote: "When 1960s idealism meets 1990s cynicism, the stage is set for a violent confrontation between good intentions and evil results." Hap Collins and Leonard return in *Mucho Mojo.* After Leonard inherits a house from his uncle, the skeleton of a murdered child is discovered under the floorboards. Hap and Leonard proceed to track down the killer. Daniel Woodrow in *Village Voice* stated: "Mr. Lansdale sets his story in motion and carries through with great, sneaky skill. The individual scenes are sometimes not only funny, but also slyly offer acute commentary on matters of race, friendship and love in small-town America."

Lansdale's fiction has often been praised and blamed for the same reasons. The extreme, graphic violence he depicts can be viewed as gratuitous or as a pointed exaggeration of the violence in America. Depending on one's perspective and sensibilities, his humor on the darkest subjects can be perceived as poor taste or as satire on American popular culture. Critics do agree that there is far more to his work than run-of-the-mill genre fiction written for the sake of entertainment. In summing up *Mucho Mojo* for *Locus,* Edward Bryant wrote that what "Lansdale proceeds to spin is not only a top-drawer thriller, but a social portrait of a society in painful evolution. His East Texas is a place of entrenched tradition in painful conflict with new ideas about race relations, gender politics, and more open choices in sexual preference."

Lansdale told Kevin E. Proulx in *Fear to the World: Eleven Voices in a Chorus of Horror:* "Good fiction can actually tell you how people relate to one another. How they really feel about things. What life is all about. What makes it worth living, or, for some people, not worth living. I find a lot more truth in fiction than nonfiction, and that's why I prefer to write it."

Lansdale also told *CA:* "My writing is done to entertain and to please me. And to put bread on the table. I like to think my work has something going for it besides momentum. That there is some thematic depth that will ring in the reader's head afterwards like an echo. I'm attempting to blend the pacing and color of genre fiction with the character and style of the mainstream. And maybe doing a damn bad job of it. But I'm trying."

BIOGRAPHICAL/CRITICAL SOURCES:

BOOKS

Proulx, Kevin E., *Fear to the World: Eleven Voices in a Chorus of Horror* (interview), Starmont House (Mercer Island, WA), 1992, pp. 43-58.

Twentieth-Century Science-Fiction Writers, 3rd edition, St. James Press, 1991.

Twentieth-Century Western Writers, 2nd edition, St. James Press, 1991.

Wiater, Stanley, *Dark Dreamers: Conversations with the Masters of Horror* (interview), Avon (New York City), 1990, pp. 111-18.

PERIODICALS

Antioch Review, winter, 1987, p. 117.

Armchair Detective, fall, 1989, p. 435; spring, 1991, p. 227 winter, 1996, p. 107.

Bloomsbury Review, December, 1991, p. 27; June, 1992, p. 17.

Deathrealm, fall/winter, 1988, pp. 42-44.

Horror Show, January, 1987.

Locus, April, 1993, p. 21; May, 1993, p. 23; July, 1993, p. 23; May, 1994, p. 25; January, 1995, p. 31.

Mystery Scene, August, 1987.

New York Times Book Review, December 14, 1986, p. 24; October 2, 1994, p. 37.

People Weekly, November 10, 1997, p. 44.

Small Press Review, April, 1990, p. 27.

Village Voice, February 6, 1990, pp. 57-58.*

* * *

LARSEN, Nella 1891-1964

PERSONAL: Born April 13, 1891, in Chicago, IL; died of heart failure, March 30, 1964, in New York, NY; daughter of Peter Walker (West Indian) and Mary Hanson (Danish); married Elmer S. Imes (a physicist), May 3, 1919 (divorced, 1933). *Education:* Attended Fisk University, Nashville, TN, 1909-10, and University of Copenhagen, 1910-12; studied nursing at Lincoln Hospital, New York, NY, 1912-15; attended New York Public Library training school, 1921-23.

CAREER: Tuskegee Institute, Tuskegee, AL, assistant superintendent of nurses, 1915-16; Lincoln Hospital, New York City, nurse, 1916-18; Department of Health, New York City, nurse, 1918-21; New York Public Library, Harlem branch, assistant librarian, 1922-23, children's librarian, 1924-26; worked as a night nurse and supervising nurse at hospitals on the lower east side of Manhattan, 1941-64; writer.

MEMBER: Writers' League Against Lynching (assistant secretary).

AWARDS, HONORS: Bronze medal from the Harmon Foundation, 1928, for *Quicksand;* first African-American woman to receive a Guggenheim fellowship, 1930.

WRITINGS:

Quicksand (novel), Knopf, 1928, reprinted, Negro Universities Press, 1969, also published with *Passing* (also see below).

Passing (novel), Knopf, 1929, reprinted, Negro Universities Press, 1969, also published with *Quicksand* (also see below); published with an introduction and notes by Thadious M. Davis, Penguin Books, 1997.

OMNIBUS VOLUMES

Quicksand; and, Passing, edited with an introduction by Deborah E. McDowell, Rutgers University Press, 1986.

An Intimation of Things Distant: The Collected Fiction of Nella Larsen, edited by Charles R. Larson, Anchor, 1992.

OTHER

Contributor of short stories to various periodicals.

SIDELIGHTS: Nella Larsen was a member of the coterie of African-American writers associated with the Harlem Renaissance, an era of outstanding achievement in African-American art and literature during the 1920s and 1930s. Though not as well known as many of her contemporaries, Larsen nonetheless won recognition for her two published novels, *Quicksand* and *Passing.*

Quicksand, which appeared in 1928, is the largely autobiographical story of Helga Crane, the daughter of an African-American man and a Scandinavian woman, who searches in vain for sexual and racial identity. Her quest takes her from a teaching position at a small college in the South to the elite social circles of Copenhagen and New York City to a backwoods Atlanta community pastored by the illiterate preacher she marries. The marriage fulfills Helga's longing for an uncomplicated existence and for sexual gratification, but it leaves her mired in a life of rural poverty and continual pregnancies.

Quicksand won a Harmon Foundation prize and was greeted with generally enthusiastic reviews in contemporary periodicals. Some critics faulted Larsen's characterizations as shallow and underdeveloped, but most praised the novel's complexity, sophistication, and artistry. A writer for *New York Times,* for example, called *Quicksand* "an articulate, sympathetic first novel, which tells its story and projects its heroine in a lucid, exaggerated manner." Similarly, writing in *Crisis,* W.E.B. Du Bois deemed it "the best piece of fiction that Negro America has produced since the heyday of [Charles] Chesnutt."

More than fifty years after its initial publication *Quicksand* continues to generate critical acclaim. In his volume *From the Dark Tower: Afro-American Writers, 1900 to 1960,* Arthur P. Davis described *Quicksand* as "a fascinating case study of an unhappy and unfortunate woman," calling Helga Crane a victim not so much of racial situation as of "her own inability to make the right decisions." She is, pronounced Davis, intriguing and complex, "a superb creation," and he assessed Larsen's book "one of the better novels of the Harlem Renaissance." Margaret Perry, author of *Silence to the Drums: A Survey of the Literature of the Harlem Renaissance,* lauded Larsen for her "awareness of female sexuality," and Addison Gayle, Jr., in his *The Way of the New World: The Black Novel in America,* called *Quicksand* "almost modern in its plot and conflicts. . . . It seeks to broach the wider question of identity, not the loss of it, but the search for it, and to suggest that this search in a world, race mad, must produce serious psychological problems of the spirit and soul."

Passing, like *Quicksand,* examines what *Ms.* contributor Mary Helen Washington labeled "the marginal black woman of the middle class, who was both unwilling to conform to a circumscribed existence in the black world and unable to move freely in the white world." *Passing* is the story of Clare Kendry, a beautiful, fair-skinned African-American woman who escapes likely impoverishment by passing for white. She marries a wealthy white man, who assumes that she is also white. Her passage across the color line is completely successful until "a longing for her own kind led her to take fatal risks," posited Margaret Cheney Dawson in her review of the novel for *New York Herald Tribune.* Clare renews ties with childhood friend Irene Redfield, who has married an African-American physician and is living in the upper circles of Harlem. Clare finds herself as attracted to Irene's husband as he is to her. Perceiving Clare as a threat to her own marriage and security, Irene wants Clare to disappear, a wish that comes true when Clare falls, jumps, or is pushed from an open window at a Harlem apartment party just as her husband appears to confront her with his discovery of her African-American roots.

Critics were divided in their reaction to *Passing.* Most found it less impressive than *Quicksand,* flawed by what a reviewer for *New York Times Book Review* called "its sudden and utterly unconvincing close, a close that solves most of the problems . . . by simply sweeping them out of existence through the engineered death of Clare Kendry, the girl who is passing." Those critics who defended the novel averred that its strengths outweigh its weaknesses. Among these was Addison Gayle, Jr., who judged *Passing* "superior" to *Quicksand* "in terms of character development, organization, and fidelity to language." Similarly, *Saturday Review of Literature* contributor W.B. Seabrook lauded the novel as "classically pure in outline, single in theme and in impression, and . . . powerful in its catastrophe." It is, added Seabrook, "a work so fine, sensitive, and distinguished that it rises above race categories and becomes that rare object, a good novel." Furthermore, Robert Bone wrote in his *The Negro Novel in America* that "despite a false and shoddy denouement, "*Passing* was "probably the best treatment of the subject in Negro fiction." Claudia Tate, contributor to *Black American Literature Forum,* concurred, describing *Passing* as "a skillfully executed and enduring work of art that did not receive the critical attention it deserved."

At the height of her popularity in 1930, Larsen was accused of plagiarism in a dispute over a short story published in *Forum* magazine. Although later exonerated, she seemed stifled by the accusation and the scandal. At the same time she experienced marital problems that led to a crudely sensationalized 1933 divorce from her physicist husband. Consequently, during the next several years Larsen gradually withdrew from her circle of literary friends on the lower east side of New York City until she broke all ties with them. She spent the last twenty years of her life working as a nurse in Manhattan hospitals.

Larsen's work is now generally viewed both as a reflection of a African-American world now past and as a delineation of a particular female perspective that has endured. Larsen's two novels, according to Washington, reveal a writer "who is legally black but internally identifies with both blacks and whites, who is supposed to be content as a member of the black elite, but feels suffocated by its narrowness, who is emotionally rooted in the black experience and yet wants to live in the whole world."

Several critics expressed regret that Larsen's literary career was so brief. Among them were Washington, who averred that Larsen's "perceptive inquiries speak clearly to the predicament of the middle-class black woman of our generation," and Davis, who called Larsen "a sensitive writer, with great skill in narration." Similarly, George Kent, writing in *Blackness and the Adventure of Western Culture,* mused, "Certainly one regrets that she did not write more novels and senses that she had a complexity of awareness that might have produced great works."

BIOGRAPHICAL/CRITICAL SOURCES:

BOOKS

Black Literature Criticism, Gale, Volume 2, 1992.

Bone, Robert, *The Negro Novel in America,* revised edition, Yale University Press, 1965.

Bontemps, Arna, editor, *The Harlem Renaissance Remembered,* Dodd, 1972.

Brown, Sterling, *The Negro in American Fiction,* Atheneum, 1965.

Contemporary Black Biography, Gale, 1996.

Contemporary Literary Criticism, Volume 37, Gale, 1986.

Davis, Arthur P., *From the Dark Tower: Afro-American Writers, 1900 to 1960,* Howard University Press, 1974.

Davis, Thadious M., *Nella Larson, Novelist of the Harlem Renaissance: A Woman's Life Unveiled,* Louisiana State University Press, 1994.

Dictionary of Literary Biography, Volume 51: *Afro-American Writers From the Harlem Renaissance to 1940,* Gale, 1987.

Gayle, Addison, Jr., *The Way of the New World: The Black Novel in America,* Anchor Press, 1975.

Huggins, Nathan, *Harlem Renaissance,* Oxford University Press, 1971.

Kent, George, *Blackness and the Adventure of Western Culture,* Third World Press, 1972.

Johnson, Willa and Thomas Green, editor, *Perspectives on Afro-American Women,* ECCA Publishers, 1975, pp. 112-25.

Kent, George, *Blackness and the Adventure of Western Culture,* Third World Press, 1972.

Larson, Charles R. *Invisible Darkness: Jean Toomer and Nella Larson,* University of Iowa Press, 1993.

Lewis, David Levering, *When Harlem Was in Vogue,* Knopf, 1981.

McLendon, Jacquelyn Y., *The Politics of Color in the Fiction of Jessie Fauset and Nella Larson,* University Press of Virginia, 1995.

Perry, Margaret, *Silence to the Drums: A Survey of the Literature of the Harlem Renaissance,* Greenwood Press, 1976.

Reference Guide to American Literature, St. James Press, 1994.

Singh, Amritjii, *The Novels of the Harlem Renaissance: Twelve Black Writers, 1923-1933,* Pennsylvania State University, 1976.

Wall, Cheryl A., *Women of the Harlem Renaissance,* Indiana University Press, 1995.

PERIODICALS

African American Review, spring, 1992, p. 173; fall, 1992, p. 475; winter, 1993, p. 599; spring, 1997, p. 23.

American Literature, December, 1986.

Black American Literature Forum, winter, 1980, pp. 142-46.
Bookman, June, 1929.
CLA Journal, March, 1973, pp. 285-301; December, 1974, pp. 235-41; June, 1977, pp. 475-86.
Crisis, June, 1928.
Ms., December, 1980, pp. 44-50.
New York Herald Tribune Books, May 13, 1928; April 28, 1929.
New York Times Book Review, April 8, 1928; April 28, 1929.
Opportunity, August, 1929.
Resources for American Literary Study, fall, 1978, pp. 193-99.
Saturday Review of Literature, May 19, 1928; May 18, 1929.
Voice Literary Supplement, March, 1987.
Washington Post Book World, March 29, 1992, p. 15.
Women's Review of Books, October, 1986.*

* * *

LASENBY, Jack 1931-

PERSONAL: Born March 9, 1931, in Waharoa, New Zealand; son of Owen Liberty (a secretary) and Linda (a housewife; maiden name, Bryce) Lasenby; married wife, Elizabeth, 1963 (deceased, 1969); children: Rebecca, Kimberly, Anne, Jeremy. *Education:* Attended Auckland University, 1950-51.

ADDRESSES: Home—14 A Trevor Terrace, Paremata, Plimmerton, New Zealand. *Agent*—Oxford University Press, P.O. Box 11-149, Auckland 5, New Zealand.

CAREER: Worked variously as a deer culler, possum trapper, and teacher, c. 1950-68; New Zealand Department of Education, Wellington, editor of *School Journal,* 1969-75; Wellington Teachers' College, Wellington, senior lecturer in English, 1975-87; full-time writer, 1987—.

AWARDS, HONORS: Esther Glen Award, New Zealand Library Association, 1989, for *The Mangrove Summer;* Sargeson Fellowship, 1991; Victoria University of Wellington writer's fellowship, 1993.

WRITINGS:

Charlie the Cheeky Kea (picture book), Golden Books (New York), 1976.
Rewi the Red Deer (picture book), Golden Books, 1976.
The Lake (children's novel), Oxford University Press (South Melbourne), 1987.
The Mangrove Summer (children's novel), Oxford University Press (London), 1988.
Dead Man's Head (children's novel), Oxford University Press, 1990; McIndoe (Dunedin, New Zealand), 1994.
Uncle Trev and the Great South Island Plan, Cape Catley Press (Picton, New Zealand), 1991.
Uncle Trev Stories, Cape Catley Press, 1991.
Uncle Trev and the Treaty of Waitangi, Cape Catley Press, 1992.
The Conjuror, Oxford University Press (South Melbourne), 1993.
Harry Wakatipu, McIndoe Publishers, 1993.
Uncle Trev's Teeth: and Other Stories, Cape Catley (Whatamango Bay, New Zealand), 1997.

Also author of school bulletins *Lost and Found,* 1970, and *The Chatham Islands,* 1973, both published by the New Zealand Department of Education. Contributor of poems, stories, plays, and articles to numerous magazines and journals.

SIDELIGHTS: Jack Lasenby draws heavily on the landscape of his native New Zealand for his children's books. His stories are set in rural towns as well as amid mountains, beaches, and swamps. Universal themes run through Lasenby's books, including group dynamics, political rule, and the quest for a better life.

Sexual misconduct is the focus of *The Lake,* a story about a girl named Ruth who runs away after being sexually abused by her new stepfather. She flees to a place of comfort—the lake cabin where she spent so much time with her recently deceased father, whom she loved dearly. In *Twentieth-Century Children's Writers,* Diane Hebley observed, "Lasenby lovingly evokes the beauty, majesty, and danger of Ruth's environment, which contributes to her growth in her struggle through grief and for survival." After two years in the wilderness, she returns home to confront her stepfather and protect her younger sister. The book includes other instances of incest and sexual assault, most notably in the character of Tommy. Although he helps Ruth during her stay at the lake, she must forgive him for his transgression of impregnating his daughter, who has since died.

The Mangrove Summer is set during World War II. Pearl Harbor has been attacked and New Zealanders, faced with blackouts and fuel rationing, fear an imminent Japanese invasion. The main character is George, whose family has moved to their isolated beach house in hopes of escaping harm. Six children (ages seven to adolescent) are staying at the beach house, and they have serious doubts about the adults' ability to protect them from the Japanese. George describes their escape to the mangrove swamps, where they feel secure that no one can find them. Hebley likened the deteriorating group dynamics to William Golding's *Lord of the Flies.* The power struggles cease, however, upon the death of one of the children.

In *The Conjuror,* Lasenby presents another image of totalitarian rule. With a volcanic landscape as a backdrop, a female-dominated society is depicted in which class designations are determined by eye color. With the help of her Black Sisters, the Conjuror rules with cruelty, dramatics, and superstition. The hero of the story is Johnny, who secretly educates himself by reading books, and convinces the next Conjuror-elect to escape with him.

Lasenby told *CA:* "I only regret that circumstances prevented me from becoming a full-time writer earlier. I enjoyed much of the work I did in my various jobs, but writing was always my aim. Much of my material to date has been drawn from direct experience. I choose to write for children because much of the best prose is being written for them: for example, by Cynthia Voigt, Philippa Pearce, and Margaret Mahy. I hope it's not too wild an ambition to be of their company. It seems to me that there are few authors for adults who share their competence."

BIOGRAPHICAL/CRITICAL SOURCES:

BOOKS

Something about the Author, Volume 65, Gale, 1991.
Twentieth-Century Children's Writers, 4th edition, St. James Press, 1995.

PERIODICALS

Junior Bookshelf, October, 1988; October, 1989.
Kirkus Reviews, May 15, 1989.
Publishers Weekly, May 12, 1989.
School Library Journal, August, 1989.
Times Literary Supplement, July 29, 1988.*

* * *

LASSITER, Adam
See KRAUZER, Steven M(ark)

LAUGIER, R.
See CUMBERLAND, Marten

* * *

LAZARUS, Henry
See SLAVITT, David R(ytman)

* * *

LEE, George W(ashington) 1894-1976

PERSONAL: Born January 4, 1894, in Indianola, MS; died August 1, 1976; son of George (a minister) and Hattie Lee. *Education:* Alcorn Agricultural and Mechanical College (now Alcorn State University), B.S. *Politics:* Republican.

CAREER: Worked odd jobs as an adolescent, including cotton planter and picker, grocery boy, houseboy, dray driver, and bellhop; vice-president of the Mississippi Life Insurance Co., beginning as district manager, 1927-76. Edited *Vision,* a journal for the Atlanta Life Insurance Co. Active in the Republican party. *Military service:* U.S. Army, 1917-19, served in France; became lieutenant.

MEMBER: National Association for the Advancement of Colored People, National Insurance Association, American Legion, Urban League, West Tennessee Civic and Political League, Omega Psi Phi, Elks.

WRITINGS:

Beale Street: Where the Blues Began (history), R. O. Ballou, 1934.
River George (novel), Macaulay, 1937, AMS Press, 1975.
Beale Street Sundown (short stories; includes "Beale Street Anyhow," "A Beale Street Treasure Hunt," "The First Blues Singer," "King of the Rousters," "She Made a Preacher Lay His Bible Down," "Passing," and "The Beale Street Blues I'm Singing"), House of Field, 1942.

Contributor of short stories and articles to periodicals, including *Negro Digest, World's Digest, Southern Literary Messenger, Vision, Tri- State Defender, Memphis Press Scimitar,* and *Memphis World.*

SIDELIGHTS: George W. Lee's writings immortalized the Beale Street neighborhood of Memphis, Tennessee.

As a leader in business and in his community, Lee was concerned with promoting pride in African-American business and decided in the early 1930s to write a factual book extolling African-American success in the Beale Street area. The result, 1934's *Beale Street: Where the Blues Began,* "gained wide critical acclaim," according to Edward D. Clark in *Dictionary of Literary Biography.* In spite of the fact that the book was extremely profitable for him due to its appeal to both African-American and white readers, Lee might have ended his career as an author to concentrate on the insurance business and politics if he had not been piqued by comments that it was *Beale Street*'s subject matter and not Lee's own writing ability that made it so popular. To put doubts concerning his literary ability to rest, Lee produced a novel, *River George,* in 1937. Later, he crowned his achievements with the short story collection *Beale Street Sundown.*

Beale Street: Where the Blues Began is divided into chapters about African-American individuals who contributed to the history of the neighborhood. These include Robert R. Church, Sr., who after the Civil War built up a multimillion-dollar estate and helped turn Beale Street into a commercial center for the African-American community, and other "bankers, ministers, lawyers, realtors, doctors, businesswomen, and insurance executives, all people Lee knew," reported Clark. Lee described the yellow fever epidemic of 1878 and contrasted the numerous heroic African-Americans who stayed in Memphis to help save the city with the many whites who escaped in fear of the disease; he also discussed Julia A. Hooks, who started an integrated music school that produced many gifted students, and composer W. C. Handy, whom he credits with "distinguished orchestral work." Though Lee's purpose in *Beale Street* was to instill pride in African-American accomplishment, he balanced the work by revealing the negative aspects of the community. Pimps, prostitutes, drug dealers, and the destitute who sift through garbage piles for food share pages with Lee's objects of admiration. Lee's portrayal of the African-American community is what Percy Hutchison of *New York Times Book Review* perceived as the book's greatest strength. Despite his criticism of stylistic flaws, Hutchison observed, "Far from being a purely dependent growth, parasitically clinging to the white man's culture, the Negro is here displayed as developing a culture of his own, caring for his own needs in medicine, in the law, in religion, education and recreation." Margaret Larkin of *Nation* was less impressed, criticizing "the pedestrian dullness with which Mr. Lee has handled the dramatic and heroic story of a Negro community struggling for economic and political power in the midst of the intolerant South."

Lee also intended his *River George* to promote African-American pride. Taking the man he wrote about in *Beale Street*'s third chapter and fictionalizing his past by adding some of his own experiences to it, Lee built a novel around the character of Aaron George. George goes to Lee's alma mater, Alcorn Agricultural and Mechanical College, in order to become a lawyer, but his education is interrupted by the death of his father. He returns home and becomes a sharecropper on Beaver Dam Plantation to help support his mother. Falling in love with a woman, Ada Green, who is also involved with the white postmaster, Fred Smith, George eventually has to leave the plantation because of a confrontation with Smith over the injustices suffered by the tenant farmers; this confrontation ends in Smith's death by his own gun. George runs to Memphis for safety and takes up lodgings with a Beale Street madame. Like the author, he enters the U.S. Army and becomes a lieutenant serving in Europe. When he returns to the United States, he tries to contact his mother and Ada, but he runs into trouble in Vicksburg, Mississippi, from whites who resent his officer's uniform. Temporarily turned aside, George becomes a deckhand on the Mississippi river and wins fame for his fighting prowess. Eventually, however, he returns to the plantation only to be lynched for the postmaster's murder upon his arrival. In *New York Times Book Review,* E.C. Beckwith praised *River George,* stating, "The story, told from the viewpoint of the Negro, abounds in expressive character types (nearly all of them colored), illuminating incidents and sidelights, which graphically amplify the novel's scope and human interest."

Though *River George* ends with George's death, its focus is on his struggles to succeed in a world of prejudice. By the time Lee published the short story collection *Beale Street Sundown,* however, his involvement with the Republican party had led him to place less importance on inspiring African-Americans toward achievement of their goals. Thus, in Clark's opinion, the emphasis of *Sundown* is on folklore. Lack of didactic purpose apparently gave Lee more artistic freedom; Clark declared that Sundown "is evidence of tremendous literary growth." The volume's stories include "Beale Street Anyhow," which concerns uproar over a possible name change to Beale Avenue, and *"A Beale Street Treasure Hunt,"* involving an old man's plot to make money from a fraudulent treasure hunt. Also in *Sundown* are *"She Made a Preacher Lay His Bible Down,"* about an ex-prostitute who joins a church choir to win the love of a minister, and *"Passing,"* about an

African-American woman passing for white in a bordello.

BIOGRAPHICAL/CRITICAL SOURCES:

BOOKS

Black Literature Criticism, Gale, 1992.
Contemporary Literary Criticism, Gale, Volume 52, 1989.
Dictionary of Literary Biography, Volume 51: *Afro-American Writers From the Harlem Renaissance to 1940,* Gale, 1987.
Gloster, Hugh M., *Negro Voices in American Fiction,* University of North Carolina Press, 1948.
Lee, George W., *Beale Street: Where the Blues Began,* R. O. Ballou, 1934.
Tucker, David M., *Lieutenant Lee of Beale Street,* Vanderbilt University Press, 1971.

PERIODICALS

Choice, December, 1970.
Nation, September 5, 1934.
New York Times Book Review, July 29, 1934; June 20, 1937.
Opportunity, October, 1934.
Scribner's Magazine, September, 1934.*

* * *

LEE, John (Darrell) 1931-

PERSONAL: Born March 12, 1931, in Indiahoma, OK; son of John Henry (a barber) and Lealiu (Prince) Lee; married Barbara Moore (a writer), April 14, 1957. *Education:* Texas Technological College (now Texas Tech University), B.A., 1952; West Virginia University, M.S.J., 1965. *Politics:* Democrat.

ADDRESSES: Home—Route 2, Hunter's Glen, Box 109, San Marcos, TX 78666. *Agent*—Don Congdon, Harold Matson Co., Inc., 276 Fifth Ave., New York, NY 10001.

CAREER: Fort Worth Star-Telegram, Fort Worth, TX, reporter-photographer, 1952-57; *Denver Post,* Denver, CO, reporter-photographer, 1958-60; Goodyear Tire & Rubber Co., Akron, OH, member of public relations staff, 1960-62; American University, Washington, DC, assistant professor of journalism, 1965-67; University of Arizona, Tucson, associate professor, 1967-69, professor of journalism, 1969-71; New York University, New York, NY, professor of journalism, 1972-74; California State University at Long Beach, professor of journalism, 1975-76; Memphis State University, Tennessee, professor of journalism, 1984—; full-time writer. Washington (DC) Journalism Center, assistant director, 1966-67, consultant, 1967—.

MEMBER: Association for Education in Journalism, Sigma Delta Chi, Kappa Tau Alpha.

AWARDS, HONORS: More than twenty local, state, and national photography awards.

WRITINGS:

Expatriate Press, West Virginia University Press, 1965.
Caught in the Act (novel), Morrow, 1968.
(Editor) *Diplomatic Persuaders: New Role of the Mass Media in Internal Relations,* Wiley, 1968.
Assignation in Algeria (novel), Walker & Co., 1971.
(With wife, Barbara Moore) *Monsters Among Us* (nonfiction), Pyramid Publications, 1975.
The Ninth Man (novel), Doubleday, 1976.
The Thirteenth Hour (novel), Doubleday, 1978.
Lago (novel), Doubleday, 1980.
(With Edward Jay Friedlander) *Feature Writing for Newspapers and Magazines: The Pursuit of Excellence,* Harper and Row (New York City), 1988.
(With Friedlander and John C. Merrill) *Modern Mass Media: Communication in Society,* Harper and Row, 1990.
Stalag Texas, Pocket, 1990.

Photographs have appeared in more than one hundred magazines and one thousand newspapers throughout the world; also contributor of articles to magazines.

BIOGRAPHICAL/CRITICAL SOURCES:

PERIODICALS

Choice, June, 1969, p. 496.
New York Times Book Review, March 3, 1968, p. 37; August 22, 1971, p. 31.
Publishers Weekly, December 4, 1967, p. 43; November 17, 1975, p. 95; December 6, 1976, p. 61; February 20, 1978, p. 106; April 4, 1980, p. 62.*

L'ESTRANGE, Anna
See ELLERBECK, Rosemary (Anne L'Estrange)

* * *

Le SUEUR, Meridel 1900-1996

PERSONAL: Born February 22, 1900, in Murray, IA; died November 14, 1996, in Hudson, WI; daughter of William Winston and Marion Lucy Wharton (mother later married to Alfred Le Sueur, who adopted the author); married Yasha Rabanoff, 1927 (deceased); children: Rachel Le Sueur, Deborah Le Sueur. *Education:* Attended high school in Fort Scott, KS, and at American Academy of Dramatic Art. *Politics:* "My politics is that of life." *Religion:* "My religion, the world."

CAREER: Writer; has been employed as a journalist and labor reporter. Actress during the 1920s, appeared in films *The Last of the Mohicans* and *The Perils of Pauline.* Instructor in writing courses, University of Minnesota.

AWARDS, HONORS: Awarded second prize in Works Progress Administration (WPA) writing contest; recipient of *California Quarterly* annual award, a University of Minnesota grant, and a Bush Foundation grant.

WRITINGS:

Annunciation, Platen Press, 1935.
Salute to Spring and Other Stories, International Publishers, 1940, reprinted, 1983.
North Star Country, Duell, Sloan & Pearce, 1945, University of Nebraska Press, 1984.
Little Brother of the Wilderness: The Story of Johnny Appleseed, Knopf, 1947, Holy Cow, 1988.
Nancy Hanks of Wilderness Road: A Story of Abraham Lincoln's Mother, Knopf, 1949.
Sparrow Hawk (story of an Indian boy), Knopf, 1950, Holy Cow, 1987.
Chanticleer of Wilderness Road: A Story of Davy Crockett, Knopf, 1951, Holy Cow, 1989.
The River Road: A Story of Abraham Lincoln, Knopf, 1954.
Crusaders: The Radical Legacy of Marian and Arthur Le Sueur (biography of her parents), Blue Heron, 1955, reprinted, Minnesota Historical Society, 1984.
Corn Village: A Selection, Stanton & Lee, 1970.
Conquistadores, F. Watts, 1973.
The Mound Builders, F. Watts, 1974.
Rites of Ancient Ripening (poems), edited by Mary Ellen Shaw, Vanilla Press, 1975.
Harvest: Collected Stories (also see below), West End, 1977.
Song for My Time: Stories of the Period of Repression (also see below), West End, 1977.
Women on the Breadlines, West End, 1977.
The Girl (novel), West End, 1979, reprinted, 1985.
Harvest [and] *Song for My Time,* MEP Publications, 1982.
Ripening: Selected Work, 1927-1980, edited by Elaine Hedges, Feminist Press, 1982, 2nd edition, 1986.
(With John Crawford) *Worker Writers,* West End, 1982.
Word Is Movement: Journal Notes from Atlanta to Tulsa to Wounded Knee, Cardinal Press, 1984.
I Hear Men Talking and Other Stories, West End, 1984.
Ripening: Selected Work, Feminist Press (New York City), 1990.
Winter Prairie Woman, illustrations by Sandy Spieler, Midwest Villages and Voices(Minneapolis, MN), 1990.
The River Road: A Story of Abraham Lincoln, illustrated by Susan Kiefer Hughes,Holy Cow! (Duluth, MN), 1991.

Also author of *Persephone,* 1927; *The Horse,* 1934; *We Sing Our Struggles: A Tribute to Us All,* edited by Mary McAnnally, Cardinal Press; and *America, Song We Sang Without Knowing: The Life and Ideas of Meridel Le Sueur,* Little Red Hen Press. Work represented in several anthologies, including*O. Henry Prize Short Stories,* 1946, and *O'Brien Best Stories.* Contributor of short stories and articles to magazines and newspapers. Editor, *Midwest,* 1935, and *People Together,* 1956.

ADAPTATIONS: My People Are My Home, a film based on Le Sueur's work, was produced by the Women's Film Collective of Minnesota.

SIDELIGHTS: Meridel Le Sueur's long and controversial career as a writer began in the Midwest, a region that continued to influence her work until her death in 1996. Although a highly regarded novelist and short story writer during the 1930s, Le Sueur's political views and activities were banned as "subversive" by Senator Joseph McCarthy in the early 1950s, resulting in over twenty years of literary obscurity. Since 1970, her books, frequently narrated from a woman's point of view, have found a new audience and popularity.

Le Sueur was born to Marion and William Wharton in Murray, Iowa, in 1900, and is the granddaughter of a Puritan temperance worker who helped to open the state of Oklahoma. "In 1910, my mother had to kidnap us out of Texas to get away from our father," the author told *Publishers Weekly* interviewer John F. Baker. Like most women and children of that day, she explained, "We were property,[treated] worse than slaves." Le Sueur's mother later married Alfred Le Sueur, a lawyer who founded the Industrial Workers of the World. Writing in *Nation,* Meredith Tax reports that the couple helped to bring Marxism to middle America by supporting the publication of socialist classics in the form of Haldeman-Julius Little Blue Books. "Ardent socialists, they saw 'a new world' opening before them in their Middle Western kitchen, where such eloquent radicals as Big Bill Haywood, Eugene Debs, Lincoln Steffens and Emma Goldman came and went," relates Blanche Gelfant in *New York Times Book Review.* Labor union organizers who visited the Le Sueur home often and Indian women the young writer befriended as a girl helped her to develop the communal ideals expressed in her works.

Le Sueur's writings chiefly focus on the people, history, and traditions of her native Midwest. She wrote her first stories "as a little girl on a remaining patch of the American frontier," notes Patricia Hampl in *Ms.* magazine. "I first felt in my bones the immense contradictions of American Midwestern life," she told Hampl, "and also its hidden potential strength and beauty and, above all, the democratic traditions and history of the frontier" among the farmers and Indians of the area.

This setting provides the backdrop of *The Girl,* written in 1939 but not published until 1978. It is the story of a girl who moves from her unhappy rural existence to urban Minnesota. There, she faces the ravages of the Depression and sexual and emotional abuse by men until she is rescued by a community of homeless women who are clearly associated with the Communist Party. Christine Bold of *Twentieth-Century Western Writers* observes, "Le Sueur can be read as celebrating the western landscape for its formative impact on American culture, but not in any easy or pretty sense."

Le Sueur's works, especially those written during the 1930s, reflect a strong sense of social awareness and social protest. In 1928, after a brief career in Hollywood as an actress and stuntwoman, Le Sueur returned to the Midwest, a return which, Hampl points out, "coincided with the rebirth of activity among various populist and worker groups." Le Sueur became an active participant in this proletarian movement. The commitment she made to writing during this time, as she recalls for Baker, was a commitment to exercise personal freedom and "to express the lives and thoughts of people who were unexpressed," she told Baker. She was one of the first women writers to break the code of silence about the hardships women faced on the American frontier: "My grandmother, who . . . never took a bath except in her shift, couldn't understand why I wanted to reveal what she had spent her life trying to conceal." According to a *Prairie Schooner* reviewer, Le Sueur's Midwestern depression-era stories cut through the "hypocrisy" of American culture and society. In a review of *Salute to Spring and Other Stories,* the reviewer writes, "American mythologies and truisms evaporate as she describes . . . an impoverished husband pressuring an unwilling wife to abort their child, an unemployed college honor student's death from starvation, striking factory workers gunned down by company men."

These initially well-received writings, as well as Le Sueur's association with the Communist party, later served to entangle her in what a critic for *Worker Writer* calls the events of the "red scare." Hampl explains: "While she was writing the luminous short stories of lives lived in poverty and obscurity which gave her a national reputation, she was also reporting on the strikes, unemployment struggles, breadlines, and the plight of farmers in the Dakotas. . . . Hailed throughout the thirties as a major writer, she was blacklisted during the McCarthy years, because her identity as a radical . . . made her suspect."

As a result, for nearly thirty years Le Sueur found it difficult to publish her work. *Worker Writer* reports: "Le Sueur gained only the attention of the bloodhounds sent out by the FBI, during the period of the 'Red scare' from 1946 to the mid-Fifties. She had to trade job for job . . . as the FBI visited and intimidated each new employer. Her writing was accepted only in the children's department of Alfred A. Knopf, under a nom de plume at *Seventeen* and *Mademoiselle,* and in the remaining publications of the Communist Party Press."

Since 1970, however, interest in Le Sueur's work has enjoyed a revival of sorts. She told *CA* that not only were her newer books being published, but her older ones were "re-discovered" by a new generation of readers, particularly those involved with the "women's movement." Le Sueur considered "the young women now struggling to find their creative direction" to be "the people I was writing for [who finally] got born." She added: "I have written all my life of the struggles of the people of America, and the Midwest particularly. My two grandmothers and my mother were feminists and I have written of the life and struggles of women even before it was popular. I find the present the most exciting of my long career because of the visible field of expression in the Indian, Chicano, and women's movements. I am writing more and better, and have an audience—for the first time."

BIOGRAPHICAL/CRITICAL SOURCES:

BOOKS

Boehnlein, James M., *The Sociocognitive Rhetoric of Meridel Le Sueur,* E. MellenPress (Lewiston), 1994.

Coiner, Constance, *Better Red: The Writing and Resistance of Tillie Olsen and Meridel Le Sueur,* Oxford University Press, 1995.

Le Sueur, Meridel, *Crusaders: The Radical Legacy of Marian and Arthur Le Sueur,* Minnesota Historical Society, 1984.

Roberts, Nora Ruth, *Three Radical Women Writers: Class and Gender in Meridel LeSueur, Tillie Olsen, and Josephine Herbst,* Garland Publishing (New York City), 1996.

Something about the Author, Volume 6, Gale, 1974.

Twentieth-Century Western Writers, 2nd edition, St. James Press, 1991.

PERIODICALS

Chicago Sunday Tribune, November 12, 1950.

Los Angeles Times Book Review, May 30, 1982.

Ms., August, 1975.

Nation, July 3, 1982.

New Republic, September 9, 1940.

New Yorker, June 1, 1940.

New York Herald Tribune Book Review, May 11, 1947, November 6, 1949, November 12, 1950, November 11, 1951, May 16, 1954.

New York Times, May 25, 1947, November 12, 1950, September 5, 1954.

New York Times Book Review, April 4, 1982.

Prairie Schooner, fall, 1977.

Publishers Weekly (interview), May 21, 1982.

San Francisco Chronicle, November 13, 1949.

Saturday Review of Literature, January 5, 1946, May 17, 1947.

Time, June 17, 1940.

Weekly Book Review, December 16, 1945.

Worker Writer, Volume 1, number 15, 1977.

OBITUARIES:

PERIODICALS

Monthly Review, September, 1997.

New York Times, November 24, 1996.*

* * *

LOGAN, Jane
See GARDNER, Virginia (Marberry)

M

MACADAM, Preston
See PRESTON, John

* * *

MANOR, Jason
See HALL, Oakley (Maxwell)

* * *

MARLAND, Christina
See PEMBERTON, Margaret

* * *

MARTHA, Henry
See HARRIS, Mark

* * *

MASON, Bobbie Ann 1940-

PERSONAL: Born May 1, 1940, in Mayfield, KY; daughter of Wilburn A. (a dairy farmer) and Christianna (Lee) Mason; married Roger B. Rawlings (a magazine editor and writer), April 12, 1969. *Education:* University of Kentucky, B.A., 1962; State University of New York at Binghamton, M.A., 1966; University of Connecticut, Ph.D., 1972.

ADDRESSES: Agent—Amanda Urban, International Creative Management, 40 West 57th St., New York, NY 10019.

CAREER: Writer. *Mayfield Messenger,* Mayfield, KY, writer, 1960; Ideal Publishing Co., New York City, writer for magazines, including *Movie Stars, Movie Life,* and *T.V. Star Parade,* 1962-63; Mansfield State College, Mansfield, PA, assistant professor of English, 1972-79.

AWARDS, HONORS: National Book Critics Circle Award nomination, American Book Award nomination, PEN-Faulkner Award for fiction nomination and Ernest Hemingway Foundation Award, all 1983, all for *Shiloh and Other Stories;* National Endowment for the Arts fellowship, 1983; Pennsylvania Arts Council grant, 1983; Guggenheim fellowship, 1984; American Academy and Institute of Arts and Letters Award, 1984; National Book Critics Circle Award nomination and Southern Book Award, both 1994, both for *Feather Crowns.*

WRITINGS:

Nabokov's Garden: A Guide to Ada, Ardis (Ann Arbor, MI), 1974.

The Girl Sleuth: A Feminist Guide to the Bobbsey Twins, Nancy Drew, and Their Sisters, Feminist Press (Old Westbury, NY), 1975.

Shiloh and Other Stories, Harper (New York City), 1982.

In Country (novel), Harper, 1985.

Spence + Lila (novel), Harper, 1988.

Love Life: Stories, Harper, 1989.

Feather Crowns, Harper, 1993.

Midnight Magic: Selected Stories of Bobbie Ann Mason, Ecco Press (Hopewell, NJ), 1998.

Clear Springs: A Memoir, Random House (New York City), 1999.

Contributor of short stories to anthologies, including *Best American Short Stories,* 1981 and 1983, *The Pushcart Prize,* 1983 and 1996, and *The O. Henry Awards,* 1986 and 1988. Contributor to numerous magazines, including *New Yorker, Atlantic,* and *Mother Jones;* frequent contributor to "The Talk of the Town" column, *New Yorker.*

ADAPTATIONS: In Country was filmed by Warner Brothers and directed by Norman Jewison in 1989.

SIDELIGHTS: The people and terrain of rural western Kentucky figure prominently in the fiction of Bobbie Ann Mason, a highly regarded novelist and short story writer. Herself a native Kentuckian, Mason has chronicled the changes wrought in her region by the introduction of such phenomena as television, shopping malls, popular music, and fast-food restaurants. Her characters often stand perplexed at the junction between traditionalism and modernity, between permanence and transience, between their own deep-seated need for individual expression and their obligations to family and home. As Meredith Sue Willis noted in the *Washington Post Book World,* Mason "has a reputation as a regional writer, but what she is really writing about is the numerous Americans whose dreams and goals have been uplifted and distorted by popular culture." According to David Quammen in the *New York Times Book Review,* "Loss and deprivation, the disappointment of pathetically modest hopes, are the themes Bobbie Ann Mason works and reworks. She portrays the disquieted lives of men and women not blessed with much money or education or luck, but cursed with enough sensitivity and imagination to suffer regrets."

Mason's first volume of fiction, *Shiloh and Other Stories,* established her reputation as a rising voice in Southern literature. Novelist Anne Tyler, for one, hailed her in the *New Republic* as "a full-fledged master of the short story." Most of the sixteen works in *Shiloh* originally appeared in the *New Yorker, Atlantic,* or other national magazines, a fact surprising to several critics who, like Anatole Broyard in the *New York Times Book Review,* labeled Mason's work "a regional literature that describes people and places almost unimaginably different from ourselves and the big cities in which we live." Explained Quammen: "Miss Mason writes almost exclusively about working-class and farm people coping with their muted frustrations in western Kentucky (south of Paducah, not far from Kentucky Lake, if that helps you), and the gap to be bridged empathically between her readership and her characters [is] therefore formidable. But formidable also is Miss Mason's talent, and her craftsmanship."

In an interview published in *Contemporary Literature,* Mason commented upon the fact that she seems to be read by an audience quite different from one in which her characters might find themselves. "I don't think I write fiction that's for a select group," she said. "I'm not sure a lot of people [in rural Kentucky] read my work. . . . I think a lot of people wouldn't *want* to read my work because they might find it too close to their lives. They're not interested in reading something that familiar; it would make them uncomfortable."

Most critics have attributed Mason's success to her vivid evocation of a region's physical and social geography. "As often as not," Gene Lyons reported in *Newsweek,* the author describes "a matter of town—paved roads, indoor plumbing; and above all, TV—having come to the boondocks with the force of an unannounced social revolution." In a similar vein, Emma Cobb commented in *Contemporary Southern Writers* that "along with giving voice to characters in language that reflects their backgrounds, Mason's work is important as a chronicle of the changing physical landscape of the contemporary South. Brand names and popular culture references infiltrate her characters' vocabularies as strip-malling, chain-store spreading, and convenience-promising change sweeps into previously isolated regions. Characters try to make their way amid the changes . . . often unsure of how to proceed and struggling to articulate their feelings." While the language of Mason's characters reflects their rural background, her people do not fit the Hollywood stereotype of backwoods "hillbillies" content to let the rest of the world pass by. Tyler noted that they have "an earnest faith in progress; they are as quick to absorb new brand names as foreigners trying to learn the language of a strange country they've found themselves in." "It is especially poignant," she added, "that the characters are trying to deal with changes most of us already take for granted." Mason's Kentucky is a world in transition, with the old South fast becoming the new. Suzanne Freeman commented in the *Washington Post Book World:* "Mason's characters are just trying not to get lost in the shuffle."

Mason often explores intensely personal events that lead to the acceptance of something new or the rejection—or loss—of something old. These adjustments in the characters' lives reflect a general uneasiness that pervades the cultural landscape; the forces of change and alienation are no less frightening because they are universal or unavoidable. The characters in Mason's fiction are caught between isolation and transience, and this struggle is reflected in their relationships, which are often emotionally and intellectually distant. "Some people will stay at home and be content there," the author noted in a *People Weekly* interview. "Others are born to run. It's that conflict that fascinates me."

As a result, wrote *Time* critic R. Z. Sheppard, "Mason has an unwavering bead on the relationship between instincts and individual longings. Her women have ambitions but never get too far from the nest; her men have domestic moments but spend a lot of time on wheels." Mason's characters "exist in a psychological rather than a physical environment," Broyard similarly contended, "one that has been gutted—like an abandoned building—by the movement of American life. They fall between categories, occupy a place between nostalgia and apprehension. They live, without history or politics, a life more like a linoleum than a tapestry."

Other critics, while noting Mason's ability to evoke psychological states, have emphasized her skill at depicting the material details of her "linoleum" world. Tyler pointed out that readers know precisely what dishes constitute the characters' meals, what clothes hang in their closets, and what craft projects fill their spare time. Mason intones the brand names that are infiltrating her characters' vocabularies, and the exact titles of soap operas and popular songs provide an aural backdrop for the fiction's emotional dramas. Her characters' voices, according to Tyler, "ring through our living rooms." *Dictionary of Literary Biography* contributor John D. Kalb noted that "Mason is among the first to use seriously the so-called low art of popular culture as an important underpinning to her literature and the lives of her characters. While she portrays the encroaching impact of urban America on her rural occupants . . . she usually does so not as a criticism but as a means of providing an accurate and realistic depiction of the people within their changing environments. Her inclusion of these popular elements enhances the sense of meeting real people engaged in their everyday lives."

In her first novel, *In Country,* "Mason returns to this same geographical and spiritual milieu" as her short fiction, noted *New York Times* critic Michiko Kakutani, "and she returns, too, to her earlier themes: the dislocations wrought on ordinary, blue-collar lives by recent history—in this case, recent history in the form of the Vietnam War." Seventeen-year-old Samantha Hughes doesn't remember the war, but it has profoundly affected her life: her father died in Vietnam and her uncle Emmett, with whom she lives, still bears the emotional and physical scars of his service. In the summer after her high school graduation, Sam struggles to understand the war and learn about her father. "Ten years after the end of the Vietnam War," summarized Richard Eder in the *Los Angeles Times Book Review,* "in the most prosaic and magical way possible, she stubbornly undertakes the exorcism of a ghost that almost everything in our everyday life manages to bury." In the novel Mason demonstrated the same concern for particulars that distinguishes her short fiction, as *Christian Science Monitor* contributor Marilyn Gardner observed: "She displays an ear perfectly tuned to dialogue, an eye that catches every telling detail and quirky mannerism. Tiny, seemingly insignificant observations and revelations accumulate almost unnoticed until something trips them, turning them into literary grenades explosive with meaning."

Detroit Free Press writer Suzanne Yeager similarly believed that the author's details contribute to the authenticity of the novel. "Mason's narrative is so extraordinarily rich with the sounds, smells and colors of daily life in the '80s that Sam and her family and friends take on an almost eerie reality." As a result, the critic added, *In Country* "becomes less a novel and more a diary of the unspoken observations of ordinary America." Jonathan Yardley, however, faulted the novel for the "dreary familiarity" of its Vietnam themes. Writing in the *Washington Post Book World,* he asserted that Mason "has failed to transform these essentially political questions into the stuff of fiction; none of her characters come to life, the novel's structure is awkward and its narrative herky-jerky, her prose wavers uncertainly between adult and teenaged voices." But other critics found Mason's work successful; *Chicago Tribune Book World* contributor Bruce Allen, for instance, said that the novel's "real triumph . . . is Mason's deep and honest portrayal of her two protagonists," especially Sam. "More than any other character in our recent fiction," the critic continued, Sam "is a real person who grows more and more real the better we come to know her—and the novel that affords us the opportunity to is, clearly, the year's most gratifying reading experience." "[Mason's] first novel, although it lacks the page-by-page abundance of her best stories," concluded Joel Conarroe in the *New York Times Book Review,* "is an exceptional achievement, at once humane, comic and moving."

Mason told *CA* that she had been most rewarded by the reaction real Vietnam veterans had to *In Country.* "It's been personally very gratifying to hear from them, to know that they took the trouble to write to me and tell me that the book meant something to them," she said. "Most of the Vietnam vets who wrote me didn't write at length; they just seemed to say thank you. It was very moving to hear from those people."

Spence + Lila, Mason's second novel, "is a love story that explores both human love and a love for life," wrote Jill McCorkle in the *Washington Post.* "It is a short novel with a simple plot, the limited space enriched by characters whose voices and situations are realistic and memorable." Spence and Lila are a Kentucky farm couple who have been married for over forty years. Lila's upcoming surgery is forcing them to face the prospect of being separated for the first time since World War II. Also, as in her other work, Mason looks at the changes in the larger environment as well as those in her characters' lives—as Kalb put it, "the changes of attitudes and values in the modern world that has intruded in [an] isolated haven." "The chapters alternate between Spence's and Lila's point of view, and such resonances [in their thoughts] range freely through the past and present," described *Los Angeles Times Book Review* contributor Nancy Mairs. Despite the potential for sentimentality in the story, Mason "manages to avoid the gooey and patronizing muck that is usually described as heartwarming," remarked a *Time* reviewer. "Her account is funny and deft, with plenty of gristle." Likewise, in Kalb's opinion, "*Spence + Lila* is a novel about real love—not saccharine-sweet sentimentality, but the well-aged version of love between two people who have shared a long, sometimes difficult and trying, life together."

Newsweek writer Peter S. Prescott, however, found *Spence + Lila* a "gently tedious" book saved only by Mason's skillful writing. But Kakutani, although acknowledging that the book "suffers from a melodramatic predictability absent from Ms. Mason's earlier works," thought that the author treated her subject "without ever becoming sentimental or cliched." The critic went on to praise Mason's "lean stripped-down language" and "nearly pitch-perfect ear for the way her characters speak," and added: "Mainly, however, it's her sure-handed ability to evoke Spence and Lila's life together that lends their story such poignance and authenticity." *New York Times Book Review* contributor Frank Conroy likewise commended Mason's dialogue, but admitted that "one wishes she had risked a bit more in this book, taking us under the surface of things instead of lingering there so lovingly and relentlessly." "Awkward silence in the face of ideas and feelings is a common frailty," elaborated Mairs, "but it represents a limitation in 'Spence + Lila,' constraining Mason to rush her story and keep to its surface. . . . If I perceive any defect in 'Spence + Lila,' " the critic continued, "it's that this is a short novel which could well have been long." "As soon as [Mason's] characters open their mouths, they come to life and move to center stage," McCorkle similarly concluded. "If there is a weakness it would be the reader's desire to prolong their talk and actions before moving to an ending that is both touching and satisfying."

Despite the author's success with *In Country* and *Spence + Lila,* "Mason's strongest form may be neither the novel nor the story, but the story *collection,*" Lorrie Moore maintained in her *New York Times Book Review* assessment of *Love Life: Stories.* "It is there, picking up her pen every 20 pages to start anew, gathering layers through echo and overlap, that Ms. Mason depicts most richly a community of contemporary lives." Jack Fuller, however, believed that *Love Life* has a weakness. "Mason is a strong enough writer to make you believe her people, but she does not allow them any escape from the cliches that surround them," the Chicago *Tribune Books* writer noted, adding that her characters have "no exit" from their problems. While Kakutani likewise remarked that "few of Ms. Mason's characters ever resolve their dilemmas—or if they do, their decisions take place . . . beyond the knowledge of the reader," she asserted that the stories "are not simply minimalist 'slice-of-life' exercises, but finely crafted tales that manage to invest inarticulate, small-town lives with dignity and intimations of meaning." Mason's "stories work like parables, small in scale and very wise, tales wistfully told by a masterful stylist whose voice rises purely from the heart of the country," stated Judith Freeman in the *Los Angeles Times Book Review.* A *Chicago Tribune Book World* critic similarly concluded that Mason "is a writer of immense sensitivity, a true seer; technically, in terms of the making of sentences, she is a near virtuoso."

Reference Guide to Short Fiction contributor Laurie Clancy opined that this collection and *Shiloh* have shown Mason to be "a regional writer par excellence"; however, she cautioned, "the best of Mason's work has a gritty authenticity and dry humor, but at times the monotony and limitations of the figures she writes about seep into the prose as well." Mason, she observed, offers "little or no analysis of the characters' inner consciousness," and *New York Times Book Review* critic Michael Gorra remarked on this as well, in his review of *Midnight Magic: Selected Stories of Bobbie Ann Mason,* which republished several stories from *Shiloh* and *Love Life.* This collection, he contended, "demonstrates . . . Mason's narrow range—narrow in terms of the characters and situations on which she draws; narrow too in her reliance on a tight and impersonal third-person voice. . . . I admire Bobbie Ann Mason's craft, her precise eye, the vivid dialogue that stops just short of turning down the road toward local color. But after reading so much of her uninflected prose, I can't help longing for something a bit more full throated."

Mason's third novel marked a departure from her tendency to set her fiction in present times. *Feather Crowns* is set in turn-of-the-century Kentucky and tells the story of a farm wife named Christianna Wheeler who gives birth to quintuplets. Overnight the modest Wheeler tobacco farm becomes a mecca for the curious of every stripe as people flock to see—and hold—the tiny babies. As events unfold, Christie and her husband find themselves drawn away from home as a literal carnival sideshow attraction. The book is a meditation upon fame, self-determination, and the conflict between superstition and science. *New York Times Book Review* correspondent Jill McCorkle noted that in *Feather Crowns,* "Mason's attention to the microscopic detail of everyday life is, as always, riveting. . . . Along with the authentically colorful, often humorous dialogue, there are wonderful descriptions of churning and nursing and chopping dark-fire tobacco. And always there are subtle reminders of life's fragility, our uncertainty about what lies ahead." McCorkle concluded: "Thematically, *Feather Crowns* is a rich extension of Ms. Mason's other works. . . . The life of Christianna Wheeler and her babies is memorable and complete."

Mason told the *San Francisco Review of Books* that, far from being a diversion for her, *Feather Crowns* represented a new way of looking at her Kentucky culture, filtered through her grandmother's generation. "Right now it's hard to know what's going on in America and where we're all going," she said. "It's gotten so complex, with so many people and our constant awareness of everybody globally, that it's bewildering. I think there must always be stages in history when we feel this way, but in order to get our bearings today we have to go back and get a clearer sense of where we came from and what formed us. To remember what is important. I think basically that is Christie's quest in the book. . . . It's about being faced with a bewildering set of circumstances. She tries to make sense of all of it and tries to rise above it and be herself, a survivor. I think that's also the challenge for us in this part of the twentieth century."

Women's Review of Books critic Michele Clark declared that in *Feather Crowns* Mason successfully depicts a moment of epiphany for its central character. "Christie Wheeler becomes empowered through her capacity to ask questions and her ability to experience each moment of daily life to its fullest," the critic stated. "And this long, satisfying novel offers readers who are willing to slow down the same chance to see ordinary life anew." In the *Los Angeles Times Book Review,* Lisa Alther called *Feather Crowns* "a brilliantly sustained and grimly humorous parable about fame in 20th-Century America," adding: "Mason's stunning morality tale about the process by which . . . degradation can overtake innocent people who simply need cash or long for some excitement is extremely illuminating—and especially for anyone alive today who has ever pondered the ravages of our modern publicity juggernaut."

Having used her rural Kentucky background in fiction, Mason explored it autobiographically in *Clear Springs: A Memoir.* "She uses this memoir of growing up in the 1950's to provide a tantalizing glimpse into the origins of her fiction," noted Josephine Humphreys in the *New York Times Book Review.* "And in the process of taking a close look at her own beginnings, Mason gets to the heart of a whole generation—those of us born, roughly speaking, between Pearl Harbor and television. Behind us lay an old way, unchanged (we thought) for centuries; springing up before us was a world no one had predicted or imagined." Mason makes clear that the changes in her world—something she has explored so extensively in her fiction—are neither totally positive nor completely negative, as the old days were not idyllic. She observes that on their farm, her family had "independence, stability, authenticity . . . along with mind-numbing, backbreaking labor and crippling social isolation." Commented Humphreys: "Because Bobbie Ann Mason's language is spare and her eye unsparing, she's able to handle matters that ordinarily invite sentimentality or romanticism. She can write the hard truth about home, love, loss and the terrifying passage of time." Still, remarked a *Publishers Weekly* reviewer, Mason makes the book "a loving embrace" of her roots and "a richly textured portrait of a rapidly disappearing way of life."

Mason once told the Mervyn Rothstein in the *New York Times:* "I basically consider myself an exile. . . . And I have been one for years. And that's what gives me the distance to look back to where I'm from and to be able to write about it with some kind of perceptiveness. . . . It seems to me that an exile has a rather peculiar sensibility—you're straddling a fence and you don't know which side you belong on. I don't know if that comes through in the fiction, but I think it's probably what gives the strength to the fiction."

BIOGRAPHICAL/CRITICAL SOURCES:

BOOKS

Authors and Artists for Young Adults, Volume 5, Gale (Detroit), 1989.
Contemporary Literary Criticism, Gale, Volume 28, 1984, Volume 43, 1987, Volume 82, 1994.
Contemporary Southern Writers, St. James Press, 1999.
Dictionary of Literary Biography, Volume 173: *American Novelists since World War II, Fifith Series,* Gale, TK.
Dictionary of Literary Biography Yearbook: 1987, Gale, 1988.
Prenshaw, Peggy Whitman, editor, *Women Writers of the South,* University Press of Mississippi (Jackson, MS), 1984.
Reference Guide to Short Fiction, 2nd edition, St. James Press, 1999.
Short Story Criticism, Volume 4, Gale, 1990.
Wilhelm, Albert, *Bobbie Ann Mason: A Study of the Short Fiction,* Twayne, 1998.

PERIODICALS

Boston Globe, October 20, 1993, p. 73.
Chicago Tribune Book World, January 23, 1983; September 1, 1985.
Christian Science Monitor, September 6, 1985.
Contemporary Literature, winter, 1991, pp. 449-470.
Detroit Free Press, October 13, 1985.
Globe and Mail (Toronto), November 9, 1985; July 30, 1988.
Los Angeles Times Book Review, September 22, 1985; June 19, 1988; March 19, 1989; October 24, 1993, pp. 2, 8.
Louisville Courier-Journal Magazine, January 29, 1989.
Nation, January 18, 1986.
New Republic, November 1, 1982.
Newsweek, November 15, 1982; September 30, 1985; August 1, 1988.
New York Review of Books, November 7, 1985.
New York Times, November 23, 1982; September 4, 1985; May 15, 1988; June 11, 1988; March 3, 1989.
New York Times Book Review, November 21, 1982; December 19, 1982; September 15, 1985; June 26, 1988; March 12, 1989; September 26, 1993, p. 7; August 9, 1998; May 30, 1999, p. 5.
New York Times Magazine, May 15, 1988, p. 50.
People Weekly, October 28, 1985.
Publishers Weekly, August 30, 1985; March 15, 1999, p. 34.
San Francisco Review of Books, February/March, 1994, pp. 12-13.
Southern Quarterly, fall, 1992, pp. 85-118.
Time, January 3, 1983; September 16, 1985; July 4, 1988.
Times (London), August 11, 1983; March 6, 1986.
Times Literary Supplement, August 12, 1983; April 18, 1986.
Tribune Books (Chicago), June 26, 1988; February 19, 1989.
Voice Literary Supplement, November 1982; February 1986; May 1989, p. 13.
Washington Post, February 5, 1976; July 1, 1988.
Washington Post Book World, October 31, 1982; September 8, 1985; March 26, 1989.
Women's Review of Books, March, 1994, p. 19.*

* * *

MCCRAY, Mike
See PRESTON, John

* * *

MCDOWELL, Michael P(aul) Kube
See KUBE-MCDOWELL, Michael P(aul)

* * *

MCGINNIS, Duane
See NIATUM, Duane

* * *

McGIVERN, Maureen Daly
See DALY, Maureen

* * *

MEYER, Lynn
See SLAVITT, David R(ytman)

MIKES, George 1912-1987

PERSONAL: Born February 15, 1912, in Siklos, Hungary; died of leukemia, August 30, 1987, in London, England; son of Alfred (a lawyer) and Margit Alice (Gal) Mikes; married Lea Hanak, January 2, 1948; children: Martin Alfred, Judith Pamela. *Education:* University of Budapest, LL.D., 1933. *Religion:* Roman Catholic. *Avocational interests:* Tennis.

CAREER: Writer; governor of London Oratory School.

MEMBER: PEN in Exile (president, 1973-80); Garrick Club and Hurlingham Club (both London).

WRITINGS:

The Epic of Lofoten, Hutchinson, 1941.

Darlan: A Study, Constable, 1943.

We Were There to Escape: The True Story of a Jugoslav Officer, Nicholson & Watson, 1945.

Pont ugye mint az angolok (songs and verses), Londoni Podium, 1945.

How to Be an Alien: A Handbook for Beginners and More Advanced Pupils, Deutsch, 1946.

How to Scrape Skies: The United States Explored, Rediscovered, and Explained, Deutsch, 1948, published as *How to Be a Swell Guy: The United States Explored, Rediscovered, and Explained,* Doubleday, 1959.

Wisdom for Others, Deutsch, 1950.

Milk and Honey: Israel Explored, Deutsch, 1950, Transatlantic, 1965.

Talicska: Humoreszkek, esszek, sohajtasok, Big Ben Kiadasa, c. 1950.

Down With Everybody!: A Cautionary Tale for Children over Twenty-One, and Other Stories, Deutsch, 1951, British Book Centre, 1952.

Shakespeare and Myself, Deutsch, 1952, British Book Centre, 1953.

Uber Alles: Germany Explored, Deutsch, 1953.

Eight Humorists, Deutsch, 1954.

Leap through the Curtain: The Story of Nora Kovach and Istvan Rabovsky, Weidenfeld & Nicolson, 1955, Dutton, 1956.

Little Cabbages, Deutsch, 1955.

Italy for Beginners, Deutsch, 1956, Transatlantic, 1965.

The Hungarian Revolution, Deutsch, 1957.

East Is East, Deutsch, 1958.

A Study in Infamy: The Operations of the Hungarian Secret Police, Deutsch, 1959.

How to Be Inimitable: Coming of Age in England, Deutsch, 1961, Transatlantic, 1966.

As Others See You, Newman Neame, 1961.

Tango: A Solo across South America, Deutsch, 1961, Transatlantic, 1965.

The Best of Mikes, Pan Books, 1962.

Switzerland for Beginners, Deutsch, 1962, Transatlantic, 1965.

Mortal Passion, Deutsch, 1963, Transatlantic, 1966.

How to Unite Nations, Deutsch, 1963, Transatlantic, 1965.

(Editor) *Prison: A Symposium,* Routledge & Kegan Paul, 1963, Horizon Press, 1964.

How to Be an Alien: In Britain, France, Italy, Germany, Switzerland, Israel, Japan, Basic Books, 1964.

(With John R.R. Bedford) *The Duke of Bedford's Book of Snobs,* P. Owen, 1965, published as *The Book of Snobs,* Coward, 1966.

Eureka!: Rummaging in Greece, Deutsch, 1965.

(Editor) *Germany Laughs at Herself: German Cartoons since 1848,* Bassermann (Stuttgart), 1965.

How to Be Affluent, Deutsch, 1966, James Heineman, 1967.

Not By Sun Alone, Deutsch, 1967.

Boomerang: Australia Rediscovered, Deutsch, 1968.

Coat of Many Colors: Israel, Gambit, 1969 (published in England as *The Prophet Motive: Israel Today and Tomorrow,* Deutsch, 1969).

Humour in Memoriam, Routledge & Kegan Paul, 1970.

The Land of the Rising Yen: Japan, Gambit, 1970.

Laughing Matter, Library Press, 1971.

Any Souvenirs?, Gambit, 1972.

(With Bedford) *How to Run a Stately Home,* Transatlantic, 1972.

The Spy Who Died of Boredom, Deutsch, 1973, Harper, 1974.

Charlie, Deutsch, 1976.

How to Be Decadent, Deutsch, 1977.

Tsi-Tsa, the Biography of a Cat, Deutsch, 1978.

English Humour for Beginners, Deutsch, 1980.

(Author of introduction) Manfred Hamm, *Coffee Houses of Europe,* Thames &Hudson (London), 1980.

How to be Seventy: An Autobiography, Deutsch, 1982.

Arthur Koestler: The Story of a Friendship, Deutsch, 1983.

How to be Poor, cartoons by Larry, Deutsch, 1983.

How to be a Guru, illustrated by Larry, Deutsch, 1984.

How to be a Brit: A Mikes Minibus, illustrated by Nicholas Bentley, Deutsch, 1984.

How to be God, illustrated by Marie-Helene Jeeves, Deutsch, 1986.

The Riches of the Poor: Who's Who, A Journey Round the World Health Organisation, Deutsch, 1987.

Contributor to *Observer, Encounter, Times Literary Supplement,* and other periodicals.

SIDELIGHTS: A school governor, journalist, editor, and author, George Mikes was known as the author of *How to Be an Alien: A Handbook for Beginners and More Advanced Pupils,* which offered an immigrant's satiric perspective on life in England. He arrived there in 1938 and found work as a war correspondent for the Hungarian-language service of the British Broadcasting Corporation (BBC). In his later years he was governor of the London Oratory School. *How to Be an Alien* was only the first of many satires by Mikes. His canon, however, also includes volumes of serious nonfiction. Among his many writings are *Milk and Honey: Israel Explored, Uber Alles: Germany Explored, The Spy Who Died of Boredom, Arthur Koestler: The Story of a Friendship,* and *How to Be a Brit.* He also edited such works as *Germany Laughs at Herself: German Cartoons Since 1848.*

A *Times Literary Supplement* reviewer stated: "[George] Mikes has made a profession of the paradox, and some twenty books reflect his special gift of observing human behaviour—especially when the humans are English—from the acute angle of the adopted Englishman. Cynical, amused, determined not to be taken in, he is that man with the heavy accent in the corner taking notes: for him face values are no values at all." Mikes's books have been translated into twenty-one languages.

BIOGRAPHICAL/CRITICAL SOURCES:

BOOKS

Mikes, George, *How to be Seventy: An Autobiography,* Deutsch, 1982.

Mikes, *Arthur Koestler: The Story of a Friendship,* Deutsch, 1983.

PERIODICALS

Books and Bookmen, December, 1968.

Christian Science Monitor, January 18, 1968.

Listener, December 31, 1970.

New Statesman, March 17, 1967.

Observer Review, October 20, 1968.

Punch, March 18, 1970.

Times Literary Supplement, April 27, 1967.

OBITUARIES:

BOOKS

The Writers Directory: 1986-88, St. James Press, 1986.

PERIODICALS

New York Times, September 4, 1987.

Times (London), September 3, 1987.*

* * *

MITCHISON, Naomi Margaret (Haldane) 1897-

PERSONAL: Born November 1, 1897, in Edinburgh, Scotland; daughter of John Scott (a physiologist and philosopher) and Kathleen (Trotter) Haldane; married Gilbert Richard Mitchison (a lawyer and member of Parliament), February, 1916 (died, 1970); children: Denis Antony, Murdoch, Lois Godfrey, Avrion, Valentine Arnold-Forster. *Education:* Attended St. Anne's College, Oxford. *Politics:* British Labour Party.

ADDRESSES: *Home*—Carradale House, Carradale, Campbeltown, Argyll, Scotland.

CAREER: Writer. Labour candidate for Parliament for the Scottish Universities Constituency, 1935; member of Argyll County Council, 1945-1966; member of Highland Panel, Scotland, 1947-65; member of the Highland and Island Advisory Council, Scotland, 1966-76. *Military service:* Served as a volunteer nurse during World War I.

MEMBER: PEN.

AWARDS, HONORS: Palmes de l'Academie Francaise, 1921; named officer of Academie Francaise, 1924; D. Univ., Sterling University, 1979; honorary fellowship, St. Anne's, Oxford, 1980, and Wolfson College, 1983; D.Litt., Strathclyde University, 1983; named commander of Order of British Empire, 1985.

WRITINGS:

NOVELS

The Conquered, Harcourt (New York City), 1923.

Cloud Cuckoo Land, J. Cape (London), 1925, Harcourt, 1926.

The Corn King and the Spring Queen, Harcourt, 1931, published as *The Barbarian,* Cameron (New York City), 1961.

The Powers of Light, illustrations by Eric Kennington, Peter Smith (New York City), 1932.
(With Wyndham Lewis) *Beyond This Limit,* J. Cape, 1935.
We Have Been Warned, Constable (London), 1935, Vanguard (New York City), 1936.
The Blood of the Martyrs, Constable, 1939, McGraw (New York City), 1948, with introduction by Donald Smith, Canongate (Edinburgh), 1988, edited and introduced by James S. Bell, Jr., Moody Press (Chicago, IL), 1994.
The Bull Calves, illustrations by Louise Richard Annand, J. Cape, 1947.
Lobsters on the Agenda, Gollancz (London), 1952.
Travel Light, Faber (London), 1952, with introduction by Elizabeth Longford, Virago, 1987.
To the Chapel Perilous, Allen & Unwin (London), 1955.
Behold Your King, Muller (London), 1957.
Memoirs of a Space Woman, Gollancz, 1962.
When We Become Men, Collins, 1965 (London).
Cleopatra's People, Heinemann (London), 1972.
Solution Three, Warner (New York City), 1975, with afterword by Susan M. Squier, Feminist Press at the City University of New York, 1995.
Not by Bread Alone, Marion Boyars (London), 1983.

STORY COLLECTIONS

When the Bough Breaks, and Other Stories, Harcourt, 1924.
Black Sparta: Greek Stories, Harcourt, 1928.
Barbarian Stories, Harcourt, 1929.
The Delicate Fire: Short Stories and Poems, Harcourt, 1933.
The Fourth Pig: Stories and Verses, Constable, 1936.
The Big House, Faber, 1950.
Five Men and a Swan: Short Stories and Poems, Allen & Unwin, 1958.
Images of Africa, Canongate (Edinburgh, Scotland), 1980.
What Do You Think Yourself? Scottish Short Stories, Harris Publishing (Edinburgh), 1982.
Early in Orcadia, Drew (Glasgow, Scotland), 1987.
A Girl Must Live, Drew (Glasgow), 1990.

PLAYS

Nix-Nought-Nothing: Four Plays for Children (includes *My Ain Sel', Hobyah! Hobyah!,* and *Elfen Hill*), J. Cape, 1928.
Kate Crackernuts: A Fairy Play, Alden Press (London), 1931.
(With Lewis E. Gielgud) *The Price of Freedom* (three-act; produced in 1949), J. Cape, 1931.
(With Gielgud) *Full Fathom Five,* produced in 1932.
An End and a Beginning, and Other Plays (includes *The City and the Citizens, For This Man Is a Roman, In the Time of Constantine, Wild Men Invade the Roman Empire, Charlemagne and His Court, The Thing That Is Plain, Cortez in Mexico, Akbar, But Still It Moves, The New Calendar,* and *American Britons*)J. Cape, 1937, published as *Historical Plays for Schools,* two volumes, 1939.
(With Gielgud) *As It Was in the Beginning* (three-act), J. Cape, 1939.
(With Brian Easdale) *The Corn King* (musical; book by Mitchison, music by Easdale; adapted from Mitchison's novel; produced in 1950, Samuel French (London), 1951.
(With Denis Macintosh) *Spindrift* (three-act; produced in 1951), Samuel French, 1951.

POETRY

The Laburnum Branch, J. Cape, 1926.
The Alban Goes Out, Raven Press (Harrow, Middlesex, England), 1939.
The Cleansing of the Knife, and Other Poems, Canongate, 1978.

CHILDREN'S BOOKS

The Hostages, and Other Stories for Boys and Girls, illustrations by Logi Southby, J. Cape, 1930, Harcourt, 1931.
Boys and Girls and Gods, F. Watts, 1931.
The Big House, Faber, 1950.
Graeme and the Dragon, illustrations by Pauline Baynes, Faber, 1954.
The Swan's Road, illustrations by Leonard Huskinson, Naldrett Press (London), 1954.
The Land the Ravens Found, illustrations by Brian Alderidge, Collins, 1955.
Little Boxes, illustrations by Annand, Faber, 1956.
The Far Harbour, illustrations by Martin Thomas, Collins, 1957.
Judy and Lakshmi, illustrations by Avinash Chandra, Collins, 1959.
The Rib of the Green Umbrella, illustrations by Edward Ardizzone, Collins, 1960.
The Young Alexander the Great, illustration by Betty Middleton-Sandford, Parrish (London), 1960, Roy (New York City), 1961.
Karensgaard: The Story of a Danish Farm, Collins, 1961.

The Young Alfred the Great, illustrations by Shirley Farrow, Parrish, 1962, Roy, 1963.

The Fairy Who Couldn't Tell a Lie, illustrations by Jane Paton, Collins, 1963.

Alexander the Great, illustrations by Rosemary Grimble, Longmans, Green (London), 1964.

Henny and Crispies, New Zealand School Publications (Wellington, New Zealand, 1964.

Ketse and the Chief, illustrations by Christine Bloomer, Thomas Nelson, 1965.

A Mochudi Family, New Zealand School Publications, 1965.

Friends and Enemies, illustrations by Caroline Sassoon, Collins, 1966, Day (New York City), 1968.

Highland Holiday, New Zealand School Publications, 1967.

The Big Surprise, Kaye & Ward (London), 1967.

African Heroes, illustrations by William Stobbs, Bodley Head (London), 1968, Farrar, Straus, 1969.

Don't Look Back, Kaye & Ward, 1969.

The Family at Ditlabeng, illustrations by Joanna Stubbs, Collins, 1969, Farrar, Straus, 1970.

Sun and Moon, illustrations by Barry Wilkinson, Bodley Head, 1970, Thomas Nelson, 1973.

The Danish Teapot, illustrations by Patricia Frost, Kaye & Ward, 1973.

Snake!, illustrations by Polly Loxton, Collins, 1976.

(With Ian Kirby and Keetla Masogo) *The Little Sister,* Oxford University Press (Cape Town, South Africa), 1976.

(With Megan Biesele) *The Wild Dogs,* Oxford University Press, 1977.

The Brave Nurse, and Other Stories, Oxford University Press, 1977.

The Two Magicians, illustrations by Danuta Laskowska, Dobson (London), 1978.

The Vegetable War, illustrations by Polly Loxton, Hamish Hamilton (London), 1980.

EDITOR

An Outline for Boys and Girls and Their Parents, Gollancz, 1932.

(With Robert Britton and George Kilgour) *Re-Educating Scotland,* Scoop Books, 1944.

What the Human Race Is Up To, Gollancz, 1962.

OTHER

Anna Comnena, Howe (London), 1928.

Comments on Birth Control, Faber, 1930.

The Home and a Changing Civilization, John Lane (London), 1934.

Naomi Mitchison's Vienna Diary, H. Smith & R. Haas (New York City), 1934.

(With Richard H. S. Crossman) *Socrates,* Hogarth (London), 1937, Stackpole (Harrisburg, PA), 1938.

The Moral Basis of Politics, Constable, 1938.

The Kingdom of Heaven, Heinemann, 1939.

(With Macintosh) *Men and Herring,* Serif Books (Edinburgh), 1949.

Other People's Worlds, Secker & Warburg (London), 1958.

Presenting Other People's Children, P. Hamlyn (London), 1961.

(With George W. L. Paterson) *A Fishing Village on the Clyde,* Oxford University Press, 1961.

Return to the Fairy Hill (autobiography/sociology), J. Day, 1966.

The Africans: A History, Blond, 1970.

Sunrise Tomorrow: A Story of Botswana, Farrar, Straus, 1973.

Small Talk: Memories of an Edwardian Childhood, Bodley Head, 1973 (London).

A Life for Africa: The Story of Bram Fischer, Carrier Pigeon (Boston, MA), 1973.

Oil for the Highlands?, Fabian Society (London), 1974.

All Change Here: Girlhood and Marriage (autobiography), Bodley Head, 1975.

You May Well Ask: A Memoir, 1920-1940, Gollancz, 1980.

Mucking Around: Five Continents over Fifty Years, Gollancz, 1981.

(With John Parker and John Saville) *Margaret Cole, 1893-1980,* Fabian Society, 1982.

Among You Taking Notes: The Wartime Diary of Naomi Mitchison, 1939-1945, edited by Dorothy Sheridan, V. Gollancz, 1985.

Naomi Mitchison (autobiography), Saltire Society (Edinburgh), 1986.

As It Was, Drew, 1988.

Work represented in anthologies, including *The Year 2000,* Collier Macmillan, 1970; *Scottish Short Stories,* Oxford University Press, 1970; and *Nova 1,* Dell, 1971.

SIDELIGHTS: Naomi Mitchison is an extremely prolific writer whose career spans eight decades and includes the publication of nearly twenty novels, several collections of short stories, and dozens of children's books and nonfiction volumes. Carol Y. Long, writing in the *Dictionary of Literary Biography,* called Mitchison a "journalist, poet, storyteller, novelist, and essayist." Long acknowledged Mitchison's various social-political activities, including the lifelong opposition to nuclear weapons, and affirmed that the writer's many works "reflect her likes and are as diverse in nature as they are in kind."

Mitchison was born in 1897 in Edinburgh, Scotland, and she studied at St. Anne's College, Oxford. She worked as a nurse during World War I, at which time she became increasingly involved in social and political causes. In 1916 she married G. Richard Mitchison, a barrister and political figure who shared her liberalism. Mitchison eventually helped establish the first birth control clinics in London, and she became involved in such far-away events as the 1934 counter-revolution in Austria and the Depression-era sharecroppers' plight in the United States. Her activities also took her, on two occasions, to the Soviet Union.

Mitchison began her novel-writing career in the early 1920s with *The Conquered,* which Alexander Scott described in *Contemporary Novelists* as a tale about the "conflict of loyalties . . . in Gaul at the time of Caesar's conquest." Among the novel's enthusiasts was a *Saturday Review* critic who wrote: "[Mitchison] has, as it were by miracle, got back into the air and mood of the time she writes about: she creates and re-creates. The splendour and the mystery come easy to her. . . . And she rises without effort to eloquence and, beyond eloquence, to poetry." More praise came from a *New York Times* reviewer who affirmed that Mitchison "has made an interesting story against a colorful background, a background that in its essentials seems as accurately as it is graphically pictured."

The theme of conflicting loyalties is also prominent in Mitchison's next novel, *Cloud Cuckoo Land,* in which inhabitants of an Aegean island find themselves drawn into the war between Athens and Sparta in ancient Greece. In *Romance and Historical Writers,* Geoffrey Sadler contended, "*Cloud Cuckoo Land* marks an advance on *The Conquered,* its insights more skilfully developed, its psychology more subtle."

In her ensuing novel, *The Corn King and the Spring Queen* (later published as *The Barbarian*), Mitchison continues to probe the notion of conflicting loyalties by depicting events in the Crimea, ancient Greece, and ancient Egypt. Scott contends that *The Corn King and the Spring Queen* is "unsurpassed in 20th-century British historical fiction for range and variety of scene and characterization, for political awareness, and for religious depth." Writing in *Romance and Historical Writers,* Sadler likewise observed that *The Corn King and the Spring Queen* "is without doubt one of the most significant historical novels," and he hailed it as "Mitchison's masterpiece."

In her ensuing historical fiction, Mitchison sometimes exhibits what Sadler calls "an overt religious belief." Among these tales are *Blood of the Martyrs,* which details the trials and tribulations suffered by Christians during the brief reign of Nero in Ancient Rome, and *Behold Your King,* which relates the crucifixion of Jesus Christ. Sadler noted that these works, "while often excellent, lack the complexity and depth of the earlier novels."

Mitchison's other novels include *Memoirs of a Spacewoman,* a novel in which, according to Alexander Scott in *Contemporary Novelists,* she demonstrates "a deep imaginative comprehension of extraterrestrial modes of existence, and a compassionate reverence for life." Scott described *Memoirs of a Spacewoman* as "a concentrated symbolic expression of generations of experience."

In addition to her many novels, Mitchison has published several volumes of short stories. Isobel Murray wrote in *Reference Guide to Short Fiction:* "The short stories often mirror the concerns and settings of the novels. So early collections are mainly concerned with history, especially the ancient world." Murray added, "Most of the best short fiction is historical, or science fiction." Among Mitchison's many stories are "The Wife of Aglaos," in which prominent citizens of ancient Greece suddenly find themselves enslaved by conquering forces; "Beyond This Limit," wherein a woman discovers her lover's plans to wed someone else; and "The Coming of the New God," which relates the pleasures enjoyed by the various wives of an African chieftain prior to the intervention of Christian missionaries. Noting Mitchison's versatility as a short-story writer, Murray wrote: "The stories often have first person narrators, most but not all female, most but not all human. Their voices are urgent or gentle; insistent or comic."

Another significant portion of Mitchison's sizable literary achievement is her work as a children's writer. Her earliest works for children include *Nix-Nought-Nothing: Four Plays for Children,* which derive from the Brothers Grimm's collection of fairy tales. She also produced many volumes of historical fiction for children. These publications include *The Hostages, and Other Stories,* which features tales recounting the development of various youths. Long wrote, "What is so compelling about the stories in *The Hostages* is Mitchison's presentation of individual lives of Greek, Roman, and Gaelic boys in their struggles to come to terms with their physical and emotional surroundings, while pointing out the obvious resemblances to present time."

Another of Mitchison's children's books is *Young Alexander the Great,* which won praise from a *Horn Book* reviewer as a work with "much to offer the student of ancient history." The *Horn Book* critic proclaimed *Young Alexander the Great* "authentic and interesting."

Africa features prominently in many of Mitchison's children's writings. "She wrote about Africa in the same way that she wrote about Scotland," contended Jenni Calder in *New Statesman and Society,* "and perhaps to English readers her descriptions of lifting potatoes in the rain . . . were as exotic as her accounts of drought-bound Botswana." Calder noted that "over a dozen of [Mitchison's] books—fiction, history, the retelling of traditional African tales—were inspired by Botswana."

Aside from her many volumes of fiction, Mitchison has generated an impressive number of nonfiction volumes. Among these work is *Mucking Around: Five Continents over Fifty Years,* an autobiographical volume in which she relates some of her experiences in various remote and exotic locations. In the *Times Literary Supplement,* Nesta Roberts stated that Mitchison "writes enviably, with the kind of apparently casual precision which though, if rarely, it can be achieved by effort, far more often comes by grace; but what gives [*Mucking Around*] its quality is the author's capacity for relating to her fellow creatures, irrespective of differences of language and culture."

Mitchison told *CA:* "A writer today must be fully aware of the contemporary problems, social and political. But these must be handled delicately. Ideas which appeal specially to the writer, for instance the threat of nuclear war and the importance of the peace movement across all national boundaries, or the position of women and the changes which seem essential, or the difficulties of race relations or the moral problems which arise from some recent scientific advances: none of these should be put forward head-on unless in deliberate propaganda writing. A skilled and capable writer may well have more effect if his or her point of view is never expressed as such but is introduced in such a way that it soaks gently into the reader's mind. This is what I have tried to do, but I must be the last to know if it works."

BIOGRAPHICAL/CRITICAL SOURCES:

BOOKS

Benton, Jill, *Naomi Mitchison: A Century of Experiment in Life and Letters,* Pandora, 1990.

Contemporary Novelists, 6th edition, St. James Press (Detroit), 1996, pp. 711-13.

Dictionary of Literary Biography, Volume 160: *British Children's Writers, 1914-1960,* Gale (Detroit), 1996, pp. 189-96.

Mitchison, Naomi, *Mucking Around: Five Continents over Fifty Years,* Gollancz, 1981.

Mitchison, *Among You Taking Notes—: The Wartime Diary of Naomi Mitchison,* V. Gollancz, 1985.

Reference Guide to Short Fiction, St. James Press, 1994, pp. 364-66.

Twentieth-Century Romance and Historical Writers, 3rd edition, St. James Press, 1994, pp. 459-62.

PERIODICALS

Horn Book, June, 1961.

New Statesman and Society, December 16, 1994.

New York Times, October 28, 1923.

New York Times Book Review, May 28, 1961.

Publishers Weekly, March 30, 1990.

Saturday Review, May 26, 1923.

Times Literary Supplement, June 5, 1980; July 24, 1981.*

* * *

MOFFETT, Judith 1942-

PERSONAL: Born August 30, 1942, in Louisville, KY; daughter of James S. (a commercial artist) and Margaret (a secretary; maiden name, Cowherd) Moffett; married Edward B. Irving, Jr., March 17, 1983. *Education:* Hanover College, A.B. (cum laude), 1964; Colorado State University, M.A., 1966; University of Wisconsin—Madison, post-graduate study, 1966-67; University of Pennsylvania, M.A., 1970, Ph.D., 1971.

ADDRESSES: Home—951 East Laird Ave., Salt Lake City, UT 84105.

CAREER: Writer. Pennsylvania State University, Behrend College, Erie, assistant professor of English, 1971-75; University of Iowa, Iowa City, teacher of writing, 1977-78; University of Pennsylvania, Philadelphia, assistant professor, 1978-86, adjunct assistant professor, 1987-88, adjunct associate professor, 1988-93, adjunct professor of English, 1993.

AWARDS, HONORS: Fulbright grants, 1967 and 1973; Eunice Tietjens Memorial Prize from *Poetry,* 1973; grants from Pennsylvania State Institute for the Arts and Humanistic Studies, 1973, American Philosophical Association, 1973, Nathhorsts Foundation, 1973,

Swedish Institute, 1973 and 1976, and Ingram Merrill Foundation, 1976, 1980, and 1991; Borestone Mountain Poetry Award, 1975, for "Cecropia Terzine"; Levinson Prize, *Poetry,* 1976; University of Pennsylvania faculty research grant, 1979 and 1983; translation prize, Swedish Academy, 1982, for *Gentleman, Single, Refined and Selected Poems, 1937-1959* by Hjalmar Gullberg; National Endowment for the Humanities translation grant, 1983, for anthology of nineteenth-century Swedish poetry; National Endowment for the Arts creative writing fellowship, 1984; Theodore Sturgeon Memorial Award for best science fiction story of the year, 1987; nomination for Nebula Award in short science fiction, 1987, 1989, 1990; John W. Campbell Award for best new writer in science fiction, 1988; translation grant from Swedish Academy, 1993.

WRITINGS:

Keeping Time (poems), Louisiana State University Press (Baton Rouge, LA), 1976.
(Translator) Hjalmar Gullberg, *Gentleman, Single, Refined and Selected Poems, 1937-1959,* Louisiana State University Press, 1979.
James Merrill: An Introduction to the Poetry (criticism), Columbia University Press (New York City), 1984.
Whinny Moor Crossing (poems), Princeton University Press (Princeton, NJ), 1984.
Pennterra (science fiction), Davis Publications (Chicago), 1987.
The Ragged World: A Novel of the Hefn on Earth (science fiction), St. Martin's (New York City), 1991.
Two That Came True (science fiction), Pulphouse Press (Eugene, OR), 1991.
Time, Like an Ever-Rolling Stream: A Sequel to the Ragged World (science fiction), St. Martin's, 1992.
Homestead Year: Back to the Land in Suburbia (nonfiction), Lyons & Burford (New York City), 1995.

WORK IN PROGRESS: Translations, introduction, and notes for an anthology of nineteenth-century Swedish poetry; a novel.

SIDELIGHTS: Judith Moffett is an accomplished poet and science-fiction storyteller. Moffett was born in 1942 in Louisville, Kentucky, and she became drawn to poetry when she was still an adolescent. She studied at various institutions, including Colorado State University, from which she received her undergraduate degree, and the University of Pennsylvania, where she earned both her master's degree and her doctorate. Pivotal among her experiences as a student was a brief period of study with poet James Merrill, whom Moffett acknowledges as a significant influence in her development as writer. She told *Contemporary Poets* that "the experience of [Merrill's] poetry . . . had the force of revelation," and she added that "it quite literary changed my life." Through Merrill, Moffett refined her own approach to narration and meter, and she enhanced her understanding of both free and formal verse. She eventually published *James Merrill: An Introduction to the Poetry,* in which she explicated her appreciation for Merrill's verse.

Keeping Time, Moffett's first poetry collection, readily marks her as a sophisticated poet with a command of varied styles and techniques. William Matthews, writing in *Contemporary Poets,* notes Moffett's "urbane, ethical, and ultimately social tone" and her use of "a range of rhyme and stanza patterns." In addition, Matthews declares that Moffett's "affection for meditative tone and autobiographical subject matter . . . links her to the most interesting poets of her generation." Moffett's second collection, *Whinny Moor Crossing,* confirms her stature as an important poet, one whom Matthews describes as "intelligent, skillful, and deceptively full-hearted."

In addition to distinguishing herself as a poet, Moffett has received acclaim as a science-fiction writer. *Pennterra,* her first novel, concerns a faraway planet colonized by Quakers. The colonists heed the restrictions imposed on them by the telepathic natives, referred to as Hrossa, but newly arrived colonists are less inclined to accept these limits. The Hrossa thereupon warn the new colonists of the dire consequences that will ensue if cooperation is not forthcoming. Some of *Pennterra* is narrated by an adolescent boy who engages in sexual relations with both a woman and a man, thus the novel, as Kev P. McVeigh notes in *Twentieth-Century Science-Fiction Writers,* "is very clearly an adult novel." McVeigh calls *Pennterra* "an interesting ecological novel" but added that it also explores "the issue of response to conflict."

Moffett followed *Pennterra* with *The Ragged World: A Novel of the Hefn on Earth,* in which an alien race, the Hefn, invade Earth in the twenty-first century and attempt to bring greater order and stability to the planet. A *Publishers Weekly* critic describes the novel's premise as "provocative." In a sequel, *Time, Like an Ever-Rolling Stream,* a pair of teenaged mathematics experts break from their time-travel project and vacation at a naturalistic farm. A *Publishers Weekly* reviewer deems this tale "engrossing."

Among Moffett's other publications is *Homestead Year: Back to the Land in Suburbia,* a journal of her gardening endeavors undertaken while she abstained from teaching and recuperated from breast cancer. A *Booklist* reviewer calls *Homestead Year* a "down-to-earth chronicle," while a *Publishers Weekly* critic observes that the book will "strike a familiar chord" in other gardeners.

BIOGRAPHICAL/CRITICAL SOURCES:

BOOKS

Contemporary Poets, 6th edition, St. James Press (Detroit), 1996, pp. 753-55.

Twentieth-Century Science-Fiction Writers, 3rd edition, St. James Press, 1991, pp. 564-65.

PERIODICALS

Booklist, April 1, 1995.

New York Times Book Review, February 3, 1991, p. 33.

Publishers Weekly, December 21, 1990, p. 47; July 13, 1992, p. 49; March 13, 1995, p. 57.

Times Literary Supplement, November 9, 1984, p. 1290.

* * *

MOFOLO, Thomas (Mokopu) 1875(?)-1948

PERSONAL: Born August 2, 1875 (some sources say 1876), in Khojane, Basutoland (now Lesotho); died in September, 1948, in Teyateyaneng, Lesotho.

CAREER: Writer. Worked various jobs, including proofreader, secretary, interpreter, recruiter, and land manager.

WRITINGS:

NOVELS

Moeti oa bochabela, [Morija, Lesotho], 1907, translation by H. Ashton published as *The Traveller of the East,* S.P.C.K., 1934.

Pitseng [Morija, Lesotho], 1910.

Chaka [Morija, Lesotho], 1925, translation by F. H. Dutton published as *Chaka: An Historical Romance,* International Institute for African Languages and Culture, 1931.

SIDELIGHTS: Thomas Mofolo is considered the first great author of what has come to be regarded as modern African literature, and his masterpiece, *Chaka,* ranks among the most significant African works of the twentieth century. O. R. Dathorne, writing in *New African,* called Mofolo "the greatest Sotho writer," and he hailed *Chaka* as a "great novel."

Mofolo was born in Kojane, Basutoland (now Lesotho), a small country within the Republic of South Africa. He was raised in a Christian household, and he was educated at local religious schools before being sent to Morija to work as a servant for the Reverend Alfred Casalis, who headed the region's bible school, printing press, and book depot.

In 1894 Mofolo enrolled in the bible school, and in 1896 he entered the teacher training college, from which he received a teaching certificate three years later. He then found employment as an interpreter at the printing press, but his work was disrupted by the Boer War, which raged from 1899 to 1902. Mofolo studied carpentry for two years and taught at various schools until 1904, when he returned to Morija and assumed positions as proofreader and Casalis's secretary.

Through the Morija Book Depot, Mofolo made the acquaintance of religious writings, African and European histories, and novels by writers ranging from H. Rider Haggard to Marie Corelli. When several missionaries encouraged him to write his own works, Mofolo responded with *Moeti oa bochabela* (translation published as *The Traveller to the East*), which is the first novel written in Sesotho. Ezekiel Mphahlele, writing in *The African Image,* affirmed that *The Traveller to the East* "gives an account of African life in ancient days" and added: "It is about a boy [Fekisi] who wanders away from his home in search of 'the unknown Creator.' He believes that the Creator does not like the brute behavior of his people, disgust in whose drunkenness, hatred and other moral lapses has caused him to leave home." Fekisi initially realizes only futility in his quest, but after encountering a trio of white hunters, he converts to Christianity and regains his happiness. Upon receiving the sacrament, however, he suddenly dies.

O. R. Dathorne, in a *New African* essay, contended that Fekisi's death constitutes a culmination of his confusion and alienation from his tribe. According to Dathorne, Fekisi's exploits "only made him more loyal, more readily able to appreciate what he had left behind; they confirmed the superiority of the tribe." Dathorne added that Fekisi "is alienated because he has lost the ability to pivot within the consciousness of the tribe which is itself disintegrating," and the critic concluded that the hero's demise "confirms his pointless vacillations and the illogicality of alienation." But Daniel P. Kunene, in the essay collection *Neo-African Literature and Culture,* deemed Mofolo's book a "conscious rejection of Sesotho traditional values," and Albert S. Gerard, in his volume *Four African Literatures,* called *The Traveller of the East* "a Christian tract," though he conceded that the work's "somewhat obvious symbolism involves a measure of insincerity."

Mofolo followed *The Traveller of the East* with *Pitseng,* which relates the exploits of two devout children who are slated for marriage by a missionary. Although the couple are briefly separated, with the boy continuing his education while the girl finds employment, they eventually reunite. Dathorne described *Pitseng* as a "highly moral story" but dismissed it as "a disappointment" and "an attempt to pacify [Mofolo's] teachers, employers and publishers." Mphahlele, however, considered it "a classic in its language and idiom," and Gerard, while acknowledging that "Mofolo fails . . . to provide a convincing picture of the ideal syncatism he advocates," affirmed that Pitseng possesses "realistic subtlety" and showed "a clear perception of the antinomy between Christian theory and Christian practice."

While writing *Pitseng,* Mofolo also began research on the life of the Zulu warrior-king Chaka, amassing historical data, anecdotes, and legends passed on through the culture's tradition of oral storytelling. Mofolo then began writing *Chaka,* a novel about the celebrated leader. This work charts the rise and fall of the Zulu who was born out of wedlock and forced to endure considerable abuse that, in turn, spurred him to become a forceful, powerful leader whose brutal ways resulted in a reign of terror that ended only after his death at the hands of his half-brothers.

Chaka, which Mofolo published in 1925, has been hailed as a masterpiece of world literature, and although it was initially regarded, perhaps inaccurately, as an "Africanized" Christian tract, it has come to be recognized as an imposing fusion of Christian philosophy, African verse and mythology, and Western literature. Among the diverse elements comprising *Chaka* are African praise poems, which were performed to honor Bantu monarchs; African oral narratives, which traditionally served as vehicles for moral instruction; and Biblical terminology. In addition, Mofolo uses conventions derived from Western fiction.

Chaka is a complex work yielding multiple interpretations. Ben Obumselu, in *Sheffield Papers on Literature and Society,* conceded that the novel "is not an easy work to classify" and noted that Mofolo "is clearly working outside the Western conventions of tragedy and epic." Donald Burness affirmed in *African Literature* that *Chaka* "can be considered an extended praise song . . . of this heroic Zulu leader; it can be regarded as an African epic celebrating the founding of an empire; it can be treated as a five act dramatic prose tragedy." Henry Newbolt, in his introduction to F. H. Dutton's English translation of *Chaka,* called Mofolo's novel "a piece of imaginative literature" and added that it is "a serious contribution to history." Melvin Herskovitz agreed, writing in *Nation* that *Chaka* showed "the touch of a skilled hand." Herskovitz affirmed that "a reading of *Chaka* will give a point of view that no work by a European observer . . . can possibly give."

Chaka can be interpreted as a tale of good against evil, and such an interpretation holds that the hero's violent demise is apt punishment for his transgressions. But some critics contend that the work's morality actually derives from traditional African values holding nature, the tribe, and the gods as inseparable. Such critics see Chaka's illegitimacy, for example, in opposition to tribal laws adapted prior to the arrival of Christian missionaries in Africa. Such a perspective also interprets Chaka's slaying of his own mother as a self-destructive act in violation of the tribe's ultimate taboo against the killing of kin.

Critics have also addressed the sympathetic nature of Mofolo's eulogy for Chaka. Daniel P. Kunene, for instance, believed that the passage reveals Mofolo's loyalty to Sesotho culture and its traditions of heroism and virility. Albert S. Gerard likewise saw the eulogy as an opportunity for Mofolo to reflect on the Mazulu empire, pondering the "past greatness of his race and its present subjugation."

The manuscript of *Chaka* was submitted to the Morija printers around 1912, but it was initially found unacceptable for publication. Although they acknowledged the novel's extraordinary qualities, the missionaries expressed grave reservations about the book's likely influence, with those opposing publication fearing that the volume's depiction of a traditional Africa, as well as its heroic portrait of the Zulu leader, would draw indigenous readers back to a non-Christian way of life and perhaps even inspire anti-Christian sentiments. After some portions were changed, *Chaka* was finally published in 1925, thirteen years after Mofolo completed it. But by this time, Mofolo had stopped writing.

After completing *Chaka,* Mofolo held various jobs, including posts as a recruiter and labor agent for diamond mines, sugar plantations, and large farms; manager of a postal route; and trade store proprietor. In 1933 Mofolo returned to his home district, where he purchased a large farm from a white landowner. But because the farm bordered land owned by another African, it contradicted the Land Act of 1914, and it was consequently seized by the government. Mofolo squandered time and money in a futile court bid to recover his property. In 1940, poor and sick, Mofolo retired, and he lived on a pension until his death in 1948.

BIOGRAPHICAL/CRITICAL SOURCES:

BOOKS

African Literature, Three Continents Press, 1976, pp. 1-24.
Gerard, Albert s., *Four African Literatures: Xhosa, Sotho, Zulu, Amharic,* University of California Press, 1971, pp. 101-80.
Kunene, Daniel P., *The Works of Thomas Mofolo,* University of California, Los Angeles, 1967.
Kunene, Daniel P., *Thomas Mofolo and the Emergence of Written Sesotho Prose,* Ravan Press, 1989.
Lindfors, Bernth and Janheinz Jahn, editors, *Neo-African Literature and Culture: Essays in Memory of Janheinz Jahn,* B. Heymann, 1976, pp. 243-57.
Molema, Leloba Sefetogi, *The Image of Christianity in Sesotho Literature: Thomas Mofolo and His Contemporaries,* H. Buske, 1989.
Mphahlele, *The African Image,* Faber, 1962, pp. 166-203.
Twentieth-Century Literary Criticism, Volume 22, Gale (Detroit), 1987, pp. 244-65.
Wauthier, Claude, *The Literature and Thought of Modern Africa,* translation by Shrley Kay, 2nd edition, Heinemann, 1978, pp. 77-103.

PERIODICALS

English in Africa, May, 1986.
French Review, April, 1984.
Literary Criterion, Number 2, 1985.
Nation, January 27, 1932, pp. 119-120.
New African, September, 1966, pp. 152-53.
Research in African Literatures, spring, 1987.
Sheffield Papers on Literature and Society, Volume 1, 1976, pp. 33-44.
South African Journal of African Languages, No. 1, 1988; November, 1989.
Spectator, August 15, 1931, p. 222.*

MOLE, John 1941-

PERSONAL: Born October 12, 1941, in Taunton, Somerset, England; son of Edgar Douglas (a chartered accountant) and Lilian Joyce (Hook) Mole; married Mary Norman (a freelance artist), August 22, 1968; children: Simon, Benjamin. *Education:* Magdalene College, Cambridge, B.A. (with honors), 1964, M.A., 1969. *Avocational interests:* Playing jazz clarinet and alto-sax, giving poetry readings in combination with jazz performances.

ADDRESSES: Home—11 Hill St., St. Albans, Hertfordshire AL3 4QS, England.

CAREER: Haberdashers' Aske's School, Elstree, Hertfordshire, England, English teacher, 1964-73; Verulam School, St. Albans, teacher of English and head of department, 1973-81; St. Albans School, St. Albans, teacher of English and head of department, 1981—; writer. Exchange teacher in Riverdale, NY, 1969-70. Co-founder and editor of the Mandeville Press. Guest on radio programs, including *Poetry Now, Forget Tomorrow's Monday, Time for Verse, Pick of the Week,* and *Poetry Please,* all broadcast by BBC, 1983-89; critic on *Kaleidoscope.*

MEMBER: National Poetry Society (member of council), Eastern Arts Association, Ver Poets (vice-president, 1979—).

AWARDS, HONORS: Eric Gregory Award, Society of Authors, 1970; Signal Award, 1988, for *Boo to a Goose;* Cholmondeley Award, 1994.

WRITINGS:

POETRY

A Feather for Memory, Outposts Publications (London), 1961.
The Instruments, Phoenix Pamphlet Poets Press (Manchester, England), 1970.
Something about Love, Sycamore Press (Oxford, England), 1972.
The Love Horse, E. J. Morton (Manchester), 1973.
(Editor) *Poetry: A Selection,* Dacorum College (Hemel Hempstead, Hertfordshire, England), 1974.
A Partial Light, Dent (London), 1975.
Our Ship, Secker & Warburg (London), 1977.
The Mortal Room, Priapus Poets (Berkhamstead, Hertfordshire), 1977.
The Tales of Rover, Mandeville Press (Hitchin, Hertfordshire), 1977.

On the Set, Keepsake Poems (Richmond, Surrey, England), 1978.
From the House Opposite, Secker & Warburg, 1979.
(With Anthony Thwaite) *British Poetry since 1945,* Longman (London), 1981.
(With Peter Scupham) *Christmas Past,* Mandeville Press, 1981.
Feeding the Lake, Secker & Warburg, 1981.
(With Scupham) *Christmas Games,* Mandeville Press, 1983.
In and out of the Apple, Secker & Warburg, 1984.
(With Scupham) *Christmas Visits,* Mandeville Press, 1984.
Learning the Ropes, Gruffy Ground Press (Winscombe, Somerset, England), 1985.
(With Scupham) *Winter Emblems,* Mandeville Press, 1986.
(With Scupham) *Christmas Fables,* Mandeville Press, 1987.
Homing, Secker & Warburg, 1987.
(With Scupham) *Christmas Gifts,* Mandeville Press, 1988.
(With Scupham) *Christmas Books,* Mandeville Press, 1989.
Depending on the Light, Peterloo, 1993.
Selected Poems, Sinclair-Stevenson (London), 1995.

CHILDREN'S BOOKS

(With wife, Mary Norman) *Once There Were Dragons,* Deutsch (London), 1979.
(Contributor) *All Sorts of Poems,* Methuen, 1980.
(Contributor) *Over the Bridge,* Puffin Books, 1981.
Boo to a Goose, illustrated by Norman, Peterloo (Calstock, Cornwall, England), 1987.
The Mad Parrot's Countdown, Peterloo, 1990.
Catching the Spider, Blackie (London), 1990.
The Conjurer's Rabbit, Blackie (London), 1992.
Back by Midnight, Penguin (London), 1994.
Copy Cat, illustrated by Bee Willey, Kingfisher (New York City), 1997.

OTHER

(Contributor) Alberta Turner, editor, *Forty-Five Contemporary Poems: The Creative Process,* edited by Alberta Turner, Longman, 1985.
Passing Judgements: Poetry in the Eighties, Bristol Press, 1989.
(Contributor) Alan Brownjohn and Sandy Brownjohn, editors, *Meet and Write,* Hodder & Stoughton, 1985.

Author of numerous scripts for BBC-Radio. Poetry reviewer for *Encounter,* 1983-89. Contributor to periodicals, including *Times Literary Supplement, Spectator, Sunday Times, Observer,* and *Independent.*

SIDELIGHTS: John Mole is an English poet whose work is marked by intellectual liveliness and steadfast values. As John Cotton notes in *Contemporary Poets:* "There are special qualities about John Mole's poetry. One of them is wit, by which I mean the intellectual enjoyment of and interest in ideas and language. . . . The other quality . . . has roots in what we might call old-fashioned values."

For Mole, however, wit is scarcely an end in itself but rather a means of illuminating the state of things. According to Cotton, wit and humor, for Mole, serve to facilitate "penetrating observations of the human situation." An *Encounter* reviewer was especially impressed with Mole's method, affirming its effectiveness as "proof, if any were needed, that poetry is as necessary in ordinary circumstances as in times and places of crisis." The *Encounter* reviewer described Mole's poems as "light in the best sense—lucid, sharp, economical."

Mole began his poetry career in the early 1960s with *A Feather for Memory,* and in the ensuing decades he has published more than two dozen additional volumes, some—on Christmas themes—in collaboration with Peter Scupham. Among Mole's many collections is the 1987 volume *Homing,* which a *Poetry Review* critic praised as an especially significant work. The critic described Mole as "a poet at the height of his powers, finding new strength with each volume and with a considerable body of work to his name," adding that "*Homing* will make it still more difficult to fail to see him as one of the most accomplished and salutary poets of the age." Cotton, in his *Contemporary Poets* piece, likewise acknowledged *Homing* as an accomplished work, declaring that it "further establishes [Mole] as a poet of an assured, meticulous craftsmanship and with a sensitive ear for cadence."

In the late 1970s Mole also began writing children's books. "An important conscious element in my starting to write for children," he told *CA,* "was a feeling that they were being sold short by the publishers of contemporary poetry." Mole dismissed much children's poetry as "mere jokiness" and affirmed that he "wanted to more . . . resonant, well-crafted poetry—comic, serious—which would extend children's awareness of their own world."

Among Mole's key children's publications is *Boo to a Goose,* which Cotton noted as a volume which "marked out [Mole's] territory and sets his standards." Cotton added that ensuing publications "have seen Mole take his rightful place in the tradition of worthy poets writing for children." Among Mole's children's books is *Boo to a Goose,* which prompted Charles Causley to write, in the *Times Educational Supplement,* that Mole "demonstrated the rare ability to write poems that appeal simultaneously to the child and the adult."

Mole has also published various critical writings, many of which were written during his stint as poetry editor of *Encounter* in the 1980s. Some of his *Encounter* writings are collected in *Passing Judgements: Poetry in the Eighties,* which inspired Terry Eagleton to write in the *Times Literary Supplement:* "Mole is a shrewd, easy-tempered, resourceful reviewer, striking just the right balance between high critical discourse and racy journalese, adept at the judicious epithet and capable of wearing his convictions lightly."

Mole told *CA:* "Much of my work has been concerned with the experience of childhood—not in any blandly nostalgic sense, but in the attempt to dramatize the fascination and bewilderment of being young. I have also found myself moved by 'sacred' places—what the painter Paul Nash called 'charged landscapes.' This sense of the sacred is peculiarly personal, can be located anywhere but only realized in the making of poems.

"A firm believer in grace under pressure and the effectiveness of restraint in poetry, I feel nevertheless that the elegance of much of my earlier work was evasive, and that its polished surfaces were too often the be-all and end-all. When I read these poems now they seem to lack substance and to be rather wilfully oblique. An increasing political concern has, I think, resulted in my poetry becoming more declarative, more direct. Not that I value humour and lightness of touch less than I did. If anything I value it more. In the words of a character from Henry James, 'the increasing seriousness of things, that's the great opportunity of jokes,' or as the Chinese proverb runs, 'govern a country as you would cook a small fish.' Though my work has come, I hope, to take on larger, more overtly universal, themes, I should like to believe that it has done so without losing touch with the parochial. For me, the successful poem keeps the particular situation as its starting point and the individually human as its scale of reference."

BIOGRAPHICAL/CRITICAL SOURCES:

BOOKS

Contemporary Poets, 6th edition, St. James Press (Detroit), 1996, pp. 755-57.

PERIODICALS

Cambridge Review, December, 1987.
Encounter, September/October, 1984.
PN Review, Volume 16, number 5, 1990.
Poetry Review, June, 1987.
Signal 56, May, 1988.
Times Educational Supplement, March 6, 1988; August 6, 1990.
Times Literary Supplement, November 24, 1989.*

* * *

MOLLENHOFF, Clark R(aymond) 1921-1991

PERSONAL: Born April 16, 1921, in Burnside, IA; died of melanoma of the liver, March 2, 1991, in Lexington, VA; son of Raymond Eldon (a salesman) and Margaret Genevieve (Clark) Mollenhoff; married Georgia Giles Osmundson, October 13, 1939 (divorced, 1978); married Jane Cook Schurz, July 12, 1981; children: (first marriage) Gjore Jean, Jacquelin Sue (Mrs. Duane Montgomery), Clark Raymond, Jr. *Education:* Webster City Junior College, Webster City, IA, graduate, 1941; Drake University, LL.B., 1944. *Politics:* Independent. *Religion:* Roman Catholic.

CAREER: Des Moines Register and Tribune, Des Moines, IA, police and municipal court reporter, 1941-44, county courthouse and statehouse reporter, 1946-49, chief of Washington, DC. Bureau, 1970-77; admitted to Iowa Bar, 1944, Washington, DC Bar, and Bar of U.S. Supreme Court; Cowles Publications, Washington Bureau, Washington, DC, reporter, 1950-69; Washington and Lee University, Lexington, VA, professor of journalism and law, 1976-91. Special counsel to President Richard Nixon, 1969-70. Member, U.S. Advisory Commission on Information Policy, 1962-65. *Military service:* U.S. Navy, 1944-46; served in Pacific; became lieutenant junior grade.

MEMBER: American Bar Association, Investigative Reporters and Editors, Inc. (member of board of directors, 1977-83), National Press Club (governor, 1956-63; vice-president, 1964), Iowa Bar Association, Sigma Delta Chi.

AWARDS, HONORS: Nieman fellowship at Harvard University, 1949-50; Sigma Delta Chi awards, 1952, 1954, 1958; Raymond Clapper Memorial Award and Heywood Broun Memorial Award, 1955; Distinguished Alumni Award, Drake University, 1956; Pulitzer Prize for national reporting, 1958, for inquiry into labor union racketeering; National Headliner Award, 1960, for magazine article in *Atlantic Monthly;* Eisenhower exchange fellowship for study abroad, 1960-61; William Allen White Foundation Award for journalistic merit, 1964; Drew Pearson Award for investigative reporting, 1973; Oxford University exchange fellow, 1980; Sigma Delta Chi fellow, 1980. LL.D., Colby College, 1959, Simpson College, 1974; L.H.D., Cornell College, 1960; Litt.D., Drake University, 1961, and Iowa Wesleyan College, 1966.

WRITINGS:

Washington Cover-Up, Doubleday, 1962.
Tentacles of Power: The Story of Jimmy Hoffa, World Publishing, 1965.
Despoilers of Democracy: The Real Story of What Washington Propagandists, Arrogant Bureaucrats, Mismanagers, Influence Peddlars, and Outright Corrupters Are Doing to Our Federal Government, Doubleday, 1965.
The Pentagon: Politics, Profits, and Plunder, Putnam, 1967, revised edition, Pinnacle Books, 1972.
George Romney: Mormon in Politics, Meredith, 1968.
Strike Force, Prentice-Hall, 1972.
Game Plan for Disaster: An Ombudsman's Report on the Nixon Years, Norton, 1976.
The Man Who Pardoned Nixon, St. Martin's, 1976.
The President Who Failed: Carter Out of Control, Macmillan, 1980.
Investigative Reporting: From Courthouse to White House, Macmillan, 1981.
Atanasoff: Forgotten Father of the Computer, Iowa State University Press (Ames, IA), 1988.
Ballad to an Iowa Farmer and Other Reflections, illustrated by Kevin Lind and Chris Bowring, Iowa State University Press, 1991.

Contributor to national magazines.

SIDELIGHTS: An educator, investigator, journalist, and author, Clark R. Mollenhoff is remembered as the Pulitzer Prize-winning investigative reporter who, in his labor racketeering stories of the 1950s, linked ex-Teamsters union leader Jimmy Hoffa to organized crime. Except for a brief stint as personal investigator for the Nixon administration, Mollenhoff served as Washington correspondent for Cowles Publications from 1950 to 1978. In that time he earned a reputation as a zealous investigator who would challenge any government official for a story. Starting in 1976 until the time of his death, Mollenhoff also taught law and journalism at Washington and Lee University.

As an investigative reporter for the *Des Moines Register and Tribune,* Clark R. Mollenhoff uncovered and documented a number of incidents of wrongdoing in government, labor, and big business. In 1958, he won a Pulitzer Prize for his investigation into labor racketeering. In his books Mollenhoff also dealt with corruption in the Pentagon, in Congress, and in the administrations of U.S. presidents.

During his years as a Washington news reporter, Mollenhoff "was known as one tough guy," the *Washington Post Magazine* declared. Cabell Phillips wrote in the *New York Times Book Review* that Mollenhoff was "a bear of a man who [was] not easily ignored, [he]. . . heckled Presidents, Cabinet officers and others in the bureaucracy with nerve-jarring persistency." Mollenhoff was one reporter who "presidents dreaded hearing at press conferences," according to the *Washington Post Magazine.* An angry President Dwight Eisenhower once told Mollenhoff to "sit down" after he asked a particularly tough question at a press conference.

A long-time advocate of open access to government information, Mollenhoff argued in many of his books for less secrecy in public affairs. R. L. Strout wrote in the *Christian Science Monitor* that "Mollenhoff regard[ed] withholding of information as a major cause of the ills of government." In *Washington Cover-Up,* Mollenhoff outlined incidents when the Washington bureaucracy withheld information from Congressional committees by declaring the material classified. In *The Pentagon: Politics, Profits, and Plunder,* "Mollenhoff [found] too many Pentagon doors bolted and too many mouths taped," as C. R. Sheldon explained in the *Christian Science Monitor.* A wide range of bureaucratic and congressional abuses were documented in *Despoilers of Democracy: The Real Story of What Washington Propagandists, Arrogant Bureaucrats, Mismanagers, Influence Peddlars, and Outright Corrupters Are Doing to Our Federal Government.*

Mollenhoff turned his attention to Presidential corruption after serving nine months as a special counsel to the Nixon administration. Mollenhoff found that Nixon used executive privilege "to hide mismanagement and corruption," the *Washington Post Magazine* explained. He wrote of Nixon's shortcomings in *Game Plan for Disaster: An Ombudsman's Report on the Nixon Years.* Succeeding presidents fared no better with Mollenhoff. President Ford was scrutinized in *The Man Who Pardoned Nixon.* President Carter was examined in *The President Who Failed: Carter Out of Control.*

Mollenhoff looked back at his long career in *Investigative Reporting: From Courthouse to White House,* a book relating his personal experiences as a reporter. "Journalism teachers might want to use it [as a textbook]," wrote David L. Grey in *Journalism Quarterly,* "or might prefer to treat it more as fascinating history and insight into the mind of perhaps the most prolific writer of articles, columns and books about the Washington scene." Certainly, Mollenhoff 's admonition to young journalists, "When in doubt, leave it out," is widely-quoted. Grey concluded that no other book about investigative reporting "seems as detailed and almost overpowering as Mollenhoff 's effort."

BIOGRAPHICAL/CRITICAL SOURCES:

BOOKS

Behrens, John C., *Typewriter Guerrillas,* Nelson-Hall, 1977.

Dygert, James, *The Investigative Journalist: Folk Heroes of a New Era,* Prentice-Hall, 1976.

Hohenberg, John, *The Pulitzer Prize Story,* Columbia University Press, 1959.

Hohenberg, *The New Front Page,* Columbia University Press, 1966.

Mollenhoff, Clark R., *Investigative Reporting: From Courthouse to White House,* Macmillan, 1981.

PERIODICALS

Book Week, November 7, 1965.

Christian Science Monitor, September 20, 1962; March 16, 1967.

Los Angeles Times Book Review, March 16, 1980.

New Leader, December 8, 1975.

New York Times Book Review, September 9, 1962; April 27, 1980.

Saturday Review, September 29, 1962; November 20, 1965; March 4, 1967.

Virginia Quarterly Review, spring, 1976.

Washington Post Book World, March 16, 1980.

Washington Post Magazine, March 9, 1980.

OBITUARIES:

PERIODICALS

Los Angeles Times, March 12, 1991.

New York Times, March 4, 1991.

Washington Post, March 3, 1991.*

MOLNAR, Ferenc 1878-1952

PERSONAL: Original name, Ferenc Neumann; born January 12, 1878, in Budapest, Hungary; immigrated to the United States in January, 1940; naturalized U.S. citizen, 1947; died of stomach cancer, April 1, 1952, in New York, NY; buried at Linden Hill Cemetery, New York, NY; son of Mor (a physician) and Jozepha (Wallfisch) Neumann; married Margit Veszi, 1906 (divorced, 1910); married Sari Fedak (an actress), 1922 (divorced, 1924); married Lili Darvan, 1926 (separated, c. 1932); children: (first marriage) one daughter. *Education:* Studied law at University of Budapest, beginning 1895; completed legal studies at the Swiss University in Geneva.

CAREER: Writer. Worked as journalist in Budapest, Hungary, 1890s; war correspondent for *Az Est,* Budapest, during World War I.

MEMBER: Petofi Society, Kisfaludy Society.

AWARDS, HONORS: Order of Franz Josef, 1916; French Cross of the Legion of Honor, 1927.

WRITINGS:

FICTION IN ENGLISH TRANSLATION

Egy gazdatlan csonak torteenete (novel), [Budapest], 1901, translation by Emil Lengyel published as *The Derelict Boat* in *Eva [and] The Derelict Boat,* Bobbs-Merrill (Indianapolis), 1926.

Eva (novel), [Budapest], 1903, translation by Emil Lengyel published as *Eva* in *Eva [and] The Derelict Boat,* Bobbs-Merrill, 1926.

A Pal utczai fiuk (novel), [Budapest], 1907, Lampel (Budapest), 1923, translation by Louis Rittenberg published as *The Paul Street Boys,* Macy-Masius (New York City), 1927.

A zenelo angyal (novel), 1935, translation by Victor Katona and Peggy Barwell published as *Angel Making Music,* H. Smith and R. Haas (New York City), 1935.

A kekszemu (short stories), 1940, translation published as *The Blued Eyed Lady,* Viking (New York City), 1942.

Farewell My Heart (novel), Simon and Schuster (New York City), 1945.

Companion in Exile (autobiography), Gaer Associates (New York City), 1950.

Stories for Two (short stories), Horizon Press (New York City), 1950.

OTHER FICTION

"Magdolna" es egyeb elbeszelesek (short stories; title means "Magdalena, and Other Stories"), [Budapest], 1898.

"A csokok ejszakaja" es egyeb elbeszelesek (title means "The Kiss at Night, and Other Stories"), [Budapest], 1899.

Az ehes varos (novel; title means "The Hungry City"), [Budapest], 1901.

Egy pesti leany tortenete (title means "The Story of a Girl from Pest"), [Budapest], 1905.

Muzsika (short stories; title means "Music"), [Budapest], 1908.

"Baro Marczius" es egyeb elbeszekesek (title means "Baron Marczius, and Other Stories"), [Budapest], 1913.

Kis harmaskonyv (short stories; title means "Three in One"), [Budapest], 1914.

"Az orias" es egyeb elbeszelesek (title means "The Giant, and Other Stories"), [Budapest], 1917.

Szentolvajok, [Budapest], 1918.

Andor, [Budapest], 1918.

A gozoszlop (novel; title means "The Steam Chimney"), Franklin-tarsulat (Budapest), 1926.

A zold huszar (title means "The Green Hussar"), Athenaeum (Budapest), 1937.

Oszi utazas (novel; title means "Autumn Journey"), Athenaeum, 1939.

STAGE PLAYS IN ENGLISH TRANSLATION

A Doktor ur (produced in 1902), [Budapest], 1902, translation published as *The Lawyer,* in *Plays of Molnar,* Jarrolds (London), 1929.

Az ordog (produced in 1907), [Budapest], 1907, translation by Oliver Herford published as *The Devil,* M. Kennerley (New York), 1908.

Liliom (produced in 1909), [Budapest], 1909, translation by Benjamin Glazer published as *Liliom,* Boni & Liveright (London), 1921.

A vacsora (produced in 1915), [Budapest], 1909, translation published as *Dinner,* in *Smart Set,* Number 67, 1922; as *The Host,* in *One-Act Plays for Stage and Study,* 1925; and as *Anniversary Dinner,* in *Romantic Comedies,* Crown (New York City), 1952.

A testor (produced in 1910), [Budapest], 1910, translation published as *The Guardsman,* 1910.

A farkas (produced in Magyar Szinhaz, Budapest, 1912), Franklin-tarsulat, 1912, translation by Benjamin F. Glazer published as *The Tale of the Wolf* in *Plays of Molnar,* Jarrolds, 1929 (also see below); translation by Henric Hirsch and Frank Hauser published as *The Wolf,* Samuel French (London), 1975.

A fehler felho (produced in 1916), [Budapest], 1916, translation by Glazer published as *The White Cloud* in *Plays of Molnar,* Jarrolds, 1929 (also see below).

Farsang (produced in 1916), Franklin-tarsulat, 1917, translation by Glazer published as *Carnival* in *Plays of Molnar,* Jarrolds, 1929 (also see below).

Uri divat (produced in 1917), Franklin-tarsulat, 1917, translation by Glazer published as *Fashions for Men* Boni & Liveright, 1922, and in *Plays of Molnar,* Jarrolds, 1929 (also see below).

A hattyu (produced in 1920), [Budapest], 1921, translation by Glazer published as *The Swan,* Boni & Liveright, 1922, and in *Plays of Molnar,* Jarrolds, 1929 (also see below).

Szinhaz: Elojatek Lear Kiralyhoz, Marshall, and The Violet (one -act plays; produced in 1921), [Budapest], 1929, translation by Glazer published as *Prologue to "King Lear," Marshall,* and *The Violet* in *Plays of Molnar,* Jarrolds, 1929 (also see below).

Egi es foldi szerelem (produced in 1923), Pantheon (Budapest) 1922, translation by Glazer published as *Heavenly and Earthly Love* in *Plays of Molnar,* Jarrolds, 1929 (also see below).

A voros malom (produced in 1922), Franklin-tarsulat, 1923, translation by Glazer published as *Mima* in *Plays of Molnar,* Jarrolds, 1929 (also see below).

Az uvegcipo (produced in 1924), Franklin- tarsulat, 1924, translation by Glazer published as *The Glass Slipper* in *Plays of Molnar,* Jarrolds, 1929 (also see below).

Riviera (produced in 1925), [Budapest], 1926, translation by Glazer published as *Riviera* in *Plays of Molnar,* Jarrolds, 1929 (also see below).

Csendelt (produced in 1925), translation by Glazer published as *Still Life* in *Plays of Molnar,* Jarrolds, 1929 (also see below).

Jatek a kastelyban (produced in 1926), 1926, translation by P. G. Wodehouse published as *The Play's the Thing,* Brentano's, 1927; translation by Glazer published in *Plays of Molnar,* Jarrolds, 1929; adaptation by Tom Stoppard published as *Rough Crossing,* Faber & Faber (London), 1985.

A boszorkany (produced in 1927), translation by Glazer published as *The Witch* in *Plays of Molnar,* Jarrolds, 1929 (also see below).

Olympia (produced in Magyar Szinhaz, 1928), translation by Glazer published as *Olympia* in *Plays of Molnar,* Jarrolds, 1929 (also see below).

Plays of Molnar (includes *The Lawyer, The Devil, Liliom, The Tale of the Wolf, The White Cloud, Carnival, Fashions for Men, The Swan, A Prologue to "King Lear," Actor from Vienna, The Violet, Marshal, Heavenly and Earthly Love, Mima, Olympia, The Glass Slipper, Riviera,* and *Still Life*), edited by Louis Rittenberg, Jarrolds, 1929, published as *All the Plays of Molnar,* Garden City Publishing (Garden City, NY), 1937.

Egy, ketto, harom (produced in 1929), [Budapest], 1929, translation published as *President* in *Romantic Comedies,* Crown, 1952 (also see below).

A jo tunder (produced in 1930), [Budapest], 1930, translation by Jane Hinton published as *The Good Fairy,* R. Long and R. R. Smith (New York City), 1932.

Valaki (produced in 1932), Franklin-tarsulat, 1932, translation published as *Arthur* in *Romantic Comedies,* Crown, 1952 (also see below).

Harmonia (produced in 1932), Athenaeum, 1932.

A cukraszne (produced in 1935), [Budapest], 1934, translation by Gilbert Miller published as *Delicate Story,* Samuel French, 1941.

Delila (produced in 1937), translation published as *Blue Danube* in *Romantic Comedies,* Crown, 1952 (also see below).

The King's Maid, produced in 1941.

Panoptikum (produced in 1948), [Budapest], 1941, translation by Arthur Richman published as *Waxworks* in *Romantic Comedies,* Crown, 1952 (also see below).

Pit-a-Pat (produced as *Das Spiel des Herzen,* 1971), translation published as *Game of Hearts* in *Romantic Comedies,* Crown, 1952 (also see below).

Romantic Comedies (includes *Actor from Vienna, President, Waxworks, Arthur, Blue Danube, The Good Fairy, Anniversary Dinner,* and *Game of Hearts*), Crown, 1952.

Work also published in various collections and anthologies, including *Husbands and Lovers,* translation by Benjamin Glazer, Boni and Liveright, 1924.

OTHER STAGE PLAYS

Jozsi (produced in 1904), [Budapest], 1902.

Menyegzo (produced in 1935), 1933.

Csoda a hegyek kozt (title means "Miracle in the Mountains"; produced in 1936), 1933.

Az ismeretlen lany (title means "The Unknown Girl"; produced in Vigszinhaz, 1934), 1934.

Nagy szerelem (title means "Great Love"; produced in 1935), 1935.

A csaszar, produced in 1946.

OTHER WORKS IN ENGLISH TRANSLATION

Ketten beszelnek (sketches), [Budapest], 1909, translation published as *Stories for Two,* Horizon Press, 1950.

Companion in Exile: Notes for an Autobiography, translation by Barrow Mussey, 1950.

OTHER

Molnar Ferenc muvei (collected works), 20 volumes, [New York City], 1928.

Szinhaz (selected works), Szepirodalmi Konyvkiado (Budapest), 1961.

Gyerekek (title means "Children"), [Budapest], 1905.

Pesti erkolscok (title means "Metropolitan Morals"), [Budapest], 1909.

Hetagup sip (title means "Pipes of Pan"), [Budapest], 1911.

Ma, tegnap, tegnapelott (title means "Today, Yesterday, Tomorrow"; journalism), [Budapest], 1912.

Egy haditudosito emlekei (title means "A War Correspondent's Diary"), [Budapest], 1916.

Az aruvimi erdo titka' es egyeb szatirak (title means "The Secret of the Aruwim Forest, and Other Satires), 1917.

Ismerosok (title means "Acquaintances"), [Budapest], 1917.

Vacsora es egyeb jelenek (title means "Dinner, and Other Scenes"), 1917.

Toll (title means "Pen"), [Budapest], 1928.

Szulofalum, Pest (miscellany), [Budapest], 1962.

ADAPTATIONS: Liliom was adapted by Richard Rogers and Oscar Hammerstein as the musical *Carousel; Jatek a kastelyban* adapted by Tom Stoppard as *Rough Crossing,* Faber & Faber (London), 1985.

SIDELIGHTS: Ferenc Molnar was a prolific Hungarian writer who enjoyed immense acclaim for his many plays, which often concern, in humorous manner, the sometimes tenuous bond between men and women. As Peter I. Barta wrote in *Reference Guide to World Literature,* Molnar's works "depict unsuccessful human relations in a tone which ranges from the playful to the satirical, frequently containing elements of nostalgia or pure sentimentalism."

Molnar was born in 1878 in Budapest, Hungary. In his early teens, when he studied at a Calvinist school, Molnar printed and staged his own works, and while studying law at the University of Budapest and Swiss University, he continued his literary career by contributing to various periodicals. Upon completing his university studies, Molnar rejected a law career and determined to support himself as a writer. He settled in Budapest and readily established himself in the city's literary community.

In 1901 Molnar published his first novel, *Egy gazdatlan csonak torteenete* (translated as *The Derelict Boat*), in which a schoolgirl falls in love with a journalist. The novel drew the ire of local critics but nonetheless found favor with the book-buying public. The next year, Molnar completed *A doktor ur (The Doctor)*, which became his first play to receive a professional staging. The public responded favorably to *The Doctor,* as it did to many of his forthcoming plays. Thus within a few years Molnar ranked among the city's most popular, and prominent, writers.

By the early 1900s Molnar had imposed upon himself a demanding schedule that required him to write both a play and a novel each year, a story each week, and a newspaper piece each day. This hectic pace, together with Molnar's scandalous romantic endeavors, kept him a constant subject of interest in Budapest, especially since his stage works, which inevitably dealt with relations between men and women, were rumored to be largely autobiographical. Clara Gyorgyey noted as much when she wrote in *Ferenc Molnar* that "the gossip-hungry Budapest populace stormed the theaters to watch the new developments in the playwright's private life."

Among Molnar's most significant plays is *Az ordog* (*The Devil*), a 1907 drama in which Satan endeavors to turn a young woman against her husband and drive her into the arms of her true love. Writing in *Poet Lore,* O. W. Firkins described *The Devil* as a play "suggestive . . . of reckless caprice or audacious trifling," and Edmund Wilson, writing in *New Yorker,* noted that the play possesses "some psychological interest: the Devil is more or less made to represent the hidden impulses of sincere passion which are at war with the social exactions." Budapest audiences, however, chose to see the play as Molnar's efforts to end his lover's marriage.

Liliom, another of Molnar's early successes, concerns the fatal romance between a carnival worker and a servant girl. When the couple began living together, they forfeit their jobs, and when the girl becomes pregnant, her lover kills himself. In an afterlife, the late hero recalls his lover. After fifteen years pass, the hero returns to Earth with an opportunity to obtain redemption. But he fails, even managing to strike his adolescent daughter when she proves insufficiently appreciative of a gift.

Liliom ranks among Molnar's most important works. John Gassner, writing in *Masters of the Drama,* even hailed it as "a play of rare beauty, one of the most gratifying romantic plays of the twentieth century." Another enthusiast, Ludwig Lewisohn, affirmed in *Nation* that "the very form of *Liliom* has a special and exhilarating charm," while Joseph Remenyi praised *Liliom* in *PMLA,* as "a tender, touching, impressive play." Remenyi added: "What makes *Liliom* outstanding compared with [Molnar's] other plays is that in this play . . . Molnar tried to take stock of imponderables which showed an honest quest for truth transcending the horizon of his credulous plays." Frank W. Chandler, meanwhile, wrote in *Modern Continental Playwrights* that *Liliom* constituted "a masterpiece." The play inspired the team of Rodgers and Hammerstein to adapt it as a musical, *Carousel,* which proved similarly successful.

In subsequent plays such as *A testor* (*The Guardsman*), *Jatek a kastelyban* (*The Play's the Thing*), and three one-act plays published together as *Szinhaz: Elojatek Lear Kiralyhoz, Marshall, and The Violet,* Molnar continued to portray domestic triangles while also addressing the relationship between illusion and reality and their intermingling in the world of the theater. In *The Guardsman,* for instance, an actor masquerades as a Russian guard to test his wife's fidelity. Although the couple eventually reconcile, the wife's faithfulness remains difficult to determine.

The characters in *The Guardsman* are typical of Molnar's comedies: the woman is beautiful, fickle, and cunning, while the man is jealous and somewhat befuddled, and he is ultimately defeated by the woman. In Molnar's world, as Joseph Remenyi noted, "man generally suffers because of a woman and the woman almost never suffers because of a man."

Elojatek Lear Kiralyhoz (*Prologue to "King Lear"* derives from a situation similar to that in *The Guardsman:* a husband discovers his wife's infidelity and attempts to confront her lover, an actor costumed as King Lear. The actor exploits the dignity of his role and the husband thereupon finds it impossible to chastise him. As S. N. Behrman observed in *The Suspended Drawing Room,* "Molnar adorns the Shakespearean characters with so much authority that the play's actual characters are compelled to admit their own lack of substance and, after being deflated, they scramble off into their dim, makeshift reality."

While writing for the stage, Molnar also completed several volumes of fiction. Many of these works, reflecting Molnar's own romantic travails, detail sexual relationships that end poorly. The exception here is *A Pal utczai fiuk* (*The Paul Street Boys*), which has been acclaimed as a classic of juvenile literature. *The Paul Street Boys* concerns the tension between rival bands of schoolboys. When one group attempts to seize control of a playground within the other group's territory, a youth from the besieged band acquits himself in a heroic, but ultimately fatal, fashion. Peter I. Barta, in his *Reference Guide to World Literature* entry on Molnar, called *The Paul Street Boys* "the most popular piece of juvenile literature in Hungarian," and he added that the novel's "sophisticated narrative voice . . . strikes a fine balance between irony and pity."

During World War I, Molnar worked as a correspondent for *Az Est,* a Budapest newspaper. He saw combat while accompanying the Austro-Hungarian forces. Consequently, his coverage, which also appeared in the *New York Times* and the *London Morning Post,* won recognition for its vivid depictions of wartime horrors. After the war, Molnar circulated through Europe, writing prolifically and living luxuriously in a series of hotels. But as World War II approached in the 1930s, Molnar began suffering from overwhelming despair that drove him into uncharacteristic seclusion. He eventually fled Europe and immigrated to the United States, where he briefly revived and managed to writer several further works.

After a massive heart attack nearly proved fatal in 1943, Molnar once again plunged into despair. According to Gyorgyey, Molnar "became apathetic, morose, a misanthrope." As he again lapsed into depression and seclusion, he suffered further when his lover took her own life. Despite his dire mental condition, Molnar continued to write, but his works—far from detailing his characteristic sexual intrigue—reflected his shattered state. He fell further ill in the early 1950s when he became stricken with stomach cancer. That disease proved fatal, taking Molnar's life in 1952.

BIOGRAPHICAL/CRITICAL SOURCES:

BOOKS

Behrman, S. N., *The Suspended Drawing Room,* Stein & Day, 1965, pp. 191-253.

Chandler, Frank, *Modern Continental Playwrights,* Harper, 1931, pp. 438-64.

Gergely, Emro Joseph, *Hungarian Drama in New York: American Adaptations, 1908-1940,* University of Pennsylvania Press, 1947, pp. 10-60.

Gyorgyey, Clara, *Ferenc Molnar,* Twayne, 1980.

Rajec, Elizabeth Molnar, *Ferenc Molnar: Bibliograpy,* H. Bohlaus, 1986.

Reference Guide to World Literature, St. James Press (Detroit), 1995, pp. 841-43.

Twentieth-Century Literary Criticism, Volume 20, Gale (Detroit), 1986, pp. 154-79.

Varkonyi, Istvan, *Ferenc Molnar and the Austro-Hungarian "Fin de Siecle,"* P. Lang, 1991.

PERIODICALS

Nation, May 11, 1921, p. 695; November 5, 1924; August 11, 1945.

New Republic, May 4, 1921.

New Yorker, June 4, 1966, pp. 88-139.

New York Herald Tribune Books, June 6, 1926; December 4, 1927.

PMLA, December, 1946, pp. 1185-1200.

Poet Lore, November-December, 1909, pp. 438-48.

Psychoanalytic Review, January, 1922.

Sewanee Review, summer, 1953, pp. 507-14.

Spectator, October 5, 1934.*

* * *

MONJO, F(erdinand) N(icholas III) 1924-1978

PERSONAL: Born August 28, 1924, in Stamford, CT; died October 9, 1978, in New York, NY; married Louise Elaine Lyczak, 1950; children: three sons, one daughter. *Education:* Columbia University, B.A., 1946.

CAREER: Simon & Schuster, New York City, editor of Golden Books, 1953-58; American Heritage Press, New York City, editor of American Heritage Junior Library, 1958-61; Coward McCann and Geoghegan, New York City, assistant director, 1961-69, vice-president and editorial director of children's books, 1969-78; writer.

AWARDS, HONORS: F. N. Monjo Memorial Fund established by New York Society Library.

WRITINGS:

CHILDREN'S BOOKS

Indian Summer, illustrations by Anita Lobel, Harper (New York City), 1968.

The Drinking Gourd, illustrations by Fred Brenner, Harper, 1970.

The One Bad Thing about Father, illustrations by Rocco Negri, Harper, 1970.

(Translator with Nina Ignatowicz) Reiner Zimnik, *The Crane,* illustrations by Zimnik, Harper, 1970.

Pirates in Panama, illustrations by Wallace Tripp, Simon & Schuster (New York City), 1970.

The Jezebel Wolf, illustrations by John Schoenherr, Simon & Schuster, 1971.

The Vicksburg Veteran, illustrations by Douglas Gorsline, Simon & Schuster, 1971.

Slater's Mill, illustrations by Laszlo Kubinyi, Simon & Schuster, 1972.

Rudi and the Distelfink, illustrations by George Kraus, Windmill Books (New York City), 1972.

The Secret of the Sachem's Tree, illustrations by Margot Tomes, Coward McCann (New York City), 1972.

Poor Richard in France, illustrations by Brinton Turkle, Holt (New York City), 1973.

Me and Willie and Pa: The Story of Abraham Lincoln and His Son Tad, illustrations by Gorsline, Simon & Schuster, 1973.

Clarence and the Burglar, illustrations by Paul Galdone, Coward McCann, 1973.

Grand Papa and Ellen Aroon, illustrations by Richard Cuffari, Holt, 1974.

The Sea-Beggar's Son, illustrations by C. Walter Hodges, Coward McCann, 1974.

King George's Head Was Made of Lead, illustrations by Margot Tomes, Coward McCann, 1974.

Letters to Horseface: Being the Story of Wolfgang Amadeus Mozart's Journey to Italy, 1769-1770, When He Was a Boy of Fourteen, illustrations by Don Bolognese and Elaine Raphael, Viking Press (New York City), 1975.

Gettysburg: Tad Lincoln's Story, illustrations by Gorsline, Windmill Books, 1976.

Willie Jasper's Golden Eagle, illustrations by Gorsline, Doubleday (New York City), 1976.

Zenas and the Shaving Mill, illustrations by Cuffari, Coward McCann, 1976.

The Porcelain Pagoda, illustrations by Egielski, Viking Press, 1976.

A Namesake for Nathan: Being an Account of Captain Nathan Hale by His Twelve-Year-Old Sister, illustrations by Eros Keith, Coward McCann, 1977.

The House on Stink Alley: A Story about the Pilgrims in Holland, illustrations by Robert Quackenbush, Holt, 1977.

Prisoners of the Scrambling Dragon, illustrations by Arthur Geisert, Holt, 1980.

SIDELIGHTS: F. N. Monjo wrote historical fiction and nonfiction for young readers. He was inspired to write about history by his family's own colorful past. His father's family emigrated from Spain and became fur merchants who sent ships to Alaska and established trade with the Eskimos. His mother's family hailed from Mississippi and regaled Monjo with stories about the Civil War and the days of the plantations. Monjo told *Cricket Magazine:* "Listening to stories like these brought history alive so vividly for me that I was never able to read it, later, as if it were a mere collection of facts and dates. Hearing my two families discuss the past—often with considerable heat and color—made it clear to me that people like Grant and Lincoln certainly had been flesh and blood creatures."

After graduating from college, Monjo went on to become an editor with several New York publishing houses. Monjo recalled to *Horn Book:* "I began to realize that most of the fun of history lay in the details that most children's books seemed to omit. So I resolved to try writing some books for young children, limited to incidents or mere glimpses from history, but allowing enough leisure and space to be able to include the details that help so much to bring a scene to life."

Monjo's first historical fiction for children is *Indian Summer,* a 1968 publication about a family of Kentucky pioneers compelled to stave off an Indian attack. The pioneers, as Trevelyn Jones explained in *School Library Journal,* "battle for their lives and cleverly defeat the Indians." Jones called *Indian Summer* "an exciting story for the very youngest readers." Polly Goodwin expressed similar praise when she wrote, in her *Washington Post Book World* appraisal, that *Indian Summer* constitutes "an exciting tale." But Mary Gloyne Byler, writing in *American Indian Authors for Young Readers,* regarded *Indian Summer* as a distorted view of the conflict between settlers and Native Americans. The book's message, Byler contended, serves to indicate that "settlers are good, peaceful people . . . and that American Indians are menacing but stupid creatures."

Monjo followed *Indian Summer* with *The Drinking Gourd,* which concerns the Underground Railroad that helped runaway slaves gain freedom in pre-Civil War America. A *Kirkus Review* critic noted the volume's "quiet drama" while Zena Sutherland, writing in the *Bulletin of the Center for Children's Books,* commended the book for its "simplicity of dialogue and exposition." Margaret Deg, meanwhile, wrote in *Children's Book Review* that the tale "is a straight, unsentimental narrative."

In his next book, *The One Bad Thing About Father,* Monjo writes, from a child's perspective, of life in the White House during the presidency of Theodore Roosevelt. Zena Sutherland wrote in *Saturday Review* that the story "gives a real sense of both the man and the era," and she wrote in *Bulletin of the Center for Children's*

Books that Monjo's storytelling "is ingenuous and candid."

Many of Monjo's books, including *The One Bad Thing About Father,* were written from a child's point of view that serves to humanize the historical characters portrayed. "We can—if we insist upon it—overwhelm our six and eight-year-olds with vast, monolithic, unsmiling, profiles," Monjo wrote in *Horn Book.* In contrast to such profiles, Monjo sought to create more realistic historical characters. "I decided that I would try to offer some flawed, partial, impressionistic, and irreverent portraits of great Americans to children today," he explained in *Horn Book,* adding "I wanted to show their foibles and to present the hero not as a huge, remote icon—but, instead, as an intimate, palpable, fallible surprise."

In *The Jezebel Wolf,* Monjo relates a childhood experience of Israel Putnam, who became a prominent military leader. The story, which concerns Putnam's encounter with a ravenous wolf, won praise from *Horn Book* reviewer Mary M. Burns as "an engrossing narrative" and from *Bulletin of the Center for Children's Books* reviewer Zena Sutherland as a tale "full of action and suspense." A *Junior Bookshelf* critic, however, contended that "there is not much . . . to suggest a sense of history."

Monjo returned to the Civil War era for *The Vicksburg Veteran,* an account of the Vicksburg campaign from the perspective of Union general Ulysses S. Grant's son. A *Kirkus Reviews* critic proclaimed the book "flavorful," and *Horn Book* reviewer Mary M. Burns called it a "lively, fictional journal." Irving Werstein, meanwhile, confirmed in the *New York Times Book Review* that *The Vicksburg Veteran* constitutes a "compelling journal," and Susan L. Pickles wrote in *School Library Journal* that the book is "believably written."

Monjo's next work, *Slater's Mill,* relates the experiences of a Quaker inventor who devises an automated spinning wheel. A *Kirkus Reviews* critic described the book as "lovingly accurate," and Zena Sutherland wrote in *Bulletin of the Center for Children's Books* that the story provides "a great deal of [technical] information."

Rudi and the Distelfink, which follows *Slater's Mill,* details the various activities of a Pennsylvania-Dutch family in the 1820s. Sara Kay Rupnik, writing in *School Library Journal,* found *Rudi and the Distelfink* less compelling than some of Monjo's previous works, and a *Kirkus Reviews* critic noted the book's lack of narrative drive. But Zena Sutherland, in her review for *Bulletin of the Center for Children's Books,* believed that the book affords "a good picture of the . . . customs of the region."

The Secret of the Sachem's Tree, another of Monjo's many works from the early 1970s, occurs during Halloween in the days of American colonialization. *School Library Journal* reviewer Carol Chatfield proclaimed the book "an interesting piece of history," and Zena Sutherland, in another of her many reviews for the *Bulletin of the Center for Children's Books,* noted the story's "lively style."

In *Poor Richard in France,* Monjo writes about Benjamin Franklin from the viewpoint of Franklin's grandson Benny. Chatfield wrote in *School Library Journal:* "Benny's view of events is based on a skeleton of facts embellished with humorous touches," while Sutherland wrote in *Bulletin of the Center for Children's Books* that Benny's accounts "are lively and humorous." And Jane Yolen, wrote in *Twentieth-Century Children's Writers* that *Poor Richard in France* finds Monjo "at his unassailable best." She concluded, "Except for his friend and colleague Jean Fritz, Monjo had no peer in the writing of easy-reading history books."

Europe provides the setting for *The Sea Beggar's Son,* Monjo's tale of a Dutch freedom fighter in the conflict that raged between Holland and Spain in the sixteenth and seventeenth centuries. Chatfield reported in *School Library Journal* that the book is "not entirely successful," but Sutherland wrote in *Bulletin of the Center for Children's Books* that Monjo's story is "stirring."

Monjo's *Letters to Horseface* relates a tour of Italy undertaken by fourteen-year-old musical prodigy Mozart, who recounts his experiences in a series of letters home to his sister, nicknamed Horseface. "What Monjo has done," wrote Harold C. Schonberg in the *New York Times Book Review,* "is to reconstruct the trip though young Mozart's mind, and he has done a remarkable job." A critic for *Publishers Weekly* was similarly impressed, noting that Monjo proves himself "very good at evoking personalities, times and places." A *Kirkus Reviews* critic, meanwhile, pronounced *Letters to Horseface* a "skilled divertimento."

Among Monjo's other children's book is *King George's Head Was Made of Lead,* which relates the melting of King George's statue to provide bullets for colonists' weapons. A *Kirkus Reviews* critic contended that the book, which unfolds from the statue's perspective, is somewhat "overextended," but Sutherland, in her appraisal for *Bulletin of the Center for Children's Books,* acknowledged the book's "characterization" and "humor."

Grand Papa and Ellen Aroon, another of Monjo's many works, portrays Thomas Jefferson as observed by his favorite granddaughter. Joe Bearden, in his *School Library Journal* review, proclaimed *Grand Papa and Ellen Aroon* "impeccably authentic," while Sutherland wrote in *Bulletin of the Center for Children's Book* of the story's "accurate information."

Summarizing his literary skills and aims, Monjo once related, "This is what I feel I can do: give a child his first authentic taste of a great figure from the past. . . . I shall certainly not have satisfied a child's interest in T. R. Or Lincoln or Jefferson, but I may have got it started."

BIOGRAPHICAL/CRITICAL SOURCES:

BOOKS

Byler, Mary Gloyne, *American Indian Authors for Young Readers: A Selected Bibliography,* Association on American Indian Affairs, 1973, p. 8.
Children's Literature Review, Volume 2, Gale (Detroit), 1976, pp. 120- 126.
Twentieth-Century Children's Writers, 4th edition, St. James Press (Detroit), 1995, pp. 670-71.

PERIODICALS

Booklist, November 15, 1974, p. 345.
Bulletin of the Center for Children's Books, June, 1970, pp. 163-64; October, 1970, p. 163; April, 1972, p. 127; October, 1973, p. 30; February, 1973, p. 95; March, 1973, p. 110; April, 1974, p. 134; March, 1974, pp. 115-116; April, 1975, p. 135; May, 1975, pp. 151-52; October, 1975, p. 30.
Children's Book Review, October, 1971, p. 163.
Cricket Magazine, September, 1975.
Horn Book, August, 1971, p. 378; October, 1971, p. 477; February, 1974, pp. 42-43; April, 1975, p. 158; October, 1975.
Junior Bookshelf, June, 1974, p. 168.
Kirkus Reviews, April 15, 1970, p. 450; February 15, 1971, p. 174; February 15, 1972, p. 194; November 1, 1972, p. 1234; November 15, 1973, p. 1269; November 1, 1974, p. 1156; December 1, 1974, p. 1257; January 1, 1975, p. 23; October 15, 1975, p. 1190.
New York Times Book Review, April 25, 1971, p. 40; November 16, 1975, p. 33.
Publishers Weekly, November 17, 1975, p. 97.
Saturday Review, March 21, 1970, p. 39.
School Library Journal, November, 1968, p. 108; December, 1970, p. 71; September, 1971, p. 159; December, 1972, p. 73; April, 1973, pp. 57-58; December, 1973, p. 43; December, 1974, p. 42; February, 1975, p. 49.
Washington Post Book World, October 6, 1968, p. 20.*

* * *

MOON, (Susan) Elizabeth (Norris) 1945-

PERSONAL: Born March 17, 1945, in McAllen, TX; daughter of Jack M. (an engineer) and Dorothy (an engineer; maiden name, Jamerson) Norris; married Richard S. Moon (a physician), 1969; children: Michael Edwin. *Education:* Rice University, B.A. (history), 1968; University of Texas at Austin, B.A. (biology), 1975; graduate study at University of Texas at San Antonio, 1975-77. *Religion:* Episcopal.

ADDRESSES: *Home*—Florence, TX. *Agent*—Joshua Bilmes, Scott Meredith Literary Agency, Inc., 845 Third Ave., New York, NY 10022.

CAREER: Writer. Emergency Medical Service volunteer, 1979-84; member of Florence City Council, 1980-84. *Military service:* U.S. Marine Corps, 1968-71.

MEMBER: Science Fiction Writers of America, Austin Writers League.

AWARDS, HONORS: Compton Crook Award, 1988, for *Sheepfarmer's Daughter;* nomination for Hugo Award, 1997, for *Remnant Population.*

WRITINGS:

"PAKSENARRION" FANTASY NOVELS

Sheepfarmer's Daughter, Baen (New York City), 1988.
Divided Allegiance, Baen, 1988.
Oath of Gold, Baen, 1989.
The Deed of Paksenarrion (includes *Sheepfarmer's Daughter, Divided Allegiance,* and *Oath of Gold*), Baen, 1992.

"PLANET PIRATES" SERIES

(With Anne McCaffrey) *Sassinak,* Baen, 1990.
(With McCaffrey) *Generation Warriors,* Baen, 1991.

(With McCaffrey and Jody Lynn Nye) *The Planet Pirates* (includes *Sassinak* and *Generation Warriors*), Baen, 1993.

OTHER

Lunar Activity, Baen, 1990.
Surrender None: The Legacy of Gird, Baen, 1990.
Liar's Oath, Baen, 1992.
Hunting Party, Baen, 1993.
Remnant Population, Baen, 1996.
The Legacy of Gird, Baen, 1996.
Once a Hero, Baen, 1997.
Rules of Engagement, Cahners, 1998.

Also author of short fiction, poetry, and plays.

SIDELIGHTS: Elizabeth Moon is a writer who has won particular recognition for her fantasy novels, including the "Paksenarrion" series recounting the exploits of the title character, a woman warrior. "In many ways, the [Paksenarrion] novels seem like standard fantasies, set in a faraway medieval land inhabited by humans, elves, dwarves, orcs, and various practitioners of good and evil magic," reports Gary Westfahl in *St. James Guide to Fantasy Writers.* But he adds that Moon's fiction is distinguished from other fantasy works by its similarities to an unlikely volume, *The Lives of the Saints.* "It is almost as if Moon consciously reached back to *The Lives of the Saints* to provide a modernized role model for young female readers," writes Westfahl, who describes Paksenarrion as "a woman who could outfight any man while maintaining higher moral standards in her adventures."

Moon commenced the Paksenarrion series in 1988 with *Sheepfarmer's Daughter,* wherein the eventual warrior is introduced as an independent woman who defies her father's efforts to arrange her marriage, then joins a mercenary team and becomes veteran of armed conflict. While undertaking a dangerous cross-country trek, however, Paksenarrion reaffirms her strong moral values and comes to believe that a greater fate awaits her. In the next volume, *Divided Allegiance,* Paksenarrion breaks from her fellow mercenaries, whose gruesome deeds have finally grown unacceptable to her, and she pledges herself to Gird, an ancient saint. In her consequent training to better serve Gird, Paksenarrion runs afoul of black magic, which leaves her, in Westfahl's words, "a pathetic wanderer." But in the third volume, *Oath of Gold,* Paksenarrion regains her courage, and in an ensuing conflict she undergoes various tortures and degradations while fighting to restore a duke to his proper kingdom.

Moon recounts Gird's own exploits in an ensuing publication, *Surrender None: The Legacy of Gird,* which relates Gird's leading role in a peasant revolt. Unlike the utterly wholesome Paksenarrion, Gird shows some foibles, including explosive rage and a penchant for alcohol abuse. In another book, *Liar's Oath,* Moon writes of Gird's disciple Luap, who succumbs to evil only to be defeated and spiritually held by foul dwarves. Luap eventually experiences a vision in which he secures from Paksenarrion an assurance that she will one day free his soul.

Another of Moon's notable works is *Sassinak,* the initial installment of the "Planet Pirates" series. In this tale, written by Moon Ann McCaffrey, an adolescent girl, Sassinak, witnesses the extermination of her family and seeks vengeance. A *Publishers Weekly* reviewer affirms that Sassinak's ensuing adventures are "expertly recounted." Moon and McCaffrey also produced a sequel, *Generation Warriors.*

Among Moon's other novels is *Remnant Population,* in which a widowed colonist remains behind when fellow humans depart from a faraway planet. She subsequently becomes embroiled in violence between new arrivals, who are soon eliminated, and the natives, who spare her and ultimately come to accept her. *Booklist* reviewer Carl Hays describes *Remnant Population* as "a fascinating adventure." Another tale, *Once a Hero,* features a heroine who must face a military court-martial after leading a mutiny on a starship. A *Publishers Weekly* critic proclaims this novel "satisfying." A following novel, *Rules of Engagement,* concerns the same heroine, Esmay Suiza, who herein interrupts her training as a star fleet commander and determines to rescue a rival in romance. A *Publishers Weekly* critic notes the story's "smart pacing" and "lively characters."

BIOGRAPHICAL/CRITICAL SOURCES:

BOOKS

St. James Guide to Fantasy Writers, St. James Press (Detroit, MI), 1996.

PERIODICALS

Booklist, April 15, 1996, p. 1425; February 1, 1997, p. 929.
Library Journal, March 15, 1997, p. 93.
Publishers Weekly, February 9, 1990, p. 56; April 22, 1996; February 24, 1997, p. 69; November 23, 1998, p. 63.*

MOORE, C(atherine) L(ucile) 1911-1988 (Lawrence O'Donnell, Lewis Padgett, joint pseudonyms)

PERSONAL: Born January 24, 1911, in Indianapolis, IN; daughter of Otto Newman and Maude Estelle (Jones) Moore; married Henry Kuttner (a writer), June 7, 1940 (died, 1958); married Thomas Reggie, June 13, 1963. *Education:* University of Southern California, B.A. (Phi Beta Kappa), 1956, M.A., 1964.

CAREER: Fletcher Trust Co., Indianapolis, IN, 1930-40, began as writer, became president; University of Southern California, Los Angeles, instructor in writing and literature, 1958-61; writer.

MEMBER: Science Fiction Writers of America, Mystery Writers of America, Writers Guild, Phi Beta Kappa, Phi Kappa Phi.

WRITINGS:

NOVELS WITH HUSBAND, HENRY KUTTNER

(Under joint pseudonym Lawrence O'Donnell) *Fury,* Grosset & Dunlap (New York City), 1950, published as *Destination Infinity,* Avon (New York City), 1958.
(Under joint pseudonym Lewis Padgett) *Tomorrow and Tomorrow* [and] *The Fairy Chessmen,* Gnome Press (New York City), 1951, published in England as *Tomorrow and Tomorrow* [and] *The Far Reality,* two volumes, Consul (London), 1963, *The Fairy Chessmen* published as *Chessboard Planet,* Galaxy (New York City), 1956.
(Under joint pseudonym Lewis Padgett) *Well of the Worlds,* Galaxy, 1953.
(Under joint pseudonym Lewis Padgett) *Under Earth's Gates,* Ace (New York City), 1954.
Doomsday Morning, Doubleday (New York City), 1957.
Earth's Last Citadel, Ace, 1964.
Valley of the Flame, Ace, 1964.
The Time Axis, Ace, 1965.
The Dark World, Ace, 1965.
The Mask of Circe, Ace, 1971.
Scarlet Dream, [Hampton Falls, NH], 1981, published as *Northwest Smith,* Ace, 1982.
(With Robert Silverberg) *Vintage Season* [and] *In Another Country* (includes Moore and Kuttner's *Vintage Season* and Silverberg's *In Another Country*), Tor (New York City), 1990.

STORY COLLECTIONS WITH KUTTNER

(Under joint pseudonym Lewis Padgett) *A Gnome There Was, and Other Tales of Science Fiction and Fantasy,* Simon & Schuster (New York City), 1950.
(Under joint pseudonym Lewis Padgett) *Robots Have No Tails,* Gnome Press, 1952.
(Under joint pseudonym Lewis Padgett) *Line to Tomorrow,* Bantam (New York City), 1954.
(Under joint pseudonym Lewis Padgett) *Mutant,* Gnome Press, 1953.
No Boundaries, Ballantine (New York City), 1955.
Clash by Night, and Other Stories, edited by Peter Pinto, Hamlyn (London), 1980.
Chessboard Planet, and Other Stories, Hamlyn, 1983.

OTHER STORY COLLECTIONS

Judgement Night: A Collection of Science Fiction, Gnome Press, 1952.
Shambleau and Others, Gnome Press, 1953.
Northwest of Earth, Gnome Press, 1954, revised edition, Consul, 1961.
(With Robert E. Howard, Frank Belknap Long, H. P. Lovecraft, and A. Merritt) *The Challenge from Beyond,* privately printed, 1954, Necronomicon, 1978.
Jirel of Joiry, Paperback Library (New York City), 1969, as *Black God's Shadow,* Donald M. Grant (West Kingston, RI), 1977.
The Best of C. L. Moore, edited by Lester del Rey, Doubleday, 1975.
Scarlet Dream, illustrated by Alicia Austin, Donald M. Grant, 1981, published as *Northwest Smith,* Ace, 1982.

OTHER

(Under joint pseudonym Lewis Padgett) *Murder in Brass* (novel), Bantam, 1947, published in England as *The Brass Ring,* Sampson Low (London), 1947.
(Under joint pseudonym Lewis Padgett) *The Day He Died* (novel), Duell (New York City), 1947.

Writer for television shows, including *77 Sunset Strip.*

Contributor of numerous short stories—sometimes in collaboration with Kuttner and sometimes under the joint pseudonym Lewis Padgett—to periodicals, including *Astounding Science Fiction, Unknown Worlds, Weird Tales,* and *Famous Fantastic Mysteries.*

SIDELIGHTS: C. L. Moore was a prolific science-fiction/fantasy writer who produced many of her writings in collaboration with her first husband, Henry Kuttner. "To a considerable degree, their arrangement was mutually beneficial," reported William P. Kelly in the *Dictionary of Literary Biography*. "Moore's imagination far outstripped Kuttner's, while his narrative skills were superior to hers." Kelly stated that by working together, Moore and Kuttner "frequently achieved an effective synthesis of their respective talents and produced some exemplary science fiction."

Moore met Kuttner in the late 1930s after she had already begun contributing to the magazine *Weird Tales*. In the 1940s Moore and Kuttner published regularly in periodicals such as *Astounding Science Fiction* and *Unknown Worlds*. Their careers together faltered somewhat towards the end of the decade, but by the mid-1950s they were again producing a substantial amount of science fiction and fantasy fiction. The couple continued writing together until Kuttner's death in 1958.

Moore's initial fame as a writer came in the mid-1930s with several tales featuring space marauder Northwest Smith. Moore introduced Smith to *Weird Tales* readers with "Shambleau," wherein the hero encounters a psychic vampire. Don D'Ammassa wrote in *Twentieth-Century Science-Fiction Writers* that "Shambleau" is a tale "with more literary quality than most of the stories in the magazines of that period." Darrell Schweitzer noted in *St. James Guide to Fantasy Writers* that the Northwest Smith tales contained "fantastic elements which were, by *Weird Tales* standards, undeniably 'weird' and very close to the supernatural."

While producing various Northwest Smith stories, Moore also commenced a series of tales featuring warrior-queen Jirel of Joiry. Jirel first appears in "The Black God's Kiss," in which she enters another dimension to kiss an idol that will, in turn, facilitate her defeat of an unfaithful lover. Schweitzer described Moore's Jirel stories as "unambiguously fantastic" and noted that "the emphasis is on the emotional, the romantic, and the overtly sexual." D'Ammassa confirmed that the tales possess "a raw power and fervor."

Among Moore's other solo writings is *Judgment Night*, the story of a female warrior who faces considerable intrigue while waiting to ascend the throne. D'Ammassa dismissed *Judgment Night* as "overly dramatic, poorly paced, and ultimately unconvincing," but a *New York Times* critic praised it as "a perfect showcase for [Moore's] romantic imagination at its absolute best."

After she began writing with Kuttner, Moore published little work under her own name. Schweitzer confirmed in *St. James Guide to Fantasy Writers* that "the two collaborated so intimately that neither could be sure who had written what." The couple's many novels together include *Earth's Last Citadel, Valley of the Flame*, and, under the joint pseudonym Lewis Padgett, *Well of the Worlds* and *Beyond Earth's Gates*. They also teamed for "The Quest of the Starstone," a tale uniting Northwest Smith and Jirel of Joiry. After Kuttner's death in 1958, Moore wrote for television.

The extent of Moore's contribution to her collaborations with Kuttner's remains difficult to determine. Some titles credited only to Kuttner have become recognized as joint efforts, and it is likely that continued research will further illuminate Moore's literary achievement. Schweitzer concluded, however, that "her small body of solo work is . . . sufficient to keep her name alive."

BIOGRAPHICAL/CRITICAL SOURCES:

BOOKS

Dictionary of Literary Biography, Volume 8: *Twentieth-Century American Science-Fiction Writers*, Gale (Detroit), 1981.

St. James Guide to Fantasy Writers, St. James Press (Detroit), 1996.

Twentieth-Century Science-Fiction Writers, 3rd edition, Gale, 1991.

Utter, Birgil, and Gordon Benson, Jr., *Catherine Lucille Moore and Henry Kuttner: A Marriage of Souls and Talent*, V. Utter, 1986.

PERIODICALS

New York Herald Tribune Book Review, January 25, 1953.

New York Times, January 11, 1953.

Saturday Review, June 6, 1953.*

* * *

MOORE, Doris Langley 1903-1989
(A Gentlewoman; Two Ladies of England, a joint pseudonym)

PERSONAL: Born in Liverpool, England; died February 24, 1989; married Robin Sugden Moore, 1926 (divorced, 1942); children: Pandora. *Education:* Attended convent schools in South Africa; studied classical languages with a private tutor in England. *Avocational interests:* Byroniana.

CAREER: Costume designer and writer. Museum of Costumes, Assembly Rooms, Bath, England, founder and advisor, 1955-74. Lecturer.

MEMBER: Royal Society of Literature (fellow).

AWARDS, HONORS: Officer, Order of the British Empire, 1971; Royal Society of Literature fellow, 1973; Rose Mary Crawshay Prize, British Academy, 1975.

WRITINGS:

ROMANCE NOVELS

A Winter's Passion, Heinemann (London), 1932.
The Unknown Eros, Secker & Warburg (London), 1935.
They Knew Her When: A Game of Snakes and Ladders, Rich & Cowan, 1938, published as *A Game of Snakes and Ladders,* Cassell (London), 1955.
Not at Home, Cassell, 1948.
All Done by Kindness, Cassell, 1951, Lippincott (Philadelphia), 1952.
My Caravaggio Style, Lippincott, 1959.

OTHER

(Translator) *Anacreon: Twenty-Nine Odes Rendered into English Verse,* Gerald Howe (London), 1926.
(Under pseudonym A Gentlewoman) *The Technique of the Love Affair,* Simon & Schuster, 1928, revised and enlarged edition, Pantheon (New York City), 1999.
Pandora's Letter Box: Being a Discourse on Fashionable Life, Gerald Howe, 1929.
(With June Moore under joint pseudonym Two Ladies of England) *The Bride's Book; or, Young Housewife's Compendium,* Gerald Howe, 1932, revised edition published under names June Moore and Doris Langley Moore as *Our Loving Duty,* Rich & Cowan (London), 1936.
(Editor) Edward de Pomiane, *Good Fare,* Gerald Howe, 1932.
(With June Moore) *The Pleasure of Your Company: A Textbook of Hospitality,* Gerald Howe, 1934, revised edition, Rich & Cowan, 1936.
E. Nesbit (biography), Benn (London), 1936, revised and enlarged edition, Chilton (Philadelphia, PA), 1966.
The Vulgar Heart: An Enquiry into the Sentimental Tendencies of Public Opinion, Cassell, 1945.
(Translator) Serge Lifar, *Carlotta Grisi,* Lehmann (London), 1947.
The Woman in Fashion, Batsford, 1949.
Pleasure: A Discursive Guide Book, Cassell, 1953.
The Child in Fashion, Batsford (London), 1953.
The Great Byron Adventure, Lippincott, 1959.
Dancing Is for Dopes (three-act play), Dramatic Publishing, 1960.
The Late Lord Byron: Posthumous Dramas, Lippincott, 1961.
Marie and the Duke of H—: The Daydream Love Affair of Marie Bashkirtseff (biography), Lippincott, 1966.
Fashion Through Fashion Plates, 1771-1970, Ward, Lock (London), 1971, C. N. Potter (New York City), 1972.
Lord Byron: Accounts Rendered, Harper, 1974.
Ada, Countess of Lovelace: Byron's Legitimate Daughter, Murray (London), 1977.
Doris Langley Moore's Book of Scraps: New Verses for Old Pictures (children's book), A. Deutsch (London), 1984.

Also author of film scripts, including "The Diary."

SIDELIGHTS: Doris Langley Moore was a versatile costume designer and writer with expertise in subjects ranging from fashion to Lord Byron, and her publications include volumes varying from self-help to romance. She published several novels that aim, as Karen Robertson noted in *Romance and Historical Writers,* to "celebrate the pleasures of connoisseurship and the satisfaction of art." Robertson added that Moore's novels "seriously investigate the nature of love, often from a contemporary woman's point of view."

In Moore's first novel, *A Winter's Passion,* the heroine overcomes her passion for her sister's lover after realizing her own artistic potential, while in *The Unknown Eros,* Moore's next novel, an artist realizes a profound understanding of love upon hearing a schoolboy sing. Robertson described *A Winter's Passion* and *The Unknown Eros* as "more overtly serious than the dazzlingly plotted comedies that follow."

Among Moore's ensuing novels are *They Knew Her When: A Game of Snakes and Ladders* (also published as *Snakes and Ladders*), wherein an actress finds herself alone in Egypt after World War I and works at a box office before meeting, and marrying, a duke, and *Not at All Home,* in which a self-righteous botanical artist gains a greater measure of humility through her interactions with a disrespectful tenant. Robertson related that both of these novels emphasize the "confrontation between honesty and hypocrisy," and she expressed special praise for *Not at All Home* as "the most satisfying of Moore's investigations of beauty, friendship, and love."

Other novels by Moore include *All Done by Kindness,* in which an art connoisseur thwarts a grubby gang eager to obtain recently found Renaissance artworks; and *My Caravaggio Style,* wherein a forger, resentful of his fiancee's interest in Lord Byron, prepares a manuscript intended as Byron's memoirs.

In addition to writing romance novels, Moore published several volumes of nonfiction, including fashion histories, self-help, and biographies. Her fashion writings include *Gallery of Fashion, 1790-1822* and *Fashion Through Fashion Plates, 1771-1970,* while her self-help publications include *The Technique of the Love Affair,* a pseudonymous 1928 volume—originally credited to "A Gentlewoman"—in which Moore provides advice to women eager to obtain a spouse. A *Time* reviewer, appraising a reprint of this work, deemed it "charming." Among Moore's other guides to behavior are *The Bride's Book; or, Young Housewife's Compendium,* written with June Moore under the joint pseudonym Two Ladies of England, and *The Pleasure of Your Company: A Text-Book of Hospitality,* also written with Moore.

As a biographer, Moore chronicled the lives of such figures as children's writer Edith Nesbit, Marie Bashkirtseff, and Lord Byron. Her publications on Byron, including *The Great Byron Adventure, Lord Byron: Accounts Rendered,* and *Ada, Countess of Lovelace: Byron's Legitimate Daughter,* inspired J. I. M. Steward to write, "She has made the ground [covering Byron and 'his circle'] her own, and has established upon it a claim to be among the most accomplished biographers of her time."

Moore's other endeavors include the founding of the Museum of Costume, where she served as an adviser from 1955 to 1974. Moore also designed costumes for films, and she exhibited costumes—culled from her extensive collection—on various television shows.

BIOGRAPHICAL/CRITICAL SOURCES:

BOOKS

Twentieth-Century Romance and Historical Writers, 3rd edition, St. James Press (Detroit, MI), 1994.

PERIODICALS

Atlantic Monthly, June, 1974; February, 1978.
New Statesman, July 5, 1974.
New Yorker, October 8, 1966; January 16, 1978.
New York Review of Books, May 18, 1978.
New York Times Book Review, October 8, 1967; December 25, 1977.
Time, February 15, 1999, p. 80.
Times Literary Supplement, February 2, 1967; October 14, 1977.

OBITUARIES:

PERIODICALS

Times (London), March 2, 1989.*

* * *

MOORE, Lorrie
See MOORE, Marie Lorena

* * *

MOORE, Marie Lorena 1957-
(Lorrie Moore)

PERSONAL: Born January 13, 1957, in Glens Falls, NY; daughter of Henry T., Jr. (an insurance company executive) and Jeanne (Day) Moore. *Education:* St. Lawrence University, B.A. (summa cum laude), 1978; Cornell University, M.F.A., 1982.

ADDRESSES: Office—English Department, University of Wisconsin—Madison, 600 North Park St., Madison, WI 53706. *Agent*—Melanie Jackson Agency, 1500 Broadway, Suite 2805, New York, NY 10036.

CAREER: Cornell University, Ithaca, NY, lecturer in English, 1982-84; University of Wisconsin—Madison, assistant professor, 1984-87, associate professor, 1987-91, professor of English, 1991—; writer.

MEMBER: PEN, Associated Writing Programs, Authors Guild, Authors League of America, Phi Beta Kappa.

AWARDS, HONORS: First prize, *Seventeen* magazine short-story contest, 1976, for "Raspberries"; Paul L.

Wolfe Memorial Prize for literature, St. Lawrence University, 1978; A. L. Andrews Prize, Cornell University, 1982, for "What Is Seized," "How to Be an Other Woman," and "The Kid's Guide to Divorce"; Associated Writing Programs finalist for short fiction, 1983, for *Self-Help;* Granville Hicks Memorial fellow, 1983; National Endowment for the Arts fellowship, 1989; Jack I. and Lillian L. Poses Creative Arts Citation in Fiction, Brandeis University, 1991; John Simon Guggenheim Memorial Foundation fellowship.

WRITINGS:

UNDER NAME LORRIE MOORE

Self-Help (short stories), Knopf (New York City), 1985.
Anagrams (novel), Knopf, 1986.
The Forgotten Helper (juvenile), Kipling Press (New York City), 1987.
Like Life (short stories), Knopf, 1990.
(Editor) *I Know Some Things: Stories about Childhood by Contemporary Writers* (anthology), Faber & Faber (London), 1992.
Who Will Run the Frog Hospital? (novel), Random House (New York City), 1994.

Contributor of stories, essays, and reviews to periodicals, including *Cosmopolitan, Seventeen, New Yorker, New York Times Book Review, Paris Review,* and *Ms.*

WORK IN PROGRESS: A novel.

SIDELIGHTS: Self-Help, Lorrie Moore's first book, is a collection of short stories that "examines the idea that lives can be improved like golf swings," according to *New York Times Book Review* critic Jay McInerney. In her book, Moore uses what McInerney calls "a distinctive, scalpel-sharp fictional voice" to produce "cohesive and moving" stories. He went on to say that "anyone who doesn't like it should consult a doctor." In the *New York Times,* Michiko Kakutani refers to the stories in *Self-Help* as "fine, funny and very moving pictures of contemporary life among the yuppies that help establish Miss Moore as a writer of enormous talent." She adds that Moore, like her characters, "possesses a wry, crackly voice" and "an askew sense of humor."

Moore's sense of humor also won her praise for *Like Life,* her second collection of short stories. "It is [Moore's] laid back sense of humor and the note of alar that lend these accomplished stories their wit and depth," writes Anna Vaux in the *Times Literary Supplement.* Calling Moore's sense of humor "wry" and "skittish," *Los Angeles Times Book Review* critic Merle Rubin nonetheless finds that Moore has "very little ability to create convincing characters or tell stories that invite us to suspend our disbelief as we read them or to brood upon them after they've been read." Other critics find Moore's characters more convincing. *New York Times Book Review* critic Stephen McCauley sees "a new richness and variety of characters" in *Like Life,* while Vaux finds that Moore's "women are high-spirited in their disappointments and alarming in their insights; her men are rarely so accomplished in the matter of perception. Their failure to grasp what is going on makes for some of the funnier moments here as well as some of the most surreal."

Moore once told *CA:* "*Self-Help* was written between 1980 and 1983. The second-person, mock-imperative narratives, of which there are six (out of nine), were written mostly as stylistic experiments: Let's see what happens when one eliminates the subject, leaves the verb shivering at the start of a clause; what happens when one appropriates the 'how-to' form for a fiction, for an irony, for a 'how-not-to.' I was interested in whatever tensions resulted when a writer foisted fictional experience off of the 'I' of the first person and onto the more generalized 'you' of the second—the vernacular 'one.'

"The second-person stories begin, ostensibly, to tell the generic tale, give the categorical advice, but become so entrenched in their own individuated detail that they succeed in telling only their own specific story, suggesting that although life is certainly not jokeless, it probably is remediless. In *Self-Help* even suicide and death are non-solutions. The self help proffered here, then, is perhaps only that of art itself, which, if you agree with Oscar Wilde, is quite useless. The first-person narratives in the collection tend to be longer and about parent-child relations and what hope for redemption may or may not reside within them."

BIOGRAPHICAL/CRITICAL SOURCES:

PERIODICALS

Los Angeles Times, June 3, 1985.
Los Angeles Times Book Review, June 3, 1990, p. 11.
New York Times, March 6, 1985.
New York Times Book Review, March 24, 1985; May 20, 1990, p. 7.
Times Literary Supplement, August 31, 1990, p. 917.
Tribune Books (Chicago), March 24, 1985.
Vanity Fair, September, 1985.*

MOORE, (James) Mavor 1919-

PERSONAL: Born March 8, 1919, in Toronto, Ontario, Canada; son of Francis John (a clergyman) and Dora (an actress; maiden name, Mavor) Moore; married Darwina Faessler, October 14, 1943 (divorced, 1969); married Phyllis Langstaff Grosskurth (a writer), October, 1969 (marriage ended, 1978); married Alexandra Browning (a singer and teacher), August 15, 1980; children: (first marriage) Dorothea, Rosalind, Marili, Charlotte; (third marriage) Jessica. *Education:* University of Toronto, B.A. (with first class honors), 1941.

ADDRESSES: Home—176 Moore Ave., Toronto, Ontario M4T 1V8, Canada. *Agent*—Canadian Speakers and Writers Service, 44 Douglas Crescent, Toronto, Ontario, Canada; and ACTAC Ltd., 16 Cadogan Lane, London SW1, England.

CAREER: Administrator, director, producer, composer, and actor. Actor on stage, radio, television, and screen, 1933-41; Canadian Broadcasting Corp. (CBC), Toronto, Ontario, radio feature producer, 1941-43, chief producer of CBC International, Montreal, Quebec, 1945-46, radio producer for Pacific region, Vancouver, British Columbia, 1946; New Play Society, Toronto, manager, 1946-50; CBC-TV, chief producer for English Network, 1950-53, assistant program director, 1954; New Play Society, manager, 1955-58; Mavor Moore Productions Ltd., Toronto, president, 1956-74; York University, Downsview, Ontario, professor of fine arts, theater, and English, 1974-84, professor emeritus, 1984—, chair of university board of governors, 1974-75, chair of Faculty of Fine Arts Council, 1978-79; University of Victoria, Victoria, British Columbia, adjunct professor, 1984—. Teacher at Academy of Radio Arts, Toronto, 1946-49; guest lecturer at various institutions, including University of Toronto, University of Guelph, University of Lethbridge, University of Calgary, Simon Fraser University, University of British Columbia, Western University, McMaster University, Laurentian University, Memorial University of Newfoundland, Queen's University (Kingston, Ontario), Mount Allison University, Brock University, Cornell University, Oregon State University, University of North Carolina, Raleigh, State University of New York College at Plattsburgh, New School for Social Research, and Washington State University. Executive producer, Information Division of the United Nations, New York City, 1946-50 and 1955-60; producer and director at various theatres and festivals, including Crest Theatre, Vancouver Festival, Vancouver Playhouse, and Neptune Theatre (Halifax, Nova Scotia); Stratford Ontario Festival, member of board of directors, 1953-54, member of senate, 1955-74; founding president, Canadian Theatre Centre, 1955-56; producer for Canadian Players, 1957-58; stage director, Canadian Opera Company, 1959-61; governor, National Theatre School of Canada, 1960-73; general director, Confederation Centre, Charlottetown, Prince Edward Island, 1963-65; president, Legendrama (Sound and Light) Ltd., 1964-67; founding artistic director, Charlottetown Festival, 1964-68; founding general director, St. Lawrence Centre for the Arts, Toronto, 1965- 70. Host of *Performance,* CBC-TV, 1981-84; actor in motion pictures, including *Thresholds,* 1982, *The Killing Fields,* 1983, and *Shell Game,* 1985. Chair, UNESCO Conference on Education, 1949; member of executive committee, Canadian Conference of the Arts, 1962-70; co-chair, National Centennial Conference, 1965-67; member of board of directors, Fathers of Confederation Foundation, 1968-74; Canada Council, member, 1974-79, chair, 1979-83; member of advisory board, Center for Inter-American Studies (New York City), 1982-84, and Cultural Council of the Americas Society, 1983-84; member of executive committee, Canadian Music Centre, beginning in 1984; honorary chair, Canada-Israel Cultural Foundation, beginning in 1984; national president, Youth and Music Canada (Jeunesses Musicales), 1985—. *Military service:* Canadian Army Intelligence Corps, 1943-45; became captain.

MEMBER: Dramatists Guild, Guild of Canadian Playwrights (founding chair, 1977-78), Canadian Association for Adult Education (member of executive committee, 1949-52), United Nations Association of Canada (member of executive committee, 1947-50).

AWARDS, HONORS: Peabody Awards, 1947, 1949, and 1957; Television Award from Canadian Association of Authors and Artists, 1955; Canadian Centennial Medal, 1967; D.Litt., York University, 1969; Officer, Order of Canada, 1973; Queen's Medal, 1977; LL.D., Mount Allison University, 1982; John Drainie Award, Association of Canadian Television and Radio Artists, 1982; LL.D. from Memorial University of Newfoundland, 1984; D.Litt., University of Guelph, 1985; Diplome d'Honneur, Canadian Conference of the Arts, 1985; Companion, Order of Canada, 1988.

WRITINGS:

PUBLISHED PLAYS

Yesterday the Children Were Dancing (adapted from Gratien Gelinas's play; produced in Charlottetown, Prince Edward Island, 1967; broadcast by CBC-TV, 1969), Clarke, Irwin (Toronto), 1968.

(Translator) *Tit-coq,* Clarke, Irwin, 1967.

Getting In (broadcast on television, 1968; broadcast on television as *The Interviewer,* 1973), Samuel French (New York City), 1973.

The Pile (broadcast on radio, 1970), published in *A Collection of Canadian Plays,* Volume 2, edited by Rolf Kalman, Simon & Pierre, 1973.

Inside Out (broadcast on television, 1971), published in *A Collection of Canadian Plays,* Volume 2, edited by Rolf Kalman, Simon & Pierre, 1973.

The Store (play; broadcast on television, 1972), published in *A Collection of Canadian Plays,* Volume 2, edited by Rolf Kalman, Simon & Pierre, 1973.

Come Away, Come Away (broadcast on television, 1972), published in *Encounter,* edited by Eugene Benson, Methuen (Toronto), 1969.

The Argument (broadcast in 1970, published in *Performing Arts in Canada,* winter, 1973.

(With Frank R. Scott) *The Roncarelli Affair* (broadcast on television, 1974), published in *The Play's the Thing: Four Original Television Dramas* edited by Tony Gifford, Macmillan (Toronto), 1975.

La Roulotte aux poupees, published in *Joie de Vivre,* Copp Clark, 1976.

Customs (broadcast in 1973), published in *Cues and Entrances,* edited by Henry Beissel, Gage Publishing (Toronto), 1977.

Six Plays by Mavor Moore (contains *The Apology, The Store, The Pile, Getting In, The Argument,* and *Come Away, Come Away*), Talonbooks (Vancouver), 1989.

UNPUBLISHED PLAYS

"I Know You," produced in Toronto, 1944.

"Spring Thaw" (revue; includes "Togetherness"), produced in Toronto, 1947.

"Who's Who," produced in Toronto, 1949.

(And composer) "The Optimist" (musical adapted from Voltaire's *Candide*), broadcast by CBC-Radio, 1952; produced in Toronto, 1955; broadcast by CBC-TV as "The Best of All Possible Worlds," 1968.

"Sunshine Town" (musical adapted from Stephen Leacock's *Sunshine Sketches of a Little Town*), broadcast on television as "The Hero of Mariposa," 1954; produced in Toronto, 1956; broadcast by CBC-TV, 1957.

"The Ottawa Man" (adapted from Nikolai Gogol's *The Inspector General*), broadcast by CBC-TV, 1959; produced in Toronto, 1961.

(With Jacques Languirand and Harry Somers) "Louis Riel" (opera; libretto by Moore and Languirand; music by Somers), produced in Toronto, 1967; produced in Washington, DC, 1975.

"Man, Inc." (adapted from Jacques Languirand's play), produced in Toronto, 1969.

"Johnny Belinda" (musical; adapted from Elmer Harris's play), produced at Charlottetown Festival, 1969; broadcast by CBC-TV, 1976.

(With Harry Freedman) "Abracadabra" (opera; libretto by Moore; music by Freedman), performed in British Columbia, 1979.

"Love and Politics" (musical; adapted from Nicholas Flood Davin's play *The Fair Grit*), produced in St. Catharines, Ontario, 1979.

"Fauntleroy" (musical; adapted from Frances Hodgson Burnett's novel *Little Lord Fauntleroy*), produced at Charlottetown Festival, 1980.

(Translator) Moliere, "The Imaginary Invalid," produced in Vancouver at University of British Columbia, 1984.

"Ghost Dance" (opera), produced in Toronto, 1985.

"A Christmas Carol" (musical; adapted from Charles Dickens's novel), produced in Vancouver, 1988.

TELEVISION PLAYS

The Inspector General (adapted from Gogol's play), CBC-TV, 1952.

To Tell the Truth (adapted from Morley Callaghan's play), CBC-TV, 1952.

The Coventry Miracle Play, CBC, 1952.

The Black Eye (adapted from James Bridie's play), CBC-TV, 1954.

Catch a Falling Star, CBC-TV, 1955.

The Man Who Caught Bullets, CBC-TV, 1958.

The Master of Santiago (adapted from Henry de Montherlant's play, CBC-TV, 1959.

The Crucible (adapted from Arthur Miller's play), CBC-TV, 1959.

The Well, CBC, 1960.

Wise Guy (adapted from Christopher Isherwood's story), CBC-TV, 1961.

The Man Born to Be King (adapted from Dorothy L. Sayer's radio play), CBC-TV, 1961.

Mary of Scotland (adapted from Maxwell Anderson's play), CBC-TV, 1966.

The Puppet Caravan (adapted from Marie Claire Blais's play *La Roulotte aux poupees*), CBC-TV, 1967.

Enoch Soames (adapted from a story by Max Beerbohm), CBC-TV, 1967.

The Lyons Mail (adapted from the Charles Reade's play), CBC-TV, 1973.

RADIO PLAYS

Christmas Carol-1941 (adapted from Charles Dickens' novel *A Christmas Carol*), CBC Radio, 1941.
The Great Flood, CBC Radio, 1948.
William Tell (adapted from Friedrich von Schiller's play), CBC Radio, 1949.
To Tell the Truth (adapted from Morley Callaghan's play), CBC Radio, 1949.
Call It a Day (adapted from Dodie Smith's play), CBC Radio, 1950.
The First Mrs. Fraser (adapted from St. John Ervine's play), CBC Radio, 1951.
The Drums Are Out (adapted from John Coulter's play), CBC Radio, 1951.
The Son, CBC Radio, 1958.
(With others) *Old Moore's Almanac,* CBC Radio, 1958.
Don Juan in Hell (adapted from George Bernard Shaw's play *Man and Superman*), CBC Radio, 1959.
Our Emblem Dear, CBC Radio, 1959.
Catch My Death, CBC Radio, 1959.
Gulliver's Travels (adapted from Jonathan Swift's novel), CBC Radio, 1959.
Brave New World (adapted from Aldous Huxley's novel), CBC Radio, 1960.
Fact or Fancy (adapted from a work by Oscar Wilde), CBC Radio, 1961.
The Rise and Fall of Witchcraft, CBC Radio, 1961.
The Cachalot (adapted from Edwin John Pratt's poem), CBC Radio, 1961.
Fast Forward, CBC Radio, 1968.
A Matter of Timing, CBC Radio, 1971.
Freak, CBC Radio, 1975.

RECORDINGS

The Store, Earplay, 1975.
Customs, Earplay, 1975.
Inside Out, and Other Stories by Mavor Moore (includes *A Matter of Timing, Come Away, Come Away, The Pile, Inside Out,* and *Getting In*), CBC International, 1979.
(With Jacques Languirand) *Louis Riel,* Centrediscs, 1985.

OTHER

And What Do You Do?: A Short Guide to the Trades and Professions (poems), Dent (Toronto), 1960.
(Editor) *The Awkward Stage: The Ontario Theatre Report,* Methuen (Toronto), 1969.
(Author of introduction) Murray Edwards, *A Stage in Our Past,* Methuen, 1970.
(Editor with Roy Bentley) *Four Canadian Playwrights: Robertson Davies, Gratien Gelinas, James Reaney, George Ryga,* Holt (Toronto), 1973.
(Editor) *An Anthology of Canadian Plays,* New Press (Toronto), 1973.
(Author of introduction) *Two Plays by George Ryga,* Turnstone Press, 1982.
Slipping on the Verge: The Performing Arts in Canada with Theatre as a Case Study, Canadian Embassy (Washington, DC), 1983.
(Contributor) *Cultures and Writers,* Multi- Heritage Alliance of Toronto, 1983,
(Author of introduction) Arthur L. Murphy, *Three Bluenose Plays,* Lancelot Press (Hantsport, Nova Scotia), 1984.
(Contributor) *Organizational Culture,* Sage Publications, 1985.
(Contributor) *Two Hundred Years,* Queen's Printer, 1985.
Reinventing Myself (memoir), 1994.

Work represented in anthologies, including *Twentieth-Century Canadian Poetry,* Ryerson, 1953; and *The Arts in Canada,* Macmillan (Toronto), 1958. Theater critic for *Canadian Commentator,* 1956-57, and Toronto *Telegram,* 1958-60. Author of column in Toronto *Globe and Mail,* 1980s. Contributor to periodicals, including *Canadian Drama, Maclean's, Canadian Forum, Saturday Night, Connoisseur,* and *Canadian Poetry.* Member of editorial board, *Canadian Theatre Review,* 1974-78, and *On-Stage Studies,* 1982—.

SIDELIGHTS: Mavor Moore is a Canadian actor, producer, composer, and writer whose output includes dozens of plays—for stage, radio, and television—and several published works. Paula Sperdakos, writing in *Canadian Theatre Review,* described Moore as an "artistic polymath" and declared that he "has been involved in virtually all aspects of the development of theatre in [Canada] since the late 1930s." Arnold Edinborough, meanwhile, summarized him in *Contemporary Dramatists* as "Canada's most ubiquitous man-about-theatre."

Moore was born in 1919 in Toronto. His mother had worked as an actress, and she readily instilled in him a love for the theatre. While still in college, Moore began working as a writer and actor for the Canadian Broadcasting Corporation (CBC), which provides television and radio service across Canada. He also joined a theatrical troupe that his mother had founded for performing at various schools in Ontario.

In the early 1940s Moore began producing documentaries for the CBC. His work there was interrupted by a stint in the Canadian Army during World War II, after which he became a producer for CBC International in Montreal. Around this time Moore also provided various administrative services for his mother's New Play Society. With the company, Moore also acted regularly, and he even wrote the company's *Spring Thaw,* which Chris Johnson, writing in the *Dictionary of Literary Biography,* described as an "extremely popular revue [that] was an annual event for many years and launched the careers of many Canadian singers and comedians."

Moore followed *Spring Thaw* with *Who's Who,* his first full-length work, which the New Play Society produced in 1949. This play, in which a dead husband and father is depicted in wildly varying recollections, exploits notions of perspective and reality and is, as Johnson writes, "characteristic of much of Moore's subsequent work."

While involved with the New Play Society, Moore also worked as an executive producer for the United Nations. In addition, he maintained his association with the CBC, serving as chief television producer in the early 1950s and becoming an assistant program director in 1954. During this period, he also teamed with his mother to establish the Stratford Shakespeare Festival, where he appeared as a performer in 1954. Furthermore, he supplied reviews for the Toronto *Telegram* and assumed duties as founding chairman of the Canadian Theatre Center.

Despite the demands of maintaining careers as an actor, producer, and critic, Moore managed to generate a considerable amount of dramatic writing. In 1952, for instance, he adapted Voltaire's *Candide* as *The Best of All Possible Worlds,* and in 1956 he supplied both the book and music for *The Hero of Mariposa,* which he derived from Stephen Leacock's *Sunshine Sketches of a Little Town.*

In the ensuing decades, Moore became involved with other performing groups, including the Canadian Opera Company (COC), where he served as a stage director in the late 1950s and early 1960s. Only a few years after leaving the company, Moore collaborated with Jacques Languirand on the libretto for composer Harry Somers's opera *Louis Riel,* which the COC performed in 1967. Johnson, in his *Dictionary of Literary Biography* entry on Moore, calls *Louis Riel* "one of Moore's most ambitious pieces of dramatic writing."

After completing the ambitious *Louis Riel,* Moore wrote several one-act plays of a rather experimental nature. Johnson wrote that these plays "are distinguished by a focus on idea and by shifts in the audience's perception of the dramatic reality." Among these plays are *Come Away, Come Away,* wherein a man befriends a girl who is eventually revealed to be dead; *The Pile,* in which a businessman and an engineer discuss ways to eliminate an unspecified mound, which may actually be the audience; and *The Store,* wherein a store manager finds himself confronted by an angry customer, one revealed, according to Johnson, as " 'the personification of the manager's own neurosis' and blamed for her life's troubles." Sperdakos describes these plays as "the kinds of richly subtextual dramatic exercises that an actor would find challenging . . . and that would amuse and intrigue an audience."

Moore's ensuing works have encompassed more adaptations, including a musical rendering of Charles Dickens' *Christmas Carol* and a staging of Frances Hodgson Burnett's *Little Lord Fauntleroy.* But he has also continued to generate more venturesome fare, notably the two-character drama *The Apology,* which derives from Plato's account of Socrates's trial. Johnson speculates that Moore's "future writing will be divided between popular musical entertainment and pithy drama of ideas."

Among Moore's other writings is *Reinventing Myself,* an autobiography recounting his first fifty years. According to Brian Fawcett, in his *Books in Canada* review, Moore's memoir is "a fascinating book." Writing in *Quill & Quire,* Douglas Fetherling contends that thc memoir reveals "precious little about the private Mavor Moore," but he acknowledges that it contains much about "the remarkable generation that built most of today's Canadian cultural infrastructure." Fawcett, meanwhile, notes that *Reinventing Myself* addresses Moore's lifelong battle with manic depression, and he sees the autobiographical volume as "an epic tale of courage and resourcefulness."

BIOGRAPHICAL/CRITICAL SOURCES:

BOOKS

Bryden, Ronald, editor, *Whittaker's Theatre: A Critic Looks at Stages in Canada and Thereabouts,* Whittaker Project, 1985.

Contemporary Dramatists, 5th edition, St. James Press (Detroit, MI), 1993.

Dictionary of Literary Biography, Volume 88: *Canadian Writers, 1920-1959, Second Series,* Gale (Detroit, MI), 1989.

Edmonstone, Wayne, *Nathan Cohen: The Making of a Critic,* Lester & Orpen, 1977.

PERIODICALS

Books in Canada, March, 1990, pp. 34-35; summer, 1994, pp. 44-45.
Canadian Drama/L'Art Dramatique Canadien, Volume 8, 1982, pp. 129-44; Volume 9, 1983, pp. 254-67, 343-51.
Canadian Theatre Review, winter, 1978, pp. 94-98; fall, 1980, pp. 18-33; summer, 1991, pp. 111-13.
Quill & Quire, June, 1994, p. 6.
Theatre History in Canada, spring, 1991, pp. 97-104.
Theatrum, June-August, 1990, p. 33.
Variety, November 2, 1992, p. 32.*

* * *

MORGAN, Rebecca
See FORREST, Richard (Stockton)

* * *

MORSE, Philip M(cCord) 1903-1985

PERSONAL: Born August 6, 1903, in Shreveport, LA; died September 5, 1985, in Concord, MA; son of Allen Crafts (a telephone engineer) and Edith Frances (McCord) Morse; married Annabelle Hopkins, April 26, 1929; children: Conrad Philip, Annabella (Mrs. Hugh Fowler). *Education:* Case Institute of Technology (now Case Western Reserve University), B.Sc., 1926; Princeton University, M.A., 1927, Ph.D., 1929. *Politics:* Independent. *Religion:* Presbyterian. *Avocational interests:* Mountain climbing, hiking, genealogy, philately, reading history and science fiction.

CAREER: Radioelectric Shop, Cleveland, OH, in sales, 1923-24; *Cleveland Commercial,* Cleveland, author of radio column, 1924-25; University of Michigan, Ann Arbor, research assistant, 1928; research physicist at Bell Telephone Laboratories, 1929; Princeton University, Princeton, NJ, instructor in physics, 1929-30; University of Munich, Munich, Germany, Rockefeller international fellow, 1930-31; Cambridge University, Cambridge, England, Rockefeller international fellow, 1930; Massachusetts Institute of Technology, Cambridge, assistant professor, 1931-34, associate professor, 1934-39, professor of physics, 1939-73, professor emeritus, 1973-85, director of U.S. Navy underwater sound project, 1940-42, director of Computation Center, 1955-67, chairman of faculty, 1958-60, director of Operations Research Center, 1958-69; writer, 1973-85. Lecturer at University of Michigan, summer, 1930, Armed Forces Staff College, 1948, Naval War College, 1950-53, University of California, Los Angeles, 1951, Oxford University, 1957, St. Olaf College, Carleton College, Hope College, and Manhattan College, all 1958-61, University of California, Berkeley, 1962, 1966, and University of Chicago and University of North Carolina, both 1969; Sigma Xi lecturer at University of Pennsylvania, 1954, and Tufts University, 1956; Phi Beta Kappa lecturer at Duke University, 1956; visiting lecturer at University of Athens, 1961; senior Fulbright lecturer in Mexico, 1962, and Australia, 1971. Director of Brookhaven National Laboratory, 1946-48; deputy director and director of research at Weapons Systems Evaluation Group, 1949-50; member of steering committee of U.S. Navy Operations Evaluation Group, 1952-56; member of board of trustees of RAND Corp., 1948-49, 1950-62, Institute for Defense Analyses, 1956-61, Council on Library Resources, 1961-85, and Analytic Services, Inc., 1962-85; member of board of directors of Adage, Inc., 1960-68, Control Data Corp., 1966-85, and Teknekron, 1969-85. Chairman of National Research Council committee on sound control, 1940-44, and committee on revision of mathematical tables, 1954-64; member of Naval Research Advisory Committee, 1946-48; member of U.S. Army Ordnance Research Advisory Board, 1951-58, applied mathematics advisory committee of National Bureau of Standards, 1952-56 (chairman of advisory panel to Technical Analysis Division, 1967-70), National Science Foundation advisory panels (chairman of Advisory Panel on University Computing Facilities, 1961-64), and President's Conference on Automobile Traffic, 1958; chairman of North Atlantic Treaty Organization advisory panel on operations research, 1960-64, and Organization for Economic Cooperation and Development advisory panel on operations research, 1962-68 (conference chairman, 1965-66); member of computation advisory panel of Honeywell Corp., 1963-64; member of advisory panel of U.S. Army Development Command, 1965-66; member of U.S. Department of Commerce panel on telecommunication sciences, 1966; member of scientific advisory council of Texas Christian University Research Foundation, 1967-70. Speaker at international conferences; consultant to Arthur D. Little, Inc., Corning Glass Co., and Philco Corp.

MEMBER: International Federation of Operations Research Societies (secretary-general, 1961-64), American Physical Society (fellow; chairman of New England section, 1940-41; member of council, 1947-50; vice president, 1971-72; president, 1972-73), American

Academy of Arts and Sciences (fellow), Acoustical Society of America (fellow; vice president, 1946-48; president, 1950-51), American Institute of Physics (member of board of governors, 1948-50, 1953-55; chairman of board of governors, 1975-80), Research Society of America (member of board of trustees, 1951-53), Operations Research Society of America (member of founding committee, 1951-52; president, 1952-53), National Academy of Sciences (fellow), Union of Concerned Scientists (chairman of financial committee, 1969), Physical Society of London (fellow), Sigma Xi, Tau Beta Pi, Cosmos Club.

AWARDS, HONORS: Rockefeller Foundation fellowship, 1930-31; D.Sc. from Case Institute of Technology (now Case Western Reserve University), 1940; distinguished service award from U.S. Navy Bureau of Ordnance, 1945; U.S. Presidential Medal for Merit, 1946; Alfred P. Sloan Award from Massachusetts Institute of Technology, 1956; silver certificate from Acoustical Society of America, 1961, gold medal, 1973; silver medal from Operational Research Society (England), 1965; Lanchester Prize from Operations Research Society of America, 1969, Kimball Prize, 1974.

WRITINGS:

(With Edward U. Condon) *Quantum Mechanics,* McGraw, 1929.

Vibration and Sound, McGraw, 1936, 2nd edition, 1948.

(With J. A. Stratton, L. J. Chu, and R. A. Hunter) *Elliptical Cylinder and Spheroidal Wave Functions,* Wiley, 1941.

(With George E. Kimball) *Methods of Operations Research,* Wiley, revised edition, 1951.

(With Herman Feshbach) *Methods of Theoretical Physics,* Parts I-II, McGraw, 1953.

(With Huseyin Yilmaz) *Tables for the Variational Determination of Atomic Wave Functions,* M.I.T. Press, 1956.

Queues, Inventories and Maintenance, Wiley, 1958.

(Editor) *Notes on Operations Research,* M.I.T. Press, 1959.

Thermal Physics, Benjamin Co., 1962, 2nd edition, 1969.

(Editor with Laura W. Bacon) *Operations Research for Public Systems,* M.I.T. Press, 1967.

Your Ancestors, privately printed, 1967.

(With K. Uno Ingard) *Theoretical Acoustics,* McGraw, 1968.

Library Effectiveness: A Systems Approach, M.I.T. Press, 1968.

Nuclear, Particle, and Many-Body Physics, Academic Press, 1972.

In at the Beginnings: A Physicist's Life (autobiography), M.I.T. Press, 1977.

Methods of Operations Research, Peninsula, 1980.

CONTRIBUTOR

F. E. Grubbs and others, editors, *Transactions of Symposia on Pure and Applied Mathematics,* Volume II, Wiley, 1955.

Edward U. Condon and Hugh Odishaw, editors, *McGraw-Hill Handbook of Physics,* McGraw, 1958.

R. E. Langer, editor, *Frontiers of Numerical Mathematics,* University of Wisconsin Press, 1960.

Siegfried Fluegge, editor, *Handbuch der Physik,* Volume XI, Part I, Springer-Verlag, 1961.

Russell L. Ackoff, editor, *Progress in Operations Research,* Volume I, Wiley, 1961.

W. F. Freiberger and William Prager, editors, *Applications of Digital Computers,* Ginn, 1963.

Robert E. Machol, editor, *System Engineering Handbook,* McGraw, 1965.

Carl F. J. Overhage and R. Joyce Harman, *INTREX Report on a Planning Conference on Information Transfer Experiments,* M.I.T. Press, 1965.

Jacinto Steinhardt, editor, *Science and the Modern World,* Plenum, 1966.

Per Olav Lowdin, editor, *Quantum Theory of Atoms, Molecules, and the Solid State,* Academic Press, 1966.

Guenter Menges, editor, *Beitrage zur Unternehmenforschung: Gegenwartiger Stand und Entwicklungstendenzen,* Physica-Verlag, 1969.

Grace J. Kelleher, editor, *The Challenge to Systems Analysis: Public Policy and Social Change,* Wiley, 1970.

Contributor of nearly one hundred articles to scientific journals. Associate editor of *Technology Review,* 1946-50; editor of *Annals of Physics,* 1956-80; member of editorial board of *Journal of Mathematics and Physics,* 1959-68, and *Science,* 1960-64; member of board of editors of American Physical Society, 1940-42.

SIDELIGHTS: Philip M. Morse, a physicist, educator, and author, taught physics at Massachusetts Institute of Technology for more than fifty years. He also served as the first director of Brookhaven National Laboratory, the nuclear research facility affiliated with the Atomic Energy Commission. Associated with numerous military and scientific advisory organizations, Morse edited the *Annals of Physics* for more than twenty years, and served on the editorial board of *Science.* He received a U.S. Presidential Medal for Merit for his activities during World War II as head of a civilian committee organized to evaluate the U.S. anti-submarine program. His books include *Vibration and Sound, Thermal Physics, Methods of Operations Research,* and the autobiography *In at the Beginnings: A Physicist's Life.*

BIOGRAPHICAL/CRITICAL SOURCES:

BOOKS

Feshbach, Herman and K. Uno Ingard, editors, *In Honor of Philip M. Morse,* M.I.T. Press, 1969.

Morse, Philip M., *In at the Beginnings: A Physicist's Life,* M.I.T. Press, 1977.

OBITUARIES:

PERIODICALS

New York Times, September 13, 1985.*

* * *

MOYES, Patricia
See HASZARD, Patricia Moyes

* * *

MYRDAL, Alva Reimer 1902-1986

PERSONAL: Born January 31, 1902, in Uppsala, Sweden; died after a long illness, February 1, 1986, in Ersta (some sources say Stockholm), Sweden; daughter of Albert (a building contractor) and Lova (Larsson) Reimer; married Karl Gunnar Myrdal (an economist and writer), October 8, 1924; children: Jan, Sissela, Kaj. *Education:* University of Stockholm, B.A., 1924; University of Geneva, graduate study, 1930-31; University of Uppsala, M.A., 1934. *Politics:* Social Democrat. *Religion:* Lutheran ("not practicing"). *Avocational interests:* Reading, cooking, foreign travel, theater, and walking, cycling, or motor tours.

CAREER: Workers Education Association, Stockholm, Sweden, teacher, 1924-32; Central Prison, Stockholm, psychological assistant, 1932-34; Training College for Preschool Teachers, Stockholm, founder and director, 1935-48; United Nations, New York City, principal director of department of social affairs, 1949-50, director of UNESCO department of social sciences, 1951-55; Government of Sweden, ambassador to India and minister to Ceylon, 1955-61, minister to Burma, 1955-58, ambassador to Nepal, 1960-61, ambassador-at-large, 1961-66, member of Swedish Parliament (Senate), 1962-70, cabinet minister for disarmament, 1966-73, and for church affairs, 1969-73; Center for the Study of Democratic Institutions, Santa Barbara, CA, visiting fellow, 1973-74; Massachusetts Institute of Technology, Cambridge, visiting professor of sociology, 1974-75; Wellesley College, Wellesley, MA, Visiting Distinguished Slater Professor of Sociology, 1976; Institute for Research on Poverty, Madison, WI, research fellow, 1977. Service to United Nations includes member of Swedish delegation to General Assembly, 1962-73, chief of Swedish delegation to disarmament conference in Geneva, 1962-73, chairperson of expert group on South Africa, 1964, deputy leader, 1967-73, and chairperson of Committee on Disarmament and Development, 1972. Chairperson of Swedish Civic Organization for Cultural Relief in Europe, 1943-48, government committee on organization of social information services, 1946, International Peace Research Institute, 1965-66, Commission on Disestablishment of the Swedish State Church, 1968-72, Commission on Studies of the Future, 1971-72, and delegation for expanding international laws against brutality in war, 1972-73; member of board of directors of Stockholm School for Social Work, 1946-48.

MEMBER: International Federation of Business and Professional Women (vice-chairperson, 1938-47), Swedish Federation of Business and Professional Women (chairperson, 1935-38 and 1940-42), World Council on Preschool Education (chairperson, 1941-49), World Federation of United Nations Associations (executive member, 1948-50).

AWARDS, HONORS: Rockefeller Foundation fellowship, 1929-30, for travel in the United States; LL.D. from Mount Holyoke College, 1950, and University of Edinburgh, 1964; Ph.D. from University of Leeds, 1962; D.H.L. from Columbia University, 1965, and Temple University, 1968; D.D. from Gustavus Adophus University, 1971; other honorary degrees from Brandeis University, 1974, University of Gothenburg, 1975, and University of East Anglia, 1976. West German Peace Prize, 1970; Wateler Prize from Hague Academy of International Peace, 1973; prize from Royal Swedish Institute of Technology, 1975; Monismanien Prize, 1976, for protection of civil liberties; gold medal from Royal Swedish Academy of Science,

1977; Albert Einstein Peace Prize; People's Peace Prize; Nobel Peace Prize, 1982.

WRITINGS:

(With husband, Gunnar Myrdal) *Kris i befolkningsfraegan* (title means "Crisis in the Population Question"), A. Bonnier, 1934.

Nation and Family: The Swedish Experiment in Democratic Family and Population Policy, Harper, 1941, 2nd edition, M.I.T. Press, 1965.

(With Gunnar Myrdal) *Kontakt med America* (title means "Contact with America"), A. Bonnier, 1941.

Women in the Community, TARP (Copenhagen, Denmark), 1943.

Kommentarer (title means "Comments on World Affairs"), A. Bonnier, 1944.

Efterkrigsplanering (title means "Postwar Planning"), Informationsbyraan Mellanfolkligt samarbete foer fred Svenska Kommitten, 1944.

(With Paul Vincent) *Are We Too Many?,* Bureau of Current Affairs, UNESCO (London, England), 1950.

(With Arthur J. Altmeyer and Dean Rusk) *America's Role in International Social Welfare,* Columbia University Press, 1955.

(With Viola Klein) *Women's Two Roles: Home and Work,* Routledge & Kegan Paul, 1956, 2nd edition, 1968.

Vaart ansvar foer de fattiga folken: Utvecklingsproblem i social naerbild (title means "Our Responsibility for the Poor Peoples: Development Problems at Close View"), Raben & Sjoegren, 1961.

(Contributor) Andrew W. Cordier and Wilder Foote, editors, *The Quest for Peace,* Columbia University, 1962.

Disarmament and the United Nations, Columbia University Press, 1965.

(With Solly Zuckerman and Lester B. Pearson) *The Control of Proliferation: Three Views,* Institute for Strategic Studies (London, England), 1966.

Oekad jaemlikhet, Prisma, 1969, abridged edition translated by Roger Lind published as *Towards Equality,* Prisma, 1971.

A Non-Aligned Look at the Future of Disarmament, Banco d'Italio (Rome, Italy), 1970.

Stickprovt paa Storbrittanien (title means "Cross Section of Great Britain"), A. Bonnier, 1972.

The Game of Disarmament, Pantheon, 1977.

Wars, Weapons, and Everyday Violence, University of New Hampshire, 1977.

Solidaritaet im Zwischenstaatlichen und welweiten Bersich (title means, "Solidarity in the International and Worldwide Field"), Evangelischer Kirchenbag (Berlin, Germany), 1977.

(With Kalevi Sorsa) *Steps Towards European Nuclear Disarmament: Two Papers for the Rome Consultation on European Nuclear Disarmament, Sponsored by the Signatories to the Russell Appeal and the Bertrand Russell Peace Foundation,* with an introduction by Ken Coates, Spokesman (Nottingham, UK), 1981.

(With others) *Forskolan: 80-Talets Viktigaste Skola,* Tiden (Stockholm), 1982.

(With others) *80'ernes Udfordring,* Politisk Revy (Copenhagen), 1982.

Also author of *City Children,* 1935, and *Disarmament: Reality or Illusion?,* 1965. Contributor to magazines, including *Parents' Magazine, Independent Woman, Scientific American, Foreign Policy,* and *Bulletin of Atomic Scientists.* Co-editor of *Morgonbris,* 1936-38; editor of *Via Suecia,* 1945-46, and *Round Table on Social Problems,* 1946-48.

SIDELIGHTS: Alva Myrdal served as a government official, diplomat, administrator, sociologist, and educator. The author of pioneering works in women's rights, population control, and social philosophy, Myrdal also wrote on possibly the most critical subject of the 1970s and 1980s—nuclear disarmament. Critics praised Myrdal's *The Game of Disarmament,* published in 1977, as "eloquent," "magnificent," and "a disenthralling masterpiece."

Herbert Mitgang wrote in the *New York Times:* "With disarmament talks coming up again, this could be one of the turning-point studies on the international agenda. I cannot imagine a more significant book,whose theme is nothing less than life or death, coming out this year."

Mitgang called *The Game of Disarmament* "both a primer and a sophisticated work." Not only did Myrdal cut through the technical, obtuse language of the military experts to expose meanings to the people who would be, as Mitgang wrote, "on the receiving end of the newly programmed final solution," but she was commended for offering possible solutions for scaling down the arms race.

Although, according to Emma Rothschild, Myrdal admitted to "a gradually increasing feeling of near despair," Rothschild found that "her values belie this sense. Her words—and her experience as Sweden's minister of disarmament, acting with moral courage in the real world of disarmament negotiations—break the set of preconceptions that surround U.S. arms policy.

I expect that most of Carter's defense advisers will read her book. I hope they see how different her way would be."

Charles L. Mee, Jr., had unqualified praise for Myrdal. He wrote that she had "labored like Sisyphus on behalf of disarmament," and that her life was "a dignified and eloquent performance in the theatre of the absurd." He concluded: "Alva Myrdal unquestionably deserves the Nobel Prize—no matter what. And I put my trust in her, and luck, and existentialism."

Myrdal told *CA:* "The prophecies I had to make in my book, *The Game of Disarmament,* were somber, to say the least. They had to be to be true to reality. But my pessimism has rather become reinforced by experiences in 1977. SALT negotiations have proceeded so haltingly. And even if a SALT II agreement is reached, it will not stifle but may actually promote the most dangerous phase of the arms race: the qualitative, technological competition for ever more sophisticated, expressive and brutal weapons, called more 'efficient,' that is: efficient for killing fellow men.

"This arms race is conducted at accelerated speed by both superpowers. Simultaneously an enormous spread of weapons to many countries is taking place. The trade in arms is a breathtaking multi-billion dollar business where the newly rich oil countries are leading the way, but others, however poor, are not hesitant to follow. SIPRI in my home country, Sweden, as well as the UN Secretariat here, are providing the horrible documentation. The mighty ones do not listen to the warnings about the mad course of events.

"The political leaders either have no will or no capacity to hold back this evil development. To me it seems as if a kind of *collective insanity* has gripped the world. What we are living through is an era of militarization of practically all societies. In domestic affairs it makes them prone to dictatorship and repression of freedom movements. In international affairs the military build-up prepares the path for new wars. Whether they be local and small-scale, or mount to a holocaust by contending superpowers, two things are certain: (1) that they are inhuman, and (2) that they are unnecessary as they certainly will not help to solve any problems. The main result of the arms race, so visibly real already now, is that it consumes giant resources that would be needed for development."

Myrdal began her career in education, working as a teacher and as director of a training college in the 1930's and 1940's. In 1949 she became principal director of the social welfare department at the United Nations, and in the early 1950's she was director of the social sciences department of UNESCO. Myrdal began her diplomatic career in 1955 as Sweden's ambassador to India. She returned to Sweden in 1961 and became special assistant on disarmament affairs, a subject then alien to her. She eventually became a knowledgeable advocate of disarmament, however, and often criticized the United States and the Soviet Union for their aggressive development of nuclear weaponry. In 1962 Myrdal began eight years of legislative service as a member of the Swedish parliament, and in 1966 she became the third woman ever to serve the Swedish cabinet as minister, working in both disarmament and church affairs before retiring in 1973. She wrote that throughout her life she engaged in extensive reading, "not only in international affairs, but also novels and poetry in Swedish, English, French, German, and some Spanish."

Myrdal was awarded the Nobel Peace Prize in 1982 for her advocacy of world disarmament; she shared the Prize with Mexican diplomat Alfonso Garcia Robles. Among her other awards were the West German Peace Prize, the Albert Einstein Peace Prize, and the People's Peace Prize. Her many writings include *Disarmament and the United Nations, A Non-Aligned Look at the Future of Disarmament,* and *Wars, Weapons, and Everyday Violence* as well as collaborative efforts such as *Are We Too Many?, America's Role in International Social Welfare, Women's Two Roles: Home and Work,* and *The Control of Proliferation: Three Views.* Her books have been published in German, French, Italian, Japanese, Spanish, and Scandinavian languages.

BIOGRAPHICAL/CRITICAL SOURCES:

BOOKS

Bok, Sissela, *Alva Myrdal: A Daughter's Memoir,* Addison-Wesley (Reading, MA), 1991.

Carlson, Allan C., *The Swedish Experiment in Family Politics: The Myrdals and the Interwar Population Crisis,* Transaction Publishers (New Brunswick, NJ), 1990.

PERIODICALS

Horizon, March, 1977.

New York Review of Books, January 20, 1977.

New York Times, February 19, 1977.

New York Times Book Review, March 6, 1977.

OBITUARIES:

PERIODICALS

AB Bookman's Weekly, March 24, 1986.
Chicago Tribune, February 4, 1986.
Detroit Free Press, February 3, 1986.
Los Angeles Times, February 8, 1986.
Newsweek, February 17, 1986.
New York Times, February 3, 1986.
Time, February 17, 1986.
Washington Post, February 3, 1986.*

N

NAVARRE, Yves (Henri Michel) 1940-1994

PERSONAL: Born September 24, 1940, in Condom, Gascony, France; died of an overdose of barbiturates, January 24, 1994, in Paris, France; son of Rene (an engineer) and Adrienne (a homemaker; maiden name, Bax) Navarre. *Education:* Universite de Lille III, Spanish, English, and modern literature degrees, 1961 and 1964; attended Ecole des Hautes Etudes Commerciales du Nord, 1964.

CAREER: Novelist; playwright. Havas Agency, copywriter, 1965; Synergie, creative editor, 1966-67; Publicis, head of design, 1968-69; B.B.D.O. International, Inc., design director, 1969-79.

MEMBER: Societe des Auteurs et Compositeurs Dramatiques, Societe des Gens de Lettres.

AWARDS, HONORS: Goncourt Prize, Academie Goncourt, 1980, for *Le Jardin d'acclimatation;* Chevalier de l'Ordre des Arts et des Lettres, French Ministry of Culture and Communication, 1980; named Chevalier de l'Ordre Merite, 1987, and Chevalier de l'Ordre de Legion d'Honneur, 1988, both by Grande Chancellerie de Legion d'Honneur.

WRITINGS:

NOVELS

Lady Black, Flammarion (Paris), 1971.

Evolene, Flammarion, 1972.

Les Loukoums, Flammarion, 1973, translation by Donald Watson published as *Sweet Tooth,* Calder, 1976.

Le Coeur qui cogne, Flammarion, 1974.

Killer, Flammarion, 1975.

Niagarak, Le Livre de Poche, 1976.

Kurwenal; ou, La Part des etres, Laffont, 1977.

Le Petit Galopin de nos corps, Laffont, 1977, translation by Donald Watson published as *The Little Rogue in Our Flesh,* Quartet, 1989.

Je vis ou je m'attache, Laffont, 1978.

Portrait de Julien devant la fenetre, Laffont, 1979.

Le Temps voulu, Flammarion, 1979, translation by Dominic Di Bernardi and Noelle Domke published as *Our Share of Time,* Dalkey Archive Press, 1987.

Le Jardin d'acclimatation, Flammarion, 1980, translation by Howard Girven published as *Cronus' Children,* Riverrun Press, 1987.

Biographie, Flammarion, 1981.

Romances sans paroles, Flammarion, 1982.

Premieres Pages, Flammarion, 1983.

L'Esperance de beaux voyages ete/automne, Flammarion, 1984.

L'Esperance de beaux voyages hiver/printemps, Flammarion, 1984.

Louise, Flammarion, 1986.

Une Vie de chat, Albin Michel, 1986, translation by Donald Watson published as *A Cat's Life,* Quartet, 1991.

Fete des meres, Albin Michel, 1987.

Romans, un roman, Albin Michel, 1988.

Hotel Styx, Albin Michel, 1989.

La Terrasse des audience, Lemeac, 1990.

Douce France, Lemeac, 1990.

Ce sont amis que vent emporte, Flammarion, 1991.

Poudre d'or, Flammarion, 1993.

Dernier dimanche avant la fin du siecle, Flammarion, 1994.

PLAYS

Theatre 1 (contains *Il pleut si on tuait papamaman, Dialogue de sourdes, Freaks Society, Champagne,* and *Les Valises*), Flammarion, 1973.

Theatre 2 (contains *Histoire d'amour, La Guerre des piscines* [also see below], *Lucienne de Carpentras,* and *Les Dernieres clientes*), Flammarion, 1976.

La Guerre des piscines (one-act play), Flammarion, 1976, translation by Donald Watson published as *Swimming Pools at War,* Ubu Repertory Theater Publications, 1982.

Theatre 3 (contains *September Song, Le Butoir, Vue imprenable sur Paris,* and *Happy End*), Flammarion, 1979.

OTHER

Plum Parade: Vingt-quatre Hueres de la vie d'un minicirque (for children), illustrated by Francois Verdier, Flammarion, 1975.

Mon oncle est un chat (for children), Amitie, 1982.

Also author of short stories. Contributor to numerous periodicals.

Navarre's translated works have appeared in various Scandinavian and European countries, including Holland, Germany, Italy, Spain, Poland, Romania, and Bulgaria.

ADAPTATIONS: Kurwenal; ou, La Part des etres was adapted by Lea Pool for the Canadian film *A corps perdu,* released in the United States as *Straight for the Heart,* L. W. Blair Films, 1990.

SIDELIGHTS: Honored in 1992 by the French Academy for his numerous novels and plays, French author Yves Navarre also won the Goncourt prize in 1980 for his novel *Le Jardin d'acclimatation* ("The Zoological Garden"), published in the United States as *Cronus' Children.* Known for his forthright treatment of homosexuality, the human psyche, and gender restrictions in society, Navarre often utilized symbolism and stream-of-consciousness techniques to underscore his themes. His approach to such topics was formal rather than sensationalized. In a *New Statesman* review of *The Little Rogue in Our Flesh,* translated from the original *Le Petit Galopin de nos corps,* Paul Binding called the author a "relentless . . . prober of human character." In *The Little Rogue in Our Flesh,* the narrator of the story comments, "Poetry does not reside in poems. . . . Poetry is all around us." Navarre seemed intent on upholding this precept in each of his works. Indeed, several critics have commented favorably on the author's poetic descriptions, including those of nature and love affairs.

Through his writings, Navarre criticized people and institutions that hinder individuality and creative expression. He presented a scathing view of social and gender restrictions placed upon women in his play *La Guerre des piscines,* translated as *Swimming Pools at War.* In an early scene, it appears that two young women are enjoying a beach vacation, but in reality they are confined in a store-window display, posing as live models on lawn furniture. The author examined confinement and focused on age in an altogether different way in his 1978 novel *Je vis ou je m'attache.* The work functions as a psychological study of a seventy-year-old woman rendered mute by a debilitating disease. She relives her life through what could be called a mime routine, physically acting out the different stages of human development. Navarre combined her actions with narratives from her family and a nurse, in addition to providing omniscient insights, which unite to present a thorough account of the woman's life.

Navarre depicted a seamier side of life in *Les Loukoums,* published in 1973 and later translated as *Sweet Tooth.* The story involves Luc, a homosexual from Paris who travels to New York to visit a lover who is dying, supposedly from syphilis. Another character, a newly widowed woman named Lucy, takes refuge at a funeral parlor. One night, while out sight-seeing, Luc encounters a black, gay sadist and is murdered. This lurid tale culminates in an encounter between the widow and the deceased Luc. One critic suggested the work had qualities of black humor—the literary device used to express the cruel nature of the modern world through exaggerated portrayals of characters or situations—yet the same critic concluded that Navarre's reliance on a serious voice hindered immersion into the technique. Navarre told *CA* that *Sweet Tooth* might "be the first novel ever written about Acquired Immune Deficiency Syndrome (AIDS)."

Several of Navarre's works, including the 1979 novel *Le Temps voulu,* translated as *Our Share of Time,* and *Kurwenal; ou, La Part des etres,* examine the mystical powers of love. In both novels, the main characters are lifted from emotional despondency after engaging in homosexual love affairs. In *Our Share of Time,* a forty-year-old literature teacher named Pierre Forgue writes a novel based on his brief romance with a young man named Daniel Carbon. Before meeting Daniel, Pierre had attempted suicide. Although this relationship brings joy to Pierre, he becomes obsessed with the meaning of love once the affair ends. *Kurwenal* again involves a romantic association between an older man and a young boy. The main character, also named Pierre, is a photojournalist dejected over the break-up of a relationship. After a chance meeting with a young deaf-mute named Quentin, they embark on a brief but emotionally satisfying affair.

Navarre's *Le Jardin d'acclimatation,* translated as *Cronus' Children,* won France's Goncourt Prize in 1980. The unusual novel is composed of reflections from each member of the Prouillan family on the fortieth birthday of the youngest son, Bertrand, a homosexual. These narratives, all given on the twentieth anniversary of Bertrand's forced lobotomy to cure his homosexual tendencies, serve as flashbacks that try to explain the reason for the desperate measure. During the years leading up to the tragedy, the Prouillan patriarch, Henri, was a despot intent on maintaining the last vestiges of power his longstanding career as a minister in the French government accorded him. The methods he used to maintain absolute control caused his four children to despise him, yet, for most of their lives, they acquiesced to his will. As a young adult, Bertrand finally gathered up the courage to confront his father. Henri was fearful of his son's orientation because of the social stigma attached to homosexuality. In addition, Bertrand's creative and spiritual powers posed an intangible threat to his father. Thus, Henri ordered the operation to maintain his familial dominance and avoid the possibility of social embarrassment.

Cronus' Children serves as an analogue to the story in Greek mythology about a Titan named Cronus who was the father of Zeus. To draw connections between the two narratives, Navarre utilized overt as well as subtle symbolism. In the myth, Cronus, the ruler of the universe, was destined to be overthrown by one of his children. Fearful of this possible loss of power, he ate his children. Unbeknownst to him, his wife saved their infant son, Zeus, by hiding him. Thus, the prophecy came true as Zeus later became ruler of the universe by defeating his father in battle and sending him into exile. In Navarre's work, the father, Henri, also obsessively defends his power. Bertrand parallels the character of Zeus, the only offspring with the ability to defy his father. Yet, in *Cronus' Children,* the myth is reversed and the father overpowers his son. The lobotomy symbolizes the devastating loss of creative intellect and its inherent power. As Bertrand arrives home from the hospital deaf, mute, and almost completely mentally incapacitated, it is clear that his father has, in effect, killed him.

A homosexual theme is again the focus of *Le Petit Galopin de nos corps,* translated as *The Little Rogue in Our Flesh.* Set at the turn of the twentieth century, Navarre's novel examines the thirty-six-year relationship between Roland Raillac and Joseph Terrefort. According to Adam Mars-Jones in the *Times Literary Supplement,* the story, revealed in the form of a diary kept by Roland, is meant "to celebrate, understand, and mourn . . . [Roland and Joseph's] relationship." Combined with letters and documents from both men, the work acts as a transcript of the lifelong love of these two men. Despite the fact that they marry women who are sisters, Roland and Joseph remain firmly committed to each other. One critic suggested that the marriage ceremony consisted of two sets of vows, the spoken vows between each man and woman and the silent vows of the two men. Mars-Jones called *The Little Rogue in Our Flesh* an "extraordinary novel [that] bears witness to what its heroes hint at to each other—that the final logic of passion, whether sexual or literary, is not fulfillment but exhaustion."

Navarre once told *CA:* "My novel *Biographie* is the key to all my other novels and plays. I am a bachelor with two cats named Tybalt and Tibeze. I am now living in Montreal, Quebec, Canada, the second largest French-speaking city in the world. The French language is my identity. I ran away from Paris because I was fed up with the puritanical and hypocritical Parisian circles. I survived a hard stroke in 1984. I'm still writing—poems, plays, songs, novels, short stories—and reading."

BIOGRAPHICAL/CRITICAL SOURCES:

BOOKS

Navarre, Yves, *The Little Rogue in Our Flesh,* translated by Donald Watson, Quartet, 1989.

PERIODICALS

Books & Bookmen, September, 1977.
Los Angeles Times, September 28, 1990.
New Statesman, January 19, 1990.
New York Times Book Review, May 3, 1987.
Times Literary Supplement, December 22, 1989.
World Literature Today, summer, 1979.

OBITUARIES:

PERIODICALS

Los Angeles Times, January 26, 1994, p. A24.
Washington Post, January 26, 1994, p. B5.*

NEAL, Harry Edward 1906-1993

PERSONAL: Born May 4, 1906, in Pittsfield, MA; died of a stroke, June 14, 1993, in Culpeper, VA; son of Walter Carlos and Lillian (Crandall) Neal; married Helen Armstrong, May 8, 1929 (died March, 1965); married Berniece Raymer Roer, July, 1965; children: Barbara, Harry, Jr. *Education:* Attended public schools in Pittsfield, MA. *Religion:* Protestant.

CAREER: U.S. Treasury Department, Secret Service, New York, NY, and Washington, DC, 1926-57, became assistant chief; freelance writer, 1957-93. Consultant, Security-Columbian Banknote Co. Conductor of workshops or lecturer at Huckleberry Workshop, Hendersonville, NC, Christian Editors' and Writers' Conference, Green Lake, WI, St. Davids (PA) Christian Writers' Conference, Georgetown University Writers Conference, McKendree College Writers' Conference, Lebanon, IL, and LaSalle College Writer's Conference, Philadelphia, PA.

MEMBER: American Society of Journalists and Authors, Association of Former Agents of the U.S. Secret Service, Authors Guild, Authors League of America, Children's Book Guild (Washington, DC), Academy of Medicine (Kansas City, MO; fellow).

AWARDS, HONORS: U.S. Government Exceptional Civilian Service Medal, 1957.

WRITINGS:

PUBLISHED BY J. MESSNER (NEW YORK CITY), EXCEPT AS INDICATED

Writing and Selling Fact and Fiction, Funk, 1949.
The Story of the Kite, Vanguard, 1954.
Nature's Guardians: Your Career in Conservation, 1956, 2nd edition, 1963.
Pathfinders, U.S.A.: Your Career on Land, Sea, Air, 1957.
The Telescope, 1958.
Skyblazers: Your Career in Aviation, 1958, 2nd edition, 1963.
Six against Crime, 1959.
Disease Detectives: Your Career in Medical Research, 1959, revised edition, 1968.
Communication: From Stone Age to Space Age, 1960.
(With Walter S. Bowen) *The United States Secret Service,* Chilton, 1960.
Engineers Unlimited: Your Career in Engineering, 1960, revised edition, 1968.
Treasures by the Millions: The Story of the Smithsonian Institution, 1961.
Money Masters: Your Career in Banking, 1961.
The Hallelujah Army: The Salvation Army in Action, Chilton, 1961.
Diary of Democracy: The Story of Political Parties in America, 1962.
Your Career in Electronics, 1963.
Money, 1963.
From Spinning Wheel to Spacecraft: The Story of the Industrial Revolution, 1964.
Nonfiction: From Idea to Published Book, Funk, 1964.
Your Career in Foreign Service, 1965.
The Mystery of Time, 1966.
The Pennsylvania Colony, Hawthorn, 1967.
The Protectors, 1968.
The Virginia Colony, Hawthorn, 1969.
Oil, 1970.
Of Maps and Men, Funk, 1970.
The People's Giant: TVA, 1970.
The Story of the Secret Service, Grosset, 1971.
The Story of Offshore Oil, 1977.
The Secret Service in Action, Elsevier/Nelson, 1980.
Before Columbus: Who Discovered America?, 1981.

Contributor of short stories and articles to *Saturday Evening Post, Cosmopolitan, Esquire, Pageant, Changing Times,* and other national magazines.

SIDELIGHTS: Harry Edward Neal, a Secret Service agent-turned-writer, began his career with the U.S. agency in 1926 as a stenographer but was promoted to agent after assisting in a raid on counterfeiters in 1931. He began writing, and published his first book in 1949, *Writing and Selling Fact and Fiction.* Neal retired from the Service as assistant chief in 1957 to become a full-time writer, concentrating on such nonfiction topics as effective writing and the history of the kite. He also penned a series of career books for young people, focusing on conservation, aviation, engineering, banking, and medical research, among other fields. The author of more than thirty books, Neal saw his work sell in the hundreds of thousands. Among Neal's other titles are *The Story of the Secret Service, The Hallelujah Army: The Salvation Army in Action, From Spinning Wheel to Spacecraft: The Story of the Industrial Revolution* and *Before Columbus: Who Discovered America?*

Neal once told *CA:* "I was a member of the U.S. Secret Service for thirty-one years. I had never even thought about writing for publication until I was assigned by my Chief to write magazine articles (under his by-line) about ways to detect counterfeit money. We received numerous requests for more articles, which I had to do.

"On my own, I enrolled in a night course on writing articles at American University in Washington. I learned a great deal, but the course folded after one semester. A course in writing short stories was open, and I took it. When it was finished I began to write short stories (never about the Secret Service). I would finish one, mail it to a magazine, and start another. The stories kept coming back and I collected a few hundred rejection slips, but I kept sending out the manuscripts.

"One day, after I had sent a story to twelve magazines, *Esquire* bought it. A week later I sold an article to *Coronet.* I began to sell more stories and articles, but I still had many rejections. At the suggestion of a friendly editor, I acquired a literary agent. At her suggestion I began to write nonfiction books, mostly because the market for short stories was dwindling fast. As I write this I still have the same agent and I have thirty published books to my credit. And I'm at work on more.

"If you're a beginning or struggling writer, be reconciled to the fact that you're going to be disappointed many times in trying to sell your work. For one thing, the competition is very tough. If you're easily discouraged, stop writing and take up plumbing.

"The only way to learn to write *professionally* is to write and write and write. The more you write, the greater will be your facility with words, and words are the stock in trade of every professional.

"Read successful authors who write material of the kind you want to write. Analyze their approaches. But don't try to imitate styles of other writers, because if you do that you can become only a good copier. Write your own way and your style will take care of itself.

"Remember—don't be discouraged by rejections. Write something every day. If you have a steady job, write at night and on weekends. Try keeping a daily journal. But WRITE!"

BIOGRAPHICAL/CRITICAL SOURCES:

BOOKS

Farrar, Larston D., *Successful Writers and How They Work,* Hawthorn, 1959.

PERIODICALS

Culpeper Star-Exponent (Culpeper, VA), November 30, 1961; September 20, 1962.
Kansas City Times, March 19, 1960.
New York Times, April 16, 1960.
Washington Post-Times Herald, April 26, 1957.

OBITUARIES:

PERIODICALS

New York Times, June 16, 1993, p. D24.
Washington Post, June 15, 1993, p. C8.*

* * *

NEVILLE, B(arbara) Alison (Boodson) 1925-
(Edward Candy)

PERSONAL: Born August 22, 1925, in London, England; daughter of Hyman and Elizabeth (Dawe) Boodson; married Joseph Godfrey Neville (a retired children's psychiatrist), July 1, 1946; children: Jeremy, Tom, Paul, Lucy, Sarah. *Education:* University College, London, and University College Hospital Medical School, M.B. and B.S., 1948, DCH., 1950. *Politics:* "None to speak of." *Religion:* Humanist. *Avocational interests:* Reading, music, friends.

ADDRESSES: *Home*—2 Mile End Rd., Norwich, England. *Agent*—John Farquharson Ltd., Bell House, 8 Bell Yard, London WC2A 2JU, England; and Anthony Sheil Associates Ltd., 2-3 Morwell St., London WC1B 3AR, England.

CAREER: Novelist. Has held resident posts in electroencephalography in various hospitals in England.

AWARDS, HONORS: Arts Council award, 1968.

WRITINGS:

ALL NOVELS UNDER PSEUDONYM EDWARD CANDY; PUBLISHED BY GOLLANCZ, EXCEPT AS INDICATED

Which Doctor, Rinehart, 1953.
Bones of Contention, 1954, Doubleday, 1983.
The Graver Tribe, 1958.
A Lady's Hand, 1960.
A Season of Discord, 1964.
Strokes of Havoc, 1966.
Parents' Day, 1967.
Doctor Amadeus, 1969.
Word for Murder, Perhaps, 1971.
Scene Changing, 1977.
Voices of Children, David & Charles, 1980.

SIDELIGHTS: B. Alison Neville once told *CA:* "Since 1970 I have, like most of my generation, I suspect, suffered a prolonged disillusionment with political and apparently humanitarian action. My two last novels are, I fear, books of despair. *Scene Changing* is about the trading in of a mundane, insignificant private life for public adulation, and the likely cost of such an exchange. *Voices of Children* suggests that private romantic fantasy and utopian dreams may be totally inappropriate and even destructive once translated into social action. At the moment, rather than sadden my readers any further, I'm compiling an anthology of nature poems, writing poems of my own (for the first time since adolescence), and planning some short stories."

BIOGRAPHICAL/CRITICAL SOURCES:

PERIODICALS

New Statesman, July 8, 1977; January 25, 1980.
New York Times Book Review, April 14, 1985.
Observer, January 16, 1966; July 27, 1969; March 28, 1971; July 17, 1977; January 27, 1980.
Times Literary Supplement, January 20, 1966; May 11, 1967; July 24, 1969; July 15, 1977; January 25, 1980.
Washington Post Book World, August 21, 1983.*

* * *

NEVILLE, Kris (Ottman) 1925- 1980

PERSONAL: Born May 9, 1925, in Carthage, MO; died of a heart attack, December 24, 1980; son of Gilbert Orrman (a blue collar and white collar worker) and Ethyl Mae (a waitress; maiden name, Peters) Neville; married Lil Johnson (a writer), September 28, 1957; children: Nieson Ottman, Helen Arleen; (stepchildren) Lois Tyus, Freddie Marie Tyus, Leonard Tyus. *Education:* University of California, Los Angeles, B.A., 1950.

CAREER: Writer. Worked for chemical and plastics companies, including Rocketdyne and Conveyor Co., from the mid-1950s through the late 1960s; employed by Epoxylite Corp., Anaheim, CA, beginning 1965. Also worked for Merchant Navy. *Military service:* U.S. Army, Signals Corps, radio operator during World War II.

WRITINGS:

FICTION

The Unearth People (novel), Belmont, 1964.
The Mutants (novel), Belmont, 1966.
Peril of the Starmen (novel; bound with *The Flame of Iridar,* by Lin Carter), Belmont, 1967.
Special Delivery (novel; bound with *Star Gladiator,* by Dave Van Arnam), Belmont, 1967.
Bettyann (novel), Tower Publications, 1970.
Invaders on the Moon (novel), Belmont, 1970.
Mission: Manstop (stories), Leisure Books, 1971.
(With wife, Lil Neville) *Run, the Spearmaker* (novel; in Japanese), Hayakawa Shobo, 1975.
The Science Fiction of Kris Neville, Southern Illinois University Press, 1984.

Work represented in anthologies, including *Out from Ganymede,* edited by Barry N. Malzberg, Warner Books, 1974; *Universe 5,* edited by Terry Carr, Random House, 1974; *Perry Rhodan 94-96,* Ace Books, 1976. Contributor to magazines, including *Galaxy, Fantasy and Science Fiction, Amazing,* and *Imagination.*

NONFICTION

(With Henry Lee) *Epoxy Resins: Their Applications and Technology,* McGraw, 1957.
(With Lee) *Handbook of Epoxy Resins,* McGraw, 1967.
(With Lee and Donald Stoffey) *New Linear Polymers,* McGraw, 1967.
(With Lee) *Handbook of Biomedical Plastics,* Pasadena Technology Press, 1971.
(With Robert L. Ibsen) *Adhesive Restorative Dentistry,* Saunders, 1974.
(With L. J. Rejda) *Industrial Motor User's Handbook of Insulation for Rewinds,* Elsevier, new edition, 1977.
(Editor, with Lee) *Handbook of Adhesive Bonding,* McGraw Hill, 1982.

SIDELIGHTS: Kris Neville is remembered as a science-fiction writer whose work represents a variety of approaches to the genre, including adventure, fantasy, and social science fiction. His stories focus more on characters—their interactions and their responses to environmental or cultural forces—than on thrilling exploits. Daniel L. Lawler of *Twentieth-Century Science-Fiction Writers* observed that Neville "knew how to make good use of psychologically enriched characters and possessed more sensitivity toward character motivation and interaction than most of his colleagues. A predominant theme of Neville's work is alienation and its psychological dimensions. Other themes include alien invasions, as in *Special Delivery,* and the social consequences of technology, as in *The Mutants,* a book about artificial insemination."

In 1980, Neville commented to *Twentieth-Century Science-Fiction Writers:* "I wrote the majority of my stories in the early 1950s. Having just graduated from UCLA with a degree in English literature, I was interested in introducing mainstream elements into science fiction (which I had been reading avidly since 1937)—shifting the emphasis to the impact of future technology on ordinary individuals. I also tried to seek out new perspectives—using female protagonists; playing with various viewpoints; seeing the future through the eyes of the old or young; portraying Earthmen in less than favorable lights; breaking taboos; making satirical comments. (I was a socialist/humanist.) In many of my shorts, I aimed for emotional effect. I was a trailblazer in my time."

BIOGRAPHICAL/CRITICAL SOURCES:

BOOKS

Twentieth-Century Science-Fiction Writers, 3rd edition, St. James Press, 1991.

PERIODICALS

Booklist, May 1, 1984, p. 1227.
Journal of American Studies, December, 1985, p. 457.
North American Review, June, 1984, p. 65.

OBITUARIES:

BOOKS

The Writers Directory: 1984-1986, St. James Press, 1983.*

* * *

NEVINS, Francis M(ichael), Jr. 1943-

PERSONAL: Born January 6, 1943, in Bayonne, NJ; son of Francis Michael and Rosemary (Konzelmann) Nevins; married Muriel Walter, June 6, 1966 (divorced, 1978); married Patricia Brooks, February 24, 1982. *Education:* St. Peter's College, A.B. (magna cum laude), 1964; New York University, J.D. (cum laude), 1967.

ADDRESSES: Home—7045 Cornell Ave., St. Louis, MO 63130. *Office*—School of Law, St. Louis University, 3700 Lindell Blvd., St. Louis, MO 63108. *Agent*—Maureen Walters, Curtis Brown Ltd., 10 Astor Pl., New York, NY 10003.

CAREER: Admitted to the Bar of New Jersey, 1967; Clark Boardman Ltd., New York City, assistant to editor-in-chief, 1967; St. Peter's College, Jersey City, NJ, adjunct instructor in government, 1967; Middlesex County Legal Services Corp., New Brunswick, NJ, staff attorney, 1970-71; St. Louis University, School of Law, St. Louis, MO, assistant professor, 1971-75, associate professor, 1975-78, professor of law, 1978—. Advisor to the estate of mystery author Cornell Woolrich, 1970-89. Member of board of directors, St. Louis Volunteer Lawyers for the Arts, 1980-89. Member, Missouri Bar probate code revision subcommittee. *Military service:* U.S. Army Reserve, 1968-70; became captain.

MEMBER: Association of American Law Schools (various offices in Law and the Arts and other sections, 1980—), Mystery Writers of America (chair or member of various committees, 1970—).

AWARDS, HONORS: Edgar Allan Poe Award, Mystery Writers of America, 1975, for *Royal Bloodline: Ellery Queen, Author and Detective,* and 1989, for *Cornell Woolrich: First You Dream, Then You Die.*

WRITINGS:

(With Chris Steinbrunner, Charles Shibuk, Marvin Lachman, and Otto Penzler) *Detectionary,* Hammermill Paper Co., 1971, revised edition, Overlook Press, 1977.
Royal Bloodline: Ellery Queen, Author and Detective, Bowling Green University Popular Press, 1974.
Publish and Perish (novel), Putnam, 1975.
Corrupt and Ensnare (novel), Putnam, 1978.
Missouri Probate Court: Intestacy, Wills and Basic Administration, Harrison Co., 1983.
(With Ray Stanich) *The Sound of Detection: Ellery Queen's Adventures in Radio,* Brownstone, 1983.
The 120-Hour Clock (novel), Walker, 1986.
The Ninety Million Dollar Mouse (novel), Walker, 1987.
Cornell Woolrich: First You Dream, Then You Die, Mysterious Press, 1988.
The Films of Hopalong Cassidy, World of Yesterday, 1988.
Bar-20: The Life of Clarence E. Mulford, Creator of Hopalong Cassidy, McFarland, 1993.
Into the Same River Twice, Carroll and Graf (New York City), 1996.
The Films of the Cisco Kid, World Yest, 1998.

EDITOR

The Mystery Writer's Art, Bowling Green University Popular Press, 1970.

Cornell Woolrich, *Nightwebs,* Harper, 1971, revised edition, Avon, 1974.

Multiplying Villainies: Selected Mystery Criticism of Anthony Boucher, privately printed, 1973.

(With Martin H. Greenberg, Walter Shine, and Jean Shine) John D. MacDonald, *The Good Old Stuff,* Harper, 1982.

(With Greenberg) *Exeunt Murderers: The Best Mystery Stories of Anthony Boucher,* Southern Illinois University Press, 1983.

(With Greenberg) *Buffet for Unwelcome Guests: The Best Short Mystery Stories of Christianna Brand,* Southern Illinois University Press, 1983.

(With Greenberg, W. Shine, and J. Shine) MacDonald, *More Good Old Stuff,* Knopf, 1984.

(With Greenberg) *Carnival of Crime: The Best Mystery Stories of Fredric Brown,* Southern Illinois University Press, 1985.

(With Greenberg) *Leopold's Way: Detective Stories by Edward D. Hoch,* Southern Illinois University Press, 1985.

(With Greenberg) *Darkness at Dawn: Early Suspense Classics by Cornell Woolrich,* Southern Illinois University Press, 1985.

(With Greenberg) *The Best of Ellery Queen,* Beaufort Books, 1985.

(With Greenberg) *Hitchcock in Prime Time,* Avon, 1985.

(With Greenberg) *The Adventures of Henry Turnbuckle: Detective Comedies by Jack Ritchie,* Southern Illinois University Press, 1987.

Better Mousetraps: The Best Mystery Stories of John Lutz, St. Martin's Press, 1988.

(With Greenberg) *Mr. President—Private Eye,* Ballantine, 1988.

(With Greenberg) *Death on Television: The Best of Henry Slesar's Alfred Hitchcock Stories,* Southern Illinois University Press, 1989.

Little Boxes of Bewilderment: Suspense Comedies by Jack Ritchie, St. Martin's Press, 1989.

Edward D. Hoch, *The Night, My Friend: Stories of Crime and Suspense,* Ohio University Press, 1991.

Woolrich, *Schwarz lst die Farbe des Blutes,* Wilhelm Heyne Verlag (Munich), 1993.

OTHER

(Author of foreword) *Private Investigations: The Novels of Dashiell Hammett,* Southern Illinois University Press, 1984.

Contributor to *1001 Midnights,* Arbor House, 1986, and to periodicals, including *New Republic, Journal of Popular Culture, Armchair Detective, Ellery Queen's Mystery Magazine, The Saint Mystery Magazine, Woman's World,* and *Espionage.*

Member of editorial board, Bantam Books Collection of Mystery Classics and University of California (San Diego extension) Mystery Library.

SIDELIGHTS: Francis M. Nevins Jr.'s, career in the crime and mystery genre includes his work as an editor of short-story collections and nonfiction books, and as an author of novels and short stories featuring characters noted for their complexity and ability to engage the reader s imagination and intellect. George J. Thompson of *Twentieth-Century Crime and Mystery Writers* praised Nevins abilities as a storyteller: "Whether working in short fiction, with all of its restrictions and demand for economy and telling detail, or in the novel, with its demands for complex plot structure and sustained character development, he consistently produces entertaining and skillful work." Thompson added that Nevins fiction demonstrates "an attempt to balance four components: clues and deductions, visual and suspenseful elements, legal ploys, and human relationships."

Nevins once told *CA:* "I was hooked on mystery fiction at the age of thirteen, after discovering Sherlock Holmes, Charlie Chan, and Perry Mason. Before the end of my first year of high school I was reading and collecting mysteries at a fiendish pace: Ellery Queen, Cornell Woolrich and countless others whom I devoured furiously. It was only after about fifteen years of reading and three or four years of writing occasional reviews and articles about the genre and its practitioners that I took the plunge and tried to write a mystery myself. The eventual discovery that I could sell almost any story I wrote is a shock from which I still haven't recovered."

The literary and legal consultant to the estate of the suspense writer Cornell Woolrich, Nevins, who has edited three volumes of Woolrich's stories, became his biographer in 1988, when he published *Cornell Woolrich: First You Dream, Then You Die.* The book, in which Nevins designates Woolrich "the Poe of the 20th Century and the poet of its shadows," is "a long labor of devotion any author would be grateful to have done on his behalf," *Los Angeles Times Book Review*'s Charles Champlin remarked. Woolrich's work included *The Bride Wore Black, Rear Window,* and *The Night Has a Thousand Eyes.*

BIOGRAPHICAL/CRITICAL SOURCES:

BOOKS

Twentieth-Century Crime and Mystery Writers, St. Martin's, 1980, 3rd edition, St. James Press, 1991.
Steinbrunner, Chris, and Otto Penzler, *Encyclopedia of Mystery and Detection,* McGraw, 1976.

PERIODICALS

Armchair Detective, May 1, 1996, p. 646.
Los Angeles Times Book Review, November 27, 1988.
New York Times, May 6, 1988.
New York Times Book Review, February 8, 1987, p. 20; March 6, 1988, p. 22; October 9, 1988, pp. 35-36.
Washington Post Book World, September 18, 1988, p. 6.*

* * *

NIATUM, Duane 1938-
(Duane McGinnis)

PERSONAL: Born February 13, 1938, in Seattle, WA; son of Dorothy Lorraine (Patsey) Babinger; children: Marc. *Education:* University of Washington, Seattle, B.A., 1970; Johns Hopkins University, M.A., 1972.

ADDRESSES: Office—Mayo's, 4516 Northeast 50th St., Seattle, WA 98105.

CAREER: Poet and freelance editor. Johns Hopkins University, Baltimore, MD, instructor in U.S. and European literature writing seminars, 1971-72; Native American Authors Program, Harper & Row Publishers, Inc., editor, 1973-74; Immaculate High School, Seattle, WA, English and literature teacher, 1974-75; Seattle Arts Commission, Seattle, worked with elderly in artist-in-the-city program, 1977-78. Visiting instructor at University of Washington, Evergreen State College, Eastern Washington University, and Seattle Central Community College; teaching curriculum developer, College of Education, University of Washington. Has worked as an assistant librarian for over three years in libraries at University of Washington and New York Historical Society. Has read his poetry and fiction at over forty colleges and universities and at art festivals throughout the United States and Europe, including Portland Poetry Festival, Anacortes Arts Festival, Portland State University, Phoenix Indian High School, University of California, Berkeley, and University of South Dakota; invitational reading, Library of Congress, 1976; member of poet-in-the-schools programs in Arizona, New Mexico, Oregon, and Washington. Judged poetry contest for Washington Poets Association, 1975, and for King County Arts Commission. *Military service:* U.S. Navy, 1955-59.

MEMBER: PEN.

AWARDS, HONORS: Pacific Northwest Writers Conference, first prize in poetry, 1966, 1970, third prize in poetry, 1968; honorable mention in poetry, Scholastic Magazines, Inc., 1968; Mary K. Dearborn Literature Award, Seattle Music and Art Foundation, 1968; Washington Governor's Award, 1971; Carnegie Fund for Authors grant, 1975; PEN Fund for Writers grant, 1976; invited to stay at Millay Colony for the Arts, 1976, and Yaddo, Saratoga Springs, NY, 1977; Poetry in Public Places Award, American International Sculptor's Symposium, 1979; Poetry in Motion Grant Award, Allied Arts Foundation, 1981; American Book Award, Before Columbus Foundation, 1982, for *Songs for the Harvester of Dreams;* Nelson Bently Award, Department of English, University of Washington, 1982; Certificate of Literary Achievement, Book Club of Washington, 1982; invited to International Poetry Festival, Rotterdam, Netherlands, 1983.

WRITINGS:

POETRY

(Under name Duane McGinnis) *After the Death of an Elder Klallam,* Baleen Press, 1970.
A Cycle for the Woman in the Field (chapbook), illustrated by Jane Berniker, Laughing Man Press, 1973.
Taos Pueblo and Other Poems (chapbook), illustrated by Wendy Rose, Greenfield Review Press, 1973.
Ascending Red Cedar Moon, Harper, 1974.
Digging out the Roots, Harper, 1977.
Turning to the Rhythms of Her Song (chapbook), Jawbone Press, 1977.
Songs for the Harvester of Dreams, University of Washington Press, 1981.
Pieces (chapbook), Strawberry Press, 1981.
Stories of the Moons, Blue Cloud Quarterly (Marvin, SD), 1987.
Drawings of the Song Animals: New and Selected Poems, Holy Cow! Press, 1991.

EDITOR

Carriers of the Dream Wheel: Contemporary Native American Poetry, Harper, 1975.

Harper's Anthology of Twentieth-Century Native American Poetry, Harper, 1988.

OTHER

Breathless (experimental verse drama), first produced at University of Washington, Seattle, WA, 1968.
To Bridge the Dream (story chapbook), A Press, 1978.
Raven and the Fear of Growing White, Bridge Press, 1983.

Contributor to anthologies, including *From the Belly of the Shark,* edited by Walter Lowenfels, Random House, 1973; *American Indian Prose and Poetry: We Wait in the Darkness,* edited by Gloria Levitas, Frank Robert Vivelo, and Jacqueline Vivelo, Capricorn Books, 1974; *Voices from Wah'Kon-Tah: Contemporary Poetry of Native Americans,* International Publishers, 1974; *The Remembered Earth: An Anthology of Contemporary Native American Literature,* edited by Geary Hobson, Red Earth Press, 1978; *This Song Remembers: Self-Portraits of Native Americans in the Arts,* edited by Jane B. Katz, Houghton, 1980; *Songs from Turtle Island,* edited by Joseph Bruchac III, Sovremennost Press/Macedonia Review (Macedonia), 1982; *Earth Power Coming: Short Fiction in Native American Literature,* edited by Simon J. Ortiz, Navajo Community College Press, 1983; *Songs from This Earth on Turtle's Back,* edited by Bruchac, Greenfield Review Press, 1983; and *Words in the Blood,* edited by Jamake Highwater, New American Library, 1984.

Contributor of poems, short stories, and essays to over one hundred newspapers and magazines in the United States, Canada, and Europe. Guest editor of *Pacific Search,* 1975, *Niagara,* 1976, and *Western Edge,* 1978.

Niatum's work has been translated into various languages, including Dutch, Italian, Macedonian, Russian, Danish, Spanish, German, Polish, French, Icelandic, and Frisian.

SIDELIGHTS: Duane Niatum is known for his efforts in anthologizing poetry by Native Americans as well as for his own writings in the same genre. His anthology *Carriers of the Dream Wheel: Contemporary Native American Poetry,* published by Harper and Row in 1975, brought together a variety of diverse talents, including Liz Sohappy Bahe, Jim Barnes, Joseph Bruchac, Gladys Cardiff, Lance Henson, Roberta Hill, N. Scott Momaday, Dana Naone, Simon J. Ortiz, Anita Endrezze Probst, W. M. Ransom, Wendy Rose, Leslie Silko, James Welch, and Ray A. Young Bear. Thirteen years later Niatum edited *Harper's Anthology of Twentieth-Century Native American Poetry.*

Niatum's own poetry has received favorable critical attention in major periodicals. William Scammel, reviewing nine American poets for the *Times Literary Supplement,* calls Niatum's *Songs for the Harvester of Dreams,* which won the American Book Award from the Before Columbus Foundation in 1982, a type of "mythopoeic minimalism, celebrating 'the primeval voices of forest animals and cedar and salmon, of totems and legends and dreams.' " Along with the poet's examination of his culture, the critic explains, Niatum uses "Indian myth to explore his own living concerns"—particularly in a poem called "First Spring," an autobiographical piece which takes a " 'red-skin American gothic' " back through forty-odd years of personal history to look at "lost love and severed connections." Doris Grumbach, who reviewed an earlier collection of poetry, *Ascending Red Cedar Moon,* for the *New Republic,* declares that she "liked these poems: lyrical, gentle, close to natural phenomena in their rhythms and images."

Niatum mentions painters of the impressionist and post-impressionist schools and music among early influences on his writing. "I studied the painters long before I studied the poets," he writes, "and have found paintings helpful to my poetry.

"I spent two years in Japan, and its culture, especially its arts and philosophies, has had a major influence on the way I approach my work. It seems to me that there are a number of parallels that can be discovered between American Indian philosophies and those of the Orient. . . . I hope that by feeling close to the world of the Orient as well as the world of my Indian and European ancestors, I can deal with the chaos of everyday. That is why people are always in the foreground of my work. And this is related to something that my Indian grandfather and great-uncle taught me as a child, that is, to always humble my soul before the spiritual reality of things as well as man."

Niatum intends to teach for a few years "to see if I can do more than an adequate job." He commented: "I enjoy living with diversity. . . . Men and women, children and old folks, who mirror contrasting values, arts, faces, ways of being and doing, are what make me happy and sad, love, and hate, appear and vanish."

BIOGRAPHICAL/CRITICAL SOURCES:

BOOKS

Dictionary of Literary Biography, Volume 175: *Native American Writers of the United States,* Gale, 1997.

PERIODICALS

Booklist, November 15, 1991, p. 596.
Library Journal, March 1, 1988, p. 68.
Los Angeles Times, February 21, 1988, p. B8.
New Republic, May 18, 1974, pp. 31-32.
Small Press Book Review, March, 1992, p. 13.
Times Literary Supplement, May 28, 1982, p. 592.*

* * *

NI CHUILLEANAIN, Eilean 1942-

PERSONAL: Surname is pronounced "Nee-Quillenoin"; born November 28, 1942, in Cork, Ireland; daughter of Cormac (a university professor) and Eilis (a writer; maiden name, Dillon) O'Cuilleanain; married Macdara Woods (a poet and editor), June 27, 1978; children: Niall. *Education:* University College, National University of Ireland, B.A., 1962, M.A., 1964; Lady Margaret Hall, Oxford, B.Litt., 1968.

ADDRESSES: Office—Trinity College, University of Dublin, Dublin 2, Ireland. *Email*—enchullnn@tcd.ie.

CAREER: University of Dublin Trinity College, Dublin, Ireland, lecturer, beginning 1966, senior lecturer in English, 1984—. With Macdara Woods and Leland Bardwell, founder of *Cyphers* literary magazine, 1975.

AWARDS, HONORS: Irish Times Poetry Award, 1966, for poems, including "Ars Poetica"; Patrick Kavanagh Award for Poetry, 1973, for *Acts and Monuments;* Books Ireland Publishers' Award, 1975, for *Site of Ambush;* O'Shaughnessy Prize, Irish-American Cultural Foundation, 1992.

WRITINGS:

POETRY

Acts and Monuments, Gallery Books, 1972.
Site of Ambush, Gallery Books, 1975.
The Second Voyage, Wake Forest University Press (Chapel Hill, NC), 1977.
(With Brian Lalor) *Cork,* illustrations by Lalor, Gallery Books, 1977.
The Rose-Geranium, Gallery Books, 1981.
The Magdalene Sermon, Gallery Press, 1989, 2nd edition, 1994, Wake Forest University Press, 1990.
The Brazen Serpent, Wake Forest University Press, 1995.

EDITOR

Irish Women: Image and Achievement, Arlen House, 1985.
Belinda, J. M. Dent (London), 1993.
(With J. D. Pheifer) *Noble and Joyous Histories: English Romances, 1350-1650,* Irish Academic Press, 1993.

OTHER

Poems represented in anthologies, including *Choice,* edited by Desmond Egan and Michael Hartnett, Goldsmith Press, 1973, and *The Pleasures of Gaelic Poetry,* edited by Sean Mac Reamoinn, Allen Lane, 1982. Contributor to periodicals, including *Aquarius, Broadsheet, Irish Press, Irish Times,* and *Ploughshares.* Co-editor of *Cyphers,* 1975—.

SIDELIGHTS: Eilean Ni Chuilleanain, who helped found the distinguished Irish literary magazine *Cyphers,* has become known for her own "intensely imagined, private, and frequently mysterious" poetry, asserts Joseph Browne in *Dictionary of Literary Biography.* A sense of connection between past and present characterizes her work, which draws on legend and mythology in its examination of being and death as well as the poet's struggle to reveal herself. Thomas McCarthy of *Contemporary Poets* describes Ni Chuilleanain as "the least directly political of Irish poets, and one of the constant outsiders in Irish poetry, never staying in one parish long enough to collect her polling card. She is free of prejudice and pretense. It is to the mythical voyagers that she owes her allegiance." Ni Chuilleanain's distant style has drawn criticism from some reviewers, but in Browne's opinion, "Her poetry's creative vigor, thematic depth, and technical range are consistently and sufficiently evident to authenticate its artistic worth. . . . In her more than one hundred published poems, . . . [Ni Chuilleanain] has, like the Gaelic poetry she so admires, provided us with a body of work 'full of suggestions and fascinating patterns.' "

In such early poems as "The Second Voyage," which first appeared in *Acts and Monuments,* Ni Chuilleanain's awareness of history and isolation figure strongly. Her choice of the Greek hero Odysseus as a protagonist demonstrates her historical orientation;

Odysseus's isolation, as a traveler at sea, expresses one of her common themes. As Ni Chuilleanain identifies memory and connection with the earth, in her early poems the sea becomes a symbol of separation and forgetting. "The Second Voyage" bears this out through Odysseus's yearning to leave the lonely sea for a settled home on land. Remarks Browne, "Odysseus is so thoroughly realized as a human being that the poem becomes brilliantly immediate and harmonious in the poet's blending of subject, theme, language, structure, and personal vision."

The problem of self has dominated Ni Chuilleanain's poetry and criticism. Her unwillingness to identify herself with female characters or even to write in an intimate, personal voice leads some reviewers to judge her poems unemotional, asexual, and elusive. Yet in Browne's opinion, "What has been misconstrued as 'paralytic politeness' may actually be a unique blend of intentional and unintentional mystery, anonymity, and reticence." In her essays, Ni Chuilleanain expresses support for the poet's right to reveal only what she chooses in order to deal with the corresponding mystery of life. Thus, suggests Browne, the important question is whether the reader is "convinced that a poem's specific mystery reflects the general mystery of humanity."

In poems such as "The Lady's Tower," from Ni Chuilleanain's second volume, *Site of Ambush,* the poet reveals herself more fully in a feminine persona isolated from, yet caught up in, the world around her. Observes Browne, "Unlike earlier poems, which were often obscured by a vague or incompletely realized persona that excluded the reader, 'The Lady's Tower' is an entirety because its persona and her world complement and complete one another, thereby engaging the reader in their existence." Ni Chuilleanain's use of a female protagonist is considered significant; Browne quoted the poet as saying she believed she had succeeded in "partly solving the female 'I' problem" with this poem.

Written to accompany Brian Lalor's drawings, the poems in *Cork* sometimes seem to reviewers to lack the originality and vigor of Ni Chuilleanain's independent writings about humanity. "Ironically," reports Browne, "it is when she deals with the natural world in her personal, imaginative fashion that Ni Chuilleanain is at her best" in this collection. *The Rose-Geranium,* in contrast, offers a vivid and personal perspective on human concerns and relationships. "The themes of time, change, aging, and death which previously had been simply characteristics of mythology, legend, history, and the natural world, that is, of the world outside her, are now observed as an intimate part of her own being and of her relations with others," Browne writes.

Ni Chuilleanain once told *CA:* "My motivation is obscure, connected with the stimulus of mythology, folklore, and religious writing (which is also an academic interest). The problem of addressing the special (Irish) audience in a special (female) voice remains unsolved and many of my poems are attempts to solve it.

"I have traveled and lived at various times in Italy, with shorter expeditions elsewhere in Europe and Morocco. All are important to my writing. I speak Irish, Italian, and French, read Latin, and hope to learn Arabic."

BIOGRAPHICAL/CRITICAL SOURCES:

BOOKS

Contemporary Poets, 6th edition, St. James Press, 1996.

Dictionary of Literary Biography, Volume 40: *Poets of Great Britain and Ireland since 1960,* Gale, 1985.

Haberstroh, Patricia Boyle, *Women Creating Women: Contemporary Irish Women Poets,* Syracuse University Press, 1996.

PERIODICALS

Choice, December, 1991.

Irish Literary Supplement, spring, 1991.

New York Times Book Review, April 14, 1996.

Poetry Ireland Review, summer, 1995.

Prairie Schooner, summer, 1995.

Times Literary Supplement, July 27, 1973; December 25-31, 1987; July 7, 1995.

University Press Book News, December, 1991.*

* * *

NICOLL, Helen 1937-

PERSONAL: Born October 10, 1937, in Natland, Westmorland, England; married Robert Kime (an antiquarian), 1970; children: Hannah, Tom. *Education:* Attended schools in Bristol, Devon, and London, England.

ADDRESSES: *Home and Office*—Dene House, Lockeridge, Marlborough, Wiltshire, England. *Agent*—c/o Heinemann Ltd., Michelin House, 81 Fulham Road, London SW3 6RB, England.

CAREER: British Broadcasting Corp. (BBC-TV), London, England, producer and director of children's programs, 1967-71; *Puffin* and *The Egg* magazines, London, editor, 1977-79; Cover to Cover Cassettes, Wiltshire, England, producer, 1983—; writer of children's books.

WRITINGS:

"MEG AND MOG" SERIES; ILLUSTRATED BY JAN PIENKOWSKI

Meg and Mog, Heinemann (London), 1972, Atheneum (New York City), 1973.
Meg's Eggs, Atheneum, 1973.
Meg at Sea, Heinemann, 1973, Harvey House (New York City), 1976.
Meg on the Moon, Heinemann, 1973, Harvey House, 1976.
Meg's Car, Heinemann, 1975.
Meg's Castle, Heinemann, 1975.
Meg's Veg, Heinemann, 1976.
Mog's Mumps, Heinemann, 1976, Penguin (New York City), 1982.
Meg and Mog Birthday Book, Heinemann, 1979, Puffin (New York City), 1991.
Mog at the Zoo, Heinemann, 1982, Penguin, 1984.
Mog in the Fog, Heinemann, 1984.
Owl at School, Heinemann, 1984, Penguin, 1985.
Mog's Box, Heinemann, 1987.
Owl at the Vet, Penguin, 1992.

OTHER

Quest for the Gloop: The Exploits of Murfy and PHIX, illustrations by Pienkowski, Heinemann, 1980.
(Compiler) *Poems for Seven-Year-Olds and Under,* Kestrel (London), 1983.

Author of *Tom's Home,* 1987.

ADAPTATIONS: David Wood has created four plays for children based on the "Meg and Mog" series, published by Puffin, 1984. Many of the books in the Meg and Mog series, including *Meg and Mog, Meg at Sea, Meg s Eggs,* and *Meg on the Moon* have been adapted to audio.

SIDELIGHTS: Helen Nicoll is best known as the creator of Meg, a witch, her cat Mog, and Snowy the Owl. Nicoll's rhyming language is witty and simple enough for the youngest beginning reader, and the trio of witch, cat, and owl have been the focus of a fourteen-book series illustrated by Jan Pienkowski. Nicoll has also produced and directed television and radio broadcasts for children for the British Broadcasting Corporation (BBC) and for a popular series of audio cassettes that accompany her books in the United Kingdom.

The Meg and Mog series follows its characters through an intriguing array of settings, including the moon and a medieval castle. As a witch, Meg is not especially skilled at magic, which may explain her hesitation in using it. The sun she conjures in *Meg's Veg* to help crops, and the wind she creates in *Meg at Sea* for a ship, appear in extreme forms, resulting in a drought and a storm. John Churcher of *Twentieth-Century Children's Writers* notes, "To young children uncertain of their own powers and the power of household implements, Meg's hit-or-miss spells must be particularly compelling." *Times Literary Supplement* reviewer William Feaver explains that "Meg the wiry witch and Mog her familiar, a black-and-white-striped cat with a tail like a frayed bootlace, are the perfect couple. Meg and Mog stories seize hold. Meg works her magic, Mog reacts and the audience joins in." The Meg and Mog books contain about a line of text per page, "encouraging early reading attempts," writes a reviewer in *Times Literary Supplement.* A reviewer in *School Librarian* states that *Mog at the Zoo* is a "wealth of fun and language learning." The audiocassette series that accompanies the "Meg and Mog" books, produced by Cover to Cover Cassettes, augments the print volumes and provides another learning tool for children. Chris Powling, reviewing the cassettes in *Books for Keeps,* especially recommends *Meg at Sea* and *Meg on the Moon.*

Nicoll and Pienkowski also collaborated on *Quest for the Gloop: The Exploits of Murfy and PHIX,* a science fiction book for older children in which a little green man and his robot succeed in their intergalactic quest to find the life-saving Gloop. According to a reviewer in the *British Book News,* it "will no doubt please young science fiction addicts" who enjoy puns.

BIOGRAPHICAL/CRITICAL SOURCES:

BOOKS

Something about the Author, Volume 87, Gale, 1996.
Twentieth-Century Children's Writers, 4th edition, St. James Press, 1995.

PERIODICALS

Books for Keeps, January, 1986, p. 12; May, 1986, p. 19; November, 1987, p. 10.
British Book News, spring, 1981, p. 23; March, 1988, p. 7.

Growing Point, May, 1982, p. 3908.
New Statesman, May 21, 1976, pp. 689-90.
Observer Review, April 19, 1987, p. 23.
Publishers Weekly, February 18, 1983, pp. 129-30.
School Librarian, September, 1983, p. 235.
Times Educational Supplement, March 15, 1985, p. 24.
Times Literary Supplement, November 3, 1972, p. 1334; March 29, 1974, p. 331; July 27, 1984, p. 854.*

* * *

NIMMO, Jenny 1942-

PERSONAL: Born January 15, 1942 (some sources say 1944), in Windsor, Berkshire, England; married David Wynn Millward (an artist and illustrator), 1974; children: two daughters, one son. *Education:* Private boarding schools, 1950-60.

ADDRESSES: Agent—Murray Pollinger, 4 Garrick St., London WC2E 9BH, England.

CAREER: Theatre Southeast, Sussex and Kent, England, actress and assistant stage manager, 1960-63; governess in Amalfi, Italy, 1963; British Broadcasting Corp. (BBC-TV), London, England, photographic researcher, 1964-66, assistant floor manager, 1966-68, 1971-74, director and writer of children's programs for "Jackanory," 1970; full-time writer, 1975—.

AWARDS, HONORS: Smarties Prize in ages 7-11 category, Rowntree Mackintosh Co., 1986, and Tir Na n'Og Award, Welsh Arts Council, 1987, both for *The Snow Spider.*

WRITINGS:

CHILDREN'S FICTION

The Bronze Trumpeter, illustrated by Caroline Scrace, Angus & Robertson (London), 1975.
Tatty Apple, illustrated by Priscilla Lamont, Methuen (London), 1984.
The Snow Spider (first book in the "Snow Spider" trilogy), illustrated by Joanna Carey, Methuen, 1986, Dutton (New York City), 1987.
Emlyn's Moon (second book in the "Snow Spider" trilogy), illustrated by Carey, Methuen, 1987, published as *Orchard of the Crescent Moon,* Dutton, 1989.
The Red Secret, illustrated by Maureen Bradley, Hamish Hamilton (London), 1989.
The Chestnut Soldier (third book in the "Snow Spider" trilogy), Methuen, 1989.
The Bears Will Get You! Methuen, 1990.
Jupiter Boots, Heinemann, 1990.
Ultramarine, Methuen, 1990.
Delilah and the Dogspell, Methuen, 1991.
Rainbow and Mr. Zed (sequel to *Ultramarine*), Methuen, 1992, Dutton, 1994.
The Breadwitch, Heinemann, 1993.
(Reteller) *The Witches and the Singing Mice,* illustrated by Angela Barrett, Dial (New York City), 1993.
The Stone Mouse, illustrated by Helen Craig, Walker (London), 1993.
(Reteller) *The Starlight Cloak,* illustrated by Justin Todd, Dial, 1993.
Griffin's Castle, Methuen, 1994.
Wilfred's Wolf, illustrated by husband, David Wynn Millward, Bodley Head (London), 1994.
Granny Grimm's Gruesome Glasses, illustrated by Millward, A. & C. Black (London), 1995.
Ronnie and the Millipede, Walker, 1995.
Gwion and the Witch, Beekman, 1996.
Branwen, Beekman, 1998.
Delilah Alone, Galaxy, 1998.

Also author of *Delilah and the Dishwater Dogs,* 1993; *Alien on the 99th Floor* and *The Witch's Tears,* both 1996; and *The Dragon s Child* and *The Owl-Tree,* both 1997.

ADAPTATIONS: The "Snow Spider" trilogy, comprising *The Snow Spider, Emlyn's Moon,* and *The Chestnut Soldier,* has been adapted as children's programs for British television. Several of Nimmo's works have been recorded. The following titles were adapted to audio by Chivers Audio Books: *The Snow Spider,* 1988; *Emlyn's Moon,* 1989; *Delilah and the Dishwater Dogs,* 1994; and *Delilah Alone,* 1998. *The Chestnut Soldier* was adapted to audio in 1992.

SIDELIGHTS: Jenny Nimmo began to receive much notice as a children's author in the 1980s. Her first book, *The Bronze Trumpeter,* was published in 1975, and led *Times Literary Supplement* contributor Ann Thwaite to call her "a new writer of considerable imagination and skill." The responsibility of raising her three children kept her from publishing another book until 1984, and Nimmo related in *Twentieth-Century Children's Writers:* "I live and work in a rural community in Wales where my three bilingual children are growing into an old but vigorous culture. Here place names hark back to legend and it seems to me that the past is still part of the rhythm of everyday life. My books are concerned with the very real problem of growing children, and most of them are set in a landscape which is undeniably magical; they are described as fantasies." As a result, "Wales has a powerful hold on [the] imagination" of this "relative newcomer to children's fantasy," as Donna White revealed in *School Librarian.*

Nimmo has received accolades for her Welsh-inspired books. To win the Tir Na n'Og Award, as she did for *The Snow Spider,* one must present a Welsh language book or, for an English language book, depict an authentic Welsh setting while raising the standard of writing for children and young people. The protagonist of *The Snow Spider* concerns the story of ten-year-old Gwyn Griffiths, whose family is torn apart by his sister's death. In order to help heal his relationship with his parents, Gwyn is given five strange birthday gifts from his mystic grandmother which are to be used to rediscover the magical powers that have long resided in his bloodline. Gwyn is taken aback when he sees his dead sister's ghostly image appear in a spider's sorcerous web. His newfound magic creates a dichotomy, for now he must choose between returning home or joining his sister in a different world. According to *Horn Book* critic Mary M. Burns, "Gwyn is a very real ten-year-old . . . conscious that he is different from his classmates, touchingly anxious to belong and to be loved." Zena Sutherland, writing for *Bulletin of the Center for Children's Books,* found *The Snow Spider* a "cohesive and compelling" story that has "depth and nuance."

The mysterious alternate world of Gwyn's Welsh home returns in *Orchard of the Crescent Moon* (published in England as *Emlyn's Moon*); this time Gwyn's neighbor Nia is the person seeking a special talent, which she must then use to rescue her friend Emlyn. Like its predecessor, *Orchard of the Crescent Moon* demonstrates "the 'realness' of the child characters, despite their close access to ancient magical powers," David Bennett noted in *Books for Keeps.* A *Publishers Weekly* critic similarly observed that while the story has fantasy elements, it is "rooted in the miseries of family misunderstandings and sorrows." "*Emlyn's Moon* confirms all our hopes" about Nimmo's "unusual talents," Marcus Crouch asserted in *Junior Bookshelf.* "This is a rich, moving and amusing story, one which demands and receives the reader's total capitulation."

The trilogy concludes with *The Chestnut Soldier,* in which Gwyn is approaching his fourteenth birthday and still exercising his magical powers. Irresponsibility causes him to lose control of one of his powers, and his carelessness endangers a weak-spirited, wounded soldier resting at a home in the village. Since the power can thwart Gwyn, he must call on his grandmother and Uncle Gwydion to exorcise the evil force from the soldier's abducted spirit. *The Chestnut Soldier* contains the most parallels to the ancient Welsh legends known as the Mabinogion, but was favored least by critic Beth E. Andersen. In *Voice of Youth Advocates,* the reviewer faulted the "relentlessly oppressive moodiness" of the characters and the "disappointingly anti-climactic finish." *School Library Journal* contributor Virginia Golodetz, however, applauded the book and stated that "Nimmo has skillfully woven the ancient story into the modern one, making it accessible to those who do not know the legend." White also praised the concluding volume, calling it "Nimmo's best book to date," showing that the author has been "stirred to new depths."

"As her major work grows in scale and complexity, Nimmo has turned to the creation of small, simpler worlds," Crouch observed in *Twentieth-Century Children's Writers. The Red Secret,* for instance, is a simple tale of Tom, a city boy whose family moves to the country, and how he rescues a wounded fox cub and makes friends in the process. Similarly told with "quiet assurance and [Nimmo's] instinct for the right turn of phrase," according to Crouch in *Junior Bookshelf,* is *Jupiter Boots,* the story of young Timothy's encounter with fancy footwear.

Nimmo returned to a supernatural setting for *Ultramarine,* which "again combines fantasy elements with the psychological growth of her protagonists to weave solid entertainment," according to a *Publishers Weekly* critic. Ned and Nell learn the truth about their parents while staying with their aunt and grandmother, a discovery which leads them to aid a mysterious stranger in rescuing sea creatures. The result is a "tantalizing blend" of elements where the children's "realities are every bit as fascinating as their fantasies," Jody McCoy remarked in *Voice of Youth Advocates. Rainbow and Mr. Zed* continues the story of Nell, who is adjusting to life without Ned on the estate of the mysterious Mr. Zed, whom she discovers is her late mother's evil brother. "In a chilling and eerie story that weaves back and forth between fantasy and reality," as *Booklist* writer Kay Weisman described it, "Nell comes to terms with her uniqueness" and thwarts her uncle's sinister plans. *Rainbow and Mr. Zed* "is exciting, moving, and deeply committed to the preservation of the world," Crouch asserted in *Junior Bookshelf.*

In *Griffin's Castle,* Nimmo uses an urban setting for the first time in one of her longer works. Eleven-year-old Dinah and her mother move into a handsome but dilapidated old house in Cardiff that Dinah dubs Griffin s Castle. When Dinah's security is threatened by her mother's boyfriend, Gomer, who sees the house as a moneymaking opportunity for himself, she finds allies in three of the carved animals that line the walls of Griffin's Castle, and makes two school friends who share her secret that the beasts have come to life. At the end of the novel, Gomer is defeated and Dinah learns that the animals have gone. In *Junior Bookshelf,* Crouch called *Griffin's Castle* Nimmo's most substantial offering since the Ultramarine sequence and noted that all readers will surely have lost their hearts to Dinah.

In an assessment of the author's career in *Twentieth-Century Children's Writers,* Crouch further lauded Nimmo, stating that she "is a living example of the basic formula for success in an author: write what you know. She works in big ideas on a small canvas, which she fills with the figures of her own rural community. Magic or no magic, hers is a real world, viewed with a keen and understanding eye and with rich appreciation of its fun and its folly."

BIOGRAPHICAL/CRITICAL SOURCES:

BOOKS

Children's Literature Review, Volume 44, Gale, 1997.
Something about the Author, Volume 87, Gale, 1996.
St. James Guide to Fantasy Writers, 1st edition, St. James Press, 1996.
Twentieth-Century Children's Writers, 4th edition, St. James Press, 1995.

PERIODICALS

Booklist, May 1, 1993, p. 1605; August, 1994, p. 2064; February 15, 1995.
Books for Keeps, September, 1986, p. 25; March, 1989, p. 19.
Bulletin of the Center for Children's Books, July-August, 1987, p. 216; July-August, 1992, p. 301.
Growing Point, May, 1989, p. 5172; November, 1991, p. 5602.
Horn Book, September-October, 1987, p. 613; September, 1993, p. 611.
Junior Bookshelf, February, 1985, p. 28; February, 1988, p. 51; April, 1989, pp. 65-66; February, 1991; August, 1992, pp. 158-59; December, 1993, p. 235; December, 1994, pp. 229-30; December, 1995, pp. 214-15.
Observer, November 30, 1986, p. 24.
Publishers Weekly, June 9, 1989, p. 68; March 9, 1992, p. 58; August 2, 1993, p. 81.
School Librarian, February, 1988, p. 21; November, 1991, pp. 130-31; February, 1992, p. 21; November, 1993, p. 157; May, 1994, p. 62.
School Library Journal, July, 1991, p. 74; November, 1992, p. 74; February, 1995.
Times Literary Supplement, April 4, 1975, p. 362.
Voice of Youth Advocates, October, 1991, p. 248; June, 1992, p. 113.*

* * *

NOLAN, Frederick William 1931- (Frederick H. Christian, Danielle Rockfern, Donald Severn)

PERSONAL: Born in 1931, in Liverpool, Lancashire, England; married Heidi Wuermli, 1962; children: two sons. *Education:* Attended Liverpool Collegiate.

ADDRESSES: *Home*—England. *Agent*—c/o Arthur Pine Associates, 250 West 57th St., New York, NY 10019.

CAREER: Corgi Books, London, England, assistant editor, 1960-64, editorial reader, 1965; Penguin Books, London, sales representative; Fontana Books, London, worked in publicity; Granada Publishing, London, and Ballantine Books, New York, worked in marketing, director of marketing, publicity, and advertising; Warner Communications, London, publisher; writer, 1972—.

WRITINGS:

HISTORICAL ROMANCE NOVELS

Carver's Kingdom, Macmillan (London), 1978, Warner, 1980.
White Nights, Red Dawn, Macmillan (New York), 1980.
A Promise of Glory (part of the "A Call to Arms" series), Arrow, 1983, Bantam, 1984.
Blind Duty (part of the "A Call to Arms" series), Arrow, 1983, Bantam, 1985.
(Under pseudonym Danielle Rockfern) *On the Field of Honour,* Hamlyn, 1985.
Maximum Demolition, Century, 1991.
Soft Target, Century, 1992.

WESTERN NOVELS; UNDER PSEUDONYM FREDERICK H. CHRISTIAN

Sudden Strikes Back, Corgi, 1966.
Sudden Troubleshooter, Corgi, 1967.
Sudden at Bay, Corgi, 1968.
Sudden: Apache Fighter, Corgi, 1969.
Sudden: Dead or Alive, Corgi, 1970.

Find Angel, Sphere, 1973, Pinnacle, 1974.
Send Angel, Sphere, 1973, Pinnacle, 1974, published as *Ride Clear of Daranga,* Pinnacle, 1979.
Kill Angel, Sphere, 1973, Pinnacle, 1974.
Trap Angel, Sphere, 1973, Pinnacle, 1974.
Frame Angel, Pinnacle, 1974, Sphere, 1975.
Hang Angel, Pinnacle, 1975.
Hunt Angel, Pinnacle, 1975.
Warn Angel, Pinnacle, 1975, published as *Take Angel,* Sphere, 1975.
Stop Angel, Pinnacle, 1976.

SUSPENSE NOVELS

The Oshawa Project, Barker, 1974, published as *The Algonquin Project,* Morrow, 1974, and as *Brass Target,* Jove, 1979.
NYPD: No Place to Be a Cop, Barker, 1974.
The Ritter Double-Cross, Barker, 1974, Morrow, 1975.
Kill Petrosino! Barker, 1975.
The Mittenwald Syndicate, Morrow, 1976.
Wolf Trap, Piatkus, 1983, St. Martin's, 1984.
Red Center, St. Martin's, 1987.
(Under pseudonym Donald Severn) *Sweet Sister Death,* Lynx, 1989, published as *A Time to Die,* 1989.
(Under pseudonym Donald Severn) *Alert State Black,* Lynx, 1990, under pseudonym Frederick Nolan, Century, 1990.
Designated Assassins, Century, 1990.
Rat Run, Century, 1991.

NONFICTION FOR CHILDREN

Jesse James, Macdonald, 1973.
Cowboys, Macdonald, 1974.
Lewis and Clark, Macdonald, 1974.
The Wagon Train, Macdonald, 1974.
Geronimo, Macdonald, 1975.
The Pilgrim Fathers, Macdonald, 1975.
The Battle of Alamo, Macdonald, 1978.
Bad Blood: The Life and Times of the Horrel Brothers, Barbed Wire Press (Stillwater, OK), 1994.

TRANSLATOR; "LUCKY LUKE" SERIES FOR CHILDREN; BY RENE DE GOSCINNY

Jesse James, Brockhampton Press, 1972.
The Stage Coach, Brockhampton Press, 1972.
Dalton City, Brockhampton Press, 1973.
The Tenderfoot, Brockhampton Press, 1974.
Western Circus, Brockhampton Press, 1974.

Also translator of *Ma Dalton,* 1980; *Curing the Daltons,* 1982; and *The Dashing White Cowboy,* 1982.

OTHER TRANSLATIONS

Benjamin Rabier, *Gideon* [and] *Gideon's House* (for children), four volumes, Hodder & Stoughton, 1979.
Peter Heim, *The Black Forest Clinic,* Sphere, 1987.

OTHER

The Life and Death of John Henry Tunstall (biography), University of New Mexico Press, 1965.
(Editor under pseudonym Frederick H. Christian) Pat Garrett, *The Authentic Life of Billy the Kid,* Sphere, 1973.
(With Jay J. Armes) *Jay J. Armes: Investigator,* Macmillan, 1976.
The Sound of Their Music: The Story of Rodgers and Hammerstein (biography; also known as *Rodgers and Hammerstein: The Sound of Their Music*), Walker, 1978.
The Lincoln County War: A Documentary History, University of Oklahoma Press, 1989.
A Poet on Broadway: The Life and Lyrics of Lorenz Hart, Oxford University Press, 1993.

Also author of radio plays *The Richard Rodgers Story* (six one-hour programs), 1976, and screenplay *Brass Target,* 1978.

SIDELIGHTS: Once responsible for marketing the work of other authors, Frederick William Nolan began writing books of his own in the mid-1960s. He is a prolific author of books in a variety of genres, including historical romance, biography, Westerns, and spy fiction. Probably best known for his popular contemporary thrillers *The Mittenwald Syndicate* and *The Oshawa Project,* Nolan has written dozens of other books, often under pen names. Nolan has used the pseudonym Danielle Rockfern for his historical fiction, Frederick H. Christian for Westerns, and Donald Severn for counter-terrorism thrillers.

According to critics, Nolan has displayed a penchant for historical fiction. His espionage thrillers are known for their well-researched historical detail. Of his historical works, Nolan commented in *Twentieth-Century Romance and Historical Writers,* "I would like to think I take my cue from Trevelyan, who said that 'what is important about history is not what happened, but how people felt when it was happening.' "

Nolan's interest in history has led him into many diverse subject areas. His works take readers from the inner circles of Nazi Germany to Tsarist Russia as well as across the Atlantic to explore the American Revolution and the 1878 Lincoln County War—a bitter fight for New Mexico land involving Billy the Kid and a young British store owner named John Henry Tunstall, among others. In addition, Nolan's biographies of Broadway notables Rodgers, Hammerstein, and Lorenz Hart provide a glimpse into the lives and times of these composers.

Nolan has been praised for his ability to evoke accurately other times and places without ever leaving England. According to *New York Times Book Review* contributor Paula Mitchell Marks, in *The Lincoln County War: A Documentary History* "Nolan makes few missteps, writing with authority and accuracy from across the Atlantic . . . and skillfully depicting the events of one of the most bitter feuds to erupt in American frontier history." *Los Angeles Times Book Review* contributor Kristiana Gregory found *A Promise of Glory,* Nolan's historical romance about the birth of the United States, so realistic of the lives and times of American patriots and British soldiers that she commented: "This is one epic that has earned a sequel."

Although some critics fault Nolan for allowing anachronisms and cliched prose to slip into his works, they nonetheless often laud Nolan's fast-paced and engaging dramas. After voicing her criticisms of the novel *White Nights, Red Dawn, Publishers Weekly* contributor Barbara A. Bannon noted that "Nolan's evocation of a turbulent period of Russian history is otherwise absorbing." Writing in the *Los Angeles Times,* Sam Kaplan also forgave the faults of *White Nights, Red Dawn:* "Despite obvious political prejudices," Kaplan wrote, and "despite problems of structure and style that at times buries the struggle of Tatiana, her family and friends under a foot of prose, the story is absorbing."

Nolan is also sometimes criticized for producing fiction that is steeped in violence and sensationalism. Critics have noted, however, that Nolan's work remains popular, especially his spy thrillers. As Sybil Steinberg observed in a *Publishers Weekly* review of *Red Center,* "Nolan knows his politics, crime, trade-craft and people, but most of all he knows how to keep readers turning pages in this riveting, witty, even stylish treat."

BIOGRAPHICAL/CRITICAL SOURCES:

BOOKS

Twentieth-Century Romance and Historical Writers, 2nd edition, 1990, 3rd edition, 1994, St. James Press.

PERIODICALS

Kirkus Reviews, April 1, 1978, p. 419; October 1, 1984, p. 925; July 1, 1994, p. 911.

Library Journal, August, 1974, p. 1991; May 1, 1978; October 1, 1980, p. 2108; February 15, 1987, p. 162; January, 1992, p. 153.

Los Angeles Times, October 15, 1981.

Los Angeles Times Book Review, April 1, 1984; April 23, 1995, p. 10.

New York Times Book Review, April 26, 1987, p. 37; August 9, 1992, p. 9.

Observer, December 24, 1989, p. 41.

Publishers Weekly, May 27, 1974, p. 59; January 6, 1975; April 19, 1976, p. 84; April 10, 1978, p. 63; September 12, 1980, p. 59; February 6, 1987, p. 85.*

* * *

NOON, Jeff 1957-

PERSONAL: Born November 24, 1957, in Manchester, England; son of James (a presser) and Lilian (a clothing machinist; maiden name, Pearson) Noon. *Education:* Attended Manchester University, 1981-84. *Politics:* "Polymorphous diversity." *Religion:* "Diverse polymorphism." *Avocational interests:* Music, wine, science.

ADDRESSES: *Agent*—Barbara J. Zitwer Agency, 525 West End Ave. No. 7H, New York, NY 10024.

CAREER: Musician, community artist, bookseller, playwright, and author.

MEMBER: British Science Fiction Association.

AWARDS, HONORS: Third prize, Mobil Playwriting Competition for the Royal Exchange Theatre, Manchester, England, for *Woundings,* 1985; Arthur C. Clarke Award for science fiction, 1993, and Eurocon Award, 1994, both for *Vurt;* John W. Campbell Award for Best New Writer, 1995.

WRITINGS:

Woundings (play), Oberon (Birmingham, England), 1986.

Vurt (novel), Ringpull (Littleborough, England), 1993, Crown (New York City), c. 1995.

Pollen (sequel to *Vurt*), Ringpull, 1995.

Automated Alice, Crown, 1996.

Contributor of the short story "Ultra Kid and Catgirl" to *Gentlemen's Quarterly,* 1995.

ADAPTATIONS: *Vurt* was adapted to audio by Simon and Schuster, 1995.

SIDELIGHTS: Former punk rock musician Jeff Noon is the author of *Vurt,* the first work in a projected quartet of cyberpunk novels and winner of the 1993 Arthur C. Clarke Award for science fiction. The action in *Vurt* takes place in Manchester, England, of the future, and in and out of virtual reality. The main character, Scribble, loses his sister (with whom he has an incestuous relationship) when she is held captive in virtual reality and an amorphous creature is returned in exchange. The reader follows Scribble's adventures as he searches for Curious Yellow Feather, a designer drug that he believes will allow him to retrieve his sister. Unlike other science-fiction novels termed "cyberpunk," *Vurt* deemphasizes technology and focuses instead on a love story. Noon told *CA* that he describes his work as "avant pulp."

"Apart from the absence of technofetishisms, the novel diverges most radically from the cyberpunk template in its abundance of heart," remarked Richard Gehr, reviewer for *Voice Literary Supplement.* "Mythic, operatic, and throwaway at once, *Vurt* riffs between myth, kitsch, and chaos through language embodying a sometimes excruciatingly elegant pop poetics." Several critics commented on the novel's reworking of science fiction genres. "You could . . . read *Vurt* as a literary remix of cyberpunk—a dub version as important for what's been taken out as for what remains. A profound story about absence and loss," wrote Gehr. Likewise, Hal Espen remarked in *New Yorker:* "While this novel observes most of the conventions of cyberpunk fiction, its imagery is insistently organic, and owes more to the underground pharmacology of the rave scene than to the world of hardwired chips and user interfaces."

Vurt has garnered widely mixed criticism. "Despite its bizarre trappings and intriguing basic conceit, it fails to convince," stated Tom De Haven in *New York Times Book Review.* Calling Noon "a woefully clumsy writer," Espen faulted the author's handling of the plot, especially Scribble's incestuous relationship. Yet other readers have found much to admire about the novel. "*Vurt* is an astonishing novel in story, style and emotion," observed David V. Barrett in *New Statesman.* "In places it has the lyricism of Elizabeth Smart's *By Grand Central Station I Sat Down and Wept,* mixed with the weird and wild fun of Chester Anderson's cult hippy-SF novel *The Butterfly Kid* and the streetwise cynicism of Kurt Vonnegut at his best." *Locus* contributor Faren Miller concluded, "In all, *Vurt* is deserving of its prestigious award, and well worth reading, so long as you're into literary quality, convincing atmosphere, and a future animated more by age-old passions than by whatever high-tech lies behind those strange drug-feathers."

Pollen, the sequel to *Vurt,* lends Noon's dystopic vision to a murder investigation. The plot involves a psychic female police officer's attempt to determine the origin of a sweet-smelling pollen, a substance linked to a series of fatalities. Through telekinesis, the officer summons "the victims' dying thoughts and discovers that their last moments were spent in a kind of rapture, an ecstasy of blood, semen and pollen," reported Jason Cowley in *Times Literary Supplement.* The officer and her daughter are immune to the fatal effects of the pollen, which soon causes a full-blown epidemic as exotic plants flower throughout the city; together mother and daughter leave for the wilderness, seeking clues to this disastrous phenomenon. Cowley noted in his review of *Pollen* that Noon "has revitalized the science-fiction novel, bringing to it a sinister playfulness and robust experimentalism." Although the critic faulted *Pollen* for creating an ultimately unconvincing blueprint of the future, he stated that "the swagger and bravura of [Noon's] style have a certain compulsion."

BIOGRAPHICAL/CRITICAL SOURCES:

BOOKS

Contemporary Literary Criticism, Yearbook 1995, Volume 91, Gale, 1996.

PERIODICALS

Entertainment Weekly, February 10, 1995, p. 60.

Locus, September, 1994, pp. 19-20.

Magazine of Fantasy and Science Fiction, July, 1995, p. 23.

New Statesman, January 21, 1994, p. 41.

New Yorker, February 13, 1995, pp. 86-87.

New York Times Book Review, February 5, 1995, p. 19.

People Weekly, February 20, 1995, p. 22.

Times (London), December 3, 1986.

Times Literary Supplement, May 19, 1995, p. 21.

Voice Literary Supplement, February, 1995, p. 14.

Washington Post Book World, February 26, 1995, p. 8.*

NORWOOD, Warren C. 1945-

PERSONAL: Born August 21, 1945, in Philadelphia, PA; son of Warren Heller (a small business owner) and Marie (a secretary; maiden name, Drautz) Norwood; married Mary Walker, April 16, 1965 (divorced, 1972); married Margot Biery (an educator in business administration), March 17, 1973; children: Margaret Marie. *Education:* North Texas State University, B.A., 1972. *Avocational interests:* Wildflower photography and classification.

ADDRESSES: Office—2428 Las Brisas, Fort Worth, TX 76119. *Agent*—Richard Curtis Associates, Inc., 164 East 64th St., Suite 1, New York, NY 10021.

CAREER: University Bookstore, University of Texas at Arlington, assistant manager, 1973-76; Century Bookstore, Fort Worth, TX, manager, 1976-77; Ballantine Books, Inc., New York City, publisher's representative in Fort Worth, 1978-79; Bantam Books, Inc., New York City, publisher's representative in Fort Worth, 1980-83. Writer. Teacher of creative writing at Tarrant County Junior College, 1981-83. *Military service:* U.S. Army, 1966-69; served in Vietnam; became staff sergeant; received Bronze Star.

MEMBER: Science Fiction Writers of America, Science Fiction Research Association, Science Fiction Poetry Association, National Rifle Association, Sky Soldiers.

WRITINGS:

SCIENCE-FICTION NOVELS

The Windhover Tapes, Bantam, Volume I: *An Image of Voices,* 1982, Volume II: *Flexing the Warp,* 1983, Volume III: *Fize of the Gabriel Ratchets,* 1983, Volume IV: *Planet of Flowers,* 1984.

(With Ralph Mylius) *The Seren Cenacles,* Bantam, 1984.

Shudderchild, Bantam, 1987.

True Jaguar, Bantam, 1988.

Vanished, Lynx, 1988.

(With Mel Odom) *Stranded,* Lynx, 1989.

Trapped! Lynx, 1989.

ODOUBLE SPIRAL WARO TRILOGY, ALL BY BANTAM

Midway Between, 1984.

Polar Fleet, 1985.

Final Command, 1986.

Contributor of stories, poems, and articles to regional and national magazines.

SIDELIGHTS: Critics praised Warren C. Norwood's first novel, *An Image of Voices,* a complex story containing elements of space opera, obscure literary allusions, and references to characters from folklore. Michael M. Levy of *Twentieth-Century Science-Fiction Writers* describes the style of this debut novel as a blend of monologue and the eighteenth-century epistolary fiction of Samuel Richardson. The first in "The Windhover Tapes" series, *An Image of Voices* is set in the distant future in which faster-than-light travel is common and humankind has not only contacted other races but interbred with them. The central character is Gerard Hopkins Manley, a diplomat and anthropologist who has a sentient space ship called Windhover. The four novels in the series concern Manley's adventures with such strange beings as sentient flowers, feminist ghosts, and wheeled birds. Throughout the series, Norwood plants numerous references to the nineteenth-century poet Gerard Manly Hopkins (whose work includes the widely anthologized poem "The Windhover"), although the characters in the novels have no knowledge of him.

Levy observes that while "The Windhover Tapes" series is "an enjoyable piece of work," there are several flaws. Among these Levy notes "the seeming irrelevance of most of the Hopkins material, Norwood's frequent inclusion of his own not-very-good poetry (including a travesty of Hopkins' '[The] Windhover'), and the author's apparent fixation on human and humanoid mammary glands (Manley's beautiful alien wife has three)." He adds that the series is uneven, fluctuating between originality and cliche. Still, Levy praises Norwood's stylistic experimentation and his creation of an unusual science-fiction hero—"an emotional man who is not afraid to cry or dote upon his infant son and daughter, a man who is capable of space opera-style action, but who would really much rather talk things out sensibly."

Levy finds most of Norwood's work since "The Windhover Tapes" disappointing, citing *The Seren Cenacles* as an example of a less-than-satisfying novel. Set in a mining colony, it is a story of terror involving political, industrial, military, and alien forces. Levy notes weaknesses in this novel such as the improbable premise and the lack of explanation and context for the many groups vying for power.

In the fantasy novel *True Jaguar,* a man realizes that he is the reincarnation of a Mayan god. It is his task to travel to the Underworld and battle demons in order to save the Earth from a comet. Levy comments that this "engaging fantasy . . . gives some indication of what Norwood is capable of at his best."

Norwood once reported to *CA:* "I decided to become a professional writer when I was seventeen. I sold my first book when I was thirty-four. Perseverance and discipline have been the keys to my success, along with a fine high school teacher and a college professor who taught me how to make myself a writer.

"Science fiction had always been my favorite recreational reading because it challenged my imagination while it entertained me. In college my primary interest in philosophy was the philosophy of science. Consequently, when I had the opportunity to devote a full year to writing, in 1980, it seemed natural to attempt a science-fiction novel. *An Image of Voices* has already been through five printings, and since the later books have also been well received, I will continue to write in this genre. That does not mean that I will confine myself to writing science fiction in the future, but I do not expect that I will ever stop writing it either. It is too much fun.

"In the last several years I have developed an increasing interest in military history, centering on World War II and Vietnam. This is part of what led me to propose the 'Double Spiral War' series, in which I hope to show that right and wrong matter less in war than winning and losing. My personal experiences in Vietnam certainly contributed to the desire to write this series, but an even more important motivational force was the realization of how few people I met truly understood the internal nature of war and its costs in human terms."

BIOGRAPHICAL/CRITICAL SOURCES:

BOOKS

Twentieth-Century Science-Fiction Writers, 3rd edition, St. James Press, 1991.

PERIODICALS

Library Journal, September 15, 1983, p. 1811; September 15, 1984, p. 1776.

Los Angeles Times Book Review, May 23, 1982, p. 6.

Publishers Weekly, December 17, 1982, p. 71; September 9, 1983, p. 60; January 27, 1984, p. 73; August 24, 1984, p. 77.*

NWAPA, Flora 1931-1993

PERSONAL: Full name, Florence Nwanzuruahu Nkiru Nwapa; born January 18, 1931, in Oguta, East Central State, Nigeria ; died October 16, 1993; married Gogo Nwakuche (an industrialist), 1967; children: Amede, Uzoma, Ejine. *Education:* University College, Ibadan, Nigeria, B.A., 1957; University of Edinburgh, diploma in education, 1958.

CAREER: Ministry of Education, Calabar, Nigeria, education officer in inspectorate division, 1958; Queen's School, Enugu, Nigeria, education officer and teacher of English and geography, 1959-61; University of Lagos, Lagos, Nigeria, administrative officer, beginning in 1962, lecturer in creative writing and geography at International Press Institute, 1962-65, assistant registrar, until 1967; East Central State of Nigeria, member of executive council and minister of health and social welfare, 1970-71, minister of lands, survey, and urban development, 1971-74, minister of establishments, beginning in 1974; Tana Press Ltd., Ogui Enugu, Nigeria, founder, chairperson, and managing director, 1977-93. Flora Nwapa Books Ltd., founder and managing director, 1977-93. Alvan Ikoku College of Education, visiting lecturer, 1976-77; University of Maiduguri, visiting professor, 1989-90; East Carolina University, visiting professor, 1993; lecturer at colleges and universities, including New York University, Trinity College (Hartford, CT), Episcopal Divinity School (Cambridge, MA), University of Minnesota—Twin Cities, Sarah Lawrence College, Kalamazoo College, University of Michigan, University of Oregon, and University of Colorado, Denver. University of Ilorin, member of governing council, 1986. Commission on Review of Higher Education in Nigeria, member, 1990.

MEMBER: International PEN, African Literature Association, Association of Nigerian Authors (vice president, 1981; president for Borno State, 1989), Children's Literature Association of Nigeria, African Studies Association (U.S.).

AWARDS, HONORS: Recipient of numerous grants; Certificate of Merit, Nigeria Association of University Women, 1980; named Officer of the Order of the Niger, Federal Government of Nigeria, 1982; fellow at University of Iowa, 1984; Merit Awards for literary achievement from University of Ife, 1985, and Solidra Circle, Lagos, Nigeria, and Octagon Club, Owerri, Nigeria, both 1987.

WRITINGS:

NOVELS

Efuru, Heinemann Educational, 1966.
Idu, Heinemann Educational, 1971.
Never Again, Tana Press, 1975, Africa World Press, 1991.
One Is Enough, Tana Press, 1982, Africa World Press, 1991.
Women Are Different, Tana Press, 1986, Africa World Press, 1991.

FOR CHILDREN

Emeka, Driver's Guard, illustrated by Roslyn Isaacs, University of London Press, 1972.
My Animal Number Book, Flora Nwapa Books, 1977.
My Tana Colouring Book, Flora Nwapa Books, 1978.
Mammywater, illustrated by Obiora Udechukwu, Tana Press, 1979.
Journey to Space, illustrated by Chinwe Orieke, Tana Press, 1980.
The Miracle Kittens, illustrated by Emeka Onwudinjo, Tana Press, 1980.
The Adventures of Deke, Flora Nwapa Books, 1982.

OTHER

This Is Lagos and Other Stories, Tana Press, 1971, Africa World Press, 1991.
Wives at War and Other Stories, Tana Press, 1986, Africa World Press, 1991.
Cassava Song and Rice Song (poems), Tana Press, 1986.

SIDELIGHTS: As a teacher, government official, businesswoman, and writer, Flora Nwapa expressed an avid interest in the traditions and momentous changes taking place in Nigeria. Such interests are a focus of her writing, whether she is educating children about the myths and spiritual beliefs of the Igbo in *Mammywater* and *Cassava Song and Rice Song* or depicting the impact of change on the women characters in her novels and short stories. All of Nwapa's works are grounded in Igbo life and culture. Her characters are drawn, like many in the African literary tradition, from the outside in, so that the orality, or the richness of African dialogue, emerges. For her talent in dramatizing the special nature of Igbo women's talk, she is praised by such critics as Lloyd Brown in *Women Writers of Black Africa* and Gay Wilentz in *Binding Cultures, Black Women Writers in Africa and the Diaspora.* In her obituary in *Guardian,* fellow author Chinua Achebe writes that Nwapa placed the "specific experiences of women squarely at the center of story-making, without apologies or the trendy self-consciousness of many later practitioners," adding that she will be missed "especially as a writer who celebrated ordinary women overcoming the constraints placed on them."

Nwapa's adult fiction comprises a transformational whole, as her women characters begin by operating within the accepted traditions of Igbo society, but move outside its codes when their social, economic and spiritual needs grow beyond the Igbo ideal of how a woman should behave. Hence, as the women protagonists in *Efuru* and *Idu* maintain individual will, they "demonstrate the ability of women to transform both motherhood and childlessness into positive, self-defined and powerful experiences," notes Jane Bryce-Okunla in *Motherlands.* Greater movement outside these traditions is depicted in *Wives at War and Other Stories.* This new direction is signaled first by the title, which—when related to some of the stories—means not only women's participation in the Nigerian Civil War between Igbos and opposing tribal groups (also called the Biafran War), but also women's direct confrontation with men for political rights; their private bonding against paternalism and the male who cannot think realistically; and their determination to avoid being regarded solely as sexual objects.

Nwapa later wrote the novels *One Is Enough* and *Women Are Different.* In *One Is Enough,* Amaku, the protagonist, relinquishes the predetermined role of wife against the wishes of her mother, the father of her children, and her community. In short, Amaku's transformation is typical of a number of Nwapa's previous women characters because she begins by endorsing her community's belittlement of her childless status but ends by questioning any standards which she feels may demean her self-image. *Women Are Different* follows the development of three women who begin as schoolmates, each looking to the future for husbands and family. Like Amaku they find that, as adults, their dreams of a stable family life are unfulfilled and they must work hard to achieve financial independence without their errant husbands' help.

Transformation and transition of women characters lie at the center of Nwapa's themes. The struggle of women as wives and mothers is interwoven with their change and emergence. In *Efuru* and *Idu* the theme of the relationship between women and their communities is essential to understanding Nwapa's portraits of the traditional wife whose status is achieved through childbirth; of the woman who achieves rank and power in seeing to it that traditions are maintained, no matter how restrictive; and of the aggressive woman who is the protector of other women as she openly and brazenly challenge the men for fair treatment. In *One Is Enough* and *Women Are Different* Nwapa celebrates the strength, imagination, and energy of women who become economically and spiritually independent in Nigeria's fast-paced urban centers. One underlying theme in both *This Is Lagos and Other Stories* and *Women Are Different* is the loss of some traditions brought about by westernization and changes in economics and political structure. In *Kunapipi* Kirsten Holst Petersen also observes that in *This Is Lagos, Never Again,* and *Wives at War* the shift in environments causes women to lose "the secure moral universe of the village" and instead be confronted by "problems of individual survival in a city jungle with no guidelines except those provided by success, modern life and wealth, exemplified by cars, drink, wigs, etc."

Nwapa's themes clearly have a feminine slant. The power of feminine bonding is a theme present in *Women Are Different, Wives at War and Other Stories,* and *One Is Enough.* Nwapa does not dehumanize or reject her male characters, but as upholders of paternalistic values, they are sometimes blind or indifferent to women's needs; they impede women's progress and exploit them economically or sexually. Commenting on Nwapa's feminism in *Efuru,* critic Adewale Maja-Pearce concludes in *World Literature Written in English* that Nwapa's feminism "isn't of the strident kind. Far from hating men, she doesn't even dislike them. The women in the novel [*Efuru*] possess some extra quality that the men lack: her women are 'good' in a way that her men never are." Underscoring this theme of feminine power Brenda Berrian in the *College Language Association Journal* (*CLAJ*) says that "Nwapa insists that although the African woman may be vulnerable to men, she does not play a subordinate role."

While women are still at the center of these texts, *This Is Lagos, Never Again,* and *Wives at War* depict the Biafran War in terms of how it affects soldiers, women, families, villages, and towns in Biafra. Biafra, so called by the Igbos of Nigeria's Eastern Region, seceded from Nigeria on May 30, 1967, as a result of massacres of thousands of Igbos by two other tribal groups, the Yorubas and Hausas, who believed the rumor that Igbos were attempting to control all of Nigeria. In *This Is Lagos,* the story "My Soldier Brother" is one of the few told from a male perspective. An adoring youth joins his Igbo militia unit to avenge his brother's death. The irony in the story captures Nwapa's sense of tragedy in all of her war stories: those Igbos most enthusiastic about an Igbo victory seem to lose sight of the fact that they were not only losing the war but also suffering the loss of entire generations of Igbos. It is this irony of fanatic patriotism amid tremendous loss and suffering that Nwapa's heroine, Kate, observes in *Never Again.* "In Nwapa's novel, the refrain 'never again' becomes the expressed resolve that such suffering, the dehumanization, and the fragmentation would no longer be tolerated," explains Maxine Sample in *Modern Fiction Studies.* In "Wives at War" and "A Certain Death" Nwapa depicts the vital role of women in the war. They organized kitchens for starving soldiers, and they were the main force behind the Biafran Red Cross. In the case of the woman character in "A Certain Death," they saved the lives of the remaining men in their families by paying substitutes to go to war. Nwapa notes in *Never Again* and *One Is Enough* that women participated in the "attack trade." Using their acquired skills in market trade, these women bargained with the enemy, the Nigerians, for items of which the starving Biafrans were in dire need.

Often referred to as Africa's first woman novelist to publish in English, Flora Nwapa is remembered as a literary voice of the African woman during a period when African literature was dominated by men. She enriched the English language with Igbo folk idioms spoken largely by and about women. In her early novels Nwapa offers a view of women's lives in precolonial times; through Nwapa the African woman is no longer silent. As Elleke Boehmer observes in *Motherlands,* Nwapa gives voice to texts which challenge the conventional literary image of women created by the African male writer and which depict the evolution of female characters who define their own lives, whether or not they are mothers or wives.

Nwapa once told *CA:* "I have been writing for nearly thirty years. My interest has been on both the rural and the urban woman in her quest for survival in a fast-changing world dominated by men.

"My fascination with the goddess of the lake, or the water spirit, shows up in most of my writings, especially in the children's book *Mammywater.* In research for a paper on priestesses and power among the Riverine Igbo, I came across interesting aspects of the call of power of a priestess of the Lake Goddess. The novel *The Lake Goddess* is based on my findings.

"I am interested in the ancestral worship of my people, and how it has affected their Christian beliefs. This interest was rekindled by the ceremonies I had to perform, as the first daughter, when my Christian father died.

"I would like to teach African literature, as well as work on the myth of the Lake Goddess and the Christian religion in a community whose ancestors mean so much to them."

BIOGRAPHICAL/CRITICAL SOURCES:

BOOKS

Brown, Lloyd, *Women Writers of Black Africa,* Greenwood, 1981.

Dictionary of Literary Biography, Volume 125: *Twentieth-Century Caribbean and Black African Writers, Second Series,* Gale, 1993.

James, Adeola, editor, *In Their Own Voices, African Women Writers Talk,* Heinemann, 1990.

Nasta, Susheila, editor, *Motherlands: Black Women's Writing from Africa, the Caribbean and South Asia,* Rutgers, 1992.

Twentieth-Century Children's Writers, 4th edition, St. James Press, 1995.

Umeh, Marie, *Emerging Perspectives on Flora Nwapa,* Africa World Press (Trenton, NJ), 1997.

Wilentz, Gay, *Binding Cultures, Black Women Writers in Africa and the Diaspora,* Indiana University Press, 1992.

PERIODICALS

Africa Woman, July/August, 1977.

African Literature Today, number 7, 1975.

College Language Association Journal, Volume 25, number 3, 1982.

Kunapipi, Volume 7, numbers 2-3, 1985.

Magazine of Fantasy and Science Fiction, autumn, 1991.

Modern Fiction Studies, autumn, 1991.

Nigeria Magazine, June, 1966.

Presence Africaine, Volume 82, 1972.

World Literature Written in English, spring, 1985.

OBITUARIES:

PERIODICALS

Guardian (London), November 4, 1993.*

O

O'BRIEN, Sean 1952-

PERSONAL: Born December 19, 1952, in London, England. *Education:* Selwyn College, Cambridge, B.A. (English), 1974; Birmingham University, M.A., 1977; attended Hull University, 1976-79; Leeds University, post-graduate certificate in education, 1981.

ADDRESSES: Home—56 Mafeking Rd., Brighton BN2 4EL, East Sussex, England.

CAREER: Beacon School, Crowborough, East Sussex, teacher, 1981-89; University of Dundee, fellow in creative writing, 1989-90; *The Printer's Devil* literary magazine, Brighton, East Sussex, founding editor, with Stephen Plaice, 1990.

AWARDS, HONORS: Eric Gregory award, 1979; Somerset Maugham award, 1984; Cholmondeley award, 1988.

WRITINGS:

POETRY

The Indoor Park, Bloodaxe (Newcastle upon Tyne), 1983.
The Frighteners, Bloodaxe, 1987.
Boundary Beach, Ulsterman (Belfast), 1989.
HMS Glasshouse, Oxford University Press (Oxford and New York), 1991.
A Rarity, Carnivorous Arpeggio Press (Hull), 1993.
Ghost Train, Oxford University Press (New York), 1995.
(Editor) *The Firebox: Poetry in Britain and Ireland after 1945,* Pan Books, 1998.

OTHER

Bloody Ambassadors: The Gruesome Stories of Irish People Tried for Murder Abroad, Poolbeg (Dublin), 1993.
The Deregulated Muse: Essays in Contemporary British and Irish Poetry, Bloodaxe, 1998.

SIDELIGHTS: Sean O'Brien's poetry rose to prominence in the 1980s with its unique blend of realism, social observation, and imagination. A sense of place, both symbolic and literal, is of great importance in O'Brien's poems. R. J. C. Watt of *Contemporary Poets* noted the influence of W. H. Auden's "polymorphous gifts . . . which show up in O'Brien's predilection for switching between the panoramic view and the telling local detail, and in his ability to capture the menacing suggestiveness of something out of view waiting to happen." Once he evokes a setting, O'Brien depicts confused and often restless lives shaped by their environment. Although travel represents the possibility of escape, his characters rarely pursue it. O'Brien also makes frequent references to maps and atlases to suggest the meeting of the tangible world with the imaginative world.

While O'Brien appreciates his English roots, he often condemns things that have been done in England's name. In *The Frighteners,* for example, the poet addresses the consequences of war by depicting its impact on the lives of children as a metaphor for its effects on future generations. At the same time, he demonstrates how the brutalities of past wars continue into the present in such forms as hypocrisy and police attitudes. As are most of O'Brien's poetry collections, *The Frighteners* is rich in imagery, leading Watt to observe, "At times the richness of his imagination becomes cryptic and inscrutable, but the clarity of his best images is shining."

O'Brien commented in *Contemporary Poets,* "I am particularly interested in history, politics, and place. My early poems drew heavily on Hull, the city where I grew up, and northern loyalties have continued to figure in my work since moving to the south in the early 1980s. . . . The conditions of the 1980s seem to me to have presented poets with a problem which has gone largely unaddressed, that of writing poetry which confronts moral and economic barbarism while remaining art. . . . In my own experience, the largely implicit political concerns of my first book, *The Indoor Park,* became a good deal more vocal in its successor, *The Frighteners,* partly through satire and historical reflections but also in the effort to use the resources of fantasy and image to bind the personal and political together."

BIOGRAPHICAL/CRITICAL SOURCES:

BOOKS

Contemporary Poets, 6th edition, St. James Press, 1996.

PERIODICALS

London Review of Books, July 23, 1987, p. 16; March 12, 1992, p. 27.

Observer, June 14, 1987, p. 22; March 1, 1992, p. 63.

Times Literary Supplement, November 20, 1987, p. 1275; January 31, 1992, p. 26; October 27, 1995, p. 27.*

* * *

O'DONNELL, Lawrence
See MOORE, C(atherine) L(ucile)

* * *

O'DRISCOLL, Dennis 1954-

PERSONAL: Born January 1, 1954, in Thurles, County Tipperary, Ireland; son of James F. (a salesman and horticulturist) and Catherine (a homemaker; maiden name, Lahart) O'Driscoll; married Julie O'Callaghan (a writer), September, 1985. *Education:* Institute of Public Administration, Certificate of Public Administration, 1972; attended National University of Ireland, University College, Dublin, 1972-75.

ADDRESSES: *Office*—c/o International Customs Branch, Castle House, South Great George's St., Dublin 2, Ireland.

CAREER: Revenue Commissioners, Dublin, Ireland, executive officer, 1970-76, higher executive officer, 1976-83, assistant principal officer, 1983—. Writer-in-residence at National University of Ireland, University College, Dublin, 1987-88; literary organizer of Dublin Arts Festival, 1977-79.

MEMBER: Irish United Nations Association (member of council, c. 1975-80).

AWARDS, HONORS: Grants from Irish Arts Council, 1985 and 1996.

WRITINGS:

(Editor with Peter Fallon) *The First Ten Years: Dublin Arts Festival Poetry,* Dublin Arts Festival, 1979.

Kist (poems), Dolmen Press (Mountrath, Ireland), 1982.

Hidden Extras (poems), Anvil Press/Dedalus Press, 1987.

(With others) *Five Irish Poets,* White Pine Press (Buffalo, NY), 1990.

Long Story Short (poems), Anvil Press/Dedalus Press, 1993.

The Bottom Line (poem), Dedalus Press, 1994.

Quality Time (poems), HarperCollins Publishers (London), 1996.

As the Poet Said, Poetry Ireland, 1998.

Contributor of about 200 articles and reviews to periodicals, including *Poetry, London Magazine, Harvard Review, Southern Review,* and *Poetry Review.* Editor of *Poetry Ireland Review,* 1986-87.

SIDELIGHTS: Dennis O'Driscoll told *CA:* "I have a demanding (and not very interesting!) full-time job. As a result, much of my literary activity is concentrated on weekends. I therefore write only the poems that absolutely insist on being written, that will not go away however much I may initially resist them. Although I dislike my job, I am suspicious in certain respects of poetry as a career, if it leads to a lot of unnecessary (and unconvincing) poems being written. I prefer to write *criticism* in my 'uninspired' periods.

"Many of my poems are about the physical frailty of people and the tenuous hold we have on life. Other themes include the small frustrations of everyday life and the drabness and monotony of routines involving unfulfilling jobs and suburban neighborhoods. Although my themes are often serious, even grim, the poetry tends to undercut solemnity through irony."

Prior to publishing his own verse, O'Driscoll was well known as a poetry reviewer. Bernard O'Donoghue of *Contemporary Poets* noted that O'Driscoll's "notably discriminating eye" soon made him a respected critic whose comments often made the reputations of the poets whose work he reviewed. At the age of twenty-eight, he published his first volume of poetry, *Kist,* which contains references to the works of such noted writers as Franz Kafka and Boris Pasternak. O'Donoghue commented that what was especially "striking was an insistent consistency of theme, indicated by the volume's archaizing title (meaning 'coffin' as well as the Elizabethan 'kissed'—as in 'Farewell unkist!') and by the cover illustration, Munch's 'The Kiss of Death.' " The poet's exploration of mortality may be linked to the early deaths of both of his parents and, as O'Donoghue continued, "The theme is carried with an extraordinary, paradoxical energy. Even while the insistent pathology threatens to become stifling, the immediacy of the plain language used is focused on the physical elements of life while they are being lost."

O'Driscoll's later work takes everyday life as its subject—people at work, family, and locale. He commented on the course of his writing in *Contemporary Poets:* "The primary impulse behind my early poetry was a sense of bewilderment, sometimes bordering on disbelief, at the human condition: the tenuous hold we have on life, the humiliation and uncertainties experienced during that life, and the degradations of illness and death. Thematically, the work has broadened, stylistically, it has become less raw with an increased irony and black humor. Themes occurring more frequently include some associated with the monotonous routines involved in earning a living. The poems are written out of—though not necessarily about—personal experiences (the early deaths of my parents; the office job I have held since I was sixteen).

"I like to use the most economic language possible in my poetry, unless the theme prompts otherwise. In this respect, I have learned a great deal from the East European poets about whom I have written a considerable amount of critical prose. A concise style is also appropriate to a life which is dominated by non-literary demands."

BIOGRAPHICAL/CRITICAL SOURCES:

BOOKS

Contemporary Poets, 6th edition, St. James Press, 1996.

PERIODICALS

Cobweb (Maynootu), number 10, 1994.
Irish Literary Supplement, Volume 2, number 2, 1983.
New Statesman, January 2, 1998.
Observer, June 15, 1997.
Sunday Tribune (Dublin), September 19, 1982; August 2, 1987; March 13, 1994.
Times Literary Supplement, March 4, 1988; October 1, 1993.*

* * *

O'HARA, Kevin
See CUMBERLAND, Marten

* * *

OKIMOTO, Jean Davies 1942-

PERSONAL: Born December 14, 1942, in Cleveland, OH; daughter of Norman Hugh (in business) and Edith (Williams) Davies; married Peter C. Kirkman, August 26, 1961 (divorced, 1971); married Joseph T. Okimoto (a psychiatrist), May 19, 1973; children: (first marriage) Katherine, Amy; (stepchildren) Stephen, Dylan. *Education:* Attended DePauw University, 1960-63, and University of Washington, Seattle, 1971-72; Antioch College, M.A., 1977. *Avocational interests:* Swimming, sailing, painting.

ADDRESSES: *Office*—2700 East Madison, Seattle, WA 98112. *Agent*—Ruth Cohen, P.O. Box 7626, Menlo Park, CA 94025.

CAREER: High school teacher of remedial reading in Seattle, WA, 1972-73; University of Washington, Seattle, editorial consultant in child psychiatry, 1973-74; Mount Baker Youth Service Bureau, Seattle, chairman, 1973, assistant to director, 1974-75; private practice of psychotherapy in Seattle, 1975—. Mount Baker Community Club, vice president, 1968; Seattle Public Schools, volunteer tutor, 1969; Franklin Area School

Council, chairman, 1970. Creator and chairperson of Mayor's Reading Awards.

MEMBER: American Personnel and Guidance Association, PEN, Authors Guild, Authors League of America, Pacific Northwest Writers' Conference, Seattle Freelancers.

AWARDS, HONORS: Washington State Governor's Writers' Award, 1982, for *It's Just Too Much;* American Library Association Best Book for Young Adults and International Reading Association Choice Book, both 1987, both for *Jason's Women.*

WRITINGS:

My Mother Is Not Married to My Father (children's novel), Putnam, 1979.
It's Just Too Much (children's novel), Putnam, 1980.
Norman Schnurman, Average Person (children's novel), Putnam, 1982.
Who Did It, Jenny Lake? (young adult novel), Putnam, 1983.
Jason's Women, Atlantic Monthly Press, 1986.
Boomerang Kids, Little, Brown, 1987.
Blumpoe the Grumpoe Meets Arnold the Cat, Little, Brown, 1990.
Take a Chance, Gramps! Little, Brown, 1990.
Molly By Any Other Name, Scholastic, 1990.
Hum It Again, Jeremy (one-act play), published in *Center Stage,* edited by Don Gallo, Harper, 1990.
A Place for Grace, Sasquatch Books (Seattle, WA), 1993.
Talent Night, Scholastic (New York City), 1995.
No Dear, Not Here: The Marbled Murrelets' Quest for a Nest in the Pacific Northwest, Sasquatch Books, 1995.
Uncle Hideki, Rain City (Seattle, WA), 1995.
The Eclipse of Moonbeam Dawson, TOR (New York City) 1997.

Contributor of short stories to books, including *Visions,* edited by Gallo, Delacorte, 1988; and *Connections,* edited by Gallo, Delacorte, 1989.

SIDELIGHTS: Jean Davies Okimoto's novels for young adults address common problems and situations faced by modern teenagers. As a psychotherapist and a twice-married woman in a blended family, Okimoto is able to draw on both her personal and professional experiences to write realistic stories for adolescents. The simple, easy style of her writing and the brevity of her novels (about one hundred pages long) make her books accessible to her young audience. Generally, her novels begin by setting up the problem of her main character; this might be divorce, fear of failure, conflict with stepsiblings, or loss of friends. The novel then follows the protagonist as he or she works through the problem and finally resolves it. Bill Buchanan of *Twentieth-Century Young Adult Writers* commented, "Occasionally, Okimoto has a tendency to allow her fiction to become subservient to her psychotherapeutic interests; consequently, at times one gets the feeling that the story has been created as a means of showcasing a problem, and then the story begins to sound like a case study." He added that while Okimoto's novels are "well-rendered and enjoyable," and while she presents "viable solutions to many problems teens are likely to encounter during the arduous process of growing up, her determination to sew everything up neatly and produce a happy ending results in her plots becoming fairly predictable." Still, he recommends Okimoto's "problem" novels to anyone counseling adolescents through difficulties at home or at school.

Okimoto's first novel, *My Mother Is Not Married to My Father,* is the story of eleven-year-old Cynthia, whose parents are getting a divorce. Through the course of the book, the parents separate, Cynthia comes to understand that the divorce is not her fault, and both parents begin new lives complete with new loves. *It's Just Too Much* is the sequel to *My Mother Is Not Married to My Father* and portrays the challenges facing Cynthia as her mother remarries. Her new stepfather has children who visit on the weekends, and Cynthia feels that they receive preferential treatment.

Okimoto compares the awkward adjustments of adolescence with the problems of aging in *Take a Chance, Gramps!* When Janie's best friend, Alicia, moves to another town just as Janie is starting junior high school, Janie feels helpless and alone. Similarly, Janie's grandfather (who lives with Janie's family) has felt alone since the death of his wife. The novel shows how these two characters help each other conquer their fears and enjoy life again. Janie and Gramps happen upon a weekly senior citizens' dance where they meet an elderly woman and her grandson. The four of them attend the dance regularly and romance ensues for young and old. Janie takes Gramps's advice and starts making an effort to meet people at school. By the end of the first term, Janie is elected to the student council.

In *Norman Schnurman, Average Person* sixth-grader Norman seeks his own identity apart from his former football star father. Uninterested in football, Norman prefers to scavenge junk stores and play with P. W., his best friend. Buchanan observed, "The character development in this novel is perhaps the strongest in [Okimoto's] writing to date, with the relationship between Norman and P. W. being particularly well realized."

Okimoto once wrote: "I had my first newspaper when I was in the sixth grade. It lasted for three issues, until it was censored by my mother, and it folded.

"In my other life (first marriage) I was an Air Force officer's wife. I wrote satire and funny articles for the Officers' Wives Club magazine, which the general's wife did not think were funny. My husband was almost kicked out of the Air Force because of my writing. I will write a novel about this someday. Revenge is an important motivation in my career.

"I coached a thirteen-year-old-girls' soccer team for two years. We lost most of our games but we had a great time. I would tell them that it didn't matter if they won or lost but how they played the game. I think they would have preferred winning. I love soccer, the Seattle Sonics and Seattle Seahawks. The only spectator sports I don't like are car racing, boxing, and bull-fighting.

"I think the world is sad and funny. Being a psychotherapist probably influences my writing. I am interested in writing about family relationships, although I might write a very commercial and somewhat disgusting book someday to make money."

BIOGRAPHICAL/CRITICAL SOURCES:

BOOKS

Something about the Author, Volume 34, Gale, 1984.
Twentieth-Century Young Adult Writers, 1st edition, St. James Press, 1994.

PERIODICALS

Kliatt Young Adult Paperback Book Guide, September, 1993.
Publishers Weekly, April 19, 1993; January 30, 1995.
School Library Journal, August, 1993; May, 1995; December, 1995.
Seattle Times, November 15, 1981.*

* * *

ORLINSKY, Harry M(eyer) 1908-1992

PERSONAL: Born March 14, 1908, in Owen Sound, Ontario, Canada; immigrated to United States, 1931, naturalized citizen, 1938; died of cancer, March 21, 1992, in Owings Mills, MD (one source says Baltimore; son of Isaac Moses and Libby Elizabeth (Ardy) Orlinsky; married Donya Fein, September 2, 1934; children: Walter Sidney, Seymour Ivan. *Education:* University of Toronto, B.A., 1931; graduate study at University of Pennsylvania, 1931-35; Dropsie College, Ph.D., 1935; postdoctoral study at Hebrew University of Jerusalem, 1935-36. *Avocational interests:* Classical music, sports, humor, and independent thinking.

CAREER: American Schools of Oriental Research, Jerusalem, Israel, Nies scholar, 1935-36; Baltimore Hebrew College, Baltimore, MD, professor of Biblical literature and Jewish history, 1936-44; Hebrew Union College—Jewish Institute of Religion, New York, NY, assistant professor, 1944-45, professor of Bible, 1945-92. Fellow of Johns Hopkins University, 1936-41; visiting instructor at Hebrew Union College—Jewish Institute of Religion, 1943-44; lecturer at New School for Social Research, 1947-49; visiting professor at Dropsie College, summers, 1951, 1953, and 1955, Brandeis University, summers, 1959 and 1960, Hebrew University of Jerusalem, 1962, and Graduate Theological Union, Berkeley, CA, 1969; Grinfield Lecturer at Oxford University, 1973-75; Horace Kallen Lecturer at Herzlia Hebrew Teachers Institute—Jewish Teachers Seminary, 1976; Albright Memorial Lecturer at Johns Hopkins University, 1977. Associate trustee of American Schools of Oriental Research; member of Yivo Institute of Jewish Research; committee member of Pseudepigraphique Grecque d'Ancient Testament, 1967-92; member of Herausgeberkollegium of Arbeiten zur Literatur und Geschichte des Hellenistischen Judentums; member of Hebrew University of Jerusalem excavations at Ramat Gan, 1936.

MEMBER: International Organization for Septuagint and Cognate Studies (co-founder; president, 1968-73), International Organization for Masoretic Studies (founder; president, 1972-92), American Oriental Society (member of executive committee, 1953), Society of Biblical Literature (vice president, 1969; president, 1970), Academy for Jewish Research (fellow), Jewish Book Council (delegate-at-large), Old Testament Society, American Standard Bible Committee (Revised Standard Version), Jewish Academy of Arts and Sciences, British Society for Old Testament Studies, American Friends of Israel Exploration Society (co-founder; president, 1953-92), American Friends of Hebrew University (member of board of directors).

AWARDS, HONORS: Frank L. Weil Award from National Jewish Welfare Board, 1959; Guggenheim fellow, 1968-69; fellow of Princeton University Council of the Humanities, 1965-92; Harry M. Orlinsky Institute of Biblical and Archaeological Research at Baltimore Hebrew College, 1979; Dr. Bernard Heller Prize from Hebrew Union College-Jewish Institute of Religion, for interdisciplinary contributions to religious studies, 1991. D.H.L. from Baltimore Hebrew College, 1972, and Spertus College of Judaica, 1979.

WRITINGS:

The Septuagint: The Oldest Translation of the Bible, Union of American Hebrew Congregations, 1949.

(Translator with A. ben Isaiah and B. Sharfman), *The Pentateuch and Rashi's Commentary: A Linear Translation,* 5 volumes, S.S. & R. Publishing Co., 1949-50.

(Translator with other members of American Standard Bible Committee) *The Holy Bible, Revised Standard Version,* Thomas Nelson, 1952.

Ancient Israel, Cornell University Press, 1954, 2nd edition, 1960.

(Editor) Solomon Goldman, *From Slavery to Freedom,* Abelard, 1958.

(Editor-in-chief) *The Torah: The Five Books of Moses,* Jewish Publication Society of America, 1962, 2nd edition, 1967.

(Author of prolegomenon) C.D. Ginsburg, *Introduction to the . . . Hebrew Bible,* Ktav, 1965.

Genesis (New Jewish Version), Harper Torchbook, 1966.

(Editor) *Notes on the New (Jewish) Translation of "The Torah,"* Jewish Publication Society, 1969.

(Editor and author of prolegomenon) A. B. Ehrlich, *Mikre ki-Pheschuto* (title means "The Bible According to Its Literal Meaning"), 3 volumes, Ktav, 1969.

(With others) *The Five Megilloth and Jonah,* Jewish Publication Society, 1969.

(Editor and co-author) *Interpreting the Prophetic Tradition,* Hebrew Union College Press and Ktav, 1969.

Understanding the Bible through History and Archaeology, Ktav, 1972.

Essays in Biblical Culture and Bible Translation, Ktav, 1974.

(With others) *The Prophets,* Jewish Publication Society, 1978.

Israel Exploration Journal Reader, 2 volumes, Ktav, 1980.

Harry M. Orlinsky Volume, edited by Baruch A. Levine, Abraham Malamat, Israel Exploration Society in cooperation with Hebrew Union College/Jewish Institute of Religion (Jerusalem), 1982.

(With Robert G. Bratcher) *A History of Bible Translation and the North American Contribution,* Scholars Press (Atlanta, GA), 1991.

CONTRIBUTOR

Edward C. Hobbs, editor, *A Stubborn Faith: Papers on Old Testament and Related Subjects Presented to Honor William Andrew Irwin,* Southern Methodist University Press, 1956.

G. E. Wright, editor, *The Bible and the Ancient Near East: Essays in Honor of W. F. Albright,* Doubleday, 1961.

P. Ramsey, editor, *Religion,* Prentice-Hall, 1965.

Studies on the Second Part of the Book of Isaiah, E. J. Brill, 1967.

Interpreter's Dictionary of the Bible, supplementary volume, Abingdon, 1976.

Editor of *Library of Biblical Studies,* Ktav, 1966-92, and of *Septuagint and Cognate Studies* and *Masoretic Studies,* Society of Biblical Literature and Scholars Press, 1974-92. Contributor to theology journals. Member of editorial board of *Journal of Biblical Literature, Israel Exploration Journal, Jewish Apocryphal Literature, Jewish Quarterly Review,* and *Old Testament Abstracts.*

SIDELIGHTS: An internationally esteemed scholar, Harry M. Orlinsky was appointed in 1952 as the only Jew to help prepare the Revised Standard Version of the Bible for Protestant Christians, and nearly forty years later he helped prepare the New Revised Standard Version. Also, Israel called upon Orlinsky to determine the authenticity of four of the Dead Sea Scrolls. The educator, editor, translator, and author began his academic career at the American Schools of Oriental Research in Jerusalem and moved on to be a professor of biblical literature and Jewish history at Baltimore Hebrew College. In 1944 he accepted a position as an assistant professor at the Hebrew Union College-Jewish Institute of Religion, becoming a professor of the Bible the following year. In 1991 the Hebrew Union College-Jewish Institute of Religion bestowed on Orlinsky the Dr. Bernard Heller Prize for his interdisciplinary contributions to religious studies, which involved archaeology, philology, comparative linguistics, and comparative religion. His works include *Ancient Israel* and a book based on it titled *Understanding the Bible through History and Archaeology, Essays in Biblical Culture and Bible Translation,* and, with Robert G. Bratcher, the 1991 book *A History of Bible Translation and the North American Contribution.* Orlinsky was a co-translator for *The Pentateuch and Rashi's Commentary: A Linear*

Translation and editor in chief for *The Torah: The Five Books of Moses.*

Orlinsky strove for accuracy and faithfulness to the original texts in all his work, but made a great effort to gear his work to the sensitivities of today's readers. His public and professional lectures dealt with the use of nonsexist language in current translations as well as the difficulty of translating from a rich expressive language to English, which he considered inadequate for the purpose.

"In the attempt to comprehend Biblical concepts and history," Orlinsky told *CA,* "I have been careful to let the Hebrew text speak for itself (exgesis) and to exclude the many later interpretations that were read back into it (eisegesis). Thus I have argued that it is simply 'wind' rather than traditional 'Spirit' (or 'spirit') that correctly renders the Hebrew *ru'ah* in Genesis 1:2, and that it is 'young woman' rather than traditional 'virgin' that correctly reproduced the meaning of the Hebrew *almah* in Isaiah 7:14. Scholarly concensus had opted since the twenties for an amphictyony in the period preceding the rise of the Hebrew monarchy (10th century B.C.E.), the period of the so-called 'Judges' (actually military chieftains). I was the first scholar to argue against this notion in detail, and the theory is now all but rejected. Most scholars still hold that the prophets and other biblical writers conceived of the God of Israel as an international God; I have long held that He was both a national God (of Israel alone) and a Universal God (sole creator, master of all the universe and its natural phenomena and inhabitants—in the sky and on the earth and in the seas); but He was never conceived as an international God.

"There is a long-held scholarly belief that the Second Isaiah (author of chapters 40-55 and much of 56-66), especially in chapter 53, speaks of a 'Servant of the Lord who suffered vicariously for sinful Israel and mankind'; I have argued in detail that this belief is a post-Jesus innovation (Philip to the Ethiopian eunuch, chapter 8 of the Book of Acts) that was read back into the Bible. Scholars have long asserted that the Hebrew text of the Bible was fixed in the first millennium by Jewish scribes known as Masorets, and hence the term 'the Masoretic text.' I have argued that the Hebrew text of the Bible was never fixed, and that the definite article 'the' in 'the Masoretic text' is a scholarly fiction; many Masoretes were responsible for many Hebrew manuscripts of the Bible coming into being, each manuscript containing *a* masoretic text. None of these texts can lay claim to ultimate authority."

Orlinsky was selected to examine the four Dead Sea scrolls that the Israeli government purchased in 1954. He discussed the story of the scrolls in *Essays in Biblical Culture and Bible Translation.* He commented: "I have published a number of articles in which I have argued against the sensational claims made by the majority of scholars for the value of the text of the scrolls, especially the complete Isaiah text of the Bible; this is the burden of my chapter on 'The Textual Criticism of the Old Testament' in *The Bible and the Ancient Near East.*"

BIOGRAPHICAL/CRITICAL SOURCES:

BOOKS

Levine, Baruch A. and Abraham Malamat, editors, *The Harry M. Orlinsky Volume,* Israel Exploration Society in cooperation with Hebrew Union College/ Jewish Institute of Religion, 1982.

PERIODICALS

Baltimore Jewish Times, April 23, 1976.
Baltimore Sun, May 17, 1976; November 15, 1977.
Jerusalem Post, August 4, 1965.
Johns Hopkins Magazine, March, 1978.
New Orleans Times-Picayune, November 19, 1978.
New York Times, May 21, 1973; November 26, 1977.

OBITUARIES:

PERIODICALS

New York Times, March 24, 1992, p. D22.
Times (London), April 4, 1992, p. 19.*

P-R

PADGETT, Lewis
See MOORE, C(atherine) L(ucile)

* * *

PALEY, William S(amuel) 1901-1990

PERSONAL: Born September 28, 1901, in Chicago, IL; died of an apparent heart attack while suffering from pneumonia, October 26, 1990, in New York, NY; son of Samuel (a cigar manufacturer) and Gold (Drell) Paley; married Dorothy Hart Hearst, May 11, 1932 (divorced July, 1947); married Barbara Cushing Mortimer, July 28, 1947 (died July 6, 1978); children: (first marriage) Jeffrey, Hilary Paley Byers; (second marriage) William Cushing, Kate Cushing. *Education:* Attended University of Chicago, 1918-19; University of Pennsylvania, B.S., 1922.

CAREER: Congress Cigar Co., Philadelphia, PA, in charge of production, 1922-28, vice president, 1923-28, secretary, 1925-28; United Independent Broadcasters (later Columbia Broadcasting System; now CBS, Inc.), New York City, president, 1928-46, chief executive officer, 1928-1977, chairman of board of directors, 1946-83, executive committee chairman, 1983-90; Whitcom Investment Co., New York City, partner, 1983-90. Chairman of President's Materials Policy Commission, 1951-52; Resources for the Future, member of executive committee, 1952-69, chairman, 1966-69, and honorary director, 1969-90; member of committee for White House Conference on Education, 1954-56; chairman of New York City Task Force on Urban Design, 1967; chairman of New York City Urban Design Council, 1968-71. President and director of William S. Paley Foundation; Museum of Modern Art, trustee, 1937-90, president, 1968-72, chairman, 1972-90; North Shore University Hospital, member of board of directors, 1949-73, co-chairman of board of trustees, 1954-73; Columbia University, life trustee, 1950-73, trustee emeritus, 1973-90; founding member of Bedford-Stuyvesant D & S Corp., 1967-72; Commission for Cultural Affairs, City of New York, member of Commission of Critical Choices for America, 1973-77; director of International Executive Service Corps; life trustee of Federation of Jewish Philanthropies. *Wartime service:* Supervisor of Office of War Information, 1943-44; chief of radio operations for Psychological Warfare Division, SHAEF, 1944-45; deputy chief of Information Control, division of USGCC, 1945; U.S. Army, 1945, served as deputy chief of Psychological Warfare Division; became colonel; received Medal of Merit and Legion of Merit; also received numerous foreign awards, including Croix de Guerre with Palm from France.

MEMBER: France-United States Association, National Institute of Social Scientists, Pilgrims of the United States, Academy of Political Scientists, Economic Club (New York), Metropolitan Club (Washington, DC), Turf and Field Club, National Golf Club, Meadowbrook Golf Club, Lyford Cay (Nassau, Bahamas).

AWARDS, HONORS: Medallion of Honor of the City of New York, 1965; Gold Achievement medal from Poor Richard Club; Keynote Award from National Association of Broadcasters; special award from Broadcast Pioneers; Concert Artist Guild Award; Skowhegan Gertrude Vanderbilt Whitney Award; gold medal from National Planning Association.

WRITINGS:

As It Happened: A Memoir (autobiography), Doubleday (Garden City, NY), 1979.

SIDELIGHTS: Broadcasting executive William S. Paley's autobiography, *As It Happened,* "operates on three levels: as a personal chronicle, as an effort to set the record straight on old controversies, and as a 50-year history of CBS and broadcasting in America as seen from the top," wrote *New York Times* television reporter Les Brown in a *New York Times Book Review* critique. "The book is most effective, and most valuable, in the last capacity."

Paley first developed an interest in broadcasting while working in his family's cigar manufacturing business. He purchased air time on the small United Independent Broadcasters network and put together "The La Palina Smoker," a show named after one of the family enterprise's more successful cigar lines. Paley bought the floundering network in 1928 for half a million dollars, changed its name to Columbia Broadcasting System, and began an expansion program that within months had increased the size of the network from sixteen to forty-nine stations.

Paley was one of the first to recruit stars from other areas of entertainment for radio appearances. For example, he convinced such people as Will Rogers and Paul Whiteman that radio exposure would aid their careers when the growing popularity of the media became evident. Paley also pioneered educational, cultural, and religious programming and during the early 1930s began building the network's news department, which featured such journalists as Edward R. Murrow, Howard K. Smith, and Howard Shirer.

Paley's interest in broadcasting was not limited to radio, however. In 1931 CBS became the first American network to establish regularly scheduled television broadcasting and by 1940 had developed a field sequential system for color television. CBS offered fifteen hours of television black-and-white programming per week in 1941, but the U.S. entry into World War II halted all programming and development.

In 1943 Paley went overseas as a civilian working for the Office of War Information, leaving Paul Kesten in charge of CBS. Paley reorganized Allied radio activities in North Africa and restored radio service in Italy after German forces were driven out. He was commissioned a colonel in the U.S. Army in April, 1945, and served as deputy chief of the Psychological Warfare Division of General Dwight D. Eisenhower's headquarters staff. Paley was discharged from active duty in November, 1945, and upon his return to New York began a reorganization of CBS that resulted in Frank Stanton taking over the presidency and Paley being named chairman of the board.

During the late 1940s Paley decided to challenge the ratings supremacy of the National Broadcasting Company (NBC). He secured a $5 million bank loan and in a series of bold moves signed some of NBC's top stars, including Jack Benny, Red Skelton, Edgar Bergen and Charlie McCarthy, Frank Sinatra, and Amos 'n' Andy. The coup, coming at the dawn of commercial television broadcasting, propelled CBS into the ratings lead, a position the network held until 1976.

The programming success CBS enjoyed during the early days of television was not equaled in the corporation's other ventures. Paley's purchase of Hytron Radio and Electronics Corporation in an attempt to manufacture television sets during the early 1950s reportedly cost CBS $50 million before the project was abandoned in 1956. And a 1953 ruling by the Federal Communications Commission (FCC) rejected the rotating disc system for color television that CBS had developed because—unlike the system advanced by the Radio Corporation of America (RCA), parent company of NBC—it was not compatible with existing black-and-white sets. Other ill-fated ventures included a brief period of ownership of the New York Yankees baseball team during the late 1960s and the Electronic Video Recording (EVR) system, an early attempt to open the home video recording market.

Despite these setbacks, CBS continued to prosper and grow, diversifying into a variety of areas, including musical instrument manufacturing, cable television, video discs and cassettes, and publishing. The corporation went through a series of managerial changes during the 1970s as it sought Paley's successor. Paley relinquished the title of chief executive officer in April, 1977, but retained chairmanship of the corporation until 1983 when he became executive committee chairman of the board of CBS. In 1983 Paley joined the Whitcom Investment Company as a partner.

"The story of CBS is never less than fascinating," wrote Gerald Clarke in a *Time* review, "but Paley's memoir, alas, tends to falter towards the end. Once he leaves the glory days of radio, the book becomes increasingly guarded and corporate in tone." Brown was also interested in the accounts covered in Paley's autobiography but disappointed with the personal insight afforded by it. As he explained: "The personal skin is scarcely penetrated and the corporate veneer never stripped away. Mr. Paley's book reveals little about him beyond the broad outlines of his life, his philosophy of broadcasting and his intense pursuit of 'the good life, enjoyed with good friends.' "

BIOGRAPHICAL/CRITICAL SOURCES:

BOOKS

Paley, William S., *As It Happened: A Memoir,* Doubleday, 1979.
Paley, Kate, *The Original Bill Paley,* Smallwood and Stewart (New York City), 1996.
Paper, Lewis J., *Empire: William S. Paley and the Making of CBS,* St. Martin's Press (New York City), 1987.
Smith, Sally Bedell, *In All His Glory: The Life of William S. Paley, the Legendary Tycoon and His Brilliant Circle,* Simon and Schuster (New York City), 1990.

PERIODICALS

New York Times, July 7, 1978; February 26, 1980; September 12, 1982; October 31, 1982; April 20, 1983.
New York Times Book Review, March 11, 1979.
Time, March 26, 1979.*

OBITUARIES:

PERIODICALS

Chicago Tribune, October 27, 1990.
Los Angeles Times, October 29, 1990.
New York Times, October 28, 1990.
Times (London), October 29, 1990.
Washington Post, October 28, 1990.*

* * *

PARKINSON, Thomas (Francis) 1920-1992

PERSONAL: Born February 24, 1920, in San Francisco, CA; died of a heart attack, January 14, 1992, in Berkeley (one source says San Francisco), CA; son of Thomas Francis and Catherine (Green) Parkinson; married Ariel Reynolds, December 23, 1948; children: Katherine, Chrysa. *Education:* University of California, Berkeley, A.B., 1945, M.A., 1946, Ph.D., 1948.

CAREER: University of California, Berkeley, instructor, 1948-50, assistant professor, 1950-53, associate professor, 1953-60, professor of English, 1960-91, special assistant to the chancellor, 1979-81. Visiting professor, Wesleyan University, Middletown, CT, 1951-52, University of Washington, 1968, and University of York (England), 1970; Fulbright professor, Universities of Bordeaux, Toulouse, and Frankfurt, 1953-54, Universities of Grenoble and Nice, 1965-66, and University of Rome, 1970; visiting lecturer, Yeats Summer School, 1965 and 1968. Member of literary panel, National Endowment for the Arts, 1971-74. Honorary fellow, St. Peter's College, Oxford University, 1969-70. *Military service:* U.S. Army Air Forces, 1943.

MEMBER: Modern Language Association of America, American Association of University Professors, Phi Beta Kappa.

AWARDS, HONORS: Guggenheim fellow and American Philosophical Society grantee in Ireland, England, and Italy, 1957-58; Institute of Creative Art fellow, 1963-64; Berkeley Citation.

WRITINGS:

W. B. Yeats, Self-Critic: A Study of His Early Verse (also see below), University of California Press, 1951.
Men, Women, Vines (poems), Harmon, 1959.
(Editor) *A Casebook on the Beat,* Crowell, 1961.
(Editor) *Masterworks of Prose,* Bobbs-Merrill, 1962.
W. B. Yeats: The Later Poetry (also see below), University of California Press, 1964.
Thanatos (poems), Oyez Press, 1965, 2nd edition, 1976.
(Editor) *Robert Lowell: A Collection of Critical Essays,* Prentice-Hall, 1968.
Homage to Jack Spicer and Other Poems: Poems 1965-1969, Ark Press, 1970.
Protect the Earth, City Light Books, 1970.
W. B. Yeats, Self-Critic: A Study of His Early Verse [and] *The Later Poetry,* University of California Press, 1971.
What the Blindman Saw; or, Twenty-Five Years of the Endless War (play), Thorp Springs Press, 1974.
Hart Crane and Yvor Winters: Their Literary Correspondence, University of California Press, 1978.
From the Grand Chartreuse (verse), Oyez Press, 1980.
Collected Poems, Oyez Press, 1980.
Poets, Poems, Movements, UMI Research Press (Ann Arbor, MI), 1987.
Poems: New and Selected, National Poetry Foundation, University of Maine (Orono, ME), 1988.

(Editor with Anne Brannen) W. B. Yeats, *Michael Robartes and the Dancer: Manuscript Materials,* Cornell University Press (Ithaca, NY), 1994.

Also author of two books of poetry, *Letter to a Young Lady,* 1946, and *The Canters of Thomas Parkinson,* 1977. Contributor of articles, poems, and reviews to *Modern Philology, Nation, Poetry, Horizon, Kenyon Review, Listener,* and other periodicals.

SIDELIGHTS: An educator, poetry scholar, editor, and writer, Thomas Parkinson was a respected intrepreter of the Irish poet William Butler Yeats. He was also recognized as one of the first critics to focus scholarly attention on the beat poets, members of a group of U.S. writers in the 1950s who rejected conventional values. He retired as a professor of English from the University of California at Berkeley in 1991, following a distinguished tenure of more than forty years; for his service there he received the Berkeley Citation. Parkinson was also a published poet whose collections include *Men, Women, Vines* and *Thanatos.* As a scholar he wrote several texts, including *W. B. Yeats, Self-Critic: A Study of His Early Verse* and *W. B. Yeats: The Later Poetry.* He edited *A Casebook on the Beat.*

After spending brief periods in his late teens and early twenties alternately attending college and working at a wide assortment of jobs, Parkinson reported that he did not settle down and become "what my poetic friends sometimes humorously call an academic square" until the late 1940s. "But how did I become what my academic friends call a bohemian anarchist?," Parkinson continued. "I had been writing verse for years, and while studying at Berkeley met Josephine Miles (this was in 1939) who was just starting her career as instructor. I also met Richard Moore, who still writes but does not publish poetry; he is best known for his films of poets and novelists done for the Public Broadcasting System. In 1944 I met Robert Duncan and got into the habit of attending Kenneth Rexroth's Friday evenings at home. In 1945, a group of us formed a circle that met every week to discuss anarchist theory, but since none of us believed in violence and most of us took a skeptical view of the ballot, we ended up talking about Balke and Yeats and Lawrence and William Morris. Among the people who attended those meetings and went to the anarchist parties thrown by San Francisco's then large group of Italian anarchists were Rexroth, Duncan, Pauline Kael, William Everson, briefly William Stafford, and the founders of the first listener supported radio station, KPFA.

"KPFA gave an audience for poets. Two of its founders, Lewis Hill and Richard Moore, were poets, and a high proportion of the programs were literary. The intellectual ferment off campus at Berkeley during that period was immense. Since English literature in the view of the university ended with the publication of *Jude the Obscure* in 1895, this left us with *our* literature, meaning Yeats, Eliot, Pound, Williams, Stevens, Mann, Proust, Joyce, Lawrence, Brecht, Pirandello, Apollinaire, George, Neruda, Lorca, Valery, Desnos—in short, all the great literature of the twentieth century. So we had weekly seminars on one or another poet.

"We had readings of our own poetry. George Leite had a wonderful modern book store and published *Circle* Magazine, which at one time had a circulation of over 10,000, until George's incapacity for dealing with money forced him into bankruptcy. But by then, the bloom had gone. The Korean War and the Cold War and the loyalty oath at the university chilled everybody. Besides, we had learned from each other what we needed. Everson joined the Catholic Church, I joined the university, Spicer wouldn't sign the loyalty oath and left Berkeley for first Minneapolis then Boston, Robin Blaser went to Boston (really Cambridge) as a librarian, Rexroth travelled in Europe, Duncan went to Majorca, later I went to Connecticut, then France. We all remained friends, but the party had really broken up.

"In 1955, Allen Ginsberg came to town, and a new party started. All the so-called beat writers came to see me and talk with me, and we became and remained good friends. They didn't all come to see me; I went to see some of them. And I never got along with Kerouac.

"So it has gone. My life is quite simply devoted to two institutions: the tradition of poetry; the greatest institution of higher learning that is, relatively speaking, public and open. . . . My wife and I are what is called responsible citizens and we are productive artists (taking critical scholarship to be an art as is poetry; I think it is) with a rewarding past and bright future. I don't even mind working for the chancellor. Maybe my teaching days are past, but I do enjoy being able to do something for the institution that provided a great opportunity to the son of an impoverished artisan."

OBITUARIES:

PERIODICALS

Los Angeles Times, January 20, 1992, p. A29.
New York Times, January 18, 1992, p. 10.
Times (London), February 12, 1992, p. 15.
Washington Post, January 21, 1992, p. B7.*

**PATON WALSH, Gillian 1937-
(Jill Paton Walsh)**

PERSONAL: Born April 29, 1937, in London, England; daughter of John Llewellyn (an engineer) and Patricia (Dubern) Bliss; married Antony Edmund Paton Walsh (a chartered secretary), August 12, 1961; children: Edmund Alexander, Margaret Ann, Helen Clare. *Education:* St. Anne's College, Oxford, Dip.Ed., 1959, M.A. (honors) in English. *Politics:* None. *Religion:* "Skepticism." *Avocational interests:* Photography, gardening, cooking, carpentry, reading.

ADDRESSES: Home—72 Water Lane, Histon, Cambridge CB4 4LR, England.

CAREER: Enfield Girls Grammar School, Middlesex, English teacher, 1959-62; writer, 1962—. Whittall Lecturer, Library of Congress, Washington, DC, 1978. Visiting Faculty Member, Center for the Study of Children's Literature, Simmons College, Boston, 1978-86. Founder, with John Rowe Townsend, of Green Bay Publishers, 1986.

MEMBER: Society of Authors (member of Management Committee), Children's Writers Group.

AWARDS, HONORS: Book World Festival award, 1970, for *Fireweed;* Whitbread Prize (shared with Russell Hoban), 1974, for *The Emperor's Winding Sheet;* Boston *Globe-Horn Book* Award, 1976, for *Unleaving;* Arts Council creative writing fellowship, 1976-77, and 1977-78; Universe Prize, 1984, for *A Parcel of Patterns;* Smarties Prize Grand Prix, 1984, for *Gaffer Samson's Luck.*

WRITINGS:

JUVENILE FICTION; UNDER NAME JILL PATON WALSH

Hengest's Tale, illustrated by Janet Margrie, St. Martin's Press, 1966.
The Dolphin Crossing, St. Martin's Press, 1967.
Fireweed, Macmillan, 1969, Farrar, Straus (New York City), 1970.
Goldengrove, Farrar, Straus, 1972.
Toolmaker, illustrated by Jeroo Roy, Heinemann, 1973, Seabury Press, 1974.
The Dawnstone, illustrated by Mary Dinsdale, London, Hamish Hamilton, 1973.
The Emperor's Winding Sheet, Farrar, Straus, 1974.
The Huffler, Farrar, Straus, 1975, published in England as *The Butty Boy,* illustrated by Juliette Palmer, Macmillan, 1975.
Unleaving, Farrar, Straus, 1976.
Crossing to Salamis (first novel in trilogy; also see below), illustrated by David Smee, Heinemann, 1977.
The Walls of Athens (second novel in trilogy; also see below), illustrated by Smee, Heinemann, 1977.
Persian Gold (third novel in trilogy; also see below), illustrated by Smee, Heinemann, 1978.
Children of the Fox (contains *Crossing to Salamis, The Walls of Athens,* and *Persian Gold*), Farrar, Straus, 1978.
A Chance Child, Farrar, Straus, 1978.
The Green Book, illustrated by Joanna Stubbs, Macmillan, 1981, illustrated by Lloyd Bloom, Farrar, Straus, 1982, published as *Shine,* Macdonald, 1988.
Babylon, illustrated by Jenny Northway, Deutsch, 1982.
A Parcel of Patterns, Farrar, Straus, 1983.
Lost and Found, illustrated by Mary Rayner, Deutsch, 1984.
Gaffer Samson's Luck, illustrated by Brock Cole, Farrar, Straus, 1984.
Torch, Viking, 1987.
Birdy and the Ghosties, illustrated by Alan Marks, Macdonald, 1989.
Can I Play Farmer, Farmer? Bodley Head, 1992.
Can I Play Wolf? Bodley Head, 1992.
Grace, Viking (New York City), 1991.
When Grandma Came (picture book), illustrated by Sophie Williams, Viking, 1992.
Matthew and the Sea Singer, Farrar, Straus, 1993.
Pepi and the Secret Names, Lee and Shepard (New York City), 1995.
Connie Came to Play, Viking, 1995.
When I Was Little Like You, Viking, 1997.

Also author of *Thomas and the Tinners,* 1995, *Can I Play Jenny Jones?* and *Can I Play Queenie?*

OTHER; UNDER NAME JILL PATON WALSH

(With Kevin Crossley Holland) *Wordhoard: Anglo-Saxon Stories,* Farrar, Straus, 1969.
Farewell, Great King (adult novel), Coward McCann, 1972.
(Editor) *Beowulf* (structural reader), Longman, 1975.
The Island Sunrise: Prehistoric Britain, Deutsch, 1975, published as *The Island Sunrise: Prehistoric Culture in the British Isles,* Seabury Press, 1976.
Five Tides (short stories), Green Bay, 1986.
Lapsing (adult novel), Weidenfeld & Nicolson, 1986, St. Martin's Press, 1987.
A School for Lovers (adult novel), Weidenfeld & Nicolson, 1989.

The Wyndham Case, St. Martin's Press (New York City), 1993.

Knowledge of Angels, Houghton Mifflin (Boston), 1994.

A Piece of Justice: An Imogen Quy Mystery, St. Martin's Press, 1995.

A School for Lovers, Black Swan (London), 1996.

The Serpentine Cave, St. Martin's Press, 1997.

(Completed by Paton Walsh) Dorothy Sayers, *Thrones, Dominations,* St. Martin's Press, 1998.

Some of Paton Walsh's manuscripts and papers may be found in the Kerlan Collection, University of Minnesota, Minneapolis.

ADAPTATIONS: Gaffer Samson's Luck was adapted to audio in 1987; *Knowledge of Angels* was adapted to audio in 1996 by Isis Audio; *A Parcel of Patterns* was adapted to audio in 1996 by Listening Library.

SIDELIGHTS: Jill Paton Walsh is noted for her works which deal realistically with life, death, and maturation. While her novels vary widely in terms of genre and style, Judith Atkinson of *Twentieth-Century Children's Writers* notes, "The most immediately attractive features of these novels . . . are their absorbing plots and believable settings." "Of [the many] skilled and sensitive writers [for young people]," declares Sheila Egoff in *Thursday's Child,* "[Paton] Walsh is the most formally literary. Her writing is studded with allusions to poetry, art and philosophy that give it an intellectual framework unmatched in children's literature." Paton Walsh's works examine eras and topics such as life, death, and honor in Anglo-Saxon England (*Hengest's Tale* and *Wordhoard*), Victorian child labor in England (*A Chance Child*), growing up in World War II England (*The Dolphin Crossing* and *Fireweed*), life in the Early Stone Age (*Toolmaker*), and loyalty in the midst of destruction in fifteenth-century Byzantium (*The Emperor's Winding Sheet*). She has also written several novels that center on the Cornish coast, where she spent part of her childhood.

Paton Walsh was born Gillian Bliss, a member of a loving family living in suburban London. Her father was an engineer, one of the earliest experimenters with television, and he and his wife actively stimulated their children to enjoy learning. "For the whole of our childhoods," Paton Walsh writes in her *Something about the Author Autobiography Series* (*SAAS*) entry, "I, and my brothers and sister—I am the eldest of four—were surrounded by love and encouragement on a lavish scale. . . . And to an unusual degree everyone was without prejudices against, or limited ambitions for, girls. As much was expected of me as of my brothers."

Paton Walsh's early novels *Fireweed* and *The Dolphin Crossing* are based on her childhood experiences during World War II. The characters experience danger and insecurity along with new friendships. "For five crucial years of my childhood—from the year I was three to the year I was eight—the war dominated and shaped everything around me," Paton Walsh explains in *SAAS,* "and then for many years, until well into my teens, postwar hardships remained.""I do not know if there was a plan of evacuation there when the war began, which my parents did not join in, or if Finchley did not seem a likely target," she continues. Finally her mother's stepfather, upset by a bombing raid, moved the family to his place in Cornwall, in the far west of England. Although Jill's mother soon returned with her younger children to her husband in London, Jill herself remained in Cornwall for the next five years, returning to her family only after her grandmother suffered a fatal heart attack.

The author used the familiar setting of Cornwall in *Goldengrove,* a book about the awkwardness that often accompanies growing up. The heroine is Madge, who, although almost fully grown, still eagerly anticipates her yearly visit to see her grandmother and cousin in Cornwall. When, one year, the visit proves disappointing, the grandmother understands that Madge's maturation is changing their relationship. Further, Madge must deal with two revelations that force her to question her faith in adults.

"I left St. Ives when I was just eight," Paton Walsh explains in *SAAS.* "A part of me is still rooted on that rocky shore, and it appears again and again in what I write." She stepped out of the comfortable world she had known directly into wartime London. "That first night back," she recalls, "I lay awake listening to the clanging sounds, like dustbins rolling round the night sky, made by German rockets falling somewhere a little distance off.

"The children I talk to nowadays are very interested in the Second World War," Paton Walsh remarks in her *SAAS* essay. "They think it must have been a time of excitement and danger, whereas it was actually dreadfully boring." Wartime restrictions and shortages meant that normal childhood activities—movies, television, radio, and even outdoor play—were severely limited. "I remember, in short, a time of discomfort and gloom, and, above all, upheaval." Part of the upheaval was caused by her mother's relatives, who had been wealthy colonists in Southeast Asia before the war, and who returned to England, newly impoverished, to live with her family. Because they had their own ideas of proper female behavior, Paton Walsh writes, she never knew "whether it was good and clever to give voice to my opinions, or pushy and priggish; not knowing from one day to the next what sort of behavior would be expected of me." "Yet in the long run," Paton Walsh concludes, "I have benefited greatly from all this. I protected myself. I learned not to care what other people think. I would say what I liked, read what I was interested in, go on my own way, and ignore what the invading hoards of aunts and uncles thought, about me, or about anything else."

Paton Walsh attended a Catholic girl's school in North Finchley, whose environment was quite different from the liberality of her home life. "The nuns who taught me were suspicious of me," she declares in her *SAAS* entry. "They liked girls who worked very hard, not those who found it easy." When Paton Walsh left the school, it was to take a place at Oxford University. "I enjoyed myself vastly at Oxford, made friends, talked late into the night, and even worked sometimes, and work included lectures by both C. S. Lewis and J. R. R. Tolkien. The subject of the lectures and tutorials was always literature or philology—we wouldn't have dared ask those great men about their own work!—but the example they set by being both great and serious scholars, and writers of fantasy and books for children was not lost on me."

By the time Paton Walsh completed her degree, she was engaged to a man she had met at school. She obtained a teaching position, but soon discovered that she disliked being a teacher. "I didn't teach long," she explains in her *SAAS* entry. "I got married in my second year as a teacher, and eighteen months later was expecting a child." The life of a housewife, however, did not suit her either: "I was bored frantic. I went nearly crazy, locked up alone with a howling baby all day and all night. . . . As plants need water and light, as the baby needed milk, I needed something intellectual, cheap, and quiet." So, she says, "I began to write a book. It was a children's book. It never occurred to me to write any other kind.

"Until the moment I began to write I did not know that I was a writer," Paton Walsh explains in *SAAS.* The book she began to work on in those day, she says, "was, unfortunately, a dreadfully bad book. It had twelve chapters of equal length, with a different bit of historical background in each one." Eventually Kevin Crossley Holland, an editor with Macmillan, explained to Paton Walsh that to publish this particular book might be a bad idea. He then offered her an option on her next work. "I set to work joyfully on *Hengest's Tale,*" she recalls, "a gory epic retold out of fragments of *Beowulf,* and I stopped work only for a fortnight—between chapter three and chapter four— when my second child, my daughter Margaret, was born. *Hengest's Tale* was my first published book. And I have never forgotten the difference it made to be able to say, to others, certainly, but above all, to myself, 'I am a writer.'

"This whole question of where ideas for books come from is very intriguing," Paton Walsh states in her *SAAS* entry. "I suppose 'Where do you get your ideas?' is the question most often asked by the children I meet. I think they are hoping for useful guidance on how to get ideas for their English homework, and I am a bit ashamed to be so hopeless at helping. But I don't really know where I get ideas from; each one in turn seems like an accident. It's a question of being on the lookout for the kind of accident that makes the idea for a book. . . . But I can say that a large part of it is giving loving attention to places; not necessarily beautiful places, just anywhere. Most of my books really have begun with thinking about the places they are set in." For example, she continues, "I went to Greece to find the landscapes for a classical historical novel, written for adults, called *Farewell, Great King,* but when I got there I found Byzantine things, the marvelous mountaintop deserted city of Mistra above all, and the result of that was *The Emperor's Winding Sheet.* And there are more places singing to me."

Critics celebrate Paton Walsh's ability to evoke both character and setting, and through them to say something meaningful about growing up. She "has an astonishing ability to create appealing personalities," declares Elizabeth S. Coolidge in *Washington Post Book World.* In reviewing *Unleaving,* in which Paton Walsh continues the story of Madge, the heroine of *Goldengrove,* Coolidge continues, "She has written a book about death, and what this means to a philosopher, a teenager, a grandmother and a very small child. Yet *Unleaving* is in no way a gloomy book, but one that leaves the reader with a warm and optimistic view of humankind." "[Paton] Walsh doesn't tidy up the blight for which man was born," states Alice Bach in a *New York Times Book Review* critique of the same book. "She's too wise to attempt answers about growing, living, dying, ethical choices. She exalts the mystery, the unknowing itself." "As time has gone by," Paton Walsh concludes in her *SAAS* entry, "I have won the friendship of many other writers and readers and book-lovers. I feel lucky in this, beyond my deserts. . . . A writer is what I shall be as long as there is a daydream in my head, and I have strength to sit up and type."

BIOGRAPHICAL/CRITICAL SOURCES:

BOOKS

Children's Literature Review, Volume 2, Gale, 1976.

Contemporary Literary Criticism, Volume 35, Gale, 1985.

Egoff, Sheila A., *Thursday's Child: Trends and Patterns in Contemporary Children's Literature,* American Library Association, 1981.

Something about the Author, Volume 72, Gale, 1993.

Something about the Author Autobiography Series, Volume 3, Gale, 1987.

Twentieth-Century Young Adult Writers, 1st edition, St. James Press, 1994.

PERIODICALS

New Statesman, October 31, 1986, p. 31; February 20, 1998, p. 47.

New York Times Book Review, August 8, 1976, p. 18; June 16, 1985, p. 30; June 14, 1992, p. 31; March 15, 1998, p. 16.

New Yorker, November 27, 1989, p. 142.

Times Literary Supplement, March 29, 1985, p. 349; November 29, 1985, p. 1358; November 28, 1986, p. 1347; November 22, 1991, p. 24.

Washington Post Book World, May 2, 1976, p. L13.*

* * *

PATON WALSH, Jill
See PATON WALSH, Gillian

* * *

PAUL, Leslie (Allen) 1905-1985

PERSONAL: Born April 30, 1905, in Dublin, Ireland; died July 8, 1985; son of Fred and Lottie (Burton) Paul. *Education:* Brockley Central School, M.A. *Avocational interests:* Photography, bird-watching, making lawns, teaching children chess.

CAREER: Began work as journalist at age of seventeen; *Open Road,* London, England, editor, 1923; *Cambria Daily Leader,* Swansea, Wales, London correspondent, 1925-29; *Plan,* London, editor, 1934-39; tutor in adult education, London, and worker in underground movement in Europe, 1933-40; Ashridge College of Citizenship, Berkhampsted, England, assistant director of studies, 1947-48; Brasted Place (college), Kent, England, director of studies, 1953-57; Leverhulme research fellow, 1957-59; King George's Jubilee Trust and Industrial Welfare Society, London, research fellow, 1959-61; English Church Assembly, London, research director, 1962-64; Kenyon College, Gambier, Ohio, resident fellow, 1964; Queen's College, Birmingham, England, lecturer in ethics and social studies, 1965-70; University of Birmingham, Birmingham, England, lecturer in department of theology, 1965-70. British Council lecturer in Turkey and Israel, 1959; Selwyn Lecturer, St. John's College and Christchurch University, both New Zealand, 1969; lecturer, Townsville University, Australia, 1969; Hale Lecturer, Seabury-Western Theological Seminary, 1970; Lilly Scholar-in-Residence, Eastern College, 1970; Bloemfontein Diocesan Lecturer, South Africa, 1977; Stuart-Asbury Lecturer, University Church, Oxford, 1978; writer-in-residence, St. Paul and St. Mary College, Cheltenham, 1981. Member of Departmental Committee on Youth Services, 1958-60; member of General Synod, Church of England, 1965-70; chairman of Hereford Diocesan Council of Social Action, 1972-78. Regular broadcaster, especially on European and overseas services, British Broadcasting Corp., 1929-65. Adviser to Diocese of Melbourne, Australia, 1969. *Military service:* British Army, Royal Artillery, 1941; Army Education Corps, 1942-46, served as tutor in modern studies at Middle East Forces college in Palestine; became captain.

MEMBER: Royal Society of Literature (fellow), Society of Authors, Institute of Liturgy and Architecture (honorary fellow).

AWARDS, HONORS: Atlantic Award in literature, 1946; honorary Doctor of Canon Law, Seabury-Western Theological Seminary, 1970; D.Litt., Geneva Theological College, 1974; West Midlands Arts Award, 1977.

WRITINGS:

The Pipes of Pan (poems), C. W. Daniel, 1927.

The Folk Trail: An Outline of the Philosophy and Activities of Woodcraft Fellowships, Noel Douglas, 1929.

The Ashen Stave, W. C. Boone, 1930.

The Green Company: Pow-wows on Pioneering for Boys and Girls, C. W. Daniel, 1931.

A Green Love and Other Poems, privately printed, 1931.

Fugitive Morning (novel), Denis Archer, 1932.

Two One-Act Plays, C. W. Daniel, 1933.

Periwake, His Odyssey (novel), Denis Archer, 1934.

Co-operation in the U.S.S.R.: A Study of the Consumers' Movement, Gollancz, 1934.

Story without End: The Junior Book of Co-operation, Co-operative Union, 1935.

Men in May (novel), Gollancz, 1936.

(Contributor) *Britain and the Soviets,* Martin Lawrence, 1936.

The Republic of Children, Allen & Unwin, 1938.

The Annihilation of Man: A Study of the Crisis in the West, Faber, 1944, Harcourt, 1945.

The Living Hedge (autobiography), Faber, 1946.

The Soviet Union (bibliography), Ashridge College Press, 1947.

Heron Lake (autobiography), Batchworth, 1948.

The Meaning of Human Existence, Faber, 1949, Lippincott, 1950.

The Age of Terror, Faber, 1950, Beacon Press, 1951.

Angry Young Man (autobiography), Faber, 1951.

(Author of foreword) Emmanuel Mounier, *Be Not Afraid,* translation by Cynthia Rowland, Rockliff, 1951.

Exile and Other Poems, Caravel, 1951.

The English Philosophers, Faber, 1953.

Sir Thomas More, Faber, 1953, Books for Libraries Press, 1970.

The Adventure of Man (geography text), four volumes, Newnes, 1954.

The Jealous God, Bles, 1955.

The Boy Down Kitchener Street, Faber, 1957.

Nature into History, Faber, 1957.

(With others) *The Youth Service in England and Wales,* H.M.S.O., 1960.

Persons and Perceptions, Faber, 1961.

Son of Man: The Life of Christ, Dutton, 1961.

The Transition from School to Work, Industrial Welfare Society, 1962.

Traveller on Sacred Ground, Hodder & Stoughton, 1963.

Deployment and Payment of the Clergy, Church Information Office, 1964.

Alternatives to Christian Belief, Doubleday, 1967.

The Death and Resurrection of the Church, Hodder & Stoughton, 1968.

Coming to Terms with Sex, Collins, 1969.

Eros Rediscovered: Restoring Sex to Humanity, Association Press, 1970.

(With Donald Swann) *This is the Story of Bontzye Shweig,* Galliard, 1970.

A Patti Col Sesso, Edizione Paoline, 1971.

Journey to Connemara (poems), Outposts, 1972.

A Church by Daylight, Chapman, 1973.

The Waters and the Wild (novel), St. Martin's, 1975.

First Love, S.P.C.K., 1977.

The Bulgarian Horse (novel), Cassell, 1979.

Springs of Good and Evil, Bible Reading Fellowship, 1979.

MONOGRAPHS, PAMPHLETS

The Child and the Race, Royal Arsenal Co-operative Society, 1926.

(Editor) *Russia 1931,* Co-operative Union, 1931.

The Training of Pioneers, National Council of Woodcraft Folk, 1936.

Portrait of an Angry Saint: The Poet Peguy, Burning Glass Press, 1949.

(Editor) *Christians and War,* Christian Action, 1951.

The Rebellion of Youth, Westminster Abbey, 1961.

Hot House, Newman Neame, 1961.

Values in Modern Society, Co-operative Union, 1962.

The Church as an Institution, Prism Pamphlets, 1967.

Colloquium, [New Zealand], 1969.

Man's Understanding of Himself, Seabury-Western Theological Seminary, 1971.

Where after Welfare?: The Welfare State Considered, Hereford Diocesan Council of Social Action, 1976.

Seeking the Christ to Celebrate, Celebration Council, 1978.

The Early Days of the Woodcraft Folk, Woodcraft Folk National Council, 1980.

Also author of *Blood and Soil,* published by Plan Press, and *Studies in the Sociology of Religion.* Contributor of stories to anthologies, including *English Story,* Collins, 1941, and *English Country Short Stories,* Elek, 1949; contributor to *Encyclopedia Americana.* Author of scripts for British Broadcasting Corp. and for Associated Television. Contributor to periodicals, including *Kenyon Review, Reporter,* and *Sunday Times* (London).

SIDELIGHTS: An educator, social philosopher, group organizer, journalist, and author, Leslie Paul wrote numerous books in various genres, including poetry, prose fiction, biographies, and sociological studies. He began his career as a journalist, worked in the British underground during World War II, and afterwards held a variety of research, writing, and lecturing posts at colleges, seminaries, and other institutions throughout the world. Paul early embraced left-wing tenets; he wrote a book titled *Cooperation in the U.S.S.R.* following a trip to the Soviet Union in 1931, and based a novel, *Men in May,* on a general strike in Britain. He subsequently focused on other social, philosophical, and ethical issues in his writings and lectures and served on several ecclesiastical advisory councils.

At the age of twenty, Paul founded a youth movement known as the Woodcraft Folk, emphasizing communal living. In 1975, the movement celebrated its fiftieth anniversary with an international camp of 3,000 children and young people at Stanford Hall, Loughborough, England. According to Paul, "the youth movements of the twenties are now exciting the interest of historians," and at his suggestion, University College, University of Wales, established a Youth Movement Archives Department which planned to publish a series of monographs on the subject.

Paul's best-known book is the autobiographical *Angry Young Man;* published in 1951, the book's title came to symbolize an entire generation of youth. But Paul was most famous as a sociologist in the field of religion. His works included *Deployment and Payment of the Clergy,* also known as "The Paul Report," which proposed vast organizational changes in the Anglican ministry; *Alternatives to Christian Belief;* and a 1974 follow up to the *Paul Report,* titled *A Church by Daylight.*

BIOGRAPHICAL/CRITICAL SOURCES:

BOOKS

Paul, Leslie, *The Living Hedge* (autobiography), Faber, 1946.

Paul, *Heron Lake* (autobiography), Batchworth, 1948.

Paul, *Angry Young Man* (autobiography), Faber, 1951.

PERIODICALS

Best Sellers, January 1, 1971.

Times Literary Supplement, September 29, 1961; November, 1961; August 17, 1967.

OBITUARIES:

BOOKS

The Writers Directory: 1982-1984, St. James Press, 1981.

PERIODICALS

Times (London), July 12, 1985.*

PAULSEN, Gary 1939-

PERSONAL: Born May 17, 1939, in Minneapolis, MN; son of Oscar (an Army officer) and Eunice Paulsen; married third wife, Ruth Ellen Wright (an artist), May 5, 1971; children: two children from first marriage, James Wright from third marriage. *Education:* Attended Bemidji College, 1957-58; and University of Colorado, 1976. *Politics:* "As Solzhenitsyn has said, 'If we limit ourselves to political structures we are not artists.' " *Religion:* "I believe in spiritual progress."

ADDRESSES: Home—Leonard, MI. *Agent*—Jonathan Lazear, 430 First Ave., N., Suite 516, Minneapolis, MN 55401.

CAREER: Has worked variously as a teacher, electronics field engineer, soldier, actor, director, farmer, rancher, truck driver, trapper, professional archer, migrant farm worker, singer, and sailor; currently a full-time writer. *Military service:* U.S. Army, 1959-62; became sergeant.

AWARDS, HONORS: Central Missouri Award for Children's Literature, 1976; *The Green Recruit* was chosen one of New York Public Library's Books for the Teen Age, 1980, 1981, and 1982, and *Sailing: From Jibs to Jibing* was chosen in 1982; *Dancing Carl* was selected one of American Library Association's Best Young Adult Books, 1983, and *Tracker* was selected in 1984; Society of Midland Authors Award, 1985, for *Tracker;* Parents' Choice Award, Parents' Choice Foundation, 1985; *Dogsong* was chosen one of Child Study Association of America's Children's Books of the Year, and was a Newbery Honor Book, 1986; *Hatchet* was named a Newbery Honor Book, received a *Booklist* Editor's Choice citation, both 1988, and received the Dorothy Canfield Fisher Children's Book Award, 1989; *The Voyage of the Frog* received *Parenting* magazine's Reading-Magic Award, the Teachers' Choice Award from International Reading Association (IRA), and a Best Book of the Year citation from *Learning* magazine, all 1990; *The Winter Room* was named a Newbery Honor Book, received the Judy Lopez Memorial Award, and received a *Parenting* magazine Best Book of the Year citation, all 1990; *The Boy Who Owned the School: A Comedy of Love* won a Parents' Choice award, 1991; ALAN Award, 1991; *Woodson* received the Western Writers of America Spur award, a *Booklist* Editor's Choice citation, and the Society of Midland Authors Book Award, all 1991; *The Haymeadow* received the Western Writers of America Spur Award, 1993; *Harris and Me* was named one of *Booklist*'s Books for Youth Top of the List, 1993; *Nightjohn and*

Dogteam received Children's Choice for 1994 citation from IRA/Children's Book Council, 1994; *Sisters/ Hermanas* was a PEN Center USA West Children's Literature Award finalist, 1994.

WRITINGS:

NOVELS

The Implosion Effect, Major Books (Canoga Park, CA), 1976.
The Death Specialists, Major Books, 1976.
The Foxman, Thomas Nelson (Nashville, TN), 1977.
Winterkill, Thomas Nelson, 1977.
Tiltawhirl John, Thomas Nelson, 1977.
C. B. Jockey, Major Books, 1977.
The Night the White Deer Died, Thomas Nelson, 1978.
Hope and a Hatchet, Thomas Nelson, 1978.
(With Ray Peekner) *The Green Recruit,* Independence Press (Independence, MO), 1978.
The Spitball Gang, Elsevier/Nelson, 1980.
The Sweeper, Harlequin (Tarrytown, NY), 1981.
Compkill, Pinnacle Books (New York City), 1981.
Clutterkill, Harlequin, 1982.
Popcorn Days and Buttermilk Nights, Lodestar Books (New York City), 1983.
Dancing Carl, Bradbury (Scarsdale, NY), 1983.
Tracker, Bradbury, 1984.
Dogsong, Bradbury, 1985.
Sentries, Bradbury, 1986.
The Crossing, Paperback Library, 1987.
Hatchet, Orchard Books, 1987.
Murphy (western), Walker & Co. (New York City), 1987.
The Island, Orchard Books, 1988.
Murphy's Gold (western), Walker & Co., 1988.
Murphy's Herd (western), Walker & Co., 1989.
Night Rituals, Donald I. Fine, Inc., 1989.
The Boy Who Owned the School: A Comedy of Love, Orchard Books, 1990.
Canyons, Delacorte (New York City), 1990.
Kill Fee, Donald I. Fine, Inc., 1990.
Woodsong, illustrated by Ruth Wright Paulsen, Bradbury, 1990.
The Cookcamp, Orchard Books, 1991.
Monument, Delacorte, 1991.
The River, Delacorte, 1991.
The Winter Room, Dell (New York City), 1991.
A Christmas Sonata, Delacorte, 1992.
Clabbered Dirt, Sweet Grass, paintings by R. Paulsen, Harcourt (New York City), 1992.
The Haymeadow, Doubleday (New York City), 1992.
Dogteam, Delacorte, 1993.
Murphy's Stand (western), Walker & Co., 1993.
Nightjohn, Delacorte, 1993.
Sisters/Hermanas, Harcourt, 1993.
The Car, Harcourt, 1994.
Legend of Red Horse Cavern, Dell, 1994.
Rodomonte's Revenge, Dell, 1994.
Winterdance: The Fine Madness of Running the Iditarod, Harcourt, 1994.
Call Me Francis Tucket, Delacorte, 1995.
Danger on Midnight River, Delacorte, 1995.
Hook 'Em, Snotty! Delacorte, 1995.
The Tent: A Tale in One Sitting, Harcourt, 1995.
The Rifle, Harcourt, 1995.
Murphy's Ambush, Walker & Co., 1995.
The Tortilla Factory, Harcourt, 1995.
Murphy's Trail, Walker (New York City), 1996.
Brian's Winter, Delacorte (New York City), 1996.
Worksong, Harcourt, 1997.
Sarny: A Life Remembered, Bantam, 1997.
Tucket's Ride, Delacorte, 1997.
Sarney, a Life Remembered, Delacorte, 1997.
The Schernoff Discoveries, Delacorte, 1997.

SHORT STORIES

The Madonna Stories, Van Vliet & Co., 1989.

NONFICTION

(With Raymond Friday Locke) *The Special War,* Sirkay, 1966.
Some Birds Don't Fly, Rand McNally (Chicago, IL), 1969.
The Building a New, Buying an Old, Remodeling a Used, Comprehensive Home and Shelter Book, Prentice-Hall (New York City), 1976.
Puppies, Dogs, and Blue Northers: Reflections on Being Raised by a Pack of Sled Dogs, Harcourt, 1976.
Farm: A History and Celebration of the American Farmer, Prentice-Hall, 1977.
(With John Morris) *Hiking and Backpacking,* illustrated by R. Paulsen, Simon & Schuster (New York City), 1978.
Successful Home Repair: When Not to Call the Contractor, Structures, 1978.
(With Morris) *Canoeing, Kayaking, and Rafting,* illustrated by John Peterson and Jack Storholm, Simon & Schuster, 1979.
Money-Saving Home Repair Guide, Ideals (State College, PA), 1981.
Beat the System: A Survival Guide, Pinnacle Books, 1983.
Eastern Sun, Winter Moon: An Autobiographical Odyssey, Harcourt, 1993.

Father Water, Mother Woods: Essays on Fishing and Hunting in the North Woods, Delacorte, 1994.

Pilgrimage on a Steelride: A Memoir about Men and Motorcycles, Harcourt, 1997.

JUVENILE

Mr. Tucket, Funk & Wagnall (New York City), 1968.

(With Dan Theis) *Martin Luther King: The Man Who Climbed the Mountain,* Raintree (Milwaukee, WI), 1976.

The Small Ones, illustrated by K. Goff and with photographs by W. Miller, Raintree, 1976.

The Grass Eaters: Real Animals, illustrated by Goff and with photographs by Miller, Raintree, 1976.

Dribbling, Shooting, and Scoring Sometimes, Raintree, 1976.

Hitting, Pitching, and Running Maybe, Raintree, 1976.

Tackling, Running, and Kicking—Now and Again, Raintree, 1977.

Riding, Roping, and Bulldogging—Almost, Raintree, 1977.

The Golden Stick, Raintree, 1977.

Careers in an Airport, photographs by Roger Nye, Raintree, 1977.

The CB Radio Caper, illustrated by John Asquith, Raintree, 1977.

The Curse of the Cobra, illustrated by Asquith, Raintree, 1977.

Running, Jumping, and Throwing—If You Can, photographs by Heinz Kluetmeier, Raintree, 1978.

Forehanding and Backhanding—If You're Lucky, photographs by Kluetmeier, Raintree, 1978.

Downhill, Hotdogging, and Cross-Country—If the Snow Isn't Sticky, photographs by Willis Wood and Kluetmeier, Raintree, 1979.

Facing Off, Checking, and Goaltending—Perhaps, photographs by Melchior DeGiacomo and Kluetmeier, Raintree, 1979.

Going Very Fast in a Circle—If You Don't Run out of Gas, photographs by Kluetmeier and Bob D'Olivo, Raintree, 1979.

Launching, Floating High, and Landing—If Your Pilot Light Doesn't Go Out, photographs by Kluetmeier, Raintree, 1979.

Pummeling, Falling, and Getting Up—Sometimes, photographs by Kluetmeier and Joe DiMaggio, Raintree, 1979.

Track, Enduro, and Motocross—Unless You Fall Over, photographs by Kluetmeier and others, Raintree, 1979.

(With Art Browne Jr.) *TV and Movie Animals,* Messner (New York City), 1980.

Sailing: From Jibs to Jibing, illustrated by R. Paulsen, Messner, 1981.

Voyage of the Frog, Orchard Books, 1989.

Harris and Me: A Summer Remembered, Harcourt, 1993.

The Rock Jockeys, Bantam, 1995.

My Life in Dog Years, Bantam, 1998.

"CULPEPPER ADVENTURES" SERIES

The Case of the Dirty Bird, Dell, 1992.

Dunc's Doll, Dell, 1992.

Culpepper's Cannon, Dell, 1992.

Dunc Gets Tweaked, Dell, 1992.

Dunc's Halloween, Dell, 1992.

Dunc Breaks the Record, Dell, 1992.

Dunc and the Flaming Ghost, Dell, 1992.

Amos Gets Famous, Dell, 1993.

Dunc and Amos Hit the Big Top, Dell, 1993.

Dunc's Dump, Dell, 1993.

Amos's Last Stand, Dell, 1993.

The Wild Culpepper Cruise, Dell, 1993.

Dunc's Undercover, Dell, 1993.

Dunc and Amos and the Red Tattoos, Dell, 1993.

Dunc and the Haunted House, Dell, 1993.

Cowpokes and Desperadoes, Dell, 1994.

Prince Amos, Dell, 1994.

Coach Amos, Dell, 1994.

Amos and the Alien, Dell, 1994.

Dunc and Amos Meet the Slasher, Dell, 1994.

Dunc and the Greased Sticks of Doom, Dell, 1994.

Amos's Killer Concert Caper, Dell, 1995.

Amos Gets Married, Dell, 1995.

Amos Goes Bananas, Dell, 1995.

Dunc and Amos Go to the Dogs, Dell, 1995.

Amos Gets Married, Bantam Doubleday Dell Books for Young Readers, 1995.

Amos Binder, Secret Agent, Yearling Books, 1997.

"GARY PAULSEN WORLD OF ADVENTURE" SERIES

Escape from Fire Mountain, Dell, 1995.

Rock Jockeys, Dell, 1995.

Captive! Demco Media, 1996.

Skydive! Yearling Books, 1996.

The Treasure of El Patron, Dell, 1996.

PLAYS

Communications (one-act play), produced in New Mexico, 1974.

Together-Apart (one-act play), produced at Changing Scene Theater, 1976.

Also author, with Roger Barrett, of *Athletics, Ice Hockey, Motor-Cycling, Motor Racing, Skiing,* and *Tennis,* all 1980. Also author of *Meteorite-Track 291, The Winter Stories, Murphy's War, The Meatgrinder,* and screenplay *A Cry in the Wind.* Contributor of more than 200 short stories and articles to periodicals.

ADAPTATIONS: *Dogsong* (filmstrip with cassette), Random House/Miller-Brody, 1986; *Dancing Carl* was first a narrative ballet for two dancers with original music by John Collins and choreography by Nancy Keller—a seven-minute version of it was aired on Minnesota Public Television.Bantam has adapted the following titles to audio: *Monument,* 1993, and *Brian's Winter,* 1996. Numerous other titles have been adapted to audio, including *A Christmas Sonata, The Island, Mr. Tucket, The Night the White Deer Died, Sisters/ Hermanas, Tracker,* and *The Winter Room,* all 1995; *The Foxman, Murphy's Ambush,* and *The Rifle,* all 1996; and *Captive!, Danger on Midnight River, Escape from Fire Mountain, The Legend of the Red Horse Cavern,* and *Skydive!,* all 1997.

SIDELIGHTS: A prolific writer in several genres, Gary Paulsen is acclaimed as the author of powerful young-adult fiction. Usually set in wilderness areas, Paulsen's books for young adults feature teenagers who arrive at self-awareness by way of experiences in nature—often through challenging tests of their own survival instincts. A former resident of northern Minnesota, Paulsen writes from his own experience of the outdoors, which includes dogsled racing in the Alaskan Iditarod, hunting, and trapping. *Tracker,* for instance, tells the story of a thirteen-year-old boy who must hunt alone for the first time to put meat on the table. Paulsen describes the spiritual relationship that develops between the hunter and his prey and how the deer's acceptance of death helps the boy come to terms with his grandfather's imminent death. *Dogsong* is a story of a boy's coming of age on the northern tundra. Eugene J. Lineham in *Best Sellers* praises Paulsen's writing style, noting: "There is poetic majesty in the descriptions without a touch of condescension to the young."

Commenting on his childhood in *Authors & Artists for Young Adults,* Paulsen remarked, "I was an 'army brat,' and it was a miserable life. School was a nightmare because I was unbelievably shy, and terrible at sports. I had no friends, and teachers ridiculed me. . . . One day as I was walking past the public library in twenty-below temperatures . . . I went in to get warm and to my absolute astonishment the librarian . . . asked me if I wanted a library card. . . . When she handed me the card, she handed me the world."

In Paulsen's novel *Hatchet,* the pilot of a single-engined plane has a heart attack and dies, crashing his plane in the Canadian wilderness. Brian Robeson, the sole passenger, must put aside his troubled thoughts about his parents' divorce and try to survive with just the hatchet that his mother had given him as a parting gift. Brian uses his hatchet in numerous ways, such as striking it against a rock to make sparks for a fire and using it to sharpen sticks for tools. The tension surrounding Brian's struggle to survive is enhanced by Paulsen's "staccato, repetitive style," according to a *Kirkus Reviews* contributor, who notes *Hatchet* is a "plausible, taut, . . . [and] spellbinding account." Comparing Paulsen to best-selling authors Robert Cormier and Paula Fox, *Christian Science Monitor*'s Stephen Fraser claims that *Hatchet* "deserves special attention. Written in terse, poetic prose, it is an adventure story in the best tradition."

Dancing Carl deviates from Paulsen's adventure stories and focuses on interpersonal relationships. When two twelve-year-old boys first meet Carl, the enigmatic man in the flight jacket, they think he is an alcoholic and a bum. They quickly learn that Carl is much more than that; he takes over the skating rink with the power of his presence, and over the course of the winter, he becomes the topic of the whole town's conversations. With his dance-like movements he expresses his emotions, and the people who watch are made to feel things too, such as repentance for a violent act, happy memories of someone who just died, Carl's pain and terror of his war experience, and Carl's love for a woman. "Readers will come away with a sense of having met an intriguing person," according to Jane E. Gardner in *School Library Journal.* "Filled with poetry and with life," praises Dorcas Hand in *Horn Book,* "[*Dancing Carl*] is not only an insightful, beautifully written story for children but for readers of any age."

Another book that touches on the subject of war and its effect on lives is *Sentries,* a collection of stories about four young people who are given the opportunity to make their lives a success during peacetime and three young men whose lives are destroyed by choices made during war. The peacetime tales relate the stories of a girl who chooses between her Indian heritage and the white world, a migrant worker who commits to working with beet harvesters, a daughter who proves that she is as capable as any son, and a gifted rock musician who creates a new music. These stories are juxtaposed with tales expressed through four battle hymns set during World War II and the Vietnam War. The purpose of these veterans' tales of mental and physical suffering and the looming threat of nuclear war are to ensure that readers do not take their choices and opportunities for granted and to encourage them to be sentries to protect their rights and freedoms. The juxtaposition of the war and peacetime chapters "conveys, better than philosophizing, the interconnections of life," according to *New York Times Book Review*'s Doris Orgel. Noting that *Sentries* "is strange [and] hard to pigeonhole," Orgel finds that although the protaganists do not interact and the combined tales do not create a novel, the "stories produce a unified effect." And, *Voice of Youth Advocates*' Evie Wilson hails Paulsen for his "literary excellence" in his selection of stories that serve to remind us of the potential of "the formidable human waste nuclear war promises."

Paulsen's novels continue to reflect the author's interest in nature and the people who derive their sustenance from the outdoors. In *The Cookcamp,* a young boy learns some valuable lessons about life and love from his grandmother, who works as a cook for a deep-woods road crew. "This short novel has almost unbelievable poignancy," comments Patty Campbell in *New York Times Book Review.* Susan M. Harding, writing in *School Library Journal,* concurs by noting that *The Cookcamp* offers a "depth of imagery and emotion" which makes the book "superb for readers just old enough to look back."

In books like *Nightjohn* and *Mr. Tucket,* Paulsen draws on history for literary inspiration. The twelve-year-old heroine of *Nightjohn* is a slave who awaits the day when she will be designated a "breeder" by her master. As Sarny tries to deal with this unpleasant eventuality, she surreptitiously takes reading lessons from an older slave named John. John pays a high price for being Sarny's teacher—two of his toes are cut off—but he is eventually able to escape and establish an underground school. In *Mr. Tucket,* fourteen-year-old Francis Tucket has a number of hair-raising adventures when he is captured by the Pawnee after drifting away from his family's Oregon-bound wagon train. After Francis escapes from the tribe, a one-armed fur trader named Jason Grimes continues the young teen's frontier education.

The traumas that go hand-in-hand with coming of age are also present in *The Car,* Paulsen's 1994 novel about a teen who deals with emotional upheaval by working on a car kit. Terry pours the frustration and anger he feels about his parents' separation into long hours with his tools, building the convertible his father never finished. In his review of *The Car* for *School Library Journal,* Tim Rausch calls the author's characters "interesting to [young adults] . . . the action is brisk."

Rosa and Traci of *Sisters/Hermanas* have little in common—at least on the surface. Rosa is an illegal immigrant who turns to prostitution in order to survive; Traci is a well-liked junior high schooler whose biggest concerns revolve around cheerleading tryouts and new clothes. Both teens, however, are deeply obsessed with beauty and its impact on their future happiness. The two young women's lives ultimately intersect at a mall, where both girls are forced to face some unpleasant realities. This tale of culture clash and youthful dreams is especially unique in that the entire text appears in both English and Spanish. Summing up the novel for *Los Angeles Times Book Review,* Yvonne Sapia terms the work "brief, ambitious, and told quite poetically."

In a series of Westerns, Paulsen features Al Murphy, a New Yorker in his early thirties who heads west with the army after the Civil War and becomes a lawman. David Whitehead of *Twentieth-Century Western Writers* describes Murphy: "Although he is a lawman's lawman, whose actions are dictated more by instinct than conscious thought, Murphy soon proves to be more than just another gun-fast hero. In Paulsen's hands, he is as close to human—with all the foibles and contradictions that this entails—as any fictional character is likely to get." *Murphy* introduces the character as he enforces the law in a Colorado town. When a girl is raped and murdered, Murphy's efforts to identify and capture the killer force him to consider his position in the community, which views him as a necessary evil. Murphy's hunches often amount to nothing, which, according to Whitehead, "serves only to make his dogged attempts at solving the crime all the more credible." Whitehead further praises the final resolution and the well-drawn cast of minor characters. The identity of the killer is revealed in *Murphy's Gold,* in which Murphy is still haunted by memories of the victim. The plot centers on the romantic possibilities between Murphy and Midge, the cafe owner, and Murphy's attempts to locate a Chinese woman's missing husband. In *Murphy's War,* Murphy has left the Colorado town and is keeping the peace in Fletcher, Wyoming. Tensions mount as he comes into conflict with a power-hungry storekeeper and a wealthy rancher intent on avenging the lynching death of his son.

Paulsen's own colorful life is the basis for the author's 1993 book titled *Eastern Sun, Winter Moon: An Autobiographical Odyssey.* Among the events chronicled are Paulsen's journey by car across the country to meet his long-absent father, his family's unsettling life in the Philippines, and the dissolution of his parents' marriage. While noting that the memoir lacks introspective depth, Tim Winton in *Los Angeles Times Book Review* nevertheless finds the book to be "no less powerful and dignified for its painful silences."

"I write because it's all I can do," Paulsen once commented. "Every time I've tried to do something else, I cannot." The author continues to write—even though the task is often daunting to him—because he wants his "years on this ball of earth to mean something. Writing furnishes a way for that to happen. . . . It pleases me to write—in a very literal sense of the word."

BIOGRAPHICAL/CRITICAL SOURCES:

BOOKS

Authors & Artists for Young Adults, Volume 17, Gale, 1995.

Paulsen, Gary, *Pilgrimage on a Steelride: A Memoir about Men and Motorcycles,* Harcourt, 1997.

Paulsen Gary, *Puppies, Dogs, and Blue Northers: Reflections on Being Raised by a Packof Sled Dogs,* Harcourt, 1996.

Salvner, Gary, M., *Presenting Gary Paulsen,* Twhayne (New York City), 1996.

Something about the Author, Volume 79, Gale, 1995.

Twentieth-Century Children's Writers, 4th edition, St. James Press, 1995.

Twentieth-Century Western Writers, 2nd edition, St. James Press, 1991.

Twentieth-Century Young Adult Writers, St. James Press, 1994.

PERIODICALS

Best Sellers, July, 1985.

Christian Science Monitor, November 6, 1987, p. B5.

Horn Book, August, 1983, pp. 446-47.

Kirkus Reviews, August 1, 1987, pp. 1161-62; September 15, 1997, p. 1443.

Library Journal, February 15, 1993.

London Review of Books, May 23, 1996, p. 28.

Los Angeles Times, December 12, 1987.

Los Angeles Times Book Review, March 21, 1993, pp. 1, 11; February 27, 1994, pp. 2, 13.

New York Times Book Review, June 29, 1986, p. 30; May 22, 1988; May 5, 1991, pp. 22-23; November 10, 1996, p. 46.

School Library Journal, May, 1983, p. 84; May, 1994, pp. 131-32; July, 1995, p. 50; June, 1997, p. 24.

Voice of Youth Advocates, October, 1986, p. 148; June, 1994; February, 1996, p. 375; February, 1997, p. 332.

Writer's Digest, January, 1980.*

PEARSON, Bill
See PEARSON, William Harrison

* * *

PEARSON, William Harrison 1922-
(Bill Pearson)

PERSONAL: Born January 18, 1922, in Greymouth, New Zealand; son of James (a railway clerk) and Agnes Ellen (McLean) Pearson. *Education:* Attended Otago University, 1940-41; Dunedin Teachers' College, teacher's certificate, 1941; University of Canterbury, B.A., 1947, M.A., 1948; King's College, London, Ph.D., 1952. *Politics:* Socialist.

ADDRESSES: Office—English Department, University of Auckland, Auckland, New Zealand.

CAREER: Student teacher, Dunedin Teachers Training College, 1940-41; elementary school teacher in Blackball, New Zealand, 1942, in Oxford, New Zealand, 1949; substitute teacher in London, England, 1952-53; University of Auckland, Auckland, New Zealand, lecturer in English literature, 1954-66; Australian National University, Canberra, senior research fellow, 1967-69; University of Auckland, associate professor of English literature, 1970-86. University of Auckland, patron of the Maori students' club; internal rapporteur at several Maori Leadership Conferences, 1959-63. *Military service:* New Zealand Army, 1942-46.

AWARDS, HONORS: Joint winner of *Landfall* Readers' Award for nonfiction, 1960, for essay "Fretful Sleepers"; New Zealand Prose Award for nonfiction, 1974, for *Fretful Sleepers and Other Essays;* Hubert Church Prose Award, 1975, for nonfiction.

WRITINGS:

UNDER NAME BILL PEARSON EXCEPT WHERE INDICATED

Coal Flat (novel), Angus & Robertson, 1963, revised edition, Longman Paul, 1970.

(Editor) Frank Sargeson, *Collected Stories, 1935-1963,* Blackwood & Janet Paul, 1964.

Henry Lawson among Maoris, Australian National University Press, 1968.

(Editor) Roderick Finlayson, *Brown Man's Burden and Later Stories,* Auckland University Press, 1973.

Fretful Sleepers and Other Essays, International Publications Service, 1974.

(Under the name William Pearson) *Chessplayer,* Viking Press (New York City),1984.

Rifled Sanctuaries: Some Views of the Pacific Islands in Western Literature, Oxford University Press (New York City), 1984.

Six Stories (short stories), Victoria University Press, 1991.

Contributor to journals in his field and to literary magazines.

SIDELIGHTS: William Harrison Pearson is an essayist, scholar, short-story writer, and novelist who writes under the name Bill Pearson. His only novel to date, *Coal Flat,* is set in a coal and gold mining settlement on New Zealand's West Coast. The novel depicts family and community life, evoking its narrow and puritan character in carefully drawn details. The setting is populated with a complete cast of characters that includes the parson, police officer, miners, visiting politicians, the doctor, and teachers. The novel portrays the struggle between the individual conscience and the collective will as well as personal relationships in the broader context of the community.

Commenting on *Coal Flat* in *Contemporary Novelists,* H. Winston Rhodes wrote, "The shriek of the dredge echoes and reechoes through the book and acts as an inhuman accompaniment to the bitter animosities, perverted affections, and destructive behavior of the people of Coal Flat. At another and perhaps even more significant level these become signs and portents of a wider deterioration in the quality of life extending well beyond its confines." Although there is bleakness in the lives of Pearson's characters, there is also kindness, friendship, and devotion.

Pearson wrote in *Contemporary Novelists:* "The writers in the light of whose practice my aspirations as a writer developed were those that in common with young men of my time I read with sympathy and a deep respect: Lawrence, Joyce, Forster, Faulkner, Hemingway, Koestler; and I had a series of passions for the novels of Virginia Woolf and John Dos Passos and Thomas Hardy. At the time of my novel's first conception in 1946, the novelist who most excited me was Graham Greene. What I had hoped to do when I was writing it (mostly in 1952 and 1953) was to devise a traditional structure that would be large enough to comprehend a community and sensitive enough to reflect the crises of feeling and conscience that might come to a man who was out of sympathy with the materialist values of the community. . . . My hope was to achieve an imaginative authenticity that my compatriots would immediately recognize as true, and which at the same time would be sufficiently clear of the accidents of parochiality to translate into human experience recognizable to readers from other societies. Whether I succeeded in this I cannot tell; but no one but an expatriate knows the pleasure of imaginatively recreating one's country in its detail, without sentimentality."

BIOGRAPHICAL/CRITICAL SOURCES:

BOOKS

Rhodes, H. Winston, *New Zealand Fiction since 1945,* John McIndoe, 1968.

Stevens, Joan, *The New Zealand Novel, 1860-1965,* A. H. Reed, 1966.

PERIODICALS

Choice, February, 1975.

Landfall, December, 1967.*

* * *

PECHMAN, Joseph A(aron) 1918-1989

PERSONAL: Surname is pronounced *Peck*-man; born April 2, 1918, in New York, NY; died after a heart attack, August 19, 1989; son of Gershon and Lena Pechman; married Sylvia Massow, September 29, 1943; children: Ellen Massow, Jane Elizabeth. *Education:* City College (now of the City University of New York), B.S., 1937; University of Wisconsin (now University of Wisconsin—Madison), M.A., 1938, Ph.D., 1942.

CAREER: National Research Project, Philadelphia, PA, statistician, 1937; assistant director of state income tax study, Wisconsin Tax Commission, 1938-39; Office of Price Administration, Washington, DC, economist, 1941-42; U.S. Department of the Treasury, Washington, DC, assistant director of tax advisory staff, 1946-53; Massachusetts Institute of Technology, Cambridge, associate professor of finance, 1953-54; Council of Economic Advisers, Washington, DC, economist, 1954-56; Committee for Economic Development, Washington, DC, economist, 1956-60; Brookings Institution, Washington, DC, executive director of studies of government finance, 1960-70, director of economic studies program, 1962-89. Irving Fisher Research Professor at Yale University, 1956-66; fellow of Center for Advanced Study in the Behavioral Sciences, 1975-76. *Military service:* U.S. Army, meteorologist, 1942-45.

MEMBER: American Finance Association (president, 1971), American Economic Association (vice president, 1978), National Tax Association, Phi Beta Kappa.

AWARDS, HONORS: LL.D. from University of Wisconsin—Madison, 1978.

WRITINGS:

(With Frank Allan Hanna) *Analysis of Wisconsin Income,* National Bureau of Economic Research, 1948.

(With Herbert Stein) *Essays in Federal Taxation,* Committee for Economic Development, 1959.

Financing State and Local Government, Brookings Institution (Washington, DC), 1965.

Individual Income Tax Provisions of the Revenue Act of 1964, Brookings Institution, 1965.

A New Tax Model for Revenue Estimating (pamphlet), Brookings Institution, 1965.

Federal Tax Policy, Brookings Institution, 1966, 3rd edition, 1977.

(With James Tobin) *Is a Negative Income Tax Practical?,* Brookings Institution, 1967.

(With Walter W. Heller) *Questions and Answers on Revenue Sharing,* Brookings Institution, 1967.

Report of the Canadian Royal Commission on Taxation: A Summing Up (pamphlet), Brookings Institution, 1967.

(With Henry J. Aaron and Michael K. Taussig) *Social Security: Perspectives for Reform,* Brookings Institution, 1968.

(With Aaron and Taussig) *The Objectives of Social Security* (pamphlet), Brookings Institution, 1968.

The Rich, the Poor, and the Taxes They Pay (pamphlet), Brookings Institution, 1969.

Distribution of Federal and State Income Taxes by Income Classes, Brookings Institution, 1972.

(With Benjamin A. Okner) *Individual Income Tax Erosion by Income Classes,* Brookings Institution, 1972.

International Trends in the Distribution of Tax Burdens: Implications for Tax Policy, Institute for Fiscal Studies (London, England), 1973.

(With Okner) *Who Bears the Tax Burden?,* Brookings Institution, 1974, reprinted as *How Fair Is the American Tax System?,* 1975.

(With George F. Break) *Federal Tax Reform: The Impossible Dream?,* Brookings Institution, 1975.

(Editor with Michael Timpane) *Work Incentives and Income Guarantees: The New Jersey Negative Income Tax Experiment,* Brookings Institution, 1975.

Federal Tax Reform for 1976, Fund for Public Policy Research 1976.

(Editor) *Comprehensive Income Taxation,* Brookings Institution, 1977.

Setting National Priorities: The 1978 Budget, Brookings Institution, 1977.

(Editor with John L. Palmer) *Welfare in Rural Areas: The North Carolina-Iowa Income Maintenance Experiment,* Brookings Institution, 1978.

(Editor) *What Should be Taxed, Income or Expenditure?: A Report of a Conference Sponsored by the Fund for Public Policy Research and the Brookings Institution,* Brookings Institution, 1980.

(Editor with Henry J. Aaron) *How Taxes Affect Economic Behavior,* Brookings Institution, 1981.

(Editor with N. J. Simler) *Economics in the Public Service: Papers in Honor of Walter W. Heller,* Norton (New York City), 1982.

(Editor) *Economics for Policymaking: Selected Essays of Arthur M. Okun,* MIT Press (Cambridge, MA), 1983.

(Editor) *Options for Tax Reform: Papers,* Brookings Institution, 1984.

(Contributor) *Tax Policy: New Directions and Possibilities,* introduction by Walter W. Heller, Center for National Policy (Washington, DC), 1984.

(Editor) The American Assembly, Columbia University, *The Promise of Tax Reform,* Prentice-Hall (Englewood Cliffs, NJ), 1985.

(Editor) *A Citizen's Guide to the New Tax Reforms: Fair Tax, Flat Tax, Simple Tax,* Rowman & Allanheld (Totowa, NJ), 1985.

Who Paid the Taxes, 1966-85?, Brookings Institution, 1985.

(Editor with Clair Brown) *Gender in the Workplace,* Brookings Institution, 1987.

(Editor) *Tax Reform and the U.S. Economy: Papers: Presented at a Conference at the Brookings Institution, December 2, 1986,* Brookings Institution, 1987.

(Editor) *Comparative Tax Systems: Europe, Canada, and Japan,* Tax Analysts (Arlington, VA), 1987.

(Editor) *World Tax Reform: A Progress Report,* Brookings Institution, 1988.

(Editor with Henry J. Aaron and Harvey Galper) *Uneasy Compromise: Problems of a Hybrid Income-Consumption Tax,* Brookings Institution, 1988.

(Editor) *The Role of the Economist in Government: An International Perspective,* New York University Press (Washington Square, NY), 1989.

Tax Reform: The Rich and the Poor, Brookings Institution, 1989.

(Editor, with the assistance of Michael S. McPherson) *Fulfilling America's Promise: Social Policies for the 1990's,* Cornell University Press (Ithaca, NY), 1992.

Contributor of articles and reviews to economic and finance journals. Member of board of editors of American Economic Association, 1960-63.

SIDELIGHTS: Considered the father of the 1986 Tax Reform Act, economist and author Joseph A. Pechman was influential in U.S. economic and tax policy for decades and wrote a standard reference work, *Federal Tax Policy.* After beginning his career in 1937 as a statistician with the National Research Project, he held various posts with federal government offices as well as private organizations such as the Brookings Institution, for which he was executive director of government finance studies for ten years. Pechman's books include *Financing State and Local Government; The Rich, the Poor, and the Taxes They Pay;* and *Setting National Priorities: The 1978 Budget.*

OBITUARIES:

PERIODICALS

Chicago Tribune, August 21, 1989.
New York Times, August 21, 1989.
Washington Post, August 20, 1989.*

* * *

PEMBERTON, Margaret 1943-
(Carris Carlise, Christina Harland)

PERSONAL: Born April 10, 1943, in Yorkshire, England; daughter of George Arthur (an architect) and Kathleen (an artist; maiden name, Ramsden) Hudson; married Mike Pemberton (an advertising executive), October 13, 1968; children: Amanda, Rebecca, Polly, Michael, Natasha Christina. *Education:* Attended girls' school in Bradford, Yorkshire, England. *Politics:* "Apolitical."

ADDRESSES: *Home*—13 Manor Ln., London SE13, England. *Agent*—Carol Smith Agency, 25 Hornton Ct., Kensington High St., London W8 7RT, England.

CAREER: Freelance writer, 1974—. Has worked as a secretary, actress, model, nurse, overseas telegraphist, and catering manager.

MEMBER: Romantic Novelists Association (chairman, 1989-91), Crime Writers Association.

WRITINGS:

Rendezvous with Danger, Macdonald & Jane's, 1974.
The Mystery of Saligo Bay, Macdonald & Jane's, 1975.
Shadows over Silver Sands, Berkeley, 1976.
The Guilty Secret, R. Hale, 1979.
Tapestry of Fear, R. Hale, 1979.
Vengeance in the Sun, R. Hale, 1979.
The Lion of Languedoc, Mills & Boon, 1980.
Harlot, Arrow, 1981.
Pioneer Girl, Mills & Boon, 1981.
Some Distant Shore, Pocket Books, 1981.
African Enchantment, Mills & Boon, 1982.
The Flower Garden, F. Watts, 1982.
Flight to Verechencko, Mills & Boon, 1983.
Forever, Fontana, 1983.
The Devil's Palace, Mills & Boon, 1984.
Goddess, Bantam, 1985.
Silver Shadows, Golden Dreams, Macdonald, 1985.
Never Leave Me, Transworld, 1986.
A Multitude of Sins, Transworld, 1988.
(Under pseudonym Carris Carlise) *Party in Peking,* St. Martin's, 1988.
(Under pseudonym Christina Harland) *White Christmas in Saigon,* Transworld, 1990.
(As Christina Harland) *Waiting Wives,* Bantam, 1991.
An Embarrassment of Riches, Bantam, 1992.
Moonflower Madness, Severn House, 1993.
Zadruga, Bantam, 1994.
Forget-Me-Not Bride, Severn House, 1995.
The Londoners, Corgi Books (London), 1995.
Magnolia Square, Transworld Publishers, 1996.
The Girl Who Knew Too Much, Severn House, 1997.
Yorkshire Rose, Ulverscroft Large Print, 1997.
The Last Letter, Severn House, 1998.

SIDELIGHTS: Margaret Pemberton is a versatile writer whose work includes suspense novels, historical fiction, romances, and family sagas. The settings of her novels vary from the past to the present and across the globe. Pamela Cleaver of *Twentieth-Century Romance and Historical Writers* commented that Pemberton's novels "are full of deeply felt emotion and sexual tension, her characters are lively, the women beautiful, the men devastatingly attractive, and her plots are ingenious: Just when you think you know what is going to happen, she surprises you."

Pioneer Girl is typical of Pemberton's early historical novels. Set against a thoroughly researched background, the story features few minor characters, thus focusing on the budding love affair between Polly and Major Dart Richards. Traveling with the Mormons on the Oregon Trail in 1846, Polly meets Dart when he tries to turn the Mormons back. They are determined to continue, however, and the officer travels with them. Although Polly and Dart are attracted to each other, they are kept apart by misunderstandings until she is captured by Indians. Dart reveals that he is half-Indian, rescues her, and they marry.

Silver Shadows, Golden Dreams takes place in the early days of Hollywood. Daisy grows up in an orphanage. When she is old enough to leave, she captures the attention of Vidal, a powerful, mysterious movie producer. Taking the screen name Valentina, she becomes a star. Although Daisy and Vidal are strongly attracted to each other, he cannot divorce his wife for reasons at first unknown to the reader. The plot proceeds through many exciting twists and turns until Daisy and Vidal are finally able to be together.

Never Leave Me is a lengthier book with a larger cast of characters. Set during and after World War II, the story tells of the forbidden love between Lisette, a French girl in the Resistance, and Dieter, a German officer. Upon liberation Dieter is killed, leaving Lisette alone and pregnant. When she rescues Luke, an Englishman, from a burning plane, he learns of her difficult situation and offers to marry her, but she refuses. Thinking she has lost the baby, she marries the American officer Greg with whom she has fallen in love. She soon realizes, however, that she is still carrying the baby and that Greg hates anything German. Lisette's feelings of guilt threaten her marriage, so when Greg believes that the child is Luke's, she does not correct him. Years later, Lisette's son Dominic falls in love with Luke's daughter and the truth comes out. Lisette and Greg's marriage remains strong as love triumphs over past hate.

Pemberton told *CA:* "My main passions in life are Mike Pemberton, smaller Pembertons, Shakespeare, theatre, acting, and travel, in that order. I am a keen amateur actress and will travel anywhere at the slightest excuse. I write because I love it, because it is the only thing I can do!"

BIOGRAPHICAL/CRITICAL SOURCES:

BOOKS

Twentieth-Century Romance and Historical Writers, 3rd edition, St. James Press, 1994.

PERIODICALS

Kirkus Reviews, May 15, 1987, p. 741.
Library Journal, July, 1993, p. 121; July, 1987, p. 92.
Publishers Weekly, June 5, 1987, p. 69.*

PENDLETON, Don
See KRAUZER, Steven M(ark)

* * *

PERHAM, Margery (Freda) 1895-1982

PERSONAL: Born September 6, 1895, in Bury, Lancashire, England; died February 19, 1982, in Burcot, Oxford, England; daughter of Frederick and Marion (Needell) Perham. *Education:* St. Hugh's College, Oxford, B.A. and M.A., 1919. *Religion:* Church of England. *Avocational interests:* Gardening, animal welfare.

CAREER: Assistant lecturer in history, University of Sheffield, Sheffield, England; Oxford University, St. Hugh's College, Oxford, England, fellow and tutor in modern history, 1924-29, research fellow, 1930-39; Rhodes travelling fellow in North America, Polynesia, Australia, and Africa, 1929-32; Rockefeller travelling fellow in East Africa and Sudan, 1932; Oxford University, research lecturer in colonial administration, 1935-39, reader in colonial administration, 1939-48, fellow of Nuffield College, 1939-63, honorary fellow of Nuffield College, 1963-82, vice-chairman of Summer School of Colonial Administration, 1937-38, director of Institute of Colonial Studies, 1945-48, chairman of Colonial Records Research Project, 1963-73. Member of Higher Education Commission and West Indies Higher Education Committee, 1944; member of executive committee, Inter-University Council on Higher Education Overseas, 1946-67; member of Colonial Social Science Research Council, 1947-61; president of Universities' Mission to Central Africa, 1963-64. Reith Lecturer, British Broadcasting Corp., 1961. Member of advisory committee on education in the colonies, 1939-45.

MEMBER: British Academy (fellow), Royal Commonwealth Society, American Academy of Arts and Sciences (fellow).

AWARDS, HONORS: Commander, Order of the British Empire, 1948; commander, Order of St. Michael and St. George, 1965; Gold Wellcome Medal, Royal African Society. D.C.L., University of Southampton, 1962; LL.D., University of St. Andrews, 1962, University of London, 1964, and University of Birmingham, 1969; L.H.D., Cambridge University, 1966, and Oxford University.

WRITINGS:

Major Dane's Garden, Hutchinson, 1925.

The Protectorate of South Africa: The Question of Their Transfer to the Union, Oxford University Press, 1935.

Native Administration in Nigeria, Oxford University Press, 1937.

Africans and British Rule, Oxford University Press, 1941.

The Government of Ethiopia, Faber, 1948, revised edition, Northwestern University Press, 1969.

(With Elspeth Huxley) *Race and Politics in Kenya,* Faber, 1956, revised edition, Greenwood Press, 1975.

Lugard, Collins, Volume I: *The Years of Adventure, 1858-1898,* 1956, Volume II: *The Years of Authority, 1898-1945,* 1960.

The Colonial Reckoning, Collins, 1961, Knopf, 1962, revised edition, Collins, 1963.

African Outline, Oxford University Press, 1966.

Colonial Sequence, 1930-1949, Barnes & Noble, 1967.

Colonial Sequence, 1949-1969, Methuen, 1970.

African Apprenticeship: An Autobiographical Journey in South Africa, 1929, Africana Publishing, 1974.

East African Journey: Kenya and Tanganyika, 1929-1930, Faber, 1976.

West African Passage: A Journey Through Nigeria, Chad, and the Cameroons, 1931-1932, edited with an introduction by A.H.M. Kirk-Greene, Peter Owen (London), 1983.

Pacific Prelude: A Journey to Samoa and Australasia, 1929, edited with an introduction by A.H.M. Kirk-Greene, Peter Owen, 1988.

A Catalogue of the Papers of Dame Margery Perham, 1895-1982, in Rhodes House Library, Oxford, compiled by Patricia Pugh, Bodleian Library (Oxford), 1989.

Also author of *Tribes of the Niger Delta: Their Religion and Customs.*

EDITOR

Ten Africans, Faber, 1936, 2nd edition, Northwestern University Press, 1964.

(With J. Simmons) *African Discovery: An Anthology of Exploration,* Faber, 1942, 2nd edition, 1957, Northwestern University Press, 1963.

The Economics of Tropical Dependency, Faber, Volume I: *The Native Economics of Nigeria,* 1946, Volume II: *Mining, Commerce, and Finance in Nigeria,* 1948.

J. W. Davidson, *Northern Rhodesian Legislative Council,* Faber, 1948.

Colonial Government, Oxford University Press, 1950.

The Diaries of Lord Lugard, Northwestern University Press, 1959-63, Volume I: *East Africa, November, 1889 to December, 1890,* Volume II: *East Africa, December, 1890 to December, 1891,* Volume III: *East Africa, January, 1892 to August, 1892,* Volume IV: *Nigeria, 1894-95 and 1898.*

Contributor to periodicals, including London *Times.*

SIDELIGHTS: Educator and author Margery Perham was an authority on Africa. Her 1922 visit to Somaliland inspired an interest in British policy in African colonies, the topic of most of her writing. As her opinions gained credence, more and more officials sought her advice. *Native Administration in Nigeria,* Perham's most influential book, "was . . . the first scholarly study of what is meant by indirect rule," noted a London *Times* reporter. This book introduced innovative theories which elicited the respect of British Secretary of State Creech-Jones, who thought the author equal to an "oracle." Perham was instrumental in founding the school of colonial studies at Oxford, and she won the first official fellowship at Nuffield College. Her awards were numerous, among them three honorary degrees, commander of the Order of the British Empire, and honorary fellow of St. Hugh's College. Her writings include *Africans and British Rule, The Government of Ethiopia, The Life of Lord Lugard, The Colonial Sequence,* and *East African Journey,* the source of the British Broadcasting Corporation (BBC) productions titled "The Time of My Life."

BIOGRAPHICAL/CRITICAL SOURCES:

BOOKS

Perham, Margery, *East African Journey: Kenya and Tanganyika, 1929-1930,* Faber (London), 1976.

Perham, M., *West African Pasage: A Journey through Nigeria, Chad, and the Cameroons, 1931-1932,* edited with an introduction by A.H.M. Kirk-Greene, Peter Owen, 1983.

Perham, M., *Pacific Prelude: A Journey to Samoa and Australasia, 1929,* edited with an introduction by A.H.M. Kirk-Greene, Peter Owen, 1988.

Pugh, Patricia, compiler, *A Catalogue of the Papers of Dame Margery Perham, 1895-1982, in Rhodes House Library, Oxford,* Bodleian Library, 1989.

Robinson, Kenneth, and Frederick Madden, *Essays in Imperial Government: Presented to Margery Perham,* Basil Blackwell, 1963.

Smith, Allison, and Mary Bull, editors, *Margery Perham and British Rule in Africa,* F. Cass (London), 1991.

PERIODICALS

Observer, November 26, 1961.
Times Literary Supplement, November 2, 1967.

OBITUARIES:

PERIODICALS

Chicago Tribune, February 24, 1982.
Times (London), February 22, 1982.*

* * *

PESHKOV, Alexei Maximovich 1868-1936 (Jehudil Chlamyda, Maxim Gorky)

PERSONAL: Given name also transliterated as Alexey, Aleksei, and Aleksey; also Maksimovich and Mikhaylovich; surname also transliterated as Pyeshkov; pseudonym also transliterated as Maksim; also Gorki, Gorkii, and Gor'ky; born March 28 (some sources say March 16), 1868, in Nizhny-Novgorod, Russia; died after alleged poisoning, June 18, 1936, in Moscow, USSR (now Russia); married Ekaterina Pavlovna Volzhina in 1896 (separated); children: one son, one daughter.

CAREER: Novelist, dramatist, short story writer, essayist, autobiographer, diarist, poet, and journalist. Editor, *Lifi,* St. Petersburg, 1899-1936; *Chronicles* magazine, 1915-17; *New Life* newspaper, 1917-18; *Dialogue,* Berlin, 1923-25; *Literary Apprenticeship* magazine, 1933.

AWARDS, HONORS: Order of Lenin, 1932. Gorky Literary Institute established in his honor.

WRITINGS:

SHORT STORY COLLECTIONS

Ocherki i rasskazy, three volumes, 1898-99.
Rasskazy, nine volumes, 1900-10.
Orloff and His Wife, 1901.
Dvadtsat shest' i odna, 1902, translation published as *Twenty-Six Men and a Girl,* 1928.
The Outcasts and Other Stories, 1902.
Creatures that Once Were Men, 1905.
Tales of Two Countries, 1914.
Chelkash, and Other Stories, 1915.
Through Russia, 1921.
The Story of the Novel and Other Stories, translated by M. Zakrevsky, 1925.
Best Short Stories, edited and translated by Avrahm Yarmolinsky and Moura Budberg, 1939, published as *A Book of Short Stories,* 1939.
Song of the Stormy Petrel and Other Short Stories, translated by M. Trommer, 1942.
Unrequited Love and Other Stories, 1949.
Selected Short Stories 1892-1901, translated by Margaret Wettlin, 1954.
A Sky-Blue Life and Other Stories, translated by George Reavey, 1964.
Collected Short Stories, edited by Yarmolinsky and Budberg, 1988.

NOVELS

Foma Gordeyev, 1900, published as *Foma Gordeiev,* 1901.
Troe, c. 1900s, translations published as *Three of Them,* 1902, as *Three Men,* 1902, as *The Three,* 1958.
Mat', 1907, translation published as *Mother,* 1907.
Zhizn nenuzhnovo cheloveka, 1907-08, translations published as *The Spy: The Story of a Superfluous Man,* 1908, as *The Life of a Useless Man,* 1971.
Ispoved, 1908, translation published as *A Confession,* 1910.
Gorodok Okurov, 1909.
Leto, 1909.
Stories of the Steppe, translated by H. Schnittkind and I. Goldberg, 1918.
Delo Artamonovykh, 1925, translation published as *The Artamonov Business,* 1948.
Zhizn' Klima Samgina, four volumes, 1927-36, translation published in four volumes: *Bystander,* 1930, *The Magnet,* 1931, *Other Fires,* 1933, *The Specter,* 1938.
Zhizn' Matveya Kozhemyakina, 1933.
Orphan Paul, 1946.

DRAMA

Meshchane, 1902, translation published as *The Smug Citizens,* 1906, also published as *The Petty Bourgeois,* 1972.
Na dne, 1902, translation published as *The Lower Depths,* 1912.
Dachniki, 1904, translation published as *Summer Folk,* 1905.
Deti solntsa, 1905, translation published as *Children of the Sun,* 1912.
Varvary, 1906, translation published as *The Barbarians* (also see below), 1906.
Poslednie, 1908.
Vstrecha 1910.

Starik, 1915, translations published as *The Judge,* 1924, as *The Old Man,* 1956.
Somov i drugie, 1931.
Yegor Bulychyov i drugiye, 1932, translation published as *Yegor Bulichov and Others* (also see below).
The Last Plays of Maxim Gorky (contains *Yegor Bulichov and Others*), 1937.
Seven Plays of Maxim Gorky (contains *The Barbarians*), 1945.
Five Plays, edited by Edward Braun, 1988.

AUTOBIOGRAPHY

Detstvo, 1915, translation published as *My Childhood,* 1928.
V liudiakh, 1916, translation published as *In the World* (also see below), 1917, also published as *My Apprenticeship,* 1952.
Moi universitety, 1923, translation published as *My University Days* (also see below), 1923, also published as *My Universities,* 1952.
Reminiscences, 1946.
Autobiography of Maxim Gorky (contains *My Childhood, In the World,* and *My University Days*), 1949.

OTHER

A. P. Chekhov, 1905, published as *Anton Tchekhov: Fragments of Recollections,* 1921.
Vospominaniya o Lve Nikolaieviche Tolstom' (memoirs), 1919, translation published as *Reminiscences of Leo Nicolayevitch Tolstoi,* 1920.
Revoliutsiia i kul'tura, 1920.
O russkom krest'iamstve, 1922.
V. I. Lenin, 1924, translation published as *V. I. Lenin,* 1931; as *Days with Lenin,* 1933.
Zametki iz dnevnika. Vospominaniya (diary), 1924, translation published as *Fragments from My Diary,* 1924.
Reminiscences of Leonid Andreyev, 1928.
Sobranie sochinenii (short stories, novels, dramas, essays, and poems), four volumes, 1928-30.
O literature, 1933; revised edition, 1935, 1955; as *On Literature: Selected Articles,* 1958.
On Guard for the Soviet Union, 1933.
Creative Labour and Culture, 1945.
Literature and Life: A Selection from the Writings, 1946.
History of the Civil War in the USSR, Volume 2: *The Great Proletarian Revolution, October-November 1917,* 1947.
Selected Works, translated by Margaret Wettlin and others, 2 volumes, 1948.
Letters of Maxim Gor'kij to V. F. Xodasevic, 1922-1925, edited and translated by Hugh McLean, in *Harvard Slavonic Studies,* I, 1953.
F. I. Chaliapin, 2 volumes, 1957-58; as *Chaliapin: An Autobiography,* edited by Nina Froud and James Hanley, 1967.
Letters to Gorky and Andreev 1899-1912, edited by Peter Yershov, translated by Lydia Weston, 1958.
Letters, translated by P. Cockerell, 1966.
Polnoe sobranie sochinenii: Khudozhestvennaia literatura, 25 volumes, 1968-76.
Nesvoevremennye mysli, 1971, translation published as *Untimely Thoughts,* edited by Herman Ermolaev, 1968.
The City of the Yellow Devil: Pamphlets, Articles, and Letters about America, 1972.
Rasskazy i povesti 1892-1917, 1976.
Collected Works, 10 volumes, 1978-82.
Perepiska Gor'kogo, 2 volumes, 1986.
Gorky and His Contemporaries, edited by Galina Belaya, translated by Cynthia Carlile, 1989.

SIDELIGHTS: As Maxim Gorky, author Alexei Maximovich Peshkov is recognized as one of the earliest and foremost exponents of socialist realism in literature. His brutal yet romantic portraits of Russian life and his sympathetic depictions of the working class had an inspirational effect on the oppressed people of his native land. From 1910 until his death, Gorky was considered Russia's greatest living writer. Gorky the tramp, the rebel, is as much a legend as the strong, individual characters presented in his stories. His hero was a new type in the history of Russian literature—a figure drawn from the masses of a growing industrialized society; his most famous novel, *Mat'* (1907; *Mother*), was the first in that country to portray the factory worker as a force destined to overthrow the existing order.

Gorky was orphaned at the age of ten and raised by his maternal grandparents. He was often treated harshly by his grandfather, and it was from his grandmother that Gorky received what little kindness he experienced as a child. During his thirteenth year, Gorky ran away from Nizhniy Novgorod, the city of his birth (now called Gorky), and lived a precarious existence as a tramp and vagrant, wandering from one job to another. Frequently beaten by his employers, nearly always hungry and ill-clothed, Gorky came to know the seamy side of Russian life as few writers before him. At the age of nineteen, he attempted suicide by shooting himself in the chest. The event became a turning point in Gorky's life; his outlook changed from one of despair to one of hope. Within a few years he began publishing stories in the provincial press. Written under the pseudonym

Maxim Gorky (Maxim the Bitter), these stories stressed the strength and individualism of the Russian peasant. When they were collected and published in *Ocherki i rasskazy,* (1898-99), Gorky gained recognition throughout Russia. His second volume of stories, *Rasskazy* (1900-10), along with the production of his controversial play *Na dne* (1902; *The Lower Depths*), assured his success and brought him acclaim in western Europe and the United States. Gorky's fame in the West coincided with increasing suspicion from the Russian authorities, who considered the author a source of the country's growing political unrest. In 1901 he was briefly jailed for publishing the revolutionary poem "Pesnya o burevestnike" ("Song of the Stormy Petrel") in a Marxist review. Three years later, he established the Znanie publishing firm to provide a forum for socially conscious writers. The friendship and advice of Nikolai Lenin strengthened Gorky's growing political radicalism. He was very active during the revolution of 1905, and after its failure he was forced to flee abroad. He was allowed to return home in 1913, and again he resumed his revolutionary activities. During the 1917 Revolution and the ensuing years of political chaos, Gorky saved the lives of several intellectuals by interceding on their behalf with the communist regime. He left Russia one last time and settled on the island of Capri for health reasons. In 1928 he returned to a national celebration of his literary, cultural, and moral contributions to the socialist cause, which took place on his sixtieth birthday. His death several years later, allegedly by poisoning, is still enveloped in mystery.

Gorky's work can be divided into three distinct groups. The first comprises his short stories, which many critics consider superior to his novels. In a highly romantic manner, these stories portray the subjugation of Russian peasants and vagrants. Many of these tales, such as "Makar Chudra" and "Chelkash," are based on actual peasant legends and allegories. In them Gorky championed the wisdom and self-reliance of his vagabonds over the brutality of the decadent bourgeoisie. Commenting on "Chelkash," Barry P. Scherr of *Reference Guide to Short Fiction* noted that "the vagabonds may be admirable for their ability to break away from the norm, but even the strongest among them are still misfits and seem doomed to a life apart from other human beings." One of the most accomplished of these vagabond stories is "Dvadtssat' shest' i odna" ("Twenty-Six Men and a Girl"), a tale in which Gorky described the sweatshop conditions in a provincial bakery. The second group consists of Gorky's autobiographical works, notably the trilogy *Detstvo* (1928; *My Childhood*), *V liudiakh* (1916; *In the World*), and *Moi universitety* (1923; *My Universities*); and his reminiscences of Tolstoy, *Vospominaniya o Lve Nikolaieviche Tolstom'* (1919; *Reminiscences of Leo Nicolayevitch Tolstoi*). The trilogy is considered one of the finest autobiographies in the Russian language. The work reveals Gorky as an acute observer of detail with a particular talent for describing people. The third group, by far the largest, consists of a number of novels and plays which are not as artistically successful as his short stories and autobiography. Gorky's first novel, *Foma Gordeyev* (1900; *Foma Gordeiev*), illustrates his characteristic admiration for the hard-working, honest individual. He contrasts the rising capitalist Ignat Gordeyev with his feeble, intellectual son Foma, a "seeker after the meaning of life," as are many of Gorky's other characters. The novel was the first of many in which the author portrayed the rise of Russian Capitalism. Of all Gorky's novels, *Mother* is perhaps the least artistic, though it is interesting from a historical perspective as his only long work devoted to the Bolshevik movement. Among the twelve plays Gorky wrote between 1901 and 1913, only one, *The Lower Depths,* deals with the "dregs of society." Though the play has most of the structural faults of his other dramas, primarily one-dimensional characters and a didactic tone, it is still regarded as one of the greatest proletarian dramas of the twentieth century. In *Reference Guide to World Literature,* Scherr noted, "The more heroic of . . . [the] characters may seem romanticized, but Gorky was the first to explore in detail a world which most Russians had only been vaguely aware." Scherr added that "in posing the conflicts that lie at the heart of his play—between the soothing if possibly harmful lie and the harsh if possibly liberating truth, between the dreams that enable people to cope with the severity of their lives and the danger that those very dreams will leave them passive—Gorky has expressed irresolvable dilemmas with which audiences around the world have been able to identify." Gorky's other plays, including *Meshchane* (1902; *The Smug Citizens*), *Varvary* (1906; *The Barbarians*), and *Yegor Bulychyov i drugiye* (1932; *Yegor Bulichov and Others*), focus either on the intelligentsia or on the struggle between capitalist and socialist forces in pre-Soviet Russia.

Despite his success and importance as a socialist writer, most modern critics agree that Gorky deserves little of the idolatrous attention that he has received. They argue that his work suffers from an overly dramatic quality, a coarse, careless style, and an externally imposed structure which results in fiction motivated by ideology rather than by artistry. Many critics suggest that his failure to develop his characters and his tendency to lapse into irrelevant discussions about the meaning of life greatly damage the seriousness of his subjects. However, it is in his short stories and, especially, in his autobiography that Gorky fully realized his artistic powers. In these works he managed to curb his ideology and focus on those talents for which he has been consistently lauded: realistic description and the ability to portray the brutality of his environment. It is for these that Gorky has been called by Stefan Zweig, one of "the few genuine marvels of our present world."

While critical regard for his work fluctuates, Gorky himself has passed into history not only as a remarkable personality, but also as the precursor of socialist realism and, therefore, an important stimulus in twentieth-century Russian literature. With Vladimir Mayakovsky and Aleksandr Blok, he was one of the few Russian writers who played an equally important part in his country both before and after the Bolshevik Revolution. Although Gorky was an intellectual, and thus distanced from the common people who overthrew the Czarists and Mensheviks, he used his influence and talent after October, 1917, to prevent the revolution from consuming itself in a savage blood-frenzy. As Janko Lavrin, author of *An Introduction to the Russian Novel,* has noted, "It was here that his personality and his work served as a bridge between the creative values of the old intelligentsia culture and the culture of the risen masses, anxious to build up a new world."

BIOGRAPHICAL/CRITICAL SOURCES:

BOOKS

Borras, F. M., *Maxim Gorky the Writer: An Interpretation,* Oxford University Press, 1967.

Dillon, E. J., *Maxim Gorky: His Life and Writings,* Isbister and Company Limited, 1902.

Gourfinkel, Nina, *Gorky,* Greenwood Press, 1975.

Hare, Richard, *Maxim Gorky: Romantic Realist and Conservative Revolutionary,* Greenwood Press, 1978.

Holtzman, Filia, *The Young Maxim Gorky: 1868-1902,* Columbia University Press, 1948.

Huneker, James, *Iconoclasts, a Book of Dramatists: Ibsen, Strindberg, Becque, Hauptmann, Sudermann, Heryieu, Gorky, Duse and D'Annunzio, Maeterlinck and Bernard Shaw,* Scribner, 1905.

Kaun, Alexander, *Maxim Gorky and His Russia,* Benjamin Blom Publishers, 1931.

Lavrin, Janko, *An Introduction to the Russian Novel,* third edition, Methuen, 1945.

Levin, Dan, *Stormy Petrel: The Life and Work of Maxim Gorky,* Appleton-Century, 1965.

Lewis, Allan, *The Contemporary Theatre: The Significant Playwrights of Our Time,* revised edition, Crown, 1971.

Lukacs, Georg, *Studies in European Realism: A Sociological Survey of the Writings of Balzac, Stendhal, Zola, Tolstoy, Gorki and Others,* translated by Edith Bone, Merlin Press, 1972, pp. 206-241.

Mirski, D. S., *Contemporary Russian Literature: 1881-1925,* Knopf, 1926.

Olgin, Moissaye J., *Maxim Gorky: Writer and Revolutionist,* International Publishers, 1933.

Reference Guide to Short Fiction, St. James Press, 1994.

Reference Guide to World Literature, 2nd edition, St. James Press, 1995.

Slonim, Marc, *Modern Russian Literature: From Chekhov to the Present,* Oxford University Press, 1953.

Struve, Gleb, *Soviet Russian Literature,* Routledge & Kegan Paul, 1935.

Trotsky, Leon, *Leon Trotsky on Literature and Art,* edited by Paul N. Siegel, Pathfinder Press, 1970.

Twentieth Century Authors: A Biographical Dictionary of Modern Literature, H. W. Wilson, 1942.

Weil, Irwin, *Gorky: His Literary Development and Influence on Soviet Intellectual Life,* Random House, 1966.

PERIODICALS

Nation, November 27, 1972, p. 537.

New York Review of Books, March 27, 1969, p. 20; March 23, 1972, p. 37.

New York Times Book Review, February 4, 1968, p. 8.

New Yorker, November 4, 1972, p. 196.

Newsweek, September 6, 1971, p. 70.

Observer, December 3, 1967, p. 28; June 18, 1972, p. 33; September 28, 1975, p. 22.

Times Literary Supplement, October 27, 1966, p. 982; February 1, 1968, p. 107; March 5, 1971, p. 257.

Washington Post Book World, September 1, 1968, p. 11.*

* * *

PETERKIEWICZ, Jerzy 1916-

PERSONAL: Surname originally Pietrkiewicz; born September 29, 1916, in Fabianki, Poland; son of Jan and Antonina (Politowska) Pietrkiewicz; married Christine Brooke-Rose, February 13, 1952 (divorced, 1975). *Education:* Attended University of Warsaw;

University of St. Andrews, M.A., 1944; King's College, London, Ph.D., 1947. *Religion:* Roman Catholic.

ADDRESSES: Home—7 Lyndhurst Ter., London NW3, England.

CAREER: Freelance writer until 1950; University of London, London, England, lecturer, 1950-64, reader, 1964-72, professor of Polish language and literature and chairman of department of East European languages and literatures, 1972-79.

MEMBER: International PEN.

WRITINGS:

Prowincja, [Warsaw], 1936.
Wiersze i poematy, [Warsaw], 1938.
Znaki na niebie, Mildner (London), 1940.
Po chlopsku: Powiesc, 2 volumes, Mildner, 1941.
Pokarm cierpki, Mysl Polska (London), 1943.
Umarli nie sa bexbronni, Ksiaznica (Glasgow), 1943.
Pogrzeb Europy, [London], 1946.
Sami swoi (play), produced in London, 1949.
Pity poemat, Instytut Literacki (Paris), 1950.
The Knotted Cord, Heinemann, 1953.
Loot and Loyalty, Heinemann, 1955.
(Editor) *Polish Prose and Verse* (in Polish), Athlone Press, 1956, new edition, 1970.
(Editor and translator) *Antologia liryki angielskiej,* Veritas, 1958.
Future to Let, Heinemann, 1958.
Isolation: A Novel in Five Acts, Heinemann, 1959.
(Editor and translator with Burns Singer) *Five Centuries of Polish Poetry,* Secker & Warburg, 1960, enlarged edition, Oxford University Press, 1970.
The Quick and the Dead, Macmillan, 1961.
That Angel Burning at My Left Side, Macmillan, 1963.
Poematy londynskie i wiersze przedwojenne, Kultura, 1965.
Inner Circle, Macmillan, 1966.
Green Flows the Bile, M. Joseph, 1969.
The Other Side of Silence: The Poet at the Limits of Language, Oxford University Press, 1970.
Scena ma trzy sciany (play), Wiadomosci, 1974.
The Third Adam, Oxford University Press, 1975.
(Editor and translator) Karol Wojtyla, *Easter Vigil and Other Poems,* Random House, 1979.
Kula magiczna (poems), [Warsaw], 1980.
(Translator) *Collected Poems,* by Karol Wojtyla, Random House (New York City),1982.
Literatura polska w perspektywie europejskiej (essays translated from English), Panstwowy Instytut (Warsaw), 1986.
Poezje wybrane, Ludowa Spoldzielnia (Warsaw), 1986.
Modlitwy intelektu, Pax (Warsaw, 1988.
Messianic Prophecy: A Case for Reappraisal, University of London Press, 1991.
In the Scales of Fate: An Autobiography, M. Boyars (New York City), 1993.
(Translator) *The Place Within: The Poetry of Pope John Paul II,* Random House (New York City), 1994.

Contributor of articles and poems to periodicals.

SIDELIGHTS: Jerzy Peterkiewicz is a poet, novelist, essayist, dramatist, editor, and literary critic whose work reflects his Polish upbringing. As a novelist, he has taken a wide range of subjects in a variety of situations. *The Knotted Cord* provides an account of a peasant boy's childhood in Poland. Among his struggles is escaping the cord of the scratchy cassock in which his pious mother dresses him, and all the cord represents to him. Patricia Merivale of *Contemporary Novelists* deems this "a first novel of promise." She also praises *Future to Let,* a humorous story of tortured loves and the contemporary politics of Polish emigrants such as Julian Atrament whose escape by means of his St. Bernard dog is called "Peterkiewicz's finest comic turn" by Merivale. *Isolation* is a parody of the spy novel.

Peterkiewicz is best known for *The Other Side of Silence: The Poet at the Limits of Language,* a study of the ways in which various nineteenth- and twentieth-century poets coped with the realization that they could never adequately express the feelings they wished to share with the rest of the world. According to Peterkiewicz, every poet has an inherent "death wish" that manifests itself once he reaches the limits of language, once he learns that his poetry does not have the power to change the course of events. This discovery leaves the poet with a sense of despair and disillusionment that eventually leads him to real or symbolic self-destruction. Though he may attempt to force others to listen and understand by making his voice more strident or by increasing his productivity (usually at the expense of quality), he more than likely will simply decide to abandon poetry entirely (even to the point of destroying or denying earlier works), often turning to alcohol or suicide to ease the pain of being unable to communicate. In any case, the author maintains, the poet's silence implies that poetry has either failed as a literary medium or that it has reached the sublime.

Though most critics agree that Peterkiewicz's subject is worthy of exploration, several feel that he places too much emphasis on his own belief that silence represents a near-mystical state of superiority and perfection.

Philip Toynbee of the *London Magazine,* for instance, claims that Peterkiewicz ends up confusing "poets with mystics and poetry with religion" during the course of his study. "Of course a good many poets committed suicide," the critic admits. "Of course a good many dried up fairly early in life and wrote worse in old age than they had in their youth; of course all serious writers have a love-hate relationship with words. I cannot think that any of this really justifies the high metaphysical theme of *The Other Side of Silence.*" Nevertheless, Toynbee concludes, "this is a rich and suggestive book; often a shrewd and original one."

The *Listener*'s Denis Donoghue notes that "if the book had an index of topics, the list would include prophecy, incantation, action, metaphor, silence (within speech), silence (as the word of God), darkness, the night journey, faith, mysticism and negation." As a result, says Donoghue, "many of [Peterkiewicz's] paragraphs are musings of the obscure, tropical meditations: his method is associative rather than consecutive." Furthermore, the critic states, because of the "intensity of his commitment" to the idea that silence represents the sublime in poetry, Peterkiewicz tends to be "impatient with the commonplace"—that is, he displays little regard for the poetry that precedes or follows a period of profound silence. Despite this feeling that the author "is too high to respect the low, mundane things," Donoghue calls *The Other Side of Silence* "a formidably thoughtful book. There are beautiful things in it, passages of remarkable force which strike the reader . . ., not to persuade but to entrance, like a flash of lightning. [But] when the flash has passed, the reader calls for reasons and explanations."

The *Yale Review* critic observes that Peterkiewicz's account of the problem of silence and some of the attempted solutions is "dense and intelligent." But he questions the author's choice of title for his work, insisting that "the book is concerned not with silence but with deafness, with poets who hear nothing and therefore say nothing." Nevertheless, the critic goes on to state, "in general, the book treats sensibly a subject that would seem to defy discussion. There are few things more difficult to talk about than silence, and the book has some passages whose prose, like silence, is all but impenetrable. . . . [But] the reader does not have much cause for complaint. . . . [*The Other Side of Silence*] should be read by everyone who is seriously interested in modern literature. It is a book which deserves to be wrestled with."

Concludes an *Economist* reviewer, who views Peterkiewicz's subject matter as "a problem of life as well as literature": *The Other Side of Silence* "is not [a book] that should be judged by the rigorous standards called for by an academic thesis. It is an imaginative inquiry, by a man himself a poet, into an area well worth the exploration. The reader . . . will find new vistas opening."

BIOGRAPHICAL/CRITICAL SOURCES:

BOOKS

Contemporary Novelists, 6th edition, St. James Press, 1996.

Peterkiewicz, Jerzy, *In the Scales of Fate: An Autobiography,* M. Boyars (New York City), 1993.

PERIODICALS

Books Abroad, spring, 1971.

Christian Science Monitor, June 18, 1970.

Economist, May 2, 1970.

Kultura, June, 1980.

Listener, March 26, 1970.

London Magazine, May, 1970.

New Statesman, October 10, 1959; September 30, 1966; March 27, 1970.

New Yorker, April 25, 1959.

New York Herald Tribune Book Review, May 17, 1959.

New York Herald Tribune Lively Arts, January 29, 1961.

New York Times, April 26, 1959.

New York Times Book Review, October 16, 1960.

Observer, September 8, 1963; February 23, 1969.

San Francisco Chronicle, September 8, 1953; October 23, 1960.

Spectator, October 9, 1959.

Times (London), January 9, 1964.

Times Literary Supplement, June 19, 1953; April 18, 1958; October 30, 1959; September 6, 1963; October 6, 1966; February 27, 1969; April 9, 1970; November 21, 1975.

Yale Review, autumn, 1970.*

* * *

PETERSHAM, Miska 1888-1960

PERSONAL: Given name, Petrezselyem Mihaly; born September 20, 1888, in Toeroekszemtmiklos, near Budapest, Hungary; died May 15, 1960; immigrated to United States, 1912, became naturalized citizen; married Maud Sylvia Fuller (author and illustrator of books for children), 1917 (died November 29, 1971); children: Miki (a son). *Education:* Attended Royal Academy of Art, Budapest, Hungary; additional study at art schools in Italy and England.

CAREER: Author and illustrator of books for children. Worked in art department of International Art Service (advertising agency), New York City.

AWARDS, HONORS: Runner-up, with wife, Maud Petersham, for Caldecott Medal, 1942, for *An American ABC;* Caldecott Medal, with wife, Maud Petersham, 1946, for *The Rooster Crows: A Book of American Rhymes and Jingles.*

WRITINGS:

CO-AUTHOR AND ILLUSTRATOR WITH WIFE, MAUD PETERSHAM; JUVENILE

Miki, Doubleday, Doran, 1929.
The Ark of Father Noah and Mother Noah, Doubleday, Doran, 1930.
The Christ Child, as Told by Matthew and Luke, Doubleday, Doran, 1931.
Auntie and Celia Jane and Miki, Doubleday, Doran, 1932.
The Story Book of Things We Use, Winston, 1933.
The Story Book of Houses, Winston, 1933.
The Story Book of Transportation, Winston, 1933.
The Story Book of Food, Winston, 1933.
The Story Book of Clothes, Winston, 1933.
Get-a-Way and Hary Janos, Viking, 1933.
Miki and Mary: Their Search for Treasures, Viking, 1934.
The Story Book of Wheels (also see below), Winston, 1935.
The Story Book of Ships (also see below), Winston, 1935.
The Story Book of Trains (also see below), Winston, 1935.
The Story Book of Aircraft (also see below), Winston, 1935.
The Story Book of Wheels, Ships, Trains, Aircraft (contains *The Story Book of Wheels, The Story Book of Ships, The Story Book of Trains,* and *The Story Book of Aircraft*), Winston, 1935.
The Story Book of Gold (also see below), Winston, 1935.
The Story Book of Coal (also see below), Winston, 1935.
The Story Book of Oil (also see below), Winston, 1935.
The Story Book of Iron and Steel (also see below), Winston, 1935.
The Story Book of the Earth's Treasures: Gold, Coal, Oil, Iron and Steel (contains *The Story Book of Gold, The Story Book of Coal, The Story Book of Oil,* and *The Story Book of Iron and Steel*), Winston, 1935.
The Story Book of Wheat (also see below), Winston, 1936.
The Story Book of Corn (also see below), Winston, 1936.
The Story Book of Rice (also see below), Winston, 1936.
The Story Book of Sugar (also see below), Winston, 1936, published as *Let's Learn about Sugar,* with illustrations by James E. Barry, Harvey House, 1969.
The Story Book of Foods from the Field: Wheat, Corn, Rice, Sugar (contains *The Story Book of Wheat, The Story Book of Corn, The Story Book of Rice,* and *The Story Book of Sugar*), Winston, 1936.
Joseph and His Brothers: From the Story Told in the Book of Genesis (also see below), Winston, 1938.
Moses: From the Story Told in the Old Testament (also see below), Winston, 1938.
Ruth: From the Story Told in the Book of Ruth (also see below), Winston, 1938.
David: From the Story Told in the First Book of Samuel and the First Book of Kings (also see below), Winston, 1938.
Stories from the Old Testament: Joseph, Moses, Ruth, David (contains *Joseph and His Brothers, Moses,Ruth,* and *David*), Winston, 1938.
The Story Book of Cotton (also see below), Winston, 1939.
The Story Book of Wool (also see below), Winston, 1939.
The Story Book of Rayon (also see below), Winston, 1939.
The Story Book of Silk (also see below), Winston, 1939, published as *Let's Learn about Silk,* with illustrations by Barry, Harvey House, 1939.
The Story Book of Things We Wear (contains *The Story Book of Cotton, The Story Book of Wool, The Story Book of Rayon,* and *The Story Book of Silk*) Winston, 1939.
An American ABC, Macmillan, 1941.
America's Postage Stamps: The Story of One Hundred Years of U.S. Postage Stamps, Macmillan, 1947.
My Very First Book, Macmillan, 1948.
The Box with Red Wheels, Macmillan, 1949.
The Circus Baby, Macmillan, 1950, reprinted, 1972.
The Story of the Presidents of the United States of America, Macmillan, 1953.
Off to Bed: Seven Stories for Wide-Awakes, Macmillan, 1954.

The Boy Who Had No Heart, Macmillan, 1955.

The Silver Mace: A Story of Williamsburg, Macmillan, 1956.

The Peppernuts, Macmillan, 1958.

ILLUSTRATOR WITH WIFE, MAUD PETERSHAM; JUVENILE

Franklin T. Baker and Ashley H. Thorndike, *Everyday Classics: Primer—Second Reader,* Macmillan, 1917.

Ada Maria Skinner and Frances Gillespy Wickes, compilers, *A Child's Own Book of Verse,* three volumes, Macmillan, 1917.

John Stuart Thomson, *Fil and Filippa: Story of Child Life in the Philippines,* Macmillan, 1917.

Mary Lydia Bolles Branch, *Guld the Cavern King,* Bookshop for Boys and Girls and Women's Educational and Industrial Union, 1918.

John Walter Wayland, *History Stories for Primary Grades,* Macmillan, 1919.

William Bowen, *Enchanted Forest,* Macmillan, 1920.

Elsie S. Eells, *Tales of Enchantment from Spain,* Harcourt, 1920.

Louise Lamprey, *Children of Ancient Britain,* Little, Brown, 1921, published as *Long Ago People: How They Lived in Britain before History Began,* Little, Brown, 1921.

Anna Cogswell Tyles, compiler, *Twenty-four Unusual Stories for Boys and Girls,* Harcourt, 1921.

Ethel May Gate, *The Broom Fairies,* Silver, Burdett, 1922.

Carl Sandburg, *Rootabaga Stories,* Harcourt, 1922.

Charles Lamb and Mary Lamb, *Tales from Shakespeare,* Macmillan, 1923.

Mabel Guinnip La Rue, *Under the Story Tree,* Macmillan, 1923.

Sandburg, *Rootabaga Pigeons,* Harcourt, 1923.

Sisters of Mercy (St. Xavier College, Chicago), *Marquette Readers,* Macmillan, 1924.

La Rue, *The F-U-N Book,* Macmillan, 1924.

La Rue, *In Animal Land,* Macmillan, 1924, revised edition, 1929.

Margery Clark, *Poppy Seed Cakes,* Doubleday, 1924.

Inez M. Howard, Alice Hawthorne, and Mae Howard, *Language Garden: A Primary Language Book,* Macmillan, 1924.

Harriott Fansler and Isidoro Panlasigui, *Philippine National Literature,* Macmillan, 1925.

Bessie Blackstone Coleman, Willis L. Uhl, and James Fleming Hosic, *Pathway to Reading: Primer,* Silver, Burdette, 1925.

Florence C. Coolidge, *Little Ugly Face, and Other Indian Tales,* Macmillan, 1925.

Olive Beaupre Miller, translator, *Nursery Friends from France,* Book House for Children, 1925.

Miller, editor, *Tales Told in Holland,* Book House for Children, 1926.

Jean Young Ayer, *The Easy Book: First Lessons in Reading,* Macmillan, 1926.

Howard, Hawthorne, and Howard, *Number Friends: A Primary Arithmetic,* Macmillan, 1927.

Elizabeth C. Miller, *Children of the Mountain Eagle,* Doubleday, 1927.

La Rue, *The Billy Bang Book,* Macmillan, 1927.

Everyday Canadian Primer, Macmillan, 1928.

Marguerite Clement, *Where Was Bobby?,* Doubleday, Doran, 1928.

Wilhelmina Harper and Aymer Jay Hamilton, compilers, *Pleasant Pathways,* Macmillan, 1928.

Ayer, Baker, and Thorndike, *Everyday Stories,* Macmillan, 1929.

Harper and Hamilton, compilers, *Winding Roads,* Macmillan, 1929.

Harper and Hamilton, compilers, *Heights and Highways,* Macmillan, 1929.

Harper and Hamilton, compilers, *Far Away Hills,* Macmillan, 1929.

E. Miller, *Pran of Albania,* Doubleday, Doran, 1929.

Marie, Queen of Roumania, *The Magic Doll of Roumania: A Wonder Story in which East and West Do Meet,* Stokes, 1929.

La Rue, *Little Indians,* Macmillan, 1930, revised edition, 1934.

Sydney Vanferson Rowland, William Dodge Lewis, and Elizabeth J. Marshall, compilers, *New Trails: Book IV,* Winston, 1930.

Rowland, Lewis, and Marshall, compilers, *Treasure Trove: Book V,* Winston, 1930.

Rowland, Lewis, and Marshall, compilers, *Rich Cargoes: Book VI,* Winston, 1931.

Rowland, Lewis, and Marshall, compilers, *Beckoning Road: Book VII,* Winston, 1931.

Rowland, Lewis, and Marshall, compilers, *Wings of Adventure: Book VIII,* Winston, 1931.

E. Miller, *Young Trajan,* Doubleday, Doran, 1931.

Marie Barringer, *Martin, the Goose Boy,* Doubleday, Doran, 1932.

La Rue, *Zip, the Toy Mule and Other Stories,* Macmillan, 1932.

Carlo Collodi, *Adventures of Pinocchio,* Garden City Publishing, 1932.

Johanna Spyri, *Heidi,* Garden City Publishing, 1932.

Ayer, *Picnic Book,* Macmillan, 1934.

Post Wheeler, *Albanian Wonder Tales,* Doubleday, Doran, 1936.

Barringer, *The Four and Lena,* Doubleday, Doran, 1938.

Miriam Evangeline Mason, *Susannah, the Pioneer Cow,* Macmillan, 1941.

Emilie Louise Dickey Johnson, *A Little Book of Prayers,* Viking, 1941.

Story of Jesus: A Little New Testament, Macmillan, 1942.

Ethan Allen Cross and Elizabeth Lehr, editors, *Literature: A Series of Anthologies,* seven volumes, Macmillan, 1943-46.

The Rooster Crows: A Book of American Rhymes and Jingles, Macmillan, 1945.

Told under the Christmas Tree, Macmillan, 1948.

Washington Irving, *Rip Van Winkle* [and] *The Legend of Sleepy Hollow,* Macmillan, 1951.

Benjamin Franklin, *Bird in the Hand: Sayings from "Poor Richard's Almanack" by the Wise American Benjamin Franklin,* Macmillan, 1951.

Eric P. Kelly, *In Clean Hay,* Macmillan, 1953.

Mason, *Miss Posy Longlegs,* Macmillan, 1955.

OTHER

Contributor of illustrations to children's magazines, including*St. Nicholas, Child Life, Story Parade,* and *Jack and Jill.*

SIDELIGHTS: Miska Petersham and his wife, Maud, met at an advertising agency in New York City where both worked in the art department. After their marriage in 1917 they began work as freelance illustrators of books for children. Two of the most popular books they illustrated were Olive Beaupre Miller's *Nursery Friends from France* and *Tales Told in Holland.* These volumes were part of a set published by Book House for Children that sold nearly ten thousand copies a year in the late 1920s and early 1930s.

The Petershams got their start as writers of books for children when they outlined the text and pictures for a book of their own and sent it to their editor at Doubleday. Although they thought that the book they had roughly put together would be turned over to an experienced author for rewriting, they soon learned—much to their surprise—that the book would be published just as they had planned it. *Miki,* their story of a boy who goes to Hungary, became the first book they illustrated and wrote together. The book was deemed by Rachel Field of *Saturday Review of Literature* an "altogether delightful volume," and Lynd Ward of *New York Herald Tribune* noted that Hungary will always be "an incredibly . . . romantic place to those who meet it first with Miki." *Miki,* along with the many other books they wrote and illustrated and the even larger number of books they illustrated for other authors, "established the Petershams as important, skilled craftsmen of the bookmaking art," according to *Dictionary of Literary Biography* contributor Sharyl G. Smith.

As creators of their own works, the Petershams are considered among the most distinguished American authors and artists for children of this century. They are lauded for their innovation in subject matter, approach, and artistic style. Combining their interests and backgrounds to create works acknowledged for their beauty, richness, variety, and appeal, the husband and wife team is credited with introducing an international scope to the American picture book; with developing informational books that are also attractive; and with setting a standard in book illustration through their mastery of the lithographic method, experimentation with printing processes, and emphasis on total book design. They directed their works, many of which have a patriotic or religious theme, to children and young people from preschool through the middle grades. Myra Cohn Livingston of *Twentieth-Century Children's Writers* commented that the Petershams' strength is their unique ability to effectively bridge the text with the illustrations in a manner easily understood by children. As evidence of the wide range of this ability, Livingston called attention to works as disparate as *The Christ Child, A Bird in the Hand* (which relates the wisdom of Benjamin Franklin), and *The Story Book of Things We Use.*

In an interview with Lee Bennett Hopkins appearing in *Books Are by People* Maud Petersham recalled some of the hard work that went into the production of her and her husband's books, as well as some of the lighter moments. "Miska and I had fun working on books for children," she reminisced, "for it often meant travel with sketchbook in hand. We wandered about in Palestine for three months before we made the illustrations for our book *The Christ Child.* . . . A visit to Sarasota, where the Ringling Brothers Circus made its winter quarters, gave us the idea for *Circus Baby* . . . , and the hunting lodge where we ourselves spent one summer inspired *The Peppernuts.* . . . Our life and work [were] so closely related that anyone who knows our books knows us."

BIOGRAPHICAL/CRITICAL SOURCES:

BOOKS

Children's Literature Review, Volume 24, Gale, 1991.

Dictionary of Literary Biography, Volume 22: *American Writers for Children, 1900-1960,* Gale, 1983.

Hopkins, Lee Bennett, *Books Are by People,* Citation, 1969.

Montgomery, Elizabeth Rider, *Story behind Modern Books,* Dodd, 1949.
Something about the Author, Volume 17, Gale, 1979.
Twentieth-Century Children's Writers, 4th edition, St. James Press, 1995.

PERIODICALS

Horn Book, July-August, 1946.
Library Journal, July, 1946; July, 1969.
New York Herald Tribune Book Review, November 17, 1929; May 17, 1953.
New York Times, October 1, 1950.
New York Times Book Review, December 14, 1980.
Publishers Weekly, October 20, 1934; June 22, 1946; August 29, 1980.
Saturday Review of Literature, November 16, 1929.
School Library Journal, October, 1980.*

* * *

PICKARD, Tom 1946-

PERSONAL: Born Thomas MacKenna, January 7, 1946, in Newcastle upon Tyne, Northumberland, England; son of Nicholson (a member of the Nova Scotia Air Force) and Ella MacKenna; adopted by great-uncle Robert Bambro (a railway worker) and great-aunt Catherine MacKenna Pickard (a domestic), name changed to Thomas Mariner Pickard; married Constance Davison, 1964 (divorced, 1978); married Joanna Voit (a photographer), 1979; children: (first marriage) Matthew and Catherine; (second marriage) Kuba Mieszko (son). *Education:* Attended Ruskin College, Oxford.

ADDRESSES: Home—London, England, and Warsaw, Poland. *Agent*—Judy Daish Associates Ltd., 83 Eastbourne Mews, London W2 6LQ, England.

CAREER: Poet, short-story writer, novelist, playwright, film writer, and radio and television writer. Worked variously for a construction company, a wine merchant, and Woolworth. Morden Tower poetry center, cofounder, 1963, manager, 1963-72; *King Ida's Watch Chain* (arts magazine), editor with Richard Hamilton, 1965; Ultima Thule book shop, founder, 1969-73. Founded *Eruption* magazine, with others. Has taught writing workshops and courses on twentieth-century poetics in German and American universities and colleges. Has participated in international writing festivals in Amsterdam, Belgrade, Brussels, Edinburgh, Frankfurt, Hamburg, Koln, New York City, Nowi Pasza, Paris, San Francisco, and Warsaw. Occasional articles for *Guardian, Daily Telegraph,* and *New Statesman.*

AWARDS, HONORS: Northern Arts Minor Award, 1965; Arts Council of Great Britain grant, 1969 and 1973; C. Day Lewis Writing Fellowship, Rutherford School, London, England, 1976-77; Arts Council creative writing fellowship, Warwick University, England, 1979-80.

WRITINGS:

POETRY

High on the Walls, Fulcrum Press, 1967, Horizon Press, 1968.
New Human Unisphere, Ultima Thule Bookshop, 1969.
An Armpit of Lice, Fulcrum Press, 1970.
The Order of Chance, Fulcrum Press, 1971.
Dancing under Fire, Middle Earth Books, 1973.
Hero Dust: New and Selected Poems, Schocken, 1979.
OK Tree, Pig Press, 1980.
Domestic Art, Slug Press (Vancouver), 1981.
In Search of "Ingenuous," Vancouver, 1981.
Custom and Exile, Allison & Busby, 1985, Schocken, 1986.
Shedding Her Skirts, Bloodaxe, 1985.
Tiepin Eros: New & Selected Poems, Bloodaxe Books, 1994.

OTHER

Guttersnipe (stories), City Lights Books, 1971.
(Editor) Tony Jackson, *The Lesser Known Shagg,* Ultima Thule Bookshop, 1971.
Serving My Time to a Trade, Paideuma (Orono, ME), 1980.
Jarrow March (political history), Schocken, 1981.
We Make Ships, Secker and Warburg, 1989.

Also author of *Dragon Story* (for children), 1985. Has also written for film, radio, and television, including *River Project* (documentary), Amber Films, 1973; *Squire* (short film), BBC 2, 1974; *Dancing under Fire* (reading of long poem), BBC Radio 3, 1975; *The Jarrow March* (documentary), BBC Radio 3, 1976; *Life of a Leaf* (drama), BBC Radio 3, 1979; *Great Day of His Wrath* (docudrama), BBC Radio 3, 1984; *It's a Start* (short story), BBC Radio 3, 1984; and *Merry Go Round: Making Poems* (BBC film for schools). Has researched for and acted in other productions, and established a video archive of living poets for Warwick University, 1979-80. Also adapted one of his own stories from *Guttersnipe* for BBC 2 television program *Full House.*

Pickard's work has been translated into Dutch, German, Russian, Polish, Italian, Norwegian, Spanish, and French.

SIDELIGHTS: In impoverished northeastern England, Tom Pickard co-founded and for several years managed Morden Tower, a poetry center situated on a medieval city wall in the industrial sector of Newcastle upon Tyne. As Eric Mottram commented in *Primary Sources,* there "the finest British and American poets read at a time when they were unheard elsewhere in [England]." Pickard related that in 1984, "Morden Tower celebrated its twentieth year as a center for live poetry."

Through his activity with the center, Pickard came in contact with poets such as Allen Ginsberg, Basil Bunting, and Jonathan Williams. In fact, Pickard told *CA* he "spent most of [his] adolescence and young manhood taking advantage of very long periods of unemployment to develop some writing skills under the generous tutelage of Basil Bunting," the English poet. He also noted in *Paideuma* that he "by some route . . . came across the Beat movement and first got a sniff of the Americans, discovering a punchy, taut and tender language." His introduction to the Beat poetry movement led him to also explore e. e. cummings, Walt Whitman, and Ezra Pound. Around the time he was running the Morden Tower reading series, he also edited the arts magazine *King Ida's Watch Chain* with Richard Hamilton and co-founded the magazine *Eruption* and the bookstore Ultima Thule.

Critics have commented on how the speech and song with which Pickard grew up also inform his poetry. Writing in *Montemora* about *Hero Dust: New and Selected Poems,* Kenneth Cox said, "The north-east of England . . . has together with a deep distrust of artifice a strong tradition of popular song. To the dignity, militancy and ribaldry of its industrial ballads Pickard adds a personal zest as well as emotion and craftsmanship far beyond their range." Mottram said of the 1973 book *Dancing under Fire,* "Pickard uses local words and slang authentically. . . . But throughout his work he reaches into a need for a certain strenuous innocence, a resistance to intellectualising, another way of speaking directly to an audience." He observed that the more recent poems in *Hero Dust* "retain [Pickard's] controlled vigor in familiar forms." In *Custom and Exile,* Robert Sheppard commented in *Times Literary Supplement,* Pickard "has refined his objectivism to produce the best poems he has written since the early 1970s."

Ken Smith noted in the *Dictionary of Literary Biography* that Pickard's later work in film, radio, and television plays and documentaries "bears a close relation to his poetry, both as an enlargement of his earlier work and as source and renewal of his poetry. . . . Moving from the North East of England to London, and from London to Warsaw, Tom Pickard's work has expanded with his vision into an authentic voice of experience closely felt and sharply drawn."

BIOGRAPHICAL/CRITICAL SOURCES:

BOOKS

Contemporary Poets, 6th edition, St. James Press, 1996.

Dictionary of Literary Biography, Volume 40: *Poets of Great Britain and Ireland Since 1960,* Gale, 1985.

PERIODICALS

Encounter, January, 1972.

Montemora, number 7, 1980.

New Statesman, June 18, 1971.

Paideuma, spring, 1980, pp. 155-163.

Primary Sources, Christmas issue, 1980, p. 15.

Spectator, October 27, 1967.

Times Literary Supplement, July 13, 1967; January 23, 1987, p. 92.*

* * *

PLUM, Jennifer
See KURLAND, Michael (Joseph)

* * *

PLUNKETT, James
See KELLY, James Plunkett

* * *

POPE-HENNESSY, John W(yndham) 1913-1994

PERSONAL: Born December 13, 1913, in London, England; died of a liver ailment, October 31, 1994, in

Florence, Italy; son of L. H. R. (a soldier) and Una (a writer) Pope-Hennessy. *Education:* Balliol College, Oxford, M.A., 1935. *Religion:* Roman Catholic. *Avocational interests:* Music.

CAREER: Victoria and Albert Museum, London, England, member of staff, 1938-73, keeper of the department of architecture and sculpture, 1954-66, director and secretary, 1967-73; British Museum, London, director, 1974-76; Metropolitan Museum of Art, New York City, consultative chairman of the department of European paintings, 1977-86. Slade Professor of Fine Art at Oxford University, 1956-57; Robert Sterling Clark Professor of Art at Williams College, 1961-62; Mellon Lecturer at the National Gallery of Art, 1963; Slade Professor of Fine Art and Peterhouse fellow at Cambridge University, 1964-65; Wrightsman Lecturer at New York University, 1965, professor at Institute of Fine Arts, 1977-94. *Military service:* British Air Ministry, 1939-45.

MEMBER: British Academy (fellow), American Academy of Arts and Sciences (fellow), Society of Antiquaries (fellow), Royal Society of Literature (fellow), Accademia Senese delgi Intronati, Accademia Fiorentina delle Arti del Disegno (honorary academician), Bayerische Akademie der Wissenchaften, American Philosophical Society.

AWARDS, HONORS: Commander, Order of the British Empire, 1959; Serena Medal for Italian Studies, British Academy, 1961; New York University Medal, 1965; knighted, 1971; LL.D., Aberdeen University, 1972, and Loyola University, 1979; honorary doctorate, Royal College of Arts, 1973; Pierpoint Morgan Library honorary fellow, 1975; Torch of Learning Medal, Hebrew University, 1977; Mitchell Prize for the History of Art, 1981, for *Luca della Robbia;* honorary citizen, Siena, 1982; Mangia d'Oro, 1982; Art Dealers of America Award, 1984; Jerusalem Prize for Arts and Letters, 1984; Premio Galileo Galilei, 1986; Grande Ufficiale, Order of Merit of the Republic, Italy, 1988.

WRITINGS:

Giovanni di Paolo, Chatto & Windus, 1937.
Sassetta, Chatto & Windus, 1939.
Sienese Quattrocento Painting, Phaidon Press, 1947.
A Sienese Codex of the "Divine Comedy," Phaidon Press, 1947.
The Drawings of Domeninchino at Windsor Castle, Phaidon Press, 1948.
Donatello's Ascension, H.M.S.O., 1949.
The Virgin with the Laughing Child, H.M.S.O., 1949.
(Editor) *Autobiography of Benvenuto Cellini,* Phaidon Press, 1949.
Nicholas Hilliard, Home & van Thal, 1949.
Paolo Uccello, Phaidon Press, 1950, revised edition, 1969.
Italian Gothic Sculpture in the Victoria and Albert Museum, H.M.S.O., 1952.
Fra Angelico, Phaidon Press, 1952, revised edition, Cornell University Press, 1974.
An Introduction to Italian Sculpture, Volume 1: *Italian Gothic Sculpture,* Volume 2: *Italian Renaissance Sculpture,* Volume 3: *Italian High Renaissance and Baroque Sculpture,* Phaidon Press, 1955-63, 2nd edition, Dutton, 1970-72, 3rd edition, Random House, 1985.
Catalogue of Italian Sculpture in the Victoria and Albert Museum, H.M.S.O., 1964.
Renaissance Bronzes in the Kress Collection, Phaidon Press, 1965.
The Portrait in the Renaissance (lectures), Bollingen Foundation, 1966.
Essays on Italian Sculpture, Phaidon Press, 1968.
The Frick Collection: Catalogue of Sculpture, Princeton University Press, 1970.
Raphael (lectures), New York University Press, 1970.
Luca della Robbia, Cornell University Press, 1980.
The Study and Criticism of Italian Sculpture, Metropolitan Museum of Art in association with Princeton University Press, 1981.
Cellini, photographs by David Finn, Takashi Okamura, and others, Abbeville Press, 1985.
(With Laurence B. Kantner) *The Robert Lehman Collection: Italian Paintings,* Metropolitan Museum of Art in association with Princeton University Press, 1987.
Learning to Look (autobiography), Doubleday/Heinemann, 1991.
The Piero della Francesca Trail, Thames & Hudson (London), 1992.
Donatello: Sculptor, Abbeville Press (New York City), 1993.
Paradiso: The Illuminations to Dante's Divine Comedy by Giovanni di Paolo, Random House (New York City), 1993.

Also author, with others, of *Westminster Abbey,* 1972; author of *La Scultura Italiana del Rinascimento,* 1986; contributor of book reviews to periodicals, including *New York Review of Books* and *Times Literary Supplement.*

SIDELIGHTS: A museum director, art historian, and writer, John Pope-Hennessy was considered one of the world's leading authorities on Italian Renaissance art.

Neil Baldwin described Pope-Hennessy in a *Publishers Weekly* interview as "a disarming synthesis of ultra-distinguished demeanor with a healthy and soft-spoken dash of warmth and humility." The British-born art historian knew at an early age that his interest in the history of art would become a vocation and he approached it not from the perspective of one who views art, but from the perspective of one who produces it, "to understand the way in which the work of art developed and why it took the form it did," he explained in an autobiographical essay for the *New York Times.*

After graduating from Oxford University in 1935, Pope-Hennessy privately studied art in Europe for two years. In 1938 he joined the staff of the Victoria and Albert Museum in London. Apart from service in World War II, Pope-Hennessy remained with that institution until the 1970s, serving finally as its director from 1967 to 1973. In 1974 he became director of the British Museum and in 1977 moved to New York City as chair of the department of European painting at the Metropolitan Museum of Art and professor of art history at New York University. In 1986 Pope-Hennessy retired to Florence, Italy. His writings about art world figures include *Giovanni de Paolo, Fra Angelico, Raphael, Benvenuto Cellini,* and *Donatello.* His autobiography, *Learning to Look,* was published in 1991.

Sixteenth-century sculptor and goldsmith Benvenuto Cellini constitutes the subject of Pope-Hennessy's *Cellini.* Much of what is known about Cellini comes from his autobiography, *Life,* which Suzanne B. Butters described in the *Times Literary Supplement* as "an account of self rich in external particulars and internal resonances." "Princes fell to his gun, gold melted into exquisite objects in his hand and pretty boys dressed as girls for his amusement," wrote William Wilson in the *Los Angeles Times Book Review.* Observing that "the Cellini who parades through his memoirs as a rogue, murderer, traveler, and seducer of both men and women has tended to overshadow his genius as a goldsmith and sculptor," Baldwin suggested that Pope-Hennessy's book "will do much to redress that imbalance." Although Wilson believed "any writer who undertakes to go over the same ground automatically gains points for intrepidity and concern for foolhardiness," George Steiner in the *New Yorker* praised *Cellini,* saying, "Through its own fidelity to Cellini's autobiography, it brings within our imaginative reach one of the earliest and most fascinating of modern men."

Pope-Hennessy's support of *Life* as a factual document makes *Cellini* different from other writings about the artist. Having published an edition of Cellini's autobiography, Pope-Hennessy retained its essential structure, "while adding his own generally perceptive analyses of the works of art themselves," wrote Charles Hope in the *New York Review of Books.* John Russell, a contributor to the *New York Times Book Review,* pointed out that the text is accompanied by new photographs by David Finn which "set the sculptures before us with an almost alarming immediacy." According to Hope, the full-page color photographs and illustrations give the book a lavish physical appearance, "but its real importance lies not in the seductive packaging but in the text. This is certainly the best account of the subject that has been written, and it amply fulfills the author's intention of reestablishing Cellini's reputation as one of the foremost sculptors of his generation." Russell added, "Not only is it a continual excitement to read, but it offers an esthetic adventure of the first order."

In his interview with Baldwin, Pope-Hennessy elaborated on the subject matter of his books: "Art history, to me, is made up of a continuing succession of evaluations and re-evaluations; just because something has been said or written before does not mean it can stand as the last word. I have always been interested in results, in original conclusions which will then inevitably supersede old ones—not just in the writing of others, but very much in my own work as well. I will continue to try to strike a balance between the necessity for a 'program'—an intellectual scheme applied to the work itself—and free invention. Both must coexist in order for art history and art criticism to be properly undertaken."

BIOGRAPHICAL/CRITICAL SOURCES:

PERIODICALS

London Review of Books, March 20, 1986; October 22, 1988.

Los Angeles Times Book Review, June 29, 1986.

Newsweek, December 16, 1985.

New Yorker, April 4, 1986.

New York Review of Books, September 28, 1967; May 29, 1986; April 25, 1991.

New York Times, December 8, 1985.

New York Times Book Review, December 8, 1985; May 26, 1991.

Publishers Weekly, January 24, 1986.

Time, December 16, 1985.

Times Literary Supplement, October 2, 1981; April 16, 1982; March 28, 1986; June 7, 1991.

Washington Post Book World, March 2, 1986.

OBITUARIES:

PERIODICALS

New York Times, November 1, 1994.
Times (London), November 2, 1994.*

* * *

POVOD, Reinaldo 1959-1994

PERSONAL: Born September 18, 1959, in New York, NY; died of tuberculosis, July 30, 1994; son of Reinaldo Joseph (a bartender) and Mildred (Gonzales) Povod; married Laureen Rodriguez (a hair stylist), September 15, 1986. *Education:* Attended Eastern New Mexico University and American Academy of Dramatic Arts. *Politics:* Democrat. *Religion:* Catholic.

CAREER: NuYoRican Poets Cafe, New York City, resident playwright, 1979-82; writer.

MEMBER: Writers Guild of America.

AWARDS, HONORS: George Oppenheimer/*Newsday* Playwriting Award, 1986, for *Cuba and His Teddy Bear;* Whiting Writers' Award, Mrs. Giles Whiting Foundation, 1987, for *Cuba and His Teddy Bear* and *La Puta Vida Trilogy.*

WRITINGS:

Cries and Shouts (one-act play), produced at NuYoRican Poets Cafe, 1979, produced Off-Broadway, 1981.
Cuba and His Teddy Bear (play), produced Off-Broadway, then on Broadway, 1986, adapted as a screenplay.
La Puta Vida Trilogy (three one-act plays), produced Off- Broadway, 1987.

Also co-author of "Everybody Wants to Be in Showbiz," an episode of the television series *Miami Vice,* National Broadcasting Company (NBC).

SIDELIGHTS: Playwright Reinaldo Povod is best known for the Broadway hit *Cuba and His Teddy Bear;* his other works include *Cries and Shouts* and *La Puta Vida Trilogy.* Raised by his grandmother in New York City's East Village, Povod was the son of a Puerto Rican mother and a Cuban father of Russian descent. In a *People* interview with Kristina Johnson, he recalled both loving and fearing his father, who became the model for the title character in *Cuba.* "My father was a hero to everybody on the block. He was a rough man on the streets, and he was respected and feared." Povod received his first break in theater at nineteen when his one-act play *Cries and Shouts* was being performed at the NuYoRican Poets Cafe in New York City. Bill Hart, the literary manager of Off-Broadway's Public Theater, saw the production and "was bowled over," he told Joel Rose in a *New York Times* interview. Hart recalled being surprised when he was introduced to the young playwright; he said to Rose, "This is unreal. This is a child." He returned the next week with Gail Merrifield, who was in charge of literary development at the Public Theater. Rose quoted Merrifield, "The minute I saw [*Cries and Shouts*] . . . I thought this is the strongest voice I've ever heard." Though he was an unknown, Povod's talent also seemed promising to actor Robert DeNiro. After Povod penned *Cuba,* DeNiro almost immediately decided he would take the lead role, which Povod had created with the actor in mind. DeNiro's performance in *Cuba* marked his return to the stage after sixteen years, as well as his Broadway debut.

First produced in 1986 at the Public Theater, *Cuba* moved to the Longacre Theater on Broadway later that year. Starring DeNiro as the streetwise drug dealer Cuba and Ralph Macchio as his artistic, misunderstood teenage son Teddy, *Cuba* explores the complex, volatile relationship between the two characters. While the hard-boiled Cuba openly conducts drug deals from his apartment with the aid of his sidekick Jackie (Burt Young), the sensitive Teddy aspires to be a writer. Although not what many would consider an ideal father, Cuba adores Teddy "so much he was capable of killing him," said *Cuba* producer Joseph Papp in an interview with Rose. Indeed, the conflict between any average parent and child is magnified in *Cuba* through the lenses of drugs and street violence, resulting in what reviewers considered to be a raw, explosive production.

Though many critics found the play to be too long and lacking in plot development, *Cuba* was praised as a strong first effort that was well-written and well-acted. William A. Henry III hailed the author in a *Time* review: "Povod knows his terrain, his dialogue is sharp and colorful yet fits the characters, he never bogs down in exposition, and he sentimentalizes nothing." According to *Newsday* contributor Allan Wallach, "At times [*Cuba*] becomes almost unbearable to watch, but harsh and crude as it is, the play rivets us." *Newsweek* writer Jack Kroll maintained that underneath its stark depiction of life on New York City's seamy lower East Side, *Cuba* is a play of "almost startling warmth, friendliness and humanity." *New York Post* contributor Clive Barnes deemed it "an important debut, and a play that grips you with its tendrils of actuality." Despite acknowledging flaws in *Cuba,* Wallach praised Povod as well, commenting that "even his beginner's mistakes contribute to the scorching impact of his first full-length play." Kroll called the dramatist "a writer of real promise."

Povod followed *Cuba* with *La Puta Vida Trilogy,* which translates as "This Bitch of a Life." Comprised of three one-act plays, the trilogy, like *Cuba,* focuses on the Hispanic community on New York's lower East Side. The first play features a drug-addicted Vietnam veteran, the second portrays a disturbingly likable child molester, and the third details a love-hate relationship between a stripper and her son that ends in murder. While some critics noted that the naturalistic portrayal of the trilogy's subject matter made it unsettling, *New Yorker* critic Edith Oliver asserted that "Mr. Povod . . . opened up a world unknown to many of his audience, and every line rings true." The reviewer went on to lament, however, that Povod provided "no indelible characters to stick to our ribs." Indeed, some critics found the characters to be flat vehicles for what they saw as a heavy-handed message on the effects of racism. But despite the faults of Povod's second dramatic effort, many reviewers lauded the play's powerful impact. Oliver hailed the writing and casting as "impeccable" and deemed Povod "a born dramatist." In an interview with Rose, Povod commented on his motivation for writing *La Puta Vida:* "What do people out there know about Hispanics?. . . This is my responsibility. . . . What they're unfamiliar with is our origins, our principles, our language. In the trilogy I hope to bridge that gap. Hear the voice! Recognize that there is a baby howling in the woods and the baby is Hispanic!"

Povod once told *CA:* "My motivation concerning the theater is to eliminate racism. As an Hispanic and a member of the 'Rainbow People'—we come in all colors, black, white, Oriental, blond and blue-eyed—I am not a reflection of this black and white world. Since Latin writers are not part of this world, we are treated with dismissive contempt! We are invalid. As an Hispanic in the theater I find myself trapped in a different time zone."

At the time of his death Povod was collaborating with Richard Barbour on a play titled *Super Fishbowl Sunday.*

BIOGRAPHICAL/CRITICAL SOURCES:

PERIODICALS

Nation, January 23, 1988, pp. 98-99.
Newsday, May 19, 1986.
Newsweek, June 2, 1986, p. 78.
New Yorker, June 2, 1986, p. 74; December 7, 1987, p. 165.
New York Post, May 19, 1986.
New York Times, July 17, 1986, p. C17; August 28, 1986; November 15, 1987, p. 5; November 25, 1987, p. C20.
People, September 1, 1986, p. 61.
Time, June 2, 1986, p. 77.

OBITUARIES:

PERIODICALS

New York Times, August 2, 1994, p. D18.*

* * *

PRESCOTT, Jack
See PRESTON, John

* * *

PRESTON, John 1945-1994
(Jack Hild, Mike McCray, Jack Prescott, pseudonyms; Preston MacAdam, joint pseudonym)

PERSONAL: Born December 11, 1945, in Framingham, MA; died of complications from AIDS, April 28, 1994, in Portland, ME; son of John (an engineer) and Nancy (a politician; maiden name, Blood) Preston. *Education:* Lake Forest College, B.A., 1968; University of Minnesota—Twin Cities, certified sexual health consultant, 1973.

CAREER: Gay House, Inc. (community center), Minneapolis, MN, founder and co-director, 1970-72; Gay Community Services, Minneapolis, founder and co-director, 1972-74; *Advocate,* San Francisco, CA, editor, 1975-76; full-time writer, 1976-94.

MEMBER: National Writers Union, National Book Critics Circle, Authors Guild, PEN, Maine Writers and Publishers Alliance.

AWARDS, HONORS: Franny, the Queen of Provincetown was named "Gay Novel of the Year" by the *Front Page,* and a stage adaptation won the Jane Chambers Gay Playwriting Award, both 1984; grant from Maine State Arts Commission, 1989-90.

WRITINGS:

FICTION

Mr. Benson (novel), Alternate Publishing, 1983.
Franny, the Queen of Provincetown (novel; variously produced and adapted as one-, two-, and three-act plays), Alyson, 1983.
I Once Had a Master and Other Tales of Erotic Love, Alyson, 1984.
The Mission of Alex Kane, Alyson, Volume I: *Sweet Dreams,* 1984, Volume II: *Golden Years,* 1984, Volume III: *Deadly Liars,* 1985, Volume IV: *Stolen Moments,* 1986, Volume V: *Secret Dangers,* 1986, Volume VI: *Lethal Secrets,* 1987.
(Editor) *Hot Living: Erotic Stories About Safer Sex,* Alyson, 1985.
Entertainment for a Master, Alyson, 1986.
Love of a Master, Alyson, 1987.
The Heir, Liberty Books (Austin, TX), 1988.
In Search of a Master, Lyle Stuart, 1989.
(Editor and author of introduction) *Flesh and the Word: An Anthology of Erotic Writing,* Dutton, 1992.
(Editor and author of introduction) *Flesh and the Word 2: An Anthology of Erotic Writing,* Plume, 1993.
(Editor with Michael Lowenthal) *Flesh and the Word 3: An Anthology of Erotic Writing,* Plume, 1995.
Journals of a Master: Two Classic Erotic Gay Novels (includes *Entertainment for a Master* and *The Love of a Master*), Alyson (Los Angeles), 1997.

Also author and co-author of mass-market paperback books, under the pseudonyms Jack Hild and Mike McCray, and under the joint pseudonyms Preston MacAdam and Mike McCray. Contributor of stories, sometimes under the pseudonym Jack Prescott, to periodicals, including *Drummer.*

NONFICTION

(Author of introduction) Phil Andros, *Stud,* Alyson, 1982.
(Contributor) Michael Denneny, Charles Ortleb, and Thomas Steele, editors, *The Christopher Street Reader,* Coward-McCann, 1983.
(Contributor) Patricia Case, editor, *The Alternative Press Annual,* Temple University Press, 1984.
(With Frederick Brandt) *Classified Affairs: A Gay Man's Guide to the Personals,* Alyson, 1984.
(Contributor) Eric Rofes, editor, *Gay Life,* Doubleday, 1986.
(With Glenn Swann) *Safe Sex: The Ultimate Erotic Guide,* Plume, 1987.
(Author of introduction) Lars Eighner, *How to Write and Sell Gay Erotica,* Liberty Books, 1987.
(Contributor) Michael Shernoff and William Scott, editors, *The Sourcebook on Lesbian/Gay Health Care,* National Lesbian and Gay Health Foundation, 1988.
(Editor) *Personal Dispatches: Writers Confront AIDS,* St. Martin's, 1989.
(Author of introduction) T. R. Witomski, *Kvetch,* Celestial Arts, 1989.
The Big Gay Book: A Man's Survival Guide for the 90's, Plume, 1991.
(Editor and author of introduction) *Hometowns: Gay Men Write About Where They Belong,* Dutton (New York City), 1991.
(Editor and author of introduction) *A Member of the Family: Gay Men Write About Their Families,* Dutton, 1992.
(Editor and author of introduction, with Joan Nestle) *Sister and Brother: Lesbians & Gay Men Write about Their Lives Together,* HarperSanFrancisco (San Francisco, CA), 1994.
(Editor with Michael Lowenthal) *Friends and Lovers: Gay Men Write about the Families They Create,* Dutton, 1995.
Winter's Light: Reflections of a Yankee Queer, edited with an introduction by Michael Lowenthal, foreword by Andrew Holleran, University Press of New England (Hanover, NH), 1995.

Also author of *Public Displays, Private Passions: Life in the Sexual Marketplace.* Contributor of articles to periodicals, including *Front Page, Harper's, Christopher Street, Tribe,* and *Philadelphia Gay News.*

SIDELIGHTS: A counselor, community activist, journalist, and author, John Preston worked as a sexual health consultant in Minneapolis, MN, in the early 1970s while he founded two of that city's first organizations to serve its gay community. His experiences led him to San Francisco in 1975 to undertake the editorship of the *Advocate,* a biweekly national newspaper aimed at a gay audience that later became an important magazine of progressive politics and culture. Preston became a freelance writer in 1976 and was a prolific contributor to numerous North American and European periodicals; he also wrote erotica under a variety of pseudonyms that attracted a cult readership. Preston once told *CA:* "I am a chronicler of a wide range of contemporary issues in gay life, from AIDS to sexuality, from politics to myths." His first novel, *Mr. Benson,* was published in 1983, and his second, *Franny, the Queen of Provincetown,* was both an award-winning book and adapted for stage; later works of fiction include *The Heir* and *In Search of a Master.*

In the early days of AIDS awareness Preston became an outspoken supporter of safe sex and served as editor of 1985's *Hot Living: Erotic Stories about Safer Sex* and co-wrote *Safe Sex: The Ultimate Erotic Guide.* He also authored a number of nonfiction books on gay culture, including *Classified Affairs: A Gay Man's Guide to the Personals, Hometowns: Gay Men Write about Where They Belong,* and *The Big Gay Book: A Man's Survival Guide for the 90's.* In 1992 Preston's papers and manuscripts became part of the Katzoff Collection at Brown University's John Hay Library.

BIOGRAPHICAL/CRITICAL SOURCES:

BOOKS

Antoniou, Laura, editor, *Looking for Mr. Preston,* Masquerade Books (New York City), 1995.

Preston, John, *Winter's Light: Reflections of a Yankee Queer,* edited with an introduction by Michael Lowenthal, foreword by Andrew Holleran, University Press of New England, 1995.

PERIODICALS

Voice Literary Supplement, November, 1983.

OBITUARIES:

PERIODICALS

Chicago Tribune, May 1, 1994, sec. 2, p. 8.

Los Angeles Times, April 30, 1994, p. A24.

New York Times, April 29, 1994, p. B8.*

* * *

PRICE, Vincent 1911-1993

PERSONAL: Born May 27, 1911, in St. Louis, MO; died of lung cancer, October 25, 1993, in Los Angeles, CA; son of Vincent Leonard (president of a candy company) and Marguerite Cobb (Wilcox) Price; married Edith Barrett (an actress), 1938 (divorced, 1948); married Mary Grant (a designer), August 28, 1949 (divorced, 1972); married Coral Browne (an actress), 1974; children: (first marriage) Vincent B.; (second marriage) Mary Victoria. *Education:* Yale University, B.A., 1933; graduate study at University of London, 1934-35. *Avocational interests:* Gourmet cooking, swimming, hiking, collecting drawings and paintings.

CAREER: Actor in plays, including *Chicago,* 1935, *Victoria Regina,* 1935-37, *Outward Bound,* 1939-40, *Angel Street,* 1941-42, *Cocktail Party,* 1951, *Don Juan in Hell,* 1952, *The Lady's Not for Burning,* 1952, *Darling of the Day,* 1968, and *Oliver!,* 1974; actor in over one hundred motion pictures, including *Service de Luxe,* 1938, *The House of the Seven Gables,* 1940, *The Song of Bernadette,* 1943, *The Keys of the Kingdom,* 1944, *Dragonwyck,* 1946, *The Web,* 1947, *The Three Musketeers,* 1948, *Champagne for Caesar,* 1950, *The House of Wax,* 1953, *The Ten Commandments,* 1956, *The Big Circus,* 1959, *House of Usher,* 1960, *The Pit and the Pendulum,* 1961, *Masque of the Red Death,* 1964, *The Abominable Dr. Phibes,* 1971, and *Theatre of Blood,* 1973. Appeared on radio programs, including *The Saint,* 1947-50, and *Lux Radio Theatre*; appeared on over 2,000 television shows, including *$64,000 Challenge, The Man from U.N.C.L.E., Hollywood Squares, Night Gallery, The Brady Bunch,* and *The Tonight Show.* Lecturer on primitive and modern art and on the letters of Van Gogh at colleges and universities. Member of the board of Archives of American Artists; member of Whitney Museum Friends of American Artists; president of art council of University of California, Los Angeles; member of U.S. Indian Arts and Crafts Board; art consultant to Sears, Roebuck & Co.; member of fine arts committee of the White House; member of board of directors of Center for Arts of Indian Affairs; member of advisory committee of Friends of Art, University of Southern California. Narrator of numerous sound recordings.

MEMBER: Royal Society of Art, Actors' Equity Association, Screen Actors Guild, Elizabethan Club, Yale Club.

AWARDS, HONORS: Academy award for documentary from Academy of Motion Pictures Arts and Sciences, 1963; Los Angeles Film Critics Award for life achievement, 1992.

WRITINGS:

I Like What I Know (autobiography), Doubleday (Garden City, NJ), 1959.

The Book of Joe: About a Dog and His Man, Doubleday, 1961.

(Editor with Chandler Brossard) *Eighteen Best Stories by Edgar Allan Poe,* Dell, 1965.

(With wife, Mary Price) *A Treasury of Great Recipes: Famous Specialties of the World's Foremost Restaurants Adapted for the American Kitchen,* Geis, 1965.

(With Mary Price) *Mary and Vincent Price Present a National Treasury of Cookery,* compiled by Helen Duprey Bullock, Heirloom Publishing, 1967.

(With Mary Price) *Mary and Vincent Price's Come Into the Kitchen Cook Book: A Collector's Treasury of America's Great Recipes,* Stravon, 1969.

Vincent Price: His Movies, His Plays, His Life, Doubleday, 1978.

(With V. B. Price) *Monsters,* Grosset & Dunlap (New York City), 1981.

ART

(Author of introduction and catalogue notes) *Vincent Price Collects Drawings,* Oakland Art Museum, 1957.

(Author of introduction) *Drawings of Five Centuries,* Santa Barbara Museum of Art, 1959.

(Author of introduction) Eugene Delacroix, *Drawings,* Borden, 1966.

The Vincent Price Treasury of American Art, Country Beautiful, 1972.

Also author, with wife Mary Price, of *The Michaelangelo Bible.* Author of introduction, Sears Vincent Price Gallery, *Nineteenth and Twentieth Century European Master Graphics,* [Chicago].

SIDELIGHTS: Best remembered as the master of horror and suspense for his work in classic films such as *Theatre of Blood, The Fly,* and *Masque of the Red Death,* Vincent Price devoted nearly sixty years to entertaining the young and old alike. He first began his acting career on stage, performing in dramas like *Victoria Regina.* He made a similar entree into motion pictures, starring in *The House of Seven Gables* and *The Song of Bernadette.* Price began his foray into villainous roles as a member of Orson Welles' Mercury Theater, and with films like *The House of Wax* and stage productions such as 1941's *Angel Street* on Broadway.

Reflecting on his role in *Angel Street* as a "villainous, smoking-jacketed smoothie," Price commented to Christopher Buckley: " 'I came out for my curtain call. . . and the audience just *hissed.* I knew I'd found my niche.' "

During his acting career, Price starred in more than one hundred motion pictures, most recently appearing in *Whales of August* and *Edward Scissorhands.* He also found time to appear in some 2,000 television productions, including *Night Gallery, Batman,* and *Mystery.* He continued his work on the stage, notably with the one-person-play *Diversions and Delights,* and even performed in a music video, Michael Jackson's *Thriller.*

Price starred in numerous films of the macabre. Among his most successful were a series of Edgar Allan Poe stories, including *The House of Usher* and *The Raven.* A more recent example is *Theatre of Blood,* in which he played a Shakespearean actor who murders drama critics for their harsh reviews and, as Buckley related, "avenges himself on Robert Morley by force-feeding him his two miniature poodles through a funnel."

Though the diabolical seemed to be Price's forte, he actually began his early career playing such respectable characters as Prince Albert in *Victoria Regina* and the Reverend William Duke in *Outward Bound.* Because of his careful diction he was often mistakenly labeled an Englishman. This, plus his suave manner and royal bearing, made him a popular and distinguished leading man during the 1940s. Among his later roles was that of Oscar Wilde in the one-man show, *Diversions and Delights,* in 1978, which one critic called "Price's finest work."

The versatile actor also starred in "clunkers" like *Abbott and Costello Meet Frankenstein* and *Dr. Goldfoot and the Bikini Machine.* But Price did not apologize for these films, which, as he explained to Buckley, he did for "the money, chiefly; that, and a compulsive need to be busy."

An avid fine art historian and collector, Price served on the board of various art organizations, including the Archives of American Artists and Center for Arts of Indian Affairs. Since his youth, when he bought a Rembrandt etching for $34.50 on the installment plan, Price added numerous works to his famous art collection. He was a member of the Fine Arts committee to the White House, and he was a frequent lecturer on primitive and modern art, as well as on Dutch painter Vincent Van Gogh. Price authored several books on the subject of art, including *The Vincent Price Treasury of American Art* and, with his second wife, Mary, *The Michelangelo Bible.* He also wrote his memoirs in *I Like What I Know* and *Vincent Price: His Movies, His Plays, His Life.* The author of *The Book of Joe: About a Dog and His Man* as well as several cookbooks, he also edited an anthology of stories by American writer Edgar Allan Poe. In 1992 he was awarded the Los Angeles Film Critics Award for life achievement.

BIOGRAPHICAL/CRITICAL SOURCES:

BOOKS

Brosman, John, *Horror People,* St. Martin's, 1976.
Price, Victoria, *Vincent Price: A Daughter's Biography,* St. Martin's, 1999.
Price, Vincent, *I Like What I Know* (autobiography), Doubleday, 1959.
Price, Vincent, *Vincent Price, His Movies, His Plays, His Life,* Doubleday, 1978.
Shipman, David, *Great Movie Stars,* A & W Visual Library, 1976.
Thomas, Tony, *Cads & Cavaliers,* Barnes, 1973.
Williams, Lucy Chase, *The Complete Films of Vincent Price,* introduction by Vincent Price, Carol Pub. Group (Secaucus, NJ), 1995.

PERIODICALS

Design, January, 1966.
Esquire, April 25, 1978.
House Beautiful, November, 1973.
New York Times Book Review, June 6, 1965.
Newsweek, June 14, 1971.

OBITUARIES:

PERIODICALS

Chicago Tribune, October 26, 1993, p. 11.
Los Angeles Times, October 26, 1993, p. A3.
New York Times, October 27, 1993, p. D23.
Times (London), October 27, 1993, p. 19.
Washington Post, October 27, 1993, p. D4.*

* * *

PULLER, Lewis B(urwell), Jr. 1945(?)-1994

PERSONAL: Born c. 1945; died of a self-inflicted gunshot wound, May 11, 1994, in Mount Vernon, VA; son of Lewis Burwell Puller (a career marine); married Linda Ford "Toddy" Todd (a teacher), August, 1968; children: Lewis III, Maggie. *Education:* College of William and Mary, B.A., 1967, law degree, 1974.

CAREER: Affiliated with Veteran's Administration, c. 1974; served on President Gerald Ford's Clemency Board during 1970s; Paralyzed Veterans of America, service director; Democratic Congressional candidate, 1978; U.S. Department of Defense, Washington, DC, senior attorney in office of general council, c. 1980-94; Vietnam Memorial Association, director. *Military service:* U. S. Marine Corps, 1968; served in Vietnam; became lieutenant; received Silver Star and two Purple Hearts.

AWARDS, HONORS: Pulitzer Prize in autobiography, Columbia University Graduate School of Journalism, 1992, for *Fortunate Son.*

WRITINGS:

Fortunate Son: The Autobiography of Lewis B. Puller, Jr., Grove Weidenfeld (New York City), 1991.

ADAPTATIONS: Fortunate Son was released on audio tape and narrated by the author, Soundbooks, 1992.

SIDELIGHTS: The 1992 Pulitzer Prize for autobiographical literature was awarded to Lewis B. Puller, Jr., for his book *Fortunate Son: The Autobiography of Lewis B. Puller, Jr.* Though the account was released in the wake of renewed interest in the Vietnam War—fostered in part by the release of such novels and films as *In Country* and *Born on the Fourth of July*—*Fortunate Son* is a work of singular power, concentrating not on the war but upon Puller's attempts to return to his country and family after becoming one of Vietnam's most gruesomely wounded survivors.

Though he had earned a degree in English, there was no doubt in Puller's mind that he would one day serve his country as a U.S. Marine. His father, Lewis, Sr., was the legendary "Chesty" Puller, the most decorated soldier in Marine Corps history (and himself the subject of a biography, Burke Davis's *Marine*). When it became his turn, Lewis, too, joined the Marines. He was "in country" for just three months, during which time he bore witness to the bloody atrocities committed on both sides.

Puller's tour of duty ended abruptly on the morning of October 11, 1968, when he tripped a booby-trapped howitzer shell. The explosion destroyed both his legs, took several fingers off both hands, burst one eardrum, and riddled much of his body with shrapnel. Unaware of the severity of his wounds, Puller recalled the initial wave of relief that accompanied his realization that he would be returning home to his pregnant wife, Toddy. It was not until he was transported to the combat hospital that the reality of his situation began to dawn on him; he remained in critical condition for several days, contracting a stress ulcer that made it necessary to surgically remove most of his stomach. He was then sent stateside, where he spent almost two years recuperating at the Philadelphia Naval Hospital. "These pages exude the whiff of authentic hell and are, accordingly, sometimes difficult to read," said William Styron in the *New York Times Book Review.* "But because Mr. Puller [wrote] with simplicity and candor, with touches of spontaneous humor, his outcry of agony and isolation, while harrowing, leaves one primarily overwhelmed with wonder at the torture a human being can absorb this side of madness."

It was primarily through the patience and unflagging love of his wife (to whom the book is dedicated) that Puller was able to survive his recuperation. Not that that love was untested: at their initial reunion, Puller, confined to a wheelchair, instructed his five-months-pregnant wife to divorce him rather than be burdened by a cripple. Toddy persevered, helping Puller through law school and assisting him in his unsuccessful bid for a seat in Congress. It was the failure of this Congressional run that drove Puller to heavy alcoholism and, ultimately, to attempt suicide—only to be saved, once again, by his wife. "Toddy," observed *New York Times* reviewer Herbert Mitgang, "is something of a heroine in the story; her loyalty makes the author seem like a very fortunate husband."

The bulk of Puller's autobiography details his slow psychological recuperation, coming more than a decade after the healing of his physical wounds. He joined Alcoholics Anonymous in 1981, shortly after acquiring a position as an attorney for the Department of the Defense; he later served there as a senior attorney, helping to reduce the size of the military. Later in his career, Puller went on to head the Vietnam Memorial Association, an American organization that aimed to reestablish ties between the two countries. He told *New York Times Book Review* interviewer Barth Healey: "[*Fortunate Son*] is not a Vietnam book. It's about bigger themes than just Vietnam: father-son, rite of passage, coming of age. . . . Vietnam is over with by page 200." Puller explained in the *Washington Post* that writing the book "was part of achieving an inner peace and going on living a productive life. I can't say that I've achieved it, but I've had some success." Following the success of his autobiography, Puller became a writer-in-residence at George Mason University.

Reviewers of *Fortunate Son* were most often struck by the sheer power of Puller's writing, undiluted by flowery description or grand metaphor. Styron called the book "an amazing tale but in many ways an artless one, with great cumulative power yet more compelling as a raw chronicle than a work offering literary surprises." Susan Fromberg Schaeffer concurred, writing in the *Los Angeles Times Book Review:* "[Puller's] story of his early life as the son of a military hero, his tour of duty, his return home, is, quite simply, inspirational, his survival miraculous. We cannot account for miracles. We can only be grateful for them—and to Puller, who . . . lived to tell us of them in this remarkable and unusually moving book." She concluded: "If we value peace but want to understand what happens when that precious and fragile peace is disrupted by that cataclysm we know as war, books like Lewis B. Puller Jr.'s *Fortunate Son* . . . are truly indispensable."

BIOGRAPHICAL/CRITICAL SOURCES:

BOOKS

Puller, Lewis B., Jr., *Fortunate Son: The Autobiography of Lewis B. Puller, Jr.,* Grove Weidenfeld, 1991.

PERIODICALS

Atlanta Journal, August 25, 1991, p. N8.
Boston Globe, June 23, 1991, p. 89; July 4, 1991, p. 13.
Los Angeles Times Book Review, June 16, 1991, p. 1.
New York Times, June 19, 1991, p. C16.
New York Times Book Review, June 16, 1991, p. 1.
People, fall, 1991, p. 83.
Washington Post, January 18, 1991, p. A19; July 1, 1991, p. C1; April 8, 1992, p. D1.
Washington Post Book World, June 2, 1991, p. 4.*

OBITUARIES:

PERIODICALS

Chicago Tribune, May 12, 1994, p. 12.
Los Angeles Times, May 12, 1994, p. A22.
New York Times, May 12, 1994, p. B14.*

* * *

RAMSEY, (Arthur) Michael 1904-1988

PERSONAL: Born November 14, 1904, in Cambridge, England; died April 23, 1988, in Oxford, England; son of Arthur Stanley (a mathematics don at Cambridge University) and Agnes (Wilson) Ramsey; married Joan Alice Hamilton, April 8, 1942. *Education:* Cambridge University, B.A., 1927, M.A., 1930, B.D., 1950; also attended Cuddesdon Theological College.

CAREER: Ordained deacon in Church of England, 1928, and priest, 1929; Church of St. Nicholas, Liverpool, England, curate, 1928-30; subwarden, Lincoln Theological College, 1930-36; Boston Parish Church, Lincolnshire, England, lecturer, 1936-38; St. Benedict's Church, Cambridge, England, vicar, 1938-40; University of Durham, Durham, England, Van Mildert Professor of Divinity, 1940-50; Cambridge University, Cambridge, Regius Professor of Divinity and fellow of Magdalene College, 1950-52; bishop of Durham, 1952-56; archbishop of York, 1956-61; archbishop of Canterbury, 1961-74. Examining chaplain to bishop of Chester, 1932-39. Select preacher to Cambridge University, 1934, 1940, 1948; canon, Durham Cathedral, 1940-50; select preacher to Oxford University, 1945-46; canon of Caistor and prebendary, Lincoln Cathedral, 1951-52; Hulsean Preacher, Cambridge University, 1969-70. Trustee of British Museum, 1963-69.

MEMBER: World Council of Churches (president, 1961-68), Cambridge Union (president, 1926).

AWARDS, HONORS: Doctorate in divinity from University of Durham, 1951, University of Edinburgh, University of Leeds, University of Hull, and Cambridge University, all 1957, Victoria University of Manchester, 1961, and University of London, 1962; honorary fellow of Magdalene College, Cambridge University, 1952-88, Merton College, Oxford University, 1974-88, and Keble College, Oxford University, 1975-88; D.Cl. from Oxford University, 1960, and University of Kent, 1966; honorary master of the bench, Inner Temple, 1962; D.Litt. from University of Keele, 1967.

WRITINGS:

The Gospel and the Catholic Church, Longmans, Green, 1936.

The Resurrection of Christ, Presbyterian Board of Christian Education, 1946.

The Glory of God and the Transfiguration of Christ, Longmans, Green, 1949.

F. D. Maurice and the Conflicts of Modern Theology, Cambridge University Press, 1951.

Durham Essays and Addresses, S.P.C.K., 1956.

An Era of Anglican Theology, Scribner, 1960.

Oratory and Literature, English Association, 1960.

Introducing the Christian Faith, S.C.M.P., 1961.

Unity, Truth, and Holiness, Fellowship of St. Alban and St. Serbius, 1961.

The Narratives of the Passion, Mowbray, 1962.

Christianity and the Supernatural, Althone, 1963.

Image Old and New: On the Problem of Finding New Ways to State Old Truths, Forward Movement, 1963.

Canterbury Essays and Addresses, Seabury, 1964.

Beyond Religion?, S.P.C.K., 1964.

Christ Crucified, for the World, Mowbray, 1964.

Sacred and Secular: A Study in the Other Worldly and This Worldly Aspects of Christianity, Longmans, Green, 1965.

The Meaning of Prayer, Morehouse, 1965.

Problems of Christian Belief, BBC Publications, 1966.

God, Christ, and the World: A Study in Contemporary Theology, Morehouse, 1969.

(With Leon-Joseph Cardinal Suenens) *The Future of the Christian Church,* Morehouse, 1970.

The Christian Priest Today, S.P.C.K., 1972.

(With Robert E. Terwillizer and A. M. Allchin) *The Charismatic Christ,* Morehouse, 1973.

Canterbury Pilgrim, S.P.C.K., 1974.

(With others) *Come Holy Spirit,* Morehouse, 1976.

Holy Spirit, S.P.C.K., 1977.

Jesus and the Living Past, Oxford University Press, 1980.

Be Still and Know, Collins (London), 1982.

The Anglican Spirit, edited by Dale Coleman, Cowley Publications (Cambridge, MA), 1991.

To Believe is to Pray: Readings from Michael Ramsey, edited by James E. Griffiss, Cowley Publications, 1996.

SIDELIGHTS: Educator and author Michael Ramsey was a leading figure in the Church of England, serving as archbishop of Canterbury from 1961 to 1974. He was ordained to the priesthood in 1929 and thereafter filled many church posts. He also held titled academic posts, including Van Mildert Professor of Divinity at the University of Durham throughout the 1940s.

When Ramsey succeeded to the episcopacy of York in 1956, many feared that his Anglo-Catholicism would prove a threat to Christian reunion, according to a *Newsweek* writer. But he retired as Archbishop of Canterbury eighteen years later "to a chorus of nearly unqualified praise—including comparisons with such giants of English ecclesiastical history as Saint Anselm and Thomas a Becket." The *Newsweek* writer continued: "In a fitting farewell to Ramsey's episcopacy, the House of Commons . . . approved a reform that he [advocated] since becoming Primate—the granting of ecclesiastical affairs to the Church of England. The church's historic ties with the state will remain. The Queen is still its Supreme Governor and the Prime Minister will continue to appoint its bishops. But Church officials may now reform doctrine and liturgy without approval from . . . Parliament."

One of Ramsey's dreams was to see Anglican reconciliation with Roman Catholicism. He helped further that cause in 1966 when he became the first Archbishop of Canterbury to officially visit Rome, exchanging a "kiss of peace" with Pope Paul VI.

In his writings, Ramsey was less conciliatory. For example, in "The Menace of Fundamentalism," an article published in 1956, Ramsey attacked fundamentalism as heretical, singling out American evangelist Billy Graham as a preacher of the "grossest doctrines." Most of Ramsey's full-length works, however, were either studies of the New Testament or broad expositions of Christian doctrine. His writings include *The Gospel and the Catholic Church, The Resurrection of Christ, Introducing the Christian Faith, Beyond Religion?, Sacred and Secular: A Study in the Other Worldly and This Worldly Aspects of Christianity,* and *Jesus and the Living Past.* Of his own perception of God, Ramsey said, "I enjoy Him. I think about Him, tell Him of my worries."

BIOGRAPHICAL/CRITICAL SOURCES:

BOOKS

Chadwick, Owen, *Michael Ramsey: A Life,* Clarendon Press (Oxford, UK), 1990.

De-la-Noy, Michael, *Michael Ramsey: A Portrait,* Collins, 1990.

Gill, Robin, and Lorna Kendall, editors, *Michael Ramsey as Theologian,* Cowley Publications, 1995.

Simpson, J. B., *The Hundredth Archbishop of Canterbury,* Harper, 1960.

PERIODICALS

Newsweek, December 16, 1974.

OBITUARIES:

BOOKS

The Writers Directory: 1988-1990, St. James Press, 1988.*

RANSFORD, Oliver 1914-1993

PERSONAL: Born April 25, 1914, in Bradford, England; died of a pulmonary embolism resulting from a traffic accident, August 5, 1993, in Bulawayo, Zimbabwe; son of Thomas Oliver (a clergyman) and Mabel Louise (Thomas) Ransford; married Doris Irene Galloway, July 19, 1939; children: Andrew, Carol, Charlotte. *Education:* University of London and Middlesex Hospital, M.D., F.F.A.R.C.S., and Diploma in Anaesthesia, 1936; University of London, D.Phil. (history), 1977. *Avocational interests:* Historical and archaeological research in South and Central Africa.

CAREER: In private practice as consultant anesthetist, Bulawayo, Zimbabwe, 1947-93. Consultant anesthetist to Rhodesia Railways; honorary consultant anesthetist to Bulawayo Group of Hospitals. *Military service:* British Army, Medical Corps, 1939-45; became major.

MEMBER: Rhodesian Medical Association, Bulawayo Club.

WRITINGS:

Livingstone's Lake: The Drama of Nyasa, Africa's Inland Sea, Crowell, 1966.

The Battle of Majuba Hill, Crowell, 1967.

Bulawayo: Historic Background of Rhodesia, Verry, 1968.

The Rulers of Rhodesia from Earliest Times to the Referendum, J. Murray, 1968.

The Battle of Spion Kop, J. Murray, 1969.

The Slave Trade: The Story of Transatlantic Slavery, J. Murray, 1971.

Rhodesian Tapestry, Books of Rhodesia, 1971.

The Great Trek, J. Murray, 1972.

(With T. W. Baxter) *Livingstone in Africa,* J. Cape, 1972.

David Livingstone: The Dark Interior, St. Martin's, 1978.

Bid the Sickness Cease: Disease in the History of Black Africa, J. Murray, 1983.

Contributor to journals.

SIDELIGHTS: A physician and writer, Oliver Ransford is best remembered for his work as a consultant anaesthetist and as a writer of African history. Beginning in the late 1930s he spent some six years with the British Army in its Colonial Medical Service. In 1947 he began a private practice in Zimbabwe. Ransford's interest in and travels through Africa inspired many of his books, including *Livingstone's Lake: The Drama of Nyasa, Af-*

rica's Inland Sea, The Rulers of Rhodesia from Earliest Times to the Referendum, and *Bid the Sickness Cease: Disease in the History of Black Africa.*

Ransford told *CA:* "Having travelled (and campaigned) through much of Africa during the last thirty-six years, I have become vastly interested in the history of sub-Saharan Africa, and most of my books have reflected this interest. But as an anaesthetist by profession, I have developed another interest in the development of modern anaesthesia (which I regard as one of the greatest boons ever to have been bestowed on mankind, for imagine what life would be like without the benefit of anaesthesia) and its relationship with the great mystery of normal sleep. I hope soon to embark upon a book on this subject."

In his 1978 biography *David Livingstone: The Dark Interior,* Ransford combined his interests in Africa and medicine to produce a new analysis of the famed British explorer's life and career. As the book's subtitle suggests, Ransford examined Livingstone's "dark interior"—in other words, those contradictory aspects of his personality that puzzled and angered his friends and family. Subject to extreme changes in mood, the explorer was, according to his biographer, a victim of an often-hereditary manic-depressive disorder known as cyclothymia. Once this is acknowledged and understood, wrote Ransford, "the paradoxes in [Livingstone's] career fall into place like the pieces in a jigsaw puzzle."

Commenting in the *Spectator,* Anthony Nutting noted that because Livingstone "rank[s] among the least attractive of the legendary explorers," writing a "readable biography" of him is "almost impossible." The reviewer found Ransford's medical explanation of his subject's character "interesting and very credible," but went on to note that "psychiatric diagnosis does not of itself make for readability. . . . In his introduction, Dr. Ransford asserts that the insight which he reveals into his subject's psyche shows him 'not as the saintly figure of his earlier adulatory biographers but as a man essentially human, and therefore of even greater stature than they delineated.' Yet nowhere in the ensuing narrative is this claim substantiated. On the contrary; Livingstone is shown, by his own writings and actions, to have been a fraud, a liar and a bully."

Elspeth Huxley, though impressed by Ransford's thoroughness, was also not entirely convinced that Livingstone truly suffered from a mental disorder. In her *Times Literary Supplement* review of the biography, Huxley observed: "Ransford has drawn on much unpublished material, his researches have been deep and wide, he has lived some forty years in Africa and personally followed many of Livingstone's trails. Few writers can have made a more serious effort to get inside Livingstone's complex mind." But she questioned Ransford's tendency to dwell on "the darker, more despondent aspects of Livingstone's character" while downplaying the explorer's "happier side, . . . [his] constant delight in the natural world about him and . . . his skill as an observer." In short, declared Huxley, "Livingstone undoubtably displayed many of the symptoms Dr. Ransford lists as manic depressive. Yet, at the end, doubts remain."

In her *Books and Bookmen* review, on the other hand, Judith Listowell praised Ransford's novel analysis of a person about whom much has already been written. "From Dr. Ransford's usual easy, readable style," the critic wrote, "Livingstone can be seen as the victim of a disease which in the nineteenth century was almost completely unknown, and about which even today much remains to be learnt. . . . Seen as suffering from manic depression, Livingstone's behaviour becomes comprehensible, and actions that seem harsh, brutal, or embarrassingly dishonest, fall into place." Listowell was pleased to find that Ransford provided up-to-date descriptions of the places Livingstone visited in Africa, but she was somewhat disappointed that the author did not always include adequate explanations of certain "reprehensible" actions in the explorer's life. Nevertheless, Listowell concluded, for the most part "Ransford [did] not try to gloss over Livingstone's mistakes, not to say misdeeds. . . . This book fairly recognizes [his] greatness."

BIOGRAPHICAL/CRITICAL SOURCES:

PERIODICALS

Books and Bookmen, August, 1978.
Spectator, September 16, 1978.
Times Literary Supplement, November 17, 1978.

OBITUARIES:

BOOKS

The Writers Directory: 1992-1994, St. James Press, 1991, p. 807.

PERIODICALS

Times (London), August 13, 1993, p. 15.*

REES, Dilwyn
See DANIEL, Glyn (Edmund)

* * *

ROCKFERN, Danielle
See NOLAN, Frederick William

* * *

ROUNTREE, Owen
See KRAUZER, Steven M(ark)

S-Y

SATIAFA
See GORDON, Vivian V(erdell)

* * *

SAUER, Julia Lina 1891-1983

PERSONAL: Born in 1891, in ,Rochester, NY; died June 26, 1983, in Rochester, NY. *Education:* Attended the University of Rochester, and New York State Library School.

CAREER: Writer. Worked as children's librarian at Rochester Public Library, Rochester, NY, 1921-58.

AWARDS, HONORS: University of Rochester Lillian Fairchild Prize, 1943; runner-up for the Newbery Medal and the American Library Association Notable Book citation, both 1944, for *Fog Magic,* and runner-up for the Newbery Medal, 1952, for *The Light at Tern Rock.*

WRITINGS:

(Editor) *Radio Roads to Reading: Library Book Talks Broadcast to Girls and Boys,* H. W. Wilson, 1939.
Fog Magic, Viking, 1943, new edition, Pocket Books, 1977.
The Light at Tern Rock, illustrated by Georges Schreiber, Viking, 1951, Puffin Books (New York City), 1994.
Mike's House, illustrated by Don Freeman, Viking, 1954, new edition, 1970.

SIDELIGHTS: Julia Lina Sauer's career as head of the Work with Children department of the public library in Rochester, New York, brought her in contact with the children's literature of the day and inspired her to write her first book, *Fog Magic.* Sauer spent her entire library career with the Rochester Public Library, but her name became known throughout the country in connection with library work for children. She was a pioneer in preschool reading and an authority on children's books.

All three of Sauer's children's books reflect her love of nature and of people. Commenting on her writing style and characterization, Mary Lystad of *Twentieth-Century Children's Writers* wrote, "Sauer's understanding of human nature and human development comes through clearly in her works. She has an excellent command of words and imagery. Her style, though, is didactic, and her message is labored by today's standards. Nevertheless, her obvious caring for nature, place, and especially people contributes to her continued appeal." Sauer's awareness of the dual worlds of fantasy and reality in children's lives is especially evident in *Fog Magic.* The story is about eleven-year-old Greta, who lives in a modern community on one side of a mountain and is fascinated with a lost fishing village on the other side. The story alternates between the realities of the present and what Greta imagines as the past, demonstrating the necessity of accepting both.

Speaking of *Fog Magic,* a *Book Week* critic commented, "This is not a book for every child, but to the right child it will bring beauty, magic, tenderness, and a brave philosophy of living." *Christian Science Monitor* called it "an exquisite book, one that has great rewards for the imaginative reader." Added a critic for *Saturday Review of Literature:* "Sometimes a book comes along that creates a sort of nostalgia in adults; a longing to go back to a time when it would have had free entry into their mind and imagination. Such a book is *Fog Magic*. . . . There is nothing about this book that is 'creepy' or unhealthy. Miss Sauer's feeling for Nova Scotia and its people gives the past as well as the present warmth and humor and reality."

In *The Light at Tern Rock,* Ronnie and his aunt enjoy staying in a lighthouse while the owner is away on vacation. In a review of *The Light at Tern Rock,* a *New York Times* critic wrote, "This is a quiet story, lacking inaction, and will be chiefly appreciated by thoughtful readers who are receptive to its poetic sense of the sea." Noted the *Saturday Review of Literature* contributor, "As in her *Fog Magic,* Miss Sauer's wording sets an atmosphere that is strongly reinforced here in Georges Schrieber's beautiful drawings."

BIOGRAPHICAL/CRITICAL SOURCES:

BOOKS

Something about the Author, Volume 32, Gale, 1983.
Twentieth-Century Children's Writers, 4th edition, St. James Press, 1995.

PERIODICALS

Book Week, November 21, 1943.
Christian Science Monitor, November 15, 1943.
New York Times, December 2, 1951.
Saturday Review of Literature, November 13, 1943; November 10, 1951.

OBITUARIES:

BOOKS

Something about the Author, Volume 36, Gale, 1984.

PERIODICALS

Horn Book Magazine, October, 1983.
School Library Journal, October, 1983.*

* * *

SAUNDERS, James (Arthur) 1925-

PERSONAL: Born January 8, 1925, in London, England; son of Walter Percival (a painter) and Dorcas Geraldine (a homemaker; maiden name, Warren) Saunders; married Audrey Joy Cross (a teacher), June 16, 1951; children: Sarah, Jane, Matthew. *Education:* Attended University College, Southampton, 1946-49. *Politics:* "Humanist." *Religion:* "Left Wing."

ADDRESSES: Home—24 St. Stephens Gardens, East Twickenham, Middlesex TW1 2LS, England. *Agent*—Casarolto Ramsay Ltd., 60-66 Waldorf St., London W1V 3HP, England.

CAREER: Taught English in London; taught chemistry at a private tutorial establishment, 1951-63; full-time writer, 1964—.

AWARDS, HONORS: Arts Council of Great Britain drama bursary, 1960 and 1984; *Evening Standard* Drama Award, 1963, for *Next Time I'll Sing to You;* Writers Guild Television Adaptation Award, 1966; Arts Council of Great Britain major bursary, 1984; British Broadcasting Corporation (BBC) Radio Play Award, 1986, for *Menocchio;* Moliere Award, 1990, for *Fall.*

WRITINGS:

PLAYS

Cinderella Comes of Age (three-act), produced in London at Torch Theatre, 1949.
Moonshine (three-act), produced in London at "Q" Theatre, 1955.
Dog Accident (one-act), broadcast on BBC-Radio, 1958, revised version produced in London at Marble Arch Theatre, 1969.
Alas, Poor Fred: A Duologue in the Style of Ionesco (one-act; produced in Scarborough, England, at Theatre-in-the-Round, 1959), Studio Theatre, 1960.
The Ark (two-act; music by Geoffrey Wright), produced in London at Westminster Theatre, 1959.
Barnstable (one-act; broadcast in 1959, produced in Dublin, Ireland, 1960, produced in London at Questors Theatre, 1960), Samuel French, 1961 (also see below).
Return to a City (one-act; also see below), produced in London at Questors Theatre, 1960.
Committal, (one-act; also see below), produced in London at Questors Theatre, 1960.
Ends and Echoes: Barnstable, Committal, Return to a City, produced in London at Questors Theatre, 1960.
A Slight Accident (one-act), produced in Nottingham, England, at Playhouse Theatre, 1961.
Double, Double (one-act; produced in London at Vanbrugh Theatre, 1962), Samuel French, 1964.
Who Was Hilary Maconochie? (one-act), produced in London at Questors Theatre, 1963.

Next Time I'll Sing to You (two-act; produced in London at Questors Theatre, 1962, produced in London at Criterion Theatre, 1963, produced in New York City at Phoenix Theater, 1963), Random House, 1963.

A Scent of Flowers (three-act; produced in London at Duke of York's Theatre, 1964; produced in New York City at Martinique Theater, 1969), Random House, 1965.

The Pedagogue (one-act), broadcast on BBC-Radio, 1964, produced in London at Questors Theatre, 1964.

Neighbours (one-act), produced in London at Questors Theatre, 1964.

(With others) *Triangle* (one-act), produced in Glasgow, Scotland, at Close Theatre, 1965, and in London at Mayfair Theatre, 1983.

(With Iris Murdoch) *The Italian Girl* (adapted from a novel by Murdoch; two-act; produced in Bristol, England, at Theatre Royal, 1967), Samuel French, 1969.

Trio (one-act), first produced in Edinburgh, Scotland, at Traverse Theatre, 1967.

Opus (two-act), produced in Hamburg, West Germany, at Scauspielhaus Theatre, 1967, and in Loughton, England, 1971.

The Travails of Sancho Panza (juvenile; two-act; adapted from the novel *Don Quixote* by Cervantes; produced in London at National Theatre, 1969), Heinemann, 1969.

Haven (one-act; produced in London at Comedy Theatre, 1969; later produced under the titles *A Man's Best Friend* and *Mixed Doubles*), Methuen, 1970.

The Borage Pigeon Affair (two-act; produced in London at Questors Theatre, 1969), Deutsch, 1970.

After Liverpool (one-act; broadcast on BBC-Radio, 1971; produced in London at Almost Free Theatre, 1971; produced in New York City, 1973), Samuel French, 1973.

Savoury Meringue (one-act), produced in London at Almost Free Theatre, 1971.

Games (one-act; produced in London at Almost Free Theatre, 1971; produced in New York City, 1973), Samuel French, 1973.

Hans Kohlhaas (two-act; adapted from the story by Heinrich Von Kleist), produced in London at Greenwich Theatre, 1972.

Bye Bye Blues (one-act), produced in Richmond, England, at Orange Tree Theatre, 1973.

Poor Old Simon (one-act), produced in Horsham, England, at Capitol Theatre, 1973.

Random Moments in a May Garden (one-act), broadcast by BBC-TV, 1973, produced in Richmond at Orange Tree Theatre, 1977.

A Journey to London (two-act; adapted from the play by John Vanbrugh), produced in London at Greenwich Theatre, 1975.

Play for Yesterday (one-act), produced in Richmond at Orange Tree Theatre, 1975.

The Island (two-act), produced in London at Questors Theater, 1975.

Squat (one-act), produced in Richmond at Orange Tree Theatre, 1976.

Mrs. Scout and the Future of Western Civilisation (one-act), produced in Richmond at Orange Tree Theatre, 1976.

Bodies (two-act; produced in Richmond at Orange Tree Theatre, 1977, produced in London at Ambassadors Theatre, 1984), Dramatists Play Service (New York), 1979.

Player Piano (two-act; adapted from the novel by Kurt Vonnegut, Jr.), produced in London at Almost Free Theatre, 1978.

Birdsong (one-act), produced in Richmond at Orange Tree Theatre, 1979, produced in New York City, 1989.

The Caucasian Chalk Circle (adaptation of the play by Bertolt Brecht), produced in Richmond, Surrey, 1979.

The Mountain, produced in Bristol, 1979.

The Girl in Melanie Klein (two-act), produced in Watford, England, at Palace Theatre, 1980.

Fall (two-act; produced in Richmond at Orange Tree Theatre, 1981, produced in London at Hampstead Theatre, 1984), Samuel French, 1985.

Nothing to Declare, broadcast on BBC-Radio, 1982, produced in Richmond at Orange Tree Theatre, 1983.

Scandella (two-act), produced in Richmond at Orange Tree Theatre, 1985.

Redevelopment (adaptation of the play by Vaclav Havel; produced in Richmond, Surrey, 1990), Faber (London), 1990.

Making It Better (two-act), produced in Paris, revised version produced in London at Criterion Theatre, 1992.

RADIO PLAYS

Author of radio plays *Love and a Limousine,* 1952; *The Drop Too Much,* 1952; *Nimrod's Oak,* 1953; *Women Are So Unreasonable,* 1957; *Dog Accident,* 1958; *Barnstable,* 1959; *Gimlet,* 1963; *It's Not the Game It Was,* 1964; *Pay As You Go,* 1965; *After Liverpool,* 1971; *Random Moments in a May Garden,* 1974; *The Last Black and White Midnight Movie,* 1979; *The Flower Case,* BBC-Radio, 1982; *A Suspension of Mercy,* adapted from the novel by Patricia Highsmith,

1983; *Menocchio,* 1985; *The Confidential Agent,* adapted from the novel by Graham Greene, 1987; *Headlong Hall,* adapted from the novel by Thomas Love Peacock, 1988; *Making It Better,* 1991; and *The Three Musketeers,* adapted from the novel by Alexander Dumas, 1993.

TELEVISION PLAYS

Watch Me, I'm a Bird, Granada, 1964.
Plastic People, London Weekend Television, 1969.
Bloomers, BBC-TV, 1979.

Also author of *Just You Wait,* 1963; *The White Stocking, New Eve and Old Adam, Tickets Please, Monkey Nuts, Two Blue Birds, In Love,* and *The Blue Moccasins,* all adapted from works by D. H. Lawrence, 1966-67; *The Beast in the Jungle,* adapted from the story by Henry James, 1969; *The Unconquered,* 1970; *Craven Arms,* adapted from the story by A. E. Coppard, 1972; *The Mill,* 1972; *The Black Dog,* 1972; *Blind Love,* adapted from the story by V. S. Pritchett, 1977; *The Healing Nightmare,* 1977; *People Like Us,* with Susan Pieat and Ian Curteis, adapted from the novel by R. F. Delderfield, 1978; and *The Magic Bathroom,* 1987.

SCREENPLAYS

The Sailor's Return (adapted from the novel by David Garnett), Osprey, 1970.

Also author of *The Captain's Doll,* adapted from the story by D. H. Lawrence, 1980.

COLLECTIONS

Neighbours and Other Plays, Deutsch, 1968.
Play Ten: Ten Short Plays by James Saunders, edited by Robin Rook, Edward Arnold, 1977.
Savoury Meringue and Other Plays, Amber Lane Press, 1980.
Bye Bye Blues and Other Plays, Amber Lane Press, 1980.

OTHER

Also author of *Retreat,* 1995.

SIDELIGHTS: One of Britain's leading experimental playwrights for several decades, James Saunders is known for both his absurdist comedies and his sociopolitically informed dramas. Many of his works focus on the nature of theatre and bring attention to the act of performing and the limits of an artificial form to render meaning to a theme. Saunders worked as a teacher in England during the 1950s and 1960s, and wrote plays in his spare time. He first attracted critical attention with witty one-act productions. Buoyed by the success of *Next Time I'll Sing to You,* which was produced in 1963 on London's West End, Saunders left teaching to devote himself exclusively to play writing. He has subsequently produced numerous experimental plays which have been hailed for their diversity of style. According to Dennis Brown in *Dictionary of Literary Biography,* "James Saunders is one of the most challenging experimentalists of the post-World War II new wave of British drama."

Among Saunders's early absurdist comedies is *Dog Accident.* The play, which examines the reactions of people as they pass a dog being hit by a car, explores people's unwillingness to become involved with things that do not immediately concern them. Saunders followed *Dog Accident* with such plays as 1959's *Alas, Poor Fred: A Duologue in the Style of Ionesco,* containing a dialogue between a married couple about a man who has somehow been cut in half (this symbolizes the couple's lives and love), and 1961's *A Slight Accident,* a black comedy about three people whose orderly lives are upset by an unusual occurrence.

The two-act *Next Time I'll Sing to You* was produced in 1962 and established Saunders as a prominent playwright in the English theater. Based on a theme from Raleigh Trevelyan's book *A Hermit Disclosed,* the play concerns the life of an actual hermit, Jimmy Mason, who died in 1942. The play avoids focus on any direct discussion of Mason, implying instead that one person cannot know another; the self can only know itself. Set up as a play within a play, *A Hermit Disclosed* boasts four actors who meet nightly only to discover the implausibility of unearthing the reasons for Mason's solitary existence. An unnamed actor plays Mason and periodically comments on his peers' ideas about him. Critics praised the play for its self-conscious theatricality, stylized dialogue, and existentialist humor. Deeming the play "lively, engaging, and at times very funny," Brown remarked that *Next Time I'll Sing to You* demonstrates Saunders's "place in the absurdist tradition and his eloquent originality." Similarly, Tish Dace of *Contemporary Dramatists* compared this work with Samuel Beckett's classic absurdist play, *Waiting for Godot.* She found that both use "off-beat characters and structure to raise fundamental human questions. After we wonder why Mason lived alone—or, indeed, why he lived—we come to wonder whether his solitude differs only superficially from our own."

After *Next Time I'll Sing to You* Saunders returned to writing one-act plays. *The Pedagogue,* produced in 1964, concerns a teacher who implores his students to respect authority and whose personality is eclipsed by his generic role as a teacher. *Neighbours,* also produced in 1964, examines racial tensions between a black man and a white woman who lodge in the same house. The play examines the phenomena of whites who profess to be liberals but harbor only surface tolerance and the myth of black sexual prowess. The play was praised for its convincing characterization, tight plot structure, and poignant dialogue. *Neighbours,* according to Ronald Bryden in *Observer Review,* is "sensitive [and] intelligent . . . with something genuinely profound to say about living." A Canadian Broadcasting Corporation (CBC) production of *Neighbours* elicited criticism from some white viewers who protested scenes in which the black and white actors kissed.

1964 also ushered in the production of Saunders's experimental three-act play, *A Scent of Flowers.* This work relates the story of Zoe, a young middle-class girl who at the beginning of the play commits suicide. Told in retrospect—with Zoe, dead, appearing on stage, speaking to the audience, and enacting scenes from her past—the audience learns of Zoe's failed love affair with a married college instructor. While trying to cope with her heartbreak, Zoe seeks out counseling from family members. Her father refuses to approach the topic, her stepmother tries to impose her ideals on Zoe, and her stepbrother is not an ideal candidate because he is in love with Zoe. In *A Scent of Flowers,* Zoe finally has a captive audience—ironically consisting of mortician's assistants—with whom to examine the family's indifference that led to her suicide.

A Scent of Flowers elicited mixed reviews. The comments of Julius Novick in the *Village Voice* summarized several critics' feelings: "On the whole this is an oddly uneven play. The writing, almost always self-conscious and highly wrought, is at various moments elegant, exquisite, witty, whimsical, sentimental, obvious, and finickingly pretentious." According to a writer in *Variety,* the work is "a metaphysical muddle at times, but more often a gracefully written, dramatically effective, potentially touching work." While displeased with the "monologues' occasional turgidity," Alan Bunce in *Christian Science Monitor* declared that this "unabashedly poetic play . . . lends a refreshing note of literacy and emotional sensitivity to a harsh Off-Broadway season." And, unqualified in her praise for the playwright, Marilyn Stasio in *Cue* proclaimed: "Saunders constructs an absorbing story. . . . [He] is a considerable talent."

Near the end of the 1960s, Saunders began to focus on sociopolitical concerns. His 1969 *The Borage Pigeon Affair* targets petty bureaucracy as it relates a furor amidst citizens of a small town who bicker over the merits of pigeons. Some residents consider the birds engaging pets, others think they are a nuisance. A television crew, led by a director named Loathing, documents the two town councillors debating the issue. Labeled a "bold, hilarious" satire by Brown, the play is an appeal for sane social values. Saunders's 1971 *Games* is more serious in tone. The work introduces four actors who rehearse a play based on the My Lai massacre, in which that village's Vietnamese residents were slaughtered by American soldiers during the Vietnam War. Exploring the meaning and motivation of the massacre, the characters in *Games* discuss—amongst themselves and with the members of the audience—how the reality of the event can best be conveyed through the stage reproduction.

In the early and mid-1970s, Saunders continued to produce plays, including *Bye Bye Blues, The Island,* and *Squat.* It was not until the 1977 production of *Bodies,* however, that he realized his greatest commercial success. With an absurdist perspective, the work depicts two couples who, many years earlier, had affairs with each others' mates. The first act portrays each character reminiscing about the affair and anxiously awaiting the foursome's reunion. One couple, Anne and Merwyn, is guilty and upset over lost passion and anxious about reaching middle age. David and Helen moved to the United States and took part in therapy to come to terms with the affair. This duo proclaims to be freed from emotion, adhering to the philosophy that humans are merely bodies wherein happiness and unhappiness do not exist. The play questions whether the pain of emotions and the search for meaning is preferable to the dull acceptance of life's trials.

Bodies is "one of the most stimulating new plays of the . . . season," maintained Mel Gussow in *New York Times.* Noting the work's "playfulness [that] warps into abrasiveness," Gussow compared the play to Edward Albee's *Who's Afraid of Virginia Woolf?* "Mr. Saunders," declared Gussow, "surprises with his ferocity." Although Gussow thought *Bodies* "too wordy," the critic continued, "The play is an excoriating investigation of man's responsibility to himself and to others, analyzing the conflicts between conscience and consciousness, the creative impulse and psychological adjustment." Brown also commended the work, stating: "If powerful intellectual dialectic, subtly orchestrated tension, and a commanding central character proclaim a play's worth, then *Bodies* has a strong claim to being [Saunders's] best play to date."

Saunders continued to write plays in the 1980s and into the 1990s. Among his later works is *Fall,* a study of a mother and her three daughters conversing while the father nears death. Well-received, the play "puts certain kinds of 'lifestyle' under examination, depicting the four main characters with a deliberately contrived detachment which allows us to evaluate self-involvement," commented Diana Devlin in *Drama.*

Saunders once told *CA:* "Playwrights, whether they like it or not, reflect the attitudes and concerns of their times. Thus I went through an absurdist phase with existentialist attitudes in the late 1950s to middle 1960s; a retreat from the complexities of the individual to an examination of the shell as social camouflage or protection in the middle 1960s; an interest in theatre as an instrument of democracy—in other words, as a tool for expressing views of society—in the late 1960s to early 1970s. This last interest went naturally with an interest in fringe theater, which I have kept; I have worked closely for the last ten years with a pub-theatre, The Richmond Fringe at the Orange Tree, one of the best of London's fringe theaters. As for present work, no one can encapsulate the history of their own time. I shall know, I suppose, in ten years time what I've been doing. Meanwhile, I write plays."

BIOGRAPHICAL/CRITICAL SOURCES:

BOOKS

Contemporary Dramatists, 5th edition, St. James Press, 1993.

Dictionary of Literary Biography, Volume 13: *British Dramatists since World War II,* Gale, 1982.

PERIODICALS

Christian Science Monitor, November 10, 1969; January 7, 1970.

Cue, November 1, 1969.

Drama, fall, 1985, p. 45.

Nation, November 17, 1969.

Newsweek, November 3, 1969.

New York, November 3, 1969, p. 63.

New Yorker, November 9, 1969.

New York Times, July 22, 1979.

Observer Review, May 14, 1967.

Plays and Players, February, 1970.

Punch, December 31, 1969.

Show Business, November 1, 1969.

Times (London), September 8, 1984.

Variety, November 5, 1969; January 28, 1970.

Village Voice, October 30, 1969.*

* * *

SAUNDERS, Jean 1932-
(Jean Innes, Sally Blake, Rowena Summers)

PERSONAL: Born February 8, 1932, in London, England; daughter of John Alexander and Minnie (Wheatley) Innes; married Geoffrey Saunders(a lecturer), September 20, 1952; children: Barry Clive, Janet Saunders Underhay, Ann Lesley Saunders Scribbins. *Education:* Educated in Weston-super-Mare, Avon, England.

ADDRESSES: Home—The Hayes, 23 Hobbiton Road, Weston-super-Mare, Somerset BS22 0HP, England. *Agent*—Curtis Brown Ltd., 162-168 Regent St., London W1R 5TA, England.

CAREER: Writer. Medical Research Council, Clevedon, Avon, England, assay laboratory assistant, 1948-54; writer, 1965—.

MEMBER: Romantic Novelists Association (chair, 1993—), Romance Writers of America, West Country Writers Association.

WRITINGS:

ADULT NOVELS

The Tender Trap, Woman's Weekly, 1977.

Lady of the Manor, Woman's Weekly, 1979.

Cobden's Cottage, Woman's Weekly, 1979.

Rainbow's End, Woman's Weekly, 1979.

The Enchantment of Merrowporth, Cameo, 1980.

The Kissing Time, Simon & Schuster, 1981.

Love's Sweet Music, Simon & Schuster, 1983.

The Language of Love, Simon & Schuster, 1983.

Taste the Wine, Simon & Schuster, 1984.

Partners in Love, Simon & Schuster, 1984.

Scarlet Rebel, Ballantine, 1984.

Golden Destiny, Pocket Books, 1986.

The Craft of Writing Romance (nonfiction), Allison & Busby (London), 1986.

For Better for Worse, Book Incentives for Premier Brands (London), 1988.

The Man from Venice, Book Incentives for Premier Brands, 1988.

Nightingale Valley, Book Incentives for Premier Brands, 1988.

Portrait of Sarah, Book Incentives for Premier Brands, 1988.

Writing Step by Step (nonfiction), Allison & Busby, 1988.
All in the April Morning, W. H. Allen (London), 1989; Zebra (New York), 1993.
The Bannister Girls, Grafton (London), 1991.
How to Create Fictional Characters, Allison & Busby, 1992.
To Love and Honour, Grafton, 1992.
How to Research Your Novel, Allison & Busby, 1993.
With This Ring, Grafton, 1993.
How to Write Realistic Dialogue, Allison & Busby, 1994.
Journey's End, G. K. Hall (Thorndike, ME), 1997.

Also author of *Dangerous Enchantment,* 1980; *The Spider's Web,* 1982; and *Wives, Friends and Lovers,* 1996.

YOUNG ADULT NOVELS

The Fugitives, Heinemann, 1974.
Only Yesterday, Scholastic Book Services, 1975.
Nightmare, Heinemann, 1977.
Roses All the Way, Heinemann, 1978.
The Tally-Man, Dreyers Forlag, 1979.
Anchor Man, Heinemann, 1980.

UNDER NAME JEAN INNES

Ashton's Folly, R. Hale, 1975.
Sands of Lamanna, R. Hale, 1975.
The Golden God, R. Hale, 1975.
The Whispering Dark, R. Hale, 1976.
White Blooms of Yarrow, R. Hale, 1976.
Boskelly's Bride, R. Hale, 1976.
The Wishing Stone, R. Hale, 1976.
The Dark Stranger, R. Hale, 1979.
Silver Lady, R. Hale, 1981.
Legacy of Love, R. Hale, 1982.
Seeker of Dreams, R. Hale, 1983.
Enchanted Island, Bantam, 1983.
Scent of Jasmine, Bantam, 1983.
Buccaneer's Bride, Zebra, 1989.
Blackmaddie, Zebra, 1990.
Dream Lover, Zebra, 1990.
Golden Captive, Zebra, 1990.
Secret Touch, Zebra, 1992.
Tropical Fire, Zebra, 1992.

UNDER PSEUDONYM SALLY BLAKE

The Devil's Kiss, Macdonald/Futura, 1981.
Moonlight Mirage, Macdonald/Futura, 1982.
Outback Woman, Mills & Boon (London), 1989.
Lady of Spain, Mills & Boon, 1990.
Far Distant Shores, Mills & Boon, 1991.
A Royal Summer, Mills & Boon, 1992.
House of Secrets, Mills & Boon, 1993.

UNDER PSEUDONYM ROWENA SUMMERS

Blackmaddie (historical novel), Hamlyn, 1980.
The Savage Moon, Sphere, 1982.
The Sweet Red Earth, Sphere, 1983.
Willow Harvest, Sphere, 1985.
Killigrew Clay ("Cornish Trilogy"), Sphere, 1986.
Clay Country ("Cornish Trilogy"), Severn House, 1987.
Family Ties ("Cornish Trilogy"), Severn House, 1988.
Highland Heritage, Mills & Boon, 1991.
Angel of the Evening, Severn House, 1991.
Velvet Dawn, Severn House, 1991.
Bargain Bride, Severn House, 1993.
Ellie's Island, Severn House, 1993.
Hidden Currents, Severn House, 1994.
Family Shadows, Severn House, 1995.
Safe Haven, Severn House, 1996.

Also author of *Woman of Property,* 1994.

OTHER

Contributor of more than six hundred short stories to women's magazines, including *Woman's Story, Woman's Own, My Weekly, Hers, Love Affair, True,* and *Loving.*

SIDELIGHTS: Jean Saunders's romance novels depict the atmospheres and attitudes of the historical periods in which they are set. Saunders conducts exhaustive research in preparation for her novels, and when she encounters discrepancies, she must determine which account seems most plausible. W. H. Bradley of *Twentieth-Century Romance and Historical Writers* commented that in *Scarlet Rebel,* Saunders "succeeds in conveying the feel of the period while continually progressing the gripping story of an intensely emotional romance between the fictional couple who are supporting the Young Pretender [Charles Edward Stuart] in his bid for the English throne. The graphic battle scenes add an extra dimension to the romantic storyline."

All in the April Morning begins with the 1906 San Francisco earthquake, which orphans Bridget, an Irish immigrant girl. She is determined to return to Ireland but is unable to find a way and eventually finds herself trapped and miserable in marriage. When her husband dies, leaving her with a daughter and pregnant with a son, she is finally able to return to Ireland. As the story continues into World War II, Bridget and her daughter are in constant conflict, which intensifies when her daughter falls in love with an airman from San Francisco, a place Bridget never wants to see again. During an air raid, Bridget is bombarded with painful memories of the earthquake and she and her daughter are brought closer together. The story ends with Bridget newly married and going back to San Francisco to see her grandson. Bradley observed, "This novel, which among other things explores with convincing authority and particular sensitivity the complex and moving relationship between the heroine and her daughter, demonstrates how Saunders has gradually expanded and developed her talents and ability to deal successfully with stronger themes and more complex relationships."

Saunders writes gothic novels under the pseudonym Jean Innes. Again, her trademark is her ability to evoke atmosphere. *Sands of Lamanna* takes place in nineteenth-century Cornwall, a setting characterized by rugged countryside, gray stone houses, folklore, and superstition. The characters, described by Bradley as "clear and distinct," include the young gypsy Wenna and her lover, both of whom are the objects of Wenna's father's curse. The story includes murder, a trial, and imprisonment, but in the end good wins over evil.

Saunders told *CA:* "I think 'staying power' is as vital as anything to an aspiring author. In twenty years of writing, my determination to 'get there' has never wavered, despite rejections and setbacks. I give many talks to writers' groups and always emphasize this aspect of the job. And it *is* a job for me—not a little hobby!

"When people tell me they couldn't put my book down, I know I've succeeded in what I set out to do. I have a great feel for backgrounds and really live out my characters' lives as I write. At the end of my longest novel, *The Savage Moon,* I was emotionally drained. This book is set in the United States during the Civil War, and when I recently visited Washington, D.C., and actually took a boat trip on the Potomac River, I felt extremely emotional about being where my characters had lived.

"Every year I go to the Writers Summer School in England and to various weekend conferences, both to listen and learn and to give talks myself. I think it's the biggest mistake for a writer to believe there's nothing more to learn—and there's nothing so enjoyable as meeting other writers and talking 'shop.'

"I'm told I'm a prolific writer. I don't find it difficult to keep doing a job that I love, though I admit it takes self-discipline to sit at a desk when the sun is shining outside, and there are still blank moments when the ideas don't come, but fortunately not too many. The more I write, the more receptive I become to ideas and to the way of communicating them on paper for other people's enjoyment as well as my own."

BIOGRAPHICAL/CRITICAL SOURCES:

BOOKS

Twentieth-Century Romance and Historical Writers, 3rd edition, St. James Press, 1994.

PERIODICALS

Booklist, December 15, 1996, p. 710.
Publishers Weekly, December 2, 1996, p. 42.*

* * *

SAVAGE, Ernest 1918-

PERSONAL: Born March 25, 1918, in Detroit, MI; son of Donald Ernest (in insurance) and Irene (Coleman) Savage; married Elizabeth Bissell, May 16, 1942 (divorced, 1962); married Jean Silack, February 19, 1965; children: Charlotte Anne Benabdallah. *Education:* Attended University of Michigan, 1936-38. *Politics:* Republican. *Religion:* Agnostic. *Avocational interests:* Fishing, gardening, walking, workshop projects, "things one does with one's hands and feet."

ADDRESSES: Home—6104 Oliver Rd., Paradise, CA 95969. *Agent*—Scott Meredith Literary Agency, Inc., 845 Third Ave., New York, NY 10022.

CAREER: Has worked as salesman, taxi driver, sailor, and fisherman; from 1945 to 1977 worked in real estate, land development, and city planning; was president of Hesperia Water Co.; was resident manager in Madrid, Spain, 1961-63; writer, 1977—. *Military service:* U.S. Army, 1941-44; became first lieutenant.

AWARDS, HONORS: Received nominations from Mystery Writers of America, 1981, for best short story for "Miracle Day" and 1982, for best novel for *Two If by Sea.*

WRITINGS:

Two If by Sea, Scribner, 1982.

Contributor of short stories to Ellery Queen's and Alfred Hitchcock's mystery magazines.

SIDELIGHTS: Ernest Savage's career as a writer began with short stories in the detective and mystery genres. Because he turned to writing in his fifties, Savage understands the decision to change careers relatively late in life. It is fitting, then, that Savage's series character is a detective named Sam Train who has left the police force after nineteen years of service. Train finds that violence can occur anywhere, not just in urban settings, and he frequently relies on his instincts rather than deductive reasoning to solve crimes. Recurring themes in Savage's short fiction include the plight of the elderly, sailing, and the city life of San Francisco.

Savage's novel, *Two If by Sea,* is the story of a man aboard a passenger and freight ship who seeks to avenge the deaths of his wife and child. The novel is generally considered a suspense story but, as Newgate Callendar explained in *New York Times Book Review,* "It is more than that." Callendar cited "the author's sophistication and real skill in characterization" and called *Two If by Sea* "an unusually powerful first novel, . . . written with Style," and a "tour de force." In *Twentieth-Century Crime and Mystery Writers,* Marvin Lachman added, "Like his shorter work, it [*Two If by Sea*] shows a mature writer who, in a short time, has brought new vitality to the hardboiled school."

Savage once told *CA:* "I am a writer of fiction, and as such my first obligation is to entertain. But if in the course of my turns on stage I should stumble on some fundamental truth, or transfigure a life or two, or reacquaint some lonely reader with his forgotten heart, so much the better. But still, let me be brief about it all; and if it works, humble."

BIOGRAPHICAL/CRITICAL SOURCES:

BOOKS

Twentieth-Century Crime and Mystery Writers, 3rd edition, St. James Press, 1991.

PERIODICALS

Kirkus Reviews, February 1, 1982.
New York Times Book Review, September 12, 1982.
Publishers Weekly, February 26, 1982.*

* * *

SAVILLE, (Leonard) Malcolm 1901-1982

PERSONAL: Born February 21, 1901, in Hastings, Sussex, England; died June 30, 1982; son of Ernest Vivian (a bookseller) and Fanny Ethel (Hayes) Saville; married Dorothy May McCoy, 1926; children: two sons, two daughters. *Education:* Educated in England.

CAREER: Cassell & Co. (publishers), London, England, in publicity, 1920-22; Amalgamated Press, London, sales promotion manager, 1922-36; George Newnes Co. (publishers), London, sales promotion manager, 1936-40; *My Garden* (magazine), London, associate editor, 1947-52; Kemsley Newspapers, London, writer, 1952-55; George Newnes & C. Arthur Peterson Ltd. (publishers), London, editor or "Sunny Stories" series, 1955-66, and general books editor, 1957-80; full-time writer, 1966-82.

MEMBER: Savage Club (London).

WRITINGS:

ALL JUVENILE, EXCEPT AS NOTED

Mystery at Witchend, George Newnes, 1943, published as *Spy in the Hills,* Farrar, 1945.
Country Scrap Book for Boys and Girls, National Magazine Co., 1944, 3rd edition, Gramol, 1946.
Seven White Gates, George Newnes, 1944.
The Gay Dolphin Adventure, George Newnes, 1945.
Open-Air Scrap Book for Boys and Girls, Gramol, 1945.
Trouble at Townsend, Transatlantic, 1945.
Jane's Country Year, George Newnes, 1946, 3rd edition, 1953.
Seaside Scrap Book, Gramol, 1946.
The Riddle of the Painted Box, Transatlantic, 1947.
The Secret of Grey Walls, George Newnes, 1947, revised edition, Armada, 1975.
Redshank's Warning, Lutterworth, 1948.
Two Fair Plaits, Lutterworth, 1948.
Lone Pine Five, George Newnes, 1949.
Strangers at Snowfell, Lutterworth, 1949.
The Adventure of the Life-Boat Service, Macdonald & Co., 1950.
The Flying Fish Adventure, J. Murray, 1950.
The Master of Maryknoll, Evans Bros., 1950, revised edition, Collins, 1971.
The Sign of the Alpine Rose, Lutterworth, 1950.
All Summer Through, Hodder & Stoughton, 1951.
The Elusive Grasshopper, George Newnes, 1951.
The Buckinghams at Ravenswyke, Evans Bros., 1952, revised edition, Collins, 1971.
Coronation Gift Book, Pitkin, 1952.
The Luck of Sallowby, Lutterworth, 1952.
The Ambermere Treasure, Lutterworth, 1953, published as *The Secret of the Ambermere Treasure,* Criterion, 1967.

Christmas at Nettleford, Hodder & Stoughton, 1953.
The Neglected Mountain, George Newnes, 1953.
The Secret of the Hidden Pool, J. Murray, 1953.
The Long Passage, Evans Bros., 1954.
Spring Comes to Nettleford, Hodder & Stoughton, 1954.
Saucers over the Moor, George Newnes, 1955, revised edition, Collins, 1972.
The Secret of Buzzard Scar, Hodder & Stoughton, 1955.
Where the Bus Stopped, Basil Blackwell, 1955.
Young Johnnie Bimbo, J. Murray, 1956.
Wings over Witchend, George Newnes, 1956.
The Fourth Key, J. Murray, 1957.
Lone Pine London, George Newnes, 1957.
Treasure at the Mill, George Newnes, 1957.
King of Kings, Nelson, 1958.
The Secret of the Gorge, George Newnes, 1958.
Four-and-Twenty Blackbirds, George Newnes, 1959, as *The Secret of Galleybird Pit,* Armada, 1968.
Mystery Mine, George Newnes, 1959.
Small Creatures, Edmund Ward, 1959.
Sea Witch Comes Home, George Newnes, 1960.
Malcolm Saville's Country Book, Cassell, 1961.
Malcolm Saville's Seaside Book, Cassell, 1962.
Not Scarlet but Gold, George Newnes, 1962.
A Palace for the Buckinghams, Evans Bros., 1963.
Three Towers in Tuscany, Heinemann, 1963.
The Purple Valley, Heinemann, 1964.
Treasure at Amorys, George Newnes, 1964.
Dark Danger, Heinemann, 1965.
The Man with Three Fingers, George Newnes, 1966, revised edition, Collins, 1971.
The Thin Grey Man, St. Martin's 1966.
White Fire, Heinemann, 1966.
Come to London, Heinemann, 1967.
Strange Story, Mowbray, 1967.
Power of Three, Heinemann, 1968.
Come to Cornwall, Benn, 1969.
Come to Devon, Benn, 1969.
Rye Royal, Collins, 1969.
Come to Somerset, Benn, 1970.
Dagger and the Flame, Heinemann, 1970.
Strangers at Witchend, Collins, 1970.
Good Dog Dandy, Collins, 1971.
The Secret of Villa Rosa, Collins, 1971.
Where's My Girl?, Collins, 1972.
Diamond in the Sky, Collins, 1975.
Eat What You Grow, Carousel, 1975.
Portrait of Rye (adult nonfiction), Henry Goulden, 1976.
Countryside Quiz, Carousel, 1978.
Home to Witchend, Armada, 1978.
Marston, Master Spy, Heinemann, 1978.
Wonder Why Book of Exploring a Wood, Transworld, 1978.
Wonder Why Book of Exploring the Seashore, Transworld, 1979.
(Editor) *Words for All Seasons* (anthology), Lutterworth, 1979.
Wonder Why Book of Wild Flowers through the Year, Transworld, 1980.
The Seashore Quiz, Carousel, 1981.

Also author of *El Nino Quiere Saber: Explorando Un Bosque,* 1984, *The Roman Treasure Mystery,* and *See How It Grows.* Author of "Susan and Bill" series, published by Thomas Nelson: *Susan and Bill and the Ivy Clad Oak,* 1954; *. . . and the Wolf Dog,* 1954; *. . . and the Golden Clock,* 1955; *. . . and the Vanishing Boy,* 1955; *. . . and the Saucy Kate,* 1956; *. . . and the Bright Star Circus,* 1960; *. . . and the Pirates Bold,* 1961. Also author of *Susan and Bill and the Dark Stranger.*

SIDELIGHTS: Malcolm Saville began writing books for young people in 1942. The son of a bookseller, he was exposed from childhood to books and reading. Consequently, it was no surprise when he pursued a career in publishing, later becoming a full-time writer.

Saville's first book, *Mystery at Witchend,* was written in installments while he was employed by a London publisher. Each installment was sent to his wife and children who were staying in Shropshire for the duration of World War II. When *Mystery at Witchend* was finally published, it proved to be extremely successful and was serialized by the British Broadcasting Corp. (BBC-Radio). Gary D. Schmidt of *Dictionary of Literary Biography* wrote, "This mystery set the pattern for much of [Saville's] later work. In fact, it established a group of children, the Lone Piners, who would figure in subsequent novels such as *Seven White Gates* (1944), *The Gay Dolphin Adventure* (1945), and *The Secret of Grey Walls* (1947). In each, the group of five children thwart spies (whether against Britain's wartime interests or against its industries), bedevil kidnappers and jewel thieves, and bring to justice malefactors who forge paintings or threaten Britain's people. The central crises of the novels are reached as the group, or a part of the group, is threatened because of what has been discovered. It is the ingenuity of the Lone Piners that leads to their eventual rescue and the turning of the tables." The adventures of the Lone Pine Club grew to include twenty titles, some of which were broadcast by BBC-Radio.

Besides the books featuring the Lone Piners, Saville wrote a series for younger readers featuring the characters Susan and Bill, and a series of books for adolescents about the adventures of secret agent Marston Baines. The seven-book Marston Baines series is intended to provide the excitement of adult novels without explicit sex and violence. During the course of his career, Saville wrote more than eighty books, with the foremost objectives being to entertain and inform. Not confining himself to fiction, he also wrote books on nature, travel, and gardening.

In a critical analysis of Saville's work, Schmidt observed, "His stories, though active and intriguing, always seem to take longer than they should. His characters are eternally gathering to tell and retell their stories in ways that are patently unrealistic and even, at times, silly. If Saville could create believable characters, he was unable to have them interact believably, nor could he allow a story to unfold without having his characters continually butting in to take over the narrator's job.

"In addition to the clumsy and stilted narrative technique, Saville frequently demonstrates a flaw fatal to mysteries: a lack of subtlety in both his plot situations and depiction of relationships between characters. . . . To some measure the lack of subtlety may be expected in a mystery set for children. Those who are clearly villainous are pitted against those who are clearly virtuous. . . . Yet certainly one reason for Saville's inability to produce a lasting novel is that his plots are so completely predictable." On the other hand, Schmidt noted that it is "his characterization that marks Saville's work as worthy of attention for more than mere historical purposes. . . . Saville's other strength lies in his use of setting. . . . In *Mystery at Witchend,* he used the setting as more than just a backdrop—a pattern he would follow in later novels. When he begins the novel by having a native warn against the dangers of the wild terrain, he is suggesting that the setting will itself be a character. And so it is."

The greatest share of Saville's stories are set in England—the locale most familiar to him and his readers—although some tales for older readers are set in such places as Italy, France, Holland, Luxembourg, and Spain. "All fiction is influenced by 'place,' " he once told *CA.*

BIOGRAPHICAL/CRITICAL SOURCES:

BOOKS

Dictionary of Literary Biography, Volume 160: *British Children's Writers, 1914-1960,* Gale, 1996.

Something about the Author, Volume 23, Gale, 1981.

Twentieth-Century Children's Writers, 4th edition, St. James Press, 1995.

PERIODICALS

Country Life, November 19, 1979.

Observer, July 19, 1981.

Sussex Life, September, 1978.

Times Literary Supplement, July 24, 1969; October 9, 1969; September 18, 1970; June 15, 1973.

OBITUARIES:

BOOKS

Something about the Author, Volume 31, Gale, 1983.

Twentieth Century Children's Writers, St. Martin's, 1978.

Who Was Who among English and European Authors, 1921-1939, Gale, 1976.

PERIODICALS

Times (London), July 3, 1982.*

* * *

SAWYER, Robert J(ames) 1960-

PERSONAL: Born April 29, 1960, in Ottawa, Canada; son of John Arthur (a professor of economics) and Virginia (a statistician; maiden name, Peterson) Sawyer; married Carolyn Joan Clink (a customer service representative), December 22, 1984. *Education:* Ryerson Polytechnical Institute, B.A.A., 1982. *Politics:* Liberal. *Avocational interests:* Collecting fossils, computing.

ADDRESSES: Home and Office—7601 Bathurst St., No. 617, Thornhill, Ontario, Canada L4J 4H5. *Agent*—Richard Curtis Associates, 171 East 74th St., New York, NY 10021.

CAREER: Freelance writer, Toronto, Ontario, Canada, 1983—. Teaching assistant, Ryerson Polytechnical Institute, Toronto, 1982-83; consultant to business and governmental agencies on communications issues and public relations, Toronto, 1983-89; freelance radio documentary writer and narrator, Canadian Broadcasting Corporation (CBC), 1984—.

MEMBER: Science Fiction and Fantasy Writers of America (Canadian regional director, 1992-95), Mystery Writers of America, Crime Writers of Canada, Writers Union of Canada.

AWARDS, HONORS: Critic's Choice, Best Science Fiction Novel of the Year, *Magazine of Fantasy and Science Fiction,* 1991, and Aurora Award, Canadian Science Fiction and Fantasy Association, 1992, both for *Golden Fleece;* Best Books for the Teen Age citation, New York Public Library, 1992, and HOMer Award, CompuServe Science Fiction and Fantasy Forum, 1993, both for *Far-Seer;* HOMer Award, 1993, for *Fossil Hunter;* Writer's Reserve Grant, Ontario Arts Council, 1993, for *The Terminal Experiment.*

WRITINGS:

SCIENCE FICTION

Golden Fleece, Warner, 1990.
Far-Seer, Berkley/Ace, 1992.
Fossil Hunter, Berkley/Ace, 1993.
Foreigner, Berkley/Ace, 1994.
End of an Era, Berkley/Ace, 1994.
The Terminal Experiment (first serialized in *Analog*), HarperPrism, 1995.
Starplex, Ace Books (New York City), 1996.
Illegal Alien, Ace Books, 1997.
Frameshift, Tor (New York City), 1997.
Factoring Humanity, Tor, 1998.
Flashforward, Tor, 1999.

EDITOR

(With David Skene Melvin) *Crossing the Line: Canadian Mysteries with a Fantastic Twist,* Pottersfield, 1998.

SIDELIGHTS: Robert J. Sawyer writes science fiction novels that deal variously with computers running amok, dinosaurs reliving the Age of Enlightenment, time-traveling paleontologists, and space-age detectives. But his books are much more than the sum of their parts. A self-proclaimed rationalist, Sawyer charts a course of conflict between science and superstition in each of his novels, and the reader soon understands that the author is firmly on the side of science and its ability to illuminate truth in our world. Sawyer's novels are meant to stretch a reader's horizon of knowledge and make one think. They are, according to R. John Hayes in his *Quill & Quire* review of *Fossil Hunter,* "not just wonderful sf, [but] wonderful fiction." In addition to the adult audience for which they were originally published, the author's stories have captured a large young adult readership.

Sawyer attended Ryerson Polytechnical Institute in Toronto, where he studied script writing and broadcasting. After graduating, Sawyer stayed on as a teaching assistant for a year while his high school sweetheart, Carolyn Joan Clink, was finishing her degree. They married in 1984, and Sawyer never looked back to academe. He set up as a freelance writer until 1989, working with businesses and publishers in Toronto, doing everything from corporate newsletters to radio broadcasts. This apprenticeship taught him the value of deadlines and of the need to produce daily, as well as some of the fundamentals of good writing, such as voice and narrative technique.

"By 1989 I had enough in the bank to take a year off to write my first novel," the author said. He turned in the completed manuscript of the novel *Golden Fleece* to his agent, who sold it within six weeks. "I was incredibly lucky with that first one," Sawyer remarked. "I sent it to the right person at the right time." *Golden Fleece* is a science fiction mystery narrated from the point of view of a sentient computer named Jason. Reminiscent of HAL, the computer in Arthur C. Clarke's *2001,* Jason kills a member of the crew who was jeopardizing the ship's forty-seven-light-year mission. Most of the narration and the subsequent unraveling of the death is told through the computer's numerous lenses aboard the ship. "The result," writes Gordon Graham in *Quill & Quire,* "is a well-paced page-turner replete with hard science." Other reviewers agreed. Writing in *Books in Canada,* Gary Draper thought the execution of Sawyer's first novel was done "with wit and imagination."

"I got the idea from my time at Ryerson," Sawyer commented. "Working in the control room of the television studio, I became fascinated by how different the view of the selected shot on one of the monitors was from the chaos that was really taking place on the studio floor. I thought it would be an intriguing idea to write an entire novel from the point of view of a camera. And from that, there developed the idea of Jason and his fixed camera eyes and his limited view of reality." Sawyer, who has seen the movie version of *2001* two dozen times, also gives credit to that piece of fiction, but he blends it into something new and explores themes beyond simply the confusion of computer mentality with human consciousness. "There is a tendency in most writing to have a strong protagonist and antagonist," Sawyer explained. "The white hat and the black hat. I never really believed in this dichotomy. Never really believed that somebody would be all good or all villain. With two of the characters in *Golden Fleece,* Jason and Aaron, the ex-husband of the murdered female crew member, I wanted to make it unclear just who was the good guy and who the bad. I wanted to make it more like real life."

Though the reviews were mostly positive and the book garnered the prestigious Aurora Award, sales were poor. For his next novel, Sawyer had to go hunting for a new publisher. With this next book, he turned to a staple that had been nourishing him for many years: dinosaurs. Inverting the acronym of his old high school science fiction club, he came up with the name Afsan for his protagonist, a dinosaur in a world in which such creatures—known as Quintaglios—have evolved sophisticated intellects comparable to human consciousness. In the Quintaglio civilization there are cities, religions, rulers, and a budding science. Afsan is an apprentice to the court astrologer, and on a voyage to pay homage to the god of their religion, he discovers—with the aid of a new invention called the far-seer ortelescope—that his world is not the center of the universe after all. He learns, in fact, that the Quintaglio world is only a moon which eventually will crash into the planet it orbits. This Copernican discovery, described in minute detail, is bound to make Afsan a pariah to court and priests alike, much as it did for the historical astronomers Copernicus and Galileo in their time. Afsan's attempts to convince others of the truth of his scientific discoveries and the need for resettlement of the Quintaglios provides the engine for the novel that Graham described in another *Quill & Quire* review as "refreshingly original."

Far-Seer was submitted to Sawyer's agent, Richard Curtis, who immediately saw the possibilities of a series in the book and convinced Sawyer not to kill off Afsan in the first volume. A touch of rewriting and the book was auctioned with options for the remaining volumes. This time the sales were on a par with the reviews: "A tour de force," wrote a critic in *Isaac Asimov's Science Fiction Magazine,* adding that the book is "vastly enjoyable, beautifully realized." Mainstream reviews were positive also. An article in *Toronto Star* reported that "without question, *Far-Seer* will be remembered as one of the year's outstanding books." And for the first time, young adult reviewers were looking at Sawyer's work. Katharine L. Kan, writing in *Voice of Youth Advocates,* termed the book "an enjoyable read, especially for dinosaur fans," and a reviewer in *Kliatt* wrote that "this is a truly great piece of fantasy SF."

The task remained, however, to turn the book into the first part of a trilogy. "I remembered a quote by Freud," Sawyer said. "He talked about the three great revolutions of thought in humankind: the destruction of the old Earth-oriented astronomy by Copernicus and Galileo; the theory of evolution as proposed by Darwin; and the revelation of the unconscious by himself, Freud. And I thought that would be a great framework for the books. I already had written the first revolution." The second followed in *Fossil Hunter,* where the Darwinian world was explored. The son of Afsan, Toroca, continues where his father has left off, and in searching for minerals necessary for the space-flight evacuation of the Quintaglios from their world, he uncovers their fossil record. Like Darwin, Toroca must come to terms with the implications of such a record. He concludes that the Quintaglios developed elsewhere and were transplanted onto the moon they call home. Meanwhile, an element of murder mystery creeps into Sawyer's story, for with the deaths of two of Afsan's children, the old dinosaur sets out to find the culprit. It is a blend to which Larry D. Condit, writing in *Voice of Youth Advocates,* responded positively: "Sawyer . . . has done an admirable job and has developed a world into which YA science fiction and dinosaur [fans] will enjoy a brief escape." "The characterization is brilliant," wrote Hayes in *Quill & Quire,* "the plotting enviable, and the narrative technique tight and fast-paced." And once again, *Toronto Star* gave it a thumbs up: "A superlative science-fiction novel."

The final book in the trilogy, *Foreigner,* was published in 1994, providing the end chapter to the Quintaglio world and their struggle to emigrate from their moon before it crashes into the giant planet around which it orbits. Afsan, now an old and venerated astronomer, again plays a key role in the action, as does a female dinosaur named Mokleb, who becomes a saurian Freud, examining the aggressiveness and intense feeling of territoriality that makes it so difficult for the Quintaglios to work together. Reviewers again commended Sawyer on his blend of science and action. Writing in *Booklist,* Carl Hays noted that Sawyer "deftly combines well-reasoned hard-science speculation with psychology, imaginative anthropology, and even linguistics." R. John Hayes of *Quill & Quire* wrote that *Foreigner* was "a fine end to a brilliant series, one that should vault Sawyer into the first rank of science fiction writers."

Sawyer's fifth book, *End of an Era,* again deals with dinosaurs—but this time more tangentially—as two paleontologists travel back in time to the Cretaceous Period to find out what really caused the reptiles' extinction. "The book is full of action, adventure, and humor," Sawyer said. "And it is the first time that you can recognize an alter ego in my work. In a way, I lived through my old dream of becoming a paleontologist with the writing of this book." Written before *Far-Seer, End of an Era* was held up by Sawyer's publisher until the Quintaglio trilogy was completed. Sawyer is currently at work on several different projects and story lines. "In science fiction," Sawyer commented, "it's not enough to have just one good idea. You need to blend at least half a dozen good ones to be able to weave an intriguing story together. Right now I'm playing around with the idea of genetic testing and the cloning of Neanderthal man. I need to let these ideas sort of brew for a while to see how they might come together into a workable story line." Once Sawyer's ideas have brewed sufficiently to come up with a plausible story line, he goes to the library. "I do about two solid months of research for each of my books. Everything from scientific journals to popular magazines to interviews with working scientists. After that there is about six or seven months of writing to get a finished novel. But throughout this process, I try to keep regular hours. Sort of a nine-to-five approach so that I can have a normal life apart from the writing."

In 1992, Sawyer's second book, *Far-Seer,* was put on the New York Public Library's list of Best Books for the Teen Age. It was a revelation for Sawyer. "Frankly, I hadn't thought of myself as a YA author until that moment. But when I stopped to think of it, I could see why the book and its sequels appealed to a younger audience. The protagonist in *Far-Seer* was an adolescent in terms of human years. And there was a lot of explanation of scientific matters in it, blended with good action. I was delighted to know that my writing could reach audiences across the age spectrum. With subsequent books, I took into consideration the fact that I was reaching young readers. I don't mean to say I simplified language or plot at all, but I did begin to look more closely at the moral statements my books were making." Visiting one seventh grade class that had used *Far-Seer* for a reading project, Sawyer was impressed not only by the art and science projects that the book inspired, but also by the fact that a full one-half of the class went on voluntarily to read the second book in the trilogy. "To have a bunch of young adults so enthused about my stuff that they would search out more to read, that was terrific."

"I am a great believer in science," Sawyer concluded. "A champion of rationalism. In all my works, I try to look at the battle between science and superstition. I blend science with action/adventure stories in an attempt to make you think. I, myself, am not a scientist; I have an arts degree, and I think that far too many people think of science as something irrelevant to their lives, or something so complex and arcane as to be incomprehensible. But science actually belongs to everybody and is vital to everybody. I want to bring science into everybody's daily life."

BIOGRAPHICAL/CRITICAL SOURCES:

BOOKS

Something about the Author, Volume 81, Gale, 1995.

PERIODICALS

Analog Science Fiction & Fact, March, 1994, p. 161; October, 1994, p. 161; May, 1997, p. 146; January, 1998, p. 145.
Booklist, March 15, 1994, p. 1333.
Books in Canada, March, 1991, p. 56; March, 1993, pp. 22-25.
Isaac Asimov's Science Fiction Magazine, June, 1992, p. 170.
Kliatt, April, 1991, p. 21; September, 1992, p. 23; September, 1993, p. 22.
Library Journal, November 15, 1990, p. 95; April 15, 1993, p. 130.
Locus, August, 1990, p. 21; January, 1991, p. 58; January, 1992, p. 19; June, 1993, p. 31.
Magazine of Fantasy and Science Fiction, December, 1990, p. 89; May, 1991, p. 50; October, 1996, p. 61.
Publishers Weekly, May 4, 1992, p. 54.
Quill & Quire, July, 1990, p. 55; July, 1992, p. 37; May, 1993, p. 26; January, 1994, p. 33.
Science Fiction Chronicle, September, 1993.
Toronto Star, August 22, 1992, p. H14; July 3, 1993, p. H14.
Voice of Youth Advocates, October, 1992, pp. 242-43; August, 1993, p. 170.*

* * *

SAWYER, Ruth 1880-1970

PERSONAL: Born August 5, 1880, in Boston, MA; died June 3, 1970; daughter of Francis Milton (an importer) and Ethelinda J. (Smith) Sawyer; married Albert C. Durand (a doctor), June 4, 1911; children: David, Margaret (Mrs. Robert McCloskey). *Education:* Columbia University, B.S., 1904. *Religion:* Unitarian.

CAREER: Short story writer and author of books for children. Helped organize kindergartens in Cuba, 1900; New York *Sun,* New York City, feature writer in Ireland, 1905, and 1907. Storyteller for the New York Lecture Bureau, beginning 1908, and started the first storytelling program for children at the NewYork Public Library.

AWARDS, HONORS: Newbery Medal, American Library Association, 1937, and Lewis Carroll Shelf Award, 1964, both for *Roller Skates;* Regina Medal, Catholic Library Association, 1965; Laura Ingalls Wilder Medal, American Library Association, 1965, for her "substantial and lasting contribution to literature for children."

WRITINGS:

JUVENILES

A Child's Year-Book, illustrated by the author, Harper, 1917.

The Tale of the Enchanted Bunnies, Harper, 1923.

Tono Antonio, illustrated by F. Luis Mora, Viking Press, 1934.

Picture Tales from Spain, illustrated by Carlos Sanchez, F. A. Stokes, 1936.

Roller Skates, illustrated by Valenti Angelo, Viking Press, 1936.

The Year of Jubilo, illustrated by Edward Shenton, Viking Press, 1940, published in England as *Lucinda's Year of Jubilo,* Bodley Head, 1965.

The Least One, illustrated by Leo Politi, Viking Press, 1941.

Old Con and Patrick, illustrated by Cathal O'Toole, Viking Press, 1946.

The Little Red Horse, illustrated by Jay Hyde Barnum, Viking Press, 1950.

The Gold of Bernardino, privately printed, 1952.

Journey Cake, Ho!, illustrated by Robert McCloskey, Viking Press, 1953.

A Cottage for Betsy, illustrated by Vera Bock, Harper, 1954.

The Enchanted Schoolhouse, illustrated by Hugh Tory, Viking Press, 1956.

(With Emmy Molles) *Dietrich of Berne and the Dwarf-King Laurin: Hero Tales of the Austrian Tirol,* illustrated by Frederick Chapman, Viking Press, 1963.

Daddles: The Story of a Plain Hound-Dog, illustrated by Robert Frankenberg, Little, Brown, 1964.

My Spain: A Story-Teller's Year of Collecting, Viking Press, 1967.

CHRISTMAS STORIES

This Way to Christmas, Harper, 1916, revised edition, 1970, new edition illustrated by Maginal Wright Barney, Harper, 1924.

The Long Christmas, illustrated by V. Angelo, Viking Press, 1941.

The Christmas Anna Angel, illustrated by Kate Seredy, Viking Press, 1944.

This Is the Christmas: A Serbian Folk Tale, Horn Book, 1945.

Maggie Rose: Her Birthday Christmas, illustrated by Maurice Sendak, Harper, 1952.

The Year of the Christmas Dragon, illustrated by Hugh Tory, Viking Press, 1960.

Joy to the World: Christmas Legends, illustrated by Trina S. Hyman, Little, Brown, 1966.

The Remarkable Christmas of the Cobbler's Sons, pictures by Barbara Cooney, Viking Press, 1994.

ADULT BOOKS

The Primrose Ring, Harper, 1915.

Seven Miles to Arden, Harper, 1916.

Herself, Himself, and Myself, Harper, 1917.

Doctor Danny (stories), illustrated by J. Scott Williams, Harper, 1918.

Leerie, illustrated by Clinton Balmer, Harper, 1920.

The Silver Sixpence, illustrated by James H. Crank, Harper, 1921.

Gladiola Murphy, Harper, 1923.

Four Ducks on a Pond, Harper, 1928.

Folkhouse: The Autobiography of a Home, illustrated by Allan McNab, D. Appleton, 1932.

The Luck of the Road, Appleton-Century, 1934.

Gallant: The Story of Storm Veblen (published serially as *Hillmen's Gold*), Appleton-Century, 1936.

RECORDINGS

Ruth Sawyer: Storyteller, 1965.

OTHER

The Sidhe of Ben-Mor: An Irish Folk Play, Badger,1910.

The Awakening, first produced in New York City,1918.

The Way of the Storyteller, Macmillan, 1942, revised edition, Viking Press, 1977.

How to Tell a Story, F. E. Compton, 1962.

Contributor of over two hundred articles, stories, poems, and serials to periodicals, including *Atlantic Monthly, Horn Book,* and *Outlook.* The College of

Sainte Catherine Library, St. Paul, MN, owns a collection of Sawyer's manuscripts.

ADAPTATIONS: The Primrose Ring was filmed by Lasky Feature Play Co., 1917; the story "Christmas Apple," published in *This Way to Christmas,* was adapted for the stage as a two-scene play by Margaret D. Williams and published by Samuel French, 1939; *Journey Cake, Ho!* was adapted as a filmstrip, with sound and picture-cued text booklet, by Weston Woods Studios, 1967.

SIDELIGHTS: Ruth Sawyer was known as a teller of folktales that she collected from around the world, and as a writer of stories about children from other cultures. Among her most popular books are *The Christmas Anna Angel,* about a Hungarian girl who yearns for a traditional Christmas celebration, and the Newbery Medal-winning *Roller Skates,* the story of a young girl who explores New York City.

As a child, Sawyer developed a love for stories from her Irish nurse, Johanna, who told her stories at bedtime. The nurse also gave Ruth a love for Irish folklore, an interest which later led her to study and collect folklore from around the world. At Columbia University, Sawyer majored in folklore and storytelling and after graduation, she worked for the New York Public Lecture Bureau, telling stories twice a week at different locations around the city. She also worked as a correspondent in Ireland for the *New York Sun* newspaper.

Many of Sawyer's books were inspired by folktales, especially those from Spain. Her *Picture Tales from Spain* was based on a trip she made to that country and on the stories she was told by the people she met. Another story from Spain was *Tono Antonio,* based on a young boy Sawyer met on this journey. The Spanish stories of Washington Irving had enthralled Sawyer when she was a girl, giving her a desire to visit Spain. "It may seem a far cry," she explained in *Horn Book,* "from a Maine farmhouse in midsummer fog to Granada in winter splendor. In years it spans half a lifetime. But for the child lying stomach down beside the hearth, lost in *The Tales of the Alhambra* and *The Conquest of Granada,* Washington Irving laid a starry trail across the ocean and those years."

One of Sawyer's most popular books was *Roller Skates,* the story of one year in the life of Lucinda, a young girl who is permitted to roller-skate wherever she pleases in New York City. In the course of her travels throughout the city, she meets and be friends people from all sorts of backgrounds, in the process learning something about the importance of individual freedom. In her Newbery Award acceptance speech, Sawyer explained: "If this book has any point at all it lies in that fact of freedom for every child, in his own way, that he, too, may catch the music of the spheres. . . . A free child is a happy child; and there is nothing more lovely; even a disagreeable child ceases to be disagreeable and is liked."

Roller Skates stirred a controversy when it first appeared because it dealt frankly with death. As Elizabeth Segel noted in *Horn Book,* "By confronting a sordid murder and the death of a tiny child, rather than the more easily accepted deaths of a pet or an aged grandparent, and by integrating these experiences with other aspects of Lucinda's year of discovery and growth, the book, in fact, deals more fully and frankly with the child's experience of death than do many of the books turned out these days."

Yet, most critics focus on the book's primary message of freedom. "Yes, Lucinda lives," Segel wrote, "and her vitality makes *Roller Skates* still readable and engaging. Depicted as neither a typical child nor an object-lesson heroine, Lucinda embodies a freedom as liberating to children's books as her year of roller-skating was to her own life."

The sequel to *Roller Skates, The Year of Jubilo,* resumes the story of Lucinda at age fourteen, when the death of her father has left her and her four older brothers with new challenges and responsibilities. Resettling with her family at their summer cottage in Maine, Lucinda maintains her relationships with her New York City friends and with her Uncle Earle through a series of descriptive and entertaining letters that are considered among the highlights of this book.

Journey Cake, Ho! is a story derived from folktales of the American South. When a young boy must go on a search for a new home, he is given a "journey cake" to eat along the way. But the cake falls out of his pack and rolls away, and the boy's frantic efforts to retrieve the cake form the story. "Where did *Journey Cake, Ho!* have its start?," Sawyer asked in an article for *Young Wings.* "It began a hundred years ago in the mountains of Kentucky, North Carolina, and Tennessee. The people told the story. They sang it. They laughed over it. But the story I have written is different from any versions I have heard, but the bare bones are the same. And I like it."

A large part of Sawyer's work are Christmas stories, many of them based on traditional or folk tales from around the world. *This Way to Christmas* features Sawyer's son, David, as the main character. When his parents are away, David's Irish caretakers tell Christmas stories to entertain him. These ten stories makeup *This Way to Christmas.* Included is one of Sawyer's personal favorites, "The Voyage of the Wee Red Cap," a story she heard from an elderly tinker while visiting Ireland. When she returned to New York, Anne Carroll Moore invited her to tell the story to a group of children at the New York Public Library. "I shall always remember the faces of the American-born Irish boys who came over from a nearby parochial school," Sawyer recalled in *Horn Book.* "I shall always remember Miss Moore's lighting of candles; and the Christmas wishes that came out of that first library story hour. Those candles have never gone out for me; they still burn and always will."

The Long Christmas, dedicated to Sawyer's daughter, Margaret, is a collection of thirteen holiday stories, one for each day from St. Thomas's Day to Candlemas. It contains, according to Jacqueline Overton in *Horn Book,* "Legends from many countries, ancient and modern, gentle and serious, joyous and gay, and she prefaced them with some of the traditional things that have gone into the keeping of Christmas: The good food, 'gay and of infinite variety,' the lighting, the bedecking, the festivity." Writing of *The Long Christmas* in *Horn Book,* Beryl Robinson remarked: "I return to this book yearly in anticipation of the Christmas season, rereading every tale, choosing those that will be a part of the year's festival."

Sawyer's *The Christmas Anna Angel* was inspired by a real-life experience of her Hungarian friend, Anna Kester. Anna recalled one Christmas in Hungary when she was a little girl and there was a food shortage. Despite the lack of flour and other baking essentials, Anna wanted to have a traditional Christmas cake to hang on the tree. Her desire becomes reality when she dreams of a Christmas angel and an angel appears. "Anna Kester's faithful memory, Ruth Sawyer's warm telling of the story of *The Christmas Anna Angel* and Kate Seredy's lovely pictures have worked their magic," Jacqueline Overton wrote in *Horn Book.* The book won Seredy a Caldecott Medal in 1954.

Speaking in *Horn Book,* Sawyer once stated: "So often I have heard a sharp criticism from a parent when she has found a shabby, dog-eared book on the library shelf. How shortsighted is such a parent! I rejoice over every one I find. It speaks more eloquently than all the good reviews how much beloved that book has been."

BIOGRAPHICAL/CRITICAL SOURCES:

BOOKS

Children's Literature Review, Volume 36, Gale, 1995.
Dictionary of Literary Biography, Volume 22: *American Writers for Children, 1900-1960,* Gale, 1983.
Haviland, Virginia, *Ruth Sawyer,* Walck, 1965.
Something about the Author, Volume 17, Gale, 1979.
Twentieth-Century Children's Writers, 4th edition, St. James Press, 1995.

PERIODICALS

Bulletin of the New York Public Library, November-December, 1956, pp. 593-98.
Horn Book, January, 1936, pp. 34-38; July 1937, pp. 251-56; November-December, 1944, pp. 447-60; October, 1965, pp. 474-80; August, 1979, pp. 454-58.
Young Wings, December, 1953.*

* * *

SCARRY, Richard (McClure) 1919-1994

PERSONAL: Surname rhymes with "carry"; born June 5, 1919, in Boston, MA; died April 30, 1994, in Gstaad, Switzerland; son of John James (proprietor of department stores) and Barbara (McClure) Scarry; married Patricia Murphy (a writer of children's books), September 7, 1949; children: Richard McClure II (Huck). *Education:* Boston Museum School of Fine Arts, 1938-41. *Avocational interests:* Skiing, sailing, traveling.

CAREER: Magazine and children's book illustrator, 1946-94; writer. *Military service:* U.S. Army, 1941-46; served as art director, editor, writer, and illustrator, Morale Services Section, Allied Forces Headquarters, North African and Mediterranean theaters; became captain.

AWARDS, HONORS: Edgar Allan Poe nomination for children's mystery, 1976, for *Richard Scarry's Great Steamboat Mystery.*

WRITINGS:

SELF-ILLUSTRATED

The Great Big Car and Truck Book, Simon & Schuster, 1951.
Rabbit and His Friends, Simon & Schuster, 1953.

Nursery Tales, Simon & Schuster, 1958.
Tinker and Tanker (also see below), Garden City Books, 1960.
The Hickory Dickory Clock Book, Doubleday, 1961.
Tinker and Tanker Out West (also see below), Doubleday, 1961.
Tinker and Tanker and Their Space Ship (also see below), Doubleday, 1961.
Tinker and Tanker and the Pirates (also see below), Doubleday, 1961.
Tinker and Tanker, Knights of the Round Table (also see below), Doubleday, 1963.
Tinker and Tanker in Africa (also see below), Doubleday, 1963.
Richard Scarry's Best Word Book Ever, Golden Press, 1963.
The Rooster Struts, Golden Press, 1963, published as *The Golden Happy Book of Animals,* 1964, published in England as *Animals,* Hamlyn, 1963.
Polite Elephant, Golden Press, 1964.
Feed the Hippo His ABC's, Golden Press, 1964.
Busy, Busy World, Golden Press, 1965.
Richard Scarry's Teeny Tiny Tales, Golden Press, 1965.
The Santa Claus Book, Golden Press, 1965.
The Bunny Book, Golden Press, 1965.
Is This the House of Mistress Mouse?, Golden Press, 1966.
Storybook Dictionary, Golden Press, 1966.
Planes, Golden Press, 1967, published as *Richard Scarry's Planes,* Western Pub. Co., 1992.
Trains, Golden Press, 1967, published as *Richard Scarry's Trains,* Golden Books, 1992.
Boats, Golden Press, 1967, published as *Richard Scarry's Boats,* Golden Books, 1992.
Cars, Golden Press, 1967.
Richard Scarry's Egg in the Hole Book, Golden Press, 1967.
What Animals Do, Golden Press, 1968.
Best Storybook Ever, Golden Press, 1968.
The Early Bird, Random House, 1968.
What Do People Do All Day? Random House, 1968.
The Adventures of Tinker and Tanker (contains *Tinker and Tanker, Tinker and Tanker Out West,* and *Tinker and Tanker and Their Space Ship*), Doubleday, 1968.
The Great Pie Robbery (also see below), Random House, 1969.
The Supermarket Mystery (also see below), Random House, 1969.
Richard Scarry's Great Big Schoolhouse, Random House, 1969.
More Adventures of Tinker and Tanker (contains *Tinker and Tanker and the Pirates, Tinker and Tanker, Knights of the Round Table,* and *Tinker and Tanker in Africa*),Doubleday, 1971.
ABC Word Book, Random House, 1971.
Richard Scarry's Best Stories Ever, Golden Press, 1971.
Richard Scarry's Fun with Words, Golden Press, 1971.
Richard Scarry's Going Places, Golden Press, 1971.
Richard Scarry's Great Big Air Book, Random House, 1971.
Richard Scarry's Things to Know, Golden Press, 1971.
Funniest Storybook Ever, Random House, 1972.
Nicky Goes to the Doctor, Golden Press, 1972.
Richard Scarry's Great Big Mystery Book (contains *The Great Pie Robbery* and *The Supermarket Mystery*), Random House, 1972.
Hop Aboard, Here We Go, Golden Press, 1972.
Babykins and His Family, Golden Press, 1973.
Silly Stories, Golden Press, 1973.
Richard Scarry's Find Your ABC's, Random House, 1973.
Richard Scarry's Please and Thank You Book, Random House, 1973.
Richard Scarry's Best Rainy Day Book Ever, Random House, 1974.
Cars and Trucks and Things That Go, Golden Press, 1974.
Richard Scarry's Great Steamboat Mystery, Random House, 1975.
Richard Scarry's Best Counting Book Ever, Random House, 1975.
Richard Scarry's Animal Nursery Tales, Golden Press, 1975.
Richard Scarry's Early Words, Random House, 1976.
Richard Scarry's Color Book, Random House, 1976.
Richard Scarry's Busiest People Ever, Random House, 1976.
Richard Scarry's Collins Cubs, Collins, 1976.
Richard Scarry's Picture Dictionary, Collins, 1976.
Richard Scarry's Random Laugh and Learn Library, four books, Random House, 1976.
Learn to Count, Golden Press, 1976.
All Year Long, Golden Press, 1976.
At Work, Golden Press, 1976.
Short and Tall, Golden Press, 1976.
My House, Golden Press, 1976.
On Vacation, Golden Press, 1976.
About Animals, Golden Press, 1976.
On the Farm, Golden Press, 1976.
Six Golden Look-Look Books, six volumes, Golden Press, 1977.
Richard Scarry's Lowly Worm Storybook, Random House, 1977.
Richard Scarry's Best Make-It Book Ever, Random House, 1977.

Tinker and Tanker Journey to Tootletown and Build a Space Ship, Golden Press, 1978.
Richard Scarry's Bedtime Stories, Random House, 1978.
Richard Scarry's Punch-Out Toy Book, Random House, 1978.
Richard Scarry's Postman Pig and His Busy Neighbors, Random House, 1978.
Richard Scarry's Lowly Worm Sniffy Book, Random House, 1978.
Richard Scarry's Stories to Color: With Lowly Worm and Mr. Paint Pig, Random House, 1978.
Storytime, Random House, 1978.
Little Bedtime Story, Random House, 1978.
Things to Learn, Golden Press, 1978.
Mr. Fixit and Other Stories, Random House, 1978.
Busy Town, Busy People, Random House, 1978.
Little ABC, Random House, 1978.
Richard Scarry's Mix or Match Storybook, Random House, 1979.
Richard Scarry's Best First Book Ever, Random House, 1979.
Richard Scarry's Busytown Pop-Up Book, Random House, 1979.
Richard Scarry's Huckles Book, Random House, 1979.
Richard Scarry's Tinker and Tanker Tales of Pirates and Knights, Golden Press, 1979.
Richard Scarry's to Market, to Market, Golden Press, 1979.
Richard Scarry's Peasant Pig and the Terrible Dragon, Random House, 1980.
Richard Scarry's Lowly Worm Word Book, Random House, 1981.
Richard Scarry's Best Christmas Book Ever, Random House, 1981.
Richard Scarry's Busy Houses, Random House, 1981.
Richard Scarry's Funniest Storybook Ever, Random House, 1982.
Richard Scarry's Four Busy Word Books, four volumes, Random House, 1982.
Christmas Mice, Golden Press, 1982.
Lowly Worm Coloring Book, Random House, 1983.
Lowly Worm Cars and Trucks Book, Random House, 1983.
The Best Mistake Ever! Random House, 1984.
Richard Scarry's Lowly Worm Bath Book, Random House, 1984.
Richard Scarry's Busy Fun and Learn Book, Western Publishing, 1984.
Richard Scarry's Pig Will and Pig Won't: A Book of Manners, Random House, 1984.
Richard Scarry's Biggest Word Book Ever! Random House, 1985.
My First Word Book, Random House, 1986.
Fun with Letters, Random House, 1986.
Fun with Numbers, three volumes, Random House, 1986.
Norwegian Dictionary: Min Forste Ordbok (subtitle means "My First 'Word Book' "), Arthur Vanous Co., 1986.
Fun with Words, Random House, 1986.
Fun with Reading, Random House, 1986.
Richard Scarry's Splish-Splash Sounds, Western Publishing, 1986.
Big and Little, Western Publishing, 1986.
Things to Love, Western Publishing, 1987.
Richard Scarry's Things That Go, Western Publishing, 1987.
Richard Scarry's Lowly Worm's Schoolbag, Random House, 1987.
Getting Ready for Numbers, Random House, 1987.
Getting Ready for School, Random House, 1987.
Getting Ready for Writing, Random House, 1987.
Busy Workers, Western Publishing, 1987.
Smokey the Fireman, Western Publishing, 1988.
Sniff the Detective, Western Publishing, 1988.
Play Day, Western Publishing, 1988.
Dr. Doctor, Western Publishing, 1988.
Farmer Patrick Pig, Western Publishing, 1988.
Frances Fix-It, Western Publishing, 1988.
Harry and Larry the Fishermen, Western Publishing, 1988.
Richard Scarry's Best Times Ever: A Book about Seasons and Holidays, Western Publishing, 1988.
Scarry's Best Ever, Random House, 1989.
Richard Scarry's Best Ride Ever, Western Publishing, 1989.
Richard Scarry's Best Friend Ever, Western Publishing, 1989.
Richard Scarry's Mother Goose Scratch and Sniff Book, Western Publishing, 1989.
Richard Scarry's Naughty Bunny, Western Publishing, 1989.
Richard Scarry's All about Cars, Western Publishing, 1989.
Richard Scarry's Best Two-Minute Stories Ever! Western Publishing, 1989.
Richard Scarry's Counting Book, Western Publishing, 1990.
Richard Scarry's Just Right Word Book, David McKay Co., 1990.
Be Careful, Mr. Frumble, Random House, 1990.
Best Read It Yourself Book Ever, Western Publishing, 1990.
Watch Your Step, Mr. Rabbit! Random House, 1991.
Richard Scarry's ABC's, Western Publishing, 1991.
Richard Scarry's Best Year Ever, Western Publishing, 1991.

Richard Scarry's Best Busy Year Ever, Western Publishing (Racine, WI), 1991.

Richard Scarry: Sergeant Murphy's Busiest Day Ever, Western Publishing, 1992.

Richard Scarry's Mr. Fix-It: Smallest Pop-Up Book Ever! Western Publishing, 1992.

Richard Scarry's Word Book: With Huckle Cat and Lowly Worm, Golden Book (New York City), 1992.

Richard Scarry's Biggest Pop-Up Book Ever! Golden Books, 1992.

Richard Scarry's The Cat Family's Busy Day, Western Publishing, 1992.

Richard Scarry's The Cat Family Takes a Trip, Western Publishing, 1992.

Richard Scarry's Bananas Gorilla, Golden Books, 1992.

Richard Scarry's Mr. Frumble: Smallest Pop-Up Book Ever! Western Publishing, 1992.

Richard Scarry's Best Little Word Book Ever! Western Publishing, 1992.

Richard Scarry's Busiest Fire Fighters Ever! Western Publishing, 1993.

Richard Scarry's Busytown Word Book, Western Publishing, 1993.

Richard Scarry's Floating Bananas, Western Publishing, 1993.

Richard Scarry's Colors, Western Publishing, 1993.

Richard Scarry's Little Red Riding Hood, Western Publishing, 1993.

Richard Scarry's Hilda Needs Help! Western Publishing, 1993.

Richard Scarry's Mr. Frumble's Coffee Shop Disaster, Western Publishing, 1993.

Richard Scarry's The Three Bears, Western Publishing, 1993.

Richard Scarry's The Three Little Pigs, Western Publishing, 1993.

Richard Scarry's The Little Red Hen, Western Publishing, 1993.

Huckle Cat's Busiest Day Ever, Random House (New York City), 1993.

Richard Scarry's the Wolf and the Seven Kids, Western Publishing, 1994.

Richard Scarry's Pie Rats Ahoy! Random House, 1994.

Richard Scarry's Best Balloon Ride Ever! Western Publishing, 1994.

Richard Scarry's Dingo, the Worst Driver Ever, Western Publishing, 1994.

Richard Scarry's the Snowstorm Surprise, Western Publishing, 1994.

Richard Scarry's Busy, Busy Town, Western Publishing, 1994.

Richard Scarry's One to Ten, Western Publishing, 1994.

Richard Scarry, Abdo and Daughters (Edina, MN), 1994.

Camping Out, Aladdin Paperbacks (New York City), 1995.

The Best Baby-Sitter Ever, Aladdin Paperbacks, 1995.

A Big Operation, Aladdin Paperbacks, 1995.

The Adventures of Lowly Worm, Random House, 1995.

Richard Scarry's Pop-Up Colors, Simon & Schuster (New York City), 1996.

Richard Scarry's Noisiest Day Ever! Publications International (Lincolnwood, IL), 1996.

A Trip to the Moon, Aladdin Paperbacks, 1996.

Hilda's Tea Party, Aladdin Paperbacks, 1996.

Busytown Race Day, Aladdin Paperbacks, 1996.

Richard Scarry's Pop-Up Numbers, Simon & Schuster, 1996.

Richard Scarry's Pop-Up Wheels, Little Simon (New York City), 1997.

Busytown Boat Race, Aladdin Paperbacks, 1997.

Richard Scarry's Pop-Up Time, Little Simon, 1997.

A Summer Picnic, Aladdin Paperbacks, 1997.

Lowly Worm Joins the Circus, Simon Spotlight (New York City), 1998.

Mr. Fixit's Magnet Machine, Simon Spotlight, 1998.

Mr. Fixit's Mix-Ups, Simon Spotlight, 1998.

Mr. Frumble's Pickle Car, Simon Spotlight, 1998.

Also author of *Mr. Frumble's Worst Day Ever,* 1992, *Richard Scarry's Busy Busy World,* Western Publishing, and writer and illustrator for *Richard Scarry's Best Sing-Along Mother Goose Video Ever!* and *Richard Scarry's Best Silly Stories and Songs Video Ever!,* both 1994.

ILLUSTRATOR

Kathryn Jackson, *Let's Go Fishing,* Simon & Schuster, 1949.

Jackson, *Mouse's House,* Simon & Schuster, 1949.

Jackson, *Duck and His Friends,* Simon & Schuster, 1949.

Jackson, *Brave Cowboy Bill,* Simon & Schuster, 1950.

Jackson, *The Animals' Merry Christmas,* Simon& Schuster, 1950.

Oliver O'Connor Barrett, *Little Benny Wanted a Pony,* Simon & Schuster, 1950.

Patricia Scarry, *Danny Beaver's Secret,* Simon & Schuster, 1953.

Leah Gale, *The Animals of Farmer Jones,* Simon & Schuster, 1953.

Margaret Wise Brown, *Little Indian,* Simon & Schuster, 1954.

P. Scarry, *Pierre Bear,* Golden Press, 1954.

Jane Werner, *Smokey the Bear,* Simon & Schuster, 1955.

Jackson, *Golden Bedtime Book,* Simon & Schuster, 1955.

Mary Maud Reed, *Mon petit dictionnaire geant,* Editions des deux coqs d'or, 1958.

P. Scarry, *Just for Fun,* Golden Press, 1960.

My Nursery Tale Book, Golden Press, 1961.

Selligmann and Levine Milton, *Tommy Visits the Doctor,* Western Publishing, 1962.

Edward Lear, *Nonsense Alphabet,* Doubleday, 1962.

Peggy Parish, *My Golden Book of Manners,* Golden Press, 1962.

M. Reed and E. Oswald, *My First Golden Dictionary Book,* Western Publishing, 1963.

(And editor and translator) Jean de la Fontaine, *Fables,* Doubleday, 1963.

Richard Scarry's Animal Mother Goose, Golden Press, 1964.

Barbara Shook Hazen, *Rudolph the Red-nosed Reindeer,* Golden Press, 1964, Western Publishing, 1991.

Jackson and others, *My Nursery Tale Book,* Western Publishing, 1964.

Jackson, *The Golden Book of 365 Stories,* Golden Press, 1966.

Ole Risom, *I Am a Bunny,* Golden Press, 1966.

Richard Scarry's Best Mother Goose Ever, Golden Press, 1970.

Richard Scarry's Mother Goose, Golden Press, 1972.

Roberta Miller, *Chipmunk's ABC,* Golden Press, 1976.

The Gingerbread Man, Golden Press, 1981.

My First Golden Dictionary, Western Publishing, 1983.

The Golden Treasury of Fairy Tales, Western Publishing, 1985.

Richard Scarry's Simple Simon and Other Rhymes, Western Publishing, 1988.

Richard Scarry's Little Miss Muffet and Other Rhymes, Western Publishing, 1988.

Jackson, *Richard Scarry's Best House Ever,* Western Publishing, 1989.

Richard Scarry's Cars and Trucks from A to Z, Random House, 1990.

Also illustrator of coloring activity books and children's foreign language dictionaries.

OTHER

Scarry's works are included in the Kerlan Collection at the University of Minnesota.

ADAPTATIONS: What Do People Do All Day and Other Stories was adapted to audio and read by Carol Channing, Caedmon, 1978. *What Do People Do All Day and Great Big Schoolhouse* was adapted to audio and read by Channing, Caedmon, 1979. *Richard Scarry's The Three Little Pigs* and *Richard Scarry's Little Red Riding Hood* were combined and adapted to audio in 1993. *Richard Scarry's Best Electronic Word Book Ever!* (computer software), CBS Interactive Learning, 1985.

SIDELIGHTS: Richard Scarry was "one of the world's best-selling super-stars of children's literature," according to Barbara Karlan in *West Coast Review of Books.* The skillful blend of education and entertainment found in Scarry's books makes them appealing both to children and their parents. Each book, be it a dictionary, an alphabet, or a fairy tale, features the author's bright, lively illustrations of such anthropomorphic animal characters as Huckle Cat, Lowly Worm, and Mr. Paint Pig. Publishing statistics testify to the popularity of Scarry's works. His books have been translated into twenty-eight languages and sold over one hundred million copies. Elaine Moss summarized the books' appeal in *Signal:* "Totally unpretentious, bubbling with humour, alive with activity, peppered with words of wisdom and corny jokes. . . . Scarry books are a marvellous combination of entertainment, always on a child's level, and incidental instruction. They occupy a unique place in the learning-to-read process."

Scarry was born and raised in Boston, Massachusetts, where his father was the owner of a small chain of department stores. He was not an enthusiastic student; he spent five years struggling through high school. "I couldn't even get into college because I didn't have enough credits," he recalled in *Parents* magazine. Scarry did try a short stint at a Boston business school, but soondropped out. Since he had always liked drawing and had spent every Saturday morning as a child studying art at the Boston Museum of Fine Arts, he applied to and was finally accepted at the Boston Museum School of Fine Arts.

World War II interrupted Scarry's art studies, however. He spent five years in the United States Army. "I had a bit of a problem getting in," he explained in *Third Book of Junior Authors.* "Because I wore glasses they wouldn't accept me as a volunteer but preferred to draft me instead." Although Scarry was originally scheduled to become a radio repairman, he soon secured a place at an Officer Candidate school. After graduation, he went on to serve as art director for the troops in North

Africa and Italy, where he drew maps and designed graphics.

After the war Scarry moved to New York City, originally intending to pursue a career as a commercial artist. However, in 1946 he completed illustrations for a children's book called *The Boss of the Barnyard,* published by Golden Press, and he was ensured a steady flow of work. He illustrated other authors' books for several years before beginning to write and illustrate original stories of his own. "During his free-lance period," wrote Bobbie Burch Lemontt in the *Dictionary of Literary Biography,*"he met Patsy Murphy, from Vancouver, British Columbia, who, hesays, writes kids' books, 'but can't draw.' After being married in 1949, the couple lived on a farm in Ridgefield, Connecticut, and collaborated on several books."

Scarry's first big commercial success came in 1963 with the publication of *Richard Scarry's Best Word Book Ever.* The book is filled with colorful illustrations and pages of information—it "contains more than 1,400 defined and illustrated objects which can engage a preschooler's interest by the infectious vitality and purposefulness of the selections, "stated Lemontt—and established Scarry's popularity with children. It "seems," wrote *New York Times* contributor Richard Flaste, "to identify everything children meet in their world, and some things in more exotic worlds."

Scarry's work, however, is not without its critics. Some librarians feel that Scarry's use of slapstick humor in his books, with its overtones of violence, could be dangerous for young children. But "it's not true violence, it's fun," he told Rudi Chelminski in *People.* "I have cars pile up and people get into trouble. It's the old banana peel or custard pie in the face. The only thing that really suffers is dignity. Kids love that—and they're right." "A typical 'violent' encounter," explained Edwin McDowell in *New York Times,* ". . . is likely to show, for example, canine cop Sergeant Murphy on a collision course with a birthday cake. Even then the moment of impact is left to the imagination."

Other critics object to what they see as sexual stereotyping in Scarry's work. But the author told Arthur Bell in *Publishers Weekly* that one reason he uses animals as subjects is to eliminate the problem of sexual and racial stereotypes: "Children can identify more closely with pictures of animals than they can with pictures of another child. They see an illustration of a blond girl or a dark-haired boy who they know is somebody other than themselves, and competition creeps in. With imagination—and children all have marvelous imagination—they can easily identify with an anteater who is a painter or a goat who is an Indian or a honey-bear schoolteacher."

In 1969 Scarry, his wife, and their son, Huck (an author-illustrator), moved to a mountain chalet in Gstaad, Switzerland. The decision was made after a skiing trip. "It was the usual 21-day excursion," Scarry told Bell. "But coming home, we had to pass through Lausanne in order to catch our plane from Geneva. From the train window I caught a glimpse of a child throwing a snowball—just that, nothing more—and I thought, 'Now is the time to move to Switzerland.' " "The move was not a political one—we had always hoped at sometime to live in Europe," Scarry continued, "but couldn't make plans because of Huck's being in school. But Huck was 15, and Switzerland was magnificent, and suddenly the time seemed right. . . . We settled our affairs and leased our house, and . . . with little more than the clothes on our backs, we moved to Lausanne."

From his European residence Scarry continued to produce highly popular children's books. "One of the greatest compliments any author can receive from a preschool audience," declared Lemontt, "is to have his or her booksheld together with more tape than there is paper in the book itself. Tearing is an accidental toddler pastime that often suggests a book is good enough to be reread. Richard Scarry's books usually display an abundance of such mending."

BIOGRAPHICAL/CRITICAL SOURCES:

BOOKS

Children's Literature Review, Gale, Volume 3, 1978, Volume 41, 1997.

De Montreville, Doris, and Donna Hill, editors, *Third Book of Junior Authors,* H. W. Wilson, 1972.

Dictionary of Literary Biography, Volume 61: *American Writers for Children since 1960: Poets, Illustrators, and Nonfiction Authors,* Gale, 1987.

Kingman, Lee, and others, editors, *Illustrators of Children's Books: 1957-1966,* Horn Book, 1968.

Lanes, Selma G., *Down the Rabbit Hole: Adventures and Misadventures in the Realm of Children's Literature,* Atheneum, 1972.

Retan, Walter, and Ole Risom, *The Busy, Busy World of Richard Scarry,* Harry N. Abrams (New York City), 1997.

Scarry, Richard, *Richard Scarry,* Abdo and Daughters (Edina, MN), 1994.

Something about the Author, Volume 75, Gale, 1994.

Ward, Martha E., and Dorothy A. Marquardt, *Authors of Books for Young People,* Scarecrow, 1971.

Wintle, Justin, and Emma Fisher, *The Pied Pipers: Interviews with the Influential Creators of Children's Literature,* Paddington Press, 1974.

PERIODICALS

New Yorker, December 14, 1968.
New York Times, March 16, 1976; April 27, 1980.
New York Times Book Review, November 6, 1966; December 14, 1968; April 5, 1968; October 1, 1972; May 6, 1973; November 14, 1976; May 27, 1980.
Parents, August, 1980.
People, October 15, 1979, pp. 105-10.
Publishers Weekly, October 20, 1969, pp. 41-42.
Signal, January, 1974.
Times Literary Supplement, December 3, 1971.
West Coast Review of Books, December, 1975.
Young Readers Review, September, 1968.

OBITUARIES:

PERIODICALS

Chicago Tribune, May 3, 1994, p. 13.
Los Angeles Times, May 4, 1994, p. A16.
New York Times, May 3, 1994, p. B10.
Washington Post, May 4, 1994, p. B8.*

* * *

SEED, Cecile Eugenie 1930-
(Jenny Seed)

PERSONAL: Born May 18, 1930, in Cape Town, South Africa; daughter of Ivan Washington (a draftsman) and Bessie (Dickerson) Booysen; married Edward Robert Seed (a railway employee), October 30, 1953; children: Anne, Dick, Alan, Robbie. *Religion:* Christian. *Avocational interests:* Tennis, bowling, reading, entertaining, church work.

ADDRESSES: *Home*—10 Pioneer Cres., Northdene, Kwa Zulu-Natal, Natal, 4093, South Africa.

CAREER: Roads Department, Town Planning Department, Pietarmaritzburg, South Africa, draftsman, 1947-53. Freelance writer, 1965—.

AWARDS, HONORS: M. E. R. Award for Children's Literature in South Africa, 1987, for *Place among the Stones.*

WRITINGS:

FICTION; UNDER PSEUDONYM JENNY SEED

The Dancing Mule, illustrated by Joan Sirr, Nelson, 1964.
The Always-Late Train, illustrated by Pieter de Weerdt, Nasionale Boekhandel, 1965.
Small House, Big Garden, illustrated by Lynette Hemmant, Hamish Hamilton (London), 1965.
Peter the Gardener, illustrated by Mary Russon, Hamish Hamilton, 1966.
Tombi's Song, illustrated by Dugald MacDougall, Hamish Hamilton, 1966, published as *Ntombi's Song,* illustrated by Anno Berry, Beacon Press (Boston), 1989.
To the Rescue, illustrated by Constance Marshall, Hamish Hamilton, 1966.
Stop Those Children!, illustrated by Russon, Hamish Hamilton, 1966.
Timothy and Tinker, illustrated by Hemmant, Hamish Hamilton, 1967.
The River Man, illustrated by MacDougall, Hamish Hamilton, 1968.
The Voice of the Great Elephant, illustrated by Trevor Stubley, Hamish Hamilton, 1968, Pantheon (New York City), 1969.
Canvas City, illustrated by Hemmant, Hamish Hamilton, 1968.
The Red Dust Soldiers, illustrated by Andrew Sier, Heinemann (London), 1968.
Prince of the Bay, illustrated by Stubley, Hamish Hamilton, 1970, published as *Vengeance of the Zulu King,* Pantheon, 1971.
The Great Thirst, illustrated by Stubley, Hamish Hamilton, 1971, Bradbury (Scarsdale, NY), 1973.
The Broken Spear, illustrated by Stubley, Hamish Hamilton, 1972.
Warriors on the Hills, illustrated by Pat Ludlow, Abelard Schuman (New York City), 1975.
The Unknown Land, illustrated by Jael Jordan, Heinemann, 1976.
Strangers in the Land, illustrated by Stubley, Hamish Hamilton, 1977.
The Year One, illustrated by Susan Sansome, Hamish Hamilton, 1981.
The Policeman's Button, illustrated by Joy Pritchard, Human & Rousseau (South Africa), 1981.
Gold Dust, illustrated by Bill le Fever, Hamish Hamilton, 1982.
The New Fire, illustrated by Mario Sickle, Human & Rousseau, 1983.
The 59 Cats, illustrated by Alida Carpenter, Daan Retief, 1983.

The Shell, illustrated by Ann Walton, Daan Retief, 1983.

The Sad Cat, illustrated by Marlize Groenewald, Daan Retief, 1984.

The Karoo Hen, illustrated by A. Venter, Daan Retief, 1984.

The Disappearing Rabbit, illustrated by Walton, Daan Retief, 1984.

Big Boy's Work, illustrated by Paula Collins, Daan Retief, 1984.

The Spy Hill, illustrated by Nelda Vermaak, Human & Rousseau, 1984.

The Lost Prince, illustrated by Walton, Daan Retief, 1985.

Day of the Dragon, illustrated by Collins, Daan Retief, 1985.

Bouncy Lizzie, illustrated by Esther Boshoff, Daan Retief, 1985.

The Strange Blackbird, illustrated by Hettie Saaiman, Daan Retief, 1986.

The Far-Away Valley, illustrated by Joan Rankin, Daan Retief, 1987.

The Christmas Bells, illustrated by Saaiman, Daan Retief, 1987.

Place among the Stones, illustrated by Helmut Starcke, Tafelberg (South Africa), 1987.

The Station-Master's Hen, illustrated by Elizabeth de Villiers, Human & Rousseau, 1987.

The Corner Cat, illustrated by de Villiers, Human & Rousseau, 1987.

Hurry, Hurry, Sibusiso, illustrated by Cornelia Holm, Daan Retief, 1988.

The Big Pumpkin, illustrated by Berry, Human & Rousseau, 1989.

Stowaway to Nowhere, Tafelberg, 1990.

Nobody's Cat, illustrated by Alida Bothma, Human & Rousseau, 1990.

The Wind's Song, illustrated by Rankin, Daan Retief, 1991.

The Hungry People, Tafelberg, 1992.

Old Grandfather Mantis, Tafelberg, 1992.

A Time to Scatter Stones, Macmillan (New York City), 1993.

Eyes of a Toad, Macmillan, 1993.

Run, Run, White Hen, Oxford University Press (New York City), 1994.

Lucky Boy, Excellentia Publishers, 1995.

Also author of *The Strange Large Egg,* 1996.

FOLKTALES; UNDER PSEUDONYM JENNY SEED

Kulumi the Brave: A Zulu Tale, illustrated by Stubley, Hamish Hamilton, World, 1970.

The Sly Green Lizard (Zulu folktale), illustrated by Graham Humphreys, Hamish Hamilton, 1973.

The Bushman's Dream: African Tales of the Creation, illustrated by Bernard Brett, Hamish Hamilton, 1974, Bradbury, 1975.

OTHER

Many of Seed's children's stories have been published in Canada, England, Zimbabwe, New Zealand, and Australia.

ADAPTATIONS: Some of Seed's children's stories have been adapted for broadcasts in countries around the world.

SIDELIGHTS: Cecile Eugenie Seed, best known under the pseudonym Jenny Seed, writes of her native South Africa, either in stories set in modern times or in historical periods, and retells traditional African folktales as well. Her historical novels portray the experiences and emotions of young characters, both indigenous and immigrant, as they cope with historical situations and events. Seed once explained that she began to write such works for children around the time that she discovered that her own children's history homework was dull. Seed "began to delve into old books" in the Durban reference library and "the past became real" to her. She "found that [history] was not boring at all but tremendously exciting and filled with real and interesting people just waiting to be put into books."

Seed's 1971 book *The Great Thirst,* one of her many historical novels set in the nineteenth century, chronicles the development of a conflict between the Nama Hottentots and the Hereros in West Africa in the 1830s, focusing on a young boy's attempt to avenge his father's murder. A reviewer for *Bulletin of the Center for Children's Books* finds that the characters of *The Great Thirst* possess "vitality" and that "tribal cultures" in the book are "described with dignity." Paul Heins, a critic for *Horn Book,* concludes that Seed's "historical data," "well-sustained narrative," and the "spiritual development of the protagonist" are all "skillfully interwoven."

Seed's retelling of the folktale *Kulumi the Brave: A Zulu Tale* demonstrates her talent for adapting local myths and legends handed down orally for generations. In *Kulumi the Brave,* Kulumi's father, a king, believes that his young son will grow up to defeat and unseat him; he banishes the boy from his kingdom. Kulumi thrives despite this treatment—he bravely faces a dragon, learns to use magic, and successfully challenges an ogress in order to claim his bride. According to Gertrude B. Herman, writing in *Library Journal,* "The use of Zulu words is authentic."

Tombi's Song provides an example of Seed's original fiction for young children. This story follows a six-year-old Zulu girl as she goes to the store for her mother. Tombi tries to be brave, but her neighbors have frightened her with tales of a monster. Nervous, she spills the sugar she has bought at the store when a bus roars by and startles her. Tombi begins to sing a song her mother taught her, and then she begins to dance; in appreciation, a white woman gives Tombi a coin which enables the girl to buy another bag of sugar. Lillian N. Gerhardt asserts in *School Library Journal* that the story "promote[s] at least four attitudes that derogate Negro races." A critic for *Kirkus Reviews* observes that *Tombi's Song* "may be marred for many readers by a semblance of colonial paternalism." Addressing these criticisms, the 1989 version of the book, published as *Ntombi's Song,* features illustrations that present a black tourist couple giving the girl the coin. This revised version of the story moved a critic for *Publishers Weekly* to describe *Ntombi's Song* as "a warm and lovely story of a small triumph," and a critic for *Kirkus Reviews* finds it to be a "happy, long, well-knit story."

Seed once explained that she began writing stories for young people only after she had married and had four children of her own. Nevertheless, she recalled, she had always been interested in writing as a child growing up in Cape Town, South Africa. "My father was a writer when he was younger, and as a small child I can remember rummaging through his cupboard drawers when I was allowed to play in his room, sorting through piles of his old manuscripts. And then, too, my mother was an excellent reader of stories. My sister Jewel and I would keep her busy with stories until her poor voice was reduced to a croak. It was not surprising then that from the age of about eight I too became interested in the written word and used to enjoy trying to compose little verses."

BIOGRAPHICAL/CRITICAL SOURCES:

BOOKS

Something about the Author, Volume 6, 1976; Volume 86, 1996, Gale.

Twentieth-Century Children's Writers, 4th edition, St. James Press, 1995.

PERIODICALS

Bulletin of the Center for Children's Books, May, 1975, p. 155.

Horn Book, April, 1975, pp. 154-55; December, 1975, p. 590.

Junior Bookshelf, February, 1983, p. 49.

Kirkus Reviews, March 1, 1968, p. 262; December 1, 1969, p. 1259; August 1, 1989, p. 1167.

Library Journal, July, 1968, p. 2731; May 15, 1971, p. 1806.

Publishers Weekly, July 28, 1989, p. 220.

School Library Journal, November, 1989, p. 94.

Times Literary Supplement, December 11, 1970, p. 1460; November 3, 1972, p. 1320; April 6, 1973, p. 383.*

* * *

SEED, Jenny
See SEED, Cecile Eugenie

* * *

SEIDEL, Kathleen G(illes) 1951-

PERSONAL: Born October 20, 1951, in Lawrence, KS; daughter of Paul W. (a professor of chemistry) and Helen M. (a pediatrician) Gilles; married Larry R. Seidel (a management consultant), April 14, 1973; children: two. *Education:* University of Chicago, A.B., 1973; Johns Hopkins University, M.A., 1975, Ph.D., 1978. *Politics:* Democrat. *Religion:* Unitarian-Universalist.

ADDRESSES: Home—Arlington, VA. *Agent*—Adele Leone Agency, 26 Nantucket Pl., Scarsdale, NY 10583.

CAREER: Northern Virginia Community College, Manassas, lecturer in English, 1977-82; full-time writer, 1982—.

MEMBER: Modern Language Association of America, Romance Writers of America, Washington Romance Writers (chairman, 1983-85).

WRITINGS:

ROMANCE NOVELS

The Same Last Name, Harlequin, 1983.
A Risk Worth Taking, Harlequin, 1983.
Mirrors and Mistakes, Harlequin, 1984.
After All These Years, Harlequin, 1984.
When Love Isn't Enough, Harlequin, 1984.

Don't Forget to Smile, Worldwide (Toronto), 1986.
Maybe This Time, Pocket Books (New York), 1990.
More Than You Dreamed, Pocket Books, 1991.

SIDELIGHTS: Kathleen G. Seidel began writing romance novels for Harlequin in the 1980s, when the publisher sought American writers for a series of novels in contemporary American settings. Commenting on Seidel's impressive academic background, Kay Mussell of *Twentieth-Century Romance and Historical Writers* noted, "As a specialist in the British novel, she brings to her novels an ability to adapt formal literary structures to traditional romance conventions, such as the marriage-of-convenience plot. More than many of her contemporaries, whose work is frequently loose and episodic, Seidel structures plots built on complex models of development."

The American settings of Seidel's novels play an important role in the plots and in the characters' development. In *Don't Forget to Smile* the heroine opens a bar in a logging town in rural Oregon to try to escape her past as a beauty contestant in the South. *The Same Last Name* features a successful lawyer in New York who is better understood in the context of his Virginia childhood. This novel is also an example of Seidel's ongoing portrayal of conflicted urban professionals whose careers demand family sacrifices, a choice that clashes with their traditional backgrounds.

The characters in Seidel's novels are open and honest with one another without being verbose. Seidel prefers a spare narrative style to the highly descriptive and dramatic styles of many romance writers. Conflicts generally arise from profound differences in characters' values or personalities rather than from accidents or misunderstandings. Commenting on Seidel's divergence from most conventional romance novel styles, Mussell wrote that she is "one of several talented romance writers who emerged in the early 1980s to redefine the traditional formula."

Seidel told *CA:* "When people find out that I have a Ph.D. in the theory of the novel, they ask, 'Why aren't you writing the Great American Novel?' 'I tried that,' I answer, 'but no one would read it.'

"In 1981, when I was engaged in the delightful chore of trying to sell my first novel, I realized that, as much as I wanted to be published, it was even more important to me to be read, and thirteen-dollar first novels do not get all that many readers.

"If you have something to say, you need to go where people are listening, and the 'brand name' category romance lines are where the readers are. My first book, as one of the launch titles for Harlequin's 'American Romance' line, had a press run of three hundred thousand.

"Perhaps the prevailing theme in my work is the notion that happiness is very often a choice. Some people make choices that nearly guarantee unhappiness. One of my heroines so wants people to like her that she is unable to act in her own interest; she must do what she thinks others want her to. In another book, the hero, a Vietnam veteran, thinks of himself as a failure and therefore structures situations so that he is certain to fail.

"What interests me is how such people change, and my plots usually show people going from making a set of choices that make them unhappy to making a set of choices that will make them happy. It is their success at doing this that makes my books compatible with the romance market.

"While it is true that there is a fair amount of mediocrity in the romance market, some of us writing for Harlequin today take our writing very seriously. We are writing books that we are proud of. We are well paid, our books have excellent distribution, and we have interested, loyal readers. Being ignored by the literary establishment is a small price to pay for that."

BIOGRAPHICAL/CRITICAL SOURCES:

BOOKS

Twentieth-Century Romance and Historical Writers, 3rd edition, St. James Press, 1994.

PERIODICALS

Publishers Weekly, March 4, 1983, p. 96; April 27, 1990, p. 56; October 25, 1991, p. 56.*

* * *

SELF, Will 1961-

PERSONAL: Born in 1961, in London, England; son of Peter (a college professor) and Elaine (Rosenbloom) Self (a publisher); married Kate Chancellor, June 13, 1990; children: Alexis, Madeleine. *Education:* Attended Oxford University, 1979-92, received M.A. (with honors). *Politics:* None. *Religion:* None.

ADDRESSES: Agent—Ed Victor, 162 Wardour St., London W1V 3AT, England.

CAREER: Worked as a clerk and a laborer. Full-time writer.

AWARDS, HONORS: Shortlisted for John Llewellyn Rhys Prize, 1991; Geoffrey Faber Memorial Prize, 1992, for *The Quantity Theory of Insanity;* voted one of twenty best young British writers in *Granta,* 1993.

WRITINGS:

The Quantity Theory of Insanity (short stories), Bloomsbury (London), 1991, Atlantic Monthly Press, 1995.
Cock and Bull (two novellas), Atlantic Monthly Press, 1992.
My Idea of Fun: A Cautionary Tale (novel), Bloomsbury, 1993, Atlantic Monthly Press, 1994.
Grey Area and Other Stories, Bloomsbury (London), 1994.
Junk Mail, Bloomsbury, 1995.
The Sweet Smell of Psychosis, illustrations by Martin-Rowson, Bloomsbury, 1996.
A Story for Europe, Bloomsbury, 1996.
Great Apes, Grove Press, 1997.
Tough, Tough Toys for Tough, Tough Boys, Grove Press, 1999.

Also author of *The Rock of Crack as Big as the Ritz,* 1995. Contributor of cartoons to periodicals, including *New Statesman* and *City Limits,* and of articles and reviews to periodicals, including *Esquire, Harpers,* and *Independent.*

SIDELIGHTS: The works of Will Self can be distinguished by their black humor and uncompromising themes. Self is the author of short stories, some of which are collected in *The Quantity Theory of Insanity,* as well as longer works of fiction like the two novellas which comprise *Cock and Bull.* In *Vanity Fair,* Zoe Heller observed that "the tone of *Quantity Theory*—both energetic and strangely lugubrious—was often profoundly discomfiting. And it was not difficult to guess that Self 's thematic preoccupations—madness, altered states, the sinister authority of the psychiatric establishment—refracted a painful biography." Madness is a topic that repeatedly appears within the stories of *The Quantity Theory of Insanity.* In "Ward 9," for example, an art therapist suffers a nervous breakdown and enters a mental asylum. The title story is based upon the proposition "that sanity is a finite quantity in any given social group," according to Nick Hornby in *Times Literary Supplement.* Hornby pointed out that Self 's stories are "full of dreary but threatening institutions,"and added, "Though you wouldn't want to live in the Self universe . . . in the end, you are grateful that he has gone through the agonies necessary for its creation."

The novellas in *Cock and Bull* both concern the inexplicable metamorphosis which transforms the respective main characters into the opposite sex. In *Bull,* a one-time rugby player named John Bull awakens one morning to discover that he has a vagina located behind his knee. "John Bull's behavior grows more and more feminine as he starts coping with premenstrual tension, water weight gain and hormonal ups and downs," Michiko Kakutani elaborated in *New York Times.* Seeking help from his physician, Bull visits Dr. Alan Margoulies, but the doctor becomes obsessed with Bull's condition and attempts to seduce him. "Margoulies' infatuation with Bull—or, rather, his new plaything—is a witty satire on the kind of man who is obsessed with women's sex organs and ignores the rest of them," commented Rhoda Koenig in *New York.* The reviewer also noted that "the doctor gets his comeuppance, and Bull, who also acquires feminine qualities of vulnerability, finds satisfaction in a unique homosexual relationship."

Like Bull, the protagonist of *Cock* also undergoes a sexual transformation. This time, Carol, a homemaker, grows a penis and develops increasingly masculine traits. She begins to dominate her alcoholic husband and eventually—according to Julie Wheelwright in *New Statesman*—"enacts a rape as revenge for her husband's sexual ineptitude." Kakutani pointed out the perceived "blatant sexism" of the novella, writing, "In *Cock,* we learn that the woman who stands up for herself relinquishes her femininity and literally turns into a man, in Carol's case a particularly foul-minded man filled with homicidal rage." However, Wheelright believed that the altered sex organs of Bull and Carol "appear as satirical metaphors of liberation." Self explained in *Vanity Fair* that he wrote *Cock and Bull* to voice his "anger at the way gender-based sexuality is so predetermined, the way we fit into our sex roles as surely as if we had cut them off the back of a cereal packet and pasted them onto ourselves."

In 1993 Self issued his first full-length novel, *My Idea of Fun: A Cautionary Tale.* The story is about Ian Wharton, who chooses people at random to kill and mutilate in grotesque ways. Except for his past mentor, Samuel Northcliffe, no one suspects Ian of committing such heinous crimes. The themes in *My Idea of Fun* include madness and sexual confusion. Will Blythe of *Es-*

quire commented that this "impressively deranged" book "belongs to a whole new genre devoted to the psycho killer and the severed limb." Blythe concluded, "Self 's extraordinary novel is an allegory of diseased consciousness, a parable for a decade when what trickled down was not money but scorn for those without it." A reviewer for *Publishers Weekly* observed that Self is a "master of the grotesque" whose book uses "vivid, jarringly unsavory imagery, richly erudite diction and a persuasive, engaging narrative voice."

Self reveals an intimate knowledge of drug culture in his fiction, having used marijuana, amphetamines, and cocaine while he was a teenager. Eventually, he became addicted to heroin; Self described himself in *Vanity Fair* as a "hard-core junkie" for almost eight years before he finally received treatment to end his habit. Heller noted in *Vanity Fair* that "the very texture of his prose bears the influence of his familiarity with drugs. . . . He has a gloriously vast vocabulary and a fetish for polysyllabic words. . . . It is most noticeable that where his vocabulary becomes most clotted, where his sentences require the most frequent application to the dictionary, he is often attempting to pin down the nuance of a precise psychic or physical experience—drug-derived perceptions for which no quotidian phrases are available."

Grey Area and Other Stories is a collection of nine short stories that depict the lives of people whose environments are so dull and meaningless that they escape into complex inner worlds. Self demonstrates that the distinctions between sanity and insanity are not always perfectly clear. A *Booklist* contributor called Self a "caustic yet competent critic of society," noting that in these stories, the "commonplace becomes awkward and surreal, allowing revelations and fresh insight to surface." In *New Statesman and Society* Mary Scott commented, "Self 's talent, like that of the best crime writers, is to drop . . . the clues that would enable us to reach his conclusions for ourselves—if we had his gift."

In the novel *Great Apes* London artist Simon Dykes wakes up to a world inhabited by chimpanzees. Although he notices that he seems to be turning into a chimpanzee, too, his denial lands him in a mental institution. His therapist is Dr. Zack Busner, a maverick researcher who takes his most intriguing cases onto talk shows. Barbara Hoffert of *Library Journal* noted that while Self "can be very funny," the book as a whole is not persuasive, partly due to Self 's extensive use of profanity and focus on sex. Although Gary Krist of *New York Times Book Review* admitted that this is not "a book that will delight everyone," he deemed it Self 's "most satisfying book so far." In *Booklist* a critic compared Self 's satire to the work of Franz Kafka and Jonathan Swift, adding that this novel "hypnotizes with its comic romps, existential posturings, and Shakespearean intrigues." A *Kirkus Reviews* contributor described *Great Apes* as "[v]ividly imagined, extraordinarily credible, provocative and entertaining in equal measure."

BIOGRAPHICAL/CRITICAL SOURCES:

BOOKS

Contemporary Novelists, 6th edition, St. James Press, 1996.

PERIODICALS

Booklist, December 1, 1995; August 19, 1997.

Esquire, April, 1994, p. 164.

Granta 43, spring, 1993, p. 259.

Kirkus Reviews, July 1, 1997.

Library Journal, October 1, 1997, p. 126.

London Review of Books, October 7, 1993, p. 20; June 19, 1997, p. 21.

Los Angeles Times Book Review, April 17, 1994, p. 4.

New Statesman, October 30, 1992, p. 35; November 25, 1994, p. 41; June 13, 1997, p. 44; May 1, 1998, p. 55.

New York, May 17, 1993, p. 87; September 1, 1997, p. 49.

New Yorker, April 11, 1994, p. 89.

New York Times, May 31, 1993; June 3, 1994, p. C24; September 12, 1997, p. C31.

New York Times Book Review, April 24, 1994, p. 27; February 26, 1995, p. 11; May 26, 1996, p. 9; September 21, 1997, p. 7; December 7, 1997, p. 62.

Observer, November 20, 1994, p. 19; January 12, 1997, p. 16; May 11, 1997, p. 16.

Publishers Weekly, February 7, 1994, p. 6.

Times Literary Supplement, December 20, 1991, p. 25; October 9, 1992, p. 22; November 18, 1994, p. 20; January 5, 1996, p. 32; December 20, 1996, p. 24; May 9, 1997, p. 19.

Tribune Books (Chicago), May 29, 1994, p. 5; March 5, 1995, p. 6; April 7, 1996, p. 6.

Vanity Fair, June, 1993, pp. 125-127, 148-151.

Washington Post Book World, April 3, 1994, p. 3; April 28, 1996, p. 3.*

SEREDY, Kate 1899-1975

PERSONAL: Surname sounds like *Sher-edy;* born November 10, 1899, in Budapest, Hungary; died March 7, 1975; came to United States, 1922; daughter of Louis Peter (a teacher) and Anna (Irany) Seredy. *Education:* Attended Academy of Arts, Budapest, six years, received art teacher's diploma; took summer courses in Paris, Rome, and Berlin, 1918-22.

CAREER: Ran a children's bookstore, 1933-34; owned a farm near Montgomery, NY, 1936-50s. Artist; author and illustrator of children's books, 1935-75. *Military service:* Served as a nurse in World War I.

AWARDS, HONORS: John Newbery Medal, 1938, for *The White Stag.*

WRITINGS:

FOR CHILDREN; ALL PUBLISHED BY VIKING PRESS, EXCEPT AS INDICATED

The Good Master, 1935.
Listening, 1936.
The White Stag, 1937.
The Singing Tree, 1939.
(Translator) *Who Is Johnny?,* 1939.
A Tree for Peter, 1940.
The Open Gate, 1943.
The Chestry Oak, 1948.
Gypsy, 1952.
Philomena, 1955.
The Tenement Tree, 1959.
A Brand New Uncle, 1960.
Lazy Tinka, 1962.

SIDELIGHTS: Kate Seredy believed in traditional values and harmony, and these beliefs permeate her fiction for middle-graders. Regarded as a gifted storyteller, Seredy wrote warm-hearted narratives that frequently reflect the culture of her native Hungary. Often utilizing pastoral settings in Hungary and America, Seredy employed vivid, rhythmic prose and concrete imagery to explore the feelings of her protagonists. These characters, who include Hungarian peasants and aristocrats, American farm and city dwellers, and Russian prisoners of war, are generally courageous, hard-working, altruistic, and peace-loving individuals with faith in themselves.

While critics find that her stories are occasionally didactic and border on sentimentality, they appreciate the positive values she imparts as well as her sensitivity to diverse populations and cultures. As an illustrator, Seredy incorporated realism and softness into her usually monochromatic drawings, and she has been particularly praised for her powerful depictions of horses.

Seredy once told CA that she became an author by accident. Prior to 1935 she designed book covers and greeting cards (and painted "horrible" lampshades) and also illustrated fifty or sixty textbooks and some children's books. A casual suggestion by editor May Massee of Viking Press that she write a story about her own childhood in Hungary became a challenge. "I started to write about things remembered, struggling with a recently learned strange language. Somehow—and I'll never know how—the story of *The Good Master* emerged. Written in longhand, it was a most unprofessional, bulky manuscript." Set on the Hungarian plains, the story is about the "good master" and his wife who live with their son, Jancsi, and their tomboy niece, Kate. Ann Bartholomew of *Twentieth-Century Children's Writers* noted, "Harvest festivals, household crafts, and even the local cooking add color to the warm family story." In *New York Times Book Review* Anne Thaxter Eaton deemed *The Good Master* "a genuinely joyous and beautiful book," adding that the "illustrations have beauty and vitality, the horses seem in motion and the children ready to speak."

Seredy won the Newbery Medal in 1938 for *The White Stag.* In *Dictionary of Literary Biography,* Kathy Piehl wrote, "The book retells the Hun-Magyar legends about the people who settled Hungary. Seredy's father had told her these stories about Nimrod, his sons Hunor and Magyar, Hunor's son, Bendeguz, and finally Bendeguz' son, Attila. Led by the god Hadur and the White Stag, who appears at crucial times to show them the way they should travel, the Huns eventually make the trip from Asia to the Hungarian plains. The journey involves bloodshed and destruction, and the book has sometimes been criticized for glorifying Attila the Hun." Addressing the suitability of the subject matter for children, Mary Gould Davis wrote in *Library Journal,* "Its integrity and beauty are such that they [children] get from it just exactly what its creator intended them to get: human pride and courage and loyalty, human pain and failure and defeat and, shaping it all, the superhuman strength, the selfless purpose that mark a hero." Piehl added that the "illustrations are majestic and imposing, an appropriate complement to the text. Black-and-white with gray shading, they capture the larger-than-life qualities of the heroes Seredy admired."

Seredy once commented, "Each book I've done was going to be [the] last; all these years I've felt like an impostor, a pretender, because *I still don't know how to write a book.* I think in pictures; I see life and thoughts pictorially, mostly in clean black and white. The beginning, the first spark for another story—for me—is always an excuse for making pictures. . . ." A small blond boy is seen clinging to a rusty iron fence against a rain-drenched backdrop of any "shanty town"—and *A Tree for Peter* happens. Another small boy tells his family that he's just seen a poor old dragon on Third Avenue, an old dragon "who had too much ice cream"; the author and the boy go to Third Avenue to investigate—and *The Tenement Tree* happens.

"From such small sparks were all my books written. I never really know what the story is going to be; soon after I start writing, the very people I am writing about take over and tell me what *they* want to do."

Seredy enjoyed woodcarving, sculpture, making pottery, painting children's portraits, and designing and sewing. She traveled in Austria, Italy, Germany, France, Switzerland, Great Britain, and the United States, and spoke German, French, and Hungarian.

BIOGRAPHICAL/CRITICAL SOURCES:

BOOKS

Children's Literature Review, Volume 10, Gale, 1986.
Dictionary of Literary Biography, Volume 22: *American Writers for Children, 1900-1960,* Gale, 1983.
Twentieth-Century Children's Writers, 4th edition, St. James Press, 1995.

PERIODICALS

Christian Science Monitor, October 5, 1984, p. B7.
Library Journal, June 15, 1938, p. 488.
Magpies, November, 1993, p. 16.
New York Times Book Review, November 17, 1935, p. 25.
Reading Teacher, April, 1982, p. 825.
Times Educational Supplement, March 4, 1983, p. 32; March 21, 1986, p. 27.*

* * *

SERRAILLIER, Ian (Lucien) 1912-1994

PERSONAL: Born September 24, 1912, in London, England; died November 28, 1994; son of Lucien and Mary (Rodger) Serraillier; married Anne Margaret Rogers, 1944; children: Helen, Jane, Christine Anne, Andrew. *Education:* St. Edmund Hall, Oxford, M.A., 1935.

CAREER: Wycliffe College, Stonehouse, Gloucestershire, England, schoolmaster, 1936-39; Dudley Grammar School, Dudley, Worcestershire, England, teacher, 1939-46; Midhurst Grammar School, Midhurst, Sussex, England, teacher, 1946-61.

AWARDS, HONORS: New York Times Best Illustrated Book citation, 1953, for *Florina and the Wild Bird;* Carnegie Medal commendation, 1956, Spring Book Festival Award, 1959, and Boys' Clubs of America Junior Book Award, 1960, for *The Silver Sword.*

WRITINGS:

(Contributor) *Three New Poets: Roy McFadden, Alex Comfort, Ian Serraillier,* Grey Walls Press, 1942.
The Weaver Birds (poems), Macmillan, 1944.
Thomas and the Sparrow (poems), Oxford University Press, 1946.
They Raced for Treasure, J. Cape, 1946, simplified educational edition published as *Treasure Ahead,* Heinemann, 1954.
Flight to Adventure, J. Cape, 1947, simplified educational edition published as *Mountain Rescue,* Heinemann,1955.
Captain Bounsaboard and the Pirates, J. Cape, 1949.
The Monster Horse (poems), Oxford University Press,1950.
There's No Escape, J. Cape, 1950, educational edition, Heinemann, 1952.
The Ballad of Kon-Tiki, Oxford University Press,1952.
Belinda and the Swans, J. Cape, 1952.
(Translator with wife, Anne Seraillier) S. Chonz, *Florina and the Wild Bird,* Oxford University Press, 1952.
(With Ronald Ridout) *Wide Horizon Reading Scheme,* Heinemann, fifteen volumes, including *Jungle Adventure,* Heinemann, 1953.
The Adventures of Dick Varley, Heinemann, 1954.
(Translator) *Beowulf the Warrior,* Oxford University Press, 1954, illustrated by Severin, Bethlehem Books (Vancouver, WA),1994.
Everest Climbed (poem), Oxford University Press,1955.
Making Good, Heinemann, 1955.
Guns in the Wild, Heinemann, 1956.
The Silver Sword, J. Cape, 1956, educational edition, Heinemann, 1957, Criterion, 1958, published as *Escape from Warsaw,* Scholastic, 1963.
Katy at Home, Heinemann, 1957.

Poems and Pictures, Heinemann, 1958.
(Contributor) Eleanor Graham, editor, *A Puffin Quartet of Poets: Eleanor Farjeon, James Reeves, E. V. Rieu, Ian Serraillier,* Penguin, 1958, revised edition, 1964.
Katy at School, Heinemann, 1959.
The Ivory Horn (adaptation of *The Song of Roland*), Oxford University Press, 1960, educational edition, Heinemann, 1962.
The Gorgon's Head: The Story of Perseus (also see below), Oxford University Press, 1961, Walck, 1962.
The Way of Danger: The Story of Theseus (also see below), Oxford University Press, 1962, Walck, 1963.
The Windmill Book of Ballads, Heinemann, 1962.
Happily Ever After: Poems for Children, Oxford University Press, 1963.
The Clashing Rocks: The Story of Jason, Oxford University Press, 1963, Walck, 1964.
The Midnight Thief: A Musical Story, music by Richard Rodney Bennett, BBC Publications, 1963.
The Enchanted Island: Stories from Shakespeare, Walck, 1964, educational edition, Heinemann, 1966.
Ahmet the Woodseller: A Musical Story, music by Gordon Crosse, Oxford University Press, 1965.
The Cave of Death, Heinemann, 1965.
Fight for Freedom, Heinemann, 1965.
A Fall from the Sky, Walck, 1966.
The Challenge of the Green Knight, Walck, 1966.
Robin in the Greenwood, Oxford University Press, 1967, Walck, 1968.
Chaucer and His World (nonfiction), Lutterworth, 1967, Walck, 1968.
The Turtle Drum (musical story), music by Malcolm Arnold, BBC Publications, 1967.
Havelok the Dane, Walck, 1967, published in England as *Havelok the Warrior,* Hamish Hamilton, 1968.
Robin and His Merry Men, Oxford University Press, 1969, Walck, 1970.
The Tale of Three Landlubbers, Hamish Hamilton, 1970, Coward, 1971.
Heracles the Strong, Walck, 1970.
The Ballad of St. Simeon, F. Watts, 1970.
A Pride of Lions (musical story), music by Phyllis Tate, Oxford University Press, 1971.
The Bishop and the Devil, F. Watts, 1971.
Have You Got Your Ticket?, Longman, 1972.
Marko's Wedding, Deutsch, 1972.
The Franklin's Tale, Retold, Warne, 1972.
I'll Tell You a Tale, Longman, 1973, revised edition, Kestrel Books, 1976.
Pop Festival, Longman, 1973.
Suppose You Met a Witch, Little, Brown, 1973.
The Robin and the Wren, Longman, 1974.
How Happily She Laughs, Longman, 1976.
The Sun Goes Free, Longman, 1977.
All Change at Singleton: For Charlton, Goodwood, East and West Dean (local history), Phillimore, 1979.
The Road to Canterbury, Kestrel Books, 1979.
(With Richard Pailthorpe) *Goodwood Country in Old Photographs,* Sutton, 1987.

Founder and editor with A. Serraillier, "New Windmill" series of contemporary literature, published by Heinemann. Omnibus volumes: *The Way of Danger* [and] *The Gorgon's Head,* educational edition, Heinemann, 1965.

SIDELIGHTS: Ian Serraillier was a poet with a passion for old balladry and legends. Many of his original works received less acclaim than those in which he retells classic tales. Among Serraillier's most respected works is *Beowulf the Warrior,* a retelling of *Beowulf.* Considering this work, a reviewer for *Times Literary Supplement* comments: "To venture on the story of Beowulf in verse, whether for children or adults, is a deed with its own kind of heroism. . . . There must be a hundred ways of failing; Mr. Serraillier has hit on one of the ways to succeed." The reviewer further commends Serraillier on how he has "preserved the note of royal breeding, of steadfast endeavor, and heroic resignation, which is so pronounced in the original poem."

In *The Challenge of the Green Knight,* "As usual, and most wisely, Mr. Serraillier does not attempt a translation or a paraphrase," writes a *Junior Bookshelf* reviewer. "Instead, he has written an original poem out of the roots of the remote masterpiece." In this case, again, "He keeps something of the mediaeval formality and mannerisms, preserving the grave courtliness in which this startlingly brutal tale [Sir Gawain and the Green Knight] is dressed. The result is a slow, powerful, occasionally beautiful poem, the weaknesses of which are built into the theme." Paul Heins agrees, noting that Serraillier's version "preserves the subtlety as well as the proportions of the original. . . . But beyond fantasy of event and realism of detail, the poet has caught Gawain's sensitive reactions to the testing of his character."

Serraillier takes Robin Hood as his subject in *Robin and His Merry Men.* Commenting on this choice, Brian Alderson writes: "It is not surprising to find Ian Serraillier turning to an adaptation of the ballads [about Robin Hood]. . . . It has been a characteristic of Serraillier's own poetry and of his previous adaptations that the words sound better off the tongue than they look on the page. . . . The Robin Hood ballads would seem to offer an even richer fund of material." Serraillier's versions "could only have been made by someone who loves the whole body of early ballad, carol, and lay, and knows it intimately," notes a reviewer for *Times Literary Supplement,* who adds his own praise for Serraillier's "very skillful" success "in preserving color, rhythm, and phrase while presenting a more immediately comprehensible language." In fact, one reviewer comments that "it takes some research to discover how much of this is Mr. Serraillier and how much the mediaeval balladeer. The modern poet has matched the old anonymous material with extraordinary skill." However, he points out that "while all this is extremely well done . . . readers who know Mr. Serraillier as . . . our finest poet writing for the young may feel that this is not the best use of his great talents."

A book which garnered less success for Serraillier is *The Enchanted Island.* In it, writes Aileen Peppett, he "attempts to lure children to enjoy Shakespeare on their own level of understanding. His method is to stress the humor, bypass the romance, and simplify the action as much as possible." A *Junior Bookshelf* reviewer suggests that "maybe the author tries too hard. This is a book mainly for children who don't know Shakespeare, to be read for its own sake. The child who meets Shakespeare for the first time here will take away the impression of fun, romance, heroism—all conveyed in simple words. . . . If *The Enchanted Island* does not quite succeed, this is because it attempts the impossible."

Serraillier's award-winning novel, *The Silver Sword,* was published more than forty years ago, and in comparison, many of his more recent works may be found lacking. Marcus Crouch writes that, in *The Silver Sword,* "Serraillier brought a poet's sensibility to a true story. . . . The story was written without heroics, but the heroism and endurance of the [characters] shone brightly in [his] unobtrusively lovely prose." Crouch also notes that "it is a book which one cannot read without profound emotional response and personal involvement. . . . Serraillier tells the story straight, never overstating the suffering, never adding his personal comment." As a reviewer for *Junior Bookshelf* says, the book is "touched with greatness. . . . It is obviously the work of a poet, who values words and uses them with restraint and economy, who never overplays a scene or overworks an emotion." He concludes: "It is sometimes said that children should be shielded from the harsh realities of life. . . . A book like *The Silver Sword* . . . can only enrich and ennoble the reader."

BIOGRAPHICAL/CRITICAL SOURCES:

BOOKS

Children's Literature Review, Volume II, Gale, 1976.

Crouch, Marcus, *The Nesbit Tradition: The Children's Novel in England,* Benn, 1972.

Crouch, Marcus, *Treasure Seekers and Borrowers: Children's Books in Britain, 1900-1960,* Library Association, 1962.

Dictionary of Literary Biography, Volume 161: *British Children's Writers since 1960, First Series,* Gale, 1996.

Something about the Author, Volume 73, Gale, 1993.

Something about the Author Autobiography Series, Volume 3, Gale, 1987.

Townsend, John Rowe, *Written for Children: An Outline of English-Language Children's Literature,* revised edition, Lippincott, 1974.

Twentieth-Century Young Adult Writers, 1st edition, St. James Press, 1994.

PERIODICALS

Christian Science Monitor, November 5, 1964.

Horn Book, August, 1967; June, 1968.

Junior Bookshelf, December, 1956; July, 1964; February, 1967; December, 1967; December, 1968; August, 1971.

New York Times Book Review, September 20, 1964; December 10, 1967.

School Library Journal, September, 1971.

Times Literary Supplement, November 19, 1954; November 28, 1963; November 24, 1966; November 30, 1967; July 2, 1971.

OBITUARIES:

PERIODICALS

Times (London), December 5, 1994, p. 21.*

* * *

SEVERN, Donald
See NOLAN, Frederick William

* * *

SHANLEY, John Patrick 1950-

PERSONAL: Born October 13, 1950, in New York, NY; father worked as a meat-packer and mother worked as a telephone operator; married Jayne Haynes, an actress (divorced). *Education:* New York University, B.S., 1977.

ADDRESSES: Home—New York, NY. *Agent*—Warner Bros., 4000 Warner Blvd., Burbank, CA 91522.

CAREER: Playwright, screenwriter, and director. Also worked as a bartender and house painter. *Military service:* U.S. Marines.

MEMBER: Writers Guild of America.

AWARDS, HONORS: Writers Guild of America Award and Academy Award (Oscar) from Academy of Motion Picture Arts and Sciences, both for best original screenplay, 1987, for *Moonstruck;* Los Angeles Drama Critics Circle award, 1987; special-jury prize at the Barcelona Film Festival for *Five Corners.*

WRITINGS:

PLAYS

Saturday Night at the War, produced in New York, 1978.
George and the Dragon, produced in New York, 1979.
Rockaway, produced in New York at Vineyard Theater, 1982.
Welcome to the Moon (produced in New York, 1982), published in *Welcome to the Moon and Other Plays,* Dramatists Play Service, 1985.
Savage in Limbo (produced in New York at 47th Street Theater, 1985), Dramatists Play Service, 1986.
the dreamer examines his pillow: A Heterosexual Homily (produced as a staged reading at the O'Neill Playwrights Conference, 1985, produced in New York at Double Image Theater, 1986), Dramatists Play Service, 1987.
Danny and the Deep Blue Sea (produced in Los Angeles at the Back Alley Theatre, 1986), published as *Danny and the Deep Blue Sea: An Apache Dance,* Dramatists Play Service, 1984.
Women of Manhattan, produced in New York at City Center Theater, 1986.
Italian American Reconciliation, produced Off-Broadway, 1988.
The Big Funk: A Casual Play, Dramatists Play Service (New York City), 1991.
Beggars in the House of Plenty, Dramatist Play Service, 1992.
13 by Shanley, Applause Books (New York City), 1992.
What Is This Everything?, produced in New York, 1992.
Four Dogs and a Bone; and, The Wild Goose, Dramatists Play Service, 1995.
Psychopathia Sexualis, produced in New York, 1997.

SCREENPLAYS

Moonstruck, Metro Goldwyn-Mayer, 1987.
Five Corners, Handmade Films, 1988.
The January Man, Metro Goldwyn-Mayer, 1989.
(And director) *Joe versus the Volcano,* Warner Bros., 1990.
Alive (based on the novel by Piers Paul Read), Paramount, 1993.
Congo (based on the novel by Michael Crichton), Paramount, 1995.

Also author of television scripts.

ADAPTATIONS: Several of Shanley's screenplays have been adapted into storybooks and novelizations.

SIDELIGHTS: "In order to write an effective screenplay, you have to have no distance from your material," John Patrick Shanley said in *American Film.* "You have to be in the scene with the characters. You cannot be cynical, you cannot be removed, you cannot be in a place where you think you know more than they know." Shanley continued, "Whatever you do in terms of telling a story, the most important thing that you can define is who you are. The stories are all out there; it's finding a place where *you* are in relationship to the story that will tell thc story."

A popular playwright and screenwriter, Shanley first gained national attention with the 1987 film *Moonstruck,* a highly emotional comedy about love, passion, and the relationships of an Italian family. To Charles Champlin of *Los Angeles Times, Moonstruck* "seems as nearly perfect as a script ever gets." Shanley began his career writing for the theater. His dramas, commonly set in Shanley's native New York City, feature eccentric, working-class characters and explosive dialogue. According to *New York* critic John Simon, the playwright is most effective "when he lets his characters have at one another and themselves in torrents of rage and despair, sarcasm and sudden epiphany."

While growing up in the Bronx, Shanley encountered some of the rough-and-tough types of characters found in his plays. After Shanley was expelled from high school a few times, a priest took an interest in his welfare and sent him to a private school in New Hampshire. Shanley then attended New York University, where he received a master's degree in educational theater. During the 1980s Shanley had numerous plays produced in New York, including *Danny and the Deep Blue Sea, Savage in Limbo, the dreamer examines his pillow,* and *Italian American Reconciliation.*

Though some of Shanley's plays, including *the dreamer examines his pillow* and *Italian American Reconciliation,* met with positive reception, Shanley's films have received greater critical praise and commercial success. *Moonstruck,* Shanley's first produced screenplay, was a surprise hit and won an Academy Award for best original screenplay. Set in Brooklyn, the film relates the romantic entanglements and relationships of the Castorini family. A *Newsweek* reviewer declared that almost immediately, *Moonstruck* "lets you know it knows it's going to revel in—and tease—every Italian-American stereotype in the book." Loretta Castorini, a widow in her late thirties, accepts an offer of marriage from timid, dull, but steady Johnny, although she does not love him. Her main concern is planning a traditional, by-the-book wedding to avoid the bad luck that she believes caused her first husband's death. Johnny leaves for Palermo to see his allegedly dying mother, instructing his fiance to invite his estranged younger brother, Ronny, to their wedding. Violent and passionate Ronny unfairly blames Johnny for the machinery accident that claimed his hand. Quickly infatuated, Loretta and Ronny begin an affair, which Loretta soon regrets and attempts to end. As excerpted in *American Film,* Ronny persuades Loretta to give up her plans with Johnny by explaining his views on love: "Love don't make things nice, it ruins everything, it breaks your heart, it makes things a mess. We're not here to make things perfect. Snowflakes are perfect. The stars are perfect. Not us. Not us! We are here to ruin ourselves and break our hearts and love the wrong people and die!"

Johnny unexpectedly arrives in town after his mother miraculously recovers. Ronny decides that that morning would be a good time to meet Loretta's family, and he and Loretta—with the rest of the family gathered around the breakfast table—wait tensely for Johnny's arrival. As Loretta readies to cancel the wedding, Johnny surprises everyone by announcing that he will not marry her; apparently he breaks the engagement to appease his dying mother. In the final scene, the family toasts themselves and the engagement of Ronny and Loretta.

Shanley populated *Moonstruck* with interesting minor characters, including Loretta's dog-loving grandfather and a middle-aged professor whose disastrous dinner dates with younger women at a neighborhood restaurant lead to what *People* contributor Peter Travers called "a jewel of a scene" with Mrs. Castorini. Having guessed her husband's infidelity, Mrs. Castorini questions the professor about why men are driven to affairs. "When you see that the whole cast of family members are involved in libidinal confusions," remarked Pauline Kael in *New Yorker,* "the operatic structure can make you feel close to deliriously happy."

Many other critics responded enthusiastically to the film's characters, humor, and emotional mood. Travers found the characters "full of mischievous surprise" and felt the screenplay had "a real comic edge." Praising the script as "inventively written," a reviewer for *Newsweek* described it as "a very knowing piece of comic artifice." Champlin contended that *Moonstruck* "proved beyond argument . . . that Shanley has a rare gift for dialogue. I'm not sure that an *ear* for dialogue is the way to say it. Real speech rarely has the economy, the timing, the polish that Shanley gives his talk." Summing up the film's appeal, Kael called *Moonstruck* "a giddy homage to our desire for grand passion. With its own special lushness, it's a rose-tinted black comedy."

Shanley's next two films, *Five Corners* and *The January Man,* did not receive the popular and critical acclaim awarded *Moonstruck.* Like many of Shanley's plays, *Five Corners* was considered off-beat. Set in the Bronx, the 1988 film concerns a violent and disturbed delinquent's behavior when released from jail. David Ansen of *Newsweek* described *Five Corners* as "a seriocomic meditation on American violence seen through the prism of a half-dozen blue-collar kids in the dawning era of the civil-rights movement." Ansen added that the ending is disappointing, as Shanley "feels compelled to bring events to a rip-roaring melodramatic conclusion, and the climax gets out of hand."

Released in 1989, *The January Man* is a thriller about an ex-cop who, wrongly accused of corruption, responds to a plea that he return to police work to apprehend a maniacal killer. Critics felt that film's downfall was a confusing plot. "There are moments when watching *January Man* is like trying to follow the third episode of a miniseries mystery after you've missed the first two," asserted Champlin. Yet the critic stated that the film confirmed Shanley's talents for creating interesting dialogue and characters who are "poised somewhere between the abnormal and the bizarre."

Joe versus the Volcano marked Shanley's film directing debut. Upon reading the script, filmmaker Steven Spielberg called and offered to produce the film, leaving the directing duties to Shanley. In this 1990 film Joe Banks, a hypochondriac working in a remarkably bleak plant that manufactures medical devices, discovers that he has a fatal "brain cloud." When his doctor informs him of this symptomless time bomb, Joe decides to live what life he has left to the fullest. Into the picture comes a billionaire who proposes a free trip to the South Seas if Joe will sacrifice himself afterwards by throwing himself into a volcano. The billionaire believes that this act will pacify the gods and ensure the success of a business deal concerning a mineral on the island. Joe agrees to the plan, begins to enjoy life, and falls in love with his benefactor's daughters—Angelica, an artistic flower-child, and Patricia, the brave skipper of her father's yacht.

Though critics appreciated the film, they faulted it for having a weak ending. Sheila Benson declared in *Los Angeles Times* that "there's a quickly-tied-together feeling to it blessedly missing from the rest of the movie. . . . If you wish for more depth at the ending . . . you're not alone; the trick is to savor the trip along the way and to hope that Shanley keeps his style and deepens his substance with his next film." Some critics note sentimentality and overstatement in *Joe versus the Volcano* and Shanley's other works, but Dave Kehr remarked in *Chicago Tribune:* "Shanley's charm is in the obviousness of his imagery, the naive insistence of his symbols. . . . Yet that insistence," Kehr added, "loses all its charm once it is transformed into . . . windy, philosophical speeches." Benson, however, strongly affirmed Shanley's first directing venture: "Witty, disarming and beautiful, *Joe* is the tip-off that John Patrick Shanley is at least as distinctive a director as he has already been a playwright and screenwriter."

BIOGRAPHICAL/CRITICAL SOURCES:

BOOKS

Contemporary Dramatists, 5th edition, St. James Press, 1993.
Contemporary Literary Criticism, Volume 75, Gale, 1993.

PERIODICALS

American Film, September, 1989.
Chicago Tribune, March 9, 1990.
Los Angeles Times, February 5, 1986; March 5, 1988; February 9, 1989; March 9, 1990.
Maclean's, April 4, 1988.
Nation, May 19, 1997.
National Review, March 4, 1988.
Newsweek, December 21, 1987; January 25, 1988.
New York, October 20, 1986; November 14, 1988.
New Yorker, January 25, 1988.
New York Times, October 14, 1982; November 24, 1982; September 26, 1985; May 5, 1986; April 10, 1988; January 13, 1989.
People, January 18, 1988.
Time, November 7, 1988; January 23, 1989.*

* * *

SHAPCOTT, Thomas W(illiam) 1935-

PERSONAL: Born March 21, 1935, in Ipswich, Australia; son of Harold (an accountant) and Dorothy (Gillespie) Shapcott; married Margaret Hodge (a teacher), April 18, 1960; married Judith Rodriguez, October 13, 1982; children: (first marriage) Katherine, Alison, Richard, Isabel. *Education:* University of Queensland, B.A., 1969.

ADDRESSES: Home—P.O. Box 231, Mont Albert, Victoria 3127, Australia.

CAREER: H. S. Shapcott (public accountant), Ipswich, Australia, clerk, 1951-63; Shapcott & Shapcott (accountants), Ipswich, partner, 1963-72; public accountant and sole trader in Ipswich, 1972-78. Secretary, Ipswich Fire Brigade, 1970—. Literature Board of Australia Council, deputy chairman, 1973-76, director, 1983-90. Executive director, National Book Council, 1992—. *Military service:* National Service, 1953.

AWARDS, HONORS: Grace Leven Prize for poetry, 1961, for *Time on Fire;* Sir Thomas White Memorial Prize for poetry, 1967, for *A Taste of Salt Water;* Sydney Myer Charity Trust Award, 1967, for *A Taste of Salt Water,* and 1969, for *Inwards to the Sun;* Churchill fellowship to the United States and England, 1972; Canada-Australia prize, 1979; gold wreath, Struga Poetry Festival, Yugoslavia, 1989; Christopher Brennan Award for Poetry, 1994; Officer in the Order of Australia, 1989; D.Litt., Macquarie University, 1989.

WRITINGS:

POEMS

Time on Fire, Jacaranda Press, 1961.
Twelve Bagatelles, Australian Letters, 1962.
The Mankind Thing, Jacaranda Press, 1964.
Sonnets 1960/1963, B. Donaghey, 1964.
A Taste of Salt Water, Angus & Robertson (London), 1967.

Inwards to the Sun, University of Queensland Press (St. Lucia, Queensland, Australia), 1969.
Fingers at Air: Experimental Poems, privately printed, 1969.
Begin with Walking, University of Queensland Press, 1969.
Interim Report, privately printed, 1972.
Shabbytown Calendar, University of Queensland Press, 1976.
Seventh Avenue Poems, Angus & Robertson, 1976.
Selected Poems, University of Queensland Press, 1978.
Turning Full Circle: Prose Poems, New Poetry (Sydney), 1978.
Stump and Grape and Bobble-nut, Bullion Publications, 1981.
Welcome!, University of Queensland Press, 1983.
Travel Dice, University of Queensland Press, 1987.
Poems, Misla (Skopje, Yugoslavia), 1989.
Selected Poems, 1956-88, University of Queensland Press, 1989.
In the Beginning, National Library of Australia (Canberra), 1990.
The City of Home, University of Queensland Press, 1995.

EDITOR

(With Rodney Hall) *New Impulses in Australian Poetry,* University of Queensland Press, 1969.
Australian Poetry Now, Sun Books, 1970.
Poets on Record, 14 volumes, University of Queensland Press, 1970-74.
Contemporary American and Australian Poetry, University of Queensland Press, 1976.
Consolidation: The Second Poets Anthology, University of Queensland Press, 1982.
Contemporary Australian Poetry (Macedonian edition), Skopje (Macedonia), 1989.
Pamphlet Poets Series 2, 6 volumes, National Library of Australia, 1991.
The Moment Made Marvelous: A Celebration of UQP Poetry, University of Queensland Press, 1998.

NOVELS

The Birthday Gift, University of Queensland Press, 1982.
White Stag of Exile, Allen Lane (London), 1984.
Holiday of the Ikon, Puffin Books (Harmondsworth, England), 1984.
Hotel Bellevue, Chatto & Windus (London), 1986.
The Search for Galina, Chatto & Windus, 1989.
(With Steve Spears) *Mr. Edmund,* McPhee Gribble, 1990.
(With A. R. Simpson) *His Master's Ghost,* McPhee Gribble, 1990.
Mona's Gift, Penguin (Sydney), 1993.

OTHER

Focus On Charles Blackman (art monograph), University of Queensland Press, 1967.
The Seven Deadly Sins (opera libretto), privately printed, 1970.
Flood Children (for children), Jacaranda Press, 1981.
The Literature Board: A Brief History, University of Queensland Press, 1988.
Limestone and Lemon Wine (stories), Black Swan (London), 1988.
(With Robin Burridge) *The Art of Charles Blackman,* A. Deutsh (London), 1989.
Biting the Bullet: A Literary Memoir, Simon & Schuster (Brookvale, New South Wales, Australia), 1990.
What You Own (stories), Angus & Robertson, 1991.

Also author of *Those Who Are Compelled,* 1980.

SIDELIGHTS: Thomas W. Shapcott has steadily developed a reputation as not only a formidable poet, but as a novelist and a leading editor in Australian literature. Shapcott's poetry has evolved from using traditional forms to a looser, more experimental style. His themes range from the artist's search for self-definition to the contrast between the poet's inner perceptions and the external world.

Time on Fire, Shapcott's first published collection of poetry, won the young poet the Grace Leven Prize. "Shapcott's best passages are those in which his finely attentive response to the natural scene develops inwardly: the pressure of the scene and the pressure of his own preoccupations fuse in a meaningful vision," David Moody writes in a *Meanjin* review of the book.

Shapcott's poems about the natural world continued to develop in *The Mankind Thing.* In the poem "Two and Half Acres," Carl Harrison-Ford notes in *Meanjin,* "the natural cycles of nature foster an awareness of form and of variety within it that obviously relates to [Shapcott's] aims in poetry. Shapcott sums this up succinctly yet unobtrusively: My fingers catch / at bark, twig, seed. There's no captivity / to hold them in. The act escapes from me. / Matter is form to hold such mystery."

A Taste of Salt Water won Shapcott two major Australian poetry awards and a wider critical attention. Divided into five sections, the book includes "sonnets and lyrics, a New Testament sequence, poems with various urban themes, elegies celebrating the deaths of people and things and a very polished poem entitled 'Macquarie as Father' " observes Robert Ward in *Australian Book Review.* Calling Shapcott "a mature and intelligent poetic talent," Ward praises his controlled use of language, its vividness and capacity, saying "He can surprise one by saying 'Let me sing / even the buzz of flies defines the spring' " Joining in the praise for *A Taste of Salt Water,* James Tulip calls the book "a series of adroit, sensitive ventures into a variety of subjects." In his review for *Southerly,* Tulip speaks of Shapcott's religious approach to myths, his fresh look at historical poetry and "strongest of all in my view, poems dealing with closely observed personal relations." Tulip goes on to admire Shapcott's verse as having "character . . . a tone, an honesty, a registering of personal engagement with the facts of normal living." But Tulip was not without complaints about the collection. He found that Shapcott's "lightness of tone often becomes a mildness of tone, and his attitudes soft and self-indulgent."

The frankly experimental work *Fingers at Air* found Shapcott poet breaking away from his traditional inclinations and working in more abstract forms. "Take the first sequence 'Dance, Dance'. . . .," writes S. E. Lee in *Southerly.* "It runs I think for 12 pages . . . and employs a recurring line design that one commonly observes on old-fashioned tiled floors. . . . The spaces inside and outside the diamond are gradually filled with cryptic words and chunks of sentences taken out of context until at the end we have a cluttered page." *Begin with Walking* continues Shapcott's abstract poetic experiments, this time introducing more American-influenced work, including poems with only one word per line. Some poems written on a visit to New York City were collected in *Seventh Avenue Poems.* Shapcott furthered the effects of free-form American styles on Australian writers by editing the anthology *Contemporary American and Australian Poetry,* published in 1976.

Shapcott's attempts at abstraction had value, despite some failures, Harrison-Ford states in a *Meanjin* analysis of the poet's work. "The many poems published since *Fingers at Air* suggest that those naked experiments proved fruitful," Harrison-Ford argues. "The privately produced *Interim Report* (1972) includes many of those poems and displays a style that is new and characteristic."

Following through on his poetic breakthroughs, Shapcott published *Shabbytown Calendar.* Called an "intricate and mature volume" by Christopher Pollnitz in *Southerly,* it "traces all twelve months, allotting three poems to each. Two poems deal with persons, places, flora and weathers loosely appropriate to the season, the third is a 'fugue' dedicated to the month." For Pollnitz, "The overriding concern of the *Calendar* is with time, with ways of mummifying, recapturing, regenerating, transcending or being reconciled to time." Pollnitz concludes that Shapcott "may have found a hint" for his poetic innovations in "contemporary American poetry." But Shapcott's work was also an important "discovery and achievement" for "contemporary Australian poetry." Kevin Hart, reviewing *Shabbytown Calendar* in *Southern Review,* finds a number of "inconsequential sketches" in the book. But there is also evidence of "a strong imaginative mind meditating on central human concerns." Hart contends that "*Shabbytown Calendar* must be seen as a flawed but persuasive attempt at a verse-novel."

Shapcott turned his talents to the novel form in 1983 with publication of *The Birthday Gift.* Following the lives of twins, Ben and Benno, Shapcott switches the point of view from their Queensland childhood in the 1940s to scenes from their young adulthood in the 1950s. These "jagged time fragments" make the novel "difficult to follow," Annette James writes in *Library Journal,* although she admits that the book contains "rich and sensitive prose." Tulip, writing about *The Birthday Gift* in *Southerly,* finds that it "lacks fictional freedom; it is one step from being a journal, an autobiography, a confession." But Tulip also sees the novel as proof of Shapcott's position as "a central reflecting intelligence of his generation."

In *White Stag of Exile* Shapcott tells the story of Karoly Pulszky, a nineteenth-century Hungarian art historian who immigrated to Australia when political turmoil drove him from his homeland. Shapcott tells the story in a disjointed manner, using letters and other documents to assemble a biography of Pulszky. In a review for *New Statesman,* Roger Lewis claims that *White Stag of Exile* "is hardly a novel at all" but more a "scrapbook of letters, journals and reports." Although Lewis concludes that it is an "odd book," one "that lingers uneasily in the limbo between fact and fantasy," Roger Manvell, writing in *British Book News,* calls *White Stag* "absorbing" and "a notable combination of research and invention."

A return to the past plays a role in Shapcott's novel *Hotel Bellevue* as well. In this book, Boyd Kennedy leaves a broken marriage to return to his grandmother's house in Brisbane. Confronting his past, he becomes involved in preventing the destruction of the historic hotel of the book's title. "A sense of the inevitable" motivates Shapcott's characters, Anthony Sattin notes in a *Times Literary Supplement* review, but that sense "works against the impact of the neatly constructed narrative." Sattin finds, however, that like most of Shapcott's work, the book is "a vigorous and energetic piece of writing" and contains "some serious and sensitive meditations on the past, and the price still to pay for it." Critic Margaret Walters, writing in *Observer,* explains that *Hotel Bellevue* "explores the ambiguities of memory—the need to preserve the past, but the need, as well, to recognize how it traps and destroys us." Ultimately, Walters concludes that the novel "doesn't have the symbolic resonance Shapcott clearly intends, and the book's interesting but disparate strands never quite cohere."

In his short story collection *Limestone and Lemon Wine* Shapcott invents the town of Limestone, set in the Australian countryside, to explore "those elements of life which can emerge particularly vividly in a small town," as Mansel Stimpson writes in *Times Literary Supplement.* The collection's longest story, "Water and Blood," reveals once again the author's interest in the relationships between the past and present. It covers a hundred years of family history while focusing on an adopted girl's obsession with her origins. "Built up from disparate sections," Stimpson writes, "[the story] shows Shapcott's skill at holding things together." Commenting on his ability to present stories in an unobtrusive style, Stimpson concludes that Shapcott's "is an art which conceals art, and is the more enjoyable for it."

Shapcott once told *CA:* "I am deeply interested in the development of poetry in Australia and in its wider relevance in English speaking contexts. My own development has been from lyrical celebratory beginnings, through increasing awareness of social process to (most recently) a sense of regional mythology within a world in flux. I do not see myself as a regional poet, though; rather, as one man rediscovering himself through others."

BIOGRAPHICAL/CRITICAL SOURCES:

BOOKS

Contemporary Literary Criticism, Volume 38, Gale, 1986.

Contemporary Poets, 6th edition, St. James Press, 1996.

PERIODICALS

Apollo, September, 1990, p. 211.

Australian, October 9, 1993.

Australian Book Review, October, 1967, p. 197; March, 1970, pp. 127-128; September, 1991, p. 18; September, 1993, pp. 17-18; September, 1995, p. 50.

Australian Literary Studies, October, 1990.

Australian Magazine, February 25, 1989.

British Book News, December, 1984, p. 750.

Canberra Times, August 19, 1988.

Illustrated London News, March, 1988, p. 79.

London Magazine, September, 1986.

Magpies, March, 1991, p. 30.

Meanjin, December, 1961, pp. 503-505; September, 1972, pp. 300-307; April, 1979, pp. 56-68.

New Statesman, August 3, 1984, p. 27.

Observer, July 29, 1984, p. 20; September 14, 1986, p. 27; February 14, 1988, p. 27; June 25, 1989 p. 45.

Overland, June, 1988.

Poetry, January, 1978, p. 225.

San Francisco Review of Books, winter, 1983, p. 11.

Southerly, Volume 25, number 2, 1965, pp. 131-137; Volume 28, number 1, 1968, pp. 71-73; Volume 30, number 4, 1970, pp. 306-311; Volume 31, number 1, 1971, pp. 72-73; Volume 33, number 2, 1973, p. 239; Volume 36, number 4, 1976, pp. 464-470; Volume 43, number 1, 1983, pp. 113-118.

Southern Review, March, 1977, pp. 79-80.

Times Literary Supplement, November 7, 1986, p. 1255; November 27, 1987, p. 1327; February 26, 1988, p. 215.

World Literature Today, autumn, 1979, p. 743; winter, 1984, p. 170; summer, 1984, p. 471; autumn, 1988, p. 725.*

* * *

SHAPIRO, David (Joel) 1947-

PERSONAL: Born January 2, 1947, in Newark, NJ; son of Irving (a physician) and Fraida (a singer and teacher; maiden name, Chagy) Shapiro; married Lindsay Stamm (a professor of architecture), August 30, 1970; children: Daniel Jonathan. *Education:* Columbia University, B.A. (magna cum laude), 1968, Ph.D. (with distinction), 1973; Clare College, Cambridge, B.A., 1970, M.A. (first class honors), 1974. *Religion:* Jewish.

ADDRESSES: Home—3001 Henry Hudson Pkwy., Linden House 3B, Bronx, NY 10463.

CAREER: Columbia University, New York City, instructor, 1972-73, assistant professor of English,

1973-81; William Paterson College, Wayne, NJ, professor of art history, 1981—. Visiting professor at Brooklyn College, 1979, William Paterson College, and Princeton School of Visual Arts; visiting professor and writer-in-residence (since 1980), Cooper Union; visiting lecturer, Princeton University, 1982-83. Professional violinist, 1963—; has played with New Jersey Symphony, Provincetown Symphony, and under Stokowski in Scranton, PA. Editorial associate, *New Yorker,* and *Art News,* 1970—. Collaborator with architect John Hejduk on theatrical masques and architectural projects, 1980—. Curator of poetry shows at PS 1 and the Salon des Independants. Specialist in teaching poetry to children for American Academy, New Jersey Council of the Arts, and New York Council of the Arts.

AWARDS, HONORS: Gotham Book Mart Avant Garde Poetry Award, 1962; Bread Loaf Writers Conference Robert Frost fellowship, 1965; New York Poets Foundation Award, 1966; Merrill Foundation fellowship, 1967; Kellett fellowship to Cambridge University, 1968-70; Book-of-the-Month Club grant, 1968; National Book Award nominee for poetry, 1971, for *A Man Holding an Acoustic Panel;* Columbia University Woodbridge Award for Academic Excellence, 1973; Creative Artists in Public Service award in poetry, 1974; Zabel Prize, National Academy and Institute, 1977, for poetry; National Endowment for the Arts and National Endowment for the Humanities grants, 1980, 1981.

WRITINGS:

Poems, privately printed, 1960.
A Second Winter, privately printed, 1961.
When Will the Bluebird, privately printed, 1962.
January: A Book of Poems, Holt (New York City), 1965.
Poems from Deal, Dutton (New York City), 1969.
(Editor with Ron Padgett) *An Anthology of New York Poets,* Random House (New York City), 1970.
A Man Holding an Acoustic Panel, Dutton, 1971.
The Dance of Things, Lincoln Center, 1971.
The Page-Turner (poems), Liveright (New York City), 1973.
Lateness: A Book of Poems, Overlook Press (Woodstock NY), 1977.
(Co-author) *Harrisburg Mon Amour, or Two Boys on a Bus* (play), music by Laurie Anderson, produced in New York City at Kitchen Theatre, 1978.
John Ashbery: An Introduction to the Poetry, Columbia University Press (New York City), 1979.
Unwritten, illustrated with drawings by Lucio Pozzi, Lapp Princess Press, 1979.
(Translator with Arthur Cohne) *The New Art of Color: The Writings of Sonia and Robert Delaunay,* Viking (New York City), 1979.
(With Roland Barthes and others) *Pop Art,* Alecta, 1980.
Jim Dine: Painting What One Is, Abrams (New York City), 1981.
(With Robert C. Hobbs) *Artistic Collaboration in Twentieth Century Art,* edited by Cynthia Jaffee McCabe, Smithsonian Institution Press (Washington, DC), 1984.
To an Idea: A Book of Poems, Overlook Press, 1984.
Jasper Johns: Drawings, 1954-1984, edited by Christopher Sweet, Abrams, 1984.
House (Blown Apart): A Book of Poems, Overlook Press, 1988.
Mondrian Flowers, Abrams, 1991.
(With Judith Stein) *Alfred Leslie: The Killing Cycle,* St. Louis Art Museum (St. Louis, MO), 1991.
(Translator with Gabriel Berns) Rafael Alberti, *The Eight Names of Picasso: Los 8 Nombres de Picasso,* Gas Station Editions, 1992.
The Thunder God: A Chinese Folktale, Harcourt Brace, 1992.
(Translator) Jacques Dupin, *Selected Poems,* Wake Forest University Press (Winston-Salem, NC), 1992.
After a Lost Original: A Book of Poems, Overlook Press, 1994.
Inventory: New and Selected Poems, Hard Press (West Stockbridge, MA), 1997.

Also author of numerous catalogs and monographs. Coeditor of *Learn Something, America,* 1968. Playwright of *New England Masque,* produced in Boston; coauthor of screenplay *Mobile Homes.* Contributor to various books; also contributor to numerous periodicals, including *Antioch Review, Art Forum, Paris Review, Minnesota Review, Art and Literature, Beloit Poetry Journal, Art News, Craft Horizons, Poetry, Saturday Review,* and *Atlantic Monthly.*

SIDELIGHTS: David Shapiro uses contemporary and autobiographical elements in writing his metaphysical poetry. Objects such as spaceships, violins, and automobiles are mentioned in his verse, alongside musings on the family and the modern Jewish experience. Tyrus Miller of *Contemporary Poets* observed that Shapiro's early poetry is "full of witty paradoxes and non sequiturs," whereas his later work reflects a move toward "philosophical meditation with personal or erotic overtones." Miller further noted that "Shapiro's best work springs from his reflection on the restlessness of imagination and desire."

Shapiro once told *CA:* "My grandfather, Berele Chagy, was one of the great Jewish cantors and composers and his improvisational liturgical style has been a great influence on my work. My family was a string quartet, and my art has been also profoundly marked by my life as a musician and by my aesthetic standards: Mozart's late quartets and Beethoven as well as the music of John Cage and Elliot Carter."

BIOGRAPHICAL/CRITICAL SOURCES:

BOOKS

Contemporary Poets, 6th edition, St. James Press, 1996.

PERIODICALS

Los Angeles Times Book Review, November 2, 1980, p. 18; February 3, 1985, p. 4.
Newsweek, December 21, 1981, p. 80.
New York Times Book Review, November 26, 1978, p. 60; December 2, 1984, p. 11; March 4, 1984, p. 14.
Times Literary Supplement, September 6, 1985, p. 970.
World Literature Today, spring, 1995, p. 366.*

* * *

SHAPIRO, Harvey 1924-

PERSONAL: Born January 27, 1924, in Chicago, IL; son of Jacob (a businessman) and Dorothy (Cohen) Shapiro; married Edna Lewis Kaufman (a psychologist), July 23, 1953; children: Saul, Dan. *Education:* Yale University, B.A., 1947; Columbia University, M.A., 1948.

ADDRESSES: Home—43 Pierrepont St., Brooklyn, NY 11201. *Office—New York Times,* 229 West 43rd St., New York, NY 10036.

CAREER: Cornell University, Ithaca, NY, instructor in English, 1949-50, 1951-52; Bard College, Annandale-on-Hudson, NY, creative writing fellow, 1950-51; *Commentary,* New York City, assistant editor, 1955-56; *New Yorker,* New York City, fiction editor, 1956-57; *New York Times Magazine,* New York City, member of editorial staff, 1957-64, assistant editor, 1964-75, deputy editor, 1983—; *New York Times Book Review,* New York City, editor, 1975-83. *Military service:* U.S. Army Air Forces, 1943-45; became technical sergeant; received Distinguished Flying Cross and Air Medal with three oak leaf clusters.

MEMBER: Elizabethan Club (New Haven).

AWARDS, HONORS: YMHA Poetry Center award, 1952; Swallow Press award, 1954; Rockefeller Foundation fellowship in poetry, 1968.

WRITINGS:

POETRY

The Eye, Swallow Press, 1953.
The Book and Other Poems, Cummington, 1955.
Mountain, Fire, Thornbush, Swallow Press, 1961.
Battle Report, Wesleyan University Press, 1966.
This World, Wesleyan University Press, 1971.
Lauds, Sun Press, 1975.
Lauds and Nightsounds, Sun Press, 1978.
The Light Holds, Wesleyan University Press, 1984.
National Cold Storage Company: New and Selected Poems, Wesleyan University Press, 1988.
A Day's Portion: Poems, Hanging Loose Press (Brooklyn, NY), 1994.
Selected Poems, with an introduction by James Atlas, University Press of New England, 1997.

NOVELS

(With Paulett Tumay) *Murder in Soho,* Dutton, 1987.

OTHER

Work represented in anthologies, including *The Voice That Is Great within Us,* edited by Hayden Carruth, Bantam, 1970; *Congregation: Contemporary Writers Read the Jewish Bible,* edited by David Rosenberg, Harcourt, 1987. Contributor to periodicals, including *Atlantic, Harper's, Poetry, New Yorker, Nation,* and *Midstream.*

SIDELIGHTS: Harvey Shapiro's poetry is characterized by its focus on the urban world of New York, the Jewish tradition, and domesticity. When writing about domestic life, he avoids the sentimentality that often accompanies this type of verse, addressing instead such difficulties as marital tension and generational gaps.

Martin McKinsey of *Contemporary Poets* observed that Shapiro, like William Carlos Williams, writes "the opportunistic poetics of an overworked professional. His muse speaks in spurts and snatches, late at night with a whiskey bottle, or during business hours." In her review of *National Cold Storage Company: New and Selected Poems,* Katharine Washburn of *New York Times Book Review* commented on Shapiro's relationship with his muse: "This is a poet who can talk directly and disarmingly to the muse, dissolving her into an ordinary woman—elusive, cajoling, giving and withholding sage advice and incalculable gifts." Washburn added, "And he can elevate an ordinary woman into a muse." Michael Collier remarked in his review of *A Day's Portion: Poems* that Shapiro "is best when his subject is memory and when he employs his gift for portraiture," adding that the poet's "direct and accessible style distinguishes him from many poets writing today."

In *Contemporary Poets,* Shapiro reflected on his career: "My earliest poetry (as sampled in *The Eye,* 1953) comes out of several influences, several traditions. As between Chaucer's note words, small articulations and Milton's large sounds, big lines, blocks of vowels, organ stops, etc., I was a Milton man. It was that sound that led me into poetry. And it was that sound that got me reading Hart Crane, one of the first American poets I began to study seriously. . . . It was Crane's sound and technique that interested me, not his (sadly) optimistic message, as it was his ability to cut city scenes and modern nervosities into Elizabethan blank verse.

"Concurrent interests: French symbolist poetry (Rimbaud, Baudelaire) and always a side interest in William Carlos Williams, just then beginning to emerge. This was an interest that pulled against all the others but was to become dominant. My worst poems of that period came out of my hankering for a large sound—poems of meaningless bombast—and attempts to reproduce French symbolism—just literary.

"To move on. In an attempt to work out of the literary (it was about that time I dropped teaching English at universities), I went back to my childhood and early adolescent interest in Jewish subjects and beliefs. . . . My Jewish poems were more than a celebration of Jewishness. They were also searching for the primitive, to get behind the Bible stories and Hebrew school to basic irrational primitive myth. . . . The Jewish influence remains in my constant search for the way, the way of right living. But here the way is constantly in the present and has always to be sought; it is not given. Urban mystic. My poems are private when set against the public declarations of many of my contemporaries, but I think they could only have been written today and that they are an accurate reading of our time."

Shapiro told *CA* that he accepts Hayden Carruth's description of his work as reflecting "the tension between his orthodox religious background and his experiences in war and in modern city living."

BIOGRAPHICAL/CRITICAL SOURCES:

BOOKS

Carruth, Hayden, *The Voice That Is Great within Us* (anthology), Bantam, 1970.

PERIODICALS

Nation, June 13, 1994; December 29, 1997.

New York Times Book Review, April 1, 1984; November 22, 1987; December 11, 1988; September 25, 1994; February 1, 1998.

Publishers Weekly, August 25, 1997, p. 67.*

* * *

SHARKEY, Jack

See SHARKEY, John Michael

* * *

SHARKEY, John Michael 1931-
(Jack Sharkey; pseudonyms: Rick Abbot, Mike Johnson)

PERSONAL: Born May 6, 1931, in Chicago, IL; son of John Patrick and Mary (Luckey) Sharkey; married Patricia Walsh, 1962; children: Beth Eileen, Carole Lynn, Susan Kathleen, Michael Joseph. *Education:* St. Mary's College (Winona, MN), B.A., 1953. *Religion:* Roman Catholic. *Avocational interests:* Charades, chess, playing piano, swimming, handball, reading mystery novels, doing British crossword puzzles.

CAREER: Writer, 1952—. *Military service:* U.S. Army, 1955-56.

MEMBER: Dramatists Guild, Authors League of America, Alpha Psi Omega.

WRITINGS:

ALL UNDER NAME JACK SHARKEY; NOVELS

Secret Martians, Ace, 1960.

Murder, Maestro, Please, Abelard, 1961.
Death for Auld Lang Syne, Holt, 1962.
Ultimatum in 2050 A.D., Ace, 1965.
The Addams Family, Pyramid Publications, 1965.

PLAYS; ALL PUBLISHED BY S. FRENCH EXCEPT AS NOTED

Here Lies Jeremy Troy (three-act; first produced on Broadway, 1965), 1969.
M Is for the Million (two-act), 1971.
Kiss or Make Up (three-act), 1972.
How Green Was My Brownie (three-act), 1972.
A Gentleman and a Scoundrel (three-act), 1973.
Meanwhile, Back on the Couch (three-act), 1973.
Roomies!: A New Comedy, 1974.
Spinoff: A New Comedy, 1974.
Who's on First?, 1975.
The Creature Creeps!: A Comedy in Three Acts, 1977.
My Son the Astronaut (musical), 1980.
Par for the Corpse: A Homicidal Comedy, 1980.
(With David Reiser) *The Picture of Dorian Gray* (musical adaptation), 1980.
Honestly Now!: A Crime Comedy, 1981.
(With Reiser) *Woman Overboard* (musical), 1981.
(With Reiser) *Slow Down, Sweet Chariot,* 1981.
(With Reiser) *Jekyll Hydes Again: A Screwball Musical,* 1984.
(With Reiser, authors of music and lyrics) *My Husband and the Wife,* 1984.
(With Mel Buttorff) *And Then I Wrote: A Comedy,* 1984.
(With Reiser) *And on the Sixth Day—: A Musical Drama,* 1984.
Jack Sharkey's Audition Pieces and Classroom Exercises, 1984.
One Toe in the Grave: A New Comedy, 1986.
(With Reiser) *Zingo!: The Carbonated Musical,* Baker's Plays (Boston, MA), 1986.
(Author of music and lyrics) *The 3 1/2 Musketeers,* Baker's Plays, 1987.
(Author of music and lyrics) *Sherlock Holmes and the Giant Rat of Sumatra,* Baker's Plays, 1987.
(Author of music and lyrics) *Time and Time Again,* Pioneer Drama Service (Denver, CO), 1987.
(Author of music and lyrics) *Wilkie Collins Classic Tale The Woman in White!: A Cautionary Chronicle of Monstrous Evil and Blackhearted Villainy in Song and Dance,* 1987.
(With Reiser) *Love with a Twist: Four O'Henry Musical Cocktails,* 1987.
(With Reiser) *Coping: A Musical Revue,* 1988.
(Author of music and lyrics) *Cinderella Meets the Wolfman!,* 1988.
(With Reiser) *The Pinchpenny Phantom of the Opera: An Affordable Musical Comedy,* 1988.
"Nell of the Ozarks," or, "Tobacco Island Meets Treasure Road," 1988.
While the Lights Were Out: An Off-the-Wall Murder Farce, 1988.
(With Leo W. Sears) *100 Lunches,* 1989.
(With Sears) *Sorry! Wrong Chimney!: A Yuletide Farce,* 1990.
I Take This Man: A Screwball Farce, 1991.
(With Sears) *Star on the Door,* 1992.
(Author of piano arrangements) *It's a Wonderful Life,* 1993.

UNDER PSEUDONYM RICK ABBOT

Dracula, the Musical?: Book, Music, and Lyrics, S. French, 1984.
Class Musical!, Baker's Plays (Boston, MA), 1986.
The Bride of Brackenloch!: A Ghastly Gothic Thriller?, S. French, 1987.
Allocating Annie, S. French, 1989.
Sing On!: A Comedy about a Musical, S. French, 1991.

Also author or co-author of other plays, all published by S. French, including *Saving Grace, The Murder Room, Rich Is Better, Dream Lover, Take a Number, Darling, Missing Link, Once Is Enough, Double Exposure, Turkey in the Straw* (musical), (with Reiser) *What a Spot!* (musical), (with Reiser) *Hope for the Best* (musical), (with Reiser) *Operetta!* (musical), (with Reiser) *Not the "Count of Monte Cristo"?* (musical), *Turnabout,* and *Pushover;* author under pseudonym Rick Abbot of *June Groom, Play On!,* and *A Turn for the Nurse,* and under pseudonym Mike Johnson of *The Clone People, The Perfect Murder,* and *Return of the Maniac.* Contributor of short stories and articles to mystery, science fiction, and men's magazines.*

* * *

SLATER, Ray
See LANSDALE, Joe R(ichard)

* * *

SLAVITT, David R(ytman) 1935-
(David Benjamin, Henry Lazarus, Lynn Meyer, Henry Sutton, pseudonyms)

PERSONAL: Born March 23, 1935, in White Plains, NY; son of Samuel Saul (a lawyer) and Adele Beatrice

(Rytman) Slavitt; married Lynn Nita Meyer, August 27, 1956 (divorced, December 20, 1977); married Janet Lee Abrahm (a physician), April 16, 1978; children: (first marriage) Evan Meyer, Sarah Rebecca, Joshua Rytman. *Education:* Yale University, A.B. (magna cum laude), 1956; Columbia University, M.A., 1957. *Politics:* Independent. *Religion:* Jewish.

ADDRESSES: Home—523 South 41st St., Philadelphia, PA 19104. *Agent*—William Morris Agency, 1350 Avenue of the Americas, New York, NY 10019.

CAREER: Georgia Institute of Technology, Atlanta, instructor in English, 1957-58; *Newsweek,* New York City, began as mailroom clerk, became book and film critic and associate editor, 1958-63, movie editor, 1963-65; freelance writer, 1965—. Assistant professor at the University of Maryland at College Park, 1977; associate professor of English at Temple University, 1978-80; lecturer in English at Columbia University, 1985-86; lecturer at Rutgers University, 1987—; lecturer in English and classics at University of Pennsylvania, 1991—. Visiting professor at the University of Texas at El Paso, University of Maryland, and Temple University. Has read his poetry at numerous colleges and universities and at the Folger Shakespeare Library and the Library of Congress.

AWARDS, HONORS: Pennsylvania Council on Arts award, 1985; National Endowment for the Arts fellowship in translation, 1988; Award in literature, American Academy and Institute of Arts and Letters, 1989; Rockefeller Foundation Artist's Residence, 1989.

WRITINGS:

POETRY

Suits for the Dead (Volume 8 of "Poets of Today" series), Scribner, 1961.
The Carnivore, University of North Carolina Press, 1965.
Day Sailing and Other Poems, University of North Carolina Press, 1969.
Child's Play, Louisiana State University Press, 1972.
Vital Signs: New and Selected Poems, Doubleday, 1975.
Rounding the Horn, Louisiana State University Press, 1978.
Dozens, Louisiana State University Press, 1981.
Big Nose, Louisiana State University Press, 1983.
The Elegies to Delia of Albius Tibullus, Bits Press, 1985.
The Walls of Thebes, Louisiana State University Press, 1986.
Equinox and Other Poems, Louisiana State University Press, 1989.
Eight Longer Poems, Louisiana State University Press, 1990.
Crossroads, Louisiana State University Press,1993.
A Gift: The Life of Da Ponte: A Poem, Louisiana State University Press (Baton Rouge), 1996.

NOVELS

Rochelle; or Virtue Rewarded, Chapman & Hall, 1966, Delacorte, 1967.
Feel Free, Delacorte, 1968.
Anagrams, Hodder & Stoughton, 1970, Doubleday, 1971.
ABCD, Doubleday, 1972.
The Outer Mongolian, Doubleday, 1973.
The Killing of the King, Doubleday, 1974.
(Under pseudonym Lynn Meyer) *Paperback Thriller,* Random House, 1975.
King of Hearts, Arbor House, 1976.
(Under pseudonym Henry Lazarus) *That Golden Woman,* Fawcett, 1976.
Jo Stern, Harper, 1978.
(Under pseudonym David Benjamin) *The Idol,* Putnam, 1979.
Cold Comfort, Methuen, 1980.
Ringer, Dutton, 1982.
Alice at 80, Doubleday, 1984.
The Agent (created by Bill Adler), Doubleday, 1986.
The Hussar, Louisiana State University Press, 1987.
Salazar Blinks, Atheneum, 1988.
Lives of the Saints, Atheneum, 1989.
Turkish Delights, Louisiana State University Press, 1993.
The Cliff, Louisiana State University Press, 1994.

NOVELS UNDER PSEUDONYM HENRY SUTTON

The Exhibitionist, Geis, 1967.
The Voyeur, Geis, 1969.
Vector, Geis, 1970.
The Liberated, Doubleday, 1973.
The Sacrifice: A Novel of the Occult, Grosset & Dunlap, 1978.
The Proposal, Charter, 1980.
Bank Holiday Monday, Sceptre, 1996.

Also author of *Gorleston,* 1995.

TRANSLATOR

(And adapter) *The Eclogues of Virgil,* illustrated by Raymond Davidson, Doubleday, 1971.

(And adapter) *The Eclogues and the Georgics of Virgil,* illustrated by Davidson, Doubleday, 1972.

(And adapter) *The Tristia of Ovid,* illustrated by Davidson, Bellflower Press, 1986.

(And adapter) *Ovid's Poetry of Exile,* Johns Hopkins University Press, 1990.

(And editor) *Seneca,* Volume 1: *The Tragedies,* Johns Hopkins University Press, 1992.

(And adapter) *The Fables of Avianus,* Johns Hopkins University Press, 1993.

(And adapter) *The Metamorphoses of Ovid,* Johns Hopkins University Press, 1994.

(And editor) *Seneca,* Volume 2: *The Tragedies,* Johns Hopkins University Press, 1994.

Aurelius Prudentius Clemens, *Hymns of Prudentius: The Cathemerinon, or, The Daily Round,* Johns Hopkins University Press, 1996.

(And editor) *Sixty-one Psalms of David,* Oxford University Press (New York City), 1996.

Broken Columns: Two Roman Epic Fragments, afterword by David Konstan, University of Pennsylvania Press (Philadelphia), 1997.

Epic and Epigram: Two Elizabethan Entertainments, Louisiana State University Press, 1997.

(And editor) *Aeschylus,* University of Pennsylvania Press, 1998.

Ausonius: Three Amusements, University of Pennsylvania Press, 1998.

The Poem of Queen Esther, Oxford University Press, 1998.

OTHER

King Saul (play), produced in New York City, 1967.

The Cardinal Sins (two-act play; produced in New York City, 1969), Gardner, Pimm & Blackman, 1972.

(With Paul F. Secord and Carl W. Backman) *Understanding Social Life: An Introduction to Social Psychology,* McGraw-Hill, 1976.

(Editor) Adrien Stoutenburg, *Land of Superior Mirages: New and Selected Poems,* Johns Hopkins University Press, 1986.

Physicians Observed (nonfiction), Doubleday, 1987.

Short Stories Are Not Real Life: Short Fiction, Louisiana State University Press, 1991.

Virgil (criticism and interpretation), Yale University Press, 1991.

(Editor, with Palmer Bovie) *Plautus: The Comedies,* Johns Hopkins University Press (Baltimore), 1995.

(Editor, with Palmer Bovie) *Aeschylus,* University of Pennsylvania Press, 1997.

(Editor, with Palmer Bovie) *Aristophanes,* University of Pennsylvania Press, 1998.

(Editor, with Palmer Bovie) *Euripidies,* University of Pennsylvania Press, 1998.

(Editor, with Palmer Bovie) *Menander,* University of Pennsylvania Press, 1998.

Get Thee to a Nunnery: Two Shakespearean Divertmentos, Catbird Press, 1999.

Contributor to books, including *The Girl in the Black Raincoat,* edited by George Garrett, Duell, Sloan & Pearce, 1966; *Man and the Movies,* edited by W. R. Robinson, Louisiana State University Press, 1967; *The Writer's Voice,* edited by Garrett, Morrow, 1973; *Contemporary Poetry in America,* edited by Miller Williams, Random House, 1973; *Poetry: Points of Departure,* edited by Henry Taylor, Winthrop, 1974; *Sexuality in the Movies,* edited by Thomas R. Atkins, Indiana University Press, 1975; *The Brand-X Anthology of Poetry,* edited by William Zaranka, Apple-Wood Books, 1981; and *Tygers of Wrath: Poems of Hate, Anger, and Invective,* edited by X. J. Kennedy, University of Georgia Press, 1981. Also contributor to periodicals, including *Kenyon Review, Sewanee Review, Yale Review, New Republic,* and *Esquire.* Occasional contributor of book reviews to the *New York Times, Newsday, Chicago Tribune,* and *Philadelphia Inquirer.*

ADAPTATIONS: Film rights to *The Hussar* have been sold.

SIDELIGHTS: David R. Slavitt has "lived three lives," writes Margo Jefferson in *New York Times Book Review:* "as a scrupulously genteel poet, as a serious minor novelist and as an exuberantly crass pseudonymous writer of potboilers." Despite his ventures into numerous literary genres, though, Slavitt considers himself a poet first and foremost—a poet who in fact writes novels only to support his habit of writing poetry. "Slavitt may well be unique in the contemporary American literary scene," maintains George Garrett in *Dictionary of Literary Biography,* "being able to write 'public' and 'private' novels (a distinction he now uses instead of the earlier and widely used division between 'popular' and 'serious' fiction) with apparent ease, with certainly no fall-off of energy, and, at one and the same time, to continue to be one of our most productive and independent poets."

Born in White Plains, New York, in 1935, Slavitt soon realized that he was part of "a grand scheme" of his father's to right an old wrong. At the end of his sophomore year in college, Slavitt's father was forced to withdraw from Yale because his own father had died and the family could no longer afford to pay the tuition. His hopes and dreams dashed, he was forced to finish his education through night classes at New York University, but he vowed to have a son one day and send him first to Andover and then to Yale. "Depending on how this story is told, it is either sad or else absurd and therefore funny. (Or maybe just plain nuts?)," reflects Slavitt in an essay for *Contemporary Authors Autobiography Series* (*CAAS*). "It is Faulknerian, if on a somewhat smaller scale. As far as I was concerned, though, it was grand enough to surround me and dictate the terms of much of my life."

Making his way through the public schools in White Plains, Slavitt reflects that he was, and still is, "bright, quick, and also easily bored." Constantly told that he was not applying himself and he would never get into Yale if he did not, Slavitt explains in *CAAS* how this tempered his view of himself: "I was . . . aware of my enormous *importance.* Even in these elementary grades, I was getting double messages from my parents about how proud they were of my obvious abilities, and at the same time how distressed—or furious—they often were at my indifferent performance." Finishing up at the local schools, Slavitt continued on to Andover at the age of fifteen and experienced one of his first great disappointments. "What I discovered after a while was that it was just a huge, rich, rather picky high school that looked pretty good in comparison with most public high schools where the physical safety of the students can't be guaranteed," recalls Slavitt in his autobiographical essay. "My life was again divided between a set of arbitrary external demands—whether my father's or Andover's hardly made much difference—and an inner life, the expression, or at least the fantasy, of that specialness I'd been taught I bore. What I needed to prove, both to myself and to the world, was that I was as good as my parents had always thought, but on my terms and for my reasons rather than theirs."

It was while he was at Andover that Slavitt first began to write poetry, and for a while he even thought of applying to Harvard because he thought it would provide a better atmosphere for a would-be writer. Slavitt's father would not even discuss such an idea—his son would go to Yale, and then to Harvard Law School. Going along with his father, Slavitt did attend Yale and had a much better time than anticipated; Andover had prepared him well. In his *CAAS* essay Slavitt recalls that he viewed "Yale's general indifference to artists and intellectuals [as] appropriate preparation for the great world where nobody gives much of a damn whether you're a writer or not, or, if you're a writer, whether you finish the book you're working on or not, or do today's stint or just bag it."

Graduating magna cum laude in 1956, Slavitt disappointed his father by not going on to law school, and instead got his first job in the personnel office of *Reader's Digest.* After earning enough money to buy two spots on the *Queen Elizabeth* for himself and his bride to be, Slavitt married Lynn Meyer and the two sailed for Europe. Only a week after their arrival, however, the couple learned that Lynn's mother had died and they had to return home. Slavitt then decided to go back to school for his master's, which he earned from Columbia in 1957. His son was born a month later, and Slavitt resolved to give teaching a try before going on to earn his doctorate. The best offer he received was from Georgia Tech, but the experience was so unpleasant that Slavitt lasted for just less than a year. "It was just dreadful," he explains in *CAAS.* "The students weren't stupid, or most of them weren't. But they were badly educated in rural secondary schools in Georgia. They were ambitious kids who wanted to escape the farms and get jobs where they'd wear suits and ties and do drafting for Lockheed at Marietta. But there were no English majors at Tech, and the department was a service department, was made up of hopefuls like me and desperate has-beens who, to assuage the wounds to their pride, were teaching high-class stuff—Homer, Shakespeare, and all the classy authors. Fundamentally, there were two courses, remedial writing, and remedial reading, although they were called Composition and Literature."

When his wife came down with mononucleosis and required a significant amount of bed rest, Slavitt was able to escape back to his parents' house in White Plains. Soon after, he began his seven years at *Newsweek,* eventually becoming the film critic. "I look back on those . . . years at *Newsweek* as a valuable part of my training as a writer, both for the writing itself and for the observation of the world of show biz and the arts," relates Slavitt in *CAAS.* It was near the beginning of his career at *Newsweek* that he had his first volume of poetry published in the "Poets of Today" series. "I was a published poet, but I didn't feel like one. I felt like a guy who works at *Newsweek,*" says Slavitt in *CAAS.* It wasn't until he had published a novel and completed another volume of poetry that Slavitt finally decided to leave the magazine behind and become a full-time writer.

"Since the appearance of his first collection of poems, *Suits for the Dead* (1961), in the distinguished Scribners *Poets of Today* series, Slavitt has proved himself to be one of the most adroitly versatile and productive writers in America," notes Garrett in his essay in *Dictionary of Literary Biography.* Garrett continues on to proclaim that "by most definitions and standards he would have to be regarded . . . as a major poet." In one of his principal collections, *Vital Signs: New and Selected Poems,* Slavitt collects all of his previously published poetry along with eighty-eight new pieces to create a volume of poems which "seem to be equally well-crafted, equally finished, and thus for all practical purposes, to be virtually simultaneous in the making rather than the result of a steady and discernable development," describes Garrett. The poems in this collection, which are arranged by theme and subject, combine classical figures, "lively humor," and "wry truths," asserts *Library Journal* contributor James McKenzie; and the subjects they encompass range from Slavitt's own everyday experience to the experience of ancient civilizations. Although Helen Vendler suggests in the *New York Times Book Review* that the poems are frequently flat and didactic, *Poetry* contributor Robert Holland considers *Vital Signs* to be "the kind of book one should not just read, but live with."

"Slavitt has always conceived of poetry as, essentially and by definition, an elite and hermetic art," relates Garrett. His 1978 collection *Rounding the Horn,* which contains "poems of statement and meditation, each built around a central image or metaphor, each related to all the others thematically and in sequence," says Garrett, deals with many of the same topics found in Slavitt's earlier works. Although Peter Stitt declares in *Poetry* that Slavitt "takes no artistic chances" and that the poems are "just a kind of mindless opinionizing,"William H. Pritchard maintains in *Hudson Review* that *Rounding the Horn* "is a thoroughly satisfactory book, always alive in its language, sometimes poignant and touching."

Slavitt's "special quality" in *The Walls of Thebes* is his "comic vision," remarks J. Hafley in *Choice,* adding that it is the poet's "finest volume thus far." Life and art are the themes of this book, and there is a "pervasive melancholy" which is warranted by the "personal horror" found in the poems, observes *Booklist* contributor Joseph Parisi. *Eight Longer Poems* also examines these themes, suggests a *Publishers Weekly* contributor, adding that Slavitt is able to transform "personal tragedy and individual suffering into universal circumstance." Slavitt is "a poet of almost brutally ironic contradictions," writes Garrett. "He is a learned and gifted metricist and an elegant formalist, whose use of many and various verse forms, both traditional and oddly and newly designed, book by book, could easily be taken as a textbook for the use of forms in contemporary American poetry."

Aside from writing his own poetry, Slavitt also translated and interpreted the poetry of Virgil in *The Eclogues of Virgil* and *The Eclogues and the Georgics of Virgil.* "Borrowing from the ways of Medieval and Renaissance translators, Slavitt developed a method involving sections of summary, critical interpretation, and commentary; and dramatically, and with deliberate anachronism, introducing himself, the living poet and translator, speaking directly to the present-day reader," describes Garrett. In the preface to the first volume, Slavitt justifies the liberties he takes in his translation: "My hope, in these renditions of Virgil's exciting poems, is that by taking certain liberties, I shall have been able to convey something of the experience of the originals, the exhilarating whipsaw feeling Virgil's readers must have experienced as they translated back from the bucolic pastures and fields of Meliboeus and Menalcas and Moeris to the elegant drawing rooms of Roman literary life, and then, feeling the brittleness, the sophistication, the suffocation of Rome, yearned for something else, something better—and by that yearning made the cardboard shepherds suddenly real asonly the objects of profound desire can be." Philip Murray, writing in *Poetry,* believes Slavitt is successful in his translations, creating "a bright and clever book." Murray also asserts: "The qualities Mr. Slavitt projects best are not always those most in evidence in the original although they are at times admirable in themselves. This is a 'fun' book, a funny and sad book, and eminently readable."

In addition to his poetry and his translations, Slavitt has also written a number of novels. Garrett asserts in his essay on Slavitt's novels that "if we turn back to his poetry as a kind of touchstone for all his work, we shall see that one major characteristic of his poetry has not yet appeared in his fiction. And that quality is his profound interest in history." Among the characteristics that do appear Slavitt's novels are humor and satire. "He brings to his fiction a great deal of practical knowledge of and experience in the craft of writing, ranging from poetry to reportage and made richer and complex by his educational background with its emphasis on the classics," comments Garrett.

One of Slavitt's earlier novels, *Anagrams,* published in 1970, "offers a satirical insight into the Quality Lit Biz as conducted on American campuses," explains Michael Mewshaw in *New York Times Book Review.* The novel centers on Jerome Carpenter, a young poet who writes phony doctoral theses on the side to support his struggle as a poet. "As a display of verbal pyrotechnics, the book is unbeatable," states Mewshaw. "Each page pulses with provocative opinions, puns, jokes and the sort of throwaway lines most authors parcel out for maximum mileage." Throughout the novel, the process of writing a long poem is described as Carpenter goes through it. Although a *Publishers Weekly* contributor finds *Anagrams* "dry and stifling,"Thomas Lask writes in *New York Times* that the novel "races along with comic inventiveness, like the last reel of a silent movie."

With another novel, *Alice at 80,* Slavitt blends fact and fiction. The book begins in 1932 with eighty-year-old Alice Liddell Hargreaves—the inspiration for Lewis Carroll's *Alice in Wonderland*—receiving an honorary doctorate from Columbia University. Realizing that it is really Carroll who is being honored, Liddell begins to look back at how he influenced both her life and those of other young girls. *Alice at 80* "has a hint of the dreamy magic of 'Alice,' " asserts *Los Angeles Times Book Review* contributor Richard Eder; "at the same time, it is a dangerously unsettling hypothesis about Dodgson's shy proclivities and their effect on three children that he photographed, sometimes nude." The other two girls are Isa Bowman, an actress who played Alice on stage, and Glenda Fenwick, who Carroll befriended on a beach in England. "Slavitt arranges their crossed paths and purposes in order to examine sex, fantasy and power as well as the emotionalties that bind them, the rules of age, gender and class that govern them," writes Jefferson. "*Alice at 80* is an original, an ingenious mixture of rumination and fantasy. . . . Slavitt writes with subtlety and a piercing indirection," concludes Eder.

The plot from a novel by an obscure German author is interpreted and rewritten by Slavitt in *The Hussar.* The protagonist is Stefan, a young new lieutenant in the Austro-Hungarian Empire just prior to the Seven Weeks' War. His regiment is billeted in a small, insignificant border town, and Stefan must lodge with a sophisticated widow, Sonja, and her lame, beautiful daughter Eugenie. Fantasizing about the women before he arrives, Stefan becomes involved with both of them, and is astonished when they want the relationships to continue. After impregnating and marrying Eugenie, Stefan becomes morally confused and he shoots himself. The novel "is brought to life by the characters who engage our emotions" and "its esoteric source and intent" will appeal to "more scholarly audiences," maintains *Library Journal* contributor Lawrence Rungren. Pointing to the "witty and eruditious verve" inSlavitt's writing, Christopher Zenowich adds in Chicago's *Tribune Books* that "*The Hussar* is a curiously charming and bittersweet meditation."

The narrator of *Lives of the Saints,* published in 1989, is a journalist who writes for a trashy Florida tabloid. Working on a story about the victims of a mass murder at the local Piggly-Wiggly, he focuses on the things they left behind, using the objects to get a sense of who the victims were. Throughout the novel the narrator routinely quotes Nicolas Malebranche, a French writer who did not believe in cause and effect, only random and illogical events. This is accounted for when it is explained that the narrator's wife and daughter were recently killed by a drunk driver; by spouting the philosophy of Malebranche, the journalist is saying he can find no logical explanation for the accident. "Slavitt is an original and ingenious writer," remarks Eder in *Los Angeles Times,* adding: "*Lives of the Saints* juggles with a lovely selection of paradoxes and speculations and with the silliness, comedy and grief that lie in its characters' lives." And according to Michael Upchurch in *Washington Post,* the novel "is angelically written, devilishly constructed and all too peculiarly human. Here's some impressive and entertaining fiction by a writer who deserves to be better known."

Although Slavitt suffers from anonymity under his own name, he did gain fame and recognition with his writings under the pseudonym Henry Sutton. Slavitt entered the popular literary business after publisher Bernard Geis was amused by one of his book reviews in the *New York Herald Tribune* and suggested what financial gains Slavitt could realize by writing a bestseller. "I replied," recalls Slavitt in his *CAAS* essay, "thanking him for his interest but letting him know that he had the wrong fellow. I was a high-brow low-revenue kind of author." Geis was insistent, though, and Slavitt met with him during his next trip to New York; and under the pseudonym of Henry Sutton, *The Exhibitionist* catapulted Slavitt into the world of popular fiction. The only reason for the pseudonym, explains Slavitt in his essay, was to sustain his first novel written under his own name, *Rochelle; or Virtue Rewarded,* which was to be published in the same month *The Exhibitionist* was slated to appear. In this way, book stores could carry a substantial number of both works.

Discussing the pseudonym in relation to his other work, Slavitt told *CA:* "I have had to struggle with Sutton for years. It seemed to me at the time a simple enough indication of what I was doing. No one criticizes the Chrysler for manufacturing Plymouths under a different name, or the Omega company for putting out Tissot watches. But my assumption of a second name for a different kind of writing seemed to offend a certain middle-brow sensibility. Most newspapers dismissed any Sutton book as slumming, and also dismissed anything

I did under my own name as high-brow and low-revenue and, paradoxically, just as proper to be ignored. Now that I've paid for the educations of my children, I think it extremely unlikely that I'll ever write a pseudonymous book again."

Slavitt also commented to *CA* on his relative anonymity since his Sutton books. "Even as a poet, I have been more or less ignored," he explains. "The old snobbishness about poets who wrote any fiction at all seems to have faded away. But it is not yet permissible to have written successful commercial fiction. I say this without any particular complaint. I rather like being ignored, having by now become accustomed to the freedom and the privacy that are the handmaidens to obscurity. I've come to understand that the lit biz is a silly waste of time. Literature, on the other hand, is not." And in his autobiographical essay Slavitt explains that this obscurity has enabled him "to return to a kind of amateur status as a writer, by which I mean that from here on I'm unlikely to write anything strictly or even primarily for money. It has to be a book I'd do for the fun of it. And if it doesn't get published, too bad."

BIOGRAPHICAL/CRITICAL SOURCES:

BOOKS

Contemporary Authors Autobiography Series, Volume 3,Gale, 1986.

Contemporary Literary Criticism, Gale, Volume 5, 1976, Volume 14, 1980.

Dictionary of Literary Biography, Gale, Volume 5: *American Poets since World War II,* 1980, Volume 6: *American Novelists since World War II, Second Series,* 1980.

Garrett, George, editor, *The Writer's Voice: Conversations with Contemporary Writers,* Morrow, 1973.

Garrett, *My Silk Purse and Yours,* University of Missouri Press, 1992.

Slavitt, David, translator and adapter, *The Eclogues of Virgil,* illustrated by Raymond Davidson, Doubleday, 1971.

PERIODICALS

Booklist, October 15, 1986.

Chicago Tribune, January 2, 1990.

Choice, October, 1986.

Hollins Critic, June, 1971.

Hudson Review, winter, 1975-76; summer, 1979.

Library Journal, May 15, 1975; February 15, 1981; May 15, 1987; April 15, 1990.

Life, January 26, 1968.

Los Angeles Times, December 21, 1989.

Los Angeles Times Book Review, July 15, 1984.

New Republic, August 20, 1990.

New Yorker, January 29, 1990.

New York Times, November 3, 1967; July 26, 1971.

New York Times Book Review, September 17, 1967; May 5, 1968; February 16, 1969; June 14, 1970; September 5, 1971; January 14, 1973; July 8, 1973; October 27, 1974; September 7, 1975; January 2, 1977; March 18, 1979; August 19, 1984; February 15, 1987; August 2, 1987; September 13, 1987; February 26, 1989; February 11, 1990; June 3, 1990; January 19, 1992; April 17, 1994; January 15, 1998.

Poetry, August, 1972; February, 1977; January, 1980.

Publishers Weekly, September 4, 1967; May 10, 1971; March 30, 1990.

Spectator, May 4, 1974.

Times Literary Supplement, August 11, 1966; November 6, 1970; May 3, 1974; December 29, 1995; August 23, 1996.

Tribune Books (Chicago), August 10, 1980; May 31, 1987; October 8, 1987.

Virginia Quarterly Review, winter, 1972; spring, 1973; spring, 1975; autumn, 1979.

Washington Post, January 25, 1990.

Washington Post Book World, August 22, 1971; March 18, 1973; August 26, 1984; October 25, 1987; September 25, 1994.

West Coast Review of Books, July, 1978; November, 1978.*

* * *

SLEATOR, William (Warner III) 1945-

PERSONAL: Surname is pronounced "*Slay*-tir"; born February 13, 1945, in Havre de Grace, MD; son of William Warner, Jr. (a professor) and Esther (a physician; maiden name, Kaplan) Sleator. *Education:* Harvard University, B.A., 1967; studied musical composition in London, England, 1967-68. *Politics:* Independent.

ADDRESSES: Home—77 Worcester St., Boston, MA 02118; Bangkok, Thailand. *Agent*—Sheldon Fogelman, 10 East 40th St., New York, NY 10016.

CAREER: Royal Ballet School, London, England, accompanist, 1967-68; Rambert School, London, accompanist, 1967-68; Boston Ballet Company, Boston, MA, rehearsal pianist, 1974-83; writer of books for children and young adults; composer and musician.

AWARDS, HONORS: Bread Loaf Writers' Conference fellowship, 1969; Caldecott Medal Honor Book, American Library Association, and *Boston Globe-Horn Book* Award, both 1971, (ALA) American Book Award for best paperback picture book, 1981, Notable Book citation, and *Horn Book* Honor List citation, all for *The Angry Moon;* Children's Book of the Year Award, Child Study Association of America, 1972, and ALA Notable Book citation, both for *Blackbriar;* Best Books for Young Adults citations, American Library Association, 1974, for *House of Stairs,* 1984, for *Interstellar Pig,* 1985, for *Singularity,* and 1987, for *The Boy Who Reversed Himself;* Best of the Best for Young Adults citation, ALA Notable Book citation, *Horn Book* Honor List citation, and Junior Literary Guild selection, all for *Interstellar Pig;* Children's Choice Award, International Reading Association and Children's Book Council, and Junior Literary Guild selection, both for *Into the Dream;* Best Book of the Year award, *School Library Journal,* 1981, for *The Green Futures of Tycho,* 1983, for *Fingers,* and 1984, for *Interstellar Pig;* Junior Literary Guild selection, 1985, for *Singularity;* Golden Pen Award, Spokane Washington Public Library, 1984 and 1985, both for "the author who gives the most reading pleasure."

WRITINGS:

The Angry Moon (picture book; retelling of a Tlingit Indian tale), illustrated by Blair Lent, Little, Brown, 1970.
Blackbriar (juvenile), illustrated by Lent, Dutton, 1972.
Run (mystery), Dutton, 1973.
House of Stairs (juvenile), Dutton, 1974.
Among the Dolls, illustrated by Trina Schart Hyman, Dutton, 1975.
(With William H. Redd) *Take Charge: A Personal Guide to Behavior Modification* (adult), Random House, 1977.
Into the Dream, illustrated by Ruth Sanderson, Dutton, 1979.
Once, Said Darlene, illustrated by Steven Kellogg, Dutton, 1979.
The Green Futures of Tycho (young adult), Dutton, 1981.
That's Silly (easy reader), illustrated by Lawrence DiFiori, Dutton, 1981.
Fingers (young adult), Dutton, 1983.
Interstellar Pig (young adult), Dutton, 1984.
Singularity (young adult), Dutton, 1985.
The Boy Who Reversed Himself (young adult), Dutton, 1986.
The Duplicate (young adult), Dutton, 1988.
Strange Attractors (young adult), Dutton, 1990.
The Spirit House, Dutton, 1991.
Oddballs, Dutton, 1993.
Others See Us, Dutton, 1993.
Dangerous Wishes, Dutton Children's Books (New York City), 1995.
The Night the Heads Came, Dutton Children's Books, 1996.
The Beasties, Dutton Children's Books, 1997.
The Boxes (young adult), Dutton Children's Books, 1998.

Also composer, with Lent, of musical score for animated film *Why the Sun and Moon Live in the Sky,* 1972; composer of scores for professional ballets, amateur films, and plays.

ADAPTATIONS: The Angry Moon has been recorded on audiocassette and distributed by Read-Along-House; *Interstellar Pig* has been recorded on audiocassette and distributed by Listening Library,1987.

SIDELIGHTS: Recipient of numerous literary awards, William Sleator is a popular science fiction writer for both children and young adults. Blending fantasy with reality, his stories depict ordinary teenagers going about their daily lives—gardening, for example, or vacationing at the beach. However, fantastic incidents involving aliens or clones, to name just a few, suddenly disrupt these familiar routines, and the characters are forced into action. "I prefer science fiction that has some basis in reality," Sleator once told *CA,* "psychological stories, time-travel stories, but especially stories about people."

For many years Sleator wavered between a writing career and a musical career. He entered Harvard University in 1963, for example, intent on pursuing a degree in music; however, he later changed his mind and graduated with his bachelor's degree in English. He then moved to London, England, where he resumed his study of musical composition and also worked as a pianist in ballet schools. He was drawn back into writing after he helped a coworker restore a run-down cottage and became curious about the building's bizarre history. "The place was interesting," he recalled to *CA,*"way out in the middle of the woods, and eerie with graffiti from 1756 on the walls. There were burial mounds nearby where druids [members of an ancient priesthood] were buried and festivals were held. The whole thing was like a Gothic novel. So there was my first [novel], *Blackbriar,* handed right to me." By 1974 Sleator had returned to the United States and joined the Boston Ballet Company as an accompanist. But after spending the next nine years juggling rehearsals, ballet tours, and writing, he finally quit the company to become a full-time author.

Among Sleator's more than seventeen books for children and young adults are *The Green Futures of Tycho* and *Interstellar Pig,* two stories that focus on the subjects of time travel and extraterrestrials. In the first story, a boy discovers a strange, egg-shaped object buried in his garden. Realizing it allows him to travel through time, he makes frequent trips to the future, where he meets his adult self. However, with each venture forward in time, he sees this adult self becoming more evil and distorted. Finally he realizes he must travel into the past to return the object to its original place. In *Interstellar Pig,* sixteen-year-old Barney is on vacation at the beach when three neighbors move into a nearby cottage. Invited to join their game called "Interstellar Pig," Barney readily accepts; however, he soon finds out that his neighbors are really aliens in disguise who plan to kill him. As Rosalie Byard concluded in *New York Times Book Review:* "Eery menace penetrates the humdrum normality of the summer holiday scene in a convincing evolution from unsettling situation to waking nightmare."

In his book *Singularity,* Sleator explores the existence of other universes. Sixteen-year-old twins Barry and Harry discover that a playhouse on their uncle's property is built over a singularity—a hole that connects two separate galaxies. Strange cosmic debris keeps appearing through the hole, and the twins find out that their uncle feared the arrival of a dangerous, intergalactic monster. Yet only Harry possesses the courage to venture inside and stand guard. "The details of Harry's year in the playhouse are fascinating," judged Anne A. Flowers in Horn Book, who also declared the book "an unusual, suspenseful yarn told by a master storyteller."

Sleator still harbors an interest in music and would one day like to compose more scores for films. But he continues to write books and considers his role as a science fiction author for young people to be of utmost importance. "My goal is to entertain my audience and to get them to read," he told *CA.* "I want kids to find out that reading is the best entertainment there is. If, at the same time, I'm also imparting some scientific knowledge, then that's good, too. I'd like kids to see that science is not just boring formulas. Some of the facts to be learned about the universe are very weird."

Sleator added: "I now divide my time between Boston, Massachusetts, and Bangkok, Thailand. I feel more at home in Thailand than in practically any other place I can think of. Partly this is because Thailand is so exotic that it feels almost like being on another planet. (Don't ask me why THAT should make me feel at home.) I also like Thai people because they turn almost any situation into an occasion to have fun; and because they are so pleasant and polite that you never know what is *really* going on in their minds, so they are a mysterious puzzle to try to figure out. It's also a lot of fun to be learning how to speak Thai, which is about as different a language from English as you could imagine. Try pronouncing a word that begins with the sound *ng,* and you'll begin to get an idea of how challenging it is. "

BIOGRAPHICAL/CRITICAL SOURCES:

BOOKS

Authors & Artists for Young Adults, Volume 5, Gale, 1990.

Children's Literature Review, Volume 29, Gale,1993, pp. 196- 208.

Davis, James, and Hazel Davis, *Presenting William Sleator,* Macmillan, 1992.

Roginski, Jim, *Behind the Covers: Interviews with Authors and Illustrators of Books for Children and Young Adults,* Libraries Unlimited, 1985.

Something about the Author, Volume 68, Gale, 1992.

PERIODICALS

Booklist, February 15, 1979, p. 936; April 1, 1981; January 15, 1990.

Bulletin of the Center for Children's Books, June, 1985; January, 1987; April, 1988; November, 1989.

Fantasy Review, December, 1986.

Horn Book, May, 1985, pp. 320-321; January, 1987; May, 1988.

New York Times Book Review, September 23, 1984, p. 47; April 24, 1994, p. 24.

Publishers Weekly, July 17, 1972.

School Library Journal, October, 1983; September, 1984; August, 1985; April, 1988; December, 1989.

Voice of Youth Advocates, April, 1985; October, 1985.*

* * *

SLEIGH, Barbara 1906-1982

PERSONAL: Born January 9, 1906, in Acock's Green, Worcestershire, England ; died February 13, 1982, in Winchester, England ; daughter of Bernard (an artist) and Stella (Phillip) Sleigh; married David Davis (a broadcasting executive), January 29, 1936; children:

Anthony, Hilary, Fabia. *Education:* Attended West Bromwich School of Art, Birmingham, England, 1922-25; Clapham High School Art Teacher's Training College, London, England, diploma, 1928. *Religion:* Church of England.

CAREER: Smethwick High School, Staffordshire, England, art teacher, 1928-30; Goldsmiths' College, London, England, lecturer, 1930-33; British Broadcasting Corp. (BBC), London, assistant on radio program *Children's Hour,* 1933-36; freelance broadcaster and radio writer, 1935-82; writer for children.

WRITINGS:

CHILDREN'S FICTION

Carbonel, illustrated by V. H. Drummond, Parrish (London), 1955, Bobbs-Merrill (New York City), 1958.

Patchwork Quilt, illustrated by Mary Shillabeer, Parrish, 1956.

The Singing Wreath and Other Stories, illustrated by Julia Comper, Parrish, 1957.

The Seven Days, illustrated by Susan Einzig, Parrish, 1958, Meredith, 1968.

The Kingdom of Carbonel, illustrated by D. M. Leonard, Parrish, 1958, Bobbs-Merrill, 1960.

No One Must Know, illustrated by Jillian Willett, Collins (London), 1962, Bobbs-Merrill, 1963.

North of Nowhere: Stories and Legends from Many Lands, illustrated by Victor Ambrus, Collins, 1964, Coward-McCann (New York City), 1966.

Jessamy, illustrated by Philip Gough, Bobbs-Merrill, 1967.

Pen, Penny, Tuppence, illustrated by Meg Stevens, Hamish Hamilton (London), 1968.

The Snowball, illustrated by Patricia Drew, Brockhampton Press, 1969.

West of Widdershins: A Gallimaufry of Stories Brewed in Her Own Cauldron, illustrated by Victor Ambrus, Collins, 1971, published as *Stirabout Stories,* Bobbs-Merrill, 1972.

Ninety-Nine Dragons, illustrated by Gunvor Edwards, Brockhampton Press, 1974.

Funny Peculiar: An Anthology, illustrated by Jennie Garratt, David & Charles (London), 1974.

Charlie Chumbles, illustrated by Frank Franus, Hodder & Stoughton (London), 1977.

Grimblegraw and the Wuthering Witch, illustrated by Glenys Ambrus, Hodder & Stoughton, 1978, revised edition, Penguin (London), 1979.

Carbonel and Calidor, illustrated by Charles Front, Kestrel, 1978.

Winged Magic: Legends and Stories from Many Lands Concerning Things That Fly, illustrated by John Patience, Hodder & Stoughton, 1979.

(Editor) *Broomsticks and Beasticles: Stories and Verse about Witches and Strange Creatures,* illustrated by John Patience, Hodder & Stoughton, 1981.

(Editor) Kenneth Grahame, *The Wind in the Willows,* illustrated by Philip Mendoza, Hodder & Stoughton, 1983.

Also author of *Spin Straw to Gold,* 1974. Wrote numerous radio plays, stories, and talks for children, for the BBC.

OTHER

The Smell of Privet (autobiography), Hutchinson, 1971.

SIDELIGHTS: Barbara Sleigh was well known in her native England as an author and editor of children's fantasy fiction. Her most popular works were those about the character of Carbonel, King of the Cats, who appears in *Carbonel, The Kingdom of Carbonel,* and *Carbonel and Calidor.* Sleigh's characters have been compared to those in the finest tradition of children's literature. As one *Junior Bookshelf* critic stated in a review of *Carbonel and Calidor,* "There is a Nesbit quality about Miss Sleigh's writing as there is in her manipulation of magic. . . . Miss Sleigh is the least prolific of writers, but her books are always well worth waiting for."

Beginning her career as a teacher and later a storyteller on the British Broadcasting Corp.'s *Children's Hour,* Sleigh did not start writing until later in her life, and even then she was never very prolific. Quickly gaining fans with the publication of *Carbonel* in 1955, Sleigh "added a splendidly individual contribution to the long line of fictional felines," according to Geoffrey Trease in *Times Literary Supplement.* In this first story, the author introduced her famed character as a kitten who is rescued by two children named Rosemary and John from a witch named Mrs. Cantrip. Carbonel is no ordinary cat: he is a king with whom the children can communicate through the use of a magic ring. In addition to the anthropomorphic world of Carbonel and his fellow felines into which Rosemary and John are drawn, there is also much in these books about witchcraft and its colorful practitioners, in particular the "idiosyncratic Mrs. Cantrip," whom Trease called an "unforgettable creation."

After *Carbonel* and *The Kingdom of Carbonel,* Sleigh did not return to this world of witches and intelligent cats for another twenty years, until her 1978 publication of *Carbonel and Calidor.* The central character in this story is actually Calidor, Carbonel's son and heir to the throne. Trouble arises when Carbonel falls in love with Dumpsie—a bright and feisty commoner cat who lives in the dump—and refuses to take Princess Melissa's paw in marriage. "Barbara Sleigh laces adventure with humor and has a casually expert way of twisting everyday settings and events into something bizarre and wholly entertaining," said Margery Fisher in her *Growing Point* assessment of the tale.

In addition to her Carbonel stories, Sleigh's lighthearted style of fantasy can be found in shorter works like *Ninety-Nine Dragons* and *Grimblegraw and the Wuthering Witch,* as well as in her short stories, many of which appear in *West of Widdershins: A Gallimaufry of Stories Brewed in Her Own Cauldron,* published in the United States as *Stirabout Stories.* In *Ninety-Nine Dragons,* Ben and Beth have a problem when the fifty sheep that Beth has been counting to help her go to sleep are threatened by the dragons that Ben has been dreaming about. *Grimblegraw and the Wuthering Witch* is about a giant who kidnaps people to do his housework. "This stylish tale," Fisher remarked in *Growing Point,* "looks back to Andrew Lang's comic tales of a fairy court as it unwinds."

"My own pleasure in storytelling," Sleigh once commented "stems from the time when I was a small girl. My father, who among other artistic activities designed stained glass windows, would often use me as a model for an infant angel, or perhaps a young St. John the Baptist. To stop me fidgeting, he would tell me tales which kept me riveted. I write stories in the hope that I may pass on some of this same delight to children today." In a *Twentieth-Century Children's Writers* entry, Sleigh further explained why she chose to write fantasy stories: "I largely write fantasy, but, I hope, of a down-to-earth kind, avoiding mere whimsy. I feel strongly this leads young readers to wider horizons, and later to imaginative adult reading."

BIOGRAPHICAL/CRITICAL SOURCES:

BOOKS

Something about the Author, Volume 86, Gale, 1996.
Twentieth-Century Children's Writers, 4th edition, St. James Press (Detroit), 1995.

PERIODICALS

Bulletin of the Center for Children's Books, October, 1967; December, 1969, p. 65; November, 1972, p. 49.
Growing Point, October, 1975, p. 2729; November, 1977, p. 3211; July, 1978, pp. 3354-58; January, 1979, pp. 3435-39.
Junior Bookshelf, February, 1975, pp. 50-51; April, 1978, pp. 93, 195; August, 1978, p. 195; April, 1980, p. 74; February, 1982, p. 30.
Kirkus Reviews, April 1, 1967, p. 416; October 1, 1968, p. 1165; August 15, 1972, p. 941.
Library Journal, May 15, 1967, p. 2024.
New Statesman, October 22, 1971, pp. 559-60; December 4, 1981, p. 18.
Times Educational Supplement, November 20, 1981, p. 34.
Times Literary Supplement, October 22, 1971, p. 1321; December 8, 1972, p. 1499; November 23, 1973, p. 1438; December 6, 1974, p. 1384; July 7, 1978, p. 765; November 25, 1983.

OBITUARIES:

BOOKS

Something about the Author, Volume 30, Gale, 1983.*

* * *

SLEPIAN, Jan(ice B.) 1921-

PERSONAL: Surname is pronounced "*slep*-ee-an"; born January 2,1921, in New York, NY; daughter of Louis (an engineer) and Florence (a homemaker; maiden name, Ellinger) Berek; married Urey Krasnopolsky, October, 1945 (divorced, 1948); married David Slepian (a mathematician), April 18, 1950; children: Steven, Don, Anne. *Education:* Brooklyn College, B.A., 1942; University of Washington, M.A. (clinical psychology), 1947; New York University, M.A. (speech pathology), 1964; attended University of California—Berkeley, 1979. *Avocational interests:* Mycology, reading, music, swimming.

ADDRESSES: Home and Office—212 Summit Ave., Summit, NJ 07901. *Agent*—Sheldon Fogelman, 10 East 40th St., New York, NY 10016.

CAREER: Massachusetts General Hospital, Boston, MA, language therapist, 1947-49; private speech therapist, 1952-58; Red Seal Clinic, Newton, NJ, speech therapist, 1953-55; Matheny School for Cerebral Palsy, Farhills, NJ, speech therapist, 1955-57; writer.

MEMBER: Society of Children's Book Writers, Authors Guild, Authors League of America.

AWARDS, HONORS: The Alfred Summer was named one of the best books of the year by *School Library Journal,* 1980, and was named a notable book by the American Library Association; American Book Award finalist in children's fiction, and *Boston Globe-Horn Book* Honor for fiction, both 1981, for *The Alfred Summer;* Author's awards, New Jersey Institute of Technology, 1981, for *The Alfred Summer,* 1983, for *The Night of the Bozos,* and 1988, for *Something beyond Paradise; Lester's Turn* was named one of the best books for children by the *New York Times,* and a notable children's book for older readers by *School Library Journal,* both 1981, a notable children's trade book in social studies by *Social Education,* and one of New York Public Library's books for the teen age, both 1982, and a notable book by the American Library Association; *The Night of the Bozos* was named one of the best books for young adults by the American Library Association, one of the children's books of the year by the Child Study Association of America, and one of the books of the year by the Library of Congress, all 1983; *Something beyond Paradise* was named one of the ten great books of the year for teens by *Redbook,* 1987; *The Broccoli Tapes* was named a notable book by the American Library Association, 1989; *Booklist* Editor's Choice, 1989, for *The Broccoli Tapes,* and 1990, for *Risk n' Roses; Risk n' Roses* was named one of New York Public Library's best books, 1990.

WRITINGS:

"LISTEN-HEAR" PICTURE-BOOK SERIES; ALL WITH ANN SEIDLER; ALL ILLUSTRATED BY RICHARD E. MARTIN

Alphie and the Dream Machine, Follett, 1964.
The Cock Who Couldn't Crow, Follett, 1964.
Lester and the Sea Monster, Follett, 1964.
Magic Arthur and the Giant, Follett, 1964
Mister Sipple and the Naughty Princess, Follett, 1964.
The Roaring Dragon of Redrose, Follett, 1964.

"JUNIOR LISTEN-HEAR" PICTURE BOOK SERIES; ALL WITH SEIDLER; ALL ILLUSTRATED BY MARTIN

Bendemolena, Follett, 1967, published as *The Cat Who Wore a Pot on Her Head,* Scholastic Inc., 1981.
Ding-Dong, Bing-Bong, Follett, 1967.
An Ear Is to Hear, Follett, 1967.
The Hungry Thing, Follett, 1967.
The Silly Listening Book, Follett, 1967.

FOR CHILDREN; WITH SEIDLER

The Best Invention of All, illustrated by Joseph Veno, Crowell- Collier, 1967.
The Hungry Thing Returns, illustrated by Martin, Scholastic Inc., 1990.
The Hungry Thing Goes to a Restaurant, pictures By Elroy Freem, Scholastic Inc., 1992.
Lost Moose, illustrated By Ted Lewin, Philomel Books,1995.

NOVELS FOR YOUNG ADULTS

The Alfred Summer, Macmillan, 1980.
Lester's Turn (sequel to *The Alfred Summer*), Macmillan, 1981.
The Night of the Bozos, Dutton, 1983.
Getting on with It (Junior Literary Guild selection), Four Winds, 1985.
Something beyond Paradise (Junior Literary Guild selection), Philomel, 1987.
The Broccoli Tapes, Putnam, 1989.
Risk n' Roses, Philomel, 1990.
Back to Before, Philomel (New York City), 1993.
Pinocchio's Sister, Philomel Books, 1995.
The Mind Reader, Philomel Books, 1997.
Emily Just in Time, illustrated By Glo Coalson,Philomel Books, 1997.

OTHER

Building Foundations for Better Speech and Reading (teachers' training series and cassette tape program; with twelve tapes and discussion guide), Instructional Dynamics Inc., 1974.

Contributor of advice on speech problems, with Ann Seidler, to newspaper column "Parents Ask."

Slepian's works are included in the Kerlan Collection at the University of Minnesota.

SIDELIGHTS: Jan Slepian has earned praise for her work on young-adult novels that champion society's outcasts. Her characters, many of whom are handicapped—physically, mentally, socially—undergo experiences that cause them to learn about themselves and the world around them while they cope with their afflictions. By beginning her career as a novelist at the relatively late age of fifty-seven, Slepian benefited from a wide range of exposure to different experiences and environments which she has often incorporated in her stories.

Slepian had no immediate desire to become a writer. After raising a family with her husband David, she worked with fellow speech therapist Ann Seidler on a handful of articles that discussed children's language difficulties. They submitted these articles to "Parents Ask," a newspaper column that dealt with child psychology. Excited by the ensuing publication of their advice, they collaborated on two series of picture books that dealt with various speech-related topics. Over a decade later, Slepian took an English class at the University of California—Berkeley and was exposed to the genre of young-adult novels. Her instructor, who was familiar with her student's work on picture books, asked Slepian about her current writing projects. When Slepian conceded that she was through with writing books, her teacher chided: "Oh no, you're not. You're just ready to go on to something else." This experience played an important part in her decision to write novels for young adults.

Upon completing her first novel, *The Alfred Summer,* Slepian was overcome with joy. She revealed in an autobiographical sketch for *Something about the Author Autobiography* "I've had many golden moments in my life, but this was something quite different. More than anything in the world I had wanted to write a decent book, and that night I knew that I had. I said to myself, 'You are fifty-seven years old and this is one of the most happy moments of your life.' It seemed to me remarkable that I could say that at my age." Her story details the experiences of four outcast children, including Lester, who is afflicted by cerebral palsy, and Alfred, who is mentally retarded. Together the kids work to construct a small boat, which they call the Getaway. "It is a name they all understand, each in his own terms," assessed Natalie Babbitt of *New York Times Book Review,* "for they are all prisoners of one kind or another." The inspiration for the title character was provided by Slepian's mentally retarded brother. The real-life Alfred was a source of both joy and anguish for Slepian and her family as the author was growing up in the Brighton Beach section of Brooklyn, New York." Only aware that Alfred was the cause of fights between my parents, I hated him. People acted funny around him, and he made my mother cry and my father angry," Slepian revealed in her autobiographical sketch. "Yet at the same time I was attached. He was sweet and laughed at my jokes and he was my brother. I learned early that you can hold within yourself contradictory feelings."

The initial story line of *The Alfred Summer* is rooted in an experience that Slepian recalled from her childhood. Her mother had tried to find a friend for Alfred by asking the mother of a child with cerebral palsy if the two boys could play together. The second woman refused to let her Lester associate with the mentally retarded Alfred, "saying that she wanted her son to play only with normal kids. When I remembered that," the author recounted in her autobiography, "I realized I had a what-if story. What if Lester and Alfred had become friends?" After its publication, *The Alfred Summer* received several distinctions. It was named a *Boston Globe-Horn Book* Award Honor Book and was cited as one of the best books of the year by *School Library Journal.* The critical acclaim that *The Alfred Summer* received caused Slepian to reevaluate her brother's impact on other people. "My mother and father thought his life was blasted, wasted," she explained in her autobiographical sketch. "In a sense it was, of course. He still sits in a hospital like a bundle from the lost and found. But in another sense his life wasn't a waste. Because of this book, that's all turned around. He has reached and affected many, many people, more than most of us 'normals' have. Such is the power of words."

The Alfred Summer spawned a sequel that won further praise for its author. *Lester's Turn* begins after Alfred's mother dies. The mentally retarded child is subsequently placed under the guardianship of a hospital. Distraught over the effect of institutionalization on his friend, Lester tries to kidnap Alfred but fails. The hospital eventually allows him to take Alfred out of the building on a trial basis. Alfred becomes ill, however, and is hurried back to the hospital where he dies of a burst appendix. Lester then realizes that his efforts to attend to his friend's needs merely helped him to avoid facing his own problems while Alfred was alive. Impressed by the two novels, Babbitt of *New York Times Book Review* noted that "Slepian's use of the language is rich, often funny, always fresh, and both stories are worth telling, a condition that has become increasingly rare in novels for young readers."

Just as Slepian used Lester as a model for one of her characters, she has often drawn upon characteristics of her own life and the places that she has visited to flesh out her stories. Her first two novels were both set in Slepian's home community of Brighton Beach. Her character Claire, who appears in both *The Alfred Summer* and *Lester's Turn,* inherited Slepian's methods for overcoming the timidity that the author felt as a child. In her autobiography, Slepian admitted to being a "morbidly shy" first grader—she even ran home from school one day and hid in a clothes hamper until her mother found her. As an adolescent, she began to get over her shyness. "Somehow I got the idea that if I could act as if I were confident and easy, people wouldn't know how I felt inside," she recounted in her autobiography. "I found out that when you pretend something long enough, you wind up believing it yourself. As time went by, the act became real. It was less of an act and more the true me. . . . I gave this early discovery of mine to Claire. . . . She needed it. She called it her Aziff (as if) theory, and I let her have it with my blessing."

Slepian set her third novel, *The Night of the Bozos,* around a lake in upstate New York where she spent Christmas vacations as a teenager. In her autobiography Slepian explained that "[the] book is a good example of how I put together people, or parts of people, I have known from different eras of my life." Slepian drew inspiration from her own son, Don, when creating the character of George Weiss, a reclusive adolescent musician with an obsession for sound in all of its forms. George lives with his mother and his Uncle Hibbie, a character based on a stuttering patient whom Slepian encountered while she was a speech therapist at Massachusetts General Hospital in the late 1940s. Because of his speech problem, Hibbie forms bonds with very few people other than his nephew. The two outcasts are befriended by Lolly, a teenager (modeled on one of Don's girlfriends) who escorts them to a carnival where her family works. There Hibbie gets a job as a "Bozo," a clown who sits above a tank of water and jeers at the crowd. His duty is to coax customers into paying to throw balls at a target that, when hit, will dunk him. Only as the Bozo can Hibbie overcome his stuttering problem, admitting that the urge to tease and joke with people has always been a part of him. With his identity protected by clown makeup, he is able to display the extroverted side of himself.

In her later novels Slepian continued her practice of using settings familiar to her as backdrops to her stories. Both *The Broccoli Tapes* and *Something beyond Paradise* take place in Hawaii, where Slepian and her family spent their summers from 1967 to the early 1980s. Her novel *Risk n' Roses* returns to the author's home state of New York and tells about two sisters whose relationship deteriorates when their family moves to a new neighborhood in the Bronx. Older sister Angela, who is mentally handicapped, becomes friends with Kaminsky, a man who lives across the street and cultivates roses. Younger sister Skip, who has always felt obligated to care for her older sister, falls under the influence of Jean Persico, a young girl who encourages Skip to join her and her clique of friends in wanton wrongdoing. When Jean tricks Angela into clipping the buds from Kaminsky's roses, Skip does not immediately protest: As Slepian writes in the book, "Her sister was nothing to her and Jean was everything." Skip does eventually stop Angela from causing further damage to Kaminsky's garden and comes to understand the sacrifices that must be made in choosing to be loyal to either friends or family. Martha V. Parravano of *Horn Book* commented, "The book's examination of the nature of power . . . is strong and lucid"

In her novels Slepian has celebrated the lives of a number of young adult characters who learn to cope with problems caused by their own handicaps, exposure to new environments, and shifting relationships. Concerning her decision to write for young adults, Slepian admitted in her autobiography: "Sometimes, when the writing is going well, when a character has come alive on the page, or I have found the right 'taste,' the right sentence or even the right word, then, I can tell you that there is nothing in the world to match it. I'm like a bystander watching a miracle. I count myself blessed that I'm a writer and think that that is the best possible thing to be."

BIOGRAPHICAL/CRITICAL SOURCES:

BOOKS

Authors and Artists for Young Adults, Volume 20, Gale, 1997.
Something about the Author, Volume 85, Gale, 1996.
Something about the Author Autobiography Series, Volume 8, Gale, 1989.

PERIODICALS

Horn Book, January, 1991, p. 70.
Los Angeles Times Book Review, April 23, 1989, p. 10.
New York Times Book Review, April 27, 1980, p. 52; May 27, 1981, p. 38; January 20, 1991, p. 28; July 30, 1995, p. 17.
Tribune Books (Chicago), September 10, 1989, p. 4; November 11, 1990, p. 6.*

* * *

SLOBODKIN, Louis 1903-1975

PERSONAL: Born February 19, 1903, in Albany, NY; died of cardiac arrest, May 8, 1975, in Miami Beach, FL; son of Nathan (an inventor) and Dora (Lubin) Slobodkin; married Florence Gersh (an author), September 27, 1927; children: Laurence B., Michael E. *Education:* Attended Beaux Arts Institute of Design, New York, NY, 1918-22. *Politics:* Democrat. *Religion:* Jewish.

CAREER: Sculptor; designer, illustrator, and author of children's books. Sculptor in studios in France and United States, 1931-35; Master Institute of United Arts, Roerich Museum, New York, head of Sculpture Department, 1934-37; Art League, New York, instructor of sculpture, 1935-36; head of sculpture division of New York City Art Project, 1941-42; executor of statues and panels for government buildings in Washington, DC, New York, and other cities, including "Young Abe Lincoln" for U.S. Department of the Interior Building in the capital. Exhibitor and lecturer at museums.

MEMBER: Sculptors Guild (board of directors, 1939-41), National Sculpture Society, American Group (president, 1940-42), American Institute of Graphic Arts (chairman of artists committee, 1946), Authors Guild of Authors League of America.

AWARDS, HONORS: Winner of various sculpture competitions; Caldecott Medal (for best illustrated book for children), 1944, for *Many Moons* by James Thurber.

WRITINGS:

SELF-ILLUSTRATED

Magic Michael, Macmillan, 1944.
Friendly Animals, Vanguard, 1944.
Clear the Track, Macmillan, 1945.
Fo'castle Waltz, Vanguard, 1945.
The Adventures of Arab, Macmillan, 1946.
Seaweed Hat, Macmillan, 1947.
Hustle and Bustle, Macmillan, 1948.
Bixby and the Secret Message, Macmillan, 1948.
Sculpture, Principles and Practice, World Publishing, 1949.
Mr. Mushroom, Macmillan, 1950.
Dinny and Danny, Macmillan, 1951.
Our Friendly Friends, Vanguard, 1951.
The Space Ship under the Apple Tree, Macmillan, 1952.
Circus April 1st, Macmillan, 1953.
Mr. Petersham's Cats, Macmillan, 1954.
The Horse with the High-Heeled Shoes, Vanguard, 1954.
The Amiable Giant, Macmillan, 1955.
Millions and Millions, Vanguard, 1955.
The Mermaid Who Could Not Sing, Macmillan, 1956.
One Is Good but Two Are Better, Vanguard, 1956.
Melvin, the Moose Child, Macmillan, 1957.
Thank You, You're Welcome, Vanguard, 1957.
The Space Ship Returns, Macmillan, 1958.
The Little Owl Who Could Not Sleep, Macmillan, 1958.
The First Book of Drawing, F. Watts, 1958.
Trick or Treat, Macmillan, 1959.
Excuse Me, Certainly, Vanguard, 1959.
Up High and Down Low, Macmillan, 1960.
Gogo the French Sea Gull, Macmillan, 1960.
Nomi and the Beautiful Animals, Vanguard, 1960.
A Good Place to Hide, Macmillan, 1961.
Picco, Vanguard, 1961.
The Three-Seated Space Ship, Macmillan, 1962.
The Late Cuckoo, Vanguard, 1962.
Luigi and the Long-Nosed Soldier, Macmillan, 1963.
Moon Blossom and the Golden Penny, Vanguard, 1963.
The Polka-Dot Goat, Macmillan, 1964.
Yasu and the Strangers, Macmillan, 1965.
Colette and the Princess, Dutton, 1965.
Read about the Policeman, F. Watts, 1966.
Read about the Postman, F. Watts, 1966.
Read about the Fireman, F. Watts, 1967.
Read about the Busman, F. Watts, 1967.
Round-Trip Space Ship, Macmillan, 1968.
Space Ship in the Park, Macmillan, 1972.
Wilbur the Warrior, Vanguard, 1972.
The Space Ship Returns to the Apple Tree, Macmillan, 1994.

COLLABORATOR, ILLUSTRATOR, AND DESIGNER

Eleanor Estes, *The Sun and the Wind and Mr. Todd,* Harcourt, 1942.
Estes, *The Hundred Dresses,* Harcourt, 1944.
Jacob Blanck, *Jonathan and the Rainbow,* Houghton, 1948.
Blanck, *The King and the Noble Blacksmith,* Houghton, 1950.
Margarite Glendenning, *Gertie the Horse,* McGraw, 1951.
Helen F. Bill, *The King's Shoes,* F. Watts, 1956.
Florence Slobodkin, *Too Many Mittens,* Vanguard, 1958.
Florence Slobodkin, *The Cowboy Twins,* Vanguard, 1960.
Andrew Packard, *Mr. Spindles and the Spiders,* Macmillan, 1961.
Florence Slobodkin, *Io Sono,* Vanguard, 1962.
Florence Slobodkin, *Mr. Papadilly and Willy,* Vanguard, 1964.

ILLUSTRATOR AND DESIGNER

Eleanor Estes, *The Moffats,* Harcourt, 1941.

Estes, *The Middle Moffat,* Harcourt, 1942.
James Thurber, *Many Moons,* Harcourt, 1943.
Estes, *Rufus M.*, Harcourt, 1943.
Nina Brown Baker, *Peter the Great,* Vanguard, 1943.
Baker, *Garibaldi,* Vanguard, 1944.
Mabel Leigh Hunt, *Young Man of the House,* Lippincott, 1944.
Baker, *Lenin,* Vanguard, 1945.
Mark Twain, *Tom Sawyer,* World Publishing, 1946.
J. Walter McSpadden, *Robin Hood,* World Publishing, 1946.
Edgar Eager, *Red Head,* Houghton, 1951.
Charles Dickens, *The Magic Fishbone,* Vanguard, 1953.
Edith Unnerstad, *The Saucepan Journey,* Macmillan, 1955.
Washington Irving, *The Alhambra,* Macmillan, 1953.
Irmengarde Eberle, *Evie and the Wonderful Kangaroo,* Knopf, 1955.
Unnerstad, *Pysen,* Macmillan, 1955.
Sara Kasdan, *Love and Knishes,* Vanguard, 1956.
Eberle, *Evie and Cooky,* Knopf, 1957.
Unnerstad, *Little O,* Macmillan, 1957.
Robert Murphy, *The Warm-Hearted Polar Bear,* Little, Brown, 1957.
F. Amerson Andrews, *Upside Down Town,* Little, Brown, 1958.
Reda Davis, *Martin's Dinosaur,* Crowell, 1959.
Priscilla and Otto Frederich, *Clean Clarence,* Lothrop, 1959.
Priscilla and Otto Frederich, *Marshmallow Ghost,* Lothrop, 1960.
Margaret Uppington, *The Lovely Culpeppers,* F. Watts, 1963.
Sara Kasdan, *Mazel Toy Y'all,* Vanguard, 1968.
Florence Slobodkin, *Sarah Somebody,* Vanguard, 1970.

ADAPTATIONS: Magic Michael was adapted to film and filmstrip by Weston Woods Studios, 1960, and *Dinny and Danny* was adapted to filmstrip with teacher's guide and record by Association-Sterling Films, 1975.

SIDELIGHTS: Louis Slobodkin was an accomplished sculptor who wrote and illustrated numerous children's books in addition to illustrating the works of other authors, including his wife. Slobodkin's achievements include winning a Caldecott award for his illustrations in James Thurber's *Many Moons.* In *Twentieth-Century Children's Writers* Rachel Fordyce observed that "the fact that Slobodkin was a sculptor obviously influenced his illustrating; movement, tension, and the dynamics of living figures read clearly through his illustration."

Slobodkin once recalled, "Eleanor Estes, who knew me as a sculptor, asked me to illustrate her first book, *The Moffats.* Thus, I became an illustrator. I began writing my own stories a few years later because I wanted to draw the pictures for them." Slobodkin's writing includes books that are instructional, such as the courtesy books *Thank You, You're Welcome* and *Excuse Me, Certainly.* He has also written informative books for children, such as the "Read About" books that describe the jobs of bus drivers, postal carriers, fire fighters, and police officers. Slobodkin also wrote fictional accounts of space travel and space inhabitants.

BIOGRAPHICAL/CRITICAL SOURCES:

BOOKS

Something about the Author, Volume 26, Gale, 1982.
Twentieth-Century Children's Writers, 4th edition, St. James Press, 1995.

PERIODICALS

Kirkus Reviews, September 15, 1965, p. 979; February 15, 1967, p. 205.
Library Journal, November 15, 1965, p. 5083; October 15, 1973, p. 3164.
Publishers Weekly, September 18, 1972, p. 74.
Times Literary Supplement, June 17, 1965, p. 507; November 30, 1967, p. 1152; April 6, 1973, p. 386.*

* * *

SUMMERS, Rowena
See SAUNDERS, Jean

* * *

SUTTON, Henry
See SLAVITT, David R(ytman)

* * *

THORNE, Nicola
See ELLERBECK, Rosemary (Anne L'Estrange)

TWO LADIES OF ENGLAND
See MOORE, Doris Langley

* * *

WALTON, Evangeline
See ENSLEY, Evangeline

* * *

WASHINGTON, Alex
See HARRIS, Mark

* * *

WELLS, John Jay
See COULSON, Juanita (Ruth)

WILLIAMS, Pete
See FAULKNOR, Cliff(ord Vernon)

* * *

WOODS, Stockton
See FORREST, Richard (Stockton)

* * *

WRIGHT, Jack R.
See HARRIS, Mark

* * *

YORKE, Katherine
See ELLERBECK, Rosemary (Anne L'Estrange)